Criminal Justice Today

An Introductory Text for the Twenty-First Century

FIFTH EDITION

Frank Schmalleger
Justice Research Association

—FOREWORD BY
Joan Petersilia, Ph.D.

PRENTICE HALL, UPPER SADDLE RIVER, NEW JERSEY 07458

Library of Congress Cataloging-in-Publication Data
Schmalleger, Frank.
    Criminal justice today: an introductory text for the twenty first
century: annotated instructor's edition/Frank Schmalleger:
foreword by Joan Petersilia.—5th ed.
        p.   cm.
    Includes indexes.
    ISBN 0-13-848250-0
    1. Criminal justice, Administration of —United States.   I. Title.
HV9950.S35   1999
364.973—dc21   98–19541
                                                              CIP

Editorial/production supervision
    and electronic page composition: *Janet M. McGillicuddy*
Template design: *Janet McGillicuddy*
Director of Manufacturing and production: *Bruce Johnson*
Managing editor: *Mary Carnis*
Design director: *Marianne Frasco*
Interior design: *Amy Rosen*
Cover design: *Joe Sengotta*
Cover image: *Diane Fenster*
Charts and graphs: *Freddy Flake/Precision Graphics*
Photo research: *Cathy Ringrose*
Manufacturing buyer: *Ed O'Dougherty*
Acquisitions editor: *Neil Marquardt*
Marketing manager: *Frank Mortimer, Jr.*
Editorial assistant: *Jean Auman*

Part and Chapter opening photographs: Part 1, Fort Worth Star—Telegram; Chapter 1, Jeffry Scott, Impact Visuals;
Chapter 2, Spencer, Stock Boston; Chapter 3, Eric Miller, AP/Wide World Photos; Chapter 4, Bill Gallery, Stock Boston;
Part 2, Matthew McVay, Stock Boston; Chapter 5, Peter Marlow, Magnum Photos, Inc.; Chapter 6, Betsy Herzog,
AP/Wide World Photos; Chapter 7, Brad Rickerby, Archive Photos; Part 3, Elaine Thompson, AP/Wide World Photos;
Chapter 8, Alex Webb, Magnum Photos, Inc.; Chapter 9, Stacy Pick, Stock Boston; Chapter 10, Corbis—Bettmann; Part
4, Swersey, Gamma—Liaison, Inc.; Chapter 11, Bob Daemmrich, Stock Boston; Chapter 12, Richard Falco, Black Star;
Chapter 13, Armineh Johannes, SIPA Press; Part 5, Donna Binder, Impact Visuals Photos & Graphics, Inc.; Chapter 14,
Lester Sloan, Woodfin Camp & Associates; Chapter 15, Billy Barnes, Stock Boston; Chapter 16, Larry Mulvehill, The
Image Works; Chapter 17, R. Blanshard, Sygma

© 1999, 1997, 1995, 1993, 1991 by Prentice-Hall, Inc.
A Simon & Schuster Company
Upper Saddle River, New Jersey 07458

Printed in the United States of America
10 9 8 7 6 5 4 3 2

ISBN 0-13-848250-0
ISBN 0-13-080761-3

Prentice-Hall International (UK) Limited, *London*
Prentice-Hall of Australia Pty. Limited, *Sydney*
Prentice-Hall Canada, Inc., *Toronto*
Prentice-Hall Hispanoamericana, S.A., *Mexico*
Prentice-Hall of India Private Limited, *New Delhi*
Prentice-Hall of Japan, Inc., *Tokyo*
Simon & Schuster Asia Pte. Ltd., *Singapore*
Editora Prentice-Hall do Brasil, Ltda., *Rio de Janeiro*

For
Harmonie Star-Schmalleger,
—my beautiful wife and other self

Contents

Part 1 CRIME IN AMERICA 3

Chapter 1

Chapter 2

THE CRIME PICTURE 35

Chapter 3

THE SEARCH FOR CAUSES 83

Chapter 4

CRIMINAL LAW   123

Part 2 Policing 175

Chapter 7

Policing: Legal Aspects   265

Part 3 ADJUDICATION 309

Chapter 8

THE COURTS 311

Chapter 9

THE COURTROOM WORK GROUP AND THE CRIMINAL TRIAL 341

Chapter 10

Part 4   CORRECTIONS   433

Chapter 11

PROBATION, PAROLE, AND COMMUNITY CORRECTIONS   435

Chapter 12

Chapter 13

Part 5   SPECIAL ISSUES   561

Chapter 14

JUVENILE DELINQUENCY   563

Chapter 15

Chapter 16

Chapter 17

THE FUTURE OF CRIMINAL JUSTICE   689

Preface

This is the Fifth Edition of *Criminal Justice Today*—and the one that will be in the hands of students as we enter the new millenium. The first edition appeared ten years ago. At that time I chose to subtitle this book *An Introductory Text for the Twenty-First Century*. I did so because I believed that most other introductory criminal justice textbooks were oriented toward the past rather than the future, and I wanted to indicate my belief that today's students must be prepared not only for the world of today but for the world of tomorrow as well. It is the world of tomorrow in which today's students will live and work, and it is from the world of tomorrow that today's students will continue to shape an ever-evolving future—a future in which, if we are lucky, we will all share and prosper. The purpose of this textbook is as simple as it is hopeful: to teach students of criminal justice the fundamental tried-and-true concepts of an evolving discipline, to give them the critical-thinking skills necessary to effectively apply those concepts to the real world, and to apply those concepts and skills to today's problems and to the emerging issues of tomorrow.

The world, along with the criminal justice system, has changed considerably during the past decade. The challenge for me, as an author, has been to keep *Criminal Justice Today* both current and relevant—and to have it become an ever more useful tool in the study of criminal justice. The rather widespread acceptance of this book in the marketplace, and the markedly positive reception it has received from both students and instructors, attests to the success of those efforts.

In the preface to the first edition, I summarized the themes central to *Criminal Justice Today*, saying: "Any introductory book on criminal justice, if it is to have a place in today's college and university classrooms, and in the classrooms of the future, must do three things well. First, it must provide a thorough historical coverage of the field by recognizing significant past developments and by acknowledging the individuals who have already contributed to the study of criminal justice. Second, to be relevant and to excite students, it must focus on contemporary issues and explore such issues within a useful analytical context. Last, to have value the book must provide a guide for understanding. It must be insightful in a way that will allow readers to reach conclusions about the practice of criminal justice and to apply what they have learned to their own lives as informed citizens of a dynamic society. To meet these goals, *Criminal Justice Today* draws intentionally upon the tensions created in the modern world by criminal activity and efforts at social control. The practice of criminal justice occurs within a web woven of highly valued and hard-won civil and individual rights, on the one hand, and the concerns of society for order, predictability, and safety, on the other—a fact from which the book never strays." The fifth edition remains true to these early themes, enhancing them through the use of contemporary examples, true-to-life scenarios, and an ever-growing package of supplements.

A number of other distinctive features set *Criminal Justice Today* apart from the plethora of introductory textbooks currently available. One is timeliness. Information is being produced today at a prodigious rate. In many cases published sources are out of date even before they come into print. Textbooks that rely solely or almost entirely on other "hard-copy" works, as many still do, are doubly doomed to untimeliness and social irrelevance. *Criminal Justice Today* is as much a product of the modern world as it is a guide to it. In its initial edition, it was the first introductory criminal justice textbook to take advantage of high-technology information retrieval sources and on-line criminal justice databases. Well-researched and highly regarded on-line services such as the National Criminal Justice Reference Service, Dialogue, CompuServe, AP Online, the Search Group BBS, and the U.S. Supreme Court's Project HERMES (with the Court's decisions now available through the Legal Information Institute at Cornell Law School) have all contributed to the development of *Criminal Justice Today* in a way that would not have been possible only a few short years ago.

In this edition, an even greater number of on-line sources have been culled for the latest in official statistics, research results, and court cases. Vital and new information from the Internet's World Wide Web has made this book up-to-date and timely in a way that only instant access to current materials can. Supplementing *Criminal Justice Today* is our award-winning web site (http://www.prenhall.com/cjtoday), which facilitates exploration of the

Web's vast resources to further develop ideas presented in the text. The ready availability of Web-based resources, including on-line discussion of text materials, an e-mail homework facility, and Simon and Schuster's NewsLink service, ensures that readers of *Criminal Justice Today* can easily keep abreast of the latest materials in the criminal justice arena.

A second distinguishing feature of this text is its emphasis on the multidimensional environment surrounding the criminal justice system. Legal, technical, social, and international forces are all discussed as major shapers of the American system of justice. In the area of constitutional issues, for example, most other texts discuss search and seizure primarily as they affect police agencies. *Criminal Justice Today* is more comprehensive in its approach. It covers the legal environment in which all agencies of criminal justice must function, from police through courts, corrections, and probation and parole. *Criminal Justice Today* also recognizes the impact on the justice system of social issues through coverage of American social problems, such as the abortion debate, domestic terrorism, hate crimes, the separatist movement, and the problems that drugs represent to society today. The multinational criminal-justice chapter and another on the future of criminal justice, with its comprehensive coverage of cybercrime, expand consideration of the nexus of social forces in which the modern justice system is enmeshed.

While *Criminal Justice Today* is comprehensive, it is also interesting. Attention-getting real-life stories have been a core feature of *Criminal Justice Today* since its first edition, and new stories have been added throughout this edition. True-to-life crime stories, although often gruesome in some respects, hold student interest and inspire discussion of critical concepts. The recent spate of school shootings, the murder of six-year-old JonBenet Ramsey, the killing spree attributed to Andrew Cunanan, the aftermath of the O. J. Simpson trials, the Oklahoma City bombing, abortion clinic shootings, the rebirth of chain gangs, and other contemporary narratives make this book exciting and applicable to the world in which we live.

Even though this book is future directed, it recognizes the debt any future owes to its past. Each section and every chapter begin with a series of thought-provoking quotations and ideas from famous philosophers, poets, scientists, and statesmen and stateswomen who have gone before. Quotations from contemporary thinkers are included as well—with many also found throughout the text.

Finally, this book is practical. While intended for use by students everywhere who are beginning the study of criminal justice, *Criminal Justice Today* incorporates and supports the best and most contemporary principles guiding the study of criminal justice. The discipline-specific educational principles underlying the Academy of Criminal Justice Sciences recent forays into the accreditation arena (via the ACJS Ad Hoc Committee on Minimum Standards for Criminal Justice Education), for example, are incorporated into this text, as are some of the more prominent state-specific guidelines for criminal justice education. *Criminal Justice Today* and its various supplements are also written to be consistent with and supportive of the California POST College Transition Program. The College Transition Program allows students to earn basic course law enforcement certification credits during their college studies—reducing the academy training time needed for students seeking law enforcement careers. POST standards, even when not state-specific, add a pragmatic dimension to the study of criminal justice—stressing as they do the development of useful employment-related abilities and critical thinking skills.

In summary, *Criminal Justice Today* is intended not as a simple description of what has already taken place in the field, but as a visual and thoughtful guide to the study and practice of criminal justice today, a road map to criminal justice in the twenty-first century, and a bridge between past and future. While we must build upon the lessons of the past in order to enter a better tomorrow, we cannot continue to live in the past. As a great writer once said—the future is already upon us!

Instructions to the Student for Using Software Simulations That Accompany Criminal Justice Today

A number of student-oriented computerized simulations are available for use with *Criminal Justice Today*. If your instructor has elected to assign the software simulations provided by Prentice Hall, you should be especially attentive to this symbol:

The symbol, commonly called a "disk icon," signifies that software is available for enacting a scenario relevant to the text material at the point where the icon appears. Your instructor may require you to complete the assignments keyed to text material identified by the icon and may also ask that you turn in written assignments describing your experience with the scenarios. The scenarios can be downloaded from the *Criminal Justice Today* web site at http://www.prenhall.com/cjtoday.

Instructions for Accessing the Criminal Justice Today World Wide Web Site

Anyone using this book is encouraged to visit the award-winning *Criminal Justice Today* home page on the World Wide Web. The site provides a broad range of materials of relevance to the study of criminal justice and has links to many other criminal justice-related sites. If you have a personal computer, a modem, an Internet account, and Web browser software you can easily access the *Criminal Justice Today* home page. Point your Web browser at http://www.prenhall.com/cjtoday and get ready for a cyberspace excursion through the halls of *Criminal Justice Today* on-line!

At places throughout this textbook you will encounter this symbol, which is called a Web icon:

Wherever the Web icon appears in the margin of this textbook, it is an indication that relevant materials can be found at the *Criminal Justice Today* Web site. In addition, assignments which build upon material from the Web are located at the end of each chapter.

Acknowledgments

My thanks to all who assisted in so many different ways in the development of this textbook. The sacrifice of time made by my wife, Harmonie; daughter, Nicole; and son, Jason, as I worked endlessly in my study, is heartfelt. Thanks also to Jean Auman, Robin Baliszewski, Mary Carnis, Marianne Frasco, Janet McGillicuddy, Neil Marquardt, Frank Mortimer (AKA "Krazy Elvis"), Marianne Peters-Riordan, Patrick Walsh, and all the Prentice Hall Career & Technology staff—true professionals, who make the task of manuscript development enjoyable. My supplements authors, Sheila and Gordon Armstrong, are extremely talented, and I am grateful to them for using their skills in support of this new edition.

From its inception, this edition has benefited considerably from the suggestions of Gordon Armstrong, Clem Bartollas, Terry Hutchins, Jess Maghan, Bill Ruefle, and Richard Zevitz, and from suggestions made by Herman Woltring of the United Nations' Crime Prevention and Criminal Justice Branch. I am grateful, as well, to the manuscript reviewers involved in this and previous editions for holding me to the fire when I might have opted for a less rigorous coverage of some topics—and to Bryan J. Vila, whose definitive works on criminal justice policy are as useful to me as they are to the discipline! A special thanks goes to Darl Champion of Methodist College, Gary Prawel at Monroe Community College, Jim Smith at West Valley College, and Derald D. Hunt, Associate Dean, emeritus, Coast Community College District, for their insightful suggestions as this new edition got underway. Manuscript reviewers who have contributed to the development of *Criminal Justice Today* include

Larry Bassi
Darl Champion
Alex Greenberg
Julia Hall
Nicholas H. Iron
Raymond E. Lloyd II
Richard H. Martin
Bonnie Neher
James S. E. Opolot
Roger L. Pennel
Albert Roberts
Benson Schaffer
Loretta Stalan
Robert W. Taylor
Pat Ungarino
Debra Kelley
Bryan Vila

W. Garrett Capune
Michael J. Mahaney
Armand P. Hernandez
William D. Hyatt
Galan M. Janeksela
Thomas P. McAninch
G. Larry Mays
David Neubauer
Lance Parr
Gary Prawel
Bill Ruefle
Stephen J. Schoenthaler
Morris R. Sterrett
Lawrence F. Travis III
L. Thomas Winfree, Jr.
Ellen G. Cohn

My thanks to each and every one! I would also like to extend a special thanks to the following individuals for their invaluable comments and suggestions along the way: Howard Abadinsky, Kevin Barrett, Z. G. Standing Bear, Michael Blankenship, Avon Burns, Kathy Cameron-Hahn, Art Chete, Geary Chlebus, Jon E. Clark, Warren Clark, Mark L. Dantzker, Vicky Doworth, Steve Egger, Michael Gray, Joe Graziano, Richard Guymon, Ed Heischmidt, Michael Hooper, P. Ray Kedia, Joan Luxenburg, Michael Lyman, Richard H. Martin, Robert (Bob) J. Meadows, Donald J. Melisi, Jim Mezhir, Rick Michelson, Roslyn Muraskin, Harv Morley, Charles Myles, David F. Owens, Michael J. Palmiotto, William H. Parsonage, Ken Peak, Morgan Peterson, Phil Purpura, Philip L. Reichel, John Robich, Carl E. Russell, Judith M. Sgarzi, Ira Silverman, John Sinsel, Ted Skotnicki, B. Grant Stitt, Tom Thackery, Joe Trevalino, Howard Tritt, Bill Tyrrell, Tim Veiders, Ron Vogel, John Volman, Jr., David Whelan, Lois Wims, and Bob Winslow.

Jean E. Sexton and Lucy H. Hartley, both very fine librarians, helped uncover information otherwise irretrievable. Thanks are also due everyone who assisted in artistic arrangements, including Cathy Ringrose, Precision Graphics, Michael L. Hammond of the Everett

(Washington) Police Department, Sgt. Michael Flores of New York City Police Department's Photo Unit, Assistant Chief James M. Lewis of the Bakersfield (California) Police Department, Monique Smith of the National Institute of Justice, and Tonya Matz of the University of Illinois at Chicago—all of whom were especially helpful in providing a wealth of photo resources. I am especially indebted to University of Illinois Professor Joseph L. Peterson for assistance with sections on scientific evidence.

A special "thank you" to my developmental editor Sheryl Fullerton, who has a knack of being able to say more in one or two pages than I can in hundreds. I'd also like to acknowledge J. Harper Wilson, Chief of the FBI's Uniform Crime Reporting Program; Nancy Carnes of the same program; Mark Reading of the Drug Enforcement Administration's Office of Intelligence; Kristina Rose at the National Criminal Justice Reference Service; Marilyn Marbrook and Michael Rand at the Office of Justice Programs; Wilma M. Grant of the U.S. Supreme Court's Project Hermes; Ken Kerle at the American Jail Association; Lisa Bastian, survey statistician with the National Crime Victimization Survey Program; Steve Shackelton with the U.S. Parks Service; Ronald T. Allen, Steve Chaney, Bernie Homme, and Kenneth L. Whitman, all with the California Peace Officer Standards and Training Commission; James E. (Jim) Smith at West Valley College in Saratoga, California; Dianne Martin at the Drug Enforcement Administration; and George J. Davino of the New York Police Department for their help in making this book both timely and accurate.

Last, but by no means least, Reed Adams, Gary Colboth, Taylor Davis, H. R. Delaney, Jannette O. Domingo, Al Garcia, Rodney Hennigsen, David M. Jones, Victor E. Kappeler, Robert O. Lampert, Norman G. Kittel, Robert J. Meadows, Joseph M. Pellicciotti, and Jeff Schrink should know that their writings, contributions, and valuable suggestions at the earliest stages of manuscript development continue to be very much appreciated. Thank you, each and everyone!

Frank Schmalleger, Ph.D.
Hilton Head Island, SC

About the Author

Frank Schmalleger, Ph.D., is Director of the Justice Research Association, a private consulting firm and "think-tank" focusing on issues of crime and justice. The Justice Research Association, which is based in Hilton Head Island, South Carolina, serves the needs of the nation's civil and criminal-justice planners and administrators through workshops, conferences, and grant-writing and program evaluation support. Dr. Schmalleger is also founder and co-director of the Criminal Justice Distance Learning Consortium (http://cjcentral.com /cjdlc).

Dr. Schmalleger holds degrees from the University of Notre Dame and Ohio State University, having earned both a master's (1970) and doctorate in sociology (1974) from Ohio State University with a special emphasis in criminology. From 1976 to 1994 he taught criminal justice courses at The University of North Carolina at Pembroke. For the last 16 of those years he chaired the university's Department of Sociology, Social Work, and Criminal Justice. As an adjunct professor with Webster University in St. Louis, Missouri, Schmalleger helped develop the university's graduate program in security administration and loss prevention. He taught courses in that curriculum for more than a decade. Schmalleger has also taught in the New School for Social Research's on-line graduate program, helping to build the world's first electronic classrooms in support of distance learning through computer telecommunications. An avid web surfer, Schmalleger is also the creator of a number of award winning World Wide Web sites, including one which supports this textbook (http://www.prenhall.com/cjtoday).

Frank Schmalleger is the author of numerous articles and many books, including the widely used *Criminology Today* (Prentice Hall, 1999); *Criminal Justice: A Brief Introduction* (Prentice Hall, 1999); *Criminal Law Today* (Prentice Hall, 1999); *Crime and the Justice System in America: An Encyclopedia* (Greenwood Publishing Group, 1997); *Trial of the Century: People of the State of California vs. Orenthal James Simpson* (Prentice Hall, 1996); *Computers in Criminal Justice* (Wyndham Hall Press, 1991); *Career Paths: A Guide to Jobs in Federal Law Enforcement* (Regents/Prentice Hall, 1994); *Criminal Justice Ethics* (Greenwood Press, 1991); *Finding Criminal Justice in the Library* (Wyndham Hall Press, 1991); *Ethics in Criminal Justice* (Wyndham Hall Press, 1990); *A History of Corrections* (Foundations Press of Notre Dame, 1983); and *The Social Basis of Criminal Justice* (University Press of America, 1981).

Schmalleger is also founding editor of the journal *The Justice Professional*. He serves as editor for the Prentice Hall series *Criminal Justice in the Twenty-first Century* and as Imprint Advisor for Greenwood Publishing Group's criminal justice reference series.

Schmalleger's philosophy of both teaching and writing can be summed up in these words: "In order to communicate knowledge we must first catch, then hold, a person's interest—be it student, colleague, or policymaker. Our writing, our speaking, and our teaching must be relevant to the problems facing people today, and they must—in some way—help solve those problems."

Foreword

The American public is preoccupied with crime and justice as never before. Public opinion polls show that Americans judge crime our nation's number one concern, and they believe it will get worse in the next few years. And, while they voice skepticism that government officials know how to curb crime they believe they have some solutions: Citizens overwhelmingly endorse such punitive measures as three-strikes laws, mandatory prison terms, no parole, and expanding the death penalty.

Perhaps it is the extensive media coverage about crime that has created a nation of "instant experts" on justice matters. After all, no previous generation of Americans has been subjected to saturated TV crime coverage, reality-based TV cop shows, and video cameras placed in stores and patrol cars to film crimes in progress. Considering all that, plus the unprecedented coverage of the *People* v. *O.J. Simpson* case and other celebrity crimes, one can understand why crime policy has moved out of academic circles and into the living rooms of the American public. U.S. citizens have seen the justice system "up close and personal," and they are angry and demanding change.

Of course, the public's desire to address the crime problem is admirable. Without their cooperation, needed programs cannot be funded or implemented. But allowing them to *direct* reform efforts is misguided and likely to be costly in both human and financial terms. Too much of current crime policy is being made according to what we wish or believe rather than on the basis of what is known.

Those familiar with the justice system know that the O.J. Simpson case and all of the other celebrity cases are idiosyncratic, an amalgam of individual ingredients that will never again arise. Most cases are not settled through lengthy trials, DNA is seldom brought to bear, the death penalty is almost never considered, and defenses like the battered wife syndrome are rarely alleged or proven. Information about these celebrity cases is, for most purposes, simply not relevant to most justice decision making. In short, U.S. citizens have become experts by studying the atypical.

So, we are rather in a quandary. The public's newfound energy to *do* something about crime is sorely needed, yet they possess little of the knowledge necessary to accurately address the problem. Cancer is a major problem, too, but the public does not think it should go in there and start tinkering—telling doctors what drugs to administer or when to hospitalize patients. But in criminal justice matters, the public does tinker. It votes to enact punitive sentencing legislation, abolish parole boards, and abandon treatment programs. It's almost as if we have put the public in charge of a major medical operation, and they are untrained and ill-equipped for the task.

But lest we take the doctor analogy too far, justice is different than medicine because the community is a coproducer of justice. Unlike the doctor, experts can't solve crime alone. In fact, they aren't even the critical link to the solutions. Rather they depend on citizens to identify assailants, bring them to justice, and assist in offender reintegration. So, justice experts cannot simply say to the public, "Leave us alone." Rather the goal must be to move the public away from the television set and toward more factual information. We must provide a comprehensive resource so that students and the public can learn to separate crime fiction from crime fact.

I believe that is what Frank Schmalleger's book, *Criminal Justice Today*, does so well. He provides a clear statement not only of the crime problem and explanations of the causes, but also of what strategies might work. He helps us to better understand the agencies that are responsible for processing criminal cases and supervising offenders, and the legal and moral boundaries which constrain them.

Schmalleger begins by summarizing criminal justice "reality" as it is currently known by scholars and practitioners. Students may be surprised, for example, by his description of serious crime trends. He tells us that while fear of crime is gripping the American public, actual levels of reported crime are relatively stable, concentrated in certain regions of the nation, and in some instances, declining. Students might well believe that criminal victimization rates have reached record levels. They have: They are at their *lowest* levels in 20 years! Again, Schmalleger sets us straight.

Many Americans might suspect that drive-by-shootings or drug-related gunfire or holdups are to blame for most shooting deaths. They would not be close to the truth. Schmalleger tells us that the most common shooting death in America takes place not on the street but in the home: It is a suicide. The second most common shooting death is not a random killing but someone shooting someone he or she knows, often in the home.

After succinctly describing the reality of crime, Schmalleger turns his attention to crime causation. Knowing the causes of crime seems critically important to finding an effective intervention. The bulk of *Criminal Justice Today* is appropriately devoted to discussing the laws that govern crime and describing the agencies responsible for administering justice. There are excellent chapters devoted to each component of the justice system, from police through courts, corrections, and probation and parole. Each chapter describes the roles and duties of those agencies, the practitioners who work within them, and issues regarding evaluation and program effectiveness. Importantly, the chapters also explain the relationship between justice agencies and their profound influence on one another—for example, how jail populations and procedures affect prisons, which in turn influence probation and parole policy, which in turn influences rehabilitation prospects.

But more useful than any of these specific details on crime or the justice system is the organizing theme of the entire textbook. Schmalleger writes that justice in America is ever-changing and cyclical, and at any point in time it mostly reflects how citizens have chosen to balance the justice system's two primary objectives: community safety versus individual rights. Balancing these two competing goals creates a constant and unavoidable tension in formulating justice policies and programs.

Of course, we all want community safety. But, philosophically, Americans will tend to align themselves more or less with one of these two perspectives. There are those who prioritize the protection of personal freedoms and civil rights within the justice process. Schmalleger labels these persons *individual rights advocates*. The public often refers to such persons as "liberals." On the other hand, there are those who suggest that, specifically on crime matters, the interest of society should take precedence over individual rights. Schmalleger labels such persons *public order advocates*, and they are popularly thought of as political "conservatives."

Depending on the mood of the country, either crime control or due process concerns receive higher priority. During the 1960s to 1980s, protecting individual rights and due process concerns seemed most important, whereas calls for social and individual responsibility now are paramount. Schmalleger correctly notes that it is the tension between these two perspectives that forms the basis of most policy-making, and public order advocates are currently winning the day and conservative crime policies are in vogue.

I believe Schmalleger's excellent discussion of these two perspectives in Chapter 1, and his effective weaving of the concept throughout each of the subsequent chapters, is this book's most unique contribution. Once students have mastered these two concepts, they will have learned something far more important than simply the facts and figures behind crime and justice, they will have learned *how to think about crime* and policies proposed for its reduction. Laws and details about crime and justice agencies will change, but having an understanding of how to appropriately think about crime is an educational advance that will forever be useful to students, whether they become criminal justice professionals or simply seek to be more informed citizens.

I know I join my criminological colleagues in congratulating Dr. Schmalleger for another excellent edition of *Criminal Justice Today*. It is a great service to criminal justice students and the general public.

Joan Petersilia, Ph.D.
University of California, Irvine
Former President, American Society of Criminology

Injustice anywhere is a threat to justice everywhere.
—Martin Luther King, Jr.

The freedom to die before you're a teenager
is not the freedom Martin Luther King lived and died for.
We have to make our people whole again.
—President Clinton

Goals of the Criminal Justice System

Common law, constitutional, statutory, and humanitarian rights of the accused:

- Justice for the Individual

- Personal Liberty

- Dignity as a Human Being

- The Right to Due Process

The individual rights listed must be effectively balanced against these community concerns:

- Social Justice

- Equality before the Law

- The Protection of Society

- Freedom from Fear

How does our system of justice work toward balance?

part 1
CRIME IN AMERICA

The will of the people is the best law

The great American statesman and orator Daniel Webster (1782–1852) once wrote: "Justice is the great interest of man on earth. It is the ligament which holds civilized beings and civilized nations together." While Webster may have lived in a relatively simple time with few problems and many shared rules, justice has never been easily won. Unlike Webster's era, society today is highly complex and populated by groups with a wide diversity of interests. It is within that challenging context that the daily practice of American criminal justice occurs.

The criminal justice system has three central components: police, courts, and corrections. The history, the activities, and the legal environment surrounding the police are discussed in Part 2 of this book. Part 3 describes courts, and Part 4 deals with prisons, probation, and parole. Part 5 provides a guide to the future of the justice system and of enforcement agencies. We begin here in Part 1, however, with an overview of that grand ideal which we call *justice*—and we consider how the justice ideal relates to the everyday practice of criminal justice in the United States today. To that end, in the four chapters which comprise this section, we will examine how and why laws are made. We will look at the wide array of interests which impinge upon the justice system, and we will examine closely the dichotomy which distinguishes citizens who are primarily concerned with individual rights from those who emphasize the need for individual responsibility and social accountability. In the pages that follow we will see how *justice* can mean protection from the power of the state to some, and vengeance to others. In this section we will also lay the groundwork for the rest of the text by painting a picture of crime in America today, suggesting possible causes for it, and showing how policies for dealing with crime have evolved.

As you read about the complex tapestry that is the practice of criminal justice in America today, you will see a system in flux, perhaps less sure of its values and purpose than at any time in its history. You may also catch the sense, however, that very soon a new and reborn institution of justice may emerge from the ferment that now exists. Whatever the final outcome, it can only be hoped that *justice*, as proffered by the American system of criminal justice, will be sufficient to hold our civilization together—and to allow it to prosper well into the twenty-first century.

chapter 1
WHAT IS CRIMINAL JUSTICE?

Crime does more than expose the weakness in social relationships; it undermines the social order itself, by destroying the assumptions on which it is based.

—CHARLES E. SILBERMAN[1]

We are sick and tired of playing games where innocent people are killed because we can't figure out an inexpensive, common sense method of enforcing law and order.

—HOUSE SPEAKER NEWT GINGRICH[2]

Justice and Criminal Justice

The rights guaranteed to criminal suspects, defendants, offenders, and prisoners were not included in the Bill of Rights for the benefit of criminals. They are fundamental political rights that protect all Americans from governmental abuse of power. These rights are found in the Fourth, Fifth, Sixth, Eighth and Fourteenth Amendments. They include the guarantee against unreasonable search and seizure, the right to reasonable bail, the right to due process of law; and the right to be free from cruel and unusual treatment. This "bundle of rights" is indispensable to a free society.

—ACLU (web site)
http://www.aclu.org/issues/criminal/iscj.html

Early on the morning of October 1, 1997, according to police reports, 16-year-old Luke Woodham, a soft-spoken normally polite young man, rose from sleep at 5 A.M., crept into his mother's bedroom in the small town of Pearl, Mississippi, and brutally killed her with a butcher knife taken from the family's kitchen.[3] Authorities later said that Mary Woodham, a 50-year-old divorcee who worked as a receptionist, was stabbed at least 50 times.

After killing his mother, Woodham apparently washed her blood from his hands and arms, loaded his 30/30 hunting rifle with ammunition, and drove to school. He arrived at Pearl High School just before 8 A.M. as students gathered in the commons—a modern enclosure with a chessboard-like tile floor. In the school parking lot he turned his bookbag over to a friend, Justin Sledge. Then, carrying the rifle, he entered the school. The first students he encountered were 17-year-old Lydia Kaye Drew and 16-year-old Christina Menefee—a former girlfriend. Without saying a word Woodham allegedly shot both girls. They fell to the tile floor outside of the school's counseling office.

Hearing the shots, students began to panic and run. Woodham fired into the crowd and screams filled the air. Assistant principal Joel Myreck was drawn out of his office by the commotion. Stepping through his office door, Myreck witnessed Woodham calmly walk up to three students who had hidden behind a column and shoot them. One of the boys, said Myreck, tried to shield his chest with a bookbag—but Woodham shot through the bag. "Everybody was screaming to get out, and everybody was ducking, and the noise—the sound will never get out of my mind," said one student.[4]

Myreck watched as Woodham walked toward an exit, thumbing fresh shells into his rifle. The assistant principal then ran out of a side door to his pickup truck. When he reached the vehicle, Myreck, a 12-year Army reserve veteran, grabbed his .45 caliber pistol and watched as Woodham got into his mother's car. As the shooter drove toward him, Myreck stood in the parking lot and leveled his pistol at Woodham. "Stop!" he yelled, and the young man did as he was told. Myreck then ordered the boy to the ground and stood over him with the pistol.

"Why? Why, why did you do that?" Myreck asked Woodham as he waited for police to arrive.

"Oh, Mr. Myreck," Woodham answered, "I'm the one who gave you the discount on the pizza the other night."

Incredulous, Myreck yelled: "What?! You just shot my kids! Why did you do that?"

"Well, Mr. Myreck," Woodham said, "the world has wronged me, and I just couldn't take it any more."

While Myreck and Woodham engaged in this strange dialog, Christina Menefee and Lydia Kaye Drew lay dying in their teacher's arms. A teacher prayed with Lydia, trying to offer some comfort as life flowed out of her.

Pearl, Mississippi, the town where the shootings took place, has been described as the "buckle of the Bible Belt"—a small southern town with 37 churches. Just as it's 22,000 residents were beginning to adjust to the shock of the killings, authorities announced that Woodham's actions were cult-inspired.[5]

Soon, another student, 18-year-old Grant Boyette, was identified as the leader of a gang bent on taking control of the high school and executing pre-selected students and teachers.

Recent shootings in our nation's schools have heightened citizens' concerns about crime. Shown here are Luke Woodham, 16, (top left) accused of a 1997 shooting rampage at the Pearl, Mississippi, high school in which two students died; alleged Paducah, Kentucky, shooter Michael Carneal, 14, (top right) who police say killed three students and wounded five others at a Heath High School prayer meeting in late 1997; and 11-year-old Andrew Golden (right), who along with Mitchell Johnson, 13, (not shown), is charged with luring their Jonesboro, Arkansas, middle school classmates outside with a fire alarm in March, 1998, and then gunning them down with high-powered rifles (killing five and wounding eleven).
Top left photo: *Rogelio Solis, AP/Wide World Photos*;
Right photos: *AP/Wide World Photos*

Prosecutors said they had interviewed an informant who told them of the group's plans. Woodham was to be the assassin, prosecutors revealed, and Boyette planned to drive the getaway car. The two had hoped to head to Cuba, where they thought they could live unmolested by U.S. authorities. According to prosecutors, Boyette, a local college student who had attended Pearl High School a year previously, prayed to Satan, idolized Hitler, and was called "Father" by the younger students whom he led.

Police chief Bill Slade confirmed prosecutor's claims and told reporters that he believed Woodham's act was part of a larger conspiracy orchestrated by Boyette. A report by ABC's *Primetime Live* said that Boyette boasted of satanic powers, including "powers to summon 12 generals of Satan, including one called Moloch to whom children are sacrificed." According to the televised report, Boyette named the cult "Kroth" and urged members to pray to Satan for money, power, and influence.

Authorities added that Boyette had ordered his followers to kill animals in preparation for killing people. Prosecutors released this passage they said was taken from Woodham's own diary, as proof of the practice: "On Saturday of last week, I made my first kill. After brutally beating the dog, we set her on fire. We sprayed [lighter] fluid down her throat. Her neck caught on fire inside and out. It was true beauty."

The bookbag that Woodham had given Sledge as he arrived at school on the day of the shootings provided more intriguing evidence. On one page of a notebook, Woodham had written: "I am not insane. I am angry. I am not spoiled or lazy, for murder is not weak and slow-witted. Murder is gutsy and daring. I killed because people like me are mistreated every day. I did this to show society, 'Push us and we will push back.'" The page ended with a passage from the nineteenth-century German philosopher Friedrich Nietzsche, that asked, "How shall we comfort ourselves, the murderers of all murderers?"[6]

The horrific events in Oklahoma City...show the high price we pay for our liberties.

—Senator Orrin Hatch Chairman of the Senate Judiciary Committee commenting on the 1995 bombing of the Alfred P. Murrah Federal Building

Crime Conduct in violation of the criminal laws of a state, the federal government, or of a local jurisdiction, for which there is no legally acceptable justification or excuse.

Social Control The use of sanctions and rewards available through a group to influence and shape the behavior of individual members of that group. Social control is a primary concern of social groups and communities, and it is the interest that human groups hold in the exercise of social control that leads to the creation of both criminal and civil statutes.

Individual Rights Advocates Those who seek to protect personal freedoms within the process of criminal justice.

Public Order Advocates Those who suggest that, under certain circumstances involving a criminal threat to public safety, the interests of society should take precedence over individual rights.

As this book goes to press, the case against Woodham and Boyette is still pending, and they remain in jail. Five other teenagers, including Justin Sledge, have been accused of conspiracy to murder. All have been charged as adults, and all have pled "not guilty."[7]

Although Woodham has been indicted on three counts of murder and seven counts of aggravated assault, Mississippi law only permits the death penalty in killings tied to other serious crimes—such as kidnapping or rape. The worst sentence that he could receive, if convicted, is life in prison.[8]

Crimes like the ones described here dramatically highlight the recent rise in violent **crime** among teenagers and enhance the fear of crime so many Americans have come to feel. They also challenge long-cherished beliefs about the extent of crime and **social control** in American society and call into question a number of basic values centered on the family, children, violence in the media, and child-rearing practices.

The Focus of This Book—Individual Rights and Public Order

This book, which is about the American system of criminal justice and the agencies and processes which constitute it, has an orientation which we think is especially valuable for studying criminal justice today. For many years the dominant philosophy in American criminal justice has focused on guaranteeing the rights of criminal defendants while seeking to understand the root causes of crime and violence. During the last few years, however, a growing conservative emphasis has focused on the rights and interests of crime victims and has called into question some of the fundamental premises upon which the American system of criminal justice has been built. In keeping with that realization, the materials presented in this text are built around the following theme:

> There is a growing recognition in contemporary society of the need to balance (1) the respect accorded the rights of individuals faced with criminal prosecution against (2) the valid interests of society in preventing future crimes and in reducing the harm caused by criminal activity. While the personal freedoms guaranteed to criminal suspects by the Constitution, as interpreted by the U.S. Supreme Court, must be closely guarded, so too the urgent social needs of local communities for controlling unacceptable behavior and protecting law-abiding citizens from harm must be recognized. Still to be adequately addressed are the needs and interests of victims, and the fear of crime now so prevalent in the minds of many law-abiding citizens.

Figure 1–1 represents our theme diagrammatically. Most people today who intelligently consider the criminal justice system assume either one or the other of these two perspectives. We shall refer to those who seek to protect personal freedoms and civil rights within the criminal justice process as **individual rights advocates**. Those who suggest that under certain circumstances involving criminal threats to public safety, the interests of society (especially crime control) should take precedence over individual rights, will be called **public order advocates**. In this book we seek to look at ways that the individual rights and the public order perspectives can be balanced to serve both sets of needs.

Both points of view have their roots in the values which formed our nation. However, the past 30 years have been especially important in clarifying the differences between the two

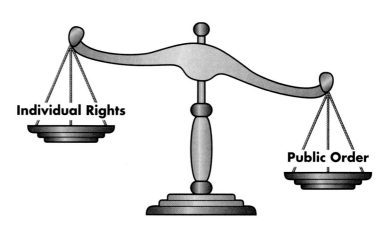

FIGURE 1–1 The theme of this book: Balancing the concern for individual rights with the need for public order through the administration of criminal justice.

points of view. The last few decades have seen a burgeoning concern with the rights of ethnic minorities, women, the physically and mentally challenged, and many other groups. The civil rights movement of the 1960s and 1970s emphasized equality of opportunity and respect for individuals regardless of race, color, creed, or personal attributes. As new laws were passed and suits filed, court involvement in the movement grew. Soon a plethora of hard-won individual rights and prerogatives, based upon the U.S. Constitution and the Bill of Rights, were recognized and guaranteed. By the 1980s the civil rights movement had profoundly affected all areas of social life—from education through employment to the activities of the criminal justice system.

This emphasis on **individual rights** was accompanied by a dramatic increase in criminal activity. "Traditional" crimes, such as murder, rape, and assault, as reported by the FBI, increased astronomically during the 1970s. Many theories were advanced to explain this virtual explosion of observed criminality. A few doubted the accuracy of "official" accounts, claiming that any actual rise in crime was much less than that portrayed in the reports. Some analysts of American culture, however, suggested that increased criminality was the result of new-found freedoms which combined with the long-pent-up hostilities of the socially and economically deprived to produce social disorganization.

By the mid-1980s, popular perceptions identified one particularly insidious form of criminal activity—the dramatic increase in the sale and use of illicit drugs—as a threat to the very fabric of American society. Cocaine, in particular, and later, laboratory-processed "crack," had spread to every corner of America. The country's borders were inundated with smugglers intent on reaping quick fortunes. Large cities became havens for drug gangs, and many inner-city areas were all but abandoned to highly armed and well-financed racketeers. Some famous personalities succumbed to the allure of drugs, and athletic teams and sporting events became focal points for drug busts. Like wildfire, drugs soon spread to younger users. Even small-town elementary schools found themselves facing the specter of campus drug dealing and associated violence.

Worse still were the seemingly ineffective governmental measures intended to stem the drug tide. Drug peddlers, because of the huge reserves of money available to them, were often able to escape prosecution or wrangle plea bargains to avoid imprisonment. Media coverage of such "miscarriages of justice" became epidemic and public anger grew.

By the close of the 1980s, neighborhoods and towns felt themselves fighting for their communal lives. City businesses faced dramatic declines in property values, and residents wrestled with the eroding quality of life. Huge rents had been torn in the national social fabric. The American way of life, long taken for granted, was under the gun. Traditional values appeared in danger of going up in smoke along with the "crack" now being smoked openly in some parks and resorts. Looking for a way to stem the tide, many took up the call for "law and order." In response, then-President Reagan initiated a "War on Drugs" and created a "drug czar" cabinet-level post to coordinate the war. Careful thought was given at the highest levels to using the military to patrol the sea lanes and air corridors through which many of the illegal drugs entered the country. President Bush, who followed President Reagan into office, quickly embraced and expanded the government's antidrug efforts.

The 1990s began with the arrest of serial murderer Jeffrey Dahmer (in 1991) and the shocking details of his crimes which later became public. Dahmer, who killed as many as 15 young men in sexually motivated encounters, cannibalized some of his victims and kept the body parts of others in his refrigerator. Dahmer's crimes, along with those of other serial killers, are discussed in more detail in Chapter 2.

In 1992, the videotaped beating of Rodney King, a black motorist, at the hands of Los Angeles-area police officers, splashed across TV screens throughout the country and shifted the public's focus onto issues of police brutality and the effective management of law enforcement personnel. As the King incident seemed to show, when financially impoverished members of "underrepresented groups" come face to face with agents of the American criminal justice system, something less than justice may be the result. Although initially acquitted by a California jury—which contained no black members—two of the officers who beat King were convicted in a 1993 federal courtroom of violating his civil rights.[9] The incident and trials are described in more detail in Chapter 7.

Individual Rights Those rights guaranteed to all members of American society by the U.S. Constitution (especially as found in the first ten amendments to the Constitution, known as the Bill of Rights). These rights are especially important to criminal defendants facing formal processing by the criminal justice system.

When you know both the accuser and the accused, as we so often do, the conflict between civil rights and victims' rights is seldom completely black or white. And it is the gray areas in between that make the debate so difficult.
—Columnist Vicki Williams, writing on crime in a small American town

The year 1993 saw an especially violent encounter in Waco, Texas, among agents of the Bureau of Alcohol, Tobacco, and Firearms, the FBI, and members of cult leader David Koresh's Branch Davidian. The fray, which began when ATF agents assaulted Koresh's fortresslike compound, leaving four agents and six cultists dead, ended 51 days later with the fiery deaths of Koresh and 71 of his followers. Many of them were children. The assault on Koresh's compound led to a congressional investigation and charges that the ATF and FBI had been ill-prepared to deal successfully with large-scale domestic resistance and had reacted more out of alarm and frustration than wisdom. Janet Reno, Attorney General under President Clinton, refused to blame agents for misjudging Koresh's intentions, although 11 Davidians were later acquitted of charges that they murdered the agents.

By the mid-1990s, however, a strong shift away from the claimed misdeeds of the criminal justice system began, and a new-found emphasis on individual accountability began to blossom among an American public fed up with crime and fearful of their own victimization. Growing calls for enhanced responsibility began to quickly replace the previous emphasis on individual rights. As a juggernaut of conservative opinion made itself felt on the political scene, Texas Senator Phil Gramm observed that the public wants to "grab violent criminals by the throat, put them in prison [and] stop building prisons like Holiday Inns."[10]

It was probably the public's perception of growing crime rates, coupled with a belief that offenders frequently went unpunished or that many received only judicial slaps on the wrists, which led to the burgeoning emphasis on responsibility and punishment. However, a few spectacular crimes which received widespread coverage in the news media heightened the public's sense that crime in the United States was out of hand and that new measures were needed to combat it. In 1993, for example, James Jordan, father of Chicago Bulls' basketball superstar Michael Jordan, was killed in a cold-blooded robbery by two young men with long criminal records. Jordan's death, which seemed the result of a chance encounter, helped rivet the nation's attention on what appeared to be the increasing frequency of random and senseless violence.

In that same year, a powerful bomb ripped apart the basement of one of the twin World Trade Center buildings in New York City. The explosion, which killed five and opened a 100-foot crater through four sublevels of concrete, displaced 50,000 workers, including employees at the commodities exchanges that handle billions of dollars worth of trade in oil, gold, coffee, and sugar. The product of terrorists with foreign links, the bombing highlighted the susceptibility of the American infrastructure to terrorist activity.[11]

Similarly, in 1993 the heart-wrenching story of Polly Klaas splashed across the national media. Twelve-year-old Polly was kidnapped from a slumber party at her home while her mother and little sister slept in the next room. Two other girls were left bound and gagged after a bearded stranger broke into the Klaas home in Petaluma, California. Despite efforts by hundreds of uniformed officers and 4,000 volunteers, attempts to find the girl proved fruitless. Nine weeks later, just before Christmas, an ex-con named Richard Allen Davis was arrested and charged with Polly's murder. Investigators found that Davis's life read like a litany of criminal activity and that Polly's death was due at least partially to failure of the criminal justice system to keep a dangerous Davis behind bars. Three years later, in 1996, Davis was convicted of Polly's murder and sentenced to death.

In 1994 the attention of the nation was riveted on proceedings in the Susan Smith case. Smith, a South Carolina mother, confessed to drowning her two young boys (ages 1 and 3 at the time) by strapping them into child-safety seats and rolling the family station wagon off a pier and into a lake. Smith, who appears to have been motivated by the demands of an extramarital love affair, had originally claimed a black man carjacked her vehicle with the boys still inside. 1994 was also the year in which 7-year-old Megan Kanka was brutally murdered by previously convicted sex offender Jesse K. Timmendequas. The New Jersey case, and the new laws that it inspired, are described in a box in this chapter.

Senseless violence linked to racial hatred stunned the nation during the 1995 trial of Colin Ferguson. Ferguson, who was eventually convicted of killing six passengers and wounding 19 others during what prosecutors claimed was a racially motivated shooting rampage on a Long Island Rail Road commuter train in 1993, maintained his innocence throughout the trial, despite the fact he was identified by more than a dozen eyewitnesses, including some he had shot. "This is a case of stereotyped victimization of a black man and subsequent conspiracy to destroy him—nothing more," Ferguson told the jury. Many were

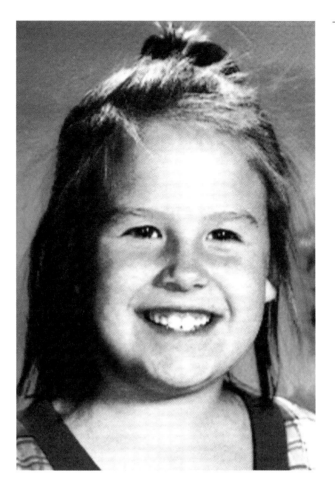

Megan Kanka, the slain child after whom New Jersey's "Megan's law" was named. Megan's law reflects America's growing conservatism toward crime and criminal offenders. *AP/Wide World Photos*

offended by the fact that Ferguson declared himself the victim when the real victims were either dead or seriously injured. Famed defense attorney William Kunstler suggested that Ferguson plead not guilty by reason of insanity, which, Kunstler argued, had been caused by "black rage" at racial injustice in America. Instead, Ferguson claimed that he had dozed off on the train and that a white man had stolen his gun and shot the passengers. Public backlash at the increasing willingness of defense attorneys to use an "offender as victim" defense contributed to growing disgust with what many saw as a hamstrung and ineffective criminal justice system.

In 1995 the double-murder trial of former football superstar and media personality O. J. Simpson received much national exposure, with daily reports on the trial appearing on television and in newspapers throughout the country. Simpson was acquitted of the brutal murders of his ex-wife, Nicole, and her associate, Ronald Goldman, after hiring a team of lawyers whom some referred to as "the million-dollar defense"—an action which many saw as akin to buying justice. In a 1997 civil trial, however, a California jury found Simpson liable for the death of Goldman and the "battery" of his former wife, and he was ordered to pay $33.5 million in damages.

Perhaps no one criminal incident gripped the psyche of the American people, and was to later galvanize the policy-making efforts of legislators, more than the 1995 bombing of the Alfred P. Murrah Federal Building in Oklahoma City by right-wing extremists. One hundred sixty-eight people died in the bombing, 19 of them children. Hundreds more were wounded and millions of dollars worth of property damage occurred. The bombing had the added impact of demonstrating just how vulnerable the United States is to terrorist assault. That attack, and a bombing during the 1996 Atlanta Olympics which killed one person and injured 111, caused many Americans to realize that the very freedoms which allow the United States to serve as a model of democracy to the rest of the world make it possible for terrorist or terrorist-affiliated groups to operate within the country relatively unencumbered.

People expect both safety and justice and do not want to sacrifice one for the other.
—Christopher Stone, President and Director, the Vera Institute of Justice

A firefighter cradles a child rescued from the Alfred P. Murrah Federal Building in Oklahoma City after a terrorist bombing there in 1995. Recent acts of domestic terrorism have raised the stakes in the battle to defend civil liberties and personal freedoms in the face of growing demands to make America safe. The child shown here later died. *Charles H. Porter, 4th, Sygma.*

The strangulation murder of six-year-old JonBenet Ramsey, the young "beauty queen" killed at Christmastime 1996 in her family's Boulder, Colorado, home added to the national sense that no one is safe. In 1997, the roadside murder of 27-year-old Ennis Cosby, well-known son of entertainer Bill Cosby, heightened the public's fear of random violence. (The Cosby case is discussed in more detail in Chapter 2.) Finally, a 1997 killing spree attributed to Andrew Cunanan, which ended in his suicide (and which claimed the life of world-renowned fashion designer Gianni Versace and five other men), galvanized the nation as the public participated in a media-led hunt for the alleged killer.

Crimes like these have changed the mood of the American public or, perhaps more accurately, have accelerated what was an already changing mood. A growing national frustration with the apparent inability of our society and its justice system to prevent crimes and to consistently hold offenders who are identified and then arrested to heart-felt standards of right and wrong has led to increased conservatism in the public policy arena. That conservative tendency, which continues to thrive today, was ushered in by the 1994 congressional elections, where get-tough-on-crime policies won the day. Since that time, numerous other public officials have joined the get-tough bandwagon. Many have stopped asking what society can do to protect individuals accused of crimes and demand to know instead how offenders can better be held accountable for violations of the criminal law. Today's national mood was recently well summarized by Paul McNulty, a former Justice Department official. "They want punishment and they want it badly," McNulty said.[12]

PERSPECTIVES ON CRIMINAL JUSTICE AND THE THEME OF THIS BOOK

While conservative sentiments still very much influence public policy, it is important to recognize that national feelings, however strong, have historically been somewhat akin to the swings of a pendulum. Hence, while the emphasis on individual rights, which rose to ascendancy a few decades ago, now appears to have been eclipsed by calls for social and individual responsibility, the tension between the two perspectives still forms the basis for most policy-making activity in the criminal justice arena. Rights advocates continue to carry on the fight for an expansion of civil and criminal rights, seeing both as necessary to an equi-

Six-year-old JonBenet Ramsey, the young "beauty queen" strangled at Christmastime 1996 in her family's Boulder, Colorado, home. JonBenet's killing, and the ensuing investigation, captured the nation's attention for years. *Dave Sartin, Gamma—Liaison, Inc.*

table and just social order. The treatment of the accused, they argue, mirrors basic cultural values. The purpose of any civilized society, they claim, should be to secure rights and freedoms for each of its citizens—including the criminally accused. Rights advocates fear unnecessarily restrictive government action and view it as an assault upon basic human dignity and individual liberty. In defense of their principles, criminal rights activists tend to recognize that it is sometimes necessary to sacrifice some degree of public safety and predictability in order to guarantee basic freedoms. Hence, rights advocates are content with a justice system which limits police powers and which holds justice agencies accountable to the highest evidentiary standards. An example of the kind of criminal justice outcome feared by individual rights advocates is the case of James Richardson, who served 21 years in a Florida prison for a crime he did not commit.[13] Following perjured testimony, Richardson was convicted in 1968 of the poisoning deaths of his seven children. He was released in 1989 after a babysitter confessed to poisoning the children's last meal because of personal jealousies. The criminal rights perspective holds that it is necessary to allow some guilty people to go free in order to reduce the likelihood of convicting the innocent.

In the present conservative environment, however, calls for system accountability are often tempered with new demands to unfetter the criminal justice system in order to make arrests easier and punishments swift and harsh. Advocates of law and order, wanting ever-greater police powers, have mounted an effective drive to abandon some of the gains made in support of the rights of criminal defendants during the civil rights era. Citing high rates of recidivism, uncertain punishments, and an inefficient courtroom maze, they claim that the criminal justice system has coddled offenders and encouraged continued law violation. Society, they say, if it is to survive, can no longer afford to accord too many rights to the individual or place the interests of any one person over that of the group.

As we enter the twenty-first century, the trick, it seems, is to balance individual rights and personal freedoms with social responsibility and respect for authority. At a recent conference sponsored by *The New York Post*, New York City Mayor Rudolph W. Giuliani identified the tension between personal freedoms and individual responsibilities as the crux of the crime problem facing his city and America today. We mistakenly look to government and elected

To participate in the very active criminal justice discussion list on the Internet, send e-mail to listserv@cunyvm.cuny.edu and type "subscribe CJUST-L your name" in the message box. Leave the subject field empty. Expect between 20 and 100 messages a day from other list members. Listserve commands are described at: http://www.lsoft.com/manuals/userindex.html.

Individual Rights Versus Group Interests —Megan's Law

In mid-1997 California authorities released to the public a CD-ROM containing detailed information on 64,000 sex offenders residing in the state. The information on the disc was mandated by a new California law requiring the publication of information on freed sex offenders. California's action reflected the conservative change sweeping through American criminal justice. Like many other states, California had recently enacted a form of "Megan's law"—a statute requiring community notification of released sex offenders. The first Megan's law was passed by the New Jersey state legislature on October 31, 1994. It was named after seven-year-old Maureen "Megan" Kanka, who was attacked, sodomized, and brutally killed by Jesse K. Timmendequas, a 33-year-old parolee living across the street from her home. Unknown to Megan or her parents, Timmendequas had been convicted twice before on charges of sexually molesting a child.

At the time the law was passed, New Jersey and 44 other states required released sex offenders to register with authorities. In passing Megan's law, however, New Jersey joined 12 states whose laws provided for some form of public notification when sex offenders were about to be released from confinement—a requirement that goes beyond mere "registration." Under New Jersey's Megan's law, the information to be released to the public includes the offender's name, a recent photograph, a physical description, a list of the offenses for which he or she was convicted, current address, place of employment or school, and the offender's automobile license plate number. As this book goes to press, Pennsylvania and a number of other jurisdictions are in the process of enacting their own versions of such laws, supported, in part, by a federal initiative advocating notification legislation. On May 17, 1996, President Clinton signed a federal "Megan's law," which was enthusiastically endorsed by Congress in a 418–0

vote. The federal version of Megan's law strengthens requirements of the Violent Crime Control and Law Enforcement Act of 1994 by requiring states not only to notify local law enforcement officials when a convicted sex offender moves into a neighborhood, but also to make that information available to the community.

One of the first court tests of New Jersey's law came on February 28, 1995, when U.S. District Judge Nicholas H. Politan ruled that the community notification provision of Megan's law was unconstitutional. A notification requirement, ruled Judge Politan, amounted to a second form of punishment—one to which the offender had not been sentenced. The judge, however, upheld New Jersey's requirement that sex offenders must register with local authorities in areas where they reside.

According to the American Civil Liberties Union, notification rules similar to New Jersey's have been thrown out by state judges in Alaska, Arizona, California, Illinois, Louisiana, and New Hampshire. Recently, however, the Supreme Court of the state of Washington upheld a statute almost identical to Megan's law, ruling that it was a regulatory measure and not a cloaked punitive device.

The New Jersey ruling against Megan's law provisions came in the case of 49-year-old Alexander A. Artway, who was convicted in 1965 of statutory rape and in 1971 of sodomizing a 21-year-old woman. The state had been supported by the U.S. Justice Department in arguing the legitimacy of the law. U.S. Attorney General Janet Reno depicted the issues involved in the case as follows: "I think we have got to balance the interests (of the public and released prisoners), and we have received studies...that there is at least a 40 percent recidivism rate among child sex offenders." "We understand," Reno said, "the necessity for striking that balance and making sure the public is protected."

Judge Politan's action led to a war of words between advocates on both sides of the issue. The judge enraged Megan's law supporters when he asked whether requiring public notification upon the release of sex offenders was similar to the Nazi practice of making Jews wear a Star of David during World War II. Supporters countered that while innocent people were forced to wear the yellow star, Artway's right to privacy ended when he committed his crimes.

Reaction from Artway himself was quick in coming. "My reaction is 'Yahoo,'" Artway said outside the courtroom building. "I jump in the air and click my heels. I can now move to another area if that becomes necessary for my protection." Artway seemed to be referring, at least in part, to the fact that a New Jersey man who had been mistaken for a released sex offender had previously suffered a beating at the hands of two men. The New Jersey Supreme Court later upheld the law, as did the U.S. Supreme Court in 1998.

In the midst of the battle over the legality of the Megan's law community notification requirements, Jesse Timmendequas was taken to trial and found guilty of murdering little Megan Kanka. The New Jersey jury that heard the case recommended death, and on June 20, 1997, Judge Andrew Smithson of state Superior Court formally sentenced Timmendequas to die. As the death sentence was read, Megan's mother buried her face in her husband's shoulder and cried. "Megan was worth a life," she told reporters. "This man will never, ever, ever get out and hurt another child."

QUESTIONS FOR DISCUSSION

1. The national debate over whether the public should be notified of the whereabouts of sex offenders after they are released from prison sets the fears of everyday citizens against the privacy and civil liberties

concerns of ex-convicts. What rights should an offender have in such cases? What rights should the community have?

2. Whose rights should be most closely guarded if a clash of interests arises? Why?

Sources: Paula Story, "California Releases CD-ROM on Criminals," The Associated Press wire services, July 1, 1997; "Jury Orders Death for Megan Kanka's Killer," Associated Press wire services, June 20, 1997; Michael Kirkland and Rick Hampson, "What's Wrong with Megan's Law," *USA Today*, May 14, 1997, p. 1A; "U.S. Defends N.J. Sex Offender Law," United Press International wire services, northeastern edition, February 9, 1995; Henry Stern, "Megan's Law," Associated Press wire services, northern edition, February 16, 1995; and Jeffrey Gold, "Megan's Law," The Associated Press wire services, March 1, 1995.

officials, Giuliani said, to assume responsibility for solving the problem of crime when, instead, it is each individual citizen who must become accountable for fixing what is wrong with our society. In the mayor's words, "We only see the oppressive side of authority…What we don't see is that freedom is not a concept in which people can do anything they want, be anything they can be. Freedom is about authority. Freedom is about the willingness of every single human being to cede to lawful authority a great deal of discretion about what you do."

This text has two basic purposes: (1) to describe in detail the criminal justice system, while (2) helping students develop an appreciation for the delicacy of the balancing act now facing it. The question for the future will be how to ensure the existence of, and effectively manage, a justice system which is as fair to the individual as it is supportive of the needs of society. Is "justice for all" a reasonable expectation of today's system of criminal justice? As the book will show, this question is complicated by the fact that individual interests and social needs frequently diverge, while at other times they parallel one another.

Social Justice

The well-known British philosopher and statesman Benjamin Disraeli (1804–1881) once defined **justice** as "truth in action." One popular dictionary definition of *justice* says that it is "the principle of moral rightness, or conformity to truth."[14]

Of special concern to anyone seeking to enact justice are **criminal justice** and **civil justice**—both of which are aspects of a wider form of equity termed **social justice**. Social justice is a concept that embraces all aspects of civilized life. It is linked to notions of fairness and to cultural beliefs about right and wrong. Questions of social justice can arise about relationships between individuals and between parties (such as corporations and agencies of government), between the rich and the poor, between the sexes, between ethnic groups and minorities, and about social linkages of all sorts. In the abstract, the concept of social justice embodies the highest personal and cultural ideals.

Civil justice, the first subcomponent of social justice, concerns itself with fairness in relationships between citizens, government agencies, and businesses in private matters—such as those involving contractual obligations, business dealings, hiring, equality of treatment, and so on. Criminal justice, in its broadest sense, refers to those aspects of social justice which concern violations of the criminal law. As mentioned earlier, community interests in the criminal justice sphere demand the apprehension and punishment of law violators. At the same time, criminal justice ideals extend to the protection of the innocent, the fair treatment of offenders, and fair play by the agencies of law enforcement, including courts and correctional institutions. Criminal justice, ideally speaking, is "truth in action" within the process that we call "the administration of justice." It is, therefore, vital to remember that *justice*, in the truest and most satisfying sense of the word, is the ultimate goal of criminal justice—and of the day-to-day practices and challenges which characterize the American criminal justice system.

Reality, unfortunately, typically falls short of the ideal and is severely complicated by the fact that justice seems to wear different guises when viewed from diverse social vantage points. To many people the criminal justice system and criminal justice agencies often seem biased in favor of the powerful. The laws they enforce seem to emanate more from well-financed, organized, and vocal interest groups than they do from any idealized sense of social

Justice The principle of fairness; the ideal of moral equity.

Criminal Justice The criminal law, the law of criminal procedure, and that array of procedures and activities having to do with the enforcement of the criminal law. Criminal justice cannot be separated from social justice because the kind of justice enacted in our nation's criminal courts is a reflection of basic American understandings of right and wrong.

Civil Justice The civil law, the law of civil procedure, and that array of procedures and activities having to do with private rights and remedies sought by civil action. Civil justice cannot be separated from social justice because the kind of justice enacted in our nation's civil courts is a reflection of basic American understandings of right and wrong.

Social Justice An ideal which embraces all aspects of civilized life and which is linked to fundamental notions of fairness and to cultural beliefs about right and wrong.

Violence has become a way of life in some parts of America. Here, a Chicago day care center class practices ducking—a skill these children will need if a gunfight breaks out on nearby streets. *Steve Leonard, Black Star*

I hope somewhere down the road I will be forgotten. . .that I will just be able to live the life I had before jail, a quiet life unknown to the world, and I'll be satisfied with that.

—Long Island shooter Colin Ferguson's comment before sentencing

justice. As a consequence, disenfranchised groups, those who do not feel as though they share in the political and economic power of society, are often wary of the agencies of justice, seeing them more as enemies than as benefactors.

On the other hand, justice practitioners, including police officers, prosecutors, judges, and correctional officials, frequently complain of unfair criticism of their efforts to uphold the law. The "realities" of law enforcement, they say, and of justice itself, are often overlooked by critics of the system who have little experience in dealing with offenders and victims. We must recognize, practitioners often tell us, that those accused of violating the criminal law face an elaborate process built around numerous legislative, administrative, and organizational concerns. Viewed realistically, the criminal justice process, while it can be fine-tuned in order to take into consideration the interests of ever wider numbers of people, rarely pleases everyone. The outcome of the criminal justice process in any particular case is a social product and, like any product which is the result of group effort, it must inevitably be a patchwork quilt of human emotions, reasoning, and concerns.

Whichever side we choose in the ongoing debate over the nature and quality of criminal justice,[15] it is vital that we recognize the plethora of pragmatic issues involved in the administration of justice, while also keeping a clear focus on the justice ideal. Was justice done, for example, in the criminal trial of O.J. Simpson or in the trials of the Los Angeles police officers who beat Rodney King? While answers to such questions may reveal a great deal about the American criminal justice system, they also have much to say about the perspective of those who provide them.

The Criminal Justice System The aggregate of all operating and administrative or technical support agencies that perform criminal justice functions. The basic divisions of the operational aspects of criminal justice are law enforcement, courts, and corrections.

American Criminal Justice: The System

THE CONSENSUS MODEL

So far we have described the agencies of law enforcement, the courts, and corrections as a **system of criminal justice**.[16] Those who speak of a system of criminal justice usually define it as consisting of the agencies of police, courts, and corrections. Each of these agencies can, in turn, be described in terms of their subsystems. Corrections, for example, includes jails,

Twenty-First Century Criminal Justice

THE NATIONAL COMMISSION ON CRIME CONTROL AND PREVENTION

Title XXVI of the Violent Crime Control and Law Enforcement Act of 1994 mandated establishment of a 28-member National Commission on Crime Control and Prevention. The commission, which is bipartisan and includes congressional as well as presidential appointees, is composed of law enforcement professionals, judges, mayors, prosecutors, professors, and former state attorneys general. Selected to chair the commission is Lee Fisher, a former Ohio state legislator and state Attorney General with a long antigun track record. Fisher is a member of the Board of Directors of the Center to Prevent Handgun Violence. The Commission is expected to release its final report in late 1999. Like the findings of its predecessors, the 1967 President's Commission on Law Enforcement and Administration of Justice and the 1973 National Advisory Commission on Criminal Justice Standards and Goals, the report of the National Commission is expected to substantially impact criminal justice activities and crime control initiatives during the first few decades of the twenty-first century. Among the Commission's mandates are:

1. To develop a comprehensive proposal for preventing and controlling crime and violence in the United States.
2. To bring attention to successful models and programs in crime prevention and crime control.
3. To reach out beyond the traditional criminal justice community for ideas for controlling and preventing crime.
4. To recommend improvements in the coordination of local, state, federal, and international crime control and prevention efforts, including efforts relating to crime near international borders.
5. To make a comprehensive study of the economic and social factors leading to or contributing to crime and violence, including the causes of illicit drug use and other substance abuse, and to develop specific proposals for legislative and administrative actions to reduce crime and violence and the factors that contribute to it.
6. To recommend means of utilizing criminal justice resources as effectively as possible, including targeting finite correctional facility space to the most serious and violent offenders, and considering increased use of intermediate sanctions for offenders who can be dealt with adequately by such means.
7. To examine distinctive crime problems and the impact of crime on members of minority groups, Native-Americans living on reservations, and other groups defined by race, ethnicity, religion, age, disability, or other characteristics, and to recommend specific responses to the distinctive crime problems of such groups.
8. To examine the problem of sexual assaults, domestic violence, and other criminal and unlawful acts that particularly affect women, and to recommend federal, state, and local strategies for more effectively preventing and punishing such crimes and acts.
9. To examine the treatment of victims in federal, state, and local criminal justice systems, and to develop recommendations to enhance and protect the rights of victims.
10. To examine the ability of federal, state, and local criminal justice systems to administer criminal law and criminal sanctions impartially without discrimination on the basis of race, ethnicity, religion, gender, or other legally proscribed grounds, and to make recommendations for correcting any deficiencies in the impartial administration of justice on these grounds.
11. To examine the nature, scope, causes, and complexities of violence in schools, and to recommend a comprehensive response to that problem.

prisons, community-based treatment programs such as "halfway houses," and programs for probation and parole. Each subarea contains still more components. Prisons, for example, can be described in terms of custody levels, inmate programs, health care, security procedures, and so on. Some prisons operate as "boot camp" facilities, designed to "shock" offenders into quick rehabilitation, while others are long-term confinement facilities designed for the most hard-core criminals who are likely to return to crime quickly if released. Students of corrections also study the process of sentencing, through which an offender's fate is

Consensus Model   A perspective on the study of criminal justice which assumes that the system's subcomponents work together harmoniously to achieve that social product we call justice.

African-American men comprise less than 6% of the U.S. population and almost one half of its criminal prisoners.

—Bureau of Justice Statistics

Conflict Model   A perspective on the study of criminal justice which assumes that the system's subcomponents function primarily to serve their own interests. According to this theoretical framework, justice is more a product of conflicts among agencies within the system than it is the result of cooperation among component agencies.

Criminal justice cannot be achieved in the absence of social justice...

—*Struggle for Justice*, American Friends' Service Committee

decided by the justice system, and examine the role of jails in holding prisoners prior to conviction and sentencing.

The systems model of criminal justice is characterized primarily by its assumption that the various parts of the justice system work together by design in order to achieve the wider purpose we have been calling *justice*. Hence, the systems perspective on criminal justice generally encompasses a larger point of view called the **consensus model**. The consensus model assumes that all the component parts of the criminal justice system strive toward a common goal and that the movement of cases and people through the system is smooth due to cooperation between the various components of the system.

The systems model of criminal justice, however, is more an analytical tool than it is a reality. Any analytical model, be it in the so-called "hard" sciences or in the social sciences, is simply a convention chosen for its explanatory power. By explaining the actions of criminal justice officials (such as arrest, prosecution, sentencing, etc.) as though they are systematically related, we are able to envision a fairly smooth and predictable process (which is described in more detail later in this chapter). The advantage we gain from this convention is a reduction in complexity, which allows us to describe the totality of criminal justice at a conceptually manageable level.

The systems model has been criticized for implying a greater level of organization and cooperation among the various agencies of justice than actually exists. The word *system* calls to mind a near-perfect form of social organization. The modern mind associates the idea of a system with machinelike precision in which wasted effort, redundancy, and conflicting actions are quickly abandoned and their causes repaired. The justice system has nowhere near this level of perfection and the systems model is admittedly an oversimplification which is primarily useful for analytical purposes. Conflicts among and within agencies are rife; immediate goals are often not shared by individual actors in the system; and the system may move in different directions depending upon political currents, informal arrangements, and personal discretionary decisions.

The Conflict Model

The **conflict model** provides another approach to the study of American criminal justice. The conflict model says that criminal justice agency interests tend to make actors within the system self-serving. Pressures for success, promotion, pay increases, and general accountability, according to this model, fragment the efforts of the system as a whole, leading to a criminal justice *non*system.[17]

Jerome Skolnick's classic study of clearance rates provides support for the idea of a criminal justice nonsystem.[18] Clearance rates are a measure of crimes solved by the police. The more crimes the police can show they have solved, the happier is the public they serve.

Skolnick discovered an instance in which an individual burglar was caught "red-handed" during the commission of a burglary. After his arrest, the police suggested that he should confess to many unsolved burglaries which they knew he had not committed. In effect they said, "Help us out, and we will try to help you out!" The burglar did confess—to over 400 other burglaries. Following the confession, the police were satisfied because they could say they had "solved" many burglaries, and the suspect was pleased as well because the police had agreed to speak on his behalf before the judge.

Both models have something to tell us. Agencies of justice with a diversity of functions (police, courts, and corrections) and at all levels (federal, state, and local) are linked closely enough for the term "system" to be meaningfully applied to them. On the other hand, the very size of the criminal justice undertaking makes effective cooperation between component agencies difficult. The police, for example, may have an interest in seeing offenders put behind bars. Prison officials, on the other hand, may be working with extremely overcrowded facilities. They may desire to see early release programs for certain categories of offenders, such as those who are judged to be nonviolent. Who wins out in the long run could be just a matter of internal politics. Everyone should be concerned, however, when the goal of justice is impacted, and sometimes even sacrificed, because of conflicts within the system.

Is the Criminal Justice System Racist?

A few years ago, Professor Lani Guinier of the University of Pennsylvania School of Law was interviewed on *Think Tank*, a public television show. Guinier was asked by Ben Wattenberg, the program's moderator, "When we talk about crime, crime, crime, are we really using a code for black, black, black?" Guinier responded this way: "To a great extent, yes, and I think that's a problem, not because we shouldn't deal with the disproportionate number of crimes that young black men may be committing, but because if we can't talk about race, then when we talk about crime, we're really talking about other things, and it means that we're not being honest in terms of acknowledging what the problem is and then trying to deal with it...."[1]

Crimes, of course, are committed by individuals of all races. The link between crime—especially violent, street, and predatory crimes—and race, however, shows a pattern that is striking in terms of its ethnic dimensions. In most crime categories, arrests of black offenders equal or exceed arrests of whites. In any given year arrests of black persons account for more than 50% of all arrests for violent crimes. Blacks, however, comprise only 12% of the U.S. population, and when *rates* (which are based upon the relative proportion of racial groups) are examined, the statistics are even more striking. The murder *rate* among blacks, for example, is ten times that of whites. Similar rate comparisons, when calculated for other violent crimes, show that far more blacks than whites are involved in other street crimes, such as assault, burglary, and robbery. Related studies show that 30% of all the young black men in America are under correctional supervision on any given *day*—far more than members of any other race in the country.

The real question for anyone interested in the justice system is how to explain such huge racial disparities. Some authors maintain that racial differences in arrest and in rates of imprisonment are due to the differential treatment of blacks at the hands of a discriminatory criminal justice system. Marvin D. Free, Jr.,[2] for example, says that the fact that blacks are *underrepresented* as criminal justice professionals results in their being *overrepresented* in arrest and confinement statistics. Some police officers, says Free, may be more prone to arrest blacks than whites, may frequently arrest blacks without sufficient evidence to support criminal charges, and may overcharge in criminal cases involving black defendants—leading to unfair and misleading statistical tabulations which depict blacks as responsible for a greater proportion of crime than is, in fact, the case.

Other writers disagree. In *The Myth of a Racist Criminal Justice System*,[3] for example, William Wilbanks claims that while the practice of American criminal justice may have been significantly racist in the past, and while some vestiges of racism may indeed remain, the system is today by-and-large objective in its processing of criminal defendants. Using statistical data, Wilbanks shows that "[a]t every point from arrest to parole there is little or no evidence of an overall racial effect, in that the percentage outcomes for blacks and whites are not very different."[4] Wilbanks claims to have reviewed "all the available studies that have examined the possible existence of racial discrimination from arrest to parole." In essence, he says, "this examination of the available evidence indicates that support for the 'discrimination thesis' is sparse, inconsistent, and frequently contradictory."

Wilbanks is careful to counter arguments advanced by those who continue to suggest the system is racist. He writes, for example, "...perhaps the black/white gap at arrest is a product of racial bias by the police in that the police are more likely to select and arrest black than white offenders. The best evidence on this question comes from the National Crime Survey which interviews 130,000 Americans each year about crime victimization.... The percent of offenders described by victims as being black is generally consistent with the percent of offenders who are black according to arrest figures."

A fundamental critique of Wilbanks' thesis comes from Coramae Richey Mann,[5] who says that his overreliance on quantitative or statistical data fails to capture the reality of racial discrimination within the justice system. White victims, says Mann, tend to overreport being victimized by black offenders because they often misperceive Hispanic and other minority offenders as black. Similarly, says Mann, black victims are sometimes reluctant to report victimization—especially at the hands of whites. Moreover, says Mann, statistics on specific crimes, such as rape, may include false accusations by white women in order to hide their involvement with black lovers. And finally, says Mann, a greater integration of black neighborhoods (in the sense that whites are less reluctant to enter black neighborhoods than blacks are to enter white neighborhoods) may result in a disproportionate but misleading number of reports by white victims.

Mann's arguments are discounted by those who point out that the statistics appear to be overwhelming. *If* they are accurate, then another question emerges: Why do blacks commit more crimes? Wilbanks says, "The assertion that the criminal justice system is not racist does not address the reasons why blacks appear to offend at higher rates than whites before coming into contact with the criminal justice system....It may be," he suggests, "that racial discrimination in American society has been responsible for conditions (for example, discrimination in employment, housing, and education) that lead to higher rates of offending by blacks."

Marvin Free, Jr., suggests that blacks are still systematically denied equal access to societal resources which would allow for full participation in American society—resulting in a higher rate of law violation. In a recent work that considers such issues in great detail, John Hagan and Ruth D. Peterson acknowledge the reality of higher crime rates among ethnic minorities, and attribute them to (1) concentrated poverty, (2) joblessness, (3) family disruption, and (4) racial segregation.[6]

The question of *actual* fairness (of the justice system) can be quite different from one of *perceived* fairness. As University of Maryland Professor Katheryn K. Russell[7] points out, "Study after study has shown that blacks and whites hold contrary views on the fairness of the criminal justice system's operation; blacks tend to be more cautious in their praise and frequently view the system as unfair and racially biased; by contrast whites have a favorable impression of the justice system....The point is not that whites are completely satisfied with the justice system, but rather that, relative to blacks, they have faith in the system." One reason for such differences may be that blacks are more likely to be victims of police harassment and brutality or may know someone who has been. Even if blacks do engage in more criminal activity than whites, says one author,[8] higher rates of offending may be due, at least in part, to their perception that members of their group have historically been treated unfairly by agents of social control—resulting in anger and defiance which express themselves in criminal activity. From this vantage point, crime—at least crimes committed by minority group members—becomes a kind of protest against a system which is perceived as fundamentally unfair.

According to Russell, inequities in the existing system may propel blacks into crime and combine with stereotypical images in the popular media to perpetuate what she calls a *criminalblackman* myth. The *criminalblackman* myth, says Russell, is a stereotypical portrayal of black men as *inherently* more sinister, evil, and dangerous than their white counterparts. The myth of the *criminalblackman*, adds Russell, is self-perpetuating—resulting in continued frustration, more crime, and growing alienation among black Americans.

QUESTIONS FOR DISCUSSION

1. What does Guinier mean when she says that if we can't talk about race, then we can't talk about crime? Is there a reluctance in our society to deal squarely with issues of race and crime? If so, why?

2. Do you think that the American criminal justice system is discriminatory? Why or why not?

3. If you think the justice system is discriminatory, what would you do to change it?

4. What is the *criminalblackman* myth? Do you think that such a myth exists in American culture? What basis, if any, does it have in reality?

[1]"For the Record," *Washington Post* wire services, March 3, 1994.

[2]Marvin D. Free, Jr., *African-Americans and the Criminal Justice System* (New York: Garland, 1996).

[3]William Wilbanks, *The Myth of a Racist Criminal Justice System* (Monterey, CA: Brooks/Cole, 1987).

[4]William Wilbanks, "The Myth of a Racist Criminal Justice System," *Criminal Justice Research Bulletin*, Vol. 3, no. 5 (Huntsville, TX: Sam Houston State University, 1987), p. 2.

[5]Coramae Richey Mann, "The Reality of a Racist Criminal Justice System," in Barry W. Hancock and Paul M. Sharp, *Criminal Justice in America: Theory, Practice, and Policy* (Upper Saddle River, NJ: Prentice Hall, 1996), pp. 51–59.

[6]John Hagan and Ruth D. Peterson, *Crime and Inequality* (Stanford, CA: Stanford University Press, 1995).

[7]Katheryn K. Russell, "The Racial Hoax as Crime: The Law as Affirmation," *Indiana Law Journal*, Vol. 71 (1996), pp. 593–621.

[8]Thomas J. Bernard, "Angry Aggression Among the 'Truly Disadvantaged,'" *Criminology*, Vol. 28, no. 1 (1990), pp. 73–96.

Source: "30% of Young Black Men Are in Corrections System, Study Finds," *Criminal Justice Newsletter*, Vol. 26, no. 19 (October 2, 1995), p. 1.

American Criminal Justice: The Process

Structurally, as we have discussed, the criminal justice system can be described in terms of its component agencies: police, courts, and corrections. Functionally, the components of the "system" may work together well or they may be in conflict. Whether system or nonsystem, however, the agencies of criminal justice must process cases which come before them. An analysis of case processing within the system provides both a useful guide to this book and a "road map" to the criminal justice system itself. Beginning with the investigation of reported crimes, Figure 1–2 illustrates the processing of a criminal case through the federal justice system.

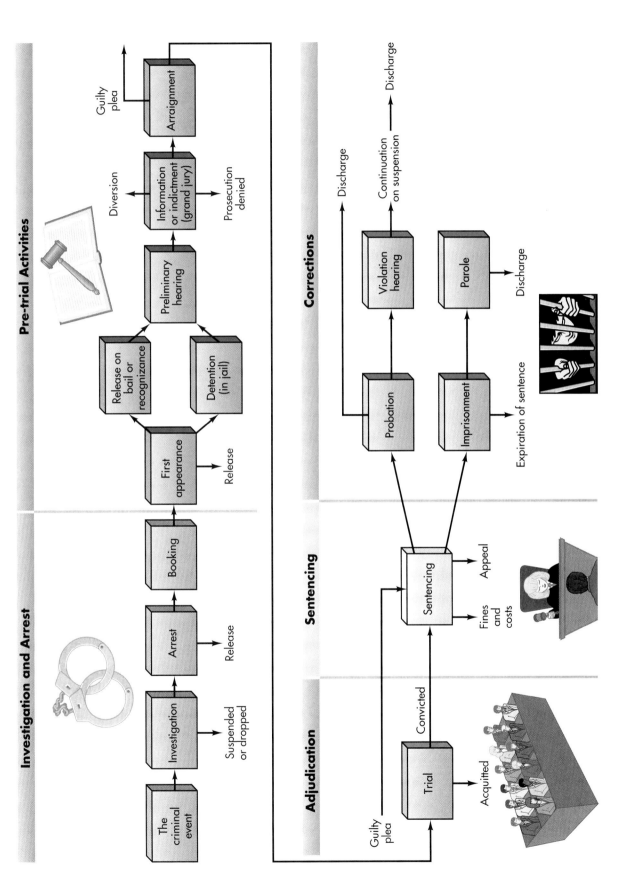

Figure 1–2 Criminal case processing. *Source:* Adapted from U.S. Department of Justice, *Compendium of Federal Justice Statistics 1989* (Washington, D.C.: Bureau of Justice Statistics, 1992), p. 3.

INVESTIGATION AND ARREST

The modern justice process begins with investigation. When a crime has been committed, it is often discovered and reported to the police. On occasion, a police officer on routine patrol discovers the crime while it is still in progress. Evidence will be gathered on the scene when possible, and a follow-up investigation will attempt to reconstruct the likely sequence of activities. A few offenders are arrested at the scene of the crime, while some are apprehended only after an extensive investigation. In such cases, arrest **warrants** issued by magistrates or other judges provide the legal basis for an apprehension by police.

An arrest involves taking a person into custody and limits their freedom. Arrest is a serious step in the process of justice and involves a discretionary decision made by the police seeking to bring criminal sanctions to bear. Most arrests are made peacefully, but some involve force when the suspect tries to resist. Only about 50% of all persons arrested are eventually convicted, and of those, only about 25% are sentenced to a year or more in prison.

During arrest and prior to questioning, defendants are usually advised of their constitutional rights as enumerated in the famous Supreme Court decision of *Miranda* v. *Arizona*.[19] Defendants are told:

(1) "You have the right to remain silent." (2) "Anything you say can and will be used against you in court." (3) "You have the right to talk to a lawyer for advice before we ask you any questions, and to have him with you during questioning." (4) "If you cannot afford a lawyer, one will be appointed for you before any questioning if you wish." (5) "If you decide to answer questions now without a lawyer present, you will still have the right to stop answering at any time. You also have the right to stop answering at any time and may talk with a lawyer before deciding to speak again." (6) "Do you wish to talk or not?" and (7) "Do you want a lawyer?"[20]

It is important to realize that although popular television programs almost always show a rights advisement at the time of arrest, the *Miranda* decision only requires police personnel to advise a person of his or her rights prior to questioning. An arrest without questioning can occur in the absence of any warning. When an officer interrupts a crime in progress, public safety considerations may make it reasonable for the officer to ask a few questions prior to a rights advisement. Many officers, however, feel on sound legal ground only by immediately following an arrest with an advisement of rights. Investigation and arrest are discussed in detail in Chapter 7, "Policing: Legal Aspects."

BOOKING

During the arrest process suspects are booked—pictures are taken, fingerprints are made, and personal information, such as address, date of birth, weight, and height, are gathered. Details of the charges are recorded, and an administrative record of the arrest is created.

During booking, suspects are again advised of their rights and are asked to sign a form on which each right is written. The written form generally contains a statement acknowledging the rights advisement and attesting to the fact that the suspect understands them.

FIRST APPEARANCE

Within hours of arrest suspects must be brought before a magistrate, (a judicial officer), for a first or initial appearance. The judge will tell them of the charges against them, will again advise them of their rights, and may sometimes provide the opportunity for **bail**.

Most defendants are released on recognizance (into their own care or the care of another) or given the chance to post bond during their first appearance. A bond may take the form of a cash deposit or a property bond in which a house or other property can serve as collateral against flight. Those who flee may be ordered to forfeit the posted cash or property. Suspects who either are not afforded the opportunity for bail because their crimes are very serious or who do not have the needed financial resources are taken to jail to await the next stage in the justice process.

If a defendant doesn't have a lawyer, one will be appointed at the first appearance. The defendant may actually have to demonstrate financial hardship or be ordered to pay for counsel. The names of assigned lawyers are usually drawn off the roster of practicing defense attorneys in the county. Some jurisdictions utilize public defenders to represent indigent defendants. All aspects of the first appearance, including bail bonds and appointed counsel, are discussed in detail in Chapter 8, "The Courts."

Warrant   Any of a number of writs issued by a judicial officer, which direct a law enforcement officer to perform a specified act and affords protection from damages if he or she performs it.

Booking   A law enforcement or correctional administrative process officially recording an entry into detention after arrest and identifying the person, the place, time, and reason for the arrest, and the arresting authority.

Bail   The money or property pledged to the court or actually deposited with the court to effect the release of a person from legal custody.

Darrel Frank, the founder of Dead Serious, Incorporated, shown with the organization's official vehicle. Reflecting the "get tough" on crime and criminals attitude now so prevalent in American society, Dead Serious offers a $5,000 reward to members who legally kill a criminal. *Fort Worth Star-Telegram*

Preliminary Hearing

The primary purpose of a **preliminary hearing**, also sometimes called a preliminary examination, is to establish whether or not sufficient evidence exists against a person to continue the justice process. At the preliminary hearing the hearing judge will seek to determine whether there is **probable cause** to believe that (1) a crime has been committed and (2) the defendant committed it. The decision is a judicial one, but the process provides the prosecutor with an opportunity to test the strength of evidence at his or her disposal.

The preliminary hearing also allows defense counsel the chance to assess the strength of the prosecution's case. As the prosecution presents evidence, the defense is said to "discover" what it is. Hence, the preliminary hearing serves a *discovery* function for the defense. If the defense attorney thinks the evidence is strong, he or she may suggest that a plea bargain be arranged. Indigent defendants have a right to be represented by counsel at the preliminary hearing.

Information Or Indictment

In some states the prosecutor may seek to continue the case against a defendant by filing an "information" with the court. An information is filed on the basis of the outcome of the preliminary hearing.

Other states require an **indictment** be returned by a **grand jury** before prosecution can proceed. The grand jury hears evidence from the prosecutor and decides whether a case should go to trial. In effect, the grand jury is the formal indicting authority. It determines whether or not probable cause exists to charge a defendant formally with a crime. Grand juries can return an indictment on less than a unanimous vote.

The grand jury system has been criticized because it is one-sided. The defense has no opportunity to present evidence; the grand jury is led only by the prosecutor, often through an appeal to emotions or in ways which will not be permitted in a trial.

At the same time, the grand jury is less bound by specific rules than a jury in a trial. For example, one member of a grand jury told the author that a rape case had been dismissed because the man had taken the woman to dinner first. Personal ignorance and subcultural biases are far more likely to be decisive in grand jury hearings than in criminal trials.

Preliminary Hearing The proceeding before a judicial officer in which three matters must be decided: whether a crime was committed, whether the crime occurred within the territorial jurisdiction of the court, and whether there are reasonable grounds to believe that the defendant committed the crime.

Probable Cause A legal criterion residing in a set of facts and circumstances which would cause a reasonable person to believe that a particular other person has committed a specific crime. Probable cause refers to the necessary level of belief which would allow for police seizures (arrests) of individuals and searches of dwellings, vehicles, and possessions.

Indictment A formal, written accusation submitted to the court by a grand jury, alleging that a specified person(s) has committed a specified offense(s), usually a felony.

Grand Jury A body of persons who have been selected according to law and sworn to hear the evidence against accused persons and to determine whether there is sufficient evidence to bring those persons to trial, to investigate criminal activity generally, and to investigate the conduct of public agencies and officials.

In defense of the grand jury, however, we should recognize that defendants who are clearly innocent will likely not be indicted. A refusal to indict can save considerable time and money by diverting poorly prepared cases from further processing by the system.

ARRAIGNMENT

Arraignment (1) The hearing before a court having jurisdiction in a criminal case, in which the identity of the defendant is established, the defendant is informed of the charge(s) and of his or her rights, and the defendant is required to enter a plea. (2) In some usages, any appearance in court prior to trial in criminal proceedings.

The **arraignment** is "the first appearance of the defendant before the court that has the authority to conduct a trial."[21] At arraignment the accused stands before a judge and hears the information, or indictment, against him or her as it is read. Defendants will again be notified of their rights and will be asked to enter a plea. Acceptable pleas generally include (1) "Not guilty"; (2) "Guilty"; and (3) "No contest" (*nolo contendere*), which may result in conviction but which can't be used later as an admission of guilt in civil proceedings. Civil proceedings, while not covered in detail in this book, provide an additional avenue of relief for victims or their survivors. Convicted offenders increasingly find themselves facing suits brought against them by victims seeking to collect monetary damages.

Federal rules of criminal procedure specify that "arraignment shall be conducted in open court and shall consist of reading the indictment or information to the defendant or stating to him the substance of the charge and calling on him to plead thereto. He shall be given a copy of the indictment or information before he is called upon to plead."[22]

Guilty pleas are not always accepted by the judge. If the judge feels a guilty plea was made under duress or because of a lack of knowledge on the part of the defendant, the plea will be rejected and a plea of "not guilty" will be substituted for it. Sometimes defendants "stand mute"; that is, they refuse to speak or enter a plea of any kind. In that case, the judge will enter a plea of "not guilty" on their behalf. The arraignment process, including pretrial motions made by the defense, is discussed in detail in Chapter 8, "The Courts."

Trial

Trial The examination in a court of the issues of fact and law in a case for the purpose of reaching a judgment of conviction or acquittal of the defendant(s).

Every criminal defendant has a right under the Sixth Amendment to the U.S. Constitution to a trial by jury. The U.S. Supreme Court, however, has held that petty offenses are not covered by the Sixth Amendment guarantee and that the seriousness of a case is determined by the way in which "society regards the offense." For the most part, "offenses for which the maximum period of incarceration is six months or less are presumptively petty."[23] In *Blanton v. North Las Vegas* (1989),[24] the Court held that "a defendant can overcome this presumption and become entitled to a jury trial, only by showing that…additional penalties [such as fines and community service] viewed together with the maximum prison term, are so severe that the legislature clearly determined that the offense is a serious one." The *Blanton* decision was further reinforced in the case of *U.S. v. Nachtigal* (1993).[25]

In most jurisdictions, many criminal cases never come to trial. The majority are "pled out" (that is, dispensed of as the result of a bargained plea) or dismissed for a variety of reasons. Some studies have found that as many as 82% of all sentences are imposed in criminal cases because of guilty pleas rather than trials.[26]

In cases which do come to trial, the procedures which govern the submission of evidence are tightly controlled by procedural law and precedent. Procedural law specifies what type of evidence may be submitted, what the credentials of those allowed to represent the state or the defendant must be, and what a jury is allowed to hear.

Precedent refers to understandings built up through common usage and also to decisions rendered by courts in previous cases. Precedent in the courtroom, for example, requires that lawyers request permission from the judge before approaching a witness. It also can mean that excessively gruesome items of evidence may not be used or must be altered in some way so that their factual value is not lost in the strong emotional reactions they may create.

Some states allow trials for less serious offenses to occur before a judge if defendants waive their right to a trial by jury. This is called a bench trial. Other states require a jury trial for all serious criminal offenses.

Trials are expensive and time consuming. They pit defense attorneys against prosecutors. Regulated conflict is the rule, and juries are required to decide the facts and apply the law as it is explained to them by the judge. In some cases, however, a jury may be unable to decide. In such cases, it is said to be deadlocked, resulting in a mistrial being declared. The defendant may then be tried again when a new jury is empaneled. The criminal trial and its participants are described fully in Chapter 9.

The criminal justice process begins with investigation. But investigations must be conducted within the law. Shown here is Richard Jewell, the former campus security guard who became the primary suspect in the 1996 Olympic park bombing. When authorities dropped their investigation of Jewell, he sued CNN, the *Atlanta Journal-Constitution*, and other organizations for libel and character defamation—and threatened suit against the FBI. *John Kuntz, Archive Photos*

SENTENCING

Once a person is convicted it becomes the responsibility of the judge to impose some form of punishment. The sentence may take the form of supervised probation in the community, a fine, a prison term or some combination of these. Defendants will often be ordered to pay the costs of court or of their own defense if they are able.

Prior to sentencing, a sentencing hearing may be held in which lawyers on both sides present information concerning the defendant. The judge may also request that a presentence report be compiled by a probation or parole officer. The report will contain information on the defendant's family and business situation, emotional state, social background, and criminal history. It will be used to assist the judge in making an appropriate sentencing decision.

Judges traditionally have had considerable discretion in sentencing, although new state and federal laws now place limits on judicial discretion in some cases, requiring that a sentence "presumed" by law be imposed. Judges still retain enormous discretion, however, in specifying whether sentences on multiple charges are to run consecutively or concurrently. Offenders found guilty of more than one charge may be ordered to serve one sentence after another is completed (a **consecutive sentence**) or be told that their sentences will run at the same time (a **concurrent sentence**).

Many sentences are appealed. The appeals process can be complex, involving both state and federal judiciaries. It is based upon the defendant's claim that rules of procedure were not properly followed at some earlier stage in the justice process or that the defendant was denied the rights accorded him by the U.S. Constitution. Chapter 10, "Sentencing," outlines modern sentencing practices and describes the many modern alternatives to imprisonment.

CORRECTIONS

Once an offender has been sentenced, the stage of "corrections" begins. Some offenders are sentenced to prison where they "do time for their crimes." Once in the correctional system,

Consecutive Sentence   (1) A sentence that is one of two or more sentences imposed at the same time, after conviction for more than one offense, and that is served in sequence with the other sentences (2) or a new sentence for a new conviction, imposed upon a person already under sentence(s) for previous offense(s), which is added to a previous sentence(s), thus increasing the maximum time the offender may be confined or under supervision.

Concurrent Sentence   (1) A sentence that is one of two or more sentences imposed at the same time after conviction for more than one offense and to be served at the same time; or (2) a new sentence imposed upon a person already under sentence(s) for a previous offense(s) to be served at the same time as one or more of the previous sentences.

they are classified according to local procedures and assigned to confinement facilities and treatment programs. Newer prisons today bear little resemblance to the massive bastions of the past which isolated offenders from society behind huge stone walls. Many modern prisons, however, still suffer from a "lock psychosis" among top- and midlevel administrators as well as a lack of significant rehabilitation programs. Chapter 12, "Prisons and Jails," discusses the philosophy behind prisons and sketches their historical development. Chapter 13, "Prison Life," portrays life on the inside and delineates the social structures which develop as a response to the pains of imprisonment.

To receive electronic mailings of the *Journal of Criminal Justice and Popular Culture* send e-mail to listserv@uacs2.albany.edu and type "subscribe CJMOVIES your name" in the message box. Leave the subject field empty.

Probation And Parole

Not everyone who is convicted of a crime and sentenced ends up in prison. Some offenders are ordered to prison only to have their sentences suspended and a probationary term imposed. They may also be ordered to perform community service activities as a condition of their probation. During the term of probation these offenders are required to submit to supervision by a probation officer and to meet other conditions set by the court. Failure to do so results in revocation of probation and imposition of the original prison sentence. Other offenders, who have served a portion of their prison sentences, may be freed on parole. They will be supervised by a parole officer and assisted in their readjustment to society. As in the case of probation, failure to meet the conditions of parole may result in parole revocation and a return to prison. Chapter 10, "Sentencing," and Chapter 11, "Probation, Parole, and Community Corrections" deal with the practice of probation and parole and with the issues surrounding it.

Due Process and Individual Rights

Imposed upon criminal justice case processing is the constitutional requirement of fairness and equity. Guaranteed by the Fifth, Sixth, and Fourteenth Amendments to the U.S. Constitution, this requirement is referred to as **due process**. The due process clause of the U.S. Constitution is succinctly stated in the Fifth Amendment, which reads "No person shall be…deprived of life, liberty, or property, without due process of law." The constitutional requirement of due process mandates the recognition of individual rights in the processing of criminal defendants when they are faced with prosecution by the states or the federal government. The guarantee of due process is found not just in the Fifth Amendment, but underlies the first ten amendments to the U.S. Constitution, which are collectively known as the Bill of Rights. The Fourteenth Amendment is of special importance, however, for it makes due process binding upon the states—that is, it requires individual states in the union to respect the due process rights of U.S. citizens who come under their jurisdiction.

The fundamental guarantees of the Bill of Rights have been interpreted and clarified by courts (especially the U.S. Supreme Court) over time. The due process standard became reality following a number of far-reaching Supreme Court decisions affecting criminal procedure which were made during the 1960s. That period was the era of the Warren Court (1953–1969), led by Chief Justice Earl Warren, a Supreme Court which is remembered for its concern with protecting the innocent against the massive power of the state in criminal proceedings.[27] As a result of the tireless efforts of the Warren Court to institutionalize the Bill of Rights, the daily practice of modern American criminal justice is now set squarely upon the due process standard. Due process requires that agencies of justice recognize these rights in their enforcement of the law, and under the due process standard rights violations may become the basis for the dismissal of evidence or criminal charges, especially at the appellate level. Table 1–1 outlines the basic rights to which defendants in criminal proceedings are generally entitled.

Due Process A right guaranteed by the Fifth, Sixth, and Fourteenth Amendments of the U.S. Constitution and generally understood, in legal contexts, to mean the due course of legal proceedings according to the rules and forms which have been established for the protection of private rights. *Annotation:* Due process of law, in criminal proceedings, is generally understood to include the following basic elements: a law creating and defining the offense, an impartial tribunal having jurisdictional authority over the case, accusation in proper form, notice and opportunity to defend, trial according to established procedure, and discharge from all restraints or obligations unless convicted.

The Role of the Courts in Defining Rights

Although the Constitution deals with many issues, what we have been calling "rights" are open to interpretation. Many modern rights, although written into the Constitution, would not exist in practice were it not for the fact that the U.S. Supreme Court decided, at some point in history, to recognize them in cases brought before it. The well-known Supreme

Table 1–1 Individual Rights Guaranteed by the Bill Of Rights*

A Right to be Assumed Innocent Until Proven Guilty

A Right Against Unreasonable Searches of Person and Place of Residence

A Right Against Arrest Without Probable Cause

A Right Against Unreasonable Seizures of Personal Property

A Right Against Self-incrimination

A Right to Fair Questioning by the Police

A Right to Protection from Physical Harm Throughout the Justice Process

A Right to an Attorney

A Right to Trial by Jury

A Right to Know the Charges

A Right to Cross-examine Prosecution Witnesses

A Right to Speak and Present Witnesses

A Right Not to be Tried Twice for the Same Crime

A Right Against Cruel or Unusual Punishment

A Right to Due Process

A Right to a Speedy Trial

A Right Against Excessive Bail

A Right Against Excessive Fines

A Right to be Treated the Same as Others, Regardless of Race, Sex, Religious Preference, and Other Personal Attributes

*As interpreted by the U.S. Supreme Court

Court case of *Gideon* v. *Wainwright*[28](1963), for example (which is discussed in detail in Chapter 9), found the Court embracing the Sixth Amendment guarantee of a right to a lawyer for all criminal defendants and mandating that states provide lawyers for defendants who are unable to pay for them. Prior to *Gideon*, court-appointed attorneys for defendants unable to afford their own counsel were practically unknown, except in capital cases and in some federal courts. After the *Gideon* decision, court-appointed counsel became commonplace, and measures were instituted in jurisdictions across the nation to select attorneys fairly for indigent defendants. It is important to note, however, that while the Sixth Amendment specifically says, among other things, that "In all criminal prosecutions, the accused shall enjoy the right to…have the Assistance of Counsel for his defence," it does *not* say, *in so many words*, that the state is *required to provide* counsel. It is the U.S. Supreme Court which, interpreting the Constitution, has said that.

Unlike the high courts of many other nations, the U.S. Supreme Court is very powerful, and its decisions often have far-reaching consequences. The decisions rendered by the justices in cases like *Gideon* become, in effect, the law of the land. For all practical purposes such decisions often carry as much weight as legislative action. For this reason some writers speak of "judge-made law" (rather than legislated law) in describing judicial precedents which impact the process of justice.

Rights which have been recognized by Court decision are often subject to continual refinement. New interpretations may broaden or narrow the scope of applicability accorded to constitutional guarantees. Although the process of change is usually very slow, we should recognize that any right is subject to continual interpretation by the courts—and especially by the U.S. Supreme Court.

Crime Control Through Due Process

Two primary goals were identified at the start of this chapter: (1) the need to enforce the law and maintain social order and (2) the need to protect individuals from injustice. The first of

Crime Control Model A criminal justice perspective that emphasizes the efficient arrest and conviction of criminal offenders.

Due Process Model A criminal justice perspective that emphasizes individual rights at all stages of justice system processing.

these principles values the efficient arrest and conviction of criminal offenders. It is often referred to as the crime control model of justice. The crime control model was first brought to the attention of the academic community in Herbert Packer's cogent analysis of the state of criminal justice in the late 1960s.[29] For that reason it is sometimes referred to as Packer's **crime control model**.

The second principle is called the **due process model** because of its emphasis on individual rights. Due process is a central and necessary part of American criminal justice. It requires a careful and informed consideration of the facts of each individual case. Under the model, police are required to recognize the rights of suspects during arrest, questioning, and handling. Prosecutors and judges must recognize constitutional and other guarantees during trial and the presentation of evidence. Due process is intended to ensure that innocent people are not convicted of crimes.

Up until now we have suggested that the dual goals of crime control and due process are in constant and unavoidable opposition to one another. Some critics of American criminal justice have argued that the practice of justice is too often concerned with crime control at the expense of due process. Other conservative analysts of the American scene maintain that our type of justice coddles offenders and does too little to protect the innocent.

While it is impossible to avoid ideological conflicts such as these, it is also realistic to think of the American system of justice as representative of *crime control through due process*. It is this model of law enforcement infused with the recognition of individual rights which provides a workable conceptual framework for understanding the American system of criminal justice—both now and into the future.

Criminal Justice and Criminology

The study of criminal justice as an academic discipline began in this country in the 1920s when August Vollmer, the former police chief of Berkeley, California, persuaded the University of California to offer courses on the subject.[30] Vollmer was joined by his student Orlando W. Wilson and by William H. Parker in calling for increased professionalism in police work through better training.[31] Early criminal justice education was practice oriented; it was a kind of extension of on-the-job training for working practitioners.

While criminal justice was often seen as a technical subject, **criminology**, on the other hand, had a firm academic base. Criminology is the interdisciplinary study of the causes of crime and of criminal motivation. It combines the academic disciplines of sociology, psychology, biology, economics, and political science in an effort to explore the mind of the offender and the social and economic conditions which give rise to criminality. The study of criminology is central to the criminal justice discipline, and courses in criminology are almost always found in criminal justice programs. Victimology is a subfield of criminology, which seeks answers to the question of why some people are victimized while others are not.

Criminology The scientific study of crime causation, prevention, and the rehabilitation and punishment of offenders.

As a separate field of study, criminal justice had fewer than 1,000 students before 1950.[32] The turbulent 1960s and 1970s brought an increasing concern with social issues and, in particular, justice. Drug use, social protests, and dramatically increasing crime rates turned the nation's attention to the criminal justice system. During the period, Congress passed two significant pieces of legislation: (1) the Law Enforcement Assistance Act of 1965, which created the Law Enforcement Assistance Administration (LEAA), and (2) the Omnibus Crime Control and Safe Streets Act of 1968. Through LEAA, vast amounts of monies were funneled into fighting crime. Law enforcement agencies received a great deal of technical assistance and new crime-fighting hardware. Students interested in the study of criminal justice often found themselves eligible for financial help under the Law Enforcement Education Program (LEEP).

LEEP monies funded a rapid growth in criminal justice offerings nationwide. In the first year of its existence, the LEEP program spent $6.5 million on 20,602 students in 485 schools around the country. By 1975 more than 100,000 students were studying criminal justice at 1,065 schools with assistance from LEEP. The federal government in that year spent in excess of $40 million on criminal justice education.[33]

The criminal justice system is composed of a sprawling bureaucracy with many separate agencies that are largely autonomous and independent.

—Gary LaFree, Ph.D., University of New Mexico

LEEP funding began to decline in 1979. Meanwhile, criminal justice programs nationwide were undergoing considerable self-examination. The direction of justice studies and the future of the discipline were open to debate. The resultant clarification of criminal justice as a discipline, combined with the recent resurgence of federal funding initiatives through the

Violent Crime Control and Law Enforcement Act of 1994, and the "block grants" and other programs it and later legislation provided, has made the field stronger and more professional than ever before.

To meet the growing needs of police officers for college-level training, the International Association of Police Professors (IAPP) was formed in 1963. The IAPP later changed its name to the Academy of Criminal Justice Sciences (ACJS) and widened its focus to include all aspects of criminal justice education. Today ACJS and it's sister organization, the American Society of Criminology (ASC), are the two largest associations of community college- and university-based criminal justice trainers and educators in the world. A few years ago, ACJS formed an Academic Review Committee charged with conducting peer reviews of academic criminal justice programs upon request. Although ACJS does not offer accreditation through its peer review process, university and community college criminal justice programs undertaking self-studies or participating in a state or regional accreditation process may find the review process helpful.[34]

Today criminal justice is well established as an academic discipline and is offered as a major course of study in well over 1,000 colleges and universities across the country. The largest criminal justice program in the United States is the John Jay College of Criminal Justice in New York City. "John Jay," as the school is called, serves over 10,000 students studying in the criminal justice area and conducts research in criminal justice organization, law enforcement, and forensic science. Other well-known criminal justice programs can be found at Sam Houston State University, the University of Illinois at Chicago, Rutgers (New Jersey), Florida State University, the State University of New York at Albany, Michigan State University, the University of Louisville, the University of Maryland, the University of Illinois, the Ohio State University, East Tennessee State University, and the University of California at Irvine.[35]

Things to Come: An Overview of this Book

This textbook is divided into five parts. Part 1, entitled *Crime in America*, provides a general introduction to the study of criminal justice, including crime statistics (Chapter 2), the causes of crime (Chapter 3), and criminal law (Chapter 4).

Part 2 is called *Policing*. Its three chapters focus on the activities of law enforcement agencies. The law enforcement field is described in Chapters 5 and 6, where historical developments are combined with modern studies to depict a dynamic profession. Precedent-setting court cases are introduced in Chapter 7 along with more recent decisions which have refined earlier ones.

Part 3, called *Adjudication*, includes chapters on the courts (Chapters 8 and 9) and sentencing (Chapter 10). Special attention is given throughout Part 4, *Corrections*, to the legal issues surrounding correctional institutions and various forms of criminal punishment. Prisons and jails (Chapter 12) and prison life (Chapter 13) are discussed, along with probation, parole, and community corrections (Chapter 11).

The final section, Part 5, *Special Issues*, looks at problems facing the justice system today. Included are "victimless" crimes and drug abuse (Chapter 15) and juvenile delinquency (Chapter 14). Chapter 16 provides a cursory overview of criminal justice systems in other nations and points out the need for international understanding. Finally, the challenges and opportunities which the future holds for the practice of American criminal justice, including computer crime and emerging investigative technologies, are discussed in the last chapter (Chapter 17).

Although this book covers many issues, its overall structure is sequential. Consecutive chapters provide a tour of criminal justice agencies and practices as they exist in the United States today. The tour begins in Part 1 with an explanation of how criminal law is created and ends in Part 4 with a discussion of problems facing corrections in the future.

Everywhere across the Nation, we are more concerned with ensuring that criminal activity does not repeat itself, rather than keeping criminal activity from occurring in the first place.

—Tony Fabelo, Executive Director, Texas Criminal Justice Policy Council

SUMMARY

In this chapter the process of American criminal justice and the agencies that contribute to it have been described as a system with three major components: police, courts, corrections.

Twenty-First Century Criminal Justice

Research and Professionalism

As an academic discipline, criminal justice made its debut in the 1930s, beginning with the work of August Vollmer (1876–1955) and continuing with the writings of his student Orlando Wilson (1900–1972). Vollmer, Wilson, and their followers were primarily interested in the application of general management principles to the administration of police agencies. Hence, in its early days, criminal justice was primarily a practical field of study—concerned with issues of organizational effectiveness. By the 1960s, however, students of criminal justice were beginning to apply the techniques of social scientific research—many of them borrowed from sister disciplines such as criminology, sociology, psychology, and political science—to the study of all aspects of the justice system. Scientific research into the operation of the criminal justice system was encouraged by the 1967 President's Commission on Law Enforcement and Administration of Justice, which influenced passage of the Safe Streets and Crime Control Act of 1968. The Safe Streets Act led to the creation of the National Institute of Law Enforcement and Criminal Justice, which later became the National Institute of Justice (NIJ). As a central part of its mission, NIJ continues to support research in the criminal justice field through substantial funding for scientific explorations into all aspects of the discipline—and funnels much of the $3 billion spent annually by the Department of Justice to help local communities fight crime.

Many early government-funded scientific studies in the criminal justice field focused on police management practices and are discussed in more detail in Chapter 5. Scientific research has since become characteristic of the entire criminal justice discipline—with studies of all aspects of criminal justice administration, practice, and ideology now routinely undertaken as well as reported at aca-demic conferences and professional meetings and in journals focusing on the profession. Such research has become a major element in the increasing professionalization of criminal justice, both as a career field and as a field of study, and can be expected to play an ever-widening role in the twenty-first century.

While space doesn't permit discussion of most scientific studies in the justice field, a recent report by Lawrence Sherman and his colleagues at the University of Maryland stands out as one of the most definitive criminal justice studies of recent times. *The New York Times* calls the "Sherman report" "the most comprehensive study ever" of the criminal justice system in this country. The Sherman study, which may set the tone for research throughout the early part of the twenty-first century, is a "meta-analysis"—or a study of other studies. Conducted at the request of the U.S. Congress and released in 1997, the report analyzes the results of hundreds of other studies conducted throughout the criminal justice enterprise over the past few decades. Entitled, "Preventing Crime: What Works, What Doesn't, What's Promising," the massive survey examined independent studies of more than 500 local crime prevention programs throughout the country in an effort to determine what programs and practices are effective at preventing or reducing crime. The study surveyed literature on gang violence prevention programs, community-based mentoring programs, after-school recreational programs, family-based crime prevention programs, school-based programs, policing programs such as neighborhood watch and community policing, drug treatment programs, and get-tough sentencing initiatives such as prison boot camps and home confinement and electronic monitoring (all of which are discussed later in this book).

The report concluded that some of the most popular programs now in widespread use, including prison boot camps, midnight basketball, neighborhood watches, and drug education classes, have little impact on crime rates in the United States. The study did find some promising results for certain programs, especially intensified police patrols in high-crime areas, drug treatment in prisons, and home visits by nurses, social workers, and others for infants in troubled families.

The most important finding of the study, however, was its conclusion that it remains difficult to assess federally-funded crime-prevention programs because there is far too little ongoing rigorous, scientific evaluation of such programs. As the study's lead author, Lawrence W. Sherman, says, "The most important finding is that we really can't tell how a majority of funding is affecting crime." The major reason for that problem, Sherman says, is that Congress has never insisted on the same kind of scientific evaluation of crime prevention programs that it does, for example, in testing new drugs before they are approved for public consumption.

The Sherman study, and others like it, hold the potential to significantly influence criminal justice research well into the next century. By pointing out the importance of rigorous and well-focused research, it is likely that Sherman's research will help move Congress to soon require well-tuned evaluations as part of the accountability process imposed upon all recipients of federal crime-fighting monies.

Fox Butterfield, (no headline), *The New York Times* News Service, April 16, 1997.

Lawrence W. Sherman, Denise Gottfredson, Doris MacKenzie, John Eck, Peter Reuter, Shawn Bushway, et al, *Preventing Crime: What Works, What Doesn't, What's Promising—A Report to the United States Congress* (Washington, D.C.: National Institute of Justice, 1997).

As we have warned, however, such a viewpoint is useful primarily for the reduction in complexity it provides. A more realistic approach to understanding criminal justice may be the nonsystem approach. As a nonsystem, criminal justice is depicted as a fragmented activity in which individuals and agencies within the process have interests and goals which at times coincide, but often conflict.

Defendants processed by the system come into contact with numerous workers in the justice process whose duty it is to enforce the law, but who also have a stake in the agencies which employ them and who hold their own personal interests and values. As they wend their way through the system, defendants may be held accountable to the law, but in the process they will also be buffeted by the personal whims of "officials," as well as by the practical needs of the system itself. A complete view of American criminal justice needs to recognize that the final outcome of any encounter with the criminal justice system will be a consequence of decisions made not just at the legislative level, but in the day-to-day activities undertaken by everyone involved in the system. Hence, in a very real sense, justice is a product whose quality depends just as much upon practical considerations as it does upon idealistic notions of right and wrong.

An alternative way of viewing the practice of criminal justice is in terms of its two goals: crime control and due process. The crime control perspective urges rapid and effective law enforcement and calls for the stiff punishment of law breakers. Due process, on the other hand, requires a recognition of the defendant's rights and holds the agents of justice accountable for any actions which might contravene those rights.

The goals of due process and crime control are often in conflict. Popular opinion may even see them as mutually exclusive. As we describe the agencies of justice in the chapters which follow, the goals of crime control and due process will appear again and again. Often they will be phrased in terms of the theme of this book, which contrasts the need to balance the rights of individuals against other valid social interests. We have presented this theme as represented by two opposing groups: individual rights advocates and public order advocates. As we shall see, however, the most fundamental challenge facing the practice of American criminal justice is one of achieving efficient enforcement of the laws while recognizing and supporting the rights of individuals. This mandate of crime control through effective due process ensures that criminal justice will remain an exciting and ever-evolving undertaking—well into the twenty-first century and beyond.

Dɪꜱᴄᴜꜱꜱɪᴏɴ Qᴜᴇꜱᴛɪᴏɴꜱ

1. What are the two models of the criminal justice process which this chapter describes? Which model do you think is more useful? Which is more accurate? Why?

2. What have we suggested are the primary goals of the criminal justice system? Do you think any one goal is more important than another? If so, which one(s)? Why?

3. What do we mean when we say that the "primary purpose of law is the maintenance of order"? Why is social order necessary? What would life be like without it?

4. Do we have too many criminal laws? Too few? Do we have enough social order or too little? How can we improve on the present situation, if at all?

5. What might a large, complex society such as our own be like without laws? Without a system of criminal justice? Would you want to live in such a society? Why or why not?

6. What do we, as individuals, have to give up to facilitate social order? Do we ever give up too much in the interest of social order? If so, when?

 WEB WATCH

To begin exploring the *Criminal Justice Today* site on the World Wide Web, point your Web browser at http://www.prenhall.com/cjtoday. Once there, click the "enter here" selection, then "Web Chapters" and finally "Chapter 1" in order to begin using the site right away. The *Criminal Justice Today* site includes a wealth of on-line criminal justice information keyed to the various chapters in this book. The material is constantly being updated, and you may later wish to revisit areas you have already explored. You may also wish to enter the Global Town Meeting which allows you to post electronic messages for others to read. Messages are arranged by topic, with new topics constantly being added. As you explore the site, you will discover that a special feature permits you to send electronic homework to your instructor. Clicking "Find the Facts" will lead you across the web in search of answers to chapter questions. Remember that if your instructor decides to use the electronic homework feature of the site, it is always a good idea to keep a copy of any homework that you submit.

NOTES

1. Charles E. Silberman, *Criminal Violence, Criminal Justice* (New York: Random House, 1978), p. 12.
2. "Gingrich Says Felons Should Be Tracked by Satellite," Reuters wire services, March 4, 1995.
3. Details for this story are taken from: "Murder in Mississippi," ABC News *Primetime Live*, October 15, 1997.
4. See "Three Slain in Mississippi Teen's Rampage," *USA Today*, October 2, 1997, 3A.
5. "Talk of Satanic Cult Follows School Shootings," the Associated Press, October 12, 1997.
6. Kevin Sack, "Town Stunned by Arrests of Seven Students in Murder Plot," *New York Times* News Service, via Simon and Schuster Newslink, October 10, 1997.
7. "Teen Pleads Innocent in High School Shootings," CNN Interactive on the World Wide Web, October 2, 1997.
8. Ibid.
9. See, "Cries of Relief," *Time*, April 26, 1993, p. 18, and "King II: What Made the Difference?" *Newsweek*, April 26, 1993, p. 26.
10. Ibid.
11. "FBI: Definitely a Bomb," *USA Today*, March 1, 1993, p. 1A.
12. Sam Vincent Meddis, "Votes Say 'Get Tough,' But Answers Not So Simple," *USA Today*, November 16, 1994, p. 6A.
13. "A Free Man," *USA Today*, April 27, 1989, p. 13A.
14. *The American Heritage Dictionary on CD-ROM* (Boston: Houghton Mifflin, 1991).
15. For a good overview of the issues involved, see, for example, Judge Harold J. Rothwax, *Guilty: The Collapse of Criminal Justice* (New York: Random House, 1996).
16. The systems model of criminal justice is often attributed to the frequent use of the term "system" by the 1967 Presidential Commission in its report, *The Challenge of Crime in a Free Society* (Washington, D.C.: U.S. Government Printing Office, 1967).
17. One of the first published works to utilize the nonsystems approach to criminal justice was the American Bar Association's *New Perspective on Urban Crime* (Washington, D.C.: ABA Special Committee on Crime Prevention and Control, 1972).
18. Jerome H. Skolnick, *Justice Without Trial* (New York: John Wiley, 1966), p. 179.
19. *Miranda* v. *Arizona,* 384 U.S. 436, 86 S.Ct. 1602, 16 L. Ed. 2d 694 (1966).
20. North Carolina Justice Academy, *Miranda Warning Card* (Salemburg, N.C.).
21. John M. Scheb and John M. Scheb II, *American Criminal Law* (St. Paul, MN: West, 1996), p. 32.
22. Federal Rules of Criminal Procedure, 10.
23. *Blanton* v. *City of North Las Vegas*, 489 U.S. 538, 103 L. Ed. 2d 550, 109 S.Ct. 1289 (1989).
24. Ibid.
25. *U.S.* v. *Nachtigal*, 122 L. Ed. 2d 374, 113 S.Ct. 1072, 1073 (1993), *per curiam*.
26. Barbara Borland and Ronald Sones, *Prosecution of Felony Arrests, 1981* (Washington, D.C.: Bureau of Justice Statistics, 1986).
27. For a complete analysis of the impact of decisions made by the Warren Court, see Fred P. Graham, *The Due Process Revolution: The Warren Court's Impact on Criminal Law* (New York: Hayden Press, 1970).

28. *Gideon* v. *Wainwright*, 372 U.S. 353 (1963).

29. Herbert Packer, *The Limits of the Criminal Sanction* (Stanford, CA: Stanford University Press, 1968).

30. For an excellent history of policing in the United States, see Edward A. Farris, "Five Decades of American Policing: 1932–1982," *The Police Chief*, November 1982, pp. 30–36.

31. Gene Edward Carte, "August Vollmer and the Origins of Police Professionalism," *Journal of Police Science and Administration*, Vol. 1, no. 1 (1973), pp. 274–281.

32. Larry L. Gaines, "Criminal Justice Education Marches On!" in Roslyn Muraskin, ed., *The Future of Criminal Justice Education* (New York: Criminal Justice Institute, Long Island University, C. W. Post Campus, 1987).

33. Ibid.

34. For more information contact ACJS at 402 Nunn Hall, Highland Heights, KY 41099-5998, or see "Academic Review of Programs," *ACJS Today*, November/December 1996, p. 9. ASC can be contacted at 1314 Kinnear Road, Suite 212, Columbus, OH 43212. Visit the *Criminal Justice Today* web site at http://www.prenhall.com/cjtoday for links to these and other professional organizations in the field.

35. This list includes schools that are well known for producing graduate students specializing in either criminal justice or criminology. Because of the liberal arts emphasis at many of the schools in the list, however, programs may be officially designated as "criminology" or even "sociology" rather than "criminal justice." One (at the University of California at Irvine) is housed within the "Program in Social Ecology."

chapter 2

THE CRIME PICTURE

It may turn out that a free society cannot really prevent crime. Perhaps its causes are locked so deeply into the human personality, the intimate processes of family life, and the subtlest aspects of the popular culture that coping is the best that we can hope for...

—JAMES Q. WILSON, UCLA[1]

No one way of describing crime describes it well enough.

—THE PRESIDENT'S COMMISSION ON LAW ENFORCEMENT AND ADMINISTRATION OF JUSTICE

Introduction: Sources of Data

We talk about the criminal justice system, but rarely does it perform as a system.

—Samuel F. Saxton, Director Prince George's County (Maryland) Dept. of Corrections

On January 16, 1997, at about one o'clock in the morning, 27-year-old Ennis Cosby, son of well-known comedian and entertainer Bill Cosby, stopped his $140,000 Mercedes-Benz convertible on the shoulder of Skirball Center Drive near Los Angeles. Cosby had been traveling on Interstate 405 on his way to visit a friend, when the car's left front tire went flat. He quickly took an exit which led him to an isolated section of Skirball. He came to a stop at the base of a hill covered with vegetation, making him virtually invisible to travelers on the busy Interstate nearby. Police say that Cosby called his friend on the car's cellular phone to report the flat tire and to say that he was going to be late. A few minutes later he was dead—killed by a single bullet fired into his brain. From what police have been able to piece together, Cosby was murdered by Mikail Markhasev, an 18-year old Ukrainian immigrant out late at night and looking for trouble. Police theorize that Markhasev was attracted to Cosby's disabled but expensive vehicle. Evidence at the scene[2] indicates that Markhasev may have approached Cosby by pretending to volunteer help,[3] and that Cosby offered him a cigarette. What happened next isn't clear. Reports surfaced months after the killing, however, revealing that Cosby had been hit in the face, perhaps in a vain attempt to resist robbery and that he was then shot at close range. Arrested when police got a tip after the *National Enquirer* offered a $100,000 reward for information in the case, Markhasev pled "not guilty" to Cosby's murder. He is awaiting trial as this book goes to press. The Los Angeles District Attorney's Office has announced that it will not pursue the death penalty in the case.

Shortly after Ennis Cosby was murdered, his father told reporters: "Our hearts go out to each and every family that has suffered such an incident. This is a life experience that is truly difficult to share." Were it not for the fact that Ennis William Cosby was Bill Cosby's son, however, his killing might have gone down in statistical reports simply as one more homicide among the nearly 24,000 that occur every year in the United States—forgotten by all but statisticians and family members left behind.

This chapter provides a statistical picture of crime in America today. It does so by examining information on reported crimes from the FBI's *Uniform Crime Reports* (UCR), as well as data from the door-to-door National Crime Victimization Survey (NCVS) conducted by the Bureau of Justice Statistics (BJS). While reading this chapter it is important to keep in mind that statistical aggregates of reported crime, whatever their source, do not readily reveal the human suffering, lost lives, lessened productivity, and reduced quality of life that crime causes. Although every murder victim like Ennis Cosby, led an intricate life and had a family, dreams, and desires, their death at the hands of another person is routinely recorded only as a numerical count in statistical reports. Such information does not contain details on the personal lives of crime victims, but represents merely a numerical compilation of reported law violations.

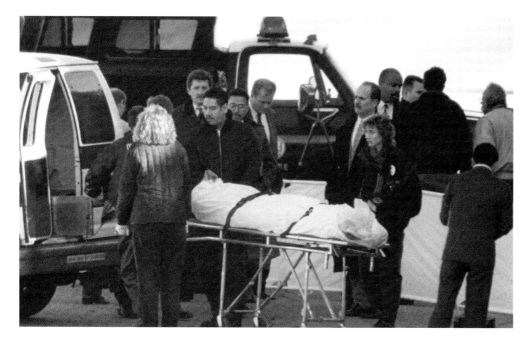

The body of Ennis Cosby, son of entertainer Bill Cosby, is removed from the spot on Interstate 405 in Los Angeles where he was murdered in the early morning hours of January 16, 1997. *Nick Ut, AP/Wide World Photos*

Crime Data And Social Policy

Crime statistics do more than merely render a picture of crime in this country. If used properly, they can provide one of the most powerful tools available to social policy decision makers. Decision makers at all levels, including legislators, elected public officials, and administrators throughout the criminal justice system, rely on crime data to analyze and evaluate existing programs, fashion and design new crime-control initiatives, develop funding requests, and plan new laws and crime-control legislation. The "get-tough" policies described in the last chapter, for example, are in large part based upon the public's perception of increasing crime rates and the measured ineffectiveness of existing programs to reduce the incidence of repeat offending.

Some, however, question just how "objective"—and therefore how useful—crime statistics are. Social events, including crime, are complex and difficult to quantify. Even the choice of which crimes should be included in statistical reports, and which should be excluded, is itself a judgment reflecting the interests and biases of policy-makers.

Moreover, public opinion about crime is not always realistic—nor is it always based on a careful consideration of statistics. As well-known criminologist Norval Morris points out, the news media does more to influence public perceptions of crime than any official data.[4] Between 1991 and 1995, for example, the frequency of crime stories reported in the national media increased by a factor of 4. From 1993–1995 crime was at the top of the list in subject matter covered in news stories at both the local and national levels. "Please note," says Morris, "that over those six years the grossly increasing preoccupation with crime stories came at a time of steadily declining crime and violence." However, as Morris adds: "Aided and abetted by this flood of misinformation, the politicians, federal and state, and local, foster the view that the public demands our present get-tough policies."

Collecting Crime Data

Generally, crime statistics come from three sources: (1) the FBI's Uniform Crime Reporting Program (UCR), (2) the **Bureau of Justice Statistics**' National Crime Victimization Survey (NCVS), and (3) offender self-reports. The most widely quoted numbers purporting to describe crime in America today probably come from the FBI's *Uniform Crime Reports* and

Bureau of Justice Statistics (BJS) A U.S. Department of Justice agency responsible for criminal justice data collection, including annual NCVS.

depend upon reports to the police by victims of crime. One problem with such summaries is that citizens do not always make official reports, sometimes because they are afraid to contact the police, or perhaps because they don't think the police can do anything about the offense. Even when reports are made, they are filtered through a number of bureaucratic levels. As Frank Hagan points out, "The government is very keen on amassing statistics. They collect them, add to them, raise them to the *n*th power, take the cube root, and prepare wonderful diagrams. But what you must never forget is that every one of these figures comes in the first instance from the *chowty dar* (village watchman), who puts down what he damn pleases."[5]

Another problem with the UCR comes from the fact that certain kinds of crimes are rarely reported, if at all. These include "victimless crimes," or crimes which, by their nature, involve willing participants. Victimless crimes (also known as social order offenses) include such things as drug use, prostitution, and gambling. Similarly, white-collar and high-technology offenses, such as embezzlement, computer crime, and corporate misdeeds, probably only rarely enter the official statistics. Hence, a relatively large amount of criminal activity in the United States probably remains unreported in the UCR, while those types of crimes which are reported may paint a misleading picture of the true nature of criminal activity by virtue of the publicity accorded to them.

A second data collection format is typified by the Bureau of Justice Statistics' (BJS) National Crime Victimization Survey (NCVS). It relies upon personal interpretations of what may (or may not) have been criminal events, and upon quasi-confidential surveys, which may selectively include data from those most willing to answer interviewer's questions. Unfortunately, the survey tends to exclude information from less gregarious and more reclusive respondents.

The NCVS suffers from other shortcomings, as well. Some victims are afraid to report crimes, even to nonpolice interviewers. Others may inaccurately interpret their own experiences or may be tempted to invent victimizations for the sake of interviewers. As the first page of the NCVS admits, "Details about the crimes come directly from the victims, and no attempt is made to validate the information against police records or any other source."[6]

A final source of crime data can be found in offender self-reports based upon surveys that ask respondents to reveal any illegal activity in which they have been involved. Offender self-reports are not discussed in detail in this chapter since surveys utilizing them are not national in scope. Similarly, offenders are often reluctant to accurately report ongoing or recent criminal involvement, making information derived from such surveys somewhat unreliable and less than current. Where information from such surveys is available, however, it tends to show that criminal activity is more widespread than most "official" surveys show.

Finally, although the FBI's UCR and the BJS's NCVS are the country's major sources of crime data, other regular publications contribute to our knowledge of crime patterns throughout the nation. Available yearly is the *Sourcebook of Criminal Justice Statistics*, a compilation of national information on crime and on the criminal justice system. The *Sourcebook* is published by BJS through support provided by the Justice System Improvement Act of 1979. A less frequent, but more concise, document is the *Report to the Nation on Crime and Justice*, issued in updated editions every few years. The National Institute of Justice (NIJ), the primary research arm of the U.S. Department of Justice, along with the Office of Juvenile Justice and Delinquency Prevention (OJJDP), the Federal Justice Research Program, and the National Victim's Resource Center, provide still more information on crime patterns.

The Uniform Crime Reports

Development of the UCR Program

In 1930 Congress authorized the attorney general of the United States to survey crime in America, and the FBI was designated to implement the program. The Bureau quickly built upon earlier efforts by the International Association of Chiefs of Police (IACP) to create a national system of uniform crime statistics. As a practical measure, IACP recommendations had utilized readily available information, and so it was that citizens's reports of crimes to the police became the basis of the plan.[7]

During its first year of operation the FBI's Uniform Crime Reporting Program received reports from 400 cities in 43 states. Twenty million people were covered by that first comprehensive survey. Today, approximately 16,000 law enforcement agencies provide crime information for the program, with data coming from city, state, and county departments. To assure uniformity in reporting, the FBI has developed standardized definitions of offenses and terminologies used in the program. A number of publications, including the *Uniform Crime Reporting Handbook* and *Manual of Law Enforcement Records*, are supplied to participating agencies, and training for effective reporting is made available through FBI-sponsored seminars and instructional literature.

Following IACP recommendations, the original UCR Program was designed to permit comparisons over time through construction of a **Crime Index**. The Index summed the total of seven major offenses—murder, forcible rape, robbery, aggravated assault, burglary, larceny-theft, and motor vehicle theft—and expressed the result as a crime rate based on population. In 1979, by congressional mandate, an eighth offense—arson—was added to the Index. Although UCR categories today parallel statutory definitions of criminal behavior, they are not legal classifications, only conveniences created for statistical reporting purposes.

Historical Trends

Since the UCR Program began there have been two major shifts in crime rates—and we are in the middle of what may now be a third. One occurred during the early 1940s, when crime decreased sharply due to the large number of young men who entered military service during World War II. Young males comprise the most "crime-prone" segment of the population, and their removal to the European and Pacific theaters of war did much to lower crime rates at home.

The other noteworthy shift in offense statistics—a dramatic increase in most forms of crime beginning in the 1960s and culminating only recently—also had a link to World War II. With the end of the war and the return of millions of young men to civilian life, birth rates skyrocketed during the period 1945–1955, creating a postwar "baby boom." By 1960, "baby boomers" were entering their teenage years. A disproportionate number of young people produced a dramatic increase in most major crimes as the baby boom generation swelled the proportion of the American population in the crime-prone age range.

Other factors contributed to the increase in reported crime during the same period. Modified reporting requirements, which reduced the stress associated with filing police reports, and the publicity associated with the rise in crime, sensitized victims to the importance of reporting. Crimes which may have gone undetected in the past began to figure more prominently in official statistics. Similarly, the growing professionalization of some police departments resulted in more accurate and increased data collection, making some of the most progressive departments appear to be associated with the largest crime increases.[8]

The 1960s were tumultuous years. The Vietnam war, a vibrant civil rights struggle, the heady growth of secularism, dramatic increases in the divorce rate, diverse forms of "liberation," and the influx of psychedelic and other drugs, all combined to fragment existing institutions. Social norms were blurred, and group control over individual behavior declined substantially. The "normless" quality of American society in the 1960s contributed greatly to the rise in crime. Crime rates continued their upward swing, with a brief respite in the early 1980s when postwar boomers began to age out of the crime-prone years and American society emerged from the cultural drift which had characterized the previous 20 years. About the same time, however, an increase in drug-related criminal activity led crime rates to soar once again, especially in the area of violent crime. Crime rates peaked about 1991 and have since begun to show what may be the start of a third major shift—with decreases in the rate of most major crimes now being reported.

Even so, a fourth shift may be discernable on the horizon—as the size of an increasingly violent teenage population is anticipated to grow over the next decade or two. John J. DiIulio, Jr., for example, warns of a coming generation of **superpredators**—young violent offenders bereft of any moral sense and steeped in violent traditions. Superpredators, according to

Crime Index An inclusive measure of the violent and property crime categories of the UCR, also known as "Part I offenses." The Crime Index has been a useful tool for geographic (state-to-state) and historical (year-to-year) comparative purposes because it employs the concept of a crime rate (the number of crimes *per* unit of population). However, the recent addition of arson as an eighth index offense and the new executive branch requirements with regard to the gathering of "hate crime" statistics have the potential to result in new crime index measurements, which may provide less than ideal comparisons.

Superpredators Juveniles who are coming of age in actual and moral poverty without the benefits of parents, teachers, coaches, or clergy to teach them right from wrong. The term is often applied to inner-city youth, socialized in violent settings without the benefit of wholesome life experiences.

DiIulio, are juveniles "who are coming of age in actual and 'moral poverty' without the benefits of parents, teachers, coaches, or clergy to teach them right from wrong and show them 'unconditional love.'"[9]

Supporting DiIulio, James A. Fox notes that, "[b]y the year 2005, the number of teens, ages 14–17, will increase by 20%, with a larger increase among blacks in this age group (26%)."[10] Such an observation, says Fox, is especially worrisome because, over the past ten years, "the rate of murder committed by teens, ages 14–17, [has] increased 172%." Indicative of a significant trend, says Fox, "black males aged 14–24," although comprising only 1% of the population, "now constitute 17% of the victims of homicide and over 30% of the perpetrators." Also, says Fox, "the differential trends by age of offender observed for homicide generalize to other violent offenses." During the last five years, for example, "the arrest rate for violent crimes (murder, rape, robbery, and aggravated assault) rose over 46% among teenagers, but only 12% among adults."

UCR Terminology

Figure 2–1 shows the UCR crime clock, which is calculated yearly as a shorthand way of diagramming crime severity in the United States. Eight "Part I offenses," also called "major crimes," are listed in the right-hand margin of the figure. Part I offenses are: (1) murder, (2) rape, (3) robbery, (4) aggravated assault, (5) burglary, (6) larceny, (7) motor vehicle theft, and (8) arson. As noted earlier, the sum total of all Part I offenses, divided by the nation's

FIGURE 2–1 FBI crime clock, 1996, showing the frequency of major crime commission.
Source: Adapted from Federal Bureau of Investigation, *Uniform Crime Reports for the United States, 1996* (Washington, D.C.: U.S. Government Printing Office, 1997).

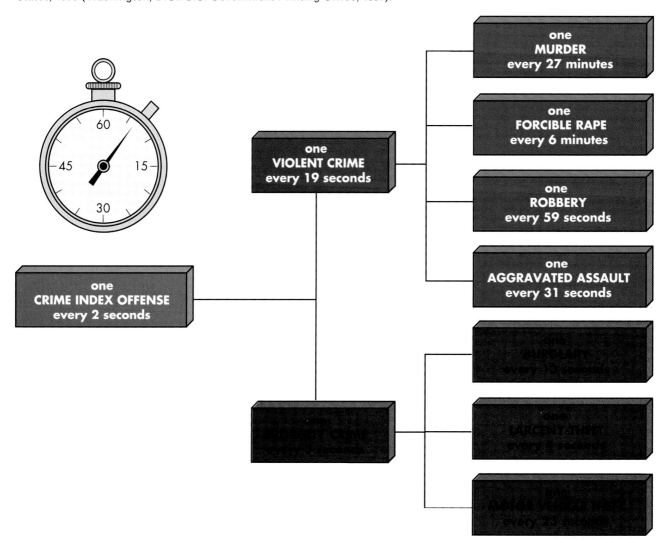

Victimless crimes, such as prostitution, are rarely reported. As a consequence, they are likely to be seriously underrepresented in the FBI's *Uniform Crime Reports*. Here, teenage prostitutes solicit a "John." *John Maher, Stock Boston*

population, comprise the UCR's widely reported crime index, which facilitates comparisons of crime rates over time. Since, however, arson was added as a Part I offense relatively late in the history of the UCR program, it is often excluded from official crime index calculations.

The crime clock distinguishes between two categories of Part I crime: **violent (or personal) crime** and **property crime**. Violent crimes include murder, forcible rape, robbery, and aggravated assault. Property crimes, as the figure shows, are burglary, larceny, and motor vehicle theft. Other than for the use of such a simple dichotomy, UCR data do not provide a clear measure of the severity of the crimes they cover.

Crime clock data are based, as are most UCR statistics, upon crimes reported to (or discovered by) the police. For a few offenses the numbers reported are probably close to the numbers which actually occur. Murder, for example, is a crime that is difficult to conceal because of its seriousness. Even where the crime is not immediately discovered, the victim is often quickly missed by friends and associates and a "missing persons" report is filed with the police.

Auto theft is another crime that is reported with a frequency similar to its actual rate of occurrence, probably because insurance companies require that a police report be filed before any claims can be collected. Unfortunately, most crimes other than murder and auto theft appear to be seriously underreported. Victims may not report for various reasons, including (1) the belief that the police can't do anything; (2) a fear of reprisal; (3) embarrassment about the crime itself or a fear of being embarrassed during the reporting process; and (4) an acceptance of criminal victimization as a normal part of life.

UCR data tend to underestimate the amount of crime which actually occurs for another reason: Built into the reporting system is the hierarchy rule—a way of "counting" crime reports such that only the most serious out of a series of events is scored. If a man and woman go on a picnic, for example, and their party is set upon by a criminal who kills the man, rapes the woman, steals the couple's car, and later burns the vehicle, the hierarchy rule dictates that only one crime will be reported in official statistics—that of murder. The offender, if apprehended, may later be charged with each of the offenses listed, but only one report of murder will appear in UCR data.

Most UCR information is reported as a *rate* of crime. Rates are computed as the number of crimes *per* some unit of population. National reports generally make use of large units of

Violent Crime An offense category which, according to the FBI's *Uniform Crime Reports* (UCR), includes murder, rape, robbery, and aggravated assault. Because the UCR depends upon *reports* (to the police) of crimes, the "official statistics" on these offenses are apt to inaccurately reflect the actual incidence of such crimes.

Property Crime An offense category which, according to the FBI's UCR program, includes burglary, larceny, auto theft, and arson. Since citizen reports of criminal incidents figure heavily in the compilation of "official statistics," the same critiques apply to tallies of these crimes as to the category of violent crime.

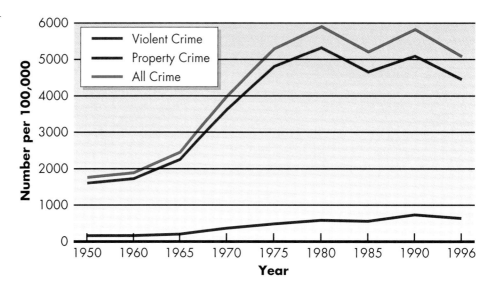

FIGURE 2–2 The rate of crime in the United States (per 100,000 inhabitants), 1960–1996. *Source:* Federal Bureau of Investigation, *Uniform Crime Reports*, various years.

In a field like criminal justice, where sensitive issues abound, none is more sensitive than the issue of race and gender bias.

—Gary LaFree, Ph.D.
University of New Mexico

population, such as 100,000 persons. Hence, the rate of rape reported by the UCR for 1996 was 36.1 forcible rapes per every 100,000 inhabitants of the United States.[11] Rates allow for a meaningful comparison over areas and across time. The rate of reported rape for 1975, for example, was about 26 per 100,000.[12] We expect the number of crimes to increase as population grows, but rate increases are cause for concern because they indicate that crimes are increasing faster than the population is growing. Rates, however, require interpretation. Since the FBI definition of rape includes only female victims, for example, the rate of victimization might be more meaningfully expressed in terms of every 100,000 female inhabitants. Similarly, although there is a tendency to judge an individual's risk of victimization based upon rates, such judgments tend to be inaccurate since they are based purely on averages and do not take into consideration individual life circumstances, such as place of residence, wealth, and educational level. While rates may tell us about aggregate conditions and trends, we must be very careful in applying them to individual cases. The crime clock, although a useful diagrammatic tool, is not a rate-based measure of criminal activity and does not allow easy comparisons over time.

Figure 2–2 shows the changes in the rate of crime in the United States between 1950 and 1996. As the figure shows, there was a substantial rise in crime between 1965–1980—a period during which crime rates tripled. Since then we have seen a leveling off of crime rates and—in recent years—what seems to be the beginning of a decline. From 1990 to 1996, for example, the rate of serious crimes reported to the FBI declined from 5,820 (per 100,000) to 5,079—a 13% decrease. The rate of property crimes, a figure which contributes substantially to overall crime index calculations, declined from 5,088 (per 100,000) to 4,445—a 13% decline: Violent crimes also decreased by 13%.

Some experts attribute the recent decline in crime rate to the aging of the baby-boom generation, which has now moved past the prime years for committing crimes. Others cite better police strategies, improved crime prevention measures, tougher gun control laws, and the recent and dramatic increase in the number of criminals now held in prison.

Any decline in crime statistics—while widely touted by politicians and criminal justice officials—may be short lived. "Right now we are at the point where there aren't a lot of people in the crime-prone years, 16–24," says James Fyfe, Temple University criminal justice professor.[13] "But we can expect in the next 10 years crime rates will increase significantly," as many more people enter the stage in life where they are most likely to commit the kinds of crimes that show up in statistical tabulations, such as those maintained by the FBI. Criminologist Jack Levin of Northeastern University in Boston agrees. Says Levin: "The baby boomers have matured into their 30s and 40s....They are graduating out of high risk violence and property crimes into white collar crimes, fraud, and embezzlement."[14]

*Table 2–1   Major Crimes Known to the Police 1996
(Part I Offenses from the UCR)*

Offense	Number	Rate per 100,000	Clearance Rate
Personal/Violent Crimes			
Murder	19,645	7.4	67%
Forcible rape	95,769	36.1	53
Robbery	537,050	202.4	27
Aggravated assault	1,029,814	388	58
Property Crimes			
Burglary	2,501,524	943.0	14
Larceny	7,894,620	2,975.9	20
Motor vehicle theft	1,395,192	525.9	14
Arson[1]	88,887	44.3	16
U.S. total	13,562,501	5,078.9	22

[1]Arson can be classified as either a property crime or a violent crime, depending upon whether or not personal injury or loss of life results from its commission. It is generally classified as a property crime, however. Arson statistics are incomplete for 1996 and do not enter in the "total" tabulations.

Source: Adapted from Federal Bureau of Investigation, *Uniform Crime Reports for the United States, 1996* (Washington, D.C.: U.S. Government Printing Office, 1997).

Moreover, as one police administrator observes, today's crime rates are still very high when measured against historical standards. Commander Dave Pettinari of the Pueblo County (Colorado) Sheriff's Department points out that: "The declining crime rate is misleading. Much has been made in the media over a 3% annual reduction during the past three years in the number of crimes reported by police to the FBI. Many think, though, that it's too early to celebrate victory. Crime rates are still many times higher today than they were in the 1950s, 1960s, or '70s. And large numbers of serious crimes today go unreported and unpunished."

A commonly used term in today's UCRs is **clearance rate**. The clearance rate of any crime refers to the proportion of reported crimes which have been "solved." Clearances are judged primarily on the basis of arrests and do not involve judicial disposition. Once an arrest has been made, a crime is regarded as "cleared" for purposes of reporting in the UCR Program. Exceptional clearances (sometimes called clearances by exceptional means) can result when law enforcement authorities believe they know who the perpetrator of a crime is but cannot make an arrest. The perpetrator may, for example, flee the country, commit suicide, or die.

For data gathering and reporting purposes, the UCR Program divides the country into four geographic regions: the Northeast, West, South, and Midwest. Unfortunately, no real attempt has been made to create divisions with nearly equal populations or similar demographic characteristics, and it is difficult to meaningfully compare one region of the country to another. Table 2–1 summarizes UCR statistics for 1996.

PART I OFFENSES

Murder

Murder is the unlawful killing of one human being by another.[15] UCR statistics on murder describe the yearly incidence of all willful and unlawful homicides within the United States. Included in the count are all cases of nonnegligent manslaughter which have been reported or discovered by the police. Not included in the count are suicides, justifiable homicides (that is, self-defense), deaths caused by negligence or accident, and attempts to murder. In 1996, some 19,645 murders came to the attention of police departments across the United

Clearance Rate   A traditional measure of investigative effectiveness that compares the number of crimes reported and/or discovered to the number of crimes solved through arrest or other means (such as the death of a suspect).

Part I Offenses (also called **Major Crimes**) Includes murder, rape, robbery, aggravated assault, burglary, larceny, and motor vehicle theft as defined under the FBI's Uniform Crime Reporting Program.

Murder   The unlawful killing of a human being. Murder is a generic term which, in common usage, may include first- and second-degree murder, as well as "manslaughter," "involuntary manslaughter," and other similar kinds of offenses.

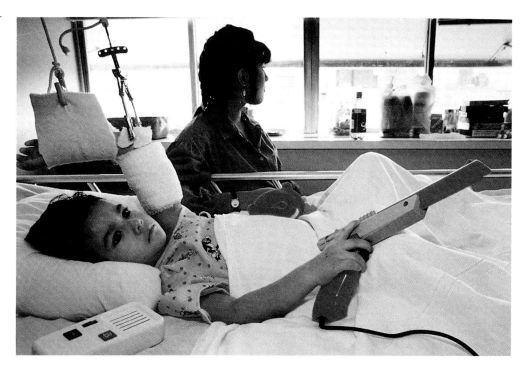

Personal violence is the type of crime which engenders the greatest fear. Here, a three-year-old in San Antonio's Santa Rosa Children's Hospital recovers after becoming the victim of a drive-by shooting. *Rick Hunter, Sygma*

States.[16] First-degree murder is a term which describes criminal homicide which is planned or involves premeditation. Second-degree murder is an intentional and unlawful killing, but one which is generally unplanned and which may happen "in the heat of passion."

Murder is the smallest numerical category in the Part I offenses. The 1994 murder rate was 7.4 homicides for every 100,000 persons in the country—a decrease of 10% over the previous year. Murder rates tend to peak annually in the warmest months. In many years, July and August show the highest number of homicides. Typically, in 1996 the month of August showed the highest number of murders.

Geographically, murder is most common in the southern states. However, because they are also the most populous, a meaningful comparison across regions of the country is difficult.

Age is no barrier to murder. Statistics for 1996 reveal that 247 infants (under the age of one) were victims of homicide, as were 320 persons aged 75 and over.[17] Persons aged 20–24 were the most likely to be murdered. Murder perpetrators were also most common in the 20- to 24-year-old age group.

Firearms are the weapon of choice in most murders. Ours is a well-armed society, and guns accounted for 68% of all killings in 1996. Handguns outnumbered shotguns 12 to 1 in the murder statistics, while rifles were a distant third. Knives were used in approximately 14% of all murders. Other weapons included explosives; poisons; narcotics overdoses; blunt objects, such as clubs; hands; feet; and fists.

Few murders are committed by strangers. Only 15% of all murders in 1996 were perpetrated by persons classified as "strangers." In 35% of all killings the relationship between the parties had not yet been determined. The largest category of killers was officially listed as "acquaintances," which probably includes a large number of former "friends." Arguments cause most murders (31%), but murders occur during commission of other crimes, such as robbery, rape, and burglary. Homicides which follow from other crimes are more likely to be impulsive rather than planned.

Murders may occur in sprees, which "involve killings at two or more locations with almost no time break between murders."[18] Andrew Cunanan, who killed fashion designer Gianni Versace in 1997, provides an example of a spree killer. Cunanan's killing spree lasted three

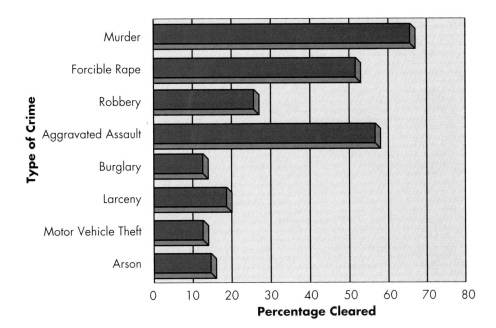

FIGURE 2–3 Crimes Cleared by Arrest, 1996. Source: Federal Bureau of Investigation, *Crime in the United States 1996*, (Washington, D.C.: Government Printing Office, 1997).

months and claimed five victims.[19] He was put on the FBI's "Ten Most Wanted" list before committing suicide aboard a Miami yacht where he had hidden. In contrast to spree killing, mass murder entails "the killing of four or more victims at one location, within one event."[20] Yet another kind of murder, serial murder, happens over time and is officially defined to "involve the killing of several victims in three or more separate events."[21] In cases of serial murder, days, months, or even years may elapse between killings. Serial killers have been frequently portrayed in the media.[22] Some of the more infamous serial killers of recent years include Jeffrey Dahmer, who received 936 years in prison for the homosexual dismemberment murders of 15 young men (and who was himself later murdered in prison); Ted Bundy, who killed many college-aged women; Henry Lee Lucas, now on death row in Texas, who was convicted of 11 murders and linked to at least 140 others;[23] Ottis Toole, Lucas' partner in crime; Charles Manson, still serving time for ordering followers to kill seven Californians, including famed actress Sharon Tate; Andrei Chikatilo, the Russian "Hannibal Lecter," who killed 52 people—mostly school children;[24] and David Berkowitz, also known as the "Son of Sam," who killed six people and wounded seven on lover's lanes around New York City.

Because murder is such a serious crime, it consumes substantial police resources. Consequently, over the years the offense has shown the highest clearance rate of any index crime. Sixty-seven percent of all homicides were cleared in 1996. Figure 2–3 shows clearance rates for all Part I offenses.

Forcible Rape

Broadly speaking, the term **rape** has been applied to a wide variety of sexual attacks and, in popular terminology, may include same-sex rape and the rape of a male by a female. Use of the term **forcible rape** for statistical reporting purposes by law enforcement agencies, however, has a specific and somewhat different meaning. The *Uniform Crime Reports* defines forcible rape as "the carnal knowledge of a female forcibly and against her will."[25] In contrast to what may be emerging social convention, in which homosexual rape is a widely recognized form of sexual assault, the latest edition of the *Uniform Crime Reporting Handbook*, which serves as a statistical reporting guide for law enforcement agencies, says: "By definition, sex attacks on males are excluded [from the crime of forcible rape] and should be classified as assaults or 'other sex offenses,' depending on the nature of the crime and the extent of the injury."[26] Although not part of UCR terminology, some jurisdictions refer to same-sex

Rape (generic) Unlawful sexual intercourse, achieved through force and without consent. Broadly speaking, the term "rape" has been applied to a wide variety of sexual attacks and may include same-sex rape and the rape of a male by a female. Some jurisdictions refer to same-sex rape as "sexual battery."

Forcible Rape (UCR) The carnal knowledge of a female forcibly and against her will. For statistical reporting purposes, however, the FBI defines forcible rape as "unlawful sexual intercourse with a female, by force and against her will, or without legal or factual consent." For statistical reporting purposes, statutory rape differs from forcible rape in that it involves sexual intercourse with a female who is under the age of consent—regardless of whether or not she is a willing partner. Date rape, or acquaintance rape, is a subcategory of rape which is of special concern today.

Sexual Battery
Intentional and wrongful physical contact with a person without his or her consent that entails a sexual component or purpose.

rape as "sexual battery." **Sexual battery**, which is not included in the UCR tally of reported rapes, is intentional and wrongful physical contact with a person without his or her consent that entails a sexual component or purpose.

Forcible rape is the least reported of all violent crimes. Typical estimates are that only one out of every four forcible rapes which actually occur are reported to the police. An even lower figure was reported by a 1992 government-sponsored study, which found that only 16% of rapes were reported.[27] The victim's fear of embarrassment has been cited as the reason most often given for nonreports. In the past, reports of rape were usually taken by seemingly hardened desk sergeants or male detectives who may not have been sensitive to the needs of the victim. In addition, the physical examination which victims had to endure was often a traumatizing experience in itself. Finally, many states routinely permitted the woman's past sexual history to be revealed in detail in the courtroom if a trial ensued. All these practices contributed to a considerable hesitancy on the part of rape victims to report their victimizations.

The last few decades have seen many changes designed to facilitate accurate reporting of rape and other sex offenses. Trained female detectives often act as victim interviewers, physicians have been better educated in handling the psychological needs of victims, and sexual histories are no longer regarded as relevant in most trials.

Rape is a complex crime involving strong emotions and injuries to the victim which often go beyond the physical. As a consequence, it is not a well-understood offense. Ronald Barri Flowers[28] has identified many cultural myths which surround the crime of rape. They include

Fallacy 1: Rape cannot occur if the woman resists.

Fact: Most victims of rape do resist.

Fallacy 2: All women secretly desire to be raped.

Fact: Although some women may fantasize about rape, none actually want to be raped.

Fallacy 3: The majority of rapes are triggered by women being out alone at night.

Fact: Most rapes occur following social encounters, such as dates.

Fallacy 4: Rape is a victim-precipitated crime.

Fact: Rape is an offender-precipitated crime.

Fallacy 5: Only young, attractive women are raped.

Fact: Women of all ages and appearances have been victims of rape.

Fallacy 6: It cannot happen to me.

Fact: Rape can happen to anyone.

Fallacy 7: Rape is motivated by the need for sexual gratification.

Fact: Most rapists appear motivated by the need to feel powerful.

Fallacy 8: Most rapes are perpetrated by strangers.

Fact: Most rapes are committed by acquaintances of the victim.

Fallacy 9: The rapist looks the part.

Fact: A rapist can be anyone.

Fallacy 10: Rape is an impulsive act.

Fact: While some rapes are impulsive, many are planned.

UCR statistics show 95,769 reported forcible rapes for 1996 (Figure 2–4), a slight decrease over the number of offenses reported for the previous year. Rape is a crime which has generally shown an increase in reporting, even in years when other personal crimes have been on the decline. By definition, rapes reported under the UCR Program are always of females. Homosexual rape is excluded from the count, as are instances of forced oral copulation, but attempts to commit rape by force or the threat of force are included. Statutory rape, where no force is involved but the female is below the age of consent, is not included in rape statistics.

The offense of rape follows homicide in its seasonal variation. The greatest number of forcible rapes in 1996 were reported in the hot summer months, while January, February, November, and December recorded the lowest number of reports.

Rape is frequently committed by a man known to the victim—as in the case of date rape. Victims may be held captive and subjected to repeated assaults.[29] In the crime of heterosexual rape, any female—regardless of age, appearance, or occupation—is a potential victim. Through personal violation, humiliation, and physical battering, rapists seek a sense of per-

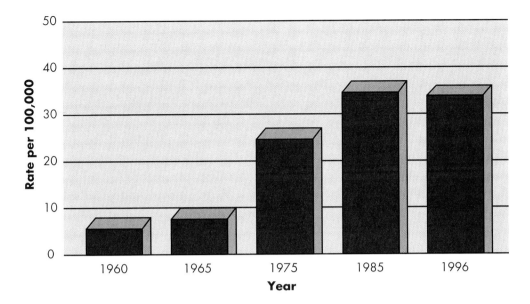

FIGURE 2–4 Rate of reported rape, 1960–1996. *Source:* Federal Bureau of Investigation, *Crime in the United States* (Washington, D.C.: U.S. Government Printing Office, various years).

sonal aggrandizement and dominance. In contrast, victims of rape often experience a lessened sense of personal worth; increased feelings of despair, helplessness, and vulnerability; a misplaced sense of guilt; and a lack of control over their personal lives.

Contemporary wisdom holds that forcible rape is often a planned violent crime which serves the offender's need for power rather than sexual gratification.[30] The "power thesis" had its origins in the writings of Susan Brownmiller, who, in 1975, argued that the primary motivation leading to rape is the male desire to "keep women in their place" and to preserve sexual role inequality through violence.[31] Although many writers on the subject of forcible rape (like Flowers, mentioned earlier) have generally accepted the power thesis, recent studies have caused some to rethink it. In a 1995 survey of the motives of serial rapists, for example, Dennis J. Stevens found that 41% of imprisoned rapists—the largest category of all—reported that "lust" was "the primary motive for predatory rape."[32]

Statistically speaking, however, most rapes are committed by acquaintances of the victims and often betray a trust or friendship. **Date rape**, which falls into this category, appears to be far more common than previously believed. Recently, the growing number of rapes perpetrated with the use of the "date rape drug" Rohypnol have alarmed law enforcement personnel. Rohypnol, which is discussed in more detail in Chapters 4 and 15, is an illegal pharmaceutical substance that is virtually tasteless. Available on the black market, it dissolves easily in drinks and can leave anyone who unknowingly consumes it unconscious for hours—making them vulnerable to sexual assault.

Rape within marriage, which has not always been recognized as a crime, is a growing area of concern in American criminal justice, and many laws have been enacted over the past few decades to deter it. Similarly, even though UCR statistics report only the rape or attempted rape of females,[33] some state statutes, by definition, allow for the rape of a male by a female. Such an offense, when it occurs, however, is typically of the statutory variety. In late 1993, for example, 24-year-old Fairfax County, Virginia, swimming coach Jean-Michelle Whitiak pleaded guilty to one count of statutory rape, admitting an affair with a 13-year-old boy. When the boy ended the relationship, Whitiak said, she had sex with two of his friends.[34] Similarly, in 1997, sixth-grade teacher Mary Kay LeTourneau, a 35-year-old married mother of four, pled guilty in Burien, Washington, to second-degree child rape after having a child by one of her students—a 13-year-old boy. Mrs. LeTourneau had known the boy since he was in the second grade. "When the sexual relationship started," she told reporters, "it seemed natural. What didn't seem natural was that there was a law forbidding such a natural thing."[35] She was sentenced to six months in jail and banned from seeing the boy or their child.

Date Rape   Unlawful forced sexual intercourse that occurs within the context of a dating relationship.

Visit the *CJToday* Web page and click on "Web Chapters," then "Chapter 2." Follow the "find the facts" links in order to explore issues of gun ownership and gun control.

The Second Amendment to the U.S. Constitution reads, "A well regulated Militia, being necessary to the security of a free State, the right of the people to keep and bear Arms, shall not be infringed." Constitutional guarantees have combined with historical circumstances to make ours a well-armed society. In a typical year approximately 12,000 murders are committed in the United States with firearms—most with handguns. Handguns are also used in many other crimes. Approximately 1 million serious violations of the law—ranging from homicide through rape, robbery, and assault—occur each year in which a handgun is used. Government statistics show that[1]

- Nonfatal handgun crimes average 4.5 offenses per year for every 1,000 people age 12 or over.
- Handguns are used in approximately 56% of all murders.
- Offenders armed with handguns commit one in every eight nonfatal violent crimes, such as rape, robbery, and assault.
- Young black males comprise the group most victimized by handgun crime. There are approximately 40 handgun crimes committed yearly against every 1,000 black males aged 16–19—a rate four times that for young white males.
- Offenders fire their weapons in 17% of all nonfatal handgun crimes, missing the victim four out of five times.
- About 21,000 victims a year are wounded by handguns.
- An average of 62,000 persons per year—about 1% of all violent crime victims—defend themselves with a firearm.
- Firearms are stolen in an estimated 340,000 crimes per year.

In 1994, in response to growing public concern over the easy availability of handguns, the U.S. Congress passed, and President Clinton signed,

the Brady Handgun Violence Prevention Act. The law was named for Reagan-era press secretary James Brady, who was shot and severely wounded in an attempt on the president's life on March 30, 1981.

The Brady law provides for a five-day waiting period before the purchase of a handgun and for the establishment of a national instant criminal background checking system to be contacted by firearms dealers before the transfer of any firearm. Applications are to be checked to determine whether receipt or possession of a handgun would be in violation of federal, state, or local law.[2]

Once the national instant criminal background check system is established (the target date for the system to be 50% operational was November 30, 1998), a licensed importer, licensed manufacturer, or licensed dealer will be required to verify the identity of the purchaser using a valid photo ID (such as a driver's license) and to contact the system in order to receive a unique identification number authorizing the purchase before transfer of the handgun can be made.

The Violent Crime Control and Law Enforcement Act of 1994 further regulated the sale of firearms within the United States, banning the manufacture of 19 military-style assault weapons, including those with specific combat features, such as high-capacity ammunition clips capable of holding more than ten rounds. This 1994 law also prohibits the sale or transfer of a gun to a juvenile, as well as the possession of a gun by a juvenile, and it prohibits gun sales to, and possession by, persons subject to family violence restraining orders.

More government regulation of gun ownership is planned. In 1995, Housing and Urban Development Secretary Henry Cisneros said that the Clinton administration was considering a ban on firearms in public housing projects in order to reduce crime and improve the quality of life there.[3]

Not everyone agrees that gun sales and gun ownership should be subject to federal regulation. The National Rifle Association (NRA), the Citizen's Committee for the Right to Keep and Bear Arms, and other pro-gun ownership groups have filed lawsuits to derail enforcement of the Brady act and the assault weapons provisions of the Violent Crime Control and Law Enforcement Act. The combined cases of *Printz* v. *U.S.* (1997)[4] and *Mack* v. *U.S.* (1997)[5], found the Court ruling that *state* officials could not be required to perform background checks on gun buyers under federal law (a requirement originally imposed by the Brady law). The NRA maintains that many existing gun control laws violate the Constitution's Second Amendment, which says that "the right of the people to keep and bear Arms shall not be infringed." Similarly, the NRA criticizes the proposed ban on guns in housing projects, again citing the Second Amendment right to bear arms and arguing that the ban would be "discriminatory" and would disarm and "single-out low-income citizens." NRA-sponsored efforts are currently underway in the House and Senate to repeal the ban on some military-style assault weapons.

In a potentially serious blow to federal efforts at gun control, the U.S. Supreme Court, in the case of *U.S.* v. *Alfonso Lopez, Jr.* (1995),[6] agreed with a lower court ruling which dismissed charges against a 12th-grade student who had carried a concealed .38-caliber handgun and five bullets into Edison High School in San Antonio, Texas. The student was charged with violating the federal Gun-Free School Zones Act of 1990, which forbids "any individual knowingly to possess a firearm at a place that [he or she] knows...is a school zone." The law had been passed to assuage parents' concerns that their children might be in mortal danger due to the presence of guns in the hands of school-aged children and interlopers on school property. The Court, however, ruled that education and the administration of educational facilities was a local and not a national function, effectively invalidating the law.

The 1996 Domestic Violence Offender Gun Ban[7] is a relatively new tool in the federal gun control arsenal. The ban prohibits individuals convicted of misdemeanor domestic violence offenses from owning or using firearms. A year after the law was passed, however, it became embroiled in controversy when hundreds of police officers across the country who had been convicted of domestic violence offenses were found to be in violation of the ban. A number of officers lost their jobs, while others were placed in positions that did not require the carrying of firearms. Beth Weaver, a spokeswoman for the National Association of Police Organizations, noted that "the [ban] is causing more chaos than almost anything I've ever seen in law enforcement..."[8] While some legislators pushed to exempt police officers and military personnel from the ban's provisions, others argued that they should be included. Feminist Majority President Eleanor Smeal was angered. "Putting guns back in the hands of wife beaters and child abusers is outrageous," she said. "Rather than trying to seek an exemption for police officers and military personnel who are abusers, we should be concerned with why we are recruiting so many abusers for these positions. One half of all 911 calls are related to domestic violence. Victims of domestic violence should expect a sympathetic officer responding to 911 calls, not one who has committed domestic violence himself,"[9] Smeal said.

QUESTIONS FOR DISCUSSION

1. This box says that "Not everyone agrees that gun sales and gun ownership should be subject to federal regulation." How do you feel? Why?

2. Do you believe that regulating the sale of handguns will lower the crime rate in the United States? Why or why not?

3. Should the Domestic Violence Offender Gun Ban be applied to police officers who have been convicted of domestic violence offenses? Why or why not?

[1]Michael J. Sniffen, "Handgun Crimes," The Associated Press wire services, May 15, 1994.

[2]18 U.S.C., Section 922(q)(1)(A).

[3]"Administration May Ban Firearms from Public Housing," United Press wire services, northern edition, February 5, 1995.

[4]Printz v. U.S. (1997), No. 95–1478. Decided June 27, 1997.

[5]Mack v. U.S. (1997), No. 95–1503. Decided June 27, 1997.

[6]U.S. v. Alfonso Lopez, Jr., 115 S.Ct. 1624, 131 L. Ed. 2d 626 (1995).

[7]PL 104–208. An amendment to Section 921(a) of Title 18, USC. Also known as the Lautenberg Amendment.

[8]Jacob R. Clark, "Police Careers May Take a Beating from Fed Domestic-Violence Law," Law Enforcement News, Vol. 23, no. 461 (February 14, 1997), p. 1.

[9]Ibid.

Robbery

Robbery, sometimes confused with burglary, is a personal crime and involves a face-to-face confrontation between victim and perpetrator. Weapons may be used, or strong-armed robbery may occur through intimidation, especially where gangs threaten victims by their sheer number. Purse snatching and pocket-picking are not classified as robbery by the UCR Program, but are included under the category "larceny-theft."

In 1996 individuals (versus businesses and banks) were typical targets of robbers. Banks, gas stations, convenience stores, and other businesses were the second most common target of robbers, with residential robberies accounting for only 10.6% of the total. In 1996, 537,050 robberies were reported to the police, and 51% of them were highway robberies (meaning that they occurred outdoors, probably as the victim was walking) or muggings. Strong-armed robberies accounted for 39% of total robberies reported. Guns were used in 41% of all robberies and knives in 9%.

Armed robbers are dangerous. Guns are actually discharged in 20% of all robberies.[36] Whenever a robbery occurs, the UCR Program scores the event as one robbery, even though there may have been a number of victims who were robbed during the event. With the move toward incident-driven reporting (discussed later in this chapter), however, the UCRs will soon make data available on the number of individuals robbed in each instance of robbery. Because statistics on crime show only the most serious offense which occurred during a particular episode, robberies are often hidden when they occur in conjunction with other, more serious, crimes. For example, in a recent year 3% of robbery victims were also raped, and a large number of homicide victims were robbed.[37]

Robbery is primarily an urban offense, and most arrestees are young males who are members of minority groups. The robbery rate in large cities in 1996 was 610 (per every 100,000 inhabitants) while it was only 18 in rural areas. Ninety percent of those arrested in 1996 were male, 65% were under the age of 25, and 60% were minorities.[38]

Robbery   The unlawful taking or attempted taking of property that is in the immediate possession of another, by force or the threat of force. Armed robbery differs from unarmed or strong-armed robbery with regard to the presence of a weapon. Contrary to popular conceptions, highway robbery does not necessarily occur on a street—and rarely in a vehicle. Highway robbery is a term applicable to any form of robbery which occurs in a public place and out of doors.

Assault   The unlawful, intentional inflicting, or attempted or threatened inflicting, of injury upon the person of another. Historically, *assault* meant only the attempt to inflict injury on another person. A completed act constituted the separate offense of battery. Under most modern penal codes, however, attempted and completed acts are put together under the generic term *assault*. While the terms "aggravated assault" and "simple assault" are standard terms for reporting purposes, most state penal codes use labels such as "first degree," "second degree," and so on to make such distinctions.

Burglary   The unlawful entry of any fixed structure, vehicle, or vessel used for regular residence, industry, or business, with or without force, with intent to commit a felony or larceny. For UCR purposes, the crime of burglary can be reported if (1) an unlawful entry of an unlocked structure has occurred, (2) a breaking and entering (of a secured structure) has taken place, or (3) a burglary has been attempted.

Aggravated Assault

Assaults are of two types: aggravated and simple. Simple assaults may involve pushing and shoving or even fistfights. Aggravated assaults are distinguished from simple assaults by the fact that they either include the use of a weapon, or the assault victim requires medical assistance. When deadly weapons are employed, even though no injury may result, aggravated assaults may be chargeable as attempted murder.[39] Hence, because of their potentially serious consequences, the UCR Program scores some cases of attempted assault as aggravated assaults.

In 1996, 1,029,814 cases of aggravated assault were reported to law enforcement agencies in the United States. The summer months evidenced the greatest frequency of assault, while February and November were the months with the lowest number of reports. Most aggravated assaults were committed with blunt objects or objects near at hand (34%), while hands, feet, and fists were also commonly used (26%). Less frequent were knives and firearms (18% and 22%, respectively), as Figure 2–5 shows. Because those who commit assaults are often known to their victims, aggravated assaults are relatively easy to solve. Fifty-eight percent of all aggravated assaults reported to the police in 1996 were cleared by arrest.

Burglary

Although it may involve personal and even violent confrontations, burglary is primarily a property crime. Burglars are interested in financial gain and usually fence (that is, illegally sell) stolen items in order to recover a fraction of their cash value. About 2.5 million burglaries were reported to the police in 1996. Dollar losses to burglary victims totaled over $3.3 billion, with an average loss per offense of $1,332.

Many people fear nighttime burglary of their residence. They imagine themselves asleep in bed as a stranger breaks into their home and then conjure up visions of a violent confrontation. While such scenarios do occur, daytime burglary is more common. Many families now have two or more breadwinners, and since children are in school during the day, some homes—and even entire neighborhoods—are virtually unoccupied during daylight hours. This shift in patterns of social activity has led to a growing burglary threat against residences during daytime.

The UCR Program employs three classifications of burglary: (1) forcible entry, (2) unlawful entry where no force is used, and (3) attempted forcible entry. In most jurisdictions, force need not be employed for a crime to be classified as burglary. Unlocked doors and open windows are invitations to burglars, and the crime of burglary consists not so much in a forcible entry as it does in the intent of the offender to trespass and steal. In a ten-year period analyzed by the Bureau of Justice Statistics, 23% of all burglaries were unlawful entries, 69% were forcible entries, and 8% were attempted forcible entries.[40] The most dangerous burglaries were those in which a household member was home (about 10% of all burglaries).[41]

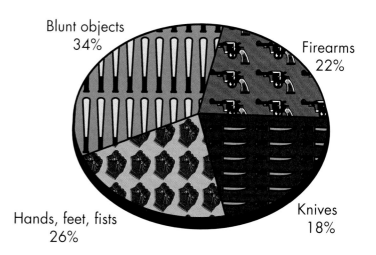

FIGURE 2–5   Aggravated assault—weapons used, 1996. *Source:* Federal Bureau of Investigation, *Crime in the United States 1996* (Washington, D.C.: U.S. Government Printing Office, 1997).

Motor vehicle theft or larceny? Even the FBI's Education and Training Services Unit in Washington, D.C., in conversations with the author, was unsure of how to classify the 1995 theft of this M-60 tank by Shawn Nelson, a former Army tank operator. Nelson drove the tank through the streets of San Diego, before being shot and killed by police who jumped on the tank and cut the hatch open with bolt cutters. In this photo, Nelson's body is being removed from the tank shortly after he was shot. *David McNew, Sygma*

Residents who were home during a burglary suffered a greater than 30% chance of becoming the victim of a violent crime.[42]

Property crimes generally involve low rates of clearance. Burglary is no exception. The clearance rate for burglary in 1996 was only 14%. Burglars are usually unknown to their victims, and, even if known, they conceal their identity by committing their crime when the victim is not present.

Larceny

Larceny is another name for theft. Some states distinguish between simple larceny and grand larceny. Grand larceny is usually defined as theft of valuables in excess of a certain set dollar amount, such as $200. Categorizing the crime by dollar amount, however, can present unique problems, as during the high fiscal inflation periods of the 1970s, when legislatures found themselves unable to enact statutory revisions fast enough to keep pace with inflation.

Larceny, as defined by the UCR Program, includes thefts of any amount. The reports specifically list the following offenses as types of larceny (listed here in order of declining frequency):

- Thefts from motor vehicles
- Shoplifting
- Thefts of motor vehicle parts and accessories
- Thefts from buildings
- Bicycle thefts
- Pocket-picking
- Purse snatching
- Thefts from coin-operated machines

Thefts of farm animals (known as rustling) and thefts of most types of farm machinery also fall into the larceny category. In fact, larceny is such a broad category that it serves as a

Larceny The unlawful taking or attempted taking of property other than a motor vehicle from the possession of another, by stealth, without force and without deceit, with intent to permanently deprive the owner of the property. Larceny is the most common of the eight major offenses—although probably only a small percentage of all larcenies which occur are actually reported to the police because of the small dollar amounts involved.

A crime of theft? Dr. Ricardo Asch, the California physician accused in 1995 of stealing frozen human embryos and illegally transferring them to infertile couples. Crime today can take many forms which traditional laws may be hard-pressed to cover. *Orange County Register, SABA Press Photos, Inc.*

kind of "catchall" in the UCR. In 1995, for example, Yale University officials filed larceny charges against 25-year-old student Lon Grammer, claiming that he had fraudulently obtained university monies.[43] The university maintained that Grammer stole his education by forging college and high-school transcripts and concocting letters of recommendation prior to admission. Grammer's alleged misdeeds, which Yale University officials said misled them into thinking that Grammer, a poor student before attending Yale, had an exceptional scholastic record, permitted him to receive $61,475 in grants and loans during the time he attended the school. Grammer was also expelled.

Larceny is a kind of catchall category, and reported thefts can involve a wide diversity of materials with values that range anywhere from pocket change to the stealing of a $100 million aircraft. As a consequence, some state laws distinguish between grand theft (or grand larceny) and petty theft. Specifically excluded from the count of larceny for reporting purposes are crimes of embezzlement, "con" games, forgery, and worthless checks. Larceny has been traditionally thought of as a crime which requires physical possession of the item appropriated. Hence, most computer crimes, including thefts engineered through on-line access or thefts of software and information itself, have typically not been scored as larcenies—unless electronic circuitry, disks, or machines themselves were actually stolen. On the other hand, the crime of larceny may count other types of high-technology thefts. In 1995, for example, Dr. Ricardo Asch, a world-renowned fertility doctor working at the University of California-Irvine, was accused of stealing frozen human embryos and implanting them into infertile women.[44] California university police reported they were investigating the egg thefts, and Dr. Asch resigned from his position at the university's Center for Reproductive Health.

Reports to the police in 1996 showed 7,894,620 larcenies nationwide, with the total value of property stolen placed at more than $4 billion. The most common form of larceny in recent years has been theft of motor vehicle parts, accessories, and contents. The theft of tires, wheels, stereos, hubcaps, radar detectors, CB radios, cassette tapes, compact discs, and cellular phones account for many of the items reported stolen.

Larceny is the most frequently reported major crime according to the UCR. It may also be the UCR's most underreported crime category because small thefts rarely come to the attention of the police. The average value of items reported stolen in 1996 was about $530.

Motor Vehicle Theft

Motor Vehicle Theft The unlawful taking or attempted taking of a self-propelled road vehicle owned by another with the intent to deprive him or her of it permanently or temporarily. The stealing of trains, planes, boats, construction equipment, and most farm machinery is classified as larceny under the UCR reporting program, *not* as motor vehicle theft.

For record-keeping purposes, the UCR Program defines motor vehicles as self-propelled vehicles which run on the ground and not on rails. Included in the definition are automobiles, motorcycles, motorscooters, trucks, buses, and snowmobiles. Excluded are trains, airplanes, bulldozers, most farm and construction machinery, ships, boats, and spacecraft—whose theft would be scored as larceny.[45] Vehicles that are temporarily taken by individuals who have lawful access to them are not scored as thefts. Hence, spouses who jointly own most property may drive the family car, even though one spouse may think of the vehicle as their exclusive personal property.

As mentioned earlier, motor vehicle theft is a crime in which most occurrences are reported to law enforcement agencies. Insurance companies require police reports before they will reimburse car owners for their losses. Some reports of motor vehicle thefts, however, may be false. People who have damaged their own vehicles in solitary crashes, or who have been unable to sell them, may try to force insurance companies to "buy" them through reports of theft.

In 1996 1.4 million motor vehicles were reported stolen. The average value per vehicle stolen was $5,372, making motor vehicle theft a $7.5 billion crime. The clearance rate for motor vehicle theft was only 14% in 1996. City agencies reported the lowest rates of clearance (13%), while rural counties had the highest rate (32%). Many stolen vehicles are routinely and quickly disassembled, with parts being resold through chop shops. Auto parts are, of course, much more difficult to identify and trace than are intact vehicles. In some parts of the country, chop shops operate like big businesses, and one shop may strip a dozen or more cars per day.

Motor vehicle theft can turn violent, such as in cases of "carjacking"—a crime in which offenders force the occupants of a car onto the street before stealing the vehicle. In an incident that brought carjacking to national prominence a few years ago, Pamela Basu of Savage, Maryland, was dragged 2 miles to her death when she became entangled in her seat belt after being pushed from her car as the carjackers drove off. The thieves had to sideswipe a chain-link fence in order to finally dislodge her. Her 2-year-old daughter, still strapped into her carseat, was apparently later tossed from the vehicle. The FBI estimates that carjackings account for slightly more than 1% of all motor vehicle thefts.[46]

Arrest reports for motor vehicle theft show that the typical offender is a young male. Fifty-nine percent of all arrestees in 1996 were under the age of 21, and 86% were male.

Arson

The UCR Program received crime reports from more than 16,000 law enforcement agencies in 1996.[47] Of these, only 8,325 submitted arson reports for all 12 months of the year. Few agencies provided complete data as to the type of arson (nature of the item burned), the estimated monetary value of the property damaged, ownership of the property, and so on.

Current arson data include only those fires which, through investigation, are determined to have been willfully or maliciously set. Fires of unknown or suspicious origin are excluded from arson statistics.[48]

The intentional and unlawful burning of structures (houses, storage buildings, manufacturing facilities, etc.) was the type of arson most often reported in 1996 (37,047 instances). The arson of vehicles was the second most common category, with 22,162 such burnings reported. The average dollar loss per instance of arson in 1996 was $10,280, and total nationwide property damage was placed at over $1 billion.[49] As with most property crimes, the clearance rate for arson was low—only 16% nationally.

The crime of arson exists in a kind of statistical limbo. In 1979 Congress ordered that it be added as an eighth Index offense. To date, however, the UCR Program has been unable to integrate statistics on arson successfully into the yearly Crime Index. The problem is twofold: (1) many law enforcement agencies have not yet begun making regular reports to the FBI on arson offenses which come under their jurisdiction, and (2) any change in the number of index offenses produces a Crime Index which will not permit meaningful comparisons to earlier crime data.

The Crime Index is a composite offense rate which provides for useful comparisons over time and between jurisdictions, so long as it retains definitional consistency. Adding a new offense to the Index, or substantially changing the definition of any of its categories, still provides a measure of "crime," but it changes the meaning of the term.

Some of these difficulties may eventually be resolved through the Special Arson Program, authorized by Congress in 1982. The FBI, in conjunction with the National Fire Data Center,

Arson The burning or attempted burning of property with or without intent to defraud. Some instances of arson are the result of malicious mischief, while others involve attempts to claim insurance monies. Still others are committed in an effort to disguise other crimes, such as murder, burglary, and larceny.

Table 2-2   UCR Part II Offenses, 1996

Offense Category	Number of Arrests
Simple assault	1,329,000
Forgery and counterfeiting	121,600
Fraud	465,000
Embezzlement	15,700
Stolen property (receiving, etc.)	151,100
Vandalism	320,900
Weapons (carrying, etc.)	216,200
Prostitution and related offenses	99,000
Sex offenses (statutory rape, etc.)	95,800
Drug law violations	1,506,200
Gambling	21,000
Offenses against the family (nonsupport, etc.)	149,800
Driving under the influence	1,467,300
Liquor law violations	677,400
Public drunkenness	718,700
Disorderly conduct	842,600
Vagrancy	27,800
Curfew/loitering	185,100
Runaways	195,700
Total	8,605,900

Source: Federal Bureau of Investigation, *Uniform Crime Reports for the United States, 1996* (Washington, D.C.: U.S. Government Printing Office, 1997).

now operates a Special Arson Reporting System, which focuses upon fire departments across the nation. The Arson Reporting system is designed to provide data which supplements yearly UCR arson tabulations.[50]

PART II OFFENSES

Part II Offenses

In Uniform Crime Reports terminology, a set of offense categories used in UCR data concerning arrests.

The *Uniform Crime Reports* also include information on what the FBI calls Part II offenses. Part II offenses are generally less serious than those that make up the Crime Index and include a number of social order, or so-called "victimless," crimes. The statistics on Part II offenses are for recorded arrests, not crimes reported to the police. The logic inherent in this form of scoring is that most Part II offenses would never come to the attention of the police were it not for arrests. Included in the Part II category are the crimes shown in Table 2–2 with the number of estimated arrests made in each category for 1996.

Part II arrests are counted each time a person is taken into custody. As a result, the statistics in Table 2-2 do not measure the number of persons arrested, but rather the number of arrests made. Some persons were arrested more than once.

NIBRS: THE NEW UCR

The *Uniform Crime Reports* are undergoing significant changes in the way in which data is gathered and reported. From 1985 to 1992 the UCR Program was comprehensively evaluated under federal contract by ABT Associates, Inc., of Cambridge, Massachusetts. The final report of the UCR study group, entitled *A Blueprint for the Future of the Uniform Crime Reporting System*, recommended a number of sweeping changes. Among them were

- Each category of offense should clearly distinguish statistics on attempts versus actual commissions.

- The rape category should be broadened to include all forcible sex offenses. Sexual battery, sodomy, and oral copulation—accomplished through the use of force—should be included.
- The "hierarchy rule" should be modified so as to count the most serious offense *for each individual victim* during an incident.[51]
- Crimes against individuals, households, and businesses should be more clearly distinguished in most categories.
- Aggravated assault should be more clearly defined in terms of the weapons used and the degree of injury suffered.
- A code of professional standards should be developed for reporting agencies and for the system as a whole.
- The UCR should be modified so as to permit easier and more meaningful comparisons with the NCVS and with Offender-Based Transaction Statistics (OBTS).

Many of these changes are now being implemented. Whereas the original UCR system was "summary based," the new "enhanced" UCR is called the National Incident-Based Reporting System, or NIBRS. The old system depended upon statistical tabulations of crime data which were often little more than frequency counts. In contrast, NIBRS is "incident driven." Under the new system, many details will be gathered about each criminal incident. Included among them will be information on place of occurrence, weapon used, type and value of property damaged or stolen, the personal characteristics of the offender and the victim, the nature of any relationship between the two, nature of the disposition of the complaint, and so on. The new reporting system replaces the old Part I and Part II offenses with 22 general offenses, including arson, assault, bribery, burglary, counterfeiting, vandalism, narcotic offenses, embezzlement, extortion, fraud, gambling, homicide, kidnapping, larceny, motor vehicle theft, pornography, prostitution, robbery, forcible sex offenses, nonforcible sex offenses, receiving stolen property, and weapons violations. Other offenses on which data will be gathered include bad checks, vagrancy, disorderly conduct, driving under the influence, drunkenness, nonviolent family offenses, liquor law violations, "peeping Tom" activity, runaway, trespass, and a general category of all "other" criminal law violations.

NIBRS also eliminates the need for the "hierarchy rule" (because multiple types of crimes can be reported within a single incident) and collects an expanded array of attributes involved in the commission of offenses, including whether the offender is suspected of using alcohol, drugs or narcotics, and/or a computer in the commission of the offense. The FBI began accepting crime data in NIBRS format in January 1989. Although NIBRS is intended to be fully in place by 1999, delays have been routine. A 1997 evaluation of the status of NIBRS implementation reported that "Although it has been a full decade since publication of the *Blueprint* recommending incident-based reporting, less than 6% of the U.S. population is represented by NIBRS contributing agencies."[52] In other words, as late as 1997, 94% of U.S. law enforcement agencies were continuing to report crime incident data under the old format. A separate study concluded that for many law enforcement "agencies, the costs of implementing changes in reporting practices to make their systems NIBRS-compliant (for example, revising offense reporting forms, department-wide training, and software re-programming), compounded by concerns over the impact NIBRS will have on the department's reported crime rate and a lack of understanding on how the data will be used at state and federal levels, create formidable impediments to NIBRS implementation."[53]

Other reporting changes, however, have already occurred. The 1990 Crime Awareness and Campus Security Act, for example, required college campuses to commence publishing annual "security reports," beginning in September 1992. Although campuses are not required by the law to share crime data with the FBI, many have begun doing just that—increasing the reported national incidence of a variety of offenses. In December 1996 the Bureau of Justice Statistics released a survey of public and private four-year institutions with 2,500 or more students. At those schools, which enrolled four out of five of the nation's nearly 9 million college students, BJS found that there were 64 violent crimes and 2,141 property crimes reported to police for every 100,000 students in 1994, the most recent year with complete data.

We are the most violent and self-destructive nation on earth...In 1990, no nation had a higher murder rate than the United States. What is worse, no nation was even close.

—From a 1991 report released by Joseph R. Biden, Jr., U.S. Senate Judiciary Committee Chairman

Burned pages of a religious book are scattered in the remains of the Rising Star Baptist Church after an arson fire in 1996. Hate crimes are officially defined as offenses "in which the defendant's conduct was motivated by hatred, bias, or prejudice, based on the actual or perceived race, color, religion, national origin, ethnicity, gender, or sexual orientation of another individual or group of individuals." *AP/Wide World Photos*

Hate Crimes Criminal offenses in which the defendant's conduct was motivated by hatred, bias, or prejudice, based on the actual or perceived race, color, religion, national origin, ethnicity, gender, or sexual orientation of another individual or group of individuals.

HATE CRIMES

A final change in reporting practices followed from the Hate Crime Statistics Act, signed into law by President Bush in April 1990. The act mandates a statistical tally of "hate crimes," and data collection under the law began in January 1991. Hate crimes have been defined by Congress as offenses "in which the defendant's conduct was motivated by hatred, bias, or prejudice, based on the actual or perceived race, color, religion, national origin, ethnicity, gender, or sexual orientation of another individual or group of individuals."[54] In 1996 police agencies reported a total of 10,702 hate crime incidents, including 12 murders, across the country. Fourteen percent of the incidents were motivated by religious bias, while 63% were caused by racial hatred. Twelve percent of all hate crimes were based on sexual orientation, and most of those were committed against males believed by their victimizers to be homosexuals.[55] Most hate crimes fell into the category of "intimidation," although vandalism, simple assault, and aggravated assault also accounted for a fair number of hate crime offenses. Notable in recent years has been a spate of church burnings throughout the south where congregations have been predominantly African-American. A few robberies and rapes were also classified under the hate crime umbrella in 1996.

Although hate crimes are popularly conceived of as crimes motivated by racial enmity, the Violent Crime Control and Law Enforcement Act of 1994 created a new definitional category of "crimes of violence motivated by gender." Congress defined a gender-motivated crime of violence to mean "a crime of violence committed because of gender or on the basis of gender, and due, at least in part, to an animus based on the victim's gender..." Even though the 1994 act did not establish separate penalties for gender-motivated crimes—anticipating, instead, that they would be prosecuted as felonies under existing laws—it did establish a federal civil rights cause of action for victims of crimes of violence motivated by gender. Under this law, anyone who suffers gender-motivated violence may sue his or her attacker to recover monetary damages. Additionally, the 1994 act mandated the addition to the hate crimes category of crimes motivated by biases against persons with disabilities.

Hate crimes are sometimes called **bias crimes.** One form of bias crime that bears special mention is homophobic homicide. Homophobic homicide is a term that refers to the

Bias Crimes Another term for hate crimes.

murder of homosexuals by those opposed to their lifestyles. A 1997 movie, *Licensed to Kill*, by producer/director Arthur Dong, for example, tells a harrowing story about homophobia and murder using police interrogation videos, crime scene photos, and courtroom footage of real-life events. Included in the movie is a detailed description of how former U.S. Army Sergeant Kenneth French, Jr., randomly killed four people in a Fayetteville, North Carolina, restaurant in response to President's Clinton's decision to allow gays into the military. According to witnesses, French shouted, "I'll show you, Clinton, about letting gays into the army" as he fired at patrons and the restaurant's owner.[56]

Even more worrisome to many enforcement agencies is the continued growth of separatist groups with their own vision of a future America. Some, like the White Aryan Resistance (WAR), hope for the start of RAHOWA, or racial holy war. Similar groups include the White Patriot Party; the Order; Aryan Nations; Posse Comitatus; the Covenant, the Sword, and the Arm of the Lord; the Ku Klux Klan; and umbrella organizations such as the Christian Conservative Church. Described variously as the "radical right," "neo-Nazis," "skinheads," "white supremacists," and "racial hate groups," indications are that these groups are organized, well financed, and extremely well armed. John R. Harrell, leader of the Christian Conservative Church, preaches that the nation is on the eve of destruction. According to some authorities, Christian patriots are exhorted to stand ready to seize control of the nation before leadership can fall into the "wrong hands."[57] Such extremist groups adhere to identity theology, a religion which claims that members of the white race are God's chosen people. Identity theology envisions an America ruled exclusively by white people under "God's law."[58] Figure 2–6 shows the location of various supremacist and survivalist groups in the United States.

Whatever we may think of them, the activities of supremacist groups may be constitutionally protected, at least in some instances. Recent authors[59] suggest, for example, that statutes intended to control hate crimes may run afoul of constitutional considerations insofar as they (1) are too vague, (2) criminalize thought more than action, (3) attempt to control what would otherwise be free speech, and (4) deny equal protection of the laws to those

FIGURE 2–6 White supremacist groups in the United States. *Source:* Klanwatch Project. Reprinted with permission.

Theory into Practice

HATE CRIMES

A decade ago, Glenn Miller, then leader of the White Patriot Party in North Carolina, declared war on ZOG—the "Zionist Occupational Government"—a conspiratorial coalition that Miller and his followers believed held the true reins of power in the United States. What follows is a portion of that strongly worded original document—authentically reproduced here to include the misspellings and typographical errors found in the original. Not long after the declaration was issued, Miller was arrested and sent to prison for his part in various crimes against the government.

DECLARATION OF WAR

Dear White Patriots:

All 5,000 White Patriots are now honor bound and duty bound to pick up the sword and do battle against the forces of evil. In the name of our Aryan God, thru His beloved son, I

Glenn Miller now this 6th day of April 1987 do hereby declare total war. I ask for no quarter. I will give none. I declare war against Niggers, Jews, Queers, assorted Mongrels, White Race traitors and despicable informants. We White Patriots will now begin the Race War and it will spread gloriously thru-out the nation. We will cleanse the land of evil, corruption, and mongrels. And, we will build a glorious future and a nation in which all our People can scream proudly, and honestly, "This is our Land. This is our People. This is our God, and this we will defend." War is the only way now, brothers and sisters. ZOG has pointed the way for us. He has left us no other choice. And, so fellow Aryan Warriors strike now. Strike for your home land. Strike for your Southern honor. Strike for the little children. Strike for your wives and loved ones. Strike for sweet

Mother Dixie. Strike for the 16 million innocent White babies murdered by Jew-legalized abortion and who cry out from their graves for vengence. Strike for the millions of your People who have been raped, assaulted, and murdered by niggers and other mongrels. Strike in vengence against the Jews for all the millions of our Race slaughtered in Jew-Wars. Strike my brothers and sisters, strike, for all the outrages committed against our People...

For God, Race, Nation and Southern Honor

Glenn Miller, Leader White Patriot Party and Loyal member of "The Order"

"THE ORDER WILL LIVE SO LONG AS ONE OF US BREATHES"

National Crime Victimization Survey (NCVS) An annual survey of selected American households conducted by the Bureau of Justice Statistics (BJS) in order to determine the extent of criminal victimization throughout the U.S.—especially unreported victimization.

who wish to express their personal biases. The U.S. Supreme Court would seem to agree. In the 1992 case of *R.A.V.* v. *City of St. Paul*,[60] which involved a burning cross on the front lawn of a black family, the Court struck down a city ordinance designed to prevent the bias-motivated display of symbols or objects, such as Nazi swastikas or burning crosses. In the same year, in the case of *Forsyth County, Ga.* v. *Nationalist Movement*,[61] the Court held that a county requirement regulating parades was unconstitutional because it regulated freedom of speech—in this case a plan by an affiliate of the Ku Klux Klan to parade in opposition to a Martin Luther King birthday celebration. In 1995, in the case of *Capitol Square Review* and *Advisory Board* v. *Pinette*, the Court reiterated its position, saying that KKK organizers in Ohio could legitimately erect an unattended cross on the Statehouse Plaza in Columbus's Capitol Square. Some laws intended to reduce the incidence of hate crimes appear to pass Supreme Court muster, however. In 1993, in the case of *Wisconsin* v. *Mitchell*,[62] for example, the Court held that Mitchell, a black man whose severe beating of a white boy was racially motivated, could be punished with additional severity as permitted by Wisconsin law because he acted out of race hatred. The Court called the assault "conduct unprotected by the First Amendment" and upheld the Wisconsin statute saying, "[since] the statute has no 'chilling effect' on free speech, it is not unconstitutionally overbroad."

The National Crime Victimization Survey

As mentioned near the beginning of this chapter, a second major source of statistical data about crime in the United States is the **National Crime Victimization Survey (NCVS)**, which is based upon victim self-reports rather than on police reports. The NCVS began operation in 1972 and

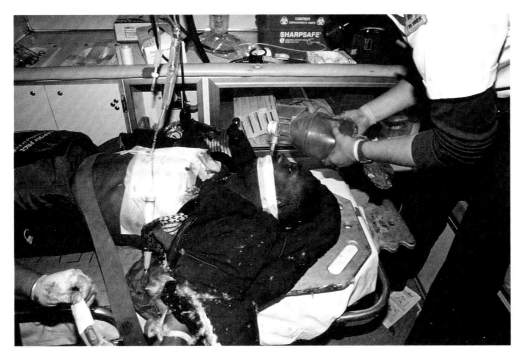

Young black males are more likely to be victims of violent crime than are members of any
other group. Here, a shooting victim receives emergency help from paramedics.
P. Cahuvel, Sygma

built upon earlier efforts by both the National Opinion Research Center and the President's
Commission on Law Enforcement and the Administration of Justice in the late 1960s to uncover
what some had been calling the "dark figure" (or unreported offenses) of crime.

Early data from the NCVS changed the way criminologists thought about crime in the
United States. The use of victim self-reports led to the discovery that crime of all types was
more prevalent than UCR statistics indicated. Many cities were shown to have victimization
rates more than twice the rate of reported offenses. Others, such as St. Louis, Missouri, and
Newark, New Jersey, were found to have rates of victimization which very nearly approximated reported crime. New York, often thought of as a "high-crime" city, was discovered to
have one of the lowest rates of self-reported victimization.

NCVS data are gathered by the Bureau of Justice Statistics (BJS) through a cooperative
arrangement with the U.S. Census Bureau.[63] NCVS interviewers work with a national sample of about 42,000 households which are interviewed twice each year. Household lists are
completely revised at the end of every three-year period. BJS statistics are published as
research briefs called "Crime and the Nation's Households" and "Criminal Victimization,"
and an annual report entitled *Criminal Victimization in the United States.*

Using definitions similar to those used by the UCR Program, the NCVS includes data on
the national incidence of rape, robbery, assault, burglary, personal and household larceny,
and motor vehicle theft. Not included are murder, kidnapping, and victimless crimes.
Commercial robbery and the burglary of businesses were dropped from NCVS reports in
1977. The NCVS employs a hierarchical counting system similar to that of the UCR: It
counts only the most "serious" incident in any series of criminal events perpetrated against
the same individual. Both completed and attempted offenses are counted, although only persons 12 years of age and older are included in household surveys. Highlights of NCVS statistics for the 1990s reveal that[64]

- Approximately 23 million American households per year are touched by crime—or 25%
  of all households.
- Nearly 35 million victimizations are reported to the NCVS per year.
- City residents are about twice as likely as rural residents to be victims of crime.
- About half of all violent crimes, two-fifths of all household crimes, and slightly more
  than one-fourth of all crimes of personal theft are reported to police.[65]

Table 2-3 A Comparison of UCR and NCVS Data, 1996

Offense	UCR	NCVS[1]
Violent Crime		
Homicide[2]	19,645	—
Forcible rape	95,769	307,000
Robbery	537,050	1,134,000
Aggravated assault	1,029,814	1,910,000
Property Crime		
Burglary	2,501,524	4,845,000
Larceny	7,894,620	21,120,000
Motor vehicle theft	1,395,192	1,387,000
Arson[3]	88,887	—
Total of all crimes recorded[4]	13,562,501	36,796,000

[1]NCVS data covers "households touched by crime," not absolute numbers of crime occurrences. More than one victimization may occur per household, but only the number of households in which victimizations occur enter the tabulations.

[2]Homicide statistics are not maintained by the NCVS.

[3]Arson data are incomplete in the UCR and not reported by NCVS.

[4]NCVS numbers include other crimes not shown in the table.

Sources: Compiled from the U.S. Department of Justice, *Criminal Victimization 1996* (Washington, D.C.: Bureau of Justice Statistics, 1997); Federal Bureau of Investigation, *Crime in the United States 1996* (Washington, D.C.: U.S. Government Printing Office, 1997).

- The total "personal cost" of crime to victims is about $13 billion per year for the United States as a whole.
- Victims of crime are more often men than women.
- Younger people are more likely than the elderly to be victims of crime.
- Blacks are more likely than whites or members of other racial groups to be victims of violent crimes.[66]
- Violent victimization rates are higher among people in lower-income families.
- Young males have the highest violent victimization rates; elderly females have the lowest.
- The chance of violent criminal victimization is much higher for young black males than for any other segment of the population. (The life chances of murder run from a high of 1 in 21 for a black male to a low of 1 in 369 for a white female.)[67]

A comparison of NCVS and UCR data for 1996 can be found in Table 2–3.

Visit the *CJToday* Web page and click on "Web Chapters," then "Chapter 2." Follow the "find the facts" links in order to explore Bureau of Justice Statistics and FBI crime information on the Web.

Problems with the NCVS

Because most researchers believe that self-reports provide a more accurate gauge of criminal incidents than do police reports, many tend to accept NCVS data over that which is provided by the UCR program. The NCVS, however, is not without its problems. Primary among them is the potential for false or exaggerated reports. False reports may be generated by overzealous interviewers or self-aggrandizing respondents and are difficult to filter out. There are no reliable estimates as to the proportion of such responses which make up NCVS totals. Unintentional inaccuracies create other problems. Respondents may suffer from faulty memories, they may misinterpret events, and they may ascribe criminal intent to accidents and mistakes. Likewise, the lapse of time between the event itself and the conduct of the interview may cause some crimes to be forgotten and others to be inaccurately reported.

Redesign of the NCVS

Just as the *Uniform Crime Reports* are undergoing change, so too is the National Crime Victimization Survey. In 1995 the NCVS began reporting data from a redesigned question-naire[68] intended to provide details on

- Interaction between victim and offender.
- Victims' crime deterrence efforts.
- Perceived effectiveness of crime deterrence efforts.
- Bystander behavior.
- Perceived alcohol and drug use by offenders.
- Suspected offender gang involvement.

The redesigned questionnaire included changes to both the survey's content and procedures used in data gathering, including

- Additional cues to help survey participants recall incidents.
- Questions encouraging respondents to report victimizations that they themselves may not define as crimes.
- More direct questions on rape, sexual assault, and other sexual crimes.
- New material to measure victimization by nonstrangers, including domestic violence.

Multiple questions and cues on crimes committed by family members, intimates, and acquaintances were added to the survey to explore domestic violence issues, and the new NCVS broadened the scope of covered sexual incidents beyond the traditional categories of rape and attempted rape to include sexual assault (other than rape), verbal threats of rape or sexual assault, and unwanted sexual contact without force but involving threats or other harm to the victim. The new questionnaire also allows for the classification of victimizations according to various life "domains," such as work or leisure, in which they occur. A 1994 NCVS report,[69] for example, showed that nearly 1 million people become victims of violent crime while at work—accounting for about 15% of all violent victimizations reported to surveyors. The same report said that more than 2 million personal thefts (about 25% of all such thefts) and over 200,000 auto thefts (about 13% of the total number of cars stolen) occur annually while persons are at work.

The most recent NCVS data indicate that 13% of violent victimizations (murders, rapes, robberies, and assaults) are committed by intimates (for example, spouses, ex-spouses, boyfriends, or girlfriends).[70] The huge majority of violent crimes committed by intimates are assaults (81% of all such crimes), while 15% of murders were committed by intimates. Thirty-three percent of victims of violent crimes believed their assailants to be under the influence of drugs or alcohol. In cases of rape, the proportion of assailants believed to be under the influence jumped to 45%, the highest reported by the survey. Seventy-one percent of violent crime victims reported taking some self-protective measure. Self-protective measures included struggling or fighting with the assailant, threats, running away, efforts at appeasement, or pleading. Sixty percent of victims who took self-protective measures reported that their actions reduced the severity of their victimization.

Justice agency response, as measured by the survey, shows that the police came to see the victim in 70% of violent crimes, 68% of household crimes (such as burglary and motor vehicle theft), and 51% of all larcenies. Police response was fastest in violent crimes, averaging under 10 minutes, and slowest where household crimes were involved.

Comparisons of the UCR and NCVS

Table 2–4 summarizes the differences between the UCR and the NCVS. Both provide estimates of crime in America. Both are limited by the type of crimes they choose to measure, by those they exclude from measurement, and by the methods they use to gather crime data.

Crime statistics from the UCR and NCVS are often used in building explanations for criminal behavior. Unfortunately, however, researchers too often forget that statistics which

62

CRIME IN AMERICA

Table 2–4   How Do the UCR and NCVS Compare?

National Crime Victimization

	Uniform Crime Reports	Survey
Offenses measured	Homicide Rape Robbery (personal and commercial) Assault (aggravated) Burglary (commercial and household) Larceny (commercial and household) Motor vehicle theft Arson	Rape Robbery (personal) Assault (aggravated and simple) Household burglary Larceny (personal and household) Motor vehicle theft
Scope	Crimes reported to the police in most jurisdictions; considerable flexibility	Crimes both reported and not reported to police; all data are available for a few large geographic areas
Collection method	Police department reports to FBI or to centralized state agencies that then report to FBI	Survey interviews; periodically measures the total number of crimes committed by asking a national sample of 49,000 households encompassing 101,000 persons age 12 and over about their experiences as victims of crime during a specified period
Kinds of information	In addition to offense counts, provides information on crime clearances, persons arrested, persons charged, law enforcement officers killed and assaulted, and characteristics of homicide victims	Provides details about victims (such as age, race, sex, education, income, and whether the victim and offender were related to each other) and about crimes (such as time and place of occurrence, whether or not reported to police, use of weapons, occurrence of injury, and economic consequences)
Sponsor	U.S. Department of Justice; Federal Bureau of Investigation	U.S. Department of Justice; Bureau of Justice Statistics

Source: Bureau of Justice Statistics, *Report to the Nation on Crime and Justice,* 2nd ed. (Washington, D.C.: U.S. Department of Justice, 1988), p. 11.

are merely descriptive can be weak in explanatory power. For example, NCVS data show that "household crime rates" are highest for households (1) headed by blacks, (2) headed by younger people, (3) with six or more members, (4) headed by renters, and (5) in central cities.[71] Such findings, combined with statistics which show that most crime occurs among members of the same race, have led some researchers to conclude that values among certain black subcultural group members both propel them into crime and make them targets of criminal victimization. The truth may be, however, that crime is more a function of geography (inner-city location) than of culture. From simple descriptive statistics, it is difficult to know which is the case.

Emerging Patterns of Criminal Activity

Planned revisions in both the NCVS and the UCR reflect the fact that patterns of criminal activity in the United States are changing. Georgette Bennett has termed the shift in crime patterns "crimewarps."[72] Crimewarps, says Bennett, represent major changes in both what society considers criminal and in who future criminal offenders will be. Some areas of coming change that she predicts are[73]

- The decline of street crime.
- The growth of white-collar crime.
- Increasing female involvement in crime.
- Increased crime commission by the elderly.
- A shift in high crime rates from the "Frost Belt" to the "Sun Belt."
- Safer cities, with increasing criminal activity in rural areas.
- The growth of high-technology crimes.

THE FEAR OF CRIME

Although we may read in newspapers or in books like Georgette Bennett's that violent street crime is decreasing, we may not believe it. In fact we may be just as afraid as ever. As Bennett has pointed out,[74] the fear of crime is often out of proportion to the likelihood of criminal victimization. Table 2–5 compares the chance of violent victimization with life chances of other serious events. For most people, the chance of accidental injury at work or at home is far greater than the chance of being criminally attacked.

Table 2–5   Life Chances of Serious Events.[1] How do Crime Rates Compare with the Rates of Other Life Events?

Events	Rate per 1,000 Adults per Year[2]
Accidental injury, all circumstances	242
Accidental injury at home	79
Personal theft	72
Accidental injury at work	58
Violent victimization	31
Assault (aggravated and simple)	24
Injury in motor vehicle accident	17
Death, all causes	11
Victimization with injury	10
Serious (aggravated) assault	9
Robbery	6
Heart disease death	4
Cancer death	2
Rape (women only)	2
Accidental death, all circumstances	0.5
Pneumonia/influenza death	0.3
Motor vehicle accidental death	0.2
Suicide	0.2
Injury from fire	0.1
Homicide/legal intervention death	0.1
Death from fire	0.03

[1]These rates approximate your chances of becoming a victim of these events. More precise estimates can be derived by taking account of such factors as your age, sex, race, place of residence, and lifestyle.

[2]These rates exclude children from the calculations (those under age 12, depending on the series). Fire injury/death data are based on the total population because no age-specific data are available in this series.

Source: National Center for Health Statistics, *Annual Report 1994* (Washington, D.C.: U.S. Government Printing Office, 1995).

The Bureau of Justice Statistics points out that "fear of crime affects many people, including some who have never been victims of crime."[75] Sources of fear are diverse. Some flow from personal experience with victimization, but most people fear crime because of dramatizations of criminal activity on television and in movies and because of frequent newspaper and media reports of crime. Feelings of vulnerability may result from learning that a friend has been victimized or from hearing that a neighbor's home has been burglarized.

A recent survey of American voters, *The Battleground Survey*,[76] found that crime topped the list of citizens' concerns. In the words of the pollsters, "Americans say crime is the No. 1 problem facing the country today...." Crime was reported to be the "top concern" of 26% of all those participating in the survey—easily outdistancing reported concerns over the economy (9%), jobs (7%), unemployment (7%), and drugs (6%). Interestingly, respondents to *The Battleground Survey*, which attempts to identify "hot" political issues, appeared to separate drug-related crimes from the threat of more personal crimes, such as murder, rape, and robbery. An independent *Washington Post* poll, conducted shortly after *The Battleground Survey*, confirmed the survey's findings, showing that 21% of Americans were more concerned about crime than about any other issue.[77]

Interestingly, the groups at highest risk of becoming crime victims are not the ones who experience the greatest fear of crime. The elderly and women report the greatest fear of victimization, even though they are among the lowest-risk groups for violent crimes. Young males, on the other hand, who stand the greatest statistical risk of victimization, often report feeling the least fear.[78] Similarly, although people most fear violent victimization by strangers, many such crimes are committed by nonstrangers or by people known to victims by sight.

WOMEN AND CRIME

Women Victims

Women are victimized far less frequently than are men in every major crime category other than rape.[79] When women are victimized, however, they are more likely than men to be injured.[80] Even though experiencing lower rates of victimization, it is realistic to acknowledge that a larger proportion of women than men make modifications in the way they live because of the threat of crime.[81] Reflecting the growing fear of crime now so pervasive in America, women, especially those living in cities, are increasingly careful about where they travel and the time of day they leave their homes—particularly if unaccompanied—and are often wary of unfamiliar males in a diversity of settings.

As in other crime-related areas, the popular media, special interest groups, and even the government have contributed to a certain degree of confusion about women's victimization.[82] Very real concerns reflected in movies, television programs, and newspaper editorial pages have properly identified date rape, familial incest, spouse abuse, and the exploitation of women through social order offenses such as prostitution and pornography as major issues facing American society today. Testimony before Congress[83] has tagged domestic violence as the largest cause of injury to American women,[84] and former Surgeon General C. Everett Koop identified violence against women by their partners as the number one health problem facing women in America today. More recently, the 1995 murder trial of O. J. Simpson focused concerns on issues of spousal abuse and on the victimization of women by spouses and ex-husbands.

When the data on women's victimization are examined closely, however, a slightly different pattern emerges. The Bureau of Justice Statistics,[85] in a detailed analysis of female victims of violent crime, found that about twice as many women who are victims of violent crimes are likely to be victimized by strangers than by people whom they know. However, when women do fall victim to violent crime, they are far more likely than men to be victimized by individuals with whom they are (or have been) in intimate relationships. When the perpetrators are known to them, women are most likely to be violently victimized by ex-spouses, boyfriends, and spouses, (in descending order of incidence). The BJS study also found that separated or divorced women are six times more likely to be victims of violent crime than widows, four and a half times more likely than married women, and three times more likely than widowers and married men. Other findings indicated that (1) women

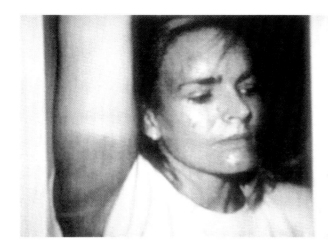

A bruised Nicole Brown Simpson after one of many alleged attacks by her husband, O. J. Simpson. According to sociologists, violence against women is perpetuated by social conditions which devalue females. *Sygma*

If people here were not getting killed on the job in homicides, we would have quite a low rate of fatalities.
—Samuel Ehrenhalt, Labor Department official commenting on findings that show murder to be the top cause of on-the-job deaths in New York City.

living in central-city areas are considerably more likely to be victimized than women residing in the suburbs; (2) suburban women, in turn, are more likely to be victimized than women living in rural areas; (3) women from low-income families experience the highest amount of violent crime; (4) the victimization of women falls as family income rises; (5) unemployed women, female students, and those in the armed forces are the most likely of all women to experience violent victimization; (6) black women are victims of violent crimes more frequently than are women of any other race; (7) Hispanic women find themselves victimized more frequently than white women; and (8) women in the age range 20–24 are most at risk for violent victimization, while those aged 16–19 comprise the second most likely group of victims.

These findings show that greater emphasis needs to be placed on alleviating the social conditions that victimize women. Suggestions already under consideration call for expansion in the number of federal and state laws designed to control domestic violence, a broadening of the federal Family Violence Prevention and Services Act, federal help in setting up state advocacy offices for battered women, increased funding for battered women's shelters, and additional monies for prosecutors and courts to develop spouse abuse units. The federal Violent Crime Control and Law Enforcement Act of 1994 was designed to meet many of these needs through a subsection entitled the "Violence Against Women Act" (VAWA). That act allocates $1.6 billion to fight violence against women. Included are funds to (1) educate police, prosecutors, and judges about the special needs of women victims; (2) encourage pro-arrest policies in cases of domestic abuse; (3) provide specialized services for female victims of crime; (4) fund battered women's shelters across the country; and (5) support rape education in a variety of settings nationwide. The law also provides for new civil rights remedies for victims of felonies motivated by gender bias and extends "rape shield law" protections to civil cases and to all criminal cases in order to bar irrelevant inquiries into a victim's sexual history.

In an insightful article built around issues in criminal justice education, Nanci Koser Wilson[86] suggests a multifaceted role for women who are interested in improving the position of women in the criminal justice system. Aspects of the role include the following:

1. *Women lobbying for change in the criminal justice system.* Wilson points to the success which has met women who have worked to change rape laws, police procedure in domestic violence cases, and the recognition of the plight of battered women in cases of spousal homicide.
2. *Women creating help for women outside the system.* The creation of rape crisis centers, centers for battered women, and the like, all point to the possibility of women helping individuals of like-gender through noncriminal justice channels.
3. *Women working in movements outside traditional crime areas.* Ecofeminism, peace work, and other social movements have done much to enhance the status of women in general and may work in the long run to reduce some of the factors which result in the criminal victimization of women.

Twenty-First Century Criminal Justice

Gender Issues I: The Growing Recognition of Women's Rights and Gender-Based Violence

The Violent Crime Control and Law Enforcement Act of 1994 included significant provisions intended to enhance gender equality throughout the criminal justice system. One especially noteworthy provision, Section 40301, is entitled the "Civil Rights Remedies for Gender-Motivated Violence Act." It establishes a "Federal civil rights cause of action for victims of crimes of violence motivated by gender." Although the section does not establish criminal penalties for gender-motivated violence (anticipating, instead, that such crimes will be punished as felonies under appropriate federal and state law) the law says that "All persons within the United States shall have the right to be free from crimes of violence motivated by gender," and mandates that "A person... who commits a crime of violence motivated by gender and thus deprives another of the right declared in [this section] shall be liable to the party injured, in an action for the recovery of compensatory and punitive damages, injunctive and declaratory relief, and such other relief as a court may deem appropriate."

In creating the Civil Rights Remedies for Gender-Motivated Violence Act, Congress found that "crimes of violence motivated by gender constitute bias crimes in violation of the victim's right to be free from discrimination on the basis of gender; current law provides a civil rights remedy for gender crimes committed in the workplace, but not for crimes of violence motivated by gender committed on the street or in the home; State and Federal criminal laws do not adequately protect against the bias element of crimes of violence motivated by gender, which separates these crimes from acts of random violence, nor do these adequately provide victims of gender-motivated crimes the opportunity to vindicate their interests; [and] existing bias and discrimination in the criminal justice system often deprives victims of crimes of violence motivated by gender of equal protection of the laws and the redress to which they are entitled..."

4. *Women producing research from a women's perspective.* Wilson points out that the tendency to dismiss the criminality of women because it is less frequent than that of males misses the opportunity to learn about crime in general via the model provided by women's criminality. Dismissing the criminality of women implies that the criminality of men is somehow "normal" and that other behavior patterns are less worthy of study. A gender-balanced approach to the study of crime should have something to teach us all.

5. *Women working within the traditional criminal justice system in woman-defined ways.* Women who choose police work or who work within correctional environments, have something to contribute to both professions by virtue of the unique perspective they bring to their jobs. Because of potential benefits to the system and to themselves, women should not be expected to automatically accept traditional masculinized understandings of criminal justice roles.

Women Offenders

In 1992, Aileen Carol Wuornos, a 35-year-old former prostitute, received multiple death sentences in Florida after confessing to a string of seven murders. Wuornos, labeled by the FBI as the "first textbook female serial killer,"[87] preyed upon men who offered her rides as she hitchhiked. Property belonging to all seven victims—most of whom were robbed, killed, and left naked—was found in a storage unit rented by Ms. Wuornos. One victim was a former police chief, another a security guard. All were white, middle-aged men with blue-collar jobs who were traveling alone. Each was killed with a small-caliber handgun.[88] In 1996 the U.S. Supreme Court turned down an appeal by Wuornos who argued that claims that she killed the men in self-defense when they became violent, raped her, and did not pay for sexual services, were not given sufficient weight before sentencing.[89]

Turn on nightly television in the United States on a typical day and you will see killing after killing, frequent acts of gruesome violence, and murder and mayhem as typical prime-time fare. The same is true whether you choose to view one of the major networks, a pay-per-view channel, or a premium service such as Home Box Office, Cinemax, or Showtime. Only a few specialized forms of programming, such as the Home Shopping Network, the Disney Channel, and Public Broadcasting, are relatively violence free.

Many argue that the networks and cable companies are simply giving viewers what they want. Violence (often tinged with sexuality or combined with explicit sexual behavior), because it is exciting, attracts audiences. And, of course, large audiences attract advertisers whose fees support the networks.

Not to be outdone by their highly visual counterparts, newspapers and newsmagazines depict real-life episodes of violent crime in every issue. For a year following the highly publicized murders of Nicole Brown Simpson and Ronald Goldman, for example, it was almost impossible to find a newspaper in the country which wasn't running a daily story about some aspect of the case, especially when O. J. Simpson, charged in the murders, went to trial. Even computer-based services, among them CompuServe and America Online, set up special O. J. Simpson sections to attract subscribers. Simpson's 1997 civil trial received almost as much publicity—limited only by the fact that the judge banned television cameras from the courtroom.

Unfortunately, what some have called the overemphasis on crime and violence, now so characteristic of the media in this country, makes it extremely difficult to separate crime fiction from crime fact. If media emphasis is any guide, it would appear that the United States is awash in crime, especially violent personal crime. The impression given is that crime is likely to strike almost anyone when they least expect it—devastating their lives (should they survive) irreparably. In fact, while there are many victims of violent crime in this country, the media's preoccupation with crime and violence is much overdone. Worse still, such preoccupation has led to an enormous fear of crime among the American public, which, for at least a substantial segment of the population, is probably misplaced.

As one social commentator points out, "Anxiety about crime grips the land but, looking at federal statistics, you have to wonder why. The FBI reports crime is merely crawling upward. Victim surveys show crime actually falling. Yet for many people, an evening stroll, an unlocked car, or going alone to the mall hint at lunacy. After tucking in their children, many parents bolt the doors, check the alarms, and pat the guns under their beds goodnight."[1] According to William Chambliss, past president of the American Society of Criminology, "[t]he best scientific evidence we have clearly shows there is no increase in crime or violent crime in the last 20 years.... The fact is, even if the crime rate was going up, the victims who were the victims remain the victims."[2]

Realistically, crime—especially violent personal crime—while it may be on the rise, appears concentrated in certain poverty-stricken population-dense regions of the nation. That is not to say that crime does not make an appearance in affluent neighborhoods and rural areas. It certainly does, but the nature and extent of criminal activity in such areas is a far cry from the inner-city areas where the daily threat of crime is a hard reality for most residents.

Yet, when surveys reporting the fear of crime are examined, Americans everywhere appear to be on guard. Fear of crime festers in people's minds like a specter haunting the land, and frightened residents routinely report taking self-protective steps. Statistics from the most recent *U.S. News*/CNN poll[3] on neighborhood crime, for example, show 37% of Americans own a gun for protection and 45% think it's unsafe to let children play unsupervised where they live. Thirty-one percent of respondents also report that there are areas within a mile of their home in which they would be afraid to walk alone at night. Other surveys, however, have found that those most afraid of crime spend more time watching television than those who are less fearful[4]—lending support to the notion that media portrayals of criminal activity lead to a heightened fear of victimization.

Efforts are currently underway to reduce the degree of crime fear induced by the mass media.[5] A recent U.S. Senate hearing, for example, stressed the need for television producers and network executives to assume a socially responsible role by lowering the amount of violence in aired programming. Unfortunately, no one knows for sure whether television merely broadcasts what viewers most want to see, or whether it presages and helps to determine what we, as a nation, are becoming.

QUESTIONS FOR DISCUSSION

1. To what extent does television influence what people think about crime? What they do?
2. Does television help shape our culture, or does it merely reflect what we, as a nation, already are?
3. Would you be supportive of more "socially responsible" television programming? Why or why not? If so, how would you change the content of television shows?

[1]Arlene Levinson, "America Behind Bars—Crime, Wanted: The True Crime Rate," the Associated Press wire services, northern edition, May 8, 1994.

[2]Ibid.

[3]CNN Online, April 2, 1995.

[4]See Arthur Spiegelman, "America's Year in Crime—Enough to Scare Anyone,"

Reuters wire services, December 15, 1994.

[5]For a good collection of articles detailing the role of the media in crime causation and social policy creation, see Ray Surette, *The Media and Criminal Justice Policy: Recent Research and Social Effects* (Springfield, IL: Charles C. Thomas, 1990), and Steven M. Chermak, *Victims in the News: Crime and the American News Media* (San Francisco: Westview Press, 1995).

The public is properly obsessed with safety. Of industrialized countries, the U.S. has the highest rate of violent crime...

—Bob Moffitt, The Heritage Foundation

In 1995 another woman, Susan Smith of Union, South Carolina, rose to prominence in the national media after she confessed to the drowning murders of her two young sons, Alex, 1, and Michael, 3. The boys died after their mother rolled their car off the end of a pier and into a lake, leaving her sons strapped in their safety seats. Smith's confession came after investigators found a letter from Smith's adulterous lover, suggesting that he felt unable to continue the relationship because of the children.

The crimes committed by Aileen Wuornos and Susan Smith, gruesome as they are, fall outside what we know of as the pattern for female criminality. Although the popular media has sometimes portrayed female criminals as similar to their male counterparts in motivation and behavior, that image is misleading. Similarly, the academic study of women's criminality has been fraught with misconceptions.

One of the first writers to attempt a definitive explanation of the criminality of women was Otto Pollak. Pollak's book, *The Criminality of Women*,[90] written in 1950, suggested that women commit the same number of offenses as men—but that most of their criminality is hidden. Pollak claimed that women's roles (at the time, primarily those of homemaker and mother) served to disguise the criminal undertakings of women. He also proposed that chivalrous treatment by a male-dominated justice system acted to bias every stage of criminal justice processing in favor of women. Hence, according to Pollak, although women are just as criminal as men, they are rarely arrested, tried, or imprisoned. In fact, while the criminality of women may approach or exceed that of men in selected offense categories, it is safe to say today that Pollak was incorrect in his assessment of the degree of female criminality.

Contemporary statistics tell us that, although females comprise 51% of the population of the United States, they are arrested for only 15% of all violent crimes and 28% of property crimes. The relatively small amount of reported female involvement in the FBI's eight major crimes can be seen in Table 2–6. The number of women committing crimes appears to be increasing faster than the number of male offenders, however. Between 1970 and 1996, crimes committed by men grew by 57%, while crimes reported to have been committed by women increased 138%. Violent crimes by males increased 130% during the period; by women 295%.[91] Property crimes perpetrated by men grew by 38%; by women 122%. Nonetheless, as the table shows, female offenders still account for only a small proportion of all reported crimes.

Statistics on the FBI's Part II offenses tell a somewhat different story. Arrests of women for embezzlement, for example, increased by more than 156% between 1970 and 1996, arrests of females for drug abuse grew by 280%, and liquor law violations by women increased 252% (versus 115% for men).[92] Such statistics are difficult to interpret, however, since reports of female involvement in crime may reflect more the growing equality of treatment accorded women in contemporary society than they do actual increases in criminal activity. In the past, when women committed crimes, they have been dealt with less officiously than is likely to be the case today. In only two officially reported categories—prostitution and runaways—do women outnumber men in the volume of offenses committed.[93] Other crimes in which significant numbers of women (relative to men) are involved include larceny-theft (where 33% of reported crimes are committed by women), forgery and counterfeiting (36%), fraud (39%), and embezzlement (41%).

Even when women commit crimes, however, they are more often followers than leaders. A 1996 study[94] of women in correctional settings, for example, found that women are far more likely to assume "secondary follower rules during criminal events," than "dominant

Table 2–6 Male/Female Involvement in Crime: Offense Patterns Differ

Percentage of All Arrests

UCR Index Crimes	Males	Females	Gender Differences
Murder and nonnegligent manslaughter	89.7%	10.3%	Men are more likely than women to be arrested for more serious crimes, such as murder, rape, robbery, or burglary
Rape	98.8	1.2	
Robbery	90.3	9.7	
Aggravated assault	82.1	17.9	
Burglary	88.7	11.3	Arrest, jail, and prison data all suggest that more women than men who commit crimes are involved in property crimes, such as larceny, forgery, fraud, and embezzlement, and in drug offenses.
Larceny-theft	66.2	33.8	
Motor vehicle theft	86.4	13.6	
Arson	85.1	14.9	

Source: Federal Bureau of Investigation, *Crime in the United States, 1996* (Washington, D.C.: U.S. Government Printing Office, 1997), p. 231.

leadership roles." Only 14% of women surveyed played primary roles, but those that did "felt that men had little influence in initiating or leading them into crime." African-American women, however, were found to be more likely to play "primary and equal crime roles" with men or with women accomplices than were white or Hispanic women. Statistics such as these dispel the myth that the female criminal in America has taken her place alongside male offenders—either in terms of leadership roles or the absolute number of crimes committed.

THE ECONOMIC COST OF CRIME

A few years ago, Florida state officials came face to face with the economic consequences of criminal activity: Three robbery-related killings of foreign visitors near Miami in the summer of 1993 caused many potential "Sunshine State" tourists to cancel their reservations and stay home. Tourism is Florida's number one industry. In a typical year, more than 40 million tourists visit the state, including 7 million foreigners. All told, they spend over $31 billion on their Florida vacations.

Following the highly publicized robbery-murder incidents, European tabloids labeled the "Sunshine State" the "State of Terror," and the British newspaper *Independent* called Florida "the main danger area" in the United States. Indicative of media sentiment across Europe, the London *Times* ran a cartoon picturing a revolver with a trigger shaped like the state of Florida, and Britain's largest newspaper, the *Sun*, ran a headline advising Florida tourists to "Get Your Butts Outta Here." The image portrayed by the media was one of a state and a nation where crime—and guns—are out of control. In response, Governor Lawton Chiles canceled foreign advertising, fearing that it would provoke only further cynicism. Although the tourism industry in Florida has begun to recover, the summer of 1993 showed state officials across the nation just how costly crime can be in terms of tourist dollars.

The national costs of crime are difficult to measure. The Bureau of Justice Statistics estimates the personal cost of crime (direct dollar losses to individuals, not including criminal justice system costs) at around $17.6 billion per year.[95] Robberies cost the nation about $500 million annually, burglaries nearly $4 billion, and larceny-thefts account for approximately $4 billion in losses per year. Not included in the Bureau's figures are the costs to crime victims of lost work, needed medical care, and the expense of new security measures they may

Female criminality has recently been the subject of much study. Shown here is Susan Smith, the Union, South Carolina, mother who confessed to the 1994 drowning deaths of her two sons, Alex, 1, and Michael, 3. Smith was sentenced to life in prison, although many felt that she should have received the death penalty, and others claimed that her "lenient" sentence revealed gender biases in the criminal justice system. *Spartan Herald Journal, Sygma (top); America Fast Photo, SABA Press Photos, Inc. (bottom)*

implement. Lost work time, for example, was reported in 12% of aggravated assaults and 17% of rapes.

In 1996 the National Institute of Justice attempted to calculate both the direct and indirect costs of criminal victimization. NIJ researchers concluded that when crimes of all types are counted "victimizations generate $105 billion annually in property and productivity losses and outlays for medical expenses. This amounts to an annual 'crime tax' of roughly $425 per man, woman, and child in the United States. When the values of pain, long-term emotional trauma, disability, and risk of death are put in dollar terms, the costs rise to $450 billion annually (or $1,800 per person)."[96] Overall, said the study authors, "rape is the costliest crime: With annual victim costs at $127 billion, it exacts a higher price than murder."[97]

Twenty-First Century Criminal Justice

Gender Issues II: The Growing Recognition of Women's Rights and Gender-Based Violence

As mentioned earlier in this chapter, the Violent Crime Control and Law Enforcement Act of 1994 included significant provisions intended to enhance gender equality throughout the criminal justice system. Section 40301, the "Civil Rights Remedies for Gender-Motivated Violence Act," is discussed in an earlier box in this chapter. Other especially notable provisions of the act are discussed here.

TITLE IV of the Violent Crime Control and Law Enforcement Act of 1994 is known as the Violence Against Women Act of 1994 (VAWA). VAWA also contains the Safe Streets for Women Act of 1994. The Safe Streets for Women Act increases federal penalties for repeat sex offenders and requires mandatory restitution for sex crimes including costs related to medical services (including physical, psychiatric, or psychological care); physical and occupational therapy or rehabilitation; necessary transportation, temporary housing, and child care expenses; lost income; attorneys' fees, plus any costs incurred in obtaining a civil protection order; and any other losses suffered by the victim as a result of the offense. The act also requires that compliance with a restitution order be made a condition of probation or supervised release (if such a sentence is imposed by the court), and provides that violation of such an order shall result in the offender's imprisonment.

Chapter 2 of the Violence Against Women Act provides funds for grants to combat violent crimes against women. The purpose of funding is to assist states "and units of local government to develop and strengthen effective law enforcement and prosecution strategies to combat violent crimes against women, and to develop and strengthen victim services in

cases involving violent crimes against women." The law also provides funds for the "training of law enforcement officers and prosecutors to more effectively identify and respond to violent crimes against women, including the crimes of sexual assault and domestic violence;" for the purpose of "developing, installing, or expanding data collection and communication systems, including computerized systems, linking police, prosecutors, and courts or for the purpose of identifying and tracking arrests, protection orders, violations of protection orders, prosecutions, and convictions for violent crimes against women, including the crimes of sexual assault and domestic violence;" and to develop and strengthen "victim services programs, including sexual assault and domestic violence programs." The act also creates the crime of crossing state lines in violation of a protection order, and another crime of crossing state lines to commit assault on a domestic partner—and sets out federal penalties for the offense of up to life in prison in cases where death results.

Chapter 3 of the Violence Against Women Act provides for monies to increase the "safety for women in public transit and public parks." The chapter authorizes up to $10 million in grants through the Department of Transportation to enhance lighting, camera surveillance, and security telephones in public transportation systems used by women.

Chapter 5 of the Violence Against Women Act provides for the creation of hotlines, educational seminars, the preparation of informational materials, and training programs for professionals intended to provide assistance to victims of sexual assault, and for the operation of a national, toll-free

telephone hotline to provide information and assistance to victims of domestic violence. Another portion of the law, titled the "Safe Homes for Women Act," increases grants for battered women's shelters, encourages arrest in cases of domestic violence, and provides for the creation of a national domestic violence hotline to provide counseling, information, and assistance to victims of domestic violence. The act also orders that any protection order issued by a state court must be recognized by another state and by the federal government, and enforced "as if it were the order of the enforcing state."

SEC. 40401, known as the "Equal Justice for Women in the Courts Act of 1994," provides monies "for the purpose of developing, testing, presenting, and disseminating model programs" to be used by states in training judges and court personnel in the laws "on rape, sexual assault, domestic violence, and other crimes of violence motivated by the victim's gender." Training is to recognize the underreporting of rape, sexual assault, and child sexual abuse; the physical, psychological, and economic impact of rape and sexual assault on the victim; and the psychology of sex offenders, their high rate of recidivism, and implications for sentencing.

The economic impact of crime is different for different groups. In 1996, for example, households reporting an annual family income of less than $7,500 suffered from almost twice the rate of burglary as did households reporting incomes over $75,000. In fact, as family income rose, the rate of reported burglaries steadily declined. The opposite was true of auto theft, where rates of auto vehicle theft rose in direct proportion to household income.[98]

The commercial costs of crime are substantial as well. Losses from commercial robberies (including bank robberies) and business burglaries have been put at $1.2 billion per year.[99] Frauds perpetrated against financial institutions in 1996 numbered 8,641 discovered cases with an associated dollar loss of nearly $3 billion.[100] The cost to businesses of white-collar crime are not known, but are thought to be substantial. To guard against crimes by employees and members of the public, private businesses spend in excess of $21 billion per year for alarms, surveillance, and private security operations.[101]

Costs to the government for the apprehension, prosecution, and disposition of offenders, including crime prevention efforts by the police, far outstrip the known dollar losses to all criminal enterprises other than drugs. Federal criminal justice expenditures for fiscal year 1996 were in excess of $16.5 billion,[102] while federal, state, and local expenditures totaled over $80 billion.[103] Nonetheless, government spending on criminal justice services amounts to only about 5% of all governmental expenditures. State and local governments absorb most of the costs of criminal justice-related activity.

Drugs and Crime

Drugs and crime are often found together. Drug law violations are themselves criminal, but more and more studies are linking drug abuse to other serious crimes. A study by the Rand Corporation found that most of the "violent predators" among prisoners had extensive histories of heroin abuse, often in combination with alcohol and other drugs.[104] Some cities report that a large percentage of their homicides are drug related.[105] Many property crimes are committed to sustain "habits," and the numbers of both violent and property crimes committed by drug users have been shown to be directly related to the level at which they use drugs.[106] Substance abuse may well be the most expensive of all illegal activities. The social cost of drug abuse has been estimated at nearly $60 billion per year, with half of that amount being in lost job productivity.[107] Drunk driving alone is thought to cost over $13 billion in property losses and medical expenses yearly.[108] Chapter 15 will examine the drug–crime link in considerable detail. Suffice it to say here that the link appears strong and shows few signs of abating.

The Elderly and Crime

UCR statistics define "older offenders" as those over 55 years of age. Relative to other age groups, older offenders rarely appear in the crime statistics. Criminality seems to decline with age, suggesting that a burnout factor applies to criminal behavior as it does to many other areas of life. In 1996 persons age 65 and over accounted for less than 1% of all arrests.[109]

The type and number of crimes committed by older people, however, appear to be changing. According to the UCR, arrests of the elderly for serious crimes decreased slightly between 1975 and 1996.[110] Overall, arrests of persons 65 and older declined by about 30% during the period, while fraud arrests jumped nearly 300%.[111] When elderly people are sent to prison, it is usually for violent crimes, though violent crimes account for far less than 50% of prison admissions among younger people. The population of prisoners age 55 and over has steadily increased, having risen from 13,800 inmates nationally in mid-1988 to 24,600 by mid-1996, an increase of more than 50%.[112]

Some authors have interpreted these statistics to presage the growth of a "geriatric delinquent" population, freed by age and retirement from jobs and responsibilities. Such people, say these authors, may turn to crime as one way of averting boredom and adding a little spice to life.[113] Statistics on geriatric offenders, however, probably require a more cautious interpretation. They are based upon relatively small numbers, and to say that "serious crime among the elderly doubled" does not mean that a geriatric crime wave is upon us. The apparent increase in criminal activity among the elderly may be due to the fact that the older population in this country is growing substantially, with even greater increases expected over the next three decades. Advances in health care have increased life expectancy and have made the added years more productive than ever before. World War II "baby boomers" will be reaching their late middle years by the year 2000, and present trends in criminal involvement among the elderly can be expected to continue. Hence, it may not be that elderly individuals in this country are committing crimes more frequently than before, but rather that the greater number of elderly in the population make for a greater prevalence of crimes committed by the elderly in the official statistics.

The elderly are also victims of crime. Although persons age 65 and older generally experience the lowest rate of victimization of any age group,[114] some aspects of serious crime against older people are worth noting. Elderly violent crime victims are more likely than younger victims to

1. Face offenders armed with guns.
2. Be victimized by total strangers.
3. Be victimized in or near their homes.
4. Report their victimization to the police

Older victims are also less likely to attempt to protect themselves than are younger ones. The older the victim, the greater the likelihood of physical injury.

Elderly people are victimized disproportionately if they fall into certain categories. Relative to their numbers in the elderly population, black men are overrepresented as victims. Similarly, separated or divorced persons and urban residents have higher rates of vic-

Mark Kohut (adjusting his collar) and 18-year-old Jeffrey Pellett, shown here in a Palm Beach, Florida, courtroom, were convicted along with a third man (Charles Rourk) in 1993 of setting fire to Chris Wilson (bottom photo) in a racially motivated hate crime. Kohut received a one-year sentence after cooperating with authorities. Pellet and Rourk were both sentenced to life in prison. *Scott Wiseman, The Palm Beach Post and Sam Mircovich, SIPA*

timization than do other elderly persons. As observed earlier, older people live in greater fear of crime than do younger people, even though their risk of victimization is considerably less. Elderly people, however, are less likely to take crime preventive measures than are any other age group. Only 6% of households headed by persons over the age of 65 have an alarm, and only 16% engrave their valuables (versus a 25% national average).

Organized Crime

Organized crime has been defined by the Organized Crime Control Act of 1970 as "the unlawful activities of the members of a highly organized, disciplined association engaged in supplying illegal goods and services, including but not limited to gambling, prostitution, loansharking, narcotics, labor racketeering, and other unlawful activities of members of such organizations."[115] Criminal organizations have existed in America since before the turn of the twentieth century. Contemporary organized crime groups are involved to some degree in just about every aspect of American life, but the manufacture, transportation, and sale of controlled substances has provided an especially lucrative form of illegal enterprise for many of them. A few such groups are thought to be among the largest businesslike enterprises in the world.

The Mafia, perhaps the best-known criminal organization in the United States, rose to power in this country largely through its exploitation of the widespread demand for consumable alcohol during prohibition years. The Mafia, now called the **Cosa Nostra**, came into existence when a group of small-time hoods, largely of Italian descent, began selling "protection" and other services, such as gambling and prostitution, in turn-of-the-century New York City. With the advent of prohibition, financial opportunities became enormous for those willing to circumvent the law, and organized gang activity spread. Soon Chicago, Detroit, Miami, San Francisco, and other major cities became gang havens. It was during this period that infamous gangsters such as Lucky Luciano and Al Capone were catapulted to the forefront of popular attention.

Today, the Cosa Nostra consists of 24 families based in various cities across the country. Their illegal take is estimated at around $60 billion per year.[116]

Families are involved in a variety of illegal activities, including drug trafficking, loansharking, gambling, shakedowns of drug dealers, killings-for-hire, and the infiltration of various labor unions. Many run legitimate businesses as fronts for money laundering and other financial activities. Such businesses are often rife with "ghost workers," paid at high rates, but who actually do no work at all. Organized crime families will stop at little to increase their influence. Nicholas Caramandi, a former member of the Philadelphia mob led by Nicodemo Scarfo, responded to a question about how high the mob reaches into American society this way: "If politicians, doctors, lawyers, entertainment people all come to us for favors, there's got to be a reason. It's because we're the best. There are no favors we can't do."[117]

The Cosa Nostra requires new members to undergo an initiation ritual, which has changed little since the days it was brought to American shores by Sicilian immigrants more than a hundred years ago. During a secretly recorded candlelit Cosa Nostra induction ceremony recently held in Medford, Massachusetts, for example, new members were required to hold a burning picture of a Catholic saint in their cupped palms and made to swear to uphold the code of *omerta* (silence). *"Come si brucia questa santa, cosi si brucera la mia anima,"* the men repeated, which means, "As burns this saint, so will burn my soul." Anyone violating the Cosa Nostra's code of silence recognizes that death is the penalty.

Crime families are hierarchically organized under a boss and consist of a number of levels, each with varying authority. Bosses exercise their power through underbosses and lieutenants. Lieutenants pass orders along to soldiers. Soldiers, the lowest level of mob operatives, are charged with directly carrying out the activities of their families. In doing so they often make use of local community members, allowing organized crime to seamlessly integrate itself into almost any locale. Hierarchical organization has frequently allowed many Cosa Nostra higher-ups to avoid arrest and prosecution. Recently, however, federal agents armed with new statutes have been able to make inroads into many such operations. For example, John Gotti, leader of New York City's infamous Gambino crime family (and once known as the "Teflon Don" for being able to beat criminal charges), was sent to federal

Although most people think of the Mafia (or Cosa Nostra) when "organized crime" is mentioned, the term actually includes a wide variety of types of groups and associated activities. Here reputed Mafia boss and head of New York's Genovese crime family, Vincent "Chin" Gigante, leaves his New York residence on June 25, 1997. Gigante was convicted a month later of conspiracy to murder and racketeering. Accused of ordering the execution of seven fellow gangsters and plotting to kill three others, Gigante was dubbed the "Oddfather" for previously appearing disheveled, and for sometimes wearing a bathrobe in public. Prosecutors claimed that he was faking mental illness. *Michael Schmelling, AP/Wide World Photos*

prison in 1992, along with underboss Frank Locascio. During the past few years, 1,170 Cosa Nostra bosses, soldiers, and associates across the nation have been convicted and sentenced.[118] Peter Milano, once boss of Los Angeles, is in prison. So, too, are leaders of Kansas City's Civella family, and a few years ago 13 members of New England's Patriarca family were convicted of murdering one of their underbosses.

In 1997, a federal jury convicted 69-year-old Vincent "The Chin" Gigante, head of New York's Genovese crime family—and one of the nation's most powerful mobsters—of racketeering and two murder conspiracies.[119] Gigante had sought to avoid prosecution by feigning mental illness, a strategy that earned him the nickname "The Oddfather." Growing disorganization among Cosa Nostra families was evident at Gigante's trial, which featured a parade of turncoat gangsters testifying for the government. Witnesses against Gigante included ex-underbosses Salvatore "Sammy the Bull" Gravano, Alphonse "Little Al" D'Arco, Philip "Crazy Phil" Leonetti, and Peter Savino, a one-time Genovese associate.

Even as the power of the Cosa Nostra wanes, other groups stand ready to take its place. There is historical precedent for such a transition. Italian-led gangs were preceded in New York City and other places by Jewish criminal organizations. One infamous Jewish gang, for example, was headed at the start of the century by Arnold Rothstein, who dreamed of becoming kingpin of all organized criminal activity in America. Ethnic succession has typified organized criminal activity. Today, gangs of Hispanics, Chinese, Japanese, Vietnamese, Puerto Ricans, Mexicans, Colombians, and African-Americans have usurped power traditionally held by the Cosa Nostra in many parts of the country. Similarly, evidence indicates that Russian-led and Arabic-speaking gangs have begun to move into New York and other cities.

On June 8, 1995, Vyacheslav Kirillovich Ivankov (known in Russian as "Yaponchik," or "The Jap") was arrested by the FBI in New York City. Ivankov is reputed to be Russia's most influential *vor*, or organized crime boss. His presence in New York was one of a number of growing signs that Russian organized crime has rapidly become a major international force. Another was a 1994 visit to Moscow by FBI Director Louis J. Freeh, who used the occasion to announce that Russian organized crime had become a new top priority for U.S. law enforcement agencies.

Russian organized crime, under the leadership of *vory* (the plural form of the word "*vor*"), has been in existence since at least the eighteenth century. With the dissolution of the Soviet Union, however, organized crime in Russia has flourished. In a speech to the Russian parliament, Russian leader Boris Yeltsin told legislators, "As the major crime networks...have grown more and more impudent, the law enforcement agencies have virtually assumed a policy of noninterference!"[1] Yeltsin charged that rampant corruption among law enforcement officials had led to the problem.

Visitors to Russia report that organized crime is in control of large sectors of Russian society—selling everything from bootlegged vodka on city street corners to stolen nuclear weapons across international borders. Bribery is a way of life in modern Russia, and interference from the police is rare. Criminal investigators are paid salaries of around $160 a month—less than city bus drivers. Many experienced police officers have left for jobs in private security, since most of Russia's new entrepreneurs willingly pay high prices for protection for themselves and the goods they manufacture. Bandits are common, and shipments of manufactured goods

must be protected by armed men as they wend their way west to European borders.

Organized crime in Russia bears striking resemblances to crime families in the West. At the uppermost level of Russian organized crime are the *vory v zakone*, a Russian phrase which can be translated as "thieves professing the code." The *vory* are the godfathers of Russian organized crime and are said to number 387 throughout Russia (about 100 of whom are currently serving prison sentences). In 1994 the Russian Ministry of Internal Affairs (MVD) detained 45 *vory* for questioning. Since the *vory* are leaders and organizers and do not commit crimes themselves, however, Russian law rarely applies to them. Russian criminal law remains virtually unchanged since Soviet days, and Russian police and prosecutors have nothing like American anti-Mafia laws, such as the Racketeer Influenced and Corrupt Organization Act (RICO). As Russian police Lt. Col. Nikolai Aulov, an anti-organized-crime official in St. Petersburg, puts it, "It's very difficult to convict someone who wasn't doing something with his own hands. The laws are imperfect."[2]

Like Mafia families, Russian organized criminal groups are hierarchically structured. With the *vor* as head, a trusted advisor, or *sovetnik*, fills a second level, channeling information between the *vor* and the group's members (*gruppa obespechenie*). The lowest-level group operatives are called *shestiorka*, or bag men and errand boys. They are often recruited from among prisoners and known street hoods and are charged with carrying out the group's dirty work.

Like Mafia chieftains, the *vor* live by a strict code. Joseph D. Serio and Vyacheslav Stepanovich Razkin, two specialists on Russian organized crime, describe the code as consisting of the following principles:[3]

1. A *vor* must turn his back on his family—mother, father, brothers, and sisters. The criminal community is his family.

2. A *vor* is forbidden to have a family, a wife, or children.

3. A *vor* is forbidden to work; a *vor* must live off the fruits of criminal activity only.

4. A *vor* must give moral and material assistance to other *vory* using the *obshchak* (the money fund of the group).

5. A *vor* must give information about accomplices and their whereabouts (for example, locations of hideouts) only in the strictest confidentiality.

6. If a *vor* is under investigation, a lower-level criminal must take responsibility upon himself to give the suspected *vor* time to flee.

7. When a conflict arises in a criminal group or among *vory*, there must be a meeting (*skhodka*) to resolve the issue.

8. When necessary, a *vor* must attend a meeting (*skhodka*) to judge another *vor* if his conduct or behavior comes into question.

9. Punishment for a *vor* decided by the meeting must be carried out.

10. A *vor* must be proficient in criminals' jargon (*fenia*).

11. A *vor* must not enter a card game if he does not have the money to pay.

12. A *vor* must teach his craft to novice thieves.

13. A *vor* should keep a gofer (*shestiorka*) under his influence.

14. A *vor* must not lose his sense when drinking alcohol.

15. A *vor* must not in any way become involved with the authorities; a *vor* must not participate in social activities, and a *vor* must not join social organizations.

16. A *vor* must not take up weapons from the hands of state authority; and a *vor* must not serve in the army.
17. A *vor* must fulfill all promises made to other *vory*.

Until Russian social disorganization is under control, it is likely that Russian organized crime will continue to flourish. Recently, U.S. State Department spokesperson Christine Shelly cautioned law enforcement personnel on the dangers of Russian organized crime. "The rise in organized crime, financial crime, nuclear materials smuggling, and drug trafficking are all aspects of that problem...which give us great concern," said Shelly. "The negative effect which crime can have on democratic and economic reform movements not only in Russia but also in the new independent states of the former Soviet Union and the potential that that has for the average citizen to equate crime with a kind of market economy—those are all serious implications of the growing crime problem," she said.[4]

QUESTIONS FOR DISCUSSION

1. What similarities does organized crime in Russia share with its counterpart in the West? Why do such similarities exist?
2. How might Russian organized crime impact the United States? What steps can American law enforcement agencies take to prevent American victimization by Russian criminals and their activities?

[1]Lee Hockstader, "Russia's War on Crime: A Lopsided, Losing Battle," *The Washington Post* on-line, February 27, 1995.
[2]Ibid.
[3]Joseph D. Serio and Vyacheslav Stepanovich Razkin, "Thieves Professing the Code: The Traditional Role of *Vory* v *Zakone* in Russia's Criminal World and Adaptations to a New Social Reality," *CJ Europe* on-line, August 14, 1995.
[4]"U.S. Concerned About Russian Crime," Reuters wire services, March 6, 1995.

SUMMARY

Two major national comprehensive crime data-gathering programs are in operation in the United States today: the FBI's *Uniform Crime Reports* (UCR) and the National Institute of Justice's National Crime Victimization Survey (NCVS). These programs provide a picture of victim characteristics through self-reports (NCVS) and reports to the police (UCR) and allow for a tabulation of the dollar costs of crime. Both programs also permit historical comparisons in crime rates and allow for some degree of predictability as to trends in crime. It is important to realize, however, that all statistics, including crime statistics, are inherently limited by the way in which they are gathered. Statistics can only portray the extent of crime according to the categories they are designed to measure and in terms understood by those whose responses they include.

Lacking in most of the crime statistics that are gathered today is any realistic appraisal of the human costs of crime—although some recent efforts by researchers at the National Institute of Justice have attempted to address this shortcoming. The trauma suffered by victims and survivors, the lowered sense of security experienced after victimization, the loss of human productivity, and reduced quality of life caused by crime are still difficult to gauge.

On the other side of the balance sheet, statistics fail to adequately identify the social costs suffered by offenders and their families. The social deprivation which may lead to crime, the fragmentation of private lives following conviction, and the loss of individuality which comes with confinement are all costs in which society must share, just as they are the culturally imposed consequences of crime and failure. Except for numbers on crimes committed, arrests, and figures on persons incarcerated, today's data-gathering strategies fall far short of gauging the human suffering and wasted human potential which both causes and follows from crime.

Even where reports do provide victim-impact measures, they may still fail to assess some of the objective costs of crime, including lowered property values in high-crime areas and inflated prices for consumer goods caused by the underground economy in stolen goods. White-collar crimes in particular are often well hidden and difficult to measure, yet many produce the largest direct dollar losses of any type of criminal activity. Hence, although modern crime statistics are useful, they do not provide the whole picture. Students of criminal justice need to be continually aware of aspects of the crime picture that fall outside of official data.

Vory v Zakone A Russian term for leaders of organized crime.

DISCUSSION QUESTIONS

1. What are the two major sources of crime statistics for the United States? How do they differ? How are they alike?

2. What can crime statistics tell us about the crime "picture" in America? How has that "picture" changed over time?

3. What are the potential sources of error in the major reports on crime? Can you think of some popular usage of those statistics that might be especially misleading?

4. Why are many crime statistics expressed as a *rate*? How does the use of crime rates improve the reporting of crime data (over a simple numerical tabulation)?

5. What is the Crime Index? Why is it difficult to add offenses to (or remove them from) the Index and still have it retain its value as a comparative tool?

6. What are the two major offense categories in Part I crimes? Are there some property crimes which might have a violent aspect? Are there any personal crimes which could be nonviolent?

7. What is the hierarchy rule in crime reporting programs? What purpose does it serve? What do you think of modifications in the hierarchy rule now occurring under NIBRS?

8. What does it mean to say that a crime has been "cleared"? Can you imagine a better way of reporting clearances?

 WEB WATCH

Access the *Criminal Justice Today* site on the World Wide Web by pointing your Web browser at http://www.prenhall.com/cjtoday. Once there, click the "enter here" selection, then "Web Chapters" and finally "Chapter 2: The Crime Picture" from the selection box. You can then access electronic information and other sites of relevance to this chapter. You may also wish to enter the Global Town Meeting, which provides facilities for the posting of electronic messages for others to read. Messages are arranged by topic, with new topics constantly being added.

NOTES

1. "Point of View," *The Chronicle of Higher Education*, June 10, 1992, p. A40.
2. See Joseph Bosco, "In the Face of Death: Fresh Details of Ennis Cosby's Final Moments Pose Additional Puzzles for a Struggling Prosecution," *Time* on-line, June 2, 1997.
3. "Actor Bill Cosby's son Found Shot to Death," CNN Interactive on the World Wide Web. Web posted, January 16, 1997.
4. Norval Morris, "Crime, the Media, and Our Public Discourse," National Institute of Justice, *Perspectives on Crime and Justice"* video series, recorded May 13, 1997.
5. As quoted in Frank Hagan, *Research Methods in Criminal Justice* (New York: Macmillan, 1982), from Eugene Webb et al., *Nonreactive Measures in the Social Sciences*, 2nd ed. (Boston: Houghton Mifflin, 1981), p. 89.
6. U.S. Bureau of Justice Statistics (BJS), *Criminal Victimization in the United States, 1985* (Washington, D.C.: U.S. Government Printing Office, 1987), p. 1.
7. Federal Bureau of Investigation (FBI), *Uniform Crime Reports for the United States, 1987* (Washington, D.C.: U.S. Government Printing Office, 1988), p. 1.

8. Hagan, *Research Methods in Criminal Justice and Criminology.*

9. John J. DiIulio, Jr., "The Question of Black Crime," *The Public Interest,* Fall 1994, pp. 3–12.

10. James Alan Fox, *Trends in Juvenile Violence: A Report to the United States Attorney General on Current and Future Rates of Juvenile Offending* (Washington, D.C.: Bureau of Justice Statistics, 1996).

11. Federal Bureau of Investigation (FBI), *Uniform Crime Reports for the United States, 1996* (Washington, D.C.: U.S. Government Printing Office, 1997), p. 16.

12. Federal Bureau of Investigation (FBI), *Uniform Crime Reports for the United States, 1975* (Washington, D.C.: U.S. Government Printing Office, 1976), p. 22.

13. "Violent Crime," The Associated Press wire services, September 18, 1996.

14. Ibid.

15. All offense definitions in this chapter are derived from those used by the UCR reporting program and are taken from the FBI, *Uniform Crime Reports: Crime in the United States, 1994* (hereafter referred to as the *Uniform Crime Reports*), or from BJS, *Criminal Justice Data Terminology,* 2nd ed. (Washington, D.C.: Bureau of Justice Statistics, 1981).

16. FBI, *Uniform Crime Reports,* 1996.

17. These and other statistics in this chapter are derived primarily from the *Uniform Crime Reports, 1996.*

18. Bureau of Justice Statistics (BJS), *Report to the Nation on Crime and Justice,* 2nd ed. (Washington, D.C.: U.S. Government Printing Office, 1988), p. 4.

19. There is no definitive "cut-off" between serial killing and spree killing in terms of time. Cunanan's three-month spree might qualify him as a serial killer in the minds of some criminologists. Nonetheless, renowned homicide investigators Robert Ressler (a former FBI criminal profiler) and Vernon Geberth (a retired New York commander of homicide investigations and noted forensic expert) both classify him as a spree killer. (See Michael Grunwald, "Cunanan Leaves Experts at Loss," *The Boston Globe* via Simon and Schuster *Newslink,* July 28, 1997.)

20. Ibid.

21. Ibid.

22. For excellent coverage of serial killers see, Steven Egger, *The Killers Among Us: An Examination of Serial Murder and Its Investigation* (Upper Saddle River, NJ: Prentice Hall, 1998); Steven A. Egger, *Serial Murder: An Elusive Phenomenon* (Westport, CT: Praeger, 1990); and, Stephen J. Giannangelo, *The Psychopathology of Serial Murder: A Theory of Violence* (New York: Praeger Publishers, 1996).

23. A few years ago Lucas recanted all of his confessions, saying he never killed anyone—except possibly his mother (a killing which he said he didn't remember). See "Condemned Killer Admits Lying, Denies Slayings," *The Washington Post,* October 1, 1995.

24. Chikatilo was executed in 1994.

25. *Uniform Crime Reports,* 1996, p. 23.

26. Federal Bureau of Investigation, *Uniform Crime Reporting Handbook* (Washington, D.C.: FBI, 1984), p. 10.

27. "Study: Rape Vastly Underreported," *The Fayetteville Observer-Times* (North Carolina), April 26, 1992, p. 16A.

28. Ronald Barri Flowers, *Women and Criminality: The Woman as Victim, Offender and Practitioner* (Westport, CT: Greenwood Press, 1987), pp. 33–36.

29. Flowers, *Women and Criminality,* p. 36.

30. A. Nichols Groth, *Men Who Rape: The Psychology of the Offender* (New York: Plenum Press, 1979).

31. Susan Brownmiller, *Against Our Will: Men, Women, and Rape* (New York: Simon and Schuster, 1975).

32. Dennis J. Stevens, "Motives of Social Rapists," Free Inquiry in *Creative Sociology,* Vol. 23, no. 2 (November 1995), pp. 117–126.

33. The latest edition of the *Uniform Crime Reporting Handbook,* which serves as a statistical reporting guide for law enforcement agencies, says, for example, "By definition, sex attacks on males are excluded and should be classified as assaults or 'other sex offenses,' depending on the nature of the crime and the extent of the injury." *Uniform Crime Reporting Handbook* (Washington, D.C.: FBI, 1984), p. 10.

34. "Swim Coach Guilty of Statutory Rape," *USA Today,* August 13, 1993, p. 3A.

35. "Teen: Teacher's Pregnancy Planned," the Associated Press wire services, August 22, 1997.

36. BJS, *Report to the Nation on Crime and Justice,* 2nd ed., p. 5.

37. Ibid.

38. FBI, *Uniform Crime Reports, 1996.* For UCR reporting purposes, "minorities" are defined as blacks, Native Americans, Asians, Pacific Islanders, and Alaskan Natives.

39. Sometimes called assault with a deadly weapon with intent to kill, or AWDWWIK.

40. BJS, *Report to the Nation on Crime and Justice,* 2nd ed., p. 6.

41. Ibid., p. 6.

42. Ibid.

43. "Yale Says Student Stole His Education," *USA Today,* April 12, 1995, p. 3A.

44. Gale Holland and Jonathan T. Lovitt, "Fertility Pioneer Is Accused of Stealing Embryos," *USA Today,* May 25, 1995, p. 8A.

45. Federal Bureau of Investigation (FBI), *Uniform Crime Reporting Handbook* (Washington, D.C.: U.S. Department of Justice, 1984), p. 28.

46. "Carjacking Case Goes to Trial," *USA Today*, April 13, 1993, p. 2A.

47. FBI, *Uniform Crime Reports, 1996.*

48. As indicated in the UCR definition of arson, *Uniform Crime Reports, 1996.*

49. FBI, *Uniform Crime Reports, 1996.*

50. Ibid.

51. While the old rule would have counted only one murder where a woman was raped and her husband murdered in the same criminal incident, the new rule would report both a murder and a rape.

52. Bureau of Justice Statistics, *Implementing the National Incident-Based Reporting System: A Project Status Report* (Washington, D.C.: Bureau of Justice Statistics, July, 1997).

53. The SEARCH Project Web Site, *NIBRS Overview*, http://www.nibrs.search.org.

54. H.R. 4797, 102d Cong. 2d Sess. (1992).

55. Uniform Crime Reports, 1996, p. 59.

56. "Grim Portraits of Homophobic Killers," *The Boston Globe* on-line, May 10, 1997.

57. Michael E. Wiggins, "Societal Changes and Right Wing Membership," paper presented at the Academy of Criminal Justice Sciences Annual Meeting, San Francisco, California, April, 1988.

58. Richard Holden, "God's Law: Criminal Process and Right Wing Extremism in America," paper presented at the annual meeting of the Academy of Criminal Justice Sciences, San Francisco, California, April 1988.

59. John Kleinig, "Penalty Enhancements for Hate Crimes," *Criminal Justice Ethics* (Summer/Fall 1992), pp. 3–6.

60. *R.A.V. v. City of St. Paul, Minn.*, 112 S.Ct. 2538 (1992).

61. *Forsyth County, Ga. v. Nationalist Movement*, 112 S.Ct. 2395 (1992).

62. *Wisconsin v. Mitchell*, 508 U.S. 47 (1993).

63. For additional information, see U.S. Department of Justice, Bureau of Justice Statistics (BJS), *Criminal Victimization in the United States, 1996* (Washington, D.C.: Bureau of Justice Statistics, 1997).

64. Bureau of Justice Statistics (BJS), *Criminal Victimization in the United States, 1991* (Washington, D.C.: Bureau of Justice Statistics, 1992).

65. Ibid.

66. Bureau of Justice Statistics, *Report to the Nation on Crime and Justice*, 2nd ed., p. 26.

67. U.S. Department of Justice, "The Risk of Violent Crime," *BJS Special Report* (Washington, D.C.: Bureau of Justice Statistics, May 1985), p. 2.

68. Bureau of Justice Statistics (BJS), "National Crime Victimization Survey Redesign," October 30, 1994.

69. Ronet Bachman, "Violence and Theft in the Workplace," A BJS Crime Data Brief, July, 1994.

70. Bureau of Justice Statistics (BJS), "Violence Between Inmates," November 1994.

71. Bureau of Justice Statistics, *Report to the Nation on Crime and Justice*, 2nd ed., p. 27.

72. Georgette Bennett, *Crimewarps: The Future of Crime in America* (Garden City, NY: Anchor/Doubleday, 1987).

73. Ibid.

74. Ibid., p. xiv.

75. *Report to the Nation on Crime and Justice*, 2nd ed., p. 24.

76. "Job Worries Persist, Poll Shows," *USA Today*, December 15, 1993, p. 4A, reporting on the 1994 *Battleground Survey* by the Tarrance Group and Mellman-Lazarus-Lake.

77. *Washington Post* wire services, December 20, 1993.

78. Bureau of Justice Statistics, *Report to the Nation on Crime and Justice*, 2nd ed., p. 32.

79. The definition of rape employed by the UCR, however, automatically excludes crimes of homosexual rape such as might occur in prisons and jails. As a consequence, the rape of males is excluded from the official count for crimes of rape.

80. Bureau of Justice Statistics, *Report to the Nation on Crime and Justice*, 2nd ed., p. 25.

81. See, for example, Elizabeth Stanko, "When Precaution Is Normal: A Feminist Critique of Crime Prevention," in Loraine Gelsthorpe and Allison Morris, *Feminist Perspectives in Criminology* (Philadelphia: Open University Press, 1990).

82. For excellent coverage of women's issues in all areas of criminal justice, see Alida V. Merlo and Joycelyn M. Pollock, eds., *Women, Law, and Social Control* (Needham Heights, MA: Allyn and Bacon, 1995), and Donna C. Hale, ed., the journal *Women and Criminal Justice*, (Binghamton, NY: The Haworth Press).

83. "Battered Women Tell Their Stories to the Senate," *The Charlotte Observer* (North Carolina), July 10, 1991, p. 3A.

84. For more information, see Eve S. Buzawa and Carl G. Buzawa, *Domestic Violence: The Criminal Justice Response* (Thousand Oaks, CA: Sage, 1996).

85. Caroline Wolf Harlow, *Female Victims of Violent Crime* (Washington, D.C.: Bureau of Justice Statistics, 1991).

86. Nanci Koser Wilson, "Feminist Pedagogy in Criminology," *Journal of Criminal Justice Education*, Vol. 2, no. 2 (Spring 1991), pp. 81–93.

87. "Florida Woman Sentenced to Death," *USA Today*, February 1, 1992, p. 3A.

88. "Fla. Slayings: Men Beware," *USA Today*, December 17, 1990, p. 3A.

89. *Wuornos* v. *Florida*, No. 96–5766.

90. Otto Pollak, *The Criminality of Women* (Philadelphia: University of Pennsylvania Press, 1950).

91. FBI, *Uniform Crime Reports, 1970* and *1996*.

92. Ibid.

93. FBI, *Uniform Crime Reports, 1996*.

94. Leanne Fiftal Alarid, James W. Marquart, Velmer S. Burton, Jr., Francis T. Cullen, and Steven J. Cuvelier, "Women's Roles in Serious Offenses: A Study of Adult Felons," *Justice Quarterly*, Vol. 13, no. 3 (September 1996), pp. 432–454.

95. Patsy A. Klaus, "The Costs of Crime to Victims," a Bureau of Justice Statistics Crime Data Brief, 1994.

96. Ted R. Miller, Mark A. Cohen, and Brian Wiersema, *Victim Costs and Consequences: A New Look* (Washington, D.C.: National Institute of Justice, February 1996).

97. Ibid.

98. Bureau of Justice Statistics, *Criminal Victimization in the United States, 1996*.

99. Bureau of Justice Statistics, *Report to the Nation on Crime and Justice*, 2nd ed.

100. Kathleen Maguire and Ann L. Pastore, eds., *Sourcebook of Criminal Justice Statistics, 1996* (Washington, D.C.: Bureau of Justice Statistics, 1997).

101. Bureau of Justice Statistics, *Report to the Nation on Crime and Justice*, 2nd ed., p. 114.

102. "President Asks for 20% Growth in Justice Department Funding," *Criminal Justice Newsletter*, February 1, 1995, p. 1.

103. Ibid.

104. J. M. Chaiken and M. R. Chaiken, *Varieties of Criminal Behavior* (Santa Monica, CA: The Rand Corporation, 1982).

105. D. McBride, "Trends in Drugs and Death," paper presented at American Society of Criminology annual meeting, Denver, Colorado, 1983.

106. B. Johnson et al., *Taking Care of Business: The Economics of Crime by Heroin Abusers* (Lexington, MA: Lexington Books, 1985). See also Bernard A. Grooper, *Research in Brief: Probing the Links Between Drugs and Crime* (Washington, D.C.: National Institute of Justice, February 1985).

107. Bureau of Justice Statistics, *Report to the Nation on Crime and Justice*, 2nd ed., p. 114.

108. Ibid.

109. Bureau of Justice Statistics, *Uniform Crime Reports, 1996*, p. 225.

110. Bureau of Justice Statistics, *Uniform Crime Reports, 1975* and *1996*.

111. Ibid.

112. *Sourcebook of Criminal Justice Statistics, 1996*, p. 527.

113. Bennett, *Crimewarps*, p. 61.

114. Much of the data in this section comes from Bureau of Justice Statistics, "Elderly Crime Victims," March 1994. See also Catherine J. Whitaker, *BJS Special Report: Elderly Victims* (Rockville, MD: Bureau of Justice Statistics, November 1987).

115. The Organized Crime Control Act of 1970.

116. Bonnie Angelo, "Wanted: A New Godfather," *Time*, April 13, 1992, Vol. 139, no. 15, p. 30.

117. Richard Behar, "In the Grip of Treachery," *Playboy*, November 1991, Vol. 38, no. 11, p. 92.

118. William Sherman, "Kingpins of the Underworld," *Cosmopolitan*, March 1992, Vol. 212, no. 3, p. 158.

119. Early reports said that Dominick Cirillo, 67—known as "Quiet Dom"—has emerged as the heir to Gigante.

chapter 3

THE SEARCH FOR CAUSES

The word needs to go out on the street. We have had it with violence. We have had it with violent people. We're tired of being told to try to understand their childhood or understand their past.

—HOUSE SPEAKER NEWT GINGRICH[1]

I could kill everyone without blinking an eye!

—CHARLIE MANSON[2]

83

Why Is There Crime?

In 1996 John Brennan Crutchley was released after spending ten years in the Florida prison system. Crutchley is the infamous "vampire rapist," so named because he abducted a 19-year-old hitchhiker in 1985, repeatedly raped her, then used an intravenous device to drain nearly half her blood so he could drink it.[3] A neighbor found the nude, bleeding, handcuffed and semiconscious woman after she escaped. She survived, and Crutchley was arrested with the woman's help.

Crimes like Crutchley's are difficult to explain. Fundamental questions about crime causation that have concerned criminologists for years are: "Why do people commit crime? Why are they deviant? What are the root causes of violence and aggression? Are people basically good, or are they motivated only by self-interest?" More precisely, we might ask, "Why does a *particular person* commit a *distinct crime* on a given occasion and under specific circumstances?" No discussion of crime and of the criminal justice system would be complete without giving some consideration to the causes of crime and deviance. That is the purpose of this chapter. Before we begin, however, some brief definitions are in order. Crime, as noted in Chapter 1, is a violation of the criminal law without acceptable legal justification;[4] while **deviant behavior** is a violation of social norms specifying appropriate or proper behavior under a particular set of circumstances. It is important to realize that deviant behavior is a broad category which often includes crime.

Many different kinds of theories have been advanced to explain all sorts of rule-violating behavior. Some observers of the contemporary scene, for example, find explanations for modern-day violence and seemingly increased rates of criminal victimization in the now widespread and commonplace episodes of violence in the American media—especially on television, in music, and in film. Experts who study the media estimate that the average American child watches 8,000 murders and 100,000 acts of violence while growing up. At a recent international conference, Suzanne Stutman, president of the Institute for Mental Health Initiatives in Washington, reported that studies consistently show that the extent of exposure to television violence in childhood is a good predictor of future criminal behavior.[5]

Deviance (also **deviant behavior**) A violation of social norms defining appropriate or proper behavior under a particular set of circumstances. Deviance often includes acts which are criminal.

Robert Brown, executive director of the Washington, D.C., Children's Trust Neighborhood Initiative, tends to lay much of the blame for contemporary violence on rap music, especially "gangsta rap." "So many of our young men," says Brown, "have accepted false icons of manhood for themselves…because the popular culture of videos and rap—Snoop Doggy Dogg and the rest—reinforces that this is the correct way to be. Guys…try to exude an aura that says, 'I am so bad that I am not afraid to take your life or to offer mine up in the process.'"[6]

A black critic of gangsta rap puts it this way: "The key element is aggression—in rappers' body language, tone, and witty rhymes—that often leaves listeners hyped, on edge, angry about…something. Perhaps the most important element in gangsta rap is its messages, which center largely around these ideas: that women are no more than 'bitches and hos,' disposable playthings who exist merely for men's abusive delight; that it's cool to use any means necessary to get the material things you want; and most importantly, it's admirable to be cold-blooded and hard."[7] The Reverend Arthur L. Cribbs, Jr., a black social critic, agrees. Cribbs, writing in a national editorial, calls gangsta rap "nothing but modern-day violence and vulgarity wrapped and packaged in blackface."[8]

Supporting such arguments are the personal lives of rappers themselves, which have frequently been anything but exemplary. On September 7, 1996, for example, rapper Tupak Shakur, well-known for his starring role in the movie *Poetic Justice*, was gunned down after leaving a Mike Tyson fight in Las Vegas. He died at a local hospital a week after being attacked. Shakur's violent past included a shooting that injured two off-duty Atlanta policemen, a conviction on sodomy charges in New York City,[9] and a previous mugging during which the rapper was shot four times. During his brief rise to stardom Shakur's brand of "gangsta rap" was condemned by former Vice President Dan Quayle, who charged that Shakur's violent lyrics had led a youth to kill a Texas state trooper.

Six months after Shakur died, the Notorious B.I.G., or Biggie Smalls—another of gangsta rap's best-known entertainers—was killed in a hail of gunfire. The 24-year-old B.I.G., whose given name was Christopher Wallace, was shot shortly after midnight on March 9, 1997, as he sat in the passenger seat of a GMC Suburban at a red light in downtown Los Angeles. He died a short time later at Cedars-Sinai Medical Center. B.I.G., a former drug dealer and street hustler from the rough Bedford-Stuyvesant section of Brooklyn, New York, had burst onto the gangsta rap scene in 1994 with his million-selling album *Ready to Die*.

About the time B.I.G. died, another infamous rapper, Snoop Doggy Dogg, and his bodyguard, McKinley Lee, were acquitted of murder charges in the 1993 slaying of Phillip Woldermariam. Woldermariam, a member of the Venice Shoreline Crips, had been shot twice in the back after meeting with Snoop. Snoop, who was born with the name Calvin Broadus in Long Beach, California, in 1971, and others like him have profited mightily by selling images of urban violence to mainstream youth. As a result of highly lucrative album sales, Snoop had no problem posting a $2 million bond following his arrest.[10] A $25 million wrongful death suit filed by Woldemariam's family was settled out of court in late 1996 for an undisclosed sum.

Unfortunately, popular rap "artists," even those who exemplify violence, may serve as role models to impressionable others. As one author puts it, "Young people bombarded with images of sex and violence often find it hard to separate fantasy from fact. And some can't resist the temptation to act out what they've seen."[11]

It is not only rap music and violent TV programming that have come under fire. Other contemporary art forms have also been called into question. A recent study, for example, of "heavy metal" music suggests that "the loud bass guitar and emotional singing of the heavy metal genre nurtures suicidal tendencies among youths already alienated and depressed by life's problems."[12] In fact, according to one 1995 survey, "57% of the public thinks violence in the media is a major factor in real-life violence" of all kinds.[13]

But whether violence in the media and depressing themes in popular music are indeed a cause of crime or of suicide, as many believe, or merely a reflection of the social conditions which exist in many American communities today is less than clear. Some, however, do not hesitate to draw such a conclusion. "What all this means to me," says *Washington Post* columnist Nathan McCall, "is that while we've been searching for complex sociological explanations for the sudden surge in violence afflicting young blacks, part of the answer may be quite simple, something dangling right under our collective noses—and ears."[14]

The political right believes that the root cause of violent crime is bad genes or bad morals. Not so, says the left. The root cause of violent crime is bad housing or dead-end jobs. And, I tell you that while doing something about the causes of violence surely requires a political ideology, the only way we can determine what those causes are in the first place is to check our ideologies at the door and to try to keep our minds open as wide, and for as long, as we can bear.

—John Monahan, Speaking at the U.S. Sentencing Commission's Inaugural Symposium on Crime and Punishment

In a rare surviving photograph, Cesare Lombroso (left) who has been dubbed the "father of modern criminology," is shown sitting with friend Louis Lombard in 1909. *Culver Pictures*

The 1996 Telecommunications Reform Act includes one possible solution to media-communicated violence. The Act contains the requirement that all 13-inch or larger television sets be equipped with a so-called "V-chip" (an antiviolence microprocessor), which will allow owners to block programming tagged as violent by an industry rating system. V-chip technology will allow parents to program their children's television sets to exclude violent programming.

Criminological Theory

Whatever the outcome of such social policy initiatives, it is important to recognize that focusing on songwriters, recording companies, and the broadcast media reflects just one way of explaining crime and criminal violence. Explanations of this sort find considerable persuasive power in emphasizing the role of economics, greed, and financial irresponsibility on the part of the nation's business leaders in crime causation. Many other types of explanations for crime can also be offered, such as genetic abnormalities which may predispose people to crime and violence or others which look to individual psychological differences or variations in patterns of early socialization. Likewise, social institutions such as the family, schools, and churches can be examined for their role in reducing or enhancing the likelihood of criminality among individuals subject to them.

Regardless of the particular mode of explanation chosen, however, there is probably no single cause of crime. Crime appears rooted in a diversity of causal factors and takes a variety of forms, depending upon the situation in which it occurs. Nonetheless, some theories of human behavior help us to understand why certain people engage in acts which society defines as criminal or deviant, while others do not.

A **theory** is a kind of model. Theories posit relationships, often of a causal sort, between events and things under study. So it is not unusual to hear someone suggest that "rap music causes crime." However, while everyone may have his or her own pet theory about crime, about the economy, or about child rearing, the word "theory" takes on a special meaning in the social sciences and in the study of criminal justice. Technically speaking, a complete theory is said to consist of a series of interrelated propositions which attempt to describe,

Theory A set of interrelated propositions that attempt to describe, explain, predict, and ultimately control some class of events. A theory gains explanatory power from inherent logical consistency and is "tested" by how well it describes and predicts reality.

Process Concludes

Steps in the Theory Building Process	Representative Activities
Theory-Based Social Policy Results	Opportunities for success are increased so that the cycle of poverty can be broken. Hence, government funded educational programs, job training, and small business support are put into place among the economically disadvantaged in order to reduce and prevent crime.
The Hypothesis Is Tested	Pilot projects to measure the impact of increased opportunities on crime rates in specific geographical locations are funded and begun. Results prove encouraging and appear to support the hypothesis.
A Theory-Based Hypothesis Develops	Breaking the cycle of poverty will reduce crime.
Theory-Based Understanding Is Achieved	Poverty is a root cause of crime.
A Theory Is Proposed	Poverty leads to lessened social opportunity. Restricted opportunity reduces success in other areas of life. Lowered success means lessened self-esteem and a reduced commitment to normative values, all of which leads to crime commission.
Questions Are Raised About Causes	Why the crime–poverty connection?
A Correlation Is Observed	High crime rates are associated with poverty.

Process Begins

FIGURE 3–1 Steps in criminal justice theory building and social policy creation.

explain, predict, and, ultimately, control some class of events. A theory's explanatory power derives primarily from its inherent logical consistency, and theories are tested by how well they describe and predict reality. In other words, a good theory provides relatively complete understanding of the phenomenon under study, while at the same time carefully made observations support predictions based upon it. A good theory fits the facts, and it stands up to continued scrutiny. Figure 3–1 diagrams the important aspects of theory creation in the social sciences and uses, by way of example, the well-known association between poverty and crime.

History is rife with theories purporting to explain rule-violating behavior. An old Roman theory, for example, based on ancient observations that nights with full moons seem to hold more crime and deviance, proposed that a kind of temporary insanity might be caused by the influence of the moon—hence the term "lunacy." The lunacy theory provided early theorists with the "ah-ha!" of understanding. According to the theory, human behavior wasn't just random, but ebbed and flowed in cadence with the lunar cycle. As a consequence, crime and deviance could be directly explained as due to the influence of the moon. The moon itself, suggested early theorists, held sway over human thought, emotions, and behavior. In fact, although modern statisticians have noted an apparent association between phases of the moon and crime rates, the precise mechanism by which the moon influences behavior has never been adequately explained.

A complete theory attempts to "flesh out" all the causal linkages between phenomena which are associated, or said to be "correlated." Hence, a comprehensive theory of lunacy might suggest, as some do, that light from the full moon stimulates the reticular activating system (RAS) in the limbic portion of the human brain, leading to easy excitement and

[The media is full of] incessant, repetitive, mindless violence and irresponsible conduct…

—President Clinton, January 1995 State of the Union Address

Hypothesis   (1) An explanation that accounts for a set of facts and that can be tested by further investigation; (2) Something that is taken to be true for the purpose of argument or investigation.

Research   The use of standardized, systematic procedures in the search for knowledge.

hyperactivity—and then to deviance and crime. Others have suggested, quite simply, that people commit more crimes when the moon is full because it is easier to see.

Theories, once created, must still be tested to tell whether or not they are true. As a consequence, modern criminology has become increasingly scientific.[15] Generally accepted research designs—coupled with careful data gathering strategies and statistical techniques for data analysis—have yielded considerable confidence in certain explanations for crime, while at the same time tending to disprove others. Theory testing usually involves the development of **hypotheses** based upon what the theory under scrutiny would predict. A theory of "lunacy," for example, might be tested in a variety of ways, including (1) observations of rates of crime and deviance on full-moon nights when the light of the moon is obscured by clouds (when we would expect no rise in such rates if proposed RAS, or visibility, explanations are correct); or (2) an examination of city crime rates on full-moon nights—especially in well-lighted city areas where the light of the moon hardly increases visibility—and so on. If the predictions made by a theory are validated by careful observation, the theory gains greater acceptability.

Unfortunately, many contemporary theories of deviant and criminal behavior are far from complete, offering only limited ideas rather than complete explanations for the behavior in question. Others are difficult to test. Moreover, when we consider the wide range of behaviors regarded as criminal—from murder to drug use to white-collar crime—it seems difficult to imagine a theory that can explain them all. Yet many past theoretical approaches to crime causation were unicausal and all inclusive. That is, they posited a single, identifiable source for all serious deviant and criminal behavior.

Theories of crime causation which have met rigorous scientific tests for acceptability provide the intellectual basis needed by policy-makers to create informed crime-control strategies. The ultimate goal of **research** and theory building in criminology is to permit the construction of models that allow for a better understanding of criminal behavior and which enhance the development of strategies intended to address the problem of crime.

Unfortunately, crime-control strategies based upon accepted theory may not always accurately reflect the causal mechanism underlying a series of observations. Early skeletal remains recently discovered by archaeologists, for example, provide evidence that some human societies believed outlandish behavior was caused by spirit possession. Skulls, dated by various techniques to approximately 30,000 years ago, show signs of early cranial surgery, apparently designed to release evil spirits thought to be residing within the heads of offenders. Surgical techniques were undoubtedly crude, and probably involved some fermented anesthesia along with flint or obsidian surgical implements. Any theory, however, gains credence if activity based upon it produces results in keeping with what that theory would predict. Spirit possession, as an explanation for deviance, probably appeared well validated by positive behavioral changes induced in those "patients" who submitted to the surgery called for by the theory. The cause of reformation may have been brain infections resulting from unsanitary conditions, slips of the stone knife, or the pain endured by those undergoing the procedure. To the uncritical observer, however, the theory of spirit possession as a cause of deviance—and cranial surgery as a treatment technique—may well have appeared supported by the "evidence."

While we will use the word *theory* in describing various explanations for crime throughout this chapter, it should be recognized that the word is only loosely applicable to some of the perspectives we will discuss. As noted, many social scientists insist that to be considered "theories," explanations must consist of sets of clearly stated, logically interrelated, and measurable propositions. The fact that few of the "theories" which follow rise above the level of organized conjecture, and that many others are not amenable to objective scrutiny through scientific testing, is one of the greatest failures of social science today.

For our purposes, explanations of criminal behavior fall into nine general categories:

- Classical
- Psychobiological
- Sociological
- Conflict
- Emergent

- Biological
- Psychological
- Social-psychological
- Phenomenological

The differences among these approaches are summarized in Table 3–1.

Table 3-1   Types of Criminological Theory

Type	Theorists	Characteristics
Classical		
Free will theories	Beccaria	Crime is caused by the individual exercise
Hedonistic calculus	Bentham	of free will. Prevention is possible
		through swift and certain punishment
		which offsets any gains to be had through
		criminal behavior.
Biological		
Phrenology	Gall	"Criminal genes" cause deviant behavior.
Atavism	Lombroso	Criminals are identifiable through
Criminal families	Dugdale	physical characteristics or genetic
	Goddard	makeup. Treatment is generally
Somatotypes	Sheldon	ineffective, but aggression may be
		usefully redirected.
Psychobiological		
Chromosome theory	Jacobs	Human DNA, environmental contaminants,
Biochemical approaches		nutrition, hormones, physical
Heredity	Mednick	trauma, and body chemistry play
	Wilson	important and interwoven roles in
	Herrnstein	producing human cognition, feeling, and
		behavior—including crime.
Psychological		
Behavioral conditioning	Pavlov	Crime is the result of inappropriate
Psychoanalysis	Freud	behavioral conditioning *or* a diseased
Psychopathology	Cleckley	mind. Treatment necessitates extensive
Behavioral theories	Skinner	behavioral therapy.
Sociological		
Social disorganization	Park	The structure of society, and its relative
Anomie	Durkheim	degree of organization or disorganization,
Subcultures	Cohen	are important factors contributing
Focal concerns	Miller	to the prevalence of criminal behavior.
	McKay	Group dynamics, group organization,
	Merton	and subgroup relationships form the
	Wolfgang	causal nexus out of which crime develops.
	Burgess	Effective social policy may require
		basic changes in patterns of socialization
		and an increase in accepted opportunities
		for success.
Social-Psychological		
Differential association	Sutherland	Crime results from the failure of
Social learning	Burgess	self-direction, inadequate social roles,
Containment	Reckless	or association with defective others.
Social control	Hirschi	Social policy places responsibility for
Neutralization	Sykes, Matza	change upon the offender.

Table 3-1 Types of Criminological Theory (continued)

Type	Theorists	Characteristics
Conflict		
Radical criminology The "new" criminology Peacemaking criminology	Turk Vold Chambliss Quinney Pepinsky	Conflict is fundamental to social life. Crime is a natural consequence of social, political, and economic inequities. Fundamental changes to the structure of society are needed for crime to disappear.
Phenomenological		
Symbolic interaction Criminal personality Career criminality Labeling	Mead Yochelson Samenow Becker	The source of criminal behavior is unknown, but an understanding of crime requires recognition of the fact that "crime" is a definition imposed upon behavior by the wider society. Individuals defined as "criminal" may be excluded by society from "normal" opportunities. Therapy requires a total reorientation of the offender.
Emergent		
Feminist criminology	Freda Adler Rita J. Simon Kathleen Daly Meda Chesney-Lind	Feminist criminology, which is representative of other new and emerging theories, emphasizes the need for gender awareness in the criminological enterprise.
Postmodern criminology	Stuart Henry Dragan Milovanovic Bruce DiCristina	Deconstructionist approaches that challenge existing theories in order to replace them with perspectives more relevant to the modern era.

The Classical School

Classical School An eighteenth-century approach to crime causation and criminal responsibility, which resulted from the Enlightenment and which emphasized the role of free will and reasonable punishments.

Classical theories of crime causation dominated criminological thought for much of the late eighteenth and early nineteenth century. A recent rebirth of classical theory has been termed "neoclassical criminology." Most classical theories of crime causation, both old and new, make certain basic assumptions. Among them are

- Crime is caused by the individual exercise of free will. Human beings are fundamentally rational, and most human behavior is the result of free will coupled with rational choice.
- Pain and pleasure are the two central determinants of human behavior.
- Crime disparages the quality of the bond which exists between individuals and society and is, therefore, an immoral form of behavior.
- Punishment, a necessary evil, is sometimes required to deter law violators and to serve as an example to others who would also violate the law.
- Crime prevention is possible through swift and certain punishment which offsets any gains to be had through criminal behavior.

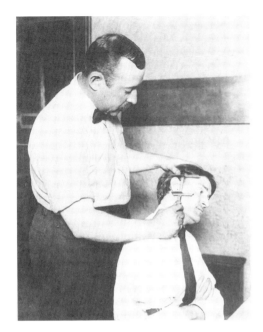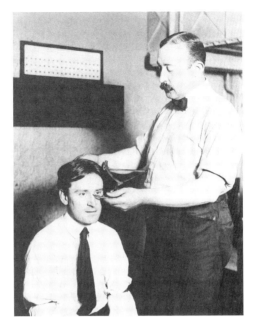

The theory of atavism, based upon the ideas of Charles Darwin, supported the use of physical anthropology in the identification of offenders. Here, the Bertillion system of identification is applied to a suspect in the years prior to the development of fingerprinting.
Courtesy of the Library of Congress

Cesare Beccaria: Crime and Punishment

In 1764 Cesare Beccaria (1738–1794) published his *Essays on Crimes and Punishment.* The book was an immediate success and stirred a hornet's nest of controversy over the treatment of criminal offenders. Beccaria proposed basic changes in the criminal laws of his day which would make them more "humanitarian." He called for abolition of physical punishment and an end to the death penalty. Beccaria believed in the thoughtful exercise of free will and is best remembered for his suggestion that punishment should be just strong enough to offset the tendency toward crime. Punishment, he said, should be sufficient to deter, but never excessive. Because Beccaria's writings stimulated many other thinkers throughout the 1700s and early 1800s, he is referred to today as the founder of the **Classical School** of criminology.

Jeremy Bentham: Hedonistic Calculus

Among those influenced by Beccaria was the Englishman Jeremy Bentham. Bentham devised a "hedonistic calculus"[16] in keeping with the idea that the individual exercise of free will would lead people to avoid crime where the benefit to be derived from committing crime was outweighed by the pain of punishment. Bentham termed his philosophy of social control "utilitarianism." Both Bentham and Beccaria agreed that punishment had to be "swift and certain"—as well as just—in order to be effective.

The Classical School of criminology represented a noteworthy advance over previous thinking about crime because it moved beyond superstition and mysticism as explanations for deviance. A product of the Enlightenment then sweeping through Europe, the Classical School demanded recognition of rationality and made possible the exercise of informed choice in human social life. Thinkers who were to follow, however, wasted little time in subjugating free will to a secondary role in the search for causal factors in crime commission. As Stephen Schafer puts it, "In the eighteenth-century individualistic orientation of criminal law, the act was judged and the man made responsible. In the next scene in the historic drama of crime, the man is judged and the search is on for finding the responsible factor."[17]

Social Policy and Classical Theory

Much of the practice of criminal justice in America today is built around a conceptual basis provided by Classical School theorists. Many contemporary programs designed to prevent crime have their philosophical roots in the classical axioms of deterrence and punishment. Modern heirs of the Classical School see punishment as a necessary central tenet of criminal justice policy and believe it to be a natural and deserved consequence of criminal activity. Such thinkers call for greater prison capacity and new prison construction. They use evidence of high crime rates to argue that punishment is a necessary crime preventative. In Chapter 1 we used the term "law and order advocates," and it can be applied to at least some modern-day proponents of classical theory who frequently seek stiffer criminal laws and enhanced penalties for criminal activity. The emphasis on punishment, however, as an appropriate response to crime, whether founded on principles of deterrence or revenge, has left many contemporary criminal justice initiatives foundering on overcrowded prisons and courtrooms packed into near paralysis.

Biological Theories

Biological School A perspective on criminological thought which holds that criminal behavior has a physiological basis. Genes, foods and food additives, hormones, and inheritance are all thought to play a role in determining individual behavior. Biological thinkers highlight the underlying animalistic aspect of being human as a major determinant of behavior.

Most early biological theories of crime causation, which built upon inherited or bodily characteristics and features, made certain fundamental assumptions. Among them are

- The basic determinants of human behavior, including criminal tendencies, are, to a considerable degree, constitutionally or genetically based.
- The basic determinants of human behavior, including criminality, may be passed on from generation to generation. In other words, a penchant for crime may be inherited.
- At least some human behavior is the result of biological propensities inherited from more primitive developmental stages in the evolutionary process. Some human beings may be further along the evolutionary ladder than others, and their behavior may reflect it.

Franz Joseph Gall: Phrenology

Phrenology The study of the shape of the head to determine anatomical correlates of human behavior.

The idea that the quality of a person could be judged by a study of the person's face is as old as antiquity. Even today we often judge people on their looks, saying, "He has an honest face" or "She has tender eyes." Horror movies have played upon unspoken cultural themes as to how a "maniac" might look. Jack Nicholson's portrayal of a crazed killer in *The Shining* and Anthony Hopkins's role as a serial killer in *Silence of the Lambs* turned that look into a fortune at the box office.

Franz Joseph Gall (1758–1828) was one of the first thinkers to present systematically the idea that bodily constitution might reflect personality. Gall was writing at a time when notions of the personality allowed for the belief that organs throughout the body determined one's mental state and behavior. People were said to be "hard hearted" or to have a "bad spleen" which filled them with bile. Gall focused instead on the head and the brain and called his approach "cranioscopy." It can be summarized in four propositions

- The brain is the organ of the mind.
- The brain consists of localized faculties or functions.
- The shape of the skull reveals the underlying development (or corresponding lack of it) of areas within the brain.
- The personality can be revealed by a study of the skull.

Gall never systematically "tested" his theory in a way that would meet contemporary scientific standards. Even so, his approach to predicting behavior, which came to be known as phrenology, quickly spread through Europe. Gall's student, Johann Gaspar Spurzheim (1776–1853), brought phrenology to America in a series of lectures and publications on the subject. By 1825, 29 phrenological journals were being produced in the United States and Britain.[18] Phrenology remained viable in America in some circles until the turn of the twentieth century, where it could still be found in some prison diagnostic schemes used to classify new prisoners.

Phrenology remains a part of popular culture today. Movies of the fictional Sherlock Holmes depict the great investigator making use of skulls inked with phrenological maps, and personality readings based upon liberal interpretations of Gall's theory are available at some county fairs, church socials, and fortune-telling booths.[19]

CESARE LOMBROSO: ATAVISM

Gall's theory was "deterministic" in the sense that it left little room for choice. What a person did depended more upon the shape of the skull than upon any exercise of choice. Other biological theories were soon to build upon that premise. One of the best known is that created by the Italian psychologist Cesare Lombroso (1835–1909).

Lombroso began his criminal anthropology with a postmortem evaluation of famous criminals, including one by the name of Vilella. Lombroso had the opportunity to interview Vilella on a number of occasions. After the man's death he correlated earlier observations of personality traits with measurable physical abnormalities. As a result of this and other studies, Lombroso reached the conclusion that criminals were atavistic human beings—throwbacks to earlier stages of evolution who were not sufficiently mentally advanced for successful life in the modern world. Atavism was identifiable in suspicious individuals, Lombroso suggested, through measures designed to reveal "primitive" physical characteristics.

In the late 1800s Darwin's theory of evolution was rapidly being applied to a diversity of fields. It was not surprising, therefore, that Lombroso would make the link between evolution and criminality. What separated Lombroso from his predecessors, however, was the continual refinement of his theory through ongoing observation. Based upon studies of known offenders, whom he compared to conformists, Lombroso identified a large number of atavistic traits, which, he claimed, could lead to crime. Among them were long arms, large lips, crooked noses, an abnormally large amount of body hair, prominent cheekbones, eyes of different colors, and ears which lacked clearly defined lobes.

Atavism implies the notion of born criminals. Throughout his life Lombroso grappled with the task of identifying the proportion of born criminals from among the total population of offenders. His estimates ranged at different times between 70% and 90%. Career criminals and criminals of opportunity without atavistic features he termed criminaloids and recognized the potential causative roles of greed, passion, and circumstance in their behavior.

Today, Lombroso is known as the founder of the **Positivist School** of criminology because of the role observation played in the formulation of his theories. Stephen Schafer calls Lombroso the "father of modern criminology,"[20] since most contemporary criminologists follow in the tradition that Lombroso began—of scientific observation and a comparison of theory with fact.

Atavism: The Evidence for and Against

After Lombroso died two English physicians, Charles Goring and Karl Pearson, decided to conduct a test of atavism. Goring and Pearson studied more than 3,000 prisoners and compared them along physiological criteria to an army detachment known as the Royal Engineers. No significant differences were found between the two groups, and Lombroso's ideas rapidly began to fall into disrepute.

A further study of atavism was published in 1939 by Ernest A. Hooton, a distinguished Harvard University anthropologist. Hooton had spent 12 years constructing anthropometric profiles of 13,873 male convicts in ten different American states. He measured each inmate in 107 different ways and compared them to 3,203 volunteers from National Guard units, firehouses, beaches, and hospitals. Surprisingly, Hooton did find some basis for Lombroso's beliefs and concluded that the inmate population in his study demonstrated a decided physical "inferiority."

Hooton never did recognize the fact, however, that the prisoners he studied were only a subgroup of the population of all offenders throughout the country. They were, in fact, the least successful offenders—the ones who had been caught and imprisoned. Other criminals

Atavism A condition characterized by the existence of features thought to be common in earlier stages of human evolution.

Positivist School An approach to criminal justice theorizing that stresses the application of scientific techniques to the study of crime and criminals.

Timothy McVeigh, convicted of the 1995 bombing of the Alfred P. Murrah Federal Building in Oklahoma City in which nearly 170 people died. McVeigh was sentenced to death. Some criminal offenders are motivated by "causes"—whether real or imaginary. *Bob Daemmrich, Sigma*

may have unknowingly been measured by Hooton among his "conformist" population, since they were the ones who had avoided capture. Hence the "inferiority" Hooton observed may have been an "artificial" product of a process of selection (arrest) by the justice system.

Criminal Families

[Television] poisons the minds of our young people…with destructive messages of casual violence and even more casual sex.

—Former Republican Presidential candidate Bob Dole

The concept of biological inheritance has been applied to "criminal families" as well as to individuals. Mental degeneration as an inherited contributor to crime was first explored by Richard Dugdale.[21] Dugdale used the family tree method to study a family he called the Jukes, publishing his findings in 1877. The Juke lineage had its beginning in America with "Max" (whose last name is unknown), a descendant of Dutch immigrants to New Amsterdam in the early 1700s. Two of Max's sons married into the notorious "Juke family of girls," six sisters, all of whom were illegitimate. Male Jukes were reputed to have been "vicious," while one of the women, named Ada, had an especially bad reputation and eventually came to be known as "the mother of criminals."

Dugdale found that, over the next 75 years, Ada's heirs included 1,200 persons, most of whom were "social degenerates." Only a handful of socially productive progeny could be identified. In 1915 Dugdale's study of the Jukes was continued by Arthur A. Estabrook, who extended the line to include 2,094 descendants and found just as few conformists.

A similar study was published by Henry Goddard in 1912.[22] Goddard examined the Kallikak family, which contained two clear lines of descent. One emanated from an affair which Martin Kallikak, a Revolutionary War soldier, had with a feeble-minded bar maid. She bore a son, and the line eventually produced 480 identifiable descendants. After the war, Kallikak returned home and married a "virtuous" Quaker girl in Philadelphia. This legitimate line produced 496 offspring by 1912, of whom only three were abnormal; none was criminal. The illegitimate group, however, contained over half "feeble-minded" or deviant progeny.

The theme which runs through these studies is that crime is an outlet for degenerate urges, produced and propagated through the social group by bad genetic material. Lacking is any recognition of the roles socialization and life circumstances play in the development of criminal behavior.

William Sheldon: Somatotypes

The last of the famous constitutional[23] theorists was William Sheldon (1893–1977). Sheldon studied 200 juvenile delinquents between the ages of 15 and 21 at the Hayden Goodwill Institute in Boston, Massachusetts, and decided that the young men possessed one of three somatotypes (or body types). The types of bodies described by Sheldon were (in his words)

Somatotyping The classification of human beings into types according to body build and other physical characteristics.

- *Mesomorphs:* with a relative predominance of muscle, bone, and connective tissue.
- *Endomorphs:* having a soft roundness throughout the various regions of the body; short tapering limbs; small bones; and soft, smooth, velvety skin.
- *Ectomorphs:* characterized by thinness, fragility, and delicacy of body.

Sheldon developed a system of measurements by which an individual's physique could be expressed as a combination of three numbers, such as 4.0–4.0–3.5 (the representation of an average male). The numbers represented the degree of endomorphy, mesomorphy, and ectomorphy present in the individual on a scale of 0 to 7, where 0 indicates a complete lack of features of one category. American females were said to average 5.0–3.0–3.5 on the scale. Although he wrote that each somatotype was possessed of a characteristic personality, Sheldon believed predominately mesomorphic individuals were most prone to aggression, violence, and delinquency.[24]

Social Policy and Biological Theories

Because traditional biological theories of crime causation attribute the cause of crime to fundamental physical characteristics which are not easily modified, they tend to suggest the need for extreme social policies. During the 1920s and early 1930s, for example, biological theories of crime causation, especially those which focused on inherited mental degeneration, led to the eugenics movement, under which mentally handicapped women were sometimes sterilized to prevent their bearing additional offspring. The eugenics movement was institutionalized by the 1927 U.S. Supreme Court case of *Buck* v. *Bell*,[25] in which Justice Oliver Wendell Holmes, Jr., writing in support of a Virginia statute permitting sterilization, said "[i]t is better for all the world, if instead of waiting to execute degenerate offspring for crime, or to let them starve for their imbecility, society can prevent those persons who are manifestly unfit from continuing their kind."

Psychobiological Theories

In recent years a more contemporary and sophisticated approach to biological theorizing about crime causation has arisen. Contemporary biochemical and physiological perspectives are sometimes termed psychobiology. The psychobiology of crime highlights the role of human DNA, environmental contaminants, nutrition, hormones, physical trauma (especially to the brain), and body chemistry in human cognition, feeling, and behavior.

Chromosome Theory

The ongoing mapping of human DNA and recent advances in the field of recombinant DNA have rekindled interest in genetic correlates of deviant behavior. More sophisticated than their historical counterparts, biological theories of today often draw upon the latest medical advances or build upon popular health concerns.

Chromosome theory became an explanation for criminal behavior in the 1960s. A normal female has a chromosome structure often diagrammed as "XX" because of how the sex-determining gene pair looks in an electron microscope. A male has a "Y" chromosome in place of the second "X," for a typical male "XY" pattern. Although it had been known for some time that a few people had abnormal patterns which included "extra" chromosomes (such as XXX females, XXY males with Klinefelter's Syndrome, and XXYY "double males"), it wasn't until the early 1960s that linkages between chromosome patterns and crime were explored. In 1965 the respected English journal *Nature* reported on the work of Patricia

Jacobs who had discovered **supermales**—men with an extra "Y" chromosome. Jacobs found that supermales were more common in prisons than in the general population.[26]

Other early studies claimed that the XYY male was more aggressive than other males and that he possessed a number of specific physical and psychological traits, such as height (over 6'1"), thinness, acne, a tendency toward homosexuality, a somewhat low IQ, and "a marked tendency to commit a succession of apparently motiveless property crimes."[27] Later studies disputed many of these findings, and the significance of the XYY pattern for behavioral prediction is today in doubt.

It is interesting to consider what chromosome theories could lead to if validated. Would males be tested at birth for an extra "Y" chromosome? If they were determined to have the extra "Y," would they be immediately institutionalized or sterilized, or worse? Would someone, perhaps, suggest that males with chromosomes for enhanced aggression be gainfully fitted into useful societal roles, for example, the military, sports, or elsewhere? Such considerations apply not only to imaginable scenarios involving chromosomes, but to all biological theories of one kind or another which imply that people are hostage to their biology.

Biochemical Factors and Imbalances

Recent research in the area of nutrition has produced some limited evidence that the old maxim "You are what you eat!" may contain more than a grain of truth. Biocriminology is a field of study which has made some strides in linking violent or disruptive behavior to eating habits, vitamin deficiencies, genetics, inheritance, and other conditions which impact body tissues.

One of the first studies to focus on chemical imbalances in the body as a cause of crime was reported in the British medical journal *Lancet* in 1943.[28] Authors of the study linked murder to hypoglycemia, or low blood sugar. Low blood sugar, produced by too much insulin in the blood or by near-starvation diets, was said to reduce the mind's capacity to reason effectively or judge the long-term consequences of behavior.

Allergic reactions to common foods have been reported as the cause of violence and homicide in a number of studies.[29] Foods said to produce allergic reactions in sensitive individuals, leading to a swelling of the brain and brain stem, include milk, citrus fruit, chocolate, corn, wheat, and eggs. Involvement of the central nervous system in such allergies, it has been suggested, reduces the amount of learning which occurs during childhood and may contribute to delinquency as well as to adult criminal behavior. Some studies have implicated food additives, such as monosodium glutamate, dyes, and artificial flavorings in producing criminal behavior.[30]

Other research has found that the amount of coffee and sugar consumed by inmates is considerably greater than in the outside population.[31] Theorists have suggested that high blood levels of caffeine and sugar produce antisocial behavior.[32] It is unclear whether inmates consume more coffee through boredom or whether "excitable" personalities feel a need for the kind of stimulation available through coffee drinking. On the other hand, habitual coffee drinkers in nonprison populations have not been linked to crime, and other studies, such as that conducted by Mortimer Gross of the University of Illinois, show no link between the amount of sugar consumed and hyperactivity.[33] Similarly, recent studies "have not yielded evidence that a change in diet will result in [a] significant reduction in aggressive or antisocial behavior" among inmate populations.[34] Nonetheless, some prison programs have been designed to limit intake of dietary stimulants through nutritional management and the substitution of artificial sweeteners for refined sugar.

Vitamins have also been examined for their impact on delinquency. Hoffer found that disruptive children consumed far less than the optimum levels of vitamins B_3 and B_6 than did nonproblem youths.[35] He claimed that the addition of these vitamins to the diets of children who were deficient in them could control unruly behavior and improve school performance.

The role of food and diet in producing criminal behavior, however, has not been well established. The American Dietetic Association and the National Council Against Health Fraud have concluded that no convincing scientific relationship between crime and diet has yet been demonstrated.[36] Both groups are becoming concerned that poor nutrition may result from programs intended to have behavioral impacts and that reduce or modify diets in prisons or elsewhere.

Hormones have also come under scrutiny as potential behavioral determinants. The male sex hormone testosterone has been linked to aggressiveness in males. Some studies of blood levels of testosterone have shown a direct relationship[37] between the amount of chemical present and the degree of violence used by sex offenders,[38] and steroid abuse among body builders has been linked to destructive urges and psychosis.[39]

Recent studies[40] of brain chemistry have led researchers to conclude that low levels of certain neurotransmitters, especially serotonin, are directly related to the inability to control aggressive impulses. The presence of adequate serotonin levels in the human brain seems to buffer irritating experiences which might otherwise result in anger and aggression. Low serotonin levels may result from the ingestion of toxic pollutants, such as the metals lead and manganese, according to one 1997 study.[41] Reduced serotonin levels, according to other studies, may also be found in men with an extra Y chromosome.[42]

HEREDITY AND ENVIRONMENT

Some contemporary biological theorists admit an environmental linkage. Sarnoff Mednick, for example, has found some basis for the claim that the autonomic nervous system (ANS) predisposes certain individuals toward criminality by limiting their ability to learn quickly.[43] Those with a slow ANS are thought to be unable to inhibit antisocial behavior quickly enough to avoid punishment and stigmatization.[44] Also, physical trauma, especially brain injury, has been shown capable of inducing severe personality changes, including aggression and violent behavior, in persons with a previous behavioral history of neither.[45] Similarly, persons born with certain abnormalities of the brain, especially frontal lobe dysfunction, may display a penchant for violence.[46] Frontal lobe dysfunction, now the subject of studies using advanced imaging techniques such as CT (computerized tomography), PET (positron emission tomography), and MRI (magnetic resonance imagery), is sometimes caused by reduced cerebral blood flow.

Studies of children adopted at birth have shown a tendency toward criminality of biological parents to be reflected in the behavior of their children, independent of the environment in which the children were raised.[47] Identical twins seem to exhibit a greater similarity in behavior than do nonidentical (or "fraternal") twins, and a number of studies have shown that identical twins are more alike in patterns and degree of criminal involvement than are fraternal twins.[48]

Perhaps the best known of modern-day biological perspectives on crime was proposed by James Q. Wilson and Richard Herrnstein in their book *Crime and Human Nature*, published in 1985.[49] Wilson and Herrnstein argue that inherited traits, such as maleness, aggressiveness, mesomorphic body type, and low intelligence, combine with environmental influences, including poor schools and strained family life, to produce crime. Although a firm determinism is rejected by the authors, who say that it is the interaction between environment and genetics that determines behavior, they do claim that children who will eventually grow up to be criminals can sometimes be identified early in their lives. The most important factor in the diversion of potential offenders from lives of crime, according to Wilson and Herrnstein, is a healthy family life in which affection for others and conscience can develop.[50] Wilson and Herrnstein also use cross-cultural data from Japan, where crime rates are very low, to suggest that inherited tendencies toward introversion among the Japanese result in fewer serious crimes than in the United States. The Wilson-Herrnstein thesis has been criticized for its failure to explain "crime" that extends beyond "traditional lower-class street crime" and for its lack of recognition of the political nature of criminal definitions.[51]

Social Policy and Psychobiological Theories

Psychobiological theories tend to suggest modifying body chemistry in order to produce desirable behavioral changes. Hence, just as researchers working with recombinant DNA techniques seek to create a "magic bullet" which might target defective chromosomes in the human immune system which allow for the growth of cancerous tissue, others envision the

Crime rates in urban areas are especially high. Some theorists argue that neighborhood lifestyles contribute to crime. *Bob Riha, Gamma-Liaison, Inc.*

day when similar techniques might be applied to the prevention and control of crime. If a gene for crime can be found, such researchers suggest, it might be turned off. In the meantime, psychobiologists have to be mostly content with medicinal approaches to the treatment of crime and violence, employing tranquilizers, antipsychotics, mood-altering substances, and other drugs.

While drug treatments fashioned after psychobiological perspectives may appear to control aggressive and criminal behavior, at least temporarily, there is little evidence to suggest that they produce lasting results. Recently, for example, all biologically based theories of crime and violence were called into question by the National Academy of Sciences, whose 1993 review of hundreds of studies on the relationship among biology, violence, and crime concluded that "No patterns precise enough to be considered reliable biological markers for violent behavior have yet been identified."[52] The study did, however, find what it called "promising leads for future research."

Psychological Theories

Psychological School A perspective on criminological thought which views offensive and deviant behavior as the products of dysfunctional personalities. The conscious, and especially the subconscious, contents of the human psyche are identified by psychological thinkers as major determinants of behavior.

Psychological theories of crime causation have an increasingly significant place in the criminological literature. Most psychological theories of crime make certain fundamental assumptions. Among them are

- The individual is the primary unit of analysis.
- Personality is the major motivational element within individuals, since it is the seat of drives and the source of motives.
- Crimes result from inappropriately conditioned behavior *or* from abnormal, dysfunctional, or inappropriate mental processes within the personality.
- Defective or abnormal mental processes may have a variety of causes, including a diseased mind and inappropriate learning or improper conditioning—often occurring in early childhood.

BEHAVIORAL CONDITIONING

A twin thread wove through early psychological theories. One emphasized **behavioral conditioning**, while the other focused mostly on personality disturbances and diseases of the mind. Taken together, these two foci constituted the early field of psychological criminology. Conditioning is a psychological principle which holds that the frequency of any behavior, including that which is criminal or deviant, can be increased or decreased through reward, punishment, and/or association with other stimuli. The concept of conditioned behavior was popularized through the work of the Russian physiologist Ivan Pavlov (1849–1936), whose work with dogs won him the Nobel Prize in physiology and medicine in 1904. The dogs, who salivated whenever food was presented to them, were always fed in the presence of a ringing bell. Soon, Pavlov found, the dogs would salivate, as if in preparation for eating, when the bell alone was rung—even when no food was present. Hence, salivation, an automatic response to the presence of food, could be conditioned to occur in response to some other stimulus—demonstrating that animal behavior could be predictably altered via association with external changes arising from the environment surrounding the organism. In like manner, behavioral psychologists suggest that criminal behavior, which may be inherently rewarding under many circumstances, tends to be more common in those who are able to avoid punishment when involved in rule-breaking behavior.

Behavioral Conditioning A psychological principle which holds that the frequency of any behavior can be increased or decreased through reward, punishment, and/or association with other stimuli.

FREUDIAN PSYCHOANALYSIS

The name most widely associated with the field of psychology is that of Sigmund Freud (1856–1939). Freud wrote very little about crime, but his followers, who developed the school of Freudian **psychoanalysis**, believed that crime could result from at least three conditions.[53]

Freudian theory posits the existence of an id, ego, and superego within the personality. The id is the source of drives which are seen as primarily sexual. The ego is a rational mental entity, which outlines paths through which the desires of the id can be fulfilled. It has often been called the "reality principle," because of the belief that it relates desires to practical behavioral alternatives. The superego is a guiding principle, often compared to conscience, which judges the quality of the alternatives presented by the ego according to the standards of right and wrong acquired by the personality of which it is a part.

Psychoanalysis A theory of human behavior, based upon the writings of Sigmund Freud, which sees personality as a complex composite of interacting mental elements.

The first possible source of criminal behavior is a weak superego, which cannot responsibly control the drives which emanate from the id. Sex crimes, crimes of passion, murder, and other violent crimes are thought to follow inadequate superego development. People who lack fully developed superegos are often called psychopaths or sociopaths, to indicate that they cannot see beyond their own interests. Freudian psychologists would probably agree with Gwynn Nettler who has observed that "[c]ivilization is paid for through development of a sense of guilt."[54]

Freud also created the concept of sublimation to explain the process by which one thing is symbolically substituted for another. He believed that sublimation was necessary when the direct pursuit of one's desires was not possible. Freud suggested, for example, that many children learned to sublimate negative feelings about their mothers. In the society where Freud developed his theories, mothers closely controlled the lives of their children, and Freud saw the developing child as continually frustrated in seeking freedom to act on his or her own. The strain produced by this conflict could not be directly expressed by the child because the mother also controlled rewards and punishments. Hence, dislike for one's mother (which Freud thought was especially strong in boys) might show itself symbolically later in life. Crimes against women could then be explained as committed by men expressing such a symbolic hatred.

A final Freudian explanation for criminality is based upon the death wish, or Thanatos, which Freud believed each of us carries. Thanatos is the desire, often unrecognized, of animate matter to return to the inanimate. Potentially self-destructive activities, including smoking, speeding, sky diving, bad diets, "picking fights," and so on, can be explained by Thanatos. The self-destructive wish may also motivate offenders to commit crimes which are themselves dangerous or self-destructive—such as burglary, assault, murder, prostitution, and drug use—or it may result in unconscious efforts to be caught. Criminals who leave evidence behind, sometimes even items of personal identification like driver's licenses and wallets, may be responding to some basic need for apprehension and punishment.

Charles Manson, one of the most photographed criminal offenders of all time, is shown here 20 years after he and his "family" shocked the world with their gruesome crimes. *Grey Villet, Black Star*

Psychopathology and Crime

From a psychiatric point of view, crime might also occur because of a diseased mind or a disordered personality—conditions which may collectively be referred to as **psychopathy** (the study of psychopathic mental conditions is called **psychopathology**). The role of a disordered personality in crime causation was central to early psychiatric theorizing. In 1944, for example, the well-known psychiatrist David Abrahamsen wrote, "[w]hen we seek to explain the riddle of human conduct in general and of antisocial behavior in particular, the solution must be sought in the personality."[55] In recent years, some psychiatrists have gone so far as to claim that criminal behavior itself is only a symptom of a more fundamental psychiatric disorder.[56]

Psychopathology The study of pathological mental conditions, that is, mental illness.

By the 1950s, psychiatrists had developed the concept of a psychopathic personality. The **psychopath**, also called a **sociopath**, is seen as perversely cruel—often without thought or feeling for his or her victims. The concept of a psychopathic personality, which by its very definition is asocial, was fully developed by Hervey Cleckley in his 1964 book *The Mask of Sanity*.[57] Cleckley described the psychopath as a "moral idiot," or as one who does not feel empathy with others, even though the person may be fully cognizant of what is objectively happening around him or her. The central defining characteristic of a psychopath is poverty of affect, or the inability to accurately imagine how others think and feel. Hence, it becomes possible for a psychopath to inflict pain and engage in cruelty without appreciation for the victim's suffering. Charles Manson, for example, whom some have called a psychopath, once told a television reporter, "I could take this book and beat you to death with it, and I wouldn't feel a thing. It'd be just like walking to the drugstore." According to Cleckley, psychopathic indicators appear early in life, often in the teenage years. They include lying, fighting, stealing, and vandalism. Even earlier signs may be found, according to some authors, in bedwetting, cruelty to animals, sleep-walking, and fire-setting.[58]

Psychopath (also **Sociopath**) A person with a personality disorder, especially one manifested in aggressively antisocial behavior, which is often said to be the result of a poorly developed superego.

While the terms *psychopath* and *criminal* are not synonymous, individuals manifesting characteristics of a psychopathic personality are likely, sooner or later, to run afoul of the law. As one writer on the topic says, "[t]he impulsivity and aggression, the selfishness in achieving one's own immediate needs, and the disregard for society's rules and laws bring these people to the attention of the criminal justice system."[59]

Although much studied, the causes of psychopathology are unclear. Somatogenic causes, or those which are based upon physiological aspects of the human organism, are said to include (1) a malfunctioning central nervous system characterized by a low state of arousal, which drives the sufferer to seek excitement, and (2) brain abnormalities, which may be present in most psychopaths from birth. Psychogenic causes, or those rooted in early interpersonal experiences, are thought to include the inability to form attachments to parents or other caregivers early in life, sudden separation from the mother during the first six months of life, and other forms of insecurity during the first few years of life. In short, a lack of love or the sensed inability to unconditionally depend upon one central loving figure (typically the mother in most psychological literature) immediately following birth is often posited as a major psychogenic factor contributing to psychopathic development.

The Psychotic Offender

Another form of mental disorder is called **psychosis**. Psychotic people, according to psychiatric definitions, are out of touch with reality in some fundamental way. They may suffer from hallucinations, delusions, or other breaks with reality. The classic psychotic thinks he is Napoleon or sees spiders covering what others perceive as only a bare wall. Individuals suffering from a psychosis are said to be psychotic. Psychoses may be either organic (that is, caused by physical damage to, or abnormalities in, the brain) or functional (that is, with no known physical cause). Psychotic persons have also been classified as schizophrenic or paranoid schizophrenic. **Schizophrenics** are said to be characterized by disordered or disjointed thinking, in which the types of logical associations they make are atypical of other people. Paranoid schizophrenics suffer from delusions and hallucinations.

Psychoses may lead to crime in a number of ways. Following the Vietnam war, for example, a number of instances were reported in which former American soldiers suffering from a kind of battlefield psychosis killed friends and family members thinking they were Viet Cong soldiers; that is, the enemy. These men, who had been traumatized by battlefield experiences in Southeast Asia, relived their past on American streets.

Psychological Profiling

Psychological profiling is the attempt to derive a composite picture of an offender's social and psychological characteristics from the crime he or she committed and from the manner in which it was committed. Psychological profiling began during World War II as an effort by William Langer (1896–1977), a government psychiatrist hired by the Office of Strategic Services, to predict Adolf Hitler's actions.[60] Profiling in the area of criminal investigations is based upon the belief that criminality, because it is a form of behavior, can be viewed as symptomatic of the offender's personality. Psychological evaluations of crime scenes, including the analysis of remaining evidence, are used to re-create the offender's frame of mind during the commission of the crime. A profile of the offender is then constructed to help in the investigation of suspects.

During the 1980s the FBI led the movement toward psychological profiling[61] through its focus on violent sex offenses[62] and arson.[63] FBI studies provided descriptions of what they termed "lust murderers" and serial arsonists. Depicted often as loners with an aversion to casual social contact, lust murderers were shown rarely to arouse suspicions in neighbors or employers. Other personality characteristics became the focus of police efforts to arrest such offenders through a prediction of what they might do next.

More recently, caregivers who suffer a disorder called the "Munchausen syndrome by proxy" (MSBP) have become the subject of profilers. MSBP, which has not yet been accepted by the courts as a defense to criminal charges, involves "subject[s] (who) injure or induce illnesses in their children in order to gain attention and sympathy for themselves." Most perpetrators are women, and the majority make their own children sick so that they can themselves receive attention from relatives, doctors, and health treatment personnel. Profilers have found that MSBP is a serial offense, although in families with multiple children only one child is usually affected at a time.[64] Most MSBP offenders have been found to possess the following characteristics: a history of self-inflicted injuries (also called "Munchausen syndrome," but involving no "proxy"); past psychiatric treatment; a history of attempted suicides; an upper-class or upper-middle-class background; a good education; and a medical background or medical education of some sort. MSBP sufferers also remain uncharacteristically calm, welcome medical tests that are painful for the child, praise medical staffs excessively, appear knowledgeable about the victim's illness, shelter the victim from school and other outside activities, allow only selected persons close to their children, stay very attentive to the victim, and find emotional satisfaction when the child is hospitalized.

Psychosis A form of mental illness in which sufferers are said to be out of touch with reality.

Schizophrenic A mentally ill individual who suffers from disjointed thinking and, possibly, delusions and hallucinations.

The crimes of some law violators seem to defy explanation. Here, Jeffrey Dahmer, accused in the dismemberment slayings of more than a dozen young men, listens as the charges against him are read. Dahmer was killed in prison by another inmate after being convicted and ordered to serve multiple life sentences.
Allan Fredrickson, Reuters/Bettmann

Other new areas for psychological profiling include hostage negotiation[65] and international terrorism.[66] Right-wing terrorist groups in the United States have also been the subject of profiling efforts.

Social Policy and Psychological Theory

Like psychological theories themselves, crime-control policies based upon psychological perspectives tend to be primarily individualistic. They are oriented toward individualized treatment, characteristically exposing the individual offender to various forms of therapy intended to overcome the person's penchant for criminality.

One special emphasis of most crime-control strategies based upon psychological theories is the attempt to assess personal **dangerousness**, a process which involves psychological testing and other efforts intended to identify personality-based characteristics which may be predictive of interpersonal aggression. Although the ability to accurately predict future dangerousness is of great concern to today's policy makers, definitions of dangerousness are fraught with difficulty. As some authors have pointed out, "dangerousness is not an objective quality like obesity or brown eyes, rather it is an ascribed quality like trustworthiness."[67] Hence, dangerousness is not necessarily a personality trait which is stable or easily identifiable. Even if it were, recent studies[68] of criminal careers seem to show that involvement in crime decreases with age. As one author puts it, if "criminality declines more or less uniformly with age, then many offenders will be 'over the hill' by the time they are old enough to be plausible candidates for preventive incarceration."[69]

Before crime control policies can be based upon present understandings of dangerousness, we need to ask: Can past behavior predict future behavior? Do former instances of criminality presage additional ones? Are there other, identifiable, characteristics which violent offenders might manifest which could serve as warning signs to criminal justice decision makers faced with the dilemma of whether or not to release convicted felons? This, like many other areas, is one in which criminologists are still learning.

Sociological Theories

Sociological theories are largely an American contribution to the study of crime causation. In the 1920s and 1930s, the famous **Chicago School** of sociology explained criminality as a

Dangerousness The likelihood that a given individual will later harm society or others. Dangerousness is often measured in terms of **recidivism**, or as the likelihood of additional crime commission within a five-year period following arrest or release from confinement.

Chicago School A type of sociological approach which emphasizes demographics (the characteristics of population groups) and geographics (the mapped location of such groups relative to one another) and sees the social disorganization which characterizes delinquency areas as a major cause of criminality and victimization.

product of society's impact upon the individual. The structure of prevailing social arrangements, the interaction between individuals and groups, and the social environment were all seen as major determinants of criminal behavior.

Sociological perspectives on crime causation are quite diverse. Most such perspectives, however, build upon certain fundamental assumptions. Among them are

- Social groups, social institutions, the arrangements of society, and social roles all provide the proper focus for criminological study.
- Group dynamics, group organization, and subgroup relationships form the causal nexus out of which crime develops.
- The structure of society, and the relative degree of social organization or **social disorganization**, are important factors contributing to the prevalence of criminal behavior.

All sociological perspectives on crime share the foregoing characteristics, but particular theories may give greater or lesser weight to the following aspects of social life:

- The clash of norms and values among variously socialized groups
- Socialization and the process of association between individuals
- The existence of subcultures and varying types of opportunities

Social disorganization A condition said to exist when a group is faced with social change, uneven development of culture, maladaptiveness, disharmony, conflict, and lack of consensus.

Social Ecology Theory

In the 1920s, during the early days of sociological theorizing, the University of Chicago brought together such thinkers as Robert Park,[70] Clifford Shaw, Henry McKay,[71] and Ernest Burgess. Park and Burgess recognized that Chicago, like most cities, could be mapped according to its social characteristics. Their map resembled a target with a bull's-eye in the center. These concentric zones were adapted by Shaw and McKay to the study of crime when they realized that zones nearest the center of the city had the highest crime rates. In particular, zone two (one removed from the center) demonstrated the consistently highest crime rate over time, regardless of the groups or nationalities inhabiting it. This "zone of transition" (so called because new immigrant groups moved into it as earlier ones became integrated into American culture) demonstrated that crime was dependent to a considerable extent upon aspects of the social structure of the city itself. Structural elements identified by Shaw and McKay included poverty, illiteracy, lack of schooling, unemployment, and illegitimacy. In combination, these elements were seen to lead to social disorganization, which, in turn, produced crime.

Anomie Theory

The French word **anomie** has been loosely translated as a condition of "normlessness." Anomie entered the literature as a sociological concept with the writings of Emile Durkheim (1858–1917) in the late 1800s.[72] Robert Merton (1910–) applied anomie to criminology in 1938 when he used the term to describe a disjuncture between socially acceptable goals and means in American society.[73]

Merton believed that while the same goals and means were held out by society as desirable for everyone to participate in, they were not equally available to all. Socially approved goals in American society, for example, include wealth, status, and political power. The acceptable means to achieve these goals lie in education, wise investment, and hard work. Unfortunately, however, opportunities are not equally distributed throughout society, and some people will turn to illegitimate means to achieve the goals they are pressured to reach. Still others will reject both the acceptable goals and the legitimate means to reach them.

Merton represented his theory with a diagram, shown in Table 3–2, in which conformists were seen to accept both the goals and means which society held out as legitimate, while innovators accepted the goals but rejected the means. It was innovators who Merton identified as criminal. They were not *inventors*, as invention is a legitimate path to success, but rather *innovators* in the use of illegal means to gain money, power, and success. The inherent logic of the table led Merton to posit other social types. Ritualists were said to be those who rejected success goals, but still performed their daily tasks in conformity with social expectations. They might hold regular jobs, but without the desire to advance in life.

Anomie A socially pervasive condition of normlessness. A disjuncture between approved goals and means.

Table 3-2   Robert Merton's Anomie Theory and Implied Types of Criminality

Category	Goals	Means	Examples
Conformist	+	+	Law-abiding behavior
Innovator	+	–	Property offenses
			White-collar crimes
Retreatist	–	–	Drug use/addiction, vagrancy, some "victimless" crimes
Ritualist	–	+	A Walter Mitty-type life
Rebel	±	±	Political crime (example: environmental activists who violate the law, violence-prone antiabortionists)

Source: From Robert K. Merton *Social Theory and Social Structure*, 1968 enlarged edition. Copyright 1967, 1968 by Robert K. Merton. Adapted with permission of The Free Press, a division of Macmillan, Inc.

An honest and fully professional police community would acknowledge in its police education the root causes of crime—poverty, unemployment, underemployment, racism, poor health care, bad housing, weak schools, mental illness, alcoholism, addiction, single-parent families, teenage pregnancy, and a society of selfishness and greed.

—Patrick V. Murphy, former commissioner of the NYC Police Department

Retreatists rejected both the goals and means and usually dropped out of society by becoming derelicts, drug users, or the like. Rebels constituted a special category—one in which the existence of both "pluses" and "minuses" indicated their desire to replace the existing system of socially approved goals and means with some other system more to their liking. They were the revolutionaries of the theory.

Merton believed that categories were not intentionally selected by the individuals who occupied them, but were imposed on people by structural aspects of society. Such factors as where they lived, how wealthy their families were, and what ethnic background they came from were all thought to be significant determinants of the "box" into which a person would be placed.

Modern writers on anomie have come to recognize that normlessness is not likely to be expressed as criminality, unless people who experience such a condition also feel that they are capable of doing something to change their lives. As Ross and Mirowsky put it, "A person who has high levels of normlessness and powerlessness is less likely to get in trouble with the law than a person who has a high level of normlessness and a high level of instrumentalism."[74]

Merton's anomie theory drew attention to the lack of equality of opportunity which existed in society at the time he was writing. An honest appraisal would probably recognize that while considerable efforts have been made to eradicate it, some of that same inequality continues today.

Subcultural Theory

Another sociological contribution to criminological theory is the idea of a subculture. A subculture is composed of a group of people who participate in a shared system of values and norms which are at variance with those in the larger culture. Subcultural explanations of crime posit the existence of group values supportive of criminal behavior. Subcultures were first recognized in the enclaves formed by immigrants who came to America during the early part of the twentieth century. Statistics have shown that certain immigrant groups had low crime rates.[75] Among them were the Scandinavians, Chinese, Dutch, Germans, and Japanese. Other immigrant groups, including Italians, Mexicans, Puerto Ricans, and Africans, demonstrated a significantly greater propensity for involvement in crime.[76]

Reaction formation   The process whereby a person openly rejects that which he or she wants, or aspires to, but cannot obtain or achieve.

Albert Cohen (1918–) coined the term **reaction formation** to encompass the rejection of middle-class values by status-seeking lower-class youths who find they are not permitted access to approved opportunities for success.[77] In Cohen's eyes, it was such a reaction which led to the development of gangs and perpetuated the existence of subcultures. Walter Miller[78] described the focal concerns of subcultural participants in terms of "trouble," "toughness,"

Twenty-First Century Criminal Justice

PHYSICAL ENVIRONMENT AND CRIME

Social ecology theory, an outgrowth of the Chicago school of sociological thought which flourished during the 1920s and 1930s, posited a link between physical location and crime. A new perspective, called Crime Prevention Through Environmental Design (CPTED), bears a strong resemblance to earlier ecological theories. CPTED, which saw its original formulation in the 1960s and 1970s, focuses on the settings in which crimes occur and on techniques for reducing vulnerability within those settings. Because defensible space concepts are being increasingly applied to the design of physical facilities, including housing, parking garages, public buildings, and even entire neighborhoods, it is highly likely that applications of CPTED will accelerate throughout the twenty-first century.

Second generation **defensible space theory**, upon which contemporary CPTED is built, developed around 1980 and considered more carefully how the impact of physical features on fear and victimization depend upon other social and cultural features in the setting. Second generation defensible space theory employed the **broken windows thesis**, which holds that physical deterioration and an increase in unrepaired buildings leads to increased concerns for personal safety among area residents. Heightened concerns, in turn, lead to further decreases in maintenance and repair and to increased delinquency, vandalism, and crime among local residents—which spawns even further deterioration in both a sense of safety and in physical deterioration. Offenders from other neighborhoods are then increasingly attracted by the area's perceived vulnerability.

Research on CPTED has shown environmental design to be effective in lowering crime or crime-related

public-order problems. Effective use of CPTED to alter features of the physical environment can affect potential offenders' perceptions about a possible crime site, their evaluations of the circumstances surrounding a potential crime site, and the availability and visibility of one or more natural guardians at or near a site. CPTED is based upon the belief that offenders decide whether or not to commit a crime in a location after they evaluate an area's features, including (1) ease of entry to the area; (2) visibility of targets to others and to the public, and the chance of being seen; (3) attractiveness or vulnerability of targets; (4) the likelihood that criminal behavior will be challenged or thwarted by people in the area if it is discovered; and (5) ease of egress (that is, the ability to quickly and easily leave the area once the crime has been committed).

According to the National Institute of Justice, CPTED suggests four approaches to making a location more resistant to crime or crime-related public-order problems, as follows:

- **Housing design or block layout**. Making it more difficult to commit crimes by (1) reducing the availability of crime targets; (2) removing barriers that prevent easy detection of potential offenders or of an offense in progress; and (3) increasing physical obstacles to committing a crime.
- **Land use and circulation patterns**. Creating safer use of neighborhood space by reducing routine exposure of potential offenders to crime targets. This can be accomplished through careful attention to walkways, paths, streets, traffic patterns, and location and hours of operation of public spaces and facilities. Street closings or revised traffic patterns that decrease

vehicular volume may, under some conditions, encourage residents to better maintain the sidewalk and street in front of their houses.
- **Territorial features**. Encouraging the use of territorial markers or fostering conditions that will lead to more extensive marking to indicate the block or site is occupied by vigilant residents. Sponsoring clean-up and beautification contests and creating controllable, semiprivate outdoor locations may encourage such activities. This strategy focuses on small-scale, private, and semipublic sites, usually within predominantly residential locales. It is most relevant at the street block level and below. It enhances the chances that residents themselves will generate semifixed features that demonstrate their involvement in and watchfulness over a particular delimited location.
- **Physical maintenance**. Controlling physical deterioration to reduce offenders' perceptions that areas are vulnerable to crime and that residents are so fearful they would do nothing to stop a crime. Physical improvements may reduce the signals of vulnerability and increase commitment to joint protective activities. Physical deterioration, in all probability, not only influences cognition and behavior of potential offenders but also shapes how residents behave and what they think about other residents.

QUESTIONS FOR DISCUSSION

1. Discuss the area that surrounds your campus. How might it be made safer by employing CPTED principles? How might your campus be made safer?

2. Even if defensible space concepts really do prevent or reduce crime, it is still necessary to pay for the physical changes and improvements required to implement the concept. How can needed renovations be made in poor neighborhoods? Who would pay the bill?

Oscar Newman, *Defensible Space* (New York: Macmillan, 1972); Oscar Newman, *Creating Defensible Space* (Washington, D.C.: Office of Housing and Urban Development, 1996); James Q. Wilson and George Kelling, "Broken Windows," *The Atlantic Monthly*, March 1982; Dan Fleissner and Fred Heinzelmann, "Crime Prevention Through Environmental Design and Community Policing," (National Institute of Justice, August 1996); Ralph B.

Taylor and Adele V. Harrell, "Physical Environment and Crime," (National Institute of Justice, May 1996); Mary S. Smith, "Crime Prevention Through Environmental Design in Parking Facilities," (National Institute of Justice, April 1996), and Corey L. Gordon and William Brill, "The Expanding Role of Crime Prevention Through Environmental Design in Premises Liability," (National Institute of Justice, April 1996).

Defensible Space Theory
The belief that an area's physical features may be modified and structured so as to reduce crime rates in that area and to lower the fear of victimization which area residents experience.

Broken Windows Thesis
A perspective on crime causation which holds that physical deterioration in an area leads to increased concerns for personal safety among area residents and to higher crime rates in that area.

Subculture of Violence   A cultural setting in which violence is a traditional, and often accepted, method of dispute resolution.

"excitement," "smartness," "fate," and "autonomy." It was a focus on such concerns, Miller suggested, that led members of criminal subcultures into violations of the law. Richard Cloward and Lloyd Ohlin proposed the existence of an illegitimate opportunity structure that permitted delinquent youths to achieve in ways which were outside of legitimate avenues to success.[79]

Subcultures of Violence

During the 1950s Marvin Wolfgang and Franco Ferracuti examined homicide rates in Philadelphia and found that murder was a way of life among certain groups.[80] They discovered a "wholesale" and a "retail" price for murder—which depended upon who was killed and who did the killing. Killings which occurred within violent subgroups were more likely to be partially excused than were those that happened elsewhere. The term **subculture of violence** has come to be associated with their work and has since been applied to other locations across the country.

Critiques of subcultural theory have been numerous. A major difficulty for these theories lies in the fact that studies involving self-reports of crime commission have shown that much violence and crime occur outside of "criminal" subcultures. It appears that many middle- and upper-class law breakers are able to avoid handling by the justice system and, therefore, do not enter the "official" crime statistics. Hence, criminal subcultures may be those in which crime is more visible rather than more prevalent.

Social Policy and Sociological Theory

Theoretical approaches which fault the social environment as the root cause of crime point in the direction of social action as a panacea. A contemporary example of intervention efforts based upon sociological theories can be had in Targeted Outreach,[81] a program now being operated by Boys and Girls Clubs of America. The club program had its origins in the 1972 implementation of a youth development strategy based upon studies undertaken at the University of Colorado which showed that at-risk youths could be effectively diverted from the juvenile justice system through the provision of positive alternatives. Utilizing a referral network comprised of local schools, police departments, and various youth-service agencies, club officials work to end what they call the "inappropriate detention of juveniles." The program, in its current form, recruits at-risk youngsters—many as young as seven years-old—and diverts them into activities which are intended to promote a sense of belonging, competence, usefulness, and power. Belonging is fostered through clubs which provide familiar settings where individuals are accepted. Competence and usefulness are developed through the provision of opportunities for meaningful activities which young people in the club program can successfully undertake. Finally, Targeted Outreach provides its youthful participants with a chance to be heard and, consequently, with the opportunity to influence decisions affecting their future (empowerment). Targeted Outreach is typical of the kinds of programs which theorists who focus on the social environment typically seek to implement. Social programs of this sort are intended to change the cultural conditions and societal arrangements which are thought to lead people into crime.

Social-Psychological Theories

While psychological approaches uncover aspects of the personality hidden even from the mind in which they reside, and sociological theories look to institutional arrangements in the social world to explain crime, social-psychological approaches to crime causation attempt to explain deviant behavior by relating it to the cultural environment in which the individual matures. Social-psychological theories add to the more structural analysis of sociological theories by including individual behavior and chosen responses to the social world.

Many social-psychological theories highlight the role of social learning. They build upon the premise that behavior—both "good" and "bad"—is learned and suggest that "bad" behavior can be unlearned. Social-psychological theories are probably the most attractive to contemporary policy makers because they demand that responsibility be placed upon the offender for actively participating in rehabilitation efforts and because they are consistent with popular cultural and religious values centered on teaching right from wrong.

Social–Psychological School A perspective on criminological thought which highlights the role played in crime causation by weakened self-esteem and meaningless social roles. Social–psychological thinkers stress the relationship of the individual to the social group as the underlying cause of behavior.

Differential Association Theory

In 1939 Edwin Sutherland (1883–1950) published the third edition of his *Principles of Criminology*. It contained, for the first time, a formalized statement of his theory of differential association, a perspective which Sutherland based upon the "laws of imitation" described by Gabriel Tarde.

Differential association viewed crime as the product of socialization and saw it as acquired by criminals according to the same principles that guided the learning of law-abiding behavior in conformists. Differential association removed criminality from the framework of the abnormal and placed it squarely within a general perspective applicable to all behavior. In the 1947 edition of his text, Sutherland wrote, "Criminal behavior is a part of human behavior, has much in common with non-criminal behavior, and must be explained within the same general framework as any other human behavior."[82] A study of the tenets of differential association (listed in Table 3–3) shows that Sutherland believed that even the sources of behavioral motivation were much the same for conformists as they were for criminals; that is, both groups strive for money and success, but choose different paths to the same goal.

Table 3-3 Sutherland's Principles of Differential Association

1. Criminal behavior is learned.
2. Criminal behavior is learned in interaction with other persons in a process of communication.
3. The principal part of the learning of criminal behavior occurs within intimate personal groups.
4. When criminal behavior is learned, the learning includes (a) techniques of committing the crime, which are sometimes very complicated, sometimes very simple, and (b) the specific direction of motives, drives, rationalizations, and attitudes.
5. The specific direction of motives and drives is learned from definitions of the legal codes as favorable or unfavorable.
6. A person becomes delinquent because of an excess of definitions favorable to violations of law over definitions unfavorable to violations of law.
7. Differential associations may vary in frequency, duration, priority, and intensity.
8. The process of learning criminal behavior by association with criminal and anticriminal patterns involves all the mechanisms that are involved in any other learning.
9. While criminal behavior is an expression of general needs and values, it is not explained by those general needs and values since noncriminal behavior is an expression of the same needs and values.

Source: Edwin Sutherland, *Principles of Criminology*, 4th ed. (Chicago: J. B. Lippincott, 1947), pp. 6–7.

FBI officials discuss the Andrew Cunanan case in 1997 before Cunanan's body was discovered. Cunanan, the prime suspect in the 1997 spree killing of five men, including internationally-acclaimed fashion designer Gianni Versace, had been on the FBI's "Most Wanted" list for two months before killing himself when Miami police surrounded the boat on which he had hidden. *Brian K. Diggs, AP/Wide World Photos*

I really truly tried to stop—but I couldn't.

—Henry Louis Wallace, accused killer of 11 women, in a tape-recorded interview with police.

The theory of differential association explained crime as a natural consequence of the interaction with criminal lifestyles. Sutherland suggested that children raised in crime-prone environments were often isolated and unable to experience the values which would otherwise lead to conformity. Some modern writers refer to this lack of socialization in conformity as a failure to train.[83]

Differential association has considerable explanative applicability even today and still provides the basis for much research in modern criminology.[84] Even popular stories of young drug pushers, for instance, often refer to the fact that inner-city youth imitate what they see. Some residents of poverty-ridden ghettos learn quickly that fast money can be had in the illicit drug trade, and they tend to follow those examples of success with which they have experience.

Differential association theory fails, however, to explain why people have the associations they do, and why some associations seem to affect certain individuals more than others. Why, for example, are most prison guards unaffected by their constant association with offenders, while a few are brought over to the inmate side and take advantage of their position to smuggle contraband and the like? The theory has also been criticized for being so general and imprecise as to allow for little testing.[85] Complete testing of the theory would require that all the associations a person has ever had be recorded and analyzed from the standpoint of the individual—a clearly impossible task.

Other theorists continue to build on Sutherland's early work. Robert L. Burgess and Ronald L. Akers, for example, have constructed a differential association-reinforcement theory, which seeks to integrate Sutherland's original propositions with B. F. Skinner's work on conditioning.[86] Burgess and Akers suggest that although values and behavior patterns are learned in association with others, the primary mechanism through which such learning occurs is operant conditioning. Reinforcement is the key, they say, to understanding any social learning as it takes place. The name **social learning theory** has been widely applied to the work of Burgess and Akers. It is somewhat a misnomer, however, since the term can easily encompass a wide range of approaches and should not be limited to one specific combination of the ideas found in differential association and reinforcement theory.

Social Learning Theory A psychological perspective that says people learn how to behave by modeling themselves after others whom they have the opportunity to observe.

Restraint Theories

Containment Theory

As we have seen consistently throughout this chapter, most criminological theories posit a cause of crime.[87] Some theories, however, focus less on causes than on constraints. Walter Reckless's (1899–1988) containment theory, for example, assumes that all of us are subject to inducements to crime.[88] Some of us resist these "pushes" toward criminal behavior, while others do not. The difference, according to Reckless, can be found in forces which contain behavior.

Reckless described two types of **containment**—inner and outer. Outer containment depends upon social roles and the norms and expectations which apply to them. People who occupy significant roles in society find themselves insulated from deviant tendencies. A corporate executive, for example, is probably less apt to hold up a liquor store than is a drifter. The difference, according to Reckless, is not due solely to income, but to the pressure to conform that the "successful" role exerts upon its occupant.

Inner containment involves a number of factors, including conscience, a positive self-image, a tolerance for frustration, and aspirations which are in line with reality. Reckless saw inner containment as more powerful than outer containment. Inner containment functions even in secret. An inner-directed person, for example, may come across a lost purse and feel compelled to locate its rightful owner and return it. If theft or greed cross the mind of the inner directed, they will say to themselves, "I'm not that kind of person. That would be wrong."

Reckless studied small, close-knit societies—including the Hutterites, Mennonites, and Amish—in developing his theory. He realized that the "containment of behavior…is…maximized under conditions of isolation and homogeneity of culture, class, and population."[89] Hence, its applicability to modern American society, with its considerable heterogeneity of values and perspectives, is questionable.

> **Containment** Those aspects of the social bond, and of the personality, which act to prevent individuals from committing crimes and keep them from engaging in deviance.

Social Control Theory

Travis Hirschi emphasizes the bond between individuals and society as the primary operative mechanism in his social control theory.[90] Hirschi identifies four components of that bond: (1) emotional attachments to significant others, (2) a commitment to appropriate lifestyles, (3) involvement or immersion in conventional values, and (4) a belief in the "correctness" of social obligations and the rules of the larger society. These components act as social controls on deviant and criminal behavior; as they weaken, social control suffers and the likelihood of crime and deviance increases. Using self-reports of delinquency from high-school students in California, Hirschi concluded that youngsters who were less attached to teachers and parents, and who had few positive attitudes toward their own accomplishments, were more likely to engage in crime and deviance than were others.[91]

Restraint theories provide only one-half of the causal picture. Since they focus primarily on why people do *not* break the law, they are especially weak in identifying the social-structural sources of motivations to commit crimes.[92] Similarly, the way in which bonds with different institutions interact with one another and with personal attributes, as well as the variety of bonds operative throughout the life cycle, have yet to be clarified.[93]

> *When internal cultures conflict, it can be as destructive as a collision between an iceberg and an ocean liner. Misunderstanding between two cultural groups can lead to conflict and, taken to the extreme, physical confrontations.*
>
> —Sherman Block, Los Angeles County Sheriff

Neutralization Techniques

Complementing restraint theory is the neutralization approach of Gresham Sykes and David Matza.[94] Sykes and Matza believed that most people drift into and out of criminal behavior but would not commit crime unless they had available to them techniques of neutralization. Such techniques are actually rationalizations which allow offenders to shed feelings of guilt and any sense of responsibility for their behavior. Sykes and Matza's study primarily concerned juveniles in whom, they suggested, neutralization techniques provided only a temporary respite from guilt. That respite, however, lasted long enough to avoid the twinges of conscience while a crime was being committed. Neutralization techniques include

- Denial of responsibility ("I'm a product of my background.")
- Denial of injury ("No one was really hurt.")
- Denial of the victim ("They deserved it.")

- Condemnation of the condemners ("The cops are corrupt.")
- Appeal to higher loyalties ("I did it for my friends.")

Restraint theories tend, as in the case of containment theory, to depend upon a general agreement as to values, or they assume that offenders are simply conformists who suffer temporary lapses. Neutralization techniques, by definition, are only needed when the delinquent has been socialized into middle-class values or where conscience is well developed. Even so, neutralization techniques do not in themselves explain crime. Such techniques are available to us all, if we make only a slight effort to conjure them up. The real question is why some people readily allow proffered neutralizations to impact their behavior, while others discount them seemingly out of hand.

Conflict Theories

Conflict Perspective   A theoretical approach which holds that crime is the natural consequence of economic and other social inequities. Conflict theorists highlight the stresses which arise among and within social groups as they compete with one another for resources and survival. The social forces which result are viewed as major determinants of group and individual behavior, including crime.

Basic to the **conflict perspective** is the belief that conflict is a fundamental aspect of social life itself and can never be fully resolved. At best, according to this perspective, formal agencies of social control merely coerce the unempowered or the disenfranchised to comply with the rules established by those in power. From the conflict point of view, laws become a tool of the powerful, useful in keeping others from wresting control over important social institutions. Social order, rather than being the result of any consensus or process of dispute resolution, rests upon the exercise of power through law. The conflict perspective can be described in terms of four key elements[95]

- Society is composed of diverse social groups, and diversity is based upon distinctions which people hold to be significant, such as gender, sexual orientation, social class, etc.
- Conflict among groups is unavoidable because of differing interests and differing values. Hence, conflict is inherent in social life.
- The fundamental nature of group conflict centers on the exercise of political power. Political power is the key to the accumulation of wealth and to other forms of power.
- Law is a tool of power and furthers the interests of those powerful enough to make it. Laws allow those in control to gain what they define (through the law) as legitimate access to scarce resources and to deny (through the law) such access to the politically disenfranchised.

Radical Criminology

Radical Criminology   A conflict perspective that sees crime as engendered by the unequal distribution of wealth, power, and other resources—which it believes is especially characteristic of capitalist societies. Also called "critical" and "Marxist" criminology.

Criminological theory took a new direction during the 1960s and 1970s, brought about in part by the turmoil which characterized American society during that period. **Radical criminology** was born and, like so many other perspectives of the time, placed the blame for criminality and deviant behavior squarely upon officially sanctioned cultural and economic arrangements. The distribution of wealth and power in society was held to be the primary cause of criminal behavior, especially among those who were disenfranchised—or left out of the "American dream." Poverty and discrimination were seen to lead to frustration and pent-up hostilities that expressed themselves in murder, rape, theft, and other crimes.

Radical criminology had its roots in earlier conflict theories and in the thought of Dutch criminologist Willem A. Bonger. Some authors have distinguished between conflict theory and radical criminology by naming them "radical conflict theory" and "conservative conflict theory."[96] The difference, however, is mostly to be found in the rhetoric of the times. Early theories saw conflict as a natural part of any society and believed that struggles for power and control would always occur. "Losers" would tend to be defined as "criminal," and constraints on their behavior would be legislated. Characteristic of this perspective are the approaches of Austin Turk (1934–   ) and George Vold[97] (1896–1967). An even earlier conflict perspective can be found in the culture conflict notions of Thorsten Sellin, who was concerned with the clash of immigrant values and traditions with those of established American culture.[98]

Radical criminology went a step farther. It recognized that the struggle to control resources is central to society, and it encompassed the notion that the law itself is a tool of the powerful. The focus of radical criminology, however, was capitalism and the evils which capitalism was believed to entail. The ideas of Karl Marx (1818–1883) decisively entered the field of criminology through the writings of William Chambliss[99] (1933–) and Richard Quinney[100] (1934–). Marxist thought assumed that the lower classes were always exploited by the "owners" in society. According to Marx, the labor of the lower classes provides the basis for the accumulated wealth of the upper classes. Marx saw the working classes as suffering under the consequences of a "false class consciousness," perpetrated by the powerful. The poor were trained to believe that capitalism was in their best interests, and, according to Marx, only when the exploited workers realized their exploitation would they rebel and change society for the better.

American radical criminology built upon the ideals of the 1960s and charged that the "establishment," controlled by the upper classes, perverted justice through the unequal application of judicial sanctions. As David Greenberg has observed, "Many researchers attributed the overrepresentation of blacks and persons from impoverished family backgrounds in arrest and conviction statistics to the discriminatory practices of the enforcement agencies. It was not that the poor stole more, but rather that when they did, the police were more likely to arrest them."[101]

The "New" Criminology

While American criminologists were applying such structural interpretations to criminal justice data, some European theorists were developing a similar school of thought, which they termed "new criminology." New criminology evolved first in the social welfare societies of Scandinavia, where it focused on the needs of the poor.[102] Both radical criminology and new criminology represented attempts to resolve the crime problem through social change. Criminologists were asked to become active agents of social change and to work for the elimination of injustice.

Gwynn Nettler, in an attack on radical criminology, has identified "epistemological, factual, sociological, moral, and promissory"[103] difficulties in the approach. Epistemological shortcomings, says Nettler, derive from the fact that radical criminologists are more political than objective and, he claims, interested in making the "world other than it is."[104] Nettler also suggests that conflict perspectives on criminology lack the evidence needed to support their most basic premises; worse still, he says, they have not "submitted their major thesis to empirical test."[105] Finally, according to Nettler, radical criminology suffers a moral debility because it reverses "the true order of affairs, as best we know them."[106] Governments are not the evildoers that radical criminology would make them out to be, nor are individual offenders innocent victims.

All conflict theories of criminality face the difficulty of realistic implementation. Radical criminology in particular is flawed by its narrow-sighted emphasis on capitalist societies. It fails to recognize adequately the role of human nature in the creation of social classes and in the perpetuation of the struggle for control of resources. Radical criminology seems to imply that some sort of utopian social arrangements—perhaps communism—would eliminate most crime. Such a belief is contrary to historical experience, as a close look at any contemporary communist society will reveal both social conflict and crime.

Peacemaking Criminology

Peacemaking criminology, or what some theorists see as a mature expression of earlier conflict theories, holds that crime-control agencies and the citizens they serve should work together to alleviate social problems and human suffering and thus reduce crime.[107] Criminology as peacemaking is only now developing, but has its roots in ancient Christian and Eastern philosophies, as well as in traditional conflict theory. Peacemaking criminology, which includes the notion of "service," has also been called "compassionate criminology," and suggests that "[c]ompassion, wisdom, and love are essential for understanding the suf-

Peacemaking Criminology
A perspective which holds that crime-control agencies and the citizens they serve should work together to alleviate social problems and human suffering and thus reduce crime.

fering of which we are all a part, and for practicing a criminology of nonviolence."[108] Peacemaking criminology also holds that official agents of social control need to work with both victimized and victimizers in order to achieve a new world order which is more just to all who live in it. In a fundamental sense, peacemaking criminologists exhort their colleagues to transcend personal dichotomies in order to end the political and ideological divisiveness which separates people. "If we ourselves cannot know peace…how will our acts disarm hatred and violence?"[109] they ask.

Peacemaking criminology is a very new undertaking, having been popularized by the works of **Harold (Hal) Pepinsky**[110] and **Richard Quinney**[111] beginning in 1986. Both Pepinsky and Quinney restate the problem of crime control from one of "how to stop crime" to one of "how to make peace" within society and among citizens and criminal justice agencies. Peacemaking criminology draws attention to many issues, among them the perpetuation of violence through the continuation of social policies based upon dominant forms of criminological theory, the role of education in peacemaking, "commonsense theories of crime," crime control as human rights enforcement, and conflict resolution within community settings.[112]

Social Policy and Conflict Theory

Because radical and conflict criminologists see crime as caused by social inequality, many such theorists have suggested that the only way to achieve real change in the rate of crime is through revolution. Revolution—because it holds the promise of greater equality for underrepresented groups and because it mandates a redistribution of wealth and power—was thought necessary for any lasting reduction in crime.

Some contemporary writers on radical criminology, however, have attempted to address the issue of what can be done under our current system—probably because they recognize that a sudden and total reversal of existing political arrangements within the United States is highly unlikely. Hence, they have begun to focus on promoting "middle-range policy alternatives" to the present system, including "equal justice in the bail system, the abolition of mandatory sentences, prosecution of corporate crimes, increased employment opportunities, and promoting community alternatives to imprisonment."[113] Likewise programs to reduce prison overcrowding, efforts to highlight injustices within the current system, the elimination of racism and other forms of inequality in the handling of both victims and offenders, growing equality in criminal justice system employment, and the like are all frequently mentioned as mid-range strategies for bringing about a justice system which is more fair and closer to the radical ideal.

Raymond Michalowski summarizes the policy directions envisioned by today's radical criminologists when he says: "[W]e cannot be free from the crimes of the poor until there are no more poor; we cannot be free from domination of the powerful until we reduce the inequalities that make domination possible; and we cannot live in harmony with others until we begin to limit the competition for material advantage over others that alienates us from one another."[114]

Phenomenological Criminology A perspective on crime causation which holds that the significance of criminal behavior is ultimately knowable only to those who participate in it. Central to this school of thought is the belief that social actors endow their behavior with meaning and purpose. Hence, a crime might mean one thing to the person who commits it, quite another to the victim, and something far different still to professional participants in the justice system.

The Phenomenological School

Phenomenological criminology built upon the ideas of George Herbert Mead[115] (1863–1931), W. I. Thomas[116] (1863–1947), and the German philosopher Alfred Schutz[117] (1899–1959). Mead propounded a theory called symbolic interaction, in which he demonstrated how people give meaning to the things around them and to their lives. Thomas explained that the significance of any human behavior is relative to the intentions behind it and to the situation in which it is interpreted. Hence, behavior which, in one place or at one time, is taken for granted may, in another place or time, be perceived as deviant or even criminal. From this viewpoint, crime, like any other social phenomenon, is more a definition imposed by society upon a particular type (or types) of activity than it is a quality inherent in the behavior itself. As a consequence, crime may mean different things to different people and is, no doubt, variously interpreted by the offender, the victim, and agents of social control. **Phenomenological criminology** is a perspective on crime causation which holds that the significance of criminal behavior varies depending upon one's interests in the crime and point of view and is ultimately knowable only to those who participate in it. Central to this school of thought are the principles that

- The significance of any behavior depends upon a social consensus about what that behavior "means."
- "Crime" is the product of an active process of interpretation and social definition.
- Continued criminal activity may be more a consequence of limited opportunities for acceptable behavior which are imposed upon individuals defined as "criminal" than it is a product of choice.

Stuart Henry and **Dragan Milovanovic,** two contemporary proponents of phenomenological criminology, use the term **constitutive criminology** to refer to the process by which human beings create "an ideology of crime that sustains it as a concrete reality."[118] A central feature of constitutive criminology is its assertion that individuals shape their world while also being shaped by it. Constitutive criminology claims that crime and crime control are not "object-like entities," but constructions produced through a social process in which offender, victim, and society are all involved.[119] "We are concerned," write Henry and Milovanovic, "with the ways in which human agents actively coproduce that which they take to be crime." For Henry and Milovanovic, the idea of crime itself is a social construction, and researchers, they say, should recognize that criminals and victims are also "emergent realities." In short, constitutive criminology focuses on the social process by which crime and criminology become cultural realities.[120]

Yochelson and Samenow: Phenomenological Methods

Some recent attempts at understanding criminality have been more descriptive than explanatory. Such efforts hold to the belief that an adequate description of any phenomenon allows for the accumulation of useful scientific knowledge through a familiarity with the thing under study. The old dictum, "It takes a thief to catch a thief," has meaning for this school of thought. Phenomenological methodology is often primarily descriptive and many phenomenological studies in the field of criminal justice have relied upon detailed study of the criminal personality.

In the 1970s Samuel Yochelson (1906–1976) and Stanton E. Samenow (1941–   ) published their multivolume work *The Criminal Personality.*[121] Yochelson had been the director of the Program for the Investigation of Criminal Behavior at St. Elizabeth's Hospital in Washington, D.C., since 1961. Samenow joined Yochelson in 1970, and the pair eventually collected detailed data on 255 criminals. Many of the offenders were hospitalized, but others were on parole; some were never arrested, but were self-admitted offenders. Yochelson and Samenow identified 53 patterns of thought and action which they said were present in all 255 offenders. They described criminals as untrustworthy, demanding, and exploitive of others, with little capacity for love. Habitual offenders were said to harbor a persistent anger, which could boil over at any time. Pride, another aspect of the criminal personality, was seen as based upon notions of what it takes to "be a man." Similarly, "superoptimism," or the belief that they could do no wrong, characterized many offenders immediately prior to the commission of crimes. This combination of pride, anger, and extreme optimism made the criminal, in the eyes of Yochelson and Samenow, dangerous indeed.[122]

Yochelson and Samenow also argued that the meaning criminal behavior had in the eyes of offenders themselves was at considerable variance with the way in which society interpreted that behavior. They found little use for the "causative" theories of criminal behavior, seeing them as further ammunition which the offender could use in defense of deviant behavior. To think of oneself, for example, as a "victim" of a bad family background provides a justification for a life of crime, with little responsibility being placed squarely on the offender to reform.

Phenomenologists, because of their avoidance of causality, provide little practical direction for treatment. As one writer on the topic says, "[Y]ou cannot change a career criminal; you must convert him."[123] Total conversion—from a criminal to a conformist mode of thought—involves a dramatic change in lifestyle and self-concept. It is, unfortunately, unachievable except possibly through an intense commitment, which must begin with the offender.

Visit the *CJToday* Web page and click on "Web Chapters," then "Chapter 3." Follow the "find the facts" links to learn more about crime causation.

Feminist criminology is especially attentive to the conditions and circumstances which contribute to the criminality of women. Shown here is Tracy Lippard, a former Miss Williamsburg (Virginia) who was accused of three counts of attempted murder in an alleged dispute with a romantic rival. *Christopher Millette*

Labeling Theory

As we saw earlier in this chapter, the worth of any theory of behavior is proven by how well it reflects the reality of the social world. In practice, however, theoretical perspectives find acceptance in the academic environment via a number of considerations. Labeling theory, for example, became fashionable in the 1960s. Its popularity, however, may have been due more to the cultural environment into which it was introduced rather than to any inherent quality of the theory itself.

In fact, labeling theory had been introduced by Frank Tannenbaum[124] (1893–1969) in 1938 under the rubric of "tagging." He wrote: "The young delinquent becomes bad because he is defined as bad and because he is not believed if he is good." He went on to say: "The process of making the criminal, therefore, is a process of tagging…it becomes a way of stimulating…and evolving the very traits that are complained of…. The person becomes the thing he is described as being."[125] Tannenbaum focused on society's power to *define* an act or individual as bad and drew attention to the group need for a "scapegoat" in explaining crime. The search for causes inherent in individuals was not yet exhausted, however, and Tannenbaum's theory fell mostly on deaf ears.

By the 1960s the social and academic environments in America had changed, and the issue of "responsibility" was seen more in terms of the group than the individual. In 1963 Howard Becker, in his book *Outsiders*, pointed out that "criminality" is not a quality inherent in an act or in a person. Crime, said Becker, results from a social definition, through law, of unacceptable behavior. That definition arises through **moral enterprise**, by which groups on both sides of an issue debate and, eventually, legislate their notion of what is moral and what is not. Becker wrote, "the central fact about deviance [is that] it is created by society…. [S]ocial groups," he said, "create deviance by making the rules whose infraction constitutes deviance."[126]

The criminal label, however, produces consequences for labeled individuals which may necessitate continued criminality. In describing the "criminal career," Becker wrote: "To be labeled a criminal one need only commit a single criminal offense…. Yet the word carries a number of connotations specifying auxiliary traits characteristic of anyone bearing the label."[127] The first time a person commits a crime, the behavior is called primary deviance and may be a merely transitory form of behavior.

Moral Enterprise The process undertaken by an advocacy group in order to have its values legitimated and embodied in law.

However, in the popular mind, a "known" criminal is not to be trusted, should not be hired because of the potential for crimes on the job, and would not be a good candidate for the military, marriage, or any position requiring responsibility. Society's tendency toward such thinking, Becker suggested, closed legitimate opportunities, ensuring that the only new behavioral alternatives available to the labeled criminal would be deviant ones. Succeeding episodes of criminal behavior were seen as a form of secondary deviance, which eventually became stabilized in the behavioral repertoire and self-concept of the labeled person.[128]

Labeling theory, like phenomenological approaches in general, can be critiqued along a number of dimensions. First, it is not really a "theory" in that labeling does not uncover the genesis of criminal behavior. It is more powerful in its description of how such behavior continues than in explaining how it originates. Second, labeling theory does not recognize the possibility that the labeled individual may make successful attempts at reform and shed the negative label. Finally, the theory does not provide an effective way of dealing with offenders. Should people who commit crimes not be arrested and tried, so as to avoid the consequences of negative labels? It would be exceedingly naive to suggest that all repeat criminal behavior would cease, as labeling theory might predict, if people who commit crimes are not officially "handled" by the system.

Labeling Theory An interactionist perspective that sees continued crime as a consequence of limited opportunities for acceptable behavior which follow from the negative responses of society to those defined as offenders.

Emergent Theories

A number of new and exciting theories of criminology hold promise for the future. Although space does not permit discussion of them all,[129] **feminist criminology** provides a useful example of the kind of emergent thought characterizing these perspectives.

As some writers in the developing field of feminist criminology have observed, "women have been virtually invisible in criminological analysis until recently and much theorizing has proceeded as though criminality is restricted to men."[130] Others put it this way: "[Traditional] criminological theory assumes a woman is like a man."[131] Feminist criminologists are now working to change long-cherished notions of crime and of criminal justice so that the role of women in both crime causation and crime control might be better appreciated.

Early works in the field of feminist criminology include **Freda Adler's** *Sisters in Crime*[132] and **Rita J. Simon's** *Women and Crime*.[133] Both books were published in 1975, and in them the authors attempted to explain existing divergences in crime rates between men and women as due primarily to socialization rather than biology. Women, claimed these authors, were taught to believe in personal limitations, faced reduced socioeconomic opportunities and, as a result, suffered from lowered aspirations. As gender equality increased, they said, it could be expected that male and female criminality would take on similar characteristics. As researchers and statisticians continue to observe, however, such has not been the case,[134] with substantial differences between the criminality of men and women remaining, even as gender equality grows.

Contemporary feminist thinking in criminology is represented by the works of writers such as **Kathleen Daly** and **Meda Chesney-Lind**.[135] Both Daly and Chesney-Lind emphasize the need for a "gender-aware" criminology and stress the usefulness of applying feminist thinking to criminological analysis. Gender, say these writers, is a central organizing principle of contemporary life. As a way of seeing the world, especially the criminal world, they suggest, it holds much promise. As a consequence, feminist thought, at least for the time being, may be more important for the way it informs and challenges existing criminology than for the new theories it offers.

In fact, much feminist thought within contemporary criminology emphasizes the need for gender-awareness. Theories of crime causation and prevention, it is suggested, must include women and more research on gender-related issues in the field is badly needed. Additionally, some authors say, "Criminologists should begin to appreciate that their discipline and its questions are a product of white, economically privileged men's experiences."[136] They suggest that rates of female criminality, which are lower than those of males, may highlight the fact that criminal behavior is not as "normal" as once thought. Because modern-day criminological perspectives were mostly developed by white middle-class males, the propositions and theories they advance fail to take into consideration women's "ways of knowing."[137] Hence, the fundamental challenge poised by feminist criminology is: Do existing the-

Feminist Criminology A developing intellectual approach which emphasizes gender issues in the subject matter of criminology.

Postmodern Criminology
A brand of criminology which developed following World War II and which builds upon the tenets inherent in postmodern social thought.

Deconstructionist Theories Emerging approaches which challenge existing criminological perspectives to debunk them and which work toward replacing them with concepts more applicable to the postmodern era.

ories of crime causation apply as well to women as they do to men? Or, as Daly and Chesney-Lind put it, given the current situation in theory development, "Do theories of men's crime apply to women?"[138]

Before concluding this chapter it is important to note that **postmodern criminology** is a term applied to a wide variety of novel perspectives which have developed over the past decade or two and which include evolving paradigms with such intriguing names as chaos theory, discourse analysis, topology theory, critical theory, realist criminology, constitutive theory, and anarchic criminology.[139] Postmodern criminology builds upon the feeling that past criminological approaches have failed to realistically assess the true causes of crime and have therefore failed to offer workable solutions for crime control—or if they have, that such theories and solutions may have been appropriate at one time, but that they are no longer applicable to the postmodern era. Because postmodern criminology challenges and debunks existing perspectives, it is referred to as deconstructionist, and such theories are sometimes called **deconstructionist theories**. Two especially notable authors in the field of postmodern criminology are Stuart Henry and Dragan Milovanovic,[140] whose work in the area of constitutive criminology was discussed earlier in this chapter.

SUMMARY

This chapter describes theoretical explanations for crime. Most of the perspectives discussed are grounded in biology, psychology, or sociology. Biological theories posit a genetic or a physiological basis for deviant and criminal behavior. The notion of a "weak" gene, which might predispose certain individuals toward criminal activity, has recently been expanded to include the impact of environmental contaminants, poor nutrition, and food additives on behavior. Studies of fraternal twins and chromosome structure have helped to lead biological theories into the modern day.

Psychological explanations of crime are individualistic. Some psychoanalytical theories see offenders as sick; others claim merely that criminal behavior is a type of conditioned response. The stimulus-response model depicts criminal behavior as the consequence of a conditioning process which extends over the entire life span of an individual.

Sociological theories hold that the individual is a product of the environment and constitute today's perspective of choice. These theories emphasize the role of social structure, inequality, and socialization in generating criminality. The danger of most sociological approaches, however, is that they tend to deny the significance of any influences beyond those which are mediated through social interaction.

An integrated perspective, which recognizes that human behavior results from a mix of biology, mental processes, and acquired traits, holds much future promise. As a consequence, our understanding of crime causation seems headed toward the day when a "unified theory" of conduct will draw upon many types of explanations in order to interpret the whole range of human behavior—including crime.

DISCUSSION QUESTIONS

1. What is a theory? Can you name or describe any theories that you use in making decisions in your daily life?

2. What is the purpose of criminological theory? Do any of the theories described in this chapter fill that purpose especially well? If so, which ones?

3. What do we mean when we say that most theories are unicausal? What would a multicausal theory be like?

4. Describe the major groups of criminological theories discussed in this chapter. What are the shortcomings of each? Which group do you think has the most explanatory power? Why?

5. Which of the major types of theories discussed in this chapter is probably the most accepted today? What dangers do you see in accepting any one type of theory over any other?

6. How do restraint theories differ from other kinds of explanations of crime causation? What do restraint theories assume is true about most of us? Are they correct?

7. Why are social policy initiatives often based upon specific criminological theories? What kinds of social policy or what form of treatment might be predicated upon phenomenological theories of crime?

8. How do radical criminologists explain crime? What form of "treatment" might be predicated upon radical theories of crime? What kinds of social policies might be derived from radical theories?

 WEB WATCH

Access the *Criminal Justice Today* site on the World Wide Web by pointing your Web browser at http://www.prenhall.com/cjtoday. Once there, click "Web Chapters," then select "Chapter 3: The Search for Causes" from the selection box in order to access electronic information and other sites of relevance to this chapter. You may also wish to enter the Global Town Meeting, which provides facilities for the posting of electronic messages for others to read. Messages are arranged by topic, with new topics constantly being added.

NOTES

1. "Gingrich Says Felons Should Be Tracked by Satellite," Reuters wire services, March 4, 1995.
2. Cited in Gwynn Nettler, *Killing One Another* (Cincinnati, OH: Anderson, 1982), p. 194.
3. Deborah Sharp, "'Vampire Rapist' Case Points Anew to Dilemma," *USA Today*, August 8, 1996, p. 3A.
4. As we shall see in Chapter 4, behavior which violates the criminal law may not be "crime" if accompanied by acceptable legal justification or excuse. Justifications and excuses that are recognized by the law may serve as defenses to a criminal charge.
5. This and many of the statistics in these opening paragraphs come from Jonathan Wright, "Media Are Mixed Blessing, Criminologists Say," Reuters wire services, May 2, 1995.
6. Ibid.
7. Nathan McCall, "My Rap Against Rap," *Washington Post* wire services, November 14, 1993.
8. Arthur L. Cribbs, Jr., "Gangsta Rappers Sing White Racists' Tune," *USA Today*, December 27, 1993, p. 9A.
9. Although charged with sodomy, Shakur was convicted on three lesser counts of sexual abuse. See Samuel Maull, "Shakur Trial," The Associated Press wire services, December 2, 1994.
10. $1 million for himself and another $1 million for his bodyguard. See "Prosecutors Mull Second Trial for Rapper," Reuters wire services, February 23, 1996.
11. Nathan McCall, "My Rap Against Rap," *Washington Post* wire services, November 14, 1993.
12. Eric Johnson, "Study Links Suicide, Heavy Metal," United Press International wire services, April 5, 1994, citing a study by Steven Stack, Jim Gundlachin, and Jimmie L. Reeves in the journal *Suicide and Life-Threatening Behavior.*
13. *U.S. News*/UCLA Survey on the Media and Violence, reported in "Hollywood: Right Face," *U.S. News and World Report*, May 15, 1995, p. 71.
14. McCall, "My Rap Against Rap."
15. The word scientific is used here to refer to the application of generally accepted research strategies designed to reject explanations which rival the one under study.

16. The term hedonistic calculus is taken from Stephen Schafer's *Theories in Criminology* (New York: Random House, 1969), p. 106.

17. Ibid., p. 109.

18. For a modern reprint of a widely read nineteenth-century work on phrenology, see Orson Squire Fowler and Lorenzo Niles Fowler, *Phrenology: A Practical Guide to Your Head* (New York: Chelsea House, 1980).

19. Ibid.

20. Schafer, *Theories in Criminology*.

21. Richard Louis Dugdale, *The Jukes: A Study in Crime, Pauperism, Disease, and Heredity*, 3d ed. (New York: G.P. Putnam's Sons, 1985).

22. Henry Herbert Goddard, *The Kallikak Family: A Study in the Heredity of Feeblemindedness* (New York: Macmillan, 1912).

23. "Constitutional" theories of crime causation refer to the *physical constitution*, or bodily characteristics, of the offenders and have nothing to do with the Constitution of the United States.

24. For more information, see Richard Herrnstein, "Crime File: Biology and Crime," a study guide (Washington, D.C.: National Institute of Justice, no date).

25. *Buck* v. *Bell*, 274 U.S. 200, 207 (1927).

26. Patricia Jacobs et al., "Aggressive Behavior, Mental Subnormality, and the XYY Male," *Nature*, Vol. 208 (1965), pp. 1351–1352.

27. Schafer, *Theories in Criminology*, p. 193.

28. D. Hill and W. Sargent, "A Case of Matricide," *Lancet*, Vol. 244 (1943), pp. 526–527.

29. See, for example, A. R. Mawson and K. J. Jacobs, "Corn Consumption, Tryptophan, and Cross-national Homicide Rates," *Journal of Orthomolecular Psychiatry*, Vol. 7 (1978), pp. 227–230, and A. Hoffer, "The Relation of Crime to Nutrition," *Humanist in Canada*, Vol. 8 (1975), p. 8.

30. See, for example, C. Hawley and R. E. Buckley, "Food Dyes and Hyperkinetic Children," *Academy Therapy*, Vol. 10 (1974), pp. 27–32, and Alexander Schauss, *Diet, Crime & Delinquency* (Berkeley, CA: Parker House, 1980).

31. "Special Report: Measuring Your Life with Coffee Spoons," *Tufts University Diet & Nutrition Letter*, Vol. 2, no. 2 (April 1984), pp. 3–6.

32. See, for example, "Special Report: Does What You Eat Affect Your Mood and Actions?" *Tufts University Diet & Nutrition Letter*, Vol. 2, no. 12 (February 1985), pp. 4–6.

33. See *Tufts University Diet & Nutrition Letter*, Vol. 2, no. 11 (January 1985), p. 2, and "Special Report: Why Sugar Continues to Concern Nutritionists," *Tufts University Diet & Nutrition Letter*, Vol. 3, no. 3 (May 1985), pp. 3–6.

34. Diana H. Fishbein and Susan E. Pease, "Diet, Nutrition, and Aggression," in Marc Hillbrand and Nathaniel J. Pallone, eds., *The Psychobiology of Aggression: Engines, Measurement, Control* (New York: The Haworth Press, 1994), pp. 117–114.

35. A. Hoffer, "Children with Learning and Behavioral Disorders," *Journal of Orthomolecular Psychiatry*, Vol. 5 (1976), p. 229.

36. "Special Report: Does What You Eat Affect Your Mood and Actions?" *Tufts University Diet & Nutrition Letter*, Vol. 2, no. 12 (February 1985), p. 4.

37. See, for example, R. T. Rada, D. R. Laws, and R. Kellner, "Plasma Testosterone Levels in the Rapist," *Psychomatic Medicine*, Vol. 38 (1976), pp. 257–268.

38. Recent studies, however, have been less than clear. See, for example, J. M. Dabbs, Jr., "Testosterone Measurements in Social and Clinical Psychology," *Journal of Social and Clinical Psychology*, Vol. 11 (1992), pp. 302–321.

39. "The Insanity of Steroid Abuse," *Newsweek*, May 23, 1988, p. 75.

40. For a summary of such studies, see Serena-Lynn Brown, Alexander Botsis, and Herman M. Van Praag, "Serotonin and Aggression," in Marc Hillbrand and Nathaniel J. Pallone, eds., *The Psychobiology of Aggression: Engines, Measurement, Control* (New York: The Haworth Press, 1994), pp. 28–39.

41. Roger D. Masters, Brian Hone, and Anil Doshi, "Environmental Pollution, Neurotoxicity, and Criminal Violence," in J. Rose, ed., *Environmental Toxicology* (London and New York: Gordon and Breach, 1997).

42. B. Bioulac, M. Benezech, B. Renaud, B. Noel, and D. Roche, "Serotonergic Functions in the XYY Syndrome," *Biological Psychiatry*, Vol. 15 (1980), pp. 917–923.

43. Sarnoff Mednick and Jan Volavka, "Biology and Crime," in Norval Morris and Michael Tonry, eds., *Crime and Justice* (Chicago: University of Chicago Press, 1980), pp. 85–159.

44. Sarnoff Mednick and S. Gloria Shaham, eds., *New Paths in Criminology* (Lexington, MA: D. C. Heath, 1979).

45. For a good survey of studies in this area, see Laurence Miller, "Traumatic Brain Injury and Aggression," in Marc Hillbrand and Nathaniel J. Pallone, eds., *The Psychobiology of Aggression: Engines, Measurement, Control* (New York: The Haworth Press, 1994), pp. 91–103.

46. For an excellent overview of such studies, see Shari Mills and Arian Raine, "Neuroimaging and Aggression," in Marc Hillbrand and Nathaniel J. Pallone, eds., *The Psychobiology of Aggression: Engines, Measurement, Control* (New York: The Haworth Press, 1994), pp. 145–158.

47. R. B. Cattell, *The Inheritance of Personality and Ability: Research Methods and Findings* (New York: Academic Press, 1982).

48. Karl Christiansen, "A Preliminary Study of Criminality Among Twins," in Sarnoff Mednick and Karl O. Christiansen, eds., *Biosocial Bases of Criminal Behavior* (New York: Gardner Press, 1977).

49. James Q. Wilson and Richard J. Herrnstein, *Crime and Human Nature* (New York: Simon & Schuster, 1985).

50. "Criminals Born and Bred," *Newsweek*, September 16, 1985, p. 69.

51. William J. Chambliss, *Exploring Criminology* (New York: Macmillan, 1988), p. 202.

52. A. Reiss and J. Roth, eds., *Understanding and Preventing Violence* (Washington, D.C.: National Academy Press, 1993).

53. Sigmund Freud, *A General Introduction to Psychoanalysis* (New York: Boni & Liveright, 1920).

54. Gwynn Nettler, *Killing One Another* (Cincinnati, OH: Anderson Publishing, 1982), p. 79.

55. David Abrahamsen, *Crime and the Human Mind* (Montclair, NJ: Patterson Smith, 1969), p. 23.

56. See Adrian Raine, *The Psychopathology of Crime: Criminal Behavior As a Clinical Disorder* (Orlando, FL: Academic Press, 1993).

57. Hervey M. Cleckley, *The Mask of Sanity*, 4th ed. (St. Louis, MO: Mosby, 1964).

58. Nettler, *Killing One Another*, p. 179.

59. Albert I. Rabin, "The Antisocial Personality—Psychopathy and Sociopathy," in Hans Toch, *Psychology of Crime and Criminal Justice* (Prospect Heights, IL: Waveland, 1979), p. 330.

60. Richard L. Ault and James T. Reese, "A Psychological Assessment of Crime Profiling," *FBI Law Enforcement Bulletin* (March 1980), pp. 22–25.

61. John E. Douglas and Alan E. Burgess, "Criminal Profiling: A Viable Investigative Tool Against Violent Crime," *FBI Law Enforcement Bulletin* (December 1986), pp. 9–13.

62. Robert R. Hazelwood and John E. Douglass, "The Lust Murderer," *FBI Law Enforcement Bulletin* (April 1980), pp. 18–22.

63. A. O. Rider, "The Firesetter—A Psychological Profile," *FBI Law Enforcement Bulletin*, Vol. 49, no. 6 (June 1980), pp. 4–11.

64. Kathryn A. Artingstall, "Munchausen Syndrome by Proxy," *FBI Law Enforcement Bulletin*, Vol. 64, no. 8 (August 1995), pp. 5–11.

65. M. Reiser, "Crime-Specific Psychological Consultation," *The Police Chief* (March 1982), pp. 53–56.

66. Thomas Strentz, "A Terrorist Psychosocial Profile: Past and Present," *FBI Law Enforcement Bulletin* (April 1988), pp. 13–19.

67. Jill Peay, "Dangerousness—Ascription or Description," in M. P. Feldman, ed., *Developments in the Study of Criminal Behavior*, Vol. Two: *Violence* (New York: John Wiley, 1982), p. 211, citing N. Walker, "Dangerous People," *International Journal of Law and Psychiatry*, Vol. 1 (1978), pp. 37–50.

68. See, for example, Michael Gottfredson and Travis Hirschi, *A General Theory of Crime* (Stanford, CA: Stanford University Press, 1990), and Travis Hirschi and Michael Gottfredson, "Age and the Explanation of Crime," *American Journal of Sociology*, Vol. 89 (1983), pp. 552–584.

69. David F. Greenberg, "Modeling Criminal Careers," *Criminology*, Vol. 29, no. 1 (1991), p. 39.

70. Robert E. Park and Ernest Burgess, *Introduction to the Science of Sociology*, 2nd ed. (Chicago: University of Chicago Press, 1924), and Robert E. Park, ed., *The City* (Chicago: University of Chicago Press, 1925).

71. Clifford R. Shaw and Henry D. McKay, "Social Factors in Juvenile Delinquency," in Vol. II of the *Report of the Causes of Crime*, National Commission on Law Observance and Enforcement Report No. 13 (Washington, D.C.: U.S. Government Printing Office, 1931), and Clifford R. Shaw, *Juvenile Delinquency in Urban Areas* (Chicago: University of Chicago Press, 1942).

72. Emile Durkheim, *Suicide* (New York: The Free Press, 1951).

73. Robert K. Merton, "Social Structure and Anomie," *American Sociological Review*, Vol. 3 (1938), pp. 672–682.

74. Catherine E. Ross and John Mirowsky, "Normlessness, Powerlessness, and Trouble with the Law," *Criminology*, Vol. 25, no. 2 (May 1987), p. 257.

75. See Nettler, *Killing One Another*, p. 58.

76. This is not to say that all members of these groups engaged in criminal behavior, but rather that statistics indicated higher average crime rates for these groups than for certain others during the period of time immediately after they immigrated to the United States.

77. Albert K. Cohen, *Delinquent Boys: The Culture of the Gang* (Glencoe, IL: The Free Press, 1958).

78. Walter B. Miller, "Lower Class Culture as a Generating Milieu of Gang Delinquency," *Journal of Social Issues*, Vol. 14 (1958), pp. 5–19.

79. Richard Cloward and Lloyd Ohlin, *Delinquency and Opportunity: A Theory of Delinquent Gangs* (New York: The Free Press, 1960).

80. Marvin Wolfgang, *Patterns in Criminal Homicide* (Philadelphia: University of Pennsylvania Press, 1958). See also Marvin Wolfgang and Franco Ferracuti, *The Subculture of Violence: Toward an Integrated Theory in Criminology* (London: Tavistock, 1967).

81. Robert W. Sweet, Jr., "Preserving Families to Prevent Delinquency," *Office of Juvenile Justice and Delinquency Prevention Model Programs 1990* (Washington, D.C.: U.S. Department of Justice, April 1992).

82. Edwin Sutherland, *Principles of Criminology*, 4th ed. (Chicago; J. B. Lippincott, 1947), p. 4.

83. Nettler, *Killing One Another.*

84. See, for example, James D. Orcutt, "Differential Association and Marijuana Use: A Closer Look at Sutherland (with a Little Help from Becker)," *Criminology*, Vol. 25, no. 2 (1987), pp. 341–358.

85. John E. Conklin, *Criminology*, 3d ed. (New York: Macmillan 1989), p. 278.

86. Robert L. Burgess and Ronald L. Akers, "A Differential Association-Reinforcement Theory of Criminal Behavior," *Social Problems*, Vol. 14 (Fall 1996), pp. 128–147.

87. Some theories are multicausal and provide explanations for criminal behavior which include a diversity of "causes."

88. Walter C. Reckless, *The Crime Problem*, 4th ed. (New York: Appleton-Century-Crofts, 1961).

89. Ibid., p. 472.

90. Travis Hirschi, *Causes of Delinquency* (Berkeley: University of California Press, 1969).

91. Ibid., p. 472.

92. For a more elaborate criticism of this sort, see John E. Conklin, *Criminology*, 3d ed. (New York: Macmillan, 1989), p. 260.

93. Ibid., p. 260.

94. Gresham Sykes and David Matza, "Techniques of Neutralization: A Theory of Delinquency," *American Sociological Review*, Vol. 22 (1957), pp. 664–670.

95. Adapted from Raymond Michalowski, "Perspectives and Paradigm: Structuring Criminological Thought," in Robert F. Meier, ed., *Theory in Criminology* (Beverly Hills, CA: Sage, 1977).

96. See George B. Vold, *Theoretical Criminology* (New York: Oxford University Press, 1986).

97. Austin T. Turk, *Criminality and the Legal Order* (Chicago: Rand McNally, 1969).

98. Thorsten Sellin, *Culture Conflict and Crime* (New York: Social Science Research Council, 1938).

99. William B. Chambliss and Robert B. Seidman, *Law, Order, and Power* (Reading, MA: Addison-Wesley, 1971).

100. Richard Quinney, *The Social Reality of Crime* (Boston: Little, Brown, 1970).

101. David F. Greenberg, *Crime and Capitalism* (Palo Alto, CA: Mayfield, 1981), p. 3.

102. See Ivan Taylor, Paul Walton, and Jock Young, *The New Criminology* (New York: Harper & Row, 1973).

103. Gwynn Nettler, *Explaining Crime*, 2nd ed. (New York: McGraw-Hill, 1978), p. 230.

104. Ibid., p. 214.

105. Ibid., p. 215.

106. Ibid., p. 221.

107. For examples of how this might be accomplished, see F. H. Knopp, "Community Solutions to Sexual Violence: Feminist/Abolitionist Perspectives," in *Criminology as Peacemaking* (Bloomington: Indiana University Press, 1991), pp. 181–193, and S. Caringella-MacDonald and D. Humphries, "Sexual Assault, Women, and the Community: Organizing to Prevent Sexual Violence," in *Criminology as Peacemaking*, pp. 98–113.

108. Richard Quinney, "Life of Crime: Criminology and Public Policy as Peacemaking," *Journal of Crime and Justice*, Vol. 16, no. 2 (1993), pp. 3–9.

109. Ram Dass and P. Gorman, *How Can I Help? Stories and Reflections on Service* (New York: Alfred A. Knopf, 1985), p. 165, as cited in *The Problem of Crime: A Peace and Social Justice Perspective*, 3rd ed., p. 116.

110. See, for example, Harold E. Pepinsky, "This Can't Be Peace: A Pessimist Looks at Punishment," in W. B. Groves and G. Newman, eds., *Punishment and Privilege* (Albany, NY: Harrow and Heston, 1986); Harold E. Pepinsky, "Violence as Unresponsiveness: Toward a New Conception of Crime," *Justice Quarterly*, Vol. 5 (1988), pp. 539–563; and Harold E. Pepinsky and Richard Quinney, eds., *Criminology as Peacemaking* (Bloomington: University of Indiana Press, 1991).

111. See, for example, Richard Quinney, "Crime, Suffering, Service: Toward a Criminology of Peacemaking," *Quest*, Vol. 1 (1988), pp. 66–75; Richard Quinney, "The Theory and Practice of Peacemaking in the Development of Radical Criminology," *Critical Criminologist*, Vol. 1, no. 5 (1989), p. 5; and Richard Quinney and John

Wildeman, *The Problem of Crime: A Peace and Social Justice Perspective*, 3d ed. (Mayfield, CA: Mountain View Press, 1991), originally published as *The Problem of Crime: A Critical Introduction to Criminology* (New York: Bantam, 1977).

112. All these themes are addressed, for example, in *Criminology as Peacemaking*.

113. Michael J. Lynch and W. Byron Groves, *A Primer in Radical Criminology*, 2nd ed. (Albany, NY: Harrow and Heston, 1989), p. 128.

114. Raymond J. Michalowski, *Order, Law, and Crime: An Introduction to Criminology* (New York: Random House, 1985), p. 410.

115. George Herbert Mead, Charles W. Morris, ed., in *Mind, Self, and Society* (Chicago: University of Chicago Press, 1934).

116. William I. Thomas and Florian Znaniecki, *The Polish Peasant in Europe and America* (Chicago: University of Chicago Press, 1918).

117. Alfred Schutz, *The Phenomenology of the Social World* (Evanston, IL: Northwestern University Press, 1967).

118. Stuart Henry and Dragan Milovanovic, "Constitutive Criminology: The Maturation of Critical Theory," *Criminology*, Vol. 29, no. 2 (May 1991), p. 293.

119. Dragan Milovanovic, *Postmodern Criminology* (Hamden, CT: Garland, 1997).

120. See also Stuart Henry and Dragan Milovanovic, *Constitutive Criminology: Beyond Postmodernism* (London: Sage, 1996).

121. Samuel Yochelson and Stanton E. Samenow, *The Criminal Personality*, 3 vols. (New York: Jason Aronson, 1976).

122. For a good summary of Yochelson and Samenow's work, see Vergil L. Williams, *Dictionary of American Penology: An Introductory Guide* (Westport, CT: Greenwood Press, 1979).

123. Frank Schmalleger, "The World of the Career Criminal," *Human Nature*, March 1979, p. 56.

124. Many of the concepts used by Howard Becker in explicating his theory of labeling, were, in fact, used previously not only by Frank Tannenbaum, but also appeared in the work of Edwin M. Lemert. Lemert wrote of "societal reaction," "primary" and "secondary deviance," and even used the word "labeling" in his book *Social Pathology* (New York: McGraw-Hill, 1951).

125. Frank Tannenbaum, *Crime and the Community* (Boston: Ginn and Co., 1938), pp. 19–20.

126. Howard Becker, *Outsiders: Studies in the Sociology of Deviance* (New York: The Free Press, 1963), pp. 8–9.

127. Ibid.

128. Ibid., p. 33.

129. For an excellent overview of feminist theory in criminology and for a comprehensive review of research regarding female offenders, see Joanne Belknap, *The Invisible Woman: Gender Crime and Justice* (Belmont, CA: Wadsworth, 1996).

130. Don C. Gibbons, *Talking About Crime and Criminals: Problems and Issues in Theory Development in Criminology* (Englewood Cliffs, NJ: Prentice Hall, 1994), p. 165, citing Loraine Gelsthorpe and Alison Morris, "Feminism and Criminology in Britain," *British Journal of Criminology*, Vol. 110.

131. Sally S. Simpson, "Feminist Theory, Crime and Justice," *Criminology*, Vol. 27, no. 4 (1989), p. 605.

132. Freda Adler, *Sisters in Crime: The Rise of the New Female Criminal* (New York: McGraw-Hill, 1975).

133. Rita J. Simon, *Women and Crime* (Lexington, MA: Lexington Books, 1975).

134. See, for example, Darrell J. Steffensmeir, "Sex Differences in Patterns of Adult Crime, 1965–1977: A Review and Assessment," *Social Forces*, Vol. 58 (1980), pp. 1098–1099.

135. See, for example, Kathleen Daly and Meda Chesney-Lind, "Feminism and Criminology," *Justice Quarterly*, Vol. 5, no. 5 (December 1988), pp. 497–535.

136. Ibid., p. 506.

137. Ibid.

138. Ibid., p. 514.

139. For an excellent and detailed discussion of many of these approaches, see Dragan Milovanovic, *Postmodern Criminology* (Hamden, CT: Garland, 1997).

140. See, for example, Stuart Henry and Dragan Milovanovic, *Constitutive Criminology: Beyond Postmodernism* (London: Sage, 1995); and Dragan Milovanovic, *Postmodern Criminology* (Hamden, CT: Garland, 1997).

chapter 4

CRIMINAL LAW

Law is the art of the good and the fair.

—ULPIAN, ROMAN JUDGE (CIRCA 200 A.D.)

Every law is an infraction of liberty.

—JEREMY BENTHAM (1784–1832)

Law should be like death, which spares no one.

—MONTESQUIEU (1689–1755)

actus reus
alibi
alter ego rule
attendant circumstances
Battered Woman's Syndrome
case law
civil law
common law
concurrence
corpus delicti
criminal law
criminal negligence
deadly force
defense
diminished capacity
double jeopardy
elements (of a crime)

entrapment
espionage
excuses
felony
guilty but mentally ill
inchoate offense
insanity defense
jural postulates
jurisprudence
justifications
law
legal cause
mala in se
mala prohibita
mens rea
misdemeanor
The M'Naghten rule

natural law
offense
penal code
penal law
precedent
procedural defense
procedural law
reasonable force
reckless behavior
self-defense
stare decisis
statutory law
strict liability
substantive criminal law
tort
treason

John Stuart Mill
Daniel M'Naghten

Nigel Walker
Roscoe Pound

Oliver Wendell Holmes
Karl Marx

Jacobson v. *U.S.*

U.S. v. *Felix*

Sources of Modern Criminal Law

Twenty years ago, as South American jungles were being cleared to make way for farmers and other settlers, a group of mercenaries brutally attacked and wiped out a small tribe of local Indians. About two dozen native men, women, and children were either hacked to death with machetes or shot. The Indians had refused to give up their land and would not move. At their arrest the killers uttered something that, to our ears, sounds frightening: "How can you arrest us?" they said. "We didn't know it was illegal to kill Indians!"

These men killed many people. But, they claimed, they were ignorant of the fact that the law forbade such a thing. In this case, these killers didn't consider their victims "human." It may seem obvious to us that what they had done was commit murder, but to them it was something else. Nevertheless, their ignorance of the law was rejected as a defense at their trial, and they were convicted of murder. All received lengthy prison sentences.

The men in this story were hardly literate, with almost no formal education. They knew very little about the law and, apparently, even less about basic moral principles. We, on the other hand, living in a modern society with highly developed means of communication, much formal schooling, and a large workforce of professionals skilled in interpreting the law, usually know what the law *says*. But do we really know what the law *is*? The job of this chapter is to discuss the law both as a product of rule creation and as a guide for behavior. We will also examine criminal law in some detail, as well as discuss defenses commonly used by defendants charged with violations of the criminal law.

THE NATURE OF LAW

Practically speaking, **laws** regulate relationships between people and also between parties (such as agencies of government and individuals). Most of us would probably agree that the law is whatever legislators, through the exercise of their politically sanctioned wisdom, tell us it is. If we hold to that belief, we would expect to be able to find the law unambiguously specified in a set of books or codes. As we shall see, however, such is not always the case.

Law A rule of conduct, generally found enacted in the form of a statute, which proscribes and/or mandates certain forms of behavior. Statutory law is often the result of moral enterprise by interest groups which, through the exercise of political power, are successful in seeing their valuative perspectives enacted into law.

Table 4-1 Sources of the Law

Historical Sources of the Law	Modern Sources of American Law
Natural law	The U.S. Constitution
Early Roman law	The Declaration of Independence
Common law	Statutes
The Old and New Testaments	Case law
The Magna Carta	
Religious belief and practice	

The laws of our nation, or of a state, are found in **statutory provisions** and constitutional enactments,[1] as well as in hundreds of years of rulings by courts at all levels. According to the authoritative *Black's Law Dictionary*, the word *law* "generally contemplates both statutory and **case law**."[2] If "the law" could be found entirely ensconced in written legal codes, it would be plain to nearly everyone, and we would need far fewer lawyers than we find practicing today. But some laws (in the sense of precedents established by courts) do not exist "on the books," and even those that do are open to interpretation.

The Development of Law

Modern law is the result of a long evolution of legal principles (see Table 4–1). A complete and accurate understanding of today's criminal law can only be had by someone who is informed as to both its history and its philosophical foundation. Before discussing further the nature of law, it will be useful to examine some of the historical sources of contemporary law. It is to such sources that our attention now turns.

The Code of Hammurabi

The Code of Hammurabi is one of the first known bodies of law to survive and be available for study today. King Hammurabi ruled the ancient city of Babylon around the year 1700 B.C. The Code of Hammurabi is a set of laws engraved on stone tablets, which were intended to establish property and other rights. Babylon was a commercial center, and the right of private property formed a crucial basis for prosperous growth. Hammurabi's laws spoke to issues of theft, ownership, sexual relationships, and interpersonal violence. Even though

Statutory Law Written or codified law. The "law on the books," as enacted by a governmental body or agency having the power to make laws.

Case Law That body of judicial precedent, historically built upon legal reasoning and past interpretations of statutory laws, which serves as a guide to decision making, especially in the courts.

The Code of Hammurabi, one of the oldest judicial codes known, was discovered inscribed on this stone obelisk, which dates from 1700 B.C. Figures at the top of the stone (a portion of which is shown here) depict King Hammurabi receiving the law from the Babylonian sun god. *Bettmann*

Hammurabi's code specified a variety of corporeal punishments—even death for a number of offenses—it routinized the practice of justice in Babylonian society by lending predictability to punishments. Prior to the Code, captured offenders often faced the most barbarous and capricious of punishments, frequently at the hands of revenge-seeking victims, no matter how minor their offenses had been. As Marvin Wolfgang has observed, "In its day, 1700 B.C., the Hammurabi Code, with its emphasis on retribution, amounted to a brilliant advance in penal philosophy mainly because it represented an attempt to keep cruelty within bounds."[3]

EARLY ROMAN LAW

The Code of Hammurabi is primarily of archeological importance. Of considerable significance for our own legal tradition, however, is early Roman law. Roman legions under the Emperor Claudius conquered England in the mid-first century. Roman authority over "Britannia" was consolidated by later rulers who built walls and fortifications to keep out the still-hostile Scots. Roman customs, law, and language were forced upon the English population during the succeeding three centuries under the Pax Romana—a peace imposed by the military of Rome.[4]

Roman law derived from the Twelve Tables, written about 450 B.C. The Twelve Tables were a collection of basic rules related to family, religious, and economic life. The Tables appear to have been based upon common and fair practices generally accepted among early tribes, which existed prior to the establishment of the Roman Republic. Unfortunately, only fragments of the Tables survive today.

The best-known legal period of Roman history occurred under the rule of the Emperor Justinian I, who ruled between 527 and 565 A.D. By the sixth century, the Roman Empire had declined substantially in size and influence and was near the end of its life. In what may have been an effort to preserve Roman values and traditions, Justinian undertook the laborious process of distilling Roman laws into a set of writings. The Justinian Code actually consisted of three lengthy legal documents: (1) the Institutes, (2) the Digest, and (3) the Code itself. Justinian's code distinguished between two major legal categories: public and private laws. Public laws dealt with the organization of the Roman state, its senate, and governmental offices. Private law concerned itself with contracts, personal possessions, the legal status of various types of persons (citizens, free persons, slaves, freedmen, guardians, husbands and wives, etc.), and injuries to citizens. It contained elements of both our modern civil and criminal law, and, no doubt, influenced Western legal thought through the Middle Ages.

COMMON LAW

Common law forms the basis of much of our modern statutory and case law. It has often been called *the* major source of modern criminal law in the United States.

Common law had its origins in early English society. The term *common law* refers to a traditional body of early unwritten legal precedents created from everyday English social customs, rules, and practices that were supported by judicial decisions during the Middle Ages. As novel situations arose and were dealt with by British justices, their reasoning and recorded declarations provided a basis for deciding similar cases in the future. These decisions generally incorporated the customs of society as they existed at the time. Eventually, this growing body of judicial pronouncements congealed into a set of legal rules widely accepted as a kind of national law, commonly applied throughout England—and common law was born. During this early stage of legal development, judges often took it upon themselves to formally criminalize actions that had previously been regarded as the basis for private disputes. Hence, many acts which we call "crimes" today, such as murder, rape, arson, and burglary, might have remained in the private sphere had it not been for such common law developments. As Howard Abadinsky says, "Common law involved the transformation of community rules into a national legal system. The controlling element (was) precedent."[5]

Common law was given considerable legitimacy upon the official declaration that it was the law of the land by the English King Edward the Confessor in the eleventh century. The authority of common law was further reinforced by the decision of William the Conqueror

Common Law Law originating from usage and custom rather than from written statutes. The term refers to non-statutory customs, traditions, and precedents that help guide judicial decision making.

to use popular customs as the basis for judicial action following his subjugation of Britain in 1066 A.D. Eventually, court decisions were recorded and made available to barristers (the English word for trial lawyers) and judges throughout England and much of the British empire.

English common law has had a substantial impact upon the development of law in the United States since the early American colonies when, like the rest of the British empire at the time, they fashioned their budding judicial systems out of principles inherent in the common law. Today, common law has been largely supplanted in all United States jurisdictions by statutory (written) law. Nonetheless, common law principles still serve as powerful interpreters of legal issues which frequently arise around the need to clarify terminology found in state codes, as well as the dictates of state law. Hence, it is not uncommon to hear of jurisdictions within the United States referred to as "common law jurisdictions," or "common law states."

The Magna Carta

The Magna Carta (literally, "great charter") is another important source of modern laws and legal procedure. The Magna Carta was signed on June 15, 1215, by King John of England at Runnymede, under pressure from British barons who took advantage of John's military defeats at the hands of Pope Innocent III and King Philip Augustus of France. The barons demanded a pledge from the king to respect their traditional rights and forced the king to agree to be bound by law.

At the time of its signing, the Magna Carta, although 63 chapters in length, was little more than a feudal document[6] listing specific royal concessions. Its wording, however, was later interpreted during a judicial revolt in 1613 to support individual rights. Sir Edward Coke, chief justice under James I, held that the Magna Carta guaranteed basic liberties for all British citizens and ruled that any acts of Parliament which contravened common law would be void. There is some evidence that this famous ruling became the basis for the rise of the U.S. Supreme Court, with its power to nullify laws enacted by Congress.[7] Similarly, one specific provision of the Magna Carta, designed originally to prohibit the king from prosecuting the barons without just cause, was expanded into the concept of "due process of law," a fundamental cornerstone of modern legal procedure. Because of these later interpretations, the Magna Carta has been called "the foundation stone of our present liberties…"[8]

The U.S. Constitution

The U.S. Constitution is one of the most significant and enduring well-springs of our modern criminal law. The Constitution was created through a long process of debate by the federal Constitutional Convention meeting in Philadelphia in 1787. The Constitution is the final authority in all questions pertaining to the rights of individuals, the power of the federal government and the states to create laws and prosecute offenders, and the limits of punishments which can be imposed for law violations.

Although the Constitution does not itself contain many specific prohibitions on behavior, it is the final authority in deciding whether new and existing laws are acceptable according to the ideals upon which our country is founded. Historically, under the principle of due process (discussed in more detail in Chapter 1), embodied in the Fifth, Sixth, and Fourteenth Amendments, it has also served to guide justices in gauging the merits of citizen's claims concerning the handling of their cases by the agencies of justice.

Natural Law

Some people believe that the basis for many of our criminal laws can be found in immutable moral principles or some identifiable aspect of the natural order. The Ten Commandments, "inborn tendencies," the idea of sin, and perceptions of various forms of order in the universe and in the social world have all provided a basis for the assertion that a "natural law" exists. **Natural law** comes from outside the social group and is thought to be knowable through some form of revelation, intuition, reason, or prophecy.

Natural Law Rules of conduct inherent in human nature and in the natural order which are thought to be knowable through intuition, inspiration, and the exercise of reason, without the need for reference to man-made laws.

Natural law was used by the early Christian church as a powerful argument in support of its interests. Secular rulers were pressed to reinforce Church doctrine in any laws they decreed. Thomas Aquinas (1225–1274) wrote in his *Summa Theologica* that any man-made law which contradicts natural law is corrupt in the eyes of God.[9] Religious practice, which strongly reflected natural law conceptions, was central to the life of early British society. Hence, natural law, as it was understood at the time, was incorporated into English common law throughout the Middle Ages.

The U.S. Declaration of Independence is built around an understanding of natural law as held by Thomas Jefferson and other signers of that important document. When Jefferson wrote of inalienable rights to "life, liberty, and the pursuit of happiness," he referred to the natural due of all men and women. Truths which are held to be "self-evident" can only be such if they are somehow available to us all through reasoning or the promptings of conscience.

Students of natural law have set for themselves the task of uncovering just what that law encompasses. The modern debate over abortion is an example of the use of natural law arguments to support both sides in the dispute. Antiabortion forces, frequently called "prolifers," claim that the unborn fetus is a person and that he or she is entitled to all the protections that we could reasonably and ethically be expected to give to any other living human being. Such protection, they suggest, is basic and humane and lies in the natural relationship of one human being to another. They are striving for passage of a law or a reinterpretation of past Supreme Court precedent that would support their position.

Supporters of the present court-supported standard (which allows abortion upon request under certain conditions) maintain that abortion is a "right" of any pregnant woman because she is the one in control of her body. Such "prochoice" groups also claim that the legal system must address the abortion question, but only by way of offering protection to this "natural right" of women. Keep in mind, however, that what we refer to as "the present law" is not so much a law "on the books," but rather a consequence of a decision rendered by the U.S. Supreme Court in the 1973 case of *Roe* v. *Wade*.[10]

Natural law advocates may well find supporters in high places. Natural law became an issue, for example, in the confirmation hearings conducted for U.S. Supreme Court judicial nominee Clarence Thomas. Because then-judge Thomas had mentioned natural law and natural rights in speeches given prior to his nomination to the Court, Senate Judiciary Committee Chairman Joseph Biden grilled him about the concept. Biden suggested that natural law was a defunct philosophical perspective, no longer worthy of serious legal consideration, and said that the duty of a U.S. Supreme Court justice was to follow the American Constitution. Thomas responded by pointing out that natural law concepts contributed greatly to the principles underlying the Constitution. It was the natural law writings of John Locke, Thomas suggested, that inspired the framers to declare: "All men are created equal."

Mala in Se/Mala Prohibita

Natural law lends credence to the belief that certain actions are wrong in themselves. These behaviors are called *mala in se*, a Latin term which generally includes crimes against humanity (such as the planned extermination of much of the Jewish population in parts of Nazi-controlled Europe during World War II) and serious personal crimes, including murder, rape, assault, arson, and other crimes of violence. Years ago, based at least partially on natural law arguments, some states legislated a special offense category called "crime against nature." Crimes against nature, as specified in laws which have been handed down from those times, mostly encompass sexual deviance, which is regarded as "contrary to the order of nature." Homosexuality, lesbianism, bestiality, and oral copulation may be prosecuted under such statutes and can carry with them quite severe potential punishments—even though large segments of the contemporary American population have experienced a shift in values whereby relatively few forms of personal choice in the sexual arena (outside of those which directly victimize nonwilling participants) are inherently condemned or seen as "unnatural."

It is easy to imagine that members of primitive societies, without a system of codified statutes, would still understand that some forms of behavior are wrong. This intuitive recognition of deviance lends support to the idea of natural law and to the classification of certain offenses as *mala in se*.

Mala in Se Acts that are regarded, by tradition and convention, as wrong in themselves.

John Salvi III, convicted in 1996 of the murders of two abortion clinic workers in the Boston area, confers with counsel. Salvi's arrest and trial demonstrated that no one is above the law, regardless of their personal or moral convictions. Salvi died in prison nine months after being sentenced to life—apparently as a result of suicide. *Sygma*

Crimes which fall outside of the "natural" category are called **mala prohibita**, meaning that they are wrong only because they are prohibited by the law (*malum prohibitum* is the term that refers to one such crime). Poaching on the king's land is an example of what was a *mala prohibita* crime under English common law. Most crimes which fall under the heading of "morals offenses" today might be called *mala prohibita*. Such offenses include prostitution, gambling, and illicit drug use.

The distinction between *mala in se* and *mala prohibita* offenses derives from common law and was an important consideration in deciding sentences in early England. *Mala prohibita* crimes were tried by justices of the peace and carried penalties which were generally far less severe than those for *mala in se* crimes.

> *Mala Prohibita* Acts that are considered "wrongs" only because there is a law against them.

Purposes of the Law

Imagine a society without laws. People would not know what to expect from one another (an area controlled by the law of contracts), nor would they be able to plan for the future with any degree of certainty (administrative law); they wouldn't feel safe (criminal law), knowing that the physically more powerful or better armed could take what they want from the less powerful; and they may not be able to exercise basic rights which would otherwise be available to them as citizens of a free nation (constitutional law). In short, laws channel human behavior while they simultaneously constrain it, and they empower individuals while contributing to social order.

A few years ago the author remembers encountering the results of a survey of attitudes among college-aged males from across the country. One of the most surprising of the survey's findings was this: Nearly 90% of the young men questioned said they would probably rape a woman if there were no laws against forced sexual behavior. These men were admitting to strong sexual drives, which they conceded they would attempt to gratify if the threat of legislated sanctions could not be applied to them. While the honesty of those responding to the questionnaire is to be appreciated, this single finding highlights the need for formal rules which put limits on the behavior of all those who comprise any society. Laws, and criminal laws in particular, are needed to prevent the victimization of innocents by those seeking purely selfish pleasures. The truth of this assertion is borne out by the lawlessness experienced in war zones, where the number of crimes of all sorts—especially rape and looting—tends to rise dramatically (as happened in Kuwait after Iraqi forces overran the country in 1991, as well as during the more recent war in Bosnia).

Max Weber (1864–1920), an eminent sociologist of the early twentieth century, said the primary purpose of law is to regulate the flow of human interaction.[11] By creating enforceable rules, laws make the behavior of others predictable. This first, and most significant, purpose of the law can be simply stated: Laws support social order.

The Assault on Abortion Clinics
—The Confusing Role of Natural Law

The origins of the natural law tradition are shrouded in antiquity. Early writings of the ancient Greek philosophers contain natural law concepts. The Greek tragedy *Antigone*, written by Sophocles, for example, emphasized the conflict between natural law inherent in an individual's conscience and in Greek statutes: Roman orators and lawyers built upon ideas they claimed to find in natural law to defend their positions.

Medieval scholars, including Thomas Aquinas, believed that natural law should bind all men and women because it can be known by reason alone. On the other hand, said Aquinas, the even more powerful divine law, which he saw as a higher aspect of natural law, can inform only the activities of the faithful since it has been revealed only to them.

Natural law scholars have long held to the tenet that codified laws and written statutes are fundamentally invalid when determined to be inconsistent with natural law. Throughout history this principle has formed the basis of much civil disobedience and conscientious objection. As the great legal scholar Ernest van den Haag points out, "It is at once the strength and the weakness of natural law that the individual conscience, not the courts, determines what its commands are."[1] Unfortunately, however, individuals can frequently disagree over the dictates of both natural law and conscience. As van den Haag points out

> Just as some philosophers inferred from natural law that slavery is wrong, others, particularly in antiquity (Aristotle among them), found that slavery is justified by natural law. Just as some will deduce from natural law that women are equal to men and ought to be treated as equals, others concluded that women are inferior and should be subordinated to men. Similarly, capital punishment can be opposed

or supported on natural-law grounds. In effect, natural law does not resolve controversies. Rather, it supplies dubious arguments to both sides.[2]

In today's active society, natural law is often cited in support of both moderate and extreme positions held by those embroiled in the ongoing controversy over abortion. A 1970 landmark proabortion source,[3] for example, claimed that women have a fundamental, inalienable, and natural right to limit their own reproduction. Without such ability, prochoice forces argue, women cannot live up to their fullest human potential. That claim found life in the following assertion, which continues to form part of the manifesto of the prochoice movement: "Our bodies are the physical bases from which we move out into the world; ignorance, uncertainty—even, at worst, shame—about our physical selves create in us an alienation from ourselves that keeps us from being the people that we could be."[4]

For its part, the U.S. Supreme Court, in *Roe* v. *Wade* (1973)[5] sided with prochoice forces in limiting the ability of states to restrict abortion. The Court based its decision upon an inherent right to privacy and personal liberty mentioned in the Fourteenth Amendment to the U.S. Constitution. Even so, the Court reasoned that a woman's right to privacy is not absolute throughout pregnancy and said that "it is not clear to us that...one has an unlimited right to do with one's body as one pleases."

Since *Roe* v. *Wade,* opponents of legalized abortion have remained active in seeking to have the Court's decision overturned. Extremists from among prolife ranks have also used natural law arguments in defense of their position. The Reverend Paul Hill, for example, sentenced in 1994 to die for the shotgun slayings of a Florida abortion clinic doctor and the doctor's security escort, frequented abortion

clinics prior to the murders carrying a sign that read, "Whoever shed unborn man's blood by man shall his blood be shed." In a statement signed by supporters and mailed by Hill to antiabortionists across the country prior to the shootings, Hill wrote, "We proclaim that whatever force is legitimate to defend the life of a born child is legitimate to defend the life of an unborn child."[6]

Hill's exhortations were echoed by others like Donald Spitz, a longtime abortion opponent in Chesapeake, Virginia, who told reporters in a telephone interview that, "I believe if an abortionist walking into the abortion mill to kill babies is killed by force, it's justifiable homicide."[7] Following Hill's sentence, the former minister was portrayed by others as a crazed zealot or a martyr—with the description often depending upon which side of the debate the speaker was on. Both sides agreed, however, that Hill was personally convinced that "righteousness will prevail" in the abortion controversy.

When Hill's trial concluded, more abortion clinics were attacked. In December 1994 two employees were shot to death in attacks at different clinics in Brookline, Massachusetts. The shooter, John Salvi III, a 22-year-old hairdresser from Hampton, New Hampshire, was arrested one day after the killings for firing at a clinic in Norfolk, Virginia. Salvi was returned to Massachusetts and convicted of murder in 1996. The toll in his two-day spree of terror was two dead and five wounded. Salvi died in prison nine months after being sentenced to a life term (Massachusetts does not have the death penalty). Prison officials said Salvi killed himself by tying a plastic trash bag around his head.

Of course, most prolifers do not advocate murdering those who practice abortion, nor does adhering to natural law principles necessarily make one a killer. "Do we look like terrorists?" asks Roy McMillan, head of a local antiabortion Christian action group and a signer of Hill's statement. "Maybe we look confrontational, like Dr. (Martin Luther) King," says McMillan. "He was willing to make things uncomfortable for society."[8]

QUESTIONS FOR DISCUSSION

1. How can natural law be used to provide a philosophical basis for opposition to abortion? For support of abortion?

2. What implications does the ongoing debate over abortion in America have for the justice system? How might it impact the criminal law?

[1]Ernest van den Haag, "Not Above the Law," *National Review*, October 7, 1991, p. 35.

[2]Ibid.

[3]Robin Morgan, *Sisterhood Is Powerful* (New York: Vintage Books, 1970).

[4]Lucinda Cisler, "Unfinished Business: Birth Control and Women's Liberation," in *Sisterhood Is Powerful*.

[5]*Roe* v. *Wade*, 410 U.S. 113 (1973).

[6]Fred Bayles, "Justifiable Homicide," The Associated Press wire services, August 10, 1994.

[7]Ibid.

[8]Ibid.

Laws also serve a variety of other purposes. They ensure that the philosophical, moral, and economic perspectives of their creators are protected and made credible. They maintain values and uphold established patterns of social privilege. They sustain existing power relationships, and, finally, they support a system for the punishment and rehabilitation of offenders. Modifications of the law, when gradually induced, promote orderly change in the rest of society.

The question of *what the law does* is quite different from the question of *what the law should do*. Writing in the mid-1800s, for example, **John Stuart Mill** (1806–1873) questioned the liberal use of the criminal law as a tool for social reform.[12] Mill objected strongly to the use of law as a "way of compulsion and control" for any purpose other than to prevent harm to others. Behavior which might be thought morally "wrong" should not be contravened by law, said Mill, unless it is also harmful to others. In similar fashion, **Nigel Walker**, a British criminologist of this century, applied what he called "a sociological eye" to the criminal codes of Western nations and concluded that criminal statutes are not appropriate when they seek to contravene behavior which lacks a clear and immediate harm to others; nor, he said, should laws be created for the purpose of compelling people to act in their own good.[13]

In reality, few legal codes live up to the Walker-Mill criteria. Most are influenced strongly by cultural conceptions of right and wrong and encompass many behaviors which are not immediately and directly harmful to anyone but those who choose to be involved with them. These illegal activities, often called victimless crimes, include drug abuse, certain forms of "deviant" sexuality, gambling, and various other legally proscribed consensual deeds. Advocates of legislation designed to curb these activities suggest that while such behavior is not always directly harmful to others, it may erode social cohesiveness and ruin the lives of those who engage in it.

Standing in strong opposition to the Walker-Mill perspective are legislators and theorists who purposefully use the law as a tool to facilitate social change. Modifications in the legal structure of a society can quickly and dramatically produce changes in the behavior of entire groups. A change in the tax laws, for example, typically sends people scrambling to their accountants to devise spending and investment strategies which can take advantage of the change. Our legal system not only condemns interpersonal violence and enforces tax codes, it also serves to support the dominant economic order (capitalism) and to protect the powerful and the wealthy (through an emphasis on private property and the rights which attach to property).

Throughout American criminal law, Judeo-Christian principles hold considerable sway. Concepts such as sin and atonement provide for a view of men and women as willful actors in a world of personal and sensual temptations. Such ideas have made possible both the legal notion of guilt and corrections-based punishment.

The realization that laws respond to the needs and interests of society at any given time was put into words by the popular jurist Oliver Wendell Holmes (1809–1894) in an address he gave at Harvard University in 1881. Holmes said, "The life of the law has not been logic; it has been experience. The felt necessities of the time, the prevalent moral and political theories, institutions of public policy, avowed or unconscious, even the prejudices which judges

Jural Postulates
Propositions developed by the famous jurist Roscoe Pound, which hold that the law reflects shared needs without which members of society could not coexist. Pound's jural postulates are often linked to the idea that the law can be used to engineer the social structure in order to ensure certain kinds of outcomes (such as property rights embodied in the law of theft do in capitalistic societies).

Jurisprudence The philosophy of law; the science and study of the law.

share with their fellowmen have had a good deal more to do than the syllogism in determining the rules by which men should be governed."[14] The "syllogism," as Holmes used the term, referred to abstract theorizing as the basis for law. The importance of such "theorizing" he thoroughly discounted.

Once law has been created it is generally slow to change because it is built upon years of tradition. The law can be thought of as a force which supports social order but which is opposed to rapid social change. When law facilitates change, that change usually proceeds in an orderly and deliberate fashion. Revolutions, on the other hand, produce near-instantaneous legal changes, but bring with them massive social disorder.

Social Engineering

One of the greatest legal scholars of modern times was **Roscoe Pound** (1870–1964), dean of the Harvard Law School during the years 1916–1936. Pound saw the law as a type of social engineering.[15] The law is a tool, he said, which meets the demands of men and women living together in society. Pound strongly believed that the law must be able to change with the times and to reflect new needs as they arise.

Pound distilled his ideas into a set of **jural postulates**. Such postulates, claimed Pound, form the basis of all law because they reflect shared needs. In 1942 Pound published his postulates in the form of five propositions.[16]

Pound's postulates form a theory of "consensus" about the origins of law—both civil and criminal. They suggest that most laws are the product of shared social needs experienced by the majority of members in the society where they arise. However, a number of writers have criticized Pound for failing to recognize the diversity of society. How, they ask, can the law address common needs in society when society consists of many different groups—each with their own set of interests and needs? As a consequence of such criticism, Pound modified his theory to include a jurisprudence of interest. Whereas the concept of **jurisprudence** refers simply to the philosophy of law or to the science and study of the law, the concept of a "jurisprudence of interest" held that one of the basic purposes of law is to satisfy "as many claims or demands of as many people as possible."[17]

Social Conflict

Opposed to Pound's theory of consensus is William Chambliss's view of law as a tool of powerful individuals and groups acting in their own interests—and often in conflict with one another.[18] Conflict theory has its roots in the writings of **Karl Marx**, who explained all of social history as the result of an ongoing conflict between the "haves" and the "have-nots."

Chambliss believes we should not see the agencies of criminal justice as "neutral." Rather, he says, government is "a weapon of the dominant classes or interest groups in society."[19] Putting it more directly, Chambliss writes, "…in one way or another, the laws which are passed, implemented, and incorporated into the legal system reflect the interests of those groups capable of having their views incorporated into the official (that is legal) views of the society."[20]

Types of Law

"Criminal" and "civil" law are the best-known types of modern law. However, scholars and philosophers have drawn numerous distinctions between categories of the law which rest upon their source, intent, and application. Laws in modern societies can be usefully described in terms of the following groups:

- Criminal law
- Civil law
- Administrative law
- Case law
- Procedural law

This typology is helpful in understanding and thinking about the law, and we will now discuss each type of law in some detail.

Theory into Practice

WHAT DOES LAW DO?
THE FUNCTIONS OF LAW

- Laws maintain order in society.
- Laws regulate human interaction.
- Laws enforce moral beliefs.
- Laws define the economic environment.
- Laws enhance predictability.
- Laws support the powerful.
- Laws promote orderly social change.
- Laws sustain individual rights.
- Laws redress wrongs.
- Laws identify evildoers.
- Laws mandate punishment and retribution.

CRIMINAL LAW

Fundamental to the concept of **criminal law** is the assumption that criminal acts injure not just individuals, but society as a whole. Hence, we can define criminal law as that body of rules and regulations which defines and specifies punishments for offenses of a public nature or for wrongs committed against the state or society. Criminal law is also called **penal law**.

Social order, as reflected in the values supported by statute, is reduced to some degree whenever a criminal act occurs. In old England (from which much of American legal tradition devolves) offenders were said to violate the "King's Peace" when they committed a crime. They offended not just their victims, but contravened the peaceful order established under the rule of the monarch. For this reason, in criminal cases the state, as the injured party, begins the official process of bringing the offender to justice. Even if the victim is dead and has no one to speak on his or her behalf, the agencies of justice will investigate the crime and file charges against the offender. Because crimes injure the fabric of society, the state, not the individual victim, becomes the plaintiff in criminal proceedings. Cases in criminal court reflect this fact by being cited as follows: *State of New York* v. *Smith* (where state law has been violated) or *U.S.* v. *Smith* (where the federal government is the injured party).

Violations of the criminal law result in the imposition of punishment. Punishment is philosophically justified by the fact that the criminal *intended* the harm and is responsible for it. Punishment serves a variety of purposes, which we will discuss later in the chapter on sentencing. When punishment is imposed in a criminal case, however, it is for one basic reason: to express society's fundamental displeasure with the offensive behavior and to hold the offender accountable for it.

Criminal law, which is built upon constitutional principles and operates within an established set of procedures applicable to the criminal justice system, is composed of both statutory and case law. Statutory law is the "law on the books." It is the result of legislative action and is often thought of as the "law of the land." Written laws exist in both criminal and civil areas and are called codes. Once laws have been written down in organized fashion, they are said to be "codified." Federal statutes are compiled in the United States Code (U.S.C.). State codes and municipal ordinances are also readily available in written, or statutory, form. The written form of the criminal law is called the **penal code**.

Written law is of two types: substantive and procedural. Substantive law deals directly with specifying the nature of, and appropriate punishment for, particular offenses. For example, every state in our country has laws against murder, rape, robbery, and assault. Differences in the law among these various jurisdictions can be studied in detail because each offense and the punishments associated with it are available in the **substantive criminal law** in written form. Procedural laws, on the other hand, specify acceptable methods for dealing with violations of substantive laws, especially within the context of a judicial setting.

Criminal Law That branch of modern law which concerns itself with offenses committed against society, members thereof, their property, and the social order. Another term for criminal law is penal law.

Penal Code The written, organized, and compiled form of the criminal laws of a jurisdiction.

Substantive Criminal Law That part of the law that defines crimes and specifies punishments.

Civil Law That part of the law that governs relationships between parties.

Tort A private or civil wrong or injury. The "unlawful violation of a private legal right other than a mere breach of contract, express or implied." (*Source:* General Statutes of Georgia, 51-1-1.)

Civil Law

Civil law provides a formal means for regulating noncriminal relationships between and among persons, businesses and other organizations, and agencies of government. In contrast to the criminal law, whose violation is an offense against the state or against the nation, civil law governs relationships between parties. Civil law contains rules for contracts, divorce, child support and custody, the creation of wills, property transfers, negligence, libel, unfair practices in hiring, the manufacture and sale of consumer goods with hidden hazards for the user, and many other contractual and social obligations. When the civil law is violated, a civil suit may follow.

Civil suits seek not punishment, but compensation, usually in the form of property or monetary damages. They may also be filed in order to achieve an injunction or a kind of judicial cease-and-desist order. A violation of the civil law may be a **tort** (for example, an unlawful violation of a private legal right other than a mere breach of contract) or a contract violation, but it is not a crime. A tort may give rise to civil liability under which the injured party may sue the person or entity who caused the injury and ask that the offending party be ordered to pay damages directly to them. Because a tort is a personal wrong, however, it is left to the aggrieved individual to set the machinery of the court in motion—that is, to bring a suit.

Civil law is more concerned with assessing liability than it is with intent. Civil suits arising from automobile crashes, for example, do not allege that either driver intended to inflict bodily harm. Nor do they claim that it was the intent of the driver to damage either vehicle. However, when someone is injured, or property damage occurs, even in an accident, civil procedures make it possible to gauge responsibility and assign liability to one party or the other. The parties to a civil suit are referred to as the plaintiff (who seeks relief) and the defendant (against whom relief is sought).

In a tragic 1995 case, which provides a good example of civil liability, Willie King, a diabetic undergoing amputation of a leg, awoke after surgery to find that surgeons at University Community Hospital in Tampa, Florida, had removed the wrong limb. King later settled out of court, and the hospital suspended all elective surgery until it could review safety procedures.[21] In a similar case, which is ongoing at the time of this writing and which may also result in a massive civil award, a Grand Rapids, Michigan, cancer patient had the wrong breast removed during a 1995 mastectomy.[22] Currently, many states award punitive damages (for example, those intended to compensate for mental anguish, degradation, shame, or hurt feelings suffered by the plaintiff) when jurors determine that the chances were better than 50% that the defendant acted with gross negligence (where gross negligence is defined as "the intentional failure to perform a manifest duty in reckless disregard of the consequences as affecting the life or property of another"[23]). Punitive damage awards may be huge. In 1996, for example, an Alabama jury awarded Alex Hardy, 37, $50 million in compensatory damages and $100 million in punitive damages after he was left partially paralyzed in the crash of his Chevrolet Blazer. Jurors found that door latches on the vehicle were defective, causing Hardy to be thrown from the vehicle.[24]

The largest civil liability action ever successfully undertaken resulted in a September 1, 1994, settlement, when a judge agreed to accept a financial agreement which had been reached between makers of silicon breast implants and members of a class action suit against the manufacturers. Under the terms of the agreement, Dow-Corning and other implant manufacturers agreed to pay members of the class of litigants more than $4.2 billion. Dow-Corning later reorganized its operations under bankruptcy protection.

Civil law pertains to injuries suffered by individuals which are unfair or unjust according to the standards operative in the social group. Breeches of contract, unfair practices in hiring, the manufacture and sale of consumer goods with hidden hazards for the user, and slanderous comments made about others have all been grounds for civil suits. Suits may, on occasion, arise as extensions of criminal action. Monetary compensation, for example, may be sought through our system of civil laws by a victim of a criminal assault after a criminal conviction has been obtained.

Following the murder a few years ago of Sandra Black, for example, her son and mother successfully sued *Soldier of Fortune* magazine, winning damages of $9.4 million.[25] *Soldier of*

Fortune had printed a classified advertisement by a "mercenary" who, as a result of the ad, eventually contracted with Mrs. Black's husband to commit the murder. In a quite different type of civil suit, Robert McLaughlin was awarded $1.9 million by a New York State Court of Claims in October 1989, after having spent six and one-half years in prison for a murder and robbery he did not commit.[26]

A 1993 civil case, which may hold considerable significance for the criminal justice system, found a Florida jury holding K-mart stores liable for selling a gun to a drunken man. The buyer, Thomas W. Knapp, used the weapon a half-hour later to shoot his girlfriend, Deborah Kitchen, in the neck—leaving her permanently paralyzed. Knapp had consumed 24 beers and nearly 25 shots of whiskey prior to purchasing the weapon. He was convicted of attempted first-degree murder and is serving a 40-year prison term. Following a civil suit brought by Kitchen, K-mart was ordered to pay her $12 million, sending a message to gun retailers across the nation. In 1997 the Florida supreme court upheld the award.[27]

In 1995, in what may eventually involve a far more massive settlement and have wide-reaching implications, a San Francisco judge ruled that a lawsuit brought by a widow of a man slain by gunfire was based upon solid legal principles and could proceed.[28] At issue was whether the handgun maker, Miami-based Navegar, Incorporated, could be sued under a legal theory which holds manufacturers liable for injuries caused by their products. In this case, Michelle Scully sued the gun manufacturer after her husband, John, was killed by an assailant who opened fire on workers in a California law office in 1993. As the shooting started, John Scully threw himself over his wife and shielded her with his body. Some criticized the judge's ruling, saying that it opened a Pandora's box of potential suits against manufacturers of all kinds of products—since lawsuits targeting products which are not defective and which function precisely as intended might result in suits against automobile manufacturers; makers of alcohol, insecticides, and high-cholesterol foods; and even against companies which make knives, gasoline, candles, and other flammable materials when irresponsible individuals choose to use those products to harm others.

Criminal action, not otherwise excusable, may even be grounds for a civil suit by the offender. In 1992, for example, a civil jury awarded $2.15 million to convicted murderer William Freeman and his family. Freeman, a former assistant chief of police from Fort Stockton, Texas, is serving a life term in prison for killing his friend, Donnie Hazelwood. A jury agreed with Freeman's claim that the sleeping pill Halcion altered his personality and caused him to kill Hazelwood.[29]

Some claim that civil suits have taken on the characteristics of a lottery—offering instant riches to those "lucky" enough to win them. In a typical year 100 million lawsuits are filed in this country—approximately one for every two living Americans. While most of these suits, which may involve divorces, wills, and bad debts, are legitimate, some are simply shots in the dark, taken by lawsuit-happy citizens hoping to win at least some limited type of fame or fortune through the courts. It is becoming increasingly clear to critics of the current system that American civil courts can unwittingly serve the get-rich-quick schemes of the greedy who feign injury.

The largest civil suit ever filed, for example, was brought by Allen and Kathy Wilson in 1994.[30] The Wilson's filed suit in Carson City, Nevada, asking the state to pay them $657 trillion—the amount the couple say they are owed on a $1,000 state-issued bond purchased in 1865. The Wilson's bought the bond in 1992 from a widow who had inherited it from her husband. They calculated the amount they claim they are owed by compounding interest at an annual rate of 24% for 130 years. The state of Nevada successfully maintained that time had run out for redeeming the bond.

In 1996 the U.S. Congress passed legislation which would have limited punitive damage claims in civil suits brought in federal and state courts to a maximum of $250,000, or three times the plaintiff's economic damages from such things as lost income and medical expenses—whichever would have been greater. Under this legislation, known as the Civil Justice Fairness Act, compensatory damages would have been awarded only for the amount of damages the plaintiff could prove were actually incurred.[31] The Act, however, was vetoed by President Clinton, and an attempted override of the presidential veto failed. Opponents of the congressional initiative argued that limits on punitive damages are inherently unfair and claimed that federal restrictions on suits filed in state courts illegally preempt state authority over such matters.

A short time later, however, the U.S. Supreme Court ruled that the U.S. Constitution does not permit "grossly excessive" damage awards in civil suits. The 1996 case[32] involved Dr. Ira Gore, Jr., who sued Bavarian Motor Works after learning that a new BMW he had bought in 1990 had been repainted before he took delivery of the car. Dr. Gore's vehicle had been damaged by acid rain during shipment to the United States from a manufacturing facility in Germany, and BMW repainted portions of the car when it arrived in the United States—without telling Dr. Gore that it had done so before selling the vehicle to him. When Gore sued, a state jury awarded him $4,000 in compensatory damages and $4 million in punitive damages. The state's supreme court reduced the award to $2 million. In overturning the huge award, the U.S. Supreme Court ruled that "the due process (fair hearing) clause of the 14th Amendment prohibits a state from imposing a 'grossly excessive' punishment on a [civil wrongdoer]." The wrongdoing in this case, said the Court, "involved a decision by a national distributor of automobiles [BMW] not to advise its dealers, and hence their customers, of predelivery damage to new cars when the cost of repair amounted to less than 3 percent of the car's suggested retail price." In wording that may hold considerable significance for future civil suits seeking large punitive damages, the Court's majority wrote: "Elementary notions of fairness enshrined in our constitutional jurisprudence dictate that a person receive fair notice not only of the conduct that will subject him to punishment but also of the severity of the penalty that a state may impose." Since the amount of punitive damages awarded in the Gore case was hundreds of times the amount of the actual damage done to the vehicle, the Court reasoned, BMW could never have anticipated having to pay such massive damages for such a relatively minor transgression. The case was sent back to the Alabama Supreme Court for a new hearing and concluded in 1997 when that court ordered BMW to pay Dr. Gore $50,000.[33]

Administrative Law

Administrative law refers to the body of *regulations* which have been created by governments to control the activities of industry, business, and individuals. Tax laws, health codes, restrictions on pollution and waste disposal, vehicle registration, building codes, and the like are examples of administrative law.

Other administrative laws cover practices in the areas of customs (imports/exports), immigration, agriculture, product safety, and most areas of manufacturing. Modern individualists claim that overregulation characterizes the American way of life, although they are in turn criticized for failing to adequately recognize the complexity of modern society. Overregulation has also been used on occasion as a rallying cry for political hopefuls who believe that many Americans wish to return to an earlier and simpler form of free enterprise.

Although the criminal law is, for the most part, separate from administrative regulations, the two may overlap. For instance, the rise in organized criminal activity in the area of toxic waste disposal—an area covered by many administrative regulations—has led to criminal prosecutions in several states. The intentional and systematic denial of civil rights in areas generally thought to be administrative in nature, such as hiring, employment, job compensation, and so forth, may also lead to criminal sanctions through the federal system of laws.

Administrative agencies will sometimes arrange settlements which fall short of court action but that are considered binding on individuals or groups who have not lived up to the intent of federal or state regulations. Education, environmental protection, and discriminatory hiring practices are all areas in which such settlements have been employed.

Case Law

Precedent A legal principle that operates to ensure that previous judicial decisions are authoritatively considered and incorporated into future cases.

Case law (which comes from judicial decisions) is also referred to as the law of **precedent**. It represents the accumulated wisdom of trial and appellate courts (those which hear appeals) in criminal, civil, and administrative law cases over the years. Once a court decision is rendered, it is written down. At the appellate level, the reasoning behind the decision is recorded as well. Under the rule of precedent, this reasoning should then be taken into consideration by other courts in settling future cases.

Willie King, shown here, agreed to settle a civil liability case out of court after doctors at University Community Hospital in Tampa, Florida, removed the wrong leg during surgery. Civil law allows individuals to pursue legal remedies when they believe they have been wronged, but not criminally victimized. *Chris O'Meara, AP/Wide World Photos*

Appellate courts have considerable power to influence new court decisions at the trial level. The court with the greatest influence, of course, is the U.S. Supreme Court. The precedents it establishes are incorporated as guidelines into the process of legal reasoning by which lower courts reach conclusions.

The principle of recognizing previous decisions as precedents to guide future deliberations is called *stare decisis* and forms the basis for our modern "law of precedent." Lief H. Carter has pointed out how precedent operates along two dimensions.[34] He calls them the vertical and the horizontal. A vertical rule requires that decisions made by a higher court be taken into consideration by lower courts in their deliberations. Under this rule, state appellate courts, for example, should be expected to follow the spirit of decisions rendered by their state supreme courts.

The horizontal dimension means that courts on the same level should be consistent in their interpretation of the law. The U.S. Supreme Court, operating under the horizontal rule, for example, should not be expected to change its ruling in cases similar to those it has already decided.

Stare decisis makes for predictability in the law. Defendants walking into a modern courtroom will have the opportunity to be represented by lawyers who are trained in legal precedents as well as procedure. As a consequence, they will have a good idea of what to expect about the manner in which their trial will proceed.

Stare Decisis The legal principle which requires that courts be bound by their own earlier decisions and by those of higher courts having jurisdiction over them regarding subsequent cases on similar issues of law and fact. The term literally means "standing by decided matters."

Procedural Law

Procedural law is another kind of statutory law. It is a body of rules which regulates the processing of an offender by the criminal justice system. **Procedural law**, for example, specifies in most jurisdictions that the testimony of one party to certain "victimless crimes" cannot be used as the sole evidence against the other party. General rules of evidence, search and seizure, procedures to be followed in an arrest, and other specified processes by which the justice system operates are also contained in procedural law.

As a great jurist once said, however, the law is like a living thing. It changes and evolves over time. Legislatures enact new statutory laws, and justices set new precedents, sometimes over-

Procedural Law That aspect of the law that specifies the methods to be used in enforcing substantive law.

WHAT IS CRIME?
THE EXAMPLE OF CRIMES AGAINST THE ENVIRONMENT

Crime can be defined simply as "a violation of the criminal law" (although this chapter and our glossary contain more complex definitions). It is important to recognize, however, that when we look behind most criminal statutes we can usually catch a glimpse of the concept of harm. Criminal activity, such as theft and assault, most of us would agree is harmful to others. Some crimes, on the other hand, such as drug abuse, prostitution, gambling, and pornography, are sometimes referred to as "victimless crimes," or social order offenses, because the harm they cause is not readily identifiable at the individual level. Statutes outlawing social order offenses are rooted in the notion of social harm—that is, although no one who participates in prostitution runs to the police to file a complaint (unless they are robbed or in some other way directly victimized), lawmakers recognize that the act somehow lessens the quality of social life. Prostitution, many lawmakers argue, is harmful to the family and (in the case of heterosexual prostitution) demeans the status of women in society.

Today, a whole new class of criminal offenses is emerging based upon the notion of environmental damage. In what may be the best known environmental catastrophe to date, the Exxon *Valdez*, a 1,000-foot supertanker, ran aground in Alaska's Prince William Sound in 1989 and spilled 11 million gallons of crude oil over 1,700 miles of pristine coastline. Animal life in the area was devastated. The U.S. Fish and Wildlife Service reported decimation of salmon spawning grounds, the death of 580,000 birds (including 144 bald eagles), and the demise of an unknown, but presumably vast amount of sea life (22 whales were known dead, along with 5,500 sea otters). The initial cleanup involved over 10,000 people and cost more than $1 billion. Damages were estimated to be much higher, and in 1994 Exxon was ordered by an Alaskan civil court to pay $5 billion in punitive damages to 14,000 fishermen and other people affected by the spill.

The *Valdez* incident, while prosecuted under both civil and criminal laws, was clearly not intended. No one (including the ship's captain, who was later prosecuted on charges akin to "drunk driving") wanted the *Valdez* to run aground. Other environmental crimes, however, some of which occur on an everyday basis, are quite intentional. Such crimes range from ecological terrorism, like that waged against Kuwait during the Gulf War by retreating Iraqi troops who set oil fields on fire throughout the country, to littering and small-scale recycling offenses, which are frequently committed by individual citizens.

Concerted efforts are now being made in the battle against environmental crime. In 1995, for example, in an effort to catch offenders who were illegally dumping hazardous waste, Florida implemented an undercover law enforcement program known as "Operation Crystal Clean." Agents of the state's attorney general's office set up a fake warehouse from which they contracted with toxic waste disposal companies to haul away numerous 55-gallon drums filled with noxious-looking water which had been mixed with a fluorescent green dye. The mixture, although harmless, looked corrosive, and the dye it contained made it easy to track—especially when illegitimate haulers dumped it into the state's rivers and waterways. Undercover air and vehicular units tracked the haulers and made note of where they left their loads. Illegal operators often dropped the barrels in wooded areas, rented warehouses, or other secluded spots. Nineteen convictions resulted from the operation, with most judges fining offenders and ordering them into community service programs in which they had to clean up illegal dump sites left by others.

At present, eight federal laws criminalize wanton acts of environmental damage. They are the Clean Air Act; the Comprehensive Environmental Response, Compensation, and Liability Act; the Federal Water Pollution Control Act; the Resource Conservation and Recovery Act; the Rivers and Harbors Act; the Safe Drinking Water Act; the Toxic Substances Control Act; and the Federal Insecticide, Fungicide, and Rodenticide Act.

As ecological awareness continues to expand, new prohibitions are legislated and previously unheard-of offenses created. Today, a highly concerned society stands increasingly ready to define abuse of the environment in criminal terms. As a consequence, words like "curbside criminals," "recycling police," and "garbage crime" are becoming commonplace. The state of Pennsylvania, for example, recently enacted a recycling law which mandates stiff sanctions, including fines and jail sentences for violators. Under the law, what had formerly been routine daily activities (throwing out the trash) become criminal offenses unless properly conducted (plastics and glass must be separated from paper products and lawn clippings and yard trash appropriately bagged).

While human beings have insulted the environment since before the dawn of history, it has only been in this century, as our dependence on the planet has become progressively obvious, that such activities have been ascribed criminal status. Hence, the question: What taken-for-granted aspects of our contemporary everyday lives, especially those which impact upon the natural environment, will become subject to criminal sanctions in the twenty-first century?

QUESTIONS FOR DISCUSSION

1. How do environmental crimes differ from other types of crime?

2. This box concludes with the question: "What taken-for-granted aspects of our contemporary everyday lives, especially those which impact upon the natural environment, will become subject to criminal sanctions in the twenty-first century?" What do you think?

Sources: P.R. Beseler, "Operation Crystal Clean," *FBI Law Enforcement Bulletin* (Washington, D.C.: FBI, May 1995), pp. 1–3; Joel Epstein and Theodore M. Hammett, *Law Enforcement Response to Environmental Crime* (Washington, D.C.: National Institute of Justice, 1995); "*Valdez* Spill Damage, Toll Much Worse," *USA Today,* April 10, 1991, p. 1A; Nanci Koser Wilson, "Recycling Offenses, the Routine Ground of Everyday Activities, and Durkheimian Functionality in Crime," paper presented at the annual meeting of the Academy of Criminal Justice Sciences, Nashville, TN, 1991; the *FBI Law Enforcement Bulletin,* special issue on environmental crime, April 1991; and "Valdez/Exxon Punished," *Time,* September 20, 1994.

ruling established ones. Many jurisdictions today, for example, because of the changed role of women in society, now allow wives to bring charges of rape against their husbands—something not permitted under the laws of most states as little as a decade or two ago. Similarly, under newly written laws in many states, wives may testify against their husbands in certain cases, even though such action is contrary to years of previously acknowledged precedent.

General Categories Of Crime

Violations of the criminal law can be of many different types and vary in severity. Five categories of violation will be discussed in the pages which follow. They are

- Felonies
- Misdemeanors
- Offenses
- Treason
- Inchoate offenses

Felonies

Violations of the criminal law can be more or less serious. **Felonies** are serious crimes. The felony category includes crimes such as murder, rape, aggravated assault, robbery, burglary, arson, and so on. Under common law, felons could be sentenced to death and/or have their property confiscated. Today, many felons receive prison sentences, although the potential range of penalties can include anything from probation and a fine to capital punishment in many jurisdictions. Following common law tradition, people who are today convicted of felonies usually lose certain privileges. Some states, for example, make conviction of a felony and incarceration grounds for uncontested divorce. Others prohibit offenders from running for public office or owning a firearm and exclude them from some professions such as medicine, law, and police work.

The federal government and many states have moved to a scheme of classifying felonies, from most to least serious, using a number or letter designation. The federal system,[35] for example, for purposes of criminal sentencing, assigns a score of 43 to first-degree murder, while the crime of theft is only rated a "base offense level" of 4. Attendant circumstances and the criminal history of the offender are also taken into consideration in sentencing decisions.

Because of differences among the states, a crime classified as a felony in one part of the country may be a misdemeanor in another, while in still other areas it may not even be a crime at all! This is especially true of some drug law violations and of certain other social order offenses such as homosexuality, prostitution, and gambling—which, in a number of jurisdictions, are perfectly legal (although such activity may still be subject to certain administrative regulations).

Misdemeanors

Misdemeanors are relatively minor crimes, consisting of offenses such as petty theft (the theft of items of little worth), simple assault (in which the victim suffers no serious injury, and in

Felony A criminal offense punishable by death or by incarceration in a prison facility for at least a year.

Misdemeanor An offense punishable by incarceration, usually in a local confinement facility, for a period of which the upper limit is prescribed by statute in a given jurisdiction, typically limited to a year or less.

Careers in Justice

Working for the U.S. Park Police

TYPICAL POSITIONS. U.S. Park Police provide enforcement services in the nation's national parks. They also serve the nation's capitol and grounds, including federal areas within the District of Columbia. Branches include the Horse-Mounted Unit, the Criminal Investigations Branch, the Traffic Safety Unit, the Special Equipment and Tactics Team, the Motor Unit (which employs motorcycles), the Canine Unit, the Marine Unit, and the Aviation Unit.

EMPLOYMENT REQUIREMENTS. Applicant must (1) be at least 21 years of age and have not reached his or her 31st birthday by the time of appoint-

ment, (2) be a U.S. citizen, (3) possess a high school diploma or equivalent, (4) have 20/60 vision or better that is correctable to 20/20, and (5) have had two years of progressively responsible experience.

OTHER REQUIREMENTS. Applicant must (1) successfully complete 18 weeks of intensive training at the Federal Law Enforcement Training Center (Glynco, Georgia) and (2) perform satisfactorily on periodic written tests.

SALARY. Agents are typically hired at federal pay grade GS-5 or GS-7, depending on education and prior work history.

BENEFITS. Benefits include (1) participation in the Federal Employee's Retirement System, (2) paid annual leave, (3) paid sick leave, (4) overtime that is compensated at the rate of time and one-half of regular pay, and (5) all uniforms and equipment, which are provided.

DIRECT INQUIRIES TO:
U.S. Park Police, Personnel Office
1100 Ohio Drive, S.W.
Washington, D.C. 20242
Phone: (202) 619-7056.

Offense (1) a violation of the criminal law, or, in some jurisdictions, (2) a minor crime, such as jaywalking, sometimes described as "ticketable."

Infraction A minor violation of state statute or local ordinance punishable by a fine or other penalty, but not by incarceration, or by a specified, usually limited term of incarceration.

Treason "[A] U.S. citizen's actions to help a foreign government overthrow, make war against, or seriously injure the United States." *Source:* Daniel Oran, *Oran's Dictionary of the Law* (St. Paul, MN: West, 1983), p. 306. Also, the attempt to overthrow the government of the society of which one is a member.

which none was intended), breaking and entering, the possession of burglary tools, disorderly conduct, disturbing the peace, filing a false crime report, and writing bad checks (although the amount for which the check is written may determine the classification of this offense).

In general, misdemeanors can be thought of as any crime punishable by a year or less in prison. In fact, most misdemeanants receive suspended sentences involving a fine and supervised probation. If an "active sentence" is received for a misdemeanor violation of the law, it probably will involve time to be spent in a local jail, perhaps on weekends, rather than imprisonment in a long-term confinement facility. Alternatively, some misdemeanants are sentenced to community service activities, requiring them to do such things as wash school buses, paint local government buildings, or clean parks and other public areas.

Normally, a police officer cannot arrest a person for a misdemeanor, unless the crime was committed in the officer's presence. If the in-presence requirement is missing, the officer will need to seek an arrest warrant from a magistrate or other judicial officer. Once a warrant has been issued, the officer may then proceed with the arrest.

Offenses

A third category of crime is the offense. Although, strictly speaking, all violations of the law can be called "criminal offenses," the term **offense** is sometimes used to specifically refer to minor violations of the law which are less serious than misdemeanors. When the term is used in that sense, it refers to such things as jaywalking, spitting on the sidewalk, littering, and certain traffic violations, including the failure to wear a seat belt. Another word used to describe such minor law violations is **infraction**. People committing infractions are typically ticketed and released, usually upon a promise to later appear in court. Court appearances may often be waived through payment of a small fine, which is often mailed in.

Treason

Felonies, misdemeanors, offenses, and the people who commit them constitute the daily work of the justice system. Special categories of crime, however, exist and should be recognized. They include treason and espionage. **Treason** has been defined as "the act of a U.S. cit-

Some crimes against the environment occur on a massive scale. Here, firefighters prepare to move in on one of the hundreds of oil well fires intentionally set in Kuwait by retreating Iraqi troops during the Gulf War. *S. Compoint, Sygma*

izen's helping a foreign government to overthrow, make war against, or seriously injure the United States."[36] Treason is also a crime under the laws of most states. Hence, treason can be more generally defined as the attempt to overthrow the government of the society of which one is a member. Some states, like California, have legislatively created the crime of treason, while in others the crime is constitutionally defined. Florida's constitution, for example, which mirrors wording in the U.S. Constitution, says that "Treason against the state shall consist only in levying war against it, adhering to its enemies, or giving them aid and comfort, and no person shall be convicted of treason except on the testimony of two witnesses to the same overt act or on confession in open court."[37]

Espionage, an offense akin to treason, refers to the "gathering, transmitting, or losing"[38] of information related to the national defense in such a manner that the information becomes available to enemies of the United States and may be used to their advantage. Espionage against the United States did not end with the Cold War. In 1994, for example, CIA agent Aldrich Hazen Ames and his wife, Rosario, were arrested and charged with conspiracy to commit espionage in a plot to sell U.S. government secrets to the Russian KGB.[39] The Ameses apparently told their Russian handlers of CIA operatives within the former Soviet Union and revealed the extent of American knowledge of KGB plans. Their activities had gone undetected for nearly a decade. Following arrest, the Ameses pleaded guilty to charges of espionage and tax fraud. Aldrich Ames was sentenced to life in prison; his wife received a five-year term.

Two years later, in 1996, CIA station chief Harold Nicholson was arrested as he was preparing to leave Washington's Dulles Airport—allegedly on his way to meet his Russian handlers. Nicholson is the highest ranking CIA employee to ever be charged with espionage. Also in 1996, 43-year-old Earl Edwin Pitts, a 13-year FBI veteran, was taken into custody at the FBI academy in Quantico, Virginia, and arraigned on charges of attempted espionage and conspiracy.[40] Pitts was charged with spying for the Russians and is said to have turned over lists of Russian agents within the United States who had been compromised. Nicholson and Pitts pled guilty to espionage charges in early 1997,[41] and both were sentenced to lengthy prison terms.

Espionage The "gathering, transmitting, or losing" of information related to the national defense in such a manner that the information becomes available to enemies of the United States and may be used to their advantage. *Source:* Henry Campbell Black, Joseph R. Nolan, and Jacqueline M. Nolan-Haley, *Black's Law Dictionary*, 6th ed. (St. Paul, MN: West, 1990), p. 24.

Treason and espionage may be committed for personal gain or for ideological reasons, or both. The Ameses received millions of dollars from the Russians for secrets they sold, Nicholson allegedly received $180,000 or more, and Pitts was charged with accepting more than $224,000 over a five-year period Both treason and espionage are often regarded as the most serious of felonies.

INCHOATE OFFENSES

Inchoate Offense   One not yet completed. Also, an offense which consists of an action or conduct which is a step toward the intended commission of another offense.

Another special category of crime is called inchoate. The word *inchoate* means incomplete or partial, and **inchoate offenses** are those which have not yet been fully carried out. Conspiracies are an example. When a person conspires to commit a crime, any action undertaken in furtherance of the conspiracy is generally regarded as a sufficient basis for arrest and prosecution. For instance, a woman who intends to kill her husband may make a phone call to find a "hit man" to carry out her plan. The call itself is evidence of her intent and can result in her imprisonment for conspiring to murder.

Another type of inchoate offense is the attempt. Sometimes an offender is not able to complete the crime. Homeowners may arrive just as a burglar is beginning to enter their residence. The burglar may drop his tools and run. Even so, in most jurisdictions, this frustrated burglar can be arrested and charged with attempted burglary.

General Features of Crime

From the perspective of Western jurisprudence, all crimes can be said to share certain features, and the notion of crime itself can be said to rest upon such general principles. Taken together, these features, which are described in the paragraphs that follow, comprise the legal essence of the concept of crime. Conventional legal wisdom holds that the essence of crime consists of three conjoined elements: (1) the criminal act (which, in legal parlance is termed the *actus reus*), (2) a culpable mental state (*mens rea*), and (3) a concurrence of the two. Hence, as we shall see in the following few pages, the essence of criminal conduct consists of a concurrence of a criminal act with a culpable mental state.

THE CRIMINAL ACT (*ACTUS REUS*)

Actus Reus   An act in violation of the law; a guilty act.

A necessary first feature of any crime is some act in violation of the law. Such an act is termed the *actus reus* of a crime. The term means a "guilty act." Generally, a person must commit some voluntary act before they are subject to criminal sanctions. Someone who admits (perhaps on a TV talk show) that they are a drug user, for example, cannot be arrested on that basis. To *be something* is not a crime—to *do something* may be. In the case of the admitted drug user, police who heard the admission might begin gathering evidence to prove some specific law violation in that person's past, or perhaps they might watch that individual for future behavior in violation of the law. An arrest might then occur. If it did, it would be based upon a specific action in violation of the law pertaining to controlled substances.

Vagrancy laws, popular in the early part of the twentieth century, have generally been invalidated by the courts because they did not specify what act violated the law. In fact, the *less* a person did, the more vagrant they were.

An *omission to act*, however, may be criminal where the person in question is required by law to do something. Child-neglect laws, for example, focus on parents and child guardians who do not live up to their responsibilities for caring for their children.

Threatening to act can itself be a criminal offense. Telling someone, "I'm going to kill you," might result in an arrest based upon the offense of "communicating threats." Threatening the President of the United States is taken seriously by the Secret Service, and individuals are regularly arrested for boasting about planned violence to be directed at the president.

Attempted criminal activity is also illegal. An attempt to murder or rape, for example, is a serious crime, even though the planned act was not accomplished.

Conspiracy statutes were mentioned earlier in this chapter. When a conspiracy unfolds, the ultimate act that it aims to bring about does not have to occur for the parties to the conspiracy to be arrested. When people plan to bomb a public building, for example, they can be legally stopped before the bombing. As soon as they take steps to "further" their plan, they have met the requirement for an act. Buying explosives, telephoning one another, or drawing plans of the building may all be actions in "furtherance of the conspiracy."

Not all conspiracy statutes require actions in furtherance of the "target crime" before an arrest can be made. Technically speaking, crimes of conspiracy can be seen as entirely distinct from the crimes which are contemplated by the conspiracy. So, for example, in 1994[42] the U.S. Supreme Court upheld the drug-related conviction of Reshat Shabani when it ruled that in the case of certain antidrug laws[43] "it is presumed that Congress intended to adopt the common law definition of conspiracy, which does not make the doing of any act other than the act of conspiring a condition of liability...." Hence, according to the Court, "the criminal agreement itself," even in the absence of actions directed toward realizing the target crime, can be grounds for arrest and prosecution.

Similar to conspiracy statutes are many newly enacted antistalking laws. Antistalking statutes are intended to prevent harassment and intimidation, even when no physical harm occurs. According to the U.S. Senate's Judiciary Committee, "there are 200,000 people in the United States who are currently 'stalking' someone...."[44] It is estimated that half of those being stalked are celebrities. Stalkers often strike after their victims have unsuccessfully complained to authorities about stalking-related activities such as harassing phone calls and letters. Antistalking statutes, however, still face a constitutional hurdle of attempting to prevent people not otherwise involved in criminal activity from walking and standing where they wish and from speaking freely. Ultimately, the U.S. Supreme Court will probably have to decide the legitimacy of such statutes.

A Guilty Mind (*Mens Rea*)

Mens rea is the second general component of crime. The term literally means "guilty mind" and refers to the specific mental state operative in the defendant at the time the behavior in question was being enacted. The importance of *mens rea* as a component of crime cannot be overemphasized and can be seen in the fact that some courts have held that "[a]ll crime exists primarily in the mind."[45] The extent to which a person can be held criminally responsible for his or her actions generally depends upon the nature of the mental state under which he or she was laboring at the time of the offense.

Mens Rea The state of mind which accompanies a criminal act. Also, guilty mind.

Four levels, or types, of *mens rea* can be distinguished: (1) purposeful (or intentional), (2) knowing, (3) reckless, and (4) negligent. *Mens rea* is most clearly present when a person acts purposefully and knowingly, but *mens rea* sufficient for criminal prosecution may also result from reckless or negligent behavior. Pure accident, however, which involves no recklessness or negligence cannot serve as the basis for either criminal or civil liability. "Even a dog," once wrote the famous Supreme Court Justice **Oliver Wendell Holmes**, "distinguishes between being stumbled over and being kicked."[46]

Nonetheless, *mens rea* is said to be present when a person *should have known better*, even if the person did not directly intend the consequences of his or her action. A person who acts negligently, and thereby endangers others, may be found guilty of **criminal negligence** when harm occurs, even though no negative consequences were intended. For example, a mother who left her 12-month-old child alone in the tub can later be prosecuted for negligent homicide if the child drowns.[47] It should be emphasized, however, that negligence in and of itself is not a crime. Negligent conduct can be evidence of crime only when it falls below some acceptable standard of care. That standard is today applied in criminal courts through the fictional creation of a *reasonable person*. The question to be asked in a given case is whether or not a reasonable person, in the same situation, would have known better and acted differently than the defendant. The reasonable person criterion provides a yardstick for juries faced with thorny issues of guilt or innocence.

Criminal Negligence Behavior in which a person fails to reasonably perceive substantial and unjustifiable risks of dangerous consequences.

 Purposeful or intentional action, in contrast to negligent action, is that which is undertaken to achieve some goal. Sometimes the harm that results from intentional action may be quite unintended—and yet fail to reduce criminal liability. The doctrine of transferred intent, for example, which operates in all U.S. jurisdictions, would hold a person guilty of murder even if he took aim and shot at an intended victim but missed, killing another person instead. The philosophical notion behind the concept of transferred intent is that the killer's intent to kill, which existed at the time of the crime, transferred from the intended victim to the person who was struck by the bullet and died.

Knowing behavior is action undertaken with awareness. Hence, a person who acts purposefully always acts knowingly, although a person may act in a knowingly criminal way but for another purpose. An airline captain, for example, who allows a flight attendant to transport cocaine aboard an airplane may do so in order to gain sexual favors from the attendant—but without having the purpose of drug smuggling in mind. Knowing behavior involves near certainty. Hence, if the flight attendant in this example carries cocaine aboard the airplane, it *will* be transported; and if an HIV-infected individual has unprotected sexual intercourse with another person, their partner *will* be exposed to the virus.

Reckless behavior, in contrast, is activity which increases the risk of harm. Although knowledge may be a part of such behavior, it exists more in the form of probability than certainty. So, for example, an old Elton John song about Marilyn Monroe says "you lived your life like a candle in the wind." The wind is, of course, a risky place to keep a lighted candle—and doing so increases the likelihood that its flame will be extinguished. But there is no certainty that the flame will be blown out, or, if so, when it might happen. As a practical example, reckless driving is a frequent charge in many jurisdictions and is generally brought when a driver engages in risky activity which endangers others.

Mens rea is a thorny concept. Not only is it philosophically and legally complex, but a person's state of mind during the commission of an offense can rarely be known directly, unless the person confesses. Hence, *mens rea* must generally be inferred from a person's actions and from all the circumstances which surround those actions. It is also important to note that *mens rea*, even in the sense of intent, is not the same thing as motive. A **motive** refers to a person's reason for committing a crime. While evidence of motive may be admissible during a criminal trial in order to help prove a crime, motive itself is not an essential element of a crime. As a result we cannot say that a bad or immoral motive makes an act a crime.

Strict Liability and *Mens Rea*

A special category of crimes, called **strict liability** offenses, requires no culpable mental state and presents a significant exception to the principle that all crimes require a conjunction of *actus reus* and *mens rea*. Strict liability offenses (also called "absolute liability offenses") make it a crime simply to *do* something, even if the offender has no intention of violating the law. Strict liability is philosophically based upon the presumption that causing harm is in itself blameworthy, regardless of the actor's intent.

Routine traffic offenses are generally considered "strict liability" offenses, which do not require intent and may be committed by someone who is unaware of what they are doing. A driver commits minor violations of his or her state motor vehicle code simply by doing that which is forbidden. Hence, driving 65 miles per hour in a 55-miles-per-hour zone is a violation of the law, even though the driver may be listening to music, thinking, or simply going with the flow of traffic—entirely unaware that his or her vehicle is exceeding the posted speed limit.

Statutory rape provides another example of the concept of strict liability.[48] The crime of statutory rape generally occurs between two consenting individuals and requires only that the offender have sexual intercourse with a person under the age of legal consent. Statutes describing the crime routinely avoid any mention of a culpable mental state. In many jurisdictions it matters little in the crime of statutory rape that the "perpetrator" knew the exact age of the "victim" or that the "victim" lied about his or her age or may have given consent, since such laws are "an attempt to prevent the sexual exploitation of persons deemed legally incapable of giving consent."[49]

CONCURRENCE

The concurrence of an unlawful act and a culpable mental state provides the third basic component of crime. **Concurrence** requires that the act and the mental state occur together in order for a crime to take place. If one precedes the other the requirements of the criminal law will not have been met. A person may intend to kill a rival, for example. As she drives to the intended victim's house, gun in hand, fantasizing about how she will commit the murder, the victim may be crossing the street on the way home from grocery shopping. If the two accidentally collide, and the intended victim dies, there has been no concurrence of act and intent.

Reckless Behavior Activity which increases the risk of harm.

Motive A person's reason for committing a crime.

Strict Liability Liability without fault or intention. Strict liability offenses do not require *mens rea*.

Concurrence The coexistence of an act in violation of the law and a culpable mental state.

Some scholars contend that the three features of crime which we have just outlined—*actus reus, mens rea,* and concurrence—are sufficient to constitute the essence of the legal concept of crime. Other scholars, however, see modern Western law as more complex. They argue that recognition of five additional principles is necessary to fully appreciate contemporary understandings of crime. These five principles are (1) causation, (2) a resulting harm, (3) the principle of legality, (4) the principle of punishment, and (5) necessary attendant circumstances. We will now discuss each of these additional features in turn.

Causation

Causation refers to the fact that the concurrence of a guilty mind and a criminal act may produce or *cause* harm. While some statutes criminalize only conduct, others subsume the notion of concurrence under causality and specify that a causality relationship is a necessary element of a given crime. Such laws require that the offender *cause* a particular result before criminal liability can be incurred. Sometimes, however, a causal link is anything but clear. A classic example of this principle involves assault with a deadly weapon with intent to kill. If a person shoots another, but the victim is seriously injured and not killed, the victim might survive for a long time in a hospital. Death may occur, perhaps a year or more later, because pneumonia sets in or because blood clots form in the injured person from lack of activity. In such cases, defense attorneys will likely argue that the defendant did not cause the death, but rather the death occurred because of disease. If a jury agrees with the defense's claim, the shooter may go free or be found guilty of a lesser charge, such as assault.

To clarify the issue of causation, the American Law Institute suggests use of the term **legal cause** in order to emphasize the notion of a legally-recognizable cause and to preclude any assumption that such a cause must be close in time and space to the result it produces. Legal causes can be distinguished from those causes which may have produced the result in question, but which may not provide the basis for a criminal prosecution because they are too complex, too indistinguishable from other causes, not knowable, or not provable in a court of law.

Legal Cause A legally-recognizable cause. The type of cause that is required to be demonstrated in court in order to hold an individual criminally liable for causing harm.

Harm

A harm occurs in any crime, although not all harms are crimes. When a person is murdered or raped, harm can clearly be identified. Some crimes, however, have come to be called "victimless." Perpetrators maintain that they are not harming anyone in committing such crimes. Rather, they say, the crime is pleasurable. Prostitution, gambling, "crimes against nature" (sexual deviance), and drug use are but a few crimes classified as "victimless." People involved in such crimes will argue that, if anyone is being hurt, it is only they. What these offenders fail to recognize, say legal theorists, is the social harm caused by their behavior. Areas afflicted with chronic prostitution, drug use, sexual deviance, and illegal gambling usually will find property values falling, family life disintegrating, and other, more traditional crimes increasing as money is sought to support the "victimless" activities and law-abiding citizens flee the area.

In a criminal prosecution, however, it is rarely necessary to prove harm as a separate element of a crime, since it is subsumed under the notion of a guilty act. In the crime of murder, for example, the "killing of a human being" brings about a harm, but is, properly speaking, an act. When done with the requisite *mens rea* it becomes a crime. A similar type of reasoning applies to the criminalization of attempts, and some writers have used the example of throwing rocks at blind people to illustrate that behavior need not actually produce harm for it to be criminal. One could imagine a scenario in which vandals decide to throw rocks at visually impaired individuals but, because of bad aim, the rocks never hit anyone and the intended targets remain blissfully unaware that anyone is trying to harm them. In such a case, shouldn't throwing rocks provide a basis for criminal liability? As one authority on the subject observes, "[c]riticism of the principle of harm has…been based on the view that the harm actually caused may be a matter of sheer accident and that the rational thing to do is to base the punishment on the *mens rea*, and the action, disregarding any actual harm or lack of harm or its degree."[50] This observation also shows why we have said that the essence of crime consists only of three things: (1) an *actus reus*, (2) *mens rea*, and (3) a concurrence of an illegal act and a culpable mental state.

LEGALITY

The principle of legality is concerned with the fact that a behavior cannot be criminal if no law exists which defines it as such. It is all right to drink beer if you are of "drinking age" because there is no statute "on the books" prohibiting it. During prohibition times, of course, the situation was quite different. (In fact, some parts of the United States are still "dry," and the purchase or public consumption of alcohol can be a law violation regardless of age.) The principle of legality also includes the notion that a law cannot be created tomorrow which will hold a person legally responsible for something he or she does today. These are called *ex post facto* laws. Laws are binding only from the date of their creation or from some future date at which they are specified as taking effect.[51]

PUNISHMENT

The principle of punishment says that no crime can be said to occur where punishment has not been specified in the law. Larceny, for example, would not be a crime if the law simply said, "It is illegal to steal." Punishment needs to be specified so that if a person is found guilty of violating the law, sanctions can be lawfully imposed.

NECESSARY ATTENDANT CIRCUMSTANCES

Attendant Circumstances The facts surrounding an event.

Finally, statutes defining some crimes specify that additional elements, called **attendant circumstances**, be present in order for a conviction to be obtained. Attendant circumstances refer to the "facts surrounding an event"[52] and include such things as time and place. Attendant circumstances, specified by law as necessary elements of an offense, are sometimes referred to as "necessary attendant circumstances" to indicate the fact that the existence of such circumstances is necessary, along with the other elements included in the relevant statute for all of the elements of a crime to be met.

Florida law, for example, makes it a crime to "Knowingly commit any lewd or lascivious act in the presence of any child under the age of 16 years…"[53] In this case, the behavior in question might not be a crime if committed in the presence of persons older than 16. Also, curfew violations are being increasingly criminalized by states shifting liability for a minor's behavior to his or her parents. In order to violate a curfew, it is necessary that a juvenile be in a public place between specified times (such as 11 P.M. or midnight, and 5 or 6 A.M.). In those states which hold parents liable for the behavior of their children, parents can be jailed or fined when such violations occur.

Sometimes attendant circumstances increase the degree, or level of seriousness, of an offense. Under Texas law, for example, the crime of burglary has two degrees, defined by state law as follows: burglary is a "(1) state jail felony if committed in a building other than a habitation; or (2) felony of the second degree [i.e., a more serious crime] if committed in a habitation." Hence, the degree of the offense of burglary changes depending upon the nature of the place burglarized.

Circumstances surrounding a crime can also be classified as aggravating or mitigating and may, by law, lessen or increase the penalty that can be imposed upon a convicted offender. Aggravating and mitigating circumstances are not elements of an offense, since they are primarily relevant at the sentencing stage of a criminal prosecution and will therefore be discussed in a later chapter.

Elements of A Specific Criminal Offense

Elements of a Crime The basic components of crime. In a specific crime, the essential features of that crime as specified by law or statute.

While we have just identified the principles which constitute the *general* notion of crime, we can also examine individual statutes in order to see what particular statutory **elements** comprise a *specific* crime. Written laws specify exactly what conditions are necessary for a person to be charged in a given instance of criminal activity, and they do so for every particular offense. Hence, elements of a crime are specific legal aspects of a criminal offense which must be proven by the prosecution in order to obtain a conviction. The crime of first-degree murder, for example, in almost every jurisdiction in the United States involves four quite distinct elements:

O.J. Simpson reacts as "not guilty" verdicts are announced at the conclusion of his 1995 double-murder trial. All of the elements of a crime must be proven beyond a reasonable doubt in order for a defendant in a criminal case to be convicted. *Sygma*

1. An unlawful killing
2. Of a human being
3. Intentionally
4. With planning (or "malice aforethought")

The elements of any specific crime are the statutory minimum without which that crime cannot be said to have occurred. In any case that goes to trial, the task of the prosecution is to prove that all the elements were indeed present and that the accused was ultimately responsible for producing them. Since statutes differ between jurisdictions, the specific elements of a particular crime, such as murder, may vary. In order to convict a defendant of a particular crime, prosecutors must prove to a judge or jury that all the required statutory elements are present.[54] If even one element of an offense cannot be established beyond a reasonable doubt, criminal liability will not have been demonstrated, and the defendant will be found not guilty.

The Example Of Murder

Every statutory element in a given instance of crime serves some purpose and is necessary. As mentioned, the crime of first-degree murder includes *an unlawful killing* as one of its required elements. Even if all the other elements of first-degree murder are present, the act will still not be first-degree murder if the initial element has not been met. In a wartime situation, for instance, killings of human beings occur. They are committed with planning and sometimes with "malice." They are certainly intentional. Yet killing in war is not unlawful, so long as the belligerents wage war according to international conventions.

The second element of first-degree murder specifies that the killing must be of a "human being." People kill all the time. They kill animals for meat, they hunt, and they practice euthanasia upon aged and injured pets. Even if the killing of an animal is planned and involves malice (perhaps a vendetta against a neighborhood dog that wrecks trash cans), it does not constitute first-degree murder. Such a killing, however, may violate statutes pertaining to cruelty to animals.

The third element of first-degree murder, "intentionality," is the basis for the defense of accident. An unintentional or nonpurposeful killing is not first-degree murder, although it may violate some other statute.

Finally, murder has not been committed unless "malice" is involved. There are different kinds of malice. Second-degree murder involves malice in the sense of hatred or spite. A more extreme form of malice is necessary for a finding of first-degree murder. Sometimes the phrase used to describe this type of feeling is "malice aforethought." This extreme kind of malice can be demonstrated by showing that planning was involved in the commission of the murder. Often, first-degree murder is described as "lying in wait," a practice which shows that thought and planning went into the illegal killing.

Whether any particular behavior meets the specific statutory minimums to qualify as a crime may be open to debate. A few years ago, for example, Adam Brown, 30, of Roseburg, Oregon, was charged with attempted first-degree murder for having knowingly exposed five children to the AIDS virus when he allegedly had unprotected sex with them. Mr. Brown, a lay minister, was informed that he had tested positive for the AIDS virus more than a year prior to the incidents. Brown was also charged with sodomy, rape, sexual penetration with a foreign object, and reckless endangerment.[55]

A charge of second-degree murder in most jurisdictions would necessitate proving that a voluntary (or intentional) killing of a human being took place—although a "crime of passion" may have been committed without the degree of malice necessary for it to be classified as first degree. Third-degree murder, or manslaughter, can be defined simply as the unlawful killing of a human being. Not only is malice lacking in third-degree murder cases, but the killer may not have even intended that any harm come to the victim. Third-degree murder statutes, however, frequently necessitate some degree of negligence on the part of the killer, and charges such as negligent homicide may result from automobile accidents resulting in death in which the driver did not exercise due care. When legally defined "gross negligence" (involving a wanton disregard for human life) is present, however, some jurisdictions permit the offender to be charged with a more serious count of murder.

In 1995, for example, in the case of Karin Smith, a grand jury returned a homicide indictment against a laboratory doctor and technician for a fatal misdiagnosis.[56] The laboratory workers had misread a Pap smear performed on Smith, returning a clean bill of health to the doctor in charge of her care. Smith died on March 8, 1995, at age 29 from cervical cancer that had spread throughout her body. Experts testifying before a grand jury said that evidence of the presence of cancer was "unequivocal" in slides from Pap smears done on Smith in 1988 and 1989, but that the laboratory which received the sample tissue had misread the test results. The prosecutor in the case claimed that laboratory personnel had demonstrated a wanton disregard for human life when they "failed to install random controls to check the quality of the Pap smear analysis; [a]nd showed indifference toward professional standards and the need for continuing education."[57]

Although most people think that homicide charges are brought primarily against those who intend to kill, the recent trend in charging negligent medical personnel with murder is evidence that the machinery of the criminal justice system is being increasingly applied outside its traditional sphere. About the time of the Smith case, for example, Denver anesthesiologist Dr. Joseph J. Verbrugge, Sr., was charged with manslaughter in the death of an eight-year-old boy undergoing ear surgery.[58] Police investigators said the doctor had fallen asleep during the surgery, allowing the boy to receive a lethal dose of anesthetic. Also in 1995 Dr. Gerald Einaugler of New York was ordered to spend 52 weekends in jail for causing the death of a nursing home patient when he mistook a dialysis tube for a feeding tube and pumped food into the patient's kidneys;[59] and New York Dr. David Benjamin faced a possible life prison sentence after being convicted of murder in the death of a woman who went to him for an abortion. Upon his August 8, 1995, conviction, Dr. Benjamin became the first doctor in New York state to be found guilty of murder for the medical mistreatment of a patient.[60] The patient, Guadalupe Negron, bled to death following a bungled abortion in the doctor's storefront clinic.

Finally, the 1997 manslaughter convictions of three youths in Tampa, Florida, who pulled up stop signs at rural intersections near Lithia, Florida, provides another clear example that criminal liability in such crimes does not require an intent to cause death. Defendants Christopher Cole, 20, Nissa Baillie, 21, and Thomas Miller, 20, were each sentenced to 30 years in prison for causing the deaths of three 18-year olds who were returning home from an evening of bowling. The victims were killed by an eight-ton truck hauling fertilizer as they crossed through an intersection where a stop sign had been removed. At sentencing Florida Circuit Judge Bob Mitchum told the defendants, "I don't believe for one minute that you…pulled these signs up with the intent of causing the death of anyone…"[61] Cole, Baillie, and Miller will be eligible for parole after 13 years.[62]

The *Corpus Delicti* of a Crime

The term *corpus delicti* literally means "body of crime." The term is often confused with the statutory elements of a crime. Sometimes the concept is mistakenly thought to mean the body of a murder victim or some other physical result of criminal activity. It actually means something quite different.

One way to understand the concept of *corpus delicti* is to realize that a person cannot be tried for a crime unless it can first be shown that the offense has, in fact, occurred. In other words, to establish the *corpus delicti* of a crime, the state has to demonstrate that a criminal law has been violated and that someone violated it. Hence, there are only two aspects to the *corpus delicti* of an offense: (1) that a certain result has been produced and (2) that a person is criminally responsible for its production. As one court said, "[c]orpus delicti consists of a showing of (1) the occurrence of the specific kind of injury and (2) someone's criminal act as the cause of the injury."[63] So, for example, the crime of larceny requires proof that the property of another has been stolen—that is, unlawfully taken by someone whose intent it was to permanently deprive the owner of its possession.[64] Hence, evidence offered to prove the *corpus delicti* in a trial for larceny is insufficient where the evidence fails to prove that any property has been stolen or where property found in a defendant's possession cannot be identified as having been stolen. Similarly, "[i]n an arson case, the *corpus delicti* consists of (1) a burned building or other property, and (2) some criminal agency which caused the burning…In other words, the *corpus delicti* includes not only the fact of burning, but it must also appear that the burning was by the willful act of some person, and not as a result of a natural or accidental cause…."[65]

We might add to the requirement to establish the *corpus delicti* of a crime before a successful prosecution can occur, the observation that the identity of the perpetrator is not an element of the *corpus delicti* of an offense. Hence, the fact that a crime has occurred can be established without having any idea who committed it or even why it was committed. This principle was clearly enunciated in a Montana case when the state's supreme court held that "the identity of the perpetrator is not an element of the *corpus delicti*." In *State* v. *Kindle* (1924),[66] the court continued, "we stated that '[i]n a prosecution for murder, proof of the *corpus delicti* does not necessarily carry with it the identity of the slain nor of the slayer'…The essential elements of the *corpus delicti* are…establishing the death and the fact that the death was caused by a criminal agency, nothing more." *Black's Law Dictionary* puts it another way: "[t]he *corpus delicti* [of a crime] is the fact of its having been actually committed."[67]

Types of Defenses to a Criminal Charge

When a person is charged with a crime, he or she typically offers some defense. A **defense** consists of evidence and arguments offered by a defendant and his or her attorneys to show why that person should not be held liable for a criminal charge. Our legal system generally recognizes four broad categories of defenses: (1) **alibi**; (2) **justifications**; (3) **excuses**; and (4) **procedural defenses**. An alibi, if shown to be valid, means that the defendant could not have committed the crime in question because he or she was somewhere else (and generally with someone else) at the time of the crime. When a defendant offers a **justification** as a defense, he or she admits committing the act in question, but claims that it was necessary in order to avoid some greater evil. A defendant who offers an **excuse** as a defense, on the other hand, claims that some personal condition or circumstance at the time of the act was such that he or she should not be held accountable under the criminal law. Procedural defenses make the claim that the defendant was in some significant way discriminated against in the justice process or that some important aspect of official procedure was not properly followed in the

Corpus Delicti The "body of crime." Facts which show that a crime has occurred.

Defenses (to a criminal charge) Evidence and arguments offered by a defendant and his or her attorney(s) to show why that person should not be held liable for a criminal charge.

Alibi A statement or contention by an individual charged with a crime that he or she was so distant when the crime was committed, or so engaged in other provable activities, that participation in commission of that crime was impossible.

Justifications A category of legal defenses in which the defendant admits committing the act in question but claims it was necessary in order to avoid some greater evil.

Excuses A category of legal defenses in which the defendant claims that some personal condition or circumstance at the time of the act was such that he or she should not be held accountable under the criminal law.

Procedural Defense A defense which claims that the defendant was in some significant way discriminated against in the justice process or that some important aspect of official procedure was not properly followed in the investigation or prosecution of the crime charged.

investigation or prosecution of the crime charged. Finally, a number of innovative defense strategies have emerged in recent years and will be discussed as a fifth category—although, technically speaking, each of the innovative defenses we shall discuss could be classified as a justification or as an excuse. Table 4–2 lists the types of defenses which fall into our five categories. Each will be discussed in the pages that follow.

Alibi

A current reference book for criminal trial lawyers says, "Alibi is different from all of the other defenses…because…it is based upon the premise that the defendant is truly innocent…"[68] The defense of alibi denies that the defendant committed the act in question. All of the other defenses we are about to discuss grant that the defendant committed the act, but they deny that he or she should be held criminally responsible. While justifications and excuses may produce findings of "not guilty," the defense of alibi claims outright innocence.

Alibi is best supported by witnesses and documentation. A person charged with a crime can use the defense of alibi to show that they were not present at the scene when the crime was alleged to have occurred. Hotel receipts, eyewitness identification, and participation in social events have all been used to prove alibis.

Justifications

As defenses, justifications claim a kind of moral high ground. Justifications may be offered by people who find themselves facing a choice between a "lesser of two evils." Generally speaking, conduct which a person believes is necessary in order to avoid a harm or evil to him- or herself or to avoid harm to another is justifiable if the harm or evil to be avoided is greater than that which the law defining the offense seeks to avoid. So, for example, a fireman might set a controlled fire in order to create a firebreak to head off a conflagration threatening a community. While intentionally setting a fire may constitute arson, doing so in order to save a town may be justifiable behavior in the eyes of the community *and* in the eyes of the law. Included under the broad category of "justifications" are (1) self-defense, (2) the defense of others, (3) defense of home and property, (4) necessity, (5) consent, and (6) resisting unlawful arrest.

Self-defense

Self-defense The protection of oneself or one's property from unlawful injury or the immediate risk of unlawful injury; the justification that the person who committed an act which would otherwise constitute an offense reasonably believed that the act was necessary to protect self or property from immediate danger.

Self-defense is probably the best known of the justifications. This defense strategy makes the claim that it was necessary to inflict some harm on another in order to ensure one's own safety in the face of near-certain injury or death. A person who harms an attacker can generally use this defense. However, the courts have held that where a "path of retreat" exists for a person being attacked, it should be taken. In other words, the safest use of self-defense is only when "cornered," with no path of escape.

Reasonable Force A degree of force that is appropriate in a given situation and is not excessive. The minimum degree of force necessary to protect oneself, one's property, a third party, or the property of another in the face of a substantial threat.

The amount of defensive force used must be proportionate to the amount of force or perceived degree of threat that one is seeking to defend against. Hence, **reasonable force** is that degree of force that is appropriate in a given situation and is not excessive. Reasonable force can also be thought of as the minimum degree of force necessary to protect oneself, one's property, a third party, or the property of another in the face of a substantial threat. **Deadly force**, the highest degree of force, is considered reasonable only when used to counter an immediate threat of death or great bodily harm. Deadly force cannot be used against non-deadly force.

Force, as the term is used within the context of self-defense, means physical force and does not extend to emotional, psychological, economic, psychic, or other forms of coercion. A person who turns the tables on a robber and assaults him during a robbery attempt, for example, may be able to claim self-defense, while the business person who physically assaults a financial rival to prevent a hostile takeover of her company will have no such recourse.

Deadly Force Force likely to cause death or great bodily harm.

Self-defense has been used recently in a spate of killings, by wives, of their abusive spouses. Killings which occur while the physical abuse is in process, especially where a history of such abuse can be shown, are likely to be accepted by juries as justified. On the other hand, wives who suffer repeated abuse but coldly plan the killing of their husbands have not fared well in court.

Table 4-2 Types of Defenses

Alibi	Justifications	Excuses	Procedural	Innovative
A claim	Self-defense	Duress	Entrapment	Abuse defense
of alibi	Defense of others	Age	Double jeopardy	Premenstrual Stress syndrome
	Defense of home and property	Mistake	*Collateral estoppel*	Other biological defenses
	Necessity	Involuntary intoxication	Selective prosecution	Black rage
	Consent	Unconsciousness	Denial of a speedy trial	Urban survival syndrome
	Accident	Provocation	Prosecutorial misconduct	
	Resisting unlawful arrest	Insanity	Police fraud	
		Diminished responsibility		

Defense of Others

The use of force to defend oneself has generally been extended to permit the use of reasonable force to defend others who are or appear to be in imminent danger. The defense of others, however, sometimes called "defense of a third person," is circumscribed in some jurisdictions by the **alter ego rule**. The alter ego rule holds that a person can only defend a third party under circumstances and only to the degree that the third party could act. In other words, a person who aids a person whom he sees being accosted may become criminally liable if that person initiated the attack or if the assault is a lawful one—for example, is being made by a law enforcement officer conducting a lawful arrest of a person who is resisting. A few jurisdictions, however, do not recognize the alter ego rule and allow a person to act in defense of another if the actor reasonably believes that his intervention is immediately necessary to protect the third person.

Defense of others cannot be claimed by an individual who joins an illegal fight merely in order to assist a friend or family member. Likewise, one who intentionally aids an offender in an assault, even though the tables have "turned" and the offender is losing the battle, cannot claim "defense of others." Under the law, defense of third persons always requires that the defender be free from fault and that he or she act to aid an innocent person who is in the process of being victimized. Also, the same restrictions that apply to self-defense also apply to the defense of a third party. Hence, a defender must only act in the face of an immediate threat to another person, cannot use deadly force against nondeadly force, and must only act to the extent and use only the degree of force needed to repel the attack.

Alter Ego Rule   A rule of law that, in some jurisdictions, holds that a person can only defend a third party under circumstances and only to the degree that the third party could act on their own behalf.

Defense of Home and Property

In most jurisdictions the owner of property can justifiably use reasonable, *nondeadly* force to prevent others from unlawfully taking or damaging it. As a general rule, however, the preservation of human life outweighs protection of property and the use of deadly force to protect property is not justified unless the perpetrator of the illegal act may intend to commit, or is in the act of committing, a violent act against another human being. A person who shoots an unarmed trespasser, for example, could not claim "defense of property" in order to avoid criminal liability. However, one who shoots and kills an armed robber while being robbed can. The difference is that a person facing an armed robber has a right to protect his or her property but is also in danger of death or serious bodily harm. An unarmed trespasser represents no such serious threat.[69]

The use of mechanical devices to protect property is a special area of law. Since, generally speaking, deadly force is not permitted in defense of property, the setting of booby traps such as spring-loaded shotguns, electrified grates, explosive devices, and the like, is generally not permitted to protect property which is unattended and unoccupied. If an individual is injured as a result of a mechanical device intended to cause death or injury in the protection of property, criminal charges may be brought against the person who set the device.

The greatest happiness of the greatest number is the foundation of morals and legislation.

—Jeremy Bentham

On the other hand, acts which would otherwise be criminal may carry no criminal liability if undertaken to protect one's home. For purposes of the law, one's "home" is one's dwelling, whether owned, rented, or merely "borrowed." Hotel rooms, rooms on board vessels, and rented rooms in houses belonging to others are all considered, for purposes of the law, one's "dwelling." The retreat rule, referred to earlier, which requires a person under attack to retreat when possible before resorting to deadly force, is subject to what some call the castle exception. The castle exception can be traced to the writings of the sixteenth-century English jurist Sir Edward Coke, who said, "A man's house is his castle—for where shall a man be safe if it be not in his house?"[70] The castle exception generally recognizes that a person has a fundamental right to be in his or her home and also recognizes the home as a final and inviolable place of retreat (that is, the home offers a place of retreat from which a person can be expected to retreat no further). Hence, it is not necessary for one to retreat from one's home in the face of an immediate threat, even where such retreat is possible, before resorting to deadly force in protection of the home. A number of court decisions have extended the castle exception to include one's place of business, such as a store or office.

Necessity

Necessity, or the claim that some illegal action was needed to prevent an even greater harm, is a useful defense in cases which do not involve serious bodily harm. One of the most famous uses of this defense occurred in *Crown* v. *Dudly & Stephens* in the late 1800s.[71] The case involved a shipwreck in which three sailors and a cabin boy were set adrift in a lifeboat. After a number of days at sea without rations, two of the sailors decided to kill and eat the cabin boy. At their trial, they argued that it was necessary to do so, or none of them would have survived. The court, however, reasoned that the cabin boy was not a direct threat to the survival of the men and rejected this defense. Convicted of murder, they were sentenced to death, although they were spared the gallows by royal intervention.

Although cannibalism is usually against the law, courts have sometimes recognized the necessity of consuming human flesh where survival was at issue. Those cases, however, involved only "victims" who had already died of natural causes.

Consent

The defense of consent claims that whatever harm was done occurred only after the injured person gave their permission for the behavior in question. A 1980s trial, for example, saw Robert Chambers plead guilty to first-degree manslaughter in the killing of 18-year-old Jennifer Levin. In what was dubbed "the Preppy Murder Case,"[72] Chambers had claimed Levin died as a result of "rough sex" during which she had tied his hands behind his back and injured his testicles. Other cases, some involving sexual asphyxia (partial suffocation designed to heighten erotic pleasures) and bondage, culminated in a headline in *Time* heralding the era of "The Rough-Sex Defense."[73] The article suggested that such a defense works best with a good-looking defendant who appears remorseful; "[a] hardened type of character...,"[74] said the story, could not effectively use the defense.

In the "condom rapist" case, Joel Valdez was found guilty of rape in 1993 after a jury in Austin, Texas, rejected his claim that the act became consensual once he complied with his victim's request to use a condom. Valdez, who was drunk and armed with a knife at the time of the offense, claimed that his victim's request was a consent to sex. After that, he said, "we were making love."[75]

Resisting Unlawful Arrest

All jurisdictions consider resistance in the face of an unlawful arrest justifiable. Some have statutory provisions detailing the limits imposed on such resistance and the conditions under which it can be used. Such laws generally state that a person may use a reasonable amount of force, other than deadly force, to resist an unlawful arrest or an unlawful search by a law enforcement officer if the officer uses or attempts to use greater force than necessary to make the arrest or search. Such laws are inapplicable in cases where the defendant is the first to resort to force. Deadly force to resist arrest is not justified unless the law enforcement officer resorts to deadly force when it is not called for.

EXCUSES

An excuse, in contrast to a justification, does not claim that the conduct in question is justified by the situation nor that it is moral. An excuse claims, rather, that the actor who engaged in the unlawful behavior was, at the time, not legally responsible for his or her actions and should not be held accountable under the law. So, for example, a person who assaults a police officer thinking that the officer is really a disguised "space alien" who has come to abduct him may be found "not guilty" of the charge of assault and battery by reason of insanity. Actions for which excuses are offered do not morally outweigh the wrong committed, but criminal liability may still be negated on the basis of some personal disability of the actor or because of some special circumstances that characterize the situation. Excuses recognized by the law include: (1) duress, (2) age, (3) mistake, (4) involuntary intoxication, (5) unconsciousness, (6) provocation, (7) insanity, and (8) diminished responsibility.

Duress

Duress is another of the defenses which depends upon an understanding of the situation. Duress has been defined as "any unlawful threat or coercion used by a person to induce another to act (or to refrain from acting) in a manner he or she otherwise would not (or would)."[76] A person may act under duress if, for example, he or she steals an employer's payroll in order to meet a ransom demand for kidnappers holding the person's children. Should the person later be arrested for larceny or embezzlement, the person can claim that he or she felt compelled to commit the crime to help ensure the safety of the children. The defense of duress is sometimes also called coercion. Duress is generally not a useful defense when the crime committed involves serious physical harm, since the harm committed may outweigh the coercive influence in the minds of jurors and judges.

Age

Age offers another kind of excuse in the face of a criminal charge, and the defense of "infancy"—as it is sometimes known in legal jargon—has its roots in the ancient belief that children cannot reason logically until around the age of seven. Early doctrine in the Christian church sanctioned that belief by declaring that rationality develops around the age of seven. As a consequence, only children past that age could be held responsible for their crimes.

The defense of infancy today has been expanded to include people well beyond the age of seven. Many states set the sixteenth birthday as the age at which a person becomes an adult for purposes of criminal prosecution. Others use the age of 17 and still others 18. When a person below the age required for adult prosecution commits a "crime," it is termed a *juvenile offense*. He or she is not guilty of a criminal violation of the law by virtue of youth.

In most jurisdictions, children below the age of seven cannot be charged even with juvenile offenses, no matter how serious their actions may appear to others. However, in a rather amazing 1994 case, prosecutors in Cincinnati, Ohio, charged a 12-year-old girl with murder after she confessed to drowning her toddler cousin 10 years previously. The cousin, 13-month-old Lamar Howell, drowned in 1984 in a bucket of bleach mixed with water. Howell's drowning had been ruled an accidental death until his cousin came forward. In discussing the charges with the media, Hamilton (Ohio) County prosecutor Joe Deters admitted that the girl could not be prosecuted. "Frankly," he said, "anything under seven cannot be an age where you form criminal intent…"[77] The prosecution's goal, claimed one of Deters's associates, was simply to "make sure she gets the counseling she needs."

Mistake

Two types of mistake may serve as a defense. One is mistake of law, and the other is mistake of fact. Rarely is the defense of mistake of law acceptable. Most people realize that it is their responsibility to know the law as it applies to them. "Ignorance of the law is no excuse" is an old dictum still heard today. On occasion, however, humorous cases do arise in which such a defense is accepted by authorities—for example, the instance of the elderly woman who raised marijuana plants because they could be used to make a tea which relieved her arthritis. When her garden was discovered she was not arrested, but advised as to how the law applied to her.

Mistake of fact is a much more useful form of the "mistake" defense. In 1987, Jerry Hall, fashion model and girlfriend of Mick Jagger, a well-known rock star, was arrested in Barbados as she attempted to leave a public airport baggage claim area after picking up a suitcase.[78] The bag contained 20 pounds of marijuana and was under surveillance by officials who were waiting for just such a pickup. Ms. Hall defended herself by arguing that she had mistook the bag for her own, which looked similar. She was released after a night in jail.

Involuntary Intoxication

The claim of involuntary intoxication may form the basis for another excuse defense. Either drugs or alcohol may produce intoxication. Voluntary intoxication itself is rarely a defense to a criminal charge because it is a self-induced condition. It is widely recognized in our legal tradition that an altered mental condition which is the product of voluntary activity cannot be used to exonerate guilty actions which follow from it. Some state statutes formalize this general principle of law and specifically state that voluntary intoxication cannot be offered as a defense to a charge of criminal behavior.[79]

Involuntary intoxication, however, is another matter. On occasion a person may be tricked into consuming an intoxicating substance. Secretly "spiked" punch, popular aphrodisiacs, or LSD-laced desserts all might be ingested unknowingly. A few years ago, for example, the Drug Enforcement Administration reported that a powerful sedative manufactured by Hoffmann-LaRoche Pharmaceuticals and sold under the brand name Rohypnol had become popular with college students and with "young men [who] put doses of Rohypnol in women's drinks without their consent in order to lower their inhibitions."[80] What other behavioral effects the pills, known variously as "roples," "roche," "ruffles," "roofies," and "rophies" on the street, might have is unknown. But a woman secretly drugged with Rohypnol might be able to offer the defense of involuntary intoxication were she to commit a crime while under the influence of the drug.

Because the effects and taste of alcohol are so widely known in our society, the defense of involuntary intoxication due to alcohol consumption can be difficult to demonstrate. A more unusual situation results from a disease caused by the yeast *Candida albicans*, occasionally found living in human intestines. A Japanese physician was the first to identify this disease, in which a person's digestive processes ferment the food they eat. Fermentation turns a portion of the food into alcohol, and people with this condition become intoxicated whenever they eat. First recognized about ten years ago, the disease has not yet been used successfully in this country to support the defense of involuntary intoxication.

Unconsciousness

A very rarely used excuse is that of unconsciousness. An individual cannot be held responsible for anything he or she does while unconscious. Because unconscious people rarely do anything at all, this defense is almost never seen in the courts. However, cases of sleepwalking, epileptic seizure, and neurological dysfunction may result in injurious, although unintentional, actions by people so afflicted. Under such circumstances a defense of unconsciousness might be argued with success.

Provocation

Provocation recognizes that a person can be emotionally enraged by another who intends to elicit just such a reaction. Should they then strike out at their tormentor, some courts have held, they may not be guilty of criminality, or they may be guilty of a lesser degree of criminality than might otherwise be the case. The defense of provocation is commonly used in barroom brawls where a person's parentage may have been called into question, although most states don't look favorably upon verbal provocation alone. It has also been used in some recent spectacular cases where wives have killed their husbands, or children their fathers, citing years of verbal and physical abuse. In these latter instances, perhaps because the degree of physical harm inflicted appears to be out of proportion to the claimed provocation, the defense of provocation has not been as readily accepted by the courts. As a rule, the defense of provocation is generally more acceptable in minor offenses than in serious violations of the law.

Insanity

The defense of insanity has received much attention from the broadcast media, where movies and shows highlighting this defense are commonplace. In practice, however, the defense of insanity is rarely raised. According to a recent eight-state study, which was funded by the National Institute of Mental Health and reported in the *Bulletin of the American Academy of Psychiatry and the Law*,[81] the insanity defense was used in less than 1% of the cases that came before county-level courts. The study showed that only 26% of all insanity pleas were argued successfully and further found that 90% of those who employed the defense had been previously diagnosed with a mental illness. As the American Bar Association says, "[t]he best evidence suggests that the mental nonresponsibility defense is raised in less than one percent of all felony cases in the United States and is successful in about a fourth of these."[82]

It is important to realize that, for purposes of the criminal law, insanity is a legal definition and not a psychiatric one. Legal definitions of insanity often have very little to do with psychological or psychiatric understandings of mental illness. Legal insanity is a concept developed over time to meet the needs of the judicial system in assigning guilt or innocence to particular defendants. It is not primarily concerned with understanding the origins of mental pathology or with its treatment, as is the idea of mental illness in psychiatry. As a consequence, medical conceptions of mental illness do not always fit well into the legal categories created by courts and legislators to deal with the phenomenon. The differences between psychiatric and legal conceptualizations of insanity often lead to disagreements among expert witnesses who, in criminal court, may appear to provide conflicting testimony as to the sanity of a defendant.

The M'Naghten Rule   Prior to the nineteenth century the **insanity defense**, as we know it today, was nonexistent. Insane people who committed crimes were punished in the same way as other law violators. It was **Daniel M'Naghten** (sometimes also spelled McNaughten or M'Naughten), a woodworker from Glasgow, Scotland, who, in 1844, became the first person to be found not guilty of a crime by reason of insanity. M'Naghten had tried to assassinate Sir Robert Peel, the British prime minister. He mistook Edward Drummond, Peel's secretary, for Peel himself, and killed Drummond instead. At his trial, defense attorneys argued that M'Naghten suffered from vague delusions centered on the idea that the Tories, a British political party, were persecuting him. Medical testimony at the trial agreed with the assertion of M'Naghten's lawyers that he didn't know what he was doing at the time of the shooting. The jury accepted M'Naghten's claim, and the insanity defense was born. The M'Naghten rule, as it has come to be called, was not so much a product of the *M'Naghten* trial, however, as it was of a later convocation of English judges assembled by the leadership of the House of Lords in order to define the criteria necessary for a finding of insanity.

The M'Naghten rule holds that *a person is not guilty of a crime if, at the time of the crime, they either didn't know what they were doing, or didn't know that what they were doing was wrong*. The inability to distinguish right from wrong must be the result of some mental defect or disability. The M'Naghten rule is still followed in many U.S. jurisdictions today. However, in most states, the burden of proving insanity falls upon the defendant. Just as defendants are assumed innocent, they are also assumed to be sane at the outset of any criminal trial.

Insanity Defense   A legal defense based on claims of mental illness or mental incapacity.

M'Naghten Rule   A rule for determining insanity which asks whether the defendant knew what he was doing or whether he knew that what he was doing was wrong.

Irresistible Impulse   The M'Naghten rule worked well for a time. Eventually, however, some cases arose in which defendants clearly knew what they were doing, and they knew it was wrong. Even so, they argued in their defense that they couldn't help themselves. They couldn't stop doing that which was wrong. Such people are said to suffer from an irresistible impulse and may be found not guilty by reason of that particular brand of insanity in 18 of the United States. Some states which do not use the irresistible impulse test in determining insanity may still allow the successful demonstration of such an impulse to be considered in sentencing decisions.

In a spectacular 1994 Virginia trial, Lorena Bobbitt successfully employed the irresistible impulse defense against charges of malicious wounding stemming from an incident in which she cut off her husband's penis with a kitchen knife as he slept. The case, which made head-lines around the world, found Bobbitt's defense attorney telling the jury, "what we have is Lorena Bobbitt's life juxtaposed against John Wayne Bobbitt's penis. The evidence will show that in her mind it was his penis from which she could not escape, that caused her the most pain, the most fear, the most humiliation."[83] The impulse to sever the organ, said the lawyer, became irresistible.

The irresistible impulse test has been criticized on a number of grounds. Primary among them is the belief that all of us suffer from compulsions. Most of us, however, learn to con-trol them. Should we give in to a compulsion, the critique goes, then why not just say it was unavoidable so as to escape any legal consequences.

The Durham Rule   A third rule for gauging insanity is called the Durham rule. It was orig-inally created in 1871 by a New Hampshire court and later adopted by Judge David Bazelon in 1954 as he decided the case of *Durham* v. *United States* for the Court of Appeals in the District of Columbia. The Durham rule states that *a person is not criminally responsible for their behavior if their illegal actions were the result of some mental disease or defect.*

Courts which follow the Durham rule will typically hear from an array of psychiatric spe-cialists as to the mental state of the defendant. Their testimony will inevitably be clouded by the need to address the question of cause. A successful defense under the Durham rule neces-sitates that jurors be able to see the criminal activity in question as the *product* of mental deficiencies harbored by the defendant. And, yet, many people who suffer from mental dis-eases or defects never commit crimes. In fact, low IQ, mental retardation, or lack of general mental capacity are not allowable as excuses for criminal behavior. Because the Durham rule is especially vague, it provides fertile grounds for conflicting claims.

The Substantial Capacity Test   Nineteen states follow another guideline—the Substantial Capacity Test—as found in the Model Penal Code of the American Law Institute.[84] Also called the ALI rule or the MPC rule, it suggests that insanity should be defined as the lack of a substantial capacity to control one's behavior. This test requires a judgment to the effect that the defendant either had, or lacked, "the mental capacity needed to understand the wrongfulness of his act or to conform his behavior to the requirements of the law."[85] The Substantial Capacity Test is a blending of the M'Naghten rule with the irresistible impulse standard. "Substantial capacity" does not require total mental incompetence, nor does the rule require the behavior in question to live up to the criterion of total irresistibility. The problem, however, of establishing just what constitutes "substantial mental capacity" has plagued this rule from its conception.

The Brawner Rule   Judge Bazelon, apparently dissatisfied with the application of the Durham rule, created a new criterion for gauging insanity in the 1972 case of *U.S.* v. *Brawner*. The Brawner rule, as it has come to be called, places responsibility for deciding insanity squarely with the jury. Bazelon suggested that the jury should be concerned with whether or not the defendant could be *justly* held responsible for the criminal act in the face of any claims of insanity. Under this proposal, juries are left with few rules to guide them other than their own sense of fairness.

Insanity and Social Reality   The insanity defense originated as a means of recognizing the social reality of mental disease. Unfortunately, the history of this defense has been rife with

Lorena Bobbitt, acquitted in 1994 of charges of malicious wounding, after she admittedly cut off her husband's penis with a razor-sharp kitchen knife as he slept. Ms. Bobbitt's attorneys successfully employed the irresistible impulse defense.
Stephen Jaffe, Reuter/Bettmann

change, contradiction, and uncertainty. Psychiatric testimony is expensive, sometimes costing thousands of dollars per day for one medical specialist. Still worse is the fact that each "expert" is commonly contradicted by another.

Public dissatisfaction with the jumble of rules defining legal insanity peaked in 1982, when John Hinckley was acquitted of trying to assassinate then-President Reagan. At his trial, Hinckley's lawyers claimed that a series of delusions brought about by a history of schizophrenia left him unable to control his behavior. Government prosecutors were unable to counter defense contentions of insanity. The resulting acquittal shocked the nation and resulted in calls for a review of the insanity defense.

One response has been to ban the insanity defense from use at trial. A ruling by the U.S. Supreme Court in support of a Montana law allows states to prohibit defendants from claiming that they were insane at the time they committed their crimes. In 1994, without comment, the high court let stand a Montana Supreme Court ruling which held that eliminating the insanity defense does not violate the U.S. Constitution. Currently, only three states—Montana, Idaho, and Utah—bar use of the insanity defense.[86]

Guilty but Insane In 1997 Pennsylvania multimillionaire John E. du Pont was found **guilty but mentally ill (GBMI)** in the shooting death of former Olympic gold medalist David Schultz during a delusional episode. Although defense attorneys were able to show that du Pont sometimes saw Nazis in his trees, heard the walls talking, and had cut off pieces of his skin to remove bugs from outer space, he was held criminally liable for Schultz's death and sentenced to 13 to 30 years in confinement.

The guilty but mentally ill verdict (in a few states the finding is guilty but insane) is now possible in at least 11 states. It is one form of response to public frustration with the insanity issue. A GBMI verdict means that a person can be held responsible for a specific criminal act even though a degree of mental incompetence may be present in his or her personality. In most GBMI jurisdictions, a jury must return a finding of "guilty but mentally ill" if (1) every element necessary for a conviction has been proven beyond a reasonable doubt, (2) the defendant is found to have been *mentally ill* at the time the crime was committed, and (3) the defendant was *not* found to have been *legally insane* at the time the crime was committed. The difference between mental illness and legal insanity is a crucial

Guilty But Mentally Ill (GBMI) Equivalent to a finding of "guilty," a GBMI verdict establishes that the defendant, although mentally ill, was in sufficient possession of his faculties to be morally blameworthy for his acts.

Multimillionaire eccentric John E. du Pont being taken into custody by SWAT team members at his Newton Square, Pennsylvania, estate in 1996. du Pont shot and killed former Olympic gold medallist David Schultz during a delusional episode, and insanity became an issue at his 1997 murder trial. Although defense attorneys were able to show that du Pont sometimes saw Nazis in his trees, heard the walls talking, and had cut off pieces of his skin to remove bugs from outer space, he was found guilty but mentally ill, and sentenced to serve 13 to 30 years in confinement. *Jim Graham, AP/Wide World Photos*

If a married woman shall be caught lying with another man, both shall be bound and thrown into the river.

—Code of Hammurabi

one, since a defendant can be mentally ill by standards of the medical profession but sane for purposes of the law.

Upon return of a GBMI verdict, a judge may impose any sentence possible under the law for the crime in question. Mandated psychiatric treatment, however, will often be part of the commitment order. The offender, once cured, will usually be placed in the general prison population to serve any remaining sentence.

As some authors have observed, the legal possibility of a guilty but mentally ill finding has three purposes: "[F]irst, to protect society; second, to hold some offenders who were mentally ill accountable for their criminal acts; (and) third, to make treatment available to convicted offenders suffering from some form of mental illness."[87]

In 1975 Michigan became the first state to pass a "guilty but mentally ill" statute, permitting a GBMI finding[88]—and the movement toward GBMI verdicts continues today among state legislatures. The U.S. Supreme Court case of *Ford* v. *Wainwright*, however, recognized an issue of a different sort.[89] The 1986 decision specified that prisoners who become insane while incarcerated cannot be executed. Hence, although insanity may not always be a successful defense to criminal prosecution, it can later become a block to the ultimate punishment.

Temporary Insanity   Temporary insanity is another possible defense against a criminal charge. Widely used in the 1940s and 1950s, temporary insanity meant that the offender claimed to be insane only at the time of the commission of the offense. If a jury agreed, the defendant virtually went free. The suspect was not guilty of the criminal action by virtue of having been insane and could not be ordered to undergo psychiatric counseling or treatment because the insanity was no longer present. This type of plea has become less popular as legislatures have regulated the circumstances under which it can be made.

The Insanity Defense Under Federal Law   In 1984 the U.S. Congress passed the federal Insanity Defense Reform Act (IDRA). The act created major revisions in the federal insanity defense. Insanity under the law is now defined as a condition in which the defendant can be shown to have been suffering under a "severe mental disease or defect" and, as a result, "was unable to appreciate the nature and quality or the wrongfulness of his acts."[90] This definition of insanity comes close to that set forth in the old M'Naghten rule.

The act also places the burden of proving the insanity defense squarely on the defendant—a provision which has been challenged a number of times since the act was passed. Such a requirement was supported by the Supreme Court prior to the act's passage. In 1983, in the case of *Jones* v. *U.S.* (1983),[91] the Court ruled that defendants can be required to prove their insanity when it becomes an issue in their defense. Shortly after the act became law, the Court in *Ake* v. *Oklahoma* (1985),[92] held that the government must assure access to a competent psychiatrist whenever a defendant indicates that insanity will be an issue at trial.

Consequences of an Insanity Ruling   The insanity defense today is not an "easy way out" of criminal prosecution, as some have assumed. Once a verdict of "not guilty by reason of insanity" is returned, the judge may order the defendant to undergo psychiatric treatment until cured. Because psychiatrists are reluctant to declare any potential criminal "cured," such a sentence may result in more time spent in an institution than would have resulted from a prison sentence. In *Foucha* v. *Louisiana*, 504 U.S. 71 (1992),[93] however, the U.S. Supreme Court held that a defendant found not guilty by reason of insanity in a criminal trial could not thereafter be institutionalized indefinitely without a showing that he or she was either dangerous or mentally ill.

Diminished Capacity

The defense of **diminished capacity**, also called diminished responsibility, is available in some jurisdictions. However, "the terms 'diminished responsibility' and 'diminished capacity' do not have a clearly accepted meaning in the courts."[94] Some defendants who offer diminished capacity defenses do so in recognition of the fact that such claims may be based on a mental condition which would not qualify as mental disease or mental defect nor be sufficient to support the defense of insanity—but which might still lower criminal culpability. According to Peter Arenella, "the defense [of diminished responsibility] was first recognized by Scottish common law courts to reduce the punishment of the 'partially insane' from murder to culpable homicide, a non-capital offense."[95]

The diminished capacity defense is similar to the defense of insanity in that it depends upon a showing that the defendant's mental state was impaired at the time of the crime. As a defense, diminished capacity is most useful where it can be shown that, because of some defect of reason or mental shortcoming, the defendant's capacity to form the *mens rea* required by a specific crime was impaired. Unlike an insanity defense, however, which can result in a finding of "not guilty," a diminished capacity defense is built upon the recognition that "[m]ental condition, though insufficient to exonerate, may be relevant to specific mental elements of certain crimes or degrees of crime."[96] So, for example, defendants might present evidence of mental abnormality in an effort to reduce first-degree murder to second-degree murder or second-degree murder to manslaughter when a killing occurs under extreme emotional disturbance. Similarly, in some jurisdictions very low intelligence will, if proved, serve to reduce first-degree murder to manslaughter.[97]

As is the case with the insanity defense, some jurisdictions have entirely eliminated the diminished capacity defense. The California Penal Code, for example, provides: "The defense of diminished capacity is hereby abolished…,"[98] and adds that "[a]s a matter of public policy there shall be no defense of diminished capacity, diminished responsibility, or irresistible impulse in a criminal action or juvenile adjudication hearing."[99]

PROCEDURAL DEFENSES

Procedural defenses make the claim that defendants were in some manner discriminated against in the justice process or that some important aspect of official procedure was not properly followed and that, as a result, they should be released from any criminal liability. The procedural defenses we shall discuss here are (1) entrapment, (2) double jeopardy, (3) *collateral estoppel*, (4) selective prosecution, (5) denial of a speedy trial, (6) prosecutorial misconduct, and (7) police fraud.

Diminished Capacity (also **Diminished Responsibility**) A defense based upon claims of a mental condition which may be insufficient to exonerate a defendant of guilt but that may be relevant to specific mental elements of certain crimes or degrees of crime.

Members of the New York City Police Department's Street Crimes Unit prepare for a day's work. Entrapment will likely not be an effective defense for muggers who attack these decoys. *Courtesy of the New York City Police Department*

Entrapment

Entrapment An improper or illegal inducement to crime by agents of enforcement. Also, a defense that may be raised when such inducements occur.

Entrapment, which can be defined as an improper or illegal inducement to crime by agents of enforcement, is a defense which limits the enthusiasm with which police officers may enforce the law. Entrapment defenses argue that enforcement agents effectively create a crime where there would otherwise have been none. For entrapment to have occurred, the idea for the criminal activity must have originated with official agents of the criminal justice system. Entrapment can also result when overzealous undercover police officers convince a defendant that the contemplated law-violating behavior is not a crime. In order to avoid claims of entrapment, officers must not engage in activity that would cause a person to commit a crime that he or she would not otherwise commit. Merely providing an opportunity for a willing offender to commit a crime, however, is *not* entrapment.

Entrapment was claimed in the still-famous case of automaker John DeLorean. DeLorean was arrested on October 19, 1982, by federal agents near the Los Angeles airport.[100] An FBI videotape, secretly made at the scene, showed him allegedly "dealing" with undercover agents and holding packets of cocaine, which he said were "better than gold." DeLorean was charged with narcotics smuggling violations involving a large amount of drugs.

At his 1984 trial, DeLorean claimed that he had been "set up" by the police to commit a crime which he would not have been involved in were it not for their urging. DeLorean's auto company had fallen upon hard times, and he was facing heavy debts. Federal agents, acting undercover, proposed to DeLorean a plan whereby he could make a great deal of money through drugs. Because the idea originated with the police, not with DeLorean, and because DeLorean was able to demonstrate successfully that he was repeatedly threatened not to "pull out" of the deal by a police informant, the jury returned a "not guilty" verdict.

The concept of entrapment is well summarized in a statement made by DeLorean's defense attorney to *Time* before the trial: "This is a fictitious crime. Without the Government there would be no crime. This is one of the most insidious and misguided law-enforcement operations in history."[101]

Double Jeopardy

The Fifth Amendment to the U.S. Constitution makes it clear that no person may be tried twice for the same offense. People who have been acquitted or found innocent may not be again put in "jeopardy of life or limb" for the same crime. The same is true of those who have been convicted: They cannot be tried again for the same offense. Cases that are dismissed for a lack of evidence also come under the double jeopardy rule and cannot result in a new trial. The U.S. Supreme Court has ruled that "the Double Jeopardy Clause protects against three distinct abuses: a second prosecution for the same offense after acquittal; a second prosecution for the same offense after conviction; and multiple punishments for the same offense."[102]

Double jeopardy does not apply in cases of trial error. Hence, convictions which are set aside because of some error in proceedings at a lower court level (for example, inappropriate instructions to the jury by the trial court judge) will permit a retrial on the same charges. Similarly, when a defendant's motion for a mistrial is successful, or members of the jury cannot agree upon a verdict (resulting in a "hung jury"), a second trial may be held.

Defendants, however, may be tried in both federal and state courts without necessarily violating the principle of double jeopardy. For example, 33-year-old Rufina Canedo pleaded guilty to possession of 50 kilograms of cocaine in 1991 and received a six-year prison sentence in a California court.[103] Federal prosecutors, however, indicted her again—this time under a federal law—for the same offense. They offered her a deal—testify against her husband or face federal prosecution and the possibility of 20 years in a federal prison. Because state and federal statutes emanate from different jurisdictions, this kind of dual prosecution has been held constitutional by the U.S. Supreme Court. To prevent abuse, the U.S. Justice Department acted in 1960 to restrict federal prosecution in such cases to situations involving a "compelling federal interest"—such as civil rights violations. However, in recent years, in the face of soaring drug law violations, the restriction has been relaxed.

In 1992, in another drug case, the U.S. Supreme Court ruled that the double jeopardy clause of the U.S. Constitution "only prevents duplicative prosecution for the same offense," but that "a substantive offense and a conspiracy to commit that offense are not the same offense for double jeopardy purposes." In that case, *U.S.* v. *Felix* (1992),[104] a Missouri man was convicted in that state of manufacturing methamphetamine and then convicted again in Oklahoma of the "separate crime" of conspiracy to manufacture a controlled substance—in part based upon his activities in Missouri. Similarly, because civil and criminal law differ as to purpose, it is possible to try someone in civil court to collect damages for a possible violation of civil law even though they have been found "not guilty" in criminal court, without violating the principle of double jeopardy. The well-known 1996–1997 California civil trial of O.J. Simpson on grounds of wrongful death resulted in widespread publicity of just such a possibility.

Collateral Estoppel

Collateral estoppel is similar to double jeopardy and applies to facts that have been determined by a "valid and final judgment."[105] Such facts cannot become the object of new litigation. Where a defendant, for example, has been acquitted of a multiple murder charge by virtue of an alibi, it would not be permissible to try that person again for the murder of a second person killed along with the first.

Selective Prosecution

The procedural defense of selective prosecution is based upon the Fourteenth Amendment's guarantee of equal protection of the laws. The defense may be available where two or more individuals are suspected of criminal involvement, but not all are actively prosecuted. Selective prosecution based fairly upon the strength of available evidence is not the object of this defense. But when prosecution proceeds unfairly on the basis of some arbitrary and discriminatory attribute, such as race, sex, friendship, age, or religious preference, protection may be feasible under it. In 1996, however, in a case that reaffirmed reasonable limits on claims of selective prosecution, the U.S. Supreme Court ruled that for a defendant to successfully "claim that he was singled out for prosecution on the basis of his race, he must make a…showing that the Government declined to prosecute similarly situated suspects of other races."[106]

Double Jeopardy A common law and constitutional prohibition against a second trial for the same offense.

Denial of Speedy Trial

The Sixth Amendment to the Constitution guarantees a right to a speedy trial. The purpose of the guarantee is to prevent unconvicted and potentially innocent people from languishing in jail. The federal government[107] and most states have laws (generally referred to as "speedy trial acts") that define the time limit necessary for a trial to be "speedy" and generally set a reasonable period, such as 90 or 120 days following arrest. Excluded from the counting procedure are delays which result from requests by the defense to prepare their case. If the limit set by law is exceeded, the defendant must be set free and no trial can occur.

Some legal experts expect speedy trial claims to be raised by defense attorneys in the case of Byron De La Beckwith, the unrepentant 75-year-old white supremacist who was recently convicted of the murder of black civil rights leader Medgar Evers in Mississippi in 1963. More than 30 years after the killing Beckwith was sentenced to life in prison, but only after two previous trials ended in hung juries.

Prosecutorial Misconduct

Another procedural defense may be found in prosecutorial misconduct. Generally speaking, prosecutorial misconduct is a term used by legal scholars to describe actions undertaken by prosecutors which give the government an unfair advantage or that prejudice the rights of a defendant or witness. Prosecutors are expected to uphold the highest ethical standards in the performance of their roles. When they knowingly permit false testimony, when they hide information that would clearly help the defense, or when they make unduly biased statements to the jury in closing arguments, the defense of prosecutorial misconduct may be available to the defendant.

The most famous instance of prosecutorial misconduct in recent history may have occurred during a convoluted 17-year-long federal case against former Cleveland autoworker John Demjanjuk. Demjanjuk, who was accused of committing war crimes as the notorious Nazi guard "Ivan the Terrible," was extradited in 1986 by the federal government to Israel to face charges there. In late 1993, however, the 6th U.S. Circuit Court of Appeals in Cincinnati, Ohio, ruled that federal prosecutors, working under what the court called a "win-at-any-cost" attitude, had intentionally withheld evidence which might have exonerated Demjanjuk (who was stripped of his U.S. citizenship when extradited, but later returned to the U.S. after the Supreme Court of Israel overturned his sentence there).[108]

No person shall be…twice put in jeopardy of life or limb…

—The Fifth Amendment to the U.S. Constitution

Police Fraud

During the 1995 double-murder trial of O. J. Simpson, defense attorneys suggested the possibility that evidence against Simpson may have been concocted and even planted by police officers with a personal dislike of the defendant. In particular, defense attorneys pointed the finger at Los Angeles police department detective Mark Fuhrman, suggesting that he may have planted a bloody glove at the Simpson estate and tampered with blood stain evidence taken from the infamous white Ford Bronco Simpson was known to drive. To support allegations that Fuhrman was motivated by racist leanings, defense attorneys subpoenaed tapes Fuhrman made over a ten-year period with a North Carolina screenwriter who had been documenting life within the LAPD.

As one observer put it, however, the defense of police fraud builds upon extreme paranoia about the government and police agencies. This type of defense, said Francis Fukuyama, carries "to extremes a distrust of government and the belief that public authorities are in a vast conspiracy to violate the rights of individuals."[109] It can also be extremely unfair to innocent people, for a strategy of this sort subjects what may otherwise be well-meaning public servants to intense public scrutiny, effectively shifting attention away from criminal defendants and onto them—sometimes with disastrous personal results. Anthony Pellicano, a private investigator hired by Fuhrman's lawyers, put it this way: "His life right now is in the toilet. He has no job, no future. People think he's a racist. He can't do anything to help himself. He's been ordered not to talk. His family and friends, he's told them not to get involved…Mark Fuhrman's life is ruined. For what? Because he found a key piece of evidence."[110] The 43-year-old Furhman retired from police work before the Simpson trial concluded.

INNOVATIVE DEFENSES

In recent years some innovative defense strategies have been employed, with varying degrees of success, in criminal cases—and it is to these that we now turn our attention. Technically speaking, the defenses listed here can be properly subsumed under the broader categories of justifications or excuses. They are discussed as a separate group, however, because each is virtually new and relatively untried. The unique and emerging character of these novel defenses, however, makes discussing them worthwhile. The innovative defenses discussed in the next few pages include: (1) the abuse defense, (2) premenstrual stress syndrome, (3) other biological defenses, (4) black rage, and (5) urban survival syndrome.

The Abuse Defense

One innovative defense which seems to be gaining in popularity with defense attorneys today, especially in murder cases, is that of abuse. Actually, the abuse defense is not new, having evolved from domestic abuse cases in the 1970s, which emphasized the inability of some battered women to escape from the demeaning situations surrounding them. **Battered woman's syndrome** (BWS), involving long-term abuse, was said to effectively prevent women from seeking divorce and, in some cases, to drive women temporarily insane—turning them into killers of their abusive spouses. BWS, sometimes also referred to as "battered spouse syndrome" or "battered person's syndrome," entered contemporary awareness with the 1979 publication of Lenore Walker's book, *The Battered Woman*.[111] Defense attorneys were quick to use Walker's slogan of "learned helplessness" to explain why battered women were unable to leave abusive situations and why they sometimes found it necessary to resort to violence in order to free themselves from it. Early versions of the abuse defense depended upon its link to the more traditional defenses of insanity and self-defense. As judges and juries increasingly accepted such defenses, however, "attorneys began to use similar arguments to defend not only wives, but also homosexual lovers, and then children, husbands, and a slew of other accused criminals."[112]

The abuse defense attempts to turn the tables on criminal prosecutors by claiming that chronic abuse sufferers may have to defend themselves at times when their abusers are most vulnerable—such as when they are asleep or otherwise distracted. This kind of argument is more frequently offered where the "victim" is weaker than the abuser, as in the case of women and children said to be abused by men.

Aspects of the abuse defense could be seen in the trials of Lorena Bobbitt, discussed earlier in this chapter, who was acquitted on charges of malicious wounding after admitting she severed her husband's penis with a kitchen knife, and Lyle and Erik Menendez, brothers whose first trial on charges of murdering their parents ended in hung juries after their attorneys claimed the boys' actions were the results of a lifetime of sexual abuse at the hands of their father. In 1996, in a second trial, however, the Menendez brothers were convicted of the murders of their parents, and sentenced to life imprisonment without parole.[113]

Some observers of the American scene say that jurors in today's society are especially sympathetic to abuse victims who act out their frustrations through crime. New York attorney Ronald L. Kuby says, for example, "One of the salutary effects of the pop psychology boom of the 1970s is that people increasingly ask, 'How did I end up like this and what can I do about it.'"[114] Popular television talk shows have probably also played a part in sensitizing people to the role of personal and family tragedies in people's lives. As a consequence, people everywhere may be ready to excuse criminal culpability if they can be shown its roots in a given situation. Southwestern University Law School professor Robert Pugsley puts it this way: "We are entering the age of the empathetic or sympathetic jury that is willing to turn the courtroom into the Oprah [Winfrey] or Phil [Donahue] show."[115]

Not everyone is enamored with the willingness of juries to consider the abuse defense, however. Los Angeles Deputy District Attorney Kathleen Cady, for example, recently saw Moosa Hanoukai convicted of voluntary manslaughter rather than first-degree murder as Cady had hoped. Hanoukai had beaten his wife to death with a wrench, but attorneys claimed he killed her because she made him sleep on the floor, called him names, and paid him a small allowance for work he did around the house. Jurors were told that Hanoukai, whose Jewish background prevented divorce, had been psychologically emasculated by his overbearing wife.

Battered Woman's Syndrome (BWS) A series of common characteristics that appear in women who are abused physically and psychologically over an extended period of time by the dominant male figure in their lives; a pattern of psychological symptoms that develop after somebody has lived in a battering relationship; or a pattern of responses and perceptions presumed to be characteristic of women who have been subjected to continuous physical abuse by their mates.

But, as Cady puts it, "Every single murderer has a reason why they killed someone…I think it sends a very frightening message to the rest of society that all you have to do is come up with some kind of excuse when you commit a crime."[116] Even a history of abuse, others say, should not be a license to kill.

Even so, the long-term trend may favor those with an abuse defense available to them. James Blatt, the attorney who defended Hanoukai says, "I think the trend is, if you can show legitimate psychological abuse over a prolonged period of time, then be prepared for a jury's reaction to that…. Whether a lot of people like it or not, it may become an inherent part of American jurisprudence."[117]

Premenstrual Stress Syndrome

The use of premenstrual stress syndrome (PMS) as a defense against criminal charges is very new and demonstrates how changing social conceptions and advancing technology may modify the way in which courts view illegal behavior. In 1980 British courts heard the case of Christine English, who killed her live-in lover when he threatened to leave her. An expert witness at the trial testified that English had been the victim of PMS for more than a decade. The witness, Dr. Katharina Dalton, advanced the claim that PMS had rendered Ms. English "irritable, aggressive…and confused, with loss of self-control."[118] The jury, apparently accepting the claim, returned a verdict of "not guilty."

PMS is not an officially acceptable defense in American criminal courts. However, in 1991 a Fairfax, Virginia, judge dismissed drunk-driving charges against a woman who cited the role PMS played in her behavior.[119] The woman, an orthopedic surgeon named Dr. Geraldine Richter, admitted to drinking four glasses of wine and allegedly kicked and cursed a state trooper who stopped her car because it was weaving down the road. A Breathalyzer test showed a blood-alcohol level of 0.13%—higher than the 0.10% needed to meet the requirement for drunk driving under Virginia law. But a gynecologist who testified on Dr. Richter's behalf said that the behavior she exhibited is characteristic of PMS. "I guess this is a new trend," said the state's attorney in commenting on the judge's ruling.

Other Biological Defenses

In all criminal prosecutions, the accused shall enjoy the right to a speedy and public trial, by an impartial jury…

—The Sixth Amendment to the U.S. Constitution

Modern nutritional science appears to be on the verge of establishing a new category of defense related to "chemical imbalances" in the human body produced by eating habits. Vitamins, food allergies, the consumption of stimulants (including coffee and nicotine), and the excessive ingestion of sugar all will probably soon be advanced by attorneys in defense of their clients.

The case of Dan White provides an example of this new direction in the development of innovative defenses.[120] In 1978, White, a former San Francisco police officer, walked into the office of Mayor Moscone and shot both the mayor and City Councilman Harvey Milk to death. It was established at the trial that White had spent the night before the murders drinking Coca-Cola and eating Twinkies, a packaged pastry. Expert witnesses testified that the huge amounts of sugar consumed by White prior to the crime substantially altered his judgment and ability to control his behavior. The jury, influenced by the expert testimony, convicted White of a lesser charge, and he served a short prison sentence.

The strategy used by White's lawyers has come to be known as the "Twinkie defense." It may well be characteristic of future defense strategies now being developed in cases across the nation.

Black Rage

The defense of "black rage" originated with the multiple-murder trial of Colin Ferguson, who was charged with killing six passengers and wounding 19 others in what authorities described as "a racially motivated attack" on the Long Island Rail Road in December 1993. In preparation for trial Ferguson's original attorneys, William Kunstler and Ronald Kuby, had planned to argue that Ferguson, who is black, was overcome by rage resulting from societywide mistreatment of blacks by whites. (All the victims in the shooting spree initiated by Ferguson were either white or Asian.)

Kunstler suggested that the "black rage" defense is fundamentally a claim of insanity. "We are mounting a traditional insanity defense, long recognized in our law, with 'black rage'

Colin Ferguson conducting his own defense. Ferguson, who rejected attorneys recommendations that he employ an innovative "black rage" defense, was convicted in 1995 of killing six people and wounding 19 others in a racially motivated shooting aboard a Long Island Rail Road commuter train. *Dick Kraus, Pool/AP/Wide World Photos*

triggering last December's massacre,"[121] Kunstler and Kuby wrote in a letter to *The New York Times.* "Without a psychiatric defense, Colin has no defense," Kunstler was quoted as saying.[122] "There was no doubt that he was there, that he fired the weapon, that he would have fired it more if he had not been wrestled to the ground. There is no doubt that Colin Ferguson, if sane, was guilty," said Kunstler.

Ferguson eventually rejected the recommendation of Kuby and Kunstler that he plead not guilty by reason of insanity caused by "black rage" at racial injustice. After conducting his own defense, in what some called a mockery of an accused's right to act as his own attorney, Ferguson was convicted of all the charges against him. Ferguson had maintained his innocence throughout the trial, despite the fact he was identified by more than a dozen eyewitnesses, including some he had shot.

Urban Survival Syndrome

A few years ago, in a Fort Worth, Texas, murder case, a mistrial was declared after jurors deadlocked over lawyers' claims that their client, 18-year-old Daimion Osby, had killed two men because he suffered from "urban survival syndrome." Although Osby admitted to shooting both unarmed men in the head in a downtown parking lot, his attorneys told jurors that he had simply staged a preemptive strike against vicious people who had been threatening him for a year.

Jurors in Osby's trial heard defense attorneys argue that urban survival syndrome is a predilection to engage in violence in order to prevent oneself from being victimized—a kind of "shoot first, ask questions later" response to the growing violence now so characteristic of many American inner cities. Lawyers described the syndrome as "a sort of mind fix that comes over a young black male living in an urban neighborhood when he's been threatened with deadly force by another black male."[123] "For young blacks to take into account what they see happening in their own neighborhoods is not being racist," said David Bays, one of Osby's lawyers. "It's being realistic." Osby, said his lawyers, had been scared into a state of "hypervigilance," convinced that he had no alternative but to kill in order to ensure his own

LAPD detective Mark Fuhrman undergoes questioning by F. Lee Bailey during the double-murder trial of O. J. Simpson. Allegations of racism and police misconduct swirled around Fuhrman both during and after the trial. *AFP, Vince Bucci, Bettmann*

Visit the *CJToday* Web page and click on "Web Chapters," then "Chapter 4." Follow the "find the facts" links in order to explore current state and federal statutes, the U.S. Constitution, and law-related links.

survival. Recently, however, Osby was tried again. This time jurors rejected urban survival syndrome as a defense. Osby was convicted and sentenced to life in prison.[124]

As one commentator on the new defense put it, "I certainly don't like the idea of using some syndrome to get someone off a murder beef. But I've met enough people who use bathtubs as bulletproof beds to know that urban survival syndrome is real. How long can people live in fear before they snap?"[125]

A similar defense, that of "urban fear syndrome," was used in the 1995 murder trial of Nathaniel Hurt. Hurt, 62, fired a .357 Magnum revolver at teenagers, killing a 13-year-old, after young people had repeatedly trashed his yard and thrown rocks at his car. His attorneys claimed that Hurt snapped under the strain of constant harassment from inner-city thugs and that his murderous reaction was excusable because he lived in constant fear. Hurt was convicted of lesser charges after the judge in the case limited application of the defense by ruling that the syndrome claimed by Hurt's lawyers was not "medically recognized."[126]

The Future of Innovative Defenses

Future years will no doubt hold many surprises for students of the criminal law as defense attorneys become ever more willing to experiment with innovative tactics. As David Rosenhan, a professor of law and psychology at Stanford University, explains it: "We're getting to see some very, very interesting things, and obviously some long shots…There are a terrific number of them."[127] To make his case, Rosenhan points to a number of situations where people who didn't file income taxes escaped IRS prosecution by arguing that traumatic life experiences gave them an aversion to forms—a condition their legal counselors termed "failure to file syndrome." Some defenses to even very serious charges seem to border on the ludicrous. In 1995, for example, the state of Texas executed John Fearance, Jr., 40, for stabbing a man 19 times during a burglary, killing him while the man's spouse watched. In his defense, Fearance had claimed that he was temporarily insane at the time of the burglary-murder, saying his "wife had baked a meat casserole" for dinner on the night of the crimes and he "likes his meat served separately."[128]

Justice in American Context

RACE ANd JUSTICE: AMERICAN ATTITUDES
IN THE WAKE OF THE O. J. SIMPSON TRIALS

The 1995 double-murder trial of O. J. Simpson was watched almost daily for a year by millions on television throughout the world. Countless others read about it in newspapers and magazines or heard about it over the radio. The Simpson trial was truly *the* megamedia event of the late twentieth century. Its sudden and dramatic close, with "not guilty" verdicts on October 3, 1995, sent social and political reverberations throughout the United States which are still being felt. At the conclusion of the trial, however, it was easy to discern a huge gap between the attitudes of white Americans and African-Americans toward the criminal justice system.

Many whites remained firmly convinced that Simpson was guilty and felt he should have been convicted. The "not guilty" verdicts (one verdict for each person Simpson was charged with killing) and his subsequent release, some felt, were a travesty of justice. This remark, which came across an on-line service shortly after the verdict was read, sums up what many whites felt at the time: "A sense of sadness overwhelms me. And I am not the only one. You can feel it all over the...building where I work...It just doesn't feel like justice." Some whites claimed that Simpson had been found "not guilty by reason of race."

A large proportion of the nation's blacks, on the other hand, celebrated Simpson's acquittal—seeing in the verdicts a triumph over racism and a vindication of the deep distrust many in the black community feel toward the justice system in this country. Reflecting on the Simpson trial, one black man put it this way: "Whether he's innocent or guilty, let him go—I think that's the way a lot of black people are feeling...."[1]

The finding by a California civil jury in 1997 that Simpson was "responsi-

ble" for the death of Goldman and the "battery" of his ex-wife, Nicole—and the jury's decision that Simpson should pay $33.5 million to the victim's families—intensified disagreement over the purpose of the American justice system and raised other questions. How could a person be acquitted in a criminal trial, some asked, and still be held financially responsible in a civil trial?

Central to the controversy were strong feelings aroused in many black Americans by charges of racism leveled against key prosecution witnesses in the criminal trial—especially LAPD Detective Mark Fuhrman. Fuhrman, a white police investigator, had gathered much of the crucial evidence against Simpson—including a bloody glove collected from a walkway at Simpson's estate. In a well-planned strategy, defense attorneys in the criminal trial were able to show that Fuhrman had lied on the stand about having repeatedly referred to black people as "niggers" during the course of his police career. While many whites saw such a revelation as irrelevant to the facts of the case, it may have convinced the mostly black jury that a racist cop could not be trusted to testify truthfully about other matters. Once Fuhrman had been successfully portrayed as a racist, it became easy for black jurors to conclude that he might have planted evidence or lied about critical issues in a case involving a black man accused of murdering a white woman and a white man.

For many black people, once the specter of racial discrimination had been raised, the underlying issue in the Simpson criminal trial became one of social justice rather than criminal justice. As one writer put it, "The Fuhrman factor evoked a powerful story in the African-American experi-

ence: of the black man fighting a system that's rigged against him. So when blacks applauded the verdict, many were cheering less for the literal event than its allegorical significance—for a different ending to the story."[2]

Some analysts suggested that the successful portrayal of Detective Mark Fuhrman as a racist by the Simpson criminal defense team effectively decided the trial. It may have been all that was needed for a jury with 9 (out of 12) black members to return a "not guilty" verdict—regardless of the apparent strength of the evidence. A public opinion poll taken just before the verdict, but after Fuhrman had been cast as a racist, showed that 77% of whites surveyed thought Simpson was guilty, but that 72% of black respondents said he was innocent.[3]

When the Simpson defense played "the race card" during the criminal trial, it built upon a distrust of the police and of the criminal justice system among African-Americans which runs deep. Recent surveys, for example, show that only 33% of black people in this country believe that police officers testify truthfully, and only 18% of blacks say they would believe a police officer over other witnesses in a criminal trial.[4] John Mack, the black president of the Los Angeles Urban League, explained that while many whites have "a user friendly relationship" with police, many black people—especially young ones—have come to distrust the police because law enforcement officers are prone to viewing them and their activities suspiciously.

Such distrust, it should be noted, can have a significant impact on the entire criminal justice process, wielding influence far beyond that of a single trial—even a highly publicized one. "Increasingly," observed a *Wall Street*

Journal article[5] published shortly after the Simpson verdict, "jury watchers are concluding that...race plays a far more significant role in jury verdicts than many people involved in the justice system prefer to acknowledge." "The willingness of many blacks...to side with African-American defendants against a mostly white-dominated justice system is a relatively new phenomenon with specific roots and ramifications," said the *Journal*.

The tenacity of those roots, some say, are founded in a realistic distrust of the justice system ingrained into the subculture of black Americans by years of experience with a system which was often biased against them. Others say that such verdicts merely reflect informal social understandings within the black community. Some jurors, for example, may simply feel that there are already too many blacks in prison, while others may not believe that prison will do any good—even though they know a suspect is guilty.

Defense attorney Johnnie Cochran echoed such sentiments near the close of the Simpson criminal trial when he told reporters that African-Americans shouldn't avoid jury summonses because their voices are needed to combat racism at all levels of the justice system.[6] "You go and you serve on jury duty," Cochran told a nearly all-black audience. "Nobody is going to save us but us." Many black jurors seem to be taking Cochran's

message to heart. In the Bronx, a New York City borough, for example, where juries are often composed mostly of African-Americans, the acquittal rate for black defendants in felony cases is nearly three times greater than the national average.[7]

Unfortunately, the Simpson verdicts in both the criminal and civil trials, and the black-white differences they revealed, may have fed a long-standing racial divide that many had thought was beginning to heal. Following the verdict in the criminal trial, 53% of blacks and 77% of whites interviewed in a *USA Today* poll said that the trial had done more to hurt race relations than to help them. The consequences of the Simpson trials for the justice system, however, may ultimately transcend racial lines. A survey conducted after the criminal trial found a large proportion of both blacks and whites reporting a heightened distrust of the justice system—and especially of police officers and defense attorneys. Echoing that feeling, a *Newsweek* article said that the problem in today's justice system is not differing attitudes among the races, but the uniquely American "license that we give lawyers to engage in truth-defending distortion and trickery at trial."[8]

What lasting changes the Simpson trials may have wrought in American criminal and civil justice are difficult to discern. However, as Georgetown

University Law School professor Paul Rothstein put it, one thing is certain: "Whites have had an unrealistic view of how perfect things function. Minorities...have had an unrealistic view of how badly they function."[9] The Simpson trials have probably made attitudes on both sides of the racial divide more realistic—and if they have done that they may serve us all well in the long run.

[1]"Nation Seeing Simpson Case in Black and White," The Associated Press, October 1, 1995.

[2]Mark Whitaker, "Whites v. Blacks," *Newsweek*, October 16, 1995, p. 34.

[3]"Nation Seeing Simpson Case in Black and White."

[4]Maria Puente, "Poll: Blacks' Confidence in Police Plummets," *USA Today, March 21, 1995, p. 3A.*

[5]Benjamin A. Holden, Laurie P. Cohen, and Eleena de Lisser, "'Color Blinded' Race Seems to Play an Increasing Role in Many Jury Verdicts," *The Wall Street Journal*, October 4, 1995, p. 1A.

[6]"Cochran," The Associated Press wire services, September 23, 1995.

[7]Holden, Cohen, and Lisser, "Color Blinded," p. 1A.

[8]John H. Langhein, "Money Talks, Clients Walk," *Newsweek,* April 17, 1995, p. 32.

[9]Joe Urschel, "74% Say O. J. Verdict Hurt Racial Ties," *USA Today,* October 9, 1995, p. 1A.

The number of new and innovative defenses being tried on juries and judges today is staggering. Some attribute the phenomenon to what they call "creative lawyering." Others, like Kent Scheidegger of the Criminal Justice Legal Foundation, calls most such defenses "outrageous." They're the tactics of lawyers "who have nothing left to argue," Scheidegger says.[129] He includes defenses like those of 37-year-old Michael Ricksgers, a Pennsylvania man who argued that sleep apnea (a disorder that causes irregular breathing during sleep) led him to pick up a .357-caliber Magnum and kill his wife; and Edward Kelly, who says he's not guilty of rape because the crime was committed by one of his 30 personalities and not by him. Ricksgers was convicted of first-degree murder in 1995, while Kelly's case is still pending.

In an insightful article,[130] Stephen J. Morse, an expert in psychiatry and the law, says that American criminal justice is now caught in the grips of a "new syndrome excuse syndrome"—meaning that new excuses are being offered on an almost daily basis for criminal activity. Many of these "excuses" are documented in the psychiatric literature as "syndromes" or conditions, and include antisocial personality disorder, posttraumatic stress disorder, intermittent explosive disorder, kleptomania, pathological gambling, postconcussional disorder, caffeine withdrawal, and premenstrual dysphoric disorder (discussed earlier as premenstrual stress syndrome). All these conditions are listed in the American Psychiatric Association's authoritative *Diagnostic and Statistical Manual of Mental Disorders*.[131] Emerging defenses, says Morse, include battered women's syndrome, Vietnam syndrome, child sexual abuse syndrome, Holocaust survivor syndrome, urban survival syndrome, rotten social background syndrome, and adopted child syndrome. "Courts," says Morse, "are increasingly inundated with claims that syndromes old and new, validated and unvalidated, should be the basis for two types of legal change:" (1) the creation of new defenses to a criminal charge and (2) "the expansion of old defenses: for example, loosening objective standards for justifications such as self-defense." Morse says that the new syndromes tend to work as defenses because they describe personal abnormalities, and most people are willing to accept abnormalities as "excusing conditions that bear on the accused's responsibility." The mistake, says Morse, is to think "that if we identify a cause for conduct, including mental or physical disorders, then the conduct is necessarily excused." "Causation," he cautions, "is not an excuse," only an explanation for the behavior.

Even so, attempts to offer novel defenses which are intended to convince jurors that even admitted criminal offenders should not be held responsible for their actions are becoming increasingly characteristic of the American way of justice. Whether such strategies will ultimately provide effective defenses may depend more upon finding juries sympathetic to them than it will upon the inherent quality of the defenses themselves.

SUMMARY

Laws regulate relationships between people and also between parties. Hence, one of the primary functions of law is the maintenance of social order. Generally speaking, laws reflect the values held by the society of which they are a part, and legal systems throughout the world reflect the experiences of the societies which created them. The emphasis placed by any law upon individual rights, personal property, and criminal reformation and punishment can tell us much about the cultural and philosophical basis of the society of which it is a part.

Although various kinds of law can be identified, this chapter has concerned itself primarily with criminal law—or that form of the law which defines and specifies punishments for offenses of a public nature or for wrongs committed against the state or society. American criminal law developed out of a long tradition of legal reasoning, extending back to the Code of Hammurabi, the earliest known codification of laws. One especially important source of modern criminal law is English "common law." Common law grew out of the customs and daily practices of English citizens during the Middle Ages and provides the basis for much of contemporary American legal practice. True to its heritage, modern criminal law generally distinguishes between serious crimes (felonies) and those which are less grave (misdemeanors). Guilt can be demonstrated, and criminal offenders convicted, only if all of the statutory elements of a particular crime can be proven in court.

Our legal system recognizes a number of defenses to a criminal charge. Primary among them are justifications and excuses. One form of excuse, the insanity defense, has recently met with considerable criticism, and efforts to reduce its application have been underway for more than a decade. Even as limits are placed on some traditional defenses, however, new and innovative defenses are emerging.

DISCUSSION QUESTIONS

1. Name and describe some of the historical sources of modern law.

2. What kinds of concerns have influenced the development of the criminal law? How are social values and power arrangements in society represented in today's laws?

3. Do you think there is a "natural" basis for laws? If so, what basis do you think is appropriate to build a system of laws upon? Do any of our modern laws appear to have a foundation in "natural law"?

4. What is "common law"? Can aspects of the common law still be found in American criminal law today? If so, where?

5. What is meant by the *corpus delicti* of a crime? How does the *corpus delicti* of a crime differ from the statutory elements that must be proven in order to convict a particular defendant of committing that crime?

6. What is the difference between *mala in se* and *mala prohibita* offenses? Do you think such a difference is practical or only theoretical? Why?

7. Does the insanity defense serve a useful function today? If you could create your own rules for determining insanity in criminal trials, what would they be? How would they differ from existing rules?

8. Near the end of this chapter Stephen J. Morse describes many emerging defenses, saying that an explanation for behavior is not the same thing as an excuse. What does Morse mean? Might an explanation be an excuse under some circumstances? If so, when?

 WEB WATCH

Access the *Criminal Justice Today* site on the World Wide Web by pointing your Web browser at http://www.prenhall.com/cjtoday. Once there, click the "enter here" selection, then "Web Chapters" and finally "Chapter 4: Criminal Law" from the selection box in order to access electronic information and other sites of relevance to this chapter. You may also wish to enter the Global Town Meeting which provides facilities for the posting of electronic messages for others to read. Messages are arranged by topic, with new topics constantly being added.

NOTES

1. Henry Campbell Black, Joseph R. Nolan, and Jacqueline M. Nolan-Haley, *Black's Law Dictionary*, 6th ed. (St. Paul, MN: West, 1990), p. 884.

2. Ibid.

3. Marvin Wolfgang, *The Key Reporter* (Phi Beta Kappa), Vol. 52, no. 1.

4. Roman influence in England had ended by 442 A.D., according to Crane Brinton, John B. Christopher, and Robert L. Wolff, in *A History of Civilization*, 3d ed., Vol. 1 (Englewood Cliffs, NJ: Prentice Hall, 1967), p. 180.

5. Howard Abadinsky, *Law and Justice* (Chicago: Nelson-Hall, 1988), p. 6.

6. Edward McNall Burns, *Western Civilization*, 7th ed. (New York: W. W. Norton, 1969), p. 339.

7. Ibid., p. 533.

8. Brinton, Christopher, and Wolf, *A History of Civilization*, p. 274.

9. Thomas Aquinas, *Summa Theologica* (Notre Dame, IN: University of Notre Dame Press, 1983).

10. *Roe v. Wade*, 410 U.S. 113 (1973).

11. Max Rheinstein, ed., *Max Weber on Law in Economy and Society* (Cambridge, MA: Harvard University Press, 1954).

12. John Stuart Mill, *On Liberty* (London: Parker, 1859).

13. Nigel Walker, *Punishment, Danger, and Stigma: The Morality of Criminal Justice* (Totowa, NJ: Barnes & Noble, 1980).

14. O. W. Holmes, *The Common Law* (Boston: Little, Brown, 1881).

15. Roscoe Pound, *Social Control Through the Law* (Hamden, CT: Archon, 1968), pp. 64–65.

16. As found in William Chambliss and Robert Seidman, *Law, Order, and Power* (Reading, MA: Addison-Wesley, 1971), pp. 141–142, 154.

17. Ibid., p. 140.

18. Ibid.

19. Ibid., p. 51

20. Ibid.

21. Deborah Sharp, "Errors Renew the Call for Doctor Review," *USA Today*, March 27, 1995, p. 1A.

22. Mary Smaragdis, "Cancer Drugs—Not Disease—Kill Illinois Man," *USA Today*, June 16, 1995, p. 3A.

23. Black, Nolan, and Nolan-Harley, *Black's Law Dictionary*, 6th ed.

24. Carrie Dowling, "Jury Awards $150 Million in Blazer Crash," *USA Today*, June 4, 1996, p. 3A.

25. *Facts on File*, 1988 (New York: Facts on File, 1988), p. 175.

26. "Man Who Spent 6 1/2 Years in Jail Is Awarded $1.9 Million by Judge," *The Fayetteville Times* (North Carolina), October 20, 1989, p. 7A.

27. While the state supreme court ruled in favor of Ms. Kitchen on the general issue of liability for gun sales, it agreed with a lower court that the case should be retried because of a procedural error.

28. Robert Davis and Tony Mauro, "Judge OKs Suit Against Gun Maker," *USA Today*, April 12, 1995, p. 3A.

29. "Jury Says Halcion Led to Murder, Awards $2.15 Million," *The Fayetteville Observer-Times* (North Carolina), November 13, 1992, p. 4A.

30. "Part-Time Carpenter Seeks $657 Trillion Payment," Reuters wire services, June 13, 1994.

31. See Liz Spayd, "America, the Plaintiff; In Seeking Perfect Equity, We've Made a Legal Lottery," *Washington Post* wire services, March 5, 1995.

32. *BMW of North America, Inc.* v. *Gore*, 116 S.Ct. 1589.

33. Phillip Rawls, "BMW Paint-Liability," Associated Press wire services, May 9, 1997.

34. Lief H. Carter, *Reason in Law*, 2nd ed. (Boston: Little, Brown, 1984).

35. United States Sentencing Commission, *Federal Sentencing Guidelines Manual* (St. Paul, MN: West, 1987).

36. Daniel Oran, *Oran's Dictionary of the Law* (St. Paul, MN: West, 1983).

37. Florida Constitution, Section 20.

38. Black, Nolan, and Nolan-Harley, *Black's Law Dictionary*, 6th ed.

39. The KGB is now defunct. It was broken up into the SVR (*Sluzhba Vneshney Razvedki*, or Federal Counterintelligence Service), the FSK (*Federal'naya sluzhba kontr-razvedky*), and a number of other agencies.

40. Steven Komarow, "FBI Agent Is Accused of Spying for Russians," *USA Today*, December 19, 1996, p. 1A.

41. "Ex-CIA Officer Pleads Guilty to Spying," Reuters wire services, March 4, 1997.

42. *United States* v. *Shabani*, No. 93-981 (1994).

43. Specifically, 21 U.S.C. 846.

44. "Senate Begins to Consider Anti-Stalking Legislation," *Criminal Justice Newsletter*, March 2, 1993, p. 2.

45. *Gordon* v. *State*, 52 Ala. 3008, 23 Am. Rep. 575 (1875).

46. Oliver Wendell Holmes, *The Common Law*, Vol. 3 (1881).

47. But not for more serious degrees of homicide, since leaving a young child alone in a tub of water, even if intentional, does not necessarily mean that the person who so acts intends the child to drown.

48. There is some disagreement, however, among jurists as to whether or not the crime of statutory rape is a strict liability offense. Some jurisdictions treat it as such and will not accept a reasonable mistake about the victim's age. Others, however, do accept such a mistake as a defense.

49. *State* v. *Stiffler*, 763 P.2d. 308 (Idaho App. 1988).

50. Ibid, p. 138.

51. The same is not true for procedures within the criminal justice system, which can be modified even after a person has been sentenced and, hence, become retroactive. See, for example, the U.S. Supreme Court case of *California Department of Corrections* v. *Morales*, 514 U.S. 499 (1995), which approved of changes in the length of time between parole hearings, even though those changes applied to offenders already sentenced.

52. *Black's Law Dictionary*, p. 127.

53. The statute also says, "A mother's breast-feeding of her baby does not under any circumstance violate this section."

54. Common law crimes, of course, are not based upon statutory elements.

55. "Murder Attempt Charged in AIDS Exposure Case," *The Fayetteville Observer-Times* (North Carolina), November 16, 1992, p. 11A.

56. James A. Carlson, "Cancer Inquest," The Associated Press wire services, April 10, 1995.

57. Ibid.

58. Ibid.

59. Ibid.

60. Lynette Holloway, "Doctor Found Guilty of Murder in Botched Abortion," *The New York Times* News Service, August 8, 1995.

61. "Three Get 15 Years in Prison," The Associated Press, June 21, 1997; Deborah Sharp, "Missing Stop Sign, Lost Lives," *USA Today*, June 19, 1997, p. 3A.

62. The judge suspended half of each 30-year sentence, resulting in a 13-year parole eligibility date.

63. *Willoughby* v. *State* (1990), Ind., 552 N.E.2d 462, 466.

64. See *Maughs* v. *Commonwealth*, 181 Va. 117, 120, 23 S.E.2d 784, 786 (1943).

65. See *State* v. *Stephenson*, Opinion No. 24403 (South Carolina, 1996), and *State* v. *Blocker*, 205 S.C. 303, 31 S.E.2d 908 (1944).

66. *State* v. *Kindle* (1924), 71 Mont. 58, 64, 227.

67. Black, Nolan, and Nolan-Harley, *Black's Law Dictionary*, 6th ed., p. 343.

68. Patrick L. McCloskey and Ronald L. Schoenberg, *Criminal Law Deskbook* (New York: Matthew Bender, 1988), Section 20.03[13].

69. The exception, of course, is that of a trespasser who trespasses in order to commit a more serious crime.

70. Sir Edward Coke, 3 *Institute*, 162.

71. *The Crown* v. *Dudly & Stephens*, 14 Q.B.D. 273, 286, 15 Cox C. C. 624, 636 (1884).

72. "The Rough-Sex Defense," *Time*, May 23, 1988, p. 55.

73. Ibid.

74. "The Preppie Killer Cops a Plea," *Time*, April 4, 1988, p. 22.

75. "Jury Convicts Condom Rapist," *USA Today*, May 14, 1993, p. 3A.

76. Black, Nolan, and Nolan-Harley, *Black's Law Dictionary*, 6th ed., p. 504.

77. "Girl Charged," The Associated Press wire services, northern edition, February 28, 1994.

78. *Facts on File, 1987* (New York: Facts on File, 1988).

79. See, for example, *Montana* v. *Egelhoff*, 116 S.Ct. 2013, 135 L. Ed. 2d 361 (1996).

80. "'Rophies' Reported Spreading Quickly Throughout the South," *Drug Enforcement Report*, June 23, 1995, pp. 1–5.

81. *Bulletin of the American Academy of Psychiatry and the Law*, Vol. 19, No. 4, 1991.

82. American Bar Association Standing Committee on Association Standards for Criminal Justice, *Proposed Criminal Justice Mental Health Standards*, (Chicago: ABA, 1984).

83. "Mrs. Bobbitt's Defense 'Life Worth More than Penis,'" Reuters world wire services, January 10, 1994.

84. American Law Institute, *Model Penal Code: Official Draft and Explanatory Notes* (Philadelphia: The Institute, 1985).

85. Ibid.

86. See Joan Biskupic, "Insanity Defense: Not a Right; In Montana Case, Justices Give States Option to Prohibit Claim," *Washington Post* wire services, March 29, 1994.

87. Ibid.

88. John Klofas and Ralph Weischeit, "Guilty but Mentally Ill: Reform of the Insanity Defense in Illinois," *Justice Quarterly*, Vol. 4, no. 1 (March 1987), pp. 40–50.

89. *Ford* v. *Wainright*, 477 U.S. 399, 106 S.Ct. 2595, 91 L. Ed. 2d 335 (1986).

90. 18 United States Code, §401.

91. *Jones* v. *U.S.*, U.S. Sup. Ct. (1983), 33 CrL 3233.

92. *Ake* v. *Oklahoma*, 470 U.S. 68, 105 S.Ct. 1087, 84 L. Ed. 2d 53.

93. *Foucha* v. *Louisiana*, 504 U.S. 71 (1992).

94. *U.S.* v. *Pohlot*, 827 F.2d 889 (1987).

95. Peter Arenella, "The Diminished Capacity and Diminished Responsibility Defenses: Two Children of a Doomed Marriage," *Columbia Law Review*, Vol. 77 (1977), p. 830.

96. *U.S.* v. *Brawner*, 471 F.2d 969 (1972).

97. *Black's Law Dictionary*, p. 458.

98. California Penal Code, Section 25 (a).

99. California Penal Code, Section 28 (b).

100. *Time*, March 19, 1984, p. 26.

101. Ibid.

102. *U.S.* v. *Halper*, 490 U.S. 435 (1989).

103. "Dual Prosecution Can Give One Crime Two Punishments," *USA Today*, March 29, 1993, p. 10A.

104. *U.S.* v. *Felix*, 112 S. Ct. 1377 (1992).

105. McCloskey and Schoenberg, *Criminal Law Deskbook*, Section 20.02[4].

106. *U.S.* v. *Armstrong*, 116 S.Ct. 1480, 134 L. Ed. 2d 687 (1996).

107. Speedy Trial Act, 18 U.S.C. §3161. Significant cases involving the U.S. Speedy Trial Act are those of *U.S.* v. *Carter*, 476 U.S. 1138, 106 S.Ct. 2241, 90 L. Ed. 2d 688 (1986), and *Henderson* v. *U.S.*, 476 U.S. 321, 106 S.Ct. 1871, 90 L. Ed. 2d 299 (1986).

108. See Jim McGee, "Judges Increasingly Question U.S. Prosecutors' Conduct," *Washington Post* wire services, November 23, 1993.

109. Francis Fukuyama, "Extreme Paranoia About Government Abounds," *USA Today*, August 24, 1995, p. 17A.

110. Lorraine Adams, "Simpson Trial Focus Shifts to Detective with Troubling Past," *Washington Post* wire services, August 22, 1995.

111. Lenore E. Walker, *The Battered Woman* (New York: Harper Collins, 1980).

112. Niko Price, "Abuse Defenses," The Associated Press wire services, May 29, 1994.

113. "Menendez Brothers Get Life Without Parole," *CNN*, Web posted July 2, 1996.

114. "Abuse Defenses," The Associated Press wire services, May 29, 1994.

115. "In S.C. Case, Reports of Abuse," *USA Today*, April 12, 1995, p. 3A.

116. "Abuse Defenses," May 29, 1994.

117. Ibid.

118. As reported in Arnold Binder, *Juvenile Delinquency: Historical, Cultural, Legal Perspectives* (New York: Macmillan, 1988), p. 494.

119. "Drunk Driving Charge Dismissed: PMS Cited," *The Fayetteville Observer-Times* (North Carolina), June 7, 1991, p. 3A.

120. *Facts on File*, 1978 (New York: Facts on File, 1979).

121. Niko Price, "Abuse Defenses," The Associated Press wire services, May 29, 1994.

122. "Train Shooting," The Associated Press wire services, August 12, 1994.

123. Courtland Milloy, "Self-Defense Goes Insane in the City," *Washington Post* wire services, May 18, 1994.

124. Robert Davis, "We Live in Age of Exotic Defenses," *USA Today*, November 22, 1994, p. 1A.

125. Ibid.

126. "Murder Acquittal in 'Urban Fear' Trial," *USA Today*, April 12, 1995, p. 3A.

127. Ibid.

128. "Nationline: Execution," *USA Today*, June 21, 1995, p. 3A.

129. Robert Davis, "We Live in Age of Exotic Defenses."

130. Stephen J. Morse, "The 'New Syndrome Excuse Syndrome,'" *Criminal Justice Ethics*, Winter-Spring, 1995, pp. 3–15.

131. American Psychiatric Association, *Diagnostic and Statistical Manual of Mental Disorders*, 4th ed. (Washington, D.C.: APA, 1994).

INDIVIDUAL RIGHTS VERSUS SOCIAL CONCERNS

The Rights of the Accused Under Investigation

Common law, constitutional, and humanitarian rights of the accused:

* A Right Against Unreasonable Searches

* A Right Against Unreasonable Arrest

* A Right Against Unreasonable Seizures of Property

* A Right to Fair Questioning by Authorities

* A Right to Protection from Personal Harm

The individual rights listed must be effectively balanced against these community concerns:

* The Efficient Apprehension of Offenders

* The Prevention of Crimes

How does our system of justice work toward balance?

NO FOOD
NO HOME
NO MONEY

part 2

POLICING

To protect and to serve

Famed police administrator and former New York City police commissioner Patrick V. Murphy once said, "It is a privilege to be a police officer in a democratic society." While Murphy's words still ring true, many of today's law enforcement officers might hear in them only the echo of a long-dead ideal, unrealistic for today's times.

America's police officers form the front line in the unending battle against crime—a battle which seems to get more sinister and demanding with each passing day. It is the police who are called when a crime is in progress or when one has been committed. The police are expected to objectively and impartially investigate law violations, gather evidence, solve crimes, and make arrests resulting in the successful prosecution of suspects—all the while adhering to strict due process standards set forth in the Constitution and enforced by the courts. The chapters in this section of *Criminal Justice Today* provide an overview of the historical development of policing; describe law enforcement agencies at the federal, state, and local levels; and discuss the due process and legal environments surrounding police activity.

As you will see, while the police are ultimately charged with protecting the public, they often feel that members of the public do not accord them the respect they deserve, and the distance between the police and the public is not easily bridged. Recently, however, a new image of policing has emerged which may do much to heal that divide. This new viewpoint, known as "community policing," goes well beyond traditional conceptions of the police as mere law enforcers and encompasses the idea that police agencies should take counsel from the communities they serve. Under this new model they are expected to prevent crime as well as to solve it and to help members of the community deal with other pressing social issues.

chapter 5

POLICING: HISTORY AND STRUCTURE

Unlike the soldier fighting a war on foreign soil, police officers, who provide for our safety at home, have never been given the honor that was their due.

—HUBERT WILLIAMS, PRESIDENT, THE POLICE FOUNDATION[1]

...[T]o introduce and implement new police ideas is not easy, but it is possible. More than that, it is essential if we are to achieve elementary public safety in American cities and confidence in the police by those who are being policed.

—JEROME H. SKOLNICK AND DAVID H. BAYLEY[2]

Historical Development of the Police

Many of the techniques used by today's police differ quite a bit from those employed in days gone by. Listen to how a policeman, writing two hundred years ago, describes the way pickpockets were caught in London around 1800: "I walked forth the day after my arrival, rigged out as the very model of a gentleman farmer, and with eyes, mouth, and pockets wide open, and a stout gold-headed cane in my hand, strolled leisurely through the fashionable thoroughfares, the pump-rooms, and the assembly-rooms, like a fat goose waiting to be plucked. I wore a pair of yellow gloves well wadded, to save me from falling, through a moment's inadvertency, into my own snare, which consisted of about fifty fish-hooks, large black hackles, firmly sewn barb downward, into each of the pockets of my brand new leather breeches. The most blundering 'prig' alive might have easily got his hand to the bottom of my pockets, but to get it out again, without tearing every particle of flesh from the bones, was a sheer impossibility…I took care never to see any of my old customers until the convulsive tug at one or other of the pockets announced the capture of a thief. I then coolly linked my arm in that of the prisoner, [and] told him in a confidential whisper who I was…"[3]

Police tactics and strategy have changed substantially since historical times, and many different kinds of police agencies—some of them highly specialized—function within the modern criminal justice system. Even so, the basic purposes of policing in democratic societies remain the same: (1) to prevent and investigate crimes, (2) to apprehend offenders, (3) to help ensure domestic peace and tranquillity, and (4) to enforce and support the laws (especially the criminal laws) of the society of which the police are a part. Simply put, as Sir Robert Peel, founder of the British system of policing, explained it in 1822: "The basic mission for which the police exist is to reduce crime and disorder."[4]

This chapter describes the development of organized policing in Western culture and discusses contemporary American police forces as they function at local, state, and federal levels. Agency examples are given at each level, and training, professionalism, and employment issues are all summarized. Finally, the promise held by private protective services and the rapid recent growth of private security organizations and the quasi-private system of justice is discussed.

English Roots

The rise of the police as an organized force in the Western world coincided with the evolution of strong centralized governments. While police forces have developed throughout the world, often in isolation from one another, the historical growth of the English police is of special significance to students of criminal justice in America, for it is upon the British model that much of early American policing was based.

Records indicate that efforts at law enforcement in early Britain, except for military intervention in the pursuit of bandits and habitual thieves, were not well organized until around the year 1200 A.D.[5] When a person committed an offense and could be identified, he or she was usually pursued by an organized posse. All able-bodied men who were in a position to hear the hue and cry raised by the victim were obligated to join the posse in a common effort to apprehend the offender. The posse was led by the Shire Reeve—"leader of the county"—or by a mounted officer—the *comes stabuli*. Our modern words "sheriff" and "constable" are derived from these early terms. The *comites stabuli* (the plural form of the term) were not uniformed, nor were they sufficient in number to perform all the tasks we associate today with law enforcement. This early system, employing a small number of mounted officers, depended for its effectiveness upon the ability to organize and direct the efforts of citizens toward criminal apprehension.

The offender, knowledgeable of a near-certain end at the hands of the posse, often sought protection from trusted friends and family. As a consequence, feuds developed among organized groups of citizens, some seeking revenge and some siding with the offender. Suspects who lacked the shelter of a sympathetic group might flee into a church and invoke the time-honored custom of sanctuary. Sanctuary was rarely an ideal escape, however, as pursuers could surround the church and wait out the offender, while preventing food and water from being carried inside. The offender, once caught, became the victim. Guilt was usually assumed, and trials were rare. Public executions, often involving torture, typified this early justice and served to provide a sense of communal solidarity as well as group retribution.

The development of law enforcement in English cities and towns grew out of an early reliance on bailiffs, or watchmen. Bailiffs were assigned the task of maintaining a night watch, primarily to detect fires and thieves. They were small in number, but only served to rouse the sleeping population, which could then deal with whatever crisis was at hand. Larger cities expanded the idea of bailiffs by creating both a "day ward" and a "**night watch**."

British police practices became codified in the **Statute of Winchester**, written in 1285. The statute specified (1) creation of the watch and the ward in cities and towns; (2) the draft of eligible males to serve either force; (3) institutionalized use of the "hue and cry," making citizens who disregarded this call for help subject to criminal penalties; and (4) that citizens must maintain weapons in their homes for answering the call to arms.

Some authors have attributed the growth of modern police forces to the gin riots which plagued London and other European cities in the 1700s and early 1800s. The invention of gin around 1720 provided, for the first time, a potent and inexpensive alcoholic drink readily available to the massed populations gathered in the early industrial ghettos of eighteenth-century cities. Seeking to drown their troubles, huge numbers of people, far beyond the ability of the bailiffs to control, began binges of drinking and rioting. These types of binges lasted for nearly a hundred years and created an immense social problem for British authorities. The bailiff system by this time had evolved into a group of woefully inadequate substitutes, hired to perform their duties in place of the original—and far more capable—draftees. Staffed by incompetents, and unable to depend upon the citizenry for help in enforcing the laws, bailiffs became targets of mob violence and were often attacked and beaten for sport.

The Bow Street Runners

The early 1700s saw the emergence in London of a large criminal organization led by Jonathan Wild. Wild ran a type of "fencing" operation built around a group of loosely organized robbers, thieves, and burglars who would turn their plunder over to him. Wild would then negotiate with the legitimate owners for a ransom of their possessions.

The police response to Wild was limited by disinterest and corruption. However, when Henry Fielding, a well-known writer, became the magistrate of the Bow Street region of London, changes began to happen. Fielding attracted a force of dedicated officers, dubbed the Bow Street Runners, who soon stood as the best and most disciplined enforcement agents that London had to offer. Fielding's personal inspiration, and his ability to communicate what he saw as the social needs of the period, may have accounted for his success.

In February 1725 Wild was arrested and arraigned on the following charges: "1.) that for many years past he had been a confederate with great numbers of highwaymen, pickpockets, housebreakers, shop-lifters, and other thieves, 2.) that he had formed a kind of corporation of thieves, of which he was the head or director…, 3.) that he had divided the town and country into so many districts, and appointed distinct gangs for each, who regularly accounted with him for their robberies…, 4.) that the persons employed by him

Comes Stabuli
Nonuniformed mounted early law enforcement officers in medieval England. Early police forces were small and relatively unorganized, but made effective use of local resources in the formation of posses, the pursuit of offenders, and the like.

Night Watch An early form of police patrol in English cities and towns.

Statute of Winchester
Written in 1285, this law created a watch and ward system in cities and towns and codified early British police practices.

Bow Street Runners An early English police unit formed under the leadership of Henry Fielding, magistrate of the Bow Street region of London.

were for the most part felon convicts…, 5.) that he had, under his care and direction, several warehouses for receiving and concealing stolen goods, and also a ship for carrying off jewels, watches, and other valuable goods, to Holland, where he had a superannuated thief for his benefactor, and 6.) that he kept in his pay several artists to make alterations, and transform watches, seals, snuff-boxes, rings, and other valuable things, that they might not be known…"[6] Convicted of these and other crimes, Wild attempted suicide by drinking a large amount of laudanum—an opium compound. The drug merely rendered him senseless, and he was hanged the following morning, having only partially recovered from its effects.

In 1754 Henry Fielding died. His brother John took over his work and occupied the position of Bow Street magistrate for another 25 years. The Bow Street Runners remain famous for quality police work to this day.

The New Police

New Police Also known as the Metropolitan Police of London and formed in 1829 under the command of Sir Robert Peel. Peel's police became the model for modern-day police forces throughout the Western world.

Bobbies The popular name given to members of Sir Robert (Bob) Peel's Metropolitan Police Force.

In 1829 Sir Robert Peel, who was later to become prime minister of England, formed what many have hailed as the world's first modern police force. Passage of the Metropolitan Police Act that same year allocated the resources for Peel's force of 1,000 uniformed, hand-picked men. The London Metropolitan Police, also known simply as the "new police," soon became a model for police forces around the world.

The Metropolitan Police were quickly dubbed "**Bobbies**," after their founder. London's Bobbies were organized around two principles: the belief that it was possible to discourage crime and the practice of preventive patrol. Peel's police patrolled the streets, walking beats. Their predecessors, the watchmen, had previously occupied fixed posts throughout the city awaiting a public outcry. The new police were uniformed, resembling a military organization, and adopted a military administrative style.

London's first two police commissioners were Colonel Charles Rowan, a career military officer, and Richard Mayne, a lawyer. Rowan brought to law enforcement the belief that mutual respect between the police and the citizenry would be crucial to the success of the new force. As a consequence, early Bobbies were chosen for their ability to reflect and inspire the highest personal ideals among young men in early nineteenth-century Britain.

Unfortunately, the new police were not well received immediately. Some elements of the population saw them as an occupying army, and open battles between the police and the citizenry ensued. The tide of sentiment turned, however, when an officer was viciously killed in the Cold Bath Fields riot of 1833. A jury, considering a murder charge against the killer, returned a verdict of not guilty, inspiring a groundswell of public support for the much-maligned force.

THE EARLY AMERICAN EXPERIENCE

Early American law enforcement efforts were based to some degree upon the British experience. Towns and cities in colonial America depended upon Americanized versions of the night watch and the day ward, but citizens intent on evading their duty dramatically reduced the quality of police service.

The unique experience of the American colonies, however, quickly differentiated the needs of colonists from the masses remaining in Europe. Huge expanses of uncharted territory, vast wealth, a widely dispersed population involved mostly with agriculture, and a sometimes ferocious frontier, all combined to mold American law enforcement in a distinctive way. Recent writers on the history of the American police have observed that policing in America was originally "decentralized," "geographically dispersed," "idiosyncratic," and "highly personalized."[7]

The Frontier

One of the major factors determining the development of American law enforcement was the frontier, which remained vast and wild until late into the nineteenth century. The backwoods areas provided a natural "haven" for outlaws and bandits. Henry Berry Lowery (the "popular outlaw" of the Carolinas), the James Gang, and many lesser-known desperadoes felt at home in the unclaimed swamps and forests.

Judge Roy Bean (seated on barrel), holding court in Langtry, Texas, circa 1900.
Culver Pictures

Only the boldest of settlers tried to police the frontier. Early among them was Charles Lynch, a Virginia farmer of the late 1700s. Lynch and his associates tracked and punished offenders, often according to the dictates of the still well-known "Lynch law," which they originated. Citizen posses and vigilante groups were often the only law available to settlers on the Western frontier. Judge Roy Bean ("the Law West of the Pecos"), "Wild Bill" Hickock, Bat Masterson, Wyatt Earp, and Pat Garrett were other popular figures of the time who took it upon themselves, sometimes in semiofficial capacities, to enforce the law on the books, along with standards of common decency.

Although **vigilantism** has today taken on a negative connotation, most of the original vigilantes of the American West were honest men and women trying to forge an organized and predictable lifestyle out of the challenging situations which they encountered. Often faced with unscrupulous, money-hungry desperadoes, they did what they could to bring the standards of civilization, as they understood them, to bear in their communities.

Law enforcement is a tool of power.
—Alvin Toffler

Vigilantism The act of taking the law into one's own hands.

Policing America's Early Cities

Small-scale, organized law enforcement came into being quite early in America's larger cities. In 1658 paid watchmen were hired by the city of New York to replace drafted citizens.[8] By 1693 the earliest uniformed officer was employed by the city, and in 1731 the first neighborhood, or precinct, station was constructed. Boston, Cincinnati, and New Orleans were among the American communities which followed the New York model and hired a force of watchmen in the early 1800s.

Peel's new police were closely studied by American leaders, and one year after their creation, Stephen Girard, a wealthy manufacturer, donated a considerable amount of money to the city of Philadelphia to create a capable police force. The city hired 120 men to staff a night watch and 24 to perform similar duties during the day.

In 1844 New York's separate day and night forces were combined into the New York City Police Department. Boston followed suit in 1855 with a similar merging of forces. Further advances in American policing, however, were precluded by the Civil War. Southern cities captured in the war found themselves under martial law and subject to policing by the military.

The turn of the century, coinciding as it did with numerous technological advances and significant social changes, brought a flood of reform. The International Association of Chiefs of Police (IACP) was formed in 1902 and immediately moved to create a nationwide clearinghouse for criminal identification. In 1915, the Fraternal Order of Police (FOP) initiated operations, patterning itself after labor unions but prohibiting strikes and accepting personnel of all ranks—from patrol officer to chief. In 1910 Alice Stebbins Wells became the first policewoman in the world, serving with the Los Angeles Police Department.[9] Prior to Wells, women had served as jail matrons and had sometimes been carried on police department payrolls as police officers (without official duties) after their officer-husbands had died in the line of duty—but had not been fully "sworn" with carrying out the duties of a police officer. Wells became an outspoken advocate for the hiring of more policewomen, and police departments across the country began to hire female officers, especially to provide police services to children and to women, as well as to "protect male officers from delicate and troublesome situations"[10]—such as the need to physically restrain female offenders. In 1915 the U.S. Census reported that 25 cities employed policewomen. In that year, coinciding with the creation of the FOP, the International Association of Policewomen (now the International Association of Women Police) formed in the city of Baltimore. In 1918 Ellen O'Grady became the first woman to hold a high administrative post in a major police organization when she was promoted to the rank of deputy police commissioner for the city of New York. As Dorothy Moses Schulz, a contemporary commentator on women's entry into policing, has observed, "The Policewomen's movement was not an isolated phenomenon, but was part of women's movement into other newly created or newly professionalized fields."[11]

During the early 1900s, automobiles, telephones, and radios all had their impact on the American police. Teddy Roosevelt, 26th president of the United States, pioneered his career by serving as a police commissioner in New York City from 1895 to 1897. While there, he promoted use of a call box system of telephones, which allowed citizens to report crimes rapidly and made it possible for officers to call quickly for assistance. As president, Roosevelt later helped to organize the FBI, which was then called the Bureau of Investigation. Federal law enforcement already existed in the form of U.S. marshals, created by an act of Congress in 1789, and in the form of postal inspectors, authorized by the U.S. Postal Act of 1829. The FBI became a national investigative service designed to quickly identify and apprehend offenders charged with a growing list of federal offenses.

Automobiles, with the affordable era of rapid transportation they created, afforded police forces with far-reaching powers, high mobility, and the ability to maintain constant communication with enforcement authorities. State police agencies arose to counter the threat of the mobile offender, with Massachusetts and Pennsylvania leading the way to statewide forces.

Prohibition and Police Corruption

A dark period began for American law enforcement agencies in 1920 with passage of a constitutional prohibition against all forms of alcoholic beverages. Until prohibition was repealed in 1933, most parts of the country were rife with criminal activity—much of it supporting the trade in bootlegged liquor. Bootleggers earned huge sums of money, and some of them became quite wealthy. Massive wealth in the hands of law violators greatly increased the potential for corruption among police officials, some of whom were "paid off" to support bootlegging operations.

Wichersham Commission
Officially called the National Commission on Law Observance and Enforcement, this body issued a 1931 report stating that prohibition was unenforceable and carried a great potential for police corruption.

In 1931 the **Wickersham Commission**, officially called the National Commission on Law Observance and Enforcement, recognized that prohibition was unenforceable and reported that it carried a great potential for police corruption.[12] The commission also established guidelines for enforcement agencies, which guided many aspects of American law enforcement until the 1970s.

The Last Half-Century

The 1960s and 1970s were a time of cultural reflection in America, which forever altered the legal and valuative environment in which the police must work. During that period, in conjunction with a burgeoning civil rights movement, the U.S. Supreme Court frequently enumerated constitutionally based personal rights for those facing arrest, investigation, and criminal prosecution within the American system of criminal justice. Although a "chipping away" at those rights, which some say is continuing today, may have begun in the 1980s, the earlier emphasis placed upon the rights of defendants undergoing criminal investigation and prosecution will have a substantial impact on law enforcement activities for many years to come.

A New York City police officer "mugging" a prisoner in the early days of police photography.
Courtesy of the Library of Congress

The 1960s and 1970s were also a period which saw intense examination of police operations, from day-to-day enforcement decisions to administrative organization and police community relations. In 1967 the President's Commission on Law Enforcement and the Administration of Justice issued its report, *The Challenge of Crime in a Free Society*,[13] which found that the police were often interpersonally isolated from the communities they served. In 1969 the Law Enforcement Assistance Administration (**LEAA**) was formed to assist police forces across the nation in acquiring the latest in technology and enforcement methods. In 1973 the National Advisory Commission on Criminal Justice Standards and Goals[14] issued a comprehensive report detailing strategies for attacking and preventing crime and for increasing the quality of law enforcement efforts at all levels. Included in the report was a call for greater participation in police work by women and ethnic minorities and the recommendation that a college degree should become a basic prerequisite for police employment by the 1980s.

> **LEAA** An acronym for the Law Enforcement Assistance Administration, which was established under Title I of the Omnibus Crime Control and Safe Streets Act of 1967.

Scientific Police Management

In 1969, with passage of the Omnibus Crime Control and Safe Streets Act, the U.S. Congress created the Law Enforcement Assistance Administration. LEAA was charged with combating crime via the expenditure of huge amounts of money in support of crime prevention and crime reduction programs. Some have compared the philosophy establishing LEAA to that which supported the American space program's goal of landing people on the moon: "Put enough money into whatever problem there is, and it will be solved!" Unfortunately, the crime problem was more difficult to address than the challenge of a moon landing; even after the expenditure of nearly $8 billion, LEAA had not come close to its goal. In 1982 LEAA expired when Congress refused it further funding.

The legacy of LEAA is an important one for police managers, however. The research-rich years of 1969–1982, supported largely through LEAA funding, have left a plethora of scientific findings of relevance to police administration and, more importantly, have established a tradition of program evaluation within police management circles. This tradition, which is known as **scientific police management**, is a natural outgrowth of LEAA's insistence that any funded program had to contain a plan for its evaluation. Scientific police management means the application of social scientific techniques to the study of police administration for the purpose of increased effectiveness, reduced frequency of citizen complaints, and enhanc-

> **Scientific Police Management** The application of social scientific techniques to the study of police administration for the purpose of increasing effectiveness, reducing the frequency of citizen complaints, and enhancing the efficient use of available resources.

ing the efficient use of available resources. The heyday of scientific police management occurred in the 1970s, when federal monies were far more readily available to support such studies than they are today.

LEAA was not alone in funding police research during the 1970s. On July 1, 1970, the Ford Foundation announced the start of a Police Development Fund totaling $30 million, to be spent over the next five years on police departments to support major crime-fighting strategies. This funding led to the establishment of the Police Foundation, which continues to exist today with the mission of "foster(ing) improvement and innovation in American policing."[15] Police Foundation-sponsored studies over the past 20 years have added to the growing body of scientific knowledge which concerns itself with policing.

Federal support for criminal justice research and evaluation continues today under the National Institute of Justice (NIJ) and the Bureau of Justice Statistics (BJS), both a part of the Office of Justice Assistance, Research, and Statistics (OJARS). OJARS was created by Congress in 1980 and functions primarily as a clearinghouse for criminal justice statistics and information. The National Criminal Justice Reference Service (NCJRS), a part of NIJ, is available to assist researchers nationwide in locating information applicable to their research projects. "Custom searches" of the NCJRS computer database can be done on line and can yield voluminous information in most criminal justice subject areas. NIJ also publishes a series of informative reports, on a monthly basis (*NIJ Reports*), which serve to keep criminal justice practitioners and researchers informed about recent findings.

Exemplary Projects

Exemplary Projects Program An LEAA-sponsored initiative designed to recognize outstanding innovative efforts to combat crime and to provide assistance to crime victims.

Beginning in 1973 LEAA established the **Exemplary Projects Program** designed to recognize outstanding innovative efforts to combat crime and provide assistance to crime victims, so that such initiatives might serve as models for the nation. One project which won exemplary status early in the program was the Street Crimes Unit of the New York City Police Department. The SCU used officers disguised as potential mugging victims and put them in areas where they were most likely to be attacked. In its first year, the SCU made nearly 4,000 arrests and averaged a successful conviction rate of around 80%. Perhaps the most telling statistic was the "average officer days per arrest." The SCU invested only 8.2 days in each arrest, whereas the department average for all uniformed officers was 167 days.[16]

Many other programs were supported and evaluated. The Hidden Cameras Project in Seattle, Washington, was one of those. The project utilized cameras hidden in convenience stores, which were triggered when a "trip" bill located in the cash register drawer was removed. Clearance rates for robberies of businesses with hidden cameras were twice that of other similar businesses. Conviction rates for photographed robbers were shown to be over twice those of suspects arrested for robbing noncamera-equipped stores. Commercial robbery in Seattle decreased by 38% in the year following the start of the project.

The Kansas City Experiment

Kansas City Experiment The first large-scale scientific study of law enforcement practices. Sponsored by The Police Foundation, it focused on the practice of preventive patrol.

By far the most famous application of social research principles to police management was the Kansas City Preventive Patrol Experiment.[17] Sponsored by The Police Foundation, the results of this year-long study were published in 1974. The study divided the southern part of Kansas City into 15 areas. Five of these "beats" were patrolled in the usual fashion. Another five beats experienced a doubling of patrol activities and had twice the normal number of patrol officers assigned to them. The final third of the beats received a novel "treatment" indeed—no patrols were assigned to them and no uniformed officers entered that part of the city unless they were called. The program was kept something of a secret, and citizens were unaware of the difference between the patrolled and "unpatrolled" parts of the city.

The results of the Kansas City experiment were surprising. Records of "preventable crimes," those toward which the activities of patrol were oriented—like burglary, robbery, auto theft, larceny, and vandalism—showed no significant differences in rate of occurrence among the three experimental beats. Similarly, citizens didn't seem to notice the change in patrol patterns in the two areas where patrol frequency was changed. Surveys conducted at the conclusion of the experiment showed no difference among citizens in the three areas as to their fear of crime before and after the study.

Table 5-1 Scientific Studies in Law Enforcement

Year	Study Name	Focus
1994	The Kansas City Gun Experiment	Supplemental police patrol to reduce gun crime
1992	The New York City Police Department's Cadet Corps Study	Level of education among officers and hiring of minority officers
1992	Metro-Dade Spouse Abuse Experiment Replication	Replication of the 1984 Minneapolis study (but conducted in Florida)
1991	Quality Policing in Madison, Wisconsin	Community policing and participatory police management
1990	Minneapolis "Hot Spot" Patrolling	Intensive patrol of problem areas
1987	Newport News (Virginia) Problem-Oriented Policing	Police solutions to community-crime problems
1986	Crime Stoppers: A National Evaluation	Media crime reduction programs
1986	Reducing Fear of Crime in Houston and Newark	Strategies for fear reduction among urban populations
1984	Minneapolis Domestic Violence Experiment	Effective police action in domestic violence situations
1981	Newark Foot Patrol Experiment	Costs versus benefits of foot patrol
1977	Cincinnati Team Policing Experiment	Team versus traditional policing
1977	Patrol Staffing in San Diego	One- versus two-officer units
1976	Police Response Time (Kansas City)	Citizen satisfaction with police response
1976	The Police and Interpersonal Conflict	Police intervention in domestic and other disputes
1976	Managing Investigations	Detective/patrol officer teams
1976	Kansas City Peer Review Panel	Improving police behavior
1974	Kansas City Patrol Study	Effectiveness of police patrol

The 1974 study can be summed up in the words of the author of the final report: "The whole idea of riding around in cars to create a feeling of omnipresence just hasn't worked…Good people with good intentions tried something that logically should have worked, but didn't."[18]

A second Kansas City study focused on "response time."[19] It found that even consistently fast police response to citizen reports of crime had little effect on either citizen satisfaction with the police or on the arrest of suspects. The study uncovered the fact that most reports made to the police came only after a considerable amount of time had passed. Hence, the police were initially handicapped by the timing of the report, and even the fastest police response was not especially effective.

The Kansas City study has been credited with beginning the now established tradition of scientific police evaluation. **Patrick V. Murphy**, former police commissioner in New York City and past president of the Police Foundation, said the Kansas City study "ranks among the very few *major* social experiments ever to be completed."[20] It, and other scientific studies of special significance to law enforcement, is summarized in Table 5–1.

Effects of the Kansas City Study on Patrol

The Kansas City studies greatly impacted managerial assumptions about the role of preventive patrol and traditional strategies for responding to citizen calls for assistance. As Joseph Lewis, then director of evaluation at the Police Foundation, said, "I think that now almost everyone would agree that almost anything you do is better than random patrol…"[21]

While some basic assumptions about patrol were called into question by the Kansas City studies, patrol remains the backbone of police work. New patrol strategies for the effective utilization of human resources have led to various kinds of **directed patrol** activities. One form of directed patrol varies the number of officers involved in patrolling according to time of day or on the basis of frequency of reported crimes within areas. The idea is to put the most officers where and when crime is most prevalent.

Directed Patrol A police management strategy designed to increase the productivity of patrol officers through the application of scientific analysis and evaluation of patrol techniques.

Other cities have prioritized calls for service,[22] ordering a quick police response only when crimes are in progress or where serious crimes have occurred. Less significant offenses, such as minor larcenies or certain citizen complaints, are handled through the mail or by having citizens come to the police station to make a report. Wilmington, Delaware, was one of the first cities to make use of split-force patrol, in which only a part of the patrol force performed routine patrol.[23] The remainder were assigned the duty of responding to calls for service, taking reports, and conducting investigations.

Recent Studies

It is a privilege to be a police officer in a democratic society.

—Patrick V. Murphy, Former Commissioner of the NYPD

Recent studies of the police have been designed to identify and probe some of the basic, and often "taken for granted," assumptions which have guided police work throughout this century. The initial response to many of these studies was, "Why should we study that? Everybody knows the answer already!" The value of applying evaluative techniques to police work, however, can be seen in the following examples:

- The 1994 Kansas City "gun experiment" was designed to "learn whether vigorous enforcement of existing gun laws could reduce gun crime." The Kansas City police department's "weed and seed" program targeted areas designated as "hot spots" within the city. These were locations identified by computer analysis as having the most gun-related crimes within the metropolitan area. A special gun detection unit was assigned to the area, and guns were removed from citizens following searches incident to arrest for other (nongun-related) crimes, traffic stops, and as the result of other legal stop-and-frisk activities. While the program was in operation gun crimes declined by 49% in the target area, while they increased slightly in a comparison area. Drive-by shootings, which dropped from seven (in the six months prior to the program) to only one (following implementation of the program), were particularly affected.[24]

- The 1984 Minneapolis domestic violence experiment was the first scientifically engineered social experiment to test the impact of the use of arrest (versus alternative forms of disposition) upon crime.[25] In this case, the crime in focus was violence in the home environment. Investigators found that offenders who were arrested were less likely to commit repeat offenses than those who were handled in some other fashion. A Police Foundation-sponsored 1992 study of domestic violence in the Metro-Dade (Florida) area reinforced the Minneapolis findings, but found that the positive effect of arrest applied almost solely to those who were employed.

- A third example of modern scientific police management comes from Newport News, Virginia.[26] In the late 1980s, the police in Newport News decided to test traditional incident-driven policing against a new approach called problem-oriented policing. Incident-driven policing mobilizes police forces to respond to citizen complaints and offenses reported by citizens. It is what the Newport News police called "the standard method for delivering police services." Problem-oriented policing, on the other hand, was developed in Newport News to identify critical crime problems in the community and to address effectively the underlying causes of crime. For example, one identified problem involved thefts from vehicles parked in the Newport News shipbuilding yard. As many as 36,000 cars were parked in those lots during the day. Applying the principles of problem-oriented policing, Newport News officers sought to explore the dimensions of the problem. After identifying theft-prone lots and a small group of frequent offenders, officers arrested one suspect in the act of breaking into a vehicle. That suspect provided the information police were seeking: It turned out that drugs were the real target of the car thieves. "Muscle cars," rock music bumper stickers, and other indicators were used by the thieves as clues to which cars had the highest potential for yielding drugs. The police learned that what seemed to be a simple problem of thefts from automobiles was really a search for drugs by a small group of "hard-core" offenders. Strategies to address the problem were developed, including wider efforts to reduce illicit drug use throughout the city.

These and other studies have established a new basis for the use of scientific evaluation in police work today. The accumulated wisdom of police management studies can be summed up in the words of Patrick Murphy, who, near retirement as director of the Police

Evaluating the Police

A few years ago the Bureau of Justice Statistics published *Performance Measures for the Criminal Justice System*, a collection of discussion papers produced by the BJS-Princeton Project group. The papers represent the best official effort to date to identify performance goals and associated measures useful in assessing the day-to-day operations of criminal justice agencies.

Historically, according to project authors, the effectiveness of policing has been measured via reported rates of crime, overall rates of arrests, clearance rates, and agency response times. However, the project also identified the following emerging goals and performance indicators in the area of policing:

Goals	Performance Indicators
Doing justice, or "treating citizens in an appropriate manner based upon their conduct."	Nature and type of patrolling strategy, number of traffic tickets issued, crimes cleared, analysis of who calls the police, quality of investigations, cases released because of police misconduct, citizen complaints, lawsuits filed, and results of dispositions and officer-initiated encounters.
Promoting secure communities, or "enabling citizens to enjoy a life without fear of crime or victimization."	The existence of programs and resources allocated to crime prevention programs, time and money dedicated to problem solving, rewards, monitoring of police, degree of public trust in the police, fear of crime, and home and business security checks by the police.
Restoring crime victims by "restoring victims' lives and welfare as much as possible."	Number of contacts with victims after initial call for assistance, types of assistance provided to victims, including information, comfort, transportation, and referrals to other agencies.
Promoting noncriminal options by "developing strong relationships with individuals in the community."	The existence of programs and resources allocated to strengthening relationships between the police and the community, including traditional community relations programs, school programs, storefront operations, and officer contacts with citizens.

Project authors also concluded that performance criteria which measure the degree of police agency orientation toward the community are becoming appropriate. Such criteria would measure "police-related and intergovernmental activities that improve the social fabric of the community, projects with the assistance of private industry that improve informal and formal social control in the community, fear of crime, [and] victimization and police service programs that help promote community spirit in those neighborhoods where none existed."

Source: Geoffrey Alpert and Mark H. Moore, "Measuring Police Performance in the New Paradigm of Policing," in John J. DiIulio, Jr., et al., *Performance Measures for the Criminal Justice System: Discussion Papers from the BJS-Princeton Project* (Washington, D.C.: Bureau of Justice Statistics, October 1993).

Foundation, stated five tenets for guiding American policing into the next century:[27]

1. Neighborhood policing programs of all kinds need to be developed, improved, and expanded.
2. More police officers need college- and graduate-level education.
3. There should be more civilianization of police departments. Civilian specialists can add to department operations and release sworn officers for police duties.
4. Departments must continue to become more representative of the communities they serve by recruiting more women and minorities.
5. Restraint in the use of force, especially deadly force, must be increased.

The FBI crime laboratory. Although a model of quality forensic analysis, the laboratory has come under severe criticism in recent years. *Courtesy FBI*

American Law Enforcement Today: From the Federal to the Local Level

The organization of American law enforcement has been called the most complex in the world. Three major legislative and judicial jurisdictions exist in the United States—federal, state, and local—and each has created a variety of police agencies to enforce its laws. Unfortunately, there has been little uniformity among jurisdictions as to the naming, function, or authority of enforcement agencies. The matter is complicated still more by the rapid growth of private security firms which operate on a profit basis and provide services which have traditionally been regarded as law enforcement activities.

FEDERAL LAW ENFORCEMENT AGENCIES

There are 21 separate federal law enforcement agencies distributed among eight U.S. government departments (see Table 5–2). In addition to the enforcement agencies listed here, dozens of other federal government offices are involved in enforcement activities through inspections, regulation, and control activities. Three of the best known federal law enforcement agencies are described in the paragraphs that follow.

Federal Bureau of Investigation

The Federal Bureau of Investigation may be the most famous law enforcement agency in the country, and in the world. Today, when mention is made of the FBI, many people immediately think of the Fox Network television show *The X-Files*. Long before there was an *X-Files*, however, the Federal Bureau of Investigation was fighting crime across America. The FBI is held in high regard by many citizens, who think of it as an example of what a law enforcement organization should be and who believe that FBI agents are exemplary police officers. William Webster, former director of the FBI, reflected this sentiment when he said: "Over the years the American people have come to expect the most professional law enforcement from the FBI. Although we use the most modern forms of management and technology in the fight against crime, our strength is in our people—in the character of the men and women

Table 5-2 American Policing: Federal Law Enforcement Agencies

Department of the Treasury
Bureau of Alcohol, Tobacco, and Firearms
Internal Revenue Service
U.S. Customs Service
U.S. Secret Service
Federal Law Enforcement Training Center

Department of Justice
Bureau of Prisons
Drug Enforcement Administration
Federal Bureau of Investigation
U.S. Marshals Service
Immigration and Naturalization Service

Department of the Interior
Fish and Wildlife Service
National Park Service
U.S. Park Police

Department of Defense
Criminal Investigation Division
Office of Special Investigations
Naval Investigative Service
Defense Criminal Investigator Service

Department of Transportation
U.S. Coast Guard

General Services Administration
Federal Protective Services

U.S. Postal Service
Postal Inspections Service

Washington, D.C.
Metropolitan Police Department

---

of the FBI. For that reason we seek only those who have demonstrated that they can perform as professional people who can, and will, carry on our tradition of fidelity, bravery, and integrity."[28]

History of the FBI   The FBI has a history which spans nearly the entire twentieth century. It began in 1908 as the Bureau of Investigation, when it was designed to serve as the investigative arm of the U.S. Department of Justice. Creation of the FBI was motivated, at least in part, by the inability of other agencies to stem the rising tide of American political and business corruption.

The Bureau began as a small organization, 35 agents originally hired to investigate crimes such as antitrust violations by businesses and bankruptcy fraud, and to pursue some federal fugitives. However, the Bureau grew quickly as passage of the White Slave Traffic Act in 1910 necessitated a coordinated interstate law enforcement effort to fight organized prostitution. Incidents of sabotage and espionage on American soil during World War I also contributed to the rapid growth of the FBI, and the Espionage Act of 1917 provided a legal basis for many Bureau investigations into subversive activities.

In 1924 J. Edgar Hoover was appointed to direct the FBI. He immediately initiated a plan to increase professionalism among agents. New agents were hired only from among college graduates, with lawyers and accountants especially sought. Training was thorough, and assignments were made on a national basis. On July 1, 1924, the Bureau opened its Identification Division to serve as a national clearinghouse for information on criminals who, with the popular availability of the automobile, were becoming increasingly mobile. The division began operations with 810,188 fingerprint cards, received from the Federal Penitentiary at Leavenworth, Kansas, and from the International Association of Chiefs of Police.

In 1932 the Bureau opened its fledgling Crime Laboratory with a borrowed microscope. Before the laboratory had completed its first year of operations, 963 analyses had been performed—most focusing on homicide-related ballistics testing and handwriting examinations in fraud cases.

During the late 1920s and early 1930s, prohibition combined with organized criminal cartels to propel the Bureau into a "war" with well-armed and violent groups. Famous gangsters of the period who made the FBI's "Ten Most Wanted" list included "Baby Face" Nelson, Clyde Barrow, Bonnie Parker, "Ma" Barker, John Dillinger, "Pretty Boy" Floyd, "Machine Gun" Kelly, and Alvin Karpis. It was during this period of its development that the Bureau's trustworthy image and the popular conception of tough "G-Men" entranced the nation.

In 1935 the Bureau of Investigation officially changed its name to the Federal Bureau of Investigation and opened its first class at the FBI National Academy. The National Academy still provides training to FBI special agents as well as to selected police officers from around the country. In 1940 the National Academy moved from Washington, D.C., to the U.S. Marine Amphibious Base at Quantico, Virginia, where it remains today.

In 1936 President Franklin Roosevelt directed the FBI to collect information on radical groups within American borders, including communist and extremist organizations. During World War II the FBI proved highly effective in combating the efforts of Nazi and Japanese saboteurs. Following the war, FBI attention focused on Soviet spy rings, which were designed to steal defense secrets, including techniques for the manufacture of atomic bombs.

During the 1960s, at the direction of Attorney General Robert F. Kennedy, the FBI became increasingly involved in investigations of civil rights violations. Some critics have charged that this era of burgeoning civil rights tarnished the image of the FBI, since FBI-sponsored investigations of rights activists were as common as those of antirights groups.[29]

The FBI Today   The official purpose of today's FBI can be found rather succinctly stated in this recently published version of the agency's mission statement: "The overall mission of the FBI is to uphold the law through the investigation of violations of federal criminal statutes; to protect the United States from hostile intelligence efforts; to provide assistance to other federal, state, and local law enforcement agencies; and to perform these responsibilities in a manner that is faithful to the Constitution and laws of the United States. This mission is further divided into five functional areas: Criminal Law Enforcement; Foreign Counterintelligence; Investigative and Operational Support; Law Enforcement Services; and Direction, Control, and Administration."[30]

Each subarea within the mission statement is further defined. For example, the criminal law enforcement function requires the agency to "investigate violations of the laws of the United States within FBI jurisdiction, collect evidence in domestic and international cases in which the United States is or may be a party of interest, conduct personnel investigations, and perform other duties imposed by law or Executive Order. Major investigative programs supporting this function include: organized crime/drugs, violent crimes, and white-collar crime."

The law enforcement services function mandates that the FBI "provide forensic, identification, information, and training services to law enforcement personnel and agencies outside the FBI. Programs supporting this function include: general law enforcement training, forensic services, non-federal fingerprint identification, as well as criminal justice data and statistics services through the National Crime Information Center (NCIC) and the Uniform Crime Reports (UCR) programs."

The foreign counterintelligence function, which is becoming increasingly important as acts of international terrorism occur with ever-greater frequency on U.S. soil, specifies that the FBI is to "conduct investigations to collect, analyze, and exploit information to identify and neutralize the activities of foreign powers and their agents that adversely affect U.S. national security through counterintelligence, counterterrorism, and security countermeasures."

The activities of today's FBI are concentrated on white-collar crime, gambling law violations, drug offenses, arson, racketeering, foreign espionage, civil rights violations, violent serial offenders, and offenses involving high technology. The FBI's UCR program gathers statistics on reported crime throughout the United States and publishes yearly summary reports. The FBI Laboratory provides significant assistance to many local and state police agencies, and the NCIC maintains millions of records on a variety of offenses in support of investigative efforts across the country. The Identification Division maintains national and international fingerprint records numbering slightly over 200 million, and the FBI National Academy now occupies 334 acres and trains over 1,000 local and state law enforcement officers every 12 months.[31]

The FBI today operates 56 field offices located throughout the United States and in Puerto Rico and employs more than 23,800 people, including 10,100 special agents. Nearly 1,200 special agents are women, and in 1992 Burdena "Birdie" Pasenelli became the first woman to head an FBI field office. With a budget of over $1 billion per year, FBI jurisdiction extends to more than 200 specific crimes and certain broad areas of criminal activity.[32]

The FBI also operates "legal attaché offices" in a number of major cities around the world, including London and Paris. Such offices permit the international coordination of enforcement activities and facilitate the flow of law enforcement-related information between the FBI and police agencies in host countries. In 1995, a few years after the end of the cold war, the FBI opened a legal attaché office in Moscow. The Moscow office assists Russian police agencies in the growing battle against organized crime in that country and helps American officials track suspected Russian criminals operating in the United States. Also in 1995 an Eastern European version of the FBI Academy, known as the International Law Enforcement Academy (ILEA) opened in Budapest, Hungary. It's purpose is to train police administrators from all of Eastern Europe in the latest crime-fighting techniques. Plans are now in the works to open a similar academy in Latin America.[33]

The FBI's recently formed National Computer Crime Squad (NCCS) investigates violations of the Federal Computer Fraud and Abuse Act of 1986 (CFAA),[34] and other federal computer crime laws. Computer crimes the NCCS investigates include (1) intrusions of public-switched networks (telephone company networks), (2) major computer network intrusions, (3) network integrity violations, (4) privacy violations, (5) industrial espionage, (6) pirated computer software, and (7) other crimes where a computer is centrally involved in committing a criminal offense. The NCCS operates out of the FBI's Washington, D.C., Metropolitan Field Office and has national jurisdiction. It coordinates many of its activities with investigative agencies in foreign countries when U.S. interests are involved. The FBI is in the process of creating individual computer crime investigation teams in each of its field offices within the United States.

During the last few years, the FBI's professional reputation has found support in a generally well-run investigation conducted in connection with the Oklahoma City bombing, the arrest of a Unabomber suspect, and the peaceful surrender of the Montana Freemen. The Bureau has been criticized, however, for its less than successful handling of the 1996 Olympic Park bombing, which led to an embarrassingly fruitless investigation of security guard Richard Jewell (see Chapter 7) and for a scandal which shook the FBI crime laboratory in 1997. The quality of work in the laboratory was called into question by whistle-blower Frederic Whitehurst, an FBI lab examiner who questioned practices at the laboratory. Whitehurst's charges were supported by an internal investigation conducted by the Justice Department's inspector general that found serious problems in the laboratory. The report documented instances in which lab examiners used faulty scientific methods, exaggerated their areas of expertise on the witness stand, and provided juries with inaccurate testimony. Defense lawyers asserted that "thousands of cases" could be tainted.[35] "The entire criminal justice system in this country has been compromised," said William Moffitt, vice president of the National Association of Criminal Defense Lawyers.[36]

Work to repair damage to the FBI's image is ongoing. FBI Deputy Director Weldon Kennedy knows the importance of maintaining a professional image, even in the face of criticism. "The single thing most responsible for the success of the FBI" says Kennedy, [is that] "people are confident that if they come to the FBI, the matter will be handled professionally and well. If that trust ever breaks down, not only is the FBI in trouble, but the American people are in trouble."[37]

The most fundamental weakness in crime control is the failure of federal and state governments to create a framework for local policing. Much of what is wrong with the police is the result of the absurd, fragmented, unworkable nonsystem of more than 17,000 local departments.

—Patrick V. Murphy, Former Commissioner of the NYC Police Department

Twenty-First Century Criminal Justice

NCIC-2000

Since its development in the 1960s, continuous improvements have been made to the FBI's National Crime Information Center (NCIC) in an ongoing effort to satisfy ever-changing law enforcement requirements and to keep pace with growing transaction volumes. Recently, the FBI announced the development of NCIC-2000, a new system intended to replace the original NCIC. Planned to be fully operational by late 1999, NCIC-2000 will perform all current NCIC functions but will add new capabilities, including increased capacity, updated technology, and enhanced fingerprint and image processing facilities. NCIC-2000's new and improved capabilities focus on immediate, on-the-scene suspect identification and include:

- Image processing (for example, mugshots, signatures, and identifying marks such as tattoos, birthmarks, and scars)
- Automated single-finger fingerprint matching via workstation and patrol car scanning devices

- Automation of some NCIC functions that are currently performed manually
- Access to new data bases, including Convicted Person on Supervised Release, the Violent Gang/Terrorist Organization File, the Protective Order File, and the Deported Felon file
- Addition of linkage fields, providing the ability to associate multiple records with the same offender or with the same offense
- Access to external data bases, including the Canadian Police Information Center (CPIC) and the Federal Bureau of Prisons' "SENTRY" database
- Automatic collection of statistics for system evaluation.

Law enforcement administrators say that NCIC-2000's enhanced ability to deliver information to on-the-scene patrol officers, including the availability of photographic images and single fingerprint technology which can pro-

vide immediate positive identification, will ensure increased officer safety while minimizing the risk of improperly detaining the wrong individual.

To take advantage of all of the features of NCIC-2000, police agencies will need a computerized workstation at a centralized site and special equipment in patrol cars. Workstation equipment standards include a 386-IBM compatible computer (or better), a flatbed scanner, a "livescan" fingerprint imaging device, an image printer, and two-way radio equipment. Patrol cars need to be equipped with a mobile display, keyboard, a one-finger "livescan" imaging device, radio interface, and a video or digital camera. According to the FBI, all law enforcement agencies are expected to install at least the minimal equipment needed to receive NCIC-2000 text responses and to send NCIC-2000 transaction formats within three years of the program's initial implementation.

Drug Enforcement Administration

History of the DEA   The U.S. Drug Enforcement Administration (DEA) had its beginnings with passage of the Harrison Narcotic Act, which was signed into law on December 17, 1914, by President Woodrow Wilson. The Harrison Act was primarily a tax law. However, Section 8 of the act made it unlawful for any "nonregistered" personnel to possess heroin, cocaine, opium, morphine, or any of their products. Enforcement began in 1915 with agents of the "Miscellaneous Division" of the Bureau of Internal Revenue finding themselves charged with precedent-setting responsibilities under the new law. During their first year of activity, agents of the Miscellaneous Division seized 44 pounds of heroin and saw 106 convictions returned (mostly of errant physicians).[38]

The 1920s saw federal narcotics enforcement activities focus on organized gangs of Chinese immigrants suspected of running much of the imported opium trade. San Francisco's Chinatown became the scene of frequent raids, and hundreds of Chinese faced deportation hearings for their alleged roles in drug running. Chief narcotics agent Joseph A. Manning identified the On Leong Tong as an organized criminal organization which employed murder-for-hire to retain control over its opium sales.

In 1919 the **Volstead Act**, designed to ensure enforcement of the Eighteenth Amendment on prohibition, was passed. The huge Prohibition Unit of the Revenue Bureau contained a smaller subelement called the Narcotics Division, headed by Levi G. Nutt, a former phar-

Careers in Justice

Working for the FBI

TYPICAL POSITIONS. Special agent, crime laboratory technician, ballistics technician, computer operator, fingerprint specialist, explosives examiner, document expert, and other nonagent technical positions.

EMPLOYMENT REQUIREMENTS. General employment requirements include (1) an age of between 23 and 37; (2) excellent physical health; (3) uncorrected vision of not less than 20/200, correctable to 20/20 in one eye, and at least 20/40 in the other eye; (4) good hearing; (5) U.S. citizenship; (6) a valid driver's license; (7) successful completion of a background investigation; (8) a law degree or a Bachelor's degree from an accredited college or university; (9) successful completion of an initial written examination; (10) an intensive formal interview; and (11)

urinalysis. A polygraph examination may also be required.

OTHER REQUIREMENTS. Five special-agent entry programs exist in the areas of law, accounting, languages, engineering/science, and a general "diversified" area, which requires a minimum of three years of full-time work experience, preferably with a law enforcement agency. The FBI emphasizes education and especially values degrees in law, graduate studies, and business and accounting. Most nonagent technical career paths also require Bachelor's or advanced degrees and U.S. citizenship.

SALARY. Special agents enter the bureau in Government Service (GS) grade 10 and can advance to grade GS-13 in field assignments and GS-15

or higher in supervisory and management positions. A high-cost area supplement ranging from 4% to 16% is paid in specified geographic areas.

BENEFITS. Benefits include (1) 13 days of sick leave annually, (2) 2-1/2 to 5 weeks of annual paid vacation and 10 paid federal holidays each year, (3) federal health and life insurance, and (4) a comprehensive retirement program.

DIRECT INQUIRIES TO:
Federal Bureau of Investigation
U.S. Department of Justice
9th Street and Pennsylvania Ave., N.W.
Washington, D.C. 20535
phone: (202) 324-4991, or check your local telephone book.
Web site: http://www.fbi.gov

---

macist. The Narcotics Division consisted of 170 agents working out of 13 offices around the country. The division was given new teeth by the Narcotic Drugs Import and Export Act of 1922, which brought into being the Federal Narcotics Control Board and strictly prohibited the importation of narcotic drugs for anything other than medical purposes.

On July 1, 1930, the Narcotics Division became the Federal Bureau of Narcotics, headed by Harry J. Anslinger, an appointee of President Herbert Hoover. Under Anslinger's leadership, the Bureau grew quickly. Marijuana abuse was identified as a serious drug problem during the 1930s, and the Marijuana Tax Act of 1937 created fines of $100 per ounce for possession of nontax-paid marijuana. The Mafia also became involved in drug trafficking. Famous criminal personalities of the times included Louis "Lepke" Buchalter, dubbed "Public Enemy Number One," whose organization allegedly smuggled 649 kilograms of pure heroin into the country from Shanghai before being broken up. His distribution network was headed by Lucky Luciano, and its investigation led to the discovery of the Mafia's enforcement arm, known as "Murder Incorporated."

Following World War II, the Bureau received legislative authority to control synthetic drugs and narcotics derivatives. The Boggs Act of 1956 made any use of heroin illegal and removed it from the shelves of pharmacies across the nation. In 1963 the President's Advisory Commission on Narcotic and Drug Abuse recommended numerous revisions in federal drug enforcement efforts. The 1960s also saw an explosion in the quantity of drugs seized in this country and overseas. The Bureau's Overseas Division, working with international police organizations, confiscated over 6 million tons of opium and its derivatives in 1964. Reorganization resulted in creation of the Bureau of Narcotics and Dangerous Drugs in 1968.

By 1970 LSD and other "designer drugs" had begun to appear, and Congress responded with passage of the Comprehensive Drug Abuse Prevention and Control Act. The act provided a firm legal basis for drug enforcement activities and established five schedules which

The work of a DEA agent can be dangerous but rewarding. Here, agents tag 4,000 pounds of cocaine seized in Key West, Florida. *Chris Brown, Stock Boston*

classified controlled substances according to their abuse potential. Finally, in July 1973, the Drug Enforcement Administration was created under federal Reorganization Plan Number 2, which merged existing federal drug enforcement activities into one centralized agency.

The DEA Today   Today the DEA is rapidly becoming the largest federal law enforcement agency. The widespread sale, transportation, and use of illicit drugs throughout the country, and the link between controlled substances and other crimes, have made enforcement of drug laws a top government priority.

Official DEA policy concentrates investigative resources on the "most significant individuals and organizations involved in drug trafficking both domestically and internationally."[39] Investigations often cross international borders, and indictments may name dozens of suspects. In the words of DEA administrators: "DEA enforces the provisions of the controlled substances and chemical diversion and trafficking laws and regulations of the United States, and operates on a nationwide basis. It presents cases to the criminal and civil justice systems of the United States—or any other competent jurisdiction—on those significant organizations and their members involved in cultivation, production, smuggling, distribution, or diversion of controlled substances appearing in or destined for illegal traffic in the United States. The DEA immobilizes these organizations by arresting their members, confiscating their drugs, and seizing their assets; and creates, manages, and supports enforcement-related programs—domestically and internationally—aimed at reducing the availability of and demand for controlled substances."

The DEA's contemporary responsibilities include

- The investigation of major narcotic violators who operate at interstate and international levels
- Seizure and forfeiture of assets derived from, traceable to, or intended to be used for illicit drug trafficking

TYPICAL POSITIONS. Special agent, criminal investigator, chemist, diversion investigator, and intelligence research specialist.

EMPLOYMENT REQUIREMENTS. Applicants for GS-5 levels must (1) be U.S. citizens, (2) be between the ages of 21 and 36 at time of hiring, (3) hold a four-year college degree, (4) be in good health, (5) pass a comprehensive background investigation, (6) hold a valid driver's license, (7) possess effective oral and written communications skills, and (8) have three years of general job experience. Applicants for GS-7 levels must also demonstrate *one* of the following: (1) a 2.9 overall college average, (2) a 3.5 grade point average in the applicant's major field of study, (3) a standing in the upper one-third of the applicant's graduating class, (4) membership in a national honorary scholastic society, (5) one year of successful graduate study, or (6) one year of specialized experience (defined as "progressively responsible investigative experience").

OTHER REQUIREMENTS. Applicants must (1) be willing to travel frequently, (2) submit to a urinalysis test designed to detect the presence of controlled substances, and (3) successfully complete a two-month formal training program at the FBI's Training Center in Quantico, Virginia. Special-agent applicants must be in excellent physical condition, possess sharp hearing, and have uncorrected vision of at least 20/200, and corrected vision of 20/20 in one eye, and at least 20/40 in the other.

SALARY. Entry-level positions for individuals with four-year college degrees begin at GS-7. Appointments are made at higher pay grades for individuals possessing additional education and experience.

BENEFITS. Benefits include (1) 13 days of sick leave annually, (2) 2-1/2 to 5 weeks of annual paid vacation and 10 paid federal holidays each year, (3) federal health and life insurance, and (4) a comprehensive retirement program.

DIRECT INQUIRIES TO:
Drug Enforcement Administration
Office of Personnel, Recruitment, and
  Placement
400 6th Street, S.W., Room 2558, N.W.
Washington, D.C. 20024
phone: (202) 401-7487
Web site: http://www.usdoj.gov/dea

- The enforcement of regulations governing the legal manufacture, distribution, and dispensing of controlled substances
- Management of a national narcotics intelligence system
- Coordination with federal, state, and local law enforcement authorities and cooperation with counterpart agencies abroad
- Training, scientific research, and information exchange in support of drug traffic prevention and control

During fiscal year 1996 DEA employed 3,710 special agents and another 420 intelligence specialists. Agents effected 26,798 arrests during 1996 and confiscated 505 kilograms of heroin, 36,163 kilograms of cocaine, and 200,819 kilograms of cannabis. Property worth $777.2 million was seized in connection with the arrests.[40]

The DEA maintains 20 field divisions and 113 resident offices within the United States and has 307 agents and 100 support personnel assigned to 71 offices in foreign countries. The agency is especially responsive to changes in the pattern of drug flow and routinely reorients its enforcement activities to deal with perceived threats. In the mid-1970s, for example, 200 new agents were added to areas along the Mexican border to stem the traffic in drugs entering the country through Mexico. Around 1980, that border traffic quieted down, while Florida's airports and harbors experienced increased illegal drug activity. The number of DEA agents in Florida rose to 300 to meet this increased threat. A shift is once again occurring in the pattern of drug flow, and the U.S.-Mexican border has become a renewed focal point of enforcement activity.

For years, the DEA and FBI shared training facilities at the FBI Academy in Quantico, Virginia. Since the expansion of both agencies, and with increasingly complex training requirements for DEA Special Agents conducting sophisticated drug investigations, the need for additional training facilities became critical. On April 21, 1997, ground was broken for a new DEA training complex on the grounds of the FBI Academy. The $29 million facility is scheduled for completion in June 1999.

U.S. Marshals Service

History of the Marshals Service   The U.S. Marshals Service (USMS) began over 200 years ago when President George Washington appointed the first 13 marshals. The offices of U.S. Marshal and Deputy Marshal had been created by the Judiciary Act of 1789, which also established the Supreme Court. Marshals hired their own deputies who served at their pleasure and who had little job security. The Marshals Service performed most federal law enforcement functions until the formation of the U.S. Department of Justice. The Service also did much more, however, since (by what may have been historical oversight) no agency was provided for in the U.S. Constitution to represent the interests of the federal government within the states. Hence, many administrative roles fell to the Service, and marshals conducted the national census, registered aliens, exchanged fugitives, and rented space from local authorities for federal courtrooms. As Frederick S. Calhoun, historian of the U.S. Marshals Service, writes, "For the American people, the marshals personified the authority of the federal government within their communities…The marshal, in effect, was the point of contact in the friction between the national government and local communities."[41]

The infamous Whiskey Rebellion of 1794, civil rights violations during post-Civil War Reconstruction, settling of the "Wild West," and desegregation efforts during the 1950s and 1960s all precipitated intensive investigations led by U.S. marshals. Labor unrest in the early part of the twentieth century was often resolved through court injunctions served by marshals. Deputy marshals provided personal protection to outstanding figures in the civil rights movement of the mid-1900s. James Meredith, the first black student at the University of Mississippi at Oxford, was shielded by marshals from hostile crowds as he registered at the school. Dr. Martin Luther King, Jr., was accompanied by deputy U.S. marshals on many of his marches and speeches.

The Marshals Service has sometimes fallen victim to differences between local and federal laws and policies. After the Civil War, for example, marshals attempting to enforce the civil rights of newly freed blacks throughout the South were often arrested and jailed by local authorities. As late as 1962 Chief Marshal James McShane was indicted in Mississippi for inciting a riot at the University of Mississippi where James Meredith was registering.[42]

The USMS has often played a quasi-military role, sometimes acting in public disorders to protect life and property. In 1973, for example, the Marshals Service was at the Sioux Indian occupation of Wounded Knee, South Dakota, and the 1970s antiwar demonstrations were policed by Marshals Service agents.

The U.S. Marshals Service received agency status in 1969. Up until that time marshals had considerable independence in their functioning, but came under close centralized administrative supervision with the change in status. While U.S. marshals are still appointed by the president, deputy marshals are now hired through the Marshals Service and are federal employees, with all the privileges and job security characteristic of such positions.

The Marshals Service Today   Today, the USMS is an enforcement arm of the office of the attorney general of the United States and is headquartered in McLean, Virginia. Ninety-five U.S. marshals direct the activities of over 2,800 deputy marshals throughout the United States and its territories. More than 1,200 other (nonsworn) employees provide support for the activities of the Marshals Service. The USMS budget is substantial, totaling more than $900 million, with $405 million earmarked in support of prisoner-related duties during fiscal year 1997.[43]

Typical tasks performed by the Marshals Service today include prisoner transportation and custody, the pursuit and arrest of fugitives, security in federal courts, personal protection for judges, and the guarding of federal witnesses. The Marshals Service Court Security Program provides protection at nearly 500 federal courtrooms and is responsible for the per-

Careers in Justice

Working as a Deputy U.S. Marshal

TYPICAL POSITIONS. Deputy U.S. marshals are involved in the following activities: (1) court security, (2) fugitive investigations, (3) personal and witness security, (4) asset seizure, (5) special operations, and (6) transportation and custody of federal prisoners.

EMPLOYMENT REQUIREMENTS. General employment requirements with the Marshals Service include (1) a comprehensive written exam, (2) a complete background investigation, (3) an oral interview, (4) excellent physical condition, and (5) a Bachelor's degree or three years of "responsible experience." Applicants must be between 21 and 36 years of age and be U.S. citizens with a valid driver's license.

OTHER REQUIREMENTS. Successful applicants must complete 16 weeks of training at the Federal Law Enforcement Training Center (FLETC) at Glynco, GA.

SALARY. Deputy U.S. Marshals are typically hired at federal pay grade GS-5 or GS-7, depending on education and prior work history.

BENEFITS. Benefits include (1) 13 days of sick leave annually, (2) 2-1/2 to 5 weeks of annual paid vacation and 10 paid federal holidays each year, (3) federal health and life insurance, and (4) a comprehensive retirement program.

DIRECT INQUIRIES TO:
U.S. Marshals Service
600 Army-Navy Drive
Arlington, Virginia 22202
phone: (202) 307-9400
Web site: http://www.usdoj.gov/
    marshals

---

sonal security of 960 federal judges and more than 200 full-time and 300 part-time U.S. magistrates. The agency made 18,250 felony arrests in 1996.[44]

The Marshals Service executes arrest warrants issued by federal courts and—through the use of numerous confiscated aircraft and other vehicles[45]—transports nearly 190,000 federal prisoners a year (including approximately 98,000 by air). Some transported prisoners, like John Hinckley, have high public profiles. Unsentenced federal prisoners are also supervised by the Marshals Service throughout the country. For that purpose the Service rents thousands of detention "spaces" in jails and other prison facilities nationwide through 1,008 intergovernmental agreements with local and state law enforcement and correctional agencies, and shepherds nearly 300,000 individuals each year who must make appearances in federal courts. The service also provides prisoner transportation for other federal agencies, including the U.S. Bureau of Prisons and the Immigration and Naturalization Service, through its Justice Prisoner and Alien Transportation System. Marshals Service investigations extend to the international extradition of fugitives wanted for prosecution in the United States, and the Service works with foreign governments through its Fugitive Investigative Strike Team (FIST).

The Marshals Service is responsible for the handling, inventorying, and safekeeping of all assets seized under federal law for all Department of Justice agencies. In addition to cars, cash, jewelry, and other "routine" items, the Marshals Service has taken possession of banks, resorts, ranches, condominiums, golf courses, restaurants, and many businesses. A few years ago, for example, the Service became responsible for the safekeeping of the "Pearl of Allah," a 14-pound pearl with a 2,000-year history, worth over $42 million, which was seized under order of the federal district of Colorado.[46] On a typical day the Service manages seized property worth about $1.3 billion, of which approximately 50% consists of confiscated vehicles. The effective operation, and possible resale, of businesses and properties requires expertise in operational areas outside of the traditional role of most law enforcement agencies.

The Witness Security Division of the Marshals Service provides physical protection for federal witnesses in cases of organized crime and major criminal activity or where significant threats to witness safety are thought to exist. The **Federal Witness Relocation Program**, run by the Marshals Service since 1971, has afforded protection to over 6,700 primary witnesses and more than 14,500 family members of witnesses since its inception.[47]

Federal Witness Relocation Program (also known as the **witness protection program**) A U.S. Marshal's Service program that protects federal witnesses and their family members in certain high-profile cases.

The Branch Davidian compound burns near Waco, Texas. In 1995 federal law enforcement agencies came under congressional scrutiny for their role in the 1993 tragedy, which caused the deaths of 82 people (many of them children). *Dallas Morning News, Gamma—Liaison, Inc.*

Changes Coming in Federal Agencies?

In addition to the 21 federal agencies whose primary duty is law enforcement, 120 other federal agencies have secondary law enforcement or quasi-enforcement responsibilities. All told, these 141 agencies are charged with enforcing more than 4,100 federal criminal laws. Recently, in what had been billed as an effort to achieve economies of scale, the Clinton administration proposed merging the DEA, the ATF, and the FBI into one federal agency. Impetus for the proposal came from the National Performance Review, also known as the "task force for reinventing government," which was headed by Vice President Al Gore. The task force concluded that consolidating agencies would end duplication and fragmentation of law enforcement efforts as well as save $187 million over a five-year period.

Other recommendations included in the report of relevance to criminal justice were proposals to

- enhance drug interdiction efforts.
- improve law enforcement computer security.
- reduce duplication in drug law enforcement intelligence systems.
- develop low-cost alternatives for housing federal prisoners.

Months after recommendations for merger were made, however, Attorney General Janet Reno, whose office oversees Justice Department law enforcement agencies, gave FBI Director Louis Freeh authority to resolve operational disputes among agencies. Mr. Freeh was also charged with ending duplication of efforts among and between agencies. Reno's action ended, at least for the time being, any possibility that FBI, DEA, ATF, and other federal agencies might merge. It can be anticipated, however, that continuing federal budget pressures will make similar moves in the future all the more likely.

State-Level Agencies

Most state police agencies were created in the late 1880s or early 1900s to meet specific needs brought about by state-level legislation. The Texas Rangers, for example, who were created

Table 5-3   American Policing: State-Level Agencies

Highway patrol	State police	State bureaus of investigation
Fish and wildlife agencies	State park services	Weigh station operations
Alcohol law enforcement agencies	State university police	Port authorities

in 1835 (before Texas gained statehood), functioned as a military organization responsible for patrolling the Republic's borders. Apprehension of Mexican cattle rustlers was one of their main concerns.[48] Massachusetts, targeting vice control, was the second state to create a law enforcement agency. The Pennsylvania Constabulary, known today as the Pennsylvania State Police, has been called the "first modern state police agency,"[49] since it was formed to meet a variety of law enforcement needs at the state level. Today, a wide diversity of policing agencies exist at the state level. Table 5–3 provides a list of typical state-sponsored law enforcement agencies.

State law enforcement agencies are usually organized after one of two models. The first, a centralized model, is well represented by agencies such as the Pennsylvania State Police, which combines the tasks of major criminal investigations with the patrol of state highways. Centralized state police agencies generally do the following:

If you want the present to be different from the past, study the past.

—Baruch Spinoza
(1632–1677)

- Assist local law enforcement departments in criminal investigations when requested to do so
- Operate identification bureaus
- Maintain a centralized criminal records repository
- Patrol the state's highways
- Provide select training for municipal and county officers

The Pennsylvania State Police was the first modern force to combine these duties and has served as a model to many states emulating the centralized model. Michigan, New Jersey, New York, Vermont, and Delaware are a few of the states which patterned their state-level enforcement activities after the Pennsylvania model.

The second state model is the decentralized model of police organization. The decentralized model tends to characterize operations in the southern United States, but is found as well in the Midwest and some western states. The model draws a clear distinction between traffic enforcement on state highways and other state-level law enforcement functions by creating at least two separate agencies. North Carolina, which is used here as an example of such a model, is one of the many states which employ both a highway patrol and a state bureau of investigation.

States which use the decentralized model usually have a number of other adjunct state-level law enforcement agencies. North Carolina, for example, has created a State Wildlife Commission with enforcement powers, a board of Alcohol Beverage Control with additional agents, and a separate Enforcement and Theft Bureau for enforcement of motor vehicle and theft laws.

North Carolina: An Example of the Decentralized Model

The Highway Patrol   The North Carolina Highway Patrol began operations on July 1, 1929. Authorized by an act of the state General Assembly, the Patrol was charged with enforcing the state's motor vehicle laws and with assisting the motoring public.[50]

Training of patrol officers was initiated in May 1929 with the return of ten men from the Pennsylvania State Police Training School. Of 400 original applicants, the Patrol accepted 67, but only 42 men successfully completed the initial training. In 1935 the North Carolina Highway Patrol was placed under the administrative auspices of the Department of Revenue and 80 new officers were hired. Silver roadsters, equipped with bulletproof windshields,

A characteristic silver and black North Carolina Highway Patrol Roadster of half a century ago. *North Carolina Highway Patrol*

became the agency's trademark. Running battles with bootleggers and gangsters soon ensued. A statewide radio communications system became operational in 1937, and by 1946 the Patrol Training School was established within the Institute of Government on the campus of the University of North Carolina at Chapel Hill. By legislative action the Patrol became a division of the Department of Crime Control and Public Safety in 1977.

The duties of the North Carolina Highway Patrol have not changed substantially since it was created. Headed by a colonel, it is administratively divided into six divisions—most under the direction of a major. The Operations Division is the largest and is further subdivided into two "zones," each with four "troops." The tasks assigned to the Operations Division are succinctly described by Directive Number Two of the North Carolina State Highway Patrol. That directive states that the division must "Provide for an effective police traffic supervision program encompassing impartial traffic law enforcement, traffic collision investigation, traffic direction and control, and related services to highway users." These duties extend to enforcement of laws against driving while impaired, breath alcohol analysis, the maintenance of needed statistics on traffic flow, violations and accidents, and the ability to respond effectively in emergency situations.

The five other major functional divisions of the Patrol are (1) Administrative Services, (2) Training, (3) Communications and Logistics, (4) Inspection and Internal Affairs, and (5) Research and Planning. Administrative Services concerns itself with hiring, promotions, time keeping, and the preparation of budgets. The Communications and Logistics Section of the Patrol coordinates the purchase and maintenance of equipment, including vehicles, and sets standards for the equipment and devices used by the patrol—including radar, VASCAR, and radiological and Breathalyzer machines. Internal Affairs develops Patrol policies and procedures, conducts investigations of charges of misconduct, and protects Patrol members against unjust accusations. The Research and Planning Section maintains a library and database to support Patrol operations. The Planning Section analyzes existing data to ensure the most effective utilization of Patrol resources.

The State Bureau of Investigation The North Carolina State Bureau of Investigation (SBI) is an agency of the North Carolina Department of Justice. The SBI was created by legislative action in 1937 for the purpose of providing law enforcement agencies across the state with investigative and laboratory assistance upon request.

The SBI also has original jurisdiction in certain drug and arson offenses, the misuse of state funds and equipment, election fraud, and mob violence within the state of North Carolina. Investigations of local government officials who misuse public funds can be con-

Table 5-4 *American Policing: Local Level Agencies*

Municipal police departments	Housing authority agents	Marine patrol agencies
Campus police	City/county agencies	Sheriff's departments
Coroner or Medical Examiner	Constables	Transit police

ducted by the SBI at the request of a regional official, such as a district attorney. Protection for visiting dignitaries is another new area of responsibility for the SBI, as is the protection of public officials who request it.

The SBI today is charged with maintaining crime statistics for the state and with the operation of a crime laboratory for the identification of offenders. Mobile crime laboratories, operated by the SBI, assist local agencies in the investigation of many offenses. An air operations wing provides the capability for airborne tracking of drug smugglers and the spotting of illegal crops.

LOCAL AGENCIES

The term *local police* encompasses agencies of wide variety. Municipal departments, rural sheriff's departments, and specialized groups such as campus police and transit police can all be grouped under the "local" rubric. A listing of conventional police agencies variously found at the local level is shown in Table 5–4.

Large municipal departments are highly visible because of their huge size, vast budgetary allotments, and innovative programs. Far greater in number, however, are local small-town and county sheriff's departments. Every incorporated municipality in the country has the authority to create its own police force. Some very small communities hire only one officer, who fills all the roles of chief, investigator, and night watch—as well as everything in between. A few communities have decided to contract with private security firms for police services, and a handful have no active police force at all, depending instead upon local sheriff's departments to deal with law violators.

City police chiefs are typically appointed by the mayor or selected by the city council. Their department's jurisdiction is limited by convention to the geographical boundaries of their communities. **Sheriffs**, on the other hand, are elected public officials whose agencies are responsible for law enforcement throughout the counties in which they function. Sheriff's deputies mostly patrol the "unincorporated" areas of the county, or those which lie between municipalities. They do, however, have jurisdiction throughout the county, and in some areas routinely work alongside municipal police to enforce laws within towns and cities.

Sheriff The elected chief officer of a county law enforcement agency, usually responsible for law enforcement in unincorporated areas and for the operation of the county jail.

Sheriff's departments are generally responsible for serving court papers, including civil summonses, and for maintaining security within state courtrooms. Sheriffs also run county jails and are responsible for more detainees awaiting trial than any other type of law enforcement department in the country. For example, the Los Angeles (L.A.) County Jail System, operated by the L.A. County Sheriff's Department, is the largest in the world.[51] In 1995, with nine separate facilities, it had an average daily population of nearly 22,000 inmates—considerably larger than the number of inmates held in many state prison systems. Over 2,500 uniformed officers and 4,000 civilian employees work in the Custody Division of the L.A. County Sheriff's Department, and that division alone operates with a yearly budget in excess of $200 million.[52]

Numbering approximately 3,100 nationwide, sheriffs' departments remain strong across most of the country, although in parts of New England deputies mostly function as court agents with limited law enforcement duties. A recent report found that most sheriffs' departments are small—with nearly two-thirds of them employing fewer than 25 sworn officers.[53] Only 12 departments were found to employ more than 1,000 officers. Even so, southern and western sheriffs are still considered the "chief law enforcement officers" in their counties.

The New York City Police Department: Big-City Law Enforcement

The New York City Police Department (NYPD) serves as a good example of a modern, progressive large-city police agency. Like many other large-city police departments, however, the NYPD has been loudly criticized in recent years for isolated failures of policy and limited instances of abuse.

New York has been described as a "World City,"[54] signifying that it is a gathering place for people of all races and nationalities from around the globe. The New York City metropolitan area is home to more than 18 million people.[55] Twenty-five percent of New York City residents were born outside the United States. In contrast to the "melting pot" image which the city earned in the early part of the twentieth century, ethnic neighborhoods are the rule today throughout the boroughs which comprise New York. Preferences in food, style of dress, customs, habits, and even language vary from block to block and street to street.

The NYPD was formed in the mid-1800s and was modeled after the London Metropolitan Police. In 1845 the force had approximately 800 sworn officers policing about a half-million city inhabitants. The Department faced its first large-scale social disorder in July 1863, with the beginning of the "Draft Riots" fueled by the Civil War. On January 1, 1898, the City of Greater New York came into being with the merger of 24 towns and villages. What had been separate municipal agencies merged into a force of 7,457 officers called the Police Department of Greater New York.[56] The NYPD today is organized around police precincts, with 76 precincts throughout New York City's five boroughs—Brooklyn, Manhattan Island, Queens, Staten Island (also known as Richmond County), and the Bronx. The department is structured into seven bureaus: (1) the Patrol Services Bureau, (2) the Transit Bureau, (3) the Housing Bureau, (4) the Detective Bureau, (5) the Organized Crime Control Bureau, (6) the Internal Affairs Bureau, and (7) the Personnel Bureau. The Patrol Services bureau, the largest and most complex of the department's subdivisions, contains the department's Special Operations Division (SOD), the Emergency Service Unit (ESU), the Mounted Unit, the Aviation Unit, the Harbor Unit, the Traffic Control Division, and the Highway Unit. The Patrol Services Bureau's nearly 26,000 members patrol more than 6,000 miles of city streets and 578 miles of waterfront, working three 8-hour shifts during each 24-hour period. Commanding the entire department is Chief Louis R. Anemone (who became chief on January 13, 1995). Civilian oversight is provided by the office of Police Commissioner Howard Safir (appointed on April 15, 1996).

In 1975 the NYPD fielded a uniformed force of 30,600 sworn officers—and was then the largest municipal police department in the world. Financial problems forced the city to reduce personnel levels in many municipal departments over the next seven years through a phased program of financial retrenchment. In January 1982, a "low" point of 21,809 uniformed officers was reached. Since then the number of sworn NYPD officers has again grown, and in mid-1997[57] the department fielded 37,745 sworn officers supported by 6,638 full-time civilian employees, along with another 1,898 part-time crossing guards. Sixty-eight percent of sworn personnel in the department are white, with 17% classifying themselves as Hispanic, 13.6% black, 1.3% Asian, and 0.1% Native American. Fourteen percent of sworn officers in the NYPD are female. The 1998 fiscal year budget for the NYPD was $2.39 billion.

Everyday [as a police officer] you get to be a different person. In that regard it is the best job in the world. You get to play many roles; rabbi, lawyer, social worker, psychiatrist.

—NYPD Police Officer Salvatore Maniscalco

NYPD Innovations   The NYPD has long been a leader in police innovation. The establishment some years ago of the Bias Incident Investigating Unit to enforce laws among those who discriminate on the basis of race, ethnicity, religion, and sexual preference against city residents and workers was the first such action by a metropolitan police department. A few years later, the NYPD New Immigrants Unit was formed to provide helpful information to immigrants in their native language. The unit's activities were designed to dispel negative images of the police, which immigrants and their children were often found to have carried with them from their homelands. Within a few years of its inception, the New Immigrants Unit was providing information to nearly 100,000 new arrivals each year.

Over a decade ago, in order to combat the problem of street drugs, the department formed Tactical Narcotics Teams (TNTs) within each borough. TNT units also worked closely with Social Club Enforcement units after the March 25, 1990, Happy Land Social Club fire—an arson incident which claimed 87 lives.

The NYPD's most noteworthy accomplishment in recent years has been a noted reduction in crime throughout the city, with decreases beginning in 1994 and exceeding similar declines in many of our nation's other cities. The decline is widely attributed to proactive strategies undertaken by the department to confront crime and disorder on a citywide basis by addressing the problem of guns, youth crime, drugs, domestic violence, disorder in public places, auto-related theft, and police corruption. Backed by sweeping changes in many department procedures and by a policy of decentralizing management to the precinct level, these strategies appear to have achieved the largest drops in felony crime in the city's modern history.

Part of the success is attributed to an increasing emphasis on community policing, which led to the formation of a Community Police Officer Program (CPOP) and to the development of precinct-level Community Policing Units (CPUs). CPUs are charged with follow-up investigations (after initial reports are taken by 911 operators or other officers), street-level narcotics enforcement, crime prevention, and with alleviating conditions within neighborhoods that can lead to crime. A departmentwide community policing emphasis has led the NYPD to target quality-of-life problems throughout the city. Solving such problems, which include public drunkenness, disorderly persons, noise complaints, "boom-box" cars, street prostitution, street-level drug dealing, blocked driveways, subway riders who ignore required fares, and what the department calls "notorious squeegee pests," is thought to have led to an overall reduction in crime by enhancing social order throughout the community. NYPD administrators appear convinced that quality-of-life policing enhances feelings of neighborhood safety and lowers the rate of serious crime. Statistics appear to support such beliefs. In the two-year period from 1994–1996, felonies throughout the city declined 28% and homicides plummeted 38%. Serious crime fell in all seven major felonies categories, in every precinct in the city.

The success of enhanced enforcement efforts is attributed in part to the NYPD's new Compstat Program, which uses crime statistics and crime tracking to quickly shift police resources to problem areas, or "hot spots," throughout the city. Computerized mapping and other contemporary crime analysis techniques function as a kind of early-warning system, allowing for the early identification of emerging crime patterns and facilitating a fast response. As Jack Maple, Deputy Commissioner of Operations for the NYPD, puts it: "We are doing something that to my knowledge has never been done before. We are fighting the war on crime as if it really were a war. You can see it in the way we gather field intelligence and adapt tactics to changing conditions, and in the way we continually assess the effectiveness of what we're doing. That's a daily process now, not an annual event. The department can make fundamental changes in its tactical approach in a few weeks instead of a few years."

The Internal Affairs Bureau   The Internal Affairs Bureau (IAB) investigates allegations of impropriety made against anyone working for the NYPD. IAB's 500 investigators are divided into individual groups working in geographic areas throughout the city, all of which report to the Chief of IAB. Several specialized groups, such as Group 51, which handles police impersonation cases, and Group 54, which investigates excessive force complaints, are housed within the IA Bureau.

NYPD's IAB regularly replicates conditions that might tempt police officers to take money or drugs, or otherwise break the law. In 1995, for example, more than 450 random integrity tests, involving over 800 department members, resulted in only eight failures. Nonetheless, in 1994 the department made 365 bribery arrests, the highest number in over a decade (arrests since then have been consistently lower). "This is an indication that the department's commitment to integrity is very clear to all," says Deputy Chief Charles Campisi, commanding officer of IAB's Corruption Prevention and Analysis Unit.

One of the IAB's most difficult challenges came in August of 1997 when four officers in Brooklyn's 70th Precinct were arrested and charged with attacking Abner Louima, a Haitian immigrant being held in police custody.[58] Witnesses said the officers beat Louima with their fists and a portable police radio after his arrest in a scuffle outside of a nightclub. In a report that shocked the city, at least one of the officers was said to have later sodomized Louima with the handle of a toilet plunger in a station house bathroom. The brutal nature of the alleged attack led to demonstrations against the department and to a reshuffling of person-

Twenty-First Century Criminal Justice

Cybercops

The term *cybercop* was first proposed in 1997 by the Software Engineering Institute at Carnegie Mellon University in its *Report to the President's Commission on Critical Infrastructure Protection*. "Cybercops," said the report, "are law enforcement personnel whose beat is cyberspace." The day-to-day work of some frontline cybercops is described in the article that follows.

When police "net" a crook these days, cops may be referring to the Internet. There was no escaping the World Wide Web for fugitive Les Rogge, a 56-year-old Seattle bank robber hiding in Guatemala. Or for Catherine Suh, a 27-year-old Chicago murderer on the lam in Hawaii from a 100-year prison sentence. Both were captured this year after tipsters spotted their mugs on "Most Wanted" electronic posters on the Internet.

From Scotland Yard to Edmonds, police have gone on-line to take a byte out of crime. On the Internet, citizens anonymously report drug dealers to the cyberpolice, check out crime in their neighborhoods, calculate their risk of being murdered, and communicate directly with the chief of police.

Police say the Internet is a powerful and versatile law-enforcement tool: Communication is immediate and crosses jurisdictional boundaries, information is just a keystroke away and the cost is commonly less than hiring a police officer. "I think it's the most effective money you can spend to prevent crime," said Bill Taylor, crime analyst for the Sacramento Police Department, which has developed one of the nation's most sophisticated Internet police sites. More than 2,000 law-enforcement agencies have gone on-line, extending the long reach of the law to millions of Internet users, said Ken Reeves, a Microsoft manager who recently established a Web site promoting new technology in law enforcement. "They're creating virtual police," he said.

But even in the land of Microsoft, authorities are struggling to keep up with the technology. Seattle and Bellevue police are just starting to look at going on-line. King County (Washington) police offer a primitive Internet site that resembles an electronic copy of a police brochure. "Some may say we're being dragged into the 21st century, technologically speaking," said King County police spokesman Jerrell Wills, who readily acknowledges that his Web page lacks content and style. "I'm a police officer, not an artist."

Many small- and medium-sized police departments are taking the lead in Internet technology. Edmonds police offer an electronic site where citizens can look up crime statistics, hiring information, minutes of police-community meetings, and tips on crime prevention. Ironically, the information is beyond the reach of the department's own officers, since none of the Edmonds police computers has Internet access. In the border town of Blaine, population 3,150, the police department's crime logs are reported each day on the Internet. A recent cybercrime log included a woman's report of being followed, the citation of an unlicensed driver at the Peace Arch, and complaints of in-line skaters obstructing traffic.

It is that kind of timely, detailed information that police have found especially well-suited for the Internet. In Virginia's Roanoke County, for example, citizens can click on a map to find out about the latest crime in their communities. "People in Roanoke County have the right to know what kind of crimes are occurring and where they are occurring so they can take steps to prevent them from happening to them," said Officer Tom Kincaid, who created his department's Web site.

Consultant Kevin Wirth also offers "Crime Online Around the Sound," a Web page that provides detailed maps

and charts of major crimes in Seattle and King County.

Some police agencies have expanded their search for fugitives to the World Wide Web. The Internet was credited for helping capture Rogge, the Seattle bank robber discovered in Guatemala, after a 14-year-old neighbor spotted the fugitive's photograph on the FBI's "10 Most Wanted" Web site. A net tipster also led authorities to Hawaii, where convicted Chicago killer Suh was living the high life under the name Tiffani Escada, a police spokeswoman said.

The Internet also has become a popular tool for police to communicate among themselves. Thousands of police officers subscribe to electronic mailing lists and read electronic bulletin boards where they can discuss ethical issues in private and exchange information about firearms, narcotics, and other sensitive topics. "These are things you don't want to make public, but you need other professionals to bounce off ideas," said Ira Wilsker, a former police officer who is leading a series of U.S. Department of Justice seminars on law enforcement and the Internet. Run for and by police officers, the computer exchanges often offer information that cannot be found elsewhere, Wilsker said. For example, police raised the alarm on the Internet about illegal use of Rohypnol, the notorious "date rape" sedative, more than a year before warnings about the drug were issued through official channels, he said. On the philosophy of know thy enemy, Wilsker said police also turn to the Internet as an intelligence source, monitoring on-line chatter by hate groups, drug users, and others who discuss their views on computer news groups. The news groups, though commonly thought of as private communications, are open to public view. The Internet also can be an effective people finder, he said.

For example, more than 90 million people and their telephone numbers and addresses can be found at the Internet site www.switchboard.com, making a nationwide search sometimes as simple as keying in a name, he said. The service is free.

With an address in hand, Wilsker advises police to turn to www.mapquest.com, which in seconds can pinpoint on a map the location of a suspect's home. "We use it for serving warrants where we don't know the area," he said.

Police officers increasingly carry portable computers in their patrol cars, providing quick access to information that could save lives, said Reeves, marketing manager for Microsoft's Justice and Public Safety division. "It's another protective device, just like the bulletproof vest," he said of computer access.

President Clinton also has been promoting the use of computers to track criminal activity. In June, Clinton called for a national computer register of sexual offenders. Last month, he announced the creation of a federal computer system to trace the illegal sale of guns to youths. "I've been in law enforcement for 25 years, and this is the most powerful law-enforcement tool I have ever seen," Joe Vince, chief of the firearms division of the federal

Bureau of Alcohol, Tobacco and Firearms, said of the new gun-tracking system.

These computer networks likely will be off-limits to the public, but most law-enforcement Internet efforts are aimed at opening communications with the public. In Northern California, Placer County citizens are invited to file complaints (or commendations) on the sheriff's department's Internet site. The Web page includes Sheriff Edward Bonner's e-mail address. The department also accepts on-line crime reports. The 2-year-old Web page, one of the nation's oldest police sites, was introduced to promote community policing, said Sgt. Bill Langton, who designed the Web site. "To make our world a whole lot safer, we have to do it as a community. We can't do it ourselves," he said. Its popularity has exceeded expectations. The Web page last month logged its 20,000th visitor.

While most law-enforcement sites are as dull as a police blotter, some departments have spiced up their Internet connections with entertaining interactive fare. In Maryland, Baltimore County police offer sound clips of the Heat, the department's all-cop rock 'n' roll band. Nashville police invite users of its Web site to calculate

their odds of being raped, robbed, stabbed, beaten, or murdered. Scotland Yard provides a historic tour of the world-famous detective agency.

Still, the response to serious attempts at on-line policing at times has been disappointing. The vast majority of people prefer to deal directly with police than go on-line to report a crime. Chicago's effort to elicit information about drug dealing over the Internet has drawn only a smattering of responses. Some departments have dropped their most-wanted postings on the Internet because they brought in so few tips.

Despite these shortcomings, police on the Web remain the envy of those just getting started. "I'm going to do my best to copy and plagiarize other people's ideas," said Wills, who views his development of King County's Web page as a long-term investment. "I don't see this as a fad, like the mood ring."

Source: Scott Maier, "Long Arm of Law is Going Online: Internet Helps Police do Their Job," the *Seattle Post-Intelligencer,* August 6, 1996. Reprinted courtesy of the *Seattle Post-Intelligencer.*

nel within the precinct involved. Zachary Carter, U.S. attorney for the Eastern District of New York, called the incident "an act of almost incomprehensible depravity." Following the officers' arrest, Louima's family announced plans to file a $55 million lawsuit against New York City, charging that negligence by the city resulted in extensive injuries to Louima.

NYPD Training NYPD training dates back to 1853, when a riot at the Astor Theater resulted in crowd-control classes being held for officers. During World War II the New York Police Academy helped train members of the Navy's Shore Patrol and the Army's Military Police. By 1955 the department was working with Baruch College in a cooperative venture leading toward credits in the school's Associate in Applied Science degree program for candidates who successfully completed the department's Recruit School. Other colleges became involved in training, and recognition of the quality of training at the NYPD was granted when the Board of Regents of the State University of New York accredited the Police Academy's Student Officer curriculum in 1974. Accreditation made possible the receipt of higher-education credits for student officers.[59]

The NYPD Police Academy is responsible for the training and professional development of all entry level and in-service uniformed and civilian members of the department. Today, under the leadership of Dr. James O'Keefe, Jr., Director of Training, the Academy offers 166 different courses, including human relations and disorder control training. All academic instructors are required to hold at least a Bachelor's degree from an accredited college or university. A graduate program has been established at the New York Institute of Technology to allow for expanded educational opportunities for instructors. A Police Cadet Corps (created in 1985), similar in purpose to military ROTC programs, is available to college students in

Careers in Justice

Working for the U.S. Secret Service

TYPICAL POSITIONS. Special agent, Uniformed Division police officers, and special officer. Clerical and administrative positions are also available.

EMPLOYMENT REQUIREMENTS. Requirements for appointment at GS-5 level include (1) successful completion of the Treasury Enforcement Agent examination, (2) a Bachelor's degree from an accredited college or university, (3) excellent physical condition, including at least 20/40 vision in each eye, correctable to 20/20, and (4) successful completion of a thorough background investigation. Appointment at the GS-7 level also requires (1) one additional year of specialized experience, (2) a Bachelor's degree with Superior Academic Achievement, or (3) one year of graduate study in a related field (police science, police administration, criminology, law, law enforcement, business administration, accounting, economics, finance, or other directly related fields).

Superior academic achievement is defined as meeting one or more of the following criteria: (1) a B average (3.0 on a 4.0 scale) for all courses completed at time of application or for all courses during the last two years of the undergraduate curriculum, (2) a B+ average (3.5 on a 4.0 scale) for all courses in the major field of study or all courses in the major during the last two years of the undergraduate curriculum, (3) rank in the upper third of the undergraduate class or major subdivision (for example, school of liberal arts), and (4) membership in an honorary scholastic society which meets the requirements of the Association of College Honor Societies.

Specialized experience is defined as responsible criminal investigative or comparable experience which required (1) the exercise of tact, resourcefulness, and judgment in collecting, assembling, and developing facts, evidence, and other pertinent data through investigative techniques which include personal interviews, (2) the ability to make oral and written reports and presentations of personally conducted or personally directed investigations, and (3) the ability to analyze and evaluate evidence and arrive at sound conclusions.

OTHER REQUIREMENTS. Valid driver's license, urinalysis test for the presence of illegal drugs prior to appointment, and the ability to qualify for top-secret security clearance.

SALARY. Special agents are appointed at the GS-5 or GS-7 level, depending upon qualifications. A high-cost area supplement ranging from 4% to 16% is paid in specified geographic areas.

BENEFITS. Benefits include (1) 13 days of sick leave annually, (2) 2-1/2 to 5 weeks of annual paid vacation and 10 paid federal holidays each year, (3) federal health and life insurance, and (4) a comprehensive retirement program.

DIRECT INQUIRIES TO:
Chief of Staffing, U.S. Secret Service
1800 G. Street, N.W., Room 912
Washington, D.C. 20223
phone: (202) 435-5800
Applications are not accepted earlier than nine months prior to graduation.
Web site:http://www.treas.gov/usss

Source: U.S. Office of Personnel Management.

the New York area who wish to enter police work following graduation. Financial incentives attach to the PCC program, including summer internships, which pay nearly $4,000 per year, and interest-free loans of $1,500 per academic year during the cadet's last two years in college. Cadets who work with the department for two years following graduation have their loans forgiven.

New NYPD police recruits undergo 27 weeks of training at the department's police academy and receive instruction in police science, the social sciences, the use and care of firearms, and emergency and pursuit driving. Following academy training, graduates are assigned to a precinct for six months of on-the-job training.

Over the last few years, a major recruitment effort has been initiated to seek better qualified candidates for NYPD police work. An age requirement of 22 was implemented and character and educational standards increased. Drug testing procedures have been changed to eliminate all advanced warnings for recruits about to undergo testing, and hair testing now complements already stringent urine analysis tests. Academy testing standards have been tightened, and physical screening and agility tests required for admission to the Academy have been made more difficult. According to the NYPD, new department standards mean that almost 5,000 officers hired between 1994 and 1996 would not have passed current physical standards required for appointment. Academic standards have been raised as well.

The June 1997 academy class was the first required to have at least 60 college credits or a minimum of two years military experience, for appointment.

Requirements for promotion have also been increased. Prior to 1988, the NYPD required no minimal educational level for promotions up to the rank of captain. Today, in contrast, aspiring sergeants must have five years as a police officer and 64 college credits to be eligible for promotion. Lieutenants must have served three years as a sergeant and hold 96 college credits. Promotion to the level of captain requires, at a minimum, two years as a lieutenant and a bachelor's degree.

Private Protective Services

Private police constitute a fourth level of enforcement activity in the United States today. Private security has been defined as "those self-employed individuals and privately funded business entities and organizations providing security-related services to specific clientele for a fee, for the individual or entity that retains or employs them, or for themselves, in order to protect their persons, private property, or interests from various hazards."[60] Public police are employed by the government and enforce public laws. Private security personnel work for corporate employers and secure private interests. The 1996 Olympics, for example, provided employment for 30,000 private security personnel—or three security officers for every one athlete that attended the Atlanta games.[61]

According to the *Hallcrest Report II*,[62] a major government-sponsored analysis of the private security industry, nearly 1.5 million people are employed in private security—more than in all local, state, and federal police agencies combined. Employment in the field of private security is anticipated to expand by around 4% per year (see Figure 5–1), while public police agencies are expected to grow by only 2.8% per year for the foreseeable future. By the year 2000, 1.9 million people will be working in private security, while only 850,000 persons will be engaged in public law enforcement.[63] Still faster growth is predicted in private security industry revenues—anticipated to increase at around 7% per year, a growth rate almost three times greater than that projected for the nation's GNP. Table 5–5 lists the ten largest private security agencies in business today. It also lists some of the types of services they offer.

Private Protective Services Independent or proprietary commercial organizations which provide protective services to employers on a contractual basis. Private security agencies, which already employ about half again as many people as public law enforcement, are expected to experience substantial growth over the next few decades.

FIGURE 5–1 Private security and law enforcement employment; projected growth to 2000 A.D. *Source:* William C. Cunningham, John J. Struchs, and Clifford W. Van Meter, "Private Security: Patterns and Trends," A National Institute of Justice *Research in Brief* (Washington, D.C.: U.S. Department of Justice, 1991).

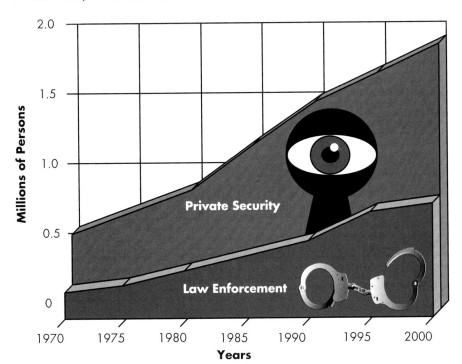

Table 5-5 American Policing: Private Police Agencies

Private Security Services

Company guards	Store/mall security	Automated teller machine services
Airport security	School security	Railroad detectives
Bank guards	Nuclear facility security	Loss prevention specialists
Executive protection agencies	Hospital security	Computer/information security

The Largest Private Security Agencies in the United States*

Security Bureau, Inc.	Globe Security	Pinkerton's, Inc.
The Wackenhut Corp.	Wells Fargo Guard Services	Allied Security, Inc.
Guardsmark, Inc.	Advance Security, Inc.	Burns International Security
American Protective Services		Services

*From *The Hallcrest Report II* (McLean, VA: Hallcrest Systems, 1990).

Private agencies provide tailored policing funded by the guarded organization rather than through the expenditure of public monies. Experts estimate that private security services cost American industries an astounding $52 billion in 1990, while monies spent on public policing totaled only $30 billion.[64] Contributing to this vast expenditure is the federal government, which is itself a major employer of private security personnel, contracting for services which range from guards to highly specialized electronic snooping and countermeasures at military installations and embassies throughout the world.

Major reasons for the quick growth of the American proprietary security sector include "(1) an increase in crimes in the workplace, (2) an increase in fear (real or perceived) of crime, (3) the fiscal crises of the states, [which] has limited public protection, and (4) an increased public and business awareness and use of...more cost-effective private security products and services."[65] In 1990, the influential yearly "Forecast Survey"[66] of private security operations identified substance abuse as the number-one worry of security managers throughout American industry—the first time in the survey's 25-year history that property crime was replaced as the industry's front-running concern.

The Development of Private Policing

Private policing in America has a long and rich history. The first security firms began operation in the mid-1800s, hired mostly by the railroad companies which were laying tracks to support the burgeoning westward expansion of our nation. Company shipments of supplies, guns, and money, as well as engineers and company officials, all needed protection from Indians, outlaws, and assorted desperadoes.

Allan Pinkerton opened his Pinkerton National Detective Agency in 1851 with the motto "We Never Sleep."[67] Pinkerton's agency specialized in railroad security and would protect shipments as well as hunt down thieves who had made a getaway. The Pinkerton service emblazoned an open eye, to signify constant vigilance, on its office doors and stationery. The term *private eye* is thought to have developed out of the use of this logo. Henry Wells and William Fargo built their still-famous Wells Fargo Company in 1852 and supplied detective and protective services to areas west of Missouri. Anyone willing to pay their fee could have a force of private guards and investigators working for them.

The early days of private security services led quickly to abuses by untrained and poorly disciplined agents. No licensing standards applied to the private security field, and security personnel sometimes became private "goons," catering only to the wishes of their employers. To cope with the situation, Pinkerton developed an elaborate code of ethics for his employees. Pinkerton's code prohibited his men and women from accepting rewards, from working for one political party against another, or from handling divorce cases (which are a primary source of revenue for private detectives today).

Private security personnel today outnumber police officers by a ratio of 5 to 3. Here, an early contingent of Pinkerton Guards is shown outside of the Kenilworth Park Race Track in Buffalo, New York, in 1907. *Culver Pictures*

Another firm, the Brinks Company, began as a general package delivery service in 1859 and grew to a fleet of 85 armored wagons by 1900. The year 1859 was a busy one for private security, for in that year Edwin Holmes began the first electronic burglar alarm firm in Boston, Massachusetts. Former law enforcement administrators began to get into the private security field in 1909 when a former director of the Bureau of Investigation formed the William J. Burns International Detective Agency. In 1954 George R. Wackenhut formed the Wackenhut Security Corporation, which has become one of the largest private security firms today.

Much has changed since the early days of private policing. Security firms today provide services for hospitals, manufacturing plants, communications industries, retirement homes, hotels, casinos, exclusive communities and clubs, nuclear storage facilities and reactors, and many other types of businesses. Physical security, loss prevention, information security, and the protection of personnel are all service areas for private security organizations.

Private security agencies have been praised for their ability to adapt to new situations and technology. While most security personnel are poorly paid and perform typical "watchmen" roles, the security industry is able to contract with experts in almost any area. Specially assembled teams, hired on a subcontractual basis, have allowed some firms to move successfully into information and technology security. As financial opportunities continue to build in high-tech security, the industry is seeing the creation of a well-educated and highly specialized cadre of workers able to meet the most exacting needs of today's large and multinational corporations. The ability of private agents to work across state lines, and even international boundaries, is an added benefit of private security to many employers.

Security personnel sometimes work undercover, blending with company employees to learn who is pilfering inventories or selling business secrets to competitors. According to the Society of Competitor Intelligence Professionals, over 80% of the *Fortune* 1000 companies have regular in-house "snoops" on the payroll.[68] Interestingly, a corporate backlash is now occurring, which has led to the hiring of even more security specialists by private industry—companies everywhere are becoming concerned with "spookproofing" their files and corporate secrets.[69]

Bodyguards, another area of private security activity, are commonplace among wealthy business executives, media stars, and successful musicians. One of the most respected executive protection programs in the world is offered by Executive Security International (ESI) in Aspen, Colorado. ESI was incorporated in 1981, and its founder, Bob Duggan, built terrorist simulation exercises into most course sequences.[70] A few years ago another firm, the Richard W. Kobetz Company, began an executive protection training program at its North Mountain Pines Training Center in Berryville, Virginia.[71] Training at Kobetz includes "offensive and escort driving techniques," threat assessment education, searches, alarms, weapons, communications, protocol, legal issues, and firearms and defensive techniques. Activities focus on "low-profile" protection utilizing limited personnel and resources, in contrast to the use of very expensive "high-profile" security as a deterrent technique, which agencies like the Secret Service are able to use.[72] The Kobetz Company offers "certification" as a personal protection specialist (PPS) following successful completion of its training.

The Private System of Justice

Security agencies work for paying clients, while law enforcement agencies are government entities. Differences between the role of private and public agencies were recently revealed in a National Institute of Justice-sponsored survey,[73] which showed that security executives order their managerial priorities as follows: (1) the protection of lives and property, (2) crime prevention, (3) loss prevention, (4) fire prevention, and (5) access control. In contrast, public law enforcement officials list a somewhat different set of priorities: (1) the protection of lives and property, (2) the arrest and prosecution of suspects, (3) the investigation of criminal incidents, (4) the maintenance of public order, and (5) crime prevention.

This difference in priorities, combined with the fact that hired security operatives serve the interest of corporate employers rather than the public, has led to charges that a private justice system operates next to the official government-sponsored system of criminal justice in America. The private system may see behavior which public police agencies would interpret as a violation of the criminal law, as merely misguided employee activity. Within the private justice system conflict resolution, economic sanctions, and retraining can supplant criminal prosecution as the most efficacious system for dealing with offending parties. According to a survey[74] published by the National Institute of Justice, "security managers in all sectors…report that the most frequently investigated crime is employee theft, and nearly half of them resolve such incidents within their own organizations."

One reason why white-collar and business crimes may be substantially underreported in official crime statistics is that unofficial resolutions, based upon investigations by proprietary security forces, may be the most frequent method of handling such offenses. As some writers have observed, the public justice system may find itself increasingly bypassed by proprietary security operations who generally find in the courts "an unsympathetic attitude…concerning business losses due to crime."[75] The *Hallcrest* report points out that not only has a "fundamental shift in protection resources…occurred from public policing to the private sector," but "this shift has also been accompanied by a shift in the character of social control."[76] According to the report, "private security defines deviance in instrumental rather than moral terms: protecting corporate interests becomes more important than fighting crime, and sanctions are applied more often against those who *create* opportunities for loss rather than those who *capitalize* on the opportunity—the traditional offenders."[77]

Hallcrest II identified the growth of the private justice system as a major source of friction between private security and public law enforcement. According to the report, "(l)aw enforcement agencies have enjoyed a dominant position in providing protective services to their communities but now foresee an erosion of their 'turf' to private security."[78] Other sources of friction between the two include (1) "moonlighting" for private agencies by public officers, (2) the fact that "(c)ases brought by private security are usually well developed, putting the law enforcement agency in the thankless position of being an information processor for the prosecutor's office,"[79] and (3) the fact that many cases developed by private security agencies are disposed of through "plea bargaining, which police officers may not understand or support, but which may suit the purposes of a company interested in (deterrence)."[80] Moonlighting by public officers is a source of conflict because, under such circumstances, (1) police authority may be seen as used for personal gain, (2) officers who moonlight long hours may not be fit for their official duties due to exhaustion, and (3) public police departments may be legally liable for the actions of their uniformed officers even though they are temporarily working for private employers.

The link between public and private police agencies has a long history. Here, Allan Pinkerton (seated, right), founder of the Pinkerton Detective Agency, is shown with Secret Service men at U.S. Army Headquarters on the Potomac River in 1862. *The Bettmann Archives*

The Professionalization of Private Security

An issue facing lawmakers across the country today is the extent of authority and the degree of force that can be legitimately used by security guards. Courts have generally held that private security personnel derive their legitimacy from the same basic authority that an employer would have in protecting his or her own property. In other words, if I have the legal right to use force to protect my home or business, then so do guards whom I have hired to act in my place. According to some courts, private security personnel, because their authority is simply an extension of private rights, are not directly bound by the legal strictures which govern the use of force, the gathering of evidence, and so on by sworn police officers.

Other courts, however, have ruled that private security personnel should be bound by the same procedural rules as sworn officers, because they are *perceived* by the public as wielding the authority of public law enforcement officers.[81] The situation is complicated by the fact that, as previously discussed, many police officers "moonlight" as private guards when they are off duty.

In order to ensure at least a minimal degree of competence among private security personnel, a number of states have moved to a licensing process for officers, although a few still require little other than an application and a small fee.[82] Twenty-three states mandate training if the security officer is to be armed, but only 14 require any training for unarmed guards.[83] Most training which does occur is relatively simplistic. Topics typically covered include (1) fire prevention, (2) first aid, (3) building safety, (4) equipment use, (5) report writing, and (6) the legal powers of private security personnel.[84] Reflecting on training and licensing requirements, one specialist has warned, "We have a vast private police force largely untrained, with few restraints, with the power to use force to take liberty and life."[85]

Most private security firms today depend upon their own training programs to prevent actionable mistakes by employees. Training in private security operations is also available from a number of schools and agencies. One is the International Foundation for Protection Officers, with offices in Cochrane, Alberta (Canada), and Midvale, Utah. Following a home-study course, successful students are accorded the status of certified protection officer (CPO). In an effort to increase the professional status of the private security industry, the 20,000-member American Society for Industrial Security (ASIS), established in 1955,

Law enforcement can ill afford to continue its traditional policy of isolating and even ignoring the activities of private security.

—National Institute of Justice, *Crime and Protection in America*

Careers in Justice

WORKING IN PROPRIETARY NUCLEAR SECURITY

TYPICAL POSITIONS. Armed guard, threat-response team member, midlevel management.

EMPLOYMENT REQUIREMENTS. Basic requirements for armed private security personnel in the nuclear area are specified by Part 73 of the Code of Federal Regulations, which mandates (1) a high-school education or equivalent, (2) an age of 21 years or older, (3) successful completion of comprehensive psychological and physical examinations, (4) corrected vision of 20/40, (5) good hearing, (6) no history of drug addiction or potentially disabling diabetes or epilepsy, and (7) a thorough background investigation. A Bachelor's degree is preferred by companies hir-

ing armed personnel in the nuclear security sector. Lateral-entry midlevel managers may be exempted from a number of the specified physical requirements, but are expected to have a substantially higher level of education (B.A. or M.A. degree) and/or experience in private security, law enforcement, or a related field.

OTHER REQUIREMENTS. New officers undergo intensive training in as many as 78 subject-matter areas specified by the federal Code.

SALARY. Armed guards earned hourly wages ranging from $6.50 to $12.00 per hour, depending on geographic location in mid-1998, with

incomes ranging to $32,000. Threat-response team (also called reactionary force team) members earned $11.50 to $15.00 per hour, depending upon employer. Midlevel managers typically earned salaries in the $30,000 to $40,000 range, although contractual commissions paid to such personnel can push salaries to six figures.

DIRECT INQUIRIES TO:
Proprietary nuclear security providers, including Burns International Security Services
387 Shuman Boulevard, Suite 120 W
Naperville, IL 60563
phone: (630) 527-4700

administers a comprehensive examination periodically in various locations across the country. Applicants who pass the examination win the coveted title of certified protection professional (CPP). CPP examinations are thorough and usually require a combination of experience and study to earn a passing grade. Examination subject areas include[86] (1) security management, (2) physical security, (3) loss prevention, (4) investigations, (5) internal/external relations, (6) protection of sensitive information, (7) personnel security, (8) emergency planning, (9) legal aspects of security, and (10) substance abuse. In addition, candidates are allowed to select from a group of specialized topic areas (such as nuclear power security, public utility security, retail security, computer security, etc.), which pertain to the fields in which they plan to work.

Visit the *CJToday* Web page and click on "Web Chapters," then "Chapter 5." Follow the "find the facts" links in order to visit law enforcement sites of interest.

ASIS also functions as a professional association, with yearly meetings held to address the latest in security techniques and equipment. ASISNET, an on-line computer bulletin board system sponsored by ASIS, provides subscribers with daily security news, up-to-date international travel briefings, and a searchable security news database. In its efforts to heighten professionalism throughout the industry, ASIS has developed a private-security code of ethics for its members which is reproduced in a "Theory Into Practice" box on page 213.

An additional sign of the increasing professionalization of private security is the ever-growing number of publications offered in the area. The *Journal of Security Administration*, published in Miami, Florida, ASIS's *Security Management* magazine, and the Security Management newsletter published semimonthly by the National Foremen's Institute in Waterford, Connecticut, along with the older journal *Security World*, serve the field as major sources of up-to-date information.

INTEGRATING PUBLIC AND PRIVATE SECURITY

As the private security field grows, its relationship to public law enforcement continues to evolve. Although competition between the sectors remains, many experts now recognize that each can help the other. A government-sponsored report[87] makes the following policy recommendations designed to maximize the cooperative crime-fighting potential of existing private and public security resources:

ETHICS IN PRIVATE SECURITY

AMERICAN SOCIETY FOR INDUSTRIAL SECURITY CODE OF ETHICS

I. A member shall perform professional duties in accordance with the law and the highest moral principles.

II. A member shall observe the precepts of truthfulness, honesty, and integrity.

III. A member shall be faithful and diligent in discharging professional responsibilities.

IV. A member shall be competent in discharging professional responsibilities.

V. A member shall safeguard confidential information and exercise due care to prevent its improper disclosure.

VI. A member shall not maliciously injure the professional reputation or practice of colleagues, clients, or employers.

Source: Courtesy of the American Society for Industrial Security.

1. The resources of proprietary and contract security should be brought to bear in cooperative, community-based crime prevention and security awareness programs.

2. An assessment should be made of (1) the basic police services the public is willing to support financially, (2) the types of police services most acceptable to police administrators and the public for transfer to the private sector, and (3) which services might be performed for a lower unit cost by the private sector with the same level of community satisfaction.

3. With special police powers, security personnel could resolve many or most minor criminal incidents prior to police involvement. State statutes providing such powers could also provide for standardized training and certification requirements, thus assuring uniformity and precluding abuses…Ideally, licensing and regulatory requirements would be the same for all states, with reciprocity for firms licensed elsewhere.

4. Law enforcement agencies should be included in the crisis-management planning of private organizations…Similarly, private security should be consulted when law enforcement agencies are developing SWAT and hostage-negotiation teams. The federal government should provide channels of communication with private security with respect to terrorist activities and threats.

5. States should enact legislation permitting private security firms access to criminal history records in order to improve the selection process for security personnel and also to enable businesses to assess the integrity of key employees.

6. Research should…attempt to delineate the characteristics of the private justice system; identify the crimes most frequently resolved; assess the types and amount of unreported crime in organizations; quantify the redirection of [the] public criminal justice workload…and examine [the]…relationships between private security and…components of the criminal justice system.

7. A federal tax credit for security expenditures, similar to the energy tax credit, might be a cost-effective way to reduce police workloads.

SUMMARY

Today's police departments owe a considerable historical legacy to Sir Robert Peel and the London Metropolitan Police. The "Met," begun in 1829 under Peel's leadership, was the world's first "modern" police force. It was organized around the practice of preventive patrol by uniformed officers.

American police agencies function to enforce the statutes created by lawmaking bodies, and differing types and levels of legislative authority are reflected in the diversity of police forces which we have in our country today. As a consequence, American policing presents a complex picture which is structured along federal, state, and local lines. All federal agencies, empowered by Congress to enforce specific statutes, have their enforcement arm, and tasks deemed especially significant by state legislatures, such as patrol of the highways, have resulted in the creation of specialized state law enforcement agencies under state jurisdiction.

For many of today's agencies, patrol retains a central role—with investigation, interrogation, and numerous support roles rounding out an increasingly specialized profession. Studies sponsored by the Police Foundation and the Law Enforcement Assistance Administration during the 1970s and 1980s brought scientific scrutiny to bear on many of the guiding assumptions of police work and have made today's police work increasingly subject to study.

Private policing, represented by the recent tremendous growth of for-hire security agencies, adds another dimension to American policing. Private security is now undergoing many of the changes which have already occurred in other law enforcement areas. Heightened training requirements, legislative regulation, court-mandated changes, and college-level educational programs in private security are all leading to increased professionalism within the security profession. Recognizing the pervasiveness of today's private security operations, many municipal departments have begun concerted efforts to involve security organizations in their crime detection and prevention efforts.

DISCUSSION QUESTIONS

1. What assumptions about police work did scientific studies of law enforcement call into question? What other assumptions are made about police work today which might be similarly questioned and/or studied?

2. What are the four levels of law enforcement described in this chapter? Why do we have so many different types of enforcement agencies in the United States? What problems, if any, do you think are created by such a diversity of levels and agencies?

3. What do you think will be the role of private police services in the United States in the future? How can the quality of such services be assured?

 WEB WATCH

Access the *Criminal Justice Today* site on the World Wide Web by pointing your Web browser at http://www.prenhall.com/cjtoday. Once there, click the "enter here" selection, then "Web Chapters," and finally "Chapter 5: Policing" from the selection box in order to access electronic information and other sites of relevance to this chapter. You may also wish to enter the Global Town Meeting, which provides facilities for the posting of electronic messages for others to read. Messages are arranged by topic, with new topics constantly being added.

NOTES

1. The Police Foundation, *Annual Report 1991* (Washington, D.C.: The Foundation, 1992).
2. Jerome H. Skolnick and David H. Bayley, *The New Blue Line: Police Innovation in Six American Cities* (New York: The Free Press, 1986), p. 229.
3. "A Reminiscence of a Bow-Street Officer," *Harper's New Monthly Magazine*, Vol. 5, no. 28 (September 1852), p. 484.
4. Andrew P. Sutor, *Police Operations: Tactical Approaches to Crimes in Progress* (St. Paul, MN: West, 1976), p. 68, citing Peel.

5. For a good discussion of the development of the modern police, see Sue Titus Reid, *Criminal Justice: Procedures and Issues* (St. Paul, MN: West, 1987), pp. 110–115, and Henry M. Wrobleski and Karen M. Hess, *Introduction to Law Enforcement and Criminal Justice*, 4th ed. (St. Paul, MN: West, 1993).

6. Camdem Pelham, *Chronicles of Crime*, Vol. 1 (London: T. Miles, 1887), p. 59.

7. Gary Sykes, "Street Justice: A Moral Defense of Order Maintenance Policing," *Justice Quarterly*, Vol. 3, no. 4 (December 1986), p. 504.

8. Law Enforcement Assistance Administration, *Two Hundred Years of American Criminal Justice: An LEAA Bicentennial Study* (Washington, D.C.: U.S. Government Printing Office, 1976), p. 15.

9. For an excellent discussion of the history of policewomen in the United States, see Dorothy Moses Schulz, *From Social Worker to Crimefighter: Women in United States Municipal Policing* (Westport, CT: Praeger, 1995), and Dorothy Moses Schulz, "Invisible No More: A Social History of Women in U.S. Policing," in Barbara R. Price and Natalie J. Sokoloff, eds., *The Criminal Justice System and Women: Offender, Victim, Worker*, 2nd ed. (New York: McGraw Hill, 1995), pp. 372–382.

10. *From Social Worker to Crimefighter*, p. 25.

11. Ibid., p. 27.

12. National Commission on Law Observance and Enforcement, *Wickersham Commission Reports*, 14 vols. (Washington, D.C.: U.S. Government Printing Office, 1931).

13. President's Commission on Law Enforcement and Administration of Justice, *The Challenge of Crime in a Free Society* (Washington, D.C.: U.S. Government Printing Office, 1967).

14. The National Advisory Commission on Criminal Justice Standards and Goals, *A National Strategy to Reduce Crime* (Washington, D.C.: U.S. Government Printing Office, 1973).

15. Thomas J. Deaken, "The Police Foundation: A Special Report," *FBI Law Enforcement Bulletin* (November 1986), p. 2.

16. National Institute of Justice, *The Exemplary Projects Program* (Washington, D.C.: U.S. Government Printing Office, 1982), p. 11.

17. George L. Kelling et al., *The Kansas City Patrol Experiment* (Washington, D.C.: The Police Foundation, 1974).

18. Kevin Krajick, "Does Patrol Prevent Crime?" *Police Magazine* (September 1978), quoting Dr. George Kelling.

19. William Bieck and David Kessler, *Response Time Analysis* (Kansas City, MO: Board of Police Commissioners, 1977). See also J. Thomas McEwen et al., *Evaluation of the Differential Police Response Field Test: Executive Summary* (Alexandria, VA: Research Management Associates, 1984), and Lawrence Sherman, "Policing Communities: What Works?" in Michael Tonry and Norval Morris, eds., *Crime and Justice: An Annual Review of Research*, Vol. 8 (Chicago: University of Chicago Press, 1986).

20. Ibid., p. 8.

21. Krajick, "Does Patrol Prevent Crime?"

22. Ibid.

23. Ibid.

24. Lawrence W. Sherman, Dennis P. Rogan, and James W. Shaw, "The Kansas City Gun Experiment—NIJ Update," *Research in Brief*, November 1994.

25. Lawrence W. Sherman and Richard A. Berk, *Minneapolis Domestic Violence Experiment*, Police Foundation Report #1 (Washington, D.C.: Police Foundation, April 1984).

26. National Institute of Justice, *Newport News Tests Problem-Oriented Policing*, National Institute of Justice Reports (Washington, D.C.: U.S. Government Printing Office, January–February 1987).

27. Adapted from Deakin, "The Police Foundation."

28. U.S. Department of Justice, *A Proud History…a Bright Future: Careers with the FBI*, FBI pamphlet (October 1986), p. 1.

29. Howard Abadinsky, *Crime and Justice: An Introduction* (Chicago: Nelson-Hall, 1987), p. 262.

30. Taken from the Federal Bureau of Investigation's Home Page on the World Wide Web, April 20, 1995.

31. Much of the information in this section comes from U.S. Department of Justice, *The FBI: The First 75 Years* (Washington, D.C.: U.S. Government Printing Office, 1986).

32. Statistical information in this section comes from the FBI site on the World Wide Web: http://www.fbi.gov.

33. Telephone conversation with FBI officials, April 21, 1995.

34. As modified in 1988 and later years.

35. Ken Foskett, "Defense Lawyers Seek Full Access to FBI Crime Lab Reports," Cox News Service wire services, April 17, 1997.

36. Ibid.

37. Michael J. Sniffen, "Freeh-FBI Image," The Associated Press wire services, February 10, 1997.

38. Drug Enforcement Administration recruitment pamphlets, 1988.

39. DEA memorandum, "Important Information for Special Agent Applicants" (Washington, D.C.: U.S. Department of Justice, DEA, no date).

40. Telephone conversation with DEA personnel, Offices of Intelligence and Public Information, August 1, 1997.

41. Frederick S. Calhoun, *The Lawmen: United States Marshals and Their Deputies, 1789 to the Present*, U.S. Marshals Service (no date), p. 3.

42. This section owes much to Calhoun, *The Lawmen*.

43. Telephone conversation with Marshals Service Public Information Office, August 1, 1997.

44. Marshall's Service, telephone conversation, August 1, 1997.

45. Aircraft and vehicles are typically acquired through the Asset Seizure and Forfeiture Program. Statistics on the Marshals Service from the pamphlet "Outline of the U.S. Marshals Service Activities," U.S. Marshals Service (no date).

46. U.S. Marshals Service, *The Pentacle*, January 1987.

47. Marshall's Service World Wide Web site, http://www.usdoj.gov/marshals/overview.html#WITNESS; as of August 1, 1997.

48. Wrobleski and Hess, Introduction to *Law Enforcement and Criminal Justice*, p. 34.

49. Ibid., p. 35.

50. Arnold W. Rector, "Creation and History of the N.C. State Highway Patrol" (Raleigh, N.C.: Department of Crime Control and Public Safety, no date).

51. Timothy J. Flanagan and Kathleen Maguire, eds., *Sourcebook of Criminal Justice Statistics 1991* (Washington, D.C.: Bureau of Justice Statistics, 1992). Note, however, that New York City jails may have average daily populations which, on a given day, exceed those of Los Angeles county.

52. Telephone conversation with Dr. John Clark, Director of Medical Services for the Los Angeles County Sheriff's Department, Custodial Division, April 20, 1995.

53. Brian A. Reaves, "Sheriffs' Departments 1990," *Bureau of Justice Statistics Bulletin* (Washington, D.C.: U.S. Department of Justice, 1992).

54. New York City Police Department, *New York City Police Department Annual Report, 1986* (New York: NYPD, 1987).

55. "Top Metro Areas," *USA Today*, September 30, 1988, p. 4B.

56. This section owes much to the New York City Police Department's *Annual Reports* (various years), to the NYPD web site (http://www.ci.nyc.ny.us/html/nypd), and to personal conversations with Jess Maghan, former NYPD director of training.

57. Staffing and budgetary information come from Michael J. Farrell, Deputy Commissioner, Policy and Planning, NYPD, August 29, 1997.

58. See Dan Barry, "2 More Police Officers Charged with Attack on Haitian," *The New York Times* news service, via Simon and Schuster Newslink, August 19, 1997. Investigation of the alleged attack is ongoing as this book goes to press.

59. Ibid.

60. *Private Security: Report of the Task Force on Private Security* (Washington, D.C.: U.S. Government Printing Office, 1976), p. 4.

61. See The Atlanta Committee for the Olympic Games, *Securing the Safest Games Ever* (Atlanta: ACOG, no date).

62. William C. Cunningham, John J. Strauchs, and Clifford W. Van Meter, *The Hallcrest Report II: Private Security Trends 1970–2000* (McLean, VA: Hallcrest Systems, 1990).

63. Includes full-time employees working for local police, sheriffs' departments, special police, and state police. See Brian A. Reaves, "Local Police Departments 1993," Bureau of Justice Statistics, April 1996.

64. Ibid., p. 229.

65. Ibid., p. 236.

66. "Forecast Survey: Executive Summary," *Security*, January 1990.

67. Dae H. Chang and James A. Fagin, eds., *Introduction to Criminal Justice: Theory and Application*, 2nd ed. (Geneva, IL: Paladin House, 1985), pp. 275–277.

68. "George Smiley Joins the Firm," *Newsweek*, May 2, 1988, pp. 46–47.

69. Ibid.

70. For more information on ESI, see E. Duane Davis, "Executive Protection: An Emerging Trend in Criminal Justice Education and Training," *The Justice Professional*, Vol. 3, no. 2 (Fall 1988).

71. "More than a Bodyguard," *Security Management*, February 10, 1986.

72. "A School for Guards of Rich, Powerful," *The Akron Beacon Journal* (Ohio), April 21, 1986.

73. National Institute of Justice, *Crime and Protection in America: A Study of Private Security and Law Enforcement Resources and Relationships*, Executive Summary (Washington, D.C.: U.S. Department of Justice, 1985), p. 42.

74. Ibid., p. 60.

75. Cunninghum, Strauch, and Van Meter, *Hallcrest II*, p. 299.

76. Ibid., p. 301.

77. Ibid. (italics added).

78. Ibid., p. 117.

79. National Institute of Justice, *Crime and Protection in America*, p. 12.

80. Ibid., p. 12.

81. *People* v. *Zelinski*, 594 P.2d 1000 (1979).

82. For additional information, see Joseph G. Deegan, "Mandated Training for Private Security," *FBI Law Enforcement Bulletin*, March 1987, pp. 6–8.

83. Cunningham, Strauchs, and Van Meter, *Hallcrest II*, p. 147.

84. National Institute of Justice, *Crime and Protection in America*, p. 37.

85. Richter Moore, "Private Police: The Use of Force and State Regulation," unpublished manuscript.

86. "The Mark of Professionalism," *Security Management*, 35th Anniversary Supplement, 1990, pp. 97–104.

87. National Institute of Justice, *Crime and Protection in America*, pp. 59–72.

chapter 6

POLICE MANAGEMENT

I liken the Los Angeles police to a business. We have 3 1/2 million customers....

—WILLIE WILLIAMS
FORMER LOS ANGELES CHIEF
OF POLICE[1]

The single most striking fact about the attitudes of citizens, black and white, toward the police is that in general those attitudes are positive, not negative.

—JAMES Q. WILSON[2]

KEY CONCEPTS

1983 Lawsuit
Bivens action
community policing
corruption
discretion
internal affairs
Knapp Commission

legalistic style
police community relations
police culture
police ethics
police management
police professionalism
police working personality

POST
problem-solving policing
service style
strategic policing
watchman style

KEY CASES

City of Canton, Ohio v. *Harris*   *Malley* v. *Briggs*   *Hunter* v. *Bryant*

Contemporary Policing: The Administrative Perspective

In November 1992 a Stanislaus County police SWAT team wearing ski masks and acting on a tip that an illegal methamphetamine lab was in operation, kicked down the doors of the Oakdale, California, home of Marian and William Hauselmann.[3] Once inside they hand-cuffed Mrs. Hauselmann, put a pillowcase over her head, and wrestled her to the floor. Her 64-year-old husband, who suffers from a heart condition, was shouted into silence. His face was cut and officers stepped on his back after throwing him down. No illegal drugs were found. Police soon realized that they had been misled by their informant and apologized to the Hauselmanns. Then they borrowed a knife from the couple's kitchen to cut the plastic handcuffs from their wrists. The county sheriff offered to pay for the broken doors. Following the incident the Hauselmanns reported being unable to sleep.

A few months prior to the Hauselmann's ordeal, multimillionaire rancher Donald Scott was fatally shot during a drug raid gone terribly wrong. His Malibu, California, property, the target of a police attack, yielded no drugs, and Scott appears to have been trying to protect himself from what he thought were intruders when he was shot.

Both these cases highlight the potentially disastrous consequences of improper police action. Effective **police management**, through which laws are enforced while the rights of suspects and of innocent people are protected, may be the single most important emerging issue facing the criminal justice system in the twenty-first century. As Dorothy Ehrlich of northern California's ACLU says, efficient enforcement of the laws is necessary, "[b]ut ter-rorizing innocent people is a price no one should have to pay."[4]

Styles of Policing

Police Management The administrative activities of controlling, directing, and coordinating police person-nel, resources, and activities in the service of crime pre-vention, the apprehension of criminals, and the recov-ery of stolen property, and the performance of a vari-ety of regulatory and help-ing services.

Police management refers to the administrative activities of controlling, directing, and coor-dinating police personnel, resources, and activities in the service of crime prevention, the apprehension of criminals, the recovery of stolen property, and the performance of a variety of regulatory and helping services.[5] Police managers include any "sworn" law enforcement personnel with administrative authority, from the rank of sergeant to captain, chief or sher-iff, and civilian personnel such as police commissioners, attorneys general, state secretaries of crime control, public safety directors, and so on.

In a recent symposium, members of Harvard University's Kennedy School of Government divided the history of American policing into three different eras.[6] Each era was distinguished from the others by the apparent dominance of a particular administrative approach to police operations. The first period, the political era, was characterized by close ties between police and public officials. It began in the 1840s and ended around 1930. Throughout the period American police agencies tended to serve the interests of powerful politicians and their cronies, while providing community order maintenance services almost as an afterthought. The second period, the reform era, began in the 1930s and lasted until

The maintenance of social order is a police function closely akin to strict law enforcement. Here, Austin, Texas, police officers remove protesters at an antiabortion sit-in.
Bob Daemmrich, Stock Boston

the 1970s. The reform era was characterized by pride in professional crime fighting. Police departments during this period focused most of their resources on solving "traditional" crimes such as murder, rape, and burglary and on capturing offenders. The final era—one which is just beginning—is the era of community problem solving. The problem-solving approach to police work stresses the service role of police officers and envisions a partnership between police agencies and their communities.

The influence of each historical phase identified by the Harvard team survives today in what James Q. Wilson calls policing styles.[7] Simply put, a style of policing describes how a particular police agency sees its purpose and the methods and techniques it undertakes to fulfill that purpose. Wilson's three types of policing—which he did not identify with a particular historical era—are (1) the watchman style (characteristic of the Harvard symposium's political era), (2) the legalistic style (professional crime fighting), and (3) the service style (which is becoming more commonplace today). These three styles, taken together, characterize nearly all municipal law enforcement agencies now operating in this country—although some departments are a mixture of two or more styles.

The Watchman Style of Policing

Police departments marked by the watchman style of policing are primarily concerned with achieving a goal that Wilson calls "order maintenance." They see their job as one of controlling illegal and disruptive behavior. The watchman style, however, as opposed to the legalistic, makes considerable use of discretion. Order in watchman-style communities may be arrived at through informal police intervention, including persuasion and threats, or even by "roughing up" a few disruptive people from time to time. Some authors have condemned this style of policing, suggesting that it is unfairly found in lower-class or lower-middle-class communities, especially where interpersonal relations may include a fair amount of violence or physical abuse.

The watchman style of policing appears to have been operative in Los Angeles, California, at the time of the well-known Rodney King beating (see Chapter 7 for details). Following the

Watchman Style A style of policing marked by a concern for order maintenance. This style of policing is characteristic of lower-class communities where informal police intervention into the lives of residents is employed in the service of keeping the peace.

riots that ensued, the Independent Commission on the Los Angeles Police Department (the Christopher Commission) determined that the Los Angeles "[p]olice placed greater emphasis on crime control over crime prevention, a policy that distanced cops from the people they serve."

The Legalistic Style of Policing

Legalistic Style A style of policing marked by a strict concern with enforcing the precise letter of the law. Legalistic departments, however, may take a "hands-off" approach to otherwise disruptive or problematic forms of behavior which are not violations of the criminal law.

Departments operating under the legalistic model are committed to enforcing the "letter of the law." Years ago, for example, when the speed limit on I-95 running north and south through North Carolina was 55 MPH, a state highway patrol official was quoted by newspapers as saying that troopers would issue tickets at 56 MPH. The law was the law, he said, and it would be enforced.

Conversely, legalistically oriented departments can be expected to routinely avoid involvement in community disputes arising from violations of social norms which do not break the law. Gary Sykes calls this enforcement style "laissez-faire policing," in recognition of its "hands-off" approach to behaviors which are simply bothersome or inconsiderate of community principles.

The Service Style of Policing

Service Style A style of policing which is marked by a concern with helping rather than strict enforcement. Service-oriented agencies are more likely to take advantage of community resources, such as drug treatment programs, than are other types of departments.

Departments which stress the goal of service reflect the felt needs of the community. In service-oriented departments, the police see themselves more as helpers than as embattled participants in a war against crime. Such departments work hand in hand with social service and other agencies to provide counseling for minor offenders and to assist community groups in preventing crimes and solving problems. Prosecutors may support the service style of policing by agreeing not to prosecute law violators who seek psychiatric help, or who voluntarily participate in programs like Alcoholics Anonymous, family counseling, drug treatment, and the like. The service style of policing is commonly found in wealthy neighborhoods, where the police are well paid and well educated. The service style is supported in part by citizen attitudes which seek to avoid the personal embarrassment which might result from a public airing of personal problems. Such attitudes reduce the number of criminal complaints filed, especially in minor disputes.

Evolving Styles of Policing

Historically, American police work has involved a fair amount of order maintenance activity. The United States a few decades ago consisted of a large number of immigrant communities, socially separated from one another by custom and language. Immigrant workers were often poorly educated, and some were prone toward displays of "manhood," which challenged police authority in the cities. Reports of police in "pitched battles" with bar-hopping laborers out for Saturday night "good times" were not uncommon. Arrests were infrequent, but "street justice" was often imposed through the use of the "billy stick" and blackjack. In these historical settings, the watchman style of policing must have seemed especially appropriate to both the police and many members of the citizenry.

As times changed, so too have American communities. Even today, however, it is probably fair to say that the style of policing which characterizes a community tends to flow, at least to some degree, from the lifestyles of those who live there. Rough-and-tumble lifestyles encourage an oppressive form of policing; refined styles produce a service emphasis with stress on working together.

Police–Community Relations

Police–Community Relations (PCR) An area of emerging police activity which stresses the need for the community and the police to work together effectively and emphasizes the notion that the police derive their legitimacy from the community they serve. PCR began to be of concern to many police agencies in the 1960s and 1970s.

In the 1960s, the legalistic style of policing, so common in America until then, began to yield to the newer service-oriented style of policing. The decade of the 1960s was one of unrest, fraught with riots and student activism. The war in Vietnam, civil rights concerns, and other burgeoning social movements produced large demonstrations and marches. The police, who were generally inexperienced in crowd control, all too often found themselves embroiled in tumultuous encounters with citizen groups. The police came to be seen by many as agents of "the establishment," and pitched battles between the police and the citizenry sometimes occurred.

Justice in American Context

The National Center for the Study of Police and Civil Disorder

In 1993, following the riots that swept Los Angeles and other American cities in the wake of the California acquittal of officers charged in the beating of black motorist Rodney King, the Police Foundation established the National Center for the Study of Police and Civil Disorder.

Hubert Williams, director of the Foundation, observed that police departments generally "possess little information on the underlying causes of civil unrest and lack standing policies and procedures detailing appropriate responses to incidents with the potential to escalate into disorder and destruction." "Moreover," said Williams, "the paramilitary crime-fighting style of many departments is based not on mutual trust and respect of police and community, but on an inbred suspicion and hostility that have served as tinder for civil disturbance." Finally, he said, "the police lack the capacity to resolve the deep-seated societal problems that form the basis for the anger and disenfranchisement felt by many in our inner cities."

Recognizing that the police cannot directly effect the fundamental social changes needed to "defuse much of this anger," Williams suggested that the police can

- "[C]ontribute to the community's sense of well being through the use of police strategies designed to build cooperative, mutually beneficial relationships between police and citizens;
- "[M]onitor indicators of community tension and take action to relieve it before it reaches explosive levels;
- "[R]espond to potentially troublesome situations in ways that defuse rather than inflame citizen hostility; and
- "[F]ace the challenge of full-scale disorder with a timely, appropriate, and effective level of force."

The National Center for the Study of Police and Civil Disorders, funded by a grant from the Ford Foundation, will develop new information on civil disorders for use by practitioners, planners, researchers, and policymakers; provide fellowships for practitioners and scholars; maintain a national information clearinghouse; convene conferences and workshops on changing aspects of the police role in contemporary society; and publish materials contributing to the body of knowledge on civil disorders. The Center will also assist police departments across the nation in developing Emergency Response Teams designed to be first-on-the-scene officers trained in diffusing potentially dangerous situations.

QUESTIONS FOR DISCUSSION:

1. Are better police–community relations an important issue in American criminal justice? Why or why not? If so, to whom are they important?
2. Other than the strategies just suggested by Hubert Williams, what else might police departments do to achieve better relations with the communities they serve?

Source: The Police Foundation, *Annual Report 1992* (Washington, D.C.: The Foundation, 1992).

As social disorganization increased, police departments across the nation sought ways to understand and deal better with the problems they faced. Significant outgrowths of this effort were the police–community relations (PCR) programs, which many departments created. Some authors have traced the development of the police–community relations concept to an annual conference begun in 1955.[8] Entitled the "National Institute of Police and Community Relations," the meetings were sponsored jointly by the National Conference of Christians and Jews and the Michigan State University Department of Police Administration and Public Safety. The emphasis on police community relations also benefited substantially from the 1967 report by the President's Commission on Law Enforcement and the Administration of Justice[9] which, as mentioned in Chapter 5, found that police agencies were often socially isolated from the communities they served.

PCR represented a movement away from an exclusive police emphasis on the apprehension of law violators and meant increasing the level of positive police–citizen interaction. At the height of the PCR movement city police departments across the country opened storefront centers where citizens could air complaints and easily interact with police representatives. As Egon Bittner recognized,[10] for PCR programs to be truly effective, they need to reach to "the grassroots of discontent," where citizen dissatisfaction with the police exists.

Contemporary police work involves a lot more than enforcing the law. *Courtesy of the New York City Police Department*

Many contemporary PCR programs involve public-relations officers appointed to provide an array of services to the community. "Neighborhood Watch" programs, drug awareness workshops, "Project ID"—which uses police equipment and expertise to mark valuables for identification in the event of theft—and police-sponsored victim's assistance programs are all examples of services embodying the spirit of PCR. Modern PCR programs, however, often fail to achieve their goal of increased community satisfaction with police services because they focus on providing services to groups who already are well satisfied with the police. On the other hand, PCR initiatives which do reach disaffected community groups are difficult to manage and may even alienate participating officers. Thus, as Bittner says, "while the first approach fails because it leaves out those groups to which the program is primarily directed, the second fails because it leaves out the police department."[11]

Team Policing

Team Policing The reorganization of conventional patrol strategies into "an integrated and versatile police team assigned to a fixed district." *Source:* Sam Souryal, *Police Administration and Management* (St. Paul, MN: West, 1977), p. 261.

During the 1960s and 1970s a number of communities began to experiment with the concept of team policing. An idea thought to have originated in Aberdeen, Scotland,[12] team policing, which in its heyday was defined as the reorganization of conventional patrol strategies into "an integrated and versatile police team assigned to a fixed district,"[13] rapidly became an extension of the PCR movement. Some authors have called team policing a "technique to deliver total police services to a neighborhood."[14] Others, however, have dismissed it as "little more than an attempt to return to the style of policing that was prevalent in the United States over a century ago."[15]

Team policing assigned officers on a semipermanent basis to particular neighborhoods, where it was expected they would become familiar with the inhabitants and with their problems and concerns. Patrol officers were given considerable authority in processing complaints from receipt through to resolution. Crimes were investigated and solved at the local level, with specialists called in only if the resources needed to continue an investigation were not locally available.

Community Policing

In recent years the police–community relations concept has undergone a substantial shift in emphasis. The old PCR model was built around the unfortunate self-image held by many police administrators of themselves as enforcers of the law who were isolated from, and often in opposition to, the communities they policed. Under such jaded administrators, PCR easily became a shallowly disguised and insecure effort to overcome public suspicion and community hostility.

In contrast, an increasing number of enlightened law enforcement administrators today are embracing the role of service provider. Modern police departments are frequently called upon to help citizens resolve a vast array of personal problems—many of which involve no law-breaking activity. Such requests may involve help for a sick child or the need to calm a distraught person, open a car with the keys locked inside, organize a community crime-prevention effort, investigate a domestic dispute, regulate traffic, or give a talk to a class of young people on the dangers of drug abuse. Calls for service today far exceed the number of calls received by the police which directly relate to law violations. As a consequence, the referral function of the police is crucial in producing effective law enforcement. Officers may make referrals, rather than arrests, for interpersonal problems to agencies as diverse as Alcoholics Anonymous, departments of social service, domestic violence centers, drug rehabilitation programs, and psychiatric clinics.

In contemporary America, according to Harvard University's Executive Session on Policing, police departments function a lot like business corporations. According to the Session, three generic kinds of "corporate strategies" guide American policing.[16] They are (1) strategic policing, (2) problem-solving policing, and (3) community policing.

The first, strategic policing, is something of a holdover from the reform era of the mid-1900s. **Strategic policing** "emphasizes an increased capacity to deal with crimes that are not well controlled by traditional methods."[17] Strategic policing retains the traditional police goal of professional crime fighting, but enlarges the enforcement target to include nontraditional kinds of criminals such as serial offenders, gangs and criminal associations, drug distribution networks, and sophisticated white-collar and computer criminals. To meet its goals, strategic policing generally makes use of innovative enforcement techniques, including intelligence operations, undercover stings, electronic surveillance, and sophisticated forensic methods.

The other two strategies give greater cognizance to the service style described by Wilson. **Problem solving** (or problem-oriented policing) takes the view that many crimes are caused by existing social conditions in the communities served by the police. To control crime, problem-oriented police managers attempt to uncover and effectively address underlying social problems. Problem-solving policing makes thorough use of other community resources such as counseling centers, welfare programs, and job-training facilities. It also attempts to involve citizens in the job of crime prevention through education, negotiation, and conflict management. Residents of poorly maintained housing areas, for example, might be asked to clean up litter, install better lighting, and provide security devices for their homes and apartments, in the belief that clean, secure, and well-lighted areas are a deterrent to criminal activity.

The third, and newest, police strategy goes a step beyond the other two. **Community policing** can be defined as "a collaborative effort between the police and the community that identifies problems of crime and disorder and involves all elements of the community in the search for solutions to these problems."[18] It has also been described as "a philosophy based on forging a partnership between the police and the community, so that they can work together on solving problems of crime, [and] fear of crime and disorder, thereby enhancing the overall quality of life in their neighborhoods."[19]

Community policing is a concept which evolved out of the early work of Robert C. Trojanowicz and George L. Kelling, who conducted studies of foot patrol programs in

Strategic Policing A style of policing which retains the traditional police goal of professional crime fighting, but enlarges the enforcement target to include nontraditional kinds of criminals such as serial offenders, gangs and criminal associations, drug distribution networks, and sophisticated white-collar and computer criminals. Strategic policing generally makes use of innovative enforcement techniques, including intelligence operations, undercover stings, electronic surveillance, and sophisticated forensic methods.

Problem-Solving Policing (also called **Problem-Oriented Policing**) A style of policing which assumes that many crimes are caused by existing social conditions within the community and that crimes can be controlled by uncovering and effectively addressing underlying social problems. Problem-solving policing makes use of other community resources such as counseling centers, welfare programs, and job-training facilities. It also attempts to involve citizens in the job of crime prevention through education, negotiation, and conflict management.

Community Policing A collaborative effort between the police and the community that identifies problems of crime and disorder and involves all elements of the community in the search for solutions to these problems.

Police officers serve food during an anti-crime rally to encourage citizen involvement in crime fighting. Activities such as this help foster the community policing ideal—through which law enforcement officers and members of the public become partners in controlling crime and keeping communities safe. *Dale Stockton*

Newark, New Jersey,[20] and Flint, Michigan,[21] showing that "police could develop more positive attitudes toward community members and could promote positive attitudes toward police if they spent time on foot in their neighborhoods."[22] The definitive work in the area is said by many to be Trojanowicz's book *Community Policing*,[23] published in 1990.

Community-policing attempts to actively involve the community with the police in the task of crime control by creating an effective working partnership between the community and the police.[24] As a consequence, community policing permits members of the community to participate more fully than ever before in defining the police role. In the words of Jerome Skolnick, community policing is "grounded on the notion that, together, police and public are more effective and more humane coproducers of safety and public order than are the police alone."[25] According to Skolnick, community policing involves at least one of four elements: (1) community-based crime prevention, (2) the reorientation of patrol activities to emphasize the importance of nonemergency services, (3) increased police accountability to the public, and (4) a decentralization of command, including a greater use of civilians at all levels of police decision making.[26] As one writer explains it, "Community policing seeks to integrate what was traditionally seen as the different law enforcement, order maintenance and social service roles of the police. Central to the integration of these roles is a working partnership with the community in determining what neighborhood problems are to be addressed, and how."[27] Table 6–1 highlights the differences between traditional and community policing.

Community policing is a two-way street. It not only requires the police to be aware of community needs, it also mandates both involvement and crime-fighting action on the part of citizens themselves. As Detective Tracie Harrison of the Denver, Colorado, police department explains it, "When the neighborhood takes stock in their community and they're serious they don't want crime, then you start to see crime go down…They're basically fed up and know the police can't do it alone."[28]

Creative approaches to policing have produced a number of innovative programs in recent years. In the early 1980s, for example, Houston's DART Program (Directed Area Responsibility Teams) emphasized problem-oriented policing; the Baltimore County, Maryland, police department began project COPE (Citizen Oriented Police Enforcement) in 1982; and Denver, Colorado, initiated its Community Service Bureau—one of the first major

Table 6-1 Traditional versus Community Policing

Question	Traditional	Community Policing
Who are the police?	A government agency principally responsible for law enforcement	Police are the public and the public are the police: The police officers are those who are paid to give full-time attention to the duties of every citizen.
What is the relationship of the police force to other public-service departments?	Priorities often conflict	The police are one department among many responsible for improving the quality of life.
What is the role of the police?	Focusing on solving crimes	A broader problem-solving approach
How is police efficiency measured?	By detection and arrest rates	By the absence of crime and disorder
What are the highest priorities?	Crimes that are high value (for example, bank robberies) and those involving violence	Whatever problems disturb the community most
What, specifically, do police deal with?	Incidents	Citizens' problems and concerns
What determines the effectiveness of police?	Response times	Public cooperation
What view do police take of service calls?	Deal with them only if there is no real police work to do	Vital function and great opportunity
What is police professionalism?	Swift, effective response to serious crime	Keeping close to the community
What kind of intelligence is most important?	Crime intelligence (study of particular crimes or series of crimes)	Criminal intelligence (information about the activities of individuals or groups)
What is the essential nature of police accountability?	Highly centralized; governed by rules, regulations, and policy directives; accountable to the law	Emphasis on local accountability to community needs
What is the role of headquarters?	To provide the necessary rules and policy directives	To preach organizational values
What is the role of the press liaison department?	To keep the "heat" off operational officers so they can get on with the job	To coordinate an essential channel of communication with the community
How do the police regard prosecutions?	As an important goal	As one tool among many

Source: Malcolm K. Sparrow, *Implementing Community Policing, National Institute of Justice* (Washington, D.C.: U.S. Department of Justice, 1988), pp. 8–9.

community-policing programs. By the late 1980s, Jerome H. Skolnick and David Bayley's study of six American cities, entitled *The New Blue Line: Police Innovation in Six American Cities*,[29] documented the growing strength of community–police cooperation throughout the nation, giving further credence to the continuing evolution of service-oriented styles of policing.

Police departments throughout the country continue to join the community-policing bandwagon. In April 1993, the city of Chicago launched a new comprehensive community-policing program called CAPS (Chicago's Alternative Policing Strategy). The Chicago plan uses rapid response teams composed of roving officers to handle emergencies, while many other officers have been put on permanent beats where they are highly visible throughout the city, with the avowed goal of maintaining and heightening citizen's perceptions of a police presence in their neighborhoods. Central to the CAPS program are monthly "beat meetings" between patrol officers and members of local neighborhoods. District Neighborhood Relations Offices provide an additional channel for communications between the police department and members of the public. CAPS actively brings other city

Crime is a community problem and stands today as one of the most serious challenges of our generation. Our citizens must...recognize their responsibilities in its suppression.
—O. W. Wilson

agencies into the process of community-order maintenance, tearing down deserted buildings, towing away abandoned cars, erasing graffiti, improving street lighting, and removing pay phones frequented by drug dealers. "Most of all," says Chicago Mayor Richard M. Daley, "we've enlisted the active participation of the people of Chicago. We have formed citizen advisory councils to track court cases and address other community issues that contribute to crime.... CAPS only works when people get involved."[30]

The CAPS program also makes innovative use of cutting-edge technology. At the start of the program, citywide cellular service providers Ameritech and Cellular One developed a plan to equip Chicago police officers and selected community members with cellular phones and voice mail to facilitate communication, and Chicago's new high-tech Emergency Communications Center is improving the department's response to emergency calls for police service. As Matt L. Rodriguez, Superintendent of Police for the city of Chicago explains it, "When most people think of community policing, they tend to focus on the interpersonal aspects of this new strategy—beat officers working with individual residents to address neighborhood problems. This type of personal partnership is certainly critical to CAPS.... In Chicago, however, we have also invested heavily in the technological aspects of community policing. We are using technology to strengthen the partnership between police and community and to help us work together on identifying and solving crime problems in our neighborhoods."[31]

Evaluations of CAPS conducted in 1995 and 1996[32] found that the program had "improved the lives of residents in virtually every area."[33] Survey-based measures showed crime-related problems declining after CAPS implementation, and official crime statistics showed a steady decline in major crimes committed in Chicago through the first half of 1997 (the latest period for which statistics are available).[34] Residents reported that street drug dealing, shootings, violence by gangs, and robbery victimization had all declined in the two years since CAPS had been implemented, although it was difficult to conclude that the decline had been entirely due to CAPS. The study did report conclusively, however, that city residents experienced a significant increase in optimism about police services since CAPS began, especially in the area of police responsiveness to neighborhood concerns.

In another example of the continuing move toward community policing, in 1994 the Los Angeles Police Department began helping residents focus on problems which provide a breeding ground for crime. Throughout the city, LAPD officers now help find jobs for teenagers, assist tenants in getting landlords to repair run-down rental property, and accompany citizen patrols in high-drug areas. The department also developed a "Community Enhancement Request" form that "enables an officer to request specific services from city agencies to handle conditions that may result in crime or community decay."[35] Their efforts appear to be paying off. FBI crime statistics released a year after the program began show that major crimes in Los Angeles fell by 12%, then declined another 11.6% from 1995 to 1996.[36]

Although community-policing programs began in the nation's metropolitan areas, the spirit of such programs, which centers on "community engagement and problem solving," has since spread to rural areas. Sheriff's departments that operate community-policing programs sometimes refer to them as "neighborhood-oriented policing" in recognition of the decentralized nature of rural communities. A report on neighborhood-oriented policing by the Bureau of Justice Assistance says that "[t]he stereotypical view is that police officers in rural areas naturally work more closely with the public than do officers in metropolitan areas."[37] Such a view, warns BJA, may not be entirely accurate, and rural departments would do well "to recognize that considerable diversity exists among rural communities and rural law enforcement agencies." Hence, as in metropolitan areas, effective community policing requires involvement of all members of the community in problem identification and problem solving.

The emphasis on community policing continues to grow. Title I of the Violent Crime Control and Law Enforcement Act of 1994, known as the Public Safety Partnership and Community Policing Act of 1994, highlights the role of community policing in combating crime nationwide and makes funding available for (among other things) "increas(ing) the number of law enforcement officers involved in activities that are focused on interaction

Community Policing in Reno, Nevada

Reno, Nevada, is a city of 120,000 with a police department of 313 sworn officers. The department also serves the needs of as many as 60,000 visitors who frequent the city's gambling districts weekly. Community policing began in Reno following a 1987 survey of public opinion that revealed that the police department suffered from a serious image problem. Public opinion described policing in Reno as "uncaring and heavy handed." At the time of the survey, the Reno police department was run via a "management by objectives" (MBO) administrative philosophy that equated high arrest rates with successful policing. The first community-policing efforts began under then-Chief R. V. Bradshaw, following the defeat of two public referendums to increase funding levels for the department.

In 1992 Richard Kirkland was appointed Reno's chief of police and immediately initiated a new program called "Community Oriented Policing and Problem Solving" (COPPS). COPPS was implemented as a departmentwide philosophy under the motto "Your police, our community." A new 40-hour training program was required of every police employee, and administrative decentralization brought about a major change in the department's organizational structure. Neighborhood advisory groups (NAGs) were developed and a Quality Assurance Bureau was created to conduct both internal and external surveys with an eye toward improving police–community relations. NAGs encouraged the sharing of ideas between police officials and community groups. Patrol officers were encouraged to identify community groups that could host NAG meetings, and NAG sessions began in earnest.

As a result of NAG meetings and community surveys, the Reno Police Department initiated a number of new police efforts. Among them were (1) an eviction program in the North/Stead area to remove drug traffickers from HUD-sponsored apartments, (2) an effort to take back control of Pat Baker Park from an army of drug dealers and users who had been using the park as a storefront for illicit transactions, (3) the use of a number of out-of-state undercover officers to eliminate "crack houses" in the Trainer Way portion of the city, (4) department-initiated towing of abandoned vehicles from Stead, an abandoned Air Force Base within the city limits, (5) establishment of a footbeat program in the Patton Drive area, where drive-by shootings and gang-related activities had been identified as problems, (6) development of the Comprehensive Mental Health Assessment Program (COMPAS) to deal effectively with the city's mentally ill and homeless populations, (7) changes in traffic enforcement procedures to use a greater number of warning tickets, and the department's acquisition of a radar trailer displaying the speed of oncoming vehicles, (8) initiation of foot, bicycle, and dirt bike patrols in downtown areas to meet the needs of Reno's many visitors, and (9) the establishment of a new communications network to better link downtown casino security operations to the police department.

Following these and other well-publicized efforts to improve the department's image, community surveys reported a considerable degree of success. While the initial 1987 survey found only 31.6% of residents feeling good about the police department, a similar 1992 survey revealed 68.7% of the populace reporting such feelings.

Similarly, the percentage of respondents reporting that officers "did not convey a feeling of concern" was cut by two-thirds between surveys. Eventually, renewed citizen satisfaction with the Reno Police Department resulted in the success of a local tax referendum that provided the department with 88 additional officers—a 39 percent increase in sworn personnel.

QUESTIONS FOR DISCUSSION

1. Why do you think more citizens reported "feeling good" about the Reno, Nevada, police department after it implemented a community-policing program? Why didn't everyone report feeling that way?

2. How do community policing programs convey a feeling that the police are concerned about citizens? What other kinds of feelings might such programs convey?

Sources: Richard Kirkland, *Community Oriented Police and Problem Solving: COPPS* (Reno, NV: Reno Police Department, 1992); Jim Weston, "Community Oriented Policing: An Approach to Traffic Management," *Law and Order*, May 1991; Robert V. Bradshaw, Ken Peak, and Ronald W. Glensor, "Community Policing Enhances Reno's Image," *The Police Chief*, October 1990; David M. Kennedy, "The Strategic Management of Police Resources," *Perspectives on Policing* (Washington, D.C.: National Institute of Justice, January 1993); and Ronald W. Glensor and Ken Peak, "Improving Perceptions of the Police with Community Policing: The Reno Experience," paper presented at the annual meeting of the Academy of Criminal Justice Sciences, March 1993.

with members of the community on proactive crime control and prevention by redeploying officers to such activities." The avowed purposes of the Community Policing Act are to (1) substantially increase the number of law enforcement officers interacting directly with members of the community (through a funded program known as "cops on the beat"); (2) provide additional and more effective training to law enforcement officers in order to enhance their problem solving, service, and other skills needed in interacting with members of the community; (3) encourage the development and implementation of innovative programs to permit members of the community to assist local law enforcement agencies in the prevention of crime in the community; and (4) encourage the development of new technologies to assist local law enforcement agencies in reorienting the emphasis of their activities from reacting to crime to preventing crime.

Also in 1994, the Community Policing Consortium, based in Washington, D.C., began operations. The Consortium, which is administered and funded by the U.S. Department of Justice's Bureau of Justice Assistance, provides a forum for training and information exchange in the area of community policing. Members of the Consortium include the International Association of Chiefs of Police, the National Sheriff's Association, the Police Executive Research Forum, the Police Foundation, and the National Organization of Black Law Enforcement Executives.

Critique of Community Policing

Unfortunately, problems remain in the community-policing area.[38] For one thing, there is evidence that not all police officers or police managers are ready to accept new images of police work. Many are loathe to take on new responsibilities as service providers whose role is increasingly defined by community needs and less by strict interpretation of the law. As one writer, a police sergeant with a Ph.D. in sociology, puts it, "It is an unrealistic leap of faith to presume that the police institution has the resources or capability to carry on all that its newly defined function will demand of it…There is no valid reason for the police to take on all of these responsibilities other than what appears to be a tacit argument that the agency of last resort is the only one that can be held strictly accountable to the public."[39] In this writer's view, the police, once their role is broadly defined by community needs, become a kind of catchall agency, or "agency of last resort," required to deal with problems ranging from handling the homeless to "worrying about the small mountains of trash on the all-too-many empty lots that once housed people and businesses."

A New York City police officer offers yet another criticism: "If we make the goals of community policing impossible to achieve, we doom the undertaking to failure. If we overwhelm police administrators with the enormity and vagueness of their proposed function, they will resist all attempts at reform."[40] He adds, "The notion of allowing the 'community' to participate in defining the police role is ill-conceived, and the most potentially explosive idea associated with community policing…If we follow the proposal that the police function is now anything the community defines it to be, it will become virtually impossible for police departments to accomplish any goals."[41]

Some authors have warned that the **police subculture** is so committed to a traditional view of police work, which is focused almost exclusively on crime fighting, that efforts to promote community policing can demoralize an entire department, rendering it ineffective at its basic tasks.[42] As the Independent Commission on the Los Angeles Police Department (the Christopher Commission) found following the "Rodney King riots," "[t]oo many…patrol officers view citizens with resentment and hostility; too many treat the public with rudeness and disrespect."[43] Some analysts warn that only when the formal values espoused by today's innovative police administrators begin to match those of rank and file officers can any police organization begin to be high performing in terms of the goals espoused by community police reformers.[44]

Nor are all public officials ready to accept community policing. Recently, for example, New York City mayor Rudolph W. Giuliani criticized the NYPD Community Police Officer Program (CPOP), saying that it "has resulted in officers doing too much social work and making too few arrests."[45] Similarly, many citizens are not ready to accept a greater involvement of the police in their personal lives. Although the turbulent protest-prone years of the 1960s and early 1970s are but a memory, some groups remain suspicious of the police. No

Police Culture (also **Subculture**) A particular set of values, beliefs, and acceptable forms of behavior characteristic of American police and with which the police profession strives to imbue new recruits. Socialization into the police subculture commences with recruit training and is ongoing thereafter.

matter how inclusive community-policing programs become, it is doubtful that the gap between the police and the public will ever be entirely bridged. The police role of restraining behavior which violates the law will always produce friction between police departments and some segments of the community.

Interestingly, as American police departments have outwardly embraced the community-policing model, they have also steadily increased their paramilitary capabilities. While only about 59% of police departments had S.W.A.T. (Special Weapons and Tactics) teams in 1982, for example, approximately 90% had such units in 1995. Moreover, a 1997 survey of police departments nationwide showed that 20% of departments without such a unit said they are planning to establish one. Hence, as the survey authors observe, "[t]hese findings reflect the aggressive turn many law enforcement agencies are assuming behind the rhetoric of community and problem-oriented policing reforms."[46]

If police agencies are to retain their relevance, however, it is likely that they will need to embrace community policing principles. In an intriguing 1997 article,[47] William F. Walsh, Director of the Southern Police Institute at the University of Louisville, "posits that policing has reached an important crossroads with organizational managers dividing their support between traditional [and] community/problem solving operational models." In order for the police to remain valuable within the society they serve, says Walsh, they must adapt their methods and their strategies to the political, social, and economic trends of emerging post-industrial society. "Community policing," Walsh writes, "requires the empowerment of patrol officers and operational supervisors who are being charged with the responsibility of developing solutions to community problems." Hence, community policing represents a shift in organizational power; that is, a movement away from centralized command and control. Walsh conceives of this shift in power as one leading to the creation of what he calls "learning organizations" staffed with "knowledge workers"—terms derived from organizational theory. "In an increasingly dynamic and unpredictable world," says Walsh, "learning organizations with the flexibility and responsiveness to adapt will be the ones most able to effectively fulfill their purpose." Information gathering and processing will emerge as the core technologies of modern police departments. As gatherers and users of information, police officers will become knowledge workers. In short, says Walsh, "the problems of the present and future call for fundamental rethinking of operational strategies if the police are to survive as a viable institution." As a result, predicts Walsh, police training and resource development in the next century "will differ drastically from what we are experiencing now." Others agree. Captain Andrew J. Harvey of the Covina, California, Police Department suggests that "in order to deal with the rapidly changing environment in the twenty-first century, law enforcement's paramilitary hierarchy, with rigid controls and strict chains of command, must give way to a structure that emphasizes network-type communication and flexibility The traditional organizational pyramid, with the chief at the top and line officers at the bottom, must become inverted."[48] Instead, says Harvey, "the community must sit at the top of the pyramid, followed by line officers, then supervisors, and finally the chief." Effective police administrators of the future, says Harvey, "will be consensus builders and agents of change." These leaders will look to the future, "anticipating trends while they perform day-to-day tasks."

Contemporary Policing: The Individual Officer

Regardless of the "official" policing style espoused by a department, individual officers retain considerable **discretion** in what they do. Police discretion refers to the exercise of choice by law enforcement officers in the decision to investigate or apprehend, the disposition of suspects, the carrying out of official duties, and in the application of sanctions. As one author has observed, "police authority can be, at once, highly specific and exceedingly vague."[49] The determination to stop and question suspects, the choice to arrest, and many other police practices are undertaken solely by individual officers acting in a decision-making capacity. Kenneth Culp Davis says, "The police make policy about what law to enforce, how much to

The police in the United States are not separate from the people. They draw their authority from the will and consent of the people, and they recruit their officers from them. The police are the instrument of the people to achieve and maintain order; their efforts are founded on principles of public service and ultimate responsibility to the public.

—The National Advisory Commission on Criminal Justice Standards and Goals

Discretion The exercise of choice, by law enforcement agents, in the disposition of suspects, in the carrying out of official duties, and in the application of sanctions.

enforce it, against whom, and on what occasions."[50] The discretionary authority exercised by individual law enforcement officers is of potentially greater significance to the individual who has contact with the police than are all department manuals and official policy statements combined.

Patrolling officers will often decide against a strict enforcement of the law, preferring instead to handle situations informally. Minor law violations, crimes committed out of the officer's presence where the victim refuses to file a complaint, and certain violations of the criminal law where the officer suspects sufficient evidence to guarantee a conviction is lacking, may all lead to discretionary action short of arrest. Although the widest exercise of discretion is more likely in routine situations involving relatively less serious violations of the law, serious and clear-cut criminal behavior may occasionally result in discretionary decisions to avoid an arrest. Drunk driving, possession of controlled substances, and assault are but a few examples of crimes in which on-the-scene officers may decide warnings or referrals are more appropriate than arrest.

A summation of various studies of police discretion tells us that a number of factors influence the discretionary decisions of individual officers. Some of these factors are

- *Background of the officer.* Law enforcement officers bring to their job all of life's previous experiences. Values shaped through early socialization in family environments, as well as attitudes acquired from ongoing socialization, impact the decisions an officer will make. If the officer has learned prejudice against certain ethnic groups, it is likely that such prejudices will manifest themselves in enforcement decisions. Officers who place a high value on the nuclear family may handle spouse abuse, child abuse, and other forms of domestic disputes in predetermined ways.

- *Characteristics of the suspect.* Some officers may treat men and women differently. A police friend of the author's has voiced the belief that women "are not generally bad…but when they do go bad, they go very bad." His official treatment of women has been tempered by this belief. Very rarely will this officer arrest a woman, but when he does, he spares no effort to see her incarcerated. Other characteristics of the suspect which may influence police decisions include demeanor, style of dress, and grooming. Belligerent suspects are often seen as "asking for it" and as challenging police authority. Well-dressed suspects are likely to be treated with deference, but poorly groomed suspects can expect less exacting treatment. Suspects sporting personal styles with a "message"—biker's attire, unkempt beards, outlandish haircuts, and other nonconformist styles—are more likely to be arrested than are others.

- *Department policy.* Discretion, while not entirely subject to control by official policy, can be influenced by it. If a department has targeted certain kinds of offenses, or if especially close control of dispatches and communications is held by supervisors who adhere to strict enforcement guidelines, discretionary release of suspects will be quite rare.

- *Community interest.* Public attitudes toward certain crimes will increase the likelihood of arrest for suspected offenders. Contemporary attitudes toward crimes involving children—including child sex abuse, the sale of drugs to minors, domestic violence involving children, and child pornography—have all led to increased and strict enforcement of laws governing such offenses across the nation. Communities may identify particular problems affecting them and ask law enforcement to respond. Fayetteville, North Carolina, adjacent to a major military base, was plagued a few years ago by a downtown area notorious for prostitution and "massage" parlors. Once the community voiced its concern over the problem and clarified its economic impact on the city, the police responded with a series of highly effective arrests, which eliminated massage parlors within the city limits. Departments which require officers to live in the areas they police are operating in recognition of the fact that community interests impact citizens and officers alike.

- *Pressures from victims.* Victims who refuse to file a complaint are commonly associated with certain crimes such as spouse abuse, the "robbery" of drug merchants, and assaults on customers of prostitutes. When victims refuse to cooperate with the police, there is often little that can be done. On the other hand, some victims are very vocal in insisting that their victimization be recognized and dealt with. Modern victim's assistance groups, including People Assisting Victims, the Victim's Assistance Network, and others, have sought to keep pressure on police departments and individual investigators to ensure the arrest and prosecution of suspects.

- *Disagreement with the law.* Some laws lack a popular consensus. Among them are many "victimless" offenses, such as homosexuality, lesbianism, drug use, gambling, pornography, and some crimes involving alcohol. Not all of these behaviors are even crimes in certain jurisdictions. Gambling is legal in Atlantic City, New Jersey, on board cruise ships, and in parts of Nevada. Many states have now legalized homosexuality and lesbianism and most forms of sexual behavior between consenting adults. Prostitution is officially sanctioned in portions of Nevada, and some drug offenses have been "decriminalized," with offenders being ticketed rather than arrested. Unpopular laws are not likely to bring much attention from law enforcement officers. Sometimes such crimes are regarded as just "part of the landscape" or as the consequence of laws which have not kept pace with a changing society. When arrests do occur, it may be because individuals investigated for more serious offenses were caught in the act of violating an unpopular statute. Drug offenders, for example, arrested in the middle of the night, may be "caught in the act" of an illegal sexual performance when the police break in. Charges may then include "crime against nature," as well as possession or sale of drugs.

  On the other hand, certain behaviors which are not law violations and which may even be protected by guarantees of free speech may be annoying, offensive, or disruptive according to the normative standards of a community or the personal standards of an officer. Where the law has been violated, and the guilty party is known to the officer, the evidence necessary for a conviction in court may be "tainted" or in other ways not usable. Sykes, in recognizing these possibilities, says, "One of the major ambiguities of the police task is that officers are caught between two profoundly compelling moral systems: justice as due process…and conversely, justice as righting a wrong as part of defining and maintaining community norms."[51] In such cases, discretionary police activity may take the form of "street justice" and approach vigilantism.

- *Available alternatives.* Police discretion can be impacted by the officer's awareness of alternatives to arrest. Community-treatment programs, including outpatient drug and alcohol counseling, psychiatric or psychological services, domestic dispute resolution centers, and other options may all be kept in mind by officers looking for a "way out" of official action.

- *Personal practices of the officer.* Some officers, because of actions undertaken in their personal lives, view potential law violations more or less seriously than other officers. The police officer who has an occasional marijuana cigarette with friends at a party may be inclined to deal less harshly with minor drug offenders than nonuser officers. The officer who routinely exceeds speed limits while driving the family car may be prone toward lenient action toward speeders encountered while on duty.

Contemporary Policing: Issues and Challenges

A number of issues hold special interest for today's police administrators and officers. Some concerns, such as police stress, danger, and the use of deadly force, derive from the very nature of police work. Others have arisen over the years due to commonplace practice, characteristic police values, and public expectations surrounding the enforcement of laws. Included here are such negatives as the potential for corruption, as well as positive efforts which focus on ethics and recruitment strategies to increase professionalism.

Police Personality and Culture

A few years ago Jerome Skolnick described what he called the "working personality" of police officers.[52] Skolnick's description was consistent with William Westley's classic study[53] of the Gary, Indiana, police department, in which he found a police culture with its own "customs,

Table 6-2 The Police Personality

Authoritarian	Individualistic	Secret
Cynical	Insecure	Prejudiced
Conservative	Loyal	
Suspicious	Efficient	
Hostile	Honorable	

laws, and morality," and with Niederhoffer's observation that cynicism was pervasive among officers in New York City.[54] More recent authors[55] have claimed that the "big curtain of secrecy" surrounding much of police work shields knowledge of the nature of the police personality from outsiders.

Skolnick found that a process of informal socialization, through which officers learn what is appropriate police behavior, occurs when new officers begin to work with seasoned veterans. Such informal socialization is often far more important than formal police academy training in determining how rookies will see police work. In everyday life, formal socialization occurs through schooling, church activities, job training, and so on. Informal socialization is acquired primarily from one's peers in less institutionalized settings and provides an introduction to value-laden subcultures. The information that passes between officers in the locker room, in a squad car, over a cup of coffee, or in many other relatively private moments produces a shared view of the world that can be best described as "streetwise." The streetwise cop may know what official department policy is, but he or she also knows the most efficient way to get a job done. By the time they become streetwise, rookie officers will know just how acceptable various informal means of accomplishing the job will be to other officers. The police subculture creates few real "mavericks," but it also produces few officers who view their job exclusively in terms of public mandates and official dictums.

Police Working Personality All aspects of the traditional values and patterns of behavior evidenced by police officers who have been effectively socialized into the police subculture. Characteristics of the police personality often extend to the personal lives of law enforcement personnel.

Skolnick says that the **police working personality** has at least six recognizable characteristics. Additional writers[56] have identified others. Taken in concert, they create the picture of the police personality shown in Table 6–2.

Some components of the police working personality are essential for survival and effectiveness. Officers are exposed daily to situations which are charged with emotions and can be potentially threatening. The need to gain control quickly over belligerent people leads to the development of authoritarian strategies for handling people. Eventually, such strategies become "second nature," and the cornerstone of the police personality is firmly set. Cynicism evolves from a constant flow of experiences which demonstrate that people and events are not always what they seem to be. The natural tendency of most suspects, even when they are clearly guilty in the eyes of the police, is denial. Repeated attempts to mislead the police in the performance of their duty creates an air of suspicion and cynicism in the minds of most officers.

The police personality has at least two sources. On the one hand, some aspects of the world view which comprise that personality can be attributed to the socialization which occurs when rookie officers are inducted into police ranks. On the other, it may be that some of the components of the police personality already exist in some individuals and lead them into police work.[57] Supporting the latter view are studies which indicate that police officers who come from conservative backgrounds continue to view themselves as defenders of middle-class morality.[58]

Police methods and the police culture are not static, however. Lawrence Sherman, for example, has reported on the modification of police tactics surrounding the use of weapons which characterized the period from 1970 to the 1980s.[59] Firearms, Sherman tells us, were routinely brought into play 25 years ago. Although not often fired, they would be frequently drawn and pointed at suspects. Few departmental restrictions were placed on the use of weapons, and officers employed them almost as they would their badge in the performance of duties. Today, the situation has changed. It is a rare officer who will unholster a weapon

Former NYPD officer Michael Dowd testifying before the Mollen Commission in 1993. The Commission investigated charges of corruption among New York City police and found instances of at least limited corruption among even senior officials. Dowd had been arrested for leading a ring of drug-dealing police officers. *Paul Hurschmann, AP/Wide World Photos*

during police work, and those who do know that only the gravest of situations can justify the public display of firearms.

Some authors attribute this shift in thinking about firearms to increased training and the growth of restrictive policies.[60] Changes in training, however, are probably more a response to a revolution in social understandings about the kind of respect due citizens. For example, the widespread change in social consciousness regarding the worth of individuals, which has taken place over the past few decades, appears to have had considerable impact upon police subculture itself.

CORRUPTION

The police role carries considerable authority, and officers are expected to exercise a well-informed discretion in all of their activities. The combination of authority and discretion, however, produces great potential for abuse.

Police deviance has been a problem in American society since the early days of policing. It is probably an ancient and natural tendency of human beings to attempt to placate or "win over" those in positions of authority over them. This tendency is complicated in today's materialistic society by greed and by the personal and financial benefits to be derived from evading the law. Hence, the temptations toward illegality offered to police range all the way from a free cup of coffee given by a small restaurant owner in the thought that one day it may be necessary to call upon the goodwill of the officer, perhaps for something as simple as a traffic ticket, to huge monetary bribes arranged by drug dealers to guarantee the police will look the other way as an important shipment of contraband arrives.

Exactly what constitutes corruption is not always clear. In recognition of what some have called corruption's "slippery slope,"[61] even the acceptance of minor gratuities is now explicitly prohibited by most police departments. The slippery slope perspective holds that even small "thank you's" which are accepted from members of the public can lead to a more ready acceptance of larger bribes. An officer who begins to accept, and then expect, gratuities may soon find that his or her practice of policing becomes influenced by such gifts and that larger ones soon follow. At that point the officer may easily slide to the bottom of the moral slope, one made slippery by previous small concessions.

Ethicists say that police corruption ranges from minor "offenses" to those which are themselves serious violations of the law. Another useful distinction is made by Barker and Carter, who distinguish between *occupational deviance* and *abuse of authority*.[62] Occupational deviance, they say, is motivated by the desire for personal benefit. Abuse of authority, however, occurs most often in order to further the organizational goals of law enforcement—including arrest, ticketing, and the successful conviction of suspects.

Examples of police deviance, ranked in what this author judges to be an increasing level of severity, are shown in Figure 6–1. Not everyone, however, would agree with this ranking.

Corruption Behavioral deviation from an accepted ethical standard.

We must strive to eliminate any racial, ethnic, or cultural bias that may exist among our ranks.
—Sherman Block, Los Angeles County Sheriff

A 1995 survey[63] of 6,982 New York City police officers found that 65% did not classify excessive force as corrupt behavior. Likewise, 71.4% of responding officers said that accepting a free meal is not a corrupt practice. Another 15% said that the use of illegal drugs should not be considered corruption.

Years ago, Frank Serpico made headlines as he testified before the Knapp Commission on police corruption in New York City.[64] Serpico, an undercover operative within the police department, revealed a complex web of corruption in which money and services routinely changed hands in "protection rackets" created by unethical officers. The Knapp Commission report distinguished between two types of corrupt officers, which they termed grass eaters and meat eaters.[65] "Grass eating," the most common form of police deviance, was described as illegitimate activity which occurs from time to time in the normal course of police work. It involves mostly small bribes or relatively minor services offered by citizens seeking to avoid arrest and prosecution. "Meat eating" is a much more serious form of corruption, involving as it does the active seeking of illicit money-making opportunities by officers. Meat eaters solicit bribes through threat or intimidation, whereas grass eaters make the simpler mistake of not refusing those which are offered.

Popular books often tell the story of police misbehavior. A few years ago, Robert Daley's best-seller *Prince of the City*[66] detailed the adventures of New York City detective Robert Leuci who walked among corrupt cops with a tape recorder hidden on his body. The more recent best-seller, *Buddy Boys*[67] by Mike McAlary is subtitled *When Good Cops Turn Bad*. McAlary, an investigative reporter with *New York Newsday*, began his efforts to uncover police corruption with a list of 13 names of officers who had been suspended in New York's

FIGURE 6–1 Types of police deviance by category and example.

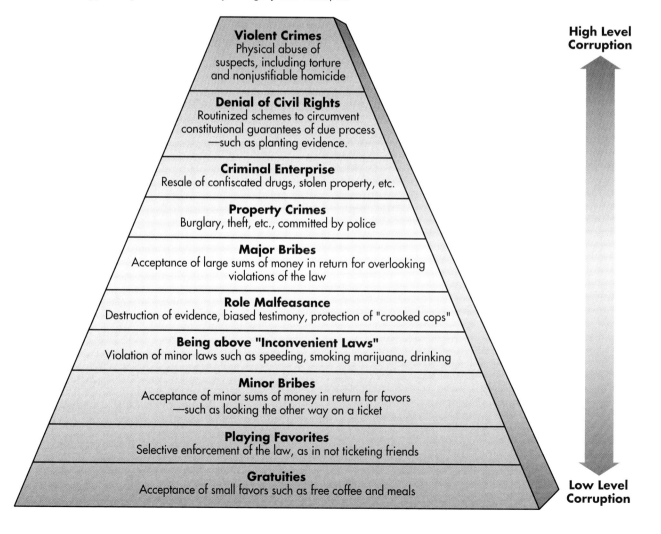

77th precinct. His book describes organized criminal activity among police in the "Big Apple," involving holdups of drug dealers, organized burglaries, fencing operations, and numerous other illegal activities conducted from behind the shield. McAlary says New York's criminal officers saw themselves as a kind of "elite" within the department and applied the name "Buddy Boys" to their gang.[68]

In 1993, during 11 days of corruption hearings reminiscent of the **Knapp Commission** era, a parade of crooked New York police officers testified before the Mollen Commission, headed by former judge and deputy mayor Milton Mollen. Among the many revelations, officers spoke of dealing drugs, stealing confiscated drug funds, stifling investigations, and beating innocent people. Officer Michael Dowd, for example, told the commission that he had run a cocaine ring out of his station house in Brooklyn and bought three homes on Long Island and a Corvette with the money he made. Most shocking of all, however, were allegations that high-level police officials attempted to hide embarrassing incidents in a "phantom file" and that many such officials may have condoned unprofessional and even criminal practices by law enforcement officers under their command. Honest officers, including internal affairs investigators, reported on how their efforts to end corruption among their fellows had been defused and resisted by higher authorities.

Spectacular as they were, however, many doubt that the Mollen hearings will have much long-term impact on policing in New York City. "The Knapp Commission exposed a form of corruption that was systemic and pervasive," said Daniel Guido, a professor at John Jay College of Criminal Justice in New York. "It involved not only the working levels of the force and plainclothes men but their supervisors. It was part of the culture of the force…. What we're seeing [with the Mollen Hearings] is not systemic, and it involves only police officers in the main. It's all been sensational and revolting, but it's important not to overgeneralize the extent to which this is going on."

Some experts say that the New York City Police Department actually has corruption under better control than most other large-city departments and that the few cases of corruption identified by the Mollen Commission were trivial relative to the size of the department. Even so, the hearings do seem to show that corruption is nearly impossible to completely stamp out and that it reemerges with each new generation of officers.

Corruption, of course, is not unique to New York. In 1992 Detroit Police Chief William Hart was sentenced to a maximum of ten years in federal prison for embezzling $2.6 million from a secret police department fund and for tax evasion. The fund, which was to be used for undercover drug buys and to pay informants, had secretly paid out nearly $10 million since its creation in 1980. Hart, who was 68 years old at the time of sentencing, had been police chief in Detroit since 1976. He resigned from office the day after his conviction, following a pension board ruling that he is entitled to receive a $53,000 annual pension despite the conviction. Hart's arrest had come on the heels of other problems for Detroit police. Two years earlier a city police officer was arrested for allegedly committing five robberies in one evening, and eight other officers were arrested for breaking and entering and assault. The *Detroit News*, a major newspaper in the city, conducted a study in which it found that Detroit police are "accused of committing crimes more often than officers in any other major U.S. city."[69]

In 1997, although not charged with corruption, Chicago Police Superintendent Matt Rodriguez resigned after a report[70] by the *Chicago Tribune* that he had violated department rules forbidding fraternization with convicted criminals. Rodriguez admitted having a long-standing friendship with Frank Milito, a former gas station owner who had served nine months in prison after pleading guilty in 1986 to charges of mail fraud. Milito was also convicted of having failed to pay $250,000 in taxes on gasoline sold by his station.

Even small cities are not immune to corruption. In 1992 former Rochester, New York, chief of police Gordon F. Urlacher was sentenced to four years in federal prison and fined $150,000 for embezzling about $300,000 from the city. Urlacher denied guilt, claiming that he was simply a bad accountant.

Money—The Root of Police Evil?

The police personality provides fertile ground for the growth of corrupt practices. Police "cynicism" develops out of continued association with criminals and problem-laden people. The cop who is "streetwise" is also ripe for corrupt influences to take root. Years ago, Edwin

Knapp Commission A committee that investigated police corruption in New York City in the early 1970s.

Sutherland applied the concept of differential association to deviant behavior.[71] You may recall from our discussion in Chapter 3 in connection with causes of crime that Sutherland suggested that continued association with one type of person, more frequently than with any other, would make the associates similar.

Sutherland was talking about criminals, not police officers. Consider, however, the dilemma of the average officer: A typical day is spent running down petty thieves, issuing traffic citations to citizens who try to talk their way out of the situation, dealing with prostitutes who feel "hassled" by the police presence, and arresting drug users who think it should be their right to do what they want as long as it "doesn't hurt anyone." The officer encounters personal hostility and experiences a constant, and often quite vocal, rejection of society's formalized norms. Bring into this environment low pay and the resulting sense that police work is not really valued, and it is easy to understand how an officer might develop a jaded attitude about the double standards of the civilization he or she is sworn to protect.

In fact, low pay may be a critical ingredient of the corruption mix. Salaries paid to police officers in this country have been notoriously low when compared to other professions involving personal dedication, extensive training, high stress, and the risk of bodily harm. As police professionalism increases, many police administrators hope that salaries will rise. No matter how much police pay grows, however, it will never be able to compete with the staggering amounts of money to be made though dealing in contraband. In *The Underground Empire: Where Crime and Governments Embrace*, James Mills[72] tells the story of a man he calls a "young American entrepreneur," whom, he writes, has "criminal operations on four continents and a daily income greater than U.S. Steel's."[73] Mills's book is about "Centac," a semisecret arm of the Drug Enforcement Administration, which coordinates the operations of various agencies in the ongoing battle against illicit drugs. Although international drug trafficking is the focus of *The Underground Empire*, the book contains details of international police corruption fostered via the vast resources available to the trade.

Working hand in hand with monetary pressures toward corruption are the moral dilemmas produced by unenforceable laws which provide the basis for criminal profit. During the Prohibition Era the Wickersham Commission warned of the potential for official corruption inherent in the legislative taboos on alcohol. The demand for drink, immense as it was, called into question the wisdom of the law, while simultaneously providing vast resources designed to circumvent the law. Today's drug scene bears some similarities to the Prohibition Era. As long as substantial segments of the population are willing to make large financial and other sacrifices to feed the drug trade, the pressures on the police to embrace corruption will remain substantial.

Combating Corruption

High moral standards, embedded into the principles of the police profession and effectively communicated to individual officers through formal training and peer group socialization, are undoubtedly the most effective way to combat corruption in police work. There are, of course, many officers of great personal integrity who hold to the highest of professional ideals. There is evidence that law enforcement training programs are becoming increasingly concerned with instruction designed to reinforce the high ideals many recruits bring to police work. As a 1995 FBI article puts it, "Ethics training must become an integral part of academy and in-service training for new and experienced officers alike."[74]

Recently, a "reframing" strategy targeting police corruption has emphasized *integrity* rather than *corruption*. In 1997, for example, the National Institute of Justice released a report entitled *Police Integrity: Public Service With Honor*.[75] The report built upon recommendations made by participants in the National Symposium on Police Integrity, which was held in Washington, D.C., in July 1996. Symposium participants included police chiefs, sheriffs, police researchers, police officers, members of other professional disciplines, community leaders, and members of other federal agencies from throughout the country. Following the lead of symposium participants, the NIJ report included many recommendations for enhancing police integrity, such as (1) integrating ethics training into the programs offered by newly funded Regional Community Policing Institutes throughout the country, (2) broadening research activities in the area of ethics through NIJ awarded grants for research on police integrity, and (3) conducting case studies of departments that have an excellent track record in the area of police integrity.

On the practical side, most large law enforcement agencies have their own **Internal Affairs** Divisions, which are empowered to investigate charges of wrongdoing made against officers. Where necessary, state police agencies may be called upon to examine reported incidents. Federal agencies, including the FBI and the DEA, involve themselves when corruption goes far enough to violate federal statutes. The U.S. Department of Justice, through various investigative offices, has the authority to examine possible violations of civil rights which may result from the misuse of police authority and is often supported by the American Civil Liberties Union, the NAACP, and other "watchdog" groups in such endeavors.

Internal Affairs That branch of a police organization tasked with investigating charges of wrongdoing against other members of the department.

Drug Testing of Police Employees

In 1997 a federal grand jury charged seven Chicago police tactical officers, considered to be among the city's finest frontline troops in the war on drugs, with plotting to arrest undercover agents posing as drug dealers and to steal their drugs. Prosecutors accused one of the indicted officers of being both a police officer and a street-gang leader. "Edward Lee Jackson," said prosecutors, "is a high-ranking leader of the Conservative Vice Lords street gang." The Jackson indictment led many to conclude that the 13,500-member Chicago Police Department had been deeply penetrated by members or associates of the city's drug gangs.[76]

On a wider scale, the widespread potential for police corruption created by illicit drugs has led to focused efforts to combat drug use by officers. Drug testing programs at the department level are an example of such efforts. When concern was at its highest, the National Institute of Justice conducted a telephone survey of 33 large police departments across the nation to determine what measures were being taken to identify officers and civilian employees who were using drugs.[77] NIJ learned that almost all departments had written procedures to test employees who were reasonably suspected of drug abuse. Applicants for police positions were being tested by 73% of the departments surveyed, and 21% of the departments were actively considering testing all officers. In what some people found a surprisingly low figure, 21% reported that they might offer treatment to identified violators rather than dismiss them, depending upon their personal circumstances.

The International Association of Chiefs of Police makes available to today's police managers a "Model Drug Testing Policy." The policy is directed toward the needs of local departments and suggests[78]

- Testing all applicants and recruits for drug or narcotics use.
- Testing current employees when performance difficulties or documentation indicate a potential drug problem.
- Testing current employees when they are involved in the use of excessive force or suffer or cause on-duty injury.
- Routine testing of all employees assigned to special "high-risk" areas such as narcotics and vice.

Drug testing based upon a reasonable suspicion that drug abuse has been or is occurring has been supported by the courts (*Maurice Turner* v. *Fraternal Order of Police*, 1985),[79] although random testing of officers was banned by the New York State Supreme Court in the case of *Philip Caruso, President of P.B.A.* v. *Benjamin Ward, Police Commissioner* (1986).[80] Citing overriding public interests, a 1989 decision by the U.S. Supreme Court upheld the testing of U.S. Customs personnel applying for transfer into positions involving drug law enforcement or carrying a firearm.[81] Many legal issues surrounding employee drug testing, however, remain to be resolved in court.

Complicating the situation is the fact that drug and alcohol addiction are "handicaps" protected by the Federal Rehabilitation Act of 1973. As such, federal law enforcement employees, as well as those working for agencies with federal contracts, are entitled to counseling and treatment before action toward termination can be taken.

The issue of employee drug testing in police departments, as in many other agencies, is a sensitive one. Some claim that existing tests for drug use are inaccurate, yielding a significant

The aftermath of the February 28, 1997 North Hollywood, California, shoot-out between police and bank robbers armed with fully automatic AK-47's. An LAPD officer walks past the body of one of the robbers, which lies covered in front of his getaway car. *Sam Mircovich, Archive Photos*

number of "false positives." Repeated testing and high "threshold" levels for narcotic substances in the blood may eliminate many of these concerns. Less easy to address, however, is the belief that drug testing intrudes upon the personal rights and professional dignity of individual employees.

The Dangers of Police Work

On October 15, 1991, the National Law Enforcement Memorial was unveiled in Washington, D.C. Initially, the memorial contained the names of 12,561 law enforcement officers killed in the line of duty. Nearly 1,000 names have since been added.[82]

Police work is, by its very nature, dangerous. While it is true that most officers throughout their careers never draw their weapons in the line of duty, it is also plain that some officers meet death while performing their jobs. On-the-job police deaths occur from stress, training accidents, and auto crashes. However, it is violent death at the hands of criminal offenders that police officers and their families fear most.

Violence in the Line of Duty

On February 28, 1997, two heavily-armed men bungled a daylight bank robbery attempt in North Hollywood, California. The men were wearing full body armor and carried automatic weapons.

LAPD Lt. Greg Meyer described the scene this way: "Imagine yourself working uniformed patrol at 9:15 A.M. on a warm sunny day and you suddenly find yourself in Beirut, Bosnia, or back in the Mekong Delta. You go from thinking about where you'll stop for that next cup of coffee, to having your black-and-white shot up with full-automatic AK-47 rounds. Within the next few minutes, officers and civilians all about you are shot down in the street by bank robbers who look like Ninja Turtles dressed to kill. And unlike the usual 'gunbattle' that lasts a few seconds, this time the shooting just keeps going, and going, and going…"[83]

The robbers didn't run when police arrived, instead standing their ground and firing bursts of armor-piercing rounds from 100-clip magazines. Covered from head to toe in full body armor, the men took numerous hits from police small arms fire without seeming to notice. Detective Gordon Hagge, one of the first officers on the scene of the shootout later told reporters for the *Los Angeles Times* that he started thinking, "I'm in the wrong place with

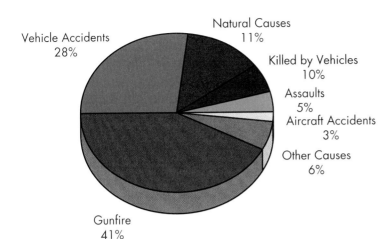

Natural Causes
11%

Vehicle Accidents
28%

Killed by Vehicles
10%

Assaults
5%

Aircraft Accidents
3%

Other Causes
6%

Gunfire
41%

FIGURE 6–2 U.S. law enforcement officers killed in the line of duty—percentage by type of incident, 1996. *Source:* Officer Down Memorial Page on the World Wide Web, http://www.odmp.org.

the wrong gun."[84] Then reality set in, said Lt. Meyer, and officers soon realized that they had "brought cap guns to World War III."[85]

Courageous officers succeeded in blocking the robbers' escape route long enough for the LAPD SWAT team's armored personnel carrier to arrive. Both would-be robbers, Larry Eugene Philips, Jr., and Emil Mataasarenanu, were finally killed in the massive exchange of gunfire that ensued. The firefight lasted nearly 20 minutes and was televised by a KTLA-TV helicopter hovering over the scene. By the time the incident ended, 18 civilians and officers had been injured.[86]

A few weeks later, in a move to give police officers heavier firepower, the Los Angeles Police Commission voted to authorize the city's officers to carry .45-caliber semi-automatic pistols in place of the 9 mm and .38-caliber revolvers that they had been using. In addition, 550 police supervisors throughout the city were given easy access to M-16 assault rifles,[87] along with "slug" ammunition (that has greater "knockdown" power when fired against suspects wearing body armor) for their shotguns.[88]

Although running gun battles are a rarity in police work, they appear to be occurring with greater regularity. Unlike the North Hollywood "incident," however, most officers are killed by lone suspects armed with a single weapon. In the early morning hours of September 30, 1992, for example, Oregon State Police Trooper Bret Clodfelter[89] stopped an intoxicated driver near Klamath Falls, Oregon. The driver was accompanied by two companions. Trooper Clodfelter arrested the car's operator, handcuffed him, and placed him in the rear of his patrol car. Since the offender's companions did not have a ride, Trooper Clodfelter offered to take them into town. After patting the men down for weapons he placed them in the rear of his patrol car, along with the arrestee. As the officer started to take the men home, one of the passengers told the killer several times (in Spanish) to shoot the trooper. Trooper Clodfelter, who did not speak Spanish, was unaware of what was being said. The killer, Francisco Mando-Hernandez, pulled out a .38 caliber handgun and shot Trooper Clodfelter four times in the back of the head. The weapon had been concealed in a coat pocket, but had not been discovered during the pat down search. All suspects fled the scene but were captured a few days later after an intensive manhunt.

Trooper Clodfelter had been married only 33 days before he died and left behind a new bride and two young children from a previous marriage. Thirteen months after his murder, Trooper Clodfelter's wife, devastated by the loss, took her own life. In 1995 Mando-Hernandez was found guilty of first-degree murder and sentenced to prison. He is currently appealing his conviction and sentence.

In 1997, 174 American law enforcement officers were killed in the line of duty.[90] Figure 6–2 shows the percentage of officers killed by circumstances. A recent study by the FBI found that slain officers appeared to be good natured and conservative in the use of physical force, "as compared to other law enforcement officers in similar situations. They were also perceived as being well-liked by the community and the department, friendly to everyone, laid back, and easy going."[91] Finally, the study also found, officers who were killed failed to wear protective vests.

Twenty-First Century Criminal Justice

"Smart Guns" and Line of Duty Deaths

Statistics show that of all officers killed feloniously in the line of duty, 16% (or one in six), are killed by a suspect with their own or another officer's service weapon. In an effort to reduce the number of such line-of-duty deaths, the National Institute of Justice (NIJ) recently funded a research project with Sandia National Laboratory intended to develop "smart gun" technology. "Smart gun" is a term used to describe a firearm that "recognizes" the user and can only be fired by an authorized user.

A variety of "smart gun" enabling mechanisms are being tested by Sandia, including those with esoteric names, such as surface acoustic wave tagging, passive radio frequency coding, touch memory, magnetic encoding, capacitive sensors/encoding, and remote radio frequency disablement. It is expected that, as a result of tests that are now ongoing, mechanical or electromechanical safing mechanisms that can be activated or deactivated by the weapon's legitimate user will soon be incorporated during the manufacturing process into firearms carried by law enforcement personnel. Working models are already available. Colt Manufacturing Company, one of the manufacturers collaborating on smart gun technology, demonstrated the first working prototype of a smart gun at a Capitol Hill press conference in late 1996.

In addition to reducing line-of-duty deaths, smart gun technology holds the potential to substantially reduce the number of children and adolescents who die each year from the accidental discharge of firearms and to reduce the likelihood that stolen weapons will be used in criminal activities.

Source: Sandia National Laboratories, World Wide Web Site.

I think I know what's wrong with the police — We're the only ticket in town. If you call the police, you get us!

—Superintendent Christopher R. Braiden, Edmonton Police Service, Alberta, Canada

For statistics on police killings to have meaning beyond the personal tragedy they entail, however, it is necessary to place them within a larger framework. There are approximately 800,000 state and local police employees in this country, and another 70,000 federal agents nationwide. Such numbers demonstrate that the rate of violent death among law enforcement officers in the line of duty is small indeed.

Risk of Disease and Infected Evidence

Not all the dangers facing law enforcement officers are as direct as outright violence and assault. The increasing incidence of serious diseases capable of being transmitted by blood and other bodily fluids, combined with the fact that crime and accident scenes are inherently dangerous, has made "caution" a necessary byword among investigators and "first-on-the-scene" officers. Potential for minor cuts and abrasions abounds in the broken glass and torn metal of a wrecked car, in the sharp edges of weapons remaining at the scene of an assault or murder, and in drug implements such as razor blades and hypodermic needles secreted in vehicles, apartments, and in pockets. Such minor injuries, previously shrugged off by many police personnel, have become a focal point for warnings about the dangers of AIDS (acquired immune deficiency syndrome), hepatitis B, tuberculosis, and other diseases spread through contact with infected blood.

In 1988 in Sonoma County, California, Sheriff Dick Michaelson became the first law enforcement supervisor to announce a clear-cut case of AIDS infection in an officer caused by interaction with a suspect. A deputy in Michaelson's department apparently contracted AIDS a few years earlier when he was pricked by a hypodermic needle during a "pat down" search.[92]

In 1992 a 46-year-old San Francisco police officer won $50,547 in disability pay and AIDS medical treatment expenses[93] and a possible $25,000-per-year permanent retirement benefit. Inspector Thomas Cady became infected with the HIV (human immunodeficiency virus) after being bitten and splashed with blood during an arrest a few years earlier.

Table 6-3 *Responses to AIDS-Related Law Enforcement Concerns*

Issue/Concern	Educational and Action Messages
Human bites	Person who bites usually receives the victim's blood; viral transmission through saliva is highly unlikely. If bitten by anyone, milk wound to make it bleed; wash the area thoroughly, and seek medical attention.
Spitting	Viral transmission through saliva is highly unlikely.
Urine/feces	Virus isolated in only very low concentrations in urine; not at all in feces; no cases of AIDS or AIDS virus infection associated with either urine or feces.
Cuts/puncture wounds	Use caution in handling sharp objects and searching areas hidden from view; needle stick studies show risk of infection is very low.
CPR/first aid	To eliminate the already minimal risk associated with CPR, use masks/airways; avoid blood-to-blood contact by keeping open wounds covered and wearing gloves when in contact with bleeding wounds.
Body removal	Observe crime scene rules: Do not touch anything. Those who must come into contact with blood or other bodily fluids should wear gloves.
Casual contact	No cases of AIDS or AIDS virus infection attributed to casual contact.
Any contact with blood or body fluids	Wear gloves if contact with blood or body fluids is considered likely. If contact occurs, wash thoroughly with soap and water; clean up spills with one part water to nine parts household bleach.
Contact with dried blood	No cases of infection have been traced to exposure to dried blood. The drying process itself appears to inactivate the virus. Despite low risk, however, caution dictates wearing gloves, a mask, and protective shoe coverings if exposure to dried blood particles is likely (for example, crime scene investigation).

Source: National Institute of Justice, Report No. 206 (November/December 1987), p. 6.

Understandably, there is much concern among officers as to how to deal with the threat of AIDS and other bloodborne diseases. However, as a manual of the New York City Police Department reminds its officers, "Police officers have a professional responsibility to render assistance to those who are in need of our services. We cannot refuse to help. Persons with infectious diseases must be treated with the care and dignity we show all citizens."[94]

The FBI has also become concerned with the use of breath alcohol instruments on infected persons, the handling of evidence of all types, seemingly innocuous implements such as staples, the emergency delivery of babies in squad cars, and with the risk of attack (especially bites) by infected individuals who are being questioned or who are in custody. The following are among the 16 recommendations made by the FBI as "defenses against exposure" to infectious substances (others are listed in Table 6–3):[95]

1. The first line of defense against infection at the crime scene is protecting the hands and keeping them away from the eyes, mouth, and nose.
2. Any person with a cut, abrasion, or any other break in the skin on the hands should never handle blood or other body fluids without protection.
3. Use gloves and replace them whenever you leave the crime scene. Wash hands thoroughly.
4. No one at the crime scene should be allowed to smoke, eat, drink, or apply makeup.

Effective police work in the emerging society will depend less on the holster and more on the head.

—Alvin Toffler

5. Use the utmost care when handling knives, razors, broken glass, nails, and the like to prevent a puncture of the skin.

6. If a puncture of the skin does occur, cleanse it thoroughly with rubbing alcohol and wash with soap and water. Then seek immediate medical assistance.

7. When possible, use disposable items at the crime scene, such as pencils, gloves, and throw-away masks. These items should be incinerated after use.

8. Nondisposable items, such as cameras, notebooks, and so on, should be decontaminated using bleach mixed with water.

The foundations of a successful community policing strategy are the close, mutually beneficial ties between police and community members.

—Bureau of Justice Statistics

The National Institute of Justice adds to this list the recommendations that suspects should be asked to empty their own pockets, where possible, and that puncture wounds should be "milked" as in the case of snakebites in order to help flush infectious agents from the wound.[96]

In order to better combat the threat of infectious diseases among health care professionals and public safety employees, the recently enacted federal Bloodborne Pathogens Act requires that police officers receive proper training in how to prevent contamination by bloodborne infectious agents. The act also requires that police officers undergo an annual refresher course on the topic.

Police departments will face an increasing number of legal challenges in the years to come in cases involving infectious diseases such as AIDS. Some predictable areas of concern will involve (1) the need to educate officers and other police employees relative to AIDS and other serious infectious diseases, (2) the responsibility of police departments to prevent the spread of AIDS in police lockups, and (3) the necessity of effective and nondiscriminatory enforcement activities and life-saving measures by police officers in AIDS environments. With regard to nondiscriminatory activities, the National Institute of Justice has suggested that legal claims in support of an officer's refusal to render assistance to people with AIDS would probably not be effective in court.[97] The reason is twofold: The officer has a basic duty to render assistance to individuals in need of it, and the possibility of AIDS transmission by casual contact has been scientifically established as extremely remote. A final issue of growing concern involves activities by police officers infected with the AIDS virus. A recent issue of *Law Enforcement News* reports, "Faced with one of the nation's largest populations of AIDS sufferers—and perhaps one of the largest cadres of AIDS-infected officers—the New York City Police Department has debuted its own AIDS awareness effort."[98] Few statistics are currently available on the number of officers with AIDS, but public reaction to those officers may be a developing problem area, which police managers will soon need to address.

Stress among Police Officers

Perhaps the most insidious and least visible of all threats facing law enforcement personnel today is debilitating stress. While some degree of stress can be a positive motivator, serious stress, over long periods of time, is generally regarded as destructive, even life threatening. Police detectives, for example, who worked around the clock in 1994 searching for two missing South Carolina boys whose mother first reported them as kidnapped but later confessed to drowning them, found the case especially stressful since it brought to mind many emotions. "I feel like I aged 10 years in 10 days,"[99] said Union County Sheriff Howard Wells, after Susan Smith confessed to her son's murders.

Stress is a natural component of police work.[100] The American Institute of Stress, based in Yonkers, New York, ranks policing among the top ten stress-producing jobs in the country.[101] Danger, frustration, paperwork, the daily demands of the job, and a lack of understanding from family members and friends contribute to the negative stresses officers experience.

Joseph Victor has identified four sources of police stress:[102] (1) external stress, which results from "real dangers," such as responding to calls involving armed suspects; (2) organizational stress, generated by the demands of police organizations themselves, such as scheduling, paperwork, training requirements, and so on; (3) personal stress, produced by interpersonal relationships among officers themselves; and (4) operational stress, which Victor defines as "the total effect of the need to combat daily the tragedies of urban life."

Some of the stressors in police work are particularly destructive. One is frustration brought on by the inability to be effective, regardless of the amount of personal effort expended. From the point of view of the individual officer, the police mandate is to bring about some change in society for the better. The crux of police work involves making arrests based upon thorough investigations which lead to convictions and the removal of individuals who are damaging to the social fabric of the community—all under the umbrella of the criminal law. Unfortunately, reality is often far from the ideal. Arrests may not lead to convictions. Evidence which is available to the officer may not be allowed in court. Sentences which are imposed may seem too "light" to the arresting officer. The feelings of powerlessness and frustration which come from seeing repeat offenders back on the streets and from experiencing numerous injustices worked upon seemingly innocent victims, may greatly stress police officers and cause them to question the purpose of their professional lives. It may also lead to desperate attempts to find relief. As Kevin Barrett observes, "The suicide rate of police officers is more than twice that of the general population."[103]

Another source of stress—that of living with constant danger—is incomprehensible to most of us, even to the family members of many officers. As one officer says, "I kick in a door and I've gotta talk some guy into putting a gun down…. And I go home, and my wife's upset because the lawn isn't cut and the kids have been bad. Now, to her that's a real problem."[104]

Stress is not unique to the police profession, but because of the "macho" attitude that has traditionally been associated with police work, denial of the stress experience may be found more often among police officers than in other occupational groups. Certain types of individuals are probably more susceptible to the negative effects of stress than are others. The Type A personality was popularized a few years ago as the category of person more likely to perceive life in terms of pressure and performance. Type B personalities were said to be more "laid back" and less likely to suffer from the negative effects of stress. Police ranks, drawn as they are from the general population, are filled with both stress-sensitive and stress-resistant personalities.

Stress Reduction   It is natural to try to reduce and control stress. Humor helps, even if it's somewhat cynical. Health-care professionals, for example, have long been noted for their ability to joke around patients who may be seriously ill or even dying. Police officers may similarly use humor to defuse their reactions to dark or threatening situations. Keeping an emotional distance from stressful events is another way of coping with them, although such distance is not always easy to maintain. Police officers who have had to deal with serious cases of physical child abuse have often reported on the emotional turmoil they experienced as a consequence of what they saw.

The support of family and friends can be crucial in developing other strategies to handle stress. Exercise, meditation, abdominal breathing, biofeedback, self-hypnosis, guided imaging, induced relaxation, subliminal conditioning, music, prayer, and diet have all been cited as techniques which can be useful in stress reduction. Devices to measure stress levels are available in the form of hand-held heart-rate monitors, blood pressure devices, "biodots" (which change color according to the amount of blood flow in the extremities), and psychological inventories.

Along with stress, fatigue can affect police officer performance. As Bryan Vila points out: "Tired, urban street cops are a national icon. Weary from overtime assignments, shift work, night school, endless hours spent waiting to testify, and the emotional and physical demands of the job, not to mention trying to patch together a family and social life during irregular islands of off-duty time, they fend off fatigue with coffee and hard-bitten humor."[105] As Vila notes, few departments set work-hour standards, and fatigue associated with the pattern and length of work hours may be expected to contribute to police accidents, injuries, and misconduct. Vila suggests controlling the work-hours of police officers, "just as we control the working hours of many other occupational groups."[106]

Pressures—from the community, from peers, from the circumstances in which police find themselves—are intense.

—James Q. Wilson, former chairman of the board, The Police Foundation

Police Civil Liability

In 1996 51-year-old Richard Kelley filed suit in federal court against the Massachusetts State Police and the Weymouth (Massachusetts) police department.[107] The suit resulted from an incident during which Kelley alleged that state troopers and Weymouth police officers treated him as a drunk, rather than recognizing the fact that he had just suffered a stroke while driving. According to Kelley, following a minor traffic accident caused by the stroke,

Adequate training can offset claims of liability. Here, a female police recruit is taught how to restrain a suspect without injuring him.
Bonnie Kamin, Comstock

officers pulled him from his car, handcuffed him, dragged him along the ground, and ignored his pleas for help—forcing him to stay at a state police barracks for seven hours before taking him for medical treatment. Drunk-driving charges against Kelley were dropped after medical tests failed to reveal the presence of any intoxicating substances in his body.

As the Kelley case demonstrates, police officers may become involved in a variety of situations which create the potential for civil suits against the officers, their superiors, and their departments. Major sources of police civil liability are listed in Table 6–4. Swanson says that the most common source of lawsuits against the police involve "assault, battery, false imprisonment, and malicious prosecution."[108]

Civil suits brought against law enforcement personnel are of two types: state or federal. Suits brought in state courts have generally been the most common form of civil litigation involving police officers. In recent years, however, an increasing number of suits are being brought in federal courts on the basis of the legal rationale that the civil rights of the plaintiff, as guaranteed by federal law, have been denied.

Common Sources of Civil Suits

Of all complaints brought against the police, assault charges are the best known, being, as they are, subject to high media visibility. Less visible, but not uncommon, are civil suits charging the police with false arrest or false imprisonment. In the 1986 case of *Malley* v. *Briggs*,[109] the U.S. Supreme Court held that a police officer who effects an arrest or conducts a search on the basis of an improperly issued warrant may be liable for monetary damages when a reasonably well-trained officer, under the same circumstances, "would have known that his affidavit failed to establish probable cause and that he should not have applied for the warrant." Significantly, the Court, in *Malley*, also ruled that an officer "cannot excuse his own default by pointing to the greater incompetence of the magistrate."[110] That is, the officer, rather than the judge who issued the warrant, is ultimately responsible for establishing the basis for pursuing the arrest or search.

Table 6-4 Major Sources of Police Civil Liability

Failure to protect property in police custody

Negligence in the care of persons in police custody

Failure to render proper emergency medical assistance

Failure to prevent a foreseeable crime

Failure to aid private citizens

Lack of due regard for the safety of others

False arrest

False imprisonment

Inappropriate use of deadly force

Unnecessary assault or battery

Malicious prosecution

Violations of constitutional rights

When an officer makes an arrest without just cause, or simply impedes an individual's right to leave the scene without good reason, he or she may also be liable for the charge of false arrest. Officers who enjoy "throwing their weight around" are especially subject to this type of suit, grounded as it is on the abuse of police authority. Because employers may generally be sued for the negligent or malicious actions of their employees, many police departments are finding themselves named as co-defendants in lawsuits today.

Negligent actions by officers may also provide the basis for suits. High-speed chases are especially dangerous because of the potential they entail for injury to innocent bystanders. Flashing blue or red lights (the color of police vehicle lights varies by state) legally only *request* the right-of-way on a highway; they do not demand it. Officers who drive in such a way as to place others in danger may find themselves the subject of suits. In the case of *Biscoe* v. *Arlington County* (1984),[111] for example, Alvin Biscoe was awarded $5 million after he lost both legs as a consequence of a high-speed chase while he was waiting to cross the street. Biscoe was an innocent bystander and was struck by a police car which had gone out of control. The fact that the police department in *Biscoe* had sanctioned high-speed chases as a part of official policy made the department especially liable. Departments may protect themselves to some degree through regulations limiting the authority of their personnel. In a 1985 case, for example, a Louisiana police department was exonerated in an accident which occurred during a high-speed chase because of its policy limiting emergency driving to no more than 20 miles over the posted speed limit. The officer, however, who drove 75 MPH in a 40-MPH zone was found to be negligent and held liable for damages.[112]

Law enforcement supervisors may find themselves the object of lawsuits by virtue of the fact that they are responsible for the actions of their officers. Where it can be shown that supervisors were negligent in hiring (as when someone with a history of alcoholism, mental problems, sexual deviance, or drug abuse is employed), or if supervisors failed in their responsibility to properly train officers before they armed and deployed them, they may be found liable for damages.

In the 1989 case of the *City of Canton, Ohio* v. *Harris*,[113] the U.S. Supreme Court ruled that a "failure to train" can become the basis for legal liability on the part of a municipality where the "failure to train amounts to deliberate indifference to the rights of persons with whom the police come in contact."[114] In that case, Geraldine Harris was arrested and taken to the Canton, Ohio, police station. While at the station she slumped to the floor several times. Officers finally decided to leave her on the floor and never called for qualified medical assistance. Upon release, Ms. Harris was taken by family members to a local hospital. She was hospitalized for a week and received follow-up outpatient treatment for the next year. The Court ruled that although municipalities could not justifiably be held liable for limited instances of unsatisfactory training, they could be held accountable where the failure to train results from a deliberate or conscious choice.

In 1997, however, the Supreme Court, in the case of *Board of the County Commissioners of Bryan County, Oklahoma* v. *Brown*,[115] ruled that to establish liability plaintiffs must show that "the municipal action in question was not simply negligent, but was taken with 'deliberate indifference' as to its known or obvious consequences." In *Brown*, a deputy named Burns was hired by the sheriff of Bryan County, Oklahoma. Burns later used excessive force in arresting a woman, and the woman sued the county for damages, claiming that Deputy Burns had been hired in spite of his having a criminal record. In fact, some years earlier Burns had pleaded guilty to various driving infractions and other misdemeanors, including assault and battery—a charge which resulted from a college fight. At trial, a spokesperson for the sheriff's department admitted to receiving Burns' driving and criminal records, but said he had not reviewed either in detail before the decision to hire Burns was made. Nonetheless, the Supreme Court held that deliberate indifference on the part of the county had not been established because it had not been demonstrated by the plaintiffs that "Burns' background made his use of excessive force in making an arrest a plainly obvious consequence of the hiring decision." According to the Court, "[o]nly where adequate scrutiny of the applicant's background would lead a reasonable policymaker to conclude that the plainly obvious consequence of the decision to hire the applicant would be the deprivation of a third party's federally protected right can the official's failure to adequately scrutinize the applicant's background constitute 'deliberate indifference.'" In other words, according to this decision, a municipality (in this case, a county) may not be held liable solely because it employs a person with an arrest record.

Federal Lawsuits

1983 Lawsuits Civil suits brought under Title 42, Section 1983 of the United States Code, against anyone denying others their constitutional rights to life, liberty, or property without due process of law.

Federal suits are often called **1983 lawsuits** because they are based upon Section 1983 of Title 42 of the United States Code—an act passed by Congress in 1871 to ensure the civil rights of men and women of all races. That act requires due process of law before any person can be deprived of life, liberty, or property and specifically provides redress for the denial of these constitutional rights by officials acting under color of state law. For example, a 1983 suit may be brought against officers who shoot suspects under questionable circumstances—thereby denying them of their right to life without due process. The 1981 case of *Prior* v. *Woods*[116] resulted in a $5.7 million judgment against the Detroit Police Department after David Prior—who was mistaken for a burglar—was shot and killed in front of his home.

***Bivens* Action** The name given to civil suits, based upon the case of *Bivens* v. *Six Unknown Federal Agents*, brought against federal government officials for denial of the constitutional rights of others.

Another type of liability action, this one directed specifically at federal officials or enforcement agents, is called a **Bivens suit**. The case of *Bivens* v. *Six Unknown Federal Agents* (1971)[117] established a path for legal action against agents enforcing federal laws, which is similar to that found in a 1983 suit. Bivens actions may be addressed against individuals, but not the United States or its agencies.[118] Federal officers have generally been granted a court-created qualified immunity and have been protected from suits where they were found to have acted in the belief that their action was consistent with federal law.[119]

In times past, the doctrine of sovereign immunity barred legal actions against state and local governments. Sovereign immunity was a legal theory which held that a governing body could not be sued because it made the law and therefore could not be bound by it. Immunity is a much more complex issue today. Some states have officially abandoned any pretext of immunity through legislative action. New York State, for example, has declared that public agencies are equally as liable as private agencies for violations of constitutional rights. Other states, like California, have enacted statutory provisions which define and place limits on governmental liability.[120] A number of state immunity statutes have been struck down by court decision. In general, states are moving in the direction of setting dollar limits on liability and adopting federal immunity principles to protect individual officers, including "good faith" and "reasonable belief" rules.

At the federal level, the concept of sovereign immunity is embodied in the Federal Tort Claims Act (FTCA),[121] which grants broad immunity to federal government agencies engaged in discretionary activities. When a federal employee is sued for a wrongful or negligent act, the Federal Employees Liability Reform and Tort Compensation Act of 1988, commonly known as the Westfall Act, empowers the attorney general to certify that the employee was acting within the scope of his or her office or employment at the time of the incident out of which the claim arose. Upon certification, the employee is dismissed from the action and the United States is substituted as defendant. The case then falls under the governance of the FTCA.

An Example of Police Civil Liability: The Case of Bernard McCummings

A 1993 U.S. Supreme Court decision in a civil suit which drew wide outrage saw convicted subway mugger Bernard McCummings awarded $4.3 million in a suit he had brought against the city of New York. McCummings was shot twice in the back in 1984 by Transit Authority officer Manuel Rodriguez as he attempted to flee a subway platform after beating and robbing a 71-year-old man. At the time of the crime McCummings had just gotten out of prison for robbery. Since the shooting, McCummings, who was 23 years old when he was injured, has remained paralyzed from the chest down. After pleading guilty to the mugging he was sentenced to prison, where he served two years. When McCummings brought suit against the city, however, a jury and appeals court found that officers had used excessive force. Before paying the award the city appealed to the Supreme Court. In upholding the cash award to McCummings, the Supreme Court reiterated earlier rulings that police officers cannot use deadly force against unarmed fleeing suspects who pose no apparent threat to officers or to the public.

McCummings's victim, Jerome Sandusky, who was carrying less than $30 at the time he was attacked, decried the ruling, saying "[i]t's justice turned upside down...and it sends a terrible message...that crime *does* pay." "Ordinarily I would be sorry for anyone that was made a cripple. But he was made a cripple because of his own action," Sandusky said. Gerald Arenberg of the National Association of Chiefs of Police sided with Sandusky. "The criminal is very well protected by the Supreme Court," Arenberg said in a national interview. Lawyers for the city were disappointed. "The message is," said one, when faced with a fleeing suspect, "it's probably wiser for a police officer to do nothing, in terms of civil liability."

Opinions on the case were, however, varied. "It was the right decision," said David Breibart, McCummings's lawyer. "It gives me great faith in the system." A *Washington Post* editorial, on the other hand, suggested that police should not be bound by the rules of fair play, when criminals are not. "What if felons knew that cops could shoot them if they fled?" the editorial asked. "More of them would likely freeze and put up their hands...[C]riminal behavior should not be treated as if it were some sort of quasi-legitimate enterprise, governed by the laws of negligence." "McCummings" said the writer, "was as much a victim of his own criminality as he was of a violation of the rules regarding the use of deadly force. Once he chose to break the law he wasn't entitled to be compensated by it." McCummings's victim agreed. Recently, Sandusky filed suit against McCummings seeking to get the $4.3 million award. Sandusky brought suit under New York's modified "Son of Sam" law, which is intended to prevent criminals from profiting from their crimes.

QUESTIONS FOR DISCUSSION

1. Do you feel McCummings should have been compensated for his injuries? Why or why not?
2. Do you agree with the assertion, in this box, that "cops should not be bound by the rules of fair play when criminals are not?" Why or why not?

Sources: "Mugger Shot by Cop to Keep $4.3 million," *USA Today*, November 30, 1993, p. 1A.; "Mugging Lawsuit," Associated Press wire services, December 15, 1993; "Compensation for a Criminal," *Washington Post* wire services, December 2, 1993; and "Scotus-Excessive Force," Associated Press wire services, November 30, 1993.

In 1995, in a case involving the FTCA, a Miami federal judge ordered the federal government to pay out more than $1 million to five crew members and a passenger on board an airplane from Belize (a small Latin American country), which was scheduled to stop in Miami after taking on additional passengers in Honduras. Testimony revealed that DEA agents had planted cocaine on the plane at its point of origin and had planned to arrest Miami dealers when they retrieved the drugs. Unfortunately, the agents had failed to notify Honduran authorities of the planted drugs, and when the plane landed in Honduras it was searched. Honduran police then arrested the six men—beating them with rubber hoses and kicking them down stairs in an effort to get confessions.[122] The judge hearing the suit against the government ruled that although the FTCA gives broad immunity to government agencies whose officials exercise discretion in everyday activities, it was not the intent of Congress to extend immunity to government agencies when the actions of their officials fail to comply with established regulations. In effect, the judge said, the failure by DEA agents to notify Honduran police of the "sting" in progress constituted a failure to perform an official duty.

For its part, the U.S. Supreme Court has supported a type of "qualified immunity" for individual officers (as opposed to the agencies for which they work) which "shields law

A successful community policing program also requires officers to be well versed in cultural diversity and competent to perform tasks needed to accomplish their duties. This, obviously, requires considerable training for officers at all levels of the department.

—Samuel D. Pratcher, Chief of Police, Wilmington, Delaware

enforcement officers from constitutional lawsuits if reasonable officers believe their actions to be lawful in light of clearly established law and the information the officers possess." The Supreme Court has also described qualified immunity as a defense "which shields public officials from actions for damages unless their conduct was unreasonable in light of clearly established law."[123] According to the Court, "the qualified immunity doctrine's central objective is to protect public officials from undue interference with their duties and from potentially disabling threats of liability…."[124] In the context of a warrantless arrest, the Court said, in *Hunter* v. *Bryant* (1991),[125] "even law enforcement officials who reasonably but mistakenly conclude that probable cause is present are entitled to immunity."[126] Most departments carry liability insurance to protect them against the severe financial damage which can result from the loss of a large suit. Some officers make it a point to acquire private policies which provide coverage in the event they are named as individuals in such suits. Both types of insurance policies generally provide for a certain amount of legal fees to be paid by the police for defense against the suit, regardless of the outcome of the case. Police departments who face civil prosecution because of the actions of an officer, however, may find that legal and financial liability extend to supervisors, city managers, and the community itself. Where insurance coverage does not exist, or is inadequate, city coffers may be nearly drained to meet the damages awarded.[127]

In a recent five-year period, for example, the city of Los Angeles, California, paid out $23 million to people who brought suits against the LAPD for civil rights violations.[128] Former Los Angeles Chief of Police Daryl Gates, in commenting on the prevalence of lawsuits against police officers today, has observed that although California cities are allowed to pay damage awards for individual officers, they do not have to. Gates continued: "Think about the chilling factor in that. [It says] 'Hey, Chief, you're on your own. We're not gonna pay anything.' Think what that does. It says, 'Hey Chief, don't open your mouth—Don't tell the public anything. Don't let them know what the real facts are in this case. Don't tell the truth.' And what does it tell the police officers? 'Don't do your work, because you're liable to wind up in court, being sued.' That, to me, is probably the most frightening thing that's happening in the United States today."[129]

Police Use of Deadly Force

The use of deadly force by police officers is one area of potential civil liability which has received considerable attention in recent years. Historically, the fleeing felon rule applied to most U.S. jurisdictions. It held that officers could use deadly force to prevent the escape of a suspected felon, even when that person represented no immediate threat to the officer or to the public. The fleeing felon rule probably stemmed from early common-law punishments, which specified death for a large number of crimes. Today, however, the death penalty is far less frequent in application, and the fleeing felon rule has been called into question in a number of courts.

The 1985 Supreme Court case of *Tennessee* v. *Garner*[130] specified the conditions under which deadly force could be used in the apprehension of suspected felons. Edward Garner, a 15-year-old suspected burglar, was shot to death by Memphis police after he refused their order to halt and attempted to climb over a chain-link fence. In an action initiated by Garner's father, who claimed that his son's constitutional rights had been violated, the Court held that the use of deadly force by the police to prevent the escape of a fleeing felon could be justified only where the suspect could reasonably be thought to represent a significant threat of serious injury or death to the public or to the officer *and* where deadly force is necessary to effect the arrest. In reaching its decision, the Court declared that "The use of deadly force to prevent the escape of *all* felony suspects, whatever the circumstances, is constitutionally unreasonable."[131]

In 1989 the Court, in the case of *Graham* v. *Connor*,[132] established the standard of "objective reasonableness" under which an officer's use of deadly force could be assessed in terms of "reasonableness at the moment." In other words, whether deadly force has been used appropriately or not should be judged, the Court said, from the perspective of a reasonable officer on the scene and not with the benefit of "20/20 hindsight." "The calculus of reasonableness," wrote the Justices, "must embody allowance for the fact that police officers are often forced to make split-second judgments—in circumstances that are tense, uncertain, and rapidly evolving—about the amount of force that is necessary in a particular situation."

Title 42, United States Code, Section 1983

Every person who, under color of any statute, ordinance, regulation, custom, or usage, of any State or Territory, subjects, or causes to be subjected, any citizen of the United States or other person within the jurisdiction thereof to the deprivation of any rights, privileges, or immunities secured by the Constitution and laws, shall be liable to the party injured in an action at law, suit in equity, or other proper proceeding for redress.

In 1995, following investigations into the actions of federal agents at the deadly siege of the Branch Davidian compound at Waco, Texas, and the tragic deaths associated with a 1992 FBI assault on antigovernment separatists in Ruby Ridge, Idaho, the federal government announced that it was adopting an "imminent danger" standard for the use of deadly force by federal agents. The federal "imminent danger" standard restricts the use of deadly force to only those situations where the lives of agents or others are in danger. As the new standard was announced, federal agencies were criticized for taking so long to adopt them. Morton Feldman, executive vice president of the National Association of Chiefs of Police, said the federal government was finally catching up with policies adopted by state and local law enforcement agencies 17 years previously. "It is totally irresponsible and reprehensible that it took the federal government so long to catch up," said Feldman. "How many hundreds of lives of officers and civilians may have been senselessly lost during the last 17 years because of this reckless, unjustifiable disregard for having an appropriate policy in place?"[133] The federal use of deadly force policy, as adopted by the FBI, is partially reproduced in a box in this section.

Studies of killings by the police have often focused on claims of discrimination, that is, that black and minority suspects are more likely to be shot than whites. Research in the area, however, has not provided solid support for such claims. While individuals shot by police are more likely to be minorities, James Fyfe[134] found that police officers will generally respond with deadly force when mortally threatened and that minorities are considerably more likely to use weapons in assaults on officers than are whites. Complicating the picture further were Fyfe's data showing that minority officers are involved in the shooting of suspects more often than other officers, a finding that may be due to the assignment of such officers to inner-city and ghetto areas. However, a more recent study by Fyfe,[135] which analyzed police shootings in Memphis, Tennessee, found that black property offenders were twice as likely as whites to be shot by police.

Although relatively few police officers will ever feel the need to fire their weapons during the course of their careers, those who do may find themselves embroiled in a web of social, legal, and personal complications. It is estimated that an average year sees 600 suspects killed by gunfire from public police in America, while another 1,200 are shot and wounded, and 1,800 individuals are shot at and missed.[136]

The personal side of police shootings is well summarized in the title of an article which appeared in *Police Magazine*. The article, "I've Killed That Man Ten Thousand Times,"[137] demonstrated how police officers who have to use their weapon may be haunted by years of depression and despair. Not long ago, according to Anne Cohen, author of the article, all departments did to help officers who had shot someone was to "give him enough bullets to reload his gun." The stress and trauma which result from shootings by officers in defense of themselves or others is only now beginning to be realized, and most departments have yet to develop mechanisms for adequately dealing with it.[138]

Especially difficult to deal with are instances of "suicide by cop," in which individuals bent on dying engage in behavior that causes responding officers to resort to deadly force. In 1997, for example, 19-year-old Moshe "Moe" Pergament, a well-mannered college student,

When a woman makes a mistake, the men can't wait to jump on the bandwagon, but if a man makes a mistake, it is covered up.

—Police Sgt. C. Lee Bennett, citing interviews with female police officers

A South Carolina SWAT team prepares for action during an inmate uprising at the Broad River Correctional Institution near Columbia. Deadly force can only be used in situations involving extreme and imminent danger. *Jamie Francis, Pool/AP/Wide World Photos*

was shot to death by Nassau County (New York) police officers after he pulled a $1.79 toy revolver from his waist band and pointed it at the officers during a traffic stop. Pergament apparently wanted to be shot by law enforcement personnel, and had planned his death. In a note found after his death and addressed to "the officer who shot me," Pergament apologized for what he had planned. "Officer," the note read, "It was a plan. I'm sorry to get you involved. I just needed to die."[139] Pergament had also written goodbye messages to friends and family members. He was apparently depressed over a $6,000 gambling debt.

In 1993 the National Institute of Justice reported on efforts begun in 1987 to develop "less than lethal weapons" for use by law enforcement officers. Questions to be answered include (1) "Can an officer stop a fleeing felon without use of deadly force?" (2) "Are there devices and substances that would rapidly subdue assailants before they could open fire or otherwise harm their hostages?" and (3) "Can technology provide devices to incapacitate assailants without also harming nearby innocent hostages and bystanders?" Chemical agents, knockout gases, stunning explosives, tranquilizing darts, and remote-delivery electronic shocks are all being studied by the agency. NIJ says it is "moving forward with research development and evaluation of devices for use by line patrol officers under a wide variety of circumstances. …[T]he goal is to give line officers effective and safe alternatives to lethal force."[140]

Professionalism and Ethics

Police administrators have responded in a variety of ways to issues of danger, liability, and the potential for corruption. Among the most significant responses have been calls for increased professionalism at all levels of policing. A profession is characterized by a body of specialized knowledge, acquired through extensive education,[141] and by a well-considered set of internal standards and ethical guidelines which hold members of the profession accountable to one another and to society. Associations of like-minded practitioners generally serve to create and disseminate standards for the profession as a whole.

Contemporary policing evidences many of the attributes of a profession. Specialized knowledge in policing includes a close familiarity with criminal law, laws of procedure, constitutional guarantees and relevant Supreme Court decisions, a working knowledge of weapons and hand-to-hand tactics, driving skills and vehicle maintenance, a knowledge of

Police Professionalism The increasing formalization of police work and the rise in public acceptance of the police which accompanies it. Any profession is characterized by a specialized body of knowledge and a set of internal guidelines which hold members of the profession accountable for their actions. A well-focused code of ethics, equitable recruitment and selection practices, and informed promotional strategies among many agencies contribute to a growing level of professionalism among American police agencies today.

Police Ethics The special responsibility for adherence to moral duty and obligation inherent in police work.

THE FBI's POLICY ON THE USE OF DEADLY FORCE

A. Defense of Life: Agents may use deadly force only when necessary, that is, when the agents have probable cause to believe that the subject of such force poses an imminent danger of death or serious physical injury to the agents or other persons.

B. Fleeing Subject: Deadly force may be used to prevent the escape of a fleeing subject if there is probable cause to believe: (1) The subject has committed a felony involving the infliction or threatened infliction of serious physical injury or death, and (2) the subject's escape would pose an imminent danger of death or serious physical injury to the agents or other persons.

C. Verbal Warnings: If feasible, and if to do so would not increase the danger to the agent or others, a verbal warning to submit to the authority of the agent shall be given prior to the use of deadly force.

D. Warning Shots: No warning shots are to be fired by agents.

E. Vehicles: Weapons may not be fired solely to disable moving vehicles. Weapons may be fired at the driver or other occupant of a moving motor vehicle only when the agents have probable cause to believe that the subject poses an imminent danger of death or serious physical injury to the agents or others, and the use of deadly force does not create a danger to the public that outweighs the likely benefits of its use.

Source: John C. Hall, "FBI Training on the New Federal Deadly Force Policy," *FBI Law Enforcement Bulletin*, April, 1996, pp. 25–32.

---

radio communications, report-writing abilities, interviewing techniques, and media and human-relations skills. Other specialized knowledge may include Breathalyzer operation, special weapons firing, polygraph operation, conflict resolution, and hostage negotiation skills. Supervisory personnel require an even wider range of skills, including administrative knowledge, management techniques, personnel administration, and department strategies for optimum utilization of officers and physical resources.

Basic law enforcement training requirements were begun in the 1950s by the state of New York and through a voluntary system of Peace Officer Standards and Training (**POST**) in California. Today, such requirements are mandated by law in every state in the nation, although they vary considerably from region to region. Modern police education involves, at a minimum, more than 100 classroom contact hours (Missouri), and in some places nearly 1,000 hours of intensive training (Hawaii),[142] in subject areas which include human relations, firearms and weapons, communications, legal aspects of policing, patrol, criminal investigations, administration, report writing, and criminal justice systems. Contemporary California POST standards are shown in a "Theory Into Practice" box in this chapter.

Federal law enforcement agents receive schooling at the Federal Law Enforcement Training Center (FLETC) at Glynco, Georgia. The Center provides training for about 60 federal law enforcement agencies (excluding the FBI, which has its own training center at Quantico, Virginia) and has begun offering advanced training to state and local police organizations (through the National Center for State and Local Law Enforcement Training, located on the FLETC campus), where such training is not available under other auspices. Specialized schools, such as Northwestern University's Traffic Institute, have also been credited with raising the level of police practice from purely operational concerns to a more professional level.[143]

Police work is guided by an ethical code originated in 1956 by the Peace Officer's Research Association of California (PORAC), in conjunction with Dr. Douglas M. Kelley of Berkeley's School of Criminology.[144] *The Law Enforcement Code of Ethics* is reproduced in a box in this chapter. Ethics training is still not well integrated into most basic law enforcement training programs, but a movement in that direction has begun and calls for expanded training in ethics are on the increase.

Professional associations abound in police work. The Fraternal Order of Police (FOP) is one of the best-known organizations of public service workers in the United States. The

POST An acronym for Peace Officer Standards and Training. All states set standards for police training and education, although not all use the term "POST."

Police Training—California's POST Standards

The California Peace Officer Standards and Training program was one of this country's first selection and training standards-setting program for law enforcement officers. Today, an updated POST program serves as a model for other similar programs in many parts of the United States. Shown here are the latest POST Regular Basic Course subject areas and required minimum hours, which took effect on July 15, 1995.

Basic POST Training (664 minimum required hours)

History, Professionalism and Ethics	8 hours	Vehicle Pullovers	14 hours
Criminal Justice System	4 hours	Crimes in Progress	16 hours
Community Relations	12 hours	Handling Disputes/Crowd Control	12 hours
Victimology/Crisis Interventions	6 hours	Domestic Violence	8 hours
Introduction to Criminal Law	6 hours	Unusual Occurrences	4 hours
Crimes Against Property	10 hours	Missing Persons	4 hours
Crimes Against Persons	10 hours	Traffic Enforcement	22 hours
General Criminal Statutes	4 hours	Traffic Accident Investigation	12 hours
Crimes Against Children	6 hours	Preliminary Investigation	42 hours
Sex Crimes	6 hours	Custody	4 hours
Juvenile Law and Procedure	6 hours	Physical Fitness/Officer Stress	40 hours
Controlled Substances	12 hours	Person Searches, Baton, etc.	60 hours
ABC Law	4 hours	First Aid and CPR	21 hours
Laws of Arrest	12 hours	Firearms/Chemical Agents	72 hours
Search and Seizure	12 hours	Information Systems	4 hours
Presentation of Evidence	8 hours	Persons with Disabilities	6 hours
Investigative Report Writing	40 hours	Crimes Against the Justice System	4 hours
Vehicle Operations	24 hours	Cultural Diversity/Discrimination	24 hours
Use of Force	12 hours	Patrol Techniques	12 hours
Gang Awareness	8 hours	Weapons Violations	4 hours
Hazardous Materials	4 hours		

Minimum Instructional Hours   599

The minimum number of hours allocated to testing in the Regular Basic Course are shown below:

Test Type	Hours
Scenario Tests	40 hours
POST-Constructed Knowledge Tests	25 hours
Total Minimum Hours	**664 hours**

Successful curriculum completion also requires that "the Law Enforcement Code of Ethics shall be administered to peace officer trainees during the basic course."

QUESTIONS FOR DISCUSSION:

1. What classes and/or subject areas would you like to see added to (or deleted from) the POST course? Why?

2. Do you believe that police training, such as POST, results in better officers? Why or why not? If so, in what way are they "better"?

Note: Every peace officer below the first middle-management level must satisfactorily complete the advanced officer course of 24 or more hours at least once every two years after completion of the basic course. This requirement may also be met by satisfactory completion of an accumulation of certified technical courses totaling 24 or more hours or satisfactory completion of an alternative method of compliance as determined by the Commission. Supervisors may also satisfy the requirement by completing supervisory or management training courses.

Source: State of California, Commission on Peace Officer Standards and Training, Commission Regulation 1005, *POST Administrative Manual*, (Sacramento, CA: POST, 1995). Reprinted with permission.

International Association of Chiefs of Police (IACP) has done much to raise professional standards in policing and continually strives for improvements in law enforcement nationwide.

Accreditation provides another channel toward police professionalism. The Commission on Accreditation for Law Enforcement Agencies (CALEA) was formed in 1979. Police departments wishing to apply for accreditation through the Commission must meet hundreds of standards relating to areas as diverse as day-to-day operations, administration, review of incidents involving the use of a weapon by officers, and evaluation and promotion of personnel. To date, few police agencies are accredited, although a number have applied to begin the process. Those agencies are now conducting self-evaluations as part of the application process. Although accreditation makes possible the identification of high-quality police departments, it is often undervalued because it carries few incentives. Accreditation is still only "icing on the cake" and does not guarantee a department any rewards beyond the recognition of peers. Today, only 2% of the nation's approximately 17,000 law enforcement agencies have been accredited by CLEA.[145]

Educational Requirements

As the concern for quality policing builds, increasing emphasis is being placed on the education of police officers. As early as 1931, the National Commission of Law Observance and Enforcement (the Wickersham Commission) highlighted the importance of a well-educated police force by calling for "educationally sound" officers.[146] In 1967 the President's Commission on Law Enforcement and the Administration of Justice voiced the belief that "[t]he ultimate aim of all police departments should be that all personnel with general enforcement powers have baccalaureate degrees." At the time, the average educational level of police officers in the United States was 12.4 years—slightly beyond a high-school degree. In 1973 the National Advisory Commission on Criminal Justice Standards and Goals made the following rather specific recommendation:[147] Every police agency should, no later than 1982, require as a condition of initial employment the completion of at least four years of education…at an accredited college or university."[148]

Recommendations, of course, do not always translate into practice. A survey of 699 police departments by PERF found that the average level of educational achievement among both black and white officers was 14 years of schooling, nearly the equivalent of an associate's degree from a "two-year" or community college.[149] Female officers (with an average level of educational achievement of 14.6 years) tend to be better educated than their male counterparts (who report an average attainment level of 13.6 years). Only 3.3% of male officers hold graduate degrees, while almost one-third (30.2%) of women officers hold such degrees. On the down side, 34.8% of male officers have no college experience, and 24.1% of female officers have none. The PERF report explained the difference between male and female educational achievement by saying that "[w]omen tend to rely on higher education more than men as a springboard for a law enforcement career…[and] [p]olice departments may utilize higher standards—consciously or unconsciously—for selecting women officers."[150]

The report also stressed the need for educated police officers, citing the following benefits which accrue to police agencies from the hiring of educated officers:[151] (1) better written reports, (2) enhanced communications with the public, (3) more effective job performance, (4) fewer citizens' complaints, (5) greater initiative, (6) a wiser use of discretion, (7) a heightened sensitivity to racial and ethnic issues, and (8) fewer disciplinary problems. On the other hand, a greater likelihood that educated officers will leave police work, and their tendency to question orders and request reassignment with relative frequency, are some education-related drawbacks.

A 1996 Bureau of Justice Report[152] found that 12% of all local police departments required that rookie officers have at least some college coursework, while 1% required new officers to have a four-year college degree, and 7% required a two-year degree. An even greater number of agencies now require the completion of at least some college-level work for officers seeking promotion. The San Diego Police Department, for example, requires two years of college work for promotion to the rank of sergeant.[153] A decade ago the Sacramento, California, police department set completion of a four-year college degree as a requirement

The Law Enforcement Code of Ethics

As a Law Enforcement Officer, my fundamental duty is to serve mankind; to safeguard lives and property; to protect the innocent against deception, the weak against oppression or intimidation, and the peaceful against violence or disorder; and to respect the Constitutional rights of all men to liberty, equality, and justice.

I will keep my private life unsullied as an example to all; maintain courageous calm in the face of danger, scorn, or ridicule; develop self-restraint; and be constantly mindful of the welfare of others. Honest in thought and deed in both my personal and official life, I will be exemplary in obeying the laws of the land and the regulations of my department. Whatever I see or hear of a confidential nature or that is confided to me in my official capacity will be kept secret unless revelation is necessary in the performance of my duty.

I will never act officiously or permit personal feelings, prejudices, animosities, or friendships to influence my decisions. With no compromise for crime and with relentless prosecution of criminals, I will enforce the law courteously and appropriately without fear or favor, malice or ill will, never employing unnecessary force or violence and never accepting gratuities.

I recognize the badge of my office as a symbol of public faith, and I accept it as a public trust to be held so long as I am true to the ethics of the police service. I will constantly strive to achieve these objectives and ideals, dedicating myself before God to my chosen profession...law enforcement.

Source: International Association of Chiefs of Police. Reprinted with Permission.

for promotion to lieutenant, and, in 1988, the New York City Police Department announced a requirement of at least 64 college credits for promotion to supervisory ranks. At the state level, a variety of plans exist for integrating college work into police careers. Minnesota now requires a college degree for new candidates taking the state's Peace Office Standards and Training Board's licensing examination. Successful completion of all POST requirements permits employment as a fully certified law enforcement officer in the state of Minnesota. In 1991 the state of New York set 60 semester hours of college-level work as a mandated minimum for hiring into the New York State Police. Finally, as the boxes on employment found in Chapter 5 show, many federal agencies require college degrees for entry-level positions. Among them are the FBI, DEA, ATF, Secret Service, the U.S. Customs Service, and the Immigration and Naturalization Service.

Recruitment and Selection

Any profession needs informed, dedicated, and competent personnel. When the National Advisory Commission on Criminal Justice Standards and Goals issued its 1973 report on the police, it bemoaned the fact that "many college students are unaware of the varied, interesting, and challenging assignments and career opportunities that exist within the police service."[154] In the intervening years, the efforts made by police departments to correct such misconceptions have had a considerable effect. Today, police organizations actively recruit new officers from college campuses, professional organizations, and two-year junior colleges and technical institutes. Education is an important criterion in selecting today's police recruits. As mentioned earlier, some departments require a minimum number of college credits for entry-level work. A policy of the Dallas, Texas, Police Department[155] requiring a minimum of 45 semester hours of successful college-level study for new recruits was upheld in 1986 by the U.S. Supreme Court in the case of *Davis* v. *Dallas*.[156]

The National Commission report stressed the setting of high standards for police recruits and recommended a strong emphasis on minority recruitment, an elimination of residence requirements (which required officers to live in the area they were hired to serve) for new officers, a decentralized application and testing procedure, and various recruiting incentives.

Justice in American Context

AMERICA'S FIRST BLACK POLICE OFFICERS?

Although the identity of the first African-American police officer may never be known, some historians trace the beginnings of African-American involvement in the police profession to the "free men of color" who were hired by the New Orleans city police department in 1805. "Free men of color were authorized by the New Orleans city council to serve as city police officers under the condition that they be commanded at all times by white officers. Although charged with traditional police duties, most of their time was spent policing the city's African-American slave population—something which few white officers were willing to do. African-American officers primarily enforced the "slave codes" of the times, which prohibited slaves from gathering in groups, possessing weapons, leaving the plantations or homes where they worked without passes, and resisting punishment. Under the codes, striking a white person was considered an especially serious offense.

In 1811 "free men of color" officers helped suppress a slave uprising and won wide acclaim throughout the city's white-run government. By 1830, however, a new "whites only" policy led to the dismissal of all African-Americans on the city's police force.

With the end of the Civil War, and the coming of Reconstruction, African-Americans were again hired to help police New Orleans. By 1868, 65% of all police officers in New Orleans were African-Americans, a percentage never again achieved by any large American city. When Reconstruction ended, the number of African-American officers serving New Orleans declined substantially, and by 1900 no black officers remained on the force.

Source: W. Marvin Dulaney, *Black Police in America* (Bloomington, IN: Indiana University Press, 1996).

The Commission also suggested that a four-year college degree should soon become a reasonable expectation for police recruits. The survey also found that 62% of responding agencies had at least one formal policy in support of officers pursuing higher education.[157]

Effective policing, however, may depend more upon personal qualities than it does upon educational attainment. O. W. Wilson once enumerated some of the "desirable personal qualities of patrol officers."[158] They include (1) initiative; (2) the capacity for responsibility; (3) the ability to deal alone with emergencies; (4) the capacity to communicate effectively with persons of diverse social, cultural, and ethnic backgrounds; (5) the ability to learn a variety of tasks quickly; (6) the attitude and ability necessary to adapt to technological changes; (7) the desire to help people in need; (8) an understanding of others; (9) emotional maturity; and (10) sufficient physical strength and endurance.

Standard procedures employed by modern departments in selecting trainees usually include basic skills tests, physical agility measurements, interviews, physical examinations, eye tests, psychological evaluations, and background investigations into the personal character of applicants. After training, successful applicants are typically placed on a period of probation approximately one year in length. The probationary period in police work has been called the "first true job-related test…in the selection procedure,"[159] providing as it does the opportunity for supervisors to gauge the new officer's response to real-life situations.

The calculus of reasonableness must embody allowance for the fact that police officers are often forced to make split-second judgments—in circumstances that are tense, uncertain, and rapidly evolving—about the amount of force that is necessary in a particular situation.

—Graham v. Connor, 490 U.S. 386, 396-397 (1989).

Ethnic and Racial Minorities and Women

In 1967 the National Advisory Commission on Civil Disorders conducted a survey of supervisory personnel in police departments.[160] They found a marked disparity between the number of black and white officers in leadership positions. One of every 26 black police officers had been promoted to the rank of sergeant, while the ratio among whites was 1 in 12. Only 1 of every 114 black officers had become a lieutenant, while among whites the ratio was 1 out of 26. At the level of captain the disparity was even greater—1 out of every 235 black officers had achieved the rank of captain, while 1 of every 53 whites had climbed to that rank.

Since then, the emphasis placed upon minority recruitment by task forces, civil rights groups, courts, and society in general, has done much to rectify the situation. In 1979, for

Women in uniform have become a common sight throughout our nation's cities and towns. Here, a female officer lectures a man who ran a red light. *Sepp Seitz, Contact Stock*

example, one of the first affirmative action disputes involving a police department was settled out of court. The settlement required the San Francisco Police Department to ensure that over the next ten years minorities would receive 50% of all promotions and that 20% of all new officers hired would be women.[161]

Today, the situation is changing. Many departments, through dedicated recruitment efforts, have dramatically increased their complement of officers from underrepresented groups. The Metropolitan Detroit Police Department, for example, now has a force that is more than 30% black. According to a 1996 report by the Bureau of Justice Statistics,[162] blacks comprise 11.3% of sworn officers, while other ethnic minorities constitute 7.7% of sworn personnel.

Unfortunately, although ethnic minorities have moved into policing in substantial numbers (see Figure 6–3), females are still significantly underrepresented. A recent study by the Police Foundation[163] found that women accounted for nearly 9% of all officers in municipal departments serving populations of 50,000 or more but that they comprised only 3% of all supervisors in city agencies, and 1% of supervisors in state police agencies. Female officers made up 10.1% of the total number of officers in departments which were functioning under court order to increase their proportion of women officers, while women constituted 8.3% of officers in agencies with voluntary affirmative action programs, and only 6.1% of officers in departments without such programs. A 1996 BJS report found that, overall, females comprise 8.8% of full-time sworn personnel in local police departments nationwide.[164]

A recent report[165] on women police officers in Massachusetts found that female officers (1) are "extremely devoted to their work," (2) "see themselves as women first, and then police officers," and (3) were more satisfied when working in nonuniformed capacities. Two groups of women officers were identified: (1) those who felt themselves to be well integrated into their departments and were confident in their jobs, and (2) those who experienced strain and on-the-job isolation. The officers' children were cited as a significant influence on their self-perceptions and on the way in which they viewed their jobs. The demands which attend child rearing in contemporary society were found to be major factors contributing to the resignation of female officers. The study also found that the longer women officers stayed on the job, the greater stress and frustration they tended to experience—primarily as a consequence of the noncooperative attitudes of male officers. Some of the female officers inter-

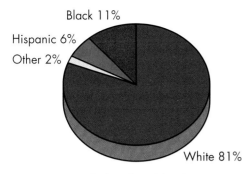

**Ethnic Minorities in
Law Enforcement**

Black 11%
Hispanic 6%
Other 2%
White 81%

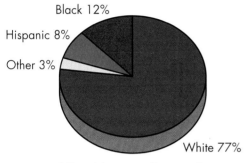

Black 12%
Hispanic 8%
Other 3%
White 77%

**Minorities as a Proportion
of the U.S. Population**

FIGURE 6–3 Ethnic minorities as a proportion of local law enforcement officers and as a proportion of the U.S. population. *Source:* Adapted from Kathleen Maquire and Ann L. Pastore, *Sourcebook of Criminal Justice Statistics 1996* (Washington, D.C.: Bureau of Justice Statistics, 1997).

viewed identified networking as a potential solution to the stresses encountered by female officers, but also said that when women get together to solve problems they are seen as "crybabies" rather than professionals. Said one of the women in the study, "[W]e've lost a lot of good women who never should have left the job. If we had helped each other maybe they wouldn't have left."[166]

Networking is a concept which is quickly taking root among the nation's women police officers, as attested to by the growth of organizations like the International Association of Women Police, based in New York City. Mentoring, another method for introducing women to police work, has been suggested by some authors.[167] Mentoring would create semiformal relationships between experienced women officers and rookies entering the profession. Through such relationships, problems could be addressed as they arose, and the experienced officer could serve to guide her junior partner through the maze of formal and informal expectations which surround the job of policing.

Other studies, like those already discussed, have found that female officers are often underutilized and that many departments are hesitant to assign women to patrol and other potentially dangerous field activities. As a consequence, some women in police work experience frustrations and a lack of satisfaction with their jobs.[168] A recent analysis of the genderization of the criminal justice workplace by Susan Ehrlich Martin and Nancy C. Jurik,[169] for example, points out that gender inequality is part of an historical pattern of entrenched forms of gender interaction relating to the division of labor, power, and culture. According to Martin and Jurik, women working the justice system are viewed in terms of such historically developed filters, causing them to be judged and treated according to normative standards developed for men rather than for women. As a consequence, formal and informal social controls continue to disenfranchise women who wish to work in the system and make it difficult to recognize the gender-specific contributions that they make as women.

Barriers, however, continue to fall. In 1979, for example, San Francisco became the first city in the world to actively recruit homosexuals for its police force. That action resulted in a reduced fear of reporting crimes among many city homosexuals, who for years had been victims of organized assaults by bikers and street gangs. Recently, Attorney General Janet Reno ordered all Justice Department agencies to end hiring discrimination based on sexual

Ethnic minorities, while still under-represented in the criminal justice system, have many opportunities for employment throughout the system. *Jeff Dunn, Stock Boston*

Visit the *CJToday* Web page and click on "Web Chapters," then "Chapter 6." Follow the "find the facts" links in order to visit the International Association of Chiefs of Police home page and other sites of interest.

orientation. Other barriers are falling as women have begun to enter the ranks of police administration. The 2,000-member International Association of Women Police estimates, for example, that there are more than 100 female chiefs of police throughout the country. A newly formed but growing organization, the Women's Police Chief Association, seeks to offer networking opportunities to women seeking and holding high rank within police departments nationwide.[170] Another organization, the National Center for Women and Policing, which is a project of the Feminist Majority Foundation, provides a nationwide resource for law enforcement agencies, community leaders, and public officials seeking to increase the numbers of women police in their communities.

In a continuing effort to increase the representation of women and ethnic minorities in police work, the Police Foundation recommends (1) involving underrepresented groups in affirmative action and long-term planning programs which are undertaken by police departments, (2) encouraging the development of an open system of promotions whereby women can feel free to apply for promotion and in which qualified individuals of any race or gender will face equity in the promotion process, and (3) using periodic audits to ensure that women officers are not being underutilized by being ineffectively tracked into clerical and support positions.[171]

SUMMARY

Police work today is characterized by the opportunity for individual officers to exercise considerable discretion, by a powerful subculture which communicates select values in support of a "police personality," and by the very real possibility of corruption and deviance. Opposed to the illegitimate use of police authority, however, are increased calls for integrity and ethical awareness in police work and for continuing growth of the professionalism ideal. Professionalism, with its emphasis on education, training, high ethical values, and personal accountability, should soon lead to greater public recognition of the significance of police work and to higher salaries for career police personnel. Increased salaries and a clear public appreciation for the work done by police officers and other police department employees should, in turn, do much to decrease corruption and deviance in law enforcement ranks.

As the environment surrounding the individual officer changes, so too will cultural expectations for the police profession. The movement away from policing as order maintenance, and a new emphasis on community policing, presage continued shifts in the police role which will likely continue well into the twenty-first century.

Twenty-First Century Criminal Justice

POLICE

In a recent speech before several civic groups, Pueblo County (Colorado) Sheriff's Department Commander Dave Pettinari predicted that law enforcement agencies of the Twenty-First Century will

- Become more, rather than less, specialized.
- Become better trained to deal with emerging threats, including blood-borne pathogens, domestic violence, increasingly sophisticated firepower available to "bad guys," and the resurgence of militias and survivalist groups.
- Become part of a communications revolution. "Our agencies will be individually wired into the World Wide Web," said Pettinari, "and each of us will have a mobile data terminal and a cellular phone in our police cars."
- Make use of identification by means of electronic telecommunications, with fingerprints, facial ratios, retinal patterns, and so on becoming part of worldwide policing. "In a world in which a person wanted in Moscow can be in New York in less than 8 hours, and fraud in Los Angeles can be committed by someone sitting at a terminal in Sao Paulo," said Pettinari, "traditional jurisdictional lines will blur."

- Become fully involved in the revolutionary changes now sweeping the workplace. "We're looking at not only privatizing jails," said Pettinari, "but perhaps contracting out law enforcement as a whole to private concerns—rent-a-cops or temp-cops to cover shifts or even whole jurisdictions."

According to Pettinari, "Law enforcement's technical knowledge and skills need to be honed to deal with future crimes; and we should not wait for these types of crimes to become rampant before we start preparing our officers. Not only is computer knowledge vital, but it is expected that a bachelor's degree from a university—not just a high-school diploma—will be the mandatory qualifier for a law enforcement career in the near future."

Pettinari attributed many of his views to an oft-cited study conducted a decade ago by police futurist Bill Tafoya[1] and noted that twenty-first century law enforcement agencies "Must begin to learn to deal with hacking, phreaking, piggybacking, data diddling, superzapping, scavenging, trapdoors, Trojan horses, logic bombs, and a whole host of other computer threats propounded not only by professionals, but also by precocious but naive youngsters. To deal with such threats,

law enforcement needs not only computer-literate officers, civilians, and managers, but a new sophistication."

"On another computer-related topic," noted the Commander, "predictions are that we will see an upswing in successful lawsuits charging invasion of privacy due to inadequacies of and inaccuracies in police computerized files." "Community involvement and self-help by citizens (community-oriented policing) will become a common practice in much of the nation..." Pettinari noted. "Even so, policing in the future may, in large part, be contracted out to private security firms." "Finally," Pettinari said, "most police executives will have to adopt a non-traditional (proactive/goal-oriented rather than top-down) leadership style."

"All in all," says Pettinari, "it's going to be a constantly changing, ever evolving dance between us and the criminals—well into the 21st century and beyond!"

[1]William L. Tafoya, "The Future of Law Enforcement? A Chronology of Events," *Criminal Justice International* (May/June 1991), p. 4.

Source: Pueblo County Sheriff's Department World Wide Web site (http://www.usa.net/~shfadm). Quoted selections reprinted with permission of the author.

DISCUSSION QUESTIONS

1. What are the central features of the police "working personality"? How does the police working personality develop? What programs might be initiated to "shape" the police personality in a more desirable way?

2. Do you think police officers exercise too much discretion in the performance of their duties? Why or why not? If it is desirable to limit discretion, how would you do it?

3. What themes run through the findings of the Knapp Commission and the Wickersham Commission? What innovative steps might police departments take to reduce or eliminate corruption among their officers?

4. Is police work a profession? Why do you think it is, or why do you think it is not? What advantages are there to viewing policing as a profession? How do you think most police officers today see their work—as a "profession" or as just a "job"?

5. Reread the Law Enforcement Code of Ethics found in this chapter. Do you think most police officers make conscious efforts to apply the code in the performance of their duties? How might ethics training in police departments be improved?

 WEB WATCH

Access the *Criminal Justice Today* site on the World Wide Web by pointing your Web browser at http://www.prenhall.com/cjtoday. Once there, click the "enter here" selection, then "Web Chapters," and finally "Chapter 6: Police Management" from the selection box in order to access electronic information and other sites of relevance to this chapter. You may also wish to enter the Global Town Meeting, which provides facilities for the posting of electronic messages for others to read. Messages are arranged by topic, with new topics constantly being added.

NOTES

1. "L.A. Police Chief: Treat People Like Customers," *USA Today*, March 29, 1993, p.13A.

2. James Q. Wilson, *Thinking About Crime* (New York: Basic Books, 1975), p. 99.

3. "Bust 180 Degrees Wrong," *USA Today*, December 1, 1992, p. 3A.

4. Ibid.

5. The elements of this definition draw upon the now-classic work by O.W. Wilson, *Police Administration* (New York: McGraw-Hill, 1950), pp. 2–3.

6. Francis X. Hartmann, "Debating the Evolution of American Policing," *Perspectives on Policing*, No. 5 (Washington, D.C.: National Institute of Justice, November 1988).

7. James Q. Wilson, *Varieties of Police Behavior: The Management of Law and Order in Eight Communities* (Cambridge, MA: Harvard University Press, 1968).

8. Louis A. Radelet, *The Police and the Community* (Encino, CA: Glencoe, 1980).

9. President's Commission on Law Enforcement and Administration of Justice, *The Challenge of Crime in a Free Society* (Washington, D.C.: U.S. Government Printing Office, 1967).

10. Egon Bittner, "Community Relations," in Alvin W. Cohn and Emilio C. Viano, eds., *Police Community Relations: Images, Roles, Realities* (Philadelphia: J. B. Lippincott, 1976), pp. 77–82.

11. Ibid.

12. Charles Hale, *Police Patrol: Operations and Management* (New York: John Wiley, 1981), p. 112.

13. Sam Souryal, *Police Administration and Management* (St. Paul, MN: West, 1977), p. 261.

14. Paul B. Weston, *Police Organization and Management* (Pacific Palisades, CA: Goodyear, 1976), p. 159.

15. Hale, *Police Patrol*.

16. Mark H. Moore and Robert C. Trojanowicz, "Corporate Strategies for Policing," *Perspectives on Policing*, No. 6 (Washington, D.C.: National Institute of Justice, November 1988).

17. Ibid., p. 6.

18. The Community Policing Consortium, "What Is Community Policing," 1995.

19. The Community Policing Consortium, "Community Policing Is Alive and Well," 1995, p. 1.

20. George L. Kelling, *The Newark Foot Patrol Experiment* (Washington, D.C.: Police Foundation, 1981).

21. Robert C. Trojanowicz, "An Evaluation of a Neighborhood Foot Patrol Program," *Journal of Police Science and Administration*, Vol. 11 (1983).

22. Bureau of Justice Assistance, *Understanding Community Policing: A Framework for Action* (Washington, D.C.: BJS, 1994), p. 10.

23. Robert C. Trojanowicz and Bonnie Bucqueroux, *Community Policing* (Cincinnati, OH: Anderson, 1990).

24. Moore and Trojanowicz, *Perspectives on Policing*, p. 8.

25. See Jerome H. Skolnick and David H. Bayley, *Community Policing: Issues and Practices Around the World* (Washington, D.C.: National Institute of Justice, 1988), and Jerome H. Skolnick and David H. Bayley, "Theme and Variation in Community Policing," in Norval Morris and Michael Tonry, eds., *Crime and Justice: An Annual Review of Research*, Vol. 10 (Chicago: University of Chicago Press, 1988), pp. 1–37.

26. Ibid.

27. William L. Goodbody, "What Do We Expect New-Age Cops to Do?" *Law Enforcement News*, April 30, 1995, pp. 14, 18.

28. Sam Vincent Meddis and Desda Moss, "Many 'Fed-Up' Communities Cornering Crime," *USA Today*, May 22, 1995, p. 8A.

29. Jerome H. Skolnick and David H. Bayley, *The New Blue Line: Police Innovation in Six American Cities* (New York: The Free Press, 1986).

30. Richard M. Daley, "A Message from the Mayor," The Chicago Police Department's World Wide Web home page, June 9, 1995.

31. Matt L. Rodriguez, "A Message from the Superintendent of Police," The Chicago Police Department's World Wide Web home page, June 9, 1995.

32. The Chicago Community Policing Evaluation Consortium, *Community Policing in Chicago: Year Three Evaluation* (Chicago: Illinois Criminal Justice Information Authority, December 1996).

33. The Chicago Community Policing Evaluation Consortium, *Community Policing in Chicago, Year Two: An Interim Report* (Chicago: Illinois Criminal Justice Information Authority, June 1995).

34. For the latest statistics, visit the CAPS program on the World Wide Web at http://www.ci.chi.il.us/CommunityPolicing.

35. Edwin Meese III, "Community Policing and the Police Officer," *Perspectives on Policing* (Washington, D.C.: National Institute of Justice, January 1993), p. 8.

36. FBI, *Uniform Crime Reports* (Washington, D.C.: U.S. Government Printing Office, various years).

37. Bureau of Justice Assistance, *Neighborhood-Oriented Policing in Rural Communities: A Program Planning Guide* (Washington, D.C.: BJA, 1994), p. 4.

38. For a good critique of community policing and of the current state of American policing in general, see Malcolm K. Sparrow, Mark H. Moore, and David M. Kennedy, *Beyond 911: A New Era for Policing* (New York: Basic Books, 1990).

39. Goodbody, "What Do We Expect New-Age Cops to Do?"

40. Ibid.

41. Ibid.

42. Malcolm K. Sparrow, "Implementing Community Policing," *Perspectives on Policing*, No. 9 (Washington, D.C.: National Institute of Justice, 1988).

43. "L.A. Police Chief: Treat People Like Customers," *USA Today*, March 29, 1993, p. 13A.

44. Robert Wasserman and Mark H. Moore, "Values in Policing," *Perspectives in Policing*, No. 8 (Washington, D.C.: National Institute of Justice, November 1988), p. 7.

45. "New York City Mayor Sparks Debate on Community Policing," *Criminal Justice Newsletter*, Vol. 25, no. 2 (January 18, 1994), p. 1.

46. Peter B. Kraska and Victor E. Kappeler, "Militarizing American Police: The Rise and Normalization of Paramilitary Units," *Social Problems*, Vol. 44, no. 1 (February 1997), pp. 1–18.

47. William F. Walsh, "Policing at the Crossroads: Changing Directions for the New Millennium," paper presented at the Academy of Criminal Justice Sciences annual meeting, Louisville, Kentucky, March 1997.

48. Andrew J. Harvey, "Building an Organizational Foundation for the Future," *FBI Law Enforcement Bulletin*, November, 1996, pp. 12–17.

49. Howard Cohen, "Overstepping Police Authority," *Criminal Justice Ethics* (Summer/Fall 1987), pp. 52–60.

50. Kenneth Culp Davis, *Police Discretion* (St. Paul, MN: West, 1975).

51. Sykes, "Street Justice," p. 505.

52. Jerome H. Skolnick, *Justice Without Trial: Law Enforcement in a Democratic Society* (New York: John Wiley, 1966).

53. William A. Westley, *Violence and the Police: A Sociological Study of Law, Custom, and Morality* (Cambridge, MA: MIT Press, 1970), and William A. Westley "Violence and the Police," *American Journal of Sociology*, Vol. 49 (1953), pp. 34–41.

54. Arthur Niederhoffer, *Behind the Shield: The Police in Urban Society* (Garden City, NY: Anchor Press, 1967).

55. Thomas Barker and David L. Carter, *Police Deviance* (Cincinnati, OH: Anderson, 1986).

56. See, for example, Michael Brown, *Working the Street: Police Discretion and the Dilemmas of Reform* (New York: Russell Sage Foundation, 1981).

57. Richard Bennett and Theodore Greenstein, "The Police Personality: A Test of the Predispositional Model," *Journal of Police Science and Administration*, Vol 3. (1975), pp. 439–445.

58. James Teevan and Bernard Dolnick, "The Values of the Police: A Reconsideration and Interpretation," *Journal of Police Science and Administration* (1973) pp. 366–369.

59. Lawrence Sherman and Robert Langworthy, "Measuring Homicide by Police Officers," *Journal of Criminal Law and Criminology*, Vol. 4 (1979), pp. 546–560, and Lawrence W. Sherman et al., *Citizens Killed by Big City Police, 1970–1984* (Washington, D.C.: Crime Control Institute, 1986).

60. Joel Samaha, *Criminal Justice* (St. Paul, MN: West, 1988), p. 235.

61. Tim Prenzler and Peta Mackay, "Police Gratuities: What the Public Thinks," *Criminal Justice Ethics*, Winter–Spring 1995, pp. 15–25.

62. Barker and Carter, *Police Deviance.*

63. "Nationline: NYC Cops—Excess Force Not Corruption," *USA Today*, June 16, 1995, p. 3A.

64. *Knapp Commission Report on Police Corruption* (New York: George Braziller, 1973).

65. Ibid.

66. Robert Daley, *Prince of the City: The Story of a Cop Who Knew Too Much* (Boston: Houghton Mifflin, 1978).

67. Mike McAlary, *Buddy Boys: When Good Cops Turn Bad* (New York: G. P. Putnam's Sons, 1987).

68. Ibid.

69. "Ex-Detroit Police Chief Sentenced," *The Fayetteville Observer-Times* (North Carolina), August 28, 1992, p. 5A.

70. Pam Belluck, "Chicago Police Steps Down After Report of Tie With Felon," New York Times News Service, Nov. 5, 1997.

71. Edwin H. Sutherland and Donald Cressey, *Principles of Criminology*, 8th ed. (Philadelphia: J. B. Lippincott, 1970).

72. James Mills, *The Underground Empire: Where Crime and Governments Embrace* (New York: Dell, 1986), p. 15.

73. Ibid.

74. Tim R. Jones, Compton Owens, and Melissa A. Smith, "Police Ethics Training: A Three-Tiered Approach," *FBI Law Enforcement Bulletin*, June, 1995, pp. 22–26.

75. Stephen J. Gaffigan and Phyllis P. McDonald, *Police Integrity: Public Service With Honor* (Washington, D.C.: National Institute of Justice, 1997).

76. Mike Robinson, "Gangbanger Cops?" The Associated Press wire services, February 10, 1997.

77. See National Institute of Justice, "Employee Drug Testing Policies in Police Departments," *National Institute of Justice Research in Brief* (Washington, D.C.: U.S. Department of Justice, 1986).

78. Ibid.

79. *Maurice Turner* v. *Fraternal Order of Police*, 500 A.2d 1005 (D.C. 1985).

80. *Philip Caruso, President of P.B.A.* v. *Benjamin Ward, Police Commissioner*, New York State Supreme Court, Pat. 37, Index no. 12632–86, 1986.

81. *National Treasury Employees Union* v. *Von Raab*, 489 U.S. 656, 659 (1989).

82. You can visit the National Law Enforcement Officers' Memorial Fund on the World Wide Web, with links to memorial listings, at http://www.1nleomf.com.

83. Greg Meyer, "LAPD Faces Urban Warfare in North Hollywood Bank Shoot-Out," *Police*, April 1997, pp. 20–23.

84. Ibid.

85. Ibid.

86. Nine police officers and two civilians were wounded by gunfire. Seven other people were injured, including a police officer and a civilian involved in a car crash. For a definitive accounting of injuries in the incident, see Lt. Greg Meyer, "40 Minutes in North Hollywood," *Police*, June 1997, p. 27–37.

87. The M-16's were military surplus. See Steve Marshall, "L.A. Cops Get 600 M-16s to Help Even Odds on Street," *USA Today*, September 17, 1997, p. 4A.

88. "Police Commission Beefs Up LAPD Firepower," CNN Interactive on the World Wide Web, March 19, 1997.

89. The incident described here comes from the World Wide Web page of the Constable Public Safety Memorial Foundation, Inc. of Bend, Oregon, from which some of the wording is taken. http://www.survival-spanish.com/foundation.htm.

90. Officer Down Memorial Home Page on the World Wide Web, http://odmp.org.

91. Anthony J. Pinizzotto and Edward F. Davis, "Cop Killers and Their Victims," *FBI Law Enforcement Bulletin*, December 1992, p. 10.

92. As reported by The Headline News Network, April 26, 1988.

93. "Homosexual Officer Wins AIDS Ruling," *The Fayetteville Observer-Times* (North Carolina), June 8, 1992, p. 5A.

94. New York City Police Department pamphlet, "AIDS and Our Workplace" (November 1987).

95. "Collecting and Handling Evidence Infected with Human Disease-Causing Organisms," *FBI Law Enforcement Bulletin* (July 1987).

96. Theodore M. Hammett, "Precautionary Measures and Protective Equipment: Developing a Reasonable Response," *National Institute of Justice Bulletin* (Washington, D.C.: U.S. Government Printing Office, 1988).

97. *National Institute of Justice Reports*, No. 206 (November/December 1987).

98. "Taking Aim at a Virus: NYPD Tackles AIDS on the Job and in the Ranks," *Law Enforcement News*, March 15, 1988, p. 1.

99. "Drowned Boys Case Takes Toll on Officers, Clergy," *The Florida Times-Union* (Jacksonville), November 10, 1994, p. A6.

100. See Kevin Barrett, "More EAPs Needed in Police Departments to Quash Officers' Superhuman Self-Image," *EA Professional Report*, January 1994, p. 3.

101. "Stress on the Job," *Newsweek*, April 25, 1988, p. 43.

102. Joseph Victor, "Police Stress: Is Anybody Out There Listening?" *New York Law Enforcement Journal* (June 1986), pp. 19–20.

103. Kevin Barrett, "Police Suicide: Is Anyone Listening," *Journal of Safe Management of Disruptive and Assaultive Behavior*, Spring 1997, pp. 6–9.

104. Ibid.

105. Bryan Vila, "Tired Cops: Probable Connections Between Fatigue and the Performance, Health, and Safety of Patrol Officers," *American Journal of Police*, Vol. 15, no. 2 (1996), pp. 51–92.

106. Bryan Vila and Erik Y. Taiji, "Fatigue and Police Officer Performance," paper presented at the annual meeting of the American Society of Criminology, Chicago, 1996.

107. "Stroke Victim Sues State Over Arrest," The Associated Press, April 24, 1996.

108. Charles R. Swanson, Leonard Territo, and Robert W. Taylor, *Police Administration: Structures, Processes, and Behavior*, 2nd ed. (New York: Macmillan, 1988).

109. *Malley* v. *Briggs*, 475 U.S. 335, 106 S.Ct. 1092 (1986).

110. Ibid., *Malley* at 4246.

111. *Biscoe* v. *Arlington County*, 238 U.S. App. D.C. 206, 738 F.2d 1352, 1362 (1984).

112. *Kaplan* v. *Lloyd's Insurance Co.*, 479 So. 2d 961 (La. App. 1985).

113. *City of Canton, Ohio* v. *Harris*, U.S. 109 S.Ct. 1197 (1989).

114. Ibid., at 1204.

115. No. 95–1100. Argued November 5, 1996—Decided April 28, 1997.

116. *Prior* v. *Woods* (1981), *National Law Journal*, November 2, 1981.

117. *Bivens* v. *Six Unknown Federal Agents*, 403 U.S. 388 (1971).

118. See *F.D.I.C.* v. *Meyer*, 510 U.S. 471 (1994), in which the U.S. Supreme Court reiterated its ruling under *Bivens*, stating that only government employees and not government agencies can be sued.

119. *Wyler* v. *U.S.*, 725 F. 2d 157 (2d Cir. 1983).

120. California Government Code, §818.

121. Federal Tort Claims Act, 28 U. S. C. 1346(b), 2671–2680.

122. "Victims of Failed DEA Sting Win More than $1 Million Judgment," *Drug Enforcement Report*, March 23, 1995, pp. 1–2.

123. *Elder* v. *Holloway*, 114 S.Ct. 1019, 127 L. Ed. 2d 344 (1994).

124. Ibid.

125. *Hunter* v. *Bryant*, 112 S.Ct. 534 (1991).

126. William U. McCormack, "Supreme Court Cases: 1991–1992 Term," *FBI Law Enforcement Bulletin*, November 1992, p. 30.

127. For more information on police liability, see Daniel L. Schofield, "Legal Issues of Pursuit Driving," *FBI Law Enforcement Bulletin* (May 1988), pp. 23–29.

128. "Playboy Interview: Daryl Gates," *Playboy*, August 1991, p. 60.

129. Ibid., p. 63.

130. *Tennessee* v. *Garner*, 471 U.S. 1 (1985).

131. Ibid.

132. *Graham* v. *Connor*, 490 U.S. 386, 396–397 (1989).

133. "NACOP Questions Delay in Federal Use of 'Imminent Danger' Standards for Deadly Force," National Association of Chiefs of Police press release, October 19, 1995.

134. James Fyfe, *Shots Fired: An Examination of New York City Police Firearms Discharges* (Ann Arbor, MI: University Microfilms, 1978).

135. James Fyfe, "Blind Justice? Police Shootings in Memphis," paper presented at the annual meeting of the Academy of Criminal Justice Sciences, Philadelphia, March 1981.

136. It is estimated that American police shoot at approximately 3,600 people every year. See William Geller "Deadly Force" study guide Crime File Series (Washington, D.C.: National Institute of Justice, no date).

137. Anne Cohen: "I've Killed That Man Ten Thousand Times," *Police Magazine* (July 1980).

138. For more information, see Joe Auten, "When Police Shoot," *North Carolina Criminal Justice Today*, Vol. 4, no. 4 (Summer 1986), pp. 9–14.

139. "Man Attracts Police Gunfire to Commit Suicide," Associated Press, Nov. 17, 1997.

140. David W. Hayeslip and Alan Preszler, "NIJ Initiative on Less-than-Lethal Weapons," *NIJ Research in Brief* (Washington, D.C.: National Institute of Justice, 1993).

141. As quoted by Michael Siegfried, "Notes on the Professionalization of Private Security," *The Justice Professional* (Spring 1989).

142. Timothy J. Flanagan and Kathleen Maguire, *Sourcebook of Criminal Justice Statistics 1989* (Washington, D.C.: U.S. Government Printing Office, 1990), p. 16.

143. See Edward A. Farris "Five Decades of American Policing, 1932–1982: The Path to Professionalism," *The Police Chief* (November 1982), p. 31.

144. Ibid., p. 34.

145. Gary W. Cordner and Gerald L. Williams, "The *CALEA* Standards: What Is the Fit with Community Policing?" *National Institute of Justice Journal*, August 1995, p. 39.

146. National Commission on Law Observance and Enforcement, *Report on Police* (Washington, D.C.: U.S. Government Printing Office, 1931).

147. National Advisory Commission on Criminal Justice Standards and Goals, *Report on the Police* (Washington, D.C.: U.S. Government Printing Office, 1973).

148. Ibid.

149. David L. Carter, Allen D. Sapp, and Darrel W. Stephens, *The State of Police Education: Policy Direction for the 21st Century* (Washington, D.C.: Police Executive Research Forum, 1989).

150. Ibid., p. xiv.

151. Ibid., pp. xxii–xxiii.

152. Brian A. Reaves, "Local Police Departments, 1993," Bureau of Justice Statistics, April 1996.

153. Ibid., p. 84.

154. National Advisory Commission on Criminal Justice Standards and Goals, *Police* (Washington, D.C.: U.S. Government Printing Office, 1973), p. 238.

155. "Dallas PD College Rule Gets Final OK," *Law Enforcement News*, July 7, 1986, pp. 1, 13.

156. *Davis* v. *Dallas*, 1986.

157. David L. Carter and Allen Sapp, *The State of Police Education: Critical Findings* (Washington, D.C.: Police Executive Research Forum, no date).

158. O. W. Wilson and Roy Clinton McLaren, *Police Administration*, 4th ed. (New York: McGraw-Hill, 1977), p. 259.

159. Ibid., p. 270.

160. Report of the National Advisory Commission on Civil Disorders, p. 332.

161. As reported in Charles Swanson and Leonard Territo, *Police Administration: Structures, Processes, and Behavior* (New York: Macmillan, 1983), p. 203, from *Affirmative Action Monthly* (February 1979), p. 22.

162. Brian A. Reaves, "Local Police Departments, 1993," Bureau of Justice Statistics, April 1996.

163. The Police Foundation, *On the Move: The Status of Women in Policing* (Washington, D.C.: The Foundation, 1990).

164. Brian A. Reaves, "Local Police Departments, 1993," Bureau of Justice Statistics, April 1996.

165. C. Lee Bennett, *Interviews with Female Police Officers in Western Massachusetts*, paper presented at the annual meeting of the Academy of Criminal Justice Sciences, Nashville, Tennessee, March 1991.

166. Ibid., p. 9.

167. See, for example, Pearl Jacobs, "Suggestions for the Greater Integration of Women into Policing," paper presented at the annual meeting of the Academy of Criminal Justice Sciences, Nashville, TN, March 1991, and Cynthia Fuchs Epstein, *Deceptive Distinctions: Sex, Gender, and the Social Order* (New Haven, CT: Yale University Press, 1988).

168. Carole G. Garrison, Nancy K. Grant, and Kenneth L. J. McCormick, "Utilization of Police Women," unpublished manuscript.

169. Susan Ehrlich Martin and Nancy C. Jurik, *Doing Justice, Doing Gender: Women in Law and Criminal Justice Occupations* (Thousand Oaks, CA: Sage, 1996).

170. See Sara Roen, "The Longest Climb," *Police*, October 1996, pp. 44–46, 66.

171. The Police Foundation, *On the Move*.

chapter 7

POLICING: LEGAL ASPECTS

"Yeah," the detective mumbled. "Fifteen guys. You might want to think about that. Only two of us."..."On the other hand..." He shook his head. "Sneaking a bunch of cops into a neighborhood like this is going to be like trying to sneak the sun past a rooster."...As he started up the stairs, Angelo reached not for his gun but for his wallet. He took out a Chase Manhattan calendar printed on a supple but firm slip of plastic. He flicked the card at Rand. "I'll open the door with this. You step in and freeze them."

"Jesus Christ, Angelo," the agent almost gasped. "We can't do that. We haven't got a warrant."

"Don't worry about it, kid," Angelo said, drawing up to the second door on the right on the second floor. "It ain't a perfect world."[1]

—LARRY COLLINS AND DOMINIQUE LAPIERRE, THE FIFTH HORSEMAN

KEY CONCEPTS

arrest
Bill of Rights
Burger court
compelling interest
due process
ECPA
emergency searches
exclusionary rule
fleeting targets exception

fruit of the poisoned tree
good faith
illegally seized evidence
inherent coercion
interrogation
landmark cases
Miranda triggers
Miranda warnings
plain view

probable cause
psychological manipulation
reasonable suspicion
Rehnquist court
search and seizure
search incident to arrest
suspicionless searches
Warren court
writ of *certiorari*

KEY CASES

Weeks v. *U.S.*
Chimel v. *California*
California v. *Hodari D.*
Mapp v. *Ohio*
Terry v. *Ohio*
Arizona v. *Fulminante*
Robinson v. *U.S.*
Brown v. *Mississippi*
Minnick v. *Mississippi*

Carroll v. *U.S.*
Escobedo v. *Illinois*
Illinois v. *Perkins*
Gideon v. *Wainwright*
Nix v. *Williams*
Alabama v. *White*
Miranda v. *Arizona*
Florida v. *Bostick*
California v. *Horton*

Silverthorne Lumber Co. v. *U.S.*
California v. *Acevedo*
Smith v. *Ohio*
U.S. Dept. of Justice v. *Landano*
Illinois v. *Condon*
Brecht v. *Abrahamson*
Wilson v. *Arkansas*
Richards v. *Wisconsin*

The Abuse of Police Power

The right of the people to be secure in their persons, houses, papers, and effects, against unreasonable searches and seizures, shall not be violated, and no warrants shall issue but upon probable cause, supported by oath or affirmation, and particularly describing the place to be searched, and the persons or things to be seized.

—Fourth Amendment to the U. S. Constitution

In August 1997, a storm of protest swirled around NYPD police officers serving Brooklyn's 70th Precinct. In the midst of the storm stood four officers accused of savagely beating and sexually assaulting Abner Louima, a 30-year-old Haitian immigrant, in a station house bathroom. Louima, a black man who worked as a security guard, had been arrested on charges of assaulting a police officer following an early morning scuffle outside a city nightclub. He claimed that after his arrival at the station house, two white officers beat him nearly senseless, then sodomized him with the handle of a toilet plunger. Louima underwent surgery to repair a torn rectum and gall bladder and remained hospitalized for weeks following the incident.

While the activities of the NYPD officers in the Louima case, if shown to be true, were indeed despicable, national publicity surrounding the incident was considerably less intense than that which centered on the videotaped 1991 beating of black motorist Rodney King by Los Angeles police officers. King, an unemployed 25-year-old black man, was stopped by LAPD officers for an alleged violation of motor vehicle laws. Police said King had been speeding and refused to stop for a pursuing patrol car. Officers claimed to have clocked King's 1988 Hyundai at 115 MPH on suburban Los Angeles' Foothill Freeway—even though the car's manufacturer later said the vehicle was not capable of speeds over 100 MPH and recordings of police radio communications surrounding the incident never mentioned excessive speed.

Eventually King did stop, but then officers of the Los Angeles Police Department attacked him—shocking him twice with electronic stun guns and striking him with nightsticks and fists. Kicked in the stomach, face, and back, he was left with 11 skull fractures, missing teeth, a crushed cheekbone, and a broken ankle. A witness told reporters she heard King begging officers to stop the beating, but that they "were all laughing, like they just had a party."[2] King eventually underwent surgery for brain injuries.

Twenty-five police officers—21 from the LAPD, 2 California Highway Patrol officers, and 2 school district officers—were involved in the incident. Four of them, who were later indicted, beat King as the other 21 watched. Los Angeles County District Attorney Ira Reiner called the behavior of the officers who watched, "irresponsible and offensive," but not criminal.[3]

There are two important differences between the King incident and the other crime stories related in this textbook: (1) this time the criminals wore police uniforms, and (2) the

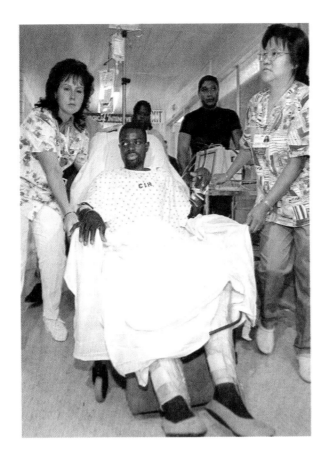

Abner Louima, the 30-year-old Haitian immigrant, around whom a storm of protest swirled in late-1997, after he claimed that four NYPD officers serving Brooklyn's 70th Precinct savagely beat and sexually assaulted him in a station house bathroom—forcing the handle of a toilet plunger up his rectum. *Todd Plitt, AP/Wide World Photos*

entire incident was captured on videotape by an amateur photographer from a nearby balcony who was trying out his new night-sensitive video camera. The two-minute videotape was repeatedly broadcast over national television and picked up by hundreds of local TV stations. The furor that erupted over the tape led to the ouster of LAPD Chief Daryl Gates and initiated a Justice Department review of law-enforcement practices across the country.[4] Some defended the police, citing the "war zone" mentality of today's inner-city crime fighters as fostering a violent mind-set. Officers involved in the beating claimed that King, at 6 feet 3 inches and 225 pounds, appeared strung out on PCP and that he and his two companions made officers feel threatened.[5]

In 1992 a California jury found the four police defendants not guilty—a verdict that resulted in days of rioting across Los Angeles. A year later, however, in the spring of 1993 two of the officers, Sergeant Stacey Koon and Officer Laurence Powell, were found guilty by a jury in federal court of denying King his constitutional right "not to be deprived of liberty without due process of law, including the right to be…free from the intentional use of unreasonable force."[6] Later that year both were sentenced to two and one-half years in prison, far less than might have been expected under federal sentencing guidelines. They were released from prison in December of 1995, and a three-year long court battle over whether federal sentencing guideline provisions were violated during sentencing was resolved in the officers' favor in 1996. Officers Theodore Briseno and Timothy Wind were exonerated at the federal level.

In 1994 King settled a civil suit against the city of Los Angeles for a reported $3.8 million. Observers later concluded that King himself was not a model citizen. At the time of the beating he was on parole after having served time in prison for robbery. Following the beating he came under investigation for another robbery and was arrested again three months after his release from the hospital for allegedly picking up a male prostitute dressed as a woman and for trying to run over police who confronted him.[7] He was sentenced in 1996 to 90 days in jail on charges of assault with a deadly weapon for trying to run over his wife during a domestic dispute,[8] and a month later was fined $1,436 and ordered to serve 30 days on a highway

There is more law at the end of the policeman's nightstick than in all the decisions of the Supreme Court.

—Alexander "Clubber" Williams, late nineteenth-century NYPD officer

The beating of Rodney King by Los Angeles police officers, captured here by a man trying out a new video camera. The 1991 incident raised many questions about police integrity, while simultaneously highlighting the power of new technology to uncover police abuses.
Rob Crandall, Picture Group

cleanup crew for violating probation on a drunk-driving conviction.[9] Regardless of King's personal life, however, the King incident, more than seven years after it occurred, continues to serve as a rallying point for individual rights activists concerned with ensuring that citizens remain protected from the abuse of police power in an increasingly conservative society.

This chapter shows how the police, like everyone else, are not above the law. It describes the legal environment surrounding police activities—from search and seizure through arrest and the interrogation of suspects. As we shall see throughout, it is democratically inspired legal restraints upon the police which help ensure individual freedoms in our society and which prevent the development of a "police state" in America. Like anything else, however, the rules by which the police are expected to operate are in constant flux, and their continuing development forms the meat of this chapter.

A Changing Legal Climate

Bill of Rights The first ten amendments to the U.S. Constitution, considered especially important in the processing of criminal defendants.

The Constitution of the United States is designed—especially in the **Bill of Rights**—to protect citizens against abuses of police power (see Table 7–1). However, the legal environment surrounding the police in modern America is much more complex than it was just 30 years ago. Up until that time, the Bill of Rights was largely given only lip service in criminal justice proceedings around the country. In practice, law enforcement, especially on the state and local level, revolved around tried and true methods of search, arrest, and interrogation, which sometimes left little room for recognition of individual rights. Police operations during that period were often far more informal than they are today, and investigating officers frequently assumed that they could come and go as they pleased, even to the extent of invading someone's personal space without the need for a search warrant. Interrogations could quickly turn violent, and the infamous "rubber hose," which was reputed to leave few marks on the body, was probably more widely used during the questioning of suspects than many would like to believe. Similarly, "doing things by the book" could mean the use of thick telephone books for beating suspects, since the books spread out the force of blows and left few visible bruises. Although such abuses were not necessarily day-to-day practices in all police agencies, and while they probably did not characterize more than a relatively small proportion of all officers, such conduct pointed to the need for greater control over police activities so that even the potential for abuse might be curtailed.

Table 7-1 Constitutional Amendments of Special Significance to the American System of Justice, from the Bill of Rights

This Right Is Guaranteed	By This Amendment
The Right Against Unreasonable Searches and Seizures	Fourth
No Arrest Without Probable Cause	Fourth
The Right Against Self-incrimination	Fifth
The Right Against "Double Jeopardy"	Fifth
The Right to Due Process of Law	Fifth, Fourteenth
The Right to a Speedy Trial	Sixth
The Right to a Jury Trial	Sixth
The Right to Know the Charges	Sixth
The Right to Cross-examine Witnesses	Sixth
The Right to a Lawyer	Sixth
The Right to Compel Witnesses on One's Behalf	Sixth
The Right to Reasonable Bail	Eighth
The Right Against Excessive Fines	Eighth
The Right Against Cruel and Unusual Punishments	Eighth
The Applicability of Constitutional Rights to All Citizens, Regardless of State Law or Procedure (not part of the Bill of Rights)	Fourteenth

It was during the 1960s that the U.S. Supreme Court, under the direction of Chief Justice Earl Warren, accelerated the process of guaranteeing individual rights in the face of criminal prosecution. Warren court rulings bound the police to strict procedural requirements in the areas of investigation, arrest, and interrogation. Later rulings scrutinized trial court procedure and enforced humanitarian standards in sentencing and punishment. The Warren court also seized upon the Fourteenth Amendment and made it a basis for judicial mandates requiring that both state and federal criminal justice agencies adhere to the Court's interpretation of the Constitution. The apex of the individual rights emphasis in Supreme Court decisions was reached in the 1966 case of *Miranda* v. *Arizona*,[10] which established the famous requirement of a police "rights advisement" of suspects. In wielding its brand of idealism, the Warren court (which held sway from 1953 until 1969) accepted the fact that a few guilty people would go free in order that the rights of the majority of Americans would be protected.

Supreme Court decisions of the last few years, however—the product of a new and still emerging conservative Court philosophy—have begun what some call a "reversal" of Warren-era advances in the area of individual rights. By creating exceptions to some of the Warren court's rules and restraints, and in allowing for the emergency questioning of suspects before they are read their rights, a changing Supreme Court has recognized the realities attending day-to-day police work and the need to ensure public safety. This practical approach to justice, which came into vogue during the Reagan–Bush political era and is still with us, is all the more interesting for the fact that it must struggle to emerge from the confines of earlier Supreme Court decisions.

Individual Rights

The Constitution of the United States provides for a system of checks and balances among the legislative, judicial, and executive (presidential) branches of government. By this we mean that one branch of government is always held accountable to the other branches. The system is designed to ensure that no *one* individual or agency can become powerful enough to usurp the rights and freedoms guaranteed under the Constitution. Without accountabil-

The "Rodney King" Trials

Until the spring of 1992 most Americans would probably have agreed that the justice system, though flawed in numerous individual instances, was the most equitable mechanism available for the apprehension of wrongdoers, for determinations of guilt or innocence, and for the imposition of punishment upon criminal offenders in an otherwise imperfect world. At the same time, most probably felt, at least intuitively, that the exercise of criminal justice occurred within a framework that was basically fair and impartial and that embodied our highest cultural ideals of social justice. In short, the symbolism of "blind justice" as equitable justice was, for many Americans, an article of faith.

This is not to say that the system was without its detractors. On the contrary, the voices of the poor, the disenfranchised, the unempowered—in particular ethnic minorities and what sociologists have come to call "underrepresented groups"—have long appealed to the conscience of the American people, chanting a litany of claimed injustices for over 200 years. The system, they said, understood only one type of justice: justice for the rich and for the powerful, justice for those who make the laws and for those who stand to benefit from them. From time to time, academicians and liberal politicians joined the fray on the side of the disenfranchised, claiming that law enforcement is fundamentally a tool of power, exercised exclusively in the service of the wealthy and the well connected. They, along with a variety of social commentators, portrayed criminal justice as one more aspect of a much broader issue—social *in*justice.

Then came an event that grabbed our nation's attention. In 1991 the videotaped police beating of a black Los Angeles motorist, Rodney King, burst upon the national scene and transfixed the American national conscience via television. And the images wouldn't fade. In 1992 a Simi Valley,

California, jury, with but one minority member, found the police officers who had been arrested for assaulting King innocent of the charges brought against them. The nation was aghast—unable to reconcile what it had perceived clearly in the media with the workings of American criminal justice. In an instant Rodney King became, to many, the symbol of justice denied. Within hours Los Angeles was embroiled in social protests, rioting, and looting. Racial tensions increased dramatically. In the spring of 1993 two of the officers, Sergeant Stacey Koon and Officer Laurence Powell, were found guilty by a jury in federal court of depriving King of his constitutional right "not to be deprived of liberty without due process of law, including the right to be...free from the intentional use of unreasonable force."[1] Officers Theodore Briseno and Timothy Wind were found not guilty of the same charge. Commenting on the differences between the two trials, *Newsweek* magazine said, "A...cynical explanation for the convictions this time is that the 12 jurors knew all too well what a full acquittal could mean. The difference between this case and last year's were the riots," says Harland Braun, Briseno's lawyer. "The Simi Valley trial surely taught the perils of a criminal justice system that's perceived to be racist. But a system that's perceived as political—one that responds to public pressure as much as evidence—isn't much better."[2] As controversy over the case continued, the American Civil Liberties Union, in heated debate, voted to protest the convictions, claiming that "repeat prosecution by different jurisdictions for the same act amounted to double jeopardy."[3]

The Rodney King "incident" was a transfiguring event in the history of American criminal justice. It brought us to realize that the strokes which paint the canvas of intergroup relations in the United States are broader than the particulars of any one case.

There is little denying that minorities are overrepresented at all stages of criminal-justice processing. Similarly, there is little denying that minority youth violate laws with considerably greater frequency than do other youths and that the violations they commit are often found to be especially socially reprehensible—typified by crimes of violence, drug dealing, and the like. And yet whose laws are these people violating? By whose standards are they being held accountable? Because crime is a social construct arising out of a nexus of legislative action, social conditions, and individual choice, it becomes possible to ask: "Whose crime is it, after all?" From the perspective of those involved in it, drug dealing may seem like a reasonable way out from poverty and violence a day-to-day necessity rooted in the will to survive. From the perspective of official agents of justice, these same behaviors confer criminal responsibility and those who engage in them are condemned—arrested and sentenced to be removed from society until such time as they are adjudged fit to return. And therein lies the rub. Return to what? To the social order understood by the lawmakers? Or to a society inherently different and populated by less forgiving foes than criminal justice policy-makers and enforcers of official law?

Ultimately we have to ask: "Is there one form of justice for the poor and another for the rich?" "Is there a separate system of justice that embodies the values of the powerful, while condemning the strivings of the underclass?" "Are the felt needs of certain people being denied by the contemporary American criminal justice system?" "Can the scales of justice be balanced?" "In a more fundamental sense, can justice be truly equitable in a society built upon the free pursuit of individual wealth and the often unbridled drive toward personal power?"

Some have suggested creating two systems of criminal justice: one for the rich and one for the poor, one for the socially downtrodden and another for the well connected. After all, they say, isn't it necessary for enforcement agents, judges, juries, and probation/parole officers to understand the backgrounds and values of the criminal-justice clients with whom they must deal? Shouldn't the system recognize the harsh realities of life in the inner city and the desperation of the indigent and the disenfranchised? But, if we lose faith in our existing system's ability to deliver justice, what is left? How do we remake a system which for over 200 years has formed the bedrock of a tenuous social order and which has held in check the excesses of the criminally compelled?

QUESTIONS FOR DISCUSSION

1. What, in your opinion, has been the significance of the Rodney King beating and subsequent trials for our nation's criminal justice system? Have those events affected the practice of criminal justice in this country? If so, how?

2. This "Theory Into Practice" box asks: "Is there one form of justice for the poor and another for the rich? Is there a separate system of justice which embodies the values of the powerful while condemning the strivings of the underclass? Are the felt needs of certain people being denied by the contemporary American criminal-justice system? Can the scales of justice be balanced? In a more fundamental sense, can justice be truly equitable in a society built upon the free pursuit of individual wealth and the often unbridled drive toward personal power?" What do you think?

[1]"Cries of Relief," *Time*, April 26, 1993, p. 18.
[2]"King II: What Made the Difference?" *Newsweek*, April 26, 1993, p. 26.
[3]"A.C.L.U.-Not All That Civil," *Time*, April 26, 1993, p. 31.

ity, it is possible to imagine a police state in which the power of law enforcement is absolute and related to political considerations and personal vendettas more than to any objective considerations of guilt or innocence.

Under our system of government, courts become the arena for dispute resolution, not just between individuals but between citizens and the agencies of government themselves. After handling by the justice system, people who feel they have not received the respect and dignity due them under the law can appeal to the courts for redress. Such appeals are usually based upon procedural issues and are independent of more narrow considerations of guilt or innocence.

In this chapter, we spend a great deal of time on cases that are important because they are famous for having clarified constitutional guarantees concerning individual liberties within the criminal justice arena. They involve issues which have come to be called "rights" by most of us. It is common to hear arrestees today say: "You can't do that! I know my rights!" Rights are concerned with procedure, that is, with how police and other actors in the criminal justice system handle each part of the process of dealing with suspects. Rights violations have often become the basis for the dismissal of charges, acquittal of defendants, or the release of convicted offenders after an appeal to a higher court.

Due Process Requirements

As you may recall from Chapter 1, due process is a requirement of the Fifth, Sixth, and Fourteenth Amendments to the U.S. Constitution which mandates that justice-system officials respect the rights of accused individuals throughout the criminal justice process. Most due process requirements of relevance to the police pertain to three major areas: (1) evidence and investigation (often called "search and seizure"), (2) arrest, and (3) interrogation. Each of these areas has been addressed by a plethora of landmark U.S. Supreme Court decisions. **Landmark cases** are recognizable by the fact that they produce substantial changes in both the understanding of the requirements of due process and in the practical day-to-day operations of the justice system. Another way to think of landmark decisions is that they help significantly in clarifying the "rules of the game"—the procedural guidelines by which the police and the rest of the justice system must abide.

The three areas we are about to discuss have been well defined by decades of court precedent. Keep in mind, however, that judicial interpretations of the constitutional requirement of due process are constantly evolving. As new decisions are rendered, and as the composition of the Court itself changes, additional refinements (and even major changes) may occur.

Landmark Cases
Precedent setting court decisions, often recognizable by the fact that they produce substantial changes in both the understanding of the requirements of due process and in the practical day-to-day operations of the justice system.

The legal environment surrounding the police helps ensure proper official conduct. In a traffic stop such as this, inappropriate behavior on the part of the officer can later become the basis for civil or criminal action against the officer and the police department. *Courtesy of the New York City Police Department*

Search and Seizure

Illegally Seized Evidence
Evidence seized in opposition to the principles of due process as described by the Bill of Rights. Most illegally seized evidence is the result of police searches conducted without a proper warrant or of improperly conducted interrogations.

The U.S. Constitution declares that people must be secure in their homes and in their persons against unreasonable searches and seizures. This right is asserted by the Fourth Amendment, which reads: "The right of the people to be secure in their persons, houses, papers, and effects, against unreasonable searches and seizures shall not be violated, and no warrants shall issue but upon probable cause, supported by oath or affirmation, and particularly describing the place to be searched, and the persons or things to be seized." This amendment, a part of the Bill of Rights, was adopted by Congress and became effective on December 15, 1791.

The language of the Fourth Amendment is familiar to all of us. "Warrants," "probable cause," and other phrases from the amendment are frequently cited in editorials, TV news shows, and daily conversation. It is the interpretation of these phrases over time by the U.S. Supreme Court, however, which has given them the impact they have on the justice system today.

The Exclusionary Rule

The first landmark case concerning search and seizure was that of *Weeks* v. *U.S.* (1914).[11] Freemont Weeks was suspected of using the U.S. mail to sell lottery tickets, a federal crime. Weeks was arrested and federal agents went to his home to conduct a search. They had no search warrant, since at the time investigators did not routinely use warrants. They confiscated many incriminating items of evidence, as well as personal possessions of the defendant, including clothes, papers, books, and even candy.

Prior to trial, Weeks's attorney asked that the personal items be returned, claiming that they had been illegally seized under Fourth Amendment guarantees. A judge agreed and ordered the materials returned. On the basis of the evidence that was retained, however, Weeks was convicted in federal court and sentenced to prison. He appealed his conviction through other courts and eventually reached the U.S. Supreme Court. There, his lawyer reasoned that if some of his client's belongings had been illegally seized, then the remainder of them were also taken improperly. The Supreme Court agreed and overturned Weeks's earlier conviction.

The *Weeks* case forms the basis of what is now called the **exclusionary rule**. The exclusionary rule means that evidence illegally seized by the police cannot be used in a trial. The rule acts as a control over police behavior and specifically focuses upon the failure of officers to obtain warrants authorizing them to either conduct searches or to effect arrests (especially where arrest may lead to the acquisition of incriminating statements or to the seizure of physical evidence).

It is important to note, incidentally, that Freemont Weeks could have been retried on the original charges following the Supreme Court decision in his case. He would not have faced double jeopardy because he was in fact not *finally convicted* on the earlier charges. His conviction was nullified on appeal, resulting in neither a conviction nor an acquittal. Double jeopardy becomes an issue only when a defendant faces retrial on the same charges following acquittal at his or her original trial or when the defendant is retried after having been convicted.

It is also important to recognize that the decision of the Supreme Court in the Weeks case was binding, at the time, only upon federal officers, because it was federal agents who were involved in the illegal seizure.

Exclusionary Rule The understanding, based on Supreme Court precedent, that incriminating information must be seized according to constitutional specifications of due process, or it will not be allowed as evidence in criminal trials.

Problems with Precedent

The *Weeks* case demonstrates the power of the Supreme Court in enforcing what we have called the "rules of the game." It also lays bare the much more significant role that the Court plays in rule creation. Until the *Weeks* case was decided, federal law enforcement officers had little reason to think they were acting in violation of due process. Common practice had not required that they obtain a warrant before conducting searches. The rule which resulted from *Weeks* was new, and it would forever alter the enforcement activities of federal officers. Yet the *Weeks* case was also retroactive, in the sense that it was applied to Weeks himself.

There is a problem in the way in which our system generates and applies principles of due process, which may be obvious from our discussion of the *Weeks* case. The problem is that the present appeals system, focusing as it does upon the "rules of the game," presents a ready-made channel for the guilty to go free. There can be little doubt but that Freemont Weeks had violated federal law. A jury had convicted him. Yet he escaped punishment because of the illegal behavior of the police—behavior which, until the Court ruled, had not been regarded as anything but legitimate.

Even if the police knowingly violate the principles of due process, which they sometimes do, our sense of justice is compromised when the guilty go free. Famed Supreme Court Justice Benjamin Cardozo (1870–1938) once complained, "The criminal is to go free because the constable has blundered."

Students of criminal justice have long considered three possible solutions to this problem. The first solution suggests that rules of due process, especially when newly articulated by the courts, should be applied only to future cases, not to the initial case in which they are stated. The justices in the *Weeks* case, for example, might have said, "We are creating the 'exclusionary rule,' based upon our realization in this case. Law enforcement officers are obligated to use it as a guide in all future searches. However, insofar as the guilt of Mr. Weeks was decided by a jury under rules of evidence existing at the time, we will let that decision stand."

A second solution would punish police officers or other actors in the criminal justice system who act illegally, but would not allow the guilty defendant to escape punishment. This solution would be useful in applying established precedent where officers and officials had the benefit of clearly articulated rules and should have known better. Under this arrangement, any officer today who intentionally violates due process guarantees might be suspended, reduced in rank, lose pay, or be fired. Some authors have suggested that "decertification" might serve as "an alternative to traditional remedies for police misconduct."[12] Departments which employed the decertification process would punish violators by removing their certification as police officers. Because, as we discussed in Chapter 6, officers in every state except Hawaii must meet the certification requirements of state boards (usually called Training and Standards Commissions or Peace Officer Standards and Training

Boards) in order to hold employment, some authors[13] argue that decertification would have a much more personal (and therefore more effective) impact on individual officers than the exclusionary rule ever could.

A third possibility would allow the Supreme Court to address theoretical questions involving issues of due process. Concerned supervisors and officials could ask how the Court would rule "if…" As things now work, the Court can only address real cases and does so on a **writ of *certiorari*,** in which the Court orders the record of a lower court case to be prepared for review.

The obvious difficulty with these solutions, however, is that they would substantially reduce the potential benefits available to defendants through the appeals process and, hence, would effectively eliminate the process itself.

Writ of *Certiorari* An order, by an appellate court, specifying whether or not that court will review the judgment of a lower court.

The Fruit of the Poisoned Tree Doctrine

The Court further built upon the rules concerning evidence with its ruling in *Silverthorne Lumber Co.* v. *U.S.*[14] In 1918 Frederick Silverthorne and his sons operated a lumber company and were accused of avoiding payment of federal taxes. When asked to turn over the company's books to federal investigators, the Silverthornes refused, citing their Fifth Amendment privilege against self-incrimination.

Shortly thereafter, federal agents, without a search warrant, descended on the lumber company and seized the wanted books. The Silverthornes' lawyer appeared in court and asked that the materials be returned, citing the need for a search warrant as had been established in the *Weeks* case. The prosecutor agreed, and the books were returned to the Silverthornes.

The Silverthornes came to trial thinking they would be acquitted because the evidence against them was no longer in the hands of prosecutors. In a surprise move, however, the prosecution introduced photocopies of incriminating evidence which they had made from the returned books. The Silverthornes were convicted in federal court. Their appeal eventually reached the Supreme Court of the United States. The Court ruled that just as illegally seized evidence cannot be used in a trial, neither can evidence be used which *derives* from an illegal seizure.[15] The conviction of the Silverthornes was overturned, and they were set free.

The *Silverthorne case* articulated a new principle of due process which we today call the **fruit of the poisoned tree doctrine.** This doctrine is potentially far reaching. Complex cases developed after years of police investigative effort may be ruined if defense attorneys are able to demonstrate that the prosecution's case, no matter how complex, was originally based upon a search or seizure which violated due process. In such cases, it is likely that all evidence will be declared "tainted" and become useless.

Fruit of the Poisoned Tree Doctrine A legal principle which excludes from introduction at trial any evidence later developed as a result of an originally illegal search or seizure.

Still, prior to the Warren court era, most U.S. Supreme Court decisions were regarded as applicable only to federal law enforcement agencies.

The Warren Court Era (1953–1969)

Before the 1960s, the U.S. Supreme Court intruded only infrequently upon the overall operation of the criminal justice system at the state and local level. As some authors have observed, however, the 1960s provided a time of youthful idealism, and "without the distraction of a depression or world war, individual liberties were examined at all levels of society."[16] Hence, while the exclusionary rule became an overriding consideration in federal law enforcement from the time that it was first defined by the Supreme Court in the *Weeks* case in 1914, it was not until 1961 that the Warren court, under Chief Justice Earl Warren, decided a case that was to change the face of American law enforcement forever. That case, *Mapp* v. *Ohio* (1961),[17] made the exclusionary rule applicable to criminal prosecutions at the state level.[18] Beginning with the now-famous *Mapp* case, the Warren court set out to chart a course which would guarantee nationwide recognition of individual rights, as it understood them, by agencies at all levels of the criminal justice system.

The Warren Court Applies the Exclusionary Rule to the States

The *Mapp* case began like many others during the protest-prone 1960s. Dolree Mapp was suspected of harboring a fugitive wanted in a bombing. When Ohio police officers arrived at her house, she refused to admit them. Eventually, they forced their way in. During the search

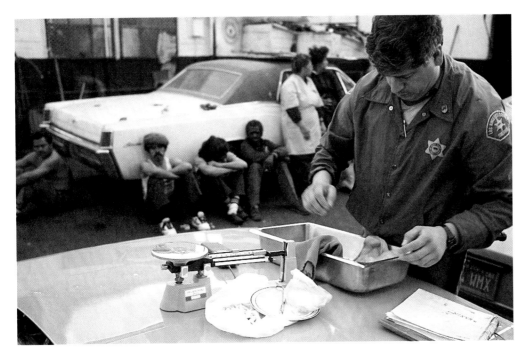

A California police officer spot checks a seized substance suspected of being cocaine. The exclusionary rule means that illegally gathered evidence cannot be used later in court, requiring that police officers pay close attention to the way in which they gather and handle evidence. *Mark Richards*

which ensued, pornographic materials, including photographs, were uncovered. Mapp was arrested, and eventually convicted, under a state law which made possession of such materials illegal.

Prior decisions by the U.S. Supreme Court, including *Wolf* v. *Colorado*,[19] had led officers to expect that the exclusionary rule did not apply to agents of state and local law enforcement. Nonetheless, in a wide-reaching and precedent-setting decision, Mapp's conviction was overturned upon appeal by a majority of Warren court justices who decided that the U.S. Constitution, under the Fourteenth Amendment's due process guarantee, mandates that state and local law enforcement officers must be held to the same standards of accountability as federal officers. There could be little doubt, said the justices, that the evidence against Mapp had been illegally obtained and therefore could not be used against her in any court of law in the United States. The precedent established in *Mapp* v. *Ohio* firmly applied the principles developed in *Weeks* and *Silverthorne* to trials in state courts, making police officers at all levels accountable to the rule of law, which, as embodied in the words of the Fourteenth Amendment, reads: "nor shall any State deprive any person of life, liberty, or property, without due process of law; nor deny to any person within its jurisdiction the equal protection of the laws."

Another important Warren-era case, that of *Chimel* v. *California* (1969)[20], involved both arrest as well as search activities by local law enforcement officers. Ted Chimel was convicted of the burglary of a coin shop, based upon evidence gathered at the scene of his arrest—his home. Officers, armed with an arrest warrant but not a search warrant, had taken Chimel into custody when they arrived at his residence and proceeded with a search of his entire three-bedroom house, including the attic, a small workshop, and the garage. Although officers realized that the search might be challenged in court, they justified it by claiming that it was conducted not so much to uncover evidence, but as part of the arrest process. Searches which are conducted incidental to arrest, they argued, are necessary for the officers' protection and should not require a search warrant. Coins taken from the burglarized coin shop were found at various places in Chimel's residence, including the garage, and provided the evidence used against him at trial.

Chimel's appeal eventually reached the U.S. Supreme Court, which ruled that the search of Chimel's residence, although incidental to arrest, became invalid when it went beyond the

Table 7-2 Implications of Chimel v. California

What Arresting Officers May Search
- The defendant
- The physical area within easy reach of the defendant

Valid Reasons for Conducting a Search
- To protect the arresting officers
- To prevent evidence from being destroyed
- To keep the defendant from escaping

When a Search Becomes Illegal
- When it goes beyond the defendant and the area within the defendant's immediate control
- When it is conducted for other than a valid reason

person arrested and the area subject to that person's "immediate control." The thrust of the Court's decision was that searches during arrest can be made to protect arresting officers, but that, without a search warrant, their scope must be strongly circumscribed. Legal implications of *Chimel v. California* are summarized in Table 7–2.

The decision in the case of Ted Chimel was predicated upon earlier reasoning by the Court in the case of *U.S.* v. *Rabinowitz* (1950).[21] Rabinowitz, a stamp collector, had been arrested and charged by federal agents with selling altered postage stamps in order to defraud other collectors. Employing a valid arrest warrant, officers arrested Rabinowitz at his place of employment and then proceeded to search his desk, file cabinets, and safe. They did not have a search warrant, but his office was small—only one room—and the officers conducted the search with a specific object in mind, the illegal stamps. Eventually, 573 altered postage stamps were seized in the search, and Rabinowitz was convicted in federal court of charges related to selling altered stamps.

Rabinowitz's appeal to the U.S. Supreme Court, based upon the claim that the warrantless search of his business was illegal, was denied. The Court ruled that the Fourth Amendment provides protection against *unreasonable* searches, but that the search, in this case, followed legally from the arrest of the suspect. In the language used by the Court, "It is not disputed that there may be reasonable searches, incident to arrest, without a search warrant. Upon acceptance of this established rule that some authority to search follows from lawfully taking the person into custody, it becomes apparent that such searches turn upon the reasonableness under all the circumstances and not upon the practicability of procuring a search warrant, for the warrant is not required."

Since the early days of the exclusionary rule, other court decisions have highlighted the fact that "the Fourth Amendment protects people, not places."[22] In other words, although the commonly heard claim that "a person's home is his or her castle" has a great deal of validity within the context of constitutional law, persons can have a reasonable expectation to privacy in "homes" of many descriptions. Apartments, duplex dwellings, motel rooms—even the cardboard boxes or makeshift tents of the homeless—can all become protected places under the Fourth Amendment. In *Minnesota v. Olson*[23] (1990), for example, the U.S. Supreme Court extended the protection against warrantless searches to overnight guests residing in the home of another. The capacity to claim the protection of the Fourth Amendment, said the Court, depends upon whether the *person* who makes that claim has a legitimate expectation of privacy in the place searched.

THE BURGER (1969–1986) AND REHNQUIST (1986–PRESENT) COURTS

The swing toward conservatism which our country experienced during the 1980s and early 1990s gave rise to "yuppies," the X-generation, designer clothes, and a renewed concern with protecting the financial and other interests of those who live within the law. The

Reagan–Bush years, and the popularity of two presidents in whom many saw the embodiment of "old-fashioned" values, reflected the tenor of a nation seeking a return to simpler times.

Throughout the late 1980s, the U.S. Supreme Court mirrored the nation's conservative tenor by distancing itself from certain earlier decisions of the Warren court. The underlying theme of the new Court, the Burger court (which held sway from 1969 until 1986), was its adherence to the principle that criminal defendants, in claiming violations of their due process rights, need to bear the bulk of responsibility in showing that police went beyond the law in the performance of their duties. That trend continues into the present day under the Rehnquist court (1986–present), led by Chief Justice William H. Rehnquist.

Good Faith Exceptions to the Exclusionary Rule

The Burger court, led by Chief Justice Warren E. Burger, began what some have called a "chipping away" at the strict application of the exclusionary rule originally set forth in the *Weeks* and *Silverthorne* cases. In the case of *Illinois* v. *Gates* (1983),[24] the Court was asked to modify the exclusionary rule to permit the use of evidence in court which had been seized in "reasonable good faith" by officers, even though the search was later ruled illegal. The Court, however, chose not to address the issue at that time.

But only a year later, in the 1984 case of *U.S.* v. *Leon*[25] the Court recognized what has now come to be called the "**good faith exception to the exclusionary rule.**" The *Leon* case involved the Burbank, California, Police Department and its investigation of a drug trafficking suspect. The suspect, Leon, was placed under surveillance following a tip from a confidential informant. Investigators applied for a search warrant based upon information gleaned through the surveillance. They believed that they were in compliance with the Fourth Amendment requirement that "no warrants shall issue but upon probable cause." **Probable cause**, a tricky but important concept, can be defined as "a legal criterion residing in a set of facts and circumstances which would cause a reasonable person to believe that a particular other person has committed a specific crime." Probable cause must be satisfactorily demonstrated by police officers in a written affidavit to a magistrate before a search warrant can be issued. Magistrates[26] are low-level judges and, under our system of checks and balances, act to ensure that the police have established the probable cause needed for warrants to be obtained.

In *U.S.* v. *Leon*, the affidavit submitted by police to a magistrate requesting a search warrant was reviewed by numerous deputy district attorneys, and the magistrate decided to issue the warrant. A search of Leon's three residences yielded a large amount of drugs and other evidence. Although Leon was convicted of drug trafficking, a later ruling in a federal district court resulted in the suppression of evidence against him on the basis that the original affidavit prepared by the police had not, in the opinion of the court, been sufficient to establish probable cause.

The government petitioned the U.S. Supreme Court to consider whether evidence gathered by officers acting in good faith as to the validity of a warrant, should fairly be excluded at trial. The impending modification of the exclusionary rule was intoned in the first sentence of that Court's written decision: "This case presents the question whether the Fourth Amendment exclusionary rule should be modified so as not to bar the use in the prosecution's case-in-chief of evidence obtained by officers acting in reasonable reliance on a search warrant issued by a detached and neutral magistrate but ultimately found to be unsupported by probable cause." The Court continued: "When law enforcement officers have acted in objective good faith or their transgressions have been minor, the magnitude of the benefit conferred on such guilty defendants offends basic concepts of the criminal justice system." Reflecting the renewed conservatism of the Burger court, the justices found for the government and reinstated the conviction of Leon.

In that same year the Supreme Court case of *Massachusetts* v. *Sheppard*[27] (1984) further reinforced the concept of "good faith." In the *Sheppard* case, officers executed a search warrant which failed to describe accurately the property to be seized. Although they were aware of the error, they had been assured by a magistrate that the warrant was valid. After the seizure was complete and a conviction had been obtained, the Massachusetts Supreme Judicial Court reversed the finding of the trial court. Upon appeal the U.S. Supreme Court reiterated the good-faith exception and let the original conviction stand.

Good Faith A possible legal basis for an exception to the exclusionary rule. Law enforcement officers who conduct a search, or seize evidence, on the basis of good faith (that is, where they believe they are operating according to the dictates of the law) and who later discover that a mistake was made (perhaps in the format of the application for a search warrant) may still use, in court, evidence seized as the result of such activities.

Probable Cause (also discussed in Chapter 1) Refers to that necessary level of belief which would allow for police seizures (arrests) of individuals and searches of dwellings, vehicles, and possessions. Probable cause can generally be found in a set of facts and circumstances which would cause a reasonable person to believe that a particular individual has committed a specific crime. Upon a demonstration of probable cause, magistrates will issue warrants authorizing law enforcement officers to effect arrests and conduct searches.

While the cases of *Leon* and *Sheppard* represented a clear reversal of Warren court philosophy, the trend continued with the 1987 case of *Illinois* v. *Krull*.[28] In *Krull*, the Court, now under the leadership of Chief Justice William H. Rehnquist, held that the good-faith exception applied to a warrantless search supported by state law even where the state statute was later found to violate the Fourth Amendment. Similarly, another 1987 Supreme Court case, *Maryland* v. *Garrison*,[29] supported the use of evidence obtained with a search warrant which was inaccurate in its specifics. In *Garrison*, officers had procured a warrant to search an apartment believing it was the only dwelling on a building's third floor. After searching the entire floor, they discovered that it housed more than one apartment. Even so, evidence acquired in the search was held to be admissible based upon the reasonable mistake of the officers.

The 1990 case of *Illinois* v. *Rodriguez*[30] further diminished the scope of the exclusionary rule. In *Rodriguez*, a badly beaten woman named Gail Fischer complained to police that she had been assaulted in a Chicago apartment. Fischer led police to the apartment—which she indicated she shared with the defendant—produced a key, and opened the door to the dwelling. Inside, investigators found the defendant, Edward Rodriguez, asleep on a bed, with drug paraphernalia and cocaine spread around him. Rodriguez was arrested and charged with assault and possession of a controlled substance.

Upon appeal, Rodriguez demonstrated that Fischer had not lived with him for at least a month—and argued that she could no longer be said to have legal control over the apartment. Hence, the defense claimed, Fischer had no authority to provide investigators with access to the dwelling. According to arguments made by the defense, the evidence, which had been obtained without a warrant, had not been properly seized. The Supreme Court disagreed, ruling that "even if Fischer did not possess common authority over the premises, there was no Fourth Amendment violation if the police *reasonably believed* at the time of their entry that Fischer possessed the authority to consent."

Legal scholars have suggested that the exclusionary rule may undergo even further modification in the near future. One analyst of the contemporary scene points to the fact that "the [Rehnquist] Court's majority is [now] clearly committed to the idea that the exclusionary rule is not directly part of the Fourth Amendment (and Fourteenth Amendment due process), but instead is an evidentiary device instituted by the Court to effectuate it."[31] In other words, if the Court should be persuaded that the rule is no longer effective, or that some other strategy could better achieve the aim of protecting individual rights, the rule could be abandoned entirely. A general listing of established exceptions to the exclusionary rule is provided in Table 7–3, including three which we will now discuss.

The Plain-View Doctrine

Plain View   A legal term describing the ready visibility of objects which might be seized as evidence during a search by police in the absence of a search warrant specifying the seizure of those objects. In order for evidence in plain view to be lawfully seized, officers must have a legal right to be in the viewing area and must have cause to believe that the evidence is somehow associated with criminal activity.

Police officers have the opportunity to begin investigations or confiscate evidence, without the need for a warrant, based upon what they find in plain view and open to public inspection. The plain view doctrine was first stated in the Supreme Court case of *Harris* v. *U.S.*[32] (1968) in which a police officer inventorying an impounded vehicle discovered evidence of a robbery. In the *Harris* case, the Court ruled that "objects falling in the plain view of an officer who has a right to be in the position to have that view are subject to seizure and may be introduced in evidence."[33]

Common situations in which the plain-view doctrine is applicable include emergencies such as crimes in progress, fires, and accidents. A police officer responding to a call for assistance, for example, might enter a residence intending to provide aid to an injured person and find drugs or other contraband in plain view. If so, he or she would be within his or her legitimate authority to confiscate the materials and effect an arrest if the owner of the substance could be identified.

The plain-view doctrine applies only to sightings by the police under legal circumstances—that is, in places where the police have a legitimate right to be and, typically, only if the sighting was coincidental. Similarly, the incriminating nature of the evidence seized must have been "immediately apparent" to the officers making the seizure.[34] If officers conspired to avoid the necessity for a search warrant by helping to create a plain-view situation through surveillance, duplicity, or other means, the doctrine likely would not apply.

Table 7-3 Established Exceptions to the Exclusionary Rule

Police Powers	Supported by
Stop and frisk	*Terry* v. *Ohio* (1968)
Warrantless searches incident to a lawful arrest	*U.S.* v. *Rabinowitz* (1950)
Seizure of evidence in "good faith," even in the face of some exclusionary rule violations	*U.S.* v. *Leon* (1984) *Illinois* v. *Krull* (1987)
Warrantless vehicle searches where probable cause exists to believe that the vehicle contains contraband and/or the occupants have been lawfully arrested	*Carroll* v. *U.S.* (1925) *New York* v. *Belton* (1981) *U.S.* v. *Ross* (1982) *California* v. *Carney* (1985) *California* v. *Acevedo* (1991) *Ornelas* v. *U.S.* (1996)
Gathering of incriminating evidence during interrogation in noncustodial circumstances	*Beckwith* v. *United States* (1976)
Authority to search incidental to arrest and/or to conduct a protective sweep in conjunction with an in-home arrest	*Chimel* v. *California* (1969) *U.S.* v. *Edwards* (1974) *Maryland* v. *Buie* (1990)
Authority to enter and/or search an "open field" without a warrant	*Hester* v. *U.S.* (1924) *Oliver* v. *U.S.* (1984) *U.S.* v. *Dunn* (1987)
Permissibility of warrantless naked-eye aerial observation of open areas and/or greenhouses	*California* v. *Ciraolo* (1986) *Florida* v. *Riley* (1989)
Warrantless seizure of abandoned materials and refuse	*California* v. *Greenwood* (1988)
Prompt action in the face of threats to public or personal safety	*Warden* v. *Hayden* (1967) *New York* v. *Quarles* (1984) *Borchardt* v. *U.S.* (1987)
Evidence in "plain view" may be seized	*Harris* v. *New York* (1968) *Coolidge* v. *New Hampshire* (1971) *Horton* v. *California* (1990)
Use of police informants in jail cells	*Kuhlman* v. *Wilson* (1986) *Illinois* v. *Perkins* (1990) *Arizona* v. *Fulminante* (1991)
Lawfulness of arrests based upon computer errors made by clerks	*Arizona* v. *Evans* (1995)

The plain-view doctrine, however, has been restricted by more recent federal court decisions. In the 1982 case of *U.S.* v. *Irizarry*[35] the First Circuit Court of Appeals held that officers could not move objects to gain a view of evidence otherwise hidden from view. Agents had arrested a number of men in a motel room in Isla Verde, Puerto Rico. A valid arrest warrant formed the legal basis for the arrest, and some quantities of plainly visible drugs were seized from the room. An agent, looking through a window into the room prior to the arrest, had seen one of the defendants with a gun. After the arrest was complete, and no gun had been found on the suspects, another officer noticed a bathroom ceiling panel out of place. The logical conclusion was that a weapon had been secreted there. Upon inspection, a substantial quantity of cocaine and various firearms were found hidden in the ceiling. The Court, however, refused to allow these weapons and drugs to be used as evidence because, it said, "the items of evidence found above the ceiling panel were not plainly visible to the agents standing in the room."[36]

In the Supreme Court case of *Arizona* v. *Hicks* (1987),[37] the requirement that evidence be in plain view, without the need for officers to move or dislodge evidence, was reiterated. In

[The police] are not perfect; we don't sign them up on some far-off planet and bring them into police service. They are products of society, and let me tell you, the human product today often is pretty weak.

—Former LAPD Chief Daryl Gates

Although the concept of plain view is difficult to define, Latasha Smith (shown here sitting on a curb) provides a personal example of the concept. After Dallas narcotics officers searched the house behind her for crack cocaine, they turned their attention to Latasha, who was arrested for failing to appear in court for a previous misdemeanor violation. *Pat Sullivan, AP/Wide World Photos*

the *Hicks* case, officers responded to a shooting in an apartment. A bullet had been fired in a second-floor apartment and had gone through the floor, injuring a man in the apartment below. The quarters of James Hicks were found to be in considerable disarray when entered by investigating officers. As officers looked for the person who might have fired the weapon, they discovered and confiscated a number of guns and a stocking mask, such as might be used in robberies. In one corner, however, officers noticed two expensive stereo sets. One of the officers, suspecting that the sets were stolen, went over to the equipment and was able to read the serial numbers of one of the components from where it rested. Some of the serial numbers, however, were not clearly visible, and the investigating officer moved some of the components in order to read the numbers. When he called the numbers into headquarters he was told that the equipment indeed had been stolen. The stereo components were seized, and James Hicks was arrested. Hicks was eventually convicted on a charge of armed robbery, based upon the evidence seized.

Upon appeal, the *Hicks* case reached the U.S. Supreme Court, which ruled that the officer's behavior had become illegal when he moved the stereo equipment to record serial numbers. The Court held that persons have a "reasonable expectation to privacy,"[38] which means that officers lacking a search warrant, even when invited into a residence, must act more like guests than inquisitors.

Most evidence seized under the plain-view doctrine is discovered "inadvertently"—that is, by accident.[39] However, in 1990, the U.S. Supreme Court, in the case of *Horton* v. *California*,[40] ruled that "even though inadvertence *is* a characteristic of most legitimate 'plain view' seizures, it *is not* a necessary condition."[41] In the *Horton* case, a warrant was issued authorizing the search of a defendant's home for stolen jewelry. The affidavit, completed by the officer who requested the warrant, alluded to an Uzi submachine gun and a stun gun—weapons purportedly used in the jewel robbery. It did not request that those weapons be listed on the search warrant. Officers searched the defendant's home, but did not find the stolen jewelry. They did, however, seize a number of weapons—among them the Uzi, two stun guns, and a .38-caliber revolver. Horton was convicted of robbery in a trial where the

In terms that apply equally to seizures of property and to seizures of persons, the Fourth Amendment has drawn a firm line at the entrance to the house. Absent exigent circumstances, that threshold may not reasonably be crossed without a warrant.

—*Payton v. New York,* 445 U.S. 573, 590 (1980).

seized weapons were introduced into evidence. He appealed his conviction, claiming that officers had reason to believe that the weapons were in his home at the time of the search and were therefore not seized inadvertently. His appeal was rejected by the Court. As a result of the *Horton* case, "inadvertence" is no longer considered a condition necessary to ensure the legitimacy of a seizure which results when evidence other than that listed in a search warrant is discovered.

Emergency Searches of Property

Certain emergencies may justify a police officer in searching a premise, even without a warrant. Recent decisions by U.S. Appeals Courts have resulted in such activities being termed exigent circumstances searches. According to the Legal Counsel Division of the FBI, there are three threats which "provide justification for emergency warrantless action."[42] They are clear dangers (1) to life, (2) of escape, and (3) of the removal or destruction of evidence. Any one of these situations may create an exception to the Fourth Amendment's requirement of a search warrant. Where emergencies necessitate a quick search of premises, however, law enforcement officers are responsible for demonstrating that a dire situation existed which justified their actions. Failure to do so successfully in court will, of course, taint any seized evidence and make it unusable.

The need for emergency searches was first recognized by the U.S. Supreme Court in 1967 in the case of *Warden* v. *Hayden*.[43] There, the Court approved the search of a residence conducted without a warrant which followed reports that an armed robber had fled into the building. In *Mincey* v. *Arizona* (1978),[44] the Supreme Court held that "the Fourth Amendment does not require police officers to delay in the course of an investigation if to do so would gravely endanger their lives or the lives of others."[45]

A 1990 decision, rendered in the case of *Maryland* v. *Buie*,[46] extended the authority of police to search locations in a house where a potentially dangerous person could hide, while an arrest warrant is being served. The *Buie* decision was meant primarily to protect investigators from potential danger and can apply even when officers lack a warrant, probable cause, or even **reasonable suspicion**.

In 1995, in the case of *Wilson* v. *Arkansas*,[47] the U.S. Supreme Court ruled that police officers generally must knock and announce their identity before entering a dwelling or other premises—even when armed with a search warrant. Under certain emergency circumstances, however, exceptions may be made, and officers may not need to knock or identify themselves prior to entering.[48] In *Wilson*, the Court added that Fourth Amendment requirements that searches be reasonable "should not be read to mandate a rigid rule of announcement that ignores countervailing law enforcement interests." Hence, officers need not announce themselves, the Court said, when suspects may be in the process of destroying evidence, officers are pursuing a recently escaped arrestee, or where officers' lives may be endangered by such an announcement. Because the *Wilson* case involved an appeal from a drug dealer, who was in fact apprehended by police officers who entered her unlocked house while she was flushing marijuana down a toilet, some say that it establishes a "drug law exception" to the knock and announce requirement.

In 1997, however, in *Richards* v. *Wisconsin*,[49] the Supreme Court clarified its position on "no knock" exceptions, saying that individual courts have the duty in each case to "determine whether the facts and circumstances of the particular entry justified dispensing with the requirement." The Court went on to say that "[a] 'no knock' entry is justified when the police have a reasonable suspicion that knocking and announcing their presence, under the particular circumstances, would be dangerous or futile, or that it would inhibit the effective investigation of the crime. This standard strikes the appropriate balance" said the Court, "between the legitimate law enforcement concerns at issue in the execution of search warrants and the individual privacy interests affected by no knock entries."[50]

Arrest

Officers seize not only property, but persons as well—a process we refer to as "arrest." Most people think of arrest in terms of what they see on popular TV crime shows. The suspect is chased, subdued, and "cuffed" after committing some loathsome act in view of the camera.

Emergency Searches
Those searches conducted by the police without a warrant, which are justified on the basis of some immediate and overriding need—such as public safety, the likely escape of a dangerous suspect, or the removal or destruction of evidence.

Reasonable Suspicion
(1) That level of suspicion which would justify an officer in making further inquiry or in conducting further investigation. Reasonable suspicion may permit stopping a person for the purpose of questioning, or a simple "patdown" search. (2) A belief, based upon a consideration of the facts at hand and upon reasonable inferences drawn from those facts, which would induce an ordinarily prudent and cautious person under the same circumstances to generally conclude that criminal activity is taking place or that criminal activity has recently occurred. Reasonable suspicion is a *general* and reasonable belief that a crime is in progress or has occurred, whereas probable cause is a reasonable belief that a *particular* person has committed a *specific* crime.

Twenty-First Century Criminal Justice

The Computer Errors Exception to the Exclusionary Rule

Over the past few decades, criminal justice agencies have become increasingly dependent upon computer technology for records management and other purposes. As we enter the twenty-first century, the use of such technology will continue to grow, further impacting the daily activities of criminal-justice agencies and bringing with it the increased likelihood of computer-generated or computer-based mistakes.

In 1995, in the case of *Arizona v. Evans*,[1] the U.S. Supreme Court created a "computer errors exception" to the exclusionary rule, by holding that a traffic stop which led to the seizure of marijuana was legal even though officers conducted the stop based upon an arrest warrant improperly stored in their computer. The case began in 1991 when Isaac Evans was stopped in Phoenix, Arizona, for driving the wrong way on a one-way street in front of a police station. A routine computer check reported an outstanding arrest warrant for Evans, and he was taken into custody. Police found marijuana in the car Evans had been driving, and he was eventually convicted on charges of possessing a controlled substance. After his arrest, however, police learned that the arrest warrant reported to them by their computer had actually been quashed a few weeks earlier but, through the clerical oversight of a court employee, had never been removed from the computer.

In upholding Evans's conviction, the high court reasoned that officers could not be held responsible for a clerical error made by a court worker and concluded that the arresting officers were acting in good faith based upon the information available to them at the time of the arrest. In addition, the majority opinion said that "the rule excluding evidence obtained without a warrant was intended to deter police misconduct, not mistakes by court employees."

In what may have been a warning to police administrators not to depend upon the excuse of computer error, however, Justice Sandra Day O'Connor, in a concurring opinion, wrote: "The police, of course, are entitled to enjoy the substantial advantages [computer] technology confers....They may not, however, rely on it blindly. With the benefits of more efficient law enforcement mechanisms comes the burden of corresponding constitutional responsibilities."

[1]*Arizona v. Isaac Evans*, 115 S.Ct. 1185, 131 L. Ed. 2d 34 (1995).

Arrest Taking an adult or juvenile into physical custody by authority of law for the purpose of charging the person with a criminal offense or a delinquent act or status offense, terminating with the recording of a specific offense. Technically, an arrest occurs whenever a person's freedom to leave is curtailed by a law enforcement officer.

Some arrests do occur that way. In reality, however, most instances of arrest are far more mundane.

In technical terms, an **arrest** occurs whenever a law enforcement officer restricts a person's freedom to leave. There may be no yelling "*You're under arrest!*" no *Miranda* warnings may be offered, and, in fact, the suspect may not even consider himself or herself to be in custody. Such arrests, and the decision to enforce them, evolve as the situation between the officer and suspect develops. They usually begin with polite conversation and a request by the officer for information. Only when the suspect tries to leave, and tests the limits of the police response, may he or she discover that he or she is really in custody. In the 1980 case of *U.S. v. Mendenhall*,[51] Justice Stewart set forth the "free to leave" test for determining whether a person has been arrested. Stewart wrote: "A person has been 'seized' within the meaning of the Fourth Amendment only if in view of all the circumstances surrounding the incident, a reasonable person would have believed that he was not free to leave." The 'free to leave' test "has been repeatedly adopted by the Court as the test for a seizure."[52] In 1994, in the case of *Stansbury v. California*,[53] the Court once again used such a test in determining the point at which an arrest had been made In *Stansbury*, where the focus was on the interrogation of a suspected child molester and murderer, the Court ruled, "In determining whether an individual was in custody, a court must examine all of the circumstances surrounding the interrogation, but the ultimate inquiry is simply whether there [was] a formal arrest or restraint on freedom of movement of the degree associated with a formal arrest."

Arrests which follow the questioning of a suspect are probably the most common type. When the decision to arrest is reached, the officer has come to the conclusion that a crime has been committed and that the suspect is probably the one who committed it. The pres-

The courts have generally held that, in order to protect themselves and the public, officers have the authority to search persons being arrested. Here, arresting officers pat down a drug suspect. *Craig Filipacchi, Gamma Liaison*

ence of these mental elements constitutes the probable cause needed for an arrest. Probable cause is the basic minimum necessary for an arrest under any circumstances.

Arrests may also occur when the officer comes upon a crime in progress. Such situations often require apprehension of the offender to ensure the safety of the public. Most arrests made during crimes in progress, however, are for misdemeanors rather than felonies. In fact, many states do not allow arrest for a misdemeanor unless it is committed in the presence of an officer. In any event, crimes in progress clearly provide the probable cause necessary for an arrest.

Most jurisdictions allow arrest for a felony without a warrant when a crime is not in progress, as long as probable cause can be established.[54] Some, however, require a warrant. In the case of *Payton* v. *New York* (1980), the U.S. Supreme Court ruled that, unless the suspect gives consent or an emergency exists, an arrest warrant is necessary if an arrest requires entry into a suspect's private residence.[55] Arrest warrants are issued by magistrates when police officers can demonstrate probable cause. Magistrates will usually require that the officers seeking an arrest warrant submit a written affidavit outlining their reason for the arrest.

Searches Incident to Arrest

The U.S. Supreme Court has established a clear rule that police officers have the right to conduct a search of a person being arrested and to search the area under the immediate control of that person in order to protect themselves from attack. This is true even if the officer and the arrestee are of different sexes.

This "rule of the game" was created in the *Rabinowitz* and *Chimel* cases cited earlier. It became firmly established in other cases involving personal searches, such as the 1973 case of *Robinson* v. *U.S.*[56] Robinson was stopped for a traffic violation when it was learned that his driver's license was expired. He was arrested for operating a vehicle without a valid license. Officers subsequently searched the defendant to be sure he wasn't carrying a weapon and discovered a substance which later proved to be heroin. He was convicted of drug possession, but appealed. When Robinson's appeal reached the U.S. Supreme Court, the Court upheld the officer's right to conduct a search without a warrant for purposes of personal protection and to use the fruits of such a search when it turns up other contraband. In the words of the Court, "A custodial arrest of a suspect based upon probable cause is a reason-

Searches Incident to an Arrest Those warrantless searches of arrested individuals which are conducted to ensure the safety of the arresting officer(s). Because individuals placed under arrest may be in the possession of weapons, courts have recognized the need for arresting officers to protect themselves by conducting an immediate and warrantless search of arrested individuals without the need for a warrant.

able intrusion under the Fourth Amendment; that intrusion being lawful, a search incident to the arrest requires no additional jurisdiction."[57]

The Court's decision in *Robinson* reinforced an earlier ruling involving a seasoned officer who conducted a "pat down" search of two men whom he suspected were "casing" a store, about to commit a robbery.[58] The officer in the case was a 39-year veteran of police work who testified that the men "did not look right." When he approached them, he suspected they might be armed. Fearing for his life, he quickly spun the men around, put them up against a wall, patted down their clothing, and found a gun on one of the men. The man, Terry, was later convicted in Ohio courts of carrying a concealed weapon.

Terry's appeal was based upon the argument that the suspicious officer had no probable cause to arrest him and therefore no cause to search him. The search, he argued, was illegal, and the evidence obtained should not have been used against him. The Supreme Court disagreed, saying: "In view of these facts, we cannot blind ourselves to the need for law enforcement officers to protect themselves and other prospective victims of violence in situations where they may lack probable cause for an arrest."[59]

The *Terry* case set the standard for brief stops and frisks based upon reasonable suspicion. Police also refer to such brief encounters as "Terry-type" stops. Reasonable suspicion can be defined as a belief, based upon a consideration of the facts at hand and upon reasonable inferences drawn from those facts, which would induce an ordinarily prudent and cautious person under the same circumstances to generally conclude that criminal activity is taking place or that criminal activity has recently occurred. It is also the level of suspicion needed to justify an officer in making further inquiry or in conducting further investigation. Reasonable suspicion, which is a *general* and reasonable belief that a crime is in progress or has occurred, should be differentiated from probable cause. Probable cause, as noted in an earlier chapter, is a reasonable belief that a *particular* person has committed a *specific* crime. It is important to note that the *Terry* case, for all the authority it conferred on officers, also made it clear that officers must have reasonable grounds for any stop or frisk that they conduct.

In 1989, the Supreme Court, in the case of *U.S.* v. *Sokolow*,[60] clarified the basis upon which law enforcement officers, lacking probable cause to believe that a crime has occurred, may stop and briefly detain a person for investigative purposes. In *Sokolow*, the Court ruled that the legitimacy of such a stop must be evaluated according to a "totality of circumstances" criteria—in which all aspects of the defendant's behavior, taken in concert, may provide the basis for a legitimate stop based upon reasonable suspicion. In this case, the defendant, Sokolow, appeared suspicious to police because, while traveling under an alias from Honolulu, he had paid $2,100 in $20 bills (from a large roll of money) for two airplane tickets after spending a surprisingly small amount of time in Miami. In addition, the defendant was obviously nervous and checked no luggage. A warrantless airport investigation by DEA agents uncovered more than 1,000 grams of cocaine in the defendant's belongings. The Court, in upholding Sokolow's conviction, ruled that, although no single activity was proof of illegal activity, taken together they created circumstances under which suspicion of illegal activity was justified.

In 1993, however, in the case of *Minnesota* v. *Dickerson*,[61] the U.S. Supreme Court placed new limits on an officer's ability to seize evidence discovered during a pat down search conducted for protective reasons when the search itself was based merely upon suspicion and failed to immediately reveal the presence of a weapon. In this case, Timothy Dickerson, who was observed leaving a building known for cocaine trafficking, was stopped by Minneapolis police officers after they noticed him acting suspiciously. The officers decided to investigate further and ordered Dickerson to submit to a pat down search. The search revealed no weapons, but the officer conducting it testified that he felt a small lump in Dickerson's jacket pocket, believed it to be a lump of crack cocaine upon examining it with his fingers, and then reached into Dickerson's pocket and retrieved a small bag of cocaine. Dickerson was arrested, tried, and convicted of possession of a controlled substance. His appeal, which claimed that the pat down search had been illegal, eventually made its way to the U.S. Supreme Court. The high court ruled that "if an officer lawfully pats down a suspect's outer clothing and feels an object whose contour or mass makes its identity immediately apparent, there has been no invasion of the suspect's privacy beyond that already authorized by the

While every person is entitled to stand silent, it is more virtuous for the wrongdoer to admit his offense and accept the punishment he deserves...it is wrong, and subtly corrosive of our criminal justice system, to regard an honest confession as a mistake.

—Justice Antonin Scalia, dissenting in *Minnick* v. *Mississippi*

Plain View Requirements

Following the opinion of the U.S. Supreme Court in the case of *Horton* v. *California* (1990), items seized under the plain-view doctrine may be admissible as evidence in a court of law if the officer who seized the evidence

1. was lawfully in the viewing area, and
2. had probable cause to believe the evidence was somehow associated with criminal activity.

officer's search for weapons." However, in *Dickerson*, the Justices ruled, "the officer never thought that the lump was a weapon, but did not immediately recognize it as cocaine." The lump was determined to be cocaine only after the officer "squeezed, slid, and otherwise manipulated the pocket's contents." Hence, the Court held, the officer's actions in this case did not qualify under what might be called a "plain feel" exception. In any case, said the Court, the search in *Dickerson* went far beyond what is permissible under *Terry*—where officer safety was the crucial issue. The Court summed up its ruling in *Dickerson* this way: "While *Terry* entitled [the officer] to place his hands on respondent's jacket and to feel the lump in the pocket, his continued exploration of the pocket after he concluded that it contained no weapon was unrelated to the sole justification for the search under Terry" and was therefore illegal.

Just as arrest must be based upon probable cause, officers may not stop and question an unwilling citizen whom they have no reason to suspect of a crime. In the case of *Brown* v. *Texas*[62] (1979), two Texas law enforcement officers stopped the defendant and asked for identification. Brown, they later testified, had not been acting suspiciously nor did they think he might have a weapon. The stop was made simply because officers wanted to know who he was. Brown was arrested under a Texas statute which required a person to identify himself properly and accurately when requested to do so by peace officers. Eventually, his appeal reached the U.S. Supreme Court which ruled that, under circumstances found in the *Brown* case, a person "may not be punished for refusing to identify himself."

In *Smith* v. *Ohio* (1990),[63] the Court held that an individual has the right to protect his or her belongings from unwarranted police inspection. In *Smith*, the defendant was approached by two officers in plain clothes who observed that he was carrying a brown paper bag. The officers asked him to "come here a minute" and, when he kept walking, identified themselves as police officers. The defendant threw the bag onto the hood of his car and attempted to protect it from the officers' intrusion. Marijuana was found inside the bag, and the defendant was arrested. Since there was little reason to stop the suspect in this case, and because control over the bag was not thought necessary for the officer's protection, the Court found that the Fourth Amendment protects both "the traveler who carries a toothbrush and a few articles of clothing in a paper bag" and "the sophisticated executive with the locked attaché case."[64]

The following year, however, in what some Court observers saw as a turnabout, the U.S. Supreme Court ruled in *California* v. *Hodari D.* (1991)[65] that suspects who flee from the police and throw away evidence as they retreat may later be arrested based upon the incriminating nature of the abandoned evidence. The case, which began in Oakland, California, centered on the behavior of a group of juveniles who had been standing around a parked car. Two city police officers, driving an unmarked car but with the word "Police" emblazoned in large letters on their jackets, approached the youths. As they came close, the juveniles apparently panicked and fled. One of them tossed away a "rock" of crack cocaine, which was retrieved by the officers. The juvenile was later arrested and convicted of the possession of a controlled substance, but the California Court of Appeals reversed his conviction, reasoning

Our police officers are high-school graduates; they are not lawyers; they are not judges.
—U.S. Representative Chuck Douglas (R.–N.H.)

that the officers did not have sufficient reasonable suspicion to make a "Terry-type stop." The Supreme Court, in reversing the finding of the California court, found that reasonable suspicion was not needed, since no "stop" was made. The suspects had not been "seized" by the police, the Court ruled. Therefore, the evidence taken was not the result of an illegal seizure within the meaning of the Fourth Amendment. The significance of *Hodari* for future police action was highlighted by California prosecutors who pointed out that cases like *Hodari* occur "almost everyday in this nation's urban areas."[66]

In a sharply worded dissenting opinion, Justices John Paul Stevens and Thurgood Marshall wrote: "It is too early to know the consequences of the court's holding. If carried to its logical conclusion, it will encourage unlawful displays of force that will frighten countless innocent citizens into surrendering whatever privacy rights they may still have."[67]

Emergency Searches of Persons

It is possible to imagine emergency situations in which officers may have to search people based upon quick decisions: a person who matches the description of an armed robber, a woman who is found lying unconscious, a man who has what appears to be blood on his shoes. Such searches can save lives by disarming fleeing felons or by uncovering a medical reason for an emergency situation. They may also prevent criminals from escaping or destroying evidence.

Emergency searches of persons, like those of premises, fall under the exigent circumstances exception to the warrant requirement of the Fourth Amendment. The Supreme Court, in the 1979 case of *Arkansas* v. *Sanders*,[68] recognized the need for such searches "where the societal costs of obtaining a warrant, such as danger to law officers or the risk of loss or destruction of evidence, outweigh the reasons for prior recourse to a neutral magistrate."[69]

The 1987 case of *Borchardt* v. *U.S.*,[70] decided by the Fifth Circuit Court of Appeals, held that Borchardt could be prosecuted for heroin uncovered during medical treatment, even though the defendant had objected to the treatment. Borchardt was a federal inmate at the time he was discovered unconscious in his cell. He was taken to a hospital where tests revealed heroin in his blood. His heart stopped, and he was revived using CPR. Borchardt was given three doses of Narcan, a drug used to counteract the effects of heroin, and he improved, regaining consciousness. The patient refused requests to pump his stomach, but began to become lethargic, indicating the need for additional Narcan. Eventually, he vomited nine plastic bags full of heroin, along with two bags which had burst. The heroin was turned over to federal officers, and Borchardt was eventually convicted of heroin possession. Attempts to exclude the heroin from evidence were unsuccessful, and the appeals court ruled that the necessity of the emergency situation overruled the defendant's objections to search his person.

The Legal Counsel Division of the FBI provides the following guidelines in conducting emergency warrantless searches of individuals, where the possible destruction of evidence is at issue (keep in mind that there may be no probable cause to *arrest* the individual being searched). All four conditions must apply:[71]

1. There was probable cause to believe at the time of the search that there was evidence concealed on the person searched.
2. There was probable cause to believe an emergency threat of destruction of evidence existed at the time of the search.
3. The officer had no prior opportunity to obtain a warrant authorizing the search.
4. The action was no greater than necessary to eliminate the threat of destruction of evidence.

Vehicle Searches

Vehicles present a special law enforcement problem. They are highly movable, and, when an arrest of a driver or an occupant occurs, the need to search them may be immediate.

The first significant Supreme Court case involving an automobile was that of *Carroll* v. *U.S.*,[72] in 1925. In the *Carroll* case a divided Court ruled that a warrantless search of an auto-

Warrantless vehicle searches such as this one, where the driver is suspected of a crime, have generally been justified by the fact that vehicles are highly mobile and can quickly leave police jurisdiction. *Craig Filipacchi, Gamma-Liaison*

mobile or other vehicle is valid if it is based upon a reasonable belief that contraband is present. In 1964, however, in the case of *Preston* v. *U.S.*[73] the limits of warrantless vehicle searches were defined. Preston was arrested for vagrancy and taken to jail. His vehicle was impounded, towed to the police garage, and later searched. Two revolvers were uncovered in the glove compartment, and more incriminating evidence was found in the trunk. Preston was convicted on weapons possession and other charges and eventually appealed to the U.S. Supreme Court. The Court held that the warrantless search of Preston's vehicle had occurred while the automobile was in secure custody and had been, therefore, illegal. Time and circumstances would have permitted, the Court reasoned, acquisition of a warrant to conduct the search.

When the search of a vehicle occurs after it has been impounded, however, that search may be legitimate if it is undertaken for routine and reasonable purposes. In the case of *South Dakota* v. *Opperman* (1976),[74] for example, the Court held that a warrantless search undertaken for purposes of the inventorying and safekeeping of personal possessions of the car's owner was not illegal, even though it turned up marijuana. The intent of the search had not been to discover contraband, but to secure the owner's belongings from possible theft. Again, in *Colorado* v. *Bertine* (1987), the Court reinforced the idea that officers may open closed containers found in a vehicle while conducting a routine search for inventorying purposes. In the words of the Court, such searches are "now a well-defined exception in the warrant requirement…"[75] In 1990, however, in the precedent-setting case of *Florida* v. *Wells*,[76] the Court agreed with a lower court's suppression of marijuana discovered in a locked suitcase in the trunk of a defendant's impounded vehicle. In *Wells*, the Court held that standardized criteria authorizing the search of a vehicle for inventorying purposes were necessary before such a discovery could be legitimate. Standardized criteria, said the Court, might take the form of department policies, written general orders, or established routines.

Generally speaking, where vehicles are concerned, an investigatory stop is permissible under the Fourth Amendment if supported by reasonable suspicion,[77] and a warrantless search of a stopped car is valid if it is based on probable cause.[78] Reasonable suspicion can

In this case, we hold that this common-law "knock and announce" principle forms a part of the reasonableness inquiry under the Fourth Amendment.

—Majority opinion in *Wilson* v. *Arkansas* (1995)

expand into probable cause when the facts in a given situation so warrant. In the 1996 case of *Ornelas* v. *U.S.*,[79] for example, two experienced police officers stopped a car driven by two men who a computer check revealed to be known or suspected drug traffickers. One of the officers noticed a loose panel above an armrest in the vehicle's backseat, and then searched the car. A package of cocaine was found beneath the panel. Following conviction the defendants appealed to the U.S. Supreme Court, claiming that no probable cause to search the car existed at the time of the stop. The majority opinion, however, noted that in the view of the court which originally heard the case, "the model, age, and source-State origin of the car, and the fact that two men traveling together checked into a motel at 4 o'clock in the morning without reservations, formed a drug-courier profile and…this profile together with the [computer] reports gave rise to a reasonable suspicion of drug-trafficking activity…[I]n the court's view, reasonable suspicion became probable cause when Deputy Luedke found the loose panel."[80] Probable cause permits a warrantless search of a vehicle under what has been called the **fleeting targets exception** to the exclusionary rule.[81]

Fleeting Targets Exception
An exception to the exclusionary rule that permits law enforcement officers to search a motor vehicle based upon probable cause but without a warrant. The fleeting targets exception is predicated upon the fact that vehicles can quickly leave the jurisdiction of a law enforcement agency.

Warrantless vehicle searches may extend to any area of the vehicle, and may include sealed containers, the trunk area, and the glove compartment if officers have probable cause to conduct a purposeful search or if officers have been given permission to search the vehicle. In the 1991 case of *Florida* v. *Jimeno*,[82] arresting officers stopped a motorist who gave them permission to search his car. The defendant was later convicted on a drug charge when a bag on the floor of the car was found to contain cocaine. Upon appeal to the Supreme Court, however, he argued that the permission given to search his car did not extend to bags and other items within the car. In a decision which may have implications beyond vehicle searches, the Court held that "[a] criminal suspect's Fourth Amendment right to be free from unreasonable searches is not violated when, after he gives police permission to search his car, they open a closed container found within the car that might reasonably hold the object of the search. The amendment is satisfied when, under the circumstances, it is objectively reasonable for the police to believe that the scope of the suspect's consent permitted them to open the particular container."[83]

In *United States* v. *Ross* (1982),[84] the Court found that officers had not exceeded their authority in opening a bag in the defendant's trunk which was found to contain heroin. The search was held to be justifiable on the basis of information developed from a search of the passenger compartment. The Court said, "If probable cause justifies the search of a lawfully stopped vehicle, it justifies the search of every part of the vehicle and its contents that may conceal the object of the search."[85] Moreover, according to the 1996 U.S. Supreme Court decision of *Whren* v. *U.S.*,[86] officers may stop a vehicle being driven suspiciously and then search it once probable cause has developed, even though their primary assignment centers on duties other than traffic enforcement *or* "if a reasonable officer would not have stopped the motorist absent some additional law enforcement objective" (which in the case of *Whren* was drug enforcement). Motorists[87] and their passengers may be ordered out of stopped vehicles in the interest of officer safety, and any evidence developed as a result of such a procedure may be used in court. In 1997, for example, in the case of *Maryland* v. *Wilson*,[88] the U.S. Supreme Court overturned a decision by a Maryland court which held that crack cocaine found during a traffic stop was seized illegally when it fell from the lap of a passenger ordered out of a stopped vehicle by a Maryland state trooper. The Maryland court reasoned that the police should not have authority to order seemingly innocent passengers out of vehicles—even those which have been stopped for legitimate reasons. The Supreme Court cited concerns for officer safety in overturning the Maryland's courts ruling and held that the activities of passengers are subject to police control.

The 1983 case of *U.S.* v. *Villamonte-Marquez*[89] widened the *Carroll* decision (discussed earlier in this chapter) to include water craft. The case involved an anchored sailboat occupied by Villamonte-Marquez which was searched by a U.S. Customs officer after one of the crew members appeared unresponsive to being hailed. The officer thought he smelled burning marijuana after boarding the vessel and saw burlap bales through an open hatch which he suspected might be contraband. A search proved him correct, and the ship's occupants were arrested. Their conviction was overturned upon appeal, but the U.S. Supreme Court reversed the appeals court. The Court reasoned that a vehicle on the water can easily leave the jurisdiction of enforcement officials, just as a car or truck can.

In *California* v. *Carney* (1985),[90] the Court extended police authority to conduct warrantless searches of vehicles to include motor homes. Earlier arguments had been advanced that a motor home, because it is more like a permanent residence, should not be considered a vehicle in the same sense of an automobile for purposes of search and seizure. The Court, in a 6-to-3 decision, rejected those arguments, reasoning that a vehicle's appointments and size do not alter its basic function of providing transportation.

Houseboats were brought under the automobile exception to the Fourth Amendment warrant requirement in the 1988 Tenth Circuit Court case of *U.S.* v. *Hill*.[91] In the *Hill* case, DEA agents developed evidence which led them to believe that methamphetamine was being manufactured on board a houseboat traversing Lake Texoma in Oklahoma. Because a storm warning had been issued for the area, agents decided to board and search the boat prior to obtaining a warrant. During the search, an operating amphetamine laboratory was discovered, and the boat was seized. In an appeal, the defendants argued that the houseboat search had been illegal because agents lacked a warrant to search their home. The appellate court, however, in rejecting the claims of the defendants, ruled that a houseboat, because it is readily mobile, may be searched without a warrant where probable cause exists to believe that a crime has been or is being committed.

Suspicionless Searches

The 1991 Supreme Court case of *Florida* v. *Bostick*,[92] which permitted warrantless "sweeps" of intercity buses, moved the Court deeply into conservative territory. The *Bostick* case came to the attention of the Court as a result of the Broward County (Florida) Sheriff Department's routine practice of boarding buses at scheduled stops and asking passengers for permission to search their bags. Terrance Bostick, a passenger on one of the buses, gave police permission to search his luggage, which was found to contain cocaine. Bostick was arrested and eventually pleaded guilty to charges of drug trafficking. The Florida Supreme Court, however, found merit in Bostick's appeal, which was based upon a Fourth Amendment claim that the search of his luggage had been unreasonable. The Florida court held that "a reasonable passenger in [Bostick's] situation would not have felt free to leave the bus to avoid questioning by the police" and overturned the conviction.

The state appealed to the U.S. Supreme Court, which held that the Florida Supreme Court erred in interpreting Bostick's *feelings* that he was not free to leave the bus. In the words of the Court, "Bostick was a passenger on a bus that was scheduled to depart. He would not have felt free to leave the bus even if the police had not been present. Bostick's movements were 'confined' in a sense, but this was the natural result of his decision to take the bus." In other words, Bostick was constrained not so much by police action as by his own feelings that he might miss the bus were he to get off. Following this line of reasoning, the Court concluded that police warrantless, suspicionless "sweeps" of buses, "trains, planes, and city streets" are permissible so long as officers (1) ask individual passengers for permission before searching their possessions, (2) do not coerce passengers to consent to a search, and (3) do not convey the message that citizen compliance with the search request is mandatory. Passenger compliance with police searches must be voluntary for the searches to be legal.

In contrast to the tone of Court decisions more than two decades earlier, the justices did not require officers to inform passengers that they were free to leave nor that they had the right to deny officers the opportunity to search (although Bostick himself was so advised by Florida officers). Any reasonable person, the Court ruled, should feel free to deny the police request. In the words of the Court, "[t]he appropriate test is whether, taking into account all of the circumstances surrounding the encounter, a reasonable passenger would feel free to decline the officers' requests or otherwise terminate the encounter." The Court continued: "[R]ejected, however, is Bostick's argument that he must have been seized because no reasonable person would freely consent to a search of luggage containing drugs, since the 'reasonable person' test presumes an innocent person."

Critics of the decision saw it as creating new "Gestapo-like" police powers in the face of which citizens on public transportation will feel compelled to comply with police requests for search authority. Dissenting Justices Blackmun, Stevens, and Marshall held that "the bus sweep at issue in this case violates the core values of the Fourth Amendment." However, in

Suspicionless Searches
Those searches conducted by law enforcement personnel without a warrant and without suspicion. Suspicionless searches are only permissible if based upon an overriding concern for public safety.

Twenty-First Century Criminal Justice

SEARCH WARRANTS by FAX

The government of Ontario recently announced the availability of search warrants by fax. The program, which began in early 1997, allows police officers across the province to use a fax machine to apply for a search warrant from a justice of the peace or local magistrate. The new service, called telewarrants, is slated to soon be available 24-hours per day, seven days a week. Other Canadian provinces, including Alberta, British Columbia, Manitoba, New Brunswick, Quebec, and the Yukon all use some form of telewarrant services.

According to Ontario's Attorney General, Charles Harnick, the telewarrant service is part of an ongoing effort to build a swifter, more effective justice system. "Often the success of a criminal investigation hinges on

timely police access to a justice of the peace to apply for a search warrant," said Harnick. "No longer will police investigations be at risk because of difficulty accessing a justice of the peace," he added. "By adopting modern technology in the justice system, we will help police crack down on criminals."

Ontario's newly established telewarrant center makes a justice of the peace available to police investigators via fax at any time. Officers fax their request for a search warrant to the center, where the justice of the peace on duty reviews the application, and faxes an approval or denial of the request back to the officers.

The telewarrant service is available to all municipal and regional police services, as well as to the

Ontario Provincial Police, the Royal Canadian Mounted Police and peace officers working for the province's ministries of transportation, natural resources, and environment and energy.

According to Trevor McCagherty, president of the Ontario Association of Chiefs of Police, "The time saved by our police officers in using the telewarrant service will translate into increased public safety for every citizen....The new telewarrant service is one more very important weapon in our arsenal against criminal activity."

Source: Press release, Office of the Ontario Attorney General, Ontario, Toronto, Canada, November 7, 1996.

words which may presage a significant change of direction for other Fourth Amendment issues, the Court defended its ruling by intoning: "[T]he Fourth Amendment proscribes unreasonable searches and seizures; it does not proscribe voluntary cooperation."

The Intelligence Function

The police role includes the need to gather information through the questioning of both suspects and informants. Even more often, the need for information leads police investigators to question potentially knowledgeable citizens who may have been witnesses or victims. Data gathering is a crucial form of intelligence, without which enforcement agencies would be virtually powerless to plan and effect arrests.

The importance of gathering information in police work cannot be overstressed. Studies have found that the one factor most likely to lead to arrest in serious crimes is the presence of a witness who can provide information to the police. Undercover operations, neighborhood watch programs, "crime stopper" groups, and organized detective work all contribute information to the police.

INFORMANTS

Information gathering is a complex process, and many ethical questions have been raised about the techniques police use to gather information. Police use of paid informants, for example, is an area of concern to ethicists who believe that informants are often paid to get away with crimes. The police practice (endorsed by some prosecutors) of agreeing not to charge one offender out of a group if he or she will "talk," and testify against others, is another concern of students of justice ethics.

As we have seen, probable cause is an important aspect of both police searches and legal arrests. The Fourth Amendment specifies, "No warrants shall issue, but upon probable cause." As a consequence, the successful use of informants in supporting requests for a warrant depends upon the demonstrable reliability of their information. The case of *Aguilar* v. *Texas* (1964)[93] clarified the use of informants and established a two-pronged test to the effect that informant information could establish probable cause if *both* of the following criteria are met:

- The source of the informant's information is made clear.
- The police officer has a reasonable belief that the informant is reliable.

The two-pronged test of *Aguilar* v. *Texas* was intended to prevent the issuance of warrants on the basis of false or fabricated information. Two later cases provided exceptions to the two-pronged test. *Harris* v. *United States* (1971)[94] recognized the fact that when an informant provided information that was damaging to him or her, it was probably true. In *Harris* an informant told police that he had purchased nontax-paid whiskey from another person. Since the information also implicated the informant in a crime, it was held to be accurate, even though it could not meet the second prong of the *Aguilar* test. The 1969 Supreme Court case of *Spinelli* v. *United States*[95] created an exception to the requirements of the first prong. In Spinelli, the Court held that some information can be so highly specific that it must be accurate, even if its source is not revealed. In 1983, in the case of *Illinois* v. *Gates*,[96] the Court adopted a totality of circumstances approach, which held that sufficient probable cause for issuing a warrant exists where an informer can be reasonably believed on the basis of everything that is known by the police. The *Gates* case involved an anonymous informant who provided incriminating information about another person through a letter to the police. Although the source of the information was not stated, and the police were unable to say whether or not the informant was reliable, the overall sense of things, given what was already known to police, was that the information supplied was probably valid.

In the 1990 case of *Alabama* v. *White*,[97] the Supreme Court ruled that an anonymous tip, even in the absence of other, corroborating information about a suspect, could form the basis for an investigatory stop where the informant accurately predicts the *future* behavior of the suspect. The Court reasoned that the ability to predict a suspect's behavior demonstrates a significant degree of familiarity with the suspect's affairs. In the words of the Court, "Because only a small number of people are generally privy to an individual's itinerary, it is reasonable for the police to believe that a person with access to such information is likely to also have access to reliable information about that individual's illegal activities."[98]

The identity of informants may be kept secret if sources have been explicitly assured of confidentiality by investigating officers or if a reasonably implied assurance of confidentiality has been made. In *U.S. Department of Justice* v. *Landano* (1993),[99] the U.S. Supreme Court required that an informant's identity be revealed through a request made under the federal Freedom of Information Act. In that case, the FBI had not specifically assured an informant of confidentiality, and the Court ruled that "the government is not entitled to a presumption that all sources supplying information to the FBI in the course of a criminal investigation are confidential sources…."

Police Interrogation

A few years ago Richard Jewell, a former campus security guard, became the primary suspect in the pipe-bombing attack that took place in Atlanta's Centennial Park during the 1996 Olympics. FBI investigators were apparently convinced that Jewell was guilty and, according to Jewell, used a ruse to try and trick him into confessing.[100] Jewell claimed that agents asked him to sign a waiver of his *Miranda* rights, even before he knew he was a suspect, by telling him that the waiver document was a prop in a training film. Agents told Jewell that they were making a film about how to interrogate suspects and that Jewell was chosen for the star role because of his heroic activities at the time of the bombing. Later, when authorities dropped their investigation of Jewell, he sued CNN, the Atlanta *Journal-Constitution*, and his former college employer for libel and character defamation—and threatened suit against the FBI. FBI Director Louis Freeh later admitted that agents had made a "major error in judgment"

Interrogation The information gathering activities of police officers which involve the direct questioning of suspects.

Theory into Practice

Public Interest and the Right to Privacy—
Suspicionless Searches

The right to privacy is a fundamental guarantee of the U.S. Constitution.[1] Most of us would probably agree that privacy is also a basic human need. Our legal system, on the other hand, has long recognized that the right to privacy must be limited in cases where individuals are reasonably suspected of having committed crimes. Arrest warrants, search warrants, and orders permitting electronic surveillance may be issued by courts upon a showing of probable cause by law enforcement officers that a crime has been committed. In two 1989 decisions, however, the U.S. Supreme Court ruled for the first time in its history that there may be instances when the need to ensure public safety provides a **compelling interest** which negates the rights of any individual to privacy, permitting searches even when a person is not suspected of a crime.

In the case of *National Treasury Employees Union* v. *Von Raab*[2] (1989), the Court, by a 5-to-4 vote, upheld a program of the U.S. Customs Service which required mandatory drug testing for all workers seeking promotions or job transfers involving drug interdiction and the carrying of firearms.

The Court's majority opinion read: "We think the government's need to conduct the suspicionless searches required by the Customs program outweighs the privacy interest of employees engaged directly in drug interdiction, and of those who otherwise are required to carry firearms."

The second case, *Skinner* v. *Railway Labor Executives' Association*[3] (1989), was decided on the same day. In *Skinner*, the justices voted 7 to 2 to permit the mandatory testing of railway crews for the presence of drugs or alcohol following serious train accidents. The *Skinner* case involved evidence of drugs in a 1987 train wreck outside of Baltimore, Maryland, in which 16 people were killed and hundreds injured.

Both decisions were decried by civil libertarians as indicating a dangerous change in high-court direction. The Court's willingness to permit suspicionless searches was condemned as infringing on the rights of innocent citizens. Justices William J. Brennan, Jr., and Thurgood Marshall summed up the concerns of many when they warned in a dissenting opinion in *Skinner* that, "the first, and worst, casualty of the war on drugs will be the precious liberties of our citizens."

QUESTIONS FOR DISCUSSION

1. Can you think of any instances, other than those mentioned here, where a "compelling interest" might justify the search of persons not considered suspects in a crime? If so, what might they be?
2. Do you agree with the assertion that "the first, and worst," casualty of the war on drugs will be the precious liberties of our citizens? Why or why not?

[1]The word used in the Fourth Amendment of the U.S. Constitution is "secure," not "private." Courts have generally equated the two terms.

[2]*National Treasury Employees Union* v. *Von Raab*, 489 U.S. 656 (1989).

[3]*Skinner* v. *Railway Labor Executives' Association*, 489 U.S. 602 (1989).

Sources: All Things Considered, National Public Radio, March 21, 1989; *Criminal Justice Newsletter*, April 3, 1989, p. 4; *Drug Enforcement Report*, March 23, 1989, p. 4; and "The High Court Weighs Drug Tests," *Newsweek*, April 3, 1989, p. 8.

Compelling Interest   A legal concept which provides a basis for suspicionless searches (urinalysis tests of train engineers, for example) when public safety is at issue. It is the concept upon which the Supreme Court cases of *Skinner* v. *Railway Labor Executives' Association* (1989) and *National Treasury Employees Union* v. *Von Raab* (1989) turned. In those cases the Court held that public safety may provide a sufficiently compelling interest such that an individual's right to privacy can be limited under certain circumstances.

when they tried to trick Jewell.[101] As the Jewell investigation was to show, police interrogators must remember that not all suspects are guilty and that everyone is entitled to constitutional rights during investigation and interrogation.

Interrogation has been defined by the U.S. Supreme Court as any behaviors by the police "that the police should know are reasonably likely to elicit an incriminating response from the suspect." Hence, interrogation may involve activities which go well beyond mere verbal questioning, and the Court has held that interrogation may include "staged lineups, reverse lineups, positing guilt, minimizing the moral seriousness of crime, and casting blame on the victim or society." It is noteworthy that the Court has also held that "police words or actions normally attendant to arrest and custody do not constitute interrogation,"[102] unless they involve pointed or directed questions. Hence, an arresting officer may instruct a suspect on what to do and may chit-chat with the offender without engaging in interrogation within the meaning of the law. Once police officers make inquiries intended to elicit information about the crime in question, however, interrogation has begun. The interrogation of suspects, like other areas of police activity, is subject to constitutional limits as interpreted by the courts, and a series of landmark decisions by the U.S. Supreme Court has focused on police interrogation.

Physical Abuse

The first in a series of significant cases was that of *Brown* v. *Mississippi*,[103] decided in 1936. The *Brown* case began with the robbery of a white store owner in Mississippi in 1934. During the robbery, the victim was killed. A posse formed and went to the home of a local black man rumored to have been one of the perpetrators. They dragged the suspect from his home, put a rope around his neck, and hoisted him into a tree. They repeated this process a number of times, hoping to get a confession from the man, but failing. The posse was headed by a deputy sheriff who then arrested other suspects in the case and laid them over chairs in the local jail and whipped them with belts and buckles until they "confessed." These confessions were used in the trial which followed, and all three defendants were convicted of murder. Their convictions were upheld by the Mississippi Supreme Court. In 1936, however, the case was reviewed by the U.S. Supreme Court, which overturned all of the convictions, saying that it was difficult to imagine techniques of interrogation more "revolting" to the sense of justice than those used in this case.

Inherent Coercion

Interrogation need not involve physical abuse for it to be contrary to constitutional principles. In the case of *Ashcraft* v. *Tennessee*,[104] the Court found that inherently coercive interrogation was not acceptable. Ashcraft had been charged with the murder of his wife, Zelma. He was arrested on a Saturday night and interrogated by relays of skilled interrogators until Monday morning, when he purportedly confessed to the murder. During questioning he had been faced by a blinding light, but not physically mistreated. Investigators later testified that when the suspect requested cigarettes, food, or water, they "kindly" provided them. The Supreme Court's ruling in this case made it plain that the Fifth Amendment guarantee against self-incrimination excludes *any* form of official coercion or pressure during interrogation.

A similar case, involving four black defendants, occurred in Florida in 1940.[105] The four men, including one whose name was Chambers, were arrested without warrants as suspects in a robbery and murder of an aged white man. After several days of questioning in a hostile atmosphere, the men confessed to the murder. The confessions were used as the primary evidence against them at a trial which ensued, and all four were sentenced to die. Upon appeal to the Supreme Court, the Court held that "the very circumstances surrounding their confinement and their questioning without any formal charges having been brought, were such as to fill petitioners with terror and frightful misgivings."[106]

Inherent Coercion Those tactics used by police interviewers which fall short of physical abuse but which, nonetheless, pressure suspects to divulge information.

Psychological Manipulation

Interrogation must not only be free of coercion and hostility, but it also cannot involve sophisticated trickery designed to ferret out a confession. While interrogators do not necessarily have to be scrupulously honest in confronting suspects, and while the expert opinions of medical and psychiatric practitioners may be sought in investigations, the use of professionals skilled in psychological manipulation to gain confessions was banned by the Court in the case of *Leyra* v. *Denno*[107] in 1954.

The early 1950s were the "heyday" of psychiatric perspectives on criminal behavior. In the *Leyra* case, detectives employed a psychiatrist to question Leyra, who had been charged with the hammer slayings of his parents. Leyra had been led to believe that the medical doctor to whom he was introduced in an interrogation room had actually been sent to help him with a sinus problem. Following a period of questioning, including subtle suggestions by the psychiatrist that he would feel better if he confessed to the murders, Leyra did indeed confess.

The Supreme Court, on appeal, ruled that the defendant had been effectively, and improperly, duped by the police. In the words of the Court, "Instead of giving petitioner the medical advice and treatment he expected, the psychiatrist by subtle and suggestive questions simply continued the police effort of the past days and nights to induce petitioner to admit his guilt. For an hour and a half or more the techniques of a highly trained psychiatrist were used to break petitioner's will in order to get him to say he had murdered his parents."[108] After a series of three trials which ended in convictions, each with less and less evidence permitted into the courtroom by appeals courts, Leyra was finally set free by a state appeals court which found insufficient evidence for the final conviction.

In 1991 the Supreme Court, in the case of *Arizona* v. *Fulminante*[109] threw an even more dampening blanket of uncertainty over the use of sophisticated techniques to gain a confes-

Psychological Manipulation Manipulative actions by police interviewers, designed to pressure suspects to divulge information, which are based upon subtle forms of intimidation and control.

Individual Rights versus Group Interests— The Fourth Amendment and Sobriety Checkpoints

The Fourth and Fourteenth Amendments to the U.S. Constitution guarantee liberty and personal security to all persons residing within the United States. Lacking probable cause to believe that a crime has been committed, the courts have generally held that police officers have no legitimate authority to detain or arrest people who are going about their business in a peaceful manner. The U.S. Supreme Court has, however, in a number of cases, decided that community interests may necessitate a temporary suspension of personal liberty, even where probable cause is lacking. One such case is that of *Michigan Department of State Police* v. *Sitz* (1990),[1] which involved the legality of highway sobriety checkpoints—even those at which nonsuspicious drivers are subjected to scrutiny.

The Court had previously established that traffic stops, including those at checkpoints along a highway, are "seizures" within the meaning of the Fourth Amendment.[2] In *Michigan Department of State Police* v. *Sitz*, however, an increasingly conservative Court ruled that such seizures are reasonable insofar as they are essential to the welfare of the community as a whole. That the Court reached its con-

clusion based upon pragmatic social interests is clear from the words used by Chief Justice Rehnquist:

No one can seriously dispute the magnitude of the drunken driving problem or the States' interest in eradicating it. Media reports of alcohol-related death and mutilation on the Nation's roads are legion. Drunk drivers cause an annual death toll of over 25,000 and in the same time span cause nearly one million personal injuries and more than five billion dollars in property damage....[t]he balance of the State's interest in preventing drunken driving, the extent to which this system can reasonably be said to advance that interest, and the degree of intrusion upon individual motorists who are briefly stopped, weighs in favor of the state program.

But, critics say, how far should the Court go in allowing officers to act without probable cause? Figures on domestic violence (child and spouse abuse, murder, incest, and other forms of victimization in the home), if compared to traffic statistics, are probably far more shocking. Using the same kind of reasoning as in *Michigan*

Department of State Police v. *Sitz*, one could imagine the chief justice writing, "the balance of the State's interest in preventing domestic violence, the extent to which preventive programs briefly inconvenience individual citizens, and the relatively small degree of intrusion upon law-abiding citizens which such a program represents, weighs in favor of random home incursions by well-intentioned police officers."

QUESTIONS FOR DISCUSSION

1. Do you agree with the assertion that "community interests may necessitate a temporary suspension of personal liberty, even where probable cause is lacking"? Why or why not? If so, under what circumstances might liberties be suspended?

2. Would you, as this box suggests, be willing to "take intrusion upon law-abiding citizens" further? If so, what areas would you consider?

[1]*Michigan Department of State Police* v. *Sitz*, 110 S.Ct. 2481 (1990).

[2]*U.S.* v. *Martinea-Fuerte*, 428 U.S. 543, 96 S.Ct. 3074 (1976), and *Brower* v. *County of Inyo*, 109 S.Ct. 1378 (1989).

sion. Oreste Fulminante was an inmate in a federal prison when he was approached secretly by a fellow inmate who was an FBI informant. The informant told Fulminante that other inmates were plotting to kill him because of a rumor that he had killed a child. He offered to protect Fulminante if he was told the details of the crime. Fulminante then described his role in the murder of his 11-year-old stepdaughter. Fulminante was arrested for that murder, tried, and convicted. Upon appeal to the U.S. Supreme Court, his lawyers argued that Fulminante's confession had been coerced because of the threat of violence communicated by the informant. The Court agreed that the confession had been coerced and ordered a new trial at which the confession could not be admitted into evidence. Simultaneously, however, the Court found that the admission of a coerced confession should be considered a harmless "trial error" which need not necessarily result in reversal of a conviction if other evidence still proves guilt. The decision was especially significant because it partially reversed the Court's earlier ruling, in *Chapman* v. *California*,[110] where it was held that forced confessions were such a basic form of constitutional error that they could never be used, and automatically invalidated any conviction to which they related.

The Right to a Lawyer at Interrogation

In 1964, in the case of *Escobedo* v. *Illinois*,[111] the right to have legal counsel present during police interrogation was recognized. Danny Escobedo was arrested without a warrant for the murder of his brother-in-law, made no statement during his interrogation, and was released the same day. A few weeks later another person identified Escobedo as the killer. Escobedo was rearrested and taken back to the police station. During the interrogation which followed, officers told him that they "had him cold" and that he should confess. Escobedo asked to see his lawyer, but was told that an interrogation was in progress and that he couldn't just go out and see his lawyer. Soon the lawyer arrived and asked to see Escobedo. Police told him that his client was being questioned and could be seen after questioning concluded. Escobedo later claimed that while he repeatedly asked for his lawyer, he was told, "Your lawyer doesn't want to see you."

Eventually, Escobedo confessed and was convicted at trial on the basis of his confession. Upon appeal to the U.S. Supreme Court, the Court overturned Escobedo's conviction, ruling that counsel is necessary at police interrogations to protect the rights of the defendant and should be provided when the defendant desires.

In 1981, the case of *Edwards* v. *Arizona*[112] established a "bright-line rule" for investigators to use in interpreting a suspect's right to counsel. In *Edwards*, the Supreme Court reiterated its *Miranda* concern that once a suspect, who is in custody and who is being questioned, has requested the assistance of counsel, all questioning must cease until an attorney is present. In 1990 the Court refined the rule in *Minnick* v. *Mississippi*, when it held that interrogation may *not* resume after the suspect has had an opportunity to consult his or her lawyer, when the lawyer is no longer present. Similarly, according to *Arizona* v. *Roberson* (1988),[113] the police may not avoid the defendant's request for a lawyer by beginning a new line of questioning, even if it is about an unrelated offense. In 1994, however, the Court, in the case of *Davis* v. *United States*,[114] "put the burden on custodial suspects to make unequivocal invocations of the right to counsel." In the Davis case, a man being interrogated in the death of a sailor waived his *Miranda* rights, but later said: "Maybe I should talk to a lawyer." Investigators asked the defendant clarifying questions, and he responded, "No, I don't want a lawyer." Upon conviction he appealed, claiming that interrogation should have ceased when he mentioned a lawyer. The Court, in affirming the conviction, stated that "it will often be good police practice for the interviewing officers to clarify whether or not (the defendant) actually wants an attorney."

Suspect Rights: The *Miranda* Decision

In the area of suspect rights, no case is as famous as that of *Miranda* v. *Arizona*,[115] which was decided in 1966. Many people regard *Miranda* as the centerpiece of Warren Court due process rulings.

The case involved Ernesto Miranda, who was arrested in Phoenix, Arizona, and accused of having kidnapped and raped a young woman. At police headquarters he was identified by the victim. After being interrogated for two hours, Miranda signed a confession which formed the basis of his later conviction on the charges.

Upon eventual appeal to the U.S. Supreme Court, the Court rendered what some regard as the most far-reaching opinion to have impacted criminal justice in the last few decades. The Court ruled that Miranda's conviction was unconstitutional because "The entire aura and atmosphere of police interrogation without notification of rights and an offer of assistance of counsel tends to subjugate the individual to the will of his examiner."

The Court continued, saying that the defendant, "must be warned prior to any questioning that he has the right to remain silent, that anything he says can be used against him in a court of law, that he has the right to the presence of an attorney, and that if he cannot afford an attorney one will be appointed for him prior to any questioning if he so desires. Opportunity to exercise these rights must be afforded to him throughout the interrogation. After such warnings have been given, and such opportunity afforded him, the individual may knowingly and intelligently waive these rights and agree to answer the questions or make a statement. But unless and until such warnings and waiver are demonstrated by the prosecution at the trial, no evidence obtained as a result of interrogation can be used against him."[116]

Miranda **Warnings** The advisement of rights due criminal suspects by the police prior to the beginning of questioning. *Miranda* warnings were first set forth by the Court in the 1966 case of *Miranda* v. *Arizona*.

Ernesto Miranda, whose conviction on rape and kidnapping charges after arresting officers failed to advise him of his rights, led to the now-famous "*Miranda* warnings." Miranda is shown here after a jury convicted him for a second time. *AP/Wide World Photos*

To ensure that proper advice is given to suspects at the time of their arrest, the now-famous *Miranda* rights are read before any questioning begins. These rights, as they appear on a *Miranda* warning card commonly used by police agencies, appear in the "Theory Into Practice" box on the next page.

Once suspects have been advised of their *Miranda* rights, they are commonly asked to sign a paper which lists each right, in order to confirm that they were advised of their rights, and that they understand each right. Questioning may then begin, but only if suspects waive their rights not to talk or to have a lawyer present during interrogation.

When the *Miranda* decision was made, some hailed it as one which ensured the protection of individual rights guaranteed under the Constitution. To guarantee those rights, they suggested, what better agency is available than the police themselves, since the police are present at the initial stages of the criminal justice process. Critics of *Miranda*, however, have argued that the decision puts police agencies in the uncomfortable and contradictory position of not only enforcing the law, but also of having to offer defendants advice on how potentially to circumvent conviction and punishment. Under *Miranda* the police partially assume the role of legal advisor to the accused. During the last years of the Reagan administration, for example, then-Attorney General Edwin Meese focused on the *Miranda* decision as the antithesis of "law and order." He pledged the resources of his office to an assault upon the *Miranda* rules to eliminate what he saw as the frequent release of guilty parties on the basis of "technicalities." Nonetheless, the *Miranda* decision survives into the present day virtually unscathed.

Waiver of *Miranda* Rights by Suspects

Suspects in police custody may legally waive their *Miranda* rights through a *voluntary* "knowing and intelligent" waiver. A *knowing waiver* can only be made if a suspect has been advised of his or her rights and was in a condition to understand the advisement. A rights advisement made in English, for example, to a Spanish-speaking defendant, cannot produce a knowing waiver. Likewise, an *intelligent waiver* of rights requires that the defendant be able to understand the consequences of not invoking the *Miranda* rights. In the case of *Moran* v. *Burbine* (1986),[117] the Supreme Court defined an intelligent and knowing waiver as one

Persons 18 years old or older who are in custody must be given this advice of rights before any questioning.

1. You have the right to remain silent.
2. Anything you say can be used against you in a court of law.
3. You have the right to talk to a lawyer and to have a lawyer present while you are being questioned.
4. If you want a lawyer before or during questioning but cannot afford to hire a lawyer, one will be appointed to represent you at no cost before any questioning.
5. If you answer questions now without a lawyer here, you still have the right to stop answering questions at any time.

WAIVER OF RIGHTS

After reading and explaining the rights of a person in custody, an officer must also ask for a waiver of those rights before any questioning. The following waiver questions must be answered affirmatively, either by express answer or by clear implication. Silence alone is not a waiver.

1. Do you understand each of these rights I have explained to you? (Answer must be YES.)
2. Having these rights in mind, do you now wish to answer questions? (Answer must be YES.)
3. Do you now wish to answer questions without a lawyer present? (Answer must be YES.)

For juveniles age 14, 15, 16, and 17, the following question must be asked:

4. Do you now wish to answer questions without your parents, guardians, or custodians present? (Answer must be YES.)

QUESTIONS FOR DISCUSSION

1. Are there any other "rights" that you would add to those listed here? If so, which ones?
2. Are there any "rights" that you would remove from those listed here? If so, which ones?

Source: N.C. Justice Academy. Reprinted with permission.

"made with a full awareness both of the nature of the right being abandoned and the consequences of the decision to abandon it."[118] Similarly, in *Colorado* v. *Spring* (1987),[119] the court held that an intelligent and knowing waiver can be made even though a suspect has not been informed of all the alleged offenses about which he or she is about to be questioned.

In 1992 *Miranda* rights were effectively extended to illegal immigrants living in the United States. In a settlement of a class-action lawsuit reached in Los Angeles with the Immigration and Naturalization Service, U.S. District Court Judge William Byrne, Jr., approved the printing of millions of notices in several languages to be given to those arrested. The approximately 1.5 million illegal aliens arrested each year must be told they may (1) talk with a lawyer, (2) make a phone call, (3) request a list of available legal services, (4) seek a hearing before an immigration judge, (5) possibly obtain release on bond, and (6) contact a diplomatic officer representing their country. This kind of thing was "long overdue," said Roberto Martinez of the American Friends Service Committee's Mexico-U.S. border program. "Up to now, we've had total mistreatment of civil rights of undocumented people."[120]

Inevitable Discovery Exception to *Miranda*

A good example of the change in Supreme Court philosophy, alluded to earlier in this chapter as a movement away from an individual rights and toward a social order perspective, can be had in the case of *Robert Anthony Williams*. The *Williams* case epitomizes what some have called a "nibbling away" at the advances in defendant rights which reached their apex in *Miranda*. The case had its beginnings in 1969, at the close of the Warren court era, when Williams was convicted of murdering a 10-year-old girl, Pamela Powers, around Christmastime. Although Williams had been advised of his rights, detectives searching for the girl's body were riding in a car with the defendant when one of them made what has since come to be known as the "Christian burial speech." The detective told Williams that, since Christmas was almost upon them, it would be "the Christian thing to do" to see to it that Pamela could have a decent burial rather than having to lay in a field somewhere.

Williams relented and led detectives to the body. However, because Williams had not been reminded of his right to have a lawyer present during his conversation with the detective, the Supreme Court in *Brewer* v. *Williams* (1977)[121] overturned Williams's conviction, saying that the detective's remarks were "a deliberate eliciting of incriminating evidence from an accused in the absence of his lawyer."

In 1977 Williams was retried for the murder, but his remarks in leading detectives to the body were not entered into evidence. The discovery of the body was itself used, however, prompting another appeal to the Supreme Court based upon the argument that the body should not have been used as evidence since it was discovered due to the illegally gathered statements. This time, in *Nix* v. *Williams* (1984),[122] the Supreme Court affirmed Williams's second conviction, holding that the body would have been found anyway, since detectives were searching in the direction where it lay when Williams revealed its location. That ruling came during the heyday of the Burger court, and clearly demonstrates a tilt by the Court away from suspect's rights and an accommodation with the imperfect world of police procedure. The *Williams* case, as it was finally resolved, is said to have created the "inevitable discovery exception" to the *Miranda* requirements.

Public Safety Exceptions to *Miranda*

In 1984 the U.S. Supreme Court also established what has come to be known as the public safety exception to the *Miranda* rule. The case *New York* v. *Quarles*,[123] centered upon an alleged rape in which the victim told police her assailant had fled, with a gun, into a nearby A&P supermarket. Two police officers entered the store and apprehended the suspect. One officer immediately noticed that the man was wearing an empty shoulder holster and, apparently fearing that a child might find the discarded weapon, quickly asked, "Where's the gun?"

Quarles was convicted of rape, but appealed his conviction, requesting that the weapon be suppressed as evidence because officers had not advised him of his *Miranda* rights before asking him about it. The Supreme Court disagreed, stating that considerations of public safety were overriding and negated the need for rights advisement prior to limited questioning which focused on the need to prevent further harm.

Where the police have not been coercive, and have issued *Miranda* warnings, the Supreme Court has held that even a later demonstration that a person may have been suffering from mental problems will not necessarily negate a confession. *Colorado* v. *Connelly* (1986)[124] involved a man who approached a Denver police officer and said he wanted to confess to the murder of a young girl. The officer immediately informed him of his *Miranda* rights, but the man waived them and continued to talk. When a detective arrived, the man was again advised of his rights and again waived them. After being taken to the local jail the man began to hear "voices" and later claimed that it was these voices which had made him confess. At the trial the defense moved to have the earlier confession negated on the basis that it was not voluntarily or freely given because of the defendant's mental condition. Upon appeal, the Supreme Court disagreed, saying that "no coercive government conduct occurred in this case."[125] Hence, "self-coercion," be it through the agency of a guilty conscience or faulty thought processes, does not appear to bar prosecution based on information revealed willingly by the defendant.

In a final refinement of *Miranda*, the lawful ability of a police informant placed in a jail cell along with a defendant to gather information for later use at trial was upheld in the 1986 case of *Kuhlmann* v. *Wilson*.[126] The passive gathering of information was judged to be acceptable, provided that the informant did not make attempts to elicit information.

In the case of *Illinois* v. *Perkins* (1990),[127] the Court expanded its position to say that, under appropriate circumstances, even the active questioning of a suspect by an undercover officer posing as a fellow inmate does not require *Miranda* warnings. In *Perkins*, the Court found that, lacking other forms of coercion, the fact that the suspect was not aware of the questioner's identity as a law enforcement officer ensured that his statements were freely given. In the words of the Court, "[t]he essential ingredients of a 'police-dominated atmosphere' and compulsion are not present when an incarcerated person speaks freely to someone that he believes to be a fellow inmate."

The public safety exception was intended to protect the police, as well as the public, from danger.

—*U.S.* v. *Brady*, 819 F2d 884 (1987)

A suspect being read his *Miranda* rights immediately after arrest. Officers often read *Miranda* rights from a card to preclude the possibility of mistake.
Bob Daemmrich, Stock Boston

Miranda and the Meaning of Interrogation

Modern interpretations of the applicability of "*Miranda* warnings" turn upon an understanding of *interrogation*. The *Miranda* decision, as originally rendered, specifically recognized the necessity for police investigators to make inquiries at crime scenes in order to determine facts or establish identities. So long as the individual questioned is not yet in custody, and so long as probable cause is lacking in the investigator's mind, such questioning can proceed without the need for *Miranda* warnings. In such cases, interrogation, within the meaning of *Miranda*, has not yet begun.

The case of *Rock* v. *Zimmerman* (1982)[128] provides a different sort of example—one in which a suspect willingly made statements to the police before interrogation began. The suspect had burned his own house and shot and killed a neighbor. When the fire department arrived, he began shooting again and killed the fire chief. Cornered later in a field, the defendant, gun in hand, spontaneously shouted at police, "How many people did I kill, how many people are dead?"[129] This spontaneous statement was held to be admissible evidence at the suspect's trial.

It is also important to recognize that the Supreme Court, in the *Miranda* decision, required that officers provide warnings only in those situations involving *both* arrest and custodial interrogation. In other words, it is generally permissible for officers to take a suspect into custody and listen without asking questions while he or she tells a story. Similarly, they may ask questions without providing a *Miranda* warning, even within the confines of a police station house, as long as the person questioned is not a suspect and is not under arrest.[130] Warnings are required only when officers begin actively to solicit responses from the defendant. Recognizing this fact, the FBI, in some of its training literature, has referred to interrogation as the *Miranda* trigger.

Officers were found to have acted properly in the case of *South Dakota* v. *Neville*, (1983)[131] in informing a DWI suspect, without reading him his rights, that he would stand to lose his

Miranda **Triggers**   The dual principles of custody and interrogation, both of which are necessary before an advisement of rights is required.

driver's license if he did not submit to a Breathalyzer test. When the driver responded, "I'm too drunk. I won't pass the test," his answer became evidence of his condition and was permitted at trial.

A third-party conversation recorded by the police after a suspect has invoked the *Miranda* right to remain silent may be used as evidence, according to a 1987 ruling in *Arizona* v. *Mauro*.[132] In *Mauro*, a man who willingly conversed with his wife in the presence of a police tape recorder, even after invoking his right to keep silent, was held to have effectively abandoned that right.

When a waiver is not made, however, in-court references to a defendant's silence following the issuing of *Miranda* warnings is unconstitutional. In 1976 (*Doyle* v. *Ohio*),[133] the U.S. Supreme Court definitively ruled that "a suspect's [post-Miranda] silence will not be used against him." Even so, according to the Court in *Brecht* v. *Abrahamson* (1993),[134] prosecution efforts to use such silence against a defendant may not invalidate a finding of guilt by a jury unless such "error had substantial and injurious effect or influence in determining the jury's verdict."[135]

Gathering Special Kinds of Nontestimonial Evidence

The police environment is complicated by the fact that suspects are often privy to special evidence of a nontestimonial sort. Nontestimonial evidence is generally physical evidence, and most physical evidence is subject to normal procedures of search and seizure. A special category of nontestimonial evidence, however, includes very personal items, which may be within or part of a person's body, such as ingested drugs, blood cells, foreign objects, medical implants, and human DNA. Also included in this category might be fingerprints and other kinds of biological residue. The gathering of such special kinds of nontestimonial evidence is a complex area rich in precedent. The Fourth Amendment guarantee that persons be secure in their homes and in their persons has been interpreted by the courts to generally mean that the improper seizure of physical evidence of any kind is illegal and will result in exclusion of that evidence at trial. When very personal kinds of nontestimonial evidence are considered, however, the issue becomes more complicated still.

The Right to Privacy

Two cases, *Hayes* v. *Florida*[136] and *Winston* v. *Lee*,[137] are examples of limits the courts have placed upon the seizure of very personal forms of nontestimonial evidence. The *Hayes* case established the right of suspects to refuse to be fingerprinted when probable cause necessary to effect an arrest does not exist. *Winston* demonstrated the inviolability of the body against surgical and other substantially invasive techniques which might be ordered by authorities against a suspect's will.

In the *Winston* case, Rudolph Lee, Jr., was found a few blocks from a store robbery with a gunshot wound in his chest. The robbery had involved an exchange of gunshots by the store owner and the robber, with the owner noting that the robber had apparently been hit by a bullet. At the hospital, the store owner identified Lee as the robber. The prosecution sought to have Lee submit to surgery to remove the bullet in his chest, arguing that the bullet would provide physical evidence linking him to the crime. Lee refused the surgery, and the Supreme Court in *Winston* v. *Lee* (1985) ruled that Lee could not be ordered to undergo

Twenty-First Century Criminal Justice

High-Technology Searches

The burgeoning use of high-technology to investigate crime and to uncover what might otherwise remain undiscovered violations of the criminal law is forcing courts throughout the nation to evaluate the applicability of constitutional guarantees in light of high-tech searches and seizures. The 1996 California appellate court decision, *People* v. *Deutsch*,[1] presages the kinds of issues likely to be encountered as the American justice system enters the twenty-first century. Excerpts from the decision are reproduced below:

This case presents the question of whether a warrantless scan made with a thermal imaging device of a private dwelling constitutes an unreasonable search within the meaning of the Fourth Amendment to the United States Constitution. We hold that it does.

Defendant, Dorian Deutsch, pleaded no contest to a single count of furnishing a room in a building for the cultivation of marijuana (Health & Safety Code, section 11366.5). On appeal she contends that the trial court erred in denying her motion to suppress evidence which was seized in a search made with a warrant issued in part upon the basis of the thermal imager scan of her home. (Penal Code, section 1538.5.) That evidence included some 200 cannabis plants which were being cultivated hydroponically under high wattage lights in two walled-off portions of the home's garage.

According to the police officer's affidavit offered in support of the search warrant, a confidential informant gave a friend a ride to defendant's home. When they arrived defendant gave the informant a small amount of dried marijuana as a thank you. The informant did not report seeing any growing cannabis plants inside the home, but did note that two doors in the

living room were "blocked off with bedsheets." The officer obtained a search warrant for utility records which showed "an unusually high electrical usage" which he concluded was "extremely consistent with the indoor cultivation of cannabis." Some four days later, without having obtained a warrant, the officer drove by the residence at 1:30 in the morning and scanned it with a thermal imager.

As described in the officer's affidavit a thermal imaging device is "a passive, non-intrusive system which detects differences in temperature at surface levels." Such devices measure radiant energy in the thermal portion of the electromagnetic spectrum[2] and display their readings showing areas which are relatively cold as nearly black, warmer areas in shades of gray and hot areas as white... With the imager the officer "observed high heat level readings, showing excessive heat release" from the "west side, north face, of the residence, which appeared to be the garage area."

DISCUSSION

Defendant maintains that use of the thermal imager on her residence was a warrantless search conducted in violation of the right, under the Fourth Amendment to the United States Constitution "of the people to be secure in their persons, houses, papers and effects, against unreasonable searches...." In *Katz* v. *United States* (1967) 389 U.S. 347 the Supreme Court rejected the notion that every impermissible governmental intrusion must involve a physical invasion or trespass. Instead, it read the protections of the amendment to foreclose a warrantless electronic interception of telephone calls made from a glass enclosed public phone booth. As articulated in Justice Harlan's concurrence the appropriate test for Fourth Amendment purposes is twofold: first,

the person must demonstrate an actual, subjective expectation of privacy in that which is searched and second, that expectation must be one our society recognizes to be reasonable... More recently the Supreme Court has restated the particular deference accorded the home characterizing as a basic "Fourth Amendment principle" the notion that "private residences are places in which the individual normally expects privacy free of governmental intrusion not authorized by a warrant, and that expectation is plainly one that society is prepared to recognize as justifiable." (*United States* v. *Karo* [1984], 468 U.S. 705, 714.)

Information or activities which are exposed to public view cannot be characterized as something in which a person has a subjective expectation of privacy, nor can they fulfill the second prong of *Katz*—as being that which society reasonably expects will remain private. A common theme of public disclosure which defeats privacy runs through many cases in which no search was found to have occurred: such as a mechanically recorded list of phone numbers dialed kept by the phone company which has been held to be as publicly disclosed as if the calls had been made through an operator (*Smith* v. *Maryland* [1979] 442 U.S. 735, 743-744), or high resolution photographs of structures in an industrial building complex viewed from the air which are as available to government inspection as to that of any airborne passerby. (*Dow Chemical Co.* v. *United States* [1986] 476 U.S. 227, 237, fn. 4, 239.) Accordingly, a warrantless thermal scan of an outbuilding located some 200–300 yards from a home has been upheld because the structure was in an "open field." (*U.S.* v. *Ishmael* [5th Cir. 1995] 48 F.3d 850, 857.)

One who discards garbage by setting it out on the public street has renounced any expectation of privacy in the contents of his garbage bin. (*California* v. *Greenwood* [1988] 486 U.S. 35, 40.) Analogizing to the discarded garbage of *Greenwood* certain thermal imaging opinions have characterized the heat signatures registered by the device as "heat waste"...The analogy is neither good law nor good physics. As a recent decision from the Tenth Circuit points out, the thermal imager does not simply measure the waste heat radiating from a structure, but it measures all temperature differentials across the exterior surface of the structure (*U.S. v. Cusumano* [10th Cir. 1995] 67 F.3d 1497). Therefore, the function of the device is to paint an infrared picture of the heat sources which permits inferences about the heat generating activities occurring within the residence. (Id. at p. 1501.) Moreover, as the *Cusumano* court notes, the thermal imager is no more directed to measuring waste heat than the electronic bug affixed to the phone booth in Katz was directed to collecting waste sound waves.

The principle that nondisclosed activities within the home are those in which society accepts a reasonable expectation of privacy and therefore activities which require a warrant for government intrusion is clearly set out in two Supreme Court beeper cases. In *United States* v. *Karo*, supra, 468 U.S. 705, drug enforcement agents arranged for a beeper to be inserted in a can of ether the agents believed was being obtained for the purpose of extracting cocaine from drug-impregnated clothing. (Id. at p. 708.) Using the signals from the beeper the agents located the can in the course of its movements to a private residence, to two different storage facilities, and then to a second residence. (Id. at pp. 708–709.) The court concluded that the monitoring of the beeper when it was inside a private residence was an unreasonable search because "[t]he beeper tells the agent that a particular article is actually located at a particular time in the private residence and is in the possession of the person or persons whose residence is being watched." (Id. at p. 715.) While the court noted that the monitoring of the beeper was less intrusive than a full-scale search would be, nonetheless the beeper revealed information to the government which would not otherwise have been obtained without a search warrant...Like the beeper signal being monitored inside the residence in *Karo* the thermal imaging scan of defendant's residence told the police something about activities within the house which they could not otherwise have learned without obtaining a warrant to search it....

Defendant demonstrated a subjective expectation of privacy in the activities she conducted inside her home. The grow rooms found in her garage were walled off, and the view by visitors into the rest of her house from the living room was blocked by bedsheets hung over the doorways. We find that society recognizes as reasonable an expectation that the heat generated from within a private residence may not be measured by the government without a warrant permitting such a search. In this instance the warrantless thermal scan of defendant's home was an unreasonable search prohibited by the Fourth Amendment...

[1]*People* v. *Dorian Odette Deutsch*, 96 C.D.O.S. 2827 (1996).

[2]The thermal imager differs from infrared devices (such as night vision goggles) in that the latter amplify the infrared spectrum of light whereas the thermal imager registers solely that portion of the infrared spectrum which we call heat.

Visit the *CJToday* Web page and click on "Web Chapters," then "Chapter 7." Follow the "find the facts" links in order to review U.S. Supreme Court decisions of relevance to policing.

surgery because such a magnitude of intrusion into his body was unacceptable under the right to privacy guaranteed by the Fourth Amendment. The *Winston* case was based upon precedent established in *Schmerber* v. *California* (1966).[138] The *Schmerber* case turned upon the extraction of a blood sample to be measured for alcohol content against the defendant's will. In *Schmerber* the Court ruled that warrants must be obtained for bodily intrusions unless fast action is necessary to prevent the destruction of evidence by natural physiological processes.

Body Cavity Searches

Body cavity searches are among the most problematic for police today. "Strip" searches of convicts in prisons, including the search of body cavities, have generally been held permissible. The 1985 Supreme Court case of *U.S.* v. *Montoya de Hernandez*[139] focused on the issue of "alimentary canal smuggling," in which the suspect typically swallows condoms filled with cocaine or heroin and waits for nature to take its course to recover the substance.

In the *Montoya* case, a woman known to be a "balloon swallower" arrived in the United States on a flight from Colombia. She was detained by customs officials and given a "pat down" search by a female agent. The agent reported that the woman's abdomen was firm and suggested that X rays be taken. The suspect refused and was given the choice of submitting to further tests or taking the next flight back to Colombia. No flight was immediately available, however, and the suspect was placed in a room for 16 hours, where she refused all food and drink. Finally, a court order for an X ray was obtained. The procedure revealed "balloons," and the woman was detained another four days, during which time she passed numerous cocaine-filled plastic condoms. The Court ruled that the woman's confinement was not unreasonable, based as it was upon the supportable suspicion that she was "body-packing" cocaine. Any discomfort she experienced, the court ruled, "resulted solely from the method that she chose to smuggle illicit drugs."[140]

Electronic Eavesdropping

Modern technology makes possible increasingly complex forms of communication. From fiber optic phone lines, microwave and cellular transmissions, and fax machines to computer communications involving modems and databases, today's global village is a close-knit weave of flowing information.

One of the first and best known of the Supreme Court decisions in the area of electronic communications was the 1928 case of *Olmstead* v. *U.S.*[141] In *Olmstead*, bootleggers used their personal telephones to discuss and transact business. Agents had tapped the lines and based their investigation and ensuing arrests upon conversations they had overheard. The defendants were convicted and eventually appealed to the high court, arguing that the agents had in effect seized information illegally without a search warrant in violation of their Fourth Amendment right to be secure in their homes. The Court ruled, however, that telephone lines were not an extension of the defendant's homes and therefore were not protected by the constitutional guarantee of security. Subsequent federal statutes (discussed shortly) have substantially modified the significance of *Olmstead*.

Recording devices carried on the body of an undercover agent or an informant were ruled to produce admissible evidence in *On Lee* v. *U.S.* (1952)[142] and *Lopez* v. *U.S.* (1963).[143] The 1967 case of *Berger* v. *New York*[144] permitted wiretaps and "bugs" in instances where state law provided for the use of such devices and where officers obtained a warrant based upon probable cause.

The Court appeared to undertake a significant change of direction in the area of electronic eavesdropping when, in 1967, it decided the case of *Katz* v. *U.S.*[145] Federal agents had monitored a number of Katz's telephone calls from a public phone using a device separate from the phone lines and attached to the glass of the phone booth. The Court, in this case, stated that what a person makes an effort to keep private, even in a public place, requires a judicial decision, in the form of a warrant issued upon probable cause, to unveil. In the words of the Court, "The government's activities in electronically listening to and recording the petitioner's words violated the privacy upon which he justifiably relied while using the telephone booth and thus constituted a 'search and seizure' within the meaning of the Fourth Amendment."

In 1968, with the case of *Lee* v. *Florida*,[146] the Court applied the Federal Communications Act[147] to telephone conversations which may be the object of police investigation and held that evidence obtained without a warrant could not be used in state proceedings if it resulted from a wiretap. The only person who has the authority to permit eavesdropping, according to that act, is the sender of the message.

The Federal Communications Act was originally passed in 1934 but did not specifically mention the potential interest of law enforcement agencies in monitoring communications. Title III of the Omnibus Crime Control and Safe Streets Act of 1968, however, mostly prohibits wiretaps but does allow officers to listen to electronic communications where (1) the officer is one of the parties involved in the communication, (2) one of the parties is not the officer, but willingly decides to share the communication with the officer, or (3) officers obtain a warrant based upon probable cause. In the 1971 case of *U.S.* v. *White*,[148] the Court held that law enforcement officers may intercept electronic information when one of the parties involved in the communication gives his or her consent, even without a warrant.

In 1984 the Supreme Court decided the case of *U.S.* v. *Karo*,[149] in which DEA agents had arrested James Karo for cocaine importation. Officers had placed a radio transmitter inside a 50-gallon drum of ether purchased by Karo for use in processing the cocaine. The transmitter was placed inside the drum with the consent of the seller of the ether but without a search warrant. The shipment of ether was followed to the Karo house, and Karo was arrested and convicted of cocaine trafficking charges. Karo appealed to the Supreme Court, claiming that the radio beeper had violated his reasonable expectation of privacy inside his premises and that, without a warrant, the evidence it produced was tainted. The Court agreed and overturned his conviction.

Minimization Requirements in Electronic Surveillance

The Supreme Court established a minimization requirement pertinent to electronic surveillance in the 1978 case of *United States* v. *Scott*.[150] Minimization means that officers must make every reasonable effort to monitor only those conversations, through the use of phone taps, body bugs, and the like, which are specifically related to criminal activity under investigation. As soon as it becomes obvious that a conversation is innocent, then the monitoring personnel are required to cease their invasion of privacy. Problems arise if the conversation occurs in a foreign language, if it is "coded," or if it is ambiguous. It has been suggested that investigators involved in electronic surveillance maintain log books of their activities which specifically show monitored conversations, as well as efforts made at "minimization."[151]

The Electronic Communications Privacy Act of 1986

ECPA An acronym for the Electronic Communications Privacy Act.

Passed by Congress in 1986, the Electronic Communications Privacy Act (**ECPA**)[152] has brought major changes in the requirements law enforcement officers must meet when using wiretaps. The ECPA deals specifically with three areas of communication: (1) wiretaps and bugs, (2) pen registers (which record the numbers dialed from a telephone), and (3) tracing devices which determine the number from which a call emanates. The act also addresses the procedures to be followed by officers in obtaining records relating to communications services, and it establishes requirements for gaining access to stored electronic communications and records of those communications.

The ECPA basically requires that investigating officers must obtain wiretap-type court orders to eavesdrop on *ongoing communications*. The use of pen registers and recording devices, however, are specifically excluded by the law from court order requirements. *Stored communications*, such as computer files made from telephonic sources, fax reproductions, digitally stored information, electronic bulletin boards, and other physical and electronic records of communications which have already occurred are categorized by the act according to the length of time they have been stored. Messages stored for fewer than 180 days are protected in the same manner as the contents of U.S. mail, and a search warrant issued upon probable cause is required to access them.[153] Information which has been on file in excess of 180 days, however, can be accessed with a court order based upon a simple showing that the information sought is relevant to an ongoing criminal investigation. Such a "showing" is less demanding than a demonstration of probable cause, which includes the claim that the information in question will provide evidence of a law violation.

A related measure, the Communications Assistance for Law Enforcement Act of 1994,[154] calls for spending $500 million to modify the United States' phone network over the next few years to allow for continued wiretapping by law-enforcement agencies. The law also specifies a standard-setting process for the redesign of existing equipment which would permit effective wiretapping in the face of coming technological advances. In the words of the FBI's Telecommunications Industry Liaison Unit (TILU), "This law requires telecommunications carriers, as defined in the Act, to ensure law enforcement's ability, pursuant to court order or other lawful authorization, to intercept communications notwithstanding advanced telecommunications technologies."[155]

The Telecommunications Act of 1996

Title V of the Telecommunications Act of 1996,[156] signed into law by President Clinton on February 8 of that year, made it a federal offense for anyone engaged in interstate or international communications to knowingly use a telecommunications device "to create, solicit, or initiate the transmission of any comment, request, suggestion, proposal, image, or other communication which is obscene, lewd, lascivious, filthy, or indecent, with intent to annoy, abuse, threaten, or harass another person." The law also provided special penalties for anyone who "makes a telephone call…without disclosing his identity and with intent to annoy, abuse, threaten, or harass any person at the called number or who receives the communication…," or "makes or causes the telephone of another repeatedly or continuously to ring, with intent to harass any person at the called number; or makes repeated telephone calls" for the purpose of harassing a person at the called number.

A section of the law, known as the Communications Decency Act[157] (CDA) criminalized the transmission to minors of "patently offensive" obscene materials over the Internet or other telecommunications services via computer. The CDA, portions of which were invalidated by the U.S. Supreme Court in the case of *Reno* v. *ACLU* (1997),[158] is discussed in greater detail in Chapter 17.

SUMMARY

This chapter described the legal environment surrounding police activities—from search and seizure through arrest and the interrogation of suspects. It is important to realize that democratically inspired legal restraints upon the police help ensure individual freedoms in our society and prevent the development of a "police state" in America. In police work and elsewhere, the principles of individual liberty and social justice are cornerstones upon which the American way of life rests. For police action to be "just," it must recognize the rights of individuals while simultaneously holding them accountable to the social obligations defined by law.

Ideally, the work of the criminal justice system is to ensure justice while guarding liberty. The liberty/justice issue is the dual thread which weaves the tapestry of the justice system together—from the simplest daily activities of police on the beat to the often complex and lengthy renderings of the U.S. Supreme Court.

For the criminal justice system as a whole, the question becomes "How can individual liberties be maintained in the face of the need for official action, including arrest, interrogation, incarceration, and the like?" The answer is far from simple, but it begins with recognition of the fact that "liberty" is a double-edged sword, entailing obligations as well as rights.

Police work gives you the test first, then the lesson.
—Anonymous

DISCUSSION QUESTIONS

1. Which Supreme Court decisions discussed in this chapter do you see as most important? Why? Are there any Supreme Court decisions discussed in this chapter with which you disagree? If so, which ones? Why do you disagree?

2. Do you agree with the theme of this chapter's summary, that "for police action to be just, it must recognize the rights of individuals, while holding citizens to the social obligations defined by law"? What is the basis for your agreement or disagreement?

3. What does the *due process environment* mean to you? How do you think we should try to ensure due process in our legal system?

4. Justice Benjamin Cardozo once complained, "The criminal is to go free because the constable has blundered." Can we afford to let some guilty people go free in order to ensure that the rights of the rest of us are protected? Is there some other (better) way to achieve the same goal?

 WEB WATCH

Access the *Criminal Justice Today* site on the World Wide Web by pointing your Web browser at http://www.prenhall.com/cjtoday. Once there, click the "enter here" selection, then "Web Chapters," and finally "Chapter 7: Policing: Legal Aspects" from the selection box in order to access electronic information and other sites of relevance to this chapter. You may also wish to enter the Global Town Meeting, which provides facilities for the posting of electronic messages for others to read. Messages are arranged by topic, with new topics constantly being added.

NOTES

1. Larry Collins and Dominique Lapierre, *The Fifth Horseman* (New York: Simon & Schuster, 1980).
2. "Police Brutality!" *Time*, March 25, 1991, p. 18.
3. "L.A. Officers Not Indicted," *The Fayetteville Observer-Times* (North Carolina), May 11, 1991, p. 10C.
4. "Police Brutality!" pp. 16–19.
5. "Police Charged in Beating Case Say They Feared for Their Lives," *The Boston Globe*, May 22, 1991, p. 22.

6. "Cries of Relief," *Time*, April 26, 1993, p. 18.

7. "Rodney King's Run-ins," *USA Today*, May 30, 1991, p. 2A.

8. "Rodney King Gets Jail Time," *The Island Packet*, August 22, 1996, p. 4A.

9. "Rodney King to Clean Streets," *The Island Packet*, September 15, 1996, p. 5A.

10. *Miranda* v. *Arizona*, 384 U.S. 436 (1966).

11. *Weeks* v. *U.S.*, 232 U.S. 383 (1914).

12. Roger Goldman and Steven Puro, "Decertification of Police: An Alternative to Traditional Remedies for Police Misconduct," *Hastings Constitutional Law Quarterly*, Vol. 15 (1988), pp. 45–80.

13. Ibid.

14. *Silverthorne Lumber Co.* v. *U.S.*, 251 U.S. 385 (1920).

15. Ibid.

16. Clemmens Bartollas, *American Criminal Justice* (New York: Macmillan, 1988), p. 186.

17. *Mapp* v. *Ohio*, 367 U.S. 643 (1961).

18. Ibid.

19. *Wolf* v. *Colorado*, 338 U.S. 25 (1949).

20. *Chimel* v. *California*, 395 U.S. 752 (1969).

21. *U.S.* v. *Rabinowitz*, 339 U.S. 56 (1950).

22. *Katz* v. *U.S.*, 389 U.S. 347, 88 S.Ct. 507 (1967).

23. *Minnesota* v. *Olson*, 110 S.Ct. 1684 (1990).

24. *Illinois* v. *Gates*, 426 U.S. 318 (1982).

25. *U.S.* v. *Leon*, 468 U.S. 897, 104 S.Ct. 3405, 82 L. Ed. 2d 677, 52 U.S.L.W. 5155 (1984).

26. Judicial titles vary between jurisdictions. Many lower-level state judicial officers are referred to as "magistrates." Federal magistrates, however, are generally regarded as functioning at a significantly higher level of judicial authority.

27. *Massachusetts* v. *Sheppard*, 104 S.Ct. 3424 (1984).

28. *Illinois* v. *Krull*, 107 S.Ct. 1160 (1987).

29. *Maryland* v. *Garrison*, 107 S.Ct. 1013 (1987).

30. *Illinois* v. *Rodriguez*, 110 S.Ct. 2793 (1990).

31. William H. Erickson, William D. Neighbors, and B. J. George, Jr., *United States Supreme Court Cases and Comments* (New York: Matthew Bender, 1987), Section 1.13 [7].

32. *Harris* v. *U.S.*, 390 U.S. 234 (1968).

33. As cited in Kimberly A. Kingston, "Look But Don't Touch: The Plain View Doctrine," *FBI Law Enforcement Bulletin* (December 1987), p. 18.

34. *Horton* v. *California*, 110 S.Ct. 2301, 47 CrL. 2135 (1990).

35. *U.S.* v. *Irizarry* (1982).

36. *FBI Law Enforcement Bulletin* (December 1987), p. 20.

37. *Arizona* v. *Hicks*, 107 S.Ct. 1149 (1987).

38. See *Criminal Justice Today*, North Carolina Justice Academy (Fall 1987), p. 24.

39. "Inadvertency" as a requirement of legitimate plain-view seizures was first cited in the U.S. Supreme Court case of *Coolidge* v. *New Hampshire*, 403 U.S. 443, 91 S.Ct. 2022 (1971).

40. *Horton* v. *California*, 110 S.Ct. 2301, 47 CrL. 2135 (1990).

41. Ibid.

42. John Gales Sauls, "Emergency Searches of Premises," Part 1, *FBI Law Enforcement Bulletin* (March 1987), p. 23.

43. *Warden* v. *Hayden*, 387 U.S. 294 (1967).

44. *Mincey* v. *Arizona*, 437 U.S. 385, 392 (1978).

45. Sauls, "Emergency Searches of Premises," p. 25.

46. *Maryland* v. *Buie*, 110 S.Ct. 1093 (1990).

47. *Wilson* v. *Arkansas*, 115 S.Ct. 1914 (1995).

48. For additional information, see Michael J. Bulzomi, "Knock and Announce: A Fourth Amendment Standard," *FBI Law Enforcement Bulletin*, Vol. 66, no. 5 (May 1997), pp. 27–31.

49. *Richards* v. *Wisconsin*, 117 S.Ct. 1416 (1997), syllabus.

50. Ibid.

51. *U.S.* v. *Mendenhall*, 446 U.S. 544 (1980).

52. A. Louis DiPietro, "Voluntary Encounters or Fourth Amendment Seizures," *FBI Law Enforcement Bulletin*, January 1992, pp. 28–32 at note 6.

53. *Stansbury* v. *California*, 114 S.Ct. 1526, 1529, 128 L. Ed. 2d 293 (1994).

54. In 1976, in the case of *Watson* v. *U.S.* (432 U.S. 411), the U.S. Supreme Court refused to impose a warrant requirement for felony arrests that occur in public places.

55. In 1981, in the case of *U.S.* v. *Steagald* (451 U.S. 204), the Court ruled that a search warrant is also necessary when the planned arrest involves entry into a third party's premises.

56. *Robinson* v. *U.S.*, 414 U.S. 218 (1973).

57. Ibid.

58. *Terry* v. *Ohio*, 392 U.S. 1 (1968).

59. Ibid.

60. *U.S.* v. *Sokolow*, 109 S.Ct. 1581 (1989).

61. *Minnesota* v. *Dickerson*, 113 S.Ct. 2130, 124 L.Ed. 2d 334 (1993).

62. *Brown* v. *Texas*, 443 U.S. 47 (1979).

63. *Smith* v. *Ohio*, 110 S.Ct. 1288 (1990).

64. Ibid., at 1289.

65. *California* v. *Hodari D.*, 111 S.Ct. 1547 (1991).

66. Criminal Justice Newsletter, May 1, 1991, p. 2.

67. Dissenting opinion in *California* v. *Hodari D.*

68. *Arkansas* v. *Sanders*, 442 U.S. 753 (1979).

69. Ibid.

70. *Borchardt* v. *U.S.*, 809 F.2d 1115 (5th Cir. 1987).

71. *FBI Law Enforcement Bulletin*, January 1988, p. 28.

72. *Carroll* v. *U.S.*, 267 U.S. 132 (1925).

73. *Preston* v. *U.S.*, 376 U.S. 364 (1964).

74. *South Dakota* v. *Opperman*, 428 U.S. 364 (1976).

75. *Colorado* v. *Bertine*, 479 U.S. 367, 107 S.Ct. 741 (1987).

76. *Florida* v. *Wells*, 110 S.Ct. 1632 (1990).

77. *Terry* v. *Ohio*, 392 U.S. 1 (1968).

78. *California* v. *Acevedo*, 500 U.S. 565 (1991).

79. *Ornelas* v. *U.S.*, 116 S.Ct. 1657 L.Ed. 2d 911 (1996).

80. Ibid.

81. The phrase is usually attributed to the 1991 U.S. Supreme Court case of *California* v. *Acevedo*. See Devallis Rutledge, "Taking an Inventory," *Police*, November, 1995, pp. 8–9.

82. *Florida* v. *Jimeno*, 111 S.Ct. 1801 (1991).

83. *Jimeno*, on-line syllabus.

84. *United States* v. *Ross*, 456 U.S. 798 (1982).

85. Ibid.

86. *Whren* v. *U.S.*, 116 S.Ct. 1769, 135 L.Ed. 2d (1996).

87. See *Pennsylvania* v. *Mimms*, 434 U.S. 106 (1977).

88. *Maryland* v. *Wilson*, 117 S.Ct. 882 (1997).

89. *U.S.* v. *Villamonte-Marquez*, 462 U.S. 579 (1983).

90. *California* v. *Carney*, 471 U.S. 386, 105 S.Ct. 2066, 85 L.Ed. 2d 406, 53 U.S.L.W. 4521 (1985).

91. *U.S.* v. *Hill*, 855 F.2d 664 (10th Cir. 1988).

92. *Florida* v. *Bostick*, 111 S.Ct. 2382 (1991).

93. *Aguilar* v. *Texas*, 378 U.S. 108 (1964).

94. *Harris* v. *United States*, 403 U.S. 573 (1971).

95. *Spinelli* v. *United States*, 393 U.S. 410 (1969).

96. *Illinois* v. *Gates*, 426 U.S. 318 (1982).

97. *Alabama* v. *White*, 110 S.Ct. 2412 (1990).

98. Ibid., at 2417.

99. *U.S. Dept. of Justice* v. *Landano*, 113 S.Ct. 2014, 124 L. Ed. 2d 84 (1993).

100. Kevin Johnson and Gary Fields, "Jewell Investigation Unmasks FBI 'Tricks,'" *USA Today*, November 8, 1996, p. 13A.

101. Gary Fields, "FBI Admits Mistake in Jewell Case," *USA Today*, April 9, 1997, p. 2A.

102. *South Dakota* v. *Neville*, 103 S.Ct. 916 (1983).

103. *Brown* v. *Mississippi*, 297 U.S. 278 (1936).

104. *Ashcraft* v. *Tennessee*, 322 U.S. 143 (1944).

105. *Chambers* v. *Florida*, 309 U.S. 227 (1940).

106. Ibid.

107. *Leyra* v. *Denno*, 347 U.S. 556 (1954).

108. Ibid.

109. *Arizona* v. *Fulminante*, 111 S.Ct. 1246 (1991).

110. *Chapman* v. *California*, 386 U.S. 18 (1967).

111. *Escobedo* v. *Illinois*, 378 U.S. 478 (1964).

112. *Edwards* v. *Arizona*, 451 U.S. 477, 101 S.Ct. 1880, 68 L. Ed. 2d 378, (1981).

113. *Arizona* v. *Roberson*, 486 U.S. 675, 108 S.Ct. 2093 (1988).

114. *Davis* v. *United States*, 114 S.Ct. 2350 (1994).

115. *Miranda* v. *Arizona*, 384 U.S. 436 (1966).

116. Ibid.

117. *Moran* v. *Burbine*, 475 U.S. 412, 421 (1986).

118. Ibid.

119. *Colorado* v. *Spring*, 479 U.S. 564, 107 S.Ct. 851 (1987).

120. "Immigrants Get Civil Rights," *USA Today*, June 11, 1992, p. 1A.

121. *Brewer* v. *Williams*, 430 U.S. 387.

122. *Nix* v. *Williams*, 104 S.Ct. 2501 (1984).

123. *New York* v. *Quarles*, 104 S.Ct. 2626, 81 L.Ed. 2d 550 (1984).

124. *Colorado* v. *Connelly*, 107 S.Ct. 515, 93 L.Ed. 2d 473 (1986).

125. Ibid.

126. *Kuhlmann* v. *Wilson*, 477 U.S., 106 S.Ct. 2616 (1986).

127. *Illinois* v. *Perkins*, 495 U.S. 292 (1990).

128. *Rock* v. *Zimmerman*, 543 F. Supp. 179 (M.D. Pa. 1982).

129. Ibid.

130. See *Oregon* v. *Mathiason*, 429 U.S. 492, 97 S.Ct. 711 (1977).

131. *South Dakota* v. *Neville*, 103 S.Ct. 916 (1983).

132. *Arizona* v. *Mauro*, 107 S.Ct. 1931, 95 L.Ed. 2d 458 (1987).

133. *Doyle* v. *Ohio*, 426 U.S. 610 (1976).

134. *Brecht* v. *Abrahamson*, 113 S.Ct. 1710, 123 L. Ed. 2d 353 (1993).

135. *Citing Kotteakos* v. *United States*, 328 U.S. 750 (1946).

136. *Hayes* v. *Florida*, 470 U.S.811, 105 S.Ct. 1643 (1985).

137. *Winston* v. *Lee*, 470 U.S.753, 105 S.Ct. 1611 (1985).

138. *Schmerber* v. *California*, 384 U.S. 757 (1966).

139. *U.S.* v. *Montoya de Hernandez*, 473 U.S. 531, 105 S.Ct. 3304 (1985).

140. Ibid.

141. *Olmstead* v. *U.S.*, 277 U.S. 438 (1928).

142. *On Lee* v. *U.S.*, 343 U.S. 747 (1952).

143. *Lopez* v. *U.S.*, 373 U.S. 427 (1963).

144. *Berger* v. *New York*, 388 U.S. 41 (1967).

145. *Katz* v. *U.S.*, 389 U.S. 347 (1967).

146. *Lee* v. *Florida*, 392 U.S. 378 (1968).

147. Federal Communications Act, 1934.

148. *U.S.* v. *White*, 401 U.S. 745 (1971).

149. Ibid.

150. *United States* v. *Scott*, 436 U.S. 128 (1978).

151. For more information, see *FBI Law Enforcement Bulletin* (June 1987), p. 25.

152. The Electronic Communications Privacy Act, 1986.

153. For more information on the ECPA, see Robert A. Fiatal, "The Electronic Communications Privacy Act: Addressing Today's Technology," *FBI Law Enforcement Bulletin* (April 1988), pp. 24–30.

154. Pub. L. 103–414.

155. Federal Bureau of Investigation, "Notice: Implementation of The Communications Assistance for Law Enforcement Act," February 23, 1995.

156. Public Law 104, 110 Statute 56.

157. Title 47, U.S.C.A., Section 223(a)(1)(B)(ii) (Supp. 1997).

158. *Reno* v. *ACLU* (1997), No. 96–511. Decided June 26, 1997.

The Rights of the Accused Before the Court

Common law, constitutional, and humanitarian rights of the accused:

* The Right to a Speedy Trial

* The Right to Legal Counsel

* The Right Against Self-incrimination

* The Right Not to Be Tried Twice for the Same Offense

* The Right to Know the Charges

* The Right to Cross-examine Witnesses

* The Right to Speak and Present Witnesses

* The Right Against Excessive Bail

The individual rights listed must be effectively balanced against these community concerns:

* Conviction of the Guilty

* Exoneration of the Innocent

* The Imposition of Appropriate Punishment

* Protection of Society

* Efficient and Cost-effective Procedures

* Seeing Justice Done

How does our system of justice work toward balance?

part 3
ADJUDICATION

Equal justice under law

The well-known British philosopher and statesman Benjamin Disraeli (1804–1881) once defined justice as "truth in action." The study of criminal case processing by courts at all levels provides perhaps the best opportunity available to us from within the criminal justice system to observe what should ideally be "truth in action." The courtroom search for truth, which is characteristic of criminal trials, pits the resources of the accused against those of the state. The ultimate outcome of such procedures, say advocates of our adversarial-based system of trial practice, should be both truth and justice.

Others are not so sure. British novelist William McIlvanney (1936–   ) once wrote: "Who thinks the law has anything to do with justice? It's what we have because we can't have justice." Indeed, many critics of the present system claim that courts at all levels have become so concerned with procedure and with sets of formalized rules that they have lost sight of truth.

The chapters which comprise this section of *Criminal Justice Today* provide an overview of American courts, including their history and present structure, and examine the multifaceted roles played by both professional and lay courtroom participants. Sentencing—the practice whereby juries recommend and judges impose sanctions on convicted offenders—is covered in the concluding chapter of this section. Whether American courts routinely uncover truth and therefore dispense justice or whether they are merely locked into a pattern of hollow procedure which does little other than mock the justice ideal will be for you to decide.

chapter 8

THE COURTS

There is no such thing as justice—in or out of court.

—CLARENCE DARROW
(1857–1938)

No person shall be held to answer for a capital or otherwise infamous crime, unless on a presentment or indictment of a grand jury...nor shall any person be subject for the same offense to be twice put in jeopardy of life or limb; nor shall be compelled in any criminal case to be a witness against himself, nor be deprived of life, liberty, or property, without due process of law...

—FIFTH AMENDMENT TO THE
U.S. CONSTITUTION

After years of twisting the Constitution into a pretzel, handcuffing cops, and drooling over the rights of killers and rapists, America's federal judges have suddenly discovered violent crime, and they're fretting that it might come to their neighborhood soon.

—*WASHINGTON TIMES* EDITORIAL

appeal
appellate jurisdiction
bail bond
circuit courts
competency to stand trial
court administrator
court of last resort
danger laws
dispute resolution center

federal court system
impeachment
initial appearance
judicial review
jurisdiction
lower court
nolo contendere
original jurisdiction
plea

plea bargaining
pretrial release
property bond
release on recognizance
state court systems
trial court
trial *de novo*
writ of *certiorari*

U.S. v. *Montalvo-Murillo*
County of Riverside (CA) v.
    McLaughlin

Keeney v. *Tamayo-Reyes*
Herrera v. *Collins*
Minnick v. *Mississippi*

United States v. *Alvarez-
    Machain*

Introduction

In January of 1997 two dynamite bombs exploded in downtown Vallejo, California, a small city of slightly more than 100,000 people located at the mouth of the Napa River in Solano County. One bomb damaged automatic teller machines at a Wells Fargo bank, while the other blew a hole in the side of the Solano County courthouse. About the same time, authorities found 30 sticks of dynamite in a backpack lying against the wall of a public library where some police evidence was kept. A few days later police arrested Kevin Lee Robinson, 29, an ex-convict who was scheduled to soon be tried on drug-related charges and accused him and five other men of the bombings. According to investigators, Robinson planned the bombings in order to derail the county's criminal justice system. Bombing the courthouse, said detectives, was an attempt by Robinson to prevent his being tried under the state's three-strikes-and-you're-out law—which could have meant a sentence of life in prison for the already twice-convicted Robinson.[1] Following the arrest, police confiscated 500 pounds of dynamite.

Robinson's alleged plan highlights the central role played by our nation's courts in the criminal justice process. Without courts to decide issues of guilt or innocence and to impose sentence on those convicted of crimes, the activities of law enforcement officials would become meaningless, and the nation's correctional facilities would serve little purpose.

There are many different kinds of courts in the United States. But courts at all levels dispense justice on a daily basis and work to ensure that all official actors in the justice system carry out their duties in recognition of the rule of law. At many points in this volume, and in three specific chapters (Chapter 7, *Policing-Legal Aspects*; Chapter 12, *Prisons and Jails*; and Chapter 11, *Probation, Parole, and Community Corrections*), we take a close look at court precedents which have defined the legality of enforcement efforts and correctional action. In Chapter 4, *Criminal Law*, we explored the lawmaking function of courts. This chapter, in order to provide readers with a picture of how courts work, will describe the American court system at both the state and federal levels. Then in Chapter 9 we will look at the roles of courtroom actors—from attorneys to victims and from jurors to judges—and examine each of the steps in a criminal trial.

Federal Court System
The three-tiered structure of federal courts, involving U.S. district courts, U.S. courts of appeal, and the U.S. Supreme Court.

State Court Systems
State judicial structures. Most states have at least three court levels, generally referred to as trial courts, appellate courts, and a state supreme court.

American Court History

Two types of courts function within the American criminal justice system: (1) state courts and (2) federal courts. Figure 8–1 outlines the structure of today's **federal court system**, while Figure 8–2 diagrams a typical **state court system**. This dual court system is the result of general agreement among the nation's founders about the need for individual states to retain significant legislative authority and judicial autonomy separate from federal control.

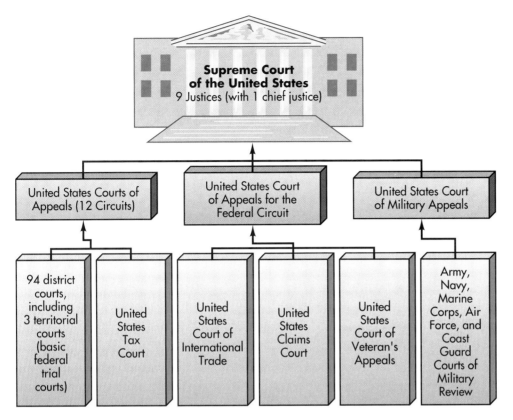

FIGURE 8–1 The structure of federal courts.

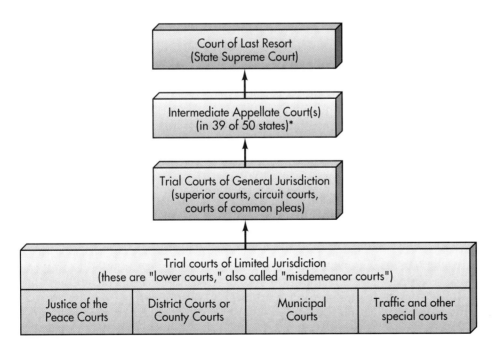

*The number of appellate courts continues to grow. As of 1996, all but 12 states had such a court, with one (North Dakota) operating one on a temporary basis to assist in handling the rising appellate caseload.

FIGURE 8–2 A typical state court system.

Although often criticized, today's criminal trial courts provide a civilized forum for exploring a variety of conflicting claims about guilt and innocence. In this old engraving dating from the time of the Spanish Inquisition, a "suspect" undergoes fire torture on "the wheel" while being questioned about alleged heretical activities. *Bettmann*

Under this concept, the United States developed as a relatively loose federation of semi-independent provinces. New states joining the union were assured of limited federal intervention into local affairs. Under this arrangement, state legislatures were free to create laws, and state court systems were needed to hear cases in which violations of those laws occurred. The last 200 years have seen a slow ebbing of states' rights relative to the power of the federal government. Even today, however, state courts do not hear cases involving alleged violations of federal law nor do federal courts involve themselves in deciding issues of state law, unless there is a conflict between local or state statutes and federal constitutional guarantees. When that happens, however, claimed violations of federal due process guarantees—especially those found in the Bill of Rights—can provide the basis for appeals made to federal courts by offenders convicted in state court systems.

This chapter describes both federal and state court systems in terms of their historical development, **jurisdiction**, and current structure. Because it is within state courts that the large majority of criminal cases originate, we turn our attention first to them.

State Court Development

Each of the original American colonies had its own court system for resolving disputes, both civil and criminal. As early as 1629 the Massachusetts Bay Colony had created a "General Court," composed of the governor, his deputy, 18 assistants, and 118 elected officials. The General Court was a combined legislature/court that made laws, held trials, and imposed sentences.[2] By 1639, as the colony grew, county courts were created, and the General Court took on as its primary job—the hearing of appeals—retaining original jurisdiction only in cases involving "tryalls of life, limm, or banishment..." (and divorce).[3]

Pennsylvania began its colonial existence with the belief that "every man could serve as his own lawyer."[4] The Pennsylvania system utilized "common peacemakers" who served as referees in disputes. Parties to a dispute, including criminal suspects, could plead their case before a common peacemaker they had chosen. The decision of the peacemaker was binding upon the parties. Although the Pennsylvania referee system ended in 1766, lower-level judges, called magistrates in many other jurisdictions, are still referred to as "justices of the peace" in Pennsylvania and a few other states.

Prior to 1776 all American colonies had established fully functioning court systems. The practice of law, however, was substantially inhibited by a lack of trained lawyers. A number

Jurisdiction The territory, subject matter, or persons over which lawful authority may be exercised by a court or other justice agency, as determined by statute or constitution.

of the early colonies even displayed a strong reluctance to recognize the practice of law as a profession. A Virginia statute, for example, enacted in 1645, provided for the removal of "mercenary attorneys" from office and prohibited the practice of law for a fee. Most other colonies retained strict control over the number of authorized barristers (another name for lawyers) by requiring formal training in English law schools and appointment by the governor. New York, which provided for the appointment of "counselors at law," permitted a total of only 41 lawyers to practice law between 1695 and 1769[5]—in large part due to the distrust of formally trained attorneys which was then widespread.

The tenuous status of lawyers in the colonies was highlighted by the 1735 New York trial of John Zenger. Zenger was editor of the *New York Journal*, a newspaper, and was accused of slandering then-governor Cosby. When Cosby threatened to disbar any lawyer who defended Zenger, he hired Pennsylvania lawyer Andrew Hamilton who was immune to the governor's threats because he was from out of state.[6]

Following the American Revolution, colonial courts provided the organizational basis for the growth of fledgling state court systems. Since there had been considerable diversity in the structure of colonial courts, state courts were anything but uniform. Initially, most states made no distinction between **original jurisdiction** (which can be defined as the lawful authority of a court to hear cases which arise within a specified geographic area or which involve particular kinds of law violations) and **appellate jurisdiction** (that is, the lawful authority of a court to review a decision made by a lower court). Many, in fact, had no provisions for appeal. Delaware, for example, did not allow for appeals in criminal cases until 1897. States which did permit appeals often lacked any established appellate courts and sometimes used state legislatures for that purpose.

By the late 1800s a dramatic increase in population, growing urbanization, the settlement of the West, and other far-reaching changes in the American way of life led to a tremendous increase in civil litigation and criminal arrests. Legislatures tried to keep pace with the rising tide of suits. They created a multiplicity of courts at the trial, appellate, and supreme court levels, calling them by a diversity of names and assigning them functions which sometimes bore little resemblance to like-sounding courts in neighboring states. City courts, which were limited in their jurisdiction by community boundaries, arose to handle the special problems of urban life, such as disorderly conduct, property disputes, and the enforcement of restrictive and regulatory ordinances. Other tribunals, such as juvenile courts, developed to handle special kinds of problems or special clients. Some, like magistrates' or small claims courts, handled only petty disputes and minor law violations. Still others, like traffic courts, were very narrow in focus. The result was a patchwork quilt of hearing bodies, some only vaguely resembling modern notions of a trial court.

State court systems did, however, have several models to follow during their development. One was the New York State Field Code of 1848, which was eventually copied by most other states. The Field Code clarified jurisdictional claims and specified matters of court procedure, but was later amended so extensively that its usefulness as a model dissolved. Another court system model was provided by the federal Judiciary Act of 1789 and later by the federal Reorganization Act of 1801. States which followed the federal model developed a three-tiered structure of (1) trial courts of limited jurisdiction, (2) trial courts of general jurisdiction, and (3) appellate courts.

Original Jurisdiction The authority of a given court over a specific geographic area or over particular types of cases. We say that a case falls "within the jurisdiction" of the court.

Appellate Jurisdiction The lawful authority of a court to review a decision made by a lower court.

State Court Systems Today

The three-tiered federal model was far from a panacea, however. Within the structure it provided, many local and specialized courts proliferated. Traffic courts, magistrates' courts, municipal courts, recorders' courts, probate courts, and courts held by justices of the peace were but a few which functioned at the lower levels. A movement toward simplification of state court structures, led primarily by the American Bar Association and the American Judicature Society, began in the early 1900s. Proponents of state court reform sought to unify redundant courts, which held overlapping jurisdiction. Most reform-minded thinkers suggested a uniform model for states everywhere which would build upon (1) a centralized court structure composed of a clear hierarchy of trial and appellate courts, (2) the consolidation of numerous lower-level courts holding overlapping jurisdiction, and (3) a centralized state court authority which would be responsible for budgeting, financing, and management of all courts within a state.

A criminal trial in progress. Courts have often been called "the fulcrum of the criminal justice system." *Michal Heron, Woodfin Camp & Associates*

The court reform movement is still ongoing today. Although it has made a substantial number of inroads in many states, there are still many differences between and among state court systems. Reform states, which early on embraced the reform movement, are now characterized by streamlined judicial systems consisting of precisely conceived trial courts of limited and general jurisdiction, supplemented by one or two appellate court levels. Nonreform, or traditional, states retain judicial systems which are a conglomeration of multilevel and sometimes redundant courts with poorly defined jurisdiction. Even in nonreform states, however, most criminal courts can be classified within the three-story structure of two trial court echelons and an appellate tier.

State Trial Courts

Trial courts are where criminal cases begin. The trial court conducts arraignments, sets bail, takes pleas, and conducts trials. (We will discuss each of these separate functions in more depth later in the chapter.) If the defendant is found guilty (or pleads guilty), the trial court imposes sentence. Trial courts of limited or special jurisdiction are also called lower courts. Lower courts are authorized to hear only less serious criminal cases, usually involving misdemeanors, or to hear special types of cases, such as traffic violations, family disputes, small claims, and so on. Courts of limited jurisdiction, which are depicted in TV shows like *Night Court* and *Family Court*, rarely hold jury trials, depending instead on the hearing judge to make determinations of both fact and law. At the lower–court level a detailed record of the proceedings is not maintained. Case files will only include information on the charge, the plea, the finding of the court, and the sentence. All but six of the United States make use of trial courts of limited jurisdiction.[7]

Lower courts are much less formal than are courts of general jurisdiction. In an intriguing analysis of court characteristics, Thomas Henderson[8] found that misdemeanor courts process cases according to what he called a "decisional model." The decisional model, said Henderson, is informal, personal, and decisive. It depends upon the quick resolution of relatively uncomplicated issues of law and fact.

Trial courts of general jurisdiction, called variously high courts, circuit courts, or superior courts, are authorized to hear any criminal case. In many states they also provide the first appellate level for courts of limited jurisdiction. In most cases, superior courts offer defendants whose cases originated in lower courts the chance for a new trial instead of a review of the record of the earlier hearing. When a new trial is held, it is referred to as **trial *de novo*.**

Trial *de Novo* Literally, a new trial. The term is applied to cases which are retried on appeal, as opposed to those which are simply reviewed on the record.

Henderson[9] describes courts of general jurisdiction according to a procedural model. Such courts, he says, make full use of juries, prosecutors, defense attorneys, witnesses, and all the other actors we usually associate with American courtrooms. The procedural model, which is far more formal than the decisional model, is fraught with numerous court appearances to ensure that all of a defendant's due process rights are protected. The procedural model makes for a long, expensive, relatively impersonal, and highly formal series of legal maneuvers involving many professional participants—a fact clearly seen in the widely televised 1995 double-murder trial of famed athlete and television personality O. J. Simpson.

Trial courts of general jurisdiction operate within a fact-finding framework called the adversarial process. That process pits the interests of the state, represented by prosecutors, against the professional skills and abilities of defense attorneys. The adversarial process is not a free-for-all, but is, rather, constrained by procedural rules specified in law and sustained through tradition.

State Appellate Courts

Most states today have an appellate division, consisting of an intermediate appellate court (often called the Court of Appeals) and a high-level appellate court (generally termed the state supreme court). High-level appellate courts are referred to as courts of last resort, to indicate that no other appellate route remains to a defendant within the state court system once the high court rules on a case. All states have supreme courts, although only 39 have intermediate appellate courts.[10]

An **appeal** by a convicted defendant asks that a higher court review the actions of a lower one. Courts within the appellate division, once they accept an appeal, do not conduct a new trial. Instead they provide a review of the case on the record. In other words, appellate courts examine the written transcript of lower-court hearings to ensure that those proceedings were carried out fairly and in accordance with proper procedure and state law. They may also allow brief oral arguments to be made by attorneys for both sides and will generally consider other briefs or information filed by the appellant (the party initiating the appeal) or appellee (the side opposed to the appeal). State statutes generally require that sentences of death or life imprisonment be automatically reviewed by the state supreme court.

Most convictions are affirmed upon appeal. Occasionally, however, an appellate court will determine that the trial court erred in allowing certain kinds of evidence to be heard or that it failed to interpret properly the significance of a relevant statute. When that happens, the verdict of the trial court will be reversed, and the case may be remanded, or sent back for a new trial. Where a conviction is overturned by an appellate court because of constitutional issues, or where a statute is determined to be invalid, the state usually has recourse to the state supreme court, or the U.S. Supreme Court (when an issue of federal law is involved, as when a state court has ruled a federal law unconstitutional).

Defendants who are not satisfied with the resolution of their case within a state court system may attempt an appeal to the U.S. Supreme Court. For such an appeal to have any chance of being heard, it must be based upon claimed violations of the defendant's rights as guaranteed under federal law or the U.S. Constitution. Under certain circumstances federal district courts may also provide a path of relief for state defendants who can show that their federal constitutional rights have been violated. However, in the 1993 case of *Keeney* v. *Tamayo-Reyes*,[11] the U.S. Supreme Court ruled that a "respondent is entitled to a federal evidentiary hearing [only] if he can show cause for his failure to develop the facts in the state-court proceedings and actual prejudice resulting from that failure, or if he can show that a fundamental miscarriage of justice would result from failure to hold such a hearing." Justice Byron White, writing for the Court, said "[i]t is hardly a good use of scarce judicial resources to duplicate fact-finding in federal court merely because a petitioner has negligently failed to take advantage of opportunities in state court proceedings." Likewise, in *Herrera* v. *Collins* (1993),[12] the Court ruled that new evidence of innocence is no reason for a federal court to order a new state trial if constitutional grounds are lacking. In *Herrera*, where the defendant was under a Texas death sentence for the murder of two police officers, the Court said: "[w]here a defendant has been afforded a fair trial and convicted of the offense for which he was charged, the constitutional presumption of innocence disappears.... Thus, claims of actual innocence based on newly discovered evidence have never been held [to be] grounds for relief, absent an independent constitutional violation occurring in the course of the underlying state criminal proceedings. To allow a federal court to grant relief...would in

Appeal Generally, the request that a court with appellate jurisdiction review the judgment, decision, or order of a lower court and set it aside (reverse it) or modify it.

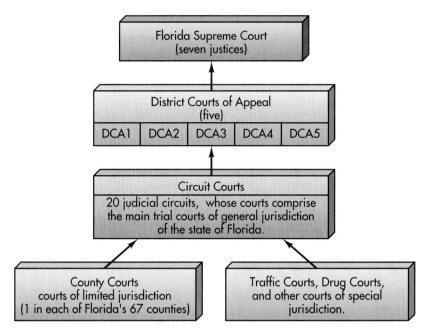

FIGURE 8–3 The court system of the state of Florida.

effect require a new trial 10 years after the first trial, not because of any constitutional violation at the first trial, but simply because of a belief that in light of his new found evidence a jury might find him not guilty at a second trial." The *Keeney* and *Herrera* decisions have had the effect of severely limiting access by state defendants to federal courts.

The Florida Court System: An Example

Florida provides an example of a reform state which has streamlined the structure of its courts. Prior to a 1973 reorganization, Florida had more different kinds of trial courts than any state except New York.[13] Today the Florida system, which is diagrammed in Figure 8–3, consists of one state supreme court, five district courts of appeal, trial courts of general jurisdiction called "circuit courts," and county courts of limited jurisdiction which hear cases involving petty offenses and civil disputes involving $15,000 or less. County courts are often called "people's courts" in Florida.

Florida's supreme court, headquartered in the Supreme Court Building in Tallahassee, is composed of seven justices, at least four of whom must agree on a decision in each case. By a majority vote of the justices, one of the justices is elected to serve as chief justice (an office which is rotated every two years). The supreme court must review final orders imposing death sentences, district court decisions declaring a state statute or provisions of the state constitution invalid, and actions of statewide agencies relating to public utilities. At its discretion, the court may also review any decision of a district court of appeal that declares invalid a state statute, interprets a provision of the state or federal constitution, affects a class of state officers, or directly conflicts with a decision of another district court or of the state supreme court on a question of law.

The bulk of trial court decisions which are appealed are never heard by the supreme court. Rather, they are reviewed by three-judge panels of the district courts of appeal. Florida's constitution provides that the legislature shall divide the state into appellate court districts and that there shall be a district court of appeal (DCA) serving each district. There are five such districts, which are headquartered in Tallahassee, Lakeland, Miami, West Palm Beach, and Daytona Beach. Fifteen judges serve in the first DCA, 14 in the second, 11 in the third, 12 in the fourth, and 9 in the fifth. Like supreme court justices, district court judges serve terms of six years and are eligible for successive terms under a merit retention vote of the electors in their districts. In each district court, a chief judge, who is selected by other district court judges, is responsible for the administrative duties of the court.

The jurisdiction of the district courts of appeal extends to appeals from judgments or orders of trial courts and to the review of certain nonfinal orders. By law, district courts in

Florida have been granted the power to review most actions taken by state agencies. As a general rule, decisions of the district courts of appeal represent the final appellate review of litigated cases. A person who is displeased with a district court's express decision may ask for review in the Florida supreme court or in the United States Supreme Court, but neither tribunal is required to accept the case for further hearing.

The majority of jury trials in Florida take place before one judge sitting as judge of a circuit court. The circuit courts are sometimes referred to as courts of general jurisdiction, in recognition of the fact that most criminal and civil cases originate at this level. Florida's constitution provides that a circuit court shall be established to serve each judicial circuit established by the legislature, of which there are 20. Within each circuit, there may be any number of judges, depending upon the population and caseload of the particular area. At present, the most judges sit in the Eleventh Judicial Circuit, and the fewest judges sit in the Sixteenth Judicial Circuit. To be eligible for the office of circuit judge, a person must be a resident elector of Florida and must have been admitted to the practice of law in the state for the preceding five years. Circuit court judges are elected by the voters of the various circuits. Circuit court judges serve six-year terms and are subject to the same disciplinary standards and procedures as Supreme Court justices and district court judges. A chief judge is chosen from among the circuit judges in each judicial circuit to carry out administrative responsibilities for all trial courts (both circuit and county courts) within the circuit.

Circuit courts have general trial jurisdiction over matters not assigned by statute to the county courts and also hear appeals from county court cases. Thus, circuit courts are simultaneously the highest trial courts and the lowest appellate courts in Florida's judicial system. The trial jurisdiction of circuit courts includes, among other matters, original jurisdiction over civil disputes involving more than $15,000; controversies involving the estates of decedents, minors, and persons adjudicated to be incompetent; cases relating to juveniles; criminal prosecutions for all felonies; tax disputes; and actions to determine the title and boundaries of real property.

County courts represent the lowest trial court level in Florida. State constitution establishes a county court in each of Florida's 67 counties. The number of judges in each county court varies with the population and caseload of the county. To be eligible for the office of county judge, a person must be a resident of the county and must have been a member of the Florida Bar for five years; in counties with a population of 40,000 or less, a person must only be a member of the Florida Bar. County judges serve four-year terms, and they are subject to the same disciplinary standards, as all other judicial officers. The trial jurisdiction of county courts is established by statute. The jurisdiction of county courts extends to civil disputes involving $15,000 or less. The majority of nonjury trials in Florida take place before one judge sitting as a judge of the county court. The county courts are sometimes referred to as "the people's courts," probably because a large part of the court's work involves high-volume citizen disputes, such as traffic offenses, less serious criminal matters (misdemeanors), and relatively small monetary disputes.

Other, special purpose, courts do exist in the state. In 1989, for example, the Florida legislature authorized the establishment of a Civil Traffic Infraction Hearing Officer Program to free up county judges for other county court work and for circuit court assignments. Initially, participation in the program was limited to those counties with a civil traffic infraction caseload of 20,000 hearings, but the threshold was subsequently lowered to 15,000. The 1990–1991 legislature expanded the magistrate's jurisdiction to include accidents resulting in property damage (not bodily injury). At the end of the year-long pilot project, the Florida supreme court recommended, and the legislature approved, the program for continuation on a local option basis.

State Court Administration

To function efficiently, courts require uninterrupted funding, adequate staffing, trained support personnel, a well-managed case flow, and coordination between levels and among jurisdictions. To oversee these and other aspects of judicial management, every state today has its own mechanism for court administration. Most make use of **state court administrators** who manage these operational functions.

The first state court administrator was appointed in New Jersey in 1948.[14] Although other states were initially slow to follow the New Jersey lead, increased federal funding for crimi-

The judicial Power of the United States shall be vested in one supreme Court, and in such inferior Courts as the Congress may from time to time ordain and establish.
—Article III, U.S. Constitution

State Court Administrators Coordinating personnel who assist with case flow management, budgeting of operating funds, and court docket administration.

nal justice administration during the 1970s and a growing realization that some form of coordinated management was necessary for effective court operation eventually led most states to create similar administrative offices.

Florida, discussed earlier, created its Office of the State Courts Administrator (OSCA) on July 1, 1972. Florida's OSCA is divided into three sections with a deputy state courts administrator heading each one. The Information Systems and Program Support section includes Research; Planning and Court Services; Alternative Dispute Resolution; and Information Systems Services. The Administrative Services section includes Finance and Accounting, Budget, Personnel Services, and General Services. The Legal Affairs and Education section includes Legal Affairs, Judiciary Education Services, and various commissions and committees authorized by the legislature and the court. As in many other states, the state courts administrator in Florida serves as the liaison between the court system and the legislative branch, the executive branch, the auxiliary agencies of the court, and national court research and planning agencies.

The following tasks are typical of state court administrators across the country today[15]

1. The preparation, presentation, and monitoring of a budget for the state court system
2. The analysis of case flows and backlogs to determine where additional resources such as judges, prosecutors, and other court personnel are needed
3. The collection and publication of statistics describing the operation of state courts
4. Efforts to streamline the flow of cases through individual courts and the system as a whole
5. Service as a liaison between state legislatures and the court system
6. The development and/or coordination of requests for federal and other outside funding
7. The management of state court personnel, including promotions for support staff and the handling of retirement and other benefits packages for court employees
8. The creation and the coordination of plans for the training of judges and other court personnel (in conjunction with local chief judges and supreme court justices)
9. The assignment of judges to judicial districts (especially in states that use rotating judgeships)
10. The administrative review of payments to legal counsel for indigent defendants

At the federal level, the federal court system is administered by the Administrative Office of the United State Courts (AO), located in Washington, D.C. The AO was created by Congress in 1939 and prepares the budget and legislative agenda for federal courts. It also performs audits of court accounts, manages funds for the operation of federal courts, compiles and publishes statistics on the volume and type of business conducted by the courts, and recommends plans and strategies to efficiently manage court business.

Dispute Resolution Centers

Dispute Resolution Centers Informal hearing infrastructures designed to mediate interpersonal disputes without need for the more formal arrangements of criminal trial courts.

Some communities have begun to recognize that it is possible to resolve at least minor disputes without the need for formal court hearings. **Dispute resolution centers**, which function to hear victim's claims of minor wrongs, such as passing bad checks, trespassing, shoplifting, and petty theft, function today in over 200 locations throughout the country.[16] Frequently staffed by volunteer mediators, such programs work to resolve disagreements (in which minor criminal offenses might otherwise be charged) without the need to assign blame. Dispute resolution programs began in the early 1970s, with the earliest being the Community Assistance Project in Chester, Pennsylvania; the Columbus, Ohio, Night Prosecutor Program; and the Arbitration as an Alternative Program in Rochester, New York. Following the lead of these programs, the U.S. Department of Justice helped promote the development of three experimental "Neighborhood Justice Centers" in Los Angeles, Kansas City, and Atlanta. Each center accepted both minor civil and criminal cases.

Mediation centers are often closely integrated with the formal criminal justice process and may substantially reduce the caseload of lower-level courts. Some centers are, in fact, run by the courts and work only with court-ordered referrals. Others are semiautonomous but may be dependent upon courts for endorsement of their decisions; others function with complete autonomy. Rarely, however, do dispute resolution programs entirely supplant the formal criminal justice mechanism, and defendants who appear before a community mediator may also later be charged with a crime.

Evaluating Courts

A few years ago the Bureau of Justice Statistics published *Performance Measures for the Criminal Justice System*, a collection of discussion papers produced by the BJS-Princeton Project group. The papers represent the best official effort to date to identify performance goals and associated measures useful in assessing the day-to-day operations of criminal justice agencies.

Following the lead of the National Center for State Courts, the Project identified, among others, the following goals and performance indicators applicable to trial courts:

Goals	Performance Indicators
Standard 1. Access to justice	
1.1 Public proceedings	Proceedings and other business are openly conducted.
1.2 Safety, accessibility, and convenience	Court facilities are safe, convenient, and accessible.
1.3 Effective participation	All who appear before the court are given the opportunity to participate
1.4 Courtesy, responsiveness, and respect	effectively, without undue hardship or inconvenience.
Standard 2. Expeditiousness and Timeliness	
2.1 Case processing	The court processes cases in a timely manner.
2.2 Compliance with schedules	The court provides reports and information according to schedules and
2.3 Prompt implementation of law and procedure	responds to requests for information in a way which assures their effective use.
Standard 3. Equity, fairness, and integrity	
3.1 Fair and reliable judicial process	Procedures adhere to law, procedural rules, and established policies.
3.2 Juries	Jury lists are representative of the jurisdiction from which they are
3.3 Court decisions and actions	drawn.
3.4 Clarity	Trial courts take responsibility for the enforcement of their orders.
3.5 Responsibility for enforcement	Records of all court decisions and actions are accurate and properly
3.6 Production and preservation of records	preserved.
Standard 4. Independence and accountability	
4.1 Independence and comity	The court maintains institutional integrity.
4.2 Accountability for public resources	The court responsibly accounts for its resources.
4.3 Personnel practices and decisions	The court uses fair employment practices.
4.4 Public education	The court informs the community of its programs.
4.5 Response to change	The court anticipates new conditions and adjusts its operations accordingly.
Standard 5. Public trust and confidence	
5.1 Accessibility	The trial court and the justice it delivers are perceived by the public as
5.2 Expeditious, fair, and reliable court functions	acceptable.
	The public has trust and confidence in the court.
5.3 Judicial independence and accountability	The trial court is not perceived to be unduly influenced by other components of government.

Source: George F. Cole, "Performance Measures for Trial Courts, Prosecution, and Public Defense," in John J. DiIulio, Jr., et al., *Performance Measures for the Criminal Justice System: Discussion Papers from the BJS-Princeton Project* (Washington, D.C.: Bureau of Justice Statistics, October 1993).

Mediation centers have been criticized for the fact that they typically work only with minor offenses, thereby denying the opportunity for mediation to victims and offenders in more serious cases, and for the fact that they may be seen by defendants as just another form of criminal sanction, rather than as a true alternative to criminal justice system processing.[17] Other critiques claim that community dispute resolution centers do little other than provide a forum for shouting matches between the parties involved.

Justice in American Context

COMMON LAW COURTS—A GROWING FORM OF DISSENT?

In 1996, a standoff between self-proclaimed "Freemen" and federal agents in Montana focused attention on the common law court movement. So-called "common law courts" are the creation of radical right-wing groups, sometimes referred to as "common law activists," who claim that official government agencies, including the criminal justice system and especially state and federal courts, are fundamentally illegal and without official power. Common law courts bear no relationship to officially recognized government-sponsored criminal justice agencies. Advocates of common law courts deny the authority of state and federal governments and have established their own courts to enforce their own laws, which are loose and mostly self-serving interpretations of early English common law. They reject almost all state and federal legislation as illegal.

Leaders of the common law courts movement claim that such courts derive their power directly from the people. Their unbridled rejection of government-sponsored courts, and of all "official" criminal justice agencies, is based upon the claim that such organizations were unfairly established through fundamentally illegal legislation. They rarely "arrest" enemies of the people, however, and almost always conduct trials *in absentia* (without the "offender" present)—

and base their "decisions" on English common law tradition. Many of those "tried" are government officials or their representatives, and law enforcement agencies fear that common law courts will become truly dangerous if and when they attempt to carry out the "sentences" they impose.

Though common law courts remain loosely organized, their advocates have forged a "common law doctrine" intended to legitimize them. The doctrine is based on snippets taken from the Magna Carta, the Bible, the Constitution, and other sources. Here are a few excerpts from a popular "common law treatise" recently being circulated:

The Common Law was recognized by Our Founding Fathers and is the basis of all law in America today...The Common Law of the States of the United States is the Common Law of England adopted by the original Constitution of the United States...

[T]he Common Law of the States may not be modified, limited nor abrogated either by an act of the legislature (Congress or State Legislature) or by a ruling of some judge or by any county board of commissioners or any other servant to the people. Federal and state bureaucracies are constantly writing and presenting code, rules or statutes in an attempt to circumvent the original Common Law foundation of Our

Constitution. A major part of the problem that we are in is a result of these unlawful attempts by legislatures, judges and bureaucracies to modify or abrogate Common Law and thus Our Constitution...

Since an unconstitutional law is void, the general principles follow that it imposes no duties, confers no rights, creates no office, bestows no power or authority on anyone, affords no protection, and justifies no acts performed under it....

A void act cannot be legally consistent with a valid one. An unconstitutional law cannot operate to supersede any existing valid law. Indeed, insofar as a statute runs counter to the fundamental law of the land, it is superseded thereby.

No one is bound to obey an unconstitutional law and no courts are bound to enforce it. The Constitution guarantees the right of a freeholder to protect his property from Criminal Trespass. Civil law or equity law is the law of the ruler; Common Law is the law of the people...

Sources: "Common Law Activist Disrupts Court," United Press International wire services, April 13, 1996; and Howard Fisher and Dale Pond, "Our American Common Law," The Constitutional Common Law Library, Enfield, Conn., via the World Wide Web. Copyright © 1992–1995 Delta Spectrum Research. Reprinted with permission.

The Rise of the Federal Courts

As we have seen, state courts had their origins in early colonial arrangements. Federal courts, however, were created by the U.S. Constitution. Section 1 of Article III of the Constitution provides for the establishment of "one supreme Court, and...such inferior Courts as the Congress may from time to time ordain and establish." Article III, Section 2, specifies that such courts are to have jurisdiction over cases arising under the Constitution, federal laws, and treaties. Federal courts are also to settle disputes between states and to have jurisdiction in cases where one of the parties is a state.

Today's federal court system represents the culmination of a series of congressional mandates which have expanded the federal judicial infrastructure so that it can continue to carry out the duties envisioned by the Constitution. Notable federal statutes which have contributed to the present structure of the federal court system include the Judiciary Act of 1789, the Judiciary Act of 1925, and the Magistrate's Act of 1968.

As a result of constitutional mandates, congressional action, and other historical developments, today's federal judiciary consists of three levels: (1) U.S. district courts, (2) U.S. courts of appeals, and (3) the U.S. Supreme Court. Each is described in turn in the following sections.

Federal District Courts

The lowest level of the federal court system consists of 94 district courts located in the 50 states (except for the District of Wyoming, which includes the Montana and Idaho portions of Yellowstone National Park); Puerto Rico; the District of Columbia; and the U.S. territories of Guam, the Virgin Islands, and the Northern Mariana Islands. District courts are the trial courts of the federal judicial system. They have original jurisdiction over all cases involving alleged violations of federal statutes. Each state has at least one U.S. district court, and some, like New York and California, have as many as four. A district may itself be divided into divisions and may have several places where the court hears cases. As just discussed, district courts were first authorized by Congress through the 1789 Judiciary Act, which allocated one federal court to each state. Because of population increases over the years, new courts have been added in a number of states.

Nearly 650 district court judges staff federal district courts. District court judges are appointed by the president, confirmed by the Senate, and serve for life. An additional 369 full-time and 110 part-time magistrate judges (referred to as "U.S. magistrates" prior to 1990) serve the district court system and assist federal judges. Magistrate judges have the power to conduct arraignments and may set bail, issue warrants, and try minor offenders.[18]

U.S. district courts handle thousands of criminal cases per year. In 1997, for example, 50,363 criminal cases and 272,027 civil cases were filed in U.S. district courts.[19] Because some courts are much busier than others, the number of district court judges varies from a low of two in some jurisdictions to a high of 27 in others. During the past 20 years the number of cases handled by the entire federal district court system has grown exponentially. The hiring of new judges has not kept pace with the increase in caseload, and questions persist as to the quality of justice that can be delivered by overworked judges.

One of the most pressing issues facing district court judges is the fact that their pay, which at $133,600 in late 1998[20] placed them in the top 1% of income-earning Americans, is small compared to what most could earn in private practice. Many federal judges, however, made substantial amounts of money from private practice before assuming the bench, while others had income from investments or held family fortunes.

U.S. Courts of Appeals

The intermediate appellate courts in the federal judicial system are the courts of appeals.[21] Twelve of these courts have jurisdiction over cases from certain geographic areas. The Court of Appeals for the Federal Circuit has national jurisdiction over specific types of cases.

The U.S. Court of Appeals for the Federal Circuit and the 12 regional courts of appeals are often referred to as circuit courts. That is because early in the nation's history, the judges of the first courts of appeals visited each of the courts in one region in a particular sequence, traveling by horseback and riding "circuit." These courts of appeals review matters from the district courts of their geographical regions, the U.S. Tax Court, and from certain federal administrative agencies. A disappointed party in a district court usually has the right to have the case reviewed in the court of appeals for the circuit. Appeals court judges are appointed for life by the president with the advice and consent of the Senate. The First through Eleventh Circuits each include three or more states, as illustrated by Figure 8–4.

Each court of appeals consists of six or more judges, depending on the caseload of the courts. The judge who has served on the court the longest and who is under 65 years of age is designated as the chief judge and performs administrative duties in addition to hearing cases. The chief judge serves for a maximum term of seven years. Each court of appeals judge is appointed for life. There are 167 judges on the 12 regional courts of appeals.

The U.S. Court of Appeals for the District of Columbia, which is often called the Twelfth Circuit, hears cases arising in the District of Columbia and has appellate jurisdiction assigned by Congress in legislation concerning many departments of the federal government. The U.S. Court of Appeals for the Federal Circuit (in effect, the thirteenth circuit) was created in 1982 by the merging of the U.S. Court of Claims and the U.S. Court of Customs

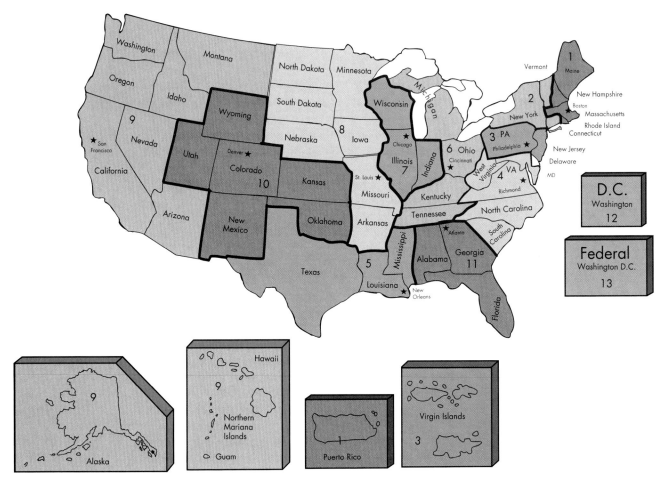

FIGURE 8–4 The 13 federal judicial circuits.

and Patent Appeals. The court hears appeals in cases from the U.S. Court of Federal Claims, the U.S. Court of International Trade, the U.S. Court of Veterans Appeals, the International Trade Commission, the Board of Contract Appeals, the Patent and Trademark Office, and the Merit Systems Protection Board. The Federal Circuit also hears appeals from certain decisions of the secretaries of the Department of Agriculture and the Department of Commerce and cases from district courts involving patents and minor claims against the federal government.

Federal appellate courts have mandatory jurisdiction over the decisions of district courts within their circuits. Mandatory jurisdiction means that U.S. courts of appeals are required to hear the cases brought to them. Criminal appeals from federal district courts are usually heard by panels of three judges sitting on a court of appeals rather than by all the judges of each circuit.

Federal appellate courts operate under the *Federal Rules of Appellate Procedure*, although each has also created its own separate Local Rules. Local Rules may mean that one circuit, such as the Second, will depend heavily upon oral arguments, while others may substitute written summary depositions in their place. Appeals generally fall into one of three categories:[22] (1) frivolous appeals, which have little substance, raise no significant new issues, and are generally quickly disposed of; (2) ritualistic appeals, which are brought primarily because of the demands of litigants, even though the probability of reversal is negligible; and (3) nonconsensual appeals, which entail major questions of law and policy and on which there is considerable professional disagreement among the courts and within the legal profession. The probability of reversal is, of course, highest in the case of nonconsensual appeals.

Because the Constitution guarantees a right to an appeal, federal circuit courts have found themselves facing an ever-increasing workload. Almost all appeals from federal district

Table 8-1 Justices of the U.S. Supreme Court

Justice	Entered Duty	Views
Chief Justice		
William H. Rehnquist[*]	January 1972	Very conservative
Associate Justices		
John Paul Stevens	December 1975	Moderate to liberal
Sandra Day O'Connor	September 1981	Moderate to conservative
Antonin Scalia	September 1986	Very conservative
Anthony M. Kennedy	February 1988	Conservative
David H. Souter	October 1990	Conservative
Clarence Thomas	October 1991	Conservative
Ruth Bader Ginsburg	August 1993	Moderate
Stephen Breyer	August 1994	Moderate

[*]Appointed Chief Justice September 1986.

courts go to the court of appeals serving the circuit in which the case was first heard. A defendant's right to appeal, however, has been interpreted to mean the right to one appeal. Hence, the U.S. Supreme Court need not necessarily hear the appeals of defendants who are dissatisfied with the decision of a federal appeals court.

The Supreme Court of the United States

At the apex of the federal court system stands the U.S. Supreme Court. The Supreme Court is located in Washington, D.C., across the street from the U.S. Capitol Building. The Court consists of nine justices, eight of whom are referred to as associate justices. The ninth presides over the Court as the chief justice of the United States. (See Table 8–1.) Supreme Court justices are nominated by the president, confirmed by the Senate, and serve for life. Lengthy terms of service are a tradition among justices. One of the earliest chief justices, John Marshall, served the Court for 34 years, from 1801 to 1835. The same was true of Justice Stephen J. Field who sat on the bench for 34 years, between 1863 and 1897. Justice Hugo Black passed the 34-year milestone, serving an additional month, before he retired in 1971. Justice William O. Douglas set a record for longevity on the bench, retiring in 1975 after 36 years and 6 months of service.

The Supreme Court of the United States wields immense power. The Court's greatest authority lies in its capacity for **judicial review** of lower court decisions and state and federal statute. By exercising its power of judicial review, the Court decides what laws and lower-court decisions are in keeping with the intent of the U.S. Constitution. The power of judicial review is not explicit in the Constitution, but was anticipated by its framers. In the *Federalist Papers*, which urged adoption of the Constitution, Alexander Hamilton wrote that, through the practice of judicial review, the Court would ensure that "the will of the whole people," as grounded in the Constitution, would be supreme over the "will of the legislature...," which might be subject to temporary whims.[23]

It was not until 1803, however, that the Court forcefully asserted its power of judicial review. In an opinion written for the case of *Marbury* v. *Madison* (1803),[24] Chief Justice John Marshall established the Court's authority as final interpreter of the U.S. Constitution, declaring that "It is emphatically the province of the judicial department to say what the law is...."

Judicial Review   The power of a court to review actions and decisions made by other agencies of government.

Increasing Complexity and the Supreme Court   The evolution of the U.S. Supreme Court provides one of the most dramatic examples of institutional development in American history. Sparsely described in the Constitution, the Court has grown from a handful of circuit-

Supreme Court Justice Ruth Bader Ginsburg, shown here with President Clinton, at her 1993 swearing-in ceremony, became the second woman to serve on the nation's highest court and the first Democratic nominee to assume the bench in 26 years.
Robert Trippett, Sipa Press

riding justices into a modern organization that wields tremendous legal power over all aspects of American life. Much of the Court's growth has been due to its increasing willingness to mediate fundamental issues of law and to act as a resort from arbitrary and capricious processing by the justice systems of the states and national government.

The *Marbury* decision established the Court as a mighty force in federal government by virtue of the power of judicial review. As we have discussed at length in Chapter 7, the Court began to apply that power during the 1960s to issues of crime and justice at the state and local levels. You may recall that the Court signaled its change in orientation in 1961 with the case of *Mapp* v. *Ohio*,[25] which extended the exclusionary rule to the states. Such extension, combined with the near-simultaneous end of the hands-off doctrine which had previously exempted state prison systems from Court scrutiny, placed the authority of the Court squarely over the activities of state criminal justice systems. From that time forward, the Court's workload became increasingly heavy and even today shows few signs of abatement.

The Supreme Court Today The Supreme Court has limited original jurisdiction and does not conduct trials except in disputes between states and some cases of attorney disbarment. The Court, rather, reviews the decisions of lower courts and may accept cases from both U.S. courts of appeals and state supreme courts. For a case to be heard, at least four justices must vote in favor of a hearing. When the Court agrees to hear a case, it will issue a **writ of certiorari** to a lower court, ordering it to send the records of the case forward for review. Once having granted *certiorari*, the justices can revoke the decision. In such cases a writ is dismissed by ruling it improvidently granted.

The U.S. Supreme Court may review any decision appealed to it which it decides is worthy of review. In fact, however, the Court elects to review only cases which involve a substantial federal question. Of approximately 5,000 requests for review received by the Court yearly, only about 200 are actually heard.

A term of the Supreme Court begins, by statute, on the first Monday in October and lasts until early July. The term is divided among sittings, when cases will be heard, and time for the writing and delivering of opinions. Between 22 and 24 cases will be heard at each sitting, with each side allotted 30 minutes for arguments before the justices. Intervening recesses

Writ of *Certiorari* A writ issued by an appellate court for the purpose of obtaining from a lower court the record of its proceedings in a particular case. In some states this writ is the mechanism for discretionary reviews. A request for review is made by petitioning for a writ of certiorari and granting of review is indicated by issuance of the writ.

The U.S. Supreme Court is the final interpreter of the U.S. Constitution and of laws passed by Congress. It is supposed to be above politics. Given the power of the Court, however, a number of observers have called it a "second legislature"—one which, with increasing frequency, steps into the middle of social issues and makes its own laws through the powerful process of judicial decree. Even the justices themselves are occasionally surprised by the Court's unchallenged ability to impose its unique interpretations upon the law. In 1990, for example, Justices Scalia and Rehnquist bemoaned what they saw as the Court's virtual and misguided independence from constitutional principles. In all too many instances, the Court, they claimed, has freely used its wide power to create ideologically driven and self-serving rules which bear little relationship to the Constitution. In a dissenting opinion in the 1990 case of *Minnick* v. *Mississippi*[1] Scalia and Rehnquist wrote: "Today's [ruling] is the latest stage of [prohibition] built upon [prohibition], producing a veritable fairyland castle of imagined constitutional restriction upon law enforcement. This newest tower, according to the Court, is needed to avoid "inconsistency with [a previous] rule,...which was needed

to protect Miranda's...right to have counsel present, which was needed to protect the right against compelled self-incrimination found—at last—in the Constitution."

If the Court does have an agenda, what kind of law is it making? During the 1970s and for part of the 1980s, the Court appeared to lean heavily in favor of the rights of criminal defendants and jealously guarded the concept of due process. By 1998, under the leadership of Chief Justice William Rehnquist, however, it had become clear that the Court has moved toward a much more conservative position. Some now charge that—with the death of Thurgood Marshall (1908–1993) and the retirements of liberal Justices William Brennan (1906–1997) and Harry Blackmun (1908–   )—a conservative juggernaut is running the Court. Many believe that a new emphasis on victims' rights and community interests is replacing the Court's historical concern with the rights of defendants. The sentiments of many individual rights advocates were captured in a *USA Today* editorial, which intoned, "The trend is worrisome. An innocent person is now far more vulnerable to harassment by police."[2]

Victims' rights advocates, however, are applauding the change. "Victims of crime and their families have a right to

a fair and speedy trial, too," says the Criminal Justice Legal Foundation's Kent Scheidegger. "The Supreme Court recognizes that. It is high time."[3] Still, more is to come. As one commentator said at the close of the Court's 1995 term, "If people think what [the Court] has done this term is bold, fasten your seat belts!"[4]

QUESTIONS FOR DISCUSSION

1. Do you agree with the assertion that the U.S. Supreme Court has begun a "swing to the right"? Why or why not?
2. Do you believe that the Supreme Court can be affected by politics or by the political leanings of the justices who serve it? If so, how?
3. Do you believe that it is possible to have a Supreme Court which is value-free and totally objective? If so, how?

[1]*Minnick* v. *Mississippi*, 111 S.Ct. 486 (1990).
[2]"Debate," *USA Today*, June 28, 1991, p. 14A.
[3]Kent S. Scheidegger, "Stop All the Fretting; Our Liberties Are Safe," *USA Today*, June 28, 1991, p. 14A.
[4]Tony Mauro, "Court's Move to the Right Confirmed," *USA Today*, June 27, 1995, p. 1A.

allow justices time to study arguments and supporting documentation and to work on their opinions.

Decisions rendered by the Supreme Court are rarely unanimous. Instead, opinions that a majority of the Court's justices agree upon become the judgment of the Court. Justices who agree with the Court's judgment, but for a different reason or because they feel that they have some new light to shed on a particular legal issue involved in the case, write concurring opinions. Justices who do not agree with the decision of the Court write dissenting opinions. Those dissenting opinions may offer new possibilities for successful appeals made at a later date.

Ideas for Change   Increasing caseloads at the federal appellate court level, combined with the many requests for Supreme Court review, have led to proposals to restructure the federal appellate court system. In 1973, a study group appointed by then-Chief Justice Burger suggested the creation of a National Court of Appeals, which would serve as a kind of "mini-Supreme Court."[26] Under the proposal, the National Court of Appeals would be staffed on a

Chambers of the United States
Supreme Court in Washington, D.C.
Doug Mills, AP/Wide World Photos

rotating basis by judges who now serve the various circuit courts of appeal. The purpose of the new court was suggested to include a review of cases awaiting hearings before the Supreme Court so that the High Court's workload might be reduced.

A similar National Court of Appeals was proposed in 1975 by the Congressional Commission on Revision of the Federal Court Appellate System. The National Court proposed by the Commission would have heard cases sent to it via transfer jurisdiction, from lower appellate courts, and through reference jurisdiction—when the Supreme Court decided to forward cases to it. The most recent version of a mini-Supreme Court was proposed by the Senate Judiciary Committee in 1986, when it called for the creation of an Intercircuit Tribunal of the U.S. courts of appeals. To date, however, no legislation to establish such a court has passed both houses of Congress.

Pretrial Activities

In the next chapter we will discuss typical stages in a criminal trial, as well as describe the many roles assumed by courtroom participants like judges, prosecutors, defense attorneys, victims, and suspects. A number of court-related pretrial activities, however, routinely take place before trial can begin. Although such activities (as well as the names given to them) vary between jurisdictions, they are generally described in the pages which follow.

First Appearance

First Appearance (also **Initial Appearance**) An appearance before a magistrate which entails the process whereby the legality of a defendant's arrest is initially assessed, and he or she is informed of the charges on which he or she is being held. At this stage in the criminal justice process, bail may be set or pretrial release arranged.

Following arrest, most defendants do not come into contact with an officer of the court until their first appearance before a magistrate, or lower-court judge.[27] A first appearance, sometimes called an initial appearance or magistrate's review, occurs when defendants are brought before a judge to be (1) given formal notice of the charges against them, (2) advised of their rights, (3) given the opportunity to retain a lawyer or to have one appointed to represent them, and (possibly) (4) afforded the opportunity for bail.

According to the procedural rules of all jurisdictions, defendants who have been taken into custody must be offered an in-court appearance before a magistrate "without unnecessary delay." The 1943 Supreme Court case of *McNabb* v. *U.S.*[28] established that any unrea-

Thurgood Marshall (1909–1993), the nation's first black U.S. Supreme Court justice.
John Ficara, Woodfin Camp & Associates

sonable delay in an initial court appearance would make confessions inadmissible if interrogating officers obtained them during the delay. Based upon the *McNabb* decision, 48 hours following arrest became the rule of thumb for reckoning the maximum time by which a first appearance should have been held.

The first appearance may also involve a probable cause hearing, although such hearings may be held separately (or may be combined, in some jurisdictions, with the preliminary hearing) since they do not require the defendant's presence. Probable cause hearings are necessary when arrests are made without a warrant, because such arrests do not require a prior judicial determination of probable cause. Such hearings ensure that probable cause for arrest and continued detention exist. During a probable cause hearing, also called a probable cause determination, a judicial officer will review police documents and reports to ensure that probable cause supported the arrest. The review of the arrest proceeds in a relatively informal fashion, with the judge seeking to decide whether, at the time of apprehension, the arresting officer had reason to believe both (1) that a crime had been or was being committed and (2) that the defendant was the person who committed it. Most of the evidence presented to the judge comes either from the arresting officer or from the victim. If probable cause is not found to exist, the suspect will be released.

In 1991, the U.S. Supreme Court, in a class-action suit entitled *County of Riverside (California)* v. *McLaughlin*,[29] imposed a promptness requirement upon probable cause determinations for in-custody arrestees. The Court held that "a jurisdiction that provides judicial determinations of probable cause within 48 hours of arrest will, as a general matter, comply with the promptness requirement…" The Court specified, however, that weekends and holidays could not be excluded from the 48-hour requirement (as they had been in Riverside County) and that, depending upon the specifics of the case, delays of fewer than two days may still be unreasonable."

During a first appearance, the suspect is not given an opportunity to present evidence, although the U.S. Supreme Court has held that defendants are entitled to representation by counsel at their first appearance.[30] Following a reading of the charges and a rights advisement, indigent defendants may have counsel appointed to represent them, and proceedings may be adjourned until counsel can be obtained.

In cases where a suspect is unruly, intoxicated, or uncooperative, a judicial review may occur in their absence. Some states waive a first appearance and proceed directly to arraignment (discussed following), especially when the defendant has been arrested on a warrant. In states which move directly to arraignment, the procedures undertaken to obtain a warrant are regarded as sufficient to demonstrate a basis for detention prior to arraignment.

Bail

A highly significant aspect of the first appearance hearing is consideration of bail or pretrial release. Defendants charged with very serious crimes, or those thought likely to escape or injure others, will usually be held in jail until trial. Such a practice is called pretrial detention.

Bail Bond An agreement guaranteeing the required appearance of a defendant in court, which records a pledge of money or property to be paid to the court if he or she does not appear and which is signed by the person to be released and any other persons acting in his or her behalf.

The majority of defendants, however, will be afforded the opportunity for release. However, since it is important to make sure that a released defendant will return for further court processing, he or she is asked to "post bail." Bail serves two purposes: (1) it helps ensure reappearance of the accused, and (2) it prevents unconvicted persons from suffering imprisonment unnecessarily.

Bail involves the posting of a bond as a pledge that the accused will return for further hearings. **Bail bonds** are usually cash deposits but may consist of property or other valuables. A fully secured bond requires the defendant to post the full amount of bail set by the court. The usual practice, however, is for a defendant to seek privately secured bail through the services of a professional bail bondsman. The bondsman will assess a percentage (usually 10–15%) of the required bond as a fee, which the defendant will have to pay up front. Those who "skip bail" by hiding or fleeing will sometimes find their bond ordered forfeit by the court. Forfeiture hearings must be held before a bond can be taken, and most courts will not order bail forfeit unless it appears that the defendant intends permanently to avoid prosecution. Bail forfeiture will often be reversed where the defendant later willingly appears to stand trial.

In many states bondsmen are empowered to hunt down and bring back defendants who have fled. In some jurisdictions bondsmen hold virtually unlimited powers and have been permitted by courts to pursue, arrest, and forcibly extradite their charges from foreign jurisdiction without concern for the due process considerations or statutory limitations which apply to law enforcement officers.[31] Recently, however, a number of states have enacted laws which eliminate for-profit bail bond businesses, replacing them instead with state-operated pretrial service agencies.

Alternatives to Bail

The Eighth Amendment to the U.S. Constitution, while it does not guarantee the opportunity for bail, does state that "Excessive bail shall not be required…." Some studies, however, have found that many defendants who are offered the opportunity for bail are unable to raise the needed money. Years ago, a report by the National Advisory Commission on Criminal

U.S. Supreme Court Justices. From front left, Antonin Scalia, John Paul Stevens, Chief Justice William H. Rehnquist, Sandra Day O'Connor, and Anthony Kennedy. Rear, from left, Ruth Bader Ginsburg, David Souter, Clarence Thomas, and Stephen Breyer. *Markel, Gamma—Liaison, Inc.*

Justice Standards and Goals found that as many as 93% of felony defendants in some juris-dictions were unable to make bail.[32]

To extend the opportunity for pretrial release to a greater proportion of nondangerous arrestees, a number of states and the federal government now make available various alter-natives to the cash bond system. Alternatives include (1) release on recognizance, (2) prop-erty bond, (3) deposit bail, (4) conditional release, (5) third-party custody, (6) unsecured or signature bond, and (7) attorney affidavit.

Release on recognizance (ROR) involves no cash bond, requiring as a guarantee only that the defendant agree in writing to return for further hearings as specified by the court. As an alternative to cash bond, release on recognizance was tested during the 1960s in a social experiment called the Manhattan Bail Project.[33] In the experiment not all defendants were eligible for release on their own recognizance. Those arrested for serious crimes, including murder, rape, robbery, and defendants with extensive prior criminal records, were excluded from participating in the project. The rest of the defendants were scored and categorized according to a number of "ideal" criteria used as indicators of both dangerousness and the likelihood of pretrial flight. Criteria included (1) no previous convictions, (2) residential sta-bility, and (3) a good employment record. Those likely to flee were not released.

Studies of the bail project revealed that it released four times as many defendants prior to trial as had been freed under the traditional cash bond system.[34] Even more surprising was the finding that only 1% of those released fled from prosecution—a figure which was the same as for those set free on cash bond.[35] Later studies, however, were unclear as to the effec-tiveness of release on recognizance, with some finding a no-show rate as high as 12%.[36]

Property bonds substitute other items of value in place of cash. Land, houses, automo-biles, stocks, and so on may be consigned to the court as collateral against pretrial flight.

An alternative form of cash bond available in some jurisdictions is **deposit bail**. Deposit bail places the court in the role of the bondsman, allowing the defendant to post a percent-age of the full bail with the court. Unlike private bail bondsmen, court-run deposit bail pro-grams usually return the amount of the deposit except for a small (perhaps 1%) adminis-trative fee. If the defendant fails to appear for court, the entire amount of court-ordered bail is forfeited.

Conditional release imposes a set of requirements upon the defendant. Requirements might include attendance at drug-treatment programs; staying away from specified others, such as potential witnesses; and regular job attendance. Release under supervision is similar to conditional release but adds the stipulation that defendants report to an officer of the court or a police officer at designated times.

Third-party custody is a bail bond alternative that assigns custody of the defendant to an individual or agency which promises to assure his or her later appearance in court.[37] Some pretrial release programs allow attorneys to assume responsibility for their clients in this fashion. If clients fail to appear, however, the attorney's privilege to participate in the pro-gram may be ended.[38]

An **unsecured bond** is based upon a court-determined dollar amount of bail. Like a credit contract, it requires no monetary deposit with the court. The defendant agrees in writing that failure to appear will result in forfeiture of the entire amount of the bond, which might then be taken in seizures of land, personal property, bank accounts, and so on.

A **signature bond** allows release based upon the defendant's written promise to appear. Signature bonds involve no particular assessment of the defendant's dangerousness or like-lihood of later appearance in court. They are used only in cases of minor offenses such as traffic law violations and some petty drug law violations. Signature bonds may be issued by the arresting officer acting on behalf of the court.

Pretrial release is common practice. Approximately 85% of all state-level criminal defen-dants[39] and 82% of all federal criminal defendants[40] are released prior to trial. Sixty-three percent of all state-level *felony* defendants[41] and 62% of federal felony defendants[42] are sim-ilarly released (see Figure 8–5). A growing movement, however, stresses the fact that defen-dants released prior to trial may be dangerous to themselves or others and seeks to reduce the number of defendants released under any conditions. This conservative policy has been promoted by an increasing concern for public safety in the face of a number of studies doc-umenting crimes committed by defendants released on bond. One such study found that 16% of defendants released before trial were rearrested, and, of those, 30% were arrested more than once.[43] Another determined that as many as 41% of those released prior to trial

Release on Recognizance (ROR) Refers to the pre-trial release of a criminal defendant on their written promise to appear. No cash or property bond is required.

Property Bond The set-ting of bail in the form of land, houses, stocks, or other tangible property. In the event the defendant absconds prior to trial, the bond becomes the property of the court.

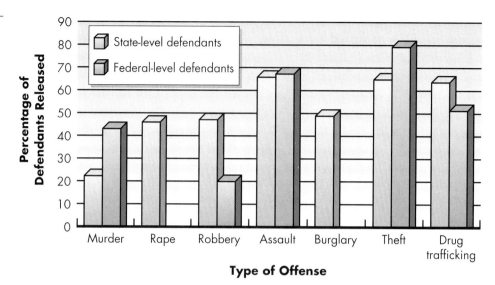

FIGURE 8–5 Proportion of state and federal felony defendants released prior to trial. *Sources:* Brian A. Reaves, *Felony Defendants in Large Urban Counties, 1994: State Court Processing Statistics* (Washington, D.C.: Bureau of Justice Statistics, 1997); Brian A. Reaves and Jacob Perez, *Pretrial Release of Felony Defendants, 1992* (Washington, D.C.: Bureau of Justice Statistics, November 1994); and Brian A. Reaves, *Pretrial Release of Federal Felony Defendants* (Washington, D.C.: Bureau of Justice Statistics, February 1994). Note: Federal pretrial release statistics are not available for the crimes of rape and burglary.

for serious crimes, such as rape and robbery, were rearrested before their trial date.[44] Not surprisingly, such studies generally find that the longer the time spent on bail prior to trial, the greater the likelihood of misconduct.

Danger Laws Those intended to prevent the pretrial release of criminal defendants judged to represent a danger to others in the community.

In response to claims like these, some states have enacted **danger laws**, which limit the right to bail for certain kinds of offenders.[45] Others, including Arizona, California, Colorado, Florida, and Illinois, have approved constitutional amendments restricting the use of bail.[46] Most such provisions exclude persons charged with certain crimes from being eligible for bail and demand that other defendants being considered for bail meet stringent conditions. Some states combine these strictures with tough release conditions designed to keep close control over defendants prior to trial.

The 1984 federal Bail Reform Act allows federal judges to assess the danger represented by an accused to the community and to deny bail to persons who are thought dangerous. In the words of the act, a suspect held in pretrial custody on federal criminal charges is required to be detained if, "after a hearing…he is found to pose a risk of flight and a danger to others or the community and if no condition of release can give reasonable assurances against these contingencies."[47] Defendants seeking bail are faced with the necessity of demonstrating a high likelihood of later court appearance. The act also requires that a defendant is entitled to a speedy first appearance and, if he or she is to be detained, that a detention hearing must be held together with the initial appearance.

In the 1990 case of *U.S. v. Montalvo-Murillo*,[48] however, a defendant who was not provided with a detention hearing at the time of his first appearance, and was subsequently released by an appeals court, was found to have no "right" to freedom because of this "minor" statutory violation. The Supreme Court held that "unless it has a substantial influence on the outcome of the proceedings…failure to comply with the Act's prompt hearing provision does not require release of a person who should otherwise be detained" because, "[a]utomatic release contravenes the statutory purpose of providing fair bail procedures while protecting the public's safety and assuring a defendant's appearance at trial."[49]

Court challenges to the constitutionality of pretrial detention legislation have not met with much success. The U.S. Supreme Court case of *U.S. v. Hazzard*[50] (1984), decided only a few months after enactment of federal bail reform, held that Congress was justified in providing for denial of bail to offenders who represent a danger to the community. Later cases have supported the presumption of flight, which federal law presupposes for certain types of defendants.[51]

A typical bail bond office. Bail bond offices such as this one are usually found near court-houses where criminal trials are held. *Mark Richards*

THE GRAND JURY

The federal government and about half of the states use grand juries as part of the pretrial process. Grand juries are composed of private citizens (often 23 in number) who hear evidence presented by the prosecution. Grand juries serve primarily as filters to eliminate from further processing cases for which there is not sufficient evidence.

In early times grand juries served a far different purpose. The grand jury system began in England in 1166 as a way of identifying law violators. Lacking a law enforcement agency with investigative authority, the government looked to the grand jury as a source of information on criminal activity in the community. Even today, grand juries in most jurisdictions may initiate prosecution independently of the prosecutor, although they rarely do.

Grand jury hearings are held in secret, and the defendant is not afforded the opportunity to appear before the grand jury.[52] Similarly, the opportunity to cross-examine prosecution witnesses is absent. Grand juries have the power to subpoena witnesses and to mandate a review of books, records, and other documents crucial to their investigations.

After hearing the evidence, the grand jury votes on the indictment presented to it by the prosecution. The indictment is a formal listing of proposed charges. If the majority of grand jury members agree to forward the indictment to the trial court, it becomes a "true bill" upon which further prosecution will turn.

THE PRELIMINARY HEARING

States which do not use grand juries rely instead upon a preliminary hearing "for charging defendants in a fashion that is less cumbersome and arguably more protective of the innocent."[53] In these jurisdictions, the prosecutor files an accusatorial document called an "information," or complaint, against the accused. A preliminary hearing is then held in order to determine whether there is probable cause to hold the defendant for trial. A few states, notably Tennessee and Georgia, use both the grand jury mechanism and a preliminary hearing as a "double check against the possibility of unwarranted prosecution."[54]

Although the preliminary hearing is not nearly as elaborate as a criminal trial, it has many of the same characteristics. The defendant is taken before a lower-court judge who will summarize the charges and review the rights to which all criminal defendants are entitled. The prosecution may present witnesses and will offer evidence in support of the complaint. The defendant will be afforded the right to testify and may also call witnesses.

Competent to Stand Trial
A finding by a court, when the defendant's sanity at the time of trial is at issue, that a defendant has sufficient present ability to consult with his lawyer with a reasonable degree of rational understanding and that he has a rational as well as factual understanding of the proceedings against him.

The primary purpose of the preliminary hearing is to give the defendant an opportunity to challenge the legal basis for his or her detention. At this point, defendants who appear or claim to be mentally incompetent may be ordered to undergo further evaluation to determine their competency to stand trial. **Competency to stand trial** may become an issue when a defendant appears to be incapable of understanding the proceedings against him or is unable to assist in his own defense due to mental disease or defect. In 1996, for example, lawyers for multimillionaire chemical heir John E. du Pont successfully argued at a pre-trial hearing that their client was psychotic and unable to work effectively with lawyers in preparing a defense to murder charges. Du Pont had been accused of shooting and killing David Schultz, an Olympic wrestler and 1984 gold medalist who had trained on du Pont's estate near Philadelphia. At the hearing, du Pont was declared schizophrenic, and his delusions of being the Dalai Lama, Jesus, and "heir to the Third Reich" were publicized in national media.[55]

Barring a finding of mental incompetence, all that is required for the wheels of justice to grind forward is a demonstration "sufficient to justify a prudent man's belief that the suspect has committed or was committing an offense"[56] within the jurisdiction of the court. If the magistrate finds enough evidence to justify a trial, the defendant is bound over to the grand jury—or sent directly to the trial court in those states which do not require grand jury review. If the complaint against the defendant cannot be substantiated, the defendant is released. A release is not a bar to further prosecution, and the defendant may be rearrested if further evidence comes to light.

Arraignment and the Plea

Plea In criminal proceedings, a defendant's formal answer in court to the charge contained in a complaint, information, or indictment that he or she is guilty of the offense charged, not guilty of the offense charged, or does not contest the charge.

Once an indictment has been returned, or an information filed, the accused will be formally arraigned. Arraignment is "the first appearance of the defendant before the court that has the authority to conduct a trial."[57] Arraignment is generally a brief process with two purposes: (1) to once again inform the defendant of the specific charges against him or her and (2) to allow the defendant to enter a **plea**. The Federal Rules of Criminal Procedure allow for one of three types of pleas to be entered: guilty, not guilty, and *nolo contendere* (no contest). A **no contest (*nolo contendere*)** plea is much the same as a plea of guilty. A defendant who pleads no contest is immediately convicted and may be sentenced just as though he or she had entered a plea of guilty. A no contest plea, however, is no admission of guilt and provides one major advantage to defendants: It may not be used as a later basis for civil proceedings which seek monetary or other damages against the defendant.

Nolo Contendere A plea of "no contest." A no contest plea may be used where the defendant does not wish to contest conviction. Because the plea does not admit guilt, however, it cannot provide the basis for later civil suits, which might follow upon the heels of a criminal conviction.

Some defendants refuse to enter any plea and are said to "stand mute." Standing mute is a defense strategy that is rarely employed by an accused. Defendants who choose this alternative simply do not answer the request for a plea. However, for procedural purposes, a defendant who stands mute is considered to have entered a plea of not guilty.

Plea Bargaining

Plea Bargaining The negotiated agreement among defendant, prosecutor, and the court as to what an appropriate plea and associated sentence should be in a given case. Plea bargaining circumvents the trial process and dramatically reduces the time required for the resolution of a criminal case.

Guilty pleas often are not as straightforward as they might seem and are typically arrived at only after complex negotiations known as plea bargaining. Plea bargaining is a process of negotiation which usually involves the defendant, prosecutor, and defense counsel. It is founded upon the mutual interests of all involved. Defense attorneys and their clients will agree to a plea of guilty when they are unsure of their ability to win acquittal at trial. Prosecutors may be willing to bargain because the evidence they have against the defendant is weaker than they would like it to be. From the prosecutorial perspective, plea bargaining results in a quick conviction without the need to commit the time and resources necessary for trial. Benefits to the accused include the possibility of reduced or combined charges, lessened defense costs, and a lower sentence than might have otherwise been anticipated.

The U.S. Supreme Court has held that a guilty plea constitutes conviction.[58] In order to validate the conviction, negotiated pleas require judicial consent. Judges are often likely to accept pleas which are the result of a bargaining process because such pleas reduce the workload of the court. Although few judges are willing to guarantee a sentence before a plea is entered, most prosecutors and criminal trial lawyers know what sentences to expect from typical pleas.

In the past, plea bargaining, though apparently common, had often been veiled in secrecy. Judicial thinking held that, for pleas to be valid, they had to be freely given. Pleas struck as the result of bargains seemed to depend upon the state's coercive power to encourage the defendant's cooperation. The 1973 National Advisory Commission on Criminal Justice Standards and Goals recommended abolishing the practice of plea negotiation.[59] That recommendation came in the midst of a national debate over the virtues of trading pleas for reductions in sentences. However, in 1970, even before the Commission's recommendation, the U.S. Supreme Court had given its consent to the informal decision-making processes of bargained pleas. In the case of *Brady* v. *U.S.*,[60] the court reasoned that such pleas were acceptable if voluntarily and knowingly made. A year later, in *Santobello* v. *New York* (1971),[61] the high court forcefully ruled that plea bargaining is an important and necessary component of the American system of justice. In the words of the Court, "The disposition of criminal charges by agreement between the prosecutor and the accused, sometimes loosely called 'plea bargaining,' is an essential component of the administration of justice. Properly administered, it is to be encouraged. If every criminal charge were subjected to a full-scale trial, the States and the Federal Government would need to multiply by many times the number of judges and court facilities."[62]

Today, bargained pleas are commonplace. Some surveys have found that 90% of all criminal cases prepared for trial are eventually resolved through a negotiated plea.[63] In a study of 37 big-city prosecutors,[64] the Bureau of Justice Statistics found that for every 100 adults arrested on a felony charge, half were eventually convicted of either a felony or a misdemeanor. Of all convictions, fully 94% were the result of a plea. Only 6% of convictions were the result of a criminal trial.

After a guilty plea has been entered, it may be withdrawn with the consent of the court. In the case of *Henderson* v. *Morgan* (1976),[65] for example, the U.S. Supreme Court permitted a defendant to withdraw a plea of guilty nine years after it had been given. In *Henderson* the defendant had originally entered a plea of guilty to second-degree murder but attempted to withdraw it before trial. Reasons for wanting to withdraw the plea included the defendant's belief that he had not been completely advised as to the nature of the charge or the sentence he might receive as a result of the plea.

Recent Supreme Court decisions, however, have enhanced the prosecutor's authority in the bargaining process by declaring that negotiated pleas cannot be capriciously withdrawn by defendants.[66] Other rulings have supported discretionary actions by prosecutors in which sentencing recommendations were retracted even after bargains had been struck.[67] Some lower-court cases have upheld the government's authority to withdraw from a negotiated plea where the defendant fails to live up to certain conditions.[68] Conditions may include requiring the defendant to provide information on other criminal involvement, criminal cartels, the activities of smugglers, and so on.

Because it is a process of negotiation involving many interests, plea bargaining may have unintended consequences. For example, while it is generally agreed that bargained pleas should relate in some way to the original charge, actual practice may not adhere to such expectations. Many plea negotiations turn on the acceptability of the anticipated sentence rather than on a close relationship between the charge and the plea. Entered pleas may be chosen for the punishments likely to be associated with them rather than for their accuracy in describing the criminal offense in which the defendant was involved.[69] This is especially true where the defendant is concerned with minimizing the socially stigmatizing impact of the offense. A charge of "indecent liberties," for example, in which the defendant is accused of sexual misconduct, may be pled out as assault. Such a plea, which takes advantage of the fact that "indecent liberties" can be thought of as a form of sexual assault, would effectively disguise the true nature of the offense.

Even though plea bargaining has been endorsed by the Supreme Court, the public continues to view it suspiciously. "Law and order" advocates, who generally favor harsh punishments and long jail terms, claim that plea bargaining results in unjustifiably light sentences. As a consequence, prosecutors who regularly engage in the practice rarely advertise it. Often unrealized is the fact that plea bargaining can be a powerful prosecutorial tool.

Power carries with it, however, the potential for misuse. Plea bargains, because they circumvent the trial process, hold the possibility of abuse by prosecutors and defense attorneys

Visit the *CJToday* Web page and click on "Web Chapters," then "Chapter 8." Follow the "find the facts" links in order to learn about the structure and function of federal courts.

A grand jury in action. Grand jury proceedings are generally very informal, as this picture shows. *Frank Fournier, Woodfin Camp & Associates*

who are more interested in a speedy resolution of cases than they are in seeing justice done. Carried to the extreme, plea bargaining may result in defendants being convicted of crimes they did not commit. Although it probably happens only rarely, it is conceivable that innocent defendants (especially those with prior criminal records) who—for whatever reason— think a jury will convict them, may plead guilty to lessened charges in order to avoid a trial. In an effort to protect defendants against hastily arranged pleas, the Federal Rules of Criminal Procedure require judges to (1) inform the defendant of the various rights he or she is surrendering by pleading guilty, (2) determine that the plea is voluntary, (3) require disclosure of any plea agreements, and (4) make sufficient inquiry to ensure there is a factual basis for the plea.[70]

Bargained pleas can take many forms and be quite inventive. The case of Steven Allen Butler is illustrative of an unusual bargained plea. In 1992 Butler, a 28-year-old Houston man, voluntarily agreed to surgical castration and a ten-year probationary sentence for repeatedly raping a 13-year-old girl while already on probation for molesting a seven-year-old. His alternative was to stand trial, facing a potential life sentence. However, after considerable public outcry over the arranged sentence, Judge Michael McSpadden withdrew the offer, saying no physician could be found to perform the surgery.[71]

SUMMARY

Throughout the United States there are two judicial systems. One consists of state and local courts established under the authority of state governments. The other is the federal court system, created by Congress under the authority of the Constitution of the United States.

State courts have virtually unlimited power to decide nearly every type of case, subject only to the limitations of the U.S. Constitution, their own state constitutions, and state law. State and local courts are located in almost every town and county across the nation and are the courts with which citizens usually have contact. These courts handle most criminal matters and the great bulk of legal business concerning wills and inheritance, estates, marital disputes, real estate and land dealings, commercial and personal contracts, and other day-to-day matters.

State criminal courts present an intriguing contrast. On the one hand, they exude an aura of highly formalized judicial procedure, while on the other they demonstrate a surprising lack of organizational uniformity. Courts in one jurisdiction may bear little resemblance to those in another state. Court reform, because it has not equally impacted all areas of the country, has in some instances exacerbated the differences between court systems.

Federal courts have power to decide only those cases over which the Constitution gives them authority. These courts are located principally in larger cities. Only carefully selected types of cases may be heard in federal courts. The highest federal court, the U.S. Supreme Court, is located in Washington, D.C., and hears cases only on appeal from lower courts.

This chapter also described pretrial practices in preparation for a detailed consideration of trial-related activities which are described in the next chapter. Prior to trial, courts often act to shield the accused from the punitive power of the state through the use of pretrial release. In doing so, they must balance the rights of the unconvicted defendant against the potential for future harm which that person may represent. A significant issue facing pretrial decision makers is how to ensure that all defendants, rich or poor, black or white, male or female, are afforded the same degree of protection.

...out of the 106 people who served on the Supreme Court, only 58 of them actually attended law school. Law schools didn't come into being or become very popular until after the Civil War.

—The Honorable Joseph F. Baca, Justice, New Mexico supreme court

DISCUSSION QUESTIONS

1. What is the "dual court system"? Why do we have a dual court system in America? Could the drive toward court unification eventually lead to a monolithic court system? Would such a system be effective?

2. This chapter says that 90% of all criminal cases carried beyond the initial stages are finally resolved through bargained pleas. What are some of the problems associated with plea bargaining? Given those problems, do you believe that plea bargaining is an acceptable practice in today's criminal justice system? Give reasons for your answer.

3. People who are accused of crimes are often granted pretrial release. Do you think all defendants accused of crimes should be so released? If not, what types of defendants might you keep in jail? Why?

4. What inequities exist in today's system of pretrial release? How might the system be improved?

 WEB WATCH

Access the *Criminal Justice Today* site on the World Wide Web by pointing your Web browser at http://www.prenhall.com/cjtoday. Once there, click the "enter here" selection, then "Web Chapters," and finally "Chapter 8: The Courts" from the selection box in order to access electronic information and other sites of relevance to this chapter. You may also wish to enter the Global Town Meeting, which provides facilities for the posting of electronic messages for others to read. Messages are arranged by topic, with new topics constantly being added.

NOTES

1. Debbie Howlett and Gary Fields, "Cluster of Bombings Touches Off Concerns," *USA Today*, February 4, 1997, p. 3A.
2. Law Enforcement Assistance Administration, *Two Hundred Years of American Criminal Justice* (Washington, D.C.: U.S. Government Printing Office, 1976), p. 31.
3. Ibid., p. 31.
4. Ibid.
5. Ibid., p. 32.
6. Ibid.
7. David B. Rottman, Carol R. Flango, and R. Shedine Lockley, *State Court Organization 1993* (Washington, D.C.: Bureau of Justice Statistics, 1995), p. 11.
8. Thomas A. Henderson, Cornelium M. Kerwin, Randall Guynes, Carl Baar, Neal Miller, Hildy Saizow, and Robert Grieser, *The Significance of Judicial Structure: The Effects of Unification on Trial Court Operations* (Washington, D.C.: National Institute of Justice, 1984).
9. Ibid.

10. As recently as 1957 only 13 states had permanent intermediate appellate courts. Now, all but 12 states have such a court, and North Dakota is operating one on a temporary basis to assist in handling the rising appellate caseload in that state. See Rottman, Flango, and Lockley, *State Court Organization 1993* , p. 5.

11. *Keeney, Superintendent, Oregon State Penitentiary* v. *Tamayo-Reyes*, 113 S.Ct. 853, 122 L. Ed. 2d 203 (1993).

12. *Herrera* v. *Collins*, 113 S.Ct. 853, 122 L. Ed. 2d 203 (1993).

13. Some of the wording in this section is taken from "Overview of the Florida State Courts System," on *Joshua*, the Florida court's World Wide Web page on the Internet, August 26, 1997.

14. H. Ted Rubin, *The Courts: Fulcrum of the Justice System* (Pacific Palisades, CA: Goodyear, 1976), p. 200.

15. Ibid., p. 198.

16. Martin Wright, *Justice for Victims and Offenders* (Bristol, PA: Open University Press, 1991), p. 56.

17. Ibid., pp. 104 and 106.

18. Administrative Office of the United States Courts, *The United States Courts: A Pictorial Summary for the Twelve Month Period Ended June 30, 1985* (Washington, D.C.: U.S. Government Printing Office, 1985), p. 16.

19. Administrative Office of the United States Courts, World Wide Web site, March 20, 1998.

20. Ibid.

21. Some of the materials in this section are adapted from the Administrative Office of the United States Courts, "Courts of Appeals," and "U.S. Court of Appeals for the Federal Circuit," Administrative Office of the United States Courts, World Wide Web site, July 27, 1995.

22. Stephen L. Wasby, *The Supreme Court in the Federal Judicial System*, 3d ed. (Chicago: Nelson-Hall, 1988), p. 58.

23. *The Supreme Court of the United States* (Washington, D.C.: U.S. Government Printing Office, no date), p. 4.

24. 1 Cranch 137 (1803).

25. *Mapp* v. *Ohio*, 367 U.S. 643 (1961).

26. Wasby, *The Supreme Court*, pp. 58–59.

27. *Arraignment* is also a term used to describe an initial appearance, although we will reserve use of that word to describe a later court appearance following the defendant's indictment by a grand jury or the filing of an information by the prosecutor.

28. *McNabb* v. *United States*, 318 U.S. 332 (1943).

29. *County of Riverside* v. *McLaughlin*, 111 S.Ct. 1661 (1991).

30. *White* v. *Maryland*, 373 U.S. 59 (1963).

31. *Taylor* v. *Taintor*, 83 U.S. 66 (1873).

32. National Advisory Commission on Criminal Justice Standards and Goals, *The Courts* (Washington, D.C.: U.S. Government Printing Office, 1973), p. 37.

33. C. Ares, A. Rankin, and H. Sturz, "The Manhattan Bail Project: An Interim Report on the Use of Pre-Trial Parole," *New York University Law Review*, Vol. 38 (January 1963), pp. 68–95.

34. H. Zeisel, "Bail Revisited," *American Bar Foundation Research Journal*, Vol. 4 (1979), pp. 769–789.

35. Ibid.

36. "12% of Those Freed on Low Bail Fail to Appear," *The New York Times*, December 2, 1983, p. 1.

37. Bureau of Justice Statistics, *Report to the Nation on Crime and Justice*, 2nd ed., (Washington, D.C.: U.S. Department of Justice, 1988) p. 76.

38. Joseph B. Vaughn and Victor E. Kappeler, "The Denial of Bail: Pre-Trial Preventive Detention," *Criminal Justice Research Bulletin*, Vol. 3, no. 6 (Huntsville, TX: Sam Houston State University, 1987), p. 1.

39. See Brian A. Reaves, *Felony Defendants in Large Urban Counties, 1994: State Court Processing Statistics* (Washington, D.C.: Bureau of Justice Statistics, 1997); and M. A. Toborg, *Pretrial Release: A National Evaluation of Practice and Outcomes* (McLean, VA: Lazar Institute, 1981).

40. Bureau of Justice Statistics, *Report to the Nation on Crime and Justice*, 2nd ed., p. 77.

41. Brian A. Reaves and Jacob Perez, *Pretrial Release of Felony Defendants 1992*, (Washington, D.C.: Bureau of Justice Statistics, November 1994).

42. Brian A. Reaves, *Pretrial Release of Federal Felony Defendants* (Washington, D.C.: Bureau of Justice Statistics, February 1994).

43. Donald E. Pryor and Walter F. Smith, "Significant Research Findings Concerning Pretrial Release," *Pretrial Issues*, Vol. 4, no. 1 (Washington, D.C.: Pretrial Services Resource Center, February 1982).

44. Bureau of Justice Statistics, *Report to the Nation on Crime and Justice*, 2nd ed., p. 77.

45. According to Vaughn and Kappeler, "The Denial of Bail," the first such legislation was the 1970 District of Columbia Court Reform and Criminal Procedure Act.

46. Ibid.

47. Bail Reform Act of 1984, 18 U.S.C. 3142(e).

48. *U.S.* v. *Montalvo-Murillo*, 495 U.S. 711 (1990).

49. *U.S.* v. *Montalvo-Murillo* (1990), syllabus.

50. *U.S.* v. *Hazzard*, 35 CrL 2217 (1984).

51. See, for example, *U.S.* v. *Motamedi*, 37 CrL 2394, CA 9 (1985).

52. A few states now have laws that permit the defendant to appear before the grand jury.

53. John M. Scheb and John M. Scheb II, *American Criminal Law* (St. Paul, MN: West, 1996), p. 31.

54. Ibid., p. 31.

55. In February 1997, following six months of treatment with anti-psychotic drugs, du Pont was found guilty of third-degree murder in the killing of Schultz and sentenced to 13 to 30 years in confinement.

56. *Federal Rules of Criminal Procedure* 5.1(a).

57. John M. Scheb and John M. Scheb II, *American Criminal Law* (St. Paul, MN: West, 1996), p. 32.

58. *Kercheval* v. *U.S.*, 274 U.S. 220, 223, 47 S.Ct. 582, 583 (1927); *Boykin* v. *Alabama*, 395 U.S. 238 (1969); and *Dickerson* v. *New Banner Institute, Inc.*, 460 U.S. 103 (1983).

59. The National Advisory Commission on Criminal Justice Standards and Goals, *Courts* (Washington, D.C.: U.S. Government Printing Office, 1973), p. 46.

60. *Brady* v. *United States*, 397 U.S. 742 (1970).

61. *Santobello* v. *New York*, 404 U.S. 257 (1971).

62. Ibid.

63. U.S. Department of Justice, Bureau of Justice Statistics, *The Prosecution of Felony Arrests* (Washington, D.C.: U.S. Government Printing Office, 1983).

64. Barbara Boland, Wayne Logan, Ronald Sones, and William Martin, *The Prosecution of Felony Arrests, 1982* (Washington, D.C.: U.S. Government Printing Office, May 1988).

65. *Henderson* v. *Morgan*, 426 U.S. 637 (1976).

66. *Santobello* v. *New York*.

67. *Mabry* v. *Johnson*, 467 U.S. 504 (1984).

68. *U.S.* v. *Baldacchino*, 762 F.2d 170 (1st Cir. 1985); *U.S.* v. *Reardon*, 787 F.2d 512 (10th Cir. 1986); and *U.S.* v. *Donahey*, 529 F.2d 831 (11th Cir. 1976).

69. For a now classic discussion of such considerations, see David Sudnow, "Normal Crimes: Sociological Features of the Penal Code in a Public Defender Office," *Social Problems*, Vol. 12 (1965), p. 255.

70. *Federal Rules of Criminal Procedure*, No. 11.

71. "Nationline," *USA Today*, March 17, 1992, p. 3A and "Man Volunteers Castration over Prison for Raping Child," *The Fayetteville Observer-Times* (North Carolina), March 7, 1992, p. 1A.

chapter 9

THE COURTROOM WORK GROUP AND THE CRIMINAL TRIAL

To hear patiently, to weigh deliberately and dispassionately, and to decide impartially; these are the chief duties of a judge.

—ALBERT PIKE (1809–1891)

A jury consists of 12 persons chosen to decide who has the better lawyer.

—ROBERT FROST

Introduction

I don't know if I ever want to try another case. I don't know if I ever want to practice law again.

—Christopher Darden, L.A. County assistant prosecutor, expressing frustration over the O. J. Simpson case

Courtroom Work Group
Professional courtroom actors, including judges, prosecuting attorneys, defense attorneys, public defenders, and others who earn a living serving the court.

"Every day, as he ambles through the cobwebbed halls of the New Orleans criminal court building, public defender Richard Teisser feels he violates his clients' constitutional rights"[1] to legal counsel. Teisser, an attorney who is paid just $18,500 per year by the state of Louisiana, has so many clients and so few resources he believes that he can't possibly do them all justice. A few years ago, in an effort to bring his plight before the public, Teisser filed suit against his own office. A local judge agreed, finding Louisiana's system of indigent defense unconstitutional. Louisiana Governor Edwin Edwards, commenting on the ruling, said that underfunding of public defenders is not limited to New Orleans but is "a state problem and a national problem."[2]

Were it not for people like Richard Teisser, few would be aware of the problems facing our nation's courts. To the public eye, criminal trials generally appear to be well managed and even dramatic events. Like plays on a stage, they involve many participants playing many different roles. Parties to the event can be divided into two categories: "professionals" and "outsiders." The "professional" category includes official courtroom actors, well versed in criminal trial practice, who set the stage for and conduct the business of the court. Judges, prosecuting attorneys, defense attorneys, public defenders, and others who earn a living serving the court fall into this category. Professional courtroom actors are also called the **courtroom work group.** Some writers[3] have pointed out that, aside from statutory requirements and ethical considerations, courtroom interaction among professionals involves an implicit recognition of informal rules of civility, cooperation, and shared goals. Hence, even within the adversarial framework of a criminal trial, the courtroom work group is dedicated to bringing the procedure to a successful close.[4]

In contrast, "outsiders" are generally unfamiliar with courtroom organization and trial procedure. Most outsiders visit the court temporarily to provide information or to serve as members of the jury. Similarly, because of their temporary involvement with the court, defendant and victim are also outsiders, even though they may have more of a personal investment in the outcome of the trial than anyone else.

This chapter continues to examine trial court activities, building upon the pretrial process described in the last chapter. In order to place the trial process within its human context, however, the various roles of the many participants in a criminal trial are first discussed.

The Courtroom Work Group: Professional Courtroom Actors

The Judge

Role of the Judge

The trial judge is probably the figure most closely associated with a criminal trial. The judge has the primary duty of ensuring justice. In the courtroom, the judge holds ultimate authority, ruling on matters of law, weighing objections from either side, deciding on the admissibility of evidence, and disciplining anyone who challenges the order of the court. In most jurisdictions, judges also sentence offenders after a verdict has been returned, and in some states judges serve to decide guilt or innocence for defendants who waive a jury trial.

Each state jurisdiction normally has a chief judge who, besides serving on the bench as a trial judge, must also manage the court system. Management includes hiring staff, scheduling sessions of court, ensuring the adequate training of subordinate judges, and coordinating activities with other courtroom actors. Chief judges usually assume their positions by virtue of seniority and rarely have any formal training in management. Hence, the managerial effectiveness of a chief judge is often a matter of personality and dedication more than anything else.

Judge An elected or appointed public official who presides over a court of law and who is authorized to hear and sometimes to decide cases and to conduct trials.

Judicial Selection

As we discussed in Chapter 8, judges at the federal level are nominated by the president of the United States and take their place on the bench only after confirmation by the Senate. At the state level, things work somewhat differently. Depending upon the jurisdiction, state judgeships are won either through popular election or political (usually gubernatorial) appointment. The processes involved in judicial selection at the state level are set by law.

Both judicial election and appointment have been criticized for the fact that each system allows politics to enter the judicial arena—although in somewhat different ways. Under the appointment system, judicial hopefuls must be in favor with incumbent politicians in order to receive appointments. Under the elective system, judicial candidates must receive the endorsement of their parties, generate contributions, and manage an effective campaign. Because partisan politics plays a role in both systems, critics have claimed that sitting judges can rarely be as neutral as they should be. They carry to the bench with them campaign promises, personal indebtedness, and possible political agendas.

To counter some of these problems, a number of states have adopted what has come to be called the Missouri Plan[5] (or the "Missouri Bar Plan") for judicial selection. The Missouri Plan combines elements of both election and appointment. It requires judicial vacancies to undergo screening by a nonpartisan state judicial nominating committee. Candidates selected by the committee are reviewed by an arm of the governor's office, which selects a final list of names for appointment. Incumbent judges must face the electorate after a specified term in office. They then run unopposed, in nonpartisan elections, in which only their records may be considered. Voters have the choice of allowing a judge to continue in office or asking that another be appointed to take his or her place. Because the Missouri Plan provides for periodic public review of judicial performance, it is also called the merit plan of judicial selection.

Qualifications of Judges

Only two decades ago many states did not require any special training, education, or other qualifications for judges. Anyone (even someone without a law degree) who won election or was appointed could assume a judgeship. Today, however, almost all states require that judges in appellate and general jurisdiction courts hold a law degree, be licensed attorneys, and be members of their state bar associations. Many states also require newly elected judges to attend state-sponsored training sessions dealing with subjects such as courtroom procedure, evidence, dispute resolution, judicial writing, administrative record keeping, and ethics.

Theory into Practice

THE FUNCTIONS OF THE TRIAL JUDGE

The American Bar Association Standards for Criminal Justice set forth the following duties of the trial judge:

1. General responsibility of the trial judge.
(a) The trial judge has the responsibility for safeguarding both the rights of the accused and the interests of the public in the administration of criminal jus-

tice. The adversary nature of the proceedings does not relieve the trial judge of the obligations of raising on his or her own initiative, at all appropriate times and in an appropriate manner, matters which may significantly promote a just determination of the trial. The only purpose of a criminal trial is to determine whether the prosecution has established the guilt of the accused as

required by law, and the trial judge should not allow the proceedings to be used for any other purpose.

Source: ABA Standards for Criminal Justice, 2nd ed., 1980. Copies of this publication are available from Service Center, American Bar Association, 750 North Lake Shore Drive, Chicago, IL 60611.

While most states provide instruction to meet the needs of trial judges, other organizations also provide specialized training. The National Judicial College, located on the campus of the University of Nevada at Reno, is one such institution. The National Judicial College was established in 1963 by the Joint Committee for the Effective Administration of Justice, chaired by Justice Tom C. Clark of the U.S. Supreme Court.[6] Courses offered by the college attract over 1,500 judges every year.

Lower-court judges, such as justices of the peace, local magistrates, and "district" court judges in some parts of the United States, may still be elected without educational and other professional requirements. Today, in 43 states some 1,300 nonlawyer judges are serving in mostly rural courts of limited jurisdiction.[7] In New York, for example, lay judges hear around three million cases each year and collect $45 million in fines.[8] The majority of cases which come before New York lay judges involve alleged traffic violations, although they may also include misdemeanors, small claims actions, and some civil cases (of up to $3,000). Some authors have defended lay judges as being closer to the citizenry in their understanding of justice.[9] Even so, in most areas there is a tendency to eliminate lay judges. States which continue to use lay judges in lower courts do require that candidates for judgeships not have criminal records and that most attend special training sessions, if elected.

Judicial Misconduct

A June 1997 West Virginia bond hearing took a turn for the worse when Pleasant County Circuit Judge Joseph Troisi allegedly bit defendant Bill Whittens on the nose.[10] The bite, said Whittens, was inflicted after he directed a derogatory remark at the judge. Whittens' nose required medical treatment at a local hospital. Judge Troisi had no comment, and the FBI was called in to investigate.

While most judges are highly professional, in and out of the courtroom, some judges occasionally overstep the limits of their authority. Poor judgment may result from bad taste or archaic attitudes, as in the case of a lower-court judge who repeatedly told a female defense counselor that she was too pretty to be a lawyer and should be at home having children. Other sexist comments resulted in calls for that judge's dismissal. Sexist behavior hasn't been confined to male judges. In 1996, for example, Cleveland Judge Shirley Strickland Saffold caused an outcry among Ohio voters when she told a woman being sentenced for misusing a credit card to "dump your boyfriend, show your legs, and marry a doctor." The judge, who is herself married to a physician, continued, "You can go sit in the bus stop, put on a short skirt, cross your legs, and pick up 25 [men]. Ten of them will give you their money."[11]

Illinois Supreme Court Justice James D. Heiple, shown here being "mugged" by the Pekin, Illinois, Police Department, was forced to resign his position as Chief Justice in 1997 after admitting that he used his office in attempts to evade traffic tickets. Most judges are highly respected members of the criminal justice system. Some, however, overstep the boundaries of judicial propriety, and can be disciplined.
AP/Wide World Photos

All states provide mechanisms for administratively dealing with complaints about judicial conduct. In 1995, for example, Pennsylvania district justice Bradford C. Timbers was suspended by the state's Judicial Conduct Board after being charged with "trying to fix a friend's speeding ticket, slapping a female co-worker's buttocks, and drinking alcohol on the job."[12] In 1997, the chief justice of the Alaska Supreme Court, Allen T. Compton, 59, stepped down from his position after being admonished for sexual harassment. He remains on the court but no longer serves as chief justice. Compton resigned his post as chief justice after receiving a private rebuke from the Alaska Commission on Judicial Conduct, which said that his conduct on two occasions in 1995 and 1996, with two different female court employees, constituted sexual harassment.[13] Also in 1997, 62-year old Illinois Supreme Court Justice James D. Heiple was forced to resign his position as chief justice after admitting that he used his office in attempts to evade traffic tickets.[14] Although he remains on the court as of this writing, a bipartisan panel of Illinois lawmakers is considering his impeachment.

At the federal level, the Judicial Councils Reform and Judicial Conduct and Disability Act, passed by Congress in 1980, specifies the procedures necessary to register complaints against federal judges and, in serious cases, to begin the process of impeachment—or forced removal from the bench. In 1987, in a rare display of its authority, Walter L. Nixon, Jr., a chief judge of the U.S. District Court for the Southern District of Mississippi, was convicted under the law on two counts of making false statements before a federal grand jury and sentenced to prison.[15] His 1993 appeal to the U.S. Supreme Court was denied.[16]

The Prosecuting Attorney

The prosecuting attorney, called variously the "solicitor," "district attorney," "state's attorney," "chief prosecutor," and so on, is responsible for presenting the state's case against the defendant. Technically speaking, the prosecuting attorney is the primary representative of the people by virtue of the belief that violations of the criminal law are an affront to the public. Except for federal prosecutors (called U.S. attorneys) and solicitors in five states, prosecutors are elected and generally serve four-year terms with the possibility of continuing reelection.[17] Widespread criminal conspiracies, whether they involve government officials or private citizens, may require the services of a special prosecutor whose office can spend the time and resources needed for efficient prosecution.[18]

Prosecutor (also **District Attorney**) An elected or appointed public official, licensed to practice law, whose job it is to conduct criminal proceedings on behalf of the state or the people against an accused person. Also called a **state's attorney.**

In many jurisdictions, because the job of prosecutor entails too many duties for one person to handle, most prosecutors supervise a staff of assistant district attorneys who do most in-court work. Assistants are trained attorneys, usually hired directly by the chief prosecutor and licensed to practice law in the states where they work. Approximately 2,300 chief prosecutors, assisted by 20,000 deputy attorneys, serve the nation's counties and independent cities.[19]

Another prosecutorial role has traditionally been that of quasi-legal advisor to local police departments. Because prosecutors are sensitive to the kinds of information needed for conviction, they may help guide police investigations and will exhort detectives to identify usable witnesses, uncover additional evidence, and the like. This role is limited, however. Police departments are independent of the administrative authority of the prosecutor and cooperation between them, although based on the common goal of conviction, is purely voluntary.[20]

Once trial begins, the job of the prosecutor is to vigorously present the state's case against the defendant. Prosecutors introduce evidence against the accused, steer the testimony of witnesses "for the people," and argue in favor of conviction. Since defendants are presumed innocent until proven guilty, the burden of demonstrating guilt beyond a reasonable doubt rests with the prosecutor.

Prosecutorial Discretion

Prosecutorial Discretion
The decision-making power of prosecutors, based upon the wide range of choices available to them, in the handling of criminal defendants, the scheduling of cases for trial, the acceptance of bargained pleas, and so on. The most important form of prosecutorial discretion lies in the power to charge, or not to charge, a person with an offense.

Prosecutors occupy a unique position in the nation's criminal justice system by virtue of the considerable discretion they exercise. As Justice Robert H. Jackson noted in 1940, "the prosecutor has more control over life, liberty, and reputation than any other person in America."[21] Before a case comes to trial, prosecutors may decide to accept a plea bargain, divert suspects to a public or private social-service agency, or dismiss the case entirely for lack of evidence or for a variety of other reasons. Various studies have found that from one-third to one-half of all felony cases are dismissed by the prosecution prior to trial or before a plea bargain is made.[22] Prosecutors also play a significant role before grand juries. States which use the grand jury system depend upon prosecutors to bring evidence before the grand jury and to be effective in seeing indictments returned against suspects.

In preparation for trial, the prosecutor decides what charges are to be brought against the defendant, examines the strength of incriminating evidence, and decides what witnesses to call. Two important Supreme Court decisions have held that it is the duty of prosecutors to, in effect, assist the defense in building its case by making available any evidence in their possession. The first case, that of *Brady* v. *Maryland*,[23] was decided in 1963. In *Brady*, the Court held that the prosecution is required to disclose to the defense exculpatory evidence that directly relates to claims of either guilt or innocence. A second, and more recent, case is that of *U.S.* v. *Bagley*,[24] decided in 1985. In *Bagley* the Court ruled that the prosecution must disclose any evidence that the defense requests. The Court reasoned that to withhold evidence, even when it does not relate directly to issues of guilt or innocence, may mislead the defense into thinking that such evidence does not exist.

One special decision the prosecutor makes concerns the filing of separate or multiple charges. The decision to try a defendant simultaneously on multiple charges can allow for the presentation of a considerable amount of evidence and permit an in-court demonstration of a complete sequence of criminal events. Such a strategy has a practical side as well; it saves time and money by substituting one trial for what might otherwise be any number of trials if each charge were to be brought separately before the court. From the prosecutor's point of view, however, trying the charges one at a time carries the advantage of allowing for another trial on a new charge if a "not guilty" verdict is returned the first time.

The activities of the prosecutor do not end with a finding of guilt or innocence. Following conviction, prosecutors usually are allowed to make sentencing recommendations to the judge. They can be expected to argue that aggravating factors (which we will discuss in Chapter 10, on sentencing), prior criminal record, or especially heinous qualities of the offense in question call for strict punishment. When convicted defendants appeal, prosecutors may need to defend their own actions and to argue, in briefs filed with appellate courts, that convictions were properly obtained. Most jurisdictions also allow prosecutors to make recommendations when defendants they have convicted are being considered for parole or early release from prison.

Until relatively recently, it has generally been held that prosecutors enjoyed much the same kind of immunity against liability in the exercise of their official duties that judges do. The 1976 Supreme Court case of *Imbler* v. *Pachtman*[25] provided the basis for such thinking

In 1976 Joe Freeman Britt, district attorney for North Carolina's rural 16th judicial district, entered the *Guiness Book of World Records* as the "world's deadliest district attorney"—a record which stands to this day. During his career as D.A., Britt, a cigar-smoking, 6-foot 6-inch mountain of a man, achieved the grim distinction of winning 46 death penalty convictions and sending 33 men and women to North Carolina's death row. One of those convicted, Velma Barfield, became the first woman executed in the United States in more than 22 years. Of all the defendants tried by Britt in death penalty cases, none have ever been acquitted, although five received life sentences rather than death.

As Britt's fame spread, press interest in the "world's deadliest district attorney" grew. Britt was soon featured in dozens of interviews and profiles. *The* (London) *Times, Newsweek, The New York Times*, the *Los Angeles Times, People* magazine, the German magazine *Stern*, and the television show *60 Minutes* all portrayed Britt as a prosecutor who gives no quarter. A "masterful orator with a deep booming voice," the *Atlanta Journal* depicted Britt this way: "He prowls the courtroom like an outraged Minotaur. He storms, scowls, gesticulates wildly and quotes the Old Testament with authority." But he doesn't shoot from the hip. Britt prepares months for each capital case. His greatest battle, he says, is with the jury. "In every prospective juror's breast there beats the flame that whispers, 'Preserve human life.' It's my job to extinguish that flame. I'll tell you, it destroys my

faith in humanity the way a prospective juror will say he believes in the death penalty and then turn around and say, 'But I ain't gonna be no part of it.'"

Surprisingly, Britt has not always favored capital punishment. As an undergraduate student at Wake Forest University, he led a campaign against the death penalty. Today, he describes himself as a "true believer." "The changeover was gradual," he says. "I had no blinding revelation." Imagine yourself "walking down a muddy ditch in the fog at daybreak...and the fog begins to lift and you find a 13-year-old girl with her dress up over her head and a bloody grin from ear to ear where someone slit her throat. Multiply that by a lot of sights and sounds and smells and see that enough times and it affects your perspective."

Britt describes himself as subscribing to a "classic" understanding

of crime. "I think punishment must have some meaning for there to be any justice," he says. "The victim's lawyer is the prosecutor.... That poor victim lying 6 feet underground has nobody to speak for him but me." Asked whether he considers himself merciless, Britt responds, "It depends on your point of view, whether you're holding a sobbing sister of the killer or (of) the victim."

What motivates Joe Freeman Britt? His closing arguments to juries can be revealing. Once he described a murder victim as someone who had been "a living, breathing human being...just like you and me...and now he's gone.... My God, it's good to be alive!" he exclaimed. "Did you watch the sun come up this morning?"

QUESTIONS FOR DISCUSSION

1. If you were a crime victim, how would you feel about having someone like Joe Freeman Britt prosecute the person who victimized you? How would you feel if you were the defendant facing Britt?

2. Do you agree with Britt's stance on capital punishment? Why or why not?

Sources: "Joe Freeman Britt, 'Deadliest Prosecutor,'" *The Fayetteville Observer-Times* (North Carolina), January 20, 1985, p. 1F; "N. Carolina Prosecutor Called World's 'Deadliest,'" *The Atlanta Journal*, March 9, 1986, p. 33A; "Controversial Britt Known as Tough," *The Charlotte Observer* (North Carolina), April 3, 1988, p. 12A; "World's Deadliest Prosecutor," *Greensboro News and Record* (North Carolina), March 29, 1987, p. 1B.

---

with its ruling that "state prosecutors are absolutely immune from liability...for their conduct in initiating a prosecution and in presenting the State's case." However, the Court, in the 1991 case of *Burns* v. *Reed*,[26] held that "[a] state prosecuting attorney is absolutely immune from liability for damages...for participating in a probable cause hearing, but not for giving legal advice to the police." The *Burns* case involved Cathy Burns of Muncie, Indiana, who allegedly shot her sleeping sons while laboring under a multiple personality disorder. In order to explore the possibility of multiple personality further, the police asked the prosecuting attorney if it would be appropriate for them to hypnotize the defendant. The prosecutor agreed that hypnosis would be a permissible avenue for investigation, and the suspect confessed to the murders while hypnotized. She later alleged in her complaint to the Supreme Court "that [the prosecuting attorney] knew or should have known that hypnotically induced testimony was inadmissible"[27] at trial.

The Abuse of Discretion

Because of the large amount of discretion prosecutors wield, there is considerable potential for them to abuse it. Discretionary decisions not to prosecute friends or political cronies or to accept guilty pleas to drastically reduced charges for personal considerations are always inappropriate and potentially dangerous possibilities. On the other hand, overzealous prosecution by district attorneys seeking heightened visibility in order to support grand political ambitions can be another source of abuse. Administrative decisions, such as case scheduling, which can wreak havoc with the personal lives of defendants and the professional lives of defense attorneys, can also be used by prosecutors to harass defendants into pleading guilty. Some forms of abuse may be unconscious. At least one study suggests that some prosecutors may have a built-in tendency toward leniency where female defendants are concerned, but tend to discriminate against minorities in deciding whether or not to prosecute.[28]

Although the electorate are the final authority to which prosecutors must answer, gross misconduct by prosecutors may be addressed by the state supreme court or by the state attorney general's office. Short of criminal misconduct, however, most of the options available to either the court or the attorney general are limited.

The Prosecutor's Professional Responsibility

From the moment you walk into the courtroom, you are the defendant's only friend.

—Austin, Texas, defense attorney Michael E. Tigar

As members of the legal profession, prosecutors are subject to the American Bar Association's (ABA) Code of Professional Responsibility. Serious violations of the code may result in a prosecutor being disbarred from the practice of law. The ABA Standard for Criminal Justice 3–1.1 describes the prosecutor's duty this way: "The duty of the prosecutor is to seek justice, not merely to convict." Hence, a prosecutor is barred by the standards of the legal profession from advocating any fact or position which he or she knows is untrue.

DEFENSE COUNSEL

Role of the Defense Attorney

Defense Counsel (also **Defense Attorney**) A licensed trial lawyer hired or appointed to conduct the legal defense of an individual accused of a crime and to represent him or her before a court of law.

The defense counsel is a trained lawyer who may specialize in the practice of criminal law. The task of the defense attorney is to represent the accused as soon as possible after arrest and to ensure that the civil rights of the defendant are not violated through processing by the criminal justice system. Other duties of the defense counsel include testing the strength of the prosecution's case, being involved in plea negotiations, and preparing an adequate defense to be used at trial. In the preparation of a defense, criminal lawyers may enlist private detectives, experts, witnesses to the crime, and character witnesses. Some will perform aspects of the role of private detective or of investigator themselves. They will also review relevant court precedents in order to determine what the best defense strategy might be.

Defense preparation may involve intense communications between lawyer and defendant. Such discussions are recognized as privileged communications, which are protected under the umbrella of lawyer-client confidentiality. In other words, lawyers cannot be compelled to reveal information which their client has confided to them.[29]

If their client is found guilty, defense attorneys will be involved in arguments at sentencing, may be asked to file an appeal, and will probably counsel the defendant and the defendant's family as to what civil matters (payment of debts, release from contractual obligations, etc.) may need to be arranged after sentence is imposed. Hence, the role of defense attorney encompasses many aspects, including attorney, negotiator, confidant, family and personal counselor, social worker, investigator, and, as we shall see, bill collector.

The Criminal Lawyer

Three major categories of defense attorneys assist criminal defendants in the United States: (1) private attorneys, usually referred to as "criminal lawyers"; (2) court-appointed counsel; and (3) public defenders.

A heated exchange between prosecutor Marcia Clark and defense attorney F. Lee Bailey during the O. J. Simpson trial. "I do not appreciate being called a liar in any court!" Bailey told the judge. The Simpson trial gave the public a bird's-eye view of the adversarial nature of our criminal justice system. *AFP/Bettmann*

Private attorneys (also called "retained counsel") either have their own legal practices or work for law firms in which they may be partners or employees. As those who have had to hire defense attorneys know, the fees of private attorneys can be high. Most privately retained criminal lawyers charge in the range of $100 to $200 per hour. Included in their bill is the time it takes to prepare for a case, as well as time spent in the courtroom. "High-powered" criminal defense attorneys who have established a regional or national reputation for successfully defending their clients can be far more expensive. A few such attorneys, such as Alan Dershowitz, Robert Shapiro, F. Lee Bailey, Johnnie Cochran (who was catapulted to fame during the O. J. Simpson criminal trial), the now-deceased civil-rights attorney William Kunstler, and Stephen Jones (who defended Timothy McVeigh), have become household names by virtue of their association with famous defendants and well-publicized trials. Fees charged by famous criminal defense attorneys may run into the hundreds of thousands of dollars—and sometimes exceed $1 million—for handling just one case!

No less an authority than Chief Justice of the U.S. Supreme Court, William H. Rehnquist, has complained that the profit motive has turned the practice of law into a business, leaving many lawyers dissatisfied and perhaps less trusted by their clients than was true in the past. At a speech two years ago to Catholic University's graduating law students, Rehnquist noted that "market capitalism has come to dominate the legal profession in a way that it did not a generation ago.... Today, the profit margin seems to be writ large in a way that it was not in the past." "[T]he practice of law is today a business where once it was a profession....," said Rehnquist.[30] Even so, the Chief Justice concluded, practicing law is still "the most satisfying way of making a living that I know of."

Although there are many high-priced criminal defense attorneys in the country, Rehnquist's comments were meant to apply mostly to civil attorneys who take a large portion of monetary awards they win for their clients. Few law students actually choose to specialize in criminal law, even though the job of a criminal lawyer may appear glamorous. Those who do often begin their careers immediately following law school, while others seek to gain experience working as assistant district attorneys or assistant public defenders for a number of years before going into private practice. In contrast to criminal lawyers whose

In all criminal prosecutions the accused shall enjoy the right to a speedy and public trial, by an impartial jury...and to be informed of the nature and cause of the accusation; to be confronted with the witnesses against him; to have compulsory process for obtaining witnesses in his favor; and to have the assistance of counsel for his defense.

—Sixth Amendment to the U.S. Constitution

names are household words, the collection of fees can be a significant source of difficulty for other defense attorneys. Most defendants are poor. Those who aren't are often reluctant to pay what may seem to them to be an exorbitant fee, and woe be it to the defense attorney whose client is convicted before the fee has been paid!

Public Defender An attorney employed by a government agency or subagency, or by a private organization under contract to a unit of government, for the purpose of providing defense services to indigents.

Criminal Defense of the Poor In 1990 state and local governments spent $1.3 billion to provide legal representation for criminal defendants unable to afford their own—and over 80% of all defendants in felony cases depend upon court-appointed attorneys, or **public defenders** to represent them.[31] A series of U.S. Supreme Court decisions have guaranteed that defendants unable to pay for private criminal defense attorneys will receive adequate representation at all stages of criminal justice processing.

In *Powell* v. *Alabama* (1932),[32] the Court held that the Fourteenth Amendment required state courts to appoint counsel for defendants in capital cases who were unable to afford their own. In 1938, in *Johnson* v. *Zerbst*,[33] the Court established the right of indigent defendants to receive the assistance of appointed counsel in all criminal proceedings in federal courts. The 1963 case of *Gideon* v. *Wainwright*[34] extended the right to appointed counsel in state courts to all indigent defendants charged with a felony. *Argersinger* v. *Hamlin* (1972)[35] saw the Court require adequate legal representation for anyone facing a potential sentence of imprisonment. Juveniles charged with delinquent acts were granted the right to appointed counsel in the case of *In re Gault* (1967),[36] which is discussed in detail in the chapter on juvenile justice.

States have responded to the federal mandate for indigent defense in a number of ways. Most now use one of three systems to deliver legal services to criminal defendants who are unable to afford their own: (1) court-assigned counsel, (2) public defenders, and (3) contractual arrangements. Most such systems are administered at the county level, although funding arrangements may involve state, county, and municipal monies.

Court-appointed defense attorneys, whose fees are paid at a rate set by the state or local government, comprise the most widely used system of indigent defense. Such defenders, also called "assigned counsel," are usually drawn from a roster of all practicing criminal attorneys within the jurisdiction of the trial court.

One problem with assigned counsel concerns degree of effort. Although most attorneys assigned by the court to indigent defense probably take their jobs seriously, some feel only a loose commitment to their clients. Paying clients, in their eyes, deserve better service and are apt to get it. The nationwide average cost per case for indigent defense in a recent year was $223, although the figure varied from a low of $63 in Arkansas to a high of $540 in New Jersey.[37]

The second type of indigent defense, the public defender program (such as the one described in the opening paragraph of this chapter), depends upon full-time salaried staff. Staff members include defense attorneys, defense investigators, and office personnel. Defense investigators gather information in support of the defense effort. They may interview friends, family members, and employers of the accused, with an eye toward effective defense. Public defender programs have become popular in recent years, with approximately 64% of counties nationwide now funding them.[38] A 1996 BJS report found that a public defender system is the primary method used to provide indigent counsel for criminal defendants and that 28% of state jurisdictions nationwide use public defender programs *exclusively* to provide indigent defense.[39] Critics charge that public defenders, because they are government employees, are not sufficiently independent from prosecutors and judges. For the same reason, clients may be suspicious of public defenders, viewing them as state functionaries. Finally, the huge caseloads typical of public defenders' offices create pressures toward an excessive use of plea bargaining.

A third type of indigent defense, contract attorney programs, arrange with local criminal lawyers to provide for indigent defense on a contractual basis. Individual attorneys, local bar associations, and multipartner law firms may all be used to provide for such arranged services. Contract defense programs are the least widely used form of indigent defense at present, although their numbers are growing.

Critics of the current system of indigent defense point out that the system is woefully underfunded. "In 1990," for example, "states spent $1.3 billion to prosecute individuals, but

GideON v. WAiNWRighT ANd INdigENT DeFENSE

Today about three-fourths of state-level criminal defendants and one-half of federal defendants are represented in court by publicly funded counsel.[1] As little as 30 years ago, however, the practice of publicly funded indigent defense was uncommon. That changed in 1963 when, in the case of *Gideon* v. *Wainwright*, the U.S. Supreme Court extended the right to legal counsel to indigent defendants charged with a criminal offense. The reasoning of the Court is well summarized in this excerpt from the majority opinion written by Justice Hugo Black:

...Governments, both state and federal, quite properly spend vast sums of money to establish machinery to try defendants accused of crime. Lawyers to prosecute are everywhere deemed essential to protect the public's interest in an orderly society.

Similarly, there are few defendants charged with crime, few indeed, who fail to hire the best lawyers they can get to prepare and present their defenses. That government hires lawyers to prosecute and defendants who have the money hire lawyers to defend are the strongest indications of the widespread belief that lawyers in criminal courts are necessities, not luxuries. The right of one charged with crime to counsel may not be deemed fundamental and essential to fair trials in some countries, but it is in ours. From the very beginning, our state and national constitutions and laws have laid great emphasis on procedural and substantive safeguards designed to assure fair trials before impartial tribunals in which every defendant stands equal before the law. This noble ideal cannot be realized if the poor man charged with crime has to face his accusers without a lawyer to assist him.

QUESTIONS FOR DISCUSSION

1. Do you agree with the Court that all indigent defendants should have the opportunity to have counsel appointed to represent them? Why or why not?
2. What would our system of criminal justice be like if court-appointed attorneys were not available to poor defendants?

[1]Steven K. Smith and Carol J. DeFrances, "Indigent Defense," Bureau of Justice Statistics, February 1996.

---

only $548 million on indigent defense; local governments spent $2.7 billion versus only $788 million; and the federal government $1.6 billion versus $408 million."[40] Overall, only 2.3% of monies spent on criminal justice activities goes to pay for indigent defense—an amount many consider too small.[41] As a consequence of such limited funding, many public defender's offices employ what critics call a "plead-'em-and-speed-'em through" strategy, often involving a heavy use of plea bargaining and initial meetings with clients in courtrooms as trials are about to begin. Mary Broderick of the National Legal Aid and Defender Association says, "We aren't being given the same weapons.... It's like trying to deal with smart bombs when all you've got is a couple of cap pistols."[42]

Of course, defendants need not accept any assigned counsel. Defendants who elect to do so may waive their right to an attorney and undertake their own defense—a right held to be inherent in the Sixth Amendment to the U.S. Constitution by the U.S. Supreme Court in the 1975 case of *Faretta* v. *California*.[43] Self-representation is uncommon, however, and only 1% of federal inmates and 3% of state inmates report having represented themselves.[44] The most famous instance of self-representation in recent years was probably the 1995 trial of Long Island Rail Road commuter train shooter Colin Ferguson, which is discussed later in this chapter.

Defendants who are not pleased with the lawyer appointed to defend them are in a somewhat different situation. They may request, through the court, that a new lawyer be assigned to represent them (as Timothy McVeigh did following his conviction and death sentence in the Oklahoma bombing case). However, unless there is clear reason for reassignment, such as an obvious personality conflict between defendant and attorney, few judges are likely to honor a request of this sort. Short of obvious difficulties, most judges will trust in the professionalism of appointed counselors.

O Lord, look down upon these the multitudes, and spread strife and dissension, so that this, Thy servant, might prosper.

—The Lawyer's Prayer (anonymous)

The Ethics of Defense

As we have discussed, the job of defense counsel at trial is to prepare and offer a vigorous defense on behalf of the accused. A proper defense often involves the presentation of evidence and the examination of witnesses, all of which requires careful thought and planning. Good attorneys, like quality craftspeople everywhere, may find themselves emotionally committed to the outcome of trials in which they are involved. Beyond the immediacy of a given trial, attorneys also realize that their reputations can be influenced by lay perceptions of their performance and that their careers and personal financial success depend upon consistently "winning" in the courtroom.

The nature of the adversarial process, fed by the emotions of the participants, conspires with the often privileged and extensive knowledge that defense attorneys have about a case, to tempt the professional ethics of some counselors. Because the defense counsel may often know more about the guilt or innocence of the defendant than anyone else prior to trial, the defense role is one which is carefully prescribed by ethical and procedural considerations. Attorneys violate both law and the standards of their own profession if they knowingly misrepresent themselves or their clients.

To help attorneys know what is expected of them, ethical standards abound. Four main groups of standards, each drafted by the American Bar Association, are especially applicable to defense attorneys

Canons of Professional Ethics
Model Code of Professional Responsibility
Model Rules of Professional Conduct
Standards for Criminal Justice

Each set of standards is revised periodically. The ABA Standard for Criminal Justice, Number 4–1.2, reads in part:

(e) Defense counsel, in common with all members of the bar, is subject to standards of conduct stated in statutes, rules, decisions of courts, and codes, canons, or other standards of professional conduct. Defense counsel has no duty to execute any directive of the accused which does not comport with law or such standards. Defense counsel is the professional representative of the accused, not the accused's alter ego.

(f) Defense counsel should not intentionally misrepresent matters of fact or law to the court.

(g) Defense counsel should disclose to the tribunal legal authority in the controlling jurisdiction known to defense counsel to be directly adverse to the position of the accused and not disclosed by the prosecutor.

(h) It is the duty of every lawyer to know and be guided by the standards of professional conduct as defined in codes and canons of the legal profession applicable in defense counsel's jurisdiction. Once representation has been undertaken, the functions and duties of defense counsel are the same whether defense counsel is assigned, privately retained, or serving in a legal aid or defender program.

Even with these directives, however, defense attorneys are under no obligation to reveal information obtained from a client without the client's permission. Sometimes, however, they may go too far. In 1992, Minneapolis multimillionaire Russell Lund, Jr., was arrested and charged with the murder of his estranged wife and her boyfriend—a former Iowa state senator. Following the murder, attention shifted to the activities of Lund's attorneys who, police claim, waited until the day after the killings before reporting the shooting, hired a private detective who may have destroyed some evidence, and checked Mr. Lund into a private psychiatric facility under a different name without telling police where he was—all activities which may have been both unethical and illegal.[45]

In 1986, the Supreme Court case of *Nix* v. *Whiteside*[46] clarified the duty of lawyers to reveal known instances of client perjury. The *Nix* case came to the Court upon the complaint of the defendant, Whiteside, who claimed that he was deprived of the assistance of effective counsel during a murder trial because his lawyer would not allow him to testify untruthfully. Whiteside wanted to testify that he had seen a gun or something metallic in his victim's hand before killing him. Before trial, however, Whiteside admitted to his lawyer that he had actually seen no weapon, but he believed that to testify to the truth would result in his convic-

Court-Appointed Counsel and the Oklahoma City Bombing

When terrorist bombers struck the Alfred P. Murrah Federal Building in Oklahoma City in the spring of 1995, they killed 168 people (19 of them children in a day care center on the building's first floor), wounded hundreds of others, and riveted national attention on two important issues facing court-appointed criminal defense counsel: (1) whether or not attorneys can be required to defend widely despised suspects and (2) whether unpopular and disdained clients can get a fair trial even if they are defended.

Timothy McVeigh, the first person to be tried in the Oklahoma City case, and a former army munitions expert, seemed guilty well before trial. Shortly after the bombing occurred the national media reported (somewhat incorrectly) that McVeigh appeared to have rented the truck used to deliver the bomb to the explosion site—even using his own name and driver's license when filling out the rental forms. Immediately after the bombing, McVeigh was arrested fleeing the scene in an old car with a missing license plate. Long before his trial began, McVeigh was reviled and hated by a large portion of the American public. He became a living symbol of a cowardly attack that killed and maimed many innocent people. Shortly after McVeigh's arrest, one lawyer sagely noted: "Across the ideological spectrum, Americans are united in hatred of him."[1]

Initially, attorneys John W. Coyle III and Susan Otto, federal public defenders in Oklahoma City, were appointed to represent McVeigh. The two soon received death threats, however, and an Oklahoma City federal judge, fearing for their safety, ordered that they be assigned 24-hour armed guards. Both attorneys quickly asked to be removed from the case, saying that they had friends among those killed in the bombing and claiming that they would find it hard to be objective. Coyle told the judge, "everyone in our city has been impacted by the explo-

sion, and counsel is no exception.... The enormous impact of this tragedy," Coyle wrote, "has caused doubt as to my ability to give Timothy McVeigh the absolutely unbiased and objective representation that everyone accused in our country deserves." More privately Coyle noted, "It's too much to ask any grand juror or trial juror to be fair in a trial like this."[2]

Finding another lawyer for McVeigh proved difficult. Miami attorney Roy Black, who successfully defended William Kennedy Smith against rape charges, turned down the case, saying he didn't think he could mount an effective defense because of his personal feelings about the crime. "Our system would not operate unless lawyers are willing to undertake the representation of the most hated and despised person," Black said.[3] But, he added, "I just think of that fireman carrying out that baby," referring to a widely published photograph which came to symbolize the horrors of the case.

The Sixth Amendment guarantees every criminal defendant the right to counsel but not the right to any particular attorney. Lawyers can and do turn down cases, but may do so legally only if they can show that there would be a genuine conflict of interest if they were to accept the case.

Finally, after a nationwide poll of possible candidates to defend McVeigh, Enid, Oklahoma, attorney Stephen Jones was called by David Russell, chief judge of the U.S. District Court for the Western District of Oklahoma, and took the job. Jones had been called after other attorneys turned the assignment down. At the time of his appointment Jones said, "I recognize that I am not the most popular person in Oklahoma..." But, he added, "[w]e honor the memory of the victims by granting the accused effective assistance of counsel, due process, a vigorous defense and trial by jury, not hysteria."[4] Jones was soon joined by Michael Tigar, a federal

appellate expert who teaches at the University of Texas School of Law, and Ronald Woods, a former FBI agent and U.S. attorney in Houston. The three were appointed through the efforts of San Antonio's Gerry Goldstein, head of the National Association of Criminal Defense Lawyers, who networked throughout the legal profession to find counsel for McVeigh. Rob Nigh, the chief federal public defender in Lincoln, Nebraska, and other attorneys later joined the defense team.

Comparing the McVeigh case with the earlier O. J. Simpson trial, one writer observed: "The test of our [criminal justice] system is not whether a rich celebrity can get justice in America, but whether a hated fanatic can."[5] Susan Estrich, a University of Southern California professor, explained it this way: "The adversary system of justice is frustrating and inefficient. But it is still the best way to get to the truth, particularly when we think we already know it. Only if the state's case is subjected to painstaking scrutiny can we be certain enough of guilt to take a man's life." Estrich added: "The job of defending a hated man should win the respect of the community, not its contempt. Not everyone can do it. But there is no more honorable task for an attorney."[6]

Prior to trial, however, some were more pragmatic in their assessment of the situation. "McVeigh's problem is not that he's despicable; it's that he's despicable and broke," said New York lawyer Ronald Kuby.[7] If he had money, Kuby claimed, lawyers "would be lined up outside his jail cell...thumping their chests about how he deserves representation...for their usual rate of X-hundred dollars an hour." Famed criminal defense attorney William Kunstler put it even more bluntly, "The law can't cope with this one...If Christ and all the angels testified [McVeigh] was innocent, he would still be found guilty."[8]

Even though McVeigh didn't have Simpson's personal resources, his defense tab—paid for by taxpayers—was huge. Near the conclusion of the trial, Jones estimated the cost of McVeigh's defense at about $3 million, while *Newsweek* magazine put the total at closer to $10 million.[9] In any case, the cost of McVeigh's defense was far higher than for that of an average federal death penalty case using public defenders—which runs about $104,000 dollars. For one thing, the costs associated with McVeigh's defense skyrocketed because he was tried in Denver—not in Oklahoma City—meaning that taxpayers had to pay for McVeigh's attorneys to set up shop away from home. Costs were also substantially increased by Jones' insistence that he needed to track down the international terrorists whom he claimed were the real culprits behind the bombing. Jones and other attorneys traveled to Europe, the Middle East, and Asia on at least nine separate occasions, visiting eight foreign countries in a fruitless effort to identify the foreign terrorists they said were responsible.

Money, however much, was not to win the day. On June 2, 1997, Kunstler's prognostication came true: Timothy McVeigh was convicted of a variety of charges, including planning the Oklahoma City bombing, carrying it out, and first-degree murder. Two weeks later, after hearing post-conviction pleas from both sides, the jury unanimously recommended that McVeigh be sentenced to death by lethal injection—a sentence that was formally imposed upon McVeigh by U.S. District Court Judge Richard Matsch on August 14, 1997.

QUESTIONS FOR DISCUSSION

1. If you were an attorney, might you have found it difficult to defend Timothy McVeigh? Why or why not?
2. Do you agree with professor Estrich that "The job of defending a hated man should win the respect of the community, not its contempt"? Explain your answer.

3. Was McVeigh's expense too costly? Why or why not? What, if anything, might have been done to reduce costs?

[1]Susan Estrich, "Fair Trial for McVeigh?" *USA Today*, April 27, 1995, p. 13A.
[2]Tony Mauro, "The Law Can't Cope with This Challenge," *USA Today*, April 27, 1995, p. 4A. Kevin Johnson, "McVeigh's Ex-Lawyer: Suspect far from 'Cool,'" *USA Today*, May 15, 1995, p. 3A.
[3]Saundra Torry, "Lawyers: Finding Counsel for McVeigh a True Test of Legal System," *The Washington Post* wire services, May 8, 1995.
[4]Laurie Asseo, "The Few & The Hated," the Associated Press wire services, May 12, 1995.
[5]Estrich, "Fair Trial for McVeigh?"
[6]Ibid.
[7]Sandra Torry, "Lawyers."
[8]Tony Mauro, "The Law Can't Cope."
[9]Robert Schmidt, "A Spare-No-Expenses Defense for McVeigh," *Legal Times*, March 31, 1997.

tion. The lawyer told Whiteside that, as a professional counselor, he would be forced to challenge Whiteside's false testimony if it occurred and to explain to the court the facts as he knew them. On the stand, Whiteside said only that he thought the victim was reaching for a gun, but did not claim to have seen one. He was found guilty of second-degree murder and appealed to the Supreme Court, on the claim of inadequate representation.

The Court, recounting the development of ethical codes in the legal profession, held that a lawyer's duty to a client "is limited to legitimate, lawful conduct compatible with the very nature of a trial as a search for truth…counsel is precluded from taking steps or in any way assisting the client in presenting false evidence or otherwise violating the law."[47]

The Bailiff

Bailiff The court officer whose duties are to keep order in the courtroom and to maintain physical custody of the jury.

Also called a court officer, **the bailiff**, another member of the professional courtroom work group, is usually an armed law enforcement officer. The job of the bailiff is to ensure order in the courtroom, announce the judge's entry into the courtroom, call witnesses, and prevent the escape of the accused (if the accused has not been released on bond). The bailiff also supervises the jury when it is sequestered and controls public and media access to the jury. Bailiffs in federal courtrooms are deputy U.S. marshals.

Courtrooms can be dangerous places. In 1993, George Lott was sentenced to die for a courtroom shooting in Tarrant County, Texas, which left two lawyers dead and three other people injured.[48] Lott said he had been frustrated by the court's handling of his divorce and by child molestation charges filed against him by his ex-wife. In a similar case, on May 5, 1992, a man opened fire with two pistols in a St. Louis courtroom during divorce proceedings, killing his wife and wounding her two lawyers and a security officer. The same day a presiding judge in Grand Forks, North Dakota, was shot to death by a man accused of failing to pay child support.[49] In 1997 a hooded man walked into an Urbana, Illinois, courtroom and lobbed a firebomb at a judge. The gas-filled bottle bounced off the judge's head and burst against a wall, setting the courtroom on fire. Three people were injured, and the judge

Defense attorney Stephen Jones (right), appointed by the court to defend suspected
Oklahoma City bomber Timothy McVeigh (center). *Kathy Roberts, AP/Wide World Photos*

suffered a cut on his head. "There's no court security in our building," explained Champaign
County (Illinois) Sheriff Dave Madigan.[50]

Local Court Administrators

Many states now employ trial court administrators whose job it is to facilitate the smooth
functioning of courts in particular judicial districts or areas. A major impetus toward the
hiring of local court administrators came from the 1967 President's Commission on Law
Enforcement and Administration of Justice. Examining state courts, the report found: "A
system that treats defendants who are charged with minor offenses with less dignity and consideration than it treats those who are charged with serious crimes."[51] A few years later, the
National Advisory Commission on Criminal Justice Standards and Goals recommended that
all courts with five or more judges should create the position of trial court administrator.[52]

Court administrators provide uniform court management, assuming many of the duties
previously performed by chief judges, prosecutors, and court clerks. Where court administrators operate, the ultimate authority for running the court still rests with the chief judge.
Administrators, however, are able to relieve the judge of many routine and repetitive tasks,
such as record keeping, scheduling, case flow analysis, personnel administration, space utilization, facilities planning, and budget management. They may also serve to take minutes at
meetings of judges and their committees.

Juror management is another area in which trial court administrators are becoming
increasingly involved. Juror utilization studies can identify such problems as the overselec-
tion of citizens for the jury pool and the reasons for what may be excessive requests to be
excluded from jury service. They can also reduce the amount of wasted time jurors spend
waiting to be called or empanelled.

Effective court administrators are able to track lengthy cases and identify bottlenecks in
court processing. They then suggest strategies to make the administration of justice increasingly efficient for courtroom professionals and more humane for lay participants.

The Court Recorder

Also called the court stenographer or court reporter, the role of the recorder is to create a
record of all that occurs during trial. Accurate records are very important in criminal trial

AMERICAN BAR ASSOCIATION STANDARDS of PROFESSIONAL RESPONSIBILITY

The intense effort of defense advocacy results, for most criminal trial lawyers, in an emotional and personal investment in the outcome of a case. To strike a balance between zealous and effective advocacy, on the one hand, and just professional conduct within the bounds of the law on the other, the American Bar Association has developed a Code of Professional Responsibility which reads in part:

In his representation of a client, a lawyer shall not:

- File a suit, assert a position, conduct a defense, delay a trial, or take other action on behalf of his client when he knows or when it is obvious that such action would serve merely to harass or maliciously injure another.
- Knowingly advance a claim or defense that is unwarranted under existing law...
- Conceal or knowingly fail to disclose that which he is required by law to reveal.
- Knowingly use perjured testimony or false evidence.
- Knowingly make a false statement of law or fact.
- Participate in the creation or preservation of evidence when he knows or it is obvious that the evidence is false.
- Counsel or assist his client in conduct that the lawyer knows to be illegal or fraudulent.

Source: Excerpted from American Bar Association, *Code of Professional Responsibility*, Disciplinary Rule 7–102. All rights reserved. Copies of this publication are available from Service Center, ABA, 750 N. Lakeshore Dr., Chicago, IL 60611.

It is the very hardest cases that truly test the system, and this is certainly one of them.

—American Bar Association President Roberta Cooper Ramo, commenting on the Oklahoma City bombing case

courts because appeals may be based entirely upon what went on in the courtroom. Especially significant are all verbal comments made in the courtroom, including testimony, objections, the rulings of the judge, the judge's instructions to the jury, arguments made by attorneys, and the results of conferences between the attorneys and the judge. Occasionally, the judge will rule that a statement should be "stricken from the record" because it is inappropriate or unfounded. The official trial record, often taken on a stenotype machine or audio recorder, may later be transcribed in manuscript form and will become the basis for any appellate review of the trial. Today's court stenographers often employ computer-aided transcription software (CAT), which translates typed stenographic shorthand into complete and readable transcripts. Court reporters may be members of the National Court Reporters Association, the United States Court Reporters Association, and the Association of Legal Administrators—all of which support the activities of these professionals.

Clerk of Court

The duties of the clerk of court (also known as the county clerk) extend beyond the courtroom. The clerk maintains all records of criminal cases, including all pleas and motions made both before and after the actual trial. The clerk also prepares a jury pool and issues jury summonses and subpoenas witnesses for both the prosecution and defense. During the trial, the clerk (or an assistant) marks physical evidence for identification as instructed by the judge and maintains custody of such evidence. The clerk also swears in witnesses and performs other functions as the judge directs.

Some states allow the clerk limited judicial duties such as the power to issue warrants and to serve as judge of probate—overseeing wills and the administration of estates and handling certain matters relating to persons declared mentally incompetent.[53]

Expert Witness A person who has special knowledge and skills recognized by the court as relevant to the determination of guilt or innocence. Expert witnesses may express opinions or draw conclusions in their testimony—unlike lay witnesses.

The Expert Witness

Most of the "insiders" we've talked about so far are either employees of the state or have ongoing professional relationships with the court (as in the case of defense counsel). Expert witnesses, however, may or may not have that kind of status, although some do. Expert witnesses are recognized for specialized skills and knowledge in an established profession or technical area. They must demonstrate their expertise through education, work experience, publications, and awards. By testifying at a trial they provide an effective way of introducing scientific evidence in such areas as medicine, psychology, ballistics, crime scene analysis, photography, and many other disciplines. An expert witness, like the other courtroom "actors" described in this chapter, is generally a paid professional. And, like all other witnesses, they are subject to cross-examination. Unlike other ("lay") witnesses, they are allowed to express opinions and draw conclusions, but only within their particular area of expertise. Expert witnesses may be veterans of many trials. Some well-known expert witnesses traverse the country and earn very high fees by testifying at one trial after another.

Expert witnesses have played significant roles in many well-known cases. The 1995 criminal trial of O. J. Simpson, for example, became a stage for a battle between experts in the analysis of human DNA, while expert testimony in the trial of John Hinckley resulted in a finding of "not guilty by reason of insanity" for the man accused of shooting then-President Reagan. Similarly, the highly publicized trial of Susan Smith, the South Carolina mother who confessed to the murder by drowning of her two young children, relied heavily upon the testimony of psychiatric experts and social workers. An important U.S. Supreme Court case addressing the admissibility of expert witness testimony is *Daubert* v. *Merrell Dow Pharmaceuticals*[54] (1993), which is discussed in greater detail in Chapter 17.

One of the difficulties with expert testimony is that it can be confusing to the jury. Sometimes the trouble is due to the nature of the subject matter and sometimes to disagreements between the experts themselves. Often, however, it arises from the strict interpretation given to expert testimony by procedural requirements. The difference between medical and legal definitions of insanity, for example, points to a divergence in both history and purpose between the law and science. Courts which attempt to apply criteria, such as the M'Naghten rule (discussed earlier), in deciding claims of "insanity" often find themselves faced with the testimony of psychiatric experts who refuse even to recognize the word. Such experts may prefer, instead, to speak in terms of psychosis and neurosis—words which have no place in judicial jargon. Legal requirements, because of the uncertainties they create, may pit experts against one another and confuse the jury.

Even so, most authorities agree that expert testimony is usually interpreted by jurors as more trustworthy than other forms of evidence. In a study of scientific evidence, one prosecutor commented that if he had to choose between presenting a fingerprint or an eyewitness at trial, he would always go with the fingerprint.[55] As a consequence of the effectiveness of scientific evidence, the National Institute of Justice recommends that "prosecutors consider the potential utility of such information in all cases where such evidence is available."[56] Some authors have called attention to the difficulties surrounding expert testimony. Procedural limitations often severely curtail the kinds of information which experts can provide.

Expert witnesses can earn substantial fees. DNA specialist John Gerdes, for example, was paid $100 per hour for his work in support of the defense in the O. J. Simpson criminal trial, and New York forensic pathologist Michael Baden charged $1,500 per day for time spent working for Simpson in Los Angeles. Baden billed Simpson more than $100,000, and the laboratory for which Gerdes worked received more than $30,000 from Simpson's defense attorneys.[57]

Outsiders: Nonprofessional Courtroom Participants

A number of people find themselves either unwilling or unwitting participants in criminal trials. Into this category fall defendants, victims, and most witnesses. Although they are "outsiders" who lack the status of paid professional participants, these are precisely the people who provide the "grist" for the judicial mill. Without them, trials could not occur, and the professional roles described earlier would be rendered meaningless.

LAY WITNESSES

Nonexpert witnesses, otherwise known as lay witnesses, may be called by either the prosecution or defense. Lay witnesses may be eyewitnesses, who saw the crime being committed

Lay Witness An eyewitness, character witness, or any other person called upon to testify who is not considered an expert. Lay witnesses must testify to facts alone and may not draw conclusions or express opinions.

The defendant's role can be crucial to the outcome of any trial, especially if they take the stand. Shown here is 19-year-old Louise Woodward, the British "nanny" convicted of second degree murder in the death of Matthew Eappen, an 8-month-old Massachussets infant in her care. Although originally sentenced to 15 years in prison after a jury did not believe her testimony, Judge Hiller Zobel ordered her conviction reduced to involuntary manslaughter and resentenced her to the time she had already served in jail. The Middlesex County district attorney's office appealed Zobel's ruling to the Massachusetts Supreme Judicial Court, arguing that the judge abused his authority, made legal errors and let his personal views influence his decision. *Jim Bourg, Gamma-Liaison, Inc.*

or who came upon the crime scene shortly after the crime had occurred. Another type of lay witness is the character witness, who provides information about the personality, family life, business acumen, and so on of the defendant in an effort to show that this is not the kind of person who would commit the crime he or she is charged with. Of course, the victim may also be a witness, providing detailed and sometimes lengthy testimony about the defendant and the event in question.

Witnesses are officially notified that they are to appear in court to testify by a written document called a **subpoena.** Subpoenas are generally "served" by an officer of the court or by a police officer, though they sometimes are mailed. Both sides in a criminal case may subpoena witnesses and might ask that persons called to testify bring with them books, papers, photographs, videotapes, or other forms of physical evidence. Witnesses who fail to appear when summoned may face contempt of court charges.

The job of a witness is to provide accurate testimony concerning only those things of which he or she has direct knowledge. Normally, witnesses will not be allowed to repeat things told to them by others unless it is necessary to do so in order to account for certain actions of their own. Since few witnesses are familiar with courtroom procedure, the task of testifying is fraught with uncertainty and can be traumatizing.

Anyone who testifies in a criminal trial must do so under oath, in which some reference to God is made, or after affirmation,[58] where a pledge to tell the truth is used by those who find either "swearing" or a reference to God objectionable. All witnesses are subject to cross-examination, a process that will be discussed in detail later in this chapter. Lay witnesses may be surprised to find that cross-examination can force them to defend their personal and moral integrity. A cross-examiner may question a witness about past vicious, criminal, or immoral acts, even where such matters have never been the subject of a criminal proceeding.[59] As long as the intent of such questions is to demonstrate to the jury that the witness may not be a person who is worthy of belief, they will normally be permitted by the judge.

Subpoena An order issued by a court of law requiring an individual to appear in court and to give testimony. Some subpoenas mandate that books, papers, and other items be surrendered to the court.

Witnesses have traditionally been shortchanged by the judicial process. Subpoenaed to attend court, they have often suffered from frequent and unannounced changes in trial dates. A witness who promptly responds to a summons to appear may find that legal maneuvering has resulted in unanticipated delays. Strategic changes by either side may make the testimony of some witnesses entirely unnecessary, and people who have prepared themselves for the psychological rigors of testifying often experience an emotional letdown.

In order to compensate witnesses for their time, and to make up for lost income, many states pay witnesses for each day that they spend in court. Payments range from $5 to $30 per day,[60] although some states pay nothing at all. In the case of *Demarest* v. *Manspeaker* (1991),[61] the U.S. Supreme Court held that federal prisoners, subpoenaed to testify, are entitled to witness fees just as nonincarcerated witnesses would be.

In another move to make the job of witnesses less onerous, 39 states and the federal government have laws or guidelines requiring that witnesses be notified of scheduling changes and cancellations in criminal proceedings.[62] In 1982 Congress passed the Victim and Witness Protection Act, which required the U.S. attorney general to develop guidelines to assist victims and witnesses in meeting the demands placed upon them by the justice system. A number of **victim assistance programs** (also called victim/witness assistance programs), described shortly, have also taken up a call for the rights of witnesses and are working to make the courtroom experience more manageable.

JURORS

Article III of the U.S. Constitution requires that "[t]he trial of all crimes…shall be by jury…" States have the authority to determine the size of criminal trial juries. Most states use juries composed of 12 persons and one or two alternates designated to fill in for jurors who are unable to continue due to accident, illness, or personal emergency. Some states allow for juries smaller than 12, and juries with as few as six members have survived Supreme Court scrutiny.[63]

Jury duty is regarded as a responsibility of citizenship. Other than juveniles and certain job occupants such as police personnel, physicians, members of the armed services on active duty, and emergency services workers, persons called for jury duty must serve unless they can convince a judge that they should be excused for overriding reasons. Aliens, those convicted of a felony, and citizens who have served on a jury within the past two years are excluded from jury service in most jurisdictions.

The names of prospective jurors are often gathered from the tax register, DMV records, or voter registration rolls of a county or municipality. Minimum qualifications for jury service include adulthood, a basic command of spoken English, citizenship, "ordinary intelligence," and local residency. Jurors are also expected to possess their "natural faculties," meaning that they should be able to hear, speak, see, move, and so forth. Some jurisdictions have recently allowed handicapped persons to serve as jurors, although the nature of the evidence to be presented in a case may preclude persons with certain kinds of handicaps from serving.

Ideally, the jury is to be a microcosm of society, reflecting the values, rationality, and common sense of the average person. The U.S. Supreme Court has held that criminal defendants have a right to have their cases heard before a jury of their peers.[64] Ideally, peer juries are those composed of a representative cross section of the community in which the alleged crime has occurred and where the trial is to be held. The idea of a peer jury stems from the Magna Carta's original guarantee of jury trials for "freemen." "Freemen" in England during the thirteenth century, however, were more likely to be of similar mind than is a cross section of Americans today. Hence, although the duty of the jury is to deliberate upon the evidence and, ultimately, determine guilt or innocence, social dynamics may play just as great a role in jury verdicts as do the facts of a case.

In a 1945 case, *Thiel* v. *Southern Pacific Company*,[65] the Supreme Court clarified the concept of a "jury of one's peers" by noting that while it is not necessary for every jury to contain representatives of every conceivable racial, ethnic, religious, gender, and economic group in the community, court officials may not systematically and intentionally exclude any juror solely because of his or her social characteristics.

The Role of the Victim in a Criminal Trial

Not all crimes have clearly identifiable victims. Some, like murder, do not have victims who survive. Where there is an identifiable surviving victim, however, he or she is often one of the

Victim Assistance Program
An organized program which offers services to victims of crime in the areas of crisis intervention and follow-up counseling and which helps victims secure their rights under the law.

Juror A member of a jury, selected for jury duty, and required to serve as an arbiter of the facts in a court of law. Jurors are expected to render verdicts of guilt or innocence as to the charges brought against an accused, although they may sometimes fail to do so (as in the case of a **hung jury**).

The O. J. Simpson Criminal Trial—The Jurors' Role

The jury is the crucial decision-making body in any criminal trial. Accordingly, the first few paragraphs of the opening statements of both the prosecution and the defense in the O. J. Simpson double-murder trial were directed at members of the jury. Here's what Los Angeles County prosecutor Christopher Darden told the jury:

> I think it's fair to say that I have the toughest job in town today except for the job that you have. Your job may just be a little bit tougher. It's your job—like my job, we both have a central focus, a single objective, and that objective is justice obviously.
>
> It's going to be a long trial and I want you to know how much we appreciate your being on the panel. We appreciate the personal sacrifices you're making by being sequestered. We understand that can be difficult.
>
> And I would like to thank you in advance for keeping the promises you made to us when you were selected for the jury initially. You promised to be fair and you promised to be open-minded and you promised to hear and see and carefully consider all the evidence in the case and you promised to...come to a verdict in this case solely on the basis of the evidence and the law given to you by Judge Ito.
>
> And you promised to do that based on the law, based on the facts and the evidence and nothing else. You promised us that you had no hidden agenda, that you only wanted to see justice done and you promised us that you would do everything you could under the law to see that justice was done.
>
> And so I thank you for that and I thank you in advance for the verdict you will at some point render in this case...

This is how defense attorney Johnnie Cochran, Jr., began the opening statement for the defense:

> We started this process of trial back on September 26, 1994, on the first day we all met, when we came down [from] the jury room up on the 11th floor. And here we are now, several months later, in this search for justice. You've heard a lot about this talk of justice. I guess Dr. Martin Luther King said it best when he said that "Injustice anywhere is a threat to justice everywhere." So we are now embarked upon a search for justice, this search for truth, this search for the facts.
>
> Each of you made a number of promises in the course of the *voir dire* examination, which is basically unprecedented and due mainly to the largess of Judge Ito in understanding the possibility of media taint associated with this case. So we know a lot about you at this point and we, of course—all sides are very, very pleased with the fact you agreed to serve as jurors, to give us your time to leave your lives, to be sequestered, as it were. That's a remarkable sacrifice. Abraham Lincoln said it best when he said that "The highest act of citizenship is jury service." And you embarked on that jury service.
>
> And it doesn't stop with just coming down and taking notes. It doesn't stop with the inconvenience of being away from your families. It stops when you can render a verdict in this case, and whether or not that verdict reflects the evidence in this case. A verdict void of sympathy for or passion against Mr. Simpson or any side in this case. You made these promises on both sides and we know you're going to keep those promises. Cicero said that "He who violates his oath profanes the faith of divinity itself." And, of course, we know that you will live up to your promises, and be fair, and keep an open mind and decide this case not on speculation, not on conjecture, not on surmise, but based upon the facts.
>
> You, as jurors, are the conscience of this community. Your verdicts set the standards of what we should have and what should happen in this community. You have this rare opportunity, it seems to me, to be participants in this search for justice and for truth. In the final analysis, hopefully by April of this year—I'm optimistic still—you'll be able to render perhaps the most important decision of your lives. So we want to keep your minds open and fresh so you can render that decision impartially on both sides, so that people all across the world can say, "This system works. This was a fair trial. These were fair people." So thank you in advance for your service, for the verdict you're likely to render and for all the things you're doing here for us....

QUESTIONS FOR DISCUSSION

1. Do you believe that a criminal trial jury is truly the conscience of a community? If so, should a jury be able to render a verdict not in keeping with the facts of a case, if it so chooses?

2. Given the length of the Simpson trial and the many inconveniences brought about by sequestering the jury, it must have taken special kinds of people to serve on the Simpson jury. What social characteristics might these jurors have had? How might such characteristics have affected the outcome of the trial?

most forgotten people in the courtroom. Although the victim may have been profoundly affected by the crime itself, and is often emotionally committed to the proceedings and trial outcome, they may not even be permitted to participate directly in the trial process. Although a powerful movement to recognize the interests of victims has begun (and is discussed in detail in the next chapter), it is still not unusual for crime victims to be totally unaware of the final outcome of a case which intimately concerns them.[66]

Hundreds of years ago the situation surrounding victims was far different. During the early Middle Ages in much of Europe, victims, or their survivors, routinely played a central role in trial proceedings and in sentencing decisions. They testified, examined witnesses, challenged defense contentions, and pleaded with the judge or jury for justice, honor, and often revenge. Sometimes they were even expected to carry out the sentence of the court, by flogging the offender or by releasing the trapdoor used for hangings. This "golden age" of the victim ended with the consolidation of power into the hands of monarchs who declared that vengeance was theirs alone.

Today, victims, like witnesses, experience many hardships as they participate in the criminal court process. Some of the rigors they endure are

1. Uncertainties as to their role in the criminal justice process.
2. A general lack of knowledge about the criminal justice system, courtroom procedure, and legal issues.
3. Trial delays which result in frequent travel, missed work, and wasted time.
4. Fear of the defendant or of retaliation from the defendant's associates.
5. The trauma of testifying and of cross-examination.

The trial process itself can make for a bitter experience. If victims take the stand, defense attorneys may test their memory, challenge their veracity, or even suggest that they were somehow responsible for their own victimization. After enduring cross-examination, some victims report feeling as though they, and not the offender, have been portrayed as the criminal to the jury. The difficulties encountered by victims have been compared to a second victimization at the hands of the criminal justice system. Additional information on victims and victim's issues, including victim's assistance programs, is provided in the next chapter.

The Role of the Defendant in a Criminal Trial

Generally, defendants must be present at their trials. Similar to state rules, federal rules of criminal procedure require that a defendant "must be present at every stage of a trial…[except that a defendant who] is initially present may…be voluntarily absent after the trial has commenced." In *Crosby* v. *U.S.* (1993),[67] the U.S. Supreme Court held that a defendant may not be tried in absentia even if he or she was present at the beginning of a trial where his or her absence is due to escape or failure to appear. In a related issue, *Zafiro* v. *U.S.* (1993)[68] held that, at least in federal courts, defendants charged with similar or related offenses may be tried together—even when their defenses differ substantially.

The majority of criminal defendants are poor, uneducated, and often alienated from the philosophy which undergirds the American justice system. A common view of the defendant in a criminal trial is that of a relatively powerless person at the mercy of judicial mechanisms. Many defendants are just that. However, such an image is often far from the truth. Defendants, especially those who seek an active role in their own defense, choreograph many courtroom activities. Experienced defendants, notably those who are career offenders, may be well versed in courtroom demeanor.

Defendants in criminal trials have a right to represent themselves and need not retain counsel nor accept the assistance of court-appointed attorneys. Such a choice, however, may not be in their best interests. The most famous instance of self-representation in recent years was probably the 1995 trial of Long Island Rail Road commuter train shooter, Colin Ferguson. Ferguson, who rejected both legal advice and in-court assistance from defense attorneys and chose to represent himself during trial, was convicted of killing six passengers and wounding 19 others during a racially motivated shooting rampage in December 1993. Some observers said that Ferguson's performance as defendant turned defense attorney "distressed his court-appointed lawyer-advisers, exacerbated the pain of the victims' family

The beauty of the jury is their morality. Tap into it.

—San Francisco defense attorney Tony Serra

An artist's depiction of a portion of the 1995 South Carolina murder trial of Susan Smith. Federal courts and some state jurisdictions still restrict the use of cameras in the courtroom. Smith was convicted of drowning her two young children by rolling the car in which they were strapped into a lake. She was sentenced to life in prison. *Yvonne Hemsey, Gamma—Liaison, Inc.*

I do not know whether the jury is useful to those who are in litigation; but I am certain it is highly beneficial to those who decide the litigation; and I look upon it as one of the most efficacious means for the education of the people which society can employ.

—Alexis de Tocqueville

members and turned the courtroom of Nassau County Judge Donald E. Belfi into a theater of the bizarre."[69] Others called it a "sham" and a "circus," but astute observers noted that it set up the possibility for a successful appeal. Following conviction, Ferguson reportedly[70] asked famed defense attorney William M. Kunstler, one of his original lawyers, to file an appeal, focusing on whether Ferguson was mentally fit to represent himself and whether the judge erred in allowing him to do so.

Even without self-representation, every defendant who chooses to do so can substantially influence events in the courtroom. Defendants exercise choice in (1) deciding whether or not to testify personally, (2) selecting and retaining counsel, (3) planning a defense strategy in coordination with their attorney, (4) deciding what information to provide to (or withhold from) the defense team, (5) deciding what plea to enter, and (6) determining whether or not to file an appeal, if convicted.

Nevertheless, even the most active defendants suffer from a number of disadvantages. One is the tendency of others to assume that anyone on trial must be guilty. Although a person is "innocent until proven guilty," the very fact that he or she is accused of an offense casts a shadow of suspicion that may foster biases in the minds of jurors and other courtroom actors. Another disadvantage lies in the often-substantial social and cultural differences which separate the offender from the professional courtroom staff. While lawyers and judges tend to identify with upper-middle-class values and lifestyles, few offenders do. The consequences of such a gap between defendant and courtroom staff may be insidious and far reaching.

The Press in the Courtroom

Often overlooked, because they do not have an official role in courtroom proceedings, are spectators and the press. At any given trial both spectators and media representatives may be present in large numbers. Spectators include members of the families of both victim and defendant, friends of either side, and curious onlookers—some of whom are avocational court watchers.

Newswriters, TV reporters, and other members of the press are apt to be present at "spectacular" trials (those involving some especially gruesome aspect or famous personality) and at those in which there is a great deal of community interest. The right of reporters and spectators to be present at a criminal trial is supported by the Sixth Amendment's insistence upon a public trial.

Press reports at all stages of a criminal investigation and trial often create problems for the justice system. Significant pretrial publicity about a case may make it difficult to find jurors who have not already formed an opinion as to the guilt or innocence of the defendant. News reports from the courtroom may influence or confuse nonsequestered jurors who hear them, especially when they contain information brought to the bench, but not heard by the jury.

In the 1976 case of *Nebraska Press Association* v. *Stuart*,[71] the U.S. Supreme Court ruled that trial court judges could not legitimately issue gag orders, preventing the pretrial publication of information about a criminal case, as long as the defendant's right to a fair trial and an impartial jury could be ensured by traditional means.[72] These means include (1) a change of venue, whereby the trial is moved to another jurisdiction less likely to have been exposed to the publicity; (2) trial postponement, which would allow for memories to fade and emotions to cool; and (3) jury selection and screening to eliminate biased persons from the jury pool. In 1986 the Court extended press access to preliminary hearings, which, it said, are "sufficiently like a trial to require public access."[73] In 1993, in the case of *Caribbean International News Corporation* v. *Puerto Rico*,[74] the Court effectively applied that requirement to territories under U.S. control.

Today, members of the press as well as video, television, and still cameras are allowed into most state courtrooms. Forty-seven states now allow courtroom cameras,[75] and organizations like Court TV have capitalized on the opportunity for live courtroom broadcasts.

The U.S. Supreme Court has been less favorably disposed to television coverage than have state courts. In 1981, a Florida defendant appealed his burglary conviction to the Supreme Court,[76] arguing that the presence of TV cameras at his trial had turned the court into a circus for attorneys and made the proceedings more a sideshow than a trial. The Supreme Court, recognizing that television cameras have an untoward effect upon many people, agreed. In the words of the Court, "Trial courts must be especially vigilant to guard against any impairment of the defendant's right to a verdict based solely upon the evidence and the relevant law."[77]

The Judicial Conference of the United States, the primary policy-making arm of the federal courts, seems to agree with the high court. A three-year pilot project which allowed television cameras into six U.S. District Courts and two appeals courts on an experimental basis closed on December 31, 1994, when the Conference voted to end the project. The Conference terminated the experiment, ruling that neither still nor video cameras would be allowed into federal courtrooms in the future. Conference members expressed concerns that cameras were a distracting influence and were having a "negative impact on jurors [and] witnesses"[78] by exposing them to possible harm by revealing their identities.

The Criminal Trial

From arrest through sentencing, the criminal justice process is carefully choreographed. Arresting officers must follow proper procedure in the gathering of evidence and in the arrest and questioning of suspects. Magistrates, prosecutors, jailers, and prison officials are all subject to similar strictures. Nowhere, however, is the criminal justice process more closely circumscribed than at the stage of the criminal trial.

Procedures in a modern courtroom are highly formalized. **Rules of evidence**, which govern the admissibility of evidence, and other procedural guidelines determine the course of a criminal hearing and trial. Rules of evidence are partially based upon tradition. All U.S. jurisdictions, however, have formalized rules of evidence in written form. Criminal trials at the federal level generally adhere to the requirements of *Federal Rules of Evidence*.

Trials are also circumscribed by informal rules and professional expectations. An important component of law school education is the teaching of rules which structure and define appropriate courtroom demeanor. In addition to statutory rules, law students are thoroughly exposed to the ethical standards of their profession as found in American Bar Association standards and other writings.

Rules of Evidence Rules of court which govern the admissibility of evidence at a criminal hearing and trial.

Adversarial System The two-sided structure under which American criminal trial courts operate, which pits the prosecution against the defense. In theory, justice is done when the most effective adversary is able to convince the judge or jury that his or her perspective on the case is the correct one.

In the next few pages we will describe the chronology of a criminal trial and comment on some of the widely accepted rules of criminal procedure. Before we begin the description, however, it is good to keep two points in mind. One is that the primary purpose of any criminal trial is the determination of the defendant's guilt or innocence. In this regard it is important to recognize the crucial distinction that scholars make between legal guilt and factual guilt. Factual guilt deals with the issue of whether or not the defendant is actually responsible for the crime of which he or she stands accused. If the defendant "did it," then he or she is, in fact, guilty. Legal guilt is not so clear. Legal guilt is established only when the prosecutor presents evidence which is sufficient to convince the judge (where the judge determines the verdict) or jury that the defendant is guilty as charged. The distinction between legal guilt and factual guilt is crucial because it points to the fact that the burden of proof rests with the prosecution, and it indicates the possibility that guilty defendants may, nonetheless, be found "not guilty."

The second point to remember is that criminal trials under our system of justice are built around an adversarial system and that central to such a system is the advocacy model. Participating in the adversarial system are advocates for the state (the prosecution or district attorney) and for the defendant (defense counsel, public defender, etc.). The philosophy behind the adversarial system holds that the greatest number of just resolutions in all foreseeable criminal trials will occur when both sides are allowed to argue their cases effectively and vociferously before a fair and impartial jury. The system requires that advocates for both sides do their utmost, within the boundaries set by law and professional ethics, to protect and advance the interests of their clients (that is, the defendant and the state). The advocacy model makes clear that it is not the job of the defense attorney or the prosecution to judge the guilt of any defendant. Hence, even defense attorneys who are convinced that their client is guilty are still exhorted to offer the best possible defense and to counsel their client as effectively as possible.

The **adversarial system** has been criticized by some thinkers who point to fundamental differences between law and science in the way the search for truth is conducted.[79] While proponents of traditional legal procedure accept the belief that truth can best be uncovered through an adversarial process, scientists adhere to a painstaking process of research and replication to acquire knowledge. Most of us would agree that scientific advances in recent years may have made factual issues less difficult to ascertain. For example, some of the new scientific techniques in evidence gathering, such as DNA fingerprinting (discussed in detail in Chapter 17), are now able to unequivocally link suspects to criminal activity. Whether scientific findings should continue to serve a subservient role to the adversarial process itself is a question now being raised. The ultimate answer will probably be couched in terms of the results either process is able to produce. If the adversarial model results in the acquittal of too many demonstrably guilty people because of legal "technicalities," or the scientific approach inaccurately identifies too many suspects, either could be restricted.

We turn now to a discussion of the steps in a criminal trial. As Figure 9–1 shows, trial chronology consists of eight stages:

Trial initiation

Jury selection

Opening statements

Presentation of evidence

Closing arguments

The judge's charge to the jury

Jury deliberations

The verdict

For purposes of brevity, jury deliberations and the verdict will be discussed jointly. If the defendant is found guilty, a sentence will be imposed by the judge at the conclusion of the trial. Sentencing is discussed in the next chapter.

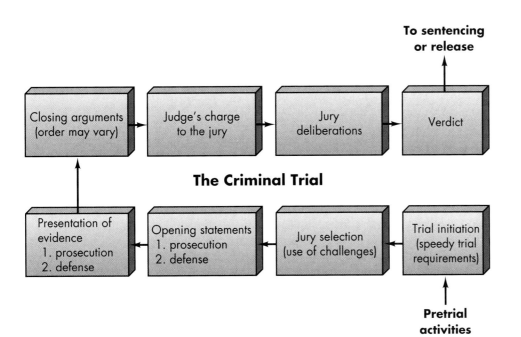

FIGURE 9–1 Stages in a criminal trial.

Trial Initiation: The Speedy Trial Act

As we mentioned in Chapter 8, the Sixth Amendment to the U.S. Constitution guarantees that "In all criminal prosecutions, the accused shall enjoy the right to a speedy and public trial." Clogged court calendars, limited judicial resources, and general inefficiency, however, often combine to produce what appears to many to be unreasonable delays in trial initiation. The attention of the Supreme Court was brought to bear on trial delays in three precedent-setting cases: *Klopfer* v. *North Carolina* (1967),[80] *Baker* v. *Wingo* (1972),[81] and *Strunk* v. *United States* (1973).[82] The *Klopfer* case involved a Duke University professor and focused on civil disobedience in a protest against segregated facilities. In Klopfer's long-delayed trial, the Court asserted that the right to a speedy trial is a fundamental guarantee of the Constitution. In the *Baker* case, the Court held that Sixth Amendment guarantees to a quick trial could be illegally violated even in cases where the accused did not explicitly object to delays. In *Strunk*, it found that denial of a speedy trial should result in a dismissal of all charges.

In 1974, against the advice of the Justice Department, the U.S. Congress passed the federal Speedy Trial Act.[83] The act, which was phased in gradually and became fully effective in 1980, allows for the dismissal of federal criminal charges in cases where the prosecution does not seek an indictment or information within 30 days of arrest (a 30-day extension is granted when the grand jury is not in session) or where a trial does not begin within 70 working days after indictment for defendants who plead not guilty. If a defendant is not available for trial, or witnesses cannot be called within the 70-day limit, the period may be extended to 180 days. Delays brought about by the defendant, through requests for a continuance or because of escape, are not counted in the specified time periods. The Speedy Trial Act has been condemned by some as shortsighted. One federal judge, for example, wrote: "The ability of the criminal justice system to operate effectively and efficiently has been severely impeded by the Speedy Trial Act. Resources are misdirected, unnecessary severances required, cases proceed to trial inadequately prepared, and in some indeterminate number of cases, indictments against guilty persons are dismissed."[84]

In an important 1988 decision, *U.S.* v. *Taylor*,[85] the U.S. Supreme Court applied the requirements of the Speedy Trial Act to the case of a drug defendant who had escaped following arrest. The Court made it clear that trial delays, when they derive from the willful actions of the defendant, do not apply to the 70-day period. The Court also held that trial delays, even when they result from government action, do not necessarily provide grounds

Speedy Trial Act A 1974 federal law requiring that proceedings in a criminal case against a defendant begin before passage of a specified period of time, such as 70 working days after indictment. Some states also have speedy trial requirements.

for dismissal if they occur "without prejudice." Delays without prejudice are those which are due to circumstances beyond the control of criminal justice agencies.

In 1993, an Indiana prisoner, William Fex, appealed a Michigan conviction on armed robbery and attempted murder charges, claiming that he had to wait 196 days after submitting a request to Indiana prison authorities for his Michigan trial to commence. In *Fex* v. *Michigan* (1993),[86] the U.S. Supreme Court ruled that "common-sense compel[s] the conclusion that the 180-day period does not commence until the prisoner's disposition request has actually been delivered to the court and prosecutor of the jurisdiction that lodged the detainer against him." In Fex's case, Indiana authorities had taken 22 days to forward his request to Michigan.

However, in a 1992 case, *Doggett* v. *U.S.*,[87] the Court held that a delay of eight and one-half years violated speedy trial provisions because it resulted from government negligence. In *Doggett*, the defendant was indicted on a drug charge in 1980, but left the country for Panama, where he lived until 1982 when he reentered the United States. He lived openly in the United States until 1988 when a credit check revealed him to authorities. He was arrested, tried, and convicted of federal drug charges stemming from his 1980 indictment. In overturning his conviction, the U.S. Supreme Court ruled: "...even delay occasioned by the Government's negligence creates prejudice that compounds over time, and at some point, as here, becomes intolerable."[88]

The federal Speedy Trial Act is applicable only to federal courts. However, the *Klopfer* case (just discussed) effectively made constitutional guarantees of a speedy trial applicable to state courts. In keeping with the trend toward reduced delays, many states have since enacted their own speedy trial legislation. Typical state legislation sets limits of 120 or 90 days as a reasonable period of time for a trial to commence.

JURY SELECTION

Jury Selection The process whereby, according to law and precedent, members of a particular trial jury are chosen.

As we mentioned in our discussion of the role of the jury in a criminal trial, the Sixth Amendment also guarantees the right to an impartial jury. An impartial jury is not necessarily an ignorant one. In other words, jurors will not always be excused from service on a jury if they have some knowledge of the case which is before them.[89] Jurors, however, who have already formed an opinion as to the guilt or innocence of a defendant are likely to be excused.

Anyone who has ever been called as a juror knows that some prospective jurors try to get excused and others who would like to serve are excused because they are not judged to be suitable. Prosecution and defense attorneys use challenges to ensure the impartiality of the jury which is being empanelled. Three types of challenges are recognized in criminal courts: (1) challenges to the array, (2) challenges for cause, and (3) **peremptory challenges**.

Peremptory Challenge A means of removing unwanted potential jurors without the need to show cause for their removal. Prosecutors and defense attorneys routinely use peremptory challenges in order to eliminate from juries individuals who, although they express no obvious bias, may be thought to hold the potential to sway the jury in an undesirable direction.

Challenges to the array signify the belief, generally by the defense attorney, that the pool from which potential jurors are to be selected is not representative of the community or is biased in some significant way. A challenge to the array is argued before the hearing judge before jury selection begins.

During the jury selection process, both prosecution and defense attorneys question potential jurors in a process known as *voir dire* examination. Jurors are expected to be unbiased and free of preconceived notions of guilt or innocence. Challenges for cause, which may arise during *voir dire* examination, make the claim that an individual juror cannot be fair or impartial. One special issue of juror objectivity has concerned the Supreme Court. It is whether jurors with philosophical opposition to the death penalty should be excluded from juries whose decisions might result in the imposition of capital punishment. In the case of *Witherspoon* v. *Illinois* (1968),[90] the Court ruled that a juror opposed to the death penalty could be excluded from such juries if it were shown that (1) the juror would automatically vote against conviction without regard to the evidence or (2) the juror's philosophical orientation would prevent an objective consideration of the evidence. The *Witherspoon* case has left unresolved a number of issues, among them the concern that it is difficult to demonstrate how a juror would automatically vote, a fact which may not even be known to the juror before trial begins.

Another area of concern which has been addressed by the Supreme Court involves the potential that jurors may be biased because of being exposed to stories about a case in the news media that appear before the start of trial. Such concerns provided an especially tricky issue for Judge Lance Ito during the double-murder trial of O. J. Simpson as Ito supervised the process of jury selection. A similar, but far less well-known case which has been reviewed by the Court is that of *Mu'Min* v. *Virginia* (1991).[91] Mu'Min was a Virginia inmate who was serving time for first-degree murder. While accompanying a work detail outside of the institution, he committed another murder. At the ensuing trial, 8 of the 12 jurors who were seated admitted that they had heard or read something about the case, although none indicated that he or she had formed an opinion in advance as to Mu'Min's guilt or innocence. Following his conviction, Mu'Min appealed to the Supreme Court, claiming that his right to a fair trial had been denied due to pretrial publicity. The Court disagreed and upheld his conviction, citing the admittedly unbiased nature of the jurors.

The third kind of challenge, the peremptory challenge, effectively removes potential jurors without the need to give a reason. Peremptory challenges, used by both the prosecution and defense, are limited in number. Federal courts allow each side up to 20 peremptory challenges in capital cases and as few as three in minor criminal cases.[92] States vary as to the number of peremptory challenges they permit.

A developing field, which seeks to take advantage of peremptory challenges, is **scientific jury selection**. Scientific jury selection uses correlational techniques from the social sciences to gauge the likelihood that potential jurors will vote for conviction or acquittal. It makes predictions based on the economic, ethnic, and other personal and social characteristics of each member of the juror pool. Intentional jury selection techniques appeared to play a significant role in the outcome of the trial of Larry Davis. Davis, who is black, was charged with the 1986 shooting of seven white New York City police officers as they attempted to arrest the heavily armed defendant for the alleged murder of four drug dealers.[93] None of the officers died, and Davis was later apprehended. At the trial, defense attorney William Kunstler assembled a jury of ten blacks and two Hispanics. On two occasions Judge Bernard Fried had dismissed previous juries before the trial could begin, saying that Kunstler was packing the panel with blacks.[94] Although many of the wounded officers testified against Davis, and no one seriously disputed the contention that Davis was the triggerman in the shooting of the officers, the jury found him innocent. The finding prompted one of the injured policemen to claim, "It was a racist verdict."[95] Explaining the jury's decision another way, a spokesperson for the NAACP Legal Defense Fund said after the trial, "The experience of blacks in the criminal justice system may make them less prone to accept the word of a police officer."[96]

Criticisms of jury selection techniques have focused on the end result of the process. Such techniques generally remove potential jurors who have any knowledge or opinions about the case to be tried. Also removed are persons trained in the law or in criminal justice. Anyone working for a criminal justice agency or anyone who has a family member working for such an agency or for a defense attorney will likely be dismissed through peremptory challenges on the chance that they may be biased in favor of one side or the other. Scientific jury selection techniques may result in the additional dismissal of educated or professionally successful individuals, to eliminate the possibility of such individuals exercising undue control over jury deliberations. The end result of the jury selection process may be to produce a jury composed of people who are uneducated, uninformed, and generally inexperienced at making any type of well-considered decision. Some of the jurors may not understand the charges against the defendant or comprehend what is required for a finding of guilt or innocence. Likewise, some selected jurors may not even possess the span of attention needed to hear all the testimony that will be offered in a case. As a consequence, decisions rendered by such a jury may be based more upon emotion than upon findings of fact.

Scientific Jury Selection
The use of correlational techniques from the social sciences to gauge the likelihood that potential jurors will vote for conviction or acquittal.

Jury Selection and Race

Juries intentionally selected so that they are racially unbalanced may soon be a thing of the past. As long ago as 1880, the U.S. Supreme Court held that "a statute barring blacks from service on grand or petit juries denied equal protection of the laws to a black man convicted of murder by an all-white jury."[97] Even so, peremptory challenges continued to tend to lead to racial imbalance. In 1965, for example, a black defendant in Alabama was convicted of rape by an all-white jury. The local prosecutor had used his peremptory challenges to exclude blacks from the jury. The case eventually reached the Supreme Court, where the conviction was upheld.[98] At that time, the Court refused to limit the practice of peremptory challenges, reasoning that to do so would place them under the same judicial scrutiny as challenges for cause.

Pre- and Posttrial Motions

A motion is defined by the *Dictionary of Criminal Justice Data Terminology*[1] as "[a]n oral or written request made to a court at any time before, during, or after court proceedings, asking the court to make a specified finding, decision, or order." Written motions are called petitions. This box lists the typical kinds of motions that may be made by both sides in a criminal case before and after trial.

MOTION FOR DISCOVERY

A motion for discovery, filed by the defense, asks the court to allow the defendant's lawyers to view the evidence which the prosecution intends to present at trial. Physical evidence, lists of witnesses, documents, photographs, and so on, which the prosecution plans to introduce in court, will usually be made available to the defense as a result of such a motion.

MOTION TO SUPPRESS EVIDENCE

In the preliminary hearing, or through pretrial discovery, the defense may learn of evidence which the prosecution intends to introduce at the trial. If some of that evidence has been, in the opinion of the defense counsel, unlawfully acquired, a motion to suppress the evidence may be filed.

MOTION TO DISMISS CHARGES

A variety of circumstances may result in the filing of a motion to dismiss. They include (1) an opinion, by defense counsel, that the indictment or information is not sound; (2) violations of speedy trial legislation; (3) a plea bargain with the defendant (which may require testimony against codefendants); (4) the death of an important witness or the destruction or disappearance of necessary evidence; (5) the confession, by a supposed victim, that the facts in the case have been fabricated; and (6) the success of a motion to suppress evidence which effectively eliminates the prosecution's case.

MOTION FOR CONTINUANCE

This motion seeks a delay in the start of the trial. Defense motions for continuance are often based upon the inability to locate important witnesses, the illness of the defendant, or a change in defense counsel immediately prior to trial.

MOTION FOR CHANGE OF VENUE

In well-known cases, pretrial publicity may lessen the opportunity for a case to be tried before an unbiased jury. A motion for a change in venue asks that the trial be moved to some other area where prejudice against the defendant is less likely to exist.

MOTION FOR SEVERANCE OF OFFENSES

Defendants charged with a number of crimes may ask to be tried separately on all or some of the charges. Although consolidating charges for trial saves time and money, some defendants may think that it is more likely to make them appear guilty.

MOTION FOR SEVERANCE OF DEFENDANTS

Similar to the preceding motion, this request asks the court to try the accused separately from any codefendants. Motions for severance are likely to be filed where the defendant believes that the jury may be prejudiced against him or her by evidence applicable only to other defendants.

MOTION TO DETERMINE PRESENT SANITY

"Present sanity," even though it may be no defense against the criminal charge, can delay trial. A person cannot be tried, sentenced, or punished while insane. If a defendant is insane at the time a trial is to begin, this motion may halt the proceedings until treatment can be arranged.

MOTION FOR A BILL OF PARTICULARS

This motion asks the court to order the prosecutor to provide detailed information about the charges which the defendant will be facing in court. Defendants charged with a number of offenses, or with a number of counts of the same offense, may make such a motion. They may, for example, seek to learn which alleged instances of an offense will become the basis for prosecution or which specific items of contraband allegedly found in their possession are held to violate the law.

MOTION FOR A MISTRIAL

A mistrial may be declared at any time, and a motion for mistrial may be made by either side. Mistrials are likely to be declared where highly prejudicial comments are made by either attorney. Defense motions for a mistrial do not provide grounds for a later claim of double jeopardy.

MOTION FOR ARREST OF JUDGMENT

After the verdict of the jury has been announced, but before sentencing, the defendant may make a motion for arrest of judgment. Such a motion means the defendant believes that some legally acceptable reason exists as to why sentencing should not occur. Defendants who are seriously ill, hospitalized, or who have gone insane prior to judgment being imposed may file such a motion.

MOTION FOR A NEW TRIAL

After a jury has returned a guilty verdict, a defense motion for a new trial may be entertained by the court. Acceptance of such a motion is most often based upon the discovery of new evidence which is of significant benefit to the defense, and will set aside the conviction.

[1]U.S. Department of Justice, *Dictionary of Criminal Justice Data Terminology*, 2nd ed. (Washington, D.C.: U.S. Government Printing Office, 1982).

This pen and ink drawing depicts one of the first jury trials on which both blacks and whites served. Circa 1867. *Courtesy of the Library of Congress*

However, in 1986, following what many claimed were widespread abuses of peremptory challenges by prosecution and defense alike, the Supreme Court was forced to overrule its earlier decision. It did so in the case of *Batson* v. *Kentucky*.[99] Batson, a black man, had been convicted of second-degree burglary and other offenses by an all-white jury. The prosecutor had used his peremptory challenges to remove all blacks from jury service at the trial. The Court agreed that the use of peremptory challenges for apparently purposeful discrimination constitutes a violation of the defendant's right to an impartial jury.

The *Batson* decision laid out the requirements which defendants seeking to establish the discriminatory use of peremptory challenges must prove. They include the need to prove that the defendant is a member of a recognized racial group which has been intentionally excluded from the jury and the need to raise a reasonable suspicion that the prosecutor used peremptory challenges in a discriminatory manner. Justice Thurgood Marshall, writing a concurring opinion in *Batson*, presaged what was to come: "The inherent potential of peremptory challenges to destroy the jury process," he wrote, "by permitting the exclusion of jurors on racial grounds should ideally lead the Court to ban them entirely from the criminal justice system."

A few years later, in *Ford* v. *Georgia* (1991),[100] the Court moved much closer to Justice Marshall's position when it remanded a case for a new trial based upon the fact that the prosecutor had used peremptory challenges to remove potential minority jurors. Nine of the ten peremptory challenges available to the prosecutor under Georgia law had been used to eliminate prospective black jurors. Following his conviction on charges of kidnapping, raping, and murdering a white woman, the black defendant, James Ford, argued that the prosecutor had demonstrated a systematic and historical racial bias in other cases as well as his own. Specifically, Ford argued that his Sixth Amendment right to an impartial jury had been violated by the prosecutor's racially based method of jury selection. His defense attorney's written appeal to the Supreme Court made the claim that "The exclusion of members of the black race in the jury when a black accused is being tried is done in order that the accused will receive excessive punishment if found guilty, or to inject racial prejudice into the fact finding process of the jury."[101] While the Court did not find a basis for such a Sixth Amendment claim, it did determine that the civil rights of the jurors themselves were violated under the Fourteenth Amendment due to a pattern of discrimination based on race.

In another 1991 case, *Powers* v. *Ohio*[102] (see "Theory Into Practice" box on Peremptory Challenges and Race in this chapter), the Court found in favor of a white defendant who claimed that his constitutional rights were violated by the intentional exclusion of blacks

Change of Venue The movement of a suit or trial from one jurisdiction to another or from one location to another within the same jurisdiction. A change of venue may be made in a criminal case to assure the defendant a fair trial.

from his jury through the use of peremptory challenges. In *Powers*, the Court held that "[a]lthough an individual juror does not have the right to sit on any particular petit jury, he or she does possess the right not to be excluded from one on account of race." In a civil case with significance for the criminal justice system, the Court held in *Edmonson* v. *Leesville Concrete Co., Inc.* (1991)[103] that peremptory challenges in *civil* suits were not acceptable if based upon race: "The importance of (*Edmonson*) lies in the Court's significant expansion of the scope of state action—the traditionally held doctrine that private attorneys are immune to constitutional requirements because they do not represent the government." Justice Anthony Kennedy, writing for the majority, said that race-based juror exclusions are forbidden in civil lawsuits because jury selection is a "unique governmental function delegated to private litigants" in a public courtroom.

Finally, in the 1992 case of *Georgia* v. *McCollum*,[104] the Court barred defendants and their attorneys from using peremptory challenges to exclude potential jurors on the basis of race. In *McCollum*, Justice Harry Blackmun writing for the majority said, "Be it at the hands of the state or defense, if a court allows jurors to be excluded because of group bias, it is a willing participant in a scheme that could only undermine the very foundation of our system of justice—our citizen's confidence in it." Soon thereafter, peremptory challenges based upon gender were similarly restricted (*J.E.B.* v. *Alabama*, 1994), although at the time of this writing the Court has refused to ban peremptory challenges which exclude jurors because of religious or sexual orientation.[105] Also, in 1996 the Court refused "to review whether potential jurors can be stricken from a trial panel because they are too fat."[106] The case involved Luis Santiago-Martinez, a drug defendant whose lawyer objected to the prosecution's use of peremptory challenges "because the government," he said, "had used such strikes to discriminate against the handicapped, specifically the obese." The attorney, who was himself obese, claimed that thin jurors might have been unfairly biased against his arguments.

After wrangling over jury selection has run its course, the jury is sworn in and alternates are selected. At this point the judge will decide whether the jury is to be sequestered during the trial. Members of **sequestered juries**, like those in the O. J. Simpson criminal trial, are not permitted to have contact with the public and are often housed in a motel or hotel until completion of the trial. Anyone who attempts to contact a sequestered jury or to influence members of a nonsequestered juror may be held accountable for jury tampering. Following jury selection, the stage is set for opening arguments[107] to begin.

Sequestered Jury One which is isolated from the public during the course of a trial and throughout the deliberation process.

Opening Statements

Opening Statement The initial statement of an attorney (or of a defendant representing himself or herself) made in a court of law to a judge, or to a judge and jury, describing the facts that he or she intends to present during trial in order to prove his or her case.

The presentation of information to the jury begins with opening statements made by the prosecution and defense (excerpts from the opening statements in the O. J. Simpson double-murder trial are included in a box earlier in this chapter). The purpose of opening statements is to advise the jury of what the attorneys intend to prove and to describe how such proof will be offered. Evidence is not itself offered during opening statements. Eventually, however, the jury will have to weigh the evidence presented during trial and decide between the effectiveness of the arguments made by both sides. When a defendant has little evidence to present, the main job of the defense attorney will be to dispute the veracity of the prosecution's version of the facts. Under such circumstances, defense attorneys may choose not to present any evidence or testimony at all, focusing instead on the burden of proof requirement facing the prosecution. Such plans will generally be made clear during opening statements. At this time the defense attorney is also likely to stress the human qualities of the defendant and to remind jurors of the awesome significance of their task.

Lawyers for both sides are bound by a "good faith" ethical requirement in their opening statements. That requirement limits the content of such statements to mentioning only that evidence which the attorneys actually believe can and will be presented as the trial progresses. Allusions to evidence which an attorney has no intention of offering are regarded as unprofessional and have been defined as "professional misconduct" by the Supreme Court.[108] When material alluded to in an opening statement cannot, for whatever reason, later be presented in court, it may offer opposing counsel an opportunity to discredit the other side.

PEREMPTORY CHALLENGES AND RACE

"[A] peremptory challenge to a juror means that one side in a trial has been given the right to throw out a certain number of possible jurors before the trial without giving any reasons."[1]

Historically, as the definition—borrowed from a legal dictionary—indicates, attorneys had been able to remove unwanted potential jurors from a criminal case during jury selection procedures through the use of a limited number of peremptory challenges without having to provide any reason whatsoever for the choices they made. (Challenges for cause, on the other hand, although not limited in number, require an acceptable rationale for juror removal.) The understanding of peremptory challenges was changed forever by the 1991 landmark U.S. Supreme Court case of *Powers* v. *Ohio*.[2] The *Powers* case dealt with a white defendant's desire to ensure a racially balanced jury. In *Powers* the Supreme Court identified three reasons why peremptory challenges may not be issued if based on race. The Court provided the following rationale for its decision:

First, the discriminatory use of peremptory challenges causes the defendant cognizable injury, and he or she has a concrete interest in challenging the practice, because racial discrimination in jury selection casts doubt on the integrity of the judicial process and places the fairness of the criminal proceeding in doubt.

Second, the relationship between the defendant and the excluded jurors is such that...both have a common interest in eliminating racial discrimination from the courtroom....

Third, it is unlikely that a juror dismissed because of race will possess sufficient incentive to set in motion the arduous process needed to vindicate his or her own rights.[3]

The Court continued:

The very fact that [members of a particular race] are singled out and expressly denied...all right to participate in the administration of the law, as jurors, because of their color, though they are citizens, and may be in other respects fully qualified, is practically a brand upon them, affixed by the law, an assertion of their inferiority, and a stimulant to that race prejudice which is an impediment to securing to individuals of that race equal justice which the law aims to secure to all others.

In a move that surprised many court watchers, the Supreme Court, near the end of its 1991 term, extended its ban on racially motivated peremptory challenges to civil cases. In *Edmonson* v. *Leesville Concrete Co., Inc.*,[4] the Court ruled: "The harms we recognized in *Powers* are not limited to the criminal sphere. A civil proceeding often implicates significant rights and interests. Civil juries, no less than their criminal counterparts, must follow the law and act as impartial factfinders. And, as we have observed, their verdicts, no less than those of their criminal counterparts, become binding judgments of the court. Racial discrimination has no place in the courtroom, whether the proceeding is civil or criminal."

Following *Powers* and *Edmonson* v. *Leesville Concrete Co., Inc.*, it is clear that neither prosecuting nor civil attorneys in the future will be able to exclude minority potential jurors consistently unless they are able to articulate clearly credible race-neutral rationales for their actions.

Even so, recent dissenting opinions indicate that considerable sentiment may exist among the justices which could lead to the return of a broader use of peremptory challenges. In a dissenting opinion in *J.E.B.* v. *Alabama* (1994)[5], Justices Scalia, Rehnquist, and Thomas wrote: "the core of the Court's reasoning [banning peremptory challenges based upon gender] is that peremptory challenges on the basis of any group characteristic subject to heightened scrutiny are inconsistent with the guarantee of the Equal Protection Clause....Since all groups are subject to the peremptory challenge...it is hard to see how any group is denied equal protection."

QUESTIONS FOR DISCUSSION

1. Do you agree with the Court's reasoning in *Powers* that peremptory challenges based upon race should not be permitted in the selection of criminal trial juries? Why or why not?

2. Review the Constitution in the appendix to this book. What support do you find in the Constitution for the *Powers* ruling? Be as specific as possible.

[1]Daniel Oran, *Oran's Dictionary of the Law* (St. Paul, MN: West, 1983), p. 312.
[2]*Powers* v. *Ohio*, 499 U.S. 400 (1991).
[3]Ibid., on-line syllabus of the majority opinion.
[4]*Edmonson* v. *Leesville Concrete Co., Inc.*, 500 U.S. (1991).
[5]*J.E.B.* v. *Alabama ex rel. T.B.*, 114 S.Ct. 1419, 128 L. Ed. 2d 89 (1994).

Lyle and Erik Menendez. Their first trial, on charges of killing their parents after an alleged lifetime of sexual abuse, resulted in "hung" juries. At a retrial in 1996, both were convicted of murder. *Nick Ut, AP/Wide World Photo*

Evidence Anything useful to a judge or jury in deciding the facts of a case. Evidence may take the form of witness testimony, written documents, videotapes, magnetic media, photographs, physical objects, and so on.

Direct Evidence Evidence which, if believed, directly proves a fact. Eyewitness testimony (and, more recently, videotaped documentation) account for the majority of all direct evidence heard in the criminal courtroom.

Circumstantial Evidence Evidence which requires interpretation or which requires a judge or jury to reach a conclusion based upon what the evidence indicates. From the close proximity of a smoking gun to the defendant, for example, the jury might conclude that she pulled the trigger.

Real Evidence Evidence consisting of physical material or traces of physical activity.

The Presentation of Evidence

The crux of the criminal trial is the presentation of evidence. The state is first given the opportunity to present evidence intended to prove the defendant's guilt. After prosecutors have rested their case, the defense is afforded the opportunity to provide evidence favorable to the defendant.

Evidence is of two types: direct and circumstantial. **Direct evidence** is that which, if believed by the judge or jury, proves a fact without needing to draw inferences. Direct evidence may consist, for example, of the information contained on a photograph or videotape. It might also consist of testimonial evidence provided by a witness on the stand. A straightforward statement by a witness, such as "I saw him do it!" is a form of direct evidence.

Circumstantial evidence is indirect. It requires the judge or jury to make inferences and draw conclusions. At a murder trial, for example, a person who heard gunshots and moments later saw someone run by with a smoking gun in hand might testify to those facts. Even though there may have been no eyewitness to the actual homicide, the jury might later conclude that the person seen with the gun was the one who pulled the trigger and committed the homicide. Contrary to popular belief, circumstantial evidence is sufficient to produce a verdict and conviction in a criminal trial. In fact, some prosecuting attorneys claim to prefer working entirely with circumstantial evidence, weaving a tapestry of the criminal act in their arguments to the jury.

Real evidence consists of physical material or traces of physical activity. Weapons, tire tracks, ransom notes, and fingerprints all fall into the category of physical evidence. Real or physical evidence is introduced into the trial process by means of exhibits. Exhibits are objects or displays which, once formally accepted as evidence by the judge, may be shown to members of the jury. Documentary evidence is another type of real evidence that includes writings such as business records, journals, written confessions, and letters. Documentary evidence can extend beyond paper and ink to include magnetic and optical storage devices used in computer operations and video and voice recordings.

One of the most significant decisions a trial court judge makes is deciding what evidence can be presented to the jury. In making that decision, judges will examine the relevance of the information in question to the case at hand. Relevant evidence is that which has a bearing on the facts at issue. For example, a decade or two ago, it was not unusual for a woman's sexual history to be brought out in rape trials. Under "rape shield statutes," most states today

The Fifth Amendment to the U.S. Constitution is one of the best-known entries in the Bill of Rights. Television shows and crime novels have popularized phrases such as "pleading the Fifth" or "taking the Fifth." As these media recognize, the Fifth Amendment is a powerful ally of any criminal defendant. When the accused, generally upon the advice of counsel, decides to invoke the Fifth Amendment right against self-incrimination, the state cannot require the defendant to testify. In the past, defendants who refused to take the stand were often denigrated by comments the prosecution made to the jury. In 1965 the U.S. Supreme Court, in the case of *Griffin* v. *California*,[1] ruled that the defendant's unwillingness to testify could not be interpreted as a sign of guilt. The Court reasoned that such interpretations forced the defendant to testify and effectively negated Fifth Amendment guarantees. Defendants who choose to testify, however, but who fail to adequately answer the questions put to them, may lawfully find themselves the target of a prosecutorial attack.

[1]*Griffin* v. *California*, 380 U.S. 609 (1965).

will not allow such a practice, recognizing that these details often have no bearing on the case. Rape shield statutes have been strengthened by recent U.S. Supreme Court decisions, including the 1991 case of *Michigan* v. *Lucas*.[109] In this case, the defendant, Lucas, had been charged with criminal sexual conduct involving his ex-girlfriend. Lucas had forced the woman into his apartment at knifepoint, beat her, and forced her to engage in several nonconsensual sex acts. At his trial, Lucas asked to have evidence introduced demonstrating that a prior sexual relationship had existed between the two. At the time, however, Michigan law required that a written motion to use such information had to be made within ten days following arraignment—a condition Lucas failed to meet. Lucas was convicted and sentenced to a term of from 44 to 180 months in prison, but appealed his conviction, claiming that the Sixth Amendment to the U.S. Constitution guaranteed him the right to confront witnesses against him. The U.S. Supreme Court disagreed, however, and ruled that the Sixth Amendment guarantee does not necessarily extend to evidence of a prior sexual relationship between a rape victim and a criminal defendant.

In evaluating evidence, judges must also weigh the probative value of an item of evidence against its potential inflammatory or prejudicial qualities. Evidence has probative value when it is useful and relevant. Even useful evidence, however, may unduly bias a jury if it is exceptionally gruesome or presented in such a way as to imply guilt. For example, gory photographs, especially in full color, may be withheld from the jury's eyes. In one recent case, a new trial was ordered when 35mm slides of the crime scene were projected on a wall over the head of the defendant as he sat in the courtroom and were found by an appellate court to have prejudiced the jury.

On occasion, some evidence will be found to have only limited admissibility. Limited admissibility means that the evidence can be used for a specific purpose, but that it might not be accurate in other details. Photographs, for example, may be admitted as evidence for the narrow purpose of showing spatial relationships between objects under discussion, even though the photographs themselves may have been taken under conditions that did not exist (such as daylight) when the offense was committed.

When judges err in allowing the use of evidence that may have been illegally or unconstitutionally gathered, grounds may be created for a later appeal if the trial concludes with a "guilty" verdict. Even when evidence is improperly introduced at trial, however, a number of Supreme Court decisions[110] have held that there may be no grounds for an effective appeal unless such introduction "had substantial and injurious effect or influence in determining the jury's verdict."[111] Called the "harmless error" rule, this standard does place the burden upon the prosecution to show that the jury's decision would most likely have been the same

In suits at common law. . .the right of trial by jury shall be preserved, and no fact tried by a jury shall be otherwise reexamined in any court of the United States, than according to the rules of the common law.

—Seventh Amendment to the U.S. Constitution

even in the absence of such inappropriate evidence. The rule is not applicable when a defendant's constitutional guarantees are violated by "structural defects in the constitution of the trial mechanism"[112] itself—as when a judge gives constitutionally improper instructions to a jury. (We'll discuss those instructions later in this chapter.)

The Testimony of Witnesses

Testimony Oral evidence offered by a sworn witness on the witness stand during a criminal trial.

Witness testimony is generally the chief means by which evidence is introduced at trial. Witnesses may include victims, police officers, the defendant, specialists in recognized fields, and others with useful information to provide. Some of these witnesses may have been present during the commission of the alleged offense, while most will have had only a later opportunity to investigate the situation or to analyze evidence.

Before a witness will be allowed to testify to any fact, the questioning attorney must establish the person's competence. Competency to testify requires that witnesses have personal knowledge of the information they will discuss and that they understand their duty to tell the truth.

One of the defense attorney's most critical decisions is whether or not to put the defendant on the stand. Defendants have a Fifth Amendment right to remain silent and to refuse to testify. In the precedent-setting case of *Griffin* v. *California* (1965),[113] the U.S. Supreme Court declared that if a defendant refuses to testify, prosecutors and judges are enjoined from even commenting on this fact, other than to instruct the jury that such a failure cannot be held to indicate guilt. Griffin was originally arrested for the beating death of a woman whose body was found in an alley. Charged with first-degree murder, he refused to take the stand when his case came to trial. At the time of the trial, Article I, Section 13, of the California Constitution provided in part: "…in any criminal case, whether the defendant testifies or not, his failure to explain or to deny by his testimony any evidence or facts in the case against him may be commented upon by the court and by counsel, and may be considered by the court or the jury." The prosecutor, remarking on the evidence in closing arguments to the jury, declared: "These things he has not seen fit to take the stand and deny or explain…Essie Mae is dead, she can't tell you her side of the story. The defendant won't." The judge then instructed the jury that they might infer from the defendant's silence his inability to deny the evidence which had been presented against him. Griffin was convicted of first-degree murder, and his appeal reached the Supreme Court. The Court ruled that the Fifth Amendment, which the Fourteenth Amendment made applicable to the states, protected the defendant from any inferences of guilt based upon a failure to testify. The verdict of the trial court was voided.

Direct examination of a witness takes place when a witness is first called to the stand. If the prosecutor calls the witness, the witness is referred to as a witness for the prosecution. Where the direct examiner is a defense attorney, witnesses are called witnesses for the defense.

The direct examiner may ask questions which require a "yes" or "no" answer but can also employ narrative questions which allow the witness to tell a story in his or her own words. During direct examination courts generally prohibit the use of leading questions, or those which suggest answers to the witness.[114] Many courts also consider questions which call for "yes" or "no" answers to be inappropriate since they are inherently suggestive.

Cross-examination refers to the examination of a witness by anyone other than the direct examiner. Anyone who offers testimony in a criminal court has the duty to submit to cross-examination.[115] The purpose of cross-examination is to test the credibility and memory of a witness.

Most states and the federal government restrict the scope of cross-examination to material covered during direct examination. Questions about other matters, even though they may relate to the case before the court, are not allowed. A small number of states allow the cross-examiner to raise any issue as long as it is deemed relevant by the court. Leading questions, generally disallowed in direct examination, are regarded as the mainstay of cross-examination. Such questions allow for a concise restatement of testimony which has already been offered and serve to focus efficiently on potential problems that the cross-examiner seeks to address.

Perjury The intentional making of a false statement as part of the testimony by a sworn witness in a judicial proceeding on a matter relevant to the case at hand.

Some witnesses offer **perjured testimony**, or statements which they know to be untrue. Reasons for perjured testimony vary, but most witnesses who lie on the stand probably do so in an effort to help friends accused of crimes. Witnesses who perjure themselves are subject to impeachment, in which either the defense counsel or prosecution demonstrates that they have intentionally offered false testimony. Such a demonstration may occur through the use of prior inconsistent statements whereby previous statements made by the witness are shown to be at odds with more recent declarations. Perjury is a serious offense in its own right, and dishonest witnesses may face fines or jail time. When it can be demonstrated that a witness has offered inaccurate or false testimony, the witness has been effectively impeached.

At the conclusion of the cross-examination, the direct examiner may again question the witness. This procedure is called redirect examination and may be followed by a recross-examination and so on, until both sides are satisfied that they have exhausted fruitful lines of questioning.

Children as Witnesses

An area of special concern involves the use of children as witnesses in a criminal trial, especially where the children may have been victims. Currently, in an effort to avoid what may be traumatizing direct confrontations between child witnesses and the accused, 37 states allow the use of videotaped testimony in their criminal courtrooms, and 32 permit the use of closed-circuit television—which allows the child to testify out of the presence of the defendant. In 1988, however, the U.S. Supreme Court, in the case of *Coy* v. *Iowa*,[116] ruled that a courtroom screen, used to shield child witnesses from visual confrontation with a defendant in a child sex abuse case, had violated the confrontation clause of the Constitution.

On the other hand, in the 1990 case of *Maryland* v. *Craig*,[117] the Court upheld the use of closed-circuit television to shield children who testify in criminal courts. The Court's decision was partially based upon the realization that "…a significant majority of States have enacted statutes to protect child witnesses from the trauma of giving testimony in child-abuse cases…[which]…attests to the widespread belief in the importance of such a policy."

The case involved Sandra Craig, a former preschool owner and administrator in Clarksville, Maryland, who had been found guilty by a trial court of 53 counts of child abuse, assault, and perverted sexual practices, which she had allegedly performed on the children under her care. During the trial, four young children, none past the age of six, had testified against Craig while separated from her in the judge's chambers. Questioned by the district attorney, the children related stories of torture, burying alive, and sexual assault with a screwdriver.[118] Sandra Craig watched the children reply over a TV monitor, which displayed the process to the jury seated in the courtroom. Following the trial, Craig appealed, arguing that her ability to communicate with her lawyer (who had been in the judge's chambers and not the courtroom during questioning of the children) had been impeded and that her right to a fair trial under the Sixth Amendment to the U.S. Constitution had been denied since she was not given the opportunity to be "confronted with the witnesses" against her. In finding against Craig, Justice Sandra Day O'Connor, writing for the Court's majority, stated, "…if the State makes an adequate showing of necessity, the State interest in protecting child witnesses from the trauma of testifying in a child-abuse case is sufficiently important to justify the use of a special procedure that permits a child witness in such cases to testify…in the absence of face-to-face confrontation with the defendant."[119]

Although a face-to-face confrontation with a child victim may not be necessary in the courtroom, until 1992 the Supreme Court had been reluctant to allow into evidence descriptions of abuse and other statements made by children, even to child-care professionals, when those statements are made outside of the courtroom. The Court, in *Idaho* v. *Wright* (1990),[120] reasoned that such "statements [are] fraught with the dangers of unreliability which the Confrontation Clause is designed to highlight and obviate."

However, in *White* v. *Illinois* (1992),[121] the Court seemed to reverse its stance, ruling that in-court testimony provided by a medical provider and the child's baby-sitter, which repeated what the child had said to them concerning White's sexually abusive behavior, was permissible. The Court rejected White's claim that out-of-court statements should be admissible only when the witness is unavailable to testify at trial, saying instead: "A finding of unavailability of an out-of-court declarant is necessary only if the out-of-court statement was made at a prior judicial proceeding." Placing *White* within the context of generally established exceptions, the court intoned: "A statement that has been offered in a moment of

No citizen possessing all other qualifications which are or may be prescribed by law shall be disqualified for service as grand or petit juror in any court of the United States, or of any State on account of race, color, or previous condition of servitude…

—18 U.S.C. 243

excitement—without the opportunity to reflect on the consequences of one's exclamation—may justifiably carry more weight with a trier of fact than a similar statement offered in the relative calm of the courtroom. Similarly, a statement made in the course of procuring medical services, where the declarant knows that a false statement may cause misdiagnosis or mistreatment, carries special guarantees of credibility that a trier of fact may not think replicated by courtroom testimony."[122]

The Hearsay Rule

One aspect of witness testimony bears special mention. **Hearsay** is anything not based upon the personal knowledge of a witness. A witness may say, for example, "John told me that Fred did it!" Such a witness becomes a hearsay declarant, and, following a likely objection by counsel, the trial judge will have to decide whether the witness's statement will be allowed to stand as evidence. In most cases the judge will instruct the jury to disregard such comments from the witness, thereby enforcing the **hearsay rule**. The hearsay rule does not permit the use of "secondhand evidence."

There are some exceptions to the hearsay rule, however, that have been established by both precedent and tradition. One is the dying declaration. Dying declarations are statements made by a person who is about to die. When heard by a second party, they may usually be repeated in court, providing that certain conditions have been met. Dying declarations are generally valid exceptions to the hearsay rule when they are made by someone who knows that they are about to die and when the statements made relate to the cause and circumstances of the impending death.

Spontaneous statements provide another exception to the hearsay rule. Statements are considered spontaneous when they are made in the heat of excitement before the person has time to make them up. For example, a defendant who is just regaining consciousness following a crime may make an utterance which could later be repeated in court by those who heard it.

Out-of-court statements made by a witness, especially when they have been recorded in writing or by some other means, may also become exceptions to the hearsay rule. The use of such statements usually requires the witness to testify that the statements were accurate at the time they were made. This "past recollection recorded" exception to the hearsay rule is especially useful in drawn-out court proceedings which occur long after the crime. Under such circumstances, witnesses may no longer remember the details of an event. Their earlier statements to authorities, however, can be introduced into evidence as past recollection recorded.

Closing Arguments

At the conclusion of a criminal trial both sides have the opportunity for a final narrative presentation to the jury in the form of closing arguments. This summation provides a review and analysis of the evidence. Its purpose is to persuade the jury to draw a conclusion favorable to the presenter. Testimony can be quoted, exhibits referred to, and attention drawn to inconsistencies in the evidence which has been presented by the other side.

States vary as to the order of closing arguments. Nearly all allow the defense attorney to speak to the jury before the prosecution makes its final points. A few permit the prosecutor the first opportunity for summation. Some jurisdictions and the *Federal Rules of Criminal Procedure*[123] authorize a defense rebuttal. Rebuttals are responses to the closing arguments of the other side.

Some specific issues may need to be addressed during summation. If, for example, the defendant has not taken the stand during the trial, the defense attorney's closing argument will inevitably stress that this failure to testify cannot be regarded as indicating guilt. Where the prosecution's case rests entirely upon circumstantial evidence, the defense can be expected to stress the lack of any direct proof, while the prosecutor is likely to argue that circumstantial evidence can be stronger than direct evidence, since it is not as easily affected by human error or false testimony.

The Judge's Charge to the Jury

After closing arguments, the judge will charge the jury to "retire and select one of your number as a foreman…and deliberate upon the evidence which has been presented until you have reached a verdict." The words of the charge will vary somewhat between jurisdictions

Hearsay Something which is not based upon the personal knowledge of a witness. Witnesses who testify, for example, about something they have heard are offering hearsay by repeating information about a matter of which they have no direct knowledge.

Hearsay Rule The long-standing American courtroom precedent that hearsay cannot be used in court. Rather than accepting testimony based upon hearsay, the American trial process asks that the person who was the original source of the hearsay information be brought into court to be questioned and cross-examined. Exceptions to the hearsay rule may occur when the person with direct knowledge is dead or otherwise unable to testify.

Closing Argument An oral summation of a case presented to a judge, or to a judge and jury, by the prosecution or by the defense in a criminal trial.

Virginia McMartin, one of the defendants in the infamous "McMartin Preschool Case"—billed as the longest-running jury trial in American history. The case, which began with 109 charges of child sexual molestation in 1984, concluded with not guilty verdicts in 1990. *Wally Fong, AP/Wide World Photos*

and among judges, but all judges will remind members of the jury of their duty to consider objectively only the evidence which has been presented and of the need for impartiality. Most judges will also remind jury members of the statutory elements of the alleged offense, of the burden of proof which rests upon the prosecution, and of the need for the prosecution to have proven guilt beyond a reasonable doubt before a guilty verdict can be returned.

In their charge many judges will also provide a summary of the evidence presented, usually from notes they have taken during the trial, as a means of refreshing the jurors' memories of events. About half of all the states allow judges the freedom to express their own views as to the credibility of witnesses and the significance of evidence. Other states only permit judges to summarize the evidence in an objective and impartial manner.

Following the charge, the jury will be removed from the courtroom and permitted to begin its deliberations. In the absence of the jury, defense attorneys may choose to challenge portions of the judge's charge. If they feel that some oversight has occurred in the original charge, they may also request that the judge provide the jury with additional instructions or information. Such objections, if denied by the judge, often become the basis for appeals when a conviction is returned.

[N]inety-five percent of the time, the only black thing a black defendant sees in the courtroom is the judge's robe.

—Delano Stewart, former chairman, Florida chapter of the National Bar Association

Jury Deliberations and the Verdict

In cases where the evidence is either very clear or very weak, jury deliberations may be brief, lasting only a matter of hours or even minutes. Some juries, however, deliberate days or sometimes weeks, carefully weighing all the nuances of the evidence they have seen and heard. Many jurisdictions require that juries reach a unanimous verdict, although the U.S. Supreme Court has ruled that unanimous verdicts are not required in noncapital cases.[124] Even so, some juries are unable to agree upon any verdict. When a jury is deadlocked, it is said to be a hung jury. Where a unanimous decision is required, juries may be deadlocked by the strong opposition of only one member to a verdict agreed upon by all the others.

In some states, judges are allowed to add a boost to nearly hung juries by recharging them under a set of instructions agreed upon by the Supreme Court in the 1896 case of *Allen* v. *United States*.[125] The Allen Charge, as it is known in those jurisdictions, urges the jury to vigorous deliberations and suggests to obstinate jurors that their objections may be ill founded if they make no impression upon the minds of other jurors.

Verdict In criminal case processing, a formal and final finding made on the charges by a jury and reported to the court, or by a trial judge when no jury is used.

Practice being a member of a jury panel. At Cyberjury, on-line panels decide real cases. Their decisions are then used by attorneys to decide whether to proceed with a jury trial. In some instances, all of the parties in a case have agreed to be bound by the decision of Cyberjury. Visit Cyberjury at: http://www.cyberjury.com.

Problems with the Jury System

Judge Harold J. Rothwax, a well-known critic of today's jury system, tells the tale of a rather startling 1991 case over which he presided. The case involved a murder defendant, a handsome young man who had been fired by a New York company that serviced automated teller machines (ATMs). After being fired, the good-looking defendant intentionally caused a machine in a remote area to malfunction. When two former colleagues arrived to fix it, he robbed them, stole the money inside the ATM, and shot both men repeatedly. One of the men survived long enough to identify his former coworker as the shooter. The man was arrested and a trial ensued; but after three weeks of hearing the case the jury deadlocked. Judge Rothwax later learned that the jury had voted 11 to 1 to convict the defendant, but the one holdout jury member just couldn't believe that "someone so good-looking could…commit such a crime."[126]

Many everyday cases, like those seen routinely by Judge Rothwax, and some highly publicized cases, like the murder trial of O.J. Simpson, which the whole world watched, have called into question the ability of the American jury system to do its job—that is, to sort through the evidence and accurately determine a defendant's guilt or innocence. Because jurors are drawn from all walks of life, many cannot be expected to understand modern legal complexities and to appreciate all the nuances of trial court practice. Some instructions to the jury are probably poorly understood and rarely observed by even the best-intentioned jurors.[127] In highly charged cases, emotions are often difficult to separate from fact, while during deliberations juries are probably dominated by one or two forceful personalities. Jurors may also become confused over legal technicalities, suffer from inattention, or be unable to understand fully the testimony of expert witnesses or the significance of technical evidence.

Many such problems became evident in the trial of Raymond Buckey and his mother, Peggy McMartin Buckey, who were tried in Los Angeles for allegedly molesting dozens of children at their family-run preschool.[128] The trial, which involved 65 counts of child sexual molestation and conspiracy and 61 witnesses, ran for more than three years. Many jurors were stressed to the breaking point by the length of time involved. Family relationships suffered as the trial droned on, and jurors were unable to accompany their spouses and children on vacation. Small-business owners, who were expected to continue paying salaries to employees serving as jurors, faced financial ruin and threatened their absent employees with termination. Careers were put on hold, and at least one juror had to be dismissed for becoming inattentive to testimony. The trial cost taxpayers more than $12 million, but was nearly negated as jury membership and the number of alternate jurors declined due to sickness and personal problems. Ultimately, the defendants were acquitted.

Another trial in which the defendants were similarly acquitted of the majority of charges against them involved state-level prosecution of the officers accused in the now-infamous Rodney King beating. Following the riots in Los Angeles (and elsewhere) which came on the heels of their verdict, jurors in the "Rodney King trial" reported being afraid for their lives. Some slept with weapons by their side, and others sent their children away to safe locales.[129] Because of the potential for harm jurors faced in the 1993 federal trial of the same officers, U.S. District Judge John G. Davies ruled that the names of jurors be forever kept secret. The secrecy order was called "an unprecedented infringement of the public's right of access to the justice system"[130] by members of the press. Similarly, in the 1993 trial of three black men charged with the beating of white truck driver Reginald Denny during the Los Angeles riots, Los Angeles Superior Court Judge John Ouderkirk ordered that the identities of jurors not be released.

Opponents of the jury system have argued that it should be replaced by a panel of judges who would both render a verdict and impose sentence. Regardless of how well considered such a suggestion may be, such a change could not occur without modification to the Constitution's Sixth Amendment right to trial by jury.

An alternative suggestion for improving the process of trial by jury has been the call for professional jurors. Professional jurors would be paid by the government, as are judges, prosecutors, and public defenders. Their job would be to sit on any jury, and they would be expected to have the expertise to do so. Professional jurors would be trained to listen objectively and would be schooled with the kinds of decision-making skills necessary to function effectively within an adversarial context. They could be expected to hear one case after another, perhaps moving between jurisdictions in cases of highly publicized crimes.

Twenty-First Century Criminal Justice

COURTROOMS OF THE FUTURE

Recently, the College of William & Mary, in conjunction with the National Center for State Courts (NCSC), unveiled Courtroom 21, the most technologically advanced courtroom in the United States. Courtroom 21, located in the McGlothlin Courtroom of the College of William & Mary, offers anyone concerned with the future of trial practice and with courtroom technology a glimpse at what American courtrooms may be like in the mid-twenty-first century. Courtroom 21 includes the following integrated capabilities:

1. Automatic video recording of proceedings using ceiling-mounted cameras with voice-initiated switching. A sophisticated voice-activation system directs cameras to tape the person speaking, to record what is said, and to tape evidence as it is being presented.
2. Recorded televised evidence display with optical disk storage. Documentary or real evidence may be presented to the judge and jury via television through the use of a video "presenter," which also makes a video record of the evidence as it is being presented for later use.
3. A remote, two-way television arrangement, which allows video and audio signals to be sent from the judge's bench to areas throughout the courtroom, including the jury box.
4. Text-, graphics-, and TV-capable jury computers. Courtroom 21's jury box contains computers for information display and animation so that jury members can easily view documents, live or prerecorded video, and other graphics such as charts, diagrams, and pictures. TV-capable jury computers also allow for the remote appearance of witnesses—that is, for questioning

witnesses who may be unable or unwilling to physically appear in the courtroom and for the display of crime scene reenactments via computer animation.

5. Access for judge and for counsel on both sides to on-line legal research databases. Available databases contain an extensive variety of state and federal statutes, case law, and other precedent which allows judges and attorneys to find answers to unanticipated legal questions which might arise during trial.
6. Built-in video playback facilities for out-of-court testimony. Because an increasing number of depositions are being video recorded by attorneys in preparation for trial, Courtroom 21 has capabilities for video deposition playback. To present expert witness testimony or to impeach a witness, video depositions can be played on court monitors.
7. Information storage with software search capabilities. Integrated software programs provide text-searching capabilities to courtroom participants. Previously transcribed testimony, as well as precedent-setting cases from other courts, can be searched and reviewed.
8. Concurrent (real-time) court reporter transcription, including the ability for each lawyer to mark an individual computerized copy for later use. A court reporter uses a self-contained computerized writing machine for real-time capture of testimony in the courtroom. When the reporter writes, the computer translates strokes into English transcripts, which are immediately distributed to the judge and counsel via their personal computers. Using this technology, the judge and attorneys can take

a copy of the day's testimony with them on their laptop computer or on a floppy diskette for evening review and trial preparation.

The technology now being demonstrated in Courtroom 21 suggests many possibilities. For one thing, court video equipment could be used by attorneys for filing remote motions and other types of hearings. As one of Courtroom 21's designers puts it, "Imagine the productivity gains if lawyers no longer need to travel across a city or county for a ten-minute appearance."

Courtroom 21 designers also suggest that the innovative use of audio and video technology can preserve far more evidence and trial detail than written records, making a comprehensive review of cases easier for appellate judges. One study, which has already been conducted by the NCSC, showed that when video records are available, appellate courts are less likely to reverse the original determinations of the trial court. Video court records, analysts say, "might also improve the performance of attorneys and judges. By preserving matters not now apparent on a written record, such as facial expressions, voice inflections, body gestures, and the like, video records may cause trial participants to be more circumspect in their behavior than at present."

High technology can also be expected to have considerable impact on the trial itself. The technology built into Courtroom 21 readily facilitates computer animations and crime scene reenactments. As one of the designers of Courtroom 21 says, "*Jurassic Park* quality computer reenactment may have enormous psychological impact" (on jurors).

While Courtroom 21 shows what a typical courtroom of the near future may be like, it also raises questions about the appropriate use of innovative courtroom technologies. As Fred Lederer, one of Courtroom 21's designers, points out, "Modern technology holds enormous promise for our courts. We must recognize, however, that technology's utility often depends upon how people will use it. Although we must continue to improve our courts via technology, we must be sensitive to technology's impact and work to recognize and minimize any negative consequences it might have on our system of justice."

An even more intriguing vision of courtrooms of the future is offered by the Technology of Justice Task Force in its 1997 draft report to the Pennsylvania Futures Commission. The task force predicted that by the year 2020, "There will be 'virtual courtrooms,' where appropriate, to provide hearings without the need for people to come to a physical courthouse." Trials via teleconferencing, public Internet access to many court documents, and payments of fines by credit card are all envisioned by the Task Force.

QUESTIONS FOR DISCUSSION

1. How might technologies such as those discussed in this box affect the outcome of criminal trials, if at all?

2. Can you imagine criminal trials in which the use of high-technology courtrooms might not be appropriate? If so, what might they be?

Sources: Court Technology Bulletin, Vol. 6, no. 1, January/February 1994; Court Technology Bulletin, Vol. 6, no. 1, March/April 1994; the National Center for State Courts World Wide Web site on the Internet (from which some of the material in this box is taken); and the Technology of Justice Task Force Draft Report to the Pennsylvania Futures Commission, February 21, 1997.

The advantages a professional jury system offers are

1. *Dependability*. Professional jurors could be expected to report to the courtroom in a timely fashion and to be good listeners, since both would be required by the nature of the job.
2. *Knowledge*. Professional jurors would be trained in the law, would understand what a finding of guilt requires, and would know what to expect from other actors in the courtroom.
3. *Equity*. Professional jurors would understand the requirements of due process and would be less likely to be swayed by the emotional content of a case, having been schooled in the need to separate matters of fact from personal feelings.

Visit the *CJToday* Web page and click on "Web Chapters," then "Chapter 9." Follow the "find the facts" links in order to visit the American Bar Association's home page.

A professional jury system would not be without difficulties. Jurors under such a system might become jaded, deciding cases out of hand as routines lead to boredom and suspects are categorized according to whether they "fit the type" for guilt or innocence developed on the basis of previous experiences. Job requirements for professional jurors would be difficult to establish without infringing on the jurors' freedom to decide cases as they understand them. For the same reason, any evaluation of the job performance of professional jurors would be a difficult call. Finally, professional jurors might not truly be peer jurors, since their social characteristics might be skewed by education, residence, and politics.

Improving the Adjudication Process

Courts today are coming under increasing scrutiny, and media-rich trials, such as those of O. J. Simpson, Susan Smith, and the Menendez brothers, have heightened awareness of problems with the American court system. One of today's most important issues involves reducing the number of jurisdictions by unifying courts. The current multiplicity of jurisdictions frequently leads to what many believe are avoidable conflicts and overlaps in the handling of criminal defendants. Problems are exacerbated by the lack of any centralized judicial authority in some states which might resolve jurisdictional and procedural disputes.[131] Proponents of unification suggest the elimination of overlapping jurisdictions, the creation of special-purpose courts, and the formulation of administrative offices in order to achieve economies of scale.[132]

Court-watch citizens groups are also rapidly growing in number. Such organizations focus on the trial court level, but they are part of a general trend toward seeking greater openness in government decision making at all levels.[133] Court-watch groups monitor court proceedings on a regular basis and attempt to document and often publicize inadequacies. They frequently focus on the handling of indigents, fairness in the scheduling of cases for trial, unnecessary court delays, the reduction of waiting time, the treatment of witnesses and jurors, and adequacy of rights advisements for defendants throughout judicial proceedings.

The statistical measurement of court performance is another area which is receiving increased attention. Research has looked at the efficiency with which prosecutors schedule cases for trial, the speed with which judges resolve issues, the amount of time judges spend on the bench, and the economic and other costs to defendants, witnesses, and communities involved in the judicial process.[134] Statistical studies of this type often attempt to measure elements of court performance as diverse as sentence variation, charging accuracy, fairness in plea bargaining, evenhandedness, delays, and attitudes toward the court by lay participants.[135]

In 1994, the Federal Judicial Center, which is the research, education, and planning agency of the federal judicial system, conducted a nationwide survey intended to gather information for the federal Judicial Conference Committee on Long Range Planning. The Center's survey reached nearly all federal judges and covered a wide range of issues. Results of the survey[136] showed that federal judges (1) were convinced that the most serious problem facing federal courts was the huge volume of criminal cases waiting to be processed; (2) believed that criminal case processing needs gravely impacted the ability of federal courts to effectively handle civil cases; (3) hoped that the concerns of federal court judges and administrators would be considered before any new federal criminal legislation was passed; and (4) wanted more discretion in sentencing and fewer rules requiring mandatory minimum sentences for criminal defendants.

SUMMARY

> *The highest act of citizenship is jury service.*
> —Abraham Lincoln

This chapter discussed activities and personnel characteristic of today's criminal courts. Although many individualized courtroom roles can be identified, the criminal trial stands as the hallmark of American criminal justice. The criminal trial owes its legacy to the development of democratic principles in western society and builds upon an adversarial process which pits prosecution against defense.

> *This is surely the first trial with 95 million jurors.*
> —Jess Maghan (University of Illinois at Chicago), commenting on the O. J. Simpson trial

Trials have historically been viewed as peer-based fact-finding processes intended to protect the rights of the accused while sifting through disputed issues of guilt or innocence. The adversarial environment, however, which has served American courts for over 200 years, is now being questioned. Well-publicized trials of the last decade or two have demonstrated apparent weaknesses in the trial process. Moreover, a plethora of far-reaching social and technological changes have recently transpired that might at least partially supplant the role of advocacy in the fact-finding process. In many cases, new technologies which were unanticipated by the framers of our present system (such as DNA fingerprinting, which is discussed in detail in Chapter 17) hold the promise to closely link suspects to criminal activity. Today's electronic media can rapidly and widely disseminate investigative findings. This combination of investigative technologies and readily available public information may eventually make courtroom debates about guilt or innocence obsolete. Whether the current adversarial system can continue to serve the interests of justice in an information-rich and technologically advanced society will be a central question for the twenty-first century.

DISCUSSION QUESTIONS

1. We described participants in a criminal trial as working together to bring about a successful close to courtroom proceedings. What do you think a "successful close" might mean to a judge? To a defense attorney? To a prosecutor? To the jury? To the defendant? To the victim?

2. What is a dying declaration? Under what circumstances might it be a valid exception to the hearsay rule? Why do most courts seem to believe that a person who is about to die is likely to tell the truth?

3. Do you think the present jury system is outmoded? Might "professional jurors" be more effective than the present system of "peer jurors"? On what do you base your opinion?

4. What is an expert witness? A lay witness? What different kinds of testimony may both provide? What are some of the difficulties in expert testimony?

5. What are the three forms of indigent defense used throughout various regions of the United States? Why might defendants prefer private attorneys over public counsel?

 WEB WATCH

Access the *Criminal Justice Today* site on the World Wide Web by pointing your Web browser at http://www.prenhall.com/cjtoday. Once there, click "Web Chapters," then select "Chapter 9: The Courtroom Work Group and the Criminal Trial" from the selection box in order to access electronic information and other sites of relevance to this chapter. You may also wish to enter the Global Town Meeting, which provides facilities for the posting of electronic messages for others to read. Messages are arranged by topic, with new topics constantly being added.

NOTES

1. Jill Smolowe, "The Trials of the Public Defender," *Time*, February 8, 1993, p. 46.
2. "Louisiana's Public Defender System Found Unconstitutional," *Criminal Justice Newsletter*, Vol. 23, no. 5, (March 3, 1992), p. 1.
3. See, for example, Jeffrey T. Ulmer, *Social Worlds of Sentencing: Court Communities Under Sentencing Guidelines* (Ithaca, NY: State University of New York Press, 1997); and Roy B. Flemming, Peter F. Nardulli, James Eisenstein, *The Craft of Justice: Politics and Work in Criminal Court Communities* (Philadelphia: University of Pennsylvania Press, 1993).
4. See, for example, Edward J. Clynch and David W. Neubauer, "Trial Courts as Organizations," *Law and Policy Quarterly*, Vol. 3 (1981), pp. 69–94.
5. In 1940 Missouri became the first state to adopt a plan for the "merit selection" of judges based upon periodic public review.
6. The National Judicial College, *1988 Course Catalog* (Reno: University of Nevada Press, 1987), p. 3.
7. Doris Marie Provine, *Judging Credentials: Nonlawyer Judges and the Politics of Professionalism* (Chicago: University of Chicago Press, 1986).
8. Ibid.
9. Ibid.
10. "Defendant Claims Judge Bit Him," Associated Press wire services, June 27, 1997.
11. Nationline: "Judge—Show Legs, Pick Up Men," *USA Today*, August 16, 1996, p. 3A.
12. Aminah Franklin, "District Justice Charged with Misconduct," *The Morning Call*, July 6, 1995, p. 1A.
13. Allen Baker, "Alaska Justice Steps Down," The Associated Press wire services, July 3, 1997.
14. Debbie Howlett, "Impeachment Sought for 'Arrogant' Judge," *USA Today*, May 6, 1997, p. 3A.
15. *U.S. v. Nixon*, 816 F.2d 1022 (1987).
16. *Nixon v. U.S.*, 506 U.S. 224, 113 S.Ct. 732, 122 L. Ed. 2d 1 (1993).
17. Bureau of Justice Statistics, *Report to the Nation on Crime and Justice: The Data* (Washington, D.C.: U.S. Department of Justice, 1983).
18. For a discussion of the resource limitations of district attorneys in combating corporate crime, see Michael L. Benson, William J. Maakestad, Francis T. Cullen, and Gilbert Geis, "District Attorneys and Corporate Crime: Surveying the Prosecutorial Gatekeepers," *Criminology*, Vol. 26, no. 3 (August 1988), pp. 505–517.
19. John M. Dawson, *Prosecutors in State Courts*, 1990 (Washington, D.C.: Bureau of Justice Statistics, 1992).
20. Many large police departments have their own legal counselors who provide advice on civil liability and who may also assist in weighing the quality of evidence which has been assembled.
21. Kenneth Culp Davis, *Discretionary Justice* (Baton Rouge: Louisiana State University Press, 1969), p. 190.
22. Barbara Borland, *The Prosecution of Felony Arrests* (Washington, D.C.: Bureau of Justice Statistics, 1983).
23. *Brady v. Maryland*, 373 U.S. 83 (1963).
24. *U.S. v. Bagley*, 473 U.S. 667 (1985).
25. *Imbler v. Pachtman*, 424 U.S. 409 (1976).
26. *Burns v. Reed*, 500 U.S. 478 (1991).

27. Ibid., complaint, p. 29.
28. Cassia Spohn, John Gruhl, and Susan Welch, "The Impact of the Ethnicity and Gender of Defendants on the Decision to Reject or Dismiss Felony Charges," *Criminology*, Vol. 25, no. 1 (1987), pp. 175–191.
29. The same is true under federal law, and in almost all of the states, of communications with clergymen and clergywomen, psychiatrists and psychologists, medical doctors, and licensed social workers in the course of psychotherapy. See, for example, *Jaffee v. Redmond*, 116 S.Ct. 1923 (1996).
30. Richard Carelli, "Rehnquist," The Associated Press wire services, May 25, 1996.
31. "Pay the Costs of Justice," *USA Today*, March 30, 1993, p. 8A.
32. *Powell v. Alabama*, 287 U.S. 45 (1932).
33. *Johnson v. Zerbst*, 304 U.S. 458 (1938).
34. *Gideon v. Wainwright*, 372 U.S. 335 (1963).
35. *Argersinger v. Hamlin*, 407 U.S. 25 (1972).
36. *In re Gault*, 387 U.S. 1 (1967).
37. Bureau of Justice Statistics, *Criminal Defense for the Poor*, 1986.
38. Steven K. Smith and Carol J. DeFrances, "Indigent Defense," Bureau of Justice Statistics, Feb. 1996.
39. Ibid.
40. "Pay the Costs of Justice," *USA Today*, March 30, 1993, p. 8A.
41. Smolowe, "The Trials of the Public Defender," p. 46.
42. Ibid.
43. *Faretta v. California*, 422 U.S. 806 (1975).
44. "Indigent Defense," pp. 2–3.
45. "Killings Spotlight Lawyers' Ethics," *The Fayetteville Observer-Times* (North Carolina), September 13, 1992, p. 11A.
46. *Nix v. Whiteside*, 475 U.S. 157 (1986).
47. Ibid.
48. "Courtroom Killings Verdict," *USA Today*, February 15, 1993, p. 3A.
49. "How Crucial Is Courtroom Security?" *Security Management* (August 1992), p. 78.
50. "Courtroom Firebomb," *USA Today*, April 9, 1997, p. 3A.
51. President's Commission on Law Enforcement and Administration of Justice, *The Challenge of Crime in a Free Society* (Washington, D.C.: U.S. Government Printing Office, 1967), p. 129.
52. National Advisory Commission on Criminal Justice Standards and Goals, *Courts* (Washington, D.C.: U.S. Government Printing Office, 1973), Standard 9.3.
53. See, for example, Joan G. Brannon, *The Judicial System in North Carolina* (Raleigh, NC: The Administrative Office of the United States Courts, 1984), p. 14.
54. *Daubert v. Merrell Dow Pharmaceuticals, Inc.*, 113 S.Ct. 2786 (1993).
55. Joseph L. Peterson, "Use of Forensic Evidence by the Police and Courts," *Research in Brief* (Washington, D.C.: National Institute of Justice, 1987), p. 3.
56. Ibid., p. 6.
57. Jennifer Bowles, "Simpson-Paid Experts," The Associated Press wire services, August 12, 1995.
58. *California v. Green*, 399 U.S. 149 (1970).
59. Patrick L. McCloskey and Ronald L. Schoenberg, *Criminal Law Deskbook* (New York: Matthew Bender, 1988), Section 17, p. 123.
60. Bureau of Justice Statistics, *Report to the Nation on Crime and Justice*, 2nd ed., p. 82.
61. *Demarest v. Manspeaker et al.*, 498 U.S. 184, 111 S.Ct. 599, 112 L. Ed. 2d 608 (1991).
62. *Report to the Nation*, p. 82.
63. *Williams v. Florida*, 399 U.S. 78, 90 S.Ct. 1893, 26 L.Ed. 2d 446 (1970).
64. *Smith v. Texas*, 311 U.S. 128 (1940). That right does not apply when the defendants are facing the possibility of a prison sentence less than six months in length or even when the potential aggregate sentence for multiple petty offenses exceeds six months [see *Lewis v. U.S.* (1996)].
65. *Thiel v. Southern Pacific Co.*, 328 U.S. 217 (1945).
66. Speaking from a personal experience, the author was himself the victim of a felony some years ago. My car was stolen in Columbus, Ohio, and recovered a year later in Cleveland. I was informed that the person who had taken it was in custody, but I never heard what happened to him nor could I learn where or whether a trial was to be held.
67. *Crosby v. U.S.*, 113 S.Ct. 748, 122 L. Ed. 2d 25 (1993).
68. *Zafiro v. U.S.*, 113 S.Ct. 933, 122 L. Ed. 2d 317 (1993).
69. Dale Russakoff, "N.Y. Defendant Keeps His Own Counsel; Alleged Killer of Six Commuter Train Passengers Shuns His Lawyers' Advice," *The Washington Post* wire services, January 27, 1995.
70. Larry McShane, "Ferguson-Why?" The Associated Press wire services, February 18, 1995.
71. *Nebraska Press Association v. Stuart*, 427 U.S. 539 (1976).
72. However, it is generally accepted that trial judges may issue limited gag orders aimed at trial participants.
73. *Press Enterprise Company v. Superior Court of California*, Riverside County, 478 U.S. 1 (1986).
74. *Caribbean International News Corporation v. Puerto Rico*, No. 92–949, May 17, 1993.
75. Dennis Cauchon, "Federal Courts Camera-Less," *USA Today*, March 10, 1993, p. 2A.
76. *Chandler v. Florida*, 499 U.S. 560 (1981).
77. Ibid.

78. Harry F. Rosenthal, "Courts-TV," The Associated Press wire services, September 21, 1994. See also "Judicial Conference Rejects Cameras in Federal Courts," *Criminal Justice Newsletter*, September 15, 1994, p. 6.

79. Marc G. Gertz and Edmond J. True, "Social Scientists in the Courtroom: The Frustrations of Two Expert Witnesses," in Susette M. Talarico, ed., *Courts and Criminal Justice: Emerging Issues* (Beverly Hills, CA: Sage Publications, 1985), pp. 81–91.

80. *Klopfer* v. *North Carolina*, 386 U.S. 213 (1967).

81. *Barker* v. *Wingo*, 407 U.S. 514 (1972).

82. *Strunk* v. *U.S.*, 412 U.S. 434 (1973).

83. The federal Speedy Trial Act, 18 U.S.C. 3161 (1974).

84. *U.S.* v. *Brainer*, 515 F. Supp. 627, 630 (D. Md.1981).

85. *U.S.* v. *Taylor*, U.S. 487 U.S. 326, 108 S.Ct. 2413, 101 L. Ed. 2d 297 (1988).

86. *Fex* v. *Michigan*, 113 S.Ct. 1085, 122 L. Ed. 2d 406 (1993).

87. *Doggett* v. *U.S.*, 112 S.Ct. 2686 (1992).

88. William U. McCormack, "Supreme Court Cases: 1991–1992 Term," *FBI Law Enforcement Bulletin*, November, 1992, pp. 28–29.

89. See, for example, the U.S. Supreme Court's decision in the case of *Murphy* v. *Florida*, 410 U.S. 525 (1973).

90. *Witherspoon* v. *Illinois*, 391 U.S. 510 (1968).

91. *Mu'Min* v. *Virginia*, 500 U.S. 415 (1991).

92. Rule 24(6) of the *Federal Rules of Criminal Procedure*.

93. "Are Juries Colorblind?" *Newsweek*, December 5, 1988, p. 94.

94. Ibid.

95. Ibid.

96. Ibid.

97. Supreme Court majority opinion in *Powers* v. *Ohio*, 499 U.S. 400 (1991), citing *Strauder* v. *West Virginia*, 100 U.S. 303 (1880).

98. *Swain* v. *Alabama*, 380 U.S. 202 (1965).

99. *Batson* v. *Kentucky*, 476 U.S. 79, 106 S.Ct. 1712 (1986).

100. *Ford* v. *Georgia*, 498 U.S. 411 (1991), footnote 2.

101. Ibid.

102. *Powers* v. *Ohio*.

103. *Edmonson* v. *Leesville Concrete Co., Inc.*, 500 U.S. 614, 111 S.Ct. 2077, 114 L. Ed. 2d 660 (1991).

104. *Georgia* v. *McCollum*, 505 U.S. 42 (1992).

105. See, for example, *Davis* v. *Minnesota*, No. 93–6577 (1994).

106. Michael Kirkland, "Court Rejects Fat Jurors Case," United Press International wire services, January 8, 1996. The case was *Santiago-Martinez* v. *U.S.*, No. 95–567, (1996).

107. Although the words *argument* and *statement* are sometimes used interchangeably in alluding to opening remarks, defense attorneys are enjoined from drawing conclusions or "arguing" to the jury at this stage in the trial. Their task, as described in the section which follows, is simply to provide information to the jury as to how the defense will be conducted.

108. *U.S.* v. *Dinitz*, 424 U.S. 600, 612 (1976).

109. *Michigan* v. *Lucas*, 500 U.S. 145 (1992).

110. *Kotteakos* v. *United States*, 328 U.S. 750 (1946); *Becht* v. *Abrahamson*, 113 S.Ct. 1710, 123 L. Ed. 2d 353 (1993); and *Arizona* v. *Fulminante*, 111 S.Ct. 1246 (1991).

111. The Court, citing *Kotteakos* v. *United States*, 328 U.S. 750 (1946) in *Brecht* v. *Abrahamson*, 113 S.Ct. 1710, 123 L. Ed. 2d 353 (1993).

112. *Sullivan* v. *Louisiana*, 113 S.Ct. 2078, 124 L. Ed. 2d 182 (1993).

113. *Griffin* v. *California*, 380 U.S. 609 (1965).

114. Leading questions may, in fact, be permitted for certain purposes, including refreshing a witness's memory, impeaching a hostile witness, introducing nondisputed material, and helping a witness with impaired faculties.

115. *In re Oliver*, 333 U.S. 257 (1948).

116. *Coy* v. *Iowa*, 487 U.S. 1012, 108 S.Ct. 2798 (1988).

117. *Maryland* v. *Craig*, 497 U.S. 836, 845-847 (1990).

118. "The Right to Confront Your Accuser," *The Boston Globe* magazine, April 7, 1991, pp. 19, 51.

119. *Maryland* v. *Craig*.

120. *Idaho* v. *Wright*, 497 U.S. 805 (1990).

121. *White* v. *Illinois*, 112 S.Ct. 736 (1992).

122. *White* v. *Illinois*, Project Hermes on-line decision.

123. Rule 29.1 of the *Federal Rules of Criminal Procedure*.

124. See *Johnson* v. *Louisiana*, 406 U.S. 356 (1972), and *Apodaca* v. *Oregon*, 406 U.S. 404 (1972).

125. *Allen* v. *U.S.*, 164 U.S. 492 (1896).

126. Judge Harold J. Rothwax, *Guilty: The Collapse of Criminal Justice* (New York: Random House, 1996).

127. Amiram Elwork, Bruce D. Sales, and James Alfini, *Making Jury Instructions Understandable* (Charlottesville, VA: Michie, 1982).

128. "Juror Hardship Becomes Critical as McMartin Trial Enters Year 3," *Criminal Justice Newsletter*, Vol. 20 (May 15, 1989), pp. 6–7.

129. "King Jury Lives in Fear from Unpopular Verdict," *The Fayetteville Observer-Times* (North Carolina), May 10, 1992, p. 7A.

130. "Los Angeles Trials Spark Debate over Anonymous Juries," *Criminal Justice Newsletter*, (February 16, 1993), pp. 3–4.

131. Some states have centralized offices called Administrative Offices of the Courts, or something similar. Such offices, however, are often primarily data-gathering agencies which have little or no authority over the day-to-day functioning of state or local courts.

132. See, for example, Larry Berkson and Susan Carbon, *Court Unification: Its History, Politics, and Implementation* (Washington, D.C.: U.S. Government Printing Office, 1978) and Thomas Henderson et al., *The Significance of Judicial Structure: The Effect of Unification on Trial Court Operators* (Alexandria, VA: Institute for Economic and Policy Studies, 1984).

133. See, for example, Kenneth Carlson, et al., *Citizen Court Watching: The Consumer's Perspectives* (Cambridge, MA: Abt Associates, 1977).

134. See, for example, Thomas J. Cook and Ronald W. Johnson, et al., *Basic Issues in Court Performance* (Washington, D.C.: National Institute of Justice, 1982).

135. See, for example, Sorrel Wildhorn et al., *Indicators of Justice: Measuring the Performance of Prosecutors, Defense, and Court Agencies Involved in Felony Proceedings* (Lexington, MA: Lexington Books, 1977).

136. Federal Judicial Center, *Planning for the Future: Results of a 1992 Federal Judicial Center Survey of United States Judges* (1994).

chapter 10

SENTENCING

aggravating circumstances
capital offense
capital punishment
determinate sentencing
deterrence
general deterrence
good time
incapacitation

indeterminate sentencing
just deserts
mandatory sentencing
mitigating circumstances
presentence investigation
presumptive sentencing
rehabilitation
restoration

retribution
sentencing
specific deterrence
structured sentencing
truth in sentencing
victim compensation
victim impact statement
writ of *habeus corpus*

Wilkerson v. *Utah*
Coker v. *Georgia*
Payne v. *Tennessee*
Furman v. *Georgia*
Woodson v. *North Carolina*

Coleman v. *Thompson*
Mistretta v. *U.S.*
Gregg v. *Georgia*
McCleskey v. *Zandt*
In re Kemmler

Booth v. *Maryland*
Stinson v. *U.S.*
Smith v. *U.S.*
Deal v. *U.S.*

Crime and Punishment: Introduction

To make punishments efficacious, two things are necessary. They must never be disproportioned to the offense, and they must be certain.

—William Sims (1806–1870)

Punishment, that is justice for the unjust.

—Saint Augustine (345–430 A.D.)

A few years ago, John Angus Smith and a friend went from Tennessee to Florida to buy cocaine. They hoped to resell it at a profit. While in Florida, they met an acquaintance of Smith's, Deborah Hoag. Hoag purchased cocaine for Smith and then accompanied him and his friend to her motel room, where they were joined by a drug dealer. While Hoag listened, Smith and the dealer discussed Smith's MAC-10 firearm, which had been modified to operate as an automatic. The MAC-10, small, compact, and lightweight, can be equipped with a silencer and is a favorite among criminals. A fully automatic MAC-10 can be devastating. It can fire more than 1,000 rounds per minute. The dealer expressed his interest in becoming the owner of a MAC-10, and Smith promised that he would discuss selling the gun if his arrangement with another potential buyer fell through.

Unfortunately for Smith, Hoag had contacts not only with narcotics traffickers but also with law enforcement officials. She was a confidential informant, and she informed the Broward County Sheriff's Office of Smith's activities. The sheriff's office responded quickly, sending an undercover officer to Hoag's motel room. Several other officers were assigned to keep the motel under surveillance. Upon arriving at Hoag's room, the undercover officer presented himself to Smith as a pawnshop dealer. Smith, in turn, presented the officer with a proposition: He had an automatic MAC-10 and silencer with which he might be willing to part if a good price could be arranged. Smith then pulled the MAC-10 out of a black canvas bag and showed it to the officer. The officer examined the gun and asked Smith what he wanted for it. Rather than asking for money, however, Smith asked for drugs. He was willing to trade his MAC-10, he said, for two ounces of cocaine. The officer told Smith that he was just a pawnshop dealer and did not distribute narcotics. Nonetheless, he indicated that he wanted the MAC-10 and would try to get the cocaine.

The undercover officer then left, promising to return within an hour, and went to the sheriff's office to arrange for Smith's arrest. But Smith did not wait. The officers who were conducting surveillance saw him leave the motel room carrying a gun bag; he then climbed into his van and drove away. The officers reported Smith's departure and began following him. When law enforcement authorities tried to stop Smith, he led them on a high-speed chase, which ended in his apprehension. Smith, it turns out, was well armed. A search of his van revealed the MAC-10, a silencer, ammunition, and a "fast-feed" mechanism. In addition, police found a MAC-11 machine gun, a loaded .45-caliber pistol, and a .22-caliber pistol with a scope and homemade silencer. Smith also had a loaded 9-millimeter handgun in his waistband.

A grand jury for the Southern District of Florida returned an indictment charging Smith with, among other offenses, two drug trafficking crimes—conspiracy to possess cocaine with intent to distribute and attempt to possess cocaine with intent to distribute. More importantly, the indictment alleged that Smith knowingly used the MAC-10 and its silencer during and in relation to a drug trafficking crime. Under federal law, a defendant who so uses a firearm must be sentenced to five years' incarceration. And where, as here, the firearm is a "machine gun" or is fitted with a silencer, the sentence is 30 years. The jury convicted Smith on all counts.

This story is taken directly from the majority opinion in the 1993 U.S. Supreme Court case of *Smith* v. *U.S.*,[1] which held that "[a] criminal who trades his firearm for drugs 'uses' it within the meaning" of federal sentencing guidelines. The plain language of the statute, the high court explained, imposes no requirement that the firearm be used as a weapon. Smith's appeal of his 30-year sentence was denied.

Sentencing is the imposition of a penalty upon a person convicted of a crime. Most sentencing decisions are made by judges, although in some cases, especially where a death sentence is possible, juries may be involved in a special sentencing phase of courtroom proceedings. The sentencing decision is one of the most difficult made by any judge or jury. Not only does it involve the future, and perhaps the very life, of the defendant, but society looks to sentencing to achieve a diversity of goals—some of which may not be fully compatible.

This chapter examines sentencing in terms of both philosophy and practice. We will describe the goals of sentencing as well as the historical development of various sentencing models in the United States. The role of victims in contemporary sentencing practices will also be discussed. This chapter contains a detailed overview of victimization and victims' rights in general—especially as they relate to courtroom procedure and to sentencing practice. Finally, federal sentencing guidelines and the significance of presentence investigations are described.

Sentencing The imposition of a criminal sanction by a judicial authority.

The Philosophy of Criminal Sentencing

Traditional sentencing options have included imprisonment, fines, probation, and—for very serious offenses—death. Limits on the range of options available to sentencing authorities are generally specified by law. Historically, those limits have shifted as understanding of crime and the goals of sentencing have changed. Sentencing philosophies, or the justifications upon which various sentencing strategies are based, are manifestly intertwined with issues of religion, morals, values, and emotions.[2] Philosophies which gained ascendancy at a particular point in history were likely to be reflections of more deeply held social values. The mentality of centuries ago, for example, held that crime was due to sin, and suffering was the culprit's due. Judges were expected to be harsh. Capital punishment, torture, and painful physical penalties served this view of criminal behavior.

An emphasis on rehabilitation became more prevalent around the time of the American and French revolutions, brought about, in part, by Enlightenment philosophies. Offenders came to be seen as highly rational beings who, more often than not, intentionally and somewhat carefully chose their course of action. Sentencing philosophies of the period stressed the need for sanctions which outweighed the benefits to be derived from making criminal choices. Severity of punishment became less important than quick and certain penalties.

Recent thinking has emphasized the need to limit offenders' potential for future harm by separating them from society. We still also believe that offenders deserve to be punished, and we have not entirely abandoned hope for their rehabilitation. Modern sentencing practices are influenced by five goals, which weave their way through widely disseminated professional and legal models, continuing public calls for sentencing reform, and everyday sentencing practice. Each goal represents a quasi-independent sentencing philosophy, since each makes distinctive assumptions about human nature and holds implications for sentencing practice. The five goals of contemporary sentencing are

1. Retribution
2. Incapacitation
3. Deterrence
4. Rehabilitation
5. Restoration

Health Alert

Issued by the Chautauqua County Sheriff's Office, Chautauqua County Health Department and Chautauqua County District Attorney

Anyone who has had unprotected sex with a man who matches this description is at risk for HIV infection.

NUSHAWN WILLIAMS

Also known as: Face Williams, "E", Shyteek Johnson, Jo Jo Williams, Lashawn Fields, Headteck Williams, Shoe Williams and Face Johnson.

Williams has been arrested for statutory rape and is currently in custody. Additional charges are pending. His birthdate is 11/1/76. He is a 5'8 black male, weighing 185 pounds. He has a 10 inch scar on his right lower arm, a stab scar behind an earlobe. He has a mustache, chin hair and wears his hair in a 2-4 inch braids.

Williams used neighborhood parks, in both urban and rural communities, to establish relationships with young women. He is reported to display a very pleasing personality. Williams is known to be a transient and has been reported to frequent other localities throughout New York State.

Anyone who thinks that they have had unprotected sex with this man should:
Call the Chautauqua County Health Department about a free confidential or anonymous HIV test immediately.

Jamestown Branch	Dunkirk Branch	Mayville Branch
110 E 4th Street	15 Lucas Avenue	Clothier Building
661-8111	366-8805	753-4491

No information about victims will be released.

In late 1997 Nushawn Williams, 20, was accused of infecting dozens of teenage girls and young women with the HIV virus in the Jamestown, New York, area. Chautauqua County, New York, District Attorney James Subjack charged Williams with reckless endangerment for each sexual encounter, and first-degree assault for each partner who subsequently became infected. The Williams case demonstrates a crucial philosophical component of sentencing: that people must be held accountable for their actions, and for the harm they cause. *Bill Sikes, AP/Wide World Photos*

RETRIBUTION

Retribution The act of taking revenge upon a criminal perpetrator.

Retribution is a call for punishment predicated upon a felt need for vengeance. Retribution is the earliest known rationale for punishment. Most early societies punished offenders whenever they could catch them. Early punishments were swift and immediate—often without the benefit of a hearing—and they were often extreme, with little thought given to whether the punishment "fit" the crime. Death and exile, for example, were commonly imposed, even on relatively minor offenders. In contrast, the Old Testament dictum of "An eye for an eye, a tooth for a tooth"—often cited as an ancient justification for retribution—was actually intended to reduce the severity of punishment for relatively minor crimes.

Just Deserts As a model of criminal sentencing, one which holds that criminal offenders deserve the punishment they receive at the hands of the law and that punishments should be appropriate to the type and severity of crime committed.

In its modern guise, retribution corresponds to the **just deserts** model of sentencing. The just deserts philosophy holds that offenders are responsible for their crimes. When they are convicted and punished, they are said to have gotten their "just deserts." Retribution sees punishment as deserved, justified, and even required[3], by the offender's behavior. The primary sentencing tool of today's just deserts model is imprisonment, but in extreme cases capital punishment (that is, death) may become the ultimate retribution.

Although it may be an age-old goal of criminal sentencing, retribution is very much in the forefront of public thinking and political policy-making today. Within the last few years, as the social order perspective with its emphasis on individual responsibility has gained ascendancy, public demands for retribution-based criminal punishments have been loud and clear. In 1994, for example, the Mississippi legislature, encouraged by Governor Kirk Fordice, voted to ban prison air conditioning, remove privately owned television sets from prison cells and dormitories, and prohibit weight lifting by inmates. Governor Fordice sent a "get-tough" proposal to the legislature, which was quickly dubbed the "Clint Eastwood Hang 'em High Bill,"[4] and required inmates to wear striped uniforms with the word "CONVICT" stamped on the back. State Representative Mac McInnis explained the state's new retribution-inspired fervor this way: "We want a prisoner to look like a prisoner, to smell like a prisoner."[5]

With public anticrime sentiment at what may be an all time high, says Jonathan Turley, director of the Prison Law Project, "It's difficult to imagine a measure draconian enough to satisfy the public desire for retribution."[6] As critics say, however, the fact that none of these measures will likely deter crime is beside the point. The goal of retribution, after all, is not deterrence, but satisfaction.[7]

INCAPACITATION

Incapacitation, the second goal of criminal sentencing, seeks to protect innocent members of society from offenders who might do them harm if they were not prevented in some way. In ancient times mutilation and amputation of the extremities were sometimes used to prevent offenders from repeating their crimes. Modern incapacitation strategies separate offenders from the community in order to reduce opportunities for further criminality. Incapacitation is sometimes called the "lock 'em up approach" and forms the basis for the movement toward prison "warehousing," discussed later in Chapter 12.

Both incapacitation and retribution are used as justifications for imprisonment. A significant difference between the two perspectives, however, lies in the fact that incapacitation requires only restraint—and not punishment. Hence advocates of the incapacitation philosophy of sentencing are sometimes also active prison reformers, seeking to humanize correctional institutions. At the forefront of technology, confinement innovations are now offering ways to achieve the goal of incapacitation without the need for imprisonment. Electronic confinement (discussed shortly) and biomedical intervention (such as "chemical castration") may be able to achieve the goals of incapacitation without the need for imprisonment.

Incapacitation The use of imprisonment or other means to reduce the likelihood that an offender will be capable of committing future offenses.

DETERRENCE

Deterrence uses punishment as an example to convince people that criminal activity is not worthwhile. Its overall goal is crime prevention. **Specific deterrence** seeks to reduce the likelihood of recidivism (repeat offenses) by convicted offenders, while **general deterrence** strives to influence the future behavior of people who have not yet been arrested and who may be tempted to turn to crime.

Deterrence is one of the more "rational" goals of sentencing. It is rational because it is an easily articulated goal, and also because it is possible to investigate objectively the amount of punishment required to deter. Jeremy Bentham's hedonistic calculus, discussed earlier in this text, laid the groundwork for many later calculations of just how harsh punishments need to be in order to deter effectively. It is generally agreed today that harsh punishments can virtually eliminate many minor forms of criminality.[8] Few traffic tickets would have to be written, for example, if minor driving offenses were punishable by death. A free society such as our own, of course, is not willing to impose extreme punishments on petty offenders, and even harsh punishments are not demonstrably effective in reducing the incidence of serious crimes such as murder and drug running.

Deterrence is compatible with the goal of incapacitation, since at least specific deterrence can be achieved through incapacitating offenders. Hugo Bedau,[9] however, points to significant differences between retribution and deterrence. Retribution is oriented toward the past, says Bedau. It seeks to redress wrongs already committed. Deterrence, in contrast, is a strategy for the future. It aims to prevent new crimes. But as H. L. A. Hart has observed,[10] retribution can be the means through which deterrence is achieved. By serving as an example of what might happen to others, punishment may have an inhibiting effect.

Deterrence A goal of criminal sentencing which seeks to prevent others from committing crimes similar to the one for which an offender is being sentenced.

Specific Deterrence A goal of criminal sentencing which seeks to prevent a particular offender from engaging in repeat criminality.

General Deterrence A goal of criminal sentencing which seeks to prevent others from committing crimes similar to the one for which a particular offender is being sentenced by making an example of the person sentenced.

REHABILITATION

Rehabilitation seeks to bring about fundamental changes in offenders and their behavior. As in the case of deterrence, the ultimate goal of rehabilitation is a reduction in the number of criminal offenses. Whereas deterrence depends upon a "fear of the law" and the consequences of violating it, rehabilitation generally works through education and psychological treatment to reduce the likelihood of future criminality.

The term *rehabilitation* however, may actually be a misnomer for the kinds of changes that its supporters seek. Rehabilitation literally means to return a person (or thing) to their previous condition. Hence, medical rehabilitation programs seek to restore functioning to atrophied limbs, rejuvenate injured organs, and mend shattered minds. In the case of criminal offenders, however, it is unlikely that restoring many to their previous state will result in anything other than a more youthful type of criminality.

Rehabilitation The attempt to reform a criminal offender. Also, the state in which a reformed offender is said to be.

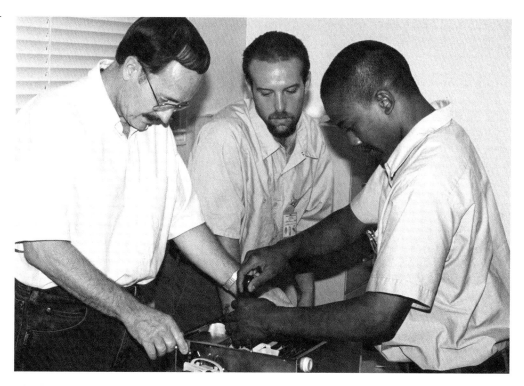

Rehabilitation is an important, if less frequently voiced, goal of modern sentencing practices. Here, inmates in a California prison learn how to work on computers. Skills acquired through such prison programs might translate into productive, noncriminal careers. *Courtesy of Robert Winslow*

In the past, rehabilitation as a sentencing strategy, if it existed at all, was primarily applied to youths. One of the first serious efforts to reform adult offenders was begun by the Pennsylvania Quakers, who initiated the development of the late-eighteenth-century penitentiary. The penitentiary, which attempted to combine enforced penance with religious instruction, proved, to be something of an aberration. Within a few decades it had been firmly supplanted by a retributive approach to corrections.

It was not until the 1930s that rehabilitation achieved a primary role in the sentencing of adult offenders in the United States. At the time, the psychological world view of therapists such as Sigmund Freud was entering popular culture. Psychology held out, as never before, the possibility of a structured approach to rehabilitation through therapeutic intervention. The rehabilitative approach of the mid-1900s became known as the medical model of corrections, since it was built around a prescriptive approach to the treatment of offenders which provided at least the appearance of clinical predictability.

The primacy of the rehabilitative goal in sentencing fell victim to a "nothing works" philosophy in the late 1970s. The nothing works doctrine was based upon studies of recidivism rates, which consistently showed that rehabilitation was more an ideal than a reality. With as many as 90% of former convicted offenders returning to lives of crime following release from prison-based treatment programs, public sentiments in favor of incapacitation grew. Although the rehabilitation ideal has clearly suffered in the public arena, some emerging evidence has begun to suggest that effective treatment programs do exist and may even be growing in number.[11]

RESTORATION

Restoration A goal of criminal sentencing which attempts to make the victim "whole again."

Victims of crime or their survivors are frequently traumatized by their experiences. Some are killed, and others receive lasting physical injuries. For many, the world is never the same. The victimized may live in constant fear—reduced in personal vigor and unable to form trusting relationships. Restoration is a sentencing goal that seeks to address this damage by making the victim and the community "whole again."

A recent report by the U.S. Department of Justice explains restoration this way: "Crime was once defined as a 'violation of the State.' This remains the case today, but we now recognize that crime is far more. It is—among other things—a violation of one person by another. While retributive justice may address the first type of violation adequately, **restorative justice** is required to effectively address the later….Thus (through restorative justice) we seek to attain a balance between the legitimate needs of the community, the…offender, and the victim."[12]

The "healing" of victims involves many aspects, ranging from victim assistance initiatives to legislation supporting victim compensation. Sentencing options which seek to restore the victim have focused primarily on restitution payments which offenders are ordered to make, either to their victims or to a general fund, which may then go to reimburse victims for suffering, lost wages, and medical expenses. In support of these goals, the 1984 Federal Comprehensive Crime Control Act specifically requires: "If sentenced to probation, the defendant must also be ordered to pay a fine, make restitution, and/or work in community service."[13]

Texas provides one example of a statewide strategy to utilize restitution as an alternative to prison.[14] The Texas Residential Restitution Program operates community-based centers, which house selected nonviolent felony offenders. Residents work at regular jobs in the community, pay for support of their families, make restitution to their victims, and pay for room and board. During nonworking hours they are required to perform community service work.

Vermont, which in 1995 began a new Sentencing Options Program built around the concept of reparative probation, provides a second example. According to state officials, the Vermont reparative options program, which "requires the offender to make reparations to the victim and to the community, marks the first time in the United States that the Restorative Justice model has been embraced by a state department of corrections and implemented on a statewide scale."[15] Vermont's reparative program builds upon "community reparative boards" consisting of five or six citizens from the community where the crime was committed and requires face-to-face public meetings between the offender and board representatives. Keeping in mind the program's avowed goals of "making the victim(s) whole again" and having the offender "make amends to the community," board members determine the specifics of the offender's sentence. Options include restitution, community service work, victim-offender mediation, victim empathy programs, driver improvement courses, and the like.

Some advocates of the restoration philosophy of sentencing point out that restitution payments and work programs which benefit the victim can also have the added benefit of rehabilitating the offender. The hope is that such sentences may teach offenders personal responsibility through structured financial obligations, job requirements, and regularly scheduled payments.

Indeterminate Sentencing

While the *philosophy* of criminal sentencing is reflected in the goals of sentencing we have just discussed, different sentencing *practices* have been linked to each goal. During most of the twentieth century, for example, the rehabilitative goal has been influential. Since rehabilitation required that individual offenders' personal characteristics be closely considered in defining effective treatment strategies, judges were generally permitted wide discretion in choosing from among sentencing options. Although incapacitation is increasingly becoming the sentencing strategy of choice, many state criminal codes still allow judges to impose fines, probation, or widely varying prison terms, all for the same offense. These sentencing practices, characterized primarily by vast judicial choice, constitute an **indeterminate sentencing model**.

Indeterminate sentencing has both an historical and a philosophical basis in the belief that convicted offenders are more likely to participate in their own rehabilitation if they can reduce the amount of time they have to spend in prison. Inmates on good behavior will be released early, while recalcitrant inmates will remain in prison until the end of their terms. For that reason, parole generally plays a significant role in states which employ the indeterminate sentencing model.

Restorative Justice A sentencing model which builds upon restitution and community participation in an attempt to make the victim "whole again."

Indeterminate Sentencing A model of criminal punishment which encourages rehabilitation via the use of general and relatively unspecific sentences (such as a term of imprisonment of "from one to ten years").

Indeterminate sentencing relies heavily upon judges' discretion to choose among types of sanctions and set upper and lower limits on the length of prison stays. Indeterminate sentences are typically imposed with wording such as "The defendant shall serve not less than five, not more than twenty-five years in the state's prison, under the supervision of the state department of correction…." Judicial discretion under the indeterminate model also extends to the imposition of concurrent or consecutive sentences, where the offender is convicted on more than one charge. Consecutive sentences are served one after the other, while concurrent sentences expire simultaneously.

The indeterminate model was also created to take into consideration detailed differences in degrees of guilt. Under this model judges could weigh minute differences among cases, situations, and offenders. All of the following could be considered before sentence was passed: (1) whether the offender committed the crime out of a need for money, for the thrill it afforded, out of a desire for revenge, or for the "hell of it"; (2) how much harm the offender intended; (3) how much the victim contributed to his or her own victimization; (4) the extent of the damages inflicted; (5) the mental state of the offender; (6) the likelihood of successful rehabilitation; (7) the degree of the offender's cooperation with authorities; and (8) a near infinity of other individual factors.

Under the indeterminate sentencing model, the inmate's behavior (while incarcerated) is the primary determinant of the amount of time served. State parole boards wield great discretion under the model, acting as the final arbiters of the actual sentence served.

A few states employ a partially indeterminate sentencing model. Partially indeterminate sentencing systems allow judges to specify only the maximum amount of time to be served. Some minimum is generally implied by law but is not under the control of the sentencing authority. General practice is to set one year as a minimum for all felonies, while a few jurisdictions assume no minimum time at all—making persons sentenced to imprisonment eligible for immediate parole.

Problems with the Indeterminate Model

Indeterminate sentencing is still the rule in many jurisdictions, including Georgia, Hawaii, Iowa, Kentucky, Massachusetts, Michigan, Nevada, New York, Oklahoma, Rhode Island, South Carolina, Texas, Utah, Vermont, West Virginia, Wyoming, and North and South Dakota.[16] By the 1970s, however, the model had come under fire for contributing to inequality in sentencing. Critics claimed that the indeterminate model allowed divergent judicial personalities, and the often too-personal philosophies of judges, to produce a wide range of sentencing practices from very lenient to very strict. The "hanging judge," who still presides in some jurisdictions, was depicted as tending to impose the maximum sentence allowable under law on anyone who comes before the bench, regardless of circumstances. Worse still, the indeterminate model was criticized for perpetuating a system under which offenders might be sentenced, at least by some judges, more on the basis of social characteristics, such as race, gender, and social class, rather than culpability.

Because of the personal nature of judicial decisions under the indeterminate model, offenders—in jurisdictions where the model is still used—often depend upon the advice and ploys of their attorneys to appear before a judge who is thought to be a good sentencing risk. Requests for delays are a commonly used defense strategy in indeterminate sentencing states where they are used in attempts to manipulate the selection of judicial personalities involved in sentencing decisions.

Good Time   The amount of time deducted from time to be served in prison on a given sentence(s) and/or under correctional agency jurisdiction, at some point after a prisoner's admission to prison, contingent upon good behavior and/or awarded automatically by application of a statute or regulation.

Another charge leveled against indeterminate sentencing is that it tends to produce dishonesty in sentencing. Because of sentence cutbacks for good behavior and other reductions available to inmates through involvement in work and study programs, punishments rarely mean what they say. A sentence of five to ten years, for example, might actually see an inmate released in a matter of months after all "gain time," **"good time,"** and other special allowances have been calculated. (Some of the same charges can be leveled against determinate sentencing schemes under which correctional officials can administratively reduce the time served by an inmate.) To ensure long prison terms within indeterminate jurisdictions, some court officials have been led to extremes. In 1994, for example, a judge in Oklahoma, an indeterminate sentencing state, followed a jury's recommendation and sentenced convicted child molester Charles Scott Robinson, aged 30, to 30,000 years in prison.[17] Judge Dan Owens, complying with the jury's efforts to ensure that Robinson would spend the rest of his

Table 10-1 *Estimated Time to be Served in State Prison versus Mean Prison Sentence*

Offense	Mean Prison Sentence	Estimated Time to Be Served in Prison
Murder	267 months	126 months
Rape	157	87
Robbery	115	55
Aggravated assault	79	39
Burglary	69	27
Larceny	45	19
Motor vehicle theft	50	23
Drug trafficking	70	33
Other felonies	41	22
Average for all felonies	**72 months**	**31 months**

Source: Patrick A. Langan and Jodi M. Brown, *Felony Sentences in the United States, 1994* (Washington, D.C.: Bureau of Justice Statistics, 1997.

life behind bars, sentenced him to serve six consecutive 5,000 year sentences. Robinson had 14 previous felony convictions.

Due largely to indeterminate sentencing practices, time served in prison is generally far less than sentences would seem to indicate. A 1995 survey[18] by the Bureau of Justice Statistics found that even violent offenders, the most serious of all, who were released from state prisons during the study period served, on average, only 48% of the sentences they originally received. Table 10–1 shows recent estimates of time served in prison versus actual sentences of felons convicted under state jurisdiction. Figure 10–1 provides a graphical representation of that data.

The Rise of Structured Sentencing

Until the 1970s, all 50 states used some form of indeterminate (or partially indeterminate) sentencing. Soon, however, calls for **equity** and **proportionality** in sentencing, heightened by claims of racial disparity in the sentencing practices[19] of some judges, led many states to move toward closer control over their sentencing systems.

Critics of the indeterminate model called for the recognition of three fundamental sentencing principles: proportionality, **equity**, and **social debt**. Proportionality refers to the belief that the severity of sanctions should bear a direct relationship to the seriousness of the crime committed. Equity is based upon a concern with social equality and means that similar crimes should be punished with the same degree of severity, regardless of the general social or personal characteristics of offenders. According to the principle of equity, for example, two bank robbers in different parts of the country, who use the same techniques and weapons, with the same degree of implied threat, even though they are tried under separate circumstances, should receive roughly the same kind of sentence. The equity principle needs to be balanced, however, against the notion of social debt. In the case of the bank robbers, the offender who has a prior criminal record can be said to have a higher level of social debt than the one-time robber, where all else is equal. Greater social debt, of course, would suggest a heightened severity of punishment or a greater need for treatment, and so on.

Beginning in the 1970s, a number of states moved to address these concerns by developing a different model of sentencing known as **structured sentencing**. One form of structured sentencing, called **determinate sentencing**, requires that a convicted offender be sentenced to a fixed term that may be reduced by good time or earned time. Determinate sentencing states eliminated the use of parole and created explicit standards to specify the amount of punishment appropriate for a given offense. Determinate sentencing practices also specify an anticipated release date for each sentenced offender.

Proportionality A sentencing principle which holds that the severity of sanctions should bear a direct relationship to the seriousness of the crime committed.

Equity A sentencing principle, based upon concerns with social equity, which holds that similar crimes should be punished with the same degree of severity, regardless of the social or personal characteristics of offenders.

Social Debt A sentencing principle which objectively counts an offender's criminal history in sentencing decisions.

Structured Sentencing A model of criminal punishment that includes determinate and commission-created presumptive sentencing schemes, as well as voluntary/advisory sentencing guidelines.

Determinate Sentencing (also called **Fixed Sentencing**) A model of criminal punishment in which an offender is given a fixed term that may be reduced by good time or earned time. Under the model, for example, all offenders convicted of the same degree of burglary would be sentenced to the same length of time behind bars.

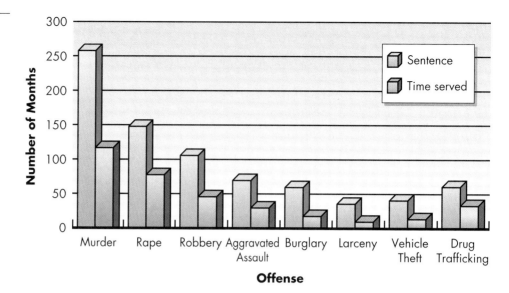

FIGURE 10–1 Time served in state prisons versus court sentence for selected offenses. *Source:* Patrick A. Langan and Jodi M. Brown, *Felony Sentences in the United States, 1994* (Washington, D.C.: Bureau of Justice Statistics, 1997).

Voluntary/Advisory Sentencing Guidelines
Recommended sentencing policies that are not required by law.

Presumptive Sentencing
A model of criminal punishment that meets the following conditions: (1) the appropriate sentence for an offender in a specific case is presumed to fall within a range of sentences authorized by sentencing guidelines that are adopted by a legislatively created sentencing body, usually a sentencing commission; (2) sentencing judges are expected to sentence within the range to provide written justification for departure; (3) the guidelines provide for some review, usually appellate, of the departure.

In a 1996 report which traced the historical development of determinate sentencing, the National Council on Crime and Delinquency (NCCD) observed that "[t]he term 'determinate sentencing' is generally used to refer to the sentencing reforms of the late 1970s. In those reforms, the legislatures of California, Illinois, Indiana, and Maine abolished the parole release decision and replaced the indeterminate penalty structure with a fixed (flat) sentence that could be reduced by a significant good-time provision. The only state that has adopted a true determinate sentencing system since 1980 is Arizona, which enacted a 'truth in sentencing law' on January 1, 1994. These five states have retained their determinate sentencing models, although no other states have adopted such a structured sentencing scheme."[20] The NCCD report continues: "In three of the states (California, Illinois, and Indiana), the legislators provided presumptive ranges of confinement. But those in Illinois and Indiana were so wide that they provided the court with extensive discretion on sentence length. For many offenses, there was no presumptive lead as to whether the sentence should be for, or against, incarceration. Thus, courts were left with extensive discretion in deciding both whether to incarcerate and the length of incarceration. It is arguable that the discretion attacked in these reforms was mainly that of parole boards and that the discretion lost by parole boards was largely shifted to the courts or to the prosecutors who control the charging function."[21]

In response to the then-growing determinate sentencing movement, a few states developed **voluntary/advisory sentencing** guidelines. Such guidelines consist of recommended sentencing policies that are not required by law. They are usually based upon past sentencing practices and serve as guides to judges. Voluntary/advisory sentencing guidelines may build upon either determinate or indeterminate sentencing structures. Florida, Maryland, Massachusetts, Michigan, Rhode Island, Utah, and Wisconsin all experimented with voluntary/advisory guidelines during the 1980s. Voluntary/advisory guidelines constitute a second form of structured sentencing.

A third model of structured sentencing employs what the NCCD calls "commission-based **presumptive sentencing** guidelines." Presumptive sentencing schemes became common in the 1980s as states began to experiment with approaches using sentencing guidelines developed by sentencing commissions. These models differed from both determinate and voluntary/advisory guidelines in three respects. First, presumptive sentencing guidelines were not developed by the legislature but by a sentencing commission that often represented a diverse array of criminal justice and sometimes private-citizen interests. Second, presumptive sentencing guidelines were explicit and highly structured, typically relying on a quantitative scoring instrument to classify the offense for which a person was to be sentenced. Third, the guidelines were not voluntary/advisory in that judges had to adhere to the sentencing system or provide a written rationale for departures. The NCCD observes, "[a]s in

A defendant stands before a judge
in Austin, Texas, for sentencing.
Bob Daemmrich, Stock Boston

the move to determinate sentencing and voluntary/advisory guidelines, the driving forces
stimulating presumptive sentencing guidelines were issues of fairness (including disparity,
certainty, and proportionality) and prison crowding. These concerns provided the impetus
for states to adopt guidelines, replace indeterminate sentencing with determinate sentencing,
and abolish or curtail discretionary parole release."[22]

The first four states to adopt presumptive sentencing guideline systems were Minnesota
(1980), Pennsylvania (1982), Washington (1983), and Florida (1983). The Minnesota model
in particular, with its focus on controlling prison population growth, has often been cited as
a successful example of controlling disparity and rising corrections costs through sentencing
guidelines. The American Bar Association has endorsed sentencing commission-based
guidelines through its Criminal Justice Standards Committee's *Sentencing Alternatives and
Procedures* (adopted by the ABA House of Delegates). In making such an endorsement, the
Standards Committee relied heavily upon the system of presumptive sentencing pioneered
in Minnesota.

The federal government and 16 states have now established commission-based sentencing guidelines. Ten of the 16 states can be classified as using presumptive sentencing guidelines. The remaining six have voluntary/advisory guideline models. As a consequence, sentencing guidelines authored by legislatively created sentencing commissions are now the
most popular form of structured sentencing.

Guideline jurisdictions, which specify a presumptive sentence for a given offense, generally
allow for "aggravating" or "mitigating" factors—indicating greater or lesser degrees of culpability—which judges can take into consideration in imposing a sentence somewhat at variance
from the presumptive term. **Aggravating circumstances** are those which appear to call for a
tougher sentence and may include especially heinous behavior, cruelty, injury to more than
one person, and so on. In death penalty cases, however, the U.S. Supreme Court has held that
aggravating factors must "provide specific and detailed guidance and make rationally reviewable the death sentencing process…. In order to decide whether a particular aggravating circumstance meets these requirements, a federal court must determine whether the statutory
language defining the circumstance is itself too vague to guide the sentencer…."[23]

Mitigating circumstances, or those which indicate that a lesser sentence is called for, are
generally similar to legal defenses, although in this case they only reduce criminal responsi-

**Aggravating
Circumstances** Those elements of an offense or of an
offender's background
which could result in a
harsher sentence under the
determinate model than
would otherwise be called
for by sentencing guide-
lines.

Mitigating Circumstances
Those elements of an
offense or of an offender's
background which could
result in a lesser sentence
under the determinate
model than would other-
wise be called for by sentencing guidelines.

Theory into Practice

Aggravating and Mitigating Factors

Listed here are some typical aggravating and mitigating factors which judges may take into consideration in arriving at sentencing decisions in presumptive sentencing jurisdictions.

AGGRAVATING FACTORS

- The defendant induced others to participate in the commission of the offense.
- The offense was especially heinous, atrocious, or cruel.
- The defendant was armed with or used a deadly weapon at the time of the crime.
- The offense was committed for the purpose of avoiding or preventing a lawful arrest or effecting an escape from custody.
- The offense was committed for hire.
- The offense was committed against a present or former law enforcement officer or correctional officer while engaged in the performance of official

duties, or because of the past exercise of official duties.
- The defendant took advantage of a position of trust or confidence to commit the offense.

MITIGATING FACTORS

- The defendant has no record of criminal convictions punishable by more than 60 days of imprisonment.
- The defendant has made substantial or full restitution.
- The defendant has been a person of good character or has had a good reputation in the community.
- The defendant aided in the apprehension of another felon or testified truthfully on behalf of the prosecution.
- The defendant acted under strong provocation, or the victim was a voluntary participant in the criminal activity, or otherwise consented to it.

- The offense was committed under duress, coercion, threat, or compulsion which was insufficient to constitute a defense but significantly reduced the defendant's culpability.
- The defendant was suffering from a mental or physical condition that was insufficient to constitute a defense but significantly reduced culpability for the offense.

QUESTIONS FOR DISCUSSION

1. What aggravating factors, if any, might you add to the list in this box? Why?
2. What mitigating factors, if any, might you add to the list in this box? Why?

---

bility, not eliminate it. Mitigating factors include such things as cooperation with the investigating authority, surrender, good character, and so on. Common aggravating and mitigating factors are listed in the above "Theory into Practice" box.

Critiques of structured sentencing

Structured sentencing models, which have generally sought to address the shortcomings of indeterminate sentencing by curtailing judicial discretion in sentencing, are not without their critics. Detractors charge that structured sentencing is (1) overly simplistic, (2) based upon a primitive concept of culpability, and (3) incapable of offering hope for rehabilitation and change. For one thing, they say, structured sentencing has built-in limitations, which render it far less able to judge the blameworthiness of individual offenders. Legislatures and sentencing commissions, say critics, simply cannot anticipate all the differences that individual cases can present. Aggravating and mitigating factors, while intended to cover most circumstances, will inevitably shortchange some defendants who don't fall neatly into the categories they provide.

A second critique of structured sentencing is that while it may reduce judicial discretion substantially, it may do nothing to hamper the huge discretionary decision-making power of prosecutors.[24] In fact, federal sentencing reformers, who have adopted a structured sentencing model, have specifically decided not to modify the discretionary power of prosecutors, citing the large number of cases which are resolved through plea bargaining. Such a shift in discretionary authority, away from judges and into the hands of prosecutors, say critics, may be misplaced.

Another criticism of structured sentencing questions its fundamental purpose. Advocates of structured sentencing inevitably cite greater equity in sentencing as the primary benefits of such a model. Reduced to its essence, this means that "those who commit the same crime get the same time." Sentencing reformers have thus couched the drive toward structured sentencing in progressive terms. Others, however, have pointed out that the philosophical underpinnings of the movement may be quite different. Albert Alschuler,[25] for example, suggests that structured sentencing is a regressive social policy which derives from American weariness with considering offenders as individuals. Describing this kind of thinking, Alschuler writes: "Don't tell us that a robber was retarded. We don't care about his problems. We don't know what to *do* about his problems, and we are no longer interested in listening to a criminal's sob stories. The most important thing about this robber is simply that he *is* a robber."[26]

A different line of thought is proposed by Christopher Link and Neal Shover[27] who found in a study of state-level economic, political, and demographic data that structured sentencing may ultimately be the result of declining economic conditions and increasing fiscal strain on state governments rather than any particular set of ideals.

A fifth critique of structured sentencing centers on its alleged inability to promote effective rehabilitation. Under indeterminate sentencing schemes, offenders have the opportunity to act responsibly and thus to participate in their own rehabilitation.[28] Lack of responsible behavior results in denial of parole and extension of the sentence. Structured sentencing schemes, by virtue of dramatic reductions in good-time allowances and parole opportunities, leave little incentive for offenders to participate in educational programs, to take advantage of opportunities for work inside of correctional institutions, to seek treatment, or to contribute in any positive way to their own change.

While these critiques may be valid, they will probably do little to stem the rising tide of structured sentencing. The growth of structured sentencing over the past few decades represents the ascendancy of the "just deserts" perspective over other sentencing goals. In a growing number of jurisdictions, punishment, deterrence, and incapacitation have replaced rehabilitation and restitution as the goals which society seeks to achieve through sentencing practices.

We will not punish a man because he hath offended, but that he may offend no more; nor does punishment ever look to the past, but to the future; for it is not the result of passion, but that the same thing be guarded against in time to come.
—Seneca (ʙ.ᴄ. 3–65 ᴀ.ᴅ.)

Mandatory Sentencing

Mandatory sentencing, which is actually another form of structured sentencing,[29] deserves special mention. **Mandatory sentencing** is just what its name implies—a structured sentencing scheme which allows no leeway in the nature of the sentence required and under which clearly enumerated punishments are mandated for specific offenses or for habitual offenders convicted of a series of crimes. Mandatory sentencing, because it is truly *mandatory*, differs from presumptive sentencing (discussed earlier) which allows for at least a limited amount of judicial discretion within ranges established by published guidelines. Some mandatory sentencing laws require only modest mandatory prison terms (for example, 3 years for armed robbery), while others are much more far-reaching

Typical of far-reaching mandatory sentencing schemes are three-strikes laws, discussed in a box in this chapter. Three-strikes laws (and, in some jurisdictions, two-strikes laws) require mandatory sentences (sometimes life in prison without the possibility of parole) for offenders convicted of a third serious felony. Such mandatory sentencing enhancements are aimed at deterring known and potentially violent offenders and are intended to incapacitate convicted criminals through long-term incarceration.

Three-strikes laws impose longer prison terms than most earlier mandatory minimum sentencing laws. California's three-strikes law, for example, requires that offenders who are convicted of a violent crime and who have had two prior convictions serve a minimum of 25 years in prison. The law doubles prison terms for offenders convicted of a second violent felony.[30] Three-strikes laws also vary in breadth. The laws of some jurisdictions stipulate that both of the prior convictions and the current offense be violent felonies; others require only that the prior felonies be violent. Some three-strikes laws count only prior adult violent felony convictions, while others permit consideration of juvenile adjudications for violent crimes.

By passing mandatory sentencing laws, legislators convey the message that certain crimes are deemed especially grave and that people who commit them deserve, and may expect,

Mandatory Sentencing A structured sentencing scheme which allows no leeway in the nature of the sentence required and under which clearly enumerated punishments are mandated for specific offenses or for habitual offenders convicted of a series of crimes.

harsh sanctions. These laws are sometimes passed in response to public outcries following heinous or well-publicized crimes.

Mandatory sentencing has had significant consequences that deserve close attention. Among them are its impact on crime and the operation of the criminal justice system. The possible differential consequences for certain groups of people also bears examination. Evaluations of mandatory sentencing have focused on two types of crimes—those committed with handguns and those related to drugs (the offenses most commonly subjected to mandatory minimum penalties in state and federal courts). An evaluation[31] of a Massachusetts law, for example, that imposed mandatory jail terms for possession of an unlicensed handgun, concluded that the law was an effective deterrent of gun crime—at least in the short term. Studies of similar laws in Michigan[32] and Florida,[33] however, found no evidence that crimes committed with firearms had been prevented by similar laws. An evaluation of mandatory gun-use sentencing enhancements in six large cities (Detroit, Jacksonville, Tampa, Miami, Philadelphia, and Pittsburgh) indicated that such laws deterred homicide but not other violent crimes.[34] A similar assessment of New York's Rockefeller drug laws was unable to support claims for their efficacy as a deterrent to drug crime.[35] None of the studies, however, examined the incapacitation effects of these laws on individual offenders.

Mandatory sentencing has also been evaluated in terms of its impact on the criminal justice system. Traditionally, criminal courts have relied on a high rate of guilty pleas to speed case processing and to avoid logjams. Officials have been able to offer inducements (by way of lowered sentences) to defendants to obtain bargained pleas. Mandatory sentencing laws, it has been found, can disrupt established plea-bargaining patterns by preventing a prosecutor from offering a short prison term in exchange for a guilty plea. However, unless policymakers enact long-term mandatory sentences that apply to many related categories of crimes, prosecutors can usually shift strategies and bargain on charges rather than on sentences—thus retaining plea bargaining as a valid option in most courtrooms.

Research findings on the impact of mandatory sentencing laws on the criminal justice system have been summarized by Michael Tonry.[36] Tonry found that under mandatory sentencing, officials tend to make earlier and more selective arrest, charging, and diversion decisions. They also tend to bargain less and to bring more cases to trial. Specifically, Tonry found that (1) criminal justice officials and practitioners (police, lawyers, and judges) exercise discretion to avoid application of laws they consider unduly harsh; (2) arrest rates for target crimes tend to decline soon after mandatory sentencing laws take effect; (3) dismissal and diversion rates increase at early stages of case processing after mandatory sentencing laws become effective; (4) for defendants whose cases are not dismissed, plea-bargain rates decline and trial rates increase; (5) for convicted defendants, sentencing delays increase; (6) enactment of mandatory sentencing laws has little impact on the probability that offenders will be imprisoned (when the effects of declining arrests, indictments, and convictions are taken into account); and (7) sentences become longer and more severe. Mandatory sentencing laws may also occasionally result in unduly harsh punishments for marginal offenders, who nonetheless meet the minimum requirements for sentencing under such laws.

In an analysis of federal sentencing guidelines, other researchers[37] found that blacks receive longer sentences than whites, not because of differential treatment by judges but because they constitute the large majority of those convicted of trafficking in crack cocaine— a crime Congress has singled out for especially harsh mandatory penalties. This pattern can be seen as constituting a "disparity in results" and, partly for this reason, the U.S. Sentencing Commission recently recommended to Congress that it eliminate the legal distinction between crack and regular cocaine for purposes of sentencing (a recommendation Congress rejected, but which is being pursued by the Clinton Administration as this book goes to press).

An alternative to mandatory minimum sentencing provisions, which would protect sentencing policy, preserve legislative control, and still toughen sentences for repeat violent offenders, is the use of presumptive sentences. Other possibilities include (1) directing mandatory sentencing laws at only a few especially serious crimes and requiring "sunset" provisions (for example, requiring geriatric inmates who have reached a specified age to be released after serving a certain minimum); (2) subjecting long mandatory sentences to periodic administrative review to determine the advisability of continued confinement in individual cases; (3) building a funding plan into sentencing legislation to ensure awareness of and responsibility for the costs of long-term imprisonment; and (4) developing policies that make more effective and systematic use of intermediate sanctions.

Truth in Sentencing

In 1984, with passage of the Comprehensive Crime Control Act, the federal government adopted presumptive sentencing for nearly all federal offenders.[38] The act also addressed the issue of honesty in sentencing. Under the old federal system, a sentence of ten years in prison might actually have meant only a few years spent behind bars before the offender was released. On average, good-time credits and parole reduced time served to about one-third of actual sentences.[39] At the time, sentencing practices of most states reflected the federal model. While sentence reductions may have benefited offenders, they often outraged victims who felt betrayed by the sentencing process. The 1984 act nearly eliminated good-time credits[40] and targeted 1992 (which was later extended to 2002) as the date for phasing out federal parole and eliminating the U.S. Parole Commission. The emphasis on honesty in sentencing created, in effect, a sentencing environment of "what you get is what you serve."

More recently, the movement toward "truth in sentencing" has accelerated. Truth in sentencing, which has been described as "a close correspondence between the sentence imposed upon those sent to prison and the time actually served prior to prison release,"[41] has become an important policy focus of many state legislatures and the federal congress. The Violent Crime Control and Law Enforcement Act of 1994 set aside $4 billion in federal prison construction funds (called "Truth in Sentencing Incentive Funds") for states which adopt truth in sentencing laws and are able to guarantee that certain violent offenders will serve 85% of their sentences. By 1996 three states—Arizona, California, and Illinois—had legislatively embraced the 85% requirement. A recent report by the Bureau of Justice Statistics[42] found that although many other states are moving toward practices which support truth in sentencing, most will need to greatly accelerate that trend if they are to be eligible for available federal monies. The report found, for example, that in 1992 violent offenders in state prisons served an average of 48% of their felony sentences prior to release. Meeting federal requirements, the study's authors found, would increase the time actually spent in prison by the average prison-bound offender by almost 50%.

Some states have chosen to approach "truth in sentencing" another way. In 1994, for example, the New Jersey supreme court imposed a "truth in sentencing" rule on New Jersey judges, which, although it doesn't require lengthened sentences, mandates that judges publicly disclose how much time a convicted defendant is likely to spend behind bars. The New Jersey court held that lower criminal court judges must "inform the public of the actual period of time" a defendant is likely to spend imprisoned. Judges must also state when a defendant can get out of prison on good behavior. "Under the truth-in-sentencing policy, the public will not be left with the mistaken impression that the sentence imposed is what the defendant will actually serve," the state's high court said. Robert Egles, executive director of the New Jersey State Parole Board called the court's decision a good one. "This is a good decision, especially for victims and crime victims' families," Egles said "The issue didn't seem to be how long the sentences were, but about the honesty of the system. If it's a 10-year sentence, but the defendant can get out in two years, it should be said," concluded Egles.[43]

Federal Sentencing Guidelines

Title II of the Comprehensive Crime Control Act, called the Sentencing Reform Act of 1984,[44] established the nine-member U.S. Sentencing Commission. The commission is composed of presidential appointees, including three federal judges. First to head the sentencing commission was William W. Wilkins, Jr., U.S. circuit judge for the Fourth Circuit.

The Sentencing Reform Act established mandatory minimum sentences for certain federal crimes, including drug offenses, and limited the discretion of federal judges by mandating the creation of federal sentencing guidelines, which federal judges are required to follow. The sentencing commission was given the task of developing structured sentencing guidelines in order to reduce disparity in sentencing, promote consistency and uniformity in sentencing, and increase sentencing fairness and equity. To guide the commission, Congress

Truth in Sentencing A close correspondence between the sentence imposed upon those sent to prison and the time actually served prior to prison release.

specified the purposes of sentencing to include (1) deterring criminals, (2) incapacitating and/or rehabilitating offenders, and (3) providing "just deserts" in punishing criminals. Congress also charged the commission with eliminating sentencing disparities and reducing confusion, and asked for a system which would permit flexibility in the face of mitigating or aggravating elements.

While developing federal sentencing guidelines, the commission analyzed thousands of past cases and enacted a scale of punishments considered typical for given types of offenses.[45] It came up with a series of federal guidelines intended to provide predictability in sentencing, but which also allow individual judges to deviate from the guidelines when specific aggravating or mitigating factors are present. The Commission also considered relevant federal law, parole guidelines, and the anticipated impact of changes upon federal prison populations. One boundary was set by statute: In creating the Sentencing Commission, Congress had also specified that the degree of discretion available in any one sentencing category could not exceed 25% of the basic penalty for that category or six months, whichever might be greater.

Guidelines established by the Commission took effect in November 1987 but quickly became embroiled in a series of legal disputes, some of which challenged Congress's authority to form the Sentencing Commission. On January 18, 1989, in the case of *Mistretta* v. *U.S.*,[46] the U.S. Supreme Court held that Congress had acted appropriately in establishing the Sentencing Commission and that the guidelines developed by the Commission could be applied in federal cases nationwide. The federal Sentencing Commission continues to meet at least once a year in order to review the effectiveness of the guidelines it created.

Federal Guideline Provisions

Federal sentencing guidelines specify a sentencing range for each criminal offense from which judges must choose. If a particular case has "atypical features," judges are allowed to depart from the guidelines. Departures are generally expected to be made only in the presence of mitigating or aggravating factors—a number of which are specified in the guidelines.[47] Aggravating circumstances may include the possession of a weapon during the commission of a crime, the degree of criminal involvement (whether the defendant was a leader or a follower in the criminal activity), and extreme psychological injury to the victim. Punishments also increase where a defendant violates a position of public or private trust, uses special skills to commit or conceal offenses, or has a criminal history. Defendants who express remorse, cooperate with authorities, or willingly make restitution may have their sentences reduced under the guidelines. Any departure from the guidelines may, however, become the basis for appellate review concerning the reasonableness of the sentence imposed, and judges who deviate from the guidelines must provide written reasons for doing so.

Federal sentencing guidelines are built around a table containing 43 rows, each corresponding to one offense level. Penalties associated with each level overlap those of levels above or below in order to discourage unnecessary litigation. A person charged with a crime involving $11,000, for example, upon conviction is unlikely to receive a penalty substantially greater than if the amount involved had been somewhat less than $10,000—a sharp contrast to the old system. A change of six levels roughly doubles the sentence imposed under the guidelines, regardless of the level at which one starts. Because of their matrix-like quality, federal sentencing provisions have also been referred to as "structured sentencing." The federal sentencing table is reproduced in Table 10–2.

The sentencing table also contains six rows, corresponding to the criminal history category into which an offender falls. Criminal history categories are determined on a point basis. Offenders earn points through previous convictions. Each prior sentence of imprisonment for more than one year and one month counts as three points. Two points are assigned for each prior prison sentence over six months, or if the defendant committed the offense while on probation, parole, or work release. The system also assigns points for other types of previous convictions and for offenses committed less than two years after release from imprisonment. Points are added together to determine the criminal history category into which an offender falls. Thirteen points or more are required for the highest category. At each offense level, sentences in the highest criminal history category are generally two to three times as severe as for the lowest category.

Table 10-2 The Federal Sentencing Table

Criminal History Category (Months)

Offense Level	I 0 or 1	II 2 or 3	III 4, 5, 6	IV 7, 8, 9	V 10, 11, 12	VI 13 or More
1	0–1	0–2	0–3	0–4	0–5	0–6
2	0–2	0–3	0–4	0–5	0–6	0–7
3	0–3	0–4	0–5	0–6	2–8	3–9
4	0–4	0–5	0–6	2–8	4–10	6–12
5	0–5	0–6	1–7	4–10	6–12	9–15
6	0–6	1–7	2–8	6–12	9–15	12–18
7	1–7	2–8	4–10	8–14	12–18	15–21
8	2–8	4–10	6–12	10–16	15–21	18–24
9	4–10	6–12	8–14	12–18	18–24	21–27
10	6–12	8–14	10–16	15–21	21–27	24–30
11	8–14	10–16	12–18	18–24	24–30	27–33
12	10–16	12–18	15–21	21–27	27–33	30–37
13	12–18	15–21	18–24	24–30	30–37	33–41
14	15–21	18–24	21–27	27–33	33–41	37–46
15	18–24	21–27	24–30	30–37	37–46	41–51
16	21–27	24–30	27–33	33–41	41–51	46–57
17	24–30	27–33	30–37	37–46	46–57	51–63
18	27–33	30–37	33–41	41–51	51–63	57–71
19	30–37	33–41	37–46	46–57	57–71	63–78
20	33–41	37–46	41–51	51–63	63–78	70–87
21	37–46	41–51	46–57	57–71	70–87	77–96
22	41–51	46–57	51–63	63–78	77–96	84–105
23	46–57	51–63	57–71	70–87	84–105	92–115
24	51–63	57–71	63–78	77–96	92–115	100–125
25	57–71	63–78	70–87	84–105	100–125	110–137
26	63–78	70–87	78–97	92–115	110–137	120–150
27	70–87	78–97	87–108	100–125	120–150	130–162
28	78–97	87–108	97–121	110–137	130–162	140–175
29	87–108	97–121	108–135	121–151	140–175	151–188
30	97–121	108–135	121–151	135–168	151–188	168–210
31	108–135	121–151	135–168	151–188	168–210	188–235
32	121–151	135–168	151–188	168–210	188–235	210–262
33	135–168	151–188	168–210	188–235	210–262	235–293
34	151–188	168–210	188–235	210–262	235–293	262–327
35	168–210	188–235	210–262	235–293	262–327	292–365
36	188–235	210–262	235–293	262–327	292–365	324–405
37	210–262	235–293	262–327	292–365	324–405	360–life
38	235–293	262–327	292–365	324–405	360–life	360–life
39	262–327	292–365	324–405	360–life	360–life	360–life
40	292–365	324–405	360–life	360–life	360–life	360–life
41	324–405	360–life	360–life	360–life	360–life	360–life
42	360–life	360–life	360–life	360–life	360–life	360–life
43	life	life	life	life	life	life

Source: U.S. Sentencing Commission, *Federal Sentencing Guideline Manual* (Washington, D.C.: U.S. Government Printing Office, 1987), p. 210.

Defendants may also move into the highest criminal history category (VI) by virtue of being designated career offenders. Under the sentencing guidelines, a defendant is a career offender if "(1) the defendant was at least 18 years old at the time of the…offense, (2) the…offense is a crime of violence or trafficking in a controlled substance, and (3) the defendant has at least two prior felony convictions of either a crime of violence or a controlled substance offense."[48]

According to the U.S. Supreme Court, an offender may be adjudged a career offender in a single hearing—even when previous convictions are lacking. In *Deal* v. *U.S.* (1993),[49] the defendant, Thomas Lee Deal, was convicted in a single proceeding of six counts of carrying and using a firearm during a series of bank robberies which occurred in the Houston, Texas, area. A federal district court sentenced him to 105 years in prison as a career offender—five years for the first count and 20 years each on the five other counts, with sentences to run consecutively. In the words of the Court, "[w]e see no reason why [the defendant should not receive such a sentence], simply because he managed to evade detection, prosecution, and conviction for the first five offenses and was ultimately tried on all six in a single proceeding."

Plea Bargaining under the Guidelines

Plea bargaining plays a major role in the federal judicial system. Approximately 90% of all federal sentences are the result of guilty pleas,[50] and the large majority of those are the result of plea negotiations. In the words of Commission Chairman Wilkins, "With respect to plea bargaining, the Commission has proceeded cautiously…the Commission did not believe it wise to stand the federal criminal justice system on its head by making too drastic and too sudden a change in these practices."[51]

Although the Commission allowed plea bargaining to continue, it did require that the agreement (1) be fully disclosed in the record of the court (unless there is an overriding and demonstrable reason why it should not) and (2) detail the actual conduct of the offense. Under these requirements defendants will no longer be able to "hide" the actual nature of their offense behind a substitute plea. The thrust of the federal rules concerning plea bargaining is to reduce the veil of secrecy that had previously surrounded the process. Information on the decision-making process itself is available to victims, the media, and the public.

In 1996, in the case of *Melendez* v. *United States*,[52] the U.S. Supreme Court held that a government motion requesting that a trial judge depart below minimum federal sentencing guidelines as part of a cooperative plea agreement does not permit imposition of a sentence below a statutory minimum specified by law. In other words, while federal judges may depart from the guidelines, they cannot accept plea bargains which would result in sentences lower than the minimum required by law for a particular type of offense.

The Sentencing Environment

If you want a small prison population, make punishment certain.

If you want a large prison population, make punishment uncertain.

—Newt Gingrich

A number of studies have attempted to investigate the decision-making process that leads to imposition of a particular sentence. Early studies[53] found a strong relationship between the informal influence of members of the courtroom work group and the severity, or lack thereof, of sentences imposed. A number suggested that minorities ran a much greater risk of imprisonment.[54] Other studies have found that sentencing variations are responsive to extralegal conditions[55] and that public opinion can play a role in the type of sentence handed down.[56] If these findings about public opinion are true, they might explain some of the increase in prison populations. A public opinion study conducted by Bowling Green State University, for example, found that 71% of respondents identified incarceration as the preferred punishment for serious offenses.[57]

More recent analyses, especially in structured sentencing jurisdictions, however, have begun to show that sentences in a number of jurisdictions are becoming more objective and, hence, predictable. A California study[58] of racial equity in sentencing, for example, found that the likelihood of going to prison was increased by

- Having multiple current conviction counts, prior prison terms, and juvenile incarcerations.
- Being on adult and/or juvenile probation or parole at the time of the offense.

- Having been released from prison within 12 months of the current offense.
- Having a history of drug and/or alcohol abuse.
- Being over 21 years of age.
- Going to trial.
- Not being released prior to trial.
- Not being represented by a private attorney.

The same study found that, perhaps partly because of the 1977 California Determinate Sentencing Act, "California courts are making racially equitable sentencing decisions."[59] Findings applied only to the crimes of assault, robbery, burglary, theft, forgery, and drug abuse, but held for sentences involving both prison and probation. Similarly, no disparities were noted in the lengths of sentences imposed.[60] Other recent studies have found that female felons are not treated substantially differently by sentencing authorities than are their male counterparts.[61]

One of the most comprehensive studies of sentencing to date was published in 1987 by Martha Myers and Susette Talarico.[62] Myers and Talarico studied sentencing practices in Georgia and found an "absence of system-wide bias or discrimination"[63] and a reliance by judges on the seriousness of offenses and statutory guidelines in arriving at sentencing decisions. Myers and Talarico also reported that the social background of judges had little direct influence on sentencing outcomes. However, older judges and those who were Baptists or religious fundamentalists were found to be generally stricter than were younger judges. One interesting result of the study was the finding that Baptist and fundamentalist judges, while they did not appear to discriminate against minority defendants, seemed to hold white defendants to a higher standard of behavior.[64]

The Presentence Investigation Report

Before imposing sentence, a judge may request information on the background of a convicted defendant. This is especially true in indeterminate sentencing jurisdictions, where judges retain considerable discretion in selecting sanctions. Traditional wisdom has held that certain factors increase the likelihood of rehabilitation and reduce the need for lengthy prison terms. These factors include a good job record, satisfactory educational attainment, strong family ties, church attendance, an arrest history of only nonviolent offenses, and psychological stability.

Presentence Investigation The examination of a convicted offender's background prior to sentencing. Presentence examinations are generally conducted by probation/parole officers and submitted to sentencing authorities.

Information about a defendant's background often comes to the judge in the form of a presentence report. The task of preparing presentence reports usually falls to the probation/parole office. Presentence reports take one of three forms: (1) a detailed written report on the defendant's personal and criminal history, including an assessment of present conditions in the defendant's life (often called the "long form"); (2) an abbreviated written report summarizing the type of information most likely to be useful in a sentencing decision (the "short form"); and (3) a verbal report to the court made by the investigating officer based on field notes but structured according to categories established for the purpose. A presentence report is much like a résumé, or *vitae*, except that it focuses on what might be regarded as negative as well as positive life experiences.

The length of the completed form is subject to great variation. One survey[65] found that Texas used one of the shortest forms of all—a one-page summary supplemented by other materials which the report writer thought might provide meaningful additional details. Orange County, California, provides an example of the opposite kind and may use the most detailed form of any jurisdiction in the country. The instructions for completing the form consist of a dozen single-spaced pages.[66]

A typical "long form" is divided into ten major informational sections, as follows: (1) personal information and identifying data describing the defendant; (2) a chronology of the current offense and circumstances surrounding it; (3) a record of the defendant's previous convictions, if any; (4) home life and family data; (5) educational background; (6) health history and current state of health; (7) military service; (8) religious preference; (9) financial condition; and (10) sentencing recommendations made by the probation/parole officer completing the report.

Justice in American Context

Three Strikes and You're Out—The Tough New Movement in Criminal Sentencing

In the spring of 1994 California legislators passed the state's now-famous "three strikes and you're out" bill. Amid much fanfare, Governor Pete Wilson signed the "three-strikes" measure into law, calling it "the toughest and most sweeping crime bill in California history."

California's law, which is retroactive (in that it counts offenses committed before the date the legislation was signed) requires a 25-year-to-life sentence for three-time felons with convictions for two or more serious or violent prior offenses. Criminal offenders facing a "second strike" can receive up to double the normal sentence for their most recent offense. Parole consideration is not available until at least 80% of the sentence has been served.

By mid-1997, 22 states had passed three-strikes legislation—and other states were considering it. Also, the federal Violent Crime Control and Law Enforcement Act of 1994 contains a three-strikes provision, which mandates life imprisonment for federal criminals convicted of three violent felonies or drug offenses.

Questions remain, however, as to the effectiveness of three-strikes legislation, and many are concerned about its impact on the justice system. One year after it was signed into law, the California three-strikes initiative was evaluated by the RAND Corporation. RAND researchers found that, in the first year, more than 5,000 defendants were convicted and sentenced under the law's provisions. The large majority of those sentenced, however, had committed nonviolent crimes such as petty theft and drug possession, causing critics of the law to argue that the law is too broad. Eighty-four percent of "two-strikes" cases and nearly 77% of "three-strikes" convictions resulted from nonviolent, drug, or property crimes. A similar 1997 study of three-strikes laws in 22 states, conducted by the Campaign for An Effective Crime Policy (CECP), concluded that such legislation results in clogged court

systems and crowded correctional facilities, while encouraging three-time felons to take dramatic risks to avoid capture.

Supporters of three-strikes laws, however, argue that those convicted under "three-strikes" provisions are career criminals being denied the opportunity to commit more violent crimes. "The real story here is the girl somewhere that did not get raped," said Mike Reynolds, a Fresno, California, photographer whose 18-year-old daughter was killed by a paroled felon. "The real story is the robbery that did not happen," he added.

Practically speaking, California's three-strikes law has had a dramatic impact on the state's criminal justice system. According to the California Youth and Adult Correctional Agency, the law has created a huge backlog of court cases, as defendants facing their third conviction opt for jury trials in the hopes of hearing an innocent verdict returned, rather than plead guilty and face certain and lengthy confinement. "'Three strikes and you're out' sounds great to a lot of people," says Alan Schuman, president of the American Probation and Parole Association. "But no one will cop a plea when it gets to the third time around. We will have more trials, and this whole country works on plea bargaining and pleading guilty, not jury trials," Schuman said at a recent meeting of the association. Some California district attorneys have responded by choosing to prosecute fewer misdemeanants in order to concentrate on the more serious three-strikes defendants.

Critics also point to the law's costs. State correctional officials say they will need to build 15 new prisons by the year 2000, when the state's prison population is expected to climb to 210,000 to accommodate "three-strikes" convicts. Currently, California's prisons, the most populous in the nation, hold around 120,000 inmates. Full enforcement of the law, reports RAND, could cost as much as

$5.5 billion annually—or $300 per California taxpayer.

Researchers at RAND conclude that while California's sweeping three-strikes legislation holds the potential to cut serious adult crime by as much as one-third throughout the state, the high cost of enforcing the law may keep it from ever being fully implemented. In 1996 the California three-strikes controversy became even more complicated following a decision by the state supreme court (in *People* v. *Superior Court of San Diego—Romero*) that California judges retain the discretion to reduce three-strike sentences as well as to avoid counting previous convictions at sentencing, "in furtherance of justice." As this book goes to press, proposals to amend California's law are being made. Some want stricter language written into the law which would require judges to follow it, while others suggest that "three-strikes" sentences should only be imposed on offenders who commit violent crimes such as murder, rape, armed robbery, and certain types of arson.

QUESTIONS FOR DISCUSSION

1. Do you think "three-strikes" laws serve a useful purpose? If so, what is that purpose? Might other sentencing arrangements meet that same purpose? If so, what arrangements might those be?
2. How will "three-strikes" laws impact state and federal spending on the criminal justice system? Do you think that such shifts in spending can be justified? If so, how?

Sources: The Campaign for an Effective Crime Policy, *The Impact of Three Strikes and You're Out Laws: What Have We Learned?* (Washington, D.C.: CECP, 1997); Bruce Smith, "Crime Solutions," The Associated Press wire services, January 11, 1995; Michael Miller, "California Gets 'Three Strikes' Anti-Crime Bill," Reuters wire services, March 7, 1994; Dion Nissenbaum, "Three-Strikes First Year Debated," United Press wire services northern edition, March 6, 1995.

The data on which a presentence report is based come from a variety of sources. Since the 1960s modern computer-based criminal information clearinghouses, such as the FBI's National Crime Information Center (NCIC), have simplified at least a part of the data gathering process. The NCIC began in 1967 and contains information on people wanted for criminal offenses throughout the United States. Individual jurisdictions also maintain criminal records repositories which are able to provide comprehensive files on the criminal history of persons processed by the justice system. In the late 1970s the federal government encouraged states to develop criminal records repositories utilizing computer technology.[67] The years that followed have been described as "the focus of a data gathering effort more massive and more coordinated than any other in criminal justice."[68]

In a presentence report, almost any third-party data are subject to ethical and legal considerations. The official records of almost any agency or organization, while they may prove to be an ideal source of information, are often protected by state and federal privacy requirements. In particular, the Federal Privacy Act of 1974[69] may limit records access. Investigators should first check on the legal availability of all records before requesting them and should receive in writing the defendant's permission to access records. Other public laws, among them the federal Freedom of Information Act,[70] may make the presentence report itself available to the defendant, although courts and court officers have generally been held to be exempt from the provision of such statutes.

Sometimes the defendant is a significant source of much of the information which appears in the presentence report. When such is the case, efforts should be made to corroborate the information provided by the defendant. Unconfirmed data will generally be marked on the report as "defendant-supplied data" or simply "unconfirmed."

The final section of a presentence report is usually devoted to the investigating officer's recommendations. A recommendation may be made in favor of probation, split sentencing, a term of imprisonment, or any other sentencing options available in the jurisdiction. Participation in community service programs may be recommended for probationers, and drug or substance abuse programs may be suggested as well. Some analysts have observed that a "judge accepts an officer's recommendation in an extremely high percentage of cases."[71] Most judges are willing to accept the report writer's recommendation because they recognize the professionalism of presentence investigators and because they know that the investigator may well be the supervising officer assigned to the defendant should a community alternative be the sentencing decision.

Jurisdictions vary in their use of presentence reports and in the form they take. Federal law mandates presentence reports in federal criminal courts and specifies 15 topical areas which each report must contain. The 1984 federal Determinate Sentencing Act directs report writers to include information on the classification of the offense and of the defendant under the offense-level and criminal history categories established by the statute.

Some states require presentence reports only in felony cases, and others in cases where defendants face the possibility of incarceration for six months. Still others may have no requirement for presentence reports beyond those ordered by a judge. Even so, report writing, rarely anyone's favorite, may seriously tax the limited resources of probation agencies. According to Andrew Klein,[72] during a recent year New York state probation officers wrote 108,408 presentence investigation reports. Most (63,902) were for misdemeanors, but 44,506 reports described the backgrounds of newly convicted felons. In the same year in New York City alone, more than 37,000 presentence investigation reports were completed, averaging 25 reports per probation officer per month.

Presentence reports may be useful sentencing tools. Many officers who prepare them take their responsibility seriously. A recent study,[73] however, shows a tendency among presentence investigators to satisfy judicial expectations about defendants by tailoring reports to fit the image the defendant projects. Prior criminal record and present offense may influence the interpretation of all the other data gathered.[74]

The Victim—Forgotten No Longer

Thanks to a grass-roots resurgence of concern for the plight of victims, which began in this country in the early 1970s and continues to grow, the sentencing environment now frequently includes consideration of the needs of victims and their survivors.[75] Unfortunately,

Developing a sentencing system that provides appropriate types and lengths of sentences for all offenders is a challenging task.
—National Conference of State Legislatures

in times past the concerns of victims were often forgotten. Although victims might testify at trial, other aspects of the victimization experience were frequently downplayed by the criminal justice system—including the psychological trauma engendered by the victimization process itself. That changed in 1982 when the President's Task Force on Victims of Crime[76] gave focus to a burgeoning victims' rights movement and urged the widespread expansion of victim assistance programs during what was then their formative period. Victim assistance programs today tend to offer services in the areas of crisis intervention and follow-up counseling and help victims secure their rights under the law.[77] Following successful prosecution, some victim assistance programs also advise victims in the filing of civil suits in order to recoup financial losses directly from the offender. A recent survey of 319 full-service victim assistance programs based in law enforcement agencies and prosecutors offices was conducted by the National Institute of Justice.[78] The survey found that "the majority of individuals seeking assistance were victims of domestic assault and the most common assistance they received was information about legal rights." Other common forms of assistance included help in applying for state victim compensation aid and referrals to social service agencies.

The 1982 President's Task Force on Victims of Crime[79] also recommended 68 programmatic and legislative initiatives for states and concerned citizens to pursue on behalf of crime victims. About the same time, voters in California approved "Proposition 8," a resolution which called for changes in the state's constitution to reflect concern for victims. A continuing thrust of victim advocacy groups turns in the direction of an amendment to the U.S. Constitution, which such groups say is needed to provide the same kind of fairness to victims that is routinely accorded to defendants. The Victims' Constitutional Amendment Network (Victims' CAN or VCAN), for example, has sought to add the phrase—"likewise, the victim, in every criminal prosecution, shall have the right to be present and to be heard at all critical stages of judicial proceedings"—to the Sixth Amendment. VCAN now advocates the addition of a new twenty-eighth amendment to the U.S. Constitution. In September 1996, a victims' rights constitutional amendment—Senate Joint Resolution 65—was proposed by a bipartisan committee in the U.S. Congress.[80] Although the plan had the support of both President Clinton and his Republican challenger, Bob Dole, the proposed amendment never cleared the committee in which it originated. Problems of wording and terminology prevented its passage. The text of the proposed amendment is reproduced in the box in page 409.

Although a victims' rights amendment to the federal Constitution may not yet be reality, 30 states had passed their own victims' rights amendments as of mid-1997,[81] and significant federal legislation has already been adopted. The 1982 Victim and Witness Protection Act,[82] for example, requires victim impact statements to be considered at federal sentencing hearings and places responsibility for their creation on federal probation officers. In 1984 the federal Victims of Crime Act (VOCA) was enacted with substantial bipartisan support. VOCA authorized federal funding to help states establish victim assistance and victim compensation programs. Under VOCA the U.S. Department of Justice's Office for Victims of Crime provides a significant source of both funding and information for victim assistance programs. The rights of victims were further strengthened under the Violent Crime Control and Law Enforcement Act of 1994, which created a federal right of allocution for victims of violent and sex crimes, permitting victims to speak at the sentencing of their assailants. The 1994 law also requires sex offenders and child molesters convicted under federal law to pay restitution to their victims and prohibits the diversion of federal victims' funds to other programs. Still more provisions of the 1994 law provide civil rights remedies for victims of felonies motivated by gender bias and extend "rape shield law" protections to civil cases and to all criminal cases as a bar to irrelevant inquiries into a victim's sexual history. A significant feature of the 1994 law can be found in a subsection titled the Violence Against Women Act (VAWA). VAWA provides financial support for police, prosecutors, and victims' services in cases involving sexual violence or domestic abuse.

Much of the philosophical basis of today's victims' movement can be found in the restorative justice model, which was discussed briefly earlier in this chapter. Restorative justice emphasizes offender accountability and victim reparation. Restorative justice also provides the basis for victim compensation programs—which are another means of recognizing the

Visit the *CJToday* Web page and click on "Web Chapters," then "Chapter 10." Follow the "find the facts" links in order to learn more about victims' issues and victims' rights.

Twenty-First Century Criminal Justice

Is a Victims' Rights Amendment at Hand?

In 1996 Senators Dianne Feinstein and Jon Kyl proposed a victims' rights amendment to the U.S. Constitution in the form of Senate Joint Resolution 65. Although the resolution failed to pass Congress, support for the amendment remains strong. A modified version of the resolution is likely to be proposed again, and many expect that it will soon pass. The text of the Kyl-Feinstein resolution follows.

IN THE SENATE OF THE UNITED STATES JOINT RESOLUTION

September 30, 1996

Proposing an amendment to the Constitution of the United States to protect the rights of crime victims.

Resolved by the Senate and House of Representatives of the United States of America in Congress assembled (two-thirds of each House concurring therein), That the following article is proposed as an amendment to the Constitution of the United States, which shall be valid for all intents and purposes as part of the Constitution when ratified by the legislatures of three-fourths of the several States within seven years from the date of its submission by the Congress:

ARTICLE

SECTION 1. Victims of crimes of violence and other crimes that Congress and the States may define by law pursuant to section 3, shall have the rights to notice of and not to be excluded from all public proceedings relating to the crime; to be heard if present and to submit a statement at a public pre-trial or trial proceeding to determine a release from custody, an acceptance of a negotiated plea, or a sentence; to these rights at a parole proceeding to the extent they are afforded to the convicted offender; to notice of a release pursuant to a public or parole proceeding or an escape; to a final disposition free from unreasonable delay; to an order of restitution from the convicted offender; to have the safety of the victim considered in determining a release from custody; and to notice of the rights established by this article.

SECTION 2. The victim shall have standing to assert the rights established by this article; however, nothing in this article shall provide grounds for the victim to challenge a charging decision or a conviction, obtain a stay of trial, or compel a new trial; nor shall anything in this article give rise to a claim for damages against the United States, a State, a political subdivision, or a public official; nor shall anything in this article provide grounds for the accused or convicted offender to obtain any form of relief.

SECTION 3. The Congress and the States shall have the power to enforce this article within their respective Federal and State jurisdictions by appropriate legislation, including the power to enact exceptions when required for compelling reasons of public safety.

SECTION 4. The rights established by this article shall be applicable to all proceedings occurring after ratification of this article.

SECTION 5. The rights established by this article shall apply in all Federal, State, military, and juvenile justice proceedings, and shall also apply to victims in the District of Columbia, and any commonwealth, territory, or possession of the United States.

---

needs of crime victims (see Table 10–3 for a comparison of restorative justice with retributive justice). Today, all 50 states have passed legislation providing for monetary payments to victims of crime. Such payments are primarily designed to compensate victims for medical expenses and lost wages. All existing programs require that applicants meet certain eligibility criteria, and most set limits on the maximum amount of compensation that can be received. Generally disallowed are claims from victims who are significantly responsible for their own victimization.

Not everyone agrees that the contemporary victims' movement is as valuable as it might seem. Robert Elias, whose book *Victims Still: The Political Manipulation of Crime Victims* provides one opposing view, argues that the movement "has supported progressively conservative legislation that attacks constitutional rights, and has adopted a retributive philosophy against offenders who themselves are victims of a repressive system."[83] Elias cites, for example, what he calls "the war on drug victims" (drug users), as symptomatic of the unfortunate policies inherent in conservative approaches to crime control.

Justice will be swift, certain, and severe.

—President Clinton, in comments made immediately following the 1995 Oklahoma City bombing

Table 10-3 Differences between Restorative and Retributive Justice

Retributive Justice	Restorative Justice
Crime is an act against the state, a violation of a law, an abstract idea.	Crime is an act against another person or the community.
The criminal justice system controls crime.	Crime control lies primarily with the community.
Offender accountability is defined as taking punishment.	Accountability is defined as assuming responsibility and taking action to repair harm.
Crime is an individual act with individual responsibility.	Crime has both individual and social dimensions of responsibility.
Victims are peripheral to the process.	Victims are central to the process of resolving a crime.
The offender is defined by deficits.	The offender is defined by the capacity to make reparation.
Emphasis is on adversarial relationships.	Emphasis is on dialog and negotiation.
Pain is imposed to punish and deter/prevent.	Restitution is a means of restoring both parties; goal of reconciliation/restoration.
Community is on sidelines, represented abstractly by the state.	Community is facilitator in restorative process.
Response is focused on offender's past behavior.	Response is focused on harmful consequences of offender's behavior; emphasis on the future and on reparation.
Dependence is upon proxy professionals.	There is direct involvement by both the offender and the victim.

Source: Adapted from Gordon Bazemore and Mark S. Umbreit, *Balanced and Restorative Justice: Program Summary* (Washington, D.C.: OJJDP, Oct. 1994), p. 7.

Victim Impact Statements

Victim Impact Statement
The in-court use of victim- or survivor-supplied information by sentencing authorities wishing to make an informed sentencing decision.

Another consequence of the national victim-witness rights movement has been a call for the use of **victim impact statements** prior to sentencing. A victim impact statement generally takes the form of a written document which describes the losses, suffering, and trauma experienced by the crime victim or the victim's survivors. Judges are expected to consider such statements in arriving at an appropriate sanction for the offender.

The drive to mandate inclusion of victim impact statements in sentencing decisions, already mandated in federal courts by the 1982 Victim and Witness Protection Act, was substantially enhanced by the "right of allocution" provision of the Violent Crime Control and Law Enforcement Act of 1994 (mentioned earlier). As a consequence, victim-impact statements played a prominent role in the sentencing of Timothy McVeigh, who was convicted of the 1995 bombing of the Murrah federal building in Oklahoma City and sentenced to die. Some states, however, have gone the federal government one better. In 1984 the state of California, for example, passed legislation[84] giving victims a right to attend and participate in sentencing and parole hearings. Approximately 20 states now have laws mandating citizen involvement in sentencing, and all 50 states and the District of Columbia "allow for some form of submission of a victim impact statement either at the time of sentencing or to be contained in the presentence investigation reports" made by court officers.[85] Where written victim impact statements are not available, courts may invite the victim to testify directly at sentencing.

The case of actress Theresa Saldana is representative of the many victims who feel they need more say in sentencing and parole decisions. Saldana, featured in such movies as *Raging Bull* and *I Want to Hold Your Hand*, and in the TV series *The Commish*, was attacked outside her apartment by a crazed drifter in 1982. She was stabbed ten times and may have been saved only by the fact that the knife her attacker was wielding bent from the force of the blows. Although seriously injured, she recovered. The man who attacked her, Arthur

Tennis superstar Monica Seles grimaces in pain after being stabbed in the back during a 1993 German tennis tournament by a knife-wielding man. German courts refused to sentence her attacker to time behind bars even though Seles complained that the attack shattered her career and left her unable to compete on the professional circuit for years. *AP/Wide World Photos*

Jackson, had a long history of psychiatric problems and claimed to be on a divine mission to unite with Ms. Saldana in heaven. Although imprisoned for the attack, Jackson continued to write his victim, promising that when he got out he would finish the job. California prison authorities claimed they were powerless to stop his letters.

In 1984, under the newly passed California's victims' right statute, Ms. Saldana testified before a resentencing body considering Jackson's case. "I will never forget the searing, ghastly pain, the grotesque and devastating experience of this person nearly butchering me to death, or the bone-chilling sight of my own blood splattered everywhere,"[86] she told the examiners. Her testimony resulted in Jackson's release being delayed until June 1989. As Jackson's release date arrived, Ms. Saldana told reporters: "It is just unbelievable that he is getting out. I feel like I am in a nightmare. I really feel my rights are being overlooked. Why is it life, liberty and the pursuit of happiness [are] being taken from me?"[87]

There is little information to date on what changes, if any, the appearance of victims at sentencing is having on the criminal justice system. At least one study, however, found that very few victims are taking advantage of their new-found opportunities. Fewer than 3% of California victims chose to appear or testify at sentencing hearings after that state's victim rights law was enacted.[88]

Hearing from victims, however, does not guarantee that a sentencing court will be sympathetic. On April 3, 1995, for example, a court in Berlin, Germany, refused to imprison Guenter Parche—the unemployed German machinist who stabbed 19-year-old tennis superstar Monica Seles in the back with a kitchen knife at the 1993 Hamburg Open. Even though Seles told the court that Parche "ruined my life" and ended my career "as the world's best tennis player,"[89] the judge ruled that a suspended sentence was appropriate because the man apparently had not intended to kill Seles—only disable her so that German star Steffi Graf could regain the number one world ranking in women's tennis. At the hearing, Seles's American psychologist had testified that Seles "felt like a bird trapped in a cage and was terrified that Parche would strike again."[90] Seles was not able to play professional tennis for more than two years following the attack, and never regained championship standing.

One 1994 study of the efficacy of victim impact statements found that sentencing decisions were rarely affected by them. In the words of the study: "These statements did not produce sentencing decisions that reflected more clearly the effects of crime on victims. Nor did we find much evidence that—with or without impact statements—sentencing decisions were influenced by our measures of the effects of crime on victims, once the charge and the defendant's prior record were taken into account."[91] The authors concluded that victim impact statements have little effect upon courts because judges and other "officials have established ways of making decisions which do not call for explicit information about the impact of crime on victims."

The Constitutionality of Victim Impact Statements

In 1987 the constitutionality of victim impact statements was called into question by the U.S. Supreme Court in the case of *Booth* v. *Maryland*.[92] The case involved Irvin Bronstein, age 78, and his wife Rose, age 75, who were robbed and brutally murdered in their home in Baltimore, Maryland, in 1983. The killers were John Booth and Willie Reid, acquaintances of the Bronstein's, caught stealing to support heroin habits. After being convicted of murder, Booth decided to allow the jury (rather than the judge) to set his sentence. The jury considered, as required by state law, a victim impact statement which was part of a presentence report prepared by probation officers. The victim impact statement used in the case was a powerful one, describing the wholesome personal qualities of the Bronsteins and the emotional suffering their children had experienced as a result of the murders.

After receiving a death sentence, Booth appealed to the U.S. Supreme Court. The Court overturned his sentence, reasoning that victim impact statements, at least in capital cases, violate the Eighth Amendment ban on cruel and unusual punishments. In a close (5-to-4) decision, the majority held that information in victim impact statements leads to the risk that the death penalty might be imposed in an arbitrary and capricious manner.

In a complete about face, affected in no small part by the gathering conservative majority among its justices, the Supreme Court held in the 1991 case of *Payne* v. *Tennessee*[93] that the *Booth* ruling had been based upon "a misreading of precedent."[94] The *Payne* case began with a 1987 double-murder, in which a 28-year-old mother and two-year-old daughter were stabbed to death in Millington, Tennessee.[95] A second child, three-year-old Nicholas Christopher, himself severely wounded in the incident, witnessed the deaths of his mother and young sister. In a trial following the killings, the prosecution claimed that Pervis Tyrone Payne, a 20-year-old retarded man, had killed the mother and child after the woman resisted his sexual advances. Payne was convicted of both murders. At the sentencing phase of the trial Mary Zvolanek, Nicholas's grandmother, testified that the boy continued to cry out daily for his dead sister. Following *Booth*, Payne's conviction was upheld by the Tennessee supreme court in an opinion which then-Justice Thurgood Marshall said did little to disguise the Tennessee court's contempt for the precedent set by *Booth*.

This time, however, the Supreme Court agreed with the Tennessee justices, holding that "[v]ictim impact evidence is simply another form or method of informing the sentencing authority about the specific harm caused by the crime in question, evidence of a general type long considered by sentencing authorities." As Chief Justice Rehnquist wrote for the majority, "[C]ourts have always taken into consideration the harm done by the defendant in imposing sentence." In a concurring opinion, Justice Antonin Scalia held that "*Booth* significantly harms our criminal justice system…" and had been decided with "plainly inadequate rational support."

Traditional Sentencing Options

Sentencing is fundamentally a risk management strategy designed to protect the public while serving the ends of rehabilitation, deterrence, retribution, and restoration. Because the goals of sentencing are difficult to agree upon, so too are sanctions. Lengthy prison terms do little for rehabilitation, while community release programs can hardly protect the innocent from offenders bent on continuing criminality.

Assorted sentencing philosophies continue to permeate state-level judicial systems. Each state has its own sentencing laws, and frequent revisions of those statutes are not uncommon. Because of huge variation from one state to another in the laws and procedures which control the imposition of criminal sanctions, sentencing has been called "the most diversified part of the Nation's criminal justice process."[96]

There is at least one common ground, however, that can be found in the four traditional sanctions which continue to dominate the thinking of most legislators and judges. The four traditional sanctions are

- Imprisonment
- Probation
- Fines
- Death

In the case of indeterminate sentencing, the first three options are widely available to judges. The option selected generally depends upon the severity of the offense and the

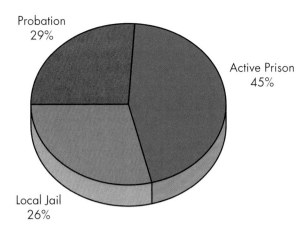

FIGURE 10–2 The sentencing of convicted felons in state courts by type of sentence. *Source:* Patrick A. Langan and Jodi M. Brown, *Felony Sentences in the United States, 1994* (Washington, D.C.: Bureau of Justice Statistics, 1997).

judge's best guess as to the likelihood of future criminal involvement on the part of the defendant. Sometimes two or more options are combined, as when an offender might be fined and sentenced to prison or placed on probation and fined in support of restitution payments.

Jurisdictions that operate under presumptive sentencing guidelines generally limit the judge's choice to only one option and often specify the extent to which that option can be applied. Dollar amounts of fines, for example, are rigidly set, and prison terms are specified for each type of offense. The death penalty remains an option in a fair number of jurisdictions, but only for a highly select group of offenders.

Recently, the Bureau of Justice Statistics reported on the sentencing practices of state felony courts.[97] Highlights of the study, using data gathered by the National Judicial Reporting Program, showed that state courts annually convict about 872,000 persons of felonies (see Figure 10–2). Of these

- Forty-five percent are sentenced to active prison terms.
- Twenty-six percent receive jail sentences, usually involving less than a year's confinement.
- Twenty-nine percent are sentenced to probation (often with fines or other special conditions).
- The average prison sentence imposed on convicted felons is six years.
- The average amount of time served in confinement for felons receiving active sentences will average about two years before release, due to considerations for good time and other credits.

The same survey revealed that 48% of those convicted in state courts of drug trafficking were sentenced to prison. Twenty-nine percent of drug trafficking convictions, however, resulted in probation, while 23% of convicted traffickers were sent to local jails for brief terms of imprisonment. Although the number of active sentences handed out to felons may seem low to some, the number of criminal defendants receiving active prison time has increased dramatically. Figure 10–3 shows that the number of court-ordered prison commitments have increased nearly eightfold in the past 40 years.

FINES

The fine is one of the oldest forms of punishment, predating even the Code of Hammurabi.[98] Until recently, however, the use of fines as criminal sanctions suffered from built-in inequities and a widespread failure to collect them. Inequities arose when offenders with vastly different financial resources were fined similar amounts. A fine of $100, for example, can place a painful economic burden upon a poor defendant but is only laughable when imposed on a wealthy offender.

Today, fines are once again receiving attention as serious sentencing alternatives. One reason for the renewed interest is the stress placed upon state resources by burgeoning prison populations. The extensive imposition of fines not only results in less crowded prisons but

[Unless the Constitution is amended] we will never correct the existing imbalance in this country between [a] defendant's irreducible constitutional rights and the current haphazard patchwork of victims' rights.

—U.S. Attorney General Janet Reno (1997)

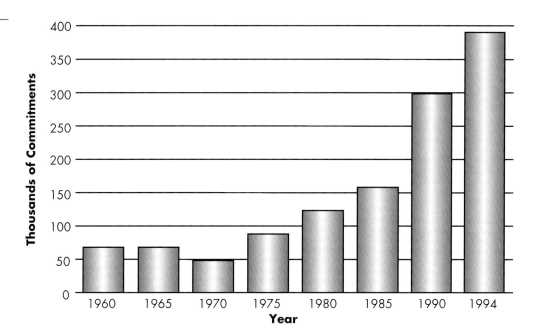

FIGURE 10–3 Court-ordered prison commitments, 1960–1994. *Source:* Patrick A. Langan and Jodi M. Brown, *Felony Sentences in the United States, 1994* (Washington, D.C.: BJS, 1997), and other years.

can contribute to state and local coffers and lower the tax burden of law-abiding citizens. Other advantages of the use of fines as criminal sanctions include the following:

- Fines can deprive offenders of the proceeds of criminal activity.
- Fines can promote rehabilitation by enforcing economic responsibility.
- Fines can be collected by existing criminal justice agencies and are relatively inexpensive to administer.
- Fines can be made proportionate to both the severity of the offense and the ability of the offender to pay.

A recent National Institute of Justice survey found that an average of 86% of convicted defendants in courts of limited jurisdiction receive fines as sentences, some in combination with another penalty.[99] Fines are also experiencing widespread use in courts of general jurisdiction, where the National Institute of Justice study found judges imposing fines in 42% of all cases which came before them for sentencing. Some studies estimate that over $1 billion in fines are collected nationwide each year.[100]

Fines are often imposed for relatively minor law violations, such as driving while intoxicated, reckless driving, disturbing the peace, disorderly conduct, public drunkenness, and vandalism. Judges in many courts, however, report the use of fines for relatively serious violations of the law, including assault, auto theft, embezzlement, fraud, and the sale and possession of various controlled substances. Fines are much more likely to be imposed, however, where the offender has both a clean record and the ability to pay.[101]

Opposition to the use of fines is based upon the following arguments:

- Fines may result in the release of convicted offenders into the community but do not impose stringent controls on their behavior.
- Fines are a relatively mild form of punishment and are not consistent with "just deserts" philosophy.
- Fines discriminate against the poor and favor the wealthy.
- Indigent offenders are especially subject to discrimination since they entirely lack the financial resources with which to pay fines.
- Fines are difficult to collect.

A number of these objections can be answered by procedures which make available to judges complete financial information on defendants. Studies have found, however, that courts of limited jurisdiction, which are the most likely to impose fines, are also the least likely to have adequate information on offenders' economic status.[102] Perhaps as a consequence, judges themselves are often reluctant to impose fines. Two of the most widely cited objections by judges to the use of fines are (1) fines allow more affluent offenders to "buy their way out" and (2) poor offenders cannot pay fines.[103]

A solution to both objections can be found in the Scandinavian system of day fines. The day-fine system is based upon the idea that fines should be proportionate to the severity of the offense but also need to take into account the financial resources of the offender. Day fines are computed by first assessing the seriousness of the offense, the defendant's degree of culpability, and his or her prior record as measured in "days." The use of days as a benchmark of seriousness is related to the fact that, without fines, the offender could be sentenced to a number of days (or months or years) in jail or prison. The number of days an offender is assessed is then multiplied by the daily wages that person earns. Hence, if two persons were sentenced to a five-day fine, but one earned only $20 per day, and the other $200 per day, the first would pay a $100 fine, and the second $1,000.

Recently, the National Institute of Justice reported on an experimental program conducted by the Richmond County Criminal Court in Staten Island, New York, which was designed to introduce and assess the use of day fines in the United States.[104] The Institute also reported on a similar 12-week experimental program involving the use of day fines by the Milwaukee Municipal Court. Both studies concluded that "the day fine can play a major…role as an intermediate sanction"[105] and that "the day-fine concept could be implemented in a typical American limited-jurisdiction court."[106]

Dᴇᴀᴛʜ: Tʜᴇ Uʟᴛɪᴍᴀᴛᴇ Sᴀɴᴄᴛɪᴏɴ

Some crimes are especially heinous and seem to cry out for extreme punishment. In 1996, for example, in what some saw as an especially atrocious murder, a Norman, Oklahoma, man decapitated his neighbor and then walked naked down an alleyway to toss the victims' head into a trash dumpster.[107] Witnesses who watched the accused killer, 33-year-old Cameron Smith, throw the head of 44-year-old Roydon Dale Major into the dumpster called police. Responding officers discovered the rest of Major's body in a room at a boarding house where both Smith and Major had lived. Major had been stabbed repeatedly before his head was severed from his body. Smith was still naked when police found him and took him into custody.

Many states today have statutory provisions that provide for a sentence of **capital punishment** for especially repugnant crimes. The death penalty itself, however, has a long and gruesome history. Civilizations have almost always put criminals to death for a variety of offenses. As times changed, so did accepted methods of execution. Under the Davidic monarchy, biblical Israel institutionalized the practice of stoning convicts to death.[108] In that practice, the entire community could participate in dispatching the offender. As an apparent aid to deterrence, the convict's deceased body could be impaled on a post at the gates of the city or otherwise exposed to public view.[109]

Athenian society, around 200 B.C., was progressive by the standards of its day. The ancient Greeks restricted the use of capital punishment and limited the suffering of the condemned through the use of poison derived from the hemlock tree. Socrates, the famous Greek orator, accused of being a political subversive, died this way.

The Romans were far less sensitive. They used beheading most often, although the law provided that arsonists should be burned alive and false witnesses thrown from a high rock.[110] Suspected witches were clubbed to death, and slaves were strangled. Even more brutal sanctions included drawing and quartering, and social outcasts, Christians, and rabble rousers were thrown to the lions or crucified. Although many people think that crucifixion was a barbarous practice that ended around the time of Christ, it survives into the present day. In 1997, for example, courts in Yemeni (a country at the southern tip of the Arabian peninsula) sentenced two convicted murderers to be publicly crucified. It was the second time in three months that Yemeni courts, in an effort to combat a spate of violent crimes, imposed crucifixion sentences.[111]

After the fall of the Roman Empire, Europe was plunged into the Dark Ages, a period of superstition marked by widespread illiteracy and political turmoil. The Dark Ages lasted

Of all the initiatives that this Congress could undertake, few will touch the heart of Americans as dearly as the measure seeking to ensure that the judicial process is just and fair for the victims of crime.
—Senator Orrin Hatch, R-Utah (1997)

Capital Punishment Another term for the death penalty. Capital punishment is the most extreme of all sentencing options.

Capital Offense A criminal offense punishable by death.

Capital punishment has stimulated debate since it was first imposed. Here children in Hopwood, Pennsylvania, protest the penalty's continued existence in many American jurisdictions. *Gene J. Puskar, AP/Wide World Photos*

There is only one basic human right, the right to do as you please unless it causes others harm. With it comes the only basic human duty, the duty to take the consequences.

—P. J. O'Rourke

from 426 A.D. until the early thirteenth century. During the Dark Ages, executions were institutionalized through the use of ordeals designed to both judge and punish. Suspects were submerged in cold water, dumped in boiling oil, crushed under huge stones, forced to do battle with professional soldiers, or thrown into bonfires. Theological arguments prevalent at the time held that innocents, protected by God and heavenly forces, would emerge from any ordeal unscathed, while guilty parties would perish. Trial by ordeal was eliminated through a decree of the Fourth Lateran Council of 1215, under the direction of Pope Innocent III, after later evidence proved that many who died in ordeals could not have committed the crimes of which they were accused.[112]

Following the Fourth Lateran Council, trials, much as we know them today, became the basis for judging guilt or innocence. The death penalty remained in widespread use. As recently as a century and a half ago, 160 crimes were punishable in England by death.[113] The young received no special privilege. In 1801 a child of 13 was hanged in Tyburn, England, for stealing a spoon.[114]

Sophisticated techniques of execution were in use by the nineteenth century. One engine of death was the guillotine, invented in France around the time of the French Revolution. The guillotine was described by its creator, Dr. Joseph-Ignace Guillotin, as "a cool breath on the back of the neck"[115] and found widespread use in eliminating opponents of the Revolution.

In America, hanging became the preferred mode of execution. It was especially popular on the frontier, since it required little by way of special materials and was a relatively efficient means of dispatch. By the early 1890s electrocution had replaced hanging as the preferred form of capital punishment in America. The appeal of electrocution was that it stopped the heart without visible signs of gross bodily trauma.

Executions: The Grim Facts

Since 1608, when records on capital punishment first became available, estimates are that more than 18,800 legal executions have been carried out in America.[116] Although capital punishment was widely used throughout the eighteenth and nineteenth centuries, the twentieth century has seen a constant decline in the number of persons legally executed in the United States. Between 1930 and 1967, when the U.S. Supreme Court ordered a nationwide stay of pending executions, nearly 3,800 persons were put to death. The years 1935 and 1936

U.S. Executions: 1976 – January 1, 1998

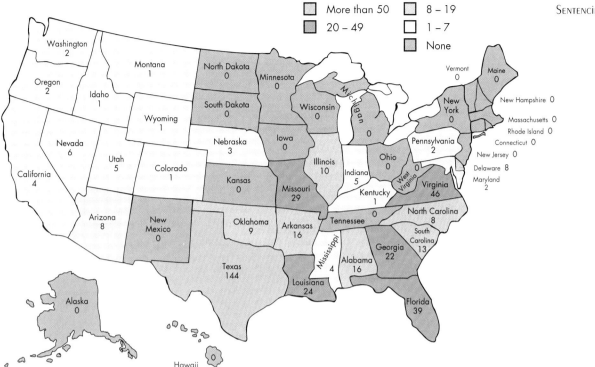

FIGURE 10–4 U.S. executions 1976–1998, by state. *Source:* Death Penalty Information Center. Data as of January 2, 1998.

were peak years, with nearly 200 legal killings each year. Executions declined substantially every year thereafter. Between 1967 and 1977 a *de facto* moratorium existed, with no executions carried out in any U.S. jurisdiction. Following the lifting of the moratorium, executions increased (see Figure 10–4). In 1993, 38 offenders were put to death, while 56 were executed nationwide in 1995. 1997 set a modern record for executions, with 74 executions—37 in Texas alone.

In 1995, the state of New York reinstated the death penalty after a 30-year hiatus. Today, 38 of the 50 states and the federal government have capital punishment laws.[117] All but New York permit execution for first-degree murder, while treason, kidnapping, the murder of a police or correctional officer, and murder while under a life sentence are punishable by death in selected jurisdictions.[118] New York allows for the imposition of a death sentence in cases involving the murder of law enforcement officers, judges, and witnesses and their families and applies the punishment to serial killers, terrorists, murderers-for-hire, and those who kill while committing another felony like robbery or rape.

The number of crimes punishable by death under federal jurisdiction increased dramatically with passage of the Violent Crime Control and Law Enforcement Act of 1994—and now includes a total of about 60 offenses. States legislators are also moving to expand the types of crime for which a sentence of death can be imposed. In 1997, for example, the Louisiana supreme court upheld the state's year-old child rape death penalty statute, which allows for the imposition of a capital sentence when the victim is under 12 years of age. The case involved an AIDS-infected father who raped his three daughters, aged five, eight, and nine years old. In upholding the father's death sentence, the Louisiana court ruled that child rape is "like no other crime."[119]

A total of 3,365 persons were under sentence of death throughout the United States on March 20, 1998. The latest statistics show that 98% of those on death row are male, 49% are classified as white, 8% are Hispanic, 42% are black, and 1% are of other races (mostly Native American and Pacific Islander).[120] Finally, methods of imposing death vary by state. The majority of death penalty states authorize execution through lethal injection. Electrocution is the second most common means of dispatch, while hanging, the gas chamber, and firing squads have survived, at least as options available to the condemned, in a few states.

If I were king, I would make every inmate that enters the system pay restitution. Citizens will not have faith in the criminal justice system until restitution is a centerpiece of our efforts.

—Samuel F. Saxton, Director, Prince George's County (Maryland) Department of Corrections

Writ of *Habeas Corpus*
The writ which directs the person detaining a prisoner to bring him or her before a judicial officer to determine the lawfulness of the imprisonment.

There can be no doubt that the taking of the life of the President creates much more societal harm than the taking of the life of a homeless person.

—Tennessee Attorney General Charles Burson, arguing before the U.S. Supreme Court in *Payne* v. *Tennessee* (1991)

Habeas Corpus Review

The legal process through which a capital sentence is carried to conclusion is fraught with problems. One serious difficulty centers on the fact that automatic review of all death sentences by appellate courts and constant legal maneuvering by defense counsel often lead to a dramatic delay between the time sentence is passed and the time it is carried out. Today, an average of nine years and five months[121] passes between the time a sentence of death is imposed and it is carried out. Such lengthy delays, compounded with uncertainty over whether a sentence will ever be finally imposed, directly contravene the generally accepted notion that punishment should be swift and certain.

Typical of delayed executions, on April 18, 1995 the Louisiana Supreme Court granted two-time killer Antonio James his fourteenth stay of execution just four hours before he was scheduled to die by lethal injection. The 39-year-old James had been sentenced to death 15 years earlier for shooting 70-year-old Henry Silver in the head during an armed robbery on New Year's Day, 1979.[122] He was later sentenced to 99 more years in prison for killing Alvin Adams, 74, during an armed robbery two weeks after the Silver killing. In granting the stay, the Louisiana Supreme Court ruled that a state district court had erred a few days earlier by not granting a hearing on new evidence James's attorneys said could prove he was not the triggerman in either killing. Before the court's ruling, Governor Edwin Edwards had refused to block the execution. James has been on Louisiana's death row since 1981—longer than any other inmate still there.

Delays in the imposition of capital sanctions have been the source of much anguish for condemned prisoners as well as for the victims and the family members of both. In 1997, for example, in a final statement just before his client was executed, the attorney for 30-year-old Dorsie Johnson-Bey told witnesses, "If the jury trying this case could see what has happened to him in the 11 years he's been on death row, they would say that he certainly doesn't pose a continuing threat to society."[123] A few minutes later, Johnson-Bey was put to death by lethal injection at the Walls Unit in Huntsville, Texas. A one-time janitor in the West Texas community of Colorado City, he had been sentenced to die for the March 1986 murder of Jack Huddleston, a 53-year-old convenience store clerk who had been shot in the head with a .25-caliber pistol after being forced to lie in the store's cooler. Huddleston had been robbed of $161 and cigarettes.

In a speech before the American Bar Association a few years ago, Chief Justice of the U.S. Supreme Court William H. Rehnquist called for reforms of the federal *habeas corpus* system which, at the time, allowed condemned prisoners virtually limitless opportunities for appeal. Writs of *habeas corpus* (Latin for "you have the body") require that a prisoner be brought into court to determine if he or she is being legally held and form the basis for many federal appeals made by prisoners on state death rows. In 1968, Chief Justice Earl Warren called the right to file *habeas* petitions, as guaranteed under the U.S. Constitution, the "symbol and guardian of individual liberty." Nearly 30 years later, however, Rehnquist claimed that writs of *habeas corpus* were being used indiscriminately by death row inmates seeking to delay executions even where grounds for such delay do not exist. "The capital defendant does not need to prevail on the merits in order to accomplish his purpose," said Rehnquist. "He wins temporary victories by postponing a final adjudication."[124]

In a move to reduce delays in the conduct of executions, the U.S. Supreme Court, in the case of *McCleskey* v. *Zandt* (1991),[125] limited the number of appeals a condemned person may lodge with the courts. Saying that repeated filings for the sole purpose of delay promotes "disrespect for the finality of convictions" and "disparages the entire criminal justice system," the Court established a two-pronged criterion for future appeals. According to *McCleskey*, in any petition beyond the first, filed with the federal court, capital defendants must demonstrate (1) good cause why the claim now being made was not included in the first filing and (2) how the absence of that claim may have harmed the petitioner's ability to mount an effective defense. Two months later, the Court reinforced *McCleskey*, when it ruled, in *Coleman* v. *Thompson*,[126] that state prisoners could not cite "procedural default," such as a defense attorney's failure to meet a state's filing deadline for appeals, as the basis for an appeal to federal court.

In 1995, in the case of *Schlup* v. *Delo*,[127] the Court continued to define standards for continued appeals from death row inmates, ruling that before appeals based upon claims of new evidence could be heard, "a petitioner must show that, in light of the new evidence, it is more likely than not that no reasonable juror would have found him guilty beyond a reasonable doubt." A "reasonable juror" was defined as one who "would consider fairly all of the evidence presented and would conscientiously obey the trial court's instructions requiring proof beyond a reasonable doubt."

Opportunities for federal appeals by death row inmates were further limited by the **Antiterrorism and Effective Death Penalty Act** of 1996, which sets a one-year postconviction deadline for state inmates filing federal *habeas corpus* appeals. The deadline is six months for state death-row inmates who were provided a lawyer for *habeas* appeals at the state level. The Act also requires federal courts to presume that the factual findings of state courts are correct, does not permit use of state court misinterpretations of the U.S. Constitution as a basis for *habeas* relief unless those misinterpretations are "unreasonable," and requires that all petitioners must show, prior to obtaining a hearing, facts sufficient to establish by clear and convincing evidence that but for constitutional error, no reasonable factfinder would have found the petitioner guilty. The act also requires approval by a three-judge panel before an inmate can file a second federal appeal raising newly discovered evidence of innocence. In 1996, in the case of *Felker* v. *Turpin*,[128] the U.S. Supreme Court ruled that limitations on the authority of federal courts to consider successive *habeas corpus* petitions imposed by the Antiterrorism and Effective Death Penalty Act of 1996 are permissible since they do not deprive the U.S. Supreme Court of its original jurisdiction over such petitions.

Some observers have objected that recent legislation, combined with the Court's own spate of decisions limiting the opportunity of convicted offenders to appeal, would swiftly and dramatically increase the rate of executions across the nation and prevent thousands of inmates, including those not on death row, from getting a fair hearing on valid appeals. "There will be many injustices which will not be corrected," warned Stephen Bright of the Southern Center for Human Rights, following passage of the 1996 Antiterrorism Act. "We'll see a lot of people in this country executed despite fundamental violations of the Constitution and despite innocence," said Bright.[129]

Opposition to Capital Punishment

Thirty years ago David Magris, who was celebrating his 21st birthday with a crime spree, shot Dennis Tapp in the back during a holdup, leaving Tapp a paraplegic. Tapp had been working a late-night shift, tending his father's quick-serve gas station. Magris went on to commit more robberies that night, killing 20-year-old Steven Tompkins in a similar crime. Although sentenced to death by a California court, the U.S. Supreme Court overturned the state's death penalty law in 1972, opening the door for Margris to be paroled in 1985. Long before Margris was freed from prison, however, Tapp had already forgiven him. A few minutes after the shooting happened, Tapp regained consciousness, dragged himself to a telephone, and called for help. The next thing he did was ask "God to forgive the man who did this to me."[130] Today, both Tapp and Margris are staunch death-penalty opponents. And he and Magris, who is president of the Northern California Coalition to Abolish the Death Penalty, have become friends. They are united by a crime that happened 30 years ago and by a heartfelt need to fight against capital punishment. "Don't get me wrong…" says Tapp, "David has a good personality. What he did was wrong…he did something stupid and he paid for it."[131]

Because of the strong emotions that state-imposed death wrings from the hearts of varied constituencies, many attempts have been made to abolish capital punishment since the founding of the United States. The first recorded effort to abolish the death penalty occurred at the home of Benjamin Franklin in 1787.[132] At a meeting on March 9 of that year, Dr. Benjamin Rush, a signer of the Declaration of Independence and leading medical pioneer, read a paper against capital punishment to a small but influential audience. Although his immediate efforts came to naught, his arguments laid the groundwork for many debates which followed. Michigan, widely regarded as the first abolitionist state, joined the Union in 1837 without a death penalty. A number of other states, including Massachusetts, West Virginia, Wisconsin, Minnesota, Alaska, and Hawaii, have since spurned death as a possible sanction for criminal acts. Many Western European countries have also rejected the death

Evolving standards of human decency will finally lead to the abolition of the death penalty in this country.

—William Brennan, Former U.S. Supreme Court Justice

penalty. As noted earlier, it remains a viable sentencing option in 38 of the states and all federal jurisdictions. As a consequence, arguments continue to rage over its value.

Today, five main rationales for abolishing capital punishment are heard

1. The death penalty can and has been inflicted on innocent people.
2. Evidence has shown that the death penalty is not an effective deterrent.
3. The imposition of the death penalty is, by the nature of our legal system, arbitrary and even discriminatory.
4. Imposition of the death penalty is far too expensive to justify its use.
5. Human life is sacred, and killing at the hands of the state is not a righteous act, but rather one which is on the same moral level as the crimes committed by the condemned.

The first four abolitionist claims are pragmatic; that is, they can be measured and verified (or disproved) by looking at the facts. The last claim is primarily philosophical and therefore not amenable to scientific investigation. Hence, we shall briefly examine only the first four.

While some evidence does exist that a few innocent people have been executed,[133] most research by far has centered on examining the deterrent effect of the death penalty. During the 1970s and 1980s[134] the deterrent effect of the death penalty became a favorite subject for debate in academic circles. Studies[135] of states which had eliminated the death penalty failed to show any increase in homicide rates. Similar studies[136] of neighboring states, in which jurisdictions retaining capital punishment were compared with those which had abandoned it, also failed to demonstrate any significant differences. Although death penalty advocates remain numerous, few any longer argue for the penalty based on its deterrent effects. Deterrent studies continue, however. In 1988, for example, a comprehensive review[137] of capital punishment in Texas, which correlated executions since 1930 with homicide rates, again failed to find any support for the use of death as a deterrent. The study was especially significant because Texas had been very active in the capital punishment arena, executing 317 persons between 1930 and 1986.[138]

The abolitionist claim that the death penalty is arbitrary is based upon the belief that access to effective representation and to the courts themselves is differentially available to people with varying financial and other resources. Access to the courts has also been restricted by a number of new state and federal laws (discussed in greater detail in Chapter 13), leading the American Bar Association's House of Delegates in 1997 to cite what it called "an erosion of legal rights of death row inmates," and to urge an immediate halt to executions in the United States until the judicial process could be overhauled.[139] ABA delegates were expressing concerns that Congress and the states have unfairly limited death row appeals through restrictive legislation. The ABA resolution also called for a halt to executions of people under 18 years old and of those who are mentally retarded.

The claim that the death penalty is discriminatory is harder to investigate. While there may be past evidence that blacks and other minorities in the United States have been disproportionately sentenced to death,[140] the present evidence is not so clear. At first glance, as one study puts it, disproportionality seems apparent: 45 of the 98 prisoners executed between January 1977 and May 1988 were black or Hispanic; 84 of the 98 had been convicted of killing whites.[141] A 1996 Kentucky study found that blacks accused of killing whites in that state between 1976 and 1991 had a higher than average probability of being charged with a capital crime and of being sentenced to die than did homicide offenders of other races.[142] For an accurate appraisal to be made, however, any claims of disproportionality must go beyond simple comparisons with racial representation in the larger population and must somehow measure both frequency and seriousness of capital crimes between and within racial groups. Following that line of reasoning, the Supreme Court, in the 1987 case of *McCleskey* v. *Kemp*[143] held that a simple showing of racial discrepancies in the application of the death penalty does not constitute a constitutional violation.

The fourth claim, that the death penalty is too expensive, is difficult to explore. Although the "official" costs associated with capital punishment are high, many death penalty supporters argue that no cost is *too* high if it achieves justice. Death penalty opponents, on the other hand, point to the huge costs to taxpayers associated with judicial appeals and with executions themselves. According to the Death Penalty Information Center (DPIC), which maintains a national database on such costs, "the death penalty costs North Carolina $2.16

On February 22, 1994, U.S. Supreme Court Justice Harry A. Blackmun used the Court's denial of an appeal by Bruce Edwin Callins, a Texas death row inmate, to explain why he would forever be opposed to the death penalty. Reproduced below are excerpts from his dissenting opinion in that case (*Callins* v. *Collins*, 114 S.Ct. 1127, 1128-38 [1994]). Shortly after the *Callins* case was decided, Justice Blackmun retired from the court, having served for 24 years. Three years later, on May 21, 1997, Edwin Callins was put to death by lethal injection at the Texas state prison at Huntsville. A box on page 422 contains a contrasting opinion provided by Justice Antonin Scalia, writing for the Court's majority.

> From this day forward, I no longer shall tinker with the machinery of death. For more than 20 years I have endeavored—indeed, I have struggled—along with a majority of this Court, to develop procedural and substantive rules that would lend more than the mere appearance of fairness to the death penalty endeavor. Rather than continue to coddle the Court's delusion that the desired level of fairness has been achieved and the need for regulation eviscerated, I feel morally and intellectually obligated simply to concede that the death penalty experiment has failed. It is virtually self-evident to me now

that no combination of procedural rules or substantive regulations ever can save the death penalty from its inherent constitutional deficiencies. The basic question—does the system accurately and consistently determine which defendants "deserve" to die?—cannot be answered in the affirmative. It is not simply that this Court has allowed vague aggravating circumstances to be employed, see, for example, *Arave* v. *Creech*, (1993), relevant mitigating evidence to be disregarded, see, for example, *Johnson* v. *Texas*, (1993), and vital judicial review to be blocked, see, for example, *Coleman* v. *Thompson*, (1991). The problem is that the inevitability of factual, legal, and moral error gives us a system that we know must wrongly kill some defendants, a system that fails to deliver the fair, consistent, and reliable sentences of death required by the Constitution.

It is the decision to sentence a defendant to death—not merely the decision to make a defendant eligible for death—that may not be arbitrary. While one might hope that providing the sentencer with as much relevant mitigating evidence as possible will lead to more rational and consistent sentences, experience has taught otherwise. It seems that the decision whether a human being should live or die is so inherently subjective—rife with all

of life's understandings, experiences, prejudices, and passion—that it inevitably defies the rationality and consistency required by the Constitution.

Perhaps one day this Court will develop procedural rules or verbal formulas that actually will provide consistency, fairness, and reliability in a capital-sentencing scheme. I am not optimistic that such a day will come. I am more optimistic, though, that this Court eventually will conclude that the effort to eliminate arbitrariness while preserving fairness "in the infliction of [death] is so plainly doomed to failure that it—and the death penalty—must be abandoned altogether." *Godfrey* v. *Georgia*, 446 U.S. 420, 442 (1980) (Marshall, J., concurring in the judgment). I may not live to see that day, but I have faith that eventually it will arrive. The path the Court has chosen lessens us all. I dissent.

QUESTIONS FOR DISCUSSION

1. Do you agree with Justice Blackmun's assessment of the death penalty as arbitrarily imposed? Why or why not?
2. If imposition of the death penalty is indeed arbitrary, as Justice Blackmun claims, how might it be made less so?

million per execution *over* the costs of a non-death penalty murder case with a sentence of imprisonment for life."[144] The DPIC also says that an average execution in Florida costs $3.2 million to carry out, and that "in Texas, a death penalty case costs an average of $2.3 million—about three times the cost of imprisoning someone in a single cell at the highest security level for 40 years."

Justifications for Capital Punishment

Shortly before Christmas 1996, New York state judge Thomas Demakos sentenced 23-year-old Joshua Torres to 58 years-to-life in prison, saying he wished that he could impose the death penalty. Torres had been convicted of abducting and burning 20-year-old Kimberly Antonakos alive after he and his partners bungled an attempt to extort ransom monies from the young woman's father. The father failed to respond to a $75,000 ransom demand made

Theory into Practice

The Death Penalty—Justice Scalia's Rebuttal

Justice Blackmun dissents from the denial of *certiorari* in this case with a statement explaining why the death penalty "as currently administered," is contrary to the Constitution of the United States. That explanation often refers to "intellectual, moral, and personal" perceptions, but never to the text and tradition of the Constitution. It is the latter rather than the former that ought to control. The Fifth Amendment provides that "[n]o person shall be held to answer for a capital...crime, unless on a presentment or indictment of a Grand Jury,...nor be deprived of life...without due process of law." This clearly permits the death penalty to be imposed, and establishes beyond doubt that the death penalty is not one of the "cruel and unusual punishments" prohibited by the Eighth Amendment.

Convictions in opposition to the death penalty are often passionate and deeply held. That would be no excuse for reading them into a Constitution that does not contain

them, even if they represented the convictions of a majority of Americans. Much less is there any excuse for using that course to thrust a minority's views upon the people. He chooses, as the case in which to make that statement, one of the less brutal of the murders that regularly come before us—the murder of a man ripped by a bullet suddenly and unexpectedly, with no opportunity to prepare himself and his affairs, and left to bleed to death on the floor of a tavern. The death-by-injection which Justice Blackmun describes looks pretty desirable next to that. It looks even better next to some of the other cases currently before us which Justice Blackmun did not select as the vehicle for his announcement that the death penalty is always unconstitutional—for example, the case of the 11-year-old girl raped by four men and then killed by stuffing her panties down her throat. See *McCollum v. North Carolina*, No. 93-7200, cert. now pending before the Court. How enviable a

quiet death by lethal injection compared with that! If the people conclude that such more brutal deaths may be deterred by capital punishment; indeed, if they merely conclude that justice requires such brutal deaths to be avenged by capital punishment; the creation of false, untextual, and unhistorical contradictions within "the Court's Eighth Amendment jurisprudence" should not prevent them.

QUESTIONS FOR DISCUSSION

1. Do you believe, as Justice Scalia seems to, that "justice requires...brutal deaths to be avenged by capital punishment"? Why or why not?
2. What recourse do opponents of the death penalty have in the face of constitutional support (Scalia mentions the Fifth Amendment) for the punishment itself?

---

by the kidnappers because his answering machine didn't record the call. According to witnesses, Torres then tied the college student to a pole, doused her with gasoline, lit a match, and set her on fire. At sentencing, Judge Demakos told those gathered in the courtroom: "I must admit that hearing this testimony (about how Kimberly was set afire) almost brought me to tears."[145] Demakos said that although the case cried out for the death penalty, he could not impose it because it was not in effect in New York state at the time the murder took place.

Judge Demakos, like many others in today's society, feels that "cold-blooded murder" justifies a sentence of death. Justifications for the death penalty are collectively referred to as the retentionist position. The three retentionist arguments are (1) revenge, (2) just deserts, and (3) protection. Those who justify capital punishment as revenge attempt to appeal to the visceral feeling that survivors, victims, and the state are entitled to "closure." Only after execution of the criminal perpetrator, they say, can the psychological and social wounds engendered by the offense begin to heal.

The just deserts argument makes the simple and straightforward claim that some people deserve to die for what they have done. Death is justly deserved; anything less cannot suffice as a sanction for the most heinous crimes. As Justice Potter Stewart once wrote, "the decision that capital punishment may be the appropriate sanction in extreme cases is an expression of the community's belief that certain crimes are themselves so grievous an affront to humanity that the only adequate response may be the penalty of death."[146]

The third retentionist claim, that of protection, asserts that offenders, once executed, can commit no further crimes. Clearly the least emotional of the retentionist claims, the protectionist argument may also be the weakest, since societal interests in protection can also be

Life is sacred. It's about the only sacred thing on earth—and no one has a right to do away with it.

—Aldona DeVetsco, mother of a murder victim, commenting on the execution of her son's killer

Drug smugglers executed in China.
Signs describe the offenders' crimes.
Xinhua, Gamma—Liaison, Inc.

met in other ways, such as incarceration. In addition, various studies have shown that there is little likelihood of repeat offenses among people convicted of murder and later released.[147] One reason for such results, however, may be that murderers generally serve lengthy prison sentences prior to release and may have lost whatever youthful propensity for criminality they previously possessed.

The Future of the Death Penalty

Because of the nature of the positions that both sides advocate, there is little common ground even for discussion between retentionists and abolitionists. Foes of the death penalty hope that its demonstrated lack of deterrent capacity will convince others that it should be abandoned. Their approach, based as it is upon statistical evidence, appears on the surface to be quite rational. However, it is doubtful that many capital punishment opponents could be persuaded to support the death penalty even if statistics showed it to be a deterrent. Likewise, the tactics of death penalty supporters are equally instinctive. Retentionists could probably not be swayed by statistical studies of deterrence, no matter what they show, since their support is bound up with emotional calls for retribution.

The future of the death penalty rests primarily with state legislatures. Short of renewed Supreme Court intervention, the future of capital punishment may depend more upon popular opinion than it does on arguments pro or con. Elected legislatures, because the careers of their members lie in the hands of their constituencies, are likely to follow the public mandate. Hence, it may be that studies of public attitudes toward the death penalty may be the most useful in predicting the sanction's future.

National opinion polls conducted by the Gallup and Harris organizations detail massive support for capital punishment as far back as 1936, but show a gradual decline in backing until 1966, when a resurgence in support began.[148] The proportion of the American public which today endorses the death penalty in national polls is at an all-time high since record keeping began, surpassing even the support of 1936.[149] When asked if they would still favor the death penalty if evidence showed conclusively that it did not deter criminals, a slim majority of Americans still say "yes."[150]

Visit the *CJToday* Web page and click on "Web Chapters," then "Chapter 10." Follow the "find the facts" links in order to learn more about the death penalty.

Demographic differences account for a considerable degree of variation in public opinion polls. Robert Bohm, for example, analyzing differences among respondents in nearly two dozen polls reports that[151] (1) "[i]n all 21 polls, the percentage of whites who favor the death penalty is greater than the percentage of blacks, while the percentage of blacks opposed and undecided is greater than the percentage of whites"; (2) "[i]n every year for which there are data, people in the top income or socioeconomic category have been more likely to support the death penalty and less likely to oppose it than people in the bottom category"; (3) "[i]n all 21 polls, the percentage of males who favor the death penalty exceeds the percentage of females, and the percentage of females opposed to the death penalty exceeds the percentage of males"; (4) "Democrats have shown the greatest opposition and the least support for the death penalty, Independents are less opposed and more supportive, and Republicans are least opposed and most supportive"; and (5) "…the South, surprisingly, has been the region least likely to support and most likely to oppose the death penalty." Other variables, such as age, religion, occupation, and city size, show less clear-cut relationships to self-avowed attitudes toward the death penalty.[152]

Some contemporary studies[153] have purported to show that support for capital punishment may be a relatively abstract form of endorsement. According to Frank P. Williams and Dennis Longmire, "A majority of citizens assert support for the general concept of the death penalty but their willingness to advocate execution as an acceptable sanction decreases as they are asked about its use in specific instances.[154] Even so, few legislators are apt to examine closely the results of polls which show such strong public leanings.

Changes in public opinion could conceivably come quickly, however. Citing the First Amendment to the U.S. Constitution, California TV station KQED filed suit in 1990 in U.S. District Court in San Francisco asking that it be allowed to provide broadcast coverage of executions. The lawsuit claimed that the current state policy of barring cameras at executions, "impedes effective reporting of executions which are events of major public and political significance."[155] The station's request was denied by the court. About the same time, Phil Donahue unsuccessfully petitioned for an opportunity to videotape the execution of North Carolina death row inmate David Lawson. Lawson was scheduled to die for killing a man during a burglary, and Donahue argued that it would be a public service to televise his death—showing people what an execution is like to help them decide whether they could morally support the penalty.

The Courts and the Death Penalty

The U.S. Supreme Court has served as a constant sounding board for issues surrounding the death penalty. One of the court's earliest cases in this area was *Wilkerson* v. *Utah* (1878),[156] which questioned shooting as a method of execution and raised Eighth Amendment claims that firing squads constituted a form of cruel and unusual punishment. The Court disagreed, however, contrasting the relatively civilized nature of firing squads with the various forms of torture often associated with capital punishment around the time the Bill of Rights was written.

In similar fashion, electrocution was supported as a permissible form of execution in *In re Kemmler* (1890).[157] In *Kemmler*, the Court defined cruel and unusual methods of execution as follows: "Punishments are cruel when they involve torture or a lingering death; but the punishment of death is not cruel, within the meaning of that word as used in the Constitution. It implies there something inhuman and barbarous, something more than the mere extinguishing of life."[158] Almost 60 years later, the Court ruled that a second attempt at the electrocution of a convicted person, when the first did not work, did not violate the Eighth Amendment.[159] The Court reasoned that the initial failure was the consequence of accident or unforeseen circumstances and not the result of an effort on the part of executioners to be intentionally cruel.

It was not until 1972, however, in the landmark case of *Furman* v. *Georgia*,[160] that the Court recognized "evolving standards of decency"[161] which might necessitate a reconsideration of Eighth Amendment guarantees. In a 5-to-4 ruling, the *Furman* decision invalidated Georgia's death penalty statute on the basis that it allowed a jury unguided discretion in the imposition of a capital sentence. The majority of justices concluded that the Georgia statute, which permitted a jury to decide simultaneously issues of guilt or innocence while it weighed sentencing options, allowed for an arbitrary and capricious application of the death penalty.

Many other states with statutes similar to Georgia's were affected by the *Furman* ruling, but moved quickly to modify their procedures. What evolved was a two-step procedure to be used in capital cases. As a consequence, death penalty trials today involve two stages. In the first stage, guilt or innocence is decided. If the defendant is convicted of a crime for which execution is possible, a second, or penalty phase, ensues. The penalty phase generally permits the introduction of new evidence that may have been irrelevant to the question of guilt but which may be relevant to punishment, such as drug use or childhood abuse. While in most death penalty jurisdictions juries determine the punishment, the trial judge sets the sentence in the second phase of capital murder trials in Arizona, Idaho, Montana, and Nebraska. Alabama, Delaware, Florida, and Indiana allow juries only to recommend a sentence to the judge.

The two-step trial procedure was specifically approved by the Court in *Gregg* v. *Georgia* (1976).[162] In *Gregg* the Court upheld the two-stage procedural requirements of Georgia's new capital punishment law as necessary for ensuring the separation of the highly personal information needed in a sentencing decision from the kinds of information reasonably permissible in a jury trial where issues of guilt or innocence alone are being decided. In the opinion written for the majority, the Court for the first time recognized the significance of public opinion in deciding upon the legitimacy of questionable sanctions.[163] Its opinion cited the strong showing of public support for the death penalty following *Furman* to mean that death was still a socially and culturally acceptable penalty.

Post-*Gregg* decisions set limits upon the use of death as a penalty for all but the most severe crimes. In 1977, in the case of *Coker* v. *Georgia*,[164] the Court struck down a Georgia law imposing the death penalty for the rape of an adult woman. The Court concluded that capital punishment under such circumstances would be "grossly disproportionate" to the crime. Somewhat later, in *Woodson* v. *North Carolina*[165] a law requiring mandatory application of the death penalty for specific crimes was overturned.

In two 1990 rulings, *Blystone* v. *Pennsylvania*[166] and *Boyde* v. *California*[167] the Court upheld state statutes which had been interpreted to dictate that death penalties must be imposed where juries find a lack of mitigating factors that could offset obvious aggravating circumstances. Similarly, in the 1990 case of R. Gene Simmons, an Arkansas mass murderer convicted of killing 16 relatives during a 1987 shooting rampage, the Court granted inmates under sentence of death the right to waive appeals. Prior to the *Simmons* case, any interested party could file a brief on behalf of condemned persons—with or without their consent.

Recently, death row inmates and those who file cases on behalf of such inmates as sounding boards to test the boundaries of statutory acceptability, have been busy bringing challenges to state capital punishment laws. Most such challenges focus upon the procedures involved in sentencing decisions. In 1995, for example, in *Harris* v. *Alabama*,[168] the U.S. Supreme Court upheld Alabama's capital sentencing system, which allows juries to recommend sentences but judges to decide them. A challenge to the constitutionality of California's capital sentencing law, which requires the jury to consider, among other things, the circumstances of the offense, prior violent crimes by the defendant, and the defendant's age, was rejected in *Tuilaepa* v. *California* (1995).[169]

Although at least one U.S. Supreme Court Justice has taken a strong position against the death penalty (see the "Theory Into Practice" box earlier), today's high court seems largely convinced of the constitutionality of a sentence of death. Open to debate, however, is the constitutionality of questionable *methods* for its imposition. In a 1993 hearing, *Poyner* v. *Murray*,[170] the U.S. Supreme Court hinted at the possibility of reopening questions first raised in *Kemmler*. The case challenged Virginia's use of the electric chair as a form of cruel and unusual punishment. Syvasky Lafayette Poyner, who originally brought the case before the Court, lost his bid for a stay of execution and was electrocuted in March 1993. Nonetheless, in *Poyner*, Justices Souter, Blackmun, and Stevens wrote: "The Court has not spoken squarely on the underlying issue since *In re Kemmler*…and the holding of that case does not constitute a dispositive response to litigation of the issue in light of modern knowledge about the method of execution in question." In a still more recent ruling, members of the Court questioned the constitutionality of hanging, suggesting that it may be a form of cruel and unusual punishment. In that case, *Campbell* v. *Wood*[171] (1994), the defendant, Charles Campbell, raped a woman, got out of prison, then came back and murdered her. His request for a stay of execution was denied since Washington state law (the state in which the

Excessive bail shall not be required, nor excessive fines imposed, nor cruel and unusual punishments inflicted.
—Eighth Amendment to the U.S. Constitution

murder occurred) offered Campbell a choice between various methods of execution and, therefore, an alternative to hanging. Similarly, in 1996 the Court upheld California's death penalty statute which provides for lethal injection as the primary method of capital punishment in that state.[172] The constitutionality of the statute had been challenged by two death row inmates who claimed that a provision in the law which permitted condemned prisoners the choice of lethal gas in lieu of injection brought the statute within the realm of allowing cruel and unusual punishments.

SUMMARY

The goals of criminal sentencing are many and varied, and include retribution, incapacitation, deterrence, rehabilitation, and restoration. The just deserts model, with its emphasis on retribution and revenge, is the ascendant sentencing philosophy in the United States today. Many citizens, however, still expect sentencing practices to provide for the other general sentencing goals. This ambivalence toward the purpose of sentencing reflects a more basic cultural uncertainty regarding the root causes of crime, the true nature of justice, and the fundamental goals of the criminal justice system.

The absence of a noticeable reduction in adult crime rates as incarceration rates have climbed raises serious questions about the efficacy of America's sentencing policies.

—The American Correctional Association

Structured sentencing, embodied in the Federal Sentencing Guidelines and in many state sentencing programs of today, is a child of the just deserts philosophy. The structured sentencing model, however, while apparently associated with a reduction in biased and inequitable sentencing practices which had characterized previous sentencing models, may not be the panacea it once seemed. Inequitable practices under the indeterminate model may never have been as widespread as opponents of that model claimed them to be. Worse still, the practice of structured sentencing may not reduce sentencing discretion but merely move it out of the hands of judges and into the ever-widening sphere of plea bargaining. Doubly unfortunate, structured sentencing, by its deemphasis of parole, weakens incentives among the correctional population for positive change and tends to swell prison populations until they're overflowing. Even so, as societywide sentiments and the social policies they support swing further in the direction of social responsibility, the interests of crime victims and the concerns of those who champion them will increasingly be recognized.

DISCUSSION QUESTIONS

1. Outline the various sentencing rationales discussed in this chapter. Which of these rationales do you find most acceptable as the primary goal of sentencing? How might your choice of rationales vary with type of offense? Can you envision any other circumstances which might make your choice less acceptable?

2. In your opinion, is the return to just deserts consistent with the structured sentencing model? Why or why not?

3. Trace the differences between structured and indeterminate sentencing. Which model holds the best long-term promise for crime reduction? Why?

 WEB WATCH

Access the *Criminal Justice Today* site on the World Wide Web by pointing your Web browser at http://www.prenhall.com/cjtoday. Once there, click on "Web Chapters," then select "Chapter 10: Sentencing" in order to access electronic information and other sites of relevance to this chapter. You may also wish to enter The Global Town Meeting, which provides facilities for the posting of electronic messages for others to read. Messages are arranged by topic, with new topics constantly being added.

NOTES

1. *Smith* v. *U.S.*, 113 S.Ct. 1178, 122 L. Ed. 2d 548 (1993).

2. For a thorough discussion of the philosophy of punishment and sentencing, see David Garland, *Punishment and Modern Society: A Study in Social Theory* (Chicago: University of Chicago Press, 1990); Ralph D. Ellis and Carol S. Ellis, *Theories of Criminal Justice: A Critical Reappraisal* (Wolfeboro, NH: Longwood Academic, 1989); and Colin Summer, *Censure, Politics, and Criminal Justice* (Bristol, PA: Open University Press, 1990).

3. The requirement for punishment is supported by the belief that social order (and the laws which represent it) could not exist for long if transgressions went unsanctioned.

4. "Back to the Chain Gang," *Newsweek*, October 17, 1994, p. 87.

5. Ibid.

6. Ibid.

7. For an excellent review of the new "get-tough" attitudes influencing sentencing decisions, see Tamasak Wicharaya, *Simple Theory, Hard Reality: The Impact of Sentencing Reforms on Courts, Prisons, and Crime* (Albany: State University of New York Press, 1995).

8. For a thorough review of the literature on deterrence, see Raymond Paternoster, "The Deterrent Effect of the Perceived Certainty and Severity of Punishment: A Review of the Evidence and Issues," *Justice Quarterly*, Vol. 4, no. 2 (June 1987), pp. 174–217.

9. Hugo Adam Bedau, "Retributivism and the Theory of Punishment," *Journal of Philosophy*, Vol. 75 (November 1978), pp. 601–620.

10. H. L. A. Hart, *Punishment and Responsibility: Essays in the Philosophy of Law* (Oxford: Clarendon Press, 1968).

11. Paul Gendreau and Robert R. Ross, "Revivification of Rehabilitation: Evidence from the 1980s," *Justice Quarterly*, Vol. 4, no. 3 (September 1987), pp. 349–408.

12. Gordon Bazemore and Mark S. Umbreit, *Balanced and Restorative Justice: Program Summary* (Washington, D.C.: OJJDP, October 1994), foreword.

13. 18 U.S.C. 3563 (a) (2).

14. See Joan Petersilia, *Expanding Options for Criminal Sentencing* (Santa Monica, CA: The Rand Corporation, 1987).

15. E-mail communications with the Office of Reparative Programs, Department of Corrections, State of Vermont, July 3, 1995.

16. Donna Hunzeker, "State Sentencing Systems and 'Truth in Sentencing,'" *State Legislative Report*, Vol. 20, no. 3 (Denver, CO: National Conference of State Legislatures, 1995).

17. "Oklahoma Rapist Gets 30,000 Years," United Press International wire services, southwest edition, December 23, 1994.

18. Lawrence A. Greenfeld, *Prison Sentences and Time Served for Violence* (Washington, D.C.: Bureau of Justice Statistics, April 1995).

19. For a thorough consideration of alleged disparities, see G. Kleck, "Racial Discrimination in Criminal Sentencing: A Critical Evaluation of the Evidence with Additional Evidence on the Death Penalty," *American Sociological Review*, no. 46 (1981), pp. 783–805, and G. Kleck, "Life Support for Ailing Hypotheses: Modes of Summarizing the Evidence for Racial Discrimination in Sentencing," *Law and Human Behavior*, no. 9 (1985), pp. 271–285.

20. National Council on Crime and Delinquency, *National Assessment of Structured Sentencing* (Washington, D.C.: BJA, 1996).

21. Ibid.

22. Ibid.

23. *Arave* v. *Creech*, 113 S.Ct. 1534, 123 L. Ed. 2d 188 (1993). See also *Richmond* v. *Lewis*, 113 S.Ct. 538, 121 L. Ed. 2d 411 (1992).

24. For an early statement of this problem, see Franklin E. Zimring, "Making the Punishment Fit the Crime: A Consumer's Guide to Sentencing Reform," in Gordon Hawkins and F. E. Zimring, eds., *The Pursuit of Criminal Justice* (Chicago: University of Chicago Press, 1984) pp. 267–275.

25. Albert W. Alschuler, "Sentencing Reform and Prosecutorial Power: A Critique of Recent Proposals for 'Fixed' and 'Presumptive' Sentencing," in Sheldon L. Messinger and Egon Bittner, Eds., *Criminology Review Yearbook*, Vol. 1 (Beverly Hills, CA: Sage Publications, 1979), pp. 416–445.

26. Ibid., p. 422.

27. Christopher T. Link and Neal Shover, "The Origins of Criminal Sentencing Reforms," *Justice Quarterly*, Vol. 3, no. 3 (September 1986), pp. 329–342.

28. For a good discussion of such issues, see Hans Toch, "Rewarding Convicted Offenders," *Federal Probation* (June 1988), pp. 42–48.

29. Much of the material in this section is derived from Dale Parent, Terence Dunworth, Douglas McDonald, and William Rhodes, "Mandatory Sentencing," *NIJ Research in Action Series* (Washington, D.C.: NIJ, January 1997).

30. In mid-1996 the California Supreme Court ruled the State's three-strikes law an undue intrusion on judges' sentencing discretion.

31. G.L. Pierce and W.J. Bowers, "The Bartley-Fox Gun Law's Short-Term Impact on Crime in Boston," *Annals of the American Academy of Political and Social Science*, Vol. 455 (1981), pp. 120–132.

32. Colin Loftin, Milton Heumann, and David McDowall, "Mandatory Sentencing and Firearms Violence: Evaluating an Alternative to Gun Control," *Law and Society Review*, Vol. 17 (1983), pp. 287–318.

33. Colin Loftin and David McDowall, "The Deterrent Effects of the Florida Felony Firearm Law," *Journal of Criminal Law and Criminology*, Vol. 75 (1984), pp. 250–259.

34. David McDowall, Colin Loftin, and Brian Wiersema, "A Comparative Study of the Preventive Effects of Mandatory Sentencing Laws for Gun Crimes," *Journal of Criminal Law and Criminology*, Vol. 83, no. 2 (Summer 1992), pp. 378–394.

35. Joint Committee on New York Drug Law Evaluation, *The Nation's Toughest Drug Law: Evaluating the New York Experience, a project of the Association of the Bar of the City of New York, the City of New York and the Drug Abuse Council, Inc.* (Washington, D.C.: U.S. Government Printing Office, 1978).

36. Michael Tonry, *Sentencing Reform Impacts* (Washington, D.C.: National Institute of Justice, 1987).

37. D.C. McDonald and K.E. Carlson, *Sentencing in the Courts: Does Race Matter? The Transition to Sentencing Guidelines, 1986–90* (Washington, D.C.: Bureau of Justice Statistics, 1993).

38. As discussed later in this chapter, federal sentencing guidelines did not become effective until 1987 and still had to meet many court challenges.

39. U.S. Sentencing Commission, *Federal Sentencing Guidelines Manual* (Washington, D.C.: U.S. Government Printing Office, 1987), p. 2.

40. A maximum of 54 days per year of good-time credit can still be earned.

41. Greenfeld, "Prison Sentences and Time Served for Violence."

42. Bureau of Justice Statistics, "Prison Sentences and Time Served for Violence," (Rockville, MD: Bureau of Justice Statistics, 1995).

43. Thomas Martello, "Truth in Sentencing," The Associated Press wire services, northern edition, April 26, 1994.

44. For an excellent review of the act and its implications, see Gregory D. Lee, "U.S. Sentencing Guidelines: Their Impact on Federal Drug Offenders," *FBI Law Enforcement Bulletin* (Washington, D.C.: FBI, May 1995) pp. 17–21.

45. U.S. Sentencing Commission, *Guidelines*, p. 10.

46. *Mistretta* v. *U.S.*, 488 U.S. 361, 371 (1989).

47. For an engaging overview of how mitigating factors might be applied under the guidelines, see *Koon* v. *U.S.*, 116 S.Ct. 2035, 135 L. Ed. 2d 392 (1996).

48. U.S. Sentencing Commission, *Guidelines*, p. 207.

49. *Deal* v. *U.S.*, 113 S.Ct. 1993, 124 L. Ed. 2d 44 (1993).

50. U.S. Sentencing Commission, *Guidelines*, p. 8.

51. "Sentencing Commission Chairman Wilkins Answers Questions on the Guidelines," National Institute of Justice, *Research in Action Report* (September 1987), p. 7.

52. *Melendez* v. *U.S.*, 117 S.Ct. 383, 136 L. Ed. 2d 301 (1996).

53. James Eisentein and Herbert Jacob, *Felony Justice* (Boston: Little, Brown, 1977).

54. Joan Petersilia, *Racial Disparities in the Criminal Justice System* (Santa Monica, CA: The Rand Corporation, 1983).

55. Anthony J. Ragona and John P. Ryan, *Beyond the Courtroom: A Comparative Analysis of Misdemeanor Sentencing—Executive Summary* (Chicago: American Judicature Society, 1983).

56. James H. Kuklinski and John E. Stanga, "Political Participation and Government Responsiveness: The Behavior of California Superior Courts," *American Political Science Review*, Vol. 73 (1979), pp. 1090–1099.

57. See Joseph Jacoby and Christopher Dunn, *National Survey on Punishment for Criminal Offenses—Executive Summary* (Washington, D.C.: Bureau of Justice Statistics, 1987). For a critique of this survey, see Barry Krisberg, "Public Attitudes About Criminal Sanctions," *The Criminologist*, Vol. 13, no. 2 (March/ April 1988), pp. 12, 16.

58. Stephen P. Klein, Susan Turner, and Joan Petersilia, *Radical Equity in Sentencing* (Santa Monica, CA: The Rand Corporation, 1988).

59. Ibid., p. 11.

60. Ibid.

61. William Wilbanks, "Are Female Felons Treated More Leniently by the Criminal Justice System?" *Justice Quarterly*, Vol. 3, no. 4 (December 1986), pp. 517–529.

62. Martha A. Myers and Susette M. Talarico, *The Social Contexts of Criminal Sentencing* (New York: Springer-Verlag, 1987).

63. Ibid., p. 170.

64. Martha A. Myers, "Sentencing Background and the Sentencing Behavior of Judges," *Criminology*, Vol. 26, no. 4 (1988), pp. 649–675.

65. Andrew Klein, *Alternative Sentencing: A Practitioner's Guide* (Cincinnati, OH: Anderson 1988), p. 23.

66. Ibid.

67. National Criminal Justice Information and Statistics Service, *Privacy and Security Planning Instructions* (Washington, D.C.: U.S. Government Printing Office, 1976).

68. U.S. Department of Justice, "State Criminal Records Repositories," Bureau of Justice Statistics, *Technical Report* (1985).

69. Privacy Act of 1974, 5 U.S.C.A. 522a, 88 Statute 1897, Public Law 93-579, December 31, 1974.

70. Freedom of Information Act, 5 U.S.C. 522, and amendments. The status of presentence investigative reports has not yet been clarified under this act to the satisfaction of all legal scholars, although generally state and federal courts are thought to be exempt from the provisions of the act.

71. Alexander B. Smith and Louis Berlin, *Introduction to Probation and Parole* (St. Paul, MN: West, 1976), p. 75.

72. Andrew Klein, *Alternative Sentencing: A Practitioner's Guide* (Cincinnati, OH: Anderson, 1988).

73. John Rosecrance, "Maintaining the Myth of Individualized Justice: Probation Presentence Reports," *Justice Quarterly*, Vol. 5, no. 2 (June 1988), pp. 237–256.

74. Ibid.

75. For a good review of the issues involved, see Robert C. Davis, Arthur J. Lurigio, and Wesley G. Skogan, *Victims of Crime*, 2nd ed. (Thousand Oaks, CA: Sage, 1997), and Leslie Sebba, *Third Parties: Victims and the Criminal Justice System* (Columbus, OH: Ohio State University Press, 1996).

76. President's Task Force on Victims of Crime, *Final Report* (Washington, D.C.: U.S. Government Printing Office, 1982).

77. Peter Finn and Beverly N. W. Lee, *Establishing and Expanding Victim-Witness Assistance Programs* (Washington, D.C.: National Institute of Justice, August 1988).

78. "Victim Assistance Programs: Whom They Service, What They Offer," A National Institute of Justice *Update* (May, 1995).

79. President's Task Force on Victims of Crime, *Final Report*.

80. SJR 65 is a major revision of an initial proposal, Sen. J. Res. 52 which Senators Kyl and Feinstein introduced on April 22, 1996. Rep. Henry Hyde introduced House Joint Resolution 174, a companion to Sen. J. Res. 52, and a similar proposal, H. J. Res. 173 on April 22, 1996.

81. Nebraska, the latest, did so in 1996. For additional information see Bill Varner, "Crime Victims' Rights, Term Limits Win Big," *USA Today*, November 7, 1996, 17A.

82. Public Law 97-291.

83. Robert J. McCormack, review of Robert Elias, *Victims Still: The Political Manipulation of Crime Victims* (Newbury Park, CA: Sage, 1993) in *Justice Quarterly*, Vol. 11, no. 4 (December 1994), pp. 725–727.

84. Proposition 8, California's Victim's Bill of Rights.

85. National Victim Center/Mothers Against Drunk Driving/American Prosecutors Research Institute, *Impact Statements: A Victim's Right to Speak: A Nation's Responsibility to Listen*, July 1994.

86. "Crazed Fan's Deadly 'Mission' Threat Terrified Actress." *The Fayetteville Observer-Times* (North Carolina), June 8, 1989, p. 11D.

87. Ibid.

88. Edwin Villmoare and Virginia V. Neto, "Victim Appearances at Sentencing Under California's Victim's Bill of Rights," National Institute of Justice, *Research in Brief* (August 1987).

89. Rick Atkinson, "Seles Says Attacker Has 'Ruined My Life': Retrial of Parche Aims At Tougher Sentence," *The Washington Post*, March 22, 1995.

90. Rick Atkinson, "Suspended Sentence Upheld for Seles' Attacker," *The Washington Post*, April 4, 1995.

91. Robert C. Davis and Barbara E. Smith, "The Effects of Victim Impact Statements on Sentencing Decisions: A Test in an Urban Setting," *Justice Quarterly*, Vol. 11, no. 3 (September 1994), pp. 453–469.

92. *Booth v. Maryland*, 107 S.Ct. 2529 (1987).

93. *Payne v. Tennessee*, 501 U.S. 808 (1991).

94. "Supreme Court Closes Term with Major Criminal Justice Rulings," Criminal Justice Newsletter, Vol. 22, no. 13 (July 1, 1991), p. 2.

95. See "What Say Should Victims Have?" *Time*, May 27, 1991, p. 61.

96. *Report to the Nation on Crime and Justice*, 2nd ed. (Washington, D.C.: U.S. Department of Justice, 1988), p. 90.

97. Patrick A. Langan and Jodi M. Brown, *Felony Sentences in State Courts, 1994* (Washington, D.C.: Bureau of Justice Statistics, 1997), and Patrick A. Langan and Jodi M. Brown, *Felony Sentences in the United States, 1994* (Washington, D.C.: Bureau of Justice Statistics, 1997).

98. Sally T. Hillsman, Barry Mahoney, George F. Cole, and Bernard Auchter, "Fines as Criminal Sanctions," National Institute of Justice, *Research in Brief* (September 1987), p. 1.

99. Ibid., p. 2.

100. Sally T. Hillsman, Joyce L. Sichel, and Barry Mahoney, *Fines in Sentencing* (New York: Vera Institute of Justice, 1983).

101. Ibid., p. 2.

102. Ibid., p. 4.

103. Ibid.

104. Douglas C. McDonald, Judith Greene, and Charles Worzella, *Day Fines in American*

Courts: The Staten Island and Milwaukee Experiments (Washington, D.C.: National Institute of Justice, 1992).

105. Ibid., p. 56.

106. Laura A. Winterfield and Sally T. Hillsman, *The Staten Island Day-Fine Project* (Washington, D.C.: National Institute of Justice, 1993), p. 1.

107. "Man Decapitates Neighbor, Tosses Head in Dumpster," Reuters wire services, May 25, 1996.

108. Herbert A. Johnson, *History of Criminal Justice*, (Cincinatti, OH: Anderson, 1988), pp. 30–31.

109. Ibid., p. 31.

110. Ibid., p. 36.

111. "Yemeni Court Upholds Crucifixions," The Associated Press wire services, August 31, 1997.

112. Ibid., p. 51.

113. Arthur Koestler, *Reflections on Hanging* (New York: Macmillan, 1957), p. xi.

114. Ibid., p. 15.

115. Merle Severy, "The Great Revolution," *National Geographic* (July 1989), p. 20.

116. Capital Punishment Research Project, University of Alabama Law School.

117. As of this writing a strong push is under way to institute the death penalty in a number of jurisdictions, including the District of Columbia. A pro-capital-punishment movement is being led in the District of Columbia by U.S. Sen. Kay Bailey Hutchison (R-Texas).

118. U.S. Department of Justice, *Capital Punishment, 1993* (Washington, D.C.: U.S. Government Printing Office, 1995).

119. Richard Willing, "Expansion of Death Penalty to Nonmurders Faces Challenges," *USA Today*, May 14, 1997, p. 6A.

120. Death Penalty Information Center Web Site, www.essential.org/dpic, March 20, 1998.

121. James Stephen and Peter Brien, *Capital Punishment 1993* (Washington, D.C.: Bureau of Justice Statistics, December 1994), p. 1. The average may be dropping, however. According to a recent report by the Death Penalty Information Center, those executed between 1977 and 1994 spent an average of eight years awaiting execution. (See Laurie Asseo, "Death-Row Appeals," The Associated Press wire services northern edition, April 18, 1996.)

122. "Killer Spared 14th Date with Execution in Louisiana," Reuters wire services, April 18, 1995.

123. Allan Turner, "Texas Executes Third and Fourth Prisoners in a Week," *The Houston Chronicle* via Simon and Schuster's NewsLink service, June 5, 1997.

124. "Chief Justice Calls for Limits on Death Row Habeas Appeals," *Criminal Justice Newsletter*, February 15, 1989, pp. 6–7.

125. *McCleskey* v. *Zandt*, 499 U. S. 467, 493–494 (1991).

126. *Coleman* v. *Thompson*, 501 U.S. 722 (1991).

127. *Schlup* v. *Delo*, 115 S.Ct. 851, 130 L. Ed. 2d 808 (1995).

128. *Felker* v. *Turpin, Warden*, 117 S.Ct. 30, 135 L. Ed. 2d 1123 (1996).

129. Laurie Asseo, "Terrorism Bill," The Associated Press wire services northern edition, April 19, 1996.

130. Michelle Locke, "Victim Forgives," The Associated Press wire services, May 19, 1996.

131. Ibid.

132. Koestler, *Reflections on Hanging*, p. xii.

133. See Radelet and Bedau, *In Spite of Innocence* (Boston: Northeastern University Press, 1992), who claim that 23 innocent people have been executed in the United States since 1900. Also, a House Judiciary Subcommittee found that 59 people have been released from the nation's death rows since 1970 because of innocence (Staff Report, House Judiciary Committee on Civil and Constitutional Rights, October, 1993).

134. Studies include S. Decker and C. Kohfeld, "A Deterrence Study of the Death Penalty in Illinois: 1933–1980," *Journal of Criminal Justice*, Vol. 12, no. 4 (1984), pp. 367–379, and S. Decker and C. Kohfeld, "An Empirical Analysis of the Effect of the Death Penalty in Missouri," *Journal of Crime and Justice*, Vol. 10, no. 1 (1987), pp. 23–46.

135. See, especially, the work of W. C. Bailey, "Deterrence and the Death Penalty for Murders in Utah: A Time Series Analysis," *Journal of Contemporary Law*, Vol. 5, no. 1 (1978), pp. 1–20, and "An Analysis of the Deterrent Effect of the Death Penalty for Murder in California," *Southern California Law Review*, Vol. 52, no. 3 (1979), pp. 743–764.

136. B. E. Forst, "The Deterrent Effect of Capital Punishment: A Cross-State Analysis of the 1960's," *Minnesota Law Review*, Vol. 61, no. 5 (1977), pp. 743–767.

137. Scott H. Decker and Carol W. Kohfeld, "Capital Punishment and Executions in the Lone Star State: A Deterrence Study," *Criminal Justice Research Bulletin* (Criminal Justice Center, Sam Houston State University), Vol. 3, no. 12 (1988).

138. Ibid.

139. "Attorneys Call for Halt to U.S. Executions," Reuters wire services, February 4, 1997.

140. As some of the evidence presented before the Supreme Court in *Furman* v. *Georgia* (408 U.S. 238, 1972) suggested.

141. *USA Today*, April 27, 1989, p. 12A.

142. Thomas J. Keil and Gennaro F. Vito, "Race and the Death Penalty in Kentucky Murder

Trials: 1976–1991, *American Journal of Criminal Justice*, Vol. 20, no. 1 (1995), pp. 17–36 (published December 1996).

143. *McCleskey* v. *Kemp*, 481 U.S. 279, 107 S.Ct. 1756, 95 L. Ed. 2d 262 (1987).

144. Death Penalty Information Center, World Wide Web site (http://www.essential. org/dpic).

145. "Judge Gives Max in Burned Alive Case," United Press International wire services, northeast edition, December 10, 1996.

146. Justice Stewart, as quoted in *USA Today*, April 27, 1989, p. 12A.

147. Koestler, *Reflections on Hanging*, pp. 147–148, and Gennaro F. Vito and Deborah G. Wilson, "Back from the Dead: Tracking the Progress of Kentucky's Furman-Commuted Death Row Population," *Justice Quarterly*, Vol. 5, no. 1 (1988), pp. 101–111.

148. P. Harris, "Over-Simplification and Error in Public Opinion Surveys on Capital Punishment," *Justice Quarterly* (1986), pp. 429–455.

149. Ibid.

150. James O. Finckenauer, "Public Support for the Death Penalty: Retribution as Just Deserts or Retribution as Revenge?" *Justice Quarterly*, Vol. 5, no. 1 (March 1988), p. 83.

151. Robert M. Bohm, *The Death Penalty in America: Current Research* (Cincinnati, OH: Anderson, 1991), pp. 119–127.

152. Ibid., p. 135.

153. Frank P. Williams III, Dennis R. Longmire, and David B. Gulick, "The Public and the Death Penalty: Opinion as an Artifact of Question Type," *Criminal Justice Research Bulletin* (Criminal Justice Center, Sam Houston State University), Vol. 3, no. 8 (1988).

154. Ibid., p. 4.

155. *Criminal Justice Newsletter*, Vol. 21, no. 23 (December 3, 1990), p. 1.

156. *Wilkerson* v. *Utah*, 99 U.S. 130 (1878).

157. *In re Kemmler*, 136 U.S. 436 (1890).

158. Ibid., p. 447.

159. *Louisiana ex rel. Francis* v. *Resweber*, 329 U.S. 459 (1947).

160. *Furman* v. *Georgia*, 408 U.S. 238 (1972).

161. A position first ascribed to in *Trop* v. *Dulles*, 356 U.S. 86 (1958).

162. *Gregg* v. *Georgia*, 428 U.S. 153 (1976).

163. Ibid., p. 173.

164. *Coker* v. *Georgia*, 433 U.S. 584 (1977).

165. *Woodson* v. *North Carolina*, 428 U.S. 280 (1976).

166. *Blystone* v. *Pennsylvania*, 494 U.S. 310 (1990).

167. *Boyde* v. *California*, 494 U.S. 370 (1990).

168. *Harris* v. *Alabama*, 513 U.S. 504, 115 S.Ct. 1031, 130 L. Ed. 2d 1004 (1995).

169. *Tuilaepa* v. *California*, 114 S.Ct. 2630, 129 L. Ed. 2d 750 (1994).

170. *Poyner* v. *Murray*, 113 S.Ct. 1573, 123 L. Ed. 2d 142 1993.

171. *Campbell* v. *Wood*, 114 S. Ct. 1337, 127 L. Ed. 2d 685 (1994).

172. U.S. Supreme Court, *Director Gomez, et al* v. *Fierro and Ruiz* (No. 95–1830), 1996.

INDIVIDUAL RIGHTS VERSUS SOCIAL CONCERNS

The Rights of the Convicted and Imprisoned

Common law, constitutional, and humanitarian rights of the convicted and imprisoned:

- A Right Against Cruel or Unusual Punishment

- A Right to Protection from Physical Harm

- A Limited Right to Legal Assistance While Imprisoned

- A Limited Right to Religious Freedom While Imprisoned

- A Limited Right to Freedom of Speech While Imprisoned

- A Right to Sanitary and Healthy Conditions of Confinement

- A Right to Due Process Prior to Denial of Privileges

The individual rights listed must be effectively balanced against these community concerns:

- Punishment of the Guilty

- Safe Communities

- The Reduction of Recidivism

- Secure Prisons

- Control over Convicts

- The Prevention of Escape

- Rehabilitation

- Affordable Prisons

How does our system of justice work toward balance?

part 4

CORRECTIONS

Punishment—that is justice for the unjust

The great Christian apologist C. S. Lewis (1898–1963) once remarked that if satisfying justice is to be the ultimate goal of Western criminal justice, then the fate of offenders cannot be dictated merely by practical considerations. "The concept of desert is the only connecting link between punishment and justice," Lewis wrote. "It is only as deserved or undeserved that a sentence can be just or unjust," he concluded.

Once a person has been arrested, tried, and sentenced, the correctional process begins. Unlike Lewis's exhortation, however, the contemporary American correctional system—which includes probation, parole, jails, prisons, capital punishment, and a plethora of innovative alternatives to traditional sentences—is tasked with far more than merely carrying out sentences. We also ask of our correctional system that it ensures the safety of law-abiding citizens, that it selects the best alternative from among the many available for handling a given offender, that it protects those under its charge, and that it guarantees fairness in the handling of all with whom it comes into contact.

This section of *Criminal Justice Today* details the development of probation, parole, community corrections, and imprisonment as correctional philosophies; describes the nuances of prison and jail life; discusses special issues in contemporary corrections (including AIDS, geriatric offenders, and female inmates); and summarizes the legal environment which both surrounds and infuses the modern-day practice of corrections. Characteristic of today's correctional emphasis is a societywide push for harsher punishments. The culmination of that strategy, however, is dramatically overcrowded correctional institutions, the problems of which are also described. As you read through this section, encountering descriptions of various kinds of criminal sanctions, you might ask yourself: "When would a punishment of this sort be deserved?" In doing so, remember to couple that thought with another question: "What are the ultimate consequences (for society and for the offender) of the kind of correctional program we are discussing here?" Unlike Lewis, you may also want to ask: "Can we afford it?"

chapter 11

PROBATION, PAROLE, AND COMMUNITY CORRECTIONS

Community corrections is an integral part of the criminal justice system and should be fully implemented and promoted in order to save expensive and scarce jail and prison space for violent and serious offenders.[1]

—NATIONAL ASSOCIATION OF COUNTIES, JUSTICE, AND PUBLIC SAFETY STEERING COMMITTEE

Introduction to Community Corrections

Despite the "get tough" image of recent legislative initiatives, the United States relies primarily on a community-based system of sentencing.[2]

—James M. Byrne, University of Lowell

...probation and parole services are characteristically poorly staffed and often poorly administered.[3]

—President's Commission on Law Enforcement and Administration of Justice

Community Corrections (also called **Community-Based Corrections**) A sentencing style that represents a movement away from traditional confinement options and an increased dependence upon correctional resources which are available in the community.

In 1996 convicted child molester Larry Don McQuay was released from a Texas prison after serving six years for sexually abusing the six-year-old son of a former girlfriend. McQuay was set free two years before the expiration of an eight-year sentence because of good behavior. His release, however, outraged many Texans because McQuay promised to rape and kill more children, saying that he was helplessly driven to have sex with kids. McQuay added, "I am doomed to eventually rape, then murder my poor little victims to keep them from telling on me."[4] McQuay requested that he be castrated prior to release, but state officials said they were unable to comply with his request. Although not able to prevent his release, officials imposed a number of stringent parole restrictions intended to limit McQuay's movements and mandated that he not associate with anyone under the age of 17.

In 1992, another parolee, 39-year-old Leslie Allen Williams, who had a 20-year history of attacks on women, confessed to killing four teenage girls in Pontiac, Michigan. Williams admitted the murders while jailed on charges he had abducted a young woman from a cemetery after she placed a wreath on her mother's grave. Before his 1992 arrest, Williams was paroled in 1990, having been in and out of prison for abducting and attacking women since 1971. Patrick Urbin, the father of 16- and 14-year-old sisters Michelle and Melissa Urbin—two of Williams's latest victims—said "[t]he system has failed us by letting this person out early...[w]e don't personally believe in the death penalty, but he should be behind bars for the rest of his life...[w]hy did they let him get so far and do so much in 20 years?"[5]

In 1995, the shocking case of Henry Marshall came to light during a television documentary[6] which detailed how the 36-year-old parolee viciously killed grill owner Dennis Griswold during a 1994 robbery of Griswold's business. Griswold's daughter, Danielle Griswold, a Tacoma, Washington, policewoman, investigated her father's murder and soon discovered that Marshall had been paroled early by Massachusetts authorities upon a request from the FBI, with whom he had agreed to work as an informant. The FBI lost track of Marshall, and he crossed the country, traveling under his own name and ending up in Washington state where he shot Griswold—later bragging to acquaintances that he loved killing more than sex and celebrating the murder with a steak cookout. Computerized background checks conducted by Officer Griswold quickly revealed that Marshall was extremely dangerous and had a lengthy record. Marshall had been charged with two attempted murders, claimed to be a hit man for a northeastern motorcycle gang, and had spent all but three months of his adult life either in prison, on parole, or out on bail awaiting trial. Prior to his early parole, in addition to the two attempted murder charges, Marshall had 23 previous criminal convictions.

Stories like these, appearing daily in papers across the country, have cast a harsh light on the early release of criminal offenders. This chapter takes a close look at the realities behind the practice of what we call "community corrections." **Community corrections**, also called **community-based corrections**, is a sentencing style that represents a movement away from traditional confinement options and an increased dependence upon correctional resources

Parole and probation are both forms of supervised release. Parole officers are shown here visiting a parolee (right) at his home. *Warren Jorgensen, AP/Wide World Photos*

which are available in the community. Community corrections can best be defined as the use of a variety of court-ordered programmatic sanctions permitting convicted offenders to remain in the community under conditional supervision as an alternative to active prison sentences. Community corrections includes a wide variety of sentencing options such as probation, parole, home confinement, the electronic monitoring of offenders, and other new and developing programs—all of which are covered in this chapter.

What Is Probation?

Probation, which is one aspect of community corrections, is "a sentence served while under supervision in the community."[7] Like other sentencing options, probation is a court-ordered sanction. Its goal is to allow for some degree of control over criminal offenders while using community programs to help rehabilitate them. Most of the alternative sanctions discussed later in this chapter are, in fact, predicated upon probationary sentences in which the offender is first placed on probation and then ordered to abide by certain conditions while remaining free in the community—such as participation in a specified program. Although probation can be directly imposed by the court in many jurisdictions, most probationers are technically sentenced first to confinement, but then immediately have their sentences suspended and are remanded into the custody of an officer of the court—the probation officer.

> **Probation** A sentence of imprisonment that is suspended. Also, the conditional freedom granted by a judicial officer to an adjudicated adult or juvenile offender, as long as the person meets certain conditions of behavior.

Probation has a long and diverse history. By the 1300s English courts had established the practice of "binding over for good behavior,"[8] in which offenders could be entrusted into the custody of willing citizens. John Augustus (1784–1859), however, is generally recognized as the world's first probation officer. Augustus, a Boston shoemaker, attended sessions of criminal court in the 1850s and would offer to take carefully selected offenders into his home as an alternative to imprisonment.[9] At first he supervised only drunkards, but by 1857 Augustus was accepting many kinds of offenders and devoting all his time to the service of the court.[10] Augustus died in 1859, having bailed out more than 2,000 convicts during his lifetime. In 1878 the Massachusetts legislature enacted a statute which authorized the city of Boston to hire a salaried probation officer. Missouri (1897) followed suit, along with Vermont (1898) and Rhode Island (1899).[11] Before the end of the nineteenth century, probation had become an accepted and widely used form of community-based supervision. By

FIGURE 11–1 Persons under correctional supervision in the United States, by type of supervision, 1995. *Source:* Bureau of Justice Statistics, *Correctional Populations in the United States* (Washington, D.C.: Bureau of Justice Statistics, 1997).

1925 all 48 states had adopted probation legislation. In the same year the National Probation Act enabled federal district court judges to appoint paid probation officers and impose probationary terms.[12]

THE EXTENT OF PROBATION

Today, probation is the most commonly used form of criminal sentencing in the United States. Between 30% and 60% of all persons found guilty of crimes are sentenced to some form of probation.[13] Figure 11–1 shows that 58% of all persons under correctional supervision in the United States on January 1, 1997, were on probation. Not shown is the fact that the number of persons supervised yearly on probation has increased from slightly over 1 million in 1980 to 3.2 million today—a 300% increase.[14] This observation has caused some writers to call "probation crowding" an "immediate threat to the criminal justice process and to community protection."[15]

Even serious offenders stand about a 1-in-4 chance of receiving a probationary term, as Figure 11–2 shows. A 1997 Bureau of Justice Statistics study[16] of felony sentences found that 3% of people convicted of homicide were placed on probation, as were 12% of convicted rapists. Twelve percent of convicted robbers and 25% of burglars were similarly sentenced to probation rather than active prison time. In a recent example,[17] 47-year-old Carrie Mote of Vernon, Connecticut, was sentenced to probation for shooting her fiancé in the chest with a .38-caliber handgun after he called off their scheduled wedding. Ms. Mote, who faced a maximum of 20 years in prison, claimed to be suffering from diminished psychological capacity at the time of the shooting because of the emotional stress brought on by the canceled wedding.

FIGURE 11–2 Percentage of convicted offenders receiving probation, by type of crime. *Source:* Patrick A. Langan and Jodi M. Brown, *Felony Sentences in the United States, 1994* (Washington, D.C.: Bureau of Justice Statistics, 1997).

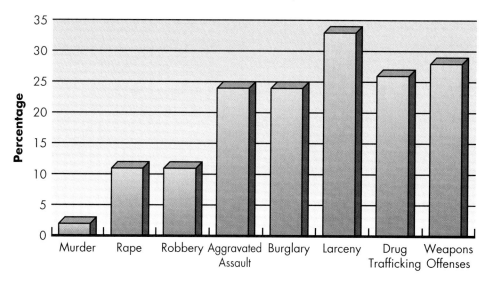

Table 11-1 *Adults on Probation and Parole in the United States, January 1, 1997*

Jurisdiction	Parolees	Probationers	Jurisdiction	Parolees	Probationers
U.S. total	704,709	3,180,363			
Federal	59,133	34,301	Montana	771	4,473
Alabama	5,213	38,764	Nebraska	706	14,503
Alaska	553	3,760	Nevada	3,216	9,760
Arizona	3,785	43,190	New Hampshire	1,066	4,414
Arkansas	5,143	38,764	New Jersey	41,547	125,881
California	97,063	292,019	New Mexico	1,426	8,928
Colorado	3,294	41,212	New York	57,137	180,580
Connecticut	1,083	55,978	North Carolina	12,358	102,483
Delaware	1,033	16,528	North Dakota	104	2,521
Florida	9,243	249,479	Ohio	6,331	102,755
Georgia	21,146	144,157	Oklahoma	2,159	28,090
Hawaii	1,733	14,238	Oregon	15,800	42,292
Idaho	692	5,855	Pennsylvania	75,013	110,532
Illinois	30,067	115,503	Rhode Island	575	20,446
Indiana	3,575	99,590	South Carolina	5,367	42,082
Iowa	2,200	15,384	South Dakota	725	3,484
Kansas	6,004	15,732	Tennessee	8,934	37,401
Kentucky	4,621	11,689	Texas	112,594	425,789
Louisiana	20,998	35,375	Utah	2,975	9,111
Maine[1]	57	7,696	Vermont	542	8,220
Maryland	16,246	70,553	Virginia	9,918	29,620
Massachusetts	4,836	44,858	Washington	560	125,317
Michigan	14,609	148,595	West Virginia	869	5,669
Minnesota	2,377	88,039	Wisconsin	8,121	51,669
Mississippi	1,513	9,999	Wyoming	364	3,432
Missouri	12,597	44,644	Washington, D.C.	7,120	9,740

[1]Maine eliminated parole in 1976.

Source: Bureau of Justice Statistics.

At the beginning of 1997, a total of 3,180,363 adults were on probation throughout the nation.[18] Individual states, however, made greater or lesser use of probation. North Dakota authorities, with the smallest probationary population, supervised only 2,521 people, while Texas reported 425,789 persons on probation (see Table 11–1). Fifty-nine percent of probationers successfully complete their probationary terms, while a small percentage abscond (about 2%), and another 3% are convicted of new crimes while on probation.[19]

Probation Conditions

Those sentenced to probation must agree to abide by court-mandated conditions of probation. Such conditions are of two types: general and specific. General conditions apply to all probationers in a given jurisdiction and usually include requirements that the probationer "obey all laws," "maintain employment," "remain within the jurisdiction of the court," "possess no firearm," "allow the probation officer to visit at home or at work," and so forth. Figure 11–3 shows a form that judges commonly use to impose general conditions of probation. Many probationers are also required to pay a fine to the court, usually in a series of installments, that is designed to reimburse victims for damages and to pay lawyers' fees and other costs of court.

STATE OF NORTH CAROLINA

File No.

_____ County _____ Seat Of Court

In The General Court Of Justice
☐ District ☐ Superior Court Division

NOTE:
(This form is not to be used for multiple offenses unless they are consolidated for judgment.)

STATE VERSUS

Defendant

Race	Sex	DOB

Attorney For State	Def. Found ☐ Not Indigent	Def. Waived ☐ Attorney	Attorney For Defendant	☐ Appointed ☐ Retained

JUDGMENT SUSPENDING SENTENCE AND COMMITMENT ON SPECIAL PROBATION

G.S. 15A-1341, 15A-1342, 15A-1343, 15A-1346

The defendant ☐ pled guilty to: ☐ was found guilty by the Court of: ☐ was found guilty by a jury of: ☐ pled no contest to:

File No.(s) And Offense(s)	Date of Offense	G.S. No.	Fel./M.	Class	Max. Term	Presumptive

The Court has considered the aggravating and mitigating factors in G.S. 15A-1340.4(a) and
☐ makes no written findings because the prison term imposed does not require such findings.
☐ makes no written findings because the prison term imposed is pursuant to a plea arrangement as to sentence.
☐ makes the Findings Of Factors In Aggravation And Mitigation Of Punishment set forth on the attached AOC-CR-303.

The Court, having considered evidence, arguments of counsel and statement of defendant, finds that the defendant's plea was freely, voluntarily, and understandingly entered, and Orders the above offenses be consolidated for judgment and the defendant be imprisoned.

for a term of _____ in the custody of the ☐ N.C. Dept. of Correction
☐ Sheriff of _____ County

The defendant shall be given credit for _____ days spent in confinement prior to the date of this Judgment as a result of this charge, to be applied toward the ☐ sentence imposed above. ☐ imprisonment required for special probation below.

SUSPENSION OF SENTENCE

With the consent of the defendant and subject to the conditions set out below, the execution of this sentence is suspended and the defendant is placed on ☐ supervised probation for _____ years. ☐ unsupervised probation for _____ years.
☐ The above period of probation shall begin: ☐ when the defendant is paroled or otherwise released from incarceration in the case referred to below. ☐ at the expiration of the sentence in the case referred to below.
(**NOTE:** *List Case Number, Date, County And Court In Which Prior Sentence Imposed.*)

SPECIAL PROBATION – G.S. 15A-1351

☐ As a condition of special probation, the defendant shall ☐ serve an active term of _____ ☐ days ☐ months in the custody of the ☐ N.C. DOC. ☐ Sheriff of this County. ☐ submit to IMPACT imprisonment per attached CR-302, Page Two. ☐ pay jail fees.
(**NOTE:** *This term shall NOT be reduced by good time, gain time or parole, or, unless provided above, by time in jail awaiting trial.*)

The defendant shall report in a sober condition to begin serving his term on:	Day	Date	Hour	☐ AM ☐ PM	and shall remain in custody until:	Day	Date	Hour	☐ AM ☐ PM

☐ The defendant shall again report in a sober condition to continue serving this term on the same day of the week for the next _____ consecutive weeks, and shall remain in custody during the same hours each week.

MONETARY CONDITIONS

The defendant shall pay to the Clerk of Superior Court the "Total Amount Due" shown below, plus the probation supervision fee set by law
☐ pursuant to a schedule determined by the probation officer. ☐ at the rate of $ _____ per _____ ,
beginning on _____ and continuing on the same day of each _____ thereafter until paid in full. ☐ Other:

Fine $	Costs $	Restitution* $	Attorney's Fee $	Community Service Fee $	Total Amount Due $

*The name(s) and address(es) and amount(s) due the person(s) to receive this restitution are:

☐ All payments received by the Clerk shall first be disbursed pro rata among the persons entitled to restitution.
☐ Upon payment of the "Total Amount Due," the probation officer may transfer the defendant to unsupervised probation.

AOC-CR-302, Rev. 7/95   Material opposite unmarked squares is to be disregarded as surplusage.

FIGURE 11–3 Probation agreement form. *Source:* Courtesy North Carolina Administrative Office of the Courts, and the North Carolina Department of Correction, Division of Adult Probation and Parole. Reprinted with permission.

REGULAR CONDITIONS OF PROBATION – G.S. 15A-1343(b)

The defendant shall: 1. Commit no criminal offense in any jurisdiction. 2. Possess no firearm, explosive device or other deadly weapon listed in G.S. 14-269. 3.Remain gainfully and suitably employed or faithfully pursue a course of study or of vocational training that will equip him for suitable employment. 4. Satisfy child support and family obligations, as required by the Court. If the defendant is on supervised probation, he shall also: 5. Remain within the jurisdiction of the Court unless granted written permission to leave by the Court or his probation officer. 6. Report as directed by the Court or his probation officer to the officer at reasonable times and places and in a reasonable manner, permit the officer to visit him at reasonable times, answer all reasonable inquiries by the officer, and obtain prior approval from the officer for, and notify the officer of, any change in address or employment. 7. Notify the probation officer if he fails to obtain or retain satisfactory employment. 8. At a time to be designated by his probation officer, visit with his probation officer at a facility maintained by the Division of Prisons. If the defendant is to serve an active sentence as a condition of special probation, he shall also: 9. Obey the rules and regulations of the Department of Correction governing the conduct of inmates while imprisoned. 10. Report to a probation officer in the State of North Carolina within 72 hours of his discharge from the active term of imprisonment.

SPECIAL CONDITIONS OF PROBATION – G.S. 15A-1343(b1), 143B-262(c)

The defendant shall also comply with the following special conditions which the Court finds are reasonably related to his rehabilitation:

☐ 11. Surrender his driver's license to the Clerk of Superior Court for transmittal to the Division of Motor Vehicles and not operate a motor vehicle for a period of _____ or until relicensed by the Division of Motor Vehicles, whichever is later.

☐ 12. Submit at reasonable times to warrantless searches by a probation officer of his person, and of his vehicle and premises while he is present, for the following purposes which are reasonably related to his probation supervision:
☐ stolen goods   ☐ controlled substances   ☐ contraband   ☐ _____

☐ 13. Not use, possess, or control any illegal drug or controlled substance unless it has been prescribed for him by a licensed physician and is in the original container with the prescription number affixed on it; not knowingly associate with any known or previously convicted users, possessors, or sellers of any illegal drugs or controlled substances; and not knowingly be present at or frequent any place where illegal drugs or controlled substances are sold, kept, or used.

☐ 14. Supply a breath, urine, and/or blood specimen for analysis of the possible presence of a prohibited drug or alcohol, when instructed by his probation officer.

☐ 15. Successfully pass the General Education Development Test (G.E.D.) during the first _____ months of the period of probation.

☐ 16. Complete _____ hours of community or reparation service during the first _____ days of the period of probation, as directed by the community service coordinator, and pay the fee prescribed by G.S. 143B-475. 1(b) ☐ pursuant to the schedule set out under monetary conditions above. ☐ within _____ days of this Judgment and before beginning service.

☐ 17. Report for initial evaluation by _____ , participate in all further evaluation, counseling, treatment, or education programs recommended as a result of that evaluation, and comply with all other therapeutic requirements of those programs until discharged.

☐ 18. Other:

☐ 19. Comply with the Additional Conditions Of Probation which are set forth on AOC-CR-302, Page Two.

☐ A hearing was held in open court in the presence of the defendant at which time a fee, including expenses, was awarded the defendant's appointed counsel or assigned public defender.

ORDER OF COMMITMENT/APPEAL ENTRIES

☐ It is ORDERED that the Clerk deliver three certified copies of this Judgment and Commitment to the Sheriff or other qualified officer, and that the officer cause the defendant to be delivered with these copies to the custody of the agency named on the reverse to serve the sentence imposed or until he shall have complied with the conditions of release pending appeal.

☐ The defendant gives notice of appeal from the judgment of the District Court to the Superior Court. The current pretrial release order shall remain in effect. ☐ except that:

☐ The defendant gives notice of appeal from the judgment of the Superior Court to the Appellate Division. Appeal entries and any conditions of post conviction release are set forth on Form AOC-CR-350.

SIGNATURE OF JUDGE

Date	Name Of Presiding Judge (Type Or Print)	Signature Of Presiding Judge

CERTIFICATION

I certify that this Judgment and the attachment(s) marked below are true copies of the originals.
☐ Judgment Suspending Sentence, Page Two [Additional Conditions Of Probation (AOC-CR-302, Page Two)]
☐ Findings Of Factors In Aggravation And Mitigation Of Punishment (AOC-CR-303)

Date Of Certification	Date Certified Copies Delivered To Sheriff	Signature And Seal
		☐ Deputy CSC ☐ Assistant CSC ☐ Clerk Of Superior Court

NOTE: *Defendant signs the following statement in all cases except unsupervised probation without community or reparation service.*
I have received a copy of this Judgment which contains all of the conditions of my probation, and I agree to them. I understand that no person who supervises me or for whom I work while performing community or reparation service is liable to me for any loss or damage which I may sustain unless my injury is caused by that person's gross negligence or intentional wrongdoing.

Date Signed	Signature Of Defendant	Witnessed By:

AOC-CR-302, Side Two, Rev. 7/95   Material opposite unmarked squares is to be disregarded as surplusage.

FIGURE 11–3 continued

Historians generally credit the Elmira Reformatory in New York as being the birthplace of parole in the United States. In this scene from the 1950s, a hopeful Elmira inmate is about to meet the state's parole board. *AP/Wide World Photos*

Special conditions may be mandated by a judge who feels that the probationary client is in need of particular guidance or control. Figure 11–3 also shows a number of special conditions that are routinely imposed upon sizable subcategories of probationers. Special condition number 11, for example, is applicable in cases of driving under the influence, while number 12 is useful in dealing with thieves, burglars, and other property offenders. The judge may also add special conditions that are tailored specifically to individual probationers. In Figure 11–3 they would be indicated under number 18—"Other." Individualized conditions may prohibit a person from associating with named others (a co-defendant, for example); they may require that the probationer be at home after dark; or they may demand that a particular treatment program be completed within a set time period.

What Is Parole?

Parole   The status of an offender conditionally released from a prison by discretion of a paroling authority prior to expiration of sentence, required to observe conditions of parole, and placed under the supervision of a parole agency.

Parole Board   A state paroling authority. Most states have parole boards (also called commissions) which decide when an incarcerated offender is ready for conditional release and which may also function as revocation hearing panels.

Parole is the supervised early release of inmates from correctional confinement. It differs from probation in both purpose and implementation. Whereas probationers generally avoid serving time in prison, offenders who are paroled have already been incarcerated. While probation is a sentencing option available to a judge who determines the form probation will take, parole, in contrast, results from an administrative decision made by a legally designated paroling authority.

States differ as to the type of parole decision-making mechanism they use, as well as the level at which it operates. Two major models prevail: (1) **Parole boards** grant parole based on their judgments and assessments. The parole board's decisions are termed *discretionary parole.* (2) Statutory decrees produce mandatory parole, with release dates usually near the completion of the inmate's prison sentence—minus time off for good behavior and other special considerations. While probation is a sentencing strategy, parole is a correctional strategy whose primary purpose is to return offenders gradually to productive lives. Parole, by making early release possible, can also act as a stimulus for positive behavioral change.

The use of parole in this country began with the Elmira Reformatory in 1876. As you may recall from Chapter 10, indeterminate sentences are a key part of a philosophy that stresses rehabilitation. The indeterminate sentence was made possible by an innovative New York law following the call of leading correctional innovators. Parole was a much-heralded tool of nineteenth-century corrections, whose advocates had been looking for a behavioral incentive to motivate youthful offenders to reform. Parole, through its promise of earned early release, seemed the ideal innovation.

Parolees comprise the smallest of the correctional categories shown in Figure 11–1 (other than "jail"). A growing reluctance to use parole seems due to the expanding realization that today's correctional routines have been generally ineffective at producing any substantial reformation among many offenders prior to their release back into the community. The abandonment of the rehabilitation goal, combined with a return to determinate sentencing in many jurisdictions—including the federal judicial system—has substantially reduced the amount of time the average correctional client spends on parole.

The Extent of Parole

Although time spent on parole is far less than it used to be, most inmates who are freed from prison are still paroled (about 75%) or are granted some other form of conditional release (about 5.5%).[20] Some states operating under determinate sentencing guidelines require that inmates serve a short period of time, such as 90 days, on reentry parole—a form of mandatory release. Mandatory releases have increased fivefold—from 6% of all releases in 1977 to over 39% today.[21] As a result, determinate sentencing schemes have changed the face of parole in America, resulting in a dramatic reduction of the average time spent under post-prison supervision, while having little impact upon the number of released inmates who experience some form of parole.

At the beginning of 1997, 704,709 people were on parole throughout the United States (see Table 11–1). States vary considerably in the use they make of parole, influenced as they are by the legislative requirements of sentencing schemes. For example, on January 1, 1997, Maine, a state which is phasing out parole, reported only 57 people under parole supervision (the lowest of all the states), and North Dakota only 104, while Texas had a parole population in excess of 112,000, and California officials were busy supervising more than 97,000 persons.

Approximately 49% of parolees successfully complete parole, while about 26% are returned to prison for parole **violations** and another 12% go back to prison for new offenses during their parole period (others may be transferred to new jurisdictions, abscond and not be caught, or die—bringing the total to 100%).[22]

Parole Conditions

In those jurisdictions which retain discretionary parole, the conditions of parole remain very similar to the conditions agreed to by probationers. Figure 11–4 shows both sides of a typical parole agreement form, which parolees must sign before their release. The general conditions of parole are listed on the back of the form and include agreements not to willfully leave the state, as well as a blanket agreement to extradition requests from other jurisdictions. Parolees must also periodically report to parole officers, and parole officers may visit parolees at their homes and places of business—often arriving unannounced.

The successful and continued employment of parolees is one of the major concerns of parole boards and their officers, and studies have found that successful employment is a major factor in reducing the likelihood of repeat offenses.[23] The importance of employment is stressed on the form in Figure 11–4, with the stricture that failure to find employment within 30 days may result in **revocation** of parole. As with probationers, working parolees can be ordered to pay fines and penalties. A provision for making **restitution** payments is included at the bottom of the first page of the agreement with the names and addresses of recipients clearly specified.

Special parole conditions have been added to the form in Figure 11–4. One of them requires the parolee to pay a "parole supervisory fee of $15" every month, a requirement now being routinely imposed in some jurisdictions (although monetary amounts may vary). A relatively new innovation, parole supervision fees shifts some of the expenses of community corrections to the offender.

Federal Parole

Federal parole decisions are made by the U.S. Parole Commission, which uses hearing examiners to visit federal prisons. Examiners typically ask inmates to describe why, in their opinion, they are ready for parole. The inmate's job readiness, home plans, past record, accom-

Probation (or Parole) Violation An act or a failure to act by a probationer (or parolee), which does not conform to the conditions of probation (or parole).

Conditions of Probation and Parole The general (state-ordered) and special (court- or board-ordered) limits imposed upon an offender who is released on either probation or parole. General conditions tend to be fixed by state statute, while special conditions are mandated by the sentencing authority and take into consideration the background of the offender and the circumstances surrounding the offense.

Probation (or Parole) Revocation The administrative action of a probation (or paroling) authority removing a person from probationary (or parole) status in response to a violation of lawfully required conditions of probation (or parole) including the prohibition against commission of a new offense and usually resulting in a return to prison.

PC -104a
10/92

STATE OF NORTH CAROLINA
PAROLE AGREEMENT BETWEEN THE NORTH CAROLINA PAROLE COMMISSION
AND

_____ , PAROLEE

In accepting this parole, I understand that the North Carolina Parole Commission may modify its terms. I also understand that I am under the legal custody of the Parole Commission until duly discharged by the Commission. I understand that should I violate parole, the Commission may cause me to be returned to custody for further action as provided by law. I understand that my term of parole shall be for no less than either (1) the remainder of the maximum term if the maximum term is less than one year, or (2) one year if the remainder of the maximum term is one year or more. I understand that I shall receive no credit for time spent on parole against the remainder of my sentence, and that in the event my parole is revoked I will be reimprisoned for the unserved portion of the maximum term of imprisonment imposed by the court. I understand that in the event of an alleged violation of parole, my parole time may be frozen at the time of the alleged violation. If my parole time is frozen, it may remain frozen until such time as the alleged violations are disposed of, even if it becomes necessary to extend my release date beyond its normal period. I further understand that if I abide by the terms and conditions of this parole, the Parole Commission will unconditionally discharge me no later than my maximum release date. In accepting this parole, I agree to abide by the following rules:

1. I will report promptly to my Probation/Parole Officer when instructed to do so, and in the manner prescribed by my Probation/Parole Officer and the Parole Commission.
2. I will work steadily at an approved job, and not change my job or my residence without permission from my Probation/Parole Officer. If I am discharged from my job or evicted from my home, I will notify my Probation/Parole Officer. I will also support any persons dependent on me to the best of my ability.
3. I will obey all municipal, county, and state and federal laws, ordinances, and orders. If I am arrested or receive a citation to appear in court while on parole, I will report this fact to my Probation/Parole Officer within 24 hours of such arrest or citation.
4. I will not leave my county of residence without obtaining permission from my Probation/Parole Officer. I will not leave the State of North Carolina without permission from the Parole Commission or my Probation/Parole Officer.
5. I will not consume alcoholic beverages to excess or use or possess drugs in violation of state and federal laws.
6. I will not own or possess any firearms or deadly weapon without written permission from the Parole Commission.
7. I will notify my Probation/Parole Officer in writing three weeks in advance of any plans to alter my marital status (marriage, separation, divorce).
8. I will allow my Probation/Parole Officer to visit my home or place of employment at any time.
9. I do hereby waive extradition to the State of North Carolina from any state of the United States and also agree that I will not contest any effort by any state to return me to the State of North Carolina.
10. I will not enter into any agreement to act as an "informer" or special agent for any law enforcement agency without permission from the Parole Commission.
11. I will not assault, or harm, or threaten to assault or harm, any person.
12. I will comply with the following Special Conditions which have been imposed by the Parole Commission:

☐ In the event (1) I do not have a plan of employment at this time, or (2) my employment plan has been found to be only temporarily suitable, I understand and agree that I must diligently seek employment which is satisfactory to the Parole Commission, and I will use my best efforts to secure the same, and will report the progress of my efforts to my Probation/Parole Officer twice weekly until satisfactory employment is obtained. I further understand and agree that if I have not obtained satisfactory employment within 30 days from today, I may be returned to prison and my parole or conditional release may be revoked, in the discretion of the Commission.

☐ I, _____ , will pay to the Department of Correction the sum

of _____ per week/month to be used to make restitution to the following named payee(s)
in the following amounts:

Name of Payee	Address	Amount to be Paid
_____	_____	_____
_____	_____	_____
_____	_____	_____

It shall be my responsibility to send my weekly/monthly payments to the Department of Correction at the following address: WORK RELEASE ACCOUNTING OFFICE, 831 West Morgan St., Raleigh, N.C. 27603.

PAYMENTS SHALL BE MADE EITHER BY CASHIER CHECK, CERTIFIED CHECK, OR POSTAL MONEY ORDER (NO PERSONAL CHECKS ACCEPTED). CHECKS SHALL BE MADE PAYABLE TO THE _DEPARTMENT OF CORRECTION_ AND INCLUDE THE NAME AND ADDRESS OF THE PAROLEE LISTED ABOVE.

GENERAL CONDITIONS

FIGURE 11–4 Parole agreement form. _Source:_ Courtesy of the North Carolina Parole Commission, and the North Carolina Department of Correction, Division of Adult Probation and Parole. Reprinted with permission.

I will accept counseling and/or treatment for drug and/or alcohol abuse at the discretion of the supervising officer.

I will not associate with known drug offenders, users, and/or pushers.

I will consent to a warrantless search of my person, premises, or any vehicle under my control by my supervising officer for any purpose reasonably related to parole supervision.

I will stay away from places where the selling and/or serving of alcohol is the primary business.

I will submit to any physical, chemical, or breathalyzer test when requested to do so by the Parole Commission, or by supervising PPO, for detection of alcohol and/or controlled substances, and pay costs thereof.

I will abide by curfew at discretion of PPO.

I will pay a parole supervision fee of $15 within 30 days after my release on parole and each month thereafter until my parole is terminated unless the Parole Commission relieves me of this obligation because of undue economic burden. I will send my parole supervision fee to the Clerk of Superior Court, Wake County, Raleigh, N.C.

I agree to:

1. Be under the Intensive Parole Supervision Program for a minimum of 6 months.

2. Obey any curfew imposed by the Parole Commission or by my Supervising Officer.

3. Submit to request for blood and urine samples for possible presence of drugs.

4. Attend and participate in counseling, treatment, or educational programs as directed by the Parole Commission or the Intensive/Parole Officer as approved by the Parole Commission, and abide by all rules, regulations, and directives of such programs.

5. Submit at reasonable times to warrantless searches by a Parole Officer of my person, vehicle, or premises while I am present for purposes which are reasonably related to parole supervision.

      I will remain at _____ School until completion of course.

      I will have no contact with _____ (co-defendant).

SPECIAL CONDITIONS—USUALLY TYPED ONTO FORM

If I violate any of the conditions or Special Conditions of parole, I may be arrested and held as a parole violator. In this event, I will be given a hearing at which time I may be represented by counsel and, if the Commission decides that I am in violation of one or more of the conditions of my parole, I may be returned to prison.

I have read or have had read to me the foregoing conditions of my parole. I fully understand them and will strictly follow them, and I understand and know what I am doing. No promises or threats have been made to me, and no pressure of any kind has been used against me at the time of signing this Parole Agreement.

DATE SIGNED _____   _____

DATE WITNESS _____   _____

DATE WITNESS _____   _____

NOTE TO CONVICTED FELONS: *The possession of a firearm by a convicted felon is a violation of both federal and state law. Also, the act of registering or voting is punishable by law until such time as these rights are restored.

PROVISION FOR PARTIAL "CIVIL DEATH"

FIGURE 11–4 continued

plishments while in prison, good behavior, and previous experiences on probation or parole form the basis for a report made by the examiners to the **parole commission**. The 1984 Comprehensive Crime Control Act, which mandated federal fixed sentencing and abolished parole for offenses committed after November 1, 1978, began a planned phase-out of the U.S. Parole Commission. Under the act, the Commission was to be abolished by 1992. The Parole Commission Phaseout Act of 1996,[24] however, extended the continued existence of the commission until 2002. Under the law, the U.S. Attorney General must annually certify to Congress that continuation of the commission is the most effective and cost-efficient method for carrying out the functions assigned to it, or they will have to propose to Congress an alternative plan for a transfer of those functions.

Probation and Parole: The Pluses and Minuses

Advantages of Probation and Parole

Restitution A court requirement that an alleged or convicted offender pay money or provide services to the victim of the crime or provide services to the community.

Probation is used to meet the needs of offenders who require some correctional supervision short of imprisonment, while at the same time providing a reasonable degree of security to the community. Parole fulfills a similar purpose for offenders released from prison. Both probation and parole provide a number of advantages over imprisonment, including

1. *Lower Cost.* Imprisonment is expensive. One study found that incarcerating a single offender in Georgia costs approximately $7,760 per year while the cost of intensive probation is as little as $985 per probationer.[25] The expense of imprisonment in some other states may be nearly three times as high as it is in Georgia. Not only do probation and parole save money, they may even help fill the public coffers. Some jurisdictions require that offenders pay a portion of the costs associated with their own supervision. Georgia, for example, charges clients between $10 and $50 per month while they are being supervised,[26] while Texas, in an innovative program which uses market-type incentives to encourage probation officers to collect fees,[27] has been able to annually recoup monies totaling more than half of the total that the state spends on probation services.

2. *Increased Employment.* Few people in prison have the opportunity to work. Work release programs, correctional industries, and inmate labor programs operate in most states, but they usually provide only low-paying jobs and require few skills. At best, such programs include only a small portion of the inmates in any given facility. Probation and parole, on the other hand, make it possible for offenders under correctional supervision to work full time at jobs in the "free" economy. They can contribute to their own and their families' support, stimulate the local economy by spending their wages, and support government through the taxes they pay.

3. *Restitution.* Offenders who are able to work are candidates for court-ordered restitution. Society's interest in restitution (sometimes called "making the victim whole again") may be better served by a probationary sentence or parole than by imprisonment. Restitution payments to victims may help restore their standard of living and personal confidence while teaching the offender responsibility.

4. *Community Support.* The decision to release a prisoner on parole, or to sentence a convicted offender to a probationary term, is often partially based upon considerations of family and other social ties. Such decisions are made in the belief that offenders will be more subject to control in the community if they participate in a web of positive social relationships. An advantage of both probation and parole is that it allows the offender to continue personal and social relationships. Probation avoids splitting up families, while parole may reunite family members separated from each other by time in prison.

5. *Reduced Risk of Criminal Socialization.* Prison has been called a "school in crime." Probation insulates adjudicated offenders, at least to some degree, from the kinds of criminal values which permeate prison. Parole, by virtue of the fact that it follows time served in prison, is less successful than probation in reducing the risk of criminal socialization.

6. *Increased Use of Community Services.* Probationers and parolees can take advantage of services offered through the community, including psychological therapy, substance abuse counseling, financial services, support groups, church outreach programs, and social services. While a few similar opportunities may be available in prison, the community environment itself can enhance the effectiveness of treatment programs by reducing the stigmatization of the offender and allowing the offender to participate in a more "normal" environment.

7. *Increased Opportunity for Rehabilitation.* Probation and parole can both be useful behavioral management tools. They reward cooperative offenders with freedom and allow for the opportunity to shape the behavior of offenders who may be difficult to reach through other programs.

Disadvantages of Probation and Parole

Any honest appraisal of probation and parole must recognize that they share a number of strategic drawbacks, such as

1. *A Relative Lack of Punishment.* The "just deserts" model of criminal sentencing insists that punishment should be a central theme of the justice process. While rehabilitation and treatment are recognized as worthwhile goals, the model suggests that punishment serves both society's need for protection and the victim's need for revenge. Probation, however, is seen as practically no punishment at all and is coming under increasing criticism as a sentencing strategy. Parole is likewise accused of unhinging the scales of justice because (1) it releases some offenders early, even when they have been convicted of serious crimes, while other, relatively minor offenders, may remain in prison, and (2) it is dishonest because it does not require completion of the offender's entire sentence behind bars.

2. *Increased Risk to the Community.* Probation and parole are strategies designed to deal with convicted *criminal* offenders. The release into the community of such offenders increases the risk that they will commit additional offenses. Community supervision can never be so complete as to eliminate such a possibility entirely, and studies on parole have pointed to the fact that an accurate assessment of offender dangerousness is beyond our present capability.[28]

   A 1992 Bureau of Justice Statistics study[29]—the nation's largest ever follow-up survey of felons on probation—found that 43% of probationers were rearrested for a felony within three years of receiving a probationary sentence, and while still on probation. Half of the arrests were for a violent crime or a drug offense. An even greater percentage of probationers, 46%, were either sent to prison or jail or had absconded.

3. *Increased Social Costs.* Some offenders placed on probation and parole will effectively and responsibly discharge their obligations. Others, however, will become social liabilities. In addition to the increased risk of new crimes, probation and parole increase the chance that added expenses will accrue to the community in the form of child support, welfare costs, housing expenses, legal aid, indigent health care, and the like.

The Legal Environment

Nine especially significant Supreme Court decisions provide a legal framework for probation and parole supervision. Among recent cases, that of *Griffin* v. *Wisconsin* (1987)[30] may be the most significant. In *Griffin*, the U.S. Supreme Court ruled that probation officers may conduct searches of a probationer's residence without the need for either a search warrant or probable cause. According to the Court, "[a] probationer's home, like anyone else's, is protected by the Fourth Amendment's requirement that searches be 'reasonable.'" However, "[a] State's operation of a probation system…presents 'special needs' beyond normal law enforcement that may justify departures from the usual warrant and probable cause requirements." Probation, the Court concluded, is similar to imprisonment because it is a "form of criminal sanction imposed upon an offender after a determination of guilt."

Other court cases focus on the conduct of parole or probation **revocation hearings**. Revocation is a common procedure. Annually, about 22% of adults on parole and 7.5% of

Revocation Hearing A hearing held before a legally constituted hearing body (such as a parole board) in order to determine whether or not a probationer or parolee has violated the conditions and requirements of his or her probation or parole.

those on probation throughout the United States have their conditional release revoked.[31] Revocation of probation or parole may be requested by the supervising officer if a client has allegedly violated the conditions of community release or has committed a new crime. The most frequent violations for which revocation occurs are (1) failure to report as required to a probation or parole office, (2) failure to participate in a stipulated treatment program, and (3) alcohol or drug abuse while under supervision.[32] Revocation hearings may result in an order that a probationer's suspended sentence be made "active" or that a parolee return to prison to complete his or her sentence in confinement.

In a 1935 decision (*Escoe* v. *Zerbst*)[33] which has since been greatly modified, the Supreme Court held that probation "comes as an act of grace to one convicted of a crime…" and that the revocation of probation without hearing or notice to the probationer was acceptable practice. By 1967, however, the case of *Mempa* v. *Rhay*[34] found the Warren court changing direction as it declared that both notice and a hearing were required. It also said that the probationer should have the opportunity for representation by counsel before a deferred prison sentence could be imposed.[35] Jerry Mempa had been convicted of riding in a stolen car at age 17 in 1959 and sentenced to prison, but his sentence was deferred and he was placed on probation. A few months later he was accused of burglary. A hearing was held, and Mempa admitted his involvement in the burglary. An active prison sentence was then imposed. At the hearing Mempa had not been offered the chance to have a lawyer represent him nor was he given the chance to present any evidence or testimony in his own defense.

Two of the most widely cited cases affecting parolees and probationers are *Morrissey* v. *Brewer* (1972)[36] and *Gagnon* v. *Scarpelli* (1973).[37] In *Morrissey*, the Court declared a need for procedural safeguards in revocation hearings involving *parolees*. After *Morrissey*, revocation proceedings would require that (1) the parolee be given written notice specifying the alleged violation; (2) evidence of the violation be disclosed; (3) a neutral and detached body constitute the hearing authority; (4) the parolee have the chance to appear and offer a defense, including testimony, documents, and witnesses; (5) the parolee have the right to cross-examine witnesses; and (6) a written statement be provided to the parolee at the conclusion of the hearing that includes the hearing body's decision, the testimony considered, and reasons for revoking parole, if such occurs.[38]

In 1973 the Court extended the procedural safeguards of *Morrissey* to *probationers* in *Gagnon* v. *Scarpelli* (1973). John Gagnon had pleaded guilty to armed robbery in Wisconsin and was sentenced to 15 years in prison. His sentence was suspended, and the judge ordered him to serve a seven-year probationary term. One month later, and only a day after having been transferred to the supervision of the Cook County, Illinois, Adult Probation Department, Gagnon was arrested by police in the course of a burglary. He was advised of his rights but confessed to officers that he was in the process of stealing money and property when discovered. His probation was revoked without a hearing. Citing its own decision a year earlier in *Morrissey* v. *Brewer*, the Supreme Court ruled that probationers, because they face a substantial loss of liberty, were entitled to two hearings—the first, a preliminary hearing, to determine whether there is "probable cause to believe that he has committed a violation of his parole," and the second, "a somewhat more comprehensive hearing prior to the making of the final revocation decision." The Court also ruled that probation revocation hearings were to be held "under the conditions specified in *Morrissey* v. *Brewer*."

The Court also dealt with a separate question centered on Gagnon's indigent status. While being careful to emphasize the narrowness of the particulars in this case, the Court added to the protections granted under *Morrissey* v. *Brewer*, ruling that probationers have the right to a lawyer, even if indigent, provided they claimed that either (1) they had not committed the alleged violation or (2) they had substantial mitigating evidence to explain their violation. In *Gagnon* and later cases, however, the Court reasserted that probation and parole revocation hearings were not a stage in the criminal prosecution process, but a simple adjunct to it, even though they might result in substantial loss of liberty. The difference is a crucial one, for it permits hearing boards and judicial review officers to function, at least to some degree, outside of the adversarial context of the trial court and with lessened attention to the rights of the criminally accused guaranteed by the Bill of Rights.

In 1997, the U.S. Supreme Court extended the rationale found in *Morrissey* and *Gagnon* to inmates set free from prison under early release programs. In a unanimous decision, the Court held that "an inmate who has been released under a program to relieve prison crowding cannot be reincarcerated without getting a chance to show at a hearing that he has met the conditions of the program and is entitled to remain free."[39] The case involved former Oklahoma inmate Ernest E. Harper, who had been released in 1990 after serving 15 years in Oklahoma prisons for murder. The program under which Harper had been set free was governed by a formula requiring the release of a certain number of inmates as the state's prison system approached capacity. Months after being released, Harper received a call from his parole officer at 5:30 A.M. telling him to report back to prison by ten o'clock that morning. Although Harper had been living according to the rules of the program under which he had been released, state officials argued that he was still a prisoner and said that they were only changing the conditions of his confinement by "recalling" him to an institution. The Supreme Court, however, disagreed, finding that Harper's release from prison was akin to parole—and that it "differed from parole in name alone." As in other situations, said the Court, inmates have a right to challenge, in a formal proceeding, any "grievous loss of liberty" under the Fourteenth Amendment's due process guarantee.

Years ago, but in a related area, the case of *Greenholtz* v. *Nebraska* (1979)[40] established that parole boards do not have to specify the evidence used in deciding to deny parole. The *Greenholtz* case focused on a Nebraska statute which required that inmates denied parole be provided with reasons for the denial. The Court held that reasons for parole denial might be provided in the interest of helping inmates prepare themselves for future review but that to require the disclosure of evidence used in the review hearing would turn the process into an adversarial proceeding.

The 1983 Supreme Court case of *Bearden* v. *Georgia*[41] established that probation could not be revoked for failure to pay a fine and make restitution if it could not be shown that the defendant was responsible for the failure. The Court also held that alternative forms of punishment must be considered by the hearing authority and be shown to be inadequate before the defendant can be incarcerated. Bearden had pleaded guilty to burglary and had been sentenced to three years probation. One of the conditions of his probation required that he pay a fine of $250 and make restitution payments totaling $500. Bearden successfully made the first two payments but then lost his job. His probation was revoked, and he was imprisoned. The Supreme Court decision stated that "If the State determines a fine or restitution to be the appropriate and adequate penalty for the crime, it may not thereafter imprison a person solely because he lacked the resources to pay it."[42] The Court held that if a defendant lacks the capacity to pay a fine or make restitution, then the hearing authority must consider any viable alternatives to incarceration prior to imposing a term of imprisonment.

In another ruling affecting restitution, *Kelly* v. *Robinson* (1986),[43] the Court held that a restitution order cannot be vacated by a filing of bankruptcy. In the *Kelly* case, a woman convicted of illegally receiving welfare benefits was ordered to make restitution in the amount of $100 per month. Immediately following the sentence, the defendant filed for bankruptcy and listed the court-ordered restitution payment as a debt from which she sought relief. The bankruptcy court discharged the debt, and a series of appeals found the U.S. Supreme Court ruling that fines and other financial penalties ordered by criminal courts are not capable of being voided by bankruptcy proceedings.

A probationer's incriminating statements to a probation officer may be used as evidence if the probationer did not specifically claim a right against self-incrimination, according to *Minnesota* v. *Murphy* (1984).[44] Marshall Murphy was sentenced to three years probation in 1980 on a charge of "false imprisonment" (kidnapping) stemming from an alleged attempted sexual attack. One condition of his probation required him to be entirely truthful with his probation officer "in all matters." Some time later Murphy admitted to his probation officer that he had confessed to a rape and murder in conversations with a counselor. He was later convicted of first-degree murder, partially on the basis of the statements made to his probation officer. Upon appeal, Murphy's lawyers claimed that their client should have been advised of his right against self-incrimination during his conversation with the probation officer. Although the Minnesota Supreme Court agreed, the U.S. Supreme Court found for the state, saying that the burden of invoking the Fifth Amendment privilege against self-incrimination in this case lay with the probationer.

An emerging legal issue today surrounds the potential liability of probation officers and parole boards and their representatives for the criminal actions of offenders they supervise or whom they have released. Some courts have held that officers are generally immune from

The abolition of parole has been tried and has failed on a spectacular scale... The absence of parole means that offenders simply walk out the door of prison at the end of a predetermined period of time, no questions asked.

—Report by the American Probation and Parole Association and the Association of Paroling Authorities International

suit because they are performing a judicial function on behalf of the state.[45] Other courts, however, have indicated that parole board members who do not carefully consider mandated criteria for judging parole eligibility could be liable for injurious actions committed by parolees.[46] In general, however, most experts agree that parole board members cannot be successfully sued unless release decisions are made in a grossly negligent or wantonly reckless manner.[47] Discretionary decisions of individual probation and parole officers which result in harm to members of the public, however, may be more actionable under civil law, especially where their decisions were not reviewed by judicial authority.[48]

In 1995, for example, Pennsylvania state officials faced the possibility of lawsuits resulting from the release of Robert "Mudman" Simon by parole board officials. "Mudman," a member of the Warlocks motorcycle gang, had been imprisoned for the murder of 19-year-old Beth Smith Dusenberg, who was shot in the face after she refused to let gang members rape her.[49] His release on parole after serving 12 years on a 10- to 20-year sentence was approved by former Pennsylvania Board of Probation and Parole member Mary Ann Stewart and parole board chairman Allen Castor, even though the sentencing judge recommended that "Mudman" not be released; a psychiatrist wrote that "he was a sociopath, lacking in remorse, and prone to kill again."[50] Three months after he was set free, "Mudman" allegedly killed New Jersey policeman Ippolito "Lee" Gonzalez, shooting the officer twice in the face at point-blank range after a routine traffic stop. As hearings in the case progressed, the Pennsylvania legislature introduced a bill which in the future would require three parole board members to approve the release of any violent inmate and would give the sentencing judge in the case the power to veto any decision by the board.[51]

...probation and parole services are characteristically poorly staffed and often poorly administered.

—President's Commission on Law Enforcement and Administration of Justice

The Federal Probation System

The Federal Probation System is just over 70 years old.[52] In 1916 the U.S. Supreme Court, in the *Killets* case[53] ruled that federal judges did not have the authority to suspend sentences and order probation. After a vigorous campaign by the National Probation Association, Congress finally passed the National Probation Act in 1925, authorizing the use of probation in federal courts. The bill came just in time to save a burgeoning federal prison system from serious overcrowding. The Mann Act, prohibition legislation, and the growth of organized crime had all led to increased arrests and a dramatic growth in the number of federal probationers in the early years of the system.

Although the 1925 act authorized one probation officer per federal judge, it allocated only $25,000 for officers' salaries. As a consequence, only eight officers were hired to serve 132 judges, and the system came to rely heavily upon voluntary probation officers. Some sources indicate that as many as 40,000 probationers were under the supervision of volunteers at the peak of the system.[54] By 1930, however, Congress provided adequate funding, and a corps of salaried professionals began to provide probation services to the U.S. courts.

In recent years the work of federal probation officers has been dramatically affected by new rules of federal procedure. Presentence investigations have been especially affected. Revised Rule 32 of the *Federal Rules of Criminal Procedure*, for example, now mandates that federal probation officers who prepare presentence reports must[55]

- Evaluate the evidence in support of facts.
- Resolve certain disputes between the prosecutor and defense attorney.
- Testify when needed to provide evidence in support of the administrative application of sentencing guidelines.
- Utilize an addendum to the report which, among other things, demonstrates that the report has been disclosed to the defense attorney, defendant, and government counsel.

Some authors have argued that these new requirements demand previously unprecedented skills from probation officers. Officers must now be capable of drawing objective conclusions based upon the facts they observe, and they must be able to make "independent judgments in the body of the report regarding which sets of facts by various observers the court should rely upon in imposing sentence."[56] They must also be effective witnesses in court during the trial phase of criminal proceedings. While in the past officers have often been called upon to provide testimony during revocation hearings, the informational role now mandated throughout the trial itself is relatively new.

The Job of a Probation/Parole Officer

Correctional personnel involved in probation/parole supervision totaled 43,198 (including approximately 2,500 federal officers) throughout the United States in 1996 according to the American Correctional Association (ACA).[57] Some 15,352 of these officers supervised probationers only, while 13,833 supervised both probationers and parolees.

The tasks performed by probation and parole officers are often quite similar. Some jurisdictions combine the roles of both into one job. This section describes the duties of probation and parole officers, whether separate or performed by the same individuals. Probation/parole work consists primarily of four functions: (1) presentence investigations, (2) intake procedures, (3) needs assessment and diagnosis, and (4) the supervision of clients.

Where probation is a possibility, intake procedures may include presentence investigations, as described in Chapter 10, which examine the offender's background in order to provide the sentencing judge with facts needed to make an informed sentencing decision. Intake procedures may also involve a dispute settlement process during which the probation officer works with the defendant and victim to resolve the complaint prior to sentencing. Intake duties tend to be more common among juvenile probation officers than they are in adult criminal court, but all officers may find themselves in the position of having to recommend to the judge what sentencing alternative would best answer the needs of the case.

Diagnosis refers to the psychological inventorying of the probation/parole client and may be done on either a formal basis involving the use of written tests administered by certified psychologists, or through informal arrangements, which typically depend upon the observational skills of the officer. Needs assessment, another area of officer responsibility, extends beyond the psychological needs of the client to a cataloging of the services necessary for a successful experience on probation or parole.

Evaluating Probation and Parole

A few years ago the Bureau of Justice Statistics published *Performance Measures for the Criminal Justice System*, a collection of discussion papers produced by the BJS–Princeton Project group. The papers represent the best official effort to date to identify performance goals and associated measures useful in assessing the day-to-day operations of criminal justice agencies.

The Project identified, among others, the following goals and performance indicators in the area of community corrections (including probation and parole):

Goals	Performance Indicators
1. Assess offender's suitability for placement	Accuracy and completeness of presentence investigation
	Timeliness of revocation and termination hearings
	Percentage of offenders recommended for probation and parole who violate their conditions or repeat offenses
2. Enforce court-ordered sanctions	Number of arrests and technical violations during supervision
	Percentage of ordered payments collected
	Number of hours/days of community service performed
	Number of favorable discharges
3. Protect the community	Number and type of supervision contacts
	Number and type of technical violations during supervision
4. Assist offenders to change	Number of times clients attend treatment or work programs
	Employment during supervision
	Number of arrests and/or other violations during supervision
	Number of drug-free and/or alcohol-free days during supervision
	Attitude change
5. Restore crime victims	Degree of payment of restitution
	Extent of victim satisfaction with services and department

Source: Joan Petersilia, "Measuring the Performance of Community Corrections," in John J. DiIulio, Jr., et al., *Performance Measures for the Criminal Justice System: Discussion Papers from the BJS–Princeton Project* (Washington, D.C.: Bureau of Justice Statistics, October 1993).

Supervision of sentenced probationers or released parolees is the most active stage of the probation/parole process, involving months (and sometimes years) of periodic meetings between the officer and client and an ongoing assessment of the success of the probation/parole endeavor in each individual case.

One special consideration affecting the work of all probation/parole officers is the need for confidentiality. The details of the presentence investigation, psychological tests, needs assessment, conversations between the officer and client, and so on should not be public knowledge. On the other hand, courts have generally held that communications between the officer and client are not privileged, as they might be between a doctor and patient or between a social worker and his or her client.[58] Hence, incriminating evidence related by a client can be shared by officers with appropriate authorities.

Difficulties with the Parole/Probation Officer Job

Perhaps the biggest difficulty that probation and parole officers face is their need to walk a fine line between two conflicting sets of duties—one of which is to provide quasi-social work services and the other to handle custodial responsibilities. In effect, two conflicting images

A boot camp correctional officer greets a new arrival. Shock incarceration programs—also called boot camp prisons—provide a sentencing alternative which is growing rapidly in popularity. *R. Maiman, Sygma*

of the officer's role coexist. The social work model stresses a service role for officers and views probationers and parolees as "clients." Officers are seen as "caregivers," who attempt to assess accurately the needs of their clients and, through an intimate familiarity with available community services—from job placement, indigent medical care, and family therapy, to psychological and substance abuse counseling—match clients and community resources. The social work model depicts probation/parole as a "helping profession," wherein officers assist their clients in meeting the conditions imposed upon them by their sentence.

The other model for officers is correctional. It sees probation/parole clients as "wards" whom officers are expected to control. This model emphasizes community protection, which officers are supposed to achieve through careful and close supervision. Custodial supervision means that officers will periodically visit their charges at work and at home, often arriving unannounced. It also means that they will be ready and willing to report clients for new offenses and for violations of the conditions of their release.

Most officers, by virtue of their personalities and experiences, probably identify more with one of the two models than with the other. They think of themselves either primarily as caregivers or as correctional officers. Regardless of the emphasis which appeals most to individual officers, however, demands of the job are bound to generate role conflict at one time or another.

A second problem in probation/parole work is high **caseloads**. The President's Commission on Law Enforcement and the Administration of Justice recommended that probation/parole caseloads should average around 35 clients per officer.[59] However, caseloads of 250 clients are common in some jurisdictions. Various authors have found that high caseloads, combined with limited training and time constraints forced by administrative and other demands, culminate in stopgap supervisory measures.[60] "Postcard probation," in which clients mail in a letter or card once a month to report on their whereabouts and circumstances, is an example of one stopgap measure that harried agencies with large caseloads use to keep track of their wards.[61]

Another difficulty with probation/parole work is the lack of opportunity for career mobility.[62] Probation and parole officers are generally assigned to small agencies, serving limited geographical areas, with one or two lead officers (usually called chief probation officers). Unless retirement or death claim the supervisors, there will be little chance for other officers to advance.

Caseload The number of probation or parole clients assigned to one probation or parole officer for supervision.

Intermediate Sanctions (also called **Alternative Sanctions**)   The use of split sentencing, shock probation and parole, home confinement, shock incarceration, and community service in lieu of other, more traditional, sanctions, such as imprisonment and fines.

Intermediate Sanctions

In 1996, 32-year-old Sia Ye Vang, a Hmong tribesman and Vietnamese immigrant living in La Crosse, Wisconsin, was convicted of sexually molesting his young stepdaughters, aged 10 and 11. Judge Ramona Gonzalez, apparently influenced by defense arguments that sex with girls is accepted practice in Vietnam, sentenced Vang to 24 years probation and ordered him to continue English classes and perform 1,000 hours of community service. The judge decided to allow Vang "the opportunity to continue his education, and his assimilation into our culture."[63] Vang could have received 80 years in prison.

Although Vang's case may be an extreme example, it illustrates the fact that significant new sentencing options have become available to judges in innovative jurisdictions over the past few decades. Many such options are called "intermediate sanctions" because they employ sentencing alternatives which fall somewhere between outright imprisonment and simple probationary release back into the community. They are also sometimes termed "alternative sentencing strategies." Michael J. Russell, former director of the National Institute of Justice, says that "intermediate punishments are intended to provide prosecutors, judges, and corrections officials with sentencing options that permit them to apply appropriate punishments to convicted offenders while not being constrained by the traditional choice between prison and probation. Rather than substituting for prison or probation, however, these sanctions—which include intensive supervision, house arrest with electronic monitoring, and shock incarceration—bridge the gap between those options and provide innovative ways to ensure swift and certain punishment."[64]

A number of citizen groups and special interest organizations are working to widen the use of sentencing alternatives. One organization of special note is the Washington, D.C.-based Sentencing Project. The Sentencing Project was formed in 1986[65] through support from foundation grants.[66] The Project is dedicated to promoting a greater use of alternatives to incarceration and provides technical assistance to public defenders, court officials, and other community organizations.

The Sentencing Project and other groups like it have contributed to the development of over 100 locally based alternative sentencing service programs. Most alternative sentencing services work in conjunction with defense attorneys to develop written sentencing plans. Such plans are basically well-considered citizen suggestions as to what appropriate sentencing in a given instance might entail. Plans are often quite detailed and may include letters of support from employers, family members, the defendant, and even victims. Sentencing plans may be used in plea bargaining sessions or presented to judges following trial and conviction. A decade ago, for example, lawyers for country and western singer Willie Nelson successfully proposed an alternative option to tax court officials, which allowed the singer to pay huge past tax liabilities by performing in concerts for that purpose. Lacking such an alternative, the tax court might have seized Nelson's property or even ordered the singer confined to a federal facility.

The basic philosophy behind intermediate sanctions is this: When judges can be offered well-planned alternatives to imprisonment, the likelihood of a prison sentence can be reduced. An analysis of alternative sentencing plans such as those sponsored by the Sentencing Project show that they are accepted by judges in up to 80% of the cases in which they are recommended, and that as many as two-thirds of offenders who receive alternative sentences successfully complete them.[67]

Intermediate, or alternative, sanctions have three distinct advantages:[68] (1) They are less expensive to operate on a per offender basis than imprisonment; (2) they are "socially cost effective," because they keep the offender in the community, thus avoiding both the breakup of the family and the stigmatization which accompanies imprisonment; and (3) they provide flexibility in terms of resources, time of involvement, and place of service. Some of these new options are described in the paragraphs that follow.

Split Sentencing

Split Sentence   A sentence explicitly requiring the convicted person to serve a period of confinement in a local, state, or federal facility followed by a period of probation.

In jurisdictions where **split sentencing** is an option, judges may impose a combination of a brief period of imprisonment and probation. Defendants sentenced under split sentencing are often ordered to serve time in a local jail rather than in a long-term confinement facility.

"Ninety days in jail, together with two years of supervised probation," would be a typical split sentence. Split sentences are frequently used with minor drug offenders and serve notice that continued law violations may result in imprisonment for much longer periods.

SHOCK PROBATION/SHOCK PAROLE

Shock probation bears a considerable resemblance to split sentencing. Again, the offender serves a relatively short period of time in custody (usually in a prison rather than jail) and is released on probation by court order. The difference is that shock probation clients must *apply* for probationary release from confinement and cannot be certain of the judge's decision. In shock probation, the court in effect makes a resentencing decision. Probation is only a statutory possibility and often little more than a vague hope of the offender as imprisonment begins. If probationary release is ordered, it may well come as a "shock" to the offender who, facing a sudden reprieve, may forswear future criminal involvement. Shock probation was first begun in Ohio in 1965[69] and is used today in about half the United States.[70]

New Jersey runs a model modern shock probation program which is administered by a specially appointed Screening Board composed of correctional officials and members of the public. The New Jersey program has served as an example to many other states. It has a stringent set of selection criteria which allow only inmates serving sentences for nonviolent crimes to apply to the Screening Board for release.[71] Inmates must have served at least 30 days before applying. Those who have served over 60 days are ineligible. Offenders must submit a personal plan describing what they will do when released, what their problems are, what community resources they need or intend to use, and what people can be relied upon to provide assistance. Part of the plan involves a community sponsor with whom the inmate must reside for a fixed period of time (usually a few months) following release. The New Jersey program is especially strict because it does not grant outright release, but rather allows only a 90-day initial period of freedom. If the inmate successfully completes the 90-day period, continued release may be requested.

Shock probation lowers the cost of confinement, maintains community and family ties, and may be an effective rehabilitative tool.[72] Similar to shock probation is shock parole. Whereas shock probation is ordered by judicial authority, shock parole is an administrative decision made by a paroling authority. Parole boards or their representatives may order an inmate's early release, hoping that brief exposure to prison may have reoriented the offender's life in a positive direction.

Shock Probation The practice of sentencing offenders to prison, allowing them to apply for probationary release, and enacting such release in surprise fashion. Offenders who receive shock probation may not be aware of the fact that they will be released on probation and may expect to spend a much longer time behind bars.

SHOCK INCARCERATION

Shock incarceration is the newest of the alternative sanctions discussed here.[73] Shock incarceration, designed primarily for young, first offenders, utilizes military-style "boot camp" prison settings to provide a highly regimented program involving strict discipline, physical training, and hard labor. Shock incarceration programs are of short duration, lasting for only 90 to 180 days. Offenders who successfully complete these programs are generally placed under community supervision. Program "failures" may be moved into the general prison population for longer terms of confinement.

The first shock incarceration program began in Georgia in 1983.[74] Since then, other programs have opened in 28 other states, and four more states are scheduled soon to begin operating shock incarceration programs.[75] The federal government and some Canadian provinces also operate shock incarceration programs. New York's program is the largest, with a capacity for 1,390 participants, while programs in Rhode Island and Wyoming can handle only 30.[76] There are other differences among the states, as well. About half provide for voluntary entry into their shock incarceration programs. A few allow inmates to decide when and whether they want to quit. Although most states allow judges to place offenders into such programs, some delegate that authority to corrections officials. Two states, Louisiana and Texas, authorize judges and corrections personnel joint authority in the decision-making process.[77] Some states, such as Massachusetts, have begun to accept classes of female inmates into boot camp settings. The Massachusetts program, which first accepted women in 1993, requires inmates to spend nearly four months undergoing the rigors of training.

The most comprehensive study of boot camp prison programs to date examined shock incarceration programs in eight states: Florida, Georgia, Illinois, Louisiana, New York,

Shock Incarceration A sentencing option which makes use of "boot camp"-type prisons in order to impress upon convicted offenders the realities of prison life.

Via an alternative sentencing program, juvenile offenders in Bellflower, California, work with children who are physically challenged. *Bart Barthalomew, Black Star*

Oklahoma, South Carolina, and Texas. The report,[78] which was issued in 1995, found that boot camp programs are especially popular today because "they are...perceived as being tough on crime," and "have been enthusiastically embraced as a viable correctional option." The report concluded, however, that "the impact of boot camp programs on offender recidivism is at best negligible."

More limited studies, such as one which focused on shock incarceration in New York state, have found that boot camp programs save money in two ways: "first by reducing expenditures for care and custody" (since the intense programs reduce time spent in custody, and participation in them is the only way New York inmates can be released from prison before their minimum parole eligibility dates) and "second, by avoiding capital costs for new prison construction."[79] A 1995 study of Oregon's Summit boot camp program reached a similar conclusion. Although they did not study recidivism, Oregon researchers found that "the Summit boot camp program is a cost-effective means of reducing prison overcrowding by treating and releasing specially selected inmates earlier than their court-determined minimum period of incarceration."[80]

Mixed Sentencing and Community Service

Mixed Sentence One which requires that a convicted offender serve weekends (or other specified periods of time) in a confinement facility (usually a jail), while undergoing probation supervision in the community.

Mixed sentences require that offenders serve weekends in jail and receive probation supervision during the week. Other types of mixed sentencing require participation in treatment or community service programs while a person is on probation. Community service programs began in Minnesota in 1972 with the Minnesota Restitution Program,[81] which gave property offenders the opportunity to work and turn over part of their pay as restitution to their victims. Courts throughout the nation quickly adopted the idea and began to build restitution orders into suspended-sentence agreements.

Community Service A sentencing alternative which requires offenders to spend at least part of their time working for a community agency.

Community service is more an adjunct to, rather than a type of, correctional sentence. Community service is compatible with most other forms of innovation in probation and parole, except, perhaps for home confinement (discussed on the following page). Even there, however, offenders could be sentenced to community service activities which might be performed in the home or at a job site during the hours they are permitted to be away from their homes. Washing police cars, cleaning school buses, refurbishing public facilities, and assisting in local government offices are typical forms of community service. Some authors have linked the development of community service sentences to the notion that work and service to others are good for the spirit.[82] Community service participants are usually minor criminals, drunk drivers, and youthful offenders.

One problem with community service sentences is that authorities rarely agree on what they are supposed to accomplish. Most people admit that offenders who work in the community are able to reduce the costs of their own supervision. There is little agreement, however, over whether such sentences reduce recidivism, provide a deterrent, or act to rehabilitate offenders.

INTENSIVE SUPERVISION

Intensive probation supervision (IPS), first implemented by Georgia in 1982, has been described as the "strictest form of probation for adults in the United States."[83] The Georgia program involves a minimum of five face-to-face contacts between the probationer and supervising officer per week, mandatory curfew, required employment, a weekly check of local arrest records, routine and unannounced alcohol and drug testing, 132 hours of community service, and automatic notification of probation officers via the State Crime Information Network whenever an IPS client is arrested.[84] Caseloads of probation officers involved in IPS are much lower than the national average. Georgia officers work as a team with one probation officer and two surveillance officers supervising about 40 probationers.[85] IPS is designed to achieve control in a community setting over offenders who would otherwise have gone to prison.

North Carolina's Intensive Supervision Program follows the model of the Georgia program and adds a mandatory "prison awareness visit" within the first three months of supervision. North Carolina selects candidates for the Intensive Supervision Program on the basis of six factors: (1) the level of risk the offender is deemed to represent to the community; (2) assessment of the candidate's potential to respond to the program; (3) existing community attitudes toward the offender; (4) the nature and extent of known substance abuse; (5) the presence or absence of favorable community conditions, such as positive family ties, the possibility of continuing meaningful employment, constructive leisure-time activities, and adequate residence; and (6) the availability of community resources relevant to the needs of the case (such as drug treatment services, mental health programs, vocational training facilities, and volunteer services).[86] Some states have extended intensive supervision to parolees, allowing the early release of some who would otherwise serve lengthy prison terms.

HOME CONFINEMENT AND ELECTRONIC MONITORING

Home confinement, also referred to as house arrest, has been defined as "a sentence imposed by the court in which offenders are legally ordered to remain confined in their own residences."[87] They may leave only to attend to medical emergencies, go to their jobs, or buy household essentials. House arrest has been cited as offering a valuable alternative to prison for offenders with special needs. Pregnant women, geriatric convicts, offenders with special handicaps, seriously or terminally ill offenders, and the mentally retarded might all be better supervised through home confinement than traditional incarceration.

Florida's Community Control Program, authorized by the state's Correctional Reform Act of 1983, is the most ambitious home confinement program in the country.[88] On any given day in Florida, as many as 5,000 offenders are restricted to their homes and supervised by community control officers who visit unannounced. Candidates for the program are required to agree to specific conditions, including (1) restitution, (2) family support payments, and (3) supervisory fees (around $50 per month). They are also obligated to fill out daily logs about their activities. Community control officers have a minimum of 20 contacts per month with each offender. Additional discussions are held by the officer with neighbors, spouses, friends, landlords, employers, and others in order to allow the earliest possible detection of program violations or renewed criminality.

Florida's most serious home confinement offenders are monitored via a computerized system of *electronic bracelets*. Random telephone calls require the offender to insert a computer chip worn in a wrist band into a specially installed modem in the home, verifying his or her presence. More modern units make it possible to record the time a supervised person enters or leaves the home and whether the phone line or equipment has been tampered with,

Intensive Supervision A form of probation supervision involving frequent face-to-face contacts between the probationary client and probation officers.

Home Confinement House arrest. Individuals ordered confined to their homes are sometimes monitored electronically to be sure they do not leave during the hours of confinement (absence from the home during working hours is often permitted).

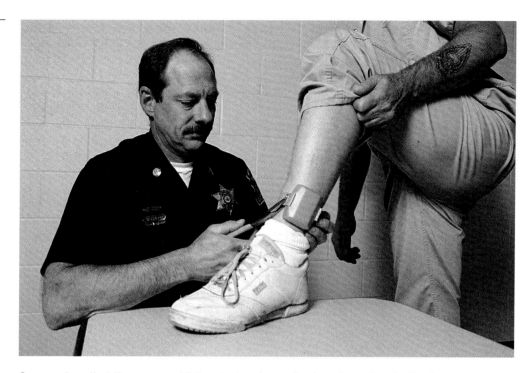

Commonly called "house arrest," the electronic monitoring of convicted offenders appears to have the capacity to dramatically reduce correctional costs for nondangerous offenders. This photograph demonstrates the use of an electronic "ankle bracelet," capable of answering a computer's call to verify that the wearer is at home. *Larry Downing, Sygma*

and to send or receive messages.[89] Electronic monitoring of offenders has undergone dramatic growth both in Florida and across the nation. A survey by the National Institute of Justice,[90] as the use of electronic monitoring was just beginning, showed only 826 offenders being monitored electronically in mid-1987. By 1989, only two years later, the number had jumped to around 6,500, while by the end of 1997 it stood at 21,375.[91] Of these, 15,373 were serving probationary sentences, and 6,002 were parolees.

In 1997 Florida lawmakers introduced legislation that would let the state's probation officers use satellites to track felons recently freed from state prisons. The satellite-tracking plan, still pending passage by the entire state senate as of this writing, would allow probation officers to keep track of every move made by convicts wearing electronic ankle bracelets.[92] If approved, Florida's satellite-tracking electronic supervision plan would be the first such program in the country.

Many states view house arrest as a cost-effective response to the rising expense of imprisonment. Estimates show that traditional home confinement programs cost about $1,500 to $7,000 per offender per year, while electronic monitoring increases the costs by at least $1,000.[93] Advocates of house arrest argue that it is also socially cost-effective,[94] as it provides no opportunity for the kinds of negative socialization which occur in prison. Opponents have pointed out that house arrest may endanger the public, that it may be illegal,[95] and that it may provide little or no punishment. Some years ago, for example, John Zaccaro, Jr., the son of former vice-presidential candidate Geraldine Ferraro, was sentenced to four months of house arrest for selling cocaine. His $1,500-a-month luxury apartment, with maid service, cable TV, and many other expensive amenities, was in a building designed for expense account businesspeople on short assignments to the Burlington, Vermont, area. Zaccaro's prosecutor observed, "This guy is a drug felon and he's living in conditions that 99.9% of the people of Vermont couldn't afford."[96]

Individualized Innovations

In an ever-growing number of cases, innovative judges have begun to use the wide discretion in sentencing available to them under the law of certain jurisdictions to impose truly unique punishments. In Memphis, Tennessee, for example, Judge Joe Brown recently began escorting burglary victims to thieves' homes, inviting them to take whatever they wanted.[97] An Arkansas judge made shoplifters walk in front of the stores they stole from, carrying signs describing their crimes. At least one Florida court began ordering those convicted of drunk driving to put a "Convicted DUI" sticker on their license plates. Similarly, two years ago, Thomas Jache, a Manchester, New Hampshire, child molester who admitted his guilt, got two years of a minimum five-year sentence suspended—but was ordered to place an advertisement in two local newspapers that included his picture, an apology, and a plea for other potential molesters to get help. In 1997, Boston courts began ordering men convicted of the crime of "sexual solicitation" to spend four hours sweeping the streets of Chinatown—an area known for prostitution. The public was invited to watch men sentenced to the city's "John Sweep" program clean up streets and alleyways littered with used condoms and sexual paraphernalia.

A common theme that carries through individualized sentencing innovations such as these is that of public shaming. The rise in shame-as-punishment harks back to "scarlet letter" days, when sentences were meant not only to punish, but also to deter wrongdoers through public humiliation. Some of today's innovative judges, faced with prison overcrowding, high incarceration costs, and public calls for retribution, have begun to employ the kinds of shaming strategies described here.

Shaming as a crime reduction strategy finds considerable support in criminal justice literature. Australian criminologist John Braithwaite,[98] for example, found shaming to be a particularly effective strategy because, he said, it holds the potential to enhance moral awareness among offenders—thereby building conscience and increasing inner control. Braithwaite distinguishes, however, between "disintegrative" (or "stigmatic") and "reintegrative" shaming. Disintegrative shaming, says Braithwaite, treats offenders like outcasts, while reintegrative shaming includes communal forgiveness and attempts to reintegrate the offender back into the community. Reintegrative shaming, which Braithwaite says is inherent in Japanese culture but not in American society, is said to be more effective at reducing recidivism. Preliminary results from a 1997 Australian study by Braithwaite and others, called the Reintegrative Shaming Experiments (RISE), appear to show that reintegrative shaming can be far more effective at producing feelings of guilt and shame in offenders than traditional criminal court processing. The RISE experiment induced feelings of shame in offenders through the use of diversionary conferencing—a technique that builds upon an intensive form of moderated interaction between victim and offender.[99]

Braithwaite is quick to point out that judges in American society are far more likely to employ disintegrative shaming techniques rather than reintegrative ones. Perhaps for that reason, critics argue that contemporary efforts at shaming by justice system officials in the United States don't work. "It's an embarrassment to the criminal justice system and all done in the guise of law and order to appease the victims,"[100] says Knoxville lawyer Jim A. H. Bell. Bell, who serves on the board of the National Association of Criminal Defense Lawyers, says "It's all done for shock value." On the other hand, Dan Kahan, a professor at the University of Chicago Law School, points out that "shame supplies the main motive why people obey the law, not so much because they're afraid of formal sanctions, but because they care what people think about them."[101]

Whether public shaming as an alternative sentencing strategy will continue to grow in popularity is unclear. What is clear, however, is that the American public and an ever-growing number of judicial officials are now looking for workable alternatives to traditional sentencing options.

QUESTIONS ABOUT ALTERNATIVE SANCTIONS

As prison populations continue to rise, alternative sentencing strategies are likely to become increasingly attractive. Many questions remain to be answered, however, before most alternative sanctions can be employed with confidence. These questions have been succinctly stated in a Rand Corporation study authored by Joan Petersilia.[102] Unfortunately, while the questions can be listed, few definitive answers are yet available. Some of the questions Petersilia poses are

- Do alternative sentencing programs threaten public safety?
- How should program participants be selected?

I understand that people want violent criminals locked up. We all do. But not every inmate is violent. We must look to supervised probation, to education. We must overcome the fear and think this out.

—Louisiana Governor Edwin Edwards

According to Australian criminologist John Braithwaite, public shaming can be a powerful tool in reshaping behavior. Here, local Afghan militiamen force a thief to undergo brutal public humiliation. The signs on the man read, "I am a thief, and this is my punishment." Braithwaite, however, would suggest more "reintegrative" and humane forms of shaming than that depicted here. *Klaus Reisiniger, Black Star*

- What are the long-term effects of community sanctions on people assigned to them?
- Are alternative sanctions cost-effective?
- Who should pay the bill for alternative sanctions?
- Who should manage stringent community-based sanctions?
- How should program outcomes be judged?
- What kind of offenders benefit most from alternative sanctions?

In order to address some of the problems raised by alternative sentencing strategies, and especially by those programs that make use of community resources and community placement, Todd R. Clear suggests reframing the idea of community corrections to include the notion of a **corrections of place**. Clear notes that although community corrections sounds much like community policing, there are important differences. "In corrections," says Clear, "the term 'community' does not stand for the problem-solving focus but instead often merely indicates that an offender happens to be living outside a correctional facility."[103] In order to develop a true corrections of place, says Clear, it is necessary to take into consideration the needs of the local community as well as the demands of the wider society for retribution, punishment, and rehabilitation. In an example from Vermont, Clear points to community boards that now assist in determining the conditions of supervision for offenders sentenced to probation and placed on parole. Suggesting that correctional officials should embrace the spirit underlying the community policing movement, Clear says that "[w]hen community members feel they can shape correctional policy by direct participation, they will also feel less estranged from the decisions made by officials, and they will feel inclined to shape their participation to be meaningful rather than antagonistic."

The Future of Probation and Parole

Parole has been widely criticized in recent years. Citizen groups claim that it unfairly reduces prison sentences imposed on serious offenders. Academicians allege that parole programs can provide no assurance that criminals will not commit further crimes. Media attacks upon parole have centered on recidivism and have highlighted the so-called "revolving prison door" as representative of the failure of parole.

Twenty-First Century Criminal Justice

CHEMICAL CASTRATION BECOMES LAW IN CALIFORNIA

In September 1996, Governor Pete Wilson signed legislation making California the first state in the nation to require regular hormone injections for convicted child molesters upon their release from prison. "Chemical castration," which went into effect in the state on January 1, 1997, requires twice-convicted child molesters to receive weekly injections of a synthetic female hormone known as Depo-Provera. The laboratory-manufactured chemical is said to lower sex drive in males. There are about 16,000 convicted child molesters in California prisons, and approximately 200 are released from custody each week. Under the law, however, judges can also mandate injections for first offenders. Treatment is to continue until state authorities determine that it is no longer necessary.

As this book goes to press, half a dozen other states are preparing simi-lar legislation. California Assembly-man Bill Hoge (R-Pasadena), the bill's author, encouraged other states to pass castration legislation. "We have now set the stage for America—and we hope you are listening America," Hoge said "We can do this all over the country. This is going to have the biggest impact on this horrible, horrible crime of any legislation ever seen."

If chemical castration survives the court challenges which are certain to come, it may establish itself in the twenty-first century as a widely used form of alternative sentencing. Opposition to the new law, however, is plentiful. Shortly after the law was signed, a spokeswoman for the American Civil Liberties Union said that the group was considering a legal challenge because the legislation sup-posedly mandates an unproven rem-edy for child molestation and is a vio-lation of civil rights. "There is no evidence, absolutely no evidence, that chemical castration will alleviate the problem," said Ann Bradley, a Los Angeles ACLU spokeswoman. "We see this as a violation of prisoners' civil liberties," she said.

Proponents of the legislation, on the other hand, cite studies in Canada and Europe where repeat offender rates of more than 80% were reduced to less than 4% among criminals treated with Depo-Provera. "I would have to say to the ACLU that there is no right to molest a child," said Governor Wilson.

Source: Dave Lesher, "Molester Castration Measure Signed: California Becomes the First State to Require That Offenders Get Periodic Injections to Suppress Sex Drive," *The Los Angeles Times*, September 18, 1996.

Some years ago, the case of Larry Singleton came to represent all that is wrong with parole. Singleton was convicted of raping 15-year-old Mary Vincent, then hacking off her forearms and leaving her for dead on a California hillside.[104] When an apparently unrepen-tant[105] Singleton was paroled after eight years in prison, public outcry was tremendous. Communities banded together to deny him residence, and he had to be paroled to the grounds of San Quentin prison until public concern lessened. Singleton's story did not end there, however. He soon moved to Florida where, in 1997, he was rearrested and charged with the murder of 31-year-old Roxanne Hayes, an alleged prostitute. Hayes' nude body was discovered in Singleton's Tampa apartment by police alerted by neighbors who heard a woman screaming. She had been stabbed many times. "It's a sad commentary on the crimi-nal justice system that a person who committed a crime this heinous was out on the street," said Tampa police spokesman Lieutenant David Gee.[106]

Official attacks upon parole have come from some powerful corners. Senator Edward Kennedy has called for the abolition of parole, as did former Attorney General Griffin Bell and former U.S. Bureau of Prisons Director Norman Carlson.[107] Prisoners have also chal-lenged the fairness of parole, saying it is sometimes arbitrarily granted and creates an undue amount of uncertainty and frustration in the lives of inmates. Parolees have complained about the unpredictable nature of the parole experience, citing their powerlessness in the parole contract. Against the pressure of official attacks and despite cases like that of Singleton, parole advocates struggle to clarify and communicate the value of parole in the correctional process.

As more and more states move toward the elimination of parole, other voices call for moderation. A 1995 report by the Center for Effective Public Policy, for example, concludes that those states which have eliminated parole "have jeopardized public safety and wasted tax

Texas has one of the tough-est parole policies in the country with the most vio-lent offenders serving 50 per-cent of their sentences in actual time and capital offenders sentenced to life serving 40 years of actual time before parole considera-tion.

—Tony Fabelo, Executive Director, Texas Criminal Justice Policy Council

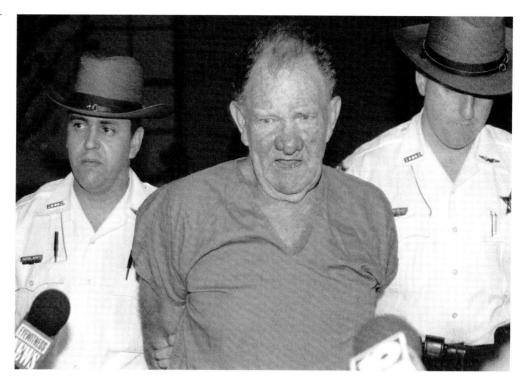

Lawrence Singleton, shown here following his 1997 arrest for the murder of a prostitute whose naked and bloody body was discovered in his Tampa apartment by police officers responding to a neighbor's call. Singleton caused a national uproar when he was paroled in California in 1986 after spending eight years in prison for the rape and mutilation of a 15-year-old girl, whose arms he cut off. *AP/Wide World Photos*

dollars." In the words of the report, "Getting rid of parole dismantles an accountable system of releasing prisoners back into the community and replaces it with a system that bases release decisions solely on whether a prison term has been completed."[108]

Probation, although it has generally fared better than parole, is not without its critics. The primary purpose of probation has always been rehabilitation. Probation is a powerful rehabilitative tool because, at least in theory, it allows the resources of a community to be focused on the offender. Unfortunately for advocates of probation, however, the rehabilitative ideal holds far less significance today than it has in the past. The contemporary demand for "just deserts" appears to have reduced the tolerance society as a whole feels for even relatively minor offenders. Also, the image of probation has not benefited from its all-too-frequent and inappropriate use with repeat or relatively serious offenders. Probation advocates themselves have been forced to admit that it is not a very powerful deterrent because it is far less punishing than a term of imprisonment. Arguments in support of probation have been weakened because some of the positive contributions probation had to offer are now being made available from other sources. Victims' compensation programs, for example, have taken the place of probationers' direct restitution payments to victims.

In an intriguing 1997 task force report on community corrections,[109] Joan Petersilia notes that the current "get-tough on criminals" attitude now sweeping the nation has resulted in increased funding for prisons, but has left stagnating budgetary allotments for probation and parole services in its wake. This result has been especially unfortunate, Petersilia says, because "[I]t has been continually shown that there is a 'highly significant statistical relationship between the extent to which probationers received needed services and the success of probation.'" "As services have dwindled," says Petersilia, "recidivism rates have climbed." Some jurisdictions, notes Petersilia, spend only a few hundred dollars per year on each probation/parole client, while successful treatment in therapeutic settings is generally acknowledged to cost nearly $15,000 per person per year. The investment of such sums in the treatment of correctional clients, argues Petersilia, is potentially worthwhile because diverting probationers and parolees from lives of continued crime will save society even more money in terms of the costs of crime and the expenses associated with eventual imprisonment.

Twenty-First Century Criminal Justice

PROBATION KIOSKS: HIGH-TECH SUPERVISION

In 1997, probation authorities in New York City began experimenting with the use of "probation kiosks" designed to lower probation officer caseloads. Fifteen electronic kiosks, similar in design to automatic teller machines, are now scattered throughout the city and allow probationers to check in with probation officers by placing their palms on a specially designed surface while answering questions presented on a flashing screen.

The kiosks identify probationers by the shape and size of their hands—which have been previously scanned into the system. Probationers are then prompted to press "yes" or "no" in response to questions such as, "Have you moved recently?" "Have you been arrested again?" "Do you need to see a probation officer?" Meetings with officers can be scheduled directly from the kiosk. Probation officers use a computer to monitor data sent from the kiosks and can zero in on individual probationers who are having problems—prompting more personal attention. By the time the system is fully operational, as many as 30,000

"low-risk" probationers—about one-third of New York City's total—will report through kiosks.

Kiosks have already yielded positive results according to NYC probation officer Genée Bogans. Before the kiosks, says Bogans, she was swamped by administrative details required to track the 250 offenders in her caseload. Kiosks allow her to track nonviolent, older offenders with a minimum of time and effort, and she now focuses most of her personal attention on the relatively few violent youths who are also part of her caseload—meeting with them and their families twice weekly in small group sessions. Bogans even goes to family funerals and graduations, making youthful offenders feel like they are getting special attention. "But it can be done only when you have 30 cases as opposed to 200," says Ms. Bogans.

New York's use of kiosks is being watched closely by other probation and parole agencies around the country as they face swelling probation caseloads and shrinking budgets. Some cities have taken other steps to automate their probation systems.

Some, like Denver and Seattle, are using 900-numbers by which probationers can report in.

Critics charge that without personal supervision probationers are more likely to reoffend—an assertion which is essentially untested. Others say kiosks are far removed from meaningful "punishment" and that offenders deserve stricter treatment. Supporters, on the other hand, say that kiosks and 900-numbers will soon become more commonplace. "New York City had no choice; it had to do something like that," says Todd Clear, associate dean of the School of Criminology at Florida State University. Clear assisted the city in restructuring its probation program. "No one wants probationers reporting to kiosks, but the alternative was even more unthinkable—a system in which nobody receives quality service," said Clear.

Source: Isabelle de Pommereau, "N.Y.C. Probation Officers To Get High-Tech Helper," *The Christian Science Monitor*, February 8, 1997, and Rice County, Minnesota, World Wide Web site.

The solution to the crisis that now exists in the probation/parole field, says Petersilia, is to "first regain the public's trust that probation and parole can be meaningful, credible sanctions." Petersilia concludes: "Once we have that in place, we need to create a public climate to support a reinvestment in community corrections. Good community corrections cost money, and we should be honest about that."

SUMMARY

Probation, simply put, is a sentence of imprisonment that is suspended. Parole, in contrast, is the conditional early release of a convicted offender from prison. Both probation and parole impose "conditions" upon defendants, requiring them to obey the law, meet with probation/parole officers, hold a job, and the like. Failure to abide by the conditions of probation or parole can result in rearrest and imprisonment.

Viewed historically, probation and parole are two of the most recent large-scale innovations in the correctional field. Both provide opportunities for the reintegration of offenders into the community through the use of resources not readily available in institutional settings. Unfortunately, however, increased freedom for criminal offenders also means some

Visit the *CJToday* Web page and click on "Web Chapters," then "Chapter 11." Follow the "find the facts" links in order to visit Vera and learn more about community corrections.

degree of increased risk for other members of society. As a consequence, contemporary "get-tough" attitudes have resulted in a lessening use of probation and parole in many jurisdictions—and an increased use of imprisonment. Until and unless probation and parole solve the problems of accurate risk assessment, reduced recidivism, and adequate supervision, they are likely to continue to be viewed with suspicion by a crime-weary public.

DISCUSSION QUESTIONS

Probation and parole have essentially shifted from legitimate correctional options in their own right to temporary diversionary strategies that we are using while we are trying to figure out how to get tough on crime, (pay) no new taxes, and not pay for any prisons at all, or to pay as little as we can, or pass it off to another generation.

—Dr. Charles M. Friel, Sam Houston State University

1. Probation is a sentence served while under supervision in the community. Do you believe that a person who commits a crime should be allowed to serve all or part of his or her sentence in the community? If so, what conditions would you impose on the offender?

2. Can you think of any other "general conditions" of probation or parole that you might add to the list of those found in the sample probation and parole forms in this chapter? If so, what would they be? Why would you want to add them?

3. Do you believe that ordering an offender to make restitution to his or her victim will teach the offender to be a more responsible person? Offer support for your opinion.

4. Do you believe that "role conflict" is a real part of most probation and parole officer's jobs? If so, do you see any way to reduce the role conflict experienced by probation and parole officers? How might you do it?

5. Do you think home confinement is a good idea? What do you think is the future of home confinement? In your opinion, does it discriminate against certain kinds of offenders? How might it be improved?

 WEB WATCH

Access the *Criminal Justice Today* site on the World Wide Web by pointing your Web browser at http://www.prenhall.com/cjtoday. Once there, click "Web Chapters" then "Chapter 11: Probation, Parole, and Community Corrections" in order to access electronic information and other sites of relevance to this chapter. You may also wish to enter the Global Town Meeting, which provides facilities for the posting of electronic messages for others to read. Messages are arranged by topic, with new topics constantly being added.

NOTES

1. As quoted in *Criminal Justice Newsletter*, January 19, 1993, p. 1.
2. James M. Byrne, *Probation, A National Institute of Justice Crime File Series Study Guide* (Washington, D.C.: U.S. Department of Justice, 1988), p. 1.
3. President's Commission on Law Enforcement and Administration of Justice, *The Challenge of Crime in a Free Society* (Washington, D.C.: U.S. Government Printing Office, 1967), p. 166.
4. Sam Howe Verhovek, "Texas Frees Child Molester Who Warned of Backsliding," *The New York Times*, April 9, 1996, p. B7.

5. "Parolee Confesses to Killing 4 Girls," *The Robesonian*, May 29, 1992, p. 1A.
6. ABC News, *Prime Time Live*, August 2, 1995.
7. *The Challenge of Crime in a Free Society.*
8. Alexander B. Smith and Louis Berlin, *Introduction to Probation and Parole* (St. Paul, MN: West, 1976), p. 75.
9. John Augustus, *John Augustus, First Probation Officer: John Augustus' Original Report on His Labors—1852* (Montclair, NJ: Patterson-Smith, 1972).
10. Smith and Berlin, *Introduction to Probation and Parole*, p. 77.

11. Ibid., p. 80.

12. George C. Killinger, Hazel B. Kerper, and Paul F. Cromwell, Jr., *Probation and Parole in the Criminal Justice System* (St. Paul, MN: West, 1976), p. 25.

13. Joan Petersilia et al., *Granting Felons Probation* (Santa Monica, CA: The Rand Corporation, 1985).

14. Bureau of Justice Statistics, "Nation's Probation and Parole Population Reached Almost 3.9 Million Last Year," BJS press release, August 14, 1997.

15. Byrne, *Probation*, p. 1.

16. Patrick A. Langan and Jodi M. Brown, *Felony Sentences in State Courts 1994* (Washington, D.C.: Bureau of Justice Statistics, 1997).

17. "Woman Gets Probation for Shooting Fiance," *The Fayetteville Observer-Times* (North Carolina), April 16, 1992, p. 9A.

18. "Nation's Probation and Parole Population Reached Almost 3.9 Million Last Year."

19. Bureau of Justice Statistics, *Correctional Populations in the United States 1995* (Washington, D.C.: Bureau of Justice Statistics, 1997).

20. Stephanie Minor-Harper and Christopher A. Innes, "Time Served in Prison and on Parole, 1984," Bureau of Justice Statistics Special Report (1987).

21. *Correctional Populations in the United States 1995*.

22. Ibid.

23. "The Effectiveness of Felony Probation: Results from an Eastern State," *Justice Quarterly* (December 1991), pp. 525–543.

24. Public Law 104–232.

25. Byrne, *Probation*.

26. Ibid., p. 3.

27. Peter Finn and Dale Parent, *Making the Offender Foot the Bill: A Texas Program* (Washington, D.C.: National Institute of Justice, 1992), and "Benefits of Probation Fees Cited in Texas Program," *Criminal Justice Newsletter* (January 19, 1993), p. 5.

28. See Andrew von Hirsch and Kathleen J. Hanrahan, *Abolish Parole?* (Washington, D.C.: Law Enforcement Assistance Administration, 1978).

29. Patrick A. Langan and Mark A. Cunniff, *Recidivism of Felons on Probation 1986–1989* (Washington, D.C.: Bureau of Justice Statistics, 1992).

30. *Griffin* v. *Wisconsin*, 483 U.S. 868, 107 S.Ct. 3164 (1987).

31. Jamie Lillis, "Twenty-two Percent of Adult Parole Cases Revoked in 1993," *Corrections Compendium*, (August 1994), pp. 7–8.

32. Ibid.

33. *Escoe* v. *Zerbst*, 295 U.S. 490 (1935).

34. *Mempa* v. *Rhay*, 389 U.S. 128 (1967).

35. A deferred sentence involves postponement of the sentencing decision, which may be made at a later time, following an automatic review of the defendant's behavior in the interim. A suspended sentence requires no review unless the probationer violates the law or conditions of probation. Both may result in imprisonment.

36. *Morrissey* v. *Brewer*, 408 U.S. 471 (1972).

37. *Gagnon* v. *Scarpelli*, 411 U.S. 778 (1973).

38. Smith and Berlin, *Introduction to Probation and Parole*, p. 143.

39. See Linda Greenhouse, *N.Y. Times* News Service, March 18, 1997 (no headline). The case is *Young* v. *Harper*, No. 95–1598 (1997).

40. *Greenholtz* v. *Inmate of Nebraska Penal and Correctional Complex*, 442 U.S. 1 (1979).

41. *Bearden* v. *Georgia*, 461 U.S. 660, 103 S.Ct. 2064, 76 L.Ed. 2d 221 (1983).

42. Ibid.

43. *Kelly* v. *Robinson*, 479 U.S. 36, 107 S.Ct. 353, 93 L. Ed. 2d 216 (1986).

44. *Minnesota* v. *Murphy*, 465 U.S. 420, 104 S.Ct. 1136, 79 L. Ed. 2d 409 (1984).

45. *Harlow* v. *Clatterbuick*, 30 CLr. 2364 (VA S.Ct. 1986); *Santangelo* v. *State*, 426 N.Y.S. 2d 931 (1980); *Welch* v. *State*, 424 N.Y.S. 2d 774 (1980); and *Thompson* v. *County of Alameda*, 614 P. 2d. 728 (1980).

46. *Tarter* v. *State of New York*, 38 CLr. 2364 (NY S.Ct. 1986); *Grimm* v. *Arizona Board of Pardons and Paroles*, 115 Arizona 260, 564 P. 2d 1227 (1977); and *Payton* v. *United States*, 636 F. 2d 132 (5th Cir.).

47. *Rolando* v. *del Carmen, Potential Liabilities of Probation and Parole Officers* (Cincinnati, OH: Anderson, 1986), p. 89.

48. See, for example, *Semler* v. *Psychiatric Institute*, 538 F. 2d 121 (4th Cir. 1976).

49. Mario F. Cattabiani, "Panel Opens Parole System Probe," *The Morning Call*, May 20, 1995, p. A6.

50. Ibid.

51. See Megan O'Matz, "System Freed 'Mudman,' Panel Hears," *The Morning Call*, June 3, 1995, p. A6, and Pamela Sampson, "Carbon Judge Testifies at 'Mudman' Hearing," *The Times News*, p. 1A.

52. This section owes much to Sanford Bates, "The Establishment and Early Years of the Federal Probation System," *Federal Probation* (June 1987), pp. 4–9.

53. *Ex parte United States*, 242 U.S. 27.

54. Bates, "The Establishment and Early Years of the Federal Probation System," p. 6.

55. As summarized by Susan Krup Grunin and Jud Watkins, "The Investigative Role of the United States Probation Officer Under Sentencing Guidelines," *Federal Probation* (December 1987), pp. 43–49.

56. Ibid., p. 46.

57. American Correctional Association, *Vital Statistics in Corrections* (Lanham, MD: ACA, 1998).

58. *Minnesota* v. *Murphy*, U.S. 104 S.Ct. 1136, 1143 (1984).

59. National Advisory Commission on Criminal Justice Standards and Goals, *Task Force Report: Corrections* (Washington,

D.C.: U.S. Government Printing Office, 1973).

60. James P. Levine, Michael C. Musheno, and Dennis J. Palumbo, *Criminal Justice in America: Law in Action* (New York: John Wiley, 1986), p. 548.

61. Ibid.

62. James A. Inciardi, *Criminal Justice*, 2nd ed. (New York: Harcourt Brace Jovanovich, 1987), p. 638.

63. "Molester Sentenced to Classes," The Associated Press, August 29, 1996.

64. From the introduction to James Austin, Michael Jones, and Melissa Bolyard, *The Growing Use of Jail Boot Camps: The Current State of the Art* (Washington, D.C.: National Institute of Justice, October 1993), p. 1.

65. Although now an independent nonprofit corporation, The Sentencing Project has its roots in a 1981 project of the National Legal Aid and Defender Association.

66. The Sentencing Project, *1989 National Directory of Felony Sentencing Services* (Washington, D.C.: The Project, 1989).

67. The Sentencing Project, *Changing the Terms of Sentencing: Defense Counsel and Alternative Sentencing Services* (Washington, D.C.: The Project, no date).

68. Joan Petersilia, *Expanding Options for Criminal Sentencing* (Santa Monica, CA: The Rand Corporation, 1987).

69. *Ohio Revised Code*, Section 2946.06.1 (July 1965).

70. Lawrence Greenfield, Bureau of Justice Statistics, *Probation and Parole 1984* (Washington, D.C.: U.S. Government Printing Office, 1986).

71. For a complete description of this program, see Petersilia, *Expanding Options for Criminal Sentencing.*

72. Harry Allen, Chris Eskridge, Edward Latessa, and Gennaro Vito, *Probation and Parole in America* (New York: The Free Press, 1985), p. 88.

73. For a good overview of such programs, see William N. Osborne, Jr., "Shock Incarceration and the Boot Camp Model: Theory and Practice," *American Jails* (July/August 1994), pp. 27–30.

74. Doris Layton MacKenzie and Deanna Bellew Ballow, "Shock Incarceration Programs in State Correctional Jurisdictions—An Update," *NIJ Reports* (May/June 1989), pp. 9–10.

75. "Shock Incarceration Marks a Decade of Expansion," *Corrections Compendium* (September 1996), pp. 10–28.

76. Ibid.

77. MacKenzie and Ballow, "Shock Incarceration Programs in State Correctional Jurisdictions."

78. National Institute of Justice, *Multisite Evaluation of Shock Incarceration* (Washington, D.C.: National Institute of Justice, 1995).

79. Cherie L. Clark, David W. Aziz, and Doris L. MacKenzie, *Shock Incarceration in New York: Focus on Treatment* (Washington, D.C.: National Institute of Justice, August 1994), p. 8.

80. "Oregon Boot Camp Is Saving the State Money, Study Finds," *Criminal Justice Newsletter* (May 1, 1995), pp. 5–6.

81. Douglas C. McDonald, "Restitution and Community Service," National Institute of Justice, *Crime File Study Guide* (1988).

82. Richard J. Maher and Henry E. Dufour, "Experimenting with Community Service: A Punitive Alternative to Imprisonment," *Federal Probation* (September 1987), pp. 22–27.

83. James P. Levine et al., *Criminal Justice in America: Law in Action* (New York: John Wiley, 1986), p. 549.

84. Billie S. Erwin and Lawrence A. Bennett, "New Dimensions in Probation: Georgia's Experience with Intensive Probation Supervision," National Institute of Justice, *Research in Brief* (1987).

85. Ibid., p. 2.

86. North Carolina Department of Correction, *Intensive Supervision Manual* (Raleigh, NC: Division of Adult Probation and Parole, 1988), pp. 3–5.

87. Joan Petersilia, "House Arrest," National Institute of Justice, *Crime File Study Guide* (1988).

88. Ibid.

89. Ibid.

90. Marc Renzema and David T. Skelton, *The Use of Electronic Monitoring by Criminal Justice Agencies 1989*, Grant Number OJP-89-M-309 (Washington, D.C.: National Institute of Justice, 1990).

91. Bureau of Justice Statistics, *Correctional Populations in the United States 1995* (Washington, D.C.: Bureau of Justice Statistics, 1997).

92. "Florida Considers Felon-Tracking Satellites," United Press International wire services, southeast edition, March, 18, 1997.

93. Petersilia, "House Arrest."

94. *BI Home Escort: Electronic Monitoring System*, advertising brochure, BI Incorporated, Boulder, Colorado (no date).

95. For additional information on the legal issues surrounding electronic home confinement, see Bonnie Berry, "Electronic Jails: A New Criminal Justice Concern," *Justice Quarterly*, Vol. 2, no. 1 (1985), pp. 1–22, and J. Robert Lilly, Richard A. Ball, and W. Robert Lotz, Jr., "Electronic Jail Revisited," *Justice Quarterly*, Vol. 3, no. 3 (September 1986), pp. 353–361.

96. "Zaccaro Serving Sentence in Luxury Apartment," *The Fayetteville Observer* (North Carolina), August 15, 1988, p. 10A.

97. Much of the information in this section is taken from Haya El Nasser, "Paying for Crime With Shame: Judges Say 'Scarlet Letter' Angle Works," *USA Today,* June 26, 1996, p. 1A.

98. John Braithwaite, *Crime, Shame, and Reintegration* (Cambridge, MA: Cambridge University Press, 1989).

99. Four papers have been released in the RISE series to date. They are: Lawrence W. Sherman and Heather Strang, *The Right Kind of Shame for Crime Prevention* (Canberra, Australia: Australian National University, 1997); Heather Strang and Lawrence W. Sherman, *The Victim's Perspective* (Canberra, Australia: Australian National University, 1997); Lawrence W. Sherman and Geoffrey C. Barnes, *Restorative Justice and Offenders' Respect for the Law* (Canberra, Australia: Australian National University, 1997); and Lawrence W. Sherman and Heather Strang, *Restorative Justice and Deterring Crime* (Canberra, Australia: Australian National University, 1997).

100. Ibid.

101. Such evidence does, in fact, exist. See, for example, Harold G. Grasmick, Robert J. Bursik, Jr., and Bruce J. Arneklev, "Reduction in Drunk Driving as a Response to Increased Threats of Shame, Embarrassment, and Legal Sanctions," *Criminology,* Vol. 31, no. 1 (1993), pp. 41–67.

102. Petersilia, "House Arrest."

103. Todd R. Clear, "Toward a Corrections of Place: The Challenge of 'Community' in Corrections," *National Institute of Justice Journal* (August 1996), pp. 52–56.

104. "A Victim's Life Sentence," *People,* April 25, 1988.

105. Ibid., p. 40.

106. Steve Morrell, "Convicted California Rapist, Mutilator, Arrested," Reuters wire services, February 20, 1997.

107. Inciardi, *Criminal Justice,* 2nd ed., p. 664.

108. The Center for Effective Public Policy, *Abolishing Parole: Why the Emperor Has No Clothes,* 1995.

109. Joan Petersilia, "A Crime Control Rationale for Reinvesting in Community Corrections," in *Critical Criminal Justice Issues: Task Force Reports From the American Society of Criminology* (Washington, D.C.: National Institute of Justice, 1997).

chapter 12
PRISONS AND JAILS

To put people behind walls and bars and do little or nothing to change them is to win a battle but lose a war. It is wrong. It is expensive. It is stupid.[1]

—FORMER CHIEF JUSTICE WARREN E. BURGER (1907–1995)

...infinite are the nine steps of a prison cell, and endless is the march of him who walks between the yellow brick wall and the red iron gate, thinking things that cannot be chained and cannot be locked...

—ARTURO GIOVANNITTI (1884–1959)

Years ago I began to recognize my kinship with all living beings....I said then, and I say now, that while there is a lower class I am in it; while there is a criminal element, I am of it; while there is a soul in prison, I am not free.

—EUGENE V. DEBS, AMERICAN SOCIALIST LEADER (1855–1926)

Early Punishments

Prison A state or federal confinement facility having custodial authority over adults sentenced to varying terms of confinement.

In the history of criminal justice, the 1990s may be remembered as the decade of imprisonment. As fear over crime grew, the concern with community protection reached a near crescendo by 1998, leading to rates of imprisonment previously unheralded. Prison populations reached the breaking point, and new facilities were being constructed everywhere. In the midst of this imprisonment frenzy, however, few took the time to reflect on the fact that the use of **prisons**, as places where convicted offenders serve time as punishment for breaking the law, is a relatively new development in the handling of offenders. In fact, the emphasis upon *time served* as the essence of criminal punishment is scarcely 200 years old.

Prior to the development of prisons, early punishments were often cruel and torturous. An example is the graphic and unsettling description of a man broken on the rack in 1721, which is provided by Camden Pelham in his *Chronicles of Crime*.[2] The offender, Nathaniel Hawes, a domestic servant in the household of a wealthy nobleman, had stolen a sheep in order to entertain a woman friend. When the "overseer" of the household discovered the offense, Hawes "shot him dead." Pelham's description of what happened next follows: "For these offences, of course, he was sentenced to be broken alive upon the rack, without the benefit of the *coup de grace*, or mercy-stroke. Informed of the dreadful sentence, he composedly laid himself down upon his back on a strong cross, on which, with his arms and legs extended, he was fastened by ropes. The executioner, having by now with a hatchet chopped off his left hand, next took up a heavy iron bar, with which, by repeated blows, he broke his bones to shivers, till the marrow, blood, and splinters flew about the field; but the prisoner never uttered a groan nor a sigh! The ropes being next unlashed, I imagined him dead…till…he writhed himself from the cross. When he fell on the grass…he rested his head on part of the timbar, and asked the by-standers for a pipe of tobacco, which was infamously answered by kicking and spitting on him. He then begged his head might be chopped off, but to no purpose." Pelham goes on to relate how the condemned man then engaged in conversation with onlookers, recounting details of his trial. At one point he asked one of those present to repay money he had loaned him, saying, "Don't you perceive, I am to be kept alive." After six hours, Pelham says, Hawes was put out of his misery by a soldier assigned to guard the proceedings. "He was knocked on the head by the…sentinel; and having been raised upon a gallows, the vultures were busy picking out the eyes of the mangled corpse, in the skull of which was clearly discernible the mark of the soldier's musket."

This gruesome tale may seem foreign to modern readers—as though it describes an event which happened in a barbarous time long ago or in a place far away. Physical punishments, often resulting in death, however, were commonplace a mere 200 years ago. Today when we think of criminal punishment, we routinely think of prisons. Because they are so commonplace, however, we tend to forget that prisons, as correctional institutions, are relatively new. Prior to the emergence of imprisonment, convicted offenders were routinely subjected to fines, physical punishment, and often death. Corporal punishments were the most common

The whipping post and pillory at New Castle, Delaware, in the early 1800s. *Courtesy of the Library of Congress*

form of criminal punishment used, and generally fit the doctrine of *lex talionis* (the law of retaliation). Under *lex talionis* the convicted offender was sentenced to suffer a punishment which most closely approximated the original injury. Also called "an eye for an eye, and a tooth for a tooth," this early rule of retaliation generally duplicated the offense, with the offender as the substitute victim. Hence, if a person blinded another, they were blinded in return. Murderers were themselves killed, with the form of execution sometimes being tailored to approximate the method they had used in committing the crime.

Lex Talionis   The law of retaliation, often expressed as "an eye for an eye," or like for like.

Flogging

Historically, the most widely used of physical punishments has been flogging.[3] The Bible mentions instances of whipping, and Christ himself was scourged. Whipping was widely used in England throughout the Middle Ages, and some offenders were said to have been beaten as they ran through streets and towns, hands tied behind their backs. American colonists carried the practice of flogging with them to the New World. The Western frontier provided the novel opportunity, quickly seized upon by settlers, of whipping convicted criminals as they were run out of town and into the hinterlands. Banishment, however, may have been little better than a death sentence, since it afforded little opportunity for the exiled offender to survive.

Whipping could be deadly. An infamous whip, the Russian knot, was fashioned out of leather thongs tipped with fishhooklike wires. A few stripes with the knot produced serious lacerations and often resulted in much blood loss. The cat-o'-nine tails, another frequently used device, was made of at least nine strands of leather or rope instead of the single strip of leather, which makes up most modern-day whips.

The last officially sanctioned flogging of a criminal offender in the United States happened in Delaware on June 16, 1952, when a burglar received 20 lashes.[4] The practice of whipping, however, is still with us. Amnesty International reports its use in various parts of the world for political and other prisoners; and in 1994 the flogging in Singapore of Michael Fay, an American teenager convicted of spray-painting parked cars, caused an international outcry from opponents of corporal punishment. The Fay flogging (called "caning" in

Singapore because it was carried out with a bamboo rod) led to a rebirth of interest in physical sanctions in this country, especially for teenagers and vandals. In 1995, following Singapore's lead, eight states[5] entertained legislation to endorse whipping or paddling as a criminal sanction. Mississippi legislators proposed paddling graffiti artists and petty thieves, Tennessee lawmakers considered punishing vandals and burglars by public caning on courthouse steps, the New Mexico Senate Judiciary Committee examined the viability of caning graffiti vandals, and Louisiana looked into the possibility of ordering parents (or a correctional officer if the parents refused) to spank their children in judicial chambers.[6] As of this writing, none of the proposals have made it into law.

Mutilation

Flogging is a painful punishment whose memory might deter repeat offenses. Mutilation, on the other hand, was primarily a strategy of specific deterrence that made it difficult or impossible for individuals to commit future crimes. Throughout history various societies have amputated the hands of thieves and robbers, blinded spies, and castrated rapists. Blasphemers have had their tongues ripped out, and pickpockets have suffered broken fingers. Extensive mutilation, which included blinding, cutting off the ears, and ripping out the tongue, was instituted in eleventh-century Britain and imposed upon hunters who poached on royal lands.[7]

Today, some countries in the Arab world, including Iran and Saudi Arabia, still rely upon a limited use of mutilation as a penalty, which incapacitates selected offenders. Mutilation also creates a general deterrent by providing potential offenders with walking examples of the consequences of crime.

Branding

In some societies branding has been used as a lesser form of mutilation. Prior to modern technology and the advent of mechanized record keeping, branding served to readily identify convicted offenders and to warn others with whom they might come into contact of their dangerous potential.

The Romans, Greeks, French, British, and many other societies have all used branding at one time or another. It was not until 1829 that the British Parliament officially eliminated branding as a punishment for crime, although the practice had probably ended somewhat earlier.

Barnes and Teeters, early writers on the history of the criminal justice system, report that branding in the American colonies was customary for certain crimes, with first offenders being branded on the hand and repeat offenders receiving an identifying mark on the forehead.[8] Women were rarely marked physically, although they may have been shamed and forced to wear marked clothing. Nathaniel Hawthorne's story of *The Scarlet Letter* is a report on that practice, where the central figure is required to wear a red letter "A," embroidered on her dress, signifying adultery.

Public Humiliation

Call Michael Fay and ask him if he'd go over there and do that again, and I bet he'd say "no."

—Tennessee state Rep. Doug Bunnels, sponsor of a 1995 state paddling bill

A number of early punishments were designed to humiliate offenders in public and to allow members of the community an opportunity for vengeance. The stocks and pillory were two such punishments. The pillory closed over the head and hands and held the offender in a standing position, while the stocks kept the person sitting with the head free. A few hundred years ago, each town had its stocks or pillory usually located in some central square or alongside a major thoroughfare.

Offenders sent to the stocks or pillory found themselves captive and on public display. They could expect to be heckled and spit upon by passers-by. Other citizens might gather to throw tomatoes or rotten eggs. On occasion, citizens who were particularly outraged by the magnitude or nature of the offense would substitute rocks for other less lethal missiles and end the offender's life. Retribution remained a community prerogative, and citizens wielded the power of final sentencing. The pillory was still used in Delaware as late as 1905.[9]

The brank and ducking stool provided other forms of public humiliation. The brank was a bird-cage-like device which fit over the offender's head. On it was a small door which, when closed, caused a razor-sharp blade to be inserted into the mouth. The ducking stool looked like a see-saw. The offender was tied to it and lowered into a river or lake, turning them nearly upside down like a duck searching for food underwater. Both devices were used in colonial times to punish gossips and were designed to fit that crime by teaching the offender to keep a shut mouth or a still tongue.

Workhouses

The sixteenth century was a time of economic upheaval in Europe, caused partly by wars and partly by the growing roots of the industrial revolution, which was soon to sweep the continent. By midcentury thousands of unemployed and vagrant people were scouring towns and villages seeking food and shelter. It was not long before they depleted the economic reserves of churches, which were the primary social relief agencies of the time.

Workhouse (or **Brideswell**) A form of early imprisonment whose purpose it was to instill habits of industry in the idle.

In the belief that poverty was caused by laziness, governments were quick to create workhouses designed to instill "habits of industry" in the unemployed. The first workhouse in Europe opened in 1557 in a former British palace called Saint Bridget's Well. The name was shortened to "Brideswell," and brideswells became a synonym for workhouses. Brideswells taught work habits, not specific skills. Inmates were made to fashion their own furniture, build additions to the facility, and raise gardens. When the number of inmates exceeded the volume of useful work to be done, "make-work" projects, including treadmills and cranks, were invented to keep them busy.

Workhouses were judged successful, if only because they were constantly filled. By 1576 Parliament decreed that every county in England should build a workhouse. Although workhouses were forerunners of our modern prisons, they did not incarcerate criminal offenders—only vagrants and the economically disadvantaged. Nor were they designed to punish convicts, but served instead to reinforce the value of hard work.

Exile

The ancient Hebrews periodically forced a sacrificial goat symbolically carrying the tribe's sins into the wilderness, a practice which has given us the modern word "scapegoating." Since then, many societies have banished "sinners" directly. The French sent criminal offenders to Devil's Island, and the Russians used Siberia for centuries for the same purpose.

England sent convicts to the American colonies beginning in 1618. The British program of exile, known as "transportation," served the dual purpose of providing a captive labor force for development of the colonies while assuaging growing English sentiments opposing corporal punishments. In 1776, however, the American Revolution forced the practice to end, and British penology shifted to the use of aging ships, called hulks, as temporary prisons. Hulks were anchored in harbors throughout England and served as floating confinement facilities even after transportation (to other parts of the globe) resumed.

In 1787, only 17 years after Captain Cook had discovered the continent, Australia became the new port of call for English prisoners. The name of Captain William Bligh, governor of the New South Wales penal colony, survives down to the present day as a symbol of the difficult conditions and rough men and women of those times.

The Emergence of Prisons

The identity of the world's first true prison may never be known, but we do know that at some point, penalties for crime came to include incarceration. During the Middle Ages, "punitive imprisonment appears to have been introduced into Europe…by the Christian Church in the incarceration of certain offenders against canon law."[10] Similarly, debtors' prisons existed throughout Europe during the 1400s and 1500s, although they housed inmates who had violated the civil law rather than criminals. John Howard, an early prison reformer, mentions prisons housing criminal offenders in Hamburg, Germany; Berne, Switzerland; and Florence, Italy, in his 1777 book, *State of Prisons*.[11] Some early efforts to imprison offenders can be found in the Hospice of San Michele, a papal prison which opened in 1704, and the Maison de Force, begun at Ghent, Belgium, in 1773. The Hospice was actually a residential school for delinquent boys and housed 60 youngsters at its opening. Both facilities stressed reformation over punishment and became early alternatives to the use of physical and public punishments.

Chaplain James Finley's Letter from the Ohio Penitentiary, 1850

It is true, there are yet two systems of prison discipline still in use, but both claim to have the two parties—the criminal and society—equally in view. The congregate system, going on the supposition that habits of labor and moral character are the chief desiderata among this class of men, set them to work at those trades for which their physical and mental powers, together with the consideration of their former occupations, may more especially adapt them; religious instruction is also given them by men appointed expressly for the purpose; and they are permitted to labor in large communities, where they can see but not converse with each other, as the friends of this system imagine that social intercourse, of some kind and to some extent, is almost as necessary to man as food. The separate system, on the other hand, looking upon all intercourse between criminals as only evil in its tendency, by which one rogue becomes the instructor or accomplice of another, secludes the convicts from each other but, to atone for this defect, it encourages the visits of good men to the cells of the prisoners; and the officers of these prisons make it a particular point of duty to visit the inmates very frequently themselves. The physical habits of the imprisoned are provided for by such trades as can be carried on by individual industry; a teacher is employed to lead them on in the study of useful branches of education; while the Gospel is regularly taught them, not only by sermons on the Sabbath, but by private efforts of the chaplain in his daily rounds.

Source: James Finley, *Memorials of Prison Life* (Cincinnati, OH: Swormstedt and Poe, 1855).

Near the end of the eighteenth century the concept of imprisonment as punishment for crime reached its fullest expression in the United States. Soon after they opened, U.S. prisons came to serve as models for European reformers searching for ways to humanize criminal punishment. For that reason, and in order to better appreciate how today's prisons operate, it is important to understand the historical development of the prison movement in the United States. Figure 12–1 depicts the stages through which American prisons progressed following introduction of the concept of incarceration as a punishment for crime around 1790. Each historical era will be discussed in the pages that follow.

The Penitentiary Era (1790–1825)

In 1790 Philadelphia's Walnut Street Jail was converted into a penitentiary by the Pennsylvania Quakers. The Quakers, following the legacy of William Penn, intended to introduce religious and humane principles into the handling of offenders. They saw in prisons the opportunity for penance—and viewed them as places wherein offenders might make amends with society and accept responsibility for their misdeeds. The philosophy of imprisonment begun by the Quakers, heavily imbued with elements of both rehabilitation and deterrence, carries over to the present day.[12]

Inmates of the Philadelphia Penitentiary were held in solitary confinement and were expected to wrestle with the evils they harbored. Penance was the primary vehicle through which rehabilitation was anticipated, and a study of the Bible was strongly encouraged. Solitary confinement was the rule, and the penitentiary was architecturally designed to minimize contact between inmates, and between inmates and staff. Exercise was allowed in small high-walled yards attached to each cell. Eventually handicrafts were introduced into the prison setting, permitting prisoners to work in their cells.

Fashioned after the Philadelphia model, the Eastern Penitentiary (1829) opened in Cherry Hill, Pennsylvania, and the Western Penitentiary (1826) in Pittsburgh. Solitary confinement and individual cells, supported by a massive physical structure with impenetrable walls became synonymous with the Pennsylvania system of imprisonment. Supporters heralded the **Pennsylvania style** as one which was both humane and provided inmates with the opportunity for rehabilitation. Many well-known figures of the day spoke out in support of

Pennsylvania Style (also **Penitentiary**)   A form of imprisonment developed by the Pennsylvania Quakers around 1790 as an alternative to corporal punishments. The style made use of solitary confinement and encouraged rehabilitation.

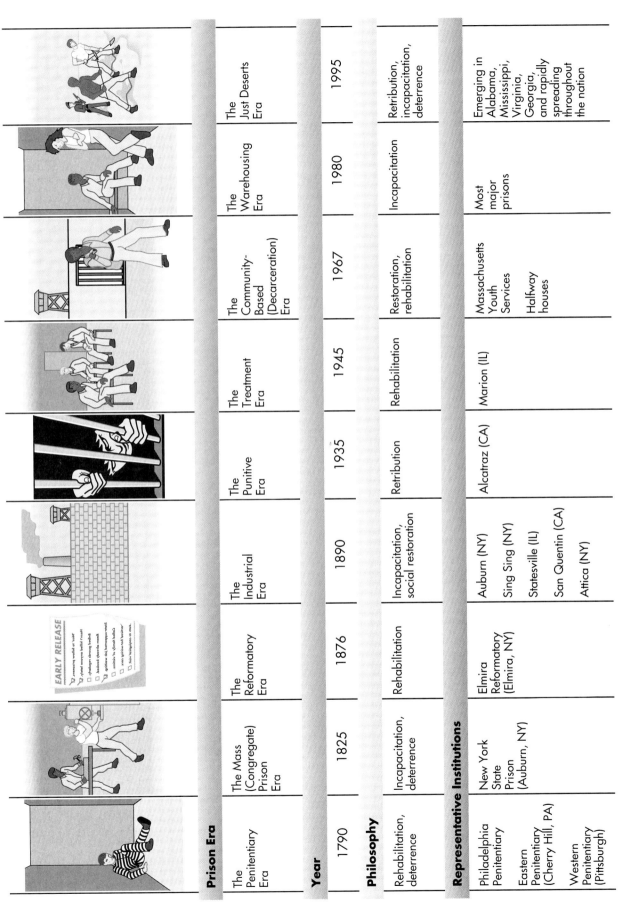

	The Penitentiary Era	The Mass (Congregate) Prison Era	The Reformatory Era	The Industrial Era	The Punitive Era	The Treatment Era	The Community-Based (Decarceration) Era	The Warehousing Era	The Just Deserts Era
Prison Era	The Penitentiary Era	The Mass (Congregate) Prison Era	The Reformatory Era	The Industrial Era	The Punitive Era	The Treatment Era	The Community-Based (Decarceration) Era	The Warehousing Era	The Just Deserts Era
Year	1790	1825	1876	1890	1935	1945	1967	1980	1995
Philosophy	Rehabilitation, deterrence	Incapacitation, deterrence	Rehabilitation	Incapacitation, social restoration	Retribution	Rehabilitation	Restoration, rehabilitation	Incapacitation	Retribution, incapacitation, deterrence
Representative Institutions	Philadelphia Penitentiary; Eastern Penitentiary (Cherry Hill, PA); Western Penitentiary (Pittsburgh)	New York State Prison (Auburn, NY)	Elmira Reformatory (Elmira, NY)	Auburn (NY); Sing Sing (NY); Statesville (IL); San Quentin (CA); Attica (NY)	Alcatraz (CA)	Marion (IL)	Massachusetts Youth Services; Halfway houses	Most major prisons	Emerging in Alabama, Mississippi, Virginia, Georgia, and rapidly spreading throughout the nation

FIGURE 12–1 Stages of Prison Development in the United States.

The Walnut Street Jail—America's first "true" prison, circa 1800. *Culver Pictures*

the Pennsylvania style, among them Benjamin Franklin and Benjamin Rush—both of whom were influential members of the Philadelphia Society for Alleviating the Miseries of Public Prisons.[13]

THE MASS PRISON ERA (1825–1876)

Vermont, Massachusetts, Maryland, and New York all built institutions modeled after Pennsylvania's penitentiaries. As prison populations began to grow, however, solitary confinement became prohibitively expensive. One of the first large prisons to abandon the Pennsylvania model was the New York State Prison at Auburn. Auburn introduced the congregate but silent system, under which inmates lived, ate, and worked together in enforced silence. This style of imprisonment, which came to be known as the **Auburn system**, relied on group workshops rather than solitary handicrafts and reintroduced corporal punishments into the handling of offenders. Whereas isolation and enforced idleness were inherent punishments under the Pennsylvania system, Auburn depended upon whipping and hard labor to maintain the rule of silence.[14]

Since even then, as now, there were competing ideas about which style of prison worked best and was most humane, Auburn prison was the site of an experiment in solitary confinement—which was the basis of the Pennsylvania style. Eighty-three men were placed in small solitary cells on Christmas Day of 1821 and released in 1823 and 1824. Five of the 83 died, 1 went insane, another attempted suicide, and the others became "seriously demoralized."[15] Although the Auburn experiment did not accurately simulate the conditions in Pennsylvania (it allowed for no handicrafts or exercise and placed prisoners in tiny cells), it provided an effective basis for condemnation of the Pennsylvania style. Partly as a result of the experiment, the Reverend Louis Dwight, an influential prison reformer of the time and leader of the prestigious Prison Discipline Society of Boston, became an advocate of the Auburn system, citing its lower cost[16] and humane conditions.[17] Lower costs resulted from the simpler facilities required by mass imprisonment, and from group workshops which provided economies of scale unachievable under solitary confinement. Dwight also believed, in large part due to the experiment in solitary confinement, that the Pennsylvania style of imprisonment was unconscionable and inhumane. As a consequence of criticisms fielded by Dwight and others like him, most American prisons built after 1825 followed the Auburn architectural style and system of prison discipline.

About the same time, however, a number of European governments sent representatives to study the virtues of the two American systems. Interestingly, most concluded that the Pennsylvania style was more conducive to reformation than was Auburn, and many European prisons adopted a strict separation of inmates. Two French visitors, Gustave de

Auburn Style (also **Congregate but Silent System**) A form of imprisonment developed in New York state around 1820 which depended upon mass prisons, where prisoners were held in congregate fashion requiring silence. This style of imprisonment was a primary competitor with the Pennsylvania style.

New York's Auburn Prison, shown here in the mid-1800s, began a congregate form of imprisonment which eventually overshadowed Pennsylvania's penitentiary style. *Culver Pictures*

Beaumont and Alexis de Tocqueville, stressed the dangers of what they called "contamination," whereby prisoners housed in Auburn-like systems could negatively influence one another.[18]

The Reformatory Era (1876–1890)

With the tension between the Auburn and Pennsylvania systems, American penology existed in an unsettled state for a half-century. That tension was resolved in 1876 with the emergence of the reformatory style, which grew out of practices innovated by two outstanding correctional leaders of the mid-1880s: Captain Alexander Maconochie and Sir Walter Crofton.

Captain Alexander Maconochie and Norfolk Island

During the 1840s Maconochie served as the warden of Norfolk Island, a prison off the coast of Australia for "doubly condemned" inmates. English prisoners sent to Australia, who committed other crimes while there, were taken to Norfolk to be segregated from less recalcitrant offenders. Prior to Maconochie's arrival, conditions at Norfolk had been atrocious. Disease on the island was rampant, fights among inmates left many dead and more injured, sanitary conditions were practically nonexistent, and physical facilities were unconducive to good supervision. Maconochie immediately set out to reform the island prison. He is still remembered for saying, "When a man keeps the key of his own prison, he is soon persuaded to fit it to the lock."[19] In that belief, he worked to create conditions which would provide incentives for prisoners to participate in their own reformation.

Maconochie developed a system of marks through which prisoners could earn enough credits to buy their freedom. Bad behavior removed marks from the inmate's ledger, while acceptable behavior added to the number of marks earned. The mark system made possible early release and led to a recognition of the indeterminate sentence as a useful tool in the reformation of offenders. Prior to Maconochie, inmates had been sentenced to determinate sentences specifying a fixed number of years they had to serve before release. The mark system squarely placed responsibility for winning an early release upon the inmate. Because of the system's similarity to the later practice of parole, it won for Maconochie the title "father of parole."

Opinion leaders in England, however, saw Maconochie's methods as too lenient. Many pointed to the fact that the indeterminate sentence made possible new lives for criminals in

Reformatory Concept A late-nineteenth-century correctional model based upon the use of the indeterminate sentence and belief in the possibility of rehabilitation, especially for youthful offenders. The reformatory concept faded with the emergence of industrial prisons around the turn of the century.

The New York State Reformatory at Elmira, circa 1876. Under the innovative leadership of Warden Zebulon Brockway, the Elmira Reformatory began the practice of earned early release. *Culver Pictures*

a world of vast opportunity (the Australian content) at the expense of the British empire, while many good citizens had to live out lives of quiet desperation and poverty back home. Amid charges that he coddled inmates, Maconochie was relieved of his duties as warden in 1844.

Sir Walter Crofton and the Irish System

Maconochie's innovations had come to the attention of Sir Walter Crofton, head of the Irish Prison System. Crofton adapted the idea of early release to his program of progressive stages. Inmates who entered Irish prisons had to work their way through four stages. The first, or entry level, involved solitary confinement and dull work. Most prisoners in the first level were housed at Mountjoy Prison in Dublin. The second stage assigned prisoners to Spike Island where they worked on fortifications. The third stage placed prisoners in field units, which worked directly in the community on public service projects. Unarmed guards supervised the prisoners. The fourth stage depended upon what Crofton called the "ticket of leave." The leave ticket allowed prisoners to live and work in the community under the occasional supervision of a "moral instructor." It could be revoked at any time up until the expiration of the offender's original sentence.

Crofton was convinced that convicts could not be rehabilitated without successful reintegration into the community. His innovations were closely watched by reformers across Europe. Unfortunately, a wave of violent robberies swept England in 1862 and led to passage of the 1863 Garrotters Act, which mandated whipping for robberies involving violence and longer prison sentences for many other crimes—effectively rolling back the clock on Crofton's innovations, at least in Europe.

The Elmira Reformatory and the Birth of Parole

In 1865 Gaylord B. Hubbell, warden of Sing Sing prison in New York, visited England and studied prisons there. He returned to the United States greatly impressed by the Irish system and recommended that indeterminate sentences be used in American prisons. The New York Prison Association, through the efforts of Theodore W. Dwight, its president, and Enoch C. Wines, its secretary, supported Hubbell and called for the creation of a "reformatory" based upon the concept of an earned early release if the inmate reformed himself.

When the new National Prison Association held its first conference in 1870 in Cincinnati, Ohio, it brought together men and women of vision. Sir Walter Crofton addressed the group,

Theory into Practice

AN EARLY TEXAS PRISON

In 1860, an unknown writer described conditions in the Texas Penitentiary at Huntsville as follows:

> By a special enactment of the Legislature, the front of the cell of any prisoner sentenced to solitary confinement for life, is painted black, and his name and sentence distinctly marked thereon. The object would seem to be to infuse a salutary dread into the minds of the other prisoners. Upon the only black-painted cell in the prison was the following inscription, in distinct white letters: William Brown, aged twenty-four years, convicted for murder in Grimes County, spring term, 1858, for which he is now suffering solitary confinement for life. Brown himself, however, was in fact at work in the factory with the other convicts! He entered the Penitentiary in May, 1859, and had been kept in close confinement in his cell, without labor, never being permitted to leave it for any purpose, until about the first of October, when his health was found to have suffered so much that, to preserve his life, he was, under a discretionary power vested in the Directors, released from the rigor of his sentence, and subjected to only the ordinary confinement of the prison. His health has since greatly improved. It is not to be wondered at that his health should decline under the strict enforcement of such a sentence. The cell in which he was confined was the same as to size, ventilation, and light as the rest; and being one of the lower tier of cells, the top of the doorway was some feet below the lower edge of the window upon the opposite side of the corridor in the outside wall. He had even less chance for fresh air than if his cell had been in almost any other location. It is the sight and knowledge of such instances of solitary unemployed confinement as this, and a willful neglect or refusal to inform themselves upon, and recognize, the very wide distinction between the terms separate and solitary, that renders many persons so violently prejudiced against, and opposed to the "Separate System."

Source: The Journal of Prison Discipline and Philanthropy, Vol. 15, no. 1 (January 1860), pp. 7–17.

and Enoch C. Wines, the meeting's organizer, called upon "all men of good will throughout the world (to) join in a plan for an ideal prison system."[20] A 37-paragraph Declaration of Principles was adopted and called for reformation to replace punishment as the goal of imprisonment. The most significant outgrowth of the conference, however, was the move to embody those principles in a reformatory built on American soil.

In 1876 the Elmira Reformatory opened in Elmira, New York, under the direction of Zebulon Brockway, a leading advocate of indeterminate sentencing and former superintendent of the Detroit House of Correction. The state of New York had passed an indeterminate sentencing bill, which made possible early release for inmates who earned it. However, because reformation was thought most likely among youths, the Elmira Reformatory accepted only first offenders between the ages of 16 and 30. A system of graded stages required inmates to meet educational, behavioral, and other goals. Schooling was mandatory, and trade training was available in telegraphy, tailoring, plumbing, carpentry, and other areas.

Unfortunately, the reformatory "proved a relative failure and disappointment."[21] Many inmates reentered lives of crime following their release, and high rates of recidivism called the success of the reformatory ideal into question. Some authors attributed the failure of the reformatory to "the ever-present jailing psychosis"[22] of the prison staff or an overemphasis on confinement and institutional security rather than reformation, which made it difficult to implement many of the ideals upon which the reformatory had been based.

Even though the reformatory was not a success, the principles which it established remain important today. Thus, indeterminate sentencing, parole, trade training, education, and primacy of reformation over punishment all serve as a foundation for ongoing debates about the purpose of punishment.

Church services in Sing Sing prison in 1906. Note the "ushers" with shotguns. *Underwood Photo Archives*

The Industrial Prison Era (1890–1935)

Industrial Prisons Those which flourished during the industrial prison era and whose intent it was to capitalize on the labor of convicts sentenced to confinement.

With the failure of the reformatory style of prison, concerns over security and discipline became dominant in American prisons. Inmate populations rose, costs soared, and states began to study practical alternatives. An especially attractive option was found in the potential profitability of inmate labor, and the era of the industrial prison in America was born.

Industrial prisons in the northern United States were characterized by thick high walls, stone or brick buildings, guard towers, and smokestacks which rose from within the walls. These prisons smelted steel, manufactured cabinets, molded tires, and turned out many other goods for the open market. Prisons in the South, which had been devastated by the Civil War, tended more toward farm labor and public works projects. The South, with its labor-intensive agricultural practices, used inmate labor to replace slaves who had been freed during the war.

The following six systems of inmate labor were in use by the early 1900s:[23]

- *Contract system.* Private businesses paid for the rent of inmate labor. They provided the raw materials and supervised the manufacturing process inside of prison facilities.
- *Piece-price system.* Goods were produced for private businesses under the supervision of prison authorities. Prisons were paid according to the number and quality of the goods manufactured.
- *Lease system.* Prisoners were taken to the work site under the supervision of armed guards. Once there, they were turned over to the private contractor who employed them and maintained discipline.
- *Public account system.* Eliminated the use of private contractors. Industries were entirely prison owned, and prison authorities managed the manufacturing process from beginning to end. Goods were sold on the free market.
- *State-use system.* Under this arrangement prisoners manufactured only goods which could be used by other state offices, or they provided labor to assist other state agencies.
- *Public works.* The maintenance of roads and highways, the cleaning of public parks and recreational facilities, and the maintenance and restoration of public buildings all came under the rubric of "public works."

State-Use System A form of inmate labor in which items produced by inmates are salable only by or to state offices. Items which only the state can sell include such things as license plates and hunting licenses, while items sold only to state offices include furniture and cleaning supplies.

Large industrial prisons that were built or converted to industrialization included San Quentin (California), Sing Sing (New York), Auburn, and the Illinois State Penitentiary at Statesville. Many prison industries were quite profitable and contributed significantly to state treasuries. Reports[24] from 1932 show that 82,276 prisoners were involved in various forms of prison labor that year, producing products with a total value of $75,369,471—a huge amount considering the worth of the dollar almost 70 years ago. Beginning as early as the 1830s, however, workers began to complain of being forced to compete with cheap prison labor. In 1834 mechanics in New York filed a petition with the state legislature asking that prison industries paying extremely low wages be eliminated. Labor unions became very well organized and powerful by the early part of the twentieth century, and the Great Depression of the 1930s, during which jobs were scarce, brought with it a call for an end to prison industries.

In 1929 union influence led Congress to pass the Hawes-Cooper Act, which required prison-made goods to conform to regulations of the states through which they were shipped. Hence, states which outlawed the manufacture of free market goods in their own prisons were effectively protected from prison-made goods which might be imported from other states. The death blow to prison industries, however, came in 1935 with passage of the **Ashurst-Sumners Act**, which specifically prohibited the interstate transportation and sale of prison goods where state laws forbade them. In consort with the Ashurst-Sumners legislation, and because of economic pressures brought on by the Depression, most states soon passed statutes which curtailed prison manufacturing within their borders, and the industrial era in American corrections came to a close.

Prison industries today, although still hampered by some federal and state laws, have begun making a comeback. Under the state-use philosophy, most states still permit the prison manufacture of goods which will be used exclusively by the prison system itself, or by other state agencies, or which only the state can legitimately sell on the open market. An example of the latter is license plates, whose sale is a state monopoly. North Carolina provides a good example of a modern state-use system. Its Correction Enterprises operates 24 inmate-run businesses, each of which is self-supporting. North Carolina inmates manufacture prison clothing (at the North Carolina Correctional Center for Women in Raleigh); raise vegetables and farm animals (at Caldonia-Odum Prison) to feed inmates throughout the state; operate an oil refinery, a forestry service, and a cannery; and manufacture soap, license plates, and some office furniture. All manufactured goods other than license plates are for use within the prison system or in other state agencies.[25]

The federal government also operates a kind of state-use system in its institutions through a government-owned corporation called Federal Prison Industries, Incorporated (also called UNICOR).[26] The corporation was established in 1934 to retain some employment programs for federal inmates in anticipation of the elimination of free market prison industries. Criticisms of UNICOR include charges that inmates are paid very low wages and are trained for jobs which do not exist in the free economy.[27] Even so, a long-term study by the Federal Bureau of Prison's Office of Research and Evaluation, whose results were published in 1994, found that federal inmates participating in work experiences through UNICOR had successful postrelease employment outcomes. The study found that inmates "who participated in UNICOR work and other vocational programming during their imprisonment showed better adjustment, were less likely to be revoked at the end of their first year back in the community, and were more likely to find employment in the halfway house and community."[28] "In addition," the study found, "they earned slightly more money in the community than inmates who had similar background characteristics, but who did not participate in work and vocational training programs."

Free market money-making prison industries are also staging a comeback, some funded by private sector investment. In 1981 under the Prison Rehabilitative Industries and Diversified Enterprises, Inc., legislation, commonly called the PRIDE Act, Florida became the first state to experiment with the wholesale transfer of its correctional industry program from public to private control.[29] PRIDE industries include sugar cane processing, construction, and automotive repair. Other states have since followed suit.

Even where prison industries are not profitable, however, some states are taking steps to ensure the productive use of inmates' time and energies. In 1995, for example, prison officials in Oregon began to implement a new state constitutional amendment which requires

An Alabama chain gang sets out to work the roads. In 1995, reflecting a renewed societywide emphasis on punishment which is reminiscent of the punitive era in corrections, Alabama became the first state to revive use of prison chain gangs. *AP/Wide World Photos*

all inmates (except those who are mentally or physically ill, or who are considered too dangerous) to work full time or to be involved in full-time education and training.[30] Since Oregon's prison regulations permit only minimum security inmates to work outside of correctional facilities, administrators have been busy creating useful job opportunities inside of prison walls. The state now uses inmates to answer phones for state agencies and employs a number of convicts in a prison industries program called Unigroup. While Oregon looks for private sector employers who can make use of the services available under its inmate labor program, it is placing inmates into public sector jobs such as state-run reforestation programs.

Florida and Oregon are not alone in their efforts to rebuild meaningful prison industries. In other states, a number of private firms have contracted with correctional institutions to manufacture office furniture and computer equipment and to provide telephone answering services for motel and hotel reservations. Indications are that we will soon see a burgeoning of privately supported prison industry. A decade ago, the National Task Force on Prison Industries, headed by former U.S. Supreme Court Chief Justice Warren E. Burger, issued a report stating five primary principles to help guide the renewal of prison industries nationwide. They are[31]

- The private sector should be involved in prison industries.
- Practices and regulations that impede the progress of prison industries should be rescinded, changed, or otherwise streamlined.
- Prison industries should provide meaningful and relevant work opportunities for inmates.
- Prison industries should operate in a businesslike manner.
- Prison industries should reduce inmate idleness.

The Task Force sought enabling legislation from the federal Congress and state legislatures to permit prison industries to flourish under controlled conditions. Movements in that direction continue today.

The Punitive Era (1935–1945)

The moratorium on free market prison industries initiated by the Ashurst-Sumners Act was to last for more than half a century. Prison administrators, caught with few ready alternatives, seized upon custody and institutional security as the long-lost central purposes of the correctional enterprise, thereby ushering in an era of punitive custody. The punitive era was characterized by an emphasis on punishment and security and by the belief that prisoners owed a debt to society which only a rigorous period of confinement could absolve. Writers of the period termed such beliefs the *convict bogey* and the *lock psychosis*,[32] referring to the fact that convicts were to be both shunned and securely locked away from society. Large maximum security institutions flourished, and the prisoner's daily routine became one of monotony and frustration. The term "stir crazy" grew out of the experience of many prisoners with the punitive era's lack of educational, treatment, and work programs. In response inmates created their own diversions, frequently attempting to escape or incite riots. One especially secure and still notorious facility of the punitive era, the federal penitentiary on Alcatraz Island, is described in a box in this chapter.

The punitive era was a lackluster time in American corrections. Innovations were rare, and an "out-of-sight, out-of-mind" philosophy characterized American attitudes toward inmates. Popular accounts of the times portrayed criminals as "mad dogs" and rehabilitation-oriented officials as "sob sisters" and "cream puffers."[33] Writing at the close of the punitive era Barnes and Teeters observed: "Even earnest administrators who sincerely believe in rehabilitation are afraid to introduce a whole-hearted program that might improve treatment procedures. Such rehabilitative treatment requires flexibility and experimentation, but these increase escape risks and even the most enlightened warden realizes that his work will be judged by newspapers, politicians, and the public on the basis of how successful he is in preventing escapes."[34] Correctional officers were even more single-minded in their security consciousness. Barnes and Teeters wrote: "The mental habits of the custodial staff revolve around the mania to keep prisoners either locked up or scrupulously accounted for. Considerations of reformation and humanity evaporate in the face of this inexorable and all-encompassing anxiety."[35]

The Era of Treatment (1945–1967)

By the late 1940s, the mood of the nation had become euphoric. Memories of World War II were dimming, industries were productive beyond the best hopes of most economic forecasters, and America's position of world leadership was fundamentally unchallenged. Nothing seemed impossible. Amid the bounty of a postwar boom economy, politicians and the public accorded themselves the additional luxury of restructuring the nation's prisons. A new interest in "corrections" and reformation, combined with the latest in behavioral techniques, ushered in an era of treatment built around what was then a prevailing psychiatric model. Inmates came to be seen more as "clients" or "patients" than as offenders, and terms like *resident* or *group member* replaced the *inmate* label. The treatment era was based upon a **medical model** of corrections—one which implied that the offender was sick and that rehabilitation was only a matter of finding the right treatment.

The Medical Model A theoretical framework for the handling of prisoners, which held that offenders were "sick" and could be "cured" through the application of behavioral and other appropriate forms of therapy.

Therapy during the period took a number of forms, many of which are still used today. Most therapeutic models assumed that the inmate had to be helped to mature psychologically and taught to assume responsibility for his or her life. Prisons built their programs around both individual treatment and group therapy approaches. In individual treatment, the offender and the therapist develop a face-to-face relationship. Most individual approaches depict the offender as someone who has not developed sufficiently to manage his or her own behavior effectively. Psychological development may have been thwarted by traumatic experiences in early life, which the therapist will try to uncover in order to produce effective behavioral change.

Group therapy relies upon the sharing of insights gleaned by members of the therapeutic group to facilitate the growth process, often by first making clear to the client the emotional basis of his or her criminal behavior. What the inmate regards as personal strengths may be shown to be really nothing more than excuses for the inability to "own up" to responsibility. Some group strategies are attack therapies, in which new group members are verbally and ideologically pummeled to rid them of old self-conceptions and criminal values in order that they might accept more positive and productive images of themselves. While individual therapy may uncover past personal traumas, group therapy may itself be traumatic in its relentless destruction of all personal armor.

One of the most famous forms of group therapy was Synanon, developed in the 1950s as a treatment for drug addiction. The word "Synanon" derived from a group member's attempt to say "seminar" and developed into a privately owned foundation providing drug treatment for addicts in Santa Monica, California. In the 1960s, Synanon-like programs became widespread and served as models for other attack therapies.

Guided group interaction (GGI) is an example of a treatment strategy which combines elements of individual treatment with group therapy. In guided group interaction, the therapist assists the group in uncovering individual fears, hidden experiences, and anxieties which act as barriers to conventional behavior. During the 1970s Florida and Georgia adopted GGI as their primary approach to the treatment of juvenile offenders, and many other states were reported to use it extensively.[36]

Other forms of therapy used in prisons have included behavior therapy, chemotherapy, aversion therapy, sensory deprivation, and neurosurgery. Prison environments based upon behavior therapy were structured so as to provide rewards for approved behavior while punishing undesirable behavior. Rewards took the form of better housing conditions, canteen allotments, or TV privileges. Chemotherapy involved the use of drugs, especially tranquilizers, to modify behavior. Neurosurgery, including the now-notorious frontal lobotomy, was used on some highly aggressive inmates to control their destructive urges. Sensory deprivation sought to calm disruptive offenders by denying them the stimulation which might set off outbursts of destructive behavior. Sensory deprivation isolated inmates in a quiet, secluded environment. Aversion therapy used drugs or electric shocks in an attempt to teach the offender to associate pain and displeasure with stimuli, which previously led to criminal behavior. Homosexual child abusers, for example, were shown pictures of nude children and simultaneously given shocks, often in especially sensitive parts of their anatomy.

Inmates have not always been happy with the treatment model. In 1972 a group of prisoners at the Marion, Illinois, federal prison joined together and demanded a right to no treatment. The group, calling itself the Federal Prisoner's Coalition, insisted that inmates

Alcatraz Federal Penitentiary. The island prison closed in 1963, a victim of changing attitudes toward corrections. It survives today as a San Francisco tourist attraction. *Paul S. Howell, Gamma—Liaison, Inc.*

ALCATRAZ FEDERAL PENITENTIARY

Alcatraz Island in San Francisco Bay is home to one of the best-known prisons of all time. The prison had its beginnings as a fort for the U.S. Army in 1854 and was used to house the Bay Area's prisoners following the great earthquake of 1906. By the 1930s, organized criminal elements were terrorizing the country, and Sanford Bates, the director of the federal prison system, began the call for one highly secure institution for the isolation of notorious offenders. Alcatraz Island was the obvious choice. The wide expanse of bay waters which separated the island from the coast were notorious for treacherous currents, making unaided escape a virtual impossibility.

During the early 1930s the island prison was built on the foundation of the old fort. Some of the first prison-used metal detectors were installed, and barbed wire perimeter fences and walls were built and reinforced with armed guards in towers at strategic points.

Alcatraz Federal Penitentiary opened in 1934 with James Johnson, former warden of San Quentin and Folsom prisons, as warden. One prisoner per cell was the rule. Cells measured 5 feet wide by 9 feet long by 7 feet high and were equipped with basic metal furniture. A rule of silence prevailed, and no newspapers or radios were permitted. Security was so strict that no original letters were delivered to inmates. Correspondence was heavily screened and retyped by the staff who then gave only a copy to the prisoner.

Alcatraz accepted inmates only from other institutions. No direct court commitments could be made. The most difficult, dangerous, and troublesome prisoners from other facilities in the federal system were sent to Alcatraz. One of the first was Al "Scarface" Capone. George "Machine Gun" Kelly, Robert Stroud (the "Birdman of Alcatraz"), "Doc" Barker, Alvin Karpis, and many others followed.

Fourteen known escapes, involving as many as 30 men, were attempted during the time Alcatraz served as a prison. Only one attempt, involving two men—Theodore Cole and Ralph Roe—may have been successful. Cole, serving a 50-year sentence for kidnapping while on the run from McAlester Penitentiary, and Roe, a career offender sentenced to 99 years for bank robbery, cut their way through the bars on a window of the prison shop. They had picked December 16, 1937, an especially foggy and damp day. Although an extensive sea and land search was underway within a half hour following the escape, Cole and Roe were never found. Official accounts point to the strong currents of the bay (which on the day of their escape were measured as swiftly flowing toward the open sea) and wintry temperatures to conclude that the attempt must have failed.

Although not successful, the most costly escape attempt came on May 2, 1946. It resulted in a three-day hostage situation which claimed the lives of two officers and three prisoners. It ended only when U.S. Marines provided demolition grenades used to flush prisoners out of occupied corridors. Seventeen guards and one prisoner were wounded. Two other inmates were sentenced to die for their role in the riot and were put to death on December 3, 1946.

By the 1950s Alcatraz Penitentiary was in a state of disrepair. The salt water of the bay had contributed to an early disintegration of the concrete used in building construction, and many of the steel rods and bars had been weakened by the corrosive air. Local residents grouped together to demand an upgrading of the environmental impact the prison was having on the bay. The final blow to Alcatraz, however, was the undermining of its purpose by a reformation-oriented society, which had moved firmly into the treatment era and away from earlier concerns with "escapeproof" institutions. As described by one writer, "Alcatraz (was) a monument to the thesis that some criminals cannot be reformed and should be repressed and disciplined by absolute inflexibility."[1] On March 21, 1963, under the direction of Attorney General Robert Kennedy, Alcatraz Penitentiary closed its doors as a prison. Today, the island institution survives as a tourist attraction and has spawned a number of shops selling prison memorabilia.

QUESTIONS FOR DISCUSSION

1. As one writer was quoted as saying, "Alcatraz (was) a monument to the thesis that some criminals cannot be reformed and should be repressed and disciplined by absolute inflexibility." Might the same be said today? If so, who would such criminals be?

2. Is there still a need for prisons like Alcatraz? Why or why not?

[1]Harry Barnes and Negley Teeters, *New Horizons in Criminology*, 3d ed. (Englewood Cliffs, NJ: Prentice Hall, 1959), p. 383.

Sources: James Fuller, *Alcatraz Federal Penitentiary, 1934–1963* (San Francisco: Asteron Production, 1987); E. E. Kirkpatrick, *Voices from Alcatraz* (San Antonio, TX: Naylor, 1947); and James A. Johnston, *Alcatraz Island Prison* (New York: Scribners, 1949).

have a basic right "to resist rehabilitation techniques designed to change their attitudes, values, or personalities."[37] Supporting the inmates' claims to no treatment was the National Prison Project of the American Civil Liberties Union. Alvin J. Bronstein, executive director of the National Prison Project, argued that personality altering techniques constituted a violation of prisoners' civil rights.[38] Other suits followed. Worried about potential liability, Donald E. Santarelli, the head of the Law Enforcement Assistance Administration, banned the expenditure of LEAA funds to support any prison programs utilizing psychosurgery, medical research, chemotherapy, and behavioral modification. Santarelli's decision was based on an LEAA report of a year earlier, which had concluded that LEAA lacked the expertise to appropriately evaluate such programs.[39]

The treatment era also suffered from attacks upon the medical model on which it depended. Academics and legal scholars pointed to a lack of evidence in support of the model[40] and began to stress individual responsibility rather than treatment in the handling of offenders. Indeterminate sentencing statutes, designed to reward inmates for improved behavior, fell before the swelling drive to replace treatment with punishment.

Any honest evaluation of the treatment era would conclude that, in practice, treatment was more an ideal than a reality. Many treatment programs existed, some of them quite intensive. Unfortunately, the correctional system in America was never capable of providing any consistent or widespread treatment because the majority of its guards and administrators were oriented primarily toward custody and were not trained to provide treatment. However, although we have identified 1967 as the end of the treatment era, many correctional rehabilitation programs continue to survive into the present day and new ones are constantly being developed.

THE COMMUNITY-BASED FORMAT (1967–1980)

Community-Based Corrections A sentencing style which represents a movement away from traditional confinement options and an increased dependence upon correctional resources which are available in the community.

Beginning in the 1960s, the realities of prison crowding combined with a renewed faith in humanity and the treatment era's belief in the possibility of behavioral change to inspire a movement away from institutionalized corrections and toward the creation of opportunities for reformation within local communities. The transition to community-based corrections (also variously called "deinstitutionalization," "diversion," and "decarceration"[41]) was based upon the premise that rehabilitation could not occur in isolation from the free social world to which inmates must eventually return. Advocates of community corrections portrayed prisons as dehumanizing, claiming they further victimized offenders who had already been negatively labeled by society. Some states strongly embraced the movement toward decarceration. In 1972, for example, under the leadership of its new director of youth services, Jerome Miller, the state of Massachusetts drew national attention when it closed all its reform schools and replaced them with group homes.[42]

Work Release A prison program in which inmates are temporarily released into the community in order to meet job responsibilities.

Decarceration, which built upon many of the alternative or intermediate sanctions discussed in the last chapter, used a variety of programs to keep offenders in contact with the community and out of prison. Among them were halfway houses, **work release** programs, and open institutions. Halfway houses have sometimes been called "halfway-in" or "halfway-out" houses, depending upon whether offenders were being given a second chance prior to incarceration or were in the process of gradual release from prison. Some early halfway houses were begun in Boston in the 1920s, but operated for only a few years.[43] It was not until 1961, however, that the Federal Bureau of Prisons opened a few experimental residential centers in support of its new prerelease programs focusing on juveniles and youthful offenders. Called prerelease guidance centers, the first of these facilities were based in Los Angeles and Chicago.[44] In 1967 the President's Commission on Law Enforcement and the Administration of Justice strongly recommended use of community-based facilities to restore ties between offenders and their families, employers, training facilities, and other social agencies.

Although the era of community-based corrections is now in decline, halfway houses and work release programs still operate in many parts of the country. A typical residential treatment facility today houses 15 to 20 residents and operates under the supervision of a director supported by a handful of counselors. The environment is nonthreatening, and residents are generally free to come and go during the workday. The building looks more like a motel or a house than it does a prison. Fences and walls are nonexistent. Transportation is provided to and from work or educational sites, and the facility retains a portion of the resident's wages to pay the costs of room and board. Residents are expected to remain in the facility following work, and some group therapy may be provided.

Today's work release programs house offenders in traditional correctional environments—usually minimum security prisons—but permit them to work at jobs in the community during the day and return to the prison at night. Inmates are usually required to pay a token amount for their room and board in the institution. The first work release law was passed by Wisconsin in 1913, but it was not until 1957 that a comprehensive program created by North Carolina spurred the development of work release programs nationwide.[45] Work release for federal prisoners was authorized by the Federal Prisoner Rehabilitation Act of 1965.[46] As work release programs grew, study release—whereby inmates attend local colleges and technical schools—was initiated in most jurisdictions as an adjunct to them.

Work release programs are still very much a part of modern corrections. Almost all states have them, and many inmates work in the community as they approach the end of their sentences. Unfortunately, work release programs are not without their social costs. Some inmates commit new crimes while in the community, and others use the opportunity to effect escapes.

The community-based format led to innovations in the use of volunteers and to the extension of inmate privileges. Open institutions were those which routinely provided inmates with a number of opportunities for community involvement and which encouraged the community to participate in the prison environment. Most open institutions, for example, made training available to citizens who wished to sponsor prisoners on day trips into the community for recreation, meals, and the like. Others allowed weekend passes or extended visits by family members and friends, while a few experimented with conjugal visiting and with prisons that housed both men and women (called "coeducational incarceration"). Based on a merit system, conjugal visiting made possible intimate visits between male inmates and their spouses in motel-like environments constructed on the prison grounds. Some writers point to unofficial conjugal visits occurring as early as 1918 at the Mississippi State Penitentiary at Parchman.[47] It was not until 1963, however, that state funding for "red houses" authorized the practice. In 1968 the California Correctional Institute at Tehachapi initiated conjugal visits in which inmates who were about to begin parole were permitted to live with their families for three days per month in apartments on the prison grounds. The practice extended to inmates at Soledad, San Quentin, and the Rehabilitation Center at Corona. By the late 1960s, conjugal visitation was under consideration in many other states, and the National Advisory Commission on Criminal Justice Standards and Goals recommended that correctional authorities should make "provisions for family visits in private surroundings conducive to maintaining and strengthening family ties."[48] In 1995, however, California, which allows about 26,000 conjugal visits a year, moved to restrict the program, prompting an outcry from inmates' families. As of mid-1995, the California Department of Corrections eliminated conjugal visits for those sentenced to death, life without parole, and those without a parole date. Rapists, sex offenders, and recently disciplined inmates also lost conjugal privileges.

Coeducational prisons housed both men and women, allowing the sexes to join in educational programs, work tasks, and certain forms of recreation, although they slept in separate dormitories and were stringently discouraged from physical intimacy. The Federal Bureau of Prisons began experimenting with coed facilities in 1971, and the Pleasanton Youth Center in California became one of the first institutions in the nation to house both men and women. A number of coed prisons continue to exist today.

Warehousing/Overcrowding (1980–1995)

During the late 1970s and into the 1980s, public disappointment, bred of high **recidivism**[49] rates coupled with dramatic news stories of inmates who committed gruesome crimes while in the community, led many legislatures to curtail the most liberal aspects of educational and work release programs. Media descriptions of institutions where inmates lounged in supposed luxury with regular visits from spouses and lovers and took frequent weekend passes infused the popular imagination with images of "prison country clubs." The failure of the rehabilitative ideal in community-based corrections, however, was due as much to changes in the individual sentencing decisions of judges as it was to citizen outrage and restrictive legislative action. Evidence points to the fact that many judges came to regard rehabilitation programs as failures and decided to implement what we have earlier called the just deserts model[50] of criminal sentencing. The just deserts model, as discussed in Chapter 10, built

The American public is alarmed about crime, and with good reason. For the past generation, state and federal crime control policies have been based on the belief that law enforcement can solve the problem: more police, harsher sentencing laws, greater use of the death penalty. But today, with an unprecedented number of people behind bars, we are no safer than before. We are, however, much less free.
—ACLU (web site)
http://www.aclu.org/issues/criminal/iscj.html

Recidivism The repetition of criminal behavior. In statistical practice, a recidivism rate may be any of a number of possible counts or instances of arrest, conviction, correctional commitment, and correctional status changes, related to counts of repetitions of these events within a given period of time.

Warehousing An imprisonment strategy based upon the desire to prevent recurrent crime but which has abandoned any hope of rehabilitation.

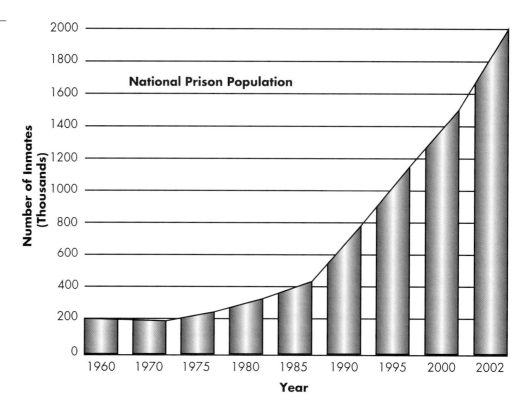

FIGURE 12–2 U.S. prison population, historical and projected growth, 1960–2000. *Sources:* Greg Wees, "Inmate Population Expected to Increase 43% by 2002," *Corrections Compendium*, April 1996; and American Correctional Association, *Vital Statistics in Corrections* (Laurel, MD: American Correctional Association, 1998).

upon a renewed belief that offenders should "get what's coming to them" and quickly led to a policy of warehousing serious offenders for the avowed purpose of protecting society—and to a rapid decline of the deinstitutionalization initiative.

Recidivism rates were widely quoted in support of the drive to warehouse offenders. One study, for example, showed that nearly 70% of young adults paroled from prison in 22 states during 1978 were rearrested for serious crimes one or more times within six years of their release.[51] The 1978 study group was estimated to have committed 36,000 new felonies within the six years following their release, including 324 murders, 231 rapes, 2,291 robberies, and 3,053 violent assaults.[52] Worse still, observed the study's authors, was the fact that 46% of recidivists would have been in prison at the time of their readmission to prison if they had fully served the maximum term to which they had been originally sentenced.[53] Those with long prior-arrest records (six or more previous adult arrests) were rearrested 90% of the time following release, and the younger the parolee was at first arrest, the greater the chance of a new crime violation. Equally intriguing was the finding that "[t]he length of time that a parolee has served in prison had no consistent impact on recidivism rates."[54]

The failure of the rehabilitative model in corrections was proclaimed emphatically by Robert Martinson in 1974.[55] Martinson and his colleagues had surveyed 231 research studies conducted to evaluate correctional treatments between 1945 and 1967. They were unable to identify any treatment program which substantially reduced recidivism. Although Martinson argued for fixed sentences, a portion of which would be served in the community, his findings were often interpreted to mean that lengthy prison terms were necessary to incapacitate offenders who could not be reformed. About the same time, the prestigious National Academy of Sciences released a report in support of Martinson, saying "we do not now know of any program or method of rehabilitation that could be guaranteed to reduce the criminal activity of released offenders."[56] This combined attack on the treatment model led to the **nothing works doctrine**, which, beginning in the late 1970s, cast a pall of doubt over the previously dominant treatment philosophy.

As a consequence, from 1975 to 1998 the American prison population grew dramatically (see Figure 12–2), and prisons everywhere became notoriously overcrowded (see

Nothing Works Doctrine
The belief, popularized by Robert Martinson in the 1970s, that correctional treatment programs have little success in rehabilitating offenders.

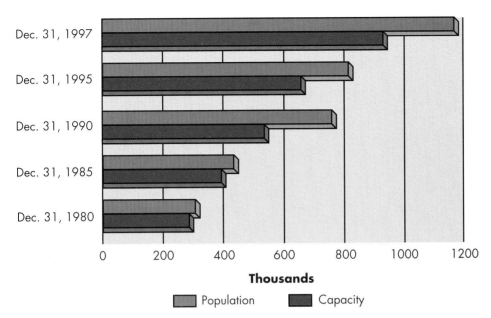

Dec. 31, 1997

Dec. 31, 1995

Dec. 31, 1990

Dec. 31, 1985

Dec. 31, 1980

0   200   400   600   800   1000   1200

Thousands

▢ Population   ▣ Capacity

FIGURE 12–3 State and federal prison populations, inmates versus capacity, 1980–1997.
Source: Bureau of Justice Statistics, *Correctional Populations in the United States*
(Washington, D.C.: Bureau of Justice Statistics, various years).

Figure 12–3), as crime rates and the fear of crime among the American public continued to rise. A survey of 1,400 criminal justice officials conducted across the country in the 1980s by the National Institute of Justice identified crowding in prisons and jails as the most serious problem facing the criminal justice system.[57] Between 1985 and 1997 state and federal prison populations increased by more than 235%,[58] with similar increases in incarceration rates for both white and black inmates. A 1990 survey of federal prisons found them 73% overcrowded,[59] and a major program of expansion, which is still ongoing, was implemented. The year 1994 saw one of the fastest increases in U.S. incarceration rates ever recorded—necessitating 1,542 additional prison beds per week.[60] The number of people imprisoned, however, continues to grow, and by the beginning of 1997 nearly 1.2 million persons were confined in prisons throughout the country (while overcrowding had dropped to approximately 20%).[61]

The incarceration of drug felons caused much of the overcrowding problem. A recent report[62] by the American Bar Association, for example, directly attributed overcrowding to a systemwide overemphasis on drug-related offenses—an emphasis which tended to imprison mostly poor, undereducated black youths who were rarely dangerous. The report pointed out that while the per capita rate of *reported* crime dropped 2.2% across the nation during the 1980s, "the incarceration rate increased more than 110 percent."[63]

An even better sense of how drug-related incarceration led to prison overcrowding can be seen in New York state's experience in enforcing its tough "Rockefeller drug laws," which were passed in 1973. In that year, New York sent 713 persons to prison for drug crimes. By 1992, as a result of the tough new laws, the state was imprisoning more than 11,000 new drug offenders every year. Recently, Thomas A. Coughlin III, Corrections Commissioner for the state of New York, told the Assembly Committee on Codes of the New York legislature, "I think we desperately need to modify our approach to the drug epidemic plaguing New York state. As of May 25 our prisons house 64,000 inmates—2,000 of them living in double bunks that were added as an emergency response to a bed shortage....If each of these 64,000 people actually belonged in prison, I would have no problem in simply asking the legislature to pay $100,000 each for all the new cells that I need. But that is not the case....Prison space is a finite resource. We should be filling it with those it was built for—the violent predator and repeat offenders. Not the guy who got caught with a few bucks worth of crack....Thus, as a simple matter of common sense, if not pure economics, we are wasting valuable and limited prison space on low-level, nonviolent offenders." "The time is long overdue," concluded Coughlin, "for the legislature to recognize this distinction and enact some basic reforms to our sentencing structure."[64]

An inmate tends plants around his quarters in a Texas tent city prison. Many prisons today are dramatically overcrowded. *Stock Boston*

As Coughlin knows, warehousing is not without its problems. For one thing, it is prohibitively expensive and has led to unmanageably overcrowded prisons. Nor does it appear to reduce the number of serious criminal offenses in society.[65] Similarly, overcrowding has led to numerous administrative difficulties, many of which continue to affect prison systems throughout the nation. By 1992, institutions in 40 states and the District of Columbia were operating under court orders to alleviate crowded conditions.[66] Entire prison systems in nine jurisdictions—Alaska, Florida, Kansas, Louisiana, Mississippi, Nevada, Rhode Island, South Carolina, and Texas—had come under court control.[67]

Some states dealt with overcrowded facilities by constructing "temporary" tent cities within prison yards. Others moved more beds into already packed dormitories, often stacking prisoners three high in triple bunk beds. A few states, following what Coughlin might suggest, declared a policy of early release for less dangerous inmates and instituted mandatory diversion programs for first-time nonviolent offenders. Others used sentence rollbacks to reduce the sentences of selected inmates by a fixed amount, usually 90 days. Early parole was similarly employed by numerous states to reduce overcrowded conditions. Almost all states shifted some of the correctional burden to local jails, and by 1996 jails were housing over 31,000 sentenced inmates because of overcrowding at long-term institutions.[68]

The Dimensions of Overcrowding

Incarceration is a crash course in extortion and criminal behavior.

—Vincent Schiraldi, National Center on Institutions and Alternatives

Even though new prisons are quickly being built throughout the nation, prison overcrowding is still very much a reality. A June 1997 report[69] by the Bureau of Justice Statistics found federal prisons operating at 25% over design capacity, while state prisons were operating an average of 20% above capacity. Experts agree that prison crowding can be measured along a number of dimensions, which include[70]

- Space available per inmate (such as square feet of floor space)
- How long inmates are confined in cells or housing units (versus time spent on recreation, etc.)
- Living arrangements (for example, single versus double bunking)
- Type of housing (use of segregation facilities, tents, etc., in place of general housing)

Complicating the crowding picture still further is the fact that prison officials have developed three definitions of prison capacity. **Rated capacity** refers to the size of the inmate population that a facility can handle according to the judgment of experts. **Operational capacity** is the number of inmates that a facility can effectively accommodate based on an appraisal of the institution's staff, programs, and services. **Design capacity** refers to the inmate population the institution was originally built to handle. Rated capacity estimates usually yield the largest inmate capacities, while design capacity (upon which observations in this chapter are based) typically shows the highest amount of overcrowding.

Crowding by itself is not cruel and unusual punishment according to the Supreme Court in *Rhodes* v. *Chapman* (1981),[71] which considered the issue of double bunking among other alleged forms of "deprivation" at the Southern Ohio correctional facility. The Ohio facility, built in 1971, was substantially overcrowded according to the original housing plans on which it was constructed. Designed to house one inmate per cell, the cells were small (only 63 square feet of floor space on the average). However, at the time the suit was filed, the facility held 2,300 inmates, 1,400 of whom were double celled. Kelly Chapman, an inmate serving a sentence as an armed robber and prison escapee, claimed that his portion of a cell was too small—smaller even than the space recommended by Ohio State Veterinarian Services for a five-week-old calf. Thirty-six states joined the case in support of the Ohio practice of double celling, while the American Medical Association and the American Public Health Association took Chapman's side.[72] The court, reasoning that overcrowding is not necessarily dangerous if other prison services are adequate, held that prison housing conditions may be "restrictive and even harsh," for they are part of the penalty that offenders pay for their crimes.

However, overcrowding combined with other negative conditions may lead to a finding against the prison system. The American Correctional Association believes that such a totality-of-conditions approach requires the court to judge the overall quality of prison life while viewing overcrowded conditions in combination with

- The prison's meeting of basic human needs.
- The adequacy of the facility's staff.
- The program opportunities available to inmates.
- The quality and strength of the prison management.

Overcrowding is the legacy of the warehousing era. Warehousing, a strategy which continues to be advocated by many, has produced record prison populations and holds the potential to expand the number of people in prison still farther. Modern advocates of incapacitation continue to find easy support for their position. Recently, for example, the Justice Department reported that new crimes committed by released prisoners cost society about $430,000 per year per offender for police work, court costs, and losses to victims. The report found that continued confinement, even in newly built prison cells, costs only around $25,000 per year per offender and was "not too expensive when weighed against the price of crimes that would otherwise be prevented by incapacitation."[73] A similar study[74] by Wisconsin found that while imprisonment costs, in that state were about $14,000 per inmate per year, the financial burden to the state of allowing the typical Wisconsin inmate "to freely roam the streets in search of victims" would be about $28,000 in new crimes per average offender each year. Researchers who conducted the study concluded that "prison pays" and suggested that "[i]mprisonment is a valuable corrections option from which the state cannot afford to shrink." In contrast to such findings, however, a comprehensive 1997 review of 500 crime prevention programs across the country found that "much [existing] research on prisons was inadequate or flawed, making it impossible to measure how much crime was actually prevented or deterred by locking up more criminals."[75]

The Just Deserts Era (1995–Present)

Warehousing and prison overcrowding have been primarily the result of both public and official frustration with rehabilitative efforts. In a sense, however, they are consequences of a strategy without a clear-cut philosophy. Since rehabilitation didn't seem to work, early advocates of warehousing—not knowing what else to do—assumed a pragmatic stance and advocated separating criminals from society by keeping them locked up for as long as possible. Their avowed goal was the protection of law-abiding citizens.

Prison Capacity A general term referring to the size of the correctional population an institution can effectively hold. There are three types of prison capacity: design, rated, and operational.

Rated Capacity The size of the inmate population a facility can handle according to the judgment of experts.

Operational Capacity The number of inmates a prison can effectively accommodate based upon management considerations.

Design Capacity The number of inmates a prison was architecturally intended to hold when it was built or modified.

The Justice Model A contemporary model of imprisonment in which the principle of just deserts forms the underlying social philosophy.

Since the early days of warehousing, however, a new philosophy which is based upon the second prong of the **justice model**—that is, an emphasis on individual responsibility—has become the operative principle underlying many correctional initiatives. This new philosophy is grounded squarely upon a just deserts theme, in which imprisonment is seen as a fully *deserved* and proper consequence of criminal and irresponsible behavior rather than just the end result of a bankrupt system unable to reform its charges. Unlike previous correctional eras, which layered other purposes upon the correctional experience (the reformatory stage, for example, was concerned with reformation, while the industrial stage sought economic gain), the current era of just deserts represents a kind of return to the root purpose of incarceration—punishment.

In many ways the current era is beginning to look like the punitive era reborn. State legislatures everywhere, encouraged in large part by their constituencies, are scrambling to limit inmate privileges and to increase the pains of imprisonment. In 1995, for example, Alabama became the first state in modern times to re-institute use of the prison chain gang.[76] Under the Alabama system, shotgun-armed guards oversaw prisoners who were chained together by the ankles while they worked the state's roadsides—picking up trash, clearing brush, and filling ditches. The system, intended primarily for parole violators who must reenter prison, was tough and unforgiving. Inmates served up to 90 days on chain gangs, during which they worked 12-hour shifts and remained chained even while using portable toilet facilities. Alabama chain gangs were discontinued in 1996 following a lawsuit against the state.

Proponents of chain gangs are adamant about the purpose such punishment serves. "If a person knows they're going to be out on the highway in chains, they are going to think twice about committing a crime," says Georgia state Prison Commissioner Ron Jones.[77] And, Jones says, officials from many other states have contacted him about beginning chain gangs elsewhere. Opponents of the chain gang, however, like ACLU National Prison Project spokeswoman Jenni Gainsborough, call it "a giant step backward"[78] or "a return to the dark ages." Some even view it as a return to slavery, especially since blacks are over-represented (on a per capita basis) among Alabama's prison population. Following Alabama's lead, in 1995 Arizona became the second state to field prison chain gangs and was followed shortly by Florida.[79] John Hallahan, warden of the prison at Douglas, Arizona, explained chain gangs this way: "The lesson is, you go to prison in Arizona and you're going to do hard labor."[80] Florida state senator Charlie Crist, nicknamed "Chain Gang Charlie" for writing the legislation reviving shackling in Florida, echoed similar sentiments. "What we want to do is tell people that if you commit a crime in Florida, if you're convicted of committing that crime in Florida, Florida will punish you, you will do your time, and it will not be pleasant."[81]

In another example of the move toward greater punishments and longer prison terms, the state of Virginia abolished parole as of January 1, 1995, increased sentences for certain violent crimes by as much as 700%, and announced it would build a dozen new prisons over the next decade. Changes in state law, initiated by the administration of Governor George Allen, were intended to move the state further in the direction of truth in sentencing and to appease the state's voters, who—reflecting what appears to be a groundswell of public opinion nationwide—demanded a get-tough stance toward criminals. William P. Barr, a former U.S. attorney general under President Bush and co-chairman of the Virginia commission which developed the state's plan, explained why no provisions for rehabilitation and crime prevention had been included: "The most effective method of prevention," he said, "is to take the rapist off the street for 12 years instead of four."[82]

Symptomatic of the shift in public attitudes in favor of the just deserts model of corrections is the virtual avalanche of state and federal legislation (much of it still pending as of this writing) intended to clamp down on prison comforts such as weight-training, adults-only films, premium cable TV channels, pornographic materials by mail, miniature golf courses, individual cells with television sets and coffee pots, personally owned computers and modems, and expensive electronic musical instruments. All would be banned under some proposed federal legislation now pending. "Some criminals have come to view jail as an almost acceptable lifestyle because amenities are better for them on the inside than on the outside. You should pay the price for your crime, not be rewarded with a vacation watching premium cable on your personal TV," says Republican congressman Dick Zimmer of New Jersey, a sponsor of the so-called "no-frills" legislation.[83]

A 1995 nationwide survey of state departments of correction by *Corrections Compendium*, a publication covering all aspects of imprisonment, found that prisons "of the present and near future are being stripped of anything that can be considered a luxury. Prison life is becoming less and less attractive with the elimination of sacred privileges like smoking and the addition of hard labor and humiliating uniforms."[84] The survey found that 60% of the 46 states which responded reported a decrease in inmate privileges during the previous 12 months, including reductions in the amount or type of personal property inmates are allowed to keep, restrictions in outside purchases and food packages from home, and the elimination of cable television and rented movies. A number of prison systems reported abolishing family visits, special occasion banquets, and the like. "The elimination of family-oriented privileges," said the publication, "reflects the extremely harsh public view towards prisoners that is currently in vogue."[85]

Other get-tough initiatives can be seen in the "three-strikes and you're out" laws now sweeping through state legislatures everywhere.[86] "Three-strikes" legislation, which is discussed in a box in Chapter 10, mandates lengthy prison terms for criminal offenders convicted of a third violent crime or felony. While "three-strikes" laws have either been enacted or are being considered in more than 30 states and by the federal government (which requires life imprisonment for federal criminals convicted of three violent felonies or drug offenses), critics of such laws say that they will not prevent crime.[87] Jerome Skolnick, of the University of California-Berkeley, for example, criticizes three-strikes legislation because, he says, while it may satisfy society's desire for retribution to "lock 'em up and throw away the key,"[88] such a practice will almost certainly not reduce the risk of victimization—especially the risk of becoming a victim of random violence. That is so, says Skolnick, because most violent crimes are committed by young men between the ages of 13 and 23. "It follows," according to Skolnick, "that if we jail them for life after their third conviction, we will get them in the twilight of their careers, and other young offenders will take their place." "Three-strikes" programs, says Skolnick, will lead to creation of "the most expensive, taxpayer-supported middle-age and old-age entitlement program in the history of the world," which will provide housing and medical care to older, burned out, law violators. Another author puts it this way: "The question…is whether it makes sense to continue to incarcerate aged prisoners beyond the time they would have served under ordinary sentences. This is unnecessary from the standpoint of public safety, and it is expensive."[89]

Alan Schuman, president of the American Probation and Parole Association, feels much the same way. While building more prisons may be a popular quick fix to crime, says Schuman, such a strategy will only cost millions of dollars without making streets safer. "The Draconian single-level approach of merely building new institutions will cause us problems for decades," Schuman said during a recent meeting.[90]

Criticisms like these, however, fail to appreciate the new sentiments underlying the correctional era now emerging. Proponents of today's get-tough policies, while no doubt interested in personal safety, lower crime rates, and balanced state and federal budgets, are keenly focused on retribution. And where retribution fuels a correctional policy, deterrence, reformation, and economic considerations play only secondary roles. The real issue for those advocating today's retribution-based correctional policies is *not* whether or not they deter, or whether or not they lower crime rates, but rather the overriding conviction that criminals *deserve* punishment. As more and more states enact three-strikes and other get-tough legislation, prison populations across the nation will swell even more, eclipsing those of the warehousing era. The new just deserts era of correctional philosophy, however, now provides what has become for many an acceptable rationale for continued prison expansion. Newman Flanagan, executive director of the National District Attorneys Association, puts it this way: "I would venture to say in all probability they (the states) will all start looking at three-strikes laws. It's the 'in' thing to do. The public is fed up with criminals."[91] In fact, it is the correctional systems of this country which will bear the burden of housing those imprisoned under such laws. One 1996 study[92] found that, as a direct consequence of three-strikes and other "get-tough" legislation now in vogue, the number of persons imprisoned in the United States can be expected to increase to nearly 2 million persons by the year 2002—adding an avalanche of new inmates on top of correctional systems already struggling to keep pace with court-ordered prison commitments. California officials estimate that by 2004 three-strikes legislation "will account for over 50% of the prison population"[93] in that state. A similar 1997

It is time for the California Department of Corrections, Governor Wilson, and others to realize that we, the families of inmates, have rights too! We work and pay taxes. And we vote. We come here today to tell you that we are fed up with being treated as second-class citizens.

—Sandra George, Pro-Family Advocates, objecting to a decision by the CDC to restrict conjugal visitation in California's prisons

Prison contraband on display in a supervisor's office. Note the handmade quality and concealability of most of the weapons. *Laimute E. Druskis*

study of three-strikes laws in 22 states concluded that such legislation results in clogged court systems and crowded correctional facilities and encourages three-time felons to take dramatic risks to avoid capture.[94]

Given studies like these, many now claim that the new retribution-based "lock 'em-up" philosophy may bode ill for the future of American corrections. "I am worried there is going to be a disaster in our prisons," says Michael Quinlan, director of the Federal Bureau of Prisons under former Presidents Bush and Reagan. The combination of burgeoning prison populations and newly popular restrictions on inmate privileges could soon have a catastrophic and disastrous effect—leading to riots, more prison violence, work stoppages, an increased number of inmate suicides, and other forms of prison disorder—says Quinlan.[95]

Selective Incapacitation—A Strategy to Reduce Overcrowding

Some authors have identified the central problem of the present era as one of selective versus collective incapacitation.[96] Collective incapacitation is a strategy which would imprison almost all serious offenders and is still found today in states which rely upon predetermined, or fixed, sentences for given offenses or for a series of specified kinds of offenses (as in the case of three-strikes legislation just discussed). Collective incapacitation is, however, prohibitively expensive as well as unnecessary in the opinion of many experts. Not all offenders need to be imprisoned because not all represent a continuing threat to society—but those who do are difficult to identify.[97]

In most jurisdictions, where the just deserts initiative holds sway, selective incapacitation is rapidly becoming the rule. Selective incapacitation seeks to identify the potentially most dangerous criminals with the goal of selectively removing them from society. Repeat offenders with records of serious and violent crimes are the most likely candidates for incapacitation—as are those who will probably commit such crimes in the future even though they have no records. But potentially violent offenders cannot be readily identified and those thought likely to commit crimes cannot be sentenced to lengthy prison terms for things they have not yet done.

In support of selective incapacitation many states have enacted career offender statutes which attempt to accurately identify potentially dangerous offenders out of known criminal populations. Selective incapacitation efforts, however, have been criticized for yielding a rate of "false positives" of over 60%,[98] and some authors have been quick to call selective incapacitation a "strategy of failure."[99] Nevertheless, in a 1996 analysis of recidivism studies,[100] Canadians Paul Gendreau, Tracy Little, and Claire Goggin found that criminal history, a history of preadult antisocial behavior, and "criminogenic needs"—which were defined as measurable antisocial thoughts, values, and behaviors—were all dependable predictors of recidivism. The article, subtitled "What Works!", was intended as a response to Martinson's "nothing works doctrine" mentioned earlier.

We are likely to see continued record overcrowding no matter how many prisons we build.

—U.S. Representative Charles B. Rangel (D.-N.Y)

Some state programs designed to reduce overcrowding, however, have run afoul of selective incarceration principles. In 1997, for example, the U.S. Supreme Court[101] ordered the state of Florida to release as many as 2,500 inmates—many of whom had been convicted of violent crimes—under a "gain time" program set up by the state in 1983. Provisions of the program allowed inmates to earn as much as two months off their sentences for every month served. Although the program was originally intended to relieve overcrowding, a change in public sentiment led Florida Attorney General Bob Butterworth to revoke gain time which had already been earned. In ordering the inmates' release, however, the U.S. Supreme Court unanimously ruled that Florida had violated constitutional guarantees against ***ex post facto*** laws and required officials to be bound by the program's original conditions. The release of hundreds of murderers, rapists, robbers, and other felons caused a statewide uproar and media furor. Lee County Sheriff John McDougall expressed dismay at the Court's decision. "A hell of a lot of innocent people are going to be robbed, raped, and murdered," he said. "How many people are going to have to die in order to pay for this blunder?"[102]

The Florida experience, and others like it, have caused states to tighten restrictions on early release programs. As the just deserts model matures, it is likely that we will see the sentencing of violent criminals to lengthy prison stays with little possibility of release and the increased use of alternative sanctions for minor offenders.

Ex post facto Latin for "after the fact." The Constitution prohibits the enactment of *ex post facto* laws, which make acts punishable as crimes which were committed before the laws in question were passed.

Prisons Today

There are approximately 1,000 state and 80 federal prisons in operation across the country today. More are quickly being built as both the states and the federal government scramble to fund and construct new facilities. America's prison population has more than tripled since 1980. On January 1, 1997, the nation's prisons (state and federal) held 1,182,169 inmates.[103] Slightly over six percent (or 74,730) of those imprisoned were women.[104]

Prisons everywhere are crowded. The incarceration rate for state and federal prisoners sentenced to more than a year has reached a record 427 prisoners per every 100,000 U.S. residents.[105] Male incarceration rates (which stand at 819 per 100,000 male residents), however, are 16 times higher than those of women (only 51 per every 100,000 females). Until 1996, the problem of overcrowding was worst in Texas, which has the nation's highest incarceration rate with 545 out of every 100,000 Texans behind prison bars. In 1996 Texas completed a $1.5 billion expansion program, moving more than 20,000 inmates into 28 new facilities across the state. The Texas prison system, which has been described as "by far the largest in the free world," is capable of housing 146,000 regular prison inmates.[106]

An examination of imprisonment statistics by race highlights the huge disparity between blacks and whites in prison. While only an estimated 461 white males are imprisoned in the United States for every 100,000 white males in the population, latest figures show an incarceration rate of 3,250 black men for every 100,000 black males.[107] Worse yet, the rate of growth in such figures shows that the imprisonment rate of blacks increased dramatically over the past ten years, while the rate of white imprisonment has grown far less. Many of these statistics are displayed graphically in Figures 12–4 and 12–5.

Federal prisons tell a similar story. On January 1, 1997, federal prisons held 105,544 inmates in facilities originally designed to accommodate only 76,897.[108]

The size of prison facilities varies greatly. One out of every four state institutions is a large, maximum security prison, with a population approaching 1,000 inmates. A few exceed that figure, but the typical state prison is small, with an inmate population of less than 500, while community-based facilities average around 50 residents.

Most people sentenced to state prisons have been convicted of violent crimes (46%), while property crimes (24%) are the second most common category for which inmates have been sentenced, and drug crimes are the reason for which 23% of "active" sentences are imposed.[109] In contrast, prisoners sentenced for drug law violations are the single largest group of federal inmates (60%), and the increase in the imprisonment of drug offenders accounts for three quarters of the total growth in the number of federal inmates since 1980.[110] The inmate population in general suffers from a low level of formal education, comes from a socially disadvantaged background, and lacks significant vocational skills.[111] Most adult inmates have served some time in juvenile correctional facilities.[112]

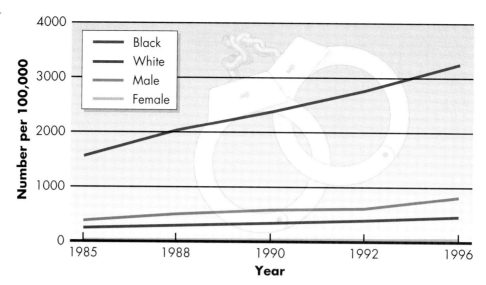

FIGURE 12–4 U.S. incarceration rates by race and sex. *Source:* Bureau of Justice Statistics.

Approximately 347,000 staff members are employed in corrections,[113] with the majority performing direct custodial tasks in state institutions. Females account for 20% of all correctional officers, with the proportion of women officers increasing at around 19% per year.[114] In an effort to encourage the increased employment of women in corrections, the American Correctional Association formally adopted a statement,[115] which reads: "Women have a right to equal employment. No person who is qualified for a particular position/assignment or for job-related opportunities should be denied such employment or opportunities because of gender." The official statement goes on to encourage correctional agencies to "ensure that recruitment, selection, and promotion opportunities are open to women."

According to a recent report by the American Correctional Association, 70% of correctional officers are white, 22% are black, and slightly over 5% are Hispanic.[116] The inmate/custody staff ratio in state prisons averages around 4.1 to 1. Incarceration costs the states an average of $11,302 per inmate per year, while the federal government spends about $13,162 to house one inmate for a year.[117] The ACA reports[118] that in 1991, entry-level correctional officers were paid between $13,520 and $33,996, depending upon the state in which they were hired. Salaries for systems administrators in adult correctional systems were as high as $131,731 (South Carolina), with institutional superintendents earning in the range of $26,436 to $93,693.

Carter, McGee, and Nelson[119] describe the typical state prison system (in relatively populous states) as consisting of

- One high-security prison for long-term, high-risk cases,
- One or more medium security institutions for the bulk of offenders who are not high risks,
- One institution for adult women,
- One or two institutions for young adults (generally under age 25),
- One or two specialized mental hospital-type security prisons for mentally ill prisoners, and
- One or more open-type institutions for low-risk nonviolent populations.

SECURITY LEVELS

Maximum-custody prisons are the institutions most often portrayed in movies and on television. They tend to be massive old prisons with large inmate populations. Some, like Central Prison in Raleigh, North Carolina, are much newer and incorporate advances in prison architecture to provide tight security without sacrificing building aesthetics. Such institutions provide a high level of security characterized by high fences, thick walls, secure

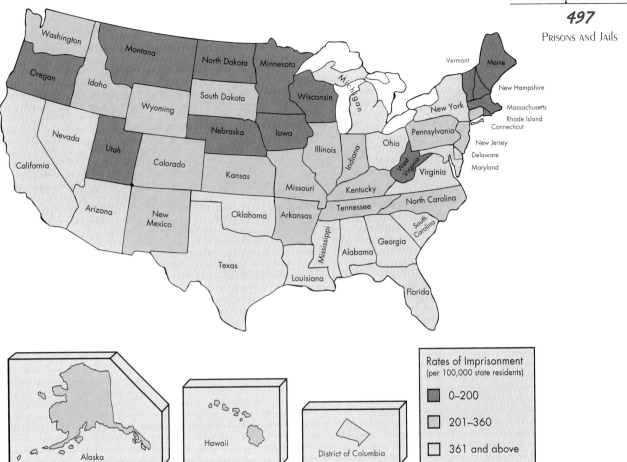

FIGURE 12–5 Rates of imprisonment in the United States.

cells, gun towers, and armed prison guards. Maximum-custody prisons tend to locate cells and other inmate living facilities at the center of the institution and place a variety of barriers between the living area and the institution's outer perimeter. Technological innovations such as electric perimeters, laser motion detectors, electronic and pneumatic locking systems, metal detectors, X-ray machines, television surveillance, radio communications, and computer information systems are frequently used today to reinforce the more traditional maximum-security strategies. These new technologies have helped to lower the cost of new prison construction, although some argue that prison electronic detection devices may be relied upon too heavily and have not yet been adequately tested.[120] Death row inmates are all maximum security prisoners, although the level of security on death row exceeds even that experienced by most prisoners held in maximum custody. Prisoners on death row must spend much of the day in single cells and are often permitted a brief shower only once a week under close supervision.

Most states today have one large centrally located maximum-security institution. Some of these prisons combine more than one custody level and may be both maximum- and medium-security facilities. Medium security is a custody level that in many ways resembles maximum security. Medium-security prisoners are generally permitted more freedom to associate with one another and can go to the prison yard, exercise room, library, and shower and bathroom facilities under less intense supervision than their maximum security counterparts. An important security tool in medium-security prisons is the count, which is literally a headcount of inmates taken at regular intervals. Counts may be taken four times a day and usually require inmates to report to designated areas to be counted. Until the count has been "cleared," all other inmate activity must cease. Medium-security prisons tend to be smaller than maximum-security institutions and often have barbed-wire-topped chain-link fences in place of the more secure stone or concrete block walls found in many of the older maximum-security facilities. Cells and living quarters tend to have more windows and are often located closer to the perimeter of the institution than is the case in maximum security. Dormitory-style housing, where prisoners live together in "ward"-like arrangements, may be employed in medium-security facilities. Medium-security facilities generally have more prison programs and opportunities for inmates to participate in recreational and other programs than do maximum-custody facilities.

Minimum-security institutions do not fit the stereotypical conception of prisons. Minimum-security inmates are generally housed in dormitory-like settings and are free to walk the yard and visit most of the prison facilities. Some newer prisons provide minimum-security inmates with private rooms, which they can decorate (within limits) according to their tastes. Inmates usually have free access to a "canteen," which sells personal products like cigarettes, toothpaste, and candy bars. Minimum-security inmates often wear uniforms of a different color from those of inmates in higher custody levels, and in some institutions may wear civilian clothes. They work under only general supervision and usually have access to recreational, educational, and skills training programs on the prison grounds. Guards are unarmed, gun towers do not exist, and fences, if they are present at all, are usually low and sometimes even unlocked. Many minimum-security prisoners participate in some sort of work or study release program, and some have extensive visitation and furlough privileges. Counts may still be taken, although most minimum-security institutions keep track of inmates through daily administrative work schedules. The primary "force" holding inmates in minimum-security institutions is their own restraint. Inmates live with the knowledge that minimum-security institutions are one step removed from close correctional supervision and that if they fail to meet the expectations of administrators they will be transferred into more secure institutions, which will probably delay their release. Inmates returning from assignments in the community may be frisked for contraband, but body cavity searches are rare in minimum custody, being reserved primarily for inmates suspected of smuggling.

Upon entry into the prison system, most states assign prisoners to initial custody levels based upon their perceived dangerousness, escape risk, and type of offense. Some inmates may enter the system at the medium- (or even minimum-) custody level. Inmates move through custody levels according to the progress they are judged to have made in self-control and demonstrated responsibility. Serious, violent criminals who begin their prison careers with lengthy sentences in maximum custody have the opportunity in most states to work their way up to minimum security, although the process usually takes a number of years. Those who "mess up" and represent continuous disciplinary problems are returned to closer custody levels. Minimum-security prisons, as a result, house inmates convicted of all types of criminal offenses.

The typical American prison today is medium or minimum custody. Some states have as many as 80 or 90 small institutions, which may originally have been located in every county to serve the needs of public works and highway maintenance. Medium- and minimum-security institutions house the bulk of the country's prison population and offer a number of programs and services designed to assist with the rehabilitation of offenders and to create the conditions necessary for a successful reentry of the inmate into society. Most prisons offer psychiatric services, academic education, vocational education, substance abuse treatment, health care, counseling, recreation, library services, religious programs, and industrial and agricultural training.[121]

The Federal Prison System

In 1895 the federal government opened a prison at Leavenworth, Kansas, for civilians convicted of violating federal law. Leavenworth had been a military prison, and control over the facility was transferred from the Department of the Army to the Department of Justice. By 1906 the Leavenworth facility had been expanded to a 1,200-inmate capacity, and another prison—in Atlanta, Georgia—had been built. McNeil Island Prison in Washington state was also functioning by the early 1900s. The first federal prison for women opened in 1927 in Alderson, West Virginia. With increasing complexity in the federal criminal code, the number of federal prisoners grew.[122]

On May 14, 1930, the Federal Bureau of Prisons (BOP) was created under the direction of Sanford Bates. The Bureau inherited a system which was dramatically overcrowded. Many federal prisoners were among the most notorious criminals in the nation, and ideals of

This new Federal Bureau of Prisons ADMAX facility in Florence, Colorado, opened in 1995. It is the only ultra-secure institution in the federal system. *AFP/Bettmann*

humane treatment and rehabilitation were all but lacking in the facilities of the 1930s. Director Bates began a program of improvements to relieve overcrowding and to increase the treatment capacity of the system. In 1933 the Medical Center for Federal Prisoners opened in Springfield, Missouri, with a capacity of around 1,000 inmates. Alcatraz Island began operations in 1934.

The federal prison system classifies its institutions according to five[123] security levels: (1) administrative maximum (ADMAX), (2) high security, (3) medium security, (4) low security, and (5) minimum security. High-security facilities are called United States Penitentiaries (USPs), medium- and low-security institutions are both called Federal Correctional Institutions (FCIs); and minimum-security prisons are termed Federal Prison Camps (FPCs).[124] Minimum-security facilities (like Eglin Air Force Base, Florida; and Maxwell Air Force Base, Alabama) are essentially honor-type camps with barracks-like housing and no fencing. Low-security facilities in the federal prison system are surrounded by double chain-link fencing and employ vehicle patrols around their perimeters to enhance security. Medium-security facilities (like those in Terminal Island, California; Lompoc, California; and Seagoville, Texas) make use of similar fencing and patrols, but supplement it with electronic monitoring of the grounds and perimeter areas. High-security facilities (USPs such as those in Atlanta, Georgia; Lewisburg, Pennsylvania; Terre Haute, Indiana; and Leavenworth, Kansas) are architecturally designed to prevent escapes and to contain disturbances. They also make use of armed patrols and intense electronic surveillance. A separate federal prison category is that of Administrative Facility, consisting of institutions with special missions, which are designed to house all types of inmates. Most administrative facilities are Metropolitan Detention Centers (MDCs). MDCs, which are generally located in large cities close to federal courthouses, are the jails of the federal correctional system and hold inmates awaiting trial in federal court. Another five administrative facilities are termed Medical Centers for Federal Prisoners (MCFPs) and function as hospitals.

As of January 1, 1997, the federal correctional system consisted of 85 facilities existing either as single institutions or as Federal Correctional Complexes—that is, sites consisting of more than one type of correctional institution (see Figure 12–6). The Federal Correctional Complex at Allenwood, Pennsylvania, for example, consists of a United States Penitentiary, a Federal Prison Camp, and two Federal Correctional Institutions (one low and one medium security), each with its own warden. Federal institutions can be classified by type as follows: 55 are Federal Prison Camps (holding 31% of all federal prisoners), 17 are low-security facilities (with 27% of the system's prisoners), 26 are medium-security facilities (23% of the pop-

ADMAX Administrative maximum; the term used by the federal government to denote ultra-high-security prisons.

FIGURE 12–6 The federal correctional system, 1997. *Source:* Federal Bureau of Prisons.

ulation), 8 are high-security prisons (10% of prisoners), and 1 is an ADMAX facility (with 1% of the prison population).

One of the most recent additions to the system is the $60 million ultra-maximum security federal prison at Florence, Colorado—the federal system's only ADMAX unit. Dubbed by some "the Alcatraz of the Rockies," the new 575-bed facility is designed to be the most secure prison ever built by the government.[125] Opened in 1995, it holds mob bosses, spies, terrorists, murderers, and escape artists. Dangerous inmates are confined to their cells 23 hours per day and are not allowed to see or associate with other inmates. Electronically controlled doors throughout the institution channel inmates to individual exercise sessions, and educational courses, religious services, and administrative matters are conducted via closed-circuit television piped directly into the prisoners' cells. Remote-controlled heavy steel doors within the prison allow correctional staff to section off the institution in the event of rioting, and the system can be controlled from outside if the entire prison is compromised.

With new facilities rapidly coming on-line, however, crowding in federal prisons is pervasive. The number of inmates held in federal prisons had risen from 24,000 in 1980 to 100,500 in 1997.[126]

In an effort to combat rising expenses, the U.S. Congress recently passed legislation that imposes a "user fee" on federal inmates able to pay the costs associated with their incarceration.[127] Under the law, inmates may be assessed a dollar amount up to the cost of a year's incarceration—currently around $20,000. The statute, which was designed so as not to impose hardships on poor defendants or their dependents, directs that collected funds, estimated to soon total $48 million per year, are to be used to improve alcohol and drug abuse programs within federal prisons.

> *If you don't like the place, don't come here.*
>
> —Maricopa County (Arizona) Sheriff Joe Arpaio, giving advice to inmates housed in his desert tent city

RECENT IMPROVEMENTS

In the midst of frequent lawsuits, court-ordered changes in prison administration, and overcrowded conditions, outstanding prison facilities are being recognized through the American Correctional Association's program of accreditation. The ACA Commission on Accreditation has developed a set of standards which correctional institutions can use in self-evaluation. Those which meet the standards can apply for accreditation under the program. Unfortunately, accreditation of prisons has few "teeth." Although unaccredited universities would not long be in business, few prisoners can choose the institution they want to be housed in.

Another avenue toward improvement of the nation's prisons can be found in the National Academy of Corrections, the training arm of the National Institute of Corrections. The

Careers in Justice

Working with the Federal Bureau of Prisons

TYPICAL POSITIONS.
Correctional officer, psychologist, physician, nurse, chaplain, correctional/drug treatment specialist, safety specialist, teacher, program officer, vocational instructor, and others.

EMPLOYMENT REQUIREMENTS.
Applicants must (1) be U.S. citizens, (2) be less than 37 years of age (although for some hard-to-fill positions an age waiver may be granted), (3) successfully complete an employee interview, (4) pass a physical examination, and (5) pass a field security investigation. Correctional officer candidates must hold a Bachelor's degree.

OTHER REQUIREMENTS.
Successful completion of in-service training at the Federal Law Enforcement Training Academy at Glynco, Georgia.

SALARY. Correctional officers are appointed at the GS-5 level, while six months or more of graduate education in criminal justice or any social science may qualify the applicant for the GS-6 level or higher. A correctional officer may be advanced to the next higher pay grade level after six months of satisfactory service.

BENEFITS. Benefits include (1) participation in the Federal Employees' Retirement System, (2) paid annual leave, (3) paid sick leave, (4) low-cost health and life insurance, and (5) paid holidays. Other benefits naturally accrue from what the Bureau describes as "strong internal merit promotion practices" and "unlimited opportunities for advancement in one of the fastest-growing government agencies."

DIRECT INQUIRIES TO:
Federal Bureau of Prisons, Room 460, 320 First Street, N.W.
Washington, D.C. 20534
Phone: (202) 307-1490
Web site: http://www.bop.gov

Academy, located in Boulder, Colorado, offers seminars and training sessions for state and local correctional managers, trainers, personnel directors, sheriffs, and state legislators.[128] Issues covered include strategies to control overcrowding, community corrections program management, prison programs, gangs and disturbances, security, and public and media relations, as well as many other topics.[129]

Jails

Jails are short-term confinement facilities which were originally intended to hold suspects following arrest and pending trial. Today, jails also house those convicted of misdemeanors who are serving relatively short sentences and felony offenders awaiting transportation to long-term confinement facilities. A 1996 report[130] by the Bureau of Justice Statistics found that the nation's jails held 455,098 men and 52,136 women, with 7,888 people held in jails being younger than 18 years old. Numerically, 50% of jail inmates are pretrial detainees or are defendants involved in some stage of the trial process.[131] While only a few years ago driving under the influence was the most common charge for jailed persons 45 years of age or older (accounting for 10% of all jail inmates), persons charged with drug law violations now account for 25% of those in jail. Bond has been set by the court, although not yet posted, for almost nine out of ten jail inmates.[132] Significantly, one of the fastest-growing sectors of today's jail population consists of sentenced offenders serving time in local jails because overcrowded prisons cannot accept them.

A total of 3,304 jails are in operation throughout the United States today, staffed by approximately 165,500 correctional workers—the equivalent of about 1 employee for every 2.8 jail inmates.[133] Overall, the jail budget is huge, and facilities are overflowing. Some $9.6 billion is spent every year by state and local governments to operate the nation's jails,[134] with more than $1 billion in additional monies earmarked for new jail construction and for facilities renovation. On average, approximately $14,667 is spent yearly to house one jail inmate.[135]

Approximately 20 million people are admitted (or readmitted) to the nation's jails each year. Some jail inmates stay for as little as one day, while others serve extended periods of jail

Jail A confinement facility administered by an agency of local government, typically a law enforcement agency, intended for adults but sometimes also containing juveniles, which holds persons detained pending adjudication and/or persons committed after adjudication (usually those committed on sentences of a year or less).

A guard walks alone along a wall at Los Angeles County's new $373 million Twin Towers Correctional Facility. Opened in 1997, it is one of the world's largest jails. *Damian Dovarganes, AP/Wide World Photos*

time. Most jails are small. Two out of three were built to house 50 or fewer inmates. Most people who spend time in jail, however, do so in larger institutions.[136] According to the National Institute of Justice, "about 6% of jail facilities housed more than half of all jail inmates..." in the nation.[137] Although there are many small and medium-sized jails across the country, a handful of "megajails" house thousands of inmates. The largest such facilities can be found in New York City's Riker's Island, the Cook County jail in Chicago, Houston's Harris County Downtown Central Jail, the New Orleans Parish Prison System, Los Angeles County's Pitchess Honor Ranch, and Los Angeles County's Men's Central Jail. Men's Central Jail was to be replaced by the new 4,000-bed Twin Towers Correctional Facility. Twin Towers, which cost $373 million to build, opened in 1997, but budget problems plaguing Los Angeles County have kept it from being fully utilized.[138] The largest employer among these huge jails is the Cook County facility, with over 1,200 personnel on its payroll.[139]

Not surprisingly, the nation's most populous states tend to have the most inmates. Almost half of the nation's jail population are housed in the jails of five states:[140] California, Texas, Florida, New York, and Georgia. Some states, however, report a much higher rate of growth in the use of local confinement facilities than others. NIJ reports that jail populations in Texas grew by 264% in the ten years between 1985 and 1995, and increased 103% in Maryland—while growing only slightly in Maine, Missouri, Nebraska, and Wyoming. Some states, such as Louisiana (with 377 jail inmates per every 100,000 residents), Georgia (328 per 100,000), and Texas (307 per 100,000), show a high *rate* of jail usage, while other states, such as Iowa, Maine, and North Dakota (with only 57 jail inmates per 100,000 state residents), and Minnesota, Montana, and South Dakota (with around 81 per 100,000), make less use of jail.[141]

Most people processed through the country's jails are members of minority groups (61%), with 44% of jail inmates classifying themselves as black, 15% as Hispanic, and another 2% as minorities belonging to other races. Thirty-nine percent of jail inmates classify themselves as white. Ninety percent are male.[142]

WOMEN AND JAIL

Although women comprise only 10% of the country's jail population, they are "virtually the largest growth group in jails nationwide."[143] Jailed women face a number of special problems. Only 25.7% of the nation's jails report having a classification system specifically designed to evaluate female inmates,[144] and, although "a large proportion of jurisdictions" report plans "to build facilities geared to the female offender,"[145] not all jurisdictions today even provide separate housing areas for female inmates. Educational levels are very low among jailed women, and fewer than half are high-school graduates.[146] Pregnancy is another problem. Nationally, 4% of female inmates are pregnant at the time they come to jail,[147] but as much as 10% of the female population of urban jails is reported to be pregnant on any given day.[148] As a consequence, a few hundred children are born in jails each year. Jailed mothers are not only separated from their children, they may have to pay for their support. Twelve percent of all jails in one study group reported requiring employed female inmates to contribute to the support of their dependent children.

Drug abuse is another significant source of difficulty for jailed women. Over 30% of women who are admitted to jail have a substance abuse problem at the time of admission, and in some parts of the country, that figure may be as high as 70%.[149] Adding to the problem is the fact that substantive medical programs for female inmates, such as obstetrics and gynecological care, are often lacking. In planning medical services for female inmates into the next century, some writers have advised jail administrators to expect to see an increasingly common kind of inmate: "[a]n opiate-addicted female who is pregnant with no prior prenatal care having one or more sexually transmitted diseases, and fitting a high-risk category for AIDS (prostitution, IV drug use)."[150]

Female inmates are only half the story. Women working in corrections are the other. In a recent study[151] Linda Zupan, one of the new generation of outstanding jail scholars, found that women comprised 22% of the correctional officer force in jails across the nation. The deployment of female personnel, however, was disproportionately skewed toward jobs in the lower ranks. Although 60% of all support staff (secretaries, cooks, and janitors) were women, only one in every ten chief administrators was female. Zupan explains this pattern by pointing to the "token-status" of women staff members in some of the nation's jails.[152] Even so, Zupan did find that women correctional employees were significantly committed to their careers and that attitudes of male workers toward female coworkers in jails were generally positive. Zupan's study uncovered 626 jails in which over 50% of the correction officer force consisted of women. On the opposite side of the coin, 954 of the nation's 3,316 jails operating at the time of the study had no female officers.[153] Zupan noted that: "An obvious problem associated with the lack of female officers in jails housing females concerns the potential for abuse and exploitation of women inmates by male staff."[154]

Jails which do hire women generally accord them equal footing with male staffers. Although cross-gender privacy is a potential area of legal liability, few jails limit the supervisory areas which may be visited by female officers working in male facilities. In three quarters of the jails studied by Zupan, women officers were assigned to supervise male housing areas. Only one in four jails which employed women restricted their access to unscreened shower and toilet facilities used by men and/or to other areas such as sexual offender units.

We are the prisoners of the prisoners we have taken.

—J. Clegg

Crowding in Jails

Jails have been called the "shame of the criminal justice system." Many are old, overcrowded, poorly funded, scantily staffed by underpaid and poorly trained employees, and given low priority in local budgets. Court-ordered caps on jail populations are increasingly common. A few years ago, for example, the Harris County Jail in Houston, Texas, was forced to release 250 inmates after missing a deadline for reducing its resident population of 6,100 people.[155] A nationwide survey, published by the Bureau of Justice Statistics, found that 46% of all jails were built more than 25 years ago and of that percentage, over half were more than 50 years old.[156]

Overcrowded jails have become a critical issue throughout the justice system.[157] A 1983 national census revealed that jails were operating at only 85% of their rated capacity.[158] By 1990, however, the nation's jails were running at 108% of capacity, and new jails could be found on drawing boards and under construction across the country. By 1995 new facilities had opened, and overall jail occupancy was reported at 93% of rated capacity, although some individual facilities were desperately overcrowded.[159] With square footage per inmate averaging only 58.3[160] in jails today, managers still cite crowding and staff shortages as the two most critical problems facing jails today.[161]

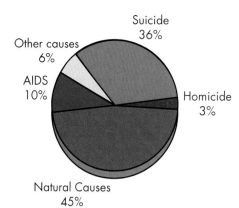

FIGURE 12–7 Causes of jail deaths in the United States. *Source:* U.S. Department of Justice.

The root cause of jail crowding can be found in a growing crime rate coupled with a punitive public attitude, which has heavily influenced correctional practice. In 1995, for example, Maricopa County, Arizona, sheriff Joe Arpaio added 25 tents to 42 others he had ordered erected two years earlier in the desert outside of Phoenix to relieve overcrowding in the county jail.[162] Arpaio, faced with 1,900 more inmates than his 3,900-capacity jail could handle, built the tent city with help from a volunteer posse, whose members work for free and pay for their own uniforms and guns. Temperatures in the desert jail, which is without air conditioning, soar to well over 100 degrees in the summer time, and wind-blown sand makes life difficult for inmates. In what some see as adding insult to injury, the tough-talking sheriff runs the desert jail frugally—replacing hot inmate meals with bologna sandwiches and requiring inmates to cut one another's hair in order to save on barber's fees. He's also put an end to violent television, forcing inmates to watch shows like *Lassie* and *Donald Duck*, rather than ones with shoot-em'-up themes.

Overcrowded prisons have also spilled over into jails. During the last few years, many states have begun using jails instead of prisons for the confinement of convicted felons, exacerbating the jail crowding problem still further. In 1993, for example, 34,200 inmates were being held in local jails because of overcrowding in state prisons. Another problem arises from the sentencing of individuals who are unable to make restitution, alimony, or child support payments to jail time—a practice which has made the local lockup at least partially a debtor's prison. Symptomatic of problems brought on by overcrowding, the National Institute of Justice reported 234 suicides in jails across the nation during a recent year.[163] Jail deaths from all causes (which total about 650 annually) are shown in Figure 12–7.

Although the societal underpinnings of overcrowding are difficult to assess, some causes of jail crowding, which can be immediately addressed, include the following:[164]

- The inability of jail inmates to make bond due to institutionalized bail bond practices and lack of funding sources for indigent defendants
- Unnecessary delays between arrest and final case disposition
- Unnecessarily limited access to vital information about defendants which could be useful in facilitating court-ordered pretrial release
- The limited ability of the criminal justice system to handle cases expeditiously due to a lack of needed resources (judges, assistant prosecuting attorneys, etc.)
- Inappropriate attorney delays in moving cases through court (motions to delay cases as part of an attorney's strategy, etc.)
- Unproductive statutes requiring that specified nonviolent offenders be jailed (including those requiring mandatory pretrial jailing of DWIs, minor drug offenders, second offense shoplifting, etc.)

Some innovative jurisdictions have already substantially reduced jail crowding. San Diego, California, for example, uses a privately operated detoxification reception program in order to divert many inebriates from the proverbial "drunk tank."[165] Officials in Galveston County, Texas, routinely divert mentally ill arrestees directly to a mental health facility.[166] Other areas use pretrial services and magistrates' offices, which are open 24 hours a day, for the purpose of setting bail, making release possible.

Inside a direct supervision jail. Inmates and officers can mingle in this Hillsborough County, New Hampshire jail. *Rick Friedman, Black Star*

Direct Supervision Jails

Some authors have suggested that the problems found in many jails today stem from "mismanagement, lack of fiscal support, heterogeneous inmate populations, overuse and misuse of detention, overemphasis on custodial goals, and political and public apathy."[167] Others propose that environmental and organizational elements inherent in traditional jail architecture and staffing have given rise to today's difficulties.[168] Traditional jails, say these observers, were built upon the assumption that inmates are inherently violent and potentially destructive. Hence, most of today's jails were constructed to give staff maximum control over inmates—through the use of thick walls, bars, and other architectural barriers to the free movement of inmates. Such institutions, however, also limit the correctional staff's visibility and access to many confinement areas. As a consequence, they tend to encourage just the kinds of inmate behavior that jails were meant to control. Efficient hallway patrols and expensive video technology help in overcoming the limits that old jail architecture places on supervision.

In an effort to solve many of the problems which have dogged jails in the past, a new jail management strategy emerged during the 1980s. Called direct supervision (or podular/direct supervision, or PDS) this contemporary approach "joins podular/unit architecture with a participative, proactive management philosophy."[169] Often built in a system of "pods," or modular self-contained housing areas linked to one another, direct supervision jails eliminate the old physical barriers which separated staff and inmates. Gone are bars and isolated secure observation areas for officers. They are replaced by an open environment, in which inmates and correctional personnel mingle with relative freedom. In a growing number of such "new-generation" jails, large reinforced Plexiglas panels have supplanted walls and serve to separate activity areas, such as classrooms and dining halls, from one another. Soft furniture is often found throughout these institutions, and individual rooms take the place of cells, allowing inmates at least a modicum of personal privacy. In today's direct supervision jails, 16 to 46 inmates typically live in one pod, with correctional staffers present among the inmate population on an around-the-clock basis.

The first direct supervision jail opened in the 1970s in Contra Costa County, California. This 386-bed facility became a model for the nation, and other new-generation jails soon opened in Las Vegas; Portland; Reno; New York City; Bucks County, Pennsylvania; Vancouver,

Direct Supervision Jails Temporary confinement facilities which eliminate many of the traditional barriers between inmates and correctional staff. Physical barriers in direct supervision jails are far less common than in traditional jails, allowing staff members the opportunity for greater interaction with, and control over, residents.

British Columbia; and Miami. The federal prison system opened PDS facilities in 1974–1975 in the Metropolitan Correctional Centers (MCCs) of San Diego, New York, and Chicago.

Direct supervision jails have been touted for their tendency to reduce inmate dissatisfaction and for their ability to deter rape and violence among the inmate population. By eliminating architectural barriers to staff/inmate interaction, direct supervision facilities are said to place officers back in control of institutions. While these innovative facilities are still too new to assess fully, a number of studies have already demonstrated their success at reducing the likelihood of inmate victimization. One such study,[170] published in 1994, found that staff morale in direct supervision jails was far higher than in traditional institutions, while inmates reported reduced stress levels, and fewer inmate-on-inmate and inmate-on-staff assaults occurred in podular jails. Similarly, sexual assault, jail rape, suicide, and escape have all been found to occur far less frequently in direct supervision facilities than in traditional institutions.[171] Significantly, new-generation jails appear to reduce substantially the number of lawsuits brought by inmates and lower the incidence of adverse court-ordered judgments against jail administrators.

The most comprehensive study of direct supervision jails to date, which reported its results in April 1995, found that 114 confinement facilities across the country could be classified as direct supervision facilities.[172] The study, which attempted to survey all such jails, found that direct supervision jails

1. range in size from small jails with 24 inmates (and 12 officers on staff), to large facilities with 2,737 (and 600 correctional officers).
2. average 591 inmates and employ 148 officers, with an inmate to officer ratio of 16.8:1 during a given shift.
3. are podular in design, with an average of 47 inmates and one officer per pod at any given time.
4. hold local, state, and federal prisoners. About 45% of the institutions surveyed held only local inmates, while the rest held mixed groups of inmates.
5. varied by security level. The majority (about 59%) held mixed-security levels, while 26% were maximum-security jails. About 13% described themselves as medium-security facilities, and another 2% fit within the minimum-security category.
6. were usually unionized. About 70% of direct supervision jails reported unionized staffs.

While the number of direct supervision jails seems to be rapidly growing, such facilities are not without their problems. In 1993, for example, the 238-bed Rensselaer County PDS jail in Troy, New York, experienced a disturbance "that resulted in a total loss of control…removal of officers from the pods—and the escape of two inmates."[173] Somewhat later, the 700-bed San Joaquin County Jail in Stockton, California, experienced numerous problems, including the escape of seven inmates.

Some authors[174] have recognized that new-generation jails are too frequently run by old-style managers and that correctional personnel sometimes lack the training needed to make the transition to the new style of supervision. Others[175] have suggested that managers of direct supervision jails, especially those at the midlevel, could benefit from clearer job descriptions and additional training. In the words of one Canadian advocate of direct supervision,[176] "training becomes particularly critical in direct supervision jails where relationships are more immediate and are more complex." Finally, recommendations have arisen from those tasked with hiring[177] that potential new staff members should be psychologically screened and that intensive use be made of preemployment interviews in order to determine the suitability of applicants for correctional officer positions in direction supervision jails.

Jails and the Future

In contrast to more visible issues confronting the justice system, such as the death penalty, gun control, the war on drugs, and big-city gangs, jails have received relatively little attention from the media and have generally escaped close public scrutiny.[178] National efforts, however, to improve the quality of jail life are under way. Some changes involve adding crucial programs for inmates. A recent American Jail Association study of drug treatment programs in jails, for example, found that "a small fraction (perhaps fewer than 10%) of inmates needing drug treatment actually receive these services."[179] Follow-up efforts were aimed at developing standards to guide jail administrators in increasing the availability of drug treatment services to inmates.

Jail industries are another growing programmatic area. The best of them serve the community while training inmates in marketable skills.[180] In an exemplary effort to humanize its megajails,[181] for example, the Los Angeles County Sheriff's Department recently opened an inmate telephone answering service. Many calls are received by the Sheriff's Department daily, requesting information about a significant number of the county's 22,000 jail inmates. These requests for information were becoming increasingly difficult to handle due to the growing fiscal constraints facing local government. To handle the huge number of calls effectively without tying up sworn law enforcement personnel, the department began using inmates specially trained to handle incoming calls. Eighty inmates were assigned to the project, with groups of different sizes covering shifts throughout the day. Each inmate staffer went through a program designed to provide coaching in proper telephone procedures and to teach each operator how to run computer terminals containing routine data on the department's inmates. The new system is now fully in place and handles 4,000 telephone inquiries a day. The time needed to answer a call and provide information has dropped from 30 minutes under the old system to a remarkable 10 seconds today.

Another innovative program operates out of the Jackson County Detention Center (JCDC) in Kansas City, Missouri.[182] The JCDC began using citizen volunteers more than a decade ago. Today, 123 volunteers work in the facility—many of them are tutors in the general education program. Others offer substance abuse counseling, marriage counseling, and chaplain's services. Citizen volunteers have contributed 50,000 hours of service time during the past six years, at a value of over half a million dollars.

Jail boot camps, like that run by the Harris County, Texas, probation department, are also growing in popularity. Boot camps in jail serve to give offenders who are sentenced to probationary terms a taste of confinement and the rigors of life behind bars. The Harris County CRIPP (Courts Regimented Intensive Probation Program) facility began operation in May 1991 and is located in Humble, Texas. Separate CRIPP programs are run for about 400 male and 50 female probationers.[183] The most recent comprehensive study[184] of jail boot camps found only 10 such jail-based programs in the country, although current numbers are probably higher.

Also capturing much recent attention are **regional jails**—that is, jails that are built and run using the combined resources of a variety of local jurisdictions and that have begun to replace smaller and often antiquated local jails in at least a few locations. One example of a regional jail is the Western Tidewater Regional Jail, serving the cities of Suffolk and Franklin, and the county of Isle of Wright in Virginia.[185] Regional jails, which are just beginning to come into their own, may develop more quickly in Virginia—where the state, recognizing the economies of consolidation, offers to reimburse localities up to 50% of the cost of building regional jails.

Regional Jails Jails that are built and run using the combined resources of a variety of local jurisdictions.

One final element in the unfolding saga of jail development should be mentioned: the emergence of state jail standards. Thirty-two states have set standards for municipal and county jails.[186] In 25 states, those standards are mandatory. The purpose of jail standards is to identify some basic minimum level of conditions necessary for inmate health and safety. On a national level, the Commission on Accreditation for Corrections, operated jointly by the American Correctional Association and the federal government, has developed its own set of jail standards,[187] as has the National Sheriff's Association. Both sets of standards are designed to ensure a minimal level of comfort and safety in local lockups. Increased standards, though, are costly. Local jurisdictions, already hard pressed to meet other budgetary demands, will probably be slow to upgrade their jails to meet such external guidelines, unless forced to. Ken Kerle, in a study[188] of 61 jails which was designed to test compliance with National Sheriff's Association guidelines, discovered that in many standards areas—especially those of tool control, armory planning, community resources, release preparation, and riot planning—the majority of jails were sorely out of compliance. Lack of a written plan was the most commonly cited reason for failing to meet the standards.

In what may be one of the best set of recommendations for the development of jails which can be used into the next century, Joel A. Thompson and G. Larry Mays[189] suggest that (1)

Twenty-First Century Criminal Justice

Jails and the Future

A number of new directions are beginning to emerge as America's jails move into the twenty-first century. Among them are:

1. A shift away from traditional publicly-run facilities to jails that are operated by private corporations under contracts with local governments. More information on the privatization of prisons and jails is provided in this chapter.

2. An increase in the proportion of inmates who are expected to pay for at least a portion of the expenses associated with their incarceration. In 1996, for example, pretrial inmates in the Broward County (Florida) jail system began paying a $2.00 per day fee for housing and meals. Charges are deducted from inmates' commissary funds, which are contributed by themselves or family members. Inmates who feel they are unable to pay the fee are required to petition jail administrators and to demonstrate why they should not be required to pay.

3. The growing use of computer-based inmate information systems that are integrated with networks used for the administration of court schedules, docket monitoring, and for coordination with other criminal justice agencies. One jail consultant has gone so far as to claim that, because of efficient and integrated information management systems, "paperwork will be a thing of the past in the 21st century jail."[1]

4. A movement toward the professionalization of jail facilities, made possible through growing opportunities for accreditation. Accreditation programs, such as those offered through the American Correctional Association, the Commission on Accreditation for Law Enforcement Agencies, and the National Commission on Correctional Health Care, are already helping shield jail administrators and local governments from the threat of lawsuits by demonstrating adherence to professional standards.

5. A movement toward the increased professionalization of jail personnel, made possible by certification programs such as the new Jail Manager Certification Program operated by the American Jail Association. "Certified Jail Manager" status became possible for the first time in 1997, when applications and certification handbooks were distributed at the AJA's annual meeting in Salt Lake City.

6. A changing public climate—one which may soon shift away from the "get-tough" policies of the past decade toward a more pragmatic emphasis on the needs of both inmates and administrators. Inmate needs in the areas of mental health counseling, suicide prevention, and opportunities for meaningful employment will be met in an effort to facilitate institutional administration.

7. A greater use of direct supervision jails, resulting in fewer internal problems and easier administration. The increased use of direct supervision jails will heighten both inmate and staff morale in most locations where such facilities are deployed.

8. A growing use of inmate labor, as counties, communities, the nonprofit sector, and corporations begin to more fully recognize the advantages to be gained from the meaningful employment of inmates. As a consequence, more inmates will work, and those who do will be involved in an ever-widening sphere of activities. The increase in inmate labor will lead to a widening of partnerships among jails, their administrators, and other community groups. Corporate employers, for example, will begin to operate more and more training programs in jails with the goal of increasing workforce efficiency.

9. A greater use of research in the field of jail operations, which will lead to better-informed and more effective programs and strategies. Research showing that more female officers mean fewer assaults overall, for example, should lead to the hiring of more women in the correctional field.

[1]Ron, Carroll, "Jails and the Criminal Justice System in the 21st Century," *American Jails*, March/April 1997, p. 31.

Sources: Ron Carroll, "Jails and the Criminal Justice System in the 21st Century," *American Jails*, March/April 1997, pp. 26–31; Susan W. McCampbell, "The Paying Prisoner," *American Jails*, March/April 1997, pp. 37–43; Cindy Malm, "AJA Jail Manager Certification Program," *American Jails*, March/April 1997, p. 99; Rod Miller, "Inmate Labor in the 21st Century," *American Jails*, March/April 1997, pp. 45–49; Joseph R. Rowan, "Corrections in the 21st Century," *American Jails*, March/April 1997, pp. 32–36.

American Jail Association Code of Ethics for Jail Officers

As an officer employed in a detention/correctional capacity, I swear (or affirm) to be a good citizen and a credit to my community, state, and nation at all times. I will abstain from all questionable behavior which might bring disrepute to the agency for which I work, my family, my community, and my associates. My lifestyle will be above and beyond reproach and I will constantly strive to set an example of a professional who performs his/her duties according to the laws of our country, state, and community and the policies, procedures, written and verbal orders, and regulations of the agency for which I work.

On the job I promise to:

Keep	The institution secure so as to safeguard my community and the lives of the staff, inmates, and visitors on the premises.
Work	With each individual firmly and fairly without regard to rank, status, or condition.
Maintain	A positive demeanor when confronted with stressful situations of scorn, ridicule, danger, and/or chaos.
Report	Either in writing or by word of mouth to the proper authorities those things which should be reported, and keep silent about matters which are to remain confidential according to the laws and rules of the agency and government.
Manage	And supervise the inmates in an evenhanded and courteous manner.
Refrain	At all times from becoming personally involved in the lives of the inmates and their families.
Treat	All visitors to the jail with politeness and respect and do my utmost to ensure that they observe the jail regulations.
Take	Advantage of all education and training opportunities designed to assist me to become a more competent officer.
Communicate	With people in or outside of the jail, whether by phone, written word, or word of mouth, in such a way so as not to reflect in a negative manner upon my agency.
Contribute	To a jail environment which will keep the inmate involved in activities designed to improve his/her attitude and character.
Support	All activities of a professional nature through membership and participation that will continue to elevate the status of those who operate our nation's jails.

Do my best through word and deed to present an image to the public at large of a jail professional, committed to progress for an improved and enlightened criminal justice system.

Source: The American Jail Association, *Code of Ethics for Jail Officers* as adopted January 10, 1991 (Hagerstown, MD: The Association, 1991). Reprinted with permission.

states should provide financial aid and/or incentives to local governments for jail construction and renovation, (2) all states must develop mandatory jail standards, (3) mandatory jail inspections should become commonplace in the enforcement of standards, (4) citizens should be educated about the function and significance of jails to increase their willingness to fund new jail construction, (5) all jails need to have written policies and procedures to be used in training and to serve as a basis for a defense against lawsuits, and (6) "[c]ommunities should explore alternatives to incarceration [because]…[m]any jail detainees are not threats to society and should not occupy scarce and expensive cell space."

Private Prisons

Throughout our nation's history, state-run prison systems have contracted with private industries for food, psychological testing, training, recreational, and other services, and it is

Private Prisons
Correctional institutions operated by private firms on behalf of local and state governments.

The Corrections Corporation of America's Houston Processing Center—one of a growing number of private prison facilities across the country. Private prisons may be the way of the future. *Brett Coomer, AP/Wide World Photos*

Privatization The movement toward the wider use of private prisons.

estimated that more than three dozen states today rely on private businesses to serve a variety of correctional needs. It was only logical, therefore, that states would at some point turn to private industry for the provision of prison space. Beginning in the early 1980s, that's exactly what they did. Although the **privatization** movement was slow to catch on, it has since grown at a rapid pace. In 1986 only 2,620 prisoners could be found in privately-run confinement facilities.[190] But by 1997 more than 74,000 prisoners were being held in 124 privately operated secure correctional facilities throughout 18 states and the District of Columbia. Today's privately-run prisons are operated by Corrections Corporation of America (CCA), U.S. Corrections Corporation, Wackenhut Corrections Corporation, and numerous other smaller companies. According to one source, the growth rate of the private prison "industry" is over 35% annually[191]— comparable to the highest growth rates anywhere in the corporate sector.

Most states that use private firms to supplement their prison resources contract with such companies to provide a full range of custodial and other correctional services. (Interest in the privatization of jails is also on the increase, although space does not permit a full discussion of the issue[192]). States contract with private companies in order to reduce overcrowding, lower operating expenses, and avoid lawsuits targeted at state officials and employees.[193] As Dale K. Sechrest and David Shichor observe, "The major arguments for privatization in the current era are economic and administrative. It is repeatedly stated that the private sector can operate prisons cheaper by providing at least the same quality of service as the public sector and [by] demonstrating more flexibility in terms of anticipating needs and devising ways to meet them."[194] A 1996 study[195] by the United States General Accounting Office, however, questioned such claims. As Sechrest and Shichor note, "The GAO study found neither cost savings nor substantial differences in the quality of services…"[196] between private and publicly-run prisons.

Many hurdles remain before the privatization movement can effectively provide large-scale custodial supervision. The "Theory Into Practice" box in this section addresses some of the questions about the movement toward private prisons. One of the most significant barriers to privatization lies in the fact that some states have old laws which prohibit private involvement in correctional management. Other practical hurdles exist as well. States which

Theory into Practice

THE DEBATE OVER PRIVATE PRISONS—SOME QUESTIONS WHICH REMAIN

- Can the government delegate its powers to incarcerate persons to a private firm?
- Can a private firm deprive persons of their liberty and exercise coercive authority, perhaps through use of deadly force?
- Who would be legally liable in the event of lawsuits?
- Who would be responsible for maintaining the prison if the private employees go on strike?
- Would a private company have the right to refuse to accept certain types of inmates, for example, those with AIDS?
- If a private firm went bankrupt, who would be responsible for the inmates and the facility?

- Could a private company reduce staff salaries or hire nonunion members as a way of reducing costs?
- Would the "profit motive" operate to the detriment of the government or the inmates, either by keeping inmates in prison who should be released or by reducing services to a point at which inmates, guards, and the public were endangered?
- What options would a government with no facility of its own have if it became dissatisfied with the performance of the private firm?
- Is it appropriate for the government to circumvent the public's

right to vote to increase its debt ceiling (to build new prisons)?

Source: Bureau of Justice Statistics. *Report to the Nation on Crime and Justice*, 2nd ed. (Washington, D.C.: U.S. Department of Justice, 1988).

do contract with private firms may face the specter of strikes by guards who do not come under state laws restricting the ability of employees to strike. Moreover, since responsibility for the protection of inmate rights still lies with the state, their liability will not transfer to private corrections.[197] In today's legal climate, it is unclear whether a state can shield itself or its employees through private prison contracting, but it would appear that such shielding is unlikely to be recognized by the courts. To limit their own liability, states will probably have to oversee private operations as well as set standards for training and custody. In 1997 the U.S. Supreme Court, in the case of *Richardson* v. *McNight*,[198] made it clear that prison guards employed by a private firm are not entitled to qualified immunity from suits by prisoners charging a violation of Section 1983 of Title 42 of the U.S. Code (see Chapter 6 for more information on "1983 lawsuits"). In the words of the Court: "While government employed prison guards may have enjoyed a kind of immunity defense arising out of their status as public employees at common law…There is no conclusive evidence of an historical tradition of immunity for private parties carrying out these functions."[199]

Some of the potentially most serious legal issues face states that contract to hold inmates outside of their own jurisdiction. In 1996, for example, two inmates escaped from a 240-man sex offender unit run by Corrections Corporation of America under contract with the state of Oregon. Problems immediately arose because the CCA unit was located near Houston, Texas—not in Oregon, where the men had been originally sentenced to confinement. Following the escape, Texas officials were unsure whether they even had arrest power over the former prisoners, since they had not committed any crimes in Texas. Moreover, while prison escape is a crime under Texas law, the law only applies to state-run facilities—not to private facilities where correctional personnel are not employed by the state nor empowered in any official capacity by state law. Harris County (Texas) prosecutor John Holmes explained the situation this way: "They have not committed the offense of escape under Texas law…and the only reason at all that they're subject to being arrested and were arrested was because during their leaving the facility, they assaulted a guard and took his motor vehicle. That we can charge them with and have."[200]

Opponents of the movement toward privatization cite these and many other issues. They claim that, aside from legal concerns, cost reductions via the use of private facilities can only

Visit the *CJToday* Web page and click on "Web Chapters," then "Chapter 12." Follow the "find the facts" links in order to learn more about corrections at the federal and state levels.

be achieved by lowering standards. They fear a return to the inhumane conditions of early jails, as private firms seek to turn prisons into profit-making operations. For states which do choose to contract with private firms, the National Institute of Justice recommends a "regular and systematic sampling" of former inmates to appraise prison conditions, as well as "on-site inspections at least every year" of each privately run institution. State personnel serving as monitors should be stationed in large facilities, says NIJ, and a "meticulous review" of all services should be conducted prior to the contract renewal date.[201]

SUMMARY

Prisons are long-term secure confinement facilities in which convicted offenders serve time as punishment for breaking the law. Jails, in contrast, are short-term confinement facilities which were originally intended to hold suspects following arrest and pending trial. Differences between the two types of institutions have begun to blur, however, as large and medium-size jails across the country are being increasingly called upon to house offenders who have been convicted of relatively minor crimes and to accommodate a portion of our country's overflowing prison population.

Today's overcrowded prisons are largely the result of historical efforts to humanize the treatment of offenders. "Doing time for crime" is our modern answer to the corporal punishments of centuries past. Even so, contemporary corrections is far from a panacea, and questions remain about the conditions of imprisonment in today's correctional facilities. Many prisons are dangerously overcrowded, and new ones are expensive to build. The emphasis upon security, which is so characteristic of correctional staff members and prison administrators, leaves little room for capable treatment programs. Moreover, an end to crowding is nowhere in sight, and a new just deserts philosophy strongly influences today's correctional policy. The just deserts philosophy is characterized by a "get-tough" attitude which continues to swell prison populations even as it reduces opportunities for change among individual inmates. It is also a highly pragmatic philosophy, based as it is upon studies demonstrating the clear likelihood of recidivism among correctional clients and upon a strong belief that "nothing works" to rehabilitate criminal offenders.

As a result of all these considerations, today's imprisonment practices rest upon a policy of frustration. Prisons exist in a kind of limbo, continuing their role as warehouses for the untrusted and the unreformable. The return of prison industries, heightened interest in efficient technologies of secure imprisonment, and court-ordered reforms are all signs that society has given up any hope of successful large-scale reformation among inmate populations.

DISCUSSION QUESTIONS

1. Trace the historical development of imprisonment, beginning with the Pennsylvania system. In what ways has correctional practice in America changed over time? What changes do you see coming?

2. In your opinion, would a return to physical punishments and public humiliation be effective deterrents to crime in today's world? Why or why not?

3. What do you think will be the future of prison industry? Describe the future you envision. On what do you base your predictions?

4. What do you see as the role of private prisons? What will be the state of private prisons two or three decades from now?

5. Explain the pros and cons of the present just deserts model of corrections. Do you believe that new rehabilitative models will be developed which will make just deserts a thing of the past? If so, on what will they be based?

6. What solutions, if any, do you see to the present overcrowded conditions of many prison systems? How might changes in the law help ease overcrowding? Are such changes a workable strategy? Why or why not?

 WEB WATCH

Access the *Criminal Justice Today* site on the World Wide Web by pointing your Web browser at http://www.prenhall.com/cjtoday. Once there, click on "Web Chapters," then select "Chapter 12: Prisons and Jails" in order to access electronic information and other sites of relevance to this chapter. You may also wish to enter the Global Town Meeting, which provides facilities for the posting of electronic messages for others to read. Messages are arranged by topic, with new topics constantly being added.

NOTES

1. As cited in the National Conference on Prison Industries, *Discussions and Recommendations* (Washington, D.C.: U.S. Government Printing Office, 1986), p. 23.

2. Camden Pelham, *Chronicles of Crime: A Series of Memoirs and Anecdotes of Notorious Characters* (London: T. Miles and Co., 1887), pp. 28–30.

3. This section owes much to Harry Elmer Barnes and Negley K. Teeters, *New Horizons in Criminology*, 3d ed. (Englewood Cliffs, NJ: Prentice Hall, 1959).

4. Ibid., p. 290.

5. See Jack Elliott, Jr., "Prison or Paddle," The Associated Press wire services, February 8, 1995.

6. Ann O'Hanlon, "New Interest in Corporal Punishment; Several States Weigh Get-Tough Measures," *The Washington Post* wire services, March 5, 1995.

7. Barnes and Teeters, *New Horizons in Criminology*, p. 292.

8. Ibid.

9. Ibid., p. 293.

10. Arthur Evans Wood and John Barker Waite, *Crime and Its Treatment: Social and Legal Aspects of Criminology* (New York: American Book Company, 1941), p. 488.

11. John Howard, *State of Prisons* (London, 1777), reprinted by E. P. Dutton, New York, 1929.

12. Although some writers hold that the Quakers originated the concept of solitary confinement for prisoners, there is evidence that the practice already existed in England prior to 1789. John Howard, for example, describes solitary confinement in use at Reading Brideswell in the 1780s.

13. Vergil L. Williams, *Dictionary of American Penology: An Introduction* (Westport, CT: Greenwood, 1979), p. 200.

14. Barnes and Teeters, *New Horizons in Criminology*, p. 348.

15. Williams, *Dictionary of American Penology*, p. 29.

16. With regard to cost, supporters of the Pennsylvania system argued that it was less expensive than the Auburn style of imprisonment because it led to reformation much faster than did the New York style.

17. Williams, *Dictionary of American Penology*, p. 30.

18. Gustave de Beaumont and Alexis de Tocqueville, *On the Penitentiary System in the United States, and Its Application in France* (Philadelphia: Carey, Lea and Blanchard, 1833).

19. As cited in Barnes and Teeters, *New Horizons in Criminology*, p. 418.

20. Frank Schmalleger, *A History of Corrections: Emerging Ideologies and Practices* (Bristol, IN: Wyndham Hall, 1986), p. 44.

21. Barnes and Teeters, *New Horizons in Criminology*, p. 428.

22. Ibid.

23. Ibid.

24. Wood and Waite, *Crime and Its Treatment*, p. 555, citing U.S. Bureau of Labor statistics.

25. Patty McQuillan, *North Carolina Department of Correction 1986* (Raleigh, NC: Correctional Enterprises Print Shop, 1986).

26. Williams, *Dictionary of American Penology*, pp. 68–70.

27. Robert Mintz, "Federal Prison Industry—The Green Monster, Part One: History and Background," *Crime and Social Justice*, Vol. 6 (Fall/Winter 1976), pp. 41–48.

28. William G. Saylor and Gerald G. Gaes, "PREP Study Links UNICOR Work Experience with Successful Post-Release Outcome," *Corrections Compendium* (October, 1994), pp. 5–6, 8.

29. Criminal Justice Associates, *Private Sector Involvement in Prison-Based Businesses: A National Assessment* (Washington, D.C.: U.S. Government Printing Office, 1985). See also National Institute of Justice (Reports), *Corrections and the Private Sector* (Washington, D.C.: U.S. Government Printing Office, 1985).

30. See "Oregon Begins to Implement Full Employment for Inmates," *Criminal Justice Newsletter*, Vol. 26, no. 6 (March 15, 1995), pp. 1–2.

31. Gail S. Funke, *National Conference on Prison Industries: Discussions and Recommendations* (Washington, D.C.: U.S. Government Printing Office, 1986).

32. Barnes and Teeters, *New Horizons in Criminology*, p. 355.

33. Ibid., p. 381.

34. Ibid., p. 357.

35. Ibid., p. 359.

36. Williams, *Dictionary of American Penology*, p. 90.

37. Ibid., p. 225.

38. Ibid., p. 64.

39. Ibid., p. 227.

40. Donal E. J. MacNamara, "Medical Model in Corrections: Requiescat in Pace," in Fred Montanino, ed., *Incarceration: The Sociology of Imprisonment* (Beverly Hills, CA: Sage Publications, 1978).

41. For a description of the community-based format in its heyday, see Andrew T. Scull, *Decarceration: Community Treatment and the Deviant—A Radical View* (Englewood Cliffs, NJ: Prentice Hall, 1977).

42. Ibid., p. 51.

43. Williams, *Dictionary of American Penology*, p. 45.

44. Ibid.

45. Clemens Bartollas, *Introduction to Corrections* (New York: Harper & Row, 1981), pp. 166–167.

46. Harry Allen, *Corrections in America: An Introduction* (Beverly Hills, CA: Glencoe, 1975), p. 468.

47. Williams, *Dictionary of American Penology*, p. 48.

48. National Advisory Commission on Criminal Justice Standards and Goals, Std. 2.17, part 2 c.

49. Recidivism can be defined in various ways according to the purpose it is intended to serve in a particular study or report. Recidivism is usually defined as rearrest (versus reconviction) and generally includes a time span of five years, although some Bureau of Justice Statistics studies have used six years and other studies one or two years as definitional criteria.

50. Various advocates of the "justice model" can be identified. For a detailed description of the two models, see Michael A. Pizzi, Jr.,

"The Medical Model and the 100 Years War," *Law Enforcement News*, July 7, 1986, pp. 8, 13; and MacNamara, "Medical Model in Corrections."

51. Bureau of Justice Statistics, *Annual Report 1987* (Washington, D.C.: Bureau of Justice Statistics, 1988), p. 70.

52. Ibid.

53. Ibid.

54. Lawrence Greenfeld, "Examining Recidivism," *BJS Special Report* (Washington, D.C.: U.S. Government Printing Office, 1985).

55. R. Martinson, "What Works: Questions and Answers About Prison Reform" *Public Interest*, no. 35 (1974), pp. 22–54. See also Douglas Lipton, Robert M. Martinson, and Judith Wilkes, *The Effectiveness of Correctional Treatment: A Survey of Treatment Evaluation Studies* (New York: Praeger, 1975).

56. L. Sechrest, S. White, and E. Brown, eds., *The Rehabilitation of Criminal Offenders: Problems and Prospects* (Washington, D.C.: The National Academy of Sciences, 1979).

57. Bureau of Justice Statistics, *Prisoners in 1987* (Washington, D.C.: U.S. Government Printing Office, 1988).

58. Christopher J. Mumola and Allen J. Beck, *Prisoners in 1996* (Washington, D.C.: Bureau of Justice Statistics, 1997).

59. Wade B. Houck, "Acquiring New Prison Sites: The Federal Experience," *NIJ Construction Bulletin* (Washington, D.C.: National Institute of Justice, 1987).

60. Allen J. Beck and Darrell K. Gilliard, *Prisoners in 1994* (Washington, D.C.: Bureau of Justice Statistics, August 1995).

61. *Prisoners in 1996* (Washington, D.C.: Bureau of Justice Statistics, 1997).

62. Lynn S. Branham, *The Use of Incarceration in the United States: A Look at the Present and the Future* (Washington, D.C.: American Bar Association, 1992).

63. "Reliance on Prisons Is Costly but Ineffective, ABA Panel Says," *Criminal Justice Newsletter*, April 15, 1992, p. 7.

64. Testimony of New York State Corrections Commissioner Thomas A. Coughlin III, "Rockefeller Drug Laws—20 Years Later," before a hearing convened by the Assembly Committee on Codes of the New York State Legislature, June 8, 1993.

65. Christy A. Visher, "Incapacitation and Crime Control: Does a 'Lock 'Em Up' Strategy Reduce Crime?" *Justice Quarterly*, Vol. 4, no. 4 (December 1987), pp. 513–543.

66. *Criminal Justice Newsletter*, Vol. 23, no. 3 (February 3, 1992), p. 8.

67. American Correctional Association, *Vital Statistics in Corrections* (Laurel, MD: ACA, 1991), p. 52.

68. Christopher J. Mumola and Allen J. Beck, *Prisoners in 1996* (Washington, D.C.: Bureau of Justice Statistics, June 1997).

69. Ibid.

70. Adapted from U.S. Department of Justice, *Report to the Nation on Crime and Justice*, 2nd ed., (Washington, D.C.: U.S. Government Printing Office, 1988), p. 108.

71. *Rhodes* v. *Chapman*, 452 U.S. 337 (1981).

72. James Lieber, "The American Prison: A Tinderbox," *The New York Times Magazine*, March 8, 1981.

73. *The Fayetteville Observer-Times* (North Carolina), July 4, 1988, p. 2A, citing James K. Stewart, director of the National Institute of Justice.

74. Wisconsin Policy Research Institute, *Crime and Punishment in Wisconsin* (Milwaukee: Wisconsin Policy Research Institute, 1990).

75. Fox Butterfield, no headline, *The New York Times* wire service, 7:06 EST, April 16, 1997, citing Office of Justice Programs, *Preventing Crime: What Works, What Doesn't, What's Promising* (Washington, D.C.: U.S. Department of Justice, 1997).

76. While many other states require inmates to work on road maintenance, and while such inmates are typically supervised by armed guards, Alabama became the first state in modern times to shackle workers.

77. Lori Sharn and Shannon Tangonan, "Chain Gangs Back in Alabama," *USA Today*, May 4, 1995, p. 3A.

78. Ibid.

79. See "Back on the Chain Gang: Florida Becomes Third State to Resurrect Forced Labor," The Associated Press, November 22, 1995.

80. "Chain Gang Hits the Road in Arizona," *USA Today*, May 16, 1995, page 3A.

81. "Back on the Chain Gang."

82. Peter Baker, "Allen Crime Plan Ends Parole; Expensive Va. Proposal Would Strain Budget, Require More Prisons," *The Washington Post* wire services, August 17, 1994.

83. "U.S. House Votes to Make Life Tougher for Prisoners," Reuters wire services, February 10, 1995.

84. "The Extinction of Inmate Privileges," *Corrections Compendium* (June 1995), p. 5.

85. Ibid.

86. The state of Washington is generally credited with having been the first state to pass a three-strikes law by voter initiative (in 1993).

87. For a good overview of the topic, see David Shichor and Dale K. Sechrest, *Three Strikes and You're Out: Vengeance as Public Policy* (Thousand Oaks, CA: Sage, 1996).

88. David S. Broder, "When Tough Isn't Smart," *The Washington Post* wire services, March 24, 1994.

89. "The Klaas Case and the Crime Bill," *The Washington Post* wire services, February 21, 1994.

90. Bruce Smith, "Crime Solutions," The Associated Press wire services, January 11, 1995.

91. Mark Jewell, "Three Strikes Laws," The Associated Press wire services, northern edition, February 21, 1994.

92. Greg Wees, "Inmate Populations Expected to Increase 43% by 2002," *Corrections Compendium* (April 1996).

93. Amanda Wunder, "Corrections Systems Must Bear the Burden of New Legislation," *Corrections Compendium* (March 1995).

94. The Campaign for an Effective Crime Policy, *The Impact of Three Strikes and You're Out Laws: What Have We Learned?* (Washington, D.C.: CECP, 1997).

95. David Lawsky, "Prison Wardens Decry Overcrowding, Survey Says," Reuters wire services, December 21, 1994.

96. D. Greenberg, "The Incapacitative Effect of Imprisonment, Some Estimates," *Law and Society Review*, Vol. 9 (1975), pp. 541–580. See also Jacqueline Cohen, "Incapacitating Criminals: Recent Research Findings," National Institute of Justice, *Research in Brief* (December 1983).

97. For information on identifying dangerous repeat offenders, see M. Chaiken and J. Chaiken "Selecting Career Criminals for Priority Prosecution," final report (Cambridge, MA: Abt Associates, 1987).

98. J. Monahan, *Predicting Violent Behavior: An Assessment of Clinical Techniques* (Beverly Hills, CA: Sage Publications, 1981).

99. S. Van Dine, J. P. Conrad, and S. Dinitz, *Restraining the Wicked: The Incapacitation of the Dangerous Offender* (Lexington, MA: Lexington Books, 1979).

100. Paul Gendreau, Tracy Little, and Claire Goggin, "A Meta-Analysis of the Predictors of Adult Offender Recidivism: What Works!" *Criminology*, Vol. 34, no. 4 (November 1996), pp. 575–607.

101. In the case of *Lynce* v. *Mathis*, No. 95–7452 (1997).

102. "Florida Releases Prisoners, Issues Warnings to Victims," The Associated Press, March 12, 1997.

103. Mumola and Beck, *Prisoners in 1996*.

104. Ibid.

105. Ibid.

106. "Prison Expansion Nears Completion," United Press International wire services, southwest edition, June 12, 1995.

107. Mumola and Beck, *Prisoners in 1996*.

108. Ibid.

109. Ibid.

110. Bureau of Justice Statistics, *National Corrections Reporting Program 1985*

(Washington, D.C.: Bureau of Justice Statistics, December 1990), p. 14.

111. Ibid., p. 54.

112. Ibid.

113. American Correctional Association, "Correctional Officers in Adult Systems," in *Vital Statistics in Corrections*, (Laurel, MD: ACA, 1998).

114. Ibid.

115. Ibid.

116. Ibid. Note: "Other" minorities round out the percentages to a total of 100%.

117. U.S. Department of Justice, *Report to the Nation on Crime and Justice*, 2nd ed. (Washington, D.C.: U.S. Government Printing Office, 1988), p. 123.

118. *Vital Statistics in Corrections*, p. 11.

119. Robert M. Carter, Richard A. McGee, and E. Kim Nelson, *Corrections in America* (Philadelphia: J. B. Lippincott, 1975), pp. 122–123.

120. Camp and Camp, "Stopping Escapes: Perimeter Security," *Prison Construction Bulletin* (Washington, D.C.: NIJ, 1987).

121. Adapted from Grizzle et al., "Measuring Corrections Performance," NIJ Grant, 78-NI-AX-O13O (1980), p. 31.

122. U.S. Bureau of Prisons, *Facilities*, Web posted at http://www.bop.gov/map.html.

123. An older system, in which the terms "Level 1," "Level 2," and so on were used, was abandoned around 1990 and officially replaced with the new terminology used here.

124. Most of the information in this section comes from telephone conversations with and faxed information from the Federal Bureau of Prisons, August 25, 1995.

125. For additional information, see Dennis Cauchon, "The Alcatraz of the Rockies," *USA Today*, November 16, 1994, p. 6A.

126. The Federal Bureau of Prisons daily count stood at 100,569 on August 30, 1997. When all inmates for whom the Bureau is responsible were counted (including juveniles, those in jail, and inmates under home confinement), the total daily population under BOP control on August 30, 1997 was 111,760. *Source:* BOP World Wide Web site, http://www.bop.gov.

127. "Congress OKs Inmates Fees to Offset Costs of Prison," *Criminal Justice Newsletter* (October 15, 1992), p. 6.

128. National Institute of Corrections, "National Academy of Corrections: Outreach Training Programs" (July 1987).

129. National Institute of Corrections, "Correctional Training Programs" (July 1987).

130. Much of the information in this section comes from Darrell K. Gilliard and Allen J. Beck, *Prison and Jail Inmates 1995* (Washington, D.C.: Bureau of Justice Statistics, 1996).

131. Ibid.

132. Bureau of Justice Statistics, *BJS Data Report*, (Washington, D.C.: USGPO, 1989), p. 63.

133. Craig A. Perkins, James J. Stephan, and Allen J. Beck, *Jails and Jail Inmates 1993–94* (Washington, D.C.: BJS, 1995).

134. Ibid.

135. Ibid.

136. U.S. Department of Justice, *Report to the Nation on Crime and Justice*, 2nd ed., p. 106.

137. Ibid.

138. See Gale Holland, "L.A. Jail Makes Delayed Debut," *USA Today*, January 27, 1997, p. 3A.

139. See Dale Stockton, "Cook County Illinois Sheriff's Office," *Police*, October 1996, pp. 40–43. The Cook County Department of Correction operates 10 separate jails which house approximately 9,000 inmates. More than 2,800 correctional officers are employed by the department.

140. U.S. Department of Justice, press release: *The Nation's Jails Hold Record 490,442 Inmates*, May 1, 1995.

141. Ibid.

142. Ibid.

143. William Reginald Mills and Heather Barrett, "Meeting the Special Challenge of Providing Health Care to Women Inmates in the '90's," *American Jails*, Vol. 4, no. 3 (September/October 1990), p. 55.

144. Ibid.

145. Ibid., p. 21.

146. Ibid.

147. American Correctional Association, *Vital Statistics in Corrections*.

148. Mills and Barrett, "Meeting the Special Challenge," p. 55.

149. Ibid.

150. Ibid.

151. Linda L. Zupan "Women Corrections Officers in the Nation's Largest Jails," *American Jails* (January/February 1991), pp. 59–62.

152. Ibid., p. 11.

153. Linda L. Zupan, "Women Corrections Officers in Local Jails," paper presented at the annual meeting of the Academy of Criminal Justice Sciences, Nashville, Tennessee, March 1991.

154. Ibid., p. 6.

155. "Jail Overcrowding in Houston Results in Release of Inmates," *Criminal Justice Newsletter*, October 15, 1990, p. 5.

156. Bureau of Justice Statistics, *Census of Local Jails 1988* (Washington, D.C.: Bureau of Justice Statistics, 1991), p. 31.

157. Kathleen Maguire and Ann L. Pastore, *Sourcebook of Criminal Justice Statistics 1994* (Washington, D.C.: U.S. Government Printing Office, 1995).

158. Ibid.

159. Bureau of Justice Statistics, *Correctional Populations in the United States 1995*

(Washington, D.C.: Bureau of Justice Statistics, 1997).

160. Bureau of Justice Statistics, *Census of Local Jails 1988* (Washington, D.C.: BJS, 1991), p. 15.

161. Randall Guynes, *Nation's Jail Managers Assess Their Problems* (Washington, D.C.: National Institute of Justice, 1988).

162. Carol J. Casteneda, "Arizona Sheriff Walking Tall, But Some Don't Like His Style," *USA Today*, May 26, 1995, p. 7A.

163. U.S. Department of Justice, *The Nation's Jails Hold Record 490,442 Inmates.*

164. As identified in George P. Wilson and Harvey L. McMurray, *System Assessment of Jail Overcrowding Assumptions*, paper presented at the annual meeting of the Academy of Criminal Justice Sciences, Nashville, Tennessee, March 1991.

165. Andy Hall, *Systemwide Strategies to Alleviate Jail Crowding* (Washington, D.C.: National Institute of Justice, 1987).

166. Ibid.

167. Linda L. Zupan and Ben A. Menke, "The New Generation Jail: An Overview," in Joel A. Thompson and G. Larry Mays, eds., *American Jails: Public Policy Issues* (Chicago: Nelson-Hall, 1991), p. 180.

168. Ibid.

169. Herbert R. Sigurdson, Billy Wayson, and Gail Funke, "Empowering Middle Managers of Direct Supervision Jails," *American Jails* (Winter 1990), p. 52.

170. Byron Johnson, "Exploring Direct Supervision: A Research Note," *American Jails* (March/April 1994), pp. 63–64.

171. H. Sigurdson, *The Manhattan House of Detention: A Study of Podular Direct Supervision* (Washington, D.C.: National Institute of Corrections, 1985). For similar conclusions, see Robert Conroy, Wantland J. Smith, and Linda L. Zupan, "Officer Stress in the Direct Supervision Jail: A Preliminary Case Study," *American Jails* (November/December 1991), p. 36.

172. Brian Dawe and James Kirby, "Direct Supervision Jails and Minimum Staffing," *American Jails* (March/April 1995), pp. 97–100.

173. W. Raymond Nelson and Russell M. Davis, "Popular Direct Supervision: The First Twenty Years," *American Jails* (July/August 1995), p. 17.

174. Jerry W. Fuqua, "New Generation Jails: Old Generation Management," *American Jails* (March/April 1991), pp. 80–83.

175. Sigurdson, Wayson, and Funke, "Empowering Middle Managers."

176. Duncan J. McCulloch and Time Stiles, "Technology and the Direct Supervision Jail," *American Jails* (Winter 1990), pp. 97–102.

177. Susan W. McCampbell, "Direct Supervision: Looking for the Right People," *American Jails* (November/December 1990), pp. 68–69.

178. For a good review of the future of American jails, see Ron Carroll, "Jails and the Criminal Justice System in the 21st Century," *American Jails*, March/April 1997, pp. 26–31.

179. Robert L. May II, Roger H. Peters, and William D. Kearns "The Extent of Drug Treatment Programs in Jails: A Summary Report," *American Jails* (September/October 1990), pp. 32–34.

180. See, for example, John W. Dietler, "Jail Industries: The Best Thing That Can Happen to a Sheriff," *American Jails* (July/August 1990), pp. 80–83.

181. Robert Osborne, "Los Angeles County Sheriff Opens New Inmate Answering Service," *American Jails* (July/August 1990), pp. 61–62.

182. Nancy E. Bond and Dave Smith, "The Challenge: Community Involvement in Corrections," *American Jails* (November/December 1992), pp. 19–20.

183. Robert J. Hunter, "A Locally Operated Boot Camp," *American Jails* (July/August 1994), pp. 13–15.

184. James Austin, Michael Jones, and Melissa Bolyard, *The Growing Use of Jail Boot Camps: The Current State of the Art* (Washington, D.C.: National Institute of Justice, October 1993).

185. See J. R. Dewan, "Regional Jail—The New Kid on the Block," *American Jails* (May/June 1995), pp. 70–72.

186. Tom Rosazza, "Jail Standards: Focus on Change," *American Jails* (November/December 1990), pp. 84–87.

187. American Correctional Association, *Manual of Standards for Adult Local Detention Facilities*, 3d ed. (College Park, MD: ACA, 1991).

188. Ken Kerle, "National Sheriff's Association Jail Audit Review," *American Jails* (Spring 1987), pp. 13–21.

189. Joel A. Thompson and G. Larry Mays, "Paying the Piper but Changing the Tune: Policy Changes and Initiatives for the American Jail," in Joel A. Thompson and G. Larry Mays, eds., *American Jails: Public Policy Issues* (Chicago: Nelson-Hall, 1991), pp. 240–246.

190. Bureau of Justice Statistics, *Report to the Nation on Crime and Justice*, p. 119. See also Judith C. Hackett et al., "Contracting for the Operation of Prisons and Jails," National Institute of Justice, *Research in Brief* (June 1987), p. 2.

191. Professor Charles Thomas, as cited in Joan Thompson, "Private Prisons," The Associated Press wire services, November 5, 1996.

192. See, for example, G. Larry Mays and Tara Gray, *Privatization and the Provision of Correctional Services: Context and*

Consequences (Cincinnati, Ohio: Anderson, 1996); Dale K. Sechrest and David Shichor, "Private Jails: Locking Down the Issues," *American Jails*, March/April 1997, pp. 9–18; R.K. Walla, "Privatization of Jails: Is It A Good Move?" *American Jails*, September/October 1995, pp. 73–74.

193. Gary Fields, "Privatized Prisons Pose Problems," *USA Today*, November 11, 1996, p. 3A.

194. Dale K. Sechrest and David Shichor, "Private Jails: Locking Down the Issues," *American Jails*, March/April 1997, pp. 9–18.

195. U.S. General Accounting Office, *Private and Public Prisons: Studies Comparing Operational Costs and/or Quality of Service* (Washington, D.C.: U.S. Government Printing Office, 1996).

196. "Private Jails: Locking Down the Issues," p. 10.

197. For a more detailed discussion of this issue, see Ira Robbins, *The Legal Dimensions of Private Incarceration* (Chicago: American Bar Foundation, 1988).

198. *Richardson et al.* v. *McKnight*, No. 96–318. Decided June 23, 1997.

199. Ibid, syllabus.

200. As quoted in Joan Thompson, "Private Prisons," The Associated Press wire services, November 5, 1996.

201. Hackett et al., "Contracting for the Operation of Prisons and Jails," p. 6.

chapter 13

PRISON LIFE

Our policy of confining large numbers of offenders seems to have been ineffective in reducing the violent crime rate.

—JOHN H. KRAMER, EXECUTIVE DIRECTOR, PENNSYLVANIA COMMISSION ON SENTENCING

The person of a prisoner sentenced to imprisonment in the State prison is under the protection of the law, and any injury to his person, not authorized by law, is punishable in the same manner as if he were not convicted or sentenced.

—CALIFORNIA PENAL CODE, SECTION 2650

519

Realities of Prison Life: The Male Inmate's World

We Must Remember Always That The "Doors Of Prisons Swing Both Ways."[1]

—Mary Belle Harris, First Federal Woman Warden

For the first 150 years of their existence, prisons and prison life could be described by the phrase "out of sight, out of mind." Very few citizens cared about prison conditions, and those unfortunate enough to be locked away were regarded as lost to the world. By the mid-1900s, beginning with the treatment era, such attitudes started to change. Concerned citizens began to offer their services to prison administrations, neighborhoods began accepting work release prisoners and halfway houses, and social scientists initiated a serious study of prison life.

This chapter describes the realities of prison life today, including prisoner lifestyles, prison subcultures, sexuality in prison, prison violence, and inmate "rights" and grievance procedures. We will discuss both the world of the inmate and the staff world. A separate section on women in prison details the social structure of women's prisons, daily life in such facilities, and the various types of female inmates. We turn now to early research on prison life and will quickly move on to a discussion of the inmate world.

RESEARCH ON PRISON LIFE—TOTAL INSTITUTIONS

In 1935 Hans Reimer, then chairman of the Department of Sociology at Indiana University, set the tone for studies of prison life when he voluntarily served three months in prison as an incognito participant observer.[2] Reimer reported the results of his studies to the American Prison Association, stimulating many other, albeit less spectacular, efforts to examine prison life. Other early studies include Donald Clemmer's *The Prison Community* (1940),[3] Gresham M. Sykes's *The Society of Captives: A Study of a Maximum Security Prison* (1958),[4] Richard A. Cloward and Donald R. Cressey's *Theoretical Studies in Social Organization of the Prison* (1960),[5] and Donald R. Cressey's *The Prison: Studies in Institutional Organization and Change* (1961).[6]

These studies and others focused primarily on maximum-security prisons for men. They treated correctional institutions as formal or complex organizations and employed the analytical techniques of organizational sociology, industrial psychology, and administrative science.[7] As modern writers on prisons have observed, "[T]he prison was compared to a primitive society, isolated from the outside world, functionally integrated by a delicate system of mechanisms, which kept it precariously balanced between anarchy and accommodation."[8]

Another approach to the study of prison life was developed by Erving Goffman who coined the term **total institutions** in a 1961 study of prisons and mental hospitals.[9] Goffman described total institutions as places where the same people work, play, eat, sleep, and recreate together on a daily basis. Such places include prisons, concentration camps, mental hospitals, seminaries, and other facilities in which residents are cut off from the larger society either forcibly or willingly. Total institutions are small societies. They evolve their own distinctive values and styles of life and place pressures on residents to fulfill rigidly proscribed behavioral roles.

Total Institutions
Enclosed facilities, separated from society both socially and physically, where the inhabitants share all aspects of their lives on a daily basis.

Custody and security remain the primary concern of prison staffers throughout the country—a fact seemingly belied by the apparent disregard of this posted notice. *Laimute E. Druskis*

Generally speaking, the work of prison researchers built upon findings of other social scientists who discovered that any group with similar characteristics, subject to confinement in the same place at the same time, develops its own subculture with specific components that govern hierarchy, behavioral patterns, values, and so on. Prison subcultures, described in the next section, also provide the medium through which prison values are communicated and expectations made known.

Prison Subcultures

Two social realities coexist in prison settings. One is the official structure of rules and procedures put in place by the wider society and enforced by prison staff. The other is the more informal but decidedly more powerful inmate world.[10] The inmate world, best described by its pervasive immediacy in the lives of inmates, is controlled by **prison subculture**. The realities of prison life—including a large and often densely packed inmate population which must look to the prison environment for all its needs—mean that prison subculture is not easily subject to the control of prison authorities.

Prison subcultures develop independently of the plans of prison administrators, and inmates entering prison discover a social world not mentioned in the handbooks prepared by correctional staff. Inmate concerns, values, roles, and even language weave a web of social reality into which new inmates step and in which they must participate. Those who try to remain aloof soon find themselves subjected to dangerous ostracism and may even be suspected of being in league with the prison administration.

The socialization of new inmates into the prison subculture has been described as a process of prisonization.[11] **Prisonization** refers to the learning of convict values, attitudes, roles, and even language. When the process is complete, new inmates have become "cons." The values of the inmate social system are embodied in a code whose violations can produce sanctions ranging from ostracism and avoidance to physical violence and homicide.[12] Sykes and Messinger[13] recognize five elements of the prison code:

1. Don't interfere with the interests of other inmates. Never rat on a con.
2. Don't lose your head. Play it cool and do your own time.
3. Don't exploit inmates. Don't steal. Don't break your word. Be right.
4. Don't whine. Be a man.
5. Don't be a sucker. Don't trust the guards or staff.

Prison Subculture The values and behavioral patterns characteristic of prison inmates. Prison subculture has been found to have surprising consistencies across the country.

Prisonization The process whereby newly institutionalized individuals come to accept prison lifestyles and criminal values. While many inmates begin their prison experience with only a modicum of values supportive of criminal behavior, the socialization experience they undergo while incarcerated leads to a much wider acceptance of such values.

Prison Argot The slang characteristic of prison subcultures and prison life.

Stanton Wheeler closely examined the concept of prisonization in a study of the Washington State Reformatory.[14] Wheeler found that the degree of prisonization experienced by inmates tends to vary over time. He described changing levels of inmate commitment to prison norms and values by way of a "U-shaped" curve. When an inmate first enters prison, Wheeler said, the conventional values of outside society are of paramount importance. As time passes, the lifestyle of the prison is adopted. However, within the half-year prior to release, most inmates begin to demonstrate a renewed appreciation for conventional values.

Different prisons share aspects of a common inmate culture,[15] so that prisonwise inmates who enter a new facility far from their home will already know the ropes. **Prison argot**, or language, provides one example of how widespread prison subculture can be. The terms used to describe inmate roles in one institution are generally understood in others. The word *rat*, for example, is prison slang for an informer. Popularized by crime movies of the 1950s, the term *rat* is understood today by members of the wider society. Other words common to prison argot are shown in the accompanying "Theory Into Practice" box.

Some criminologists have suggested that inmate codes are simply a reflection of general criminal values. If so, they are brought to the institution rather than created there. Either way, the power and pervasiveness of the inmate code require convicts to conform to the world-view held by the majority of prisoners.

The Evolution of Subcultures

Prison subculture is constantly changing. Like any other American subculture, it evolves to reflect the concerns and experiences of the wider culture, reacting to new crime-control strategies and embracing novel opportunities for crime and its commission. The AIDS epidemic of the last two decades, for example, has brought about changes in prison sexual behavior, at least for a segment of the inmate population, while the emergence of a high-tech criminal group has further differentiated convict types. Because of such changes, John Irwin, by the time he was about to complete his now-famous study entitled *The Felon* (1970), expressed worry that his book was already obsolete.[16] *The Felon*, for all its insights into prison subculture, follows in the descriptive tradition of works by Clemmer and Reimer. Irwin recognized that by 1970 prison subcultures had begun to reflect cultural changes sweeping America. A decade later other investigators of prison subculture were able to write, "It was no longer meaningful to speak of a single inmate culture or even subculture. By the time we began our field research…it was clear that the unified, oppositional convict culture, found in the sociological literature on prisons, no longer existed."[17]

Stastny and Tyrnauer, describing prison life at Washington State Penitentiary in 1982, discovered four clearly distinguishable subcultures: (1) official, (2) traditional, (3) reform, and (4) revolutionary. Official culture was promoted by the staff and by administrative rules of the institution. Enthusiastic participants in official culture were mostly correctional officers and other staff members, although inmates were also well aware of the normative expectations official culture imposed on them. Official culture impacted the lives of inmates primarily through the creation of a prisoner hierarchy based upon sentence length, prison jobs, and the "perks" which cooperation with the dictates of official culture could produce. Traditional prison culture, described by early writers on the subject, still existed, but its participants spent much of their time lamenting the decline of the convict code among younger prisoners. Reform culture was unique at Washington State Penitentiary. It was the result of a brief experiment with inmate self-government during the early 1970s. Elements of prison life which evolved during the experimental period sometimes survived the termination of self-government and were eventually institutionalized in what Stastny and Tyrnauer call reform culture. Such elements included inmate participation in civic-style clubs, citizen involvement in the daily activities of the prison, banquets, and inmate speaking tours. Revolutionary culture built upon the radical political rhetoric of the disenfranchised and found a ready audience among minority prisoners who saw themselves as victims of society's basic unfairness. Although they did not participate in it, revolutionary inmates understood traditional prison culture and generally avoided running afoul of its rules.

View an on line prisoner's dictionary (which is frequently updated) at http://www.wco.com/~aerick/lingo.htm.

THE FUNCTIONS OF PRISON SOCIETY

How do social scientists and criminologists explain the existence of prison societies? Although people around the world live in groups and create their own cultures, in few cases

Prison Argot—The Language of Confinement

Writers who have studied prison life often comment on the use by prisoners of a special language or slang, which is termed prison *argot*. This language generally refers to the roles assigned by prison culture to types of inmates as well as to prison activities. This box lists a few of the many words and phrases identified in various studies by different authors. The first group of words are characteristic of male prisons; the last few have been used in prisons for women.

MEN'S PRISON SLANG

Ace duce: Best friend

Badge (or bull, hack, "the man," or screw): A correctional officer

Banger (or burner, shank, or sticker): A knife

Billys: White men

Boneyard: Conjugal visiting area

Cat-J (or J-cat): A prisoner in need of psychological or psychiatric therapy or medication

Cellie: Cellmate

Chester: Child molester

Dog: Homeboy or friend

Fag: A male inmate who is believed to be a "natural" or "born" homosexual

Featherwood: A peckerwood's woman

Fish: A newly arrived inmate

Gorilla: An inmate who uses force to take what he wants from others

Homeboy: A prisoner from one's hometown or neighborhood

Ink: Tattoos

Lemon squeezer: An inmate who has an unattractive "girlfriend"

Man walking: A phrase used to signal that a guard is coming

Merchant (or peddler): One who sells when he should give

Peckerwood (or wood): A white prisoner

Punk: A male inmate who is forced into a submissive or feminine role during homosexual relations

Rat (or snitch): An inmate who squeals (provides information about other inmates to the prison administration)

Schooled: Knowledgeable in the ways of prison life

Shakedown: A search of a cell or of a work area

Tree jumper: Rapist

Turn out: To rape or make into a punk

Wolf: A male inmate who assumes the aggressive masculine role during homosexual relations

WOMEN'S PRISON SLANG

Cherry (or Cherrie): A female inmate who has not yet been introduced to lesbian activities

Fay Broad: A white female inmate

Femme (or Mommy): A female inmate who plays the female role during lesbian relations

Safe: The vagina, especially when used for hiding contraband

Stud Broad (or Daddy): A female inmate who assumes the role of a male during lesbian relations

Sources: Gresham Sykes, *The Society of Captives* (Princeton, NJ: Princeton University Press, 1958); Rose Giallombardo, *Society of Women: A Study of A Woman's Prison* (New York: John Wiley, 1966); and Richard A. Cloward et al., *Theoretical Studies in Social Organization of the Prison* (New York: Social Science Research Council, 1960). For a more contemporary listing of prison slang terms, see Reinhold Aman, *Hillary Clinton's Pen Pal: A Guide to Life* and *Lingo in Federal Prison.* (Santa Rosa, CA: Maledicta Press, 1996); Jerome Washington, *Iron House: Stories from the Yard* (Ann Arbor, MI: QED Press, 1994); Morrie Camhi, *The Prison Experience* (Boston: Charles Tuttle Co., 1989); and Harold Long, *Survival In Prison* (Port Townsend, WA: Loompanics Unlimited, 1990).

does the intensity of human interaction approach the level found in prisons. As we discussed in Chapter 12, today's prisons are overcrowded places where inmates can find no retreat from the constant demands of staff and the pressures brought by fellow prisoners. Prison subculture, according to some authors, is fundamentally an adaptation to deprivation and confinement. It is a way of addressing the psychological, social, physical, and sexual needs of prisoners living within the context of a highly controlled and regimented institutional setting.

What are some of the deprivations prisoners experience? In *The Society of Captives*, Gresham Sykes calls felt deprivations the "pains of imprisonment."[18] The pains of imprisonment—the frustrations induced by the rigors of confinement—form the nexus of a deprivation model of prison culture. Sykes said that prisoners are deprived of (1) liberty, (2) goods and services, (3) heterosexual relationships, (4) autonomy, and (5) personal security and that these deprivations lead to the development of subcultures intended to ameliorate the personal pains which accompany them.

In contrast to the deprivation model, the importation model of prison culture suggests that inmates bring with them values, roles, and behavior patterns from the outside world. Such external values, second nature as they are to career offenders, depend substantially

A group of male inmates dressed as women in a California institution. Homosexuality is common in both men's and women's prisons.
Rasmussen, Sipa Press

upon the criminal world view. When offenders are confined, these external elements shape the inmate social world.

The social structure of the prison, a concept that refers to accepted and relatively permanent social arrangements, is another element which shapes prisoner subculture. Donald Clemmer's early prison study recognized nine structural dimensions of inmate society. He said that prison society could be described in terms of[19]

1. The prisoner/staff dichotomy
2. The three general classes of prisoners
3. Work gangs and cellhouse groups
4. Racial groups
5. Type of offense
6. The power of inmate "politicians"
7. Degree of sexual abnormality
8. The record of repeat offenses
9. Personality differences due to preprison socialization

Clemmer's nine structural dimensions are probably still descriptive of prison life today. When applied in individual situations, they designate an inmate's position in the prison "pecking order" and create expectations of the appropriate role for that person. Prison roles serve to satisfy the needs of inmates for power, sexual performance, material possessions, individuality, and personal pleasure—and to define the status of one prisoner relative to another. For example, inmate leaders, sometimes referred to as "real men" or "toughs" by prisoners in early studies, offer protection to those who live by the rules. They also provide for a redistribution of wealth inside of prison and see to it that the rules of the complex prison-derived economic system—based on barter, gambling, and sexual favors—are observed.

Homosexuality in Prison

Homosexual behavior inside of prisons is an important area which is both constrained and encouraged by prison subculture, and Sykes's early study of prison argot found many words describing homosexual activity. Among them were the terms "wolf," "punk," and "fag." Wolves were aggressive men who assumed the masculine role in homosexual relations. Punks were forced into submitting to the female role, often by wolves. Fags described a special category of men who had a natural proclivity toward homosexual activity and effeminate mannerisms. While both wolves and punks were fiercely committed to their heterosexual identity and participated in homosexuality only because of prison conditions, fags generally engaged in homosexual lifestyles before their entry into prison and continued to emulate feminine mannerisms and styles of dress once incarcerated.

Prison homosexuality depends to a considerable degree upon the naivete of young inmates experiencing prison for the first time. Older prisoners looking for homosexual liaisons may ingratiate themselves with new arrivals by offering cigarettes, money, drugs, food, or protection. At some future time these "loans" will be "called in," with payoffs demanded in sexual favors. Because the inmate code requires the repayment of favors, the "fish" who tries to resist may quickly find himself face to face with the brute force of inmate society.

Prison rape represents a special category of homosexual behavior behind bars. Estimates of the incidence of prison rape are both rare and dated. Those that are survey-based vary considerably in their findings. One such study found 4.7% of inmates in the Philadelphia prison system willing to report sexual assaults.[20] Another survey found that 28% of prisoners had been targets of sexual aggressors at least once during their institutional careers.[21]

Rape in prison is often the result of gang activity or of inmates working together to overcome the victim. While not greatly different from other prisoners, a large proportion of sexual aggressors are characterized by low education and poverty, having grown up in a broken home headed by the mother, and having a record for violent offenses. Victims of prison rape tend to be physically slight, young, white, nonviolent offenders from nonurban areas.[22] Lee Bowker, summarizing studies of sexual violence in prison,[23] provides the following observations:

1. Most sexual aggressors do not consider themselves to be homosexuals.
2. Sexual release is not the primary motivation for sexual attack.
3. Many aggressors must continue to participate in gang rapes in order to avoid becoming victims themselves.
4. The aggressors have themselves suffered much damage to their masculinity in the past.

As in cases of heterosexual rape, sexual assaults in prison are likely to leave psychological scars long after the physical event is over.[24] The victims of prison rape live in fear, may feel constantly threatened, and can turn to self-destructive activities.[25] At the very least victims question their masculinity and undergo a personal devaluation. In some cases victims of prison sexual attacks turn to violence. Frustrations, long bottled up through abuse and fear, may explode and turn the would-be rapist into a victim of prison homicide.

Prison Lifestyles and Inmate Types

Prison society is strict and often unforgiving. Even so, inmates are able to express some individuality through the choice of a prison lifestyle. John Irwin was the first well-known author to describe prison lifestyles, viewing them (like the subcultures of which they are a part) as adaptations to the prison environment.[26] Other writers have since elaborated on these coping mechanisms. Listed in the pages that follow are some of the types of prisoners described by commentators.

1. *The Mean Dude.* Some inmates adjust to prison by being mean. They are quick to fight, and when they fight, they fight like wild men (or women). They give no quarter and seem to expect none in return. Other inmates know that such prisoners are best left alone. The mean dude receives frequent write-ups and spends much time in solitary confinement.

   The mean dude role is supported by the fact that some prisoners occupy it in prison as they did when they were free. Similarly, certain personality types, such as the psychopathic, may feel a natural attraction to this role. On the other hand, prison culture sup-

A San Diego, California, inmate shows off his physique. Some inmates attempt to adapt to prison life by acting tough. Recent attempts by both the states and the federal government to ban weight lifting programs in prison, however, may soon put a crimp in such styles of adaptation. *Armineh Johannes, Sipa Press*

ports the role of the mean dude in two ways: (a) by expecting inmates to be tough and (b) through the prevalence of a type of wisdom which says that "only the strong survive" inside prison.

A psychologist might say that the mean dude is acting out against the fact of captivity, striking out at anyone he (or she) can. This type of role performance is more common in male institutions and in maximum-security prisons. It tends to become less common as inmates progress to lower-security levels.

2. *The Hedonist.* Some inmates build their lives around the limited pleasures which can be had within the confines of prison. The smuggling of contraband, homosexuality, gambling, drug running, and other officially condemned activities provide the center of interest for prison hedonists. Hedonists generally have an abbreviated view of the future, living only for the "now." Such a temporal orientation is probably characteristic of the personality type of all hedonists and exists in many persons, incarcerated or not.

3. *The Opportunist.* The opportunist takes advantage of the positive experiences prison has to offer. Schooling, trade training, counseling, and other self-improvement activities are the focal points of the opportunist's life in prison. Opportunists are the "do-gooders" of the prison subculture. They are generally well liked by prison staff, but other prisoners shun and mistrust them because they come closest to accepting the role which the staff defines as "model prisoner." Opportunists may also be religious, a role adaptation worthy of a separate description (see number 8).

4. *The Retreatist.* Prison life is rigorous and demanding. Badgering by the staff and actual or feared assaults by other inmates may cause some prisoners to attempt psychological retreat from the realities of imprisonment. Such inmates may experience neurotic or psychotic episodes, become heavily involved in drug and alcohol abuse, or even attempt suicide. Depression and mental illness are the hallmarks of the retreatist personality in prison. The best hope for the retreatist, short of release, is protective custody combined with therapeutic counseling.

5. *The Legalist.* The legalist is the "jail house lawyer." Just like the mean dude, the legalist fights confinement. The weapons in this fight are not fists or clubs, however, but the

Whilst we have prisons it matters little which of us occupies the cells.
—George Bernard Shaw

Prison inmates adapt diverse coping strategies. Here, convicted murderer Henry Lee Lucas claims to have found God. *Bob Daemmrich, Stock Boston*

legal "writ." Convicts facing long sentences, with little possibility for early release through the correctional system, are most likely to turn to the courts in their battle against confinement.

6. *The Radical.* Radical inmates picture themselves as political prisoners. Society, and the successful conformists who populate it, are seen as oppressors who have forced criminality upon many "good people" through the creation of a system which distributes wealth and power inequitably. The radical inmate speaks a language of revolution and may be versed in the writings of the "great" revolutionaries of the past.

   The inmate who takes on the radical role is unlikely to receive much sympathy from prison staff. Radical rhetoric tends to be diametrically opposed to staff insistence on accepting responsibility for problematic behavior.

7. *The Colonist.* Some inmates think of prison as their home. They "know the ropes," have many "friends" inside, and may feel more comfortable institutionalized than on the streets. They typically hold either positions of power or respect (or both) among the inmate population. These are the prisoners who don't look forward to leaving prison. Most colonizers grow into the role gradually and only after already having spent years behind bars. Once released, some colonizers have been known to attempt new crimes in order to return to prison.

8. *The Religious.* Some prisoners profess a strong religious faith. They may be "born-again" Christians, committed Muslims, or even Hare Krishnas. Religious inmates frequently attend services, may form prayer groups, and sometimes ask the prison administration to allocate meeting facilities or create special diets to accommodate their claimed spiritual needs.

   While it is certainly true that some inmates have a strong religious faith, staff members are apt to be suspicious of the overly religious prisoner. The tendency is to view such prisoners as "faking it" in order to demonstrate a fictitious rehabilitation and thereby gain sympathy for an early release.

9. *The Realist.* The realist is a prisoner who sees confinement as a natural consequence of criminal activity. Time spent in prison is an unfortunate "cost of doing business." This stoic attitude toward incarceration generally leads the realist to "pull his (or her) own time" and to make the best of it. Realists tend to know the inmate code, are able to avoid trouble, and continue in lives of crime once released.

Realities of Prison Life: The Staff World

The flip side of inmate society can be found in the world of the prison staff, which includes many more people and professions than guard. Staff roles encompass those of warden, psychologist, counselor, area supervisor, program director, instructor, and correctional officer—and in some large prisons, physician and therapist. Officers, generally considered the bottom of the staff hierarchy, may be divided into cellbock and tower guards, while some are regularly assigned to administrative offices where they perform clerical tasks.

Like prisoners, correctional officers undergo a socialization process that helps them to function by the official and unofficial rules of staff society. Lucien Lombardo has described the process by which officers are socialized into the prison work world.[27] Lombardo interviewed 359 correctional personnel at New York's Auburn Prison and found that rookie officers had to quickly abandon preconceptions of both inmates and other staff members. According to Lombardo, new officers learn that inmates are not the "monsters" much of the public makes them out to be. On the other hand, rookies may be seriously disappointed in their experienced colleagues when they realize that ideals of professionalism, often stressed during early training, are rarely translated into reality. The pressures of the institutional work environment, however, soon force most correctional personnel to adopt a united front in relating to inmates.

One of the leading formative influences on staff culture is the potential threat that inmates pose. Inmates far outnumber correctional personnel in any institution, and the hostility they feel for guards is only barely hidden even at the best of times. Correctional personnel know that however friendly inmates may appear, a sudden change in institutional climate—as can happen in anything from simple disturbances on the yard to full-blown riots—can quickly and violently unmask deep-rooted feelings of mistrust and hatred.

As in years past, prison staffers are still most concerned with custody and control. Society, especially under the emerging just deserts philosophy of criminal sentencing, expects correctional staff to keep inmates in custody as the basic prerequisite of successful job performance. Custody is necessary before any other correctional activities, such as instruction or counseling, can be undertaken. Control, the other major staff concern, ensures order, and an orderly prison is thought to be safe and secure. In routine daily activities, control over almost all aspects of inmate behavior becomes paramount in the minds of most correctional officers. It is the twin interests of custody and control that lead to institutionalized procedures for ensuring security in most facilities. The use of strict rules, body and cell searches, counts, unannounced shakedowns, the control of dangerous items, materials, and contraband, and the extensive use of bars, locks, fencing, cameras, and alarms all support the human vigilance of the staff in maintaining security.

Types of Correctional Officers

Staff culture, in combination with naturally occurring personality types, gives rise to a diversity of officer "types." Like the inmate typology we've already discussed, correctional staff can be classified according to certain distinguishing characteristics. Among the most prevalent types are

Visit the *CJToday* Web page and click on "Web Chapters," then "Chapter 13." Follow the "find the facts" links in order to visit the International Association of Correctional Officers home page.

1. *The Dictator.* Some officers go by the book; others go beyond it, using prison rules to enforce their own brand of discipline. The guard who demands signs of inmate subservience, from constant use of the word "sir" or "ma'am" to frequent free shoeshines, is one type of dictator. Another goes beyond legality, beating or "macing" inmates even for minor infractions or perceived insults. Dictator guards are bullies. They find their counterpart in the "mean dude" inmate described earlier.

   Dictator guards may have sadistic personalities and gain ego satisfaction through the feelings of near omnipotence which come from the total control of others. Some may be fundamentally insecure and employ a false bravado to hide their fear of inmates. Officers who fit the dictator category are the most likely to be targeted for vengeance should control of the institution temporarily revert to the inmates.

2. *The Friend.* Friendly officers try to fraternize with inmates. They approach the issue of control by trying to be "one of the guys." They seem to believe that they can win inmate cooperation by being nice. Unfortunately, such guards do not recognize that fraterniza-

tion quickly leads to unending requests for special favors—from delivering mail to bending "minor" prison rules. Once a few rules have been "bent," the officer may find that inmates have the upper hand through the potential for blackmail.

Many officers have amiable relationships with inmates. In most cases, however, affability is only a convenience which both sides recognize can quickly evaporate. Friendly officers, as the term is being used here, are *overly* friendly. They may be young and inexperienced. On the other hand, they may simply be possessed of kind and idealistic personalities built on successful friendships in free society.

3. *The Merchant.* Contraband could not exist in any correctional facility without the merchant officer. The merchant participates in the inmate economy, supplying drugs, pornography, alcohol, and sometimes even weapons to inmates who can afford to pay for them.

Probably only a very few officers consistently perform the role of merchant, although a far larger proportion may occasionally turn a few dollars by smuggling some item through the gate. Low salaries create the potential for mercantile corruption among many otherwise "straight arrow" officers. Until salaries rise substantially, the merchant will remain an institutionalized feature of most prisons.

4. *The Turnkey.* The turnkey officer cares little for what goes on in the prison setting. Officers who fit this category may be close to retirement, or they may be alienated from their jobs for various reasons. Low pay, the view that inmates are basically "worthless" and incapable of changing, and the monotonous ethic of "doing time" all combine to numb the professional consciousness of even young officers.

The term "turnkey" comes from prison argot where it means a guard who is there just to open and shut doors and who cares about nothing other than getting through his or her shift. Inmates do not see the turnkey as a threat nor is such an officer likely to challenge the status quo in institutions where merchant guards operate.

5. *The Climber.* The climber is apt to be a young officer with an eye for promotion. Nothing seems impossible to the climber, who probably hopes eventually to be warden or program director or to hold some high-status position within the institutional hierarchy. Climbers are likely to be involved in schooling, correspondence courses, and professional organizations. They may lead a movement toward unionization for correctional personnel and tend to see the guard's role as a "profession" which should receive greater social recognition.

Climbers have many ideas. They may be heavily involved in reading about the latest confinement or administrative technology. If so, they will suggest many ways to improve prison routine, often to the consternation of other complacent staff members.

Like the turnkey, climbers turn a blind eye toward inmates and their problems. They are more concerned with improving institutional procedures and with their own careers than they are with the treatment or day-to-day control of inmates.

6. *The Reformer.* The reformer is the "do-gooder" among officers, the person who believes that prison should offer opportunities for personal change. The reformer tends to lend a sympathetic ear to the personal needs of inmates and is apt to offer "arm-chair" counseling and suggestions. Many reformers are motivated by personal ideals, and some of them are highly religious. Inmates tend to see the reformer guard as naive, but harmless. Because the reformer actually tries to help, even when help is unsolicited, he or she is the most likely of all the guard types to be accepted by prisoners.

The Professionalization of Correctional Officers

Correctional officers have generally been accorded low occupational status. Historically, the role of "prison guard" required minimal formal education and held few opportunities for professional growth and career advancement. Such jobs were typically low-paying, frustrating, and often boring. Growing problems in our nation's prisons, including emerging issues of legal liability, however, increasingly require a well-trained and adequately equipped force of professionals. As correctional personnel have become better trained and more proficient, the old concept of "guard" has been supplanted by that of *corrections officer.*

Many states and a growing number of large-city correctional systems make efforts to eliminate individuals with potentially harmful personality characteristics from correctional

Security is the primary concern of correctional staff. *Laimute E. Druskis*

officer applicant pools. New York, New Jersey, Ohio, Pennsylvania, and Rhode Island, for example, all use some form of psychological screening in assessing candidates for prison jobs.[28]

Although only some states utilize psychological screening, all make use of training programs intended to prepare successful applicants for prison work. New York, for example, requires trainees to complete six weeks of classroom-based instruction, as well as 40 hours of rifle range practice, followed by another six weeks of on-the-job training. Training days begin around 5 A.M. with a mile run and conclude after dark with study halls for students who need extra help. To keep pace with rising inmate populations, the state has often had to run a number of simultaneous training academies.[29]

On the federal level, a developmental model for correctional careers addresses many of the problems of correctional staffing. The Federal Bureau of Prisons' Career Development Model stands as an example of what state departments of correction can do in the area of staff training and development. The model establishes five sequential phases for the development of career correctional officers:[30] (1) Phase I, Career Assessment; (2) Phase II, Career Path Development; (3) Phase III, Career Enhancement and Management Development; (4) Phase IV, Advanced Management Development; and (5) Phase V, Senior Executive Service Development. Using a psychological personality inventory, the model seeks to identify the skills, abilities, and interests of officers and matches them with career opportunities in the federal correctional system.

Prison Riots

The ten years between 1970 and 1980 have been called the "explosive decade" of prison riots.[31] The decade began with a massive uprising at Attica Prison in New York state in September 1971. The Attica riot resulted in 43 deaths. More than 80 men were wounded. The "explosive decade" ended in 1980 at Santa Fe, New Mexico. There, in a riot at the New Mexico penitentiary, 33 inmates died, the victims of vengeful prisoners out to eliminate rats and informants. Many of the deaths involved mutilation and torture. More than 200 other inmates were beaten and sexually assaulted, and the prison was virtually destroyed.

Prison riots did not stop with the end of the explosive 1970s. For 11 days in 1987, the Atlanta (Georgia) Federal Penitentiary fell into the hands of inmates. The institution was

Code of Ethics—American Correctional Association Preamble

The American Correctional Association expects of its members unfailing honesty, respect for the dignity and individuality of human beings, and a commitment to professional and compassionate service. To this end we subscribe to the following principles:

- Members will respect and protect the civil and legal rights of all individuals.
- Members will treat every professional situation with concern for the person's welfare and with no intent of personal gain.
- Relationships with colleagues will be such that they promote mutual respect within the profession and improve the quality of service.
- Public criticisms of colleagues or their agencies will be made only when warranted, verifiable, and constructive in purpose.
- Members will respect the importance of all disciplines within the criminal justice system and work to improve cooperation with each segment.
- Subject to the individual's rights to privacy, members will honor the public's right to know and share information with the public to the extent permitted by law.

- Members will respect and protect the right of the public to be safeguarded from criminal activity.
- Members will not use their positions to secure personal privileges or advantages.
- Members will not, while acting in an official capacity, allow personal interest to impair objectivity in the performance of duty.
- No member will enter into any activity or agreement, formal or informal, which presents a conflict of interest or is inconsistent with the conscientious performance of his or her duties.
- No member will accept any gift, service, or favor that is or appears to be improper or implies an obligation inconsistent with the free and objective exercise of his or her professional duties.
- In any public statement, members will clearly distinguish between personal views and those statements or positions made on behalf of an agency or the Association.
- Each member will report to the appropriate authority any corrupt or unethical behavior where there is sufficient cause to initiate a review.

- Members will not discriminate against any individual because of race, gender, creed, national origin, religious affiliation, age, or any other type of prohibited discrimination.
- Members will preserve the integrity of private information; they will neither seek data on individuals beyond that needed to perform their responsibilities nor reveal nonpublic data unless expressly authorized to do so.
- Any member who is responsible for agency personnel actions will make all appointments, promotions, or dismissals in accordance with established civil service rules, applicable contract agreements, and individual merit, and not in furtherance of partisan interests.

Adopted August 1975 at the 105th Congress of Correction.

Revised August 1990 at the 120th Congress of Correction.

Source: American Correctional Association, *Code of Ethics* (Laurel, MD: American Correctional Association, 1990). Reprinted with permission.

"trashed," and inmates had to be temporarily relocated while it was rebuilt. The Atlanta riot followed closely on the heels of a similar, but less intense, disturbance at the federal detention center at Oakdale, Louisiana. Both outbreaks were attributed to the dissatisfaction of Cuban inmates, most of whom had arrived on the Mariel boat lift.[32] A two-night rampage in October 1989 left more than 100 people injured and the Pennsylvania prison at Camp Hill in shambles. At the time of the riot, the State Correctional Institution at Camp Hill was 45% over its capacity of 2,600 inmates.[33] Easter Sunday 1993 saw the beginning of an 11-day rebellion at the 1,800-inmate Southern Ohio Correctional Facility in Lucasville, Ohio—one of the country's toughest maximum-security prisons. The riot ended with nine inmates and one correctional officer dead. The officer had been hung. Paul W. Goldberg, executive director of the Ohio Civil Service Employees Association, told an Ohio senate panel that "[T]hose of us who deal with our prisons every day—the men and women on the front lines—know that overcrowding and understaffing are at the heart of Ohio's prison crisis...." "Lucasville is not an aberration," said Goldberg. "Every prison in Ohio is a powder keg."[34] The close of the riot—involving a parade of 450 inmates—was televised as prisoners had demanded.

A Broad River Correctional Institution (South Carolina) inmate is subdued following a riot in 1995. A new rule requiring collar-length hair sparked the riot, which resulted in five staff members being stabbed. Three others were taken hostage. *Jamie Francis, Pool/AP/Wide World Photos*

Among other demands were (1) no retaliation by officials, (2) review of medical staffing and care, (3) review of mail and visitation rules, (4) review of commissary prices, and (5) better enforcement against what the inmates called "inappropriate supervision."[35]

Riots related to inmate grievances over perceived disparities in federal drug sentencing policies and the possible loss of weight lifting equipment occurred throughout the federal prison system in October 1995. The riots, which began at Allenwood Correctional Facility in Pennsylvania and the federal prison at Talladega, Alabama, quickly spread to eight other federal prisons. Within a few days, the unrest led to a nationwide lockdown of 73 federal prisons. Although fires were set and a number of inmates and guards were injured, no deaths resulted.

CAUSES OF RIOTS

It is difficult to explain satisfactorily why prisoners riot, despite study groups which attempt to piece together the "facts" leading up to an incident. After the riot at Attica, the New York State Special Commission of Inquiry filed a report which recommended the creation of inmate advisory councils, changes in staff titles and uniforms, and other institutional improvements. The report emphasized "enhancing (the) dignity, worth, and self-confidence" of inmates. The New Mexico attorney general, in a final report on the violence at Santa Fe, placed blame upon a breakdown in informal controls and the subsequent emergence of a new group of violent inmates among the general prison population.[36]

A number of authorities[37] have suggested a variety of causes for prison riots. Among them are

1. An insensitive prison administration and neglected inmates' demands. Calls for "fairness" in disciplinary hearings, better food, more recreational opportunities, and the like may lead to riots when ignored.

2. The lifestyles most inmates are familiar with on the streets. It should be no surprise that prisoners use organized violence when many of them are violent people anyway.

Table 13-1 *Prison Gangs and Gang Membership in the Texas Prison System, 1990*

Name of Gang	Racial Composition	Membership	Year Formed
Texas Syndicate	Predominantly Hispanic	289	1975
Texas Mafia	Predominantly white	80	1982
Aryan Brotherhood of Texas	All white	170	1983
Mexican Mafia	All Hispanic	417	1984
Nuestro Carneles	All Hispanic	31	1984
Mandingo Warriors	All black	36	1985
Self-defense Family	Predominantly black	76	1985
Hermanos De Pistolero	All Hispanic	75	1985
Total		1,174	

Source: Robert S. Fong, Ronald E. Vogel and S. Buentello "Prison Gang Dynamics: A Look Inside the Texas Department of Corrections," in A. V. Merlo and P. Menekos, eds., *Dilemmas and Directions in Corrections* (Cincinnati, OH: Anderson, 1992).

3. Dehumanizing prison conditions. Overcrowded facilities, the lack of opportunity for individual expression, and other aspects of total institutions culminate in explosive situations of which riots are but one form.

4. The way that riots regulate inmate society and redistribute power balances among inmate groups. Riots provide the opportunity to "cleanse" the prison population of informers and rats and to resolve struggles among power brokers and ethnic groups within the institution.

5. "Power vacuums" created by changes in prison administration, the transfer of influential inmates, or court-ordered injunctions which significantly alter the informal social control mechanisms of the institution.

Although riots are difficult to predict in specific institutions, some state prison systems appear ripe for disorder. Texas, for example, has an overcrowded system that exhibits a number of characteristics listed above. Making matters worse, Texas prisons house a number of rapidly expanding gangs among whom turf violations can easily lead to widespread disorder. Gang membership among inmates in the Texas prison system, practically nonexistent in 1983, is now estimated at over 1,200.[38] The Texas Syndicate, the Aryan Brotherhood of Texas, and the Mexican Mafia are probably the largest gangs functioning in the Texas prison system. Each has around 300 members.[39] Table 13–1 summarizes what is known about gangs in the Texas prison system. Gangs not listed in the table, but known to operate in some prisons, include: Aryan Warriors; Black Gangster Disciples (mostly in the Midwest); the Black Guerrilla Family, an African-American prison gang; and the Nuestra Familia, an organization of Hispanic prisoners.

Gangs in Texas grew rapidly in part because of the "power vacuum" created when a court ruling ended the "building tender" system.[40] Building tenders were tough inmates who were given an almost free reign by prison administrators in keeping other inmates in line, especially in many of the state's worst prisons. The end of the building tender system dramatically increased demands on the Texas Department of Corrections for increased abilities and professionalism among its guards and other prison staff.

The "real" reasons for any riot are probably institution specific and may not allow for easy generalization. However, it is no simple coincidence that the "explosive decade" of prison riots coincided with the growth of revolutionary prisoner subcultures referred to earlier. As the old convict code began to give way to an emerging perception of social victimization among inmates, it was probably only a matter of time until those perceptions turned to militancy. Seen from this perspective, riots are more a revolutionary activity undertaken by politically motivated cliques rather than spontaneous and disorganized expressions stemming from the frustrations of prison life.

The number of women in prison is growing steadily. Because of disciplinary problems, this woman is housed in the segregation unit of a Rhode Island correctional facility. *Gal Zucker, Stock Boston*

STAGES IN RIOTS AND RIOT CONTROL

Rioting cannot be predicted.[41] Riots are generally unplanned and tend to occur spontaneously, the result of some relatively minor precipitating event. Once the stage has been set, prison riots tend to evolve through five phases:[42] (1) explosion, (2) organization (into inmate-led groups), (3) confrontation (with authority), (4) termination (through negotiation or physical confrontation), and (5) reaction and explanation (usually by investigative commissions). Donald Cressey[43] points out that the early explosive stages of a riot tend to involve "binges" during which inmates exult in their new-found freedom with virtual orgies of alcohol and drug use or sexual activity. Buildings are burned, facilities are wrecked, and old grudges between individual inmates and inmate groups are settled, often through violence. After this initial explosive stage, leadership changes tend to occur. New leaders emerge who, at least for a time, may effectively organize inmates into a force that can confront and resist official's attempts to regain control of the institution. Bargaining strategies then develop and the process of negotiation begins.

In the past, many correctional facilities depended upon informal procedures to quell disturbances—and often drew upon the expertise of seasoned correctional officers who were veterans of past skirmishes and riots. Given the large size of many of today's institutions, the rapidly changing composition of inmate and staff populations, and increasing tensions caused by overcrowding and the movement toward reduced inmate privileges, the "old guard" system can no longer be depended upon to quell disturbances. Hence, most modern facilities have incident management procedures and systems in place which are designed to be implemented in the event of disturbances. Such systems remove the burden of riot control from the individual officer, depending instead upon a systematic and deliberate approach developed to deal with a wide variety of correctional incidents.

Realities of Prison Life: Women in Prison

As Chapter 12 showed, 74,730 women are imprisoned in state and federal correctional institutions throughout the United States[44]—accounting for 6.3% of all prison inmates. A recent survey found that California has the largest number of female prisoners (10,248), exceeding

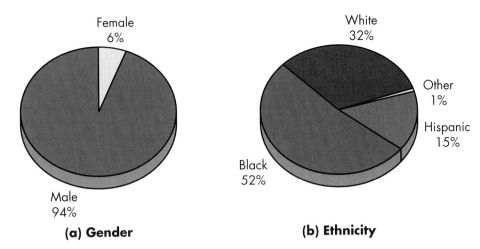

FIGURE 13–1 Prison inmates by gender and ethnicity, state and federal prisons, 1997.
Source: Christopher J. Mumola and Allen J. Beck, *Prisoners in 1996*. (Washington, D.C.: Bureau of Justice Statistics, 1997).

even the federal government (7,700).[45] Figure 13–1 provides a breakdown of the total American prison population by gender and ethnicity. Most women inmates are housed in centralized state facilities known as "women's prisons," which are dedicated exclusively to the holding of female felons. Many states, however, particularly those with small populations, continue to keep women prisoners in special wings of what are otherwise institutions for men.

While there are still far more men imprisoned across the nation than women (approximately 16 men for every woman), the number of female inmates is rising quickly.[46] In 1981 women comprised only 4% of the nation's overall prison population, but the number of female inmates nearly tripled during the 1980s and is continuing to grow at a rate far greater than that shown by male inmates.

Women's prisons are overcrowded, as are men's. The California Institution for Women at Frontera, for example, was originally designed to hold 1,011 inmates. As of this writing, it holds more than 2,500 women. At Bedford Hills Correctional Facility in Westchester County, New York, double bunking is the rule, and conditions there are so crowded that inmates barely have the room necessary to turn around in their living quarters. Even well-managed prisons with nice facades, however, can have problems. One study of a pleasant-appearing women's prison in New York concluded that it was a place of "intense hostility, frustrations, and anger."[47]

Professionals working with imprisoned women attribute the rise in female prison populations largely to drugs.[48] Figure 13–2 shows, in relative graphics, the proportion of men and women imprisoned for various kinds of offenses. While the figure shows that approximately 33% of all women in prison are there explicitly for drug offenses, other estimates say that the impact of drugs on the imprisonment of women is far greater than a simple reading of the figure indicates. Warden Robert Brennan of New York city's Rose M. Singer jail for women estimates that drugs—either directly or indirectly—account for the imprisonment of around 95% of the inmates there. Drug-related offenses committed by women include larceny, burglary, fraud, prostitution, embezzlement, and robbery, as well as other crimes stimulated by the desire for drugs. In fact, incarcerated women most frequently list (1) trying to pay for drugs, (2) attempts to relieve economic pressures, and (3) poor judgment as the reasons for their arrest.[49]

Another reason for the rapid growth in the number of women behind bars may be the demise, over the last decade or two, of the "Chivalry Factor." The Chivalry Factor, so called because it was based upon an archaic cultural stereotype that depicted women as helpless or childlike compared to men, allegedly lessened the responsibility of female offenders in the eyes of some male judges and prosecutors—resulting in fewer active prison sentences for women involved in criminal activity. Recent studies show that the Chivalry Factor is now primarily of historical interest. In jurisdictions examined, the gender of convicted offenders

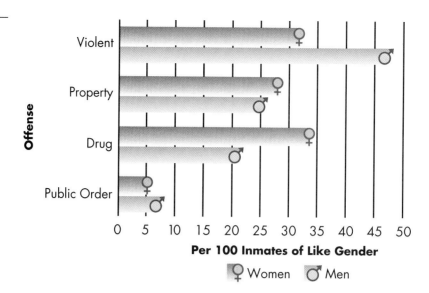

FIGURE 13–2 Men and women in prison by type of offense. *Source:* Bureau of Justice Statistics, *Survey of State Prison Inmates 1991* (Washington, D.C.: U.S. Government Printing Office, 1993).

no longer affects sentencing practices except insofar as it may be tied to other social variables. B. Keith Crew,[50] for example, in a comprehensive study of gender differences in sentencing observes, "[A] woman does not automatically receive leniency because of her status of wife or mother, but she may receive leniency if those statuses become part of the official explanation of her criminal behavior (for example, she was stealing to feed her children, or an abusive husband forced her to commit a crime)."

Although there may be no one "typical" prison for women and no perfectly "average" female inmate, the American Correctional Association's 1990 report by the Task Force on the Female Offender found that women inmates and the institutions which house them could be generally described as follows:[51]

1. Most prisons for women are located in towns with fewer than 25,000 inhabitants.
2. A significant number of facilities were not designed to house female inmates.
3. The number of female offenders being sent to prison is rising.
4. Most facilities that house female inmates also house males.
5. Not many facilities for women have programs especially designed for female offenders.
6. Very few major disturbances or escapes are reported among female inmates.
7. Substance abuse among female inmates is very high.
8. Very few work assignments are available to female inmates.
9. The number of female inmates without a high-school education is very high.

Statistics[52] show that the average age of female inmates is 29–30, most are black or Hispanic (57%), most come from single-parent or broken homes, and 50% have other family members who are incarcerated. The typical female inmate is a high-school dropout (50%), who left school either because she was bored or because of pregnancy (34%). She has been arrested an average of two to nine times (55%) and has run away from home between one and three times (65%). Thirty-nine percent report using drugs to make them feel better emotionally, while 28% have attempted suicide at least once. Sixty-two percent were single parents with one to three children prior to incarceration, and many have been physically and/or sexually abused.[53]

Eighty percent of women entering prison are mothers, and 85% of those women retain custody of their children at the time of prison admission. One out of four women entering prison has either recently given birth or is pregnant. Critics charge that women inmates face a prison system designed for male inmates and run by men. Hence, pregnant inmates, many of whom are drug users, malnourished, or sick, often receive little prenatal care—a situation that risks additional complications. Separation from their children is a significant deprivation facing incarcerated mothers. Although husbands and/or boyfriends may assume responsibility for the children of imprisoned spouses/girlfriends, such an outcome is the exception to the rule. Eventually, a large proportion of children are released by their imprisoned mothers into foster care or put up for adoption.

Some states do offer parenting classes for women inmates with children. In a national survey[54] of prisons for women, 36 states responded that they provide parenting programs which deal with caretaking, reducing violence toward children, visitation problems, and related issues. Some offer facilities as diverse as play areas complete with toys, while others attempt to alleviate difficulties attending mother/child visits. The typical program studied lasts from four to nine weeks and provides for a meeting time of two hours per week.

Other meaningful prison programs for women are often lacking—perhaps because the ones which are in place were originally based upon traditional models of female roles which left little room for substantive employment opportunities. Many trade training programs still emphasize low-paying jobs, such as cook, beautician, or laundry machine operator. Classes in homemaking are not uncommon.

It is better to prevent crimes than to punish them.

—Cesare Bonesana, Marchese Di Beccaria

Social Structure in Women's Prisons

Most studies of women's prisons have revealed a unique feature of such institutions: the way that women inmates construct organized families. Typical of such studies are Ward and Kassebaum's *Women's Prison: Sex and Social Structure*,[55] E. Heffernan's *Making It in Prison: The Square, The Cool, and the Life*,[56] and Rose Giallombardo's *Society of Women: A Study of Women's Prisons*.[57]

Giallombardo, for example, examined the Federal Reformatory for Women at Alderson, West Virginia, spending a year in gathering data (1962–1963). Focusing closely on the formation of families, she entitled one of her chapters "The Homosexual Alliance as a Marriage Unit." In it she describes in great detail the sexual identities assumed by women at Alderson and the symbols they chose to communicate those roles. Hair style, dress, language, and mannerisms were all used to signify "maleness" or "femaleness." Giallombardo details "the anatomy of the marriage relationship from courtship to 'fall out,' that is, from inception to the parting of the ways, or divorce."[58] Romantic love at Alderson was seen as of central importance to any relationship between inmates, and all homosexual relationships were described as voluntary. Through marriage the "stud broad" became the husband and the "femme" the wife.

Studies attempting to document the extent of inmate involvement in prison "families" produce varying results. Some have found as many as 71% of women prisoners involved in the phenomenon, while others have found none.[59] The kinship systems described by Giallombardo and others, however, extend beyond simple "family" ties to the formation of large, intricately related, groups involving a large number of nonsexual relationships. In these groups the roles of "children," "in-laws," "grandparents," and so on may be explicitly recognized. Even "birth order" within a family can become an issue for kinship groups.[60] Kinship groups sometimes occupy a common household—usually a prison cottage or dormitory area. The description of women's prisons provided by authors like Giallombardo show a closed society in which social interaction—including expectations, normative forms of behavior, and emotional ties—is regulated by an inventive system of artificial relationships which mirror the outside world.

Some authors have suggested that this emphasis on describing family structures in women's prisons is unfortunate because it tends to deny other structural features of those institutions.[61] The family emphasis may, in fact, be due to traditional explanations of female criminality which were intertwined with narrow understandings of the role of women in society.

Types of Female Inmates

As in institutions for men, the subculture of women's prisons is multidimensional. Esther Heffernan, for example, found that three terms used by women prisoners she studied—the "square," the "cool," and the "life"—were indicative of three styles of adaptation to prison life.[62] Square inmates had few early experiences with criminal lifestyles and tended to sym-

pathize with the values and attitudes of conventional society. Cool prisoners were more likely to be career offenders. They tended to keep to themselves and were generally supportive of inmate values. Women who participated in the "life" subculture were well familiar with lives of crime. Many had been arrested repeatedly for prostitution, drug use, theft, and so on. "Life" group members were full participants in the economic, social, and familial arrangements of the prison. Heffernan believed that "the life" offered an alternative lifestyle to women who had experienced early and constant rejection by conventional society. Within "the life" women could establish relationships, achieve status, and find meaning in their lives. The "square," the "life," and the "cool" represented subcultures to Heffernan because individuals with similar adaptive choices tended to closely relate to one another and to support the lifestyle characteristic of that type.

"Square" inmates are definitely in the minority in prisons for both men and women. Perhaps for that reason they have rarely been studied. In an insightful self-examination, however, one such inmate, Jean Harris, published her impressions of prison life after more than seven years in the maximum security Bedford Hills (New York) Correctional Facility. Harris was convicted of killing the "Scarsdale Diet Doctor," Herman Tarnower, over a romance gone sour. A successful socialite in her early fifties at the time of the crime, Harris had an eye-opening experience in prison. Her book, *They Always Call Us Ladies*,[63] argues hard for prison reform. Sounding like the "square" she was, Harris says other inmates are "hard for you and me to relate to"[64] and describes them as "childlike women without social skills."[65] Speaking to a reporter, Harris related, "There's really nobody for me to talk to here."[66] Harris was granted clemency by New York Governor Mario Cuomo on December 29, 1992—after having served 12 years in prison.[67]

Recently, the social structure of women's prison has become dichotomized by the advent of "crack kids," as they are called in prison argot. "Crack kids," whose existence highlights generational differences among female offenders, are streetwise young women with little respect for traditional prison values, for their elders, or even for their own children. Known for frequent fights and for their lack of even simple domestic skills, these young women quickly estrange many older inmates, some of whom call them "animalescents."

VIOLENCE IN WOMEN'S PRISONS

Some authors have suggested that violence in women's prisons is less frequent than it is in institutions for men. Bowker observes that "[e]xcept for the behavior of a few "guerrillas," it appears that violence is only used in women's prisons to settle questions of dominance and

A jailhouse lawyer leaves his cell in Oregon State Penitentiary en route to the prison law library. Jailhouse lawyers are not formally schooled in the law but come from the ranks of inmates and routinely assist fellow inmates in filing briefs with the court. *AP/Wide World Photos*

subordination when other manipulative strategies fail to achieve the desired effect."[68] It appears that few homosexual liaisons are forced, perhaps representing a general aversion among women to such victimization in wider society. At least one study, however, has shown the use of sexual violence in women's prisons as a form of revenge against inmates who are overly vocal in their condemnation of such practices among other prisoners.[69]

Not all abuse occurs at the hands of inmates. On November 15, 1992, 14 correctional officers, 10 men and 4 women, were indicted for the alleged abuse of female inmates at the 900-bed Women's Correctional Institute in Hardwick, Georgia. The charges resulted from affidavits filed by 90 female inmates alleging "rape, sexual abuse, prostitution, coerced abortions, sex for favors, and retaliation for refusal to participate"[70] in such activities. One inmate who was forced to have an abortion after becoming pregnant by a male staff member said "[A]s an inmate, I simply felt powerless to avoid the sexual advances of staff and to refuse to have an abortion."[71]

The Task Force on the Female Offender[72] recommends a number of changes in the administration of prisons for women. Among them are

1. Substance abuse programs should be available to women inmates.
2. Women inmates need to acquire greater literacy skills, and literacy programs should form the basis upon which other programs are built.
3. Female offenders should be housed in buildings independent of male inmates.
4. Institutions for women should develop programs for keeping children in the facility in order to "fortify the bond between mother and child."
5. To ensure equal access to assistance, institutions should be built to accommodate programs for female offenders.

Prisoner Rights

Until the 1960s American courts took a neutral approach—commonly called the **hands-off doctrine**—toward the running of prisons. Judges assumed that prison administrators were sufficiently professional in the performance of their duties to balance institutional needs

Hands-Off Doctrine An historical policy of nonintervention with regard to prison management, which American courts tended to follow until the late 1960s. For the past 30 years the doctrine has languished as judicial intervention in prison administration has dramatically increased, although there is now growing evidence of a return to a new hands-off doctrine.

Civil Death   The legal status of prisoners in some jurisdictions who are denied the opportunity to vote, hold public office, marry, or enter into contracts by virtue of their status as incarcerated felons. While civil death is primarily of historical interest, some jurisdictions still place limits on the contractual opportunities available to inmates.

with humane considerations. The hands-off doctrine rested upon the belief that defendants lost most of their rights upon conviction, suffering a kind of **civil death**. Many states defined the concept of civil death through legislation which denied inmates the right to vote, hold public office, or even marry. Some states made incarceration for a felony a basis for uncontested divorce at the request of the noncriminal spouse.

The hands-off doctrine ended in 1969 when a federal court declared the entire Arkansas prison system unconstitutional after hearing arguments that it constituted a form of cruel and unusual punishment.[73] The court's decision resulted from what it judged to be pervasive overcrowding and primitive living conditions. Stories about the system by longtime inmates claimed that a number of other inmates had been beaten or shot to death by guards and buried over the years in unmarked graves on prison property. An investigation did unearth some skeletons in old graves, but their origin was never resolved.

Detailed media coverage of the Arkansas prison system gave rise to suspicions about correctional institutions everywhere. Within a few years federal courts intervened in the running of prisons in Florida, Louisiana, Mississippi, New York City, and Virginia.[74] In 1975, in a precedent-setting decision, U.S. District Court Judge Frank M. Johnson issued an order which banned the Alabama Board of Corrections from accepting any more inmates. Citing a population which was more than double the capacity of the state's system, Judge Johnson enumerated 44 standards to be met before additional inmates could be admitted to prison. Included in the requirements were specific guidelines on living space, staff/inmate ratios, visiting privileges, the racial makeup of staff, and food service modifications.

The Legal Basis of Prisoners' Rights

In 1974, the Supreme Court case of *Pell* v. *Procunier*[75] established a "balancing test" which, although it was at the time addressed only to First Amendment rights, served to define a guideline generally applicable to all prison operations. In *Pell* the Court ruled that the "prison inmate retains those First Amendment rights that are not inconsistent with his status as a prisoner or with the legitimate penological objectives of the corrections system."[76] In other words, inmates have rights much the same as people who are not incarcerated, provided that the legitimate needs of the prison for security, custody, and safety are not compromised. Other court decisions have declared that order maintenance, security, and rehabilitation are all legitimate concerns of prison administration, but that financial exigency and convenience are not. As the **balancing test** makes clear, we see reflected in prisoner rights a microcosm of the due process versus social order dilemma found in wider society.

Balancing Test   A principle developed by the courts and applied to the corrections arena by the 1974 case of *Pell* v. *Procunier*, which attempts to weigh the rights of an individual as guaranteed by the Constitution against the authority of states to make laws or otherwise restrict a person's freedom in order to protect its interests and its citizens.

Prisoner rights, because they are constrained by the legitimate needs of imprisonment, are more conditional rights than they are absolute rights. The Second Amendment to the U.S. Constitution, for example, grants citizens the right to bear arms. The right to arms is, however, necessarily compromised by the need for order and security in prison, and we would not expect a court to rule that inmates have a right to weapons. Conditional rights, because they are subject to the exigencies of imprisonment, bear a strong resemblance to privileges, which should not be surprising since "privileges" were all that inmates officially had until the modern era. The practical difference between a privilege and a conditional right stems from the fact that privileges exist only at the convenience of granting institutions and can be revoked at any time for any reason. The rights of prisoners, on the other hand, have a basis in the Constitution and in law external to the institution. Although the institution may change them for legitimate correctional reasons, they may not be infringed without good cause that can be demonstrated in a court of law.

The past two decades have seen many lawsuits brought by prisoners challenging the constitutionality of some aspect of confinement. As mentioned in Chapter 10, suits filed by prisoners with the courts are generally called writs of *habeas corpus* and formally request that the person detaining a prisoner bring him or her before a judicial officer to determine the lawfulness of imprisonment. The American Correctional Association says that most prisoner lawsuits have been based upon: "1. the Eighth Amendment prohibition against cruel and unusual punishment; 2. the Fourteenth Amendment prohibition against the taking of life, liberty, or property without due process of law; and 3. the Fourteenth Amendment provision requiring equal protection of the laws."[77] Aside from appeals by inmates which question the propriety of their convictions and sentences, such constitutional challenges represent the bulk of legal action initiated by those imprisoned. State statutes and federal legislation, how-

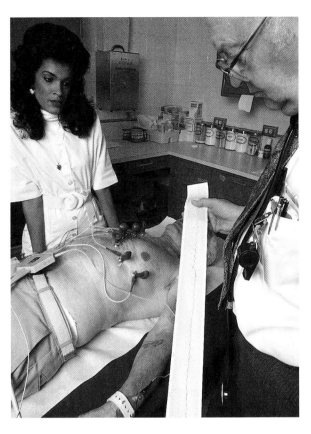

Court decisions over the years have established a firm set of inmate rights. Among them is a right to health care. Here, an inmate undergoes an EKG test in New Jersey's Riverfront Prison. *J. Griffin, The Image Works*

ever, including Section 1983 of the Civil Rights Act of 1871, provide other bases for challenges to the legality of specific prison conditions and procedures.

Precedents in Inmate Rights

To date, the Supreme Court has not spoken with finality on many questions of inmate rights, and there is some evidence of a trend back to a modified "hands-off doctrine."[78] However, high-court decisions of the last few decades can be interpreted along with a number of lower court findings to enumerate the conditional rights of prisoners shown in Table 13–2. A number of especially significant Court decisions are discussed in the pages which follow.

Communications

As previously mentioned, the rights listed in Table 13–2 are not absolute but must be balanced against the security, order maintenance, and treatment needs of the institution. The Supreme Court has indicated that institutional exigency can in fact abbreviate any right. In the case of *Procunier* v. *Martinez* (1974),[79] for example, the Court ruled that a prisoner's mail may be censored if it is necessary to do so for security purposes. On the other hand, mere institutional convenience does not provide a sufficient basis for the denial of rights. In *McNamara* v. *Moody* (1979),[80] a federal court upheld the right of an inmate to write vulgar letters to his girlfriend in which he made disparaging comments about the prison staff. The court reasoned that the letters may have been embarrassing to prison officials but that they did not affect the security or order of the institution. However, libelous materials have generally not been accorded First Amendment protection in or out of institutional contexts.

Concerning inmate publications, legal precedent has held that prisoners have no inherent right to publish newspapers or newsletters for use by other prisoners, although many institutions do permit and finance such periodicals.[81] Publications originating from outside of prison, such as newspapers, magazines, and special interest tracts, have generally been protected when mailed directly from the publisher, although magazines which depict deviant sexual behavior can be banned according to *Mallery* v. *Lewis* (1983)[82] and other precedents. Nudity by itself is not necessarily obscene, and federal courts have held that prisons cannot ban nude pictures of inmates' wives and girlfriends.[83]

Table 13-2 The Conditional Rights of Inmates

Religious Freedom

The Right of Assembly for Religious Services and Groups

The Right to Attend Services of Other Religious Groups

The Right to Receive Visits from Ministers

The Right to Correspond with Religious Leaders

A Right to Observe Religious Dietary Laws

The Right to Wear Religious Insignia

Freedom of Speech

The Right to Meet with Members of the Press[1]

The Right to Receive Publications Directly from the Publisher

The Right to Communicate with Nonprisoners

Access to Legal Assistance

A Right of Access to the Courts[2]

A Right to Visits from Attorneys

A Right to Mail Communications with Lawyers[3]

A Right to Communicate with Legal Assistance Organizations

A Right to Consult "Jail House Lawyers"[4]

A Right to Assistance in Filing Legal Papers, which should include one of the following:

    Access to an Adequate Law Library

    Paid Attorneys

    Paralegal Personnel or Law Students

Medical Treatment

A Right to Sanitary and Healthy Conditions

A Right to Medical Attention for Serious Physical Problems

A Right to Needed Medications

A Right to Treatment in Accordance with "Doctor's Orders"

Protection

A Right to Food, Water, and Shelter

A Right to Protection from Foreseeable Attack

A Right to Protection from Predictable Sexual Abuse

A Right to Protection Against Suicide

Institutional Punishment and Discipline

An Absolute Right Against Corporal Punishments (unless *sentenced* to such punishments)

A Right to Due Process Prior to Punishment, including:

    Notice of Charges

    A Fair and Impartial Hearing

    An Opportunity for Defense

    A Right to Present Witnesses

    A Written Decision

[1]But not beyond the opportunities afforded for inmates to meet with members of the general public.

[2]As restricted by the Prison Litigation Reform Act of 1996.

[3]Mail communications are generally designated as privileged or nonprivileged. Privileged communications include those between inmates and their lawyers or court officials and cannot legitimately be read by prison officials. Nonprivileged communications include most other written communications.

[4]Jail house lawyers are inmates with experience in the law, usually gained from filing legal briefs on their own behalf or on the behalf of others. Consultation with jail house lawyers was ruled permissible in the Supreme Court case of *Johnson* v. *Avery*, 393 U.S. 483 (1968), unless inmates are provided with paid legal assistance.

Theory into Practice

Religious Assembly

The following statements, excerpted from prison "rule books" of two different states, capture the essence of the court-created balancing test as it weighs prison administrative and security concerns against the right to freedom of religion, which is guaranteed by the U.S. Constitution:

Religious Services. Religious services, speeches, or addresses by inmates other than those approved by the Superintendent or designee are prohibited.

Source: Standards of Inmate Behavior, All Institutions, State of New York, Department of Correctional Services (1988).

Freedom of Religion. Inmates will be able to practice their religion in keeping with the security needs of each unit. Ministers and other religious counselors will be allowed to visit inmates. The time, place, and method of such visits are controlled by the custody and security needs of each unit.

Source: Rules and Procedures Governing the Management and Conduct of Inmates Under the Control of the Division of Prisons, North Carolina Division of Prisons (1983).

Religious Practice

The early Supreme Court case of *Cruz* v. *Beto* (1972)[84] established that inmates must be given a "reasonable opportunity" to pursue their faith even if it differs from traditional forms of worship. Meeting facilities must be provided for religious use when those same facilities are made available to other groups of prisoners for other purposes,[85] but no group can claim exclusive use of a prison area for religious reasons.[86] The right to assemble for religious purposes, however, can be denied to inmates who use such meetings to plan escapes or who take the opportunity to dispense contraband. Similarly, prisoners in segregation do not have to be permitted the opportunity to attend group religious services.[87]

Although prisoners cannot be made to attend religious services,[88] records of religious activity can be maintained in order to administratively determine dietary needs and eligibility for passes to religious services outside of the institution.[89] In *Dettmer* v. *Landon* (1985),[90] a federal court held that an inmate who claimed to practice witchcraft must be provided with the artifacts necessary for his worship services. Included were items such as sea salt, sulfur, a quartz clock, incense, candles, and a white robe without a hood. However, drugs and dangerous substances have not been considered permissible even when inmates claimed they were a necessary part of their religious services.[91] Prison regulations prohibiting the wearing of beards, even those grown for religious reasons, were held acceptable for security considerations in the 1985 federal court case of *Hill* v. *Blackwell.*[92]

The Privilege of the Writ of Habeas Corpus shall not be suspended, unless when in Cases of Rebellion or Invasion the public Safety may require it.

—Article I, section 9, clause 2, of the U.S. Constitution.

Visitation

Visitation and access to the news media are other areas which have come under court scrutiny. Maximum-security institutions rarely permit "contact" visits, and some have on occasion suspended all visitation privileges. In the case of *Block* v. *Rutherford* (1984),[93] the Supreme Court upheld the policy of the Los Angeles County Central Jail which prohibited all visits from friends and relatives. The Court agreed that the large jail population and the conditions under which visits might take place could combine to threaten the security of the jail.

In *Pell* v. *Procunier* (1974),[94] cited in the balancing test, the Court found in favor of a California law which denied prisoners the opportunity to hold special meetings with members of the press. The Court reasoned that media interviews could be conducted through regular visitation arrangements and that most of the information desired by the media could be conveyed through correspondence. In *Pell*, the Court also held that any reasonable policy of media access was acceptable so long as it was administered fairly and without bias.

In a later case, the Court ruled that news personnel cannot be denied correspondence with inmates, but also ruled that they have no constitutional right to interview inmates or to inspect correctional facilities beyond the visitation opportunities available to others.[95] This equal access policy was set forth in *Houchins v. KQED, Inc.* (1978), by Justice Stewart who wrote that "The Constitution does no more than assure the public and the press equal access once government has opened its doors."[96]

Legal Access to the Courts

A well-established right of prisoners is access to the courts[97] and to legal assistance. The right of prisoners to petition the court was recognized in *Bounds v. Smith* (1977),[98] which, at the time, was a far-reaching Supreme Court decision. While attempting to define "access," the Court in *Bounds* imposed upon the states the duty of assisting inmates in the preparation and filing of legal papers. Assistance could be provided through trained personnel knowledgeable in the law or via law libraries in each institution, which all states have since built. In 1996, however, in the case of *Lewis v. Casey*, the U.S. Supreme Court repudiated part of the *Bounds* decision, saying "[S]tatements in *Bounds* suggesting that prison authorities must also enable the prisoner to discover grievances, and to litigate effectively once in court…have no antecedent in this Court's pre-*Bounds* cases, and are now disclaimed." In *Lewis*, the Court overturned earlier decisions by a federal district court and by the Ninth Circuit Court of Appeals. Both lower courts had found in favor of Arizona inmates who had complained that state prison law libraries provided inadequate legal research facilities, thereby depriving them of their right of legal access to the courts as established by *Bounds*. In turning back portions of *Bounds*, the majority in *Lewis* wrote that inmates raising such claims need to demonstrate "widespread actual injury" to their ability to access the courts, not merely "isolated instances of actual injury." "Moreover," wrote the Justices, "*Bounds* does not guarantee inmates the wherewithal to file any and every type of legal claim, but requires only that they be provided with the tools to attack their sentences…and to challenge the conditions of their confinement."

In an earlier case, *Johnson v. Avery* (1968),[99] the Court had ruled that persons under correctional supervision have a right to consult "jail house lawyers" for advice when assistance from trained professionals is not available. Other court decisions have established that inmates have a right to correspond with their attorneys[100] and with legal assistance organizations. Such letters, however, can be opened and inspected for contraband[101] (but not read) by prison authorities in the presence of the inmate. The right to meet with hired counsel for reasonable lengths of time has also been upheld.[102] Indigent defendants must be provided with stamps for the purpose of legal correspondence,[103] and inmates cannot be disciplined for communicating with lawyers or requesting legal help. Conversations between inmates and their lawyers can be monitored, although any evidence obtained through such a process cannot be used in court.[104] Inmates do not, however, have the right to an appointed lawyer, even when indigent, if no judicial proceedings against them have been initiated.[105]

Medical Care

The historic Supreme Court case of *Estelle v. Gamble* (1976)[106] specified prison officials' duty to provide for inmates' medical care. In *Estelle*, the Court concerned itself with "deliberate indifference" on the part of the staff toward a prisoner's need for serious medical attention. "Deliberate indifference" can mean a wanton disregard for the health of inmates. Hence, while poor treatment, misdiagnosis, and the like may constitute medical malpractice, they do not necessarily constitute deliberate indifference.[107]

More recently, in *Farmer v. Brennan* (1994),[108] the Court clarified the concept of "deliberate indifference" by holding that it required both actual knowledge and disregard of risk of harm. The case involved Dee Farmer, a preoperative transsexual with obvious feminine characteristics who had been incarcerated with other males in the federal prison system. Farmer was sometimes held in the general prison population but was more often in segregation. While mixing with other inmates, however, Farmer was beaten and raped by a fellow prisoner. Subsequently, he sued correctional officials, claiming that they had acted with deliberate indifference to his safety because they knew that the penitentiary had a violent environment as well as a history of inmate assaults, and because they should have known that Farmer would be particularly vulnerable to sexual attack.

The Court sent Farmer's case back to a lower court for rehearing, after clarifying what it said was necessary to establish deliberate indifference. "Prison officials," wrote the justices, "have a duty under the Eighth Amendment to provide humane conditions of confinement. They must ensure that inmates receive adequate food, clothing, shelter, and medical care and must protect prisoners from violence at the hands of other prisoners. However, a constitutional violation occurs only where…the official has acted with 'deliberate indifference' to inmate health or safety." The Court continued: "A prison official may be held liable under the Eighth Amendment for acting with 'deliberate indifference' to inmate health or safety only if he knows that inmates face a substantial risk of serious harm and disregards that risk by failing to take reasonable measures to abate it."[109]

Two other cases, *Ruiz* v. *Estelle* (1982)[110] and *Newman* v. *Alabama* (1972)[111] have had substantial impact concerning the rights of prisoners to medical attention. In *Ruiz*, the Texas Department of Corrections was found lacking in its medical treatment programs. The court ordered an improvement in record keeping, physical facilities, and general medical care, while it continued to monitor the progress of the department. In *Newman*, Alabama's prison medical services were found so inadequate as to be "shocking to the conscience." Problems with the Alabama program included[112]

- Not enough medical personnel
- Poor physical facilities for medical treatment
- Poor administrative techniques for dispersal of medications
- Poor medical records
- A lack of medical supplies
- Poorly trained or untrained inmates who provided some medical services and performed minor surgery
- Medically untrained personnel who determined the need for treatment

Part of the issue of medical treatment is the question of whether inmates can be forced to take medication or can refuse to eat. A 1984 federal court case held that inmates could be medicated in emergency situations against their wills.[113] The court did recognize that unwanted medications designed to produce only psychological effects, such as tranquilizers, might be refused more readily than life-sustaining drugs.[114] Similarly, other courts have held that inmates do not have a right to starve themselves to death.

In 1993, the Court gave indication that environmental conditions of prison life which pose a threat to inmate health may have to be corrected. In *Helling* v. *McKinney*,[115] Nevada inmate William McKinney claimed that exposure to secondary cigarette smoke circulating in his cell was threatening his health, in violation of the Eighth Amendment's prohibition on cruel and unusual punishment. The Court, in ordering that a federal district court provide McKinney with the opportunity to prove his allegations, held that "[A]n injunction cannot be denied to inmates who plainly prove an unsafe, life-threatening condition on the ground that nothing yet has happened to them." In effect, the *Helling* case gave notice to prison officials that they are responsible not only for "inmates' current serious health problems," but also for maintaining environmental conditions under which health problems might be prevented from developing.

Privacy

Many court decisions, including the Tenth Circuit case of *U.S.* v. *Ready* (1978)[116] and the U.S. Supreme Court decisions of *Katz* v. *U.S.* (1967)[117] and *Hudson* v. *Palmer* (1984)[118] have held that inmates cannot have a reasonable expectation to privacy while incarcerated. Palmer, an inmate in Virginia, claimed that Hudson, a prison guard, had unreasonably destroyed some of his personal (noncontraband) property following a cell search. Palmer's complaint centered on the lack of due process which accompanied the destruction. The Court disagreed, saying that the need for prison officials to conduct thorough and unannounced searches precludes inmate privacy in personal possessions.

In *Block* v. *Rutherford* (1984)[119] the Court established that prisoners do not have a right to be present during a search of their cells. Some lower courts, however, have begun to indicate that body cavity searches may be unreasonable unless based upon a demonstrable suspicion or conducted after prior warning has been given to the inmate.[120] They have also indicated that searches conducted simply to "harass or humiliate" inmates are illegitimate.[121] These

Theory into Practice

Procedures for the Filing of Inmate Grievances in the State of New York

1. Inmate grievance forms shall be made available to any inmate through the facility's duty office within 24 hours of a request. The grievance complaint form shall be filled out by the inmate with the assistance of any other inmate or staff member of the inmate's choice.

2. The completed grievance form shall be transmitted to the designated staff person who shall attempt to help resolve the grievance informally.

3. If the grievance cannot be resolved informally within four working days, the designated staff shall convene an IGRC (Inmate Grievance Review Committee) hearing within seven working days from the date the grievance was received by that staff person. The IGRC shall be composed of two staff representatives appointed by the superintendent, two inmates selected by the grievant, and the nonvoting chairperson designated by the superintendent or his or her designee.

4. At the IGRC hearing, the inmate, the advisor, and the other parties shall hear the grievance and the IGRC shall render a recommendation (to the superintendent).

Source: State of New York, Department of Correctional Services, Directive 4041, *Inmate Grievance Program Modification Plan.*

---

cases may be an indication that the Supreme Court will soon recognize a limited degree of privacy in prison cell searches, especially those which uncover legal documents and personal papers prepared by the prisoner.[122]

Disciplinary and Grievance Procedures

A major area of inmate concern is the hearing of grievances. Complaints may arise in areas as diverse as food service (quality of food or special diets for religious purposes or health regimens), interpersonal relations between inmates and staff, denial of privileges, and accusations of misconduct levied against an inmate or a guard.

In 1972 the National Council on Crime and Delinquency developed a Model Act for the Protection of Rights of Prisoners, which included the opportunity for grievances to be heard. The 1973 National Advisory Commission on Criminal Justice Standards and Goals called for the establishment of responsible practices for the hearing of inmate grievances. Finally, in 1977, in the case of *Jones* v. *North Carolina Prisoners' Labor Union, Inc.,*[123] the Supreme Court held that prisons must establish some formal opportunity for the airing of inmate grievances. Soon, formal grievance plans were established in prisons in an attempt to divert inmate-originated grievances away from the courts.

Grievance Procedure
Formalized arrangements, usually involving a neutral hearing board, whereby institutionalized individuals have the opportunity to register complaints about the conditions of their confinement.

Today all sizable prisons have an established **grievance procedure** whereby an inmate files a complaint with local authorities and receives a mandated response. Modern grievance procedures range from the use of a hearing board composed of staff members and inmates to a single staff appointee charged with the resolution of complaints. Inmates who are dissatisfied with the handling of their grievance can generally appeal beyond the level of the local prison unit. The accompanying "Theory Into Practice" box outlines the procedures to be followed in the filing of grievances in the New York state correctional system.

Disciplinary actions by prison authorities may also require a formalized hearing process, especially when staff members bring charges of rule violations against inmates, which might result in some form of punishment being imposed on them. In a precedent-setting decision, the Supreme Court decided, in the case of *Wolff* v. *McDonnell* (1974),[124] that sanctions could not be levied against inmates without appropriate due process. The *Wolff* case involved an inmate who had been deprived of previously earned "good-time" credits because of misbehavior. The Court established that "good-time" credits were a form of "state-created right(s)," which, once created, could not be "arbitrarily abrogated."[125] *Wolff* was especially significant because it began an era of court scrutiny of what came to be called "state-created liberty interests." State-created liberty interests were said to be based upon the language used

Theory into Practice

Typical Rules Governing the Conduct of Prisoners— Major and Minor Offenses

1.00	All Penal Law offenses are prohibited and may be referred to law enforcement agencies for prosecution through the courts.
100.10	Inmates shall not assault, inflict, or attempt to inflict bodily harm upon any other inmate.
100.11	Inmates shall not assault, inflict, or attempt to inflict bodily harm upon any staff member.
100.13	Inmates shall not engage in fighting.
101.10	Inmates shall not engage in, encourage, solicit, or attempt to force others to engage in sexual acts.
101.21	Physical contact between inmates, including but not limited to kissing, embracing, or hand holding, is prohibited.
104.11	Inmates shall not engage in any violent conduct or conduct involving the threat of violence.
105.10	The unauthorized assembly of inmates in groups is prohibited.
105.11	Religious services, speeches, or addresses by inmates other than those approved by the superintendent or designee are prohibited.
106.10	All orders of facility personnel will be obeyed promptly and without argument.
108.10	Inmates shall not escape, attempt to escape, conspire to, or be an accessory to an escape.
113.10	Inmates shall not make, possess, sell, or exchange any item of contraband that may be classified as a weapon by description, use, or appearance.
113.12	Inmates shall not make, possess, use, sell, or exchange any narcotic, narcotic paraphernalia, or controlled substance.

Source: Excerpted from State of New York, Department of Correctional Services, *Standards of Inmate Behavior, All Institutions*, revised June 1988.

in published prison regulations, and were held, in effect, to confer due process guarantees upon prisoners. Hence, if a prison regulation said that a disciplinary hearing should be held before a prisoner could be sent to solitary confinement, and that such a hearing should permit a discussion of the evidence for and against the prisoner, courts interpreted that regulation to mean that the prisoner had a state-created right to a hearing and sending him or her to solitary confinement in violation of the regulation was a violation of a state-created liberty interest. State-created rights and privileges were also called "protected liberties" in later court decisions and were interpreted to include any significant change in a prisoner's status.

In the interest of due process, and especially where written prison regulations governing the hearing process exist, courts have generally held that inmates going before disciplinary hearing boards are entitled to (1) notice of the charges brought against them, (2) the chance to organize a defense, (3) an impartial hearing, and (4) the opportunity to present witnesses and evidence on their behalf. A written statement of the hearing board's conclusions should be provided to the inmate.[126] More recently, in the case of *Ponte* v. *Real* (1985),[127] the Supreme Court held that prison officials must provide an explanation to inmates who are denied the opportunity to have a desired witness at their hearing. The case of *Vitek* v. *Jones* (1980) extended the requirement of due process to inmates about to be transferred from prisons to mental hospitals.[128]

So that inmates can know what is expected of them as they enter prison, the American Correctional Association recommends: "A rulebook that contains all chargeable offenses, ranges of penalties and disciplinary procedures [be] posted in a conspicuous and accessible area; [and] a copy…given to each inmate and staff member."[129] A list of "major" and "minor" rule violations, typical of many prisons, are shown in the box on this page.

A Return to the Hands-Off Doctrine?

Many state-created rights and "protected liberties" may soon be a thing of the past. In June 1991, an increasingly conservative U.S. Supreme Court signaled the beginning of what appears to be at least a partial return to the "hands-off" doctrine of earlier times. The case, *Wilson* v. *Seiter*,[130] involved a 1983 suit brought against Richard P. Seiter, director of the Ohio Department of Rehabilitation and Correction, and Carl Humphreys, warden of the Hocking Correctional Facility (HCF) in Nelsonville, Ohio. In the suit, Pearly L. Wilson, a felon incarcerated at HCF, alleged that a number of the conditions of his confinement—specifically, overcrowding, excessive noise, insufficient locker storage space, inadequate heating and cooling, improper ventilation, unclean and inadequate restrooms, unsanitary dining facilities and food preparation, and housing with mentally and physically ill inmates—constituted cruel and unusual punishment in violation of the Eighth and Fourteenth Amendments to the U.S. Constitution. Wilson asked for a change in prison conditions and sought $900,000 from prison officials in compensatory and punitive damages.

Both the federal district court in which Wilson first filed affidavits and the Sixth Circuit Court of Appeals held that no constitutional violations existed because the conditions cited by Wilson were not the result of malicious intent on the part of officials. The U.S. Supreme Court agreed, noting that the "deliberate indifference" standard applied in *Estelle* v. *Gamble*[131] to claims involving medical care is similarly applicable to other cases in which prisoners challenge the conditions of their confinement. In effect, the Court created a standard which effectively means that all future challenges to prison conditions by inmates, which are brought under the Eighth Amendment, must show "deliberate indifference" by the officials responsible for the existence of those conditions before the Court will hear the complaint.

The written opinion of the Court in *Wilson* v. *Seiter* is telling. Writing for the majority, Justice Scalia observed that "if a prison boiler malfunctions accidentally during a cold winter, an inmate would have no basis for an Eighth Amendment claim, even if he suffers objectively significant harm. If a guard accidentally stepped on a prisoner's toe and broke it, this would not be punishment in anything remotely like the accepted meaning of the word."

Although the criterion of deliberate indifference is still evolving, it is likely that such indifference could be demonstrated by petitioners able to show that prison administrators have done nothing to alleviate life-threatening prison conditions after those conditions had been called to their attention. Even so, critics of *Wilson* are concerned that the decision may excuse prison authorities from the need to improve living conditions within institutions on the basis of simple budgetary constraints. Four of the justices themselves recognized the potential held by *Wilson* for a near-return to the days of the hands-off doctrine. Although concurring with the Court's majority, Justices White, Marshall, Blackmun, and Stevens noted their fear that "[t]he ultimate result of today's decision, [may be] that 'serious deprivations of basic human needs'...will go unredressed due to an unnecessary and meaningless search for 'deliberate indifference.'"

In the 1995 case of *Sandin* v. *Conner*,[132] the U.S. Supreme Court took a much more definitive stance in favor of a new type of hands-off doctrine and voted 5 to 4 to reject the argument that any state action taken for a punitive reason encroaches upon a prisoner's constitutional due process right to be free from the deprivation of liberty. The Court effectively set aside substantial portions of earlier decisions such as *Wolff* v. *McDonnell* (1974)[133] and *Hewitt* v. *Helms* (1983),[134] which, wrote the justices, focused more on procedural issues than on those of "real substance." As a consequence, the majority opinion held, past cases such as these have "impermissibly shifted the focus" away from the *nature* of a due process deprivation to one based on the language of a particular state or prison regulation. "This shift in focus," the justices wrote, "has encouraged prisoners to comb regulations in search of mandatory language on which to base entitlements to various state-conferred privileges." As a result, the Court said, cases such as *Wolff* and *Hewitt* "created disincentives for States to codify prison management procedures in [order to avoid lawsuits by inmates], and...led to the involvement of federal courts in the day-to-day management of prisons."

In *Sandin*, Demont Conner, an inmate at the Halawa Correctional Facility in Hawaii, was serving an indeterminate sentence of 30 years to life for numerous crimes, including murder, kidnapping, robbery, and burglary. Conner alleged in a lawsuit in federal court that prison officials had deprived him of procedural due process when a hearing committee refused to allow him to present witnesses during a disciplinary hearing and then sentenced him to segregation for alleged misconduct. An appellate court agreed with Conner, concluding that an existing prison regulation which instructed the hearing committee to find guilt in cases where a misconduct charge is supported by substantial evidence, meant that the committee could not impose segregation if it did not look at all the evidence available to it.

The Supreme Court, however, reversed the decision of the appellate court, holding that while "such a conclusion may be entirely sensible in the ordinary task of construing a statute defining rights and remedies available to the general public, [i]t is a good deal less sensible in the case of a prison regulation primarily designed to guide correctional officials in the administration of a prison." The Court concluded that "such regulations [are] not designed to confer rights on inmates," but are meant only to provide *guidelines* to prison staff members. Hence, based upon *Sandin*, it appears that inmates in the future will have a much more difficult time challenging the administrative regulations and procedures imposed upon them by prison officials, even when stated procedures are not explicitly followed. "The *Hewitt* approach," wrote the majority in *Sandin*, "has run counter to the view expressed in several of our cases that federal courts ought to afford appropriate deference and flexibility to state officials trying to manage a volatile environment.…The time has come" said the Court, "to return to those due process principles that were correctly established and applied in" earlier times.

The Prison Litigation Reform Act (1996)

While only about 2,000 petitions per year concerning inmate problems were being filed with the courts in 1961, by 1975 the number of filings had increased to around 17,000, and by 1996 prisoners filed 68,235 civil-rights lawsuits in federal courts nationwide.[135] Some inmate-originated suits seemed patently ludicrous and became the subject of much media coverage in the mid-1990s.[136] One such suit involved Robert Procup, a Florida State Prison inmate serving time for the murder of his business partner. Procup repeatedly sued Florida prison officials—once because he got only one roll with his dinner; again because he once didn't get a luncheon salad; a third time because prison provided TV-dinners didn't come with a drink; and a fourth time because his cell had no television. Two other well-publicized cases involved an inmate who went to court asking to be allowed to exercise religious freedom by attending prison chapel services in the nude; and an inmate who, thinking he could become pregnant via homosexual relations, sued prison doctors who wouldn't provide him with birth control pills. An infamous example of seemingly frivolous inmate lawsuits was one brought by inmates claiming religious freedoms and demanding that members of the Church of the New Song, or CONS, be provided steak and Harvey's Bristol Cream every Friday in order to celebrate communion. The CONS suit stayed in various courts for ten years before finally being thrown out.[137]

The huge number of inmate-originated lawsuits created a backlog of cases in many federal courts and was targeted by the media and some citizen's groups as an unnecessary waste of taxpayer money. The National Association of Attorneys General, which supports efforts to restrict frivolous inmate lawsuits, estimates that lawsuits filed by prisoners cost states more than $81 million a year in legal fees alone.[138]

In 1996, in an effort to restrict inmate filings to worthwhile cases and to reduce the number of suits brought by state prisoners in federal courts, Congress enacted the federal Prison Litigation Reform Act (PLRA).[139] The Act was signed into law by President Clinton in April of that year. It

- Requires inmates to pay a $120 federal-court filing fee.
- Limits the award of attorneys' fees in successful lawsuits brought by inmates.
- Requires judges to screen all inmate complaints against the federal government and to immediately dismiss those deemed frivolous or without merit.
- Revokes the good-time credits earned by federal prisoners toward early release if they file a malicious lawsuit.
- Bars prisoners from suing the federal government for mental or emotional injury unless there was also an associated physical injury.
- Mandates that court orders affecting prison administration cannot go any further than necessary to correct a violation of a particular inmate's civil rights.
- Makes it possible for state officials to have court orders lifted after two years unless there is a new finding of a continuing violation of federally guaranteed civil rights.

• Mandates that any court order requiring the release of prisoners due to overcrowding be approved by a three-member court before it can become effective.

A number of states have filed suit under PLRA, seeking to wrest control of their prison systems back from federal authorities. Federal oversight of prisons in 40 states and in the District of Columbia had been ordered during the 1980s by federal courts as a result of over-crowding or poor administration by local officials. The first successful bid to end federal oversight of an entire state system came in 1996 when control of the South Carolina prison system reverted back to state authorities. The state had yielded to federal oversight in a 1985 agreement. Iowa and Wisconsin have also sought relief under PLRA, and, as of this writing, New York, Michigan, Illinois, and Connecticut are considering filing challenges.

Opponents of PLRA fear that it might stifle the filing of meritorious suits by inmates fac-ing real deprivations. "Although the act was advertised as an attack on frivolous litigation, it actually is an attack on litigation of great merit," says Elizabeth Alexander of the American Civil Liberties Union's national prison project.[140] Ira Robbins, an American University law professor, adds: "A lot of the changes that have to be made to bring prisons up to minimum levels of decency aren't going to occur." In passing the Prison Litigation Reform Act, Robbins is concerned that "Congress has focused on efficiency at the expense of fairness."[141] Prisoners' rights organizations have vowed to challenge the PLRA in court, and Elizabeth Alexander, Executive Director of the ACLU Foundation's Prison Project, says, "We believe that the major provisions of the PLRA are unconstitutional and will be held so as a violation of the separation of powers and the due process clause of the Constitution." Ms. Alexander promised that the ACLU would "challenge PLRA in every court in which it comes up."[142]

Issues Facing Prisons Today

Prisons are society's answer to a number of social problems. They house outcasts, misfits, and some highly dangerous people. While prisons provide a part of the answer to the ques-tion of crime control, they also face problems of their own. A few of those special problems are described in what follows.

AIDS

An earlier chapter discussed the steps being taken by police agencies to deal with health threats represented by AIDS. In 1993 the Centers for Disease Control reported confirming 11,565 cases of AIDS among inmates of the nation's prisons[143]—an increase of more than five-fold since 1987. By the time of the survey, more than 3,500 inmate deaths had been attributed to HIV infection throughout prisons and jails across the nation. More recent sur-veys,[144] one reported in 1997, have estimated the number of HIV-infected inmates in the nation's prisons at much higher levels—some as high as 80,000 inmates.[145] Positive sero-prevalence rates have been found to vary from region to region—ranging between 2.1% and 7.6% of all men entering prison and between 2.5% and 14.7% of women. Some states have especially high rates. New York, for example, recently reported that 20% of all inmates it houses are HIV positive, with slightly less than 10% of those exhibiting symptoms of AIDS.

The exact number of HIV-infected inmates is difficult to assess because only 16 states and the District of Columbia require AIDS testing of all inmates. From what is known, men appear to account for 95% of all inmates affected by AIDS. Blacks, at 58%, comprise the largest racial/ethnic category; 32% of those infected are white, and 10% are Hispanic.

The incidence of HIV infection among the general population stands at 8.6 cases per 100,000 according to a recent report by the Centers for Disease Control. Among inmates, however, best estimates place the reported HIV-infection rate at 2,300 cases per 100,000[146]—many times as great; AIDS, in fact, has become the leading cause of death among prison inmates.[147] While not all inmates are infected in prison, authorities say the virus is spread behind bars through homosexual activity (including rape), intravenous drug use, and the sharing of tainted tattoo and hypodermic needles. The fact that inmates tend to have histo-ries of high-risk behavior before entering prison, especially intravenous drug use, however, probably means that many are infected before coming to prison and helps to explain much of the huge difference in infection rates.

Early studies have shown that, contrary to popular opinion, AIDS transmission inside of prisons appears minimal. In a test of inmates at a U.S. Army military prison, 542 prisoners who upon admission had tested negative for exposure to the AIDS virus were retested two years later. None showed any signs of exposure to the virus.[148] On the other hand, some authorities suggest that it is only a matter of time before widespread forms of high-risk behavior inside of prisons begin to make a more visible contribution to the spread of AIDS.[149] Similarly, prison staffers fear infection from AIDS through routine activities, such as cell searches, responding to fights, performing body searches, administering CPR, and confiscating needles or weapons.

A recent report by the National Institute of Justice[150] suggests that there are two types of strategies available to correctional systems to reduce the transmission of AIDS. One strategy relies upon medical technology to identify seropositive inmates and segregate them from the rest of the prison population. Mass screening and inmate segregation, however, may be prohibitively expensive. They may also be illegal. Some states specifically prohibit HIV antibody testing without the informed consent of the person tested.[151] The related issue of confidentiality may be difficult to manage, especially where the purpose of testing is to segregate infected inmates from others. In addition, civil liability may result where inmates are falsely labeled as infected or where inmates known to be infected are not prevented from spreading the disease. As of 1995, only two state prison systems[152] segregated all known HIV-infected inmates, but more limited forms of separation can be practiced. In 1994, for example, a federal appeals court upheld a California prison policy which bars inmates who are HIV positive from working in food service jobs.[153]

Many state prison systems routinely deny HIV-positive inmates jobs, educational opportunities, visitation privileges, conjugal visits, and home furloughs, causing some researchers to conclude that "inmates with HIV and AIDS are routinely discriminated against and denied equal treatment in ways that have no accepted medical basis."[154] Theodore Hammett, the nation's leading researcher on AIDS in prison, says, "The point is, people shouldn't be punished for having a certain medical condition."[155]

The second strategy is one of prevention through education. Educational programs teach both inmates and staff members about the dangers of high-risk behavior and offer suggestions on how to avoid HIV infection. An NIJ model program[156] recommends the use of simple, straightforward messages presented by knowledgeable and approachable trainers. Alarmism, says NIJ, is to be avoided. A recent survey[157] found that 98% of state and federal prisons provide some form of AIDS/HIV education, and that 90% of jails do as well—although most such training is oriented toward correctional staff rather than inmates.

In anticipation of court rulings which will likely prohibit the mass testing of inmates for the AIDS virus, the second strategy seems best. A third, but controversial, strategy involves issuing condoms to prisoners. Although this alternative is sometimes rejected because it implicitly condones sexual behavior among inmates, six correctional systems within the United States report that they make condoms available to inmates upon request.[158]

Geriatric Offenders

As determinate sentencing and the just deserts model take greater hold and more and more criminals are sentenced to longer prison terms, there will be increasing numbers of older prisoners among the general prison population. Although some prisoners grow old behind bars, others are old before they get there. American prisons, serving an aging population, are seeing more geriatric prisoners than ever before. At the moment, however, "It's a middle-aged bulge, rather than an increasing proportion of elderly prisoners," says Allen Beck of the Bureau of Justice Statistics.[159] The proportion of state prisoners under age 35 decreased from 73 percent in 1986 to 68 percent in 1991. Meanwhile, prisoners aged 35 to 54 increased from 25 percent to 29 percent. The proportion aged 55 and older remained the same—about 3 percent.

Soon, however, longer sentences will bring a relentless increase in the number of elderly prisoners being held at both the federal and state levels. Mandatory life without parole laws will create an ever-growing number of elderly inmates, and some experts are predicting an explosion in the number of elderly prisoners in coming decades. The "graying" of America's prison population is due to a number of causes: (1) increasing crime among those over 50; (2) the gradual aging of the society from which prisoners come; (3) a trend toward longer sentences,

Geriatric inmates are becoming an increasingly large part of the inmate population. Here, Jonathan Turley, founder of the Project for Older Prisoners (POPS), speaks with two Angola, Louisiana, inmates. *Mark Sultz, AP/Wide World Photos*

especially for violent offenders with previous records (for example, the "three-strikes" laws of many states); and (4) the gradual accumulation of older habitual offenders in prison.[160]

Crimes of violence are what bring most older inmates into the correctional system. According to one study, 52% of inmates who were over the age of 50 at the time they entered prison had committed violent crimes, compared with 41% of younger inmates.[161] Ronald Wikberg and Burk Foster provide a snapshot of long-termers in their recent study of Angola prison.[162] Wikberg and Foster described 31 inmates at the Louisiana State Penitentiary at Angola who had served a continuous sentence of 25 years or longer, as of early 1988. They found the typical long-termer to be black (27 out of 31), with many of them sentenced for raping or killing a white. Inmate ages ranged from 42 to 71. A common thread linking most of these inmates was that their release was opposed by victims' families and friends. Some had a record as prison troublemakers, but a few had been near-model prisoners.

Long-termers and geriatric inmates have special needs. They tend to suffer from handicaps, physical impairments, and illnesses not generally encountered among their more youthful counterparts. Unfortunately, few prisons are equipped to deal adequately with the medical needs of aging offenders. Some large facilities have begun to set aside special sections to care for elderly inmates with "typical" disorders, such as Alzheimer's disease, cancer, or heart disease. Unfortunately, such efforts have barely kept pace with problems. The number of inmates requiring round-the-clock care is expected to increase dramatically over the next two decades.[163]

Even the idea of rehabilitation takes on a new meaning where geriatric offenders are concerned. What kinds of programs are most likely to be useful in providing the older inmate with the needed tools for success on the outside? Which counseling strategies hold the greatest promise for introducing socially acceptable behavior patterns into the long-established lifestyles of elderly offenders about to be released? There are few answers to these questions. To date, no in-depth federal studies to answer such questions have been done which might help prepare the nation's prison system for handling the needs of older inmates.[164]

Mentally Ill Inmates

The mentally ill are another inmate category with special needs. Some inmates are neurotic or have personality problems, which increase tension in prison. Others have serious psycho-

Evaluating Prisons

A few years ago the Bureau of Justice Statistics published *Performance Measures for the Criminal Justice System*, a collection of discussion papers produced by the BJS-Princeton Project group. The papers represent the best official effort to date to identify performance goals and associated measures useful in assessing the day-to-day operations of criminal justice agencies.

The Project identified, among others, the following goals and performance indicators in the area of corrections:

Goals	Performance Indicators
1. Security: "Keep them in"	Ratings of how building design affects surveillance, frequency of shakedowns and body searches, inmate security violations, drug-related incidents, the number of escapes, and the ratio of resident population to security staff.
2. Safety: "Keep them safe"	Likelihood of an inmate being assaulted in the living area, rate of armed assaults involving inmates, rate of assault by staff, perceived danger to staff members, proportion of staff assaulted, dangerousness rating of inmate population, and frequency of accidents.
3. Order: "Keep them in line"	Perceived security of inmate personal property, number of inmates "written up," number of disturbances, number of significant incidents in which restraint was used, average number of good-time days taken away, and proportion of major report sanctions imposed.
4. Care: "Keep them healthy"	Average number of days inmates were ill or injured, number of significant incidents involving suicide attempts, clinical contacts, medical appointments, lab appointments, physicals and TB tests, dental visits, number of counseling sessions, type and rated effectiveness of counseling, and the proportion of inmates involved in counseling, substance abuse, and employment counseling.
5. Activity: "Keep them busy"	Number and type of inmate jobs, proportion of population eligible, proportion working, vocational training courses provided, grievances related to work, religious and recreational services available, and the extent of adult basic education and secondary educational opportunities available.
6. Justice: "Do it fairly"	Degree to which staff lets inmates know what is expected of them, honesty and fairness of staff, degree of force used by staff, number and rate of grievances filed, adequacy of grievance process, access to legal resources including law libraries, and the speediness of grievance and disciplinary resolutions.
7. Conditions: "Without undue suffering"	Degree of crowding; social density; availability of privacy; perceived freedom of movement for inmates; inmates per shower, sink, toilet, telephone, television, and per cell; perceived noise level; quality and variety of food; adequacy of commissary; and ease of visitation arrangements and procedures.
8. Management: "As efficiently as possible"	Perceived job satisfaction among staff, job stress index, hardening-toward-inmates index, staff turnover, staff termination, degree of supervisor-officer communications, and staff, education, and salary.

Source: Charles H. Logan, "Criminal Justice Performance Measures for Prisons," in John J. DiIulio, Jr., et al., *Performance Measures for the Criminal Justice System: Discussion Papers from the BJS-Princeton Project* (Washington, D.C.: Bureau of Justice Statistics, October 1993).

logical disorders which may have escaped earlier diagnosis (at trial) or which did not provide a legal basis for the reduction of criminal responsibility. A fair number of offenders develop psychiatric symptoms while in prison. Some news accounts of modern prisons have focused squarely on the problem: "Raging mental illness is so common it's ignored," wrote a *Newsweek* staffer visiting a women's prison.[165]

Unfortunately, few states have any substantial capacity for the psychiatric treatment of mentally disturbed inmates. In 1982 Hans Toch described the largely ineffective practice of bus therapy, whereby disturbed inmates are shuttled back and forth between mental health centers and correctional facilities.[166] In February 1990, the U.S. Supreme Court, in the case of *Washington State* v. *Harper*[167], ruled that mentally ill inmates could be required to take antipsychotic drugs, even against their wishes. The ruling stipulated that such a requirement would apply where "the inmate is dangerous to himself or others, and the treatment is in the inmate's medical interest."

Mentally deficient inmates constitute still another group with special needs. Some studies estimate the proportion of mentally deficient inmates at about 10%.[168] Retarded inmates are less likely to complete training and rehabilitative programs successfully than are other inmates. They also evidence difficulty in adjusting to the routines of prison life. As a consequence, they are likely to exceed the averages in proportion of sentence served.[169] Only seven states report special facilities or programs for the mentally retarded inmate.[170] Other state systems "mainstream" such inmates, making them participate in regular activities with other inmates.

Texas, one state which does provide special services for retarded inmates, began a Mentally Retarded Offender Program (MROP) in 1984. Inmates in Texas are given a battery of tests that measure intellectual and social adaptability skills, and prisoners who are identified as retarded are housed in special satellite correctional units. The Texas MROP program provides individual and group counseling, along with training in adult life skills.

SUMMARY

Prisons are small, self-contained societies, which are sometimes described as "total institutions." Studies of prison life have detailed the existence of prison subcultures, or inmate worlds, replete with inmate values, social roles, and lifestyles. New inmates who are socialized into prison subculture are said to undergo the process of "prisonization." Prisonization involves, among other things, learning the language of prison—commonly called prison argot.

Prison subcultures are very influential and must be reckoned with by both inmates and staff. Given the large and often densely packed inmate populations which characterize many of today's prisons, however, prison subcultures are not easily subject to the control of prison authorities. Complicating life behind bars are numerous conflicts of interest between inmates and staff. Lawsuits, riots, violence, and frequent formal grievances are symptoms of such differences.

For many years courts throughout the nation assumed a "hands-off" approach to prisons, rarely intervening in the day-to-day administration of prison facilities. That changed in the late 1960's when the hands-off era ended and the U.S. Supreme Court began to identify inmate "rights" mandated by the U.S. Constitution. Rights identified by the Court include the right to physical integrity, an absolute right to be free from unwarranted corporeal punishments, certain religious rights, and procedural rights such as those involving access to attorneys, to the courts, and so on. The conditional rights of prisoners, which have been repeatedly supported by the U.S. Supreme Court, mandate professionalism among prison administrators and require vigilance in the provision of correctional services. The era of prisoner rights was sharply curtailed, however, with passage of the 1996 Prison Litigation Reform Act, and by a growing recognition of the legal morass resulting from unregulated access to federal courts by inmates across the nation. The Prison Litigation Reform Act, in concert with other restrictions sanctioned by the U.S. Supreme Court, has substantially limited inmate access to courts at the federal level.

Today's prisons remain miniature societies—reflecting the problems and challenges which exist in the larger society of which they are a part. HIV-infected inmates, geriatric offenders, homosexual inmates, and the mentally ill all constitute special groups within the inmate population which require additional attention.

DISCUSSION QUESTIONS

1. Explain the concept of prison subcultures. What purpose do you think prison subcultures serve? Why do they develop?

2. What does "prisonization" mean? Describe the U-shaped curve developed by Stanton Wheeler as it relates to prisonization. Why do you think the curve is U-shaped?

3. What are the primary concerns of prison staff? Do you agree that those concerns are important? What other goals might staff members focus on?

4. What does it mean to say that inmates have "rights"? Where do such "rights" come from? Do you think that inmates have too many "rights"? Why or why not?

5. What does the term "state-created rights" mean within the context of corrections? What do you think might be the future of state-created rights?

6. Explain the "balancing test" established by the Supreme Court in deciding issues of prisoners' rights. How might such a test apply to the emerging area of inmate privacy?

7. What are some of the special problems facing prisons today which are discussed in this chapter? What new problems do you think the future might bring?

 WEB WATCH

Access the *Criminal Justice Today* site on the World Wide Web by pointing your Web browser at http://www.prenhall.com/cjtoday. Once there, click on "Web Chapters," then select "Chapter 13: Prison Life" in order to access electronic information and other sites of relevance to this chapter. You may also wish to enter the Global Town Meeting, which provides facilities for the posting of electronic messages for others to read. Messages are arranged by topic, with new topics constantly being added.

NOTES

1. Joseph W. Rogers, "Mary Belle Harris: Warden and Rehabilitation Pioneer," *Criminal Justice Research Bulletin*, Vol. 3, no. 9 (Huntsville, TX: Sam Houston State University, 1988), p. 8.

2. Hans Reimer, "Socialization in the Prison Community," *Proceedings of the American Prison Association 1937* (New York: American Prison Association, 1937), pp. 151–155.

3. Donald Clemmer, *The Prison Community* (Boston: Holt, Rinehart, Winston, 1940).

4. Gresham M. Sykes, *The Society of Captives: A Study of a Maximum Security Prison* (Princeton, NJ: Princeton University Press, 1958).

5. Richard A. Cloward, et al., *Theoretical Studies in Social Organization of the Prison* (New York: Social Science Research Council, 1960).

6. Donald R. Cressey, ed., *The Prison: Studies in Institutional Organization and Change* (New York: Holt, Rinehart and Winston, 1961).

7. Lawrence Hazelrigg, ed., *Prison Within Society: A Reader in Penology* (Garden City, NY: Anchor Books, 1969), preface.

8. Charles Stastny and Gabrielle Tyrnauer, *Who Rules the Joint? The Changing Political Culture of Maximum-Security Prisons in America* (Lexington, MA: Lexington Books, 1982), p. 131.

9. Erving Goffman, *Asylums: Essays on the Social Situation of Mental Patients and Other Inmates* (Garden City, NY: Anchor Books, 1961).

10. For a first-hand account of the prison experience, see Victor Hassine, *Life Without Parole: Living in Prison Today* (Los Angeles: Roxbury, 1996); and W. Rideau and R. Wikberg, *Life Sentences: Rage and Survival Behind Prison Bars* (New York: Times Books, 1992).

11. The concept of prisonization is generally attributed to Clemmer, *The Prison Community*, although Quaker penologists of the late 1700s were actively concerned with preventing "contamination" (the spread of criminal values) among prisoners.

12. Gresham M. Sykes and Sheldon L. Messinger, "The Inmate Social System," in Richard A. Cloward, et al., *Theoretical Studies in Social Organization of the Prison* (New York: Social Science Research Council, 1960), pp. 5–19.

13. Ibid., p. 5.

14. Stanton Wheeler, "Socialization in Correctional Communities," *American Sociological Review*, Vol. 26 (October 1961), pp. 697–712.

15. Sykes, *The Society of Captives*, p. xiii.

16. Stastny and Tyrnauer, *Who Rules the Joint?*, p. 135.

17. Ibid.

18. Sykes, *The Society of Captives*.

19. Clemmer, *The Prison Community* (New York: Holt, Rinehart and Winston, 1940), pp. 294–296.

20. Alan J. Davis, "Sexual Assaults in the Philadelphia Prison System and Sheriff's Vans," *Trans-Action*, Vol. 6 (December 1968), pp. 8–16.

21. Daniel Lockwood, "Sexual Aggression Among Male Prisoners," unpublished dissertation (Ann Arbor, MI: University Microfilms International, 1978).

22. Lee H. Bowker, *Prison Victimization* (New York: Elsevier, 1980).

23. Ibid., p. 42.

24. Ibid., p. 1.

25. Hans Toch, *Living in Prison: The Ecology of Survival* (New York: The Free Press, 1977), p. 151.

26. John Irwin, *The Felon* (Englewood Cliffs, NJ: Prentice Hall, 1970).

27. Lucien X. Lombardo, *Guards Imprisoned: Correctional Officers at Work* (New York: Elsevier, 1981), pp. 22–36.

28. Leonard Morgenbesser, "NY State Law Prescribes Psychological Screening for CO Job Applicants," *Correctional Training* (Newsletter of the American Association of Correctional Training Personnel, Winter 1983), p. 1.

29. "A Sophisticated Approach to Training Prison Guards," *Newsday*, August 12, 1982.

30. Rosalie Rosetti, "Charting Your Course: Federal Model Encourages Career Choices," *Corrections Today* (August 1988), pp. 34–38.

31. Stastny and Tyrnauer, *Who Rules the Joint?* p. 1.

32. See Frederick Talbott, "Reporting from Behind the Walls: Do It Before the Siren Wails," *The Quill* (February 1988), pp. 16–21.

33. "Prison Riot Leaves Injuries," *The Fayetteville Observer-Times* (North Carolina), October 28, 1989, p. 1A.

34. Lee Leonard, "Lucasville Guards Were Outnumbered 50-1 Before Riot," *Columbus Dispatch*, May 12, 1993.

35. "Ohio Prison Rebellion Is Ended," *USA Today*, April 22, 1993, p. 2A.

36. *Report of the Attorney General on the February 2 and 3, 1980 Riot at the Penitentiary of New Mexico* (two parts), June and September 1980.

37. See, for example, American Correctional Association, *Riots and Disturbances in Correctional Institutions* (College Park, MD: ACA, 1981); Michael Braswell, et al., *Prison Violence in America* (Cincinnati, OH: Anderson, 1985); and R. Conant, "Rioting, Insurrectional and Civil Disorderliness," *American Scholar*, Vol. 37 (Summer 1968), pp. 420–433.

38. Robert S. Fong, Ronald E. Vogel, and S. Buentello "Prison Gang Dynamics: A Look Inside the Texas Department of Corrections," in A. V. Merlo and P. Menekos, eds., *Dilemmas and Directions in Corrections* (Cincinnati, OH: Anderson, 1992).

39. Ibid.

40. *Ruiz v. Estelle*, 503 F.Supp. 1265 (S.D. Texas, 1980).

41. Steve Dillingham and Reid Montgomery, "Prison Riots: A Corrections Nightmare Since 1774," in Braswell, et al., *Prison Violence in America*, pp. 19–36.

42. Vernon Fox, "Prison Riots in a Democratic Society," *Police*, Vol. 26, no. 12 (December 1982), pp. 35–41.

43. Donald R. Cressey, "Adult Felons in Prison," in Lloyd E. Ohlin, ed., *Prisoners in America* (Englewood Cliffs, NJ: Prentice Hall, 1972), pp. 117–150.

44. Christopher J. Mumola and Allen J. Beck, *Prisoners in 1996* (Washington, D.C.: Bureau of Justice Statistics, 1997).

45. Ibid.

46. This section owes much to the American Correctional Association, Task Force on the Female Offender, *The Female Offender: What Does the Future Hold?* (Washington, D.C.: St. Mary's Press, 1990), and "The View from Behind Bars," *Time*, Fall 1990 (special issue), pp. 20–22.

47. James C. Fox, "Women's Prison Policy, Prisoner Activism, and the Impact of the Contemporary Feminist Movement: A Case Study," *The Prison Journal*, Vol. 64, no. 1 (Spring/Summer 1984), pp. 15–36.

48. For greater insight into the criminality of incarcerated women, see Evelyn K. Sommers, *Voices from Within: Women who have Broken the Law* (Toronto: University of Toronto Press, 1995).

49. American Correctional Association, *The Female Offender*.

50. B. Keith Crew, "Sex Differences in Criminal Sentencing: Chivalry or Patriarchy?" *Justice Quarterly*, Vol. 8, no. 1 (March 1991), pp. 59–83.

51. American Correctional Association, *The Female Offender*.

52. Ibid.

53. Mary Jeanette Clement, "National Survey of Programs for Incarcerated Women," paper presented at the Academy of Criminal Justice Sciences annual meeting, Nashville, Tennessee, March 1991.

54. Ibid., pp. 8–9.

55. D. Ward and G. Kannebaum, *Women's Prison: Sex and Social Structure* (London: Weidenfeld and Nicolson, 1966).

56. Esther Heffernan, *Making It in Prison: The Square, the Cool and the Life* (London: Wiley-Interscience, 1972).

57. Rose Giallombardo, *Society of Women: A Study of Women's Prisons* (New York: John Wiley, 1966).

58. Ibid., p. 136.

59. For a summary of such studies (including some previously unpublished), see Bowker, *Prisoner Subcultures* (Lexington, MA: Lexington Books, 1977), p. 86.

60. Giallombardo, *Society of Women*, p. 162.

61. Russell P. Dobash, P. Emerson Dobash, and Sue Gutteridge, *The Imprisonment of Women* (Oxford: Basil Blackwell, 1986), p. 6.

62. Heffernan, *Making It in Prison*.

63. Jean Harris, *They Always Call Us Ladies* (New York: Scribners, 1988).

64. "The Lady on Cell Block 112A," *Newsweek*, September 5, 1988, p. 60.

65. Ibid.

66. Ibid.

67. "Scarsdale Diet Doctor's Killer Given Clemency," *USA Today*, December 30, 1992, p. 3A.

68. Bowker, *Prison Victimization*, p. 53.

69. Giallombardo, *Society of Women*.

70. "Georgia Indictments Charge Abuse of Female Inmates," *USA Today*, November 16, 1992, p. 3A.

71. Ibid.

72. American Correctional Association, *The Female Offender*, p. 39.

73. *Holt* v. *Sarver*, 309 F.Supp. 362 (E.D. Ark 1970).

74. Vergil L. Williams, *Dictionary of American Penology: An Introduction* (Westport, CT: Greenwood, 1979), pp. 6–7.

75. *Pell* v. *Procunier*, 417 U.S. 817, 822 (1974).

76. Ibid.

77. American Correctional Association, *Legal Responsibility and Authority of Correctional Officers: A Handbook on Courts, Judicial Decisions and Constitutional Requirements* (College Park, MD: ACA, 1987), p. 8.

78. According to the ACA, *Legal Responsibility*, p. 57, "A trend may be developing in favor of less intrusive remedial orders in conditions cases in favor of allowing institutional official an opportunity to develop and implement relief with as little court involvement as possible." For further information on this and other issues in the area of prisoners' rights, see Barbara B. Knight and Stephen T. Early, Jr., *Prisoner's Rights in America* (Chicago: Nelson-Hall, 1986).

79. *Procunier* v. *Martinez*, 416 U.S. 396 (1974).

80. *McNamara* v. *Moody*, 606 F.2d 621 (5th Cir. 1979).

81. *The Luparar* v. *Stoneman*, 382 F.Supp. 495 (D. Vt. 1974).

82. *Mallery* v. *Lewis*, 106 Idaho 227 (1983).

83. See, for example, *Pepperling* v. *Crist*, 678 F. 2d 787 (9th Cir. 1981).

84. *Cruz* v. *Beto*, 405 U.S. 319 (1972).

85. *Aziz* v. *LeFevre*, 642 F.2d 1109 (2nd Cir. 1981).

86. *Glasshofer* v. *Thornburg*, 514 F.Supp. 1242 (E.D. Pa. 1981).

87. See, for example, *Smith* v. *Coughlin*, 748 F.2d 783 (2d Cir. 1984).

88. *Campbell* v. *Cauthron*, 623 F.2d 503 (8th Cir. 1980).

89. *Smith* v. *Blackledge*, 451 F.2d 1201 (4th Cir. 1971).

90. *Dettmer* v. *Landon*, 617 F.Supp. 592, 594 (D.C. Va. 1985).

91. *Lewellyn (L'Aquarius)* v. *State*, 592 P.2d 538 (Okla. Crim. App. 1979).

92. *Hill* v. *Blackwell*, 774 F.2d 338, 347 (8th Cir. 1985).

93. *Block* v. *Rutherford*, 486 U.S. 576 (1984).

94. *Pell* v. *Procunier*, 417 U.S. 817, 822 (1974).

95. *Houchins* v. *KQED, Inc.*, 438 U.S. 11 (1978).

96. Ibid.

97. For a Supreme Court review of the First Amendment right to petition the courts, see *McDonald* v. *Smith*, 105 S.Ct. 2787 (1985).

98. *Bounds* v. *Smith*, 430 U.S. 817, 821 (1977).

99. *Johnson* v. *Avery*, 393 U.S. 483 (1968).

100. *Bounds* v. *Smith.*

101. *Taylor* v. *Sterrett*, 532 F.2d 462 (5th Cir. 1976).

102. *In re Harrell*, 87 Cal. Rptr. 504, 470 P.2d 640 (1970).

103. *Guajardo* v. *Estelle*, 432 F.Supp. 1373 (S.D. Texas, 1977).

104. *O'Brien* v. *United States*, 386 U.S. 345 (1967); and *Weatherford* v. *Bursey,* 429 U.S. 545 (1977).

105. *U.S.* v. *Gouveia*, 104 S.Ct. 2292, 81 L.Ed. 2d 146 (1984).

106. *Estelle* v. *Gamble*, 429 U.S. 97 (1976).

107. Ibid., pp. 105–106

108. *Farmer* v. *Brennan*, 114 S.Ct. 1970, 128 L. Ed. 2d 811 (1994).

109. Ibid.

110. *Ruiz* v. *Estelle*, 679 F.2d 1115 (5th Cir. 1982).

111. *Newman* v. *Alabama*, 349 F.Supp. 278 (M.D. Ala. 1972).

112. Adapted from American Correctional Association, *Legal Responsibility and Authority of Correctional Officers*, pp. 25–26.

113. *In re Caulk*, 35 CrL 2532 (New Hampshire S.Ct. 1984).

114. Ibid.

115. *Helling* v. *McKinney*, 113 S.Ct. 2475, 125 L. Ed. 2d 22 (1993).

116. *U.S.* v. *Ready*, 574 F.2d 1009 (10th Cir. 1978).

117. *Katz* v. *U.S.*, 389 U.S. 347, 88 S.Ct. 507, 19 L.Ed. 2ed 576 (1967).

118. *Hudson* v. *Palmer*, 468 U.S. 517 (1984).

119. *Block* v. *Rutherford*, 104 S.Ct. 3227, 3234–35 (1984).

120. *U.S.* v. *Lilly*, 576 F.2d 1240 (5th Cir. 1978).

121. *Palmer* v. *Hudson*, 697 F.2d 1220 (4th Cir. 1983).

122. William H. Erickson, et al., *United States Supreme Court Cases and Comments* (New York: Matthew Bender, 1987), Section 10.02 2 (c), pp. 10–38.

123. *Jones* v. *North Carolina Prisoners' Labor Union, Inc.*, 433 U.S. 119, 53 L. Ed. 2d 629, 641 (1977).

124. *Wolff* v. *McDonnell*, 94 S.Ct. 2963 (1974).

125. Ibid.

126. Ibid.

127. *Ponte* v. *Real*, 471 U.S. 491, 105 S.Ct. 2192, 85 L. Ed. 2d 553 (1985).

128. *Vitek* v. *Jones*, 445 U.S. 480 (1980).

129. American Correctional Association, Standard 2-4346. See ACA, *Legal Responsibility and Authority of Correctional Officers*, p. 49.

130. *Wilson* v. *Seiter et al.*, 501 U.S. 294 (1991).

131. *Estelle* v. *Gamble*, 429 U.S. 97, 106 (1976).

132. *Sandin* v. *Conner*, 63 U.S.L.W. 4601 (1995).

133. *Wolff* v. *McDonnell*, 94 S.Ct. 2963 (1974).

134. *Hewitt* v. *Helms*, 459 U. S. 460 (1983).

135. Laurie Asseo, "Inmate Lawsuits," The Associated Press wire services, May 24, 1996; and "State and Federal Prisoners Filed 68,235 Petitions in U.S. Courts in 1996," BJS Press Release, October 29, 1997.

136. See, for example, "The Great Prison Pastime," *20/20*, ABC News, September 24, 1993, which is part of the video library available to instructor's using this textbook.

137. Ibid.

138. "Inmate Lawsuits."

139. Public Law 104-134. Although the PLRA was signed into law on April 26, 1996, and is frequently referred to as the "Prison Litigation Reform Act of 1996," the official name of the act is the "Prison Litigation Reform Act of 1995."

140. Ibid.

141. Ibid.

142. "Inmate Litigation and the PLRA," *Corrections Compendium*, December 1996, p. 2.

143. Cheryl A. Crawford, "Health Care Needs in Corrections: NIJ Responds," *National Institute of Justice Journal* (November 1994), p. 31.

144. National Research Council, *The Social Impact of AIDS in the United States* (Washington, D.C.: National Academy Press, 1993), p. 180.

145. Laura Maruschak, *HIV in Prisons and Jails* (Washington, D.C.: Bureau of Justice Statistics, 1997); and Brenda Rodriguez, "Behind Bars, Illicit Activities are Spreading AIDS Virus," *San Antonio Express-News*, via Simon & Schuster Newslink, September 14, 1997 (which puts the figure at over 24,000).

146. Laura Maruschak, *HIV in Prisons and Jails* (Washington, D.C.: Bureau of Justice Statistics, 1997).

147. Dennis Cauchon, "AIDS in Prison: Locked Up and Locked Out," *USA Today*, March 31, 1995, p. 6A.

148. Theodore M. Hammett, *AIDS in Correctional Facilities: Issues and Options*, 3d ed (Washington, D.C.: National Institute of Justice, 1988), p. 29.

149. M. A. R. Kleiman and R. W. Mockler, "AIDS, the Criminal Justice System, and Civil Liberties," *Governance: Harvard Journal of Public Policy* (Summer/Fall 1987), pp. 48–54.

150. Hammett, *AIDS in Correctional Facilities*, p. 37.

151. At the time of writing, California, Wisconsin, Massachusetts, New York, and the District of Columbia were among such jurisdictions.

152. Cheryl A. Crawford, "Health Care Needs in Corrections: NIJ Responds."

153. See "Court Allows Restriction on HIV-Positive Inmates," in *Criminal Justice Newsletter*, Vol. 25, no. 23 (December 1, 1994), pp. 2–3.

154. Cauchon, "AIDS in Prison."

155. Hammett, *AIDS in Correctional Facilities*, pp. 47–49.

156. Ibid.

157. Darrell Bryan, "Inmates, HIV and the Constitutional Right to Privacy: AIDS in Prison Facilities," *Corrections Compendium*, Vol. 19, no. 9 (September 1994), pp. 1–3.

158. Cheryl A. Crawford, "Health Care Needs in Corrections: NIJ Responds."

159. As quoted in Paula Mergenhagen, "The Prison Population Bomb," *American Demographics*, February 1996. Available on the World Wide Web at: http://www.demographics.com/Publications/AD/96_AD/9602_AD/ad880.htm.

160. Ronald Wikbert and Burk Foster, "The Longtermers: Louisiana's Longest Serving Inmates and Why They've Stayed So Long," paper presented at the annual meeting of the Academy of Criminal Justice Sciences, Washington, D.C., 1989.

161. Lincoln J. Fry, "The Older Prison Inmate: A Profile," *The Justice Professional*, Vol. 2, no. 1 (Spring 1987), pp. 1–12.

162. Wikberg and Foster, "The Longtermers."

163. Ibid., p. 51.

164. Chaneles, "Growing Old Behind Bars," p. 51.

165. "The Lady in Cell Block 112A," *Newsweek*, September, 5, 1988, p. 60.

166. Hans Toch, "The Disturbed Disruptive Inmate: Where Does the Bus Stop?" *The Journal of Psychiatry and Law*, Vol. 10 (1982), pp. 327–349.

167. *Washington* v. *Harper*, 494 U.S. 210 (1990).

168. Robert O. Lampert, "The Mentally Retarded Offender in Prison," *The Justice Professional*, Vol. 2, no. 1 (Spring 1987), p. 61.

169. Ibid., p. 64.

170. George C. Denkowski and Kathryn M. Denkowski, "The Mentally Retarded Offender in the State Prison System: Identification, Prevalence, Adjustment, and Rehabilitation," *Criminal Justice and Behavior*, Vol. 12 (1985), pp. 55–75.

INDIVIDUAL RIGHTS VERSUS SOCIAL CONCERNS

Issues for the Future

Common law, constitutional, and humanitarian rights of the accused which may soon be threatened by technological advances and other developments:

* A Right to Privacy
* A Right to Be Assumed Innocent
* A Right Against Self-incrimination
* A Right to Equal Protection of the Laws
* A Right Against Cruel and Unusual Punishment

The individual rights listed must be effectively balanced against these present and emerging community concerns:

* Widespread Drug Abuse Among Youth
* The Threat of Juvenile Crime
* Urban Gang Violence
* High-Technology and Computer Crimes (Cybercrime)
* Terrorism and Narco-terrorism
* Occupational and White-Collar Crime

How does our system of justice work toward balance?

part 5
SPECIAL ISSUES

THE FUTURE COMES ONE DAY AT A TIME

No one can truly say what the future holds. Will the purveyors of individual rights or social order advocates ultimately claim the day? We cannot say for sure. This much is certain, however: Things change. The American system of criminal justice in the next century, and the century after that, will not be quite the same system we know today. Many of the coming changes, however, are now discernible—and hints at what is to come appear on the horizon with increasing frequency and growing clarity. Some of the more obvious of the coming changes are already upon us. They include (1) a restructuring of the juvenile justice system in the face of growing concerns about violent juvenile crime and spreading youth gang warfare; (2) the increased bankruptcy of a war against drugs whose promises seem increasingly hollow; (3) a growing recognition of America's international role as both victim and purveyor of worldwide criminal activity; and (4) the quickly unfolding potential of cybercrimes—those which both employ high-technology in their commission and target the fruits of such technology

This, the last part of *Criminal Justice Today*, discusses each of these issues in the chapters which follow. It also draws your attention back to the bedrock underlying the American system of justice—the Constitution, the Bill of Rights, and the demands of due process, all of which can be expected to continue to structure the justice system well into the future.

chapter 14

JUVENILE DELINQUENCY

America's best hope for reducing crime is to reduce juvenile delinquency and youth crime.

—PRESIDENT'S COMMISSION (1967)

Our society's fearful of our kids. I think we don't know how to set limits on them. They begin to behave in severely outrageous ways, and nobody stops them.

—DAVID YORK, CO-FOUNDER OF TOUGHLOVE INTERNATIONAL[1]

abused child
adjudicatory hearing
cohort
delinquency
delinquent act
delinquent child
dependent child

dispositionary hearing
intake
juvenile disposition
juvenile justice system
juvenile petition
neglected child
parens patriae

social disorganization
social ecology
status offender
status offense
teen court
undisciplined child

KEY CASES

In re Gault
McKeiver v. *Penna.*

Schall v. *Martin*
Kent v. *U.S.*

In re Winship
Breed v. *Jones*

Introduction

On September 7, 1994, 11-year-old Robert "Yummy" Sandifer was buried in Chicago—a young victim of the city's "gang problem." Yummy, whose nickname was given to him by his grandmother because he loved cookies, had been sought by police who suspected him of the cold-blooded killing of a 14-year-old girl in a gang ritual. Four other children were wounded in the incident. Fearing that Yummy might implicate them in the shooting, gang leaders apparently ordered him killed. A few days later, his body was discovered near a railroad underpass with two bullets through the head.

Sandifer's funeral became a rallying point for antigang sentiments and a forum for those wanting to express their frustration with the conditions many of today's children live under. "Every child in the city should be here to see that if you're in a gang, if you're in the wrong crowd, this could be you,"[2] said one mourner.

Yummy Sandifer, although still a child when he died, never lived the life of a child. When he was 22 months old, Sandifer came to the attention of the Illinois Department of Children and Family Services after being treated at a hospital emergency room for scratches and bruises which covered his body. He was later moved to his grandmother's home. Although his grandmother abhorred the idea, Sandifer became a tough street kid, growing up within a gang, in the middle of a neighborhood terrorized by gangs. By the time of his death, Sandifer had appeared in juvenile court at least eight times, charged with various counts of robbery, burglary, auto theft, and arson. "Yet," as one news account of the funeral described him, "it was still a boy lying in the casket. Dressed in a beige suit, surrounded by a stuffed rabbit and pig, Yummy lay on a satin bed, his face bathed in the rosy glow of a lamp clamped to the lid."[3] As Yummy's casket was wheeled to the waiting hearse, a teenager rapped, "Children are dying, rapidly, day after day; Maybe it's time we open our eyes and make it a better place to stay; From the older generation to the younger generation, please put down the guns."[4] Two boys, ages 14 and 16, were arrested and charged with Sandifer's murder.

The sad case of Yummy Sandifer reflects much of what faces American youngsters today. All too many of our nation's children live as outcasts in a society which has neglected its responsibility for the care and training of its young and has left them to grow up—often far too fast—as best they can. On the other hand, some children appear to be willing participants in criminal activity, and crime statistics show that a significant proportion of all illegal activity today is committed by juveniles. Although states vary as to the age at which a person enters adulthood, statistics on crime make it clear that young people are involved disproportionately in certain offenses. A recent report, for example, found that persons aged 12 to 18 account for over 19% of all violent crimes and 35% of property crimes, while comprising only 9% of the population of the United States.[5] On the average, about 20% of all arrests in any year are of juveniles,[6] and juveniles under the age of 18 have a higher likelihood of being arrested for robbery and UCR index property crimes than any other age group. One estimate places the number of males who will be arrested at least once before their eighteenth birthday at 27%.[7] Figure 14–1 shows *Uniform Crime Report* statistics on juvenile arrests for selected offense categories.

A sweeping report[8] on juvenile crime and on the juvenile justice system in America which was recently released by the Office of Juvenile Justice and Delinquency Prevention (OJJDP) found that

Juvenile violence is rampant, juvenile crime is exploding, juvenile killers are threatening the fabric of our society, and it's only going to get worse—much worse.

—Senator John Aschroft (R.-Mo.), introducing legislation to change the federal juvenile justice program

Children view the body of 11-year-old Robert "Yummy" Sandifer. Sandifer was executed by fellow Chicago gang members after being suspected of the killing of a 14-year-old girl in a gang ritual. Younger criminals are committing more violent crimes, which is posing questions about when and how they should be prosecuted. *Jose More, Sygma*

- 69 million Americans—more than one in four—are under the age of 18.
- The juvenile population in America is growing and will reach 74 million by the year 2010.
- A juvenile's risk of becoming a victim of violent crime has increased substantially in recent years.
- Homicide is the second leading cause of death among juveniles (next only to motor vehicle accidents).
- Almost 2,600 juveniles are murdered in the United States yearly—an average of seven per day.
- Juveniles are responsible for about one in every five violent crimes reported to the NCVS.

FIGURE 14–1 Juvenile involvement in crime versus system totals, 1996. *Source:* Federal Bureau of Investigation, *Crime in the United States 1996* (Washington, D.C.: U.S. Government Printing Office, 1997).

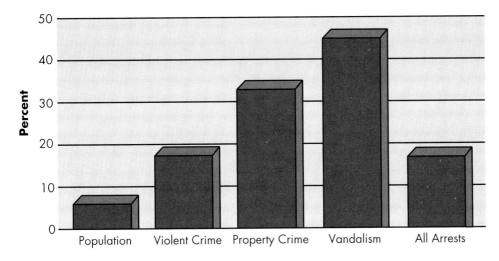

- Age, sex, and race are closely associated with the risk of violent victimization—black males aged 14 to 17, for example, are 29 times more likely to be murdered than are white females of the same age.
- Black juveniles are far more likely to come into contact with the juvenile justice system than are whites (although they comprise 15% of the juvenile population, blacks account for 49% of all juvenile arrests for violent crime index offenses).
- If trends continue as they have, juvenile arrests for violent crime will increase 100% between 1985 and 2010.

The study also found that:

- Most juveniles (perhaps as many as 90%) have committed at least one delinquent act.
- A small number of juvenile offenders (perhaps 6% of all boys) are chronic or persistent offenders.
- Serious adult offenders are likely to have had more serious juvenile careers.
- Most juveniles who come into contact with the juvenile justice system do so only once.
- More than half of juvenile homicide victims are killed with a firearm.
- Nearly 35% of male juveniles report carrying a gun at least "now and then."
- Juvenile gangs are widespread, and gang activity has increased substantially in the past 20 years.
- For every two youths murdered in 1991, one youth committed suicide.
- In 1992, 14.6 million juveniles lived below the poverty level—42% more than in 1976.
- More than 200,000 children are born to mothers below the age of 18 every year—four out of five of whom are unmarried.
- Fewer children now live with both parents than ever before.
- Child protective service agencies receive nearly 2 million reports of child maltreatment yearly.
- Childhood abuse and neglect significantly increase a child's odds of future delinquency and adult criminality.

An even more recent report, prepared for the Bureau of Justice Statistics by James Alan Fox,[9] found that black males ages 14–17 constitute just over 1% of the population but make up over 30% of the perpetrators of criminal homicide. Moreover, said the report, "by the year 2005, the number of teens ages 14–17 will increase by 20% with a larger increase among blacks in this age group (26%)." The report included a graph (Figure 14–2) forecasting the number of homicides that can be expected to be committed by offenders aged 14–17 through 2005 "if recent trends in offending rates persist."

One reason for studying juvenile delinquency is that juvenile crime accounts for a relatively large percentage of all crimes committed in this country. Moreover, reports indicate that many adult criminals began their illegal activities while young. The case of Fort Lauderdale, Florida's 12-year-old "Crime Boy" is illustrative. Crime Boy, so dubbed by the local media who cannot legally release his name, committed his first crime—a burglary—at the age of eight. Since then he has been arrested for a variety of offenses—57 in all—and chances are that he has committed many other crimes which will never come to light.[10] Crime Boy lives with his 41-year-old grandmother. His mother is serving time in prison for murder, and his father's whereabouts are unknown. A brief review of records in Crime Boy's hometown revealed that he is not the only juvenile with a long string of offenses. Another 12-year-old has accumulated 58 charges, and a 13-year-old living there has been arrested 78 times.

Not all crimes are committed by disadvantaged youth. In 1997, for example, 18-year-old Melissa Drexler, an indulged only child bent on becoming a fashion designer,[11] was arrested following her high-school prom and charged with murder. Drexler had allegedly given birth in a bathroom stall at New Jersey's Lacey Township High, wrapped her newborn in plastic, and placed it in a trash bag where it died.[12] Witnesses said they heard groans from the stall after Drexler entered it, but that she called out to them, saying "Go tell the boys we'll be right out." Drexler returned to the dance floor and ate a salad before leaving the prom.

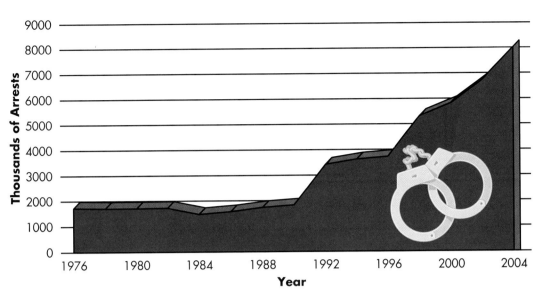

FIGURE 14-2 Number of homicides by offenders aged 14-17, projections through 2004. *Source:* James Alan Fox, *Trends in Juvenile Violence* (Washington, D.C.: Bureau of Justice Statistics, 1996), p. 15.

A similar crime shocked suburban Wyckoff, New Jersey, an enclave of wealthy and upper-middle-class families, where Amy Grossberg, 18, and boyfriend Brian Peterson, 19, stand accused of murdering their newborn son on November 12, 1996. According to authorities, Amy, a University of Delaware freshman, began experiencing labor pains in her dorm room around midnight. She had hidden her pregnancy from her parents for its entire term. Frightened, she called her boyfriend, Brian, at his college in Gettysburg, Pennsylvania. Three hours later he picked Amy up in his black Toyota Celica and drove her to a nearby Comfort Inn. Amy's baby, a healthy 6 pound 2 ounce boy, was born around dawn. Brian reportedly told authorities that he then put the child in a plastic bag and dropped him into a dumpster near the hotel. Amy and Brian might have been able to return to relatively normal lives, and their crime might have remained unnoticed, except for the fact that Amy experienced serious complications the next day. Following a rushed trip to the hospital, doctors determined that the placenta had been retained in Amy's uterus. She broke down emotionally and told investigators about the motel birth and her boyfriend's disposal of the baby. Arrests followed. One family friend described both Amy and Brian as "good kids." "They were two wealthy kids who had so many options in life," said Constantine Maroulis.[13] Some believe that the charges against Drexler, Grossberg, and Peterson are indicative of an eroding moral sense characteristic of today's privileged teens. Jerry Capone, a Wilmington, Delaware, attorney, put it this way: "These kids from strong family backgrounds should have the proper moral background. [This] really frightens me. It means this lack of respect for human life cuts across all economic classes."

This chapter has four purposes. First, we will describe the **juvenile justice system** from its historical beginnings to the present. The juvenile justice system has its roots in the adult system. In the juvenile system, however, we find a more uniform philosophical base and a generally clear agreement about the system's purpose. Both may be due to the system's relative newness and to the fact that society generally agrees that young people who have gone wrong are worthwhile salvaging. However, as a box in this chapter shows, the philosophy which underlies the juvenile justice system in America is being increasingly called into question by "get-tough" advocates of law and order, many of whom are fed up with violent juvenile crime.

Our second purpose will be to compare the juvenile and adult systems as they currently operate. The philosophy behind the juvenile justice system has led to administrative and other procedures which, in many jurisdictions, are not found in the adult system. The juvenile justice process, for example, is frequently not as open as the adult system. Hearings may be held in secret, the names of offenders are not published, and records of juvenile proceedings may be destroyed later.[14]

Juvenile Justice System Government agencies which function to investigate, supervise, adjudicate, care for, or confine youthful offenders and other children subject to the jurisdiction of the juvenile court.

Melissa Drexler and date John Lewis arrive at a high-school prom on June 6, 1997. Minutes later, authorities say Drexler gave birth in a bathroom stall, stuffed the baby in a trash can, and returned to the dance floor. The child died. *AP/Wide World Photos*

Our third focus will be to describe in detail the agencies, processes, and problems of the juvenile justice system itself. Although each state may have variations, a common system structure is shared by all.

Of course, the juvenile justice system is not without its critics. As conservative attitudes began to bring changes in the adult criminal justice system over the last decade or so, the juvenile justice system remained one of the last surviving bastions of tradition. Based upon premises quite different from those of the adult system, juvenile justice has long been a separate decision-making arena, in which the best interests of the child have been accorded great importance. Near the end of this chapter we will turn to our fourth focus and will consider some of the issues raised by critics of the current system. As we will see, substantial changes are now afoot.

Juvenile Justice Throughout History

EARLIEST TIMES

The history of the Western world reveals that children who committed crimes in past centuries could expect no preferential treatment because of their youth. They were adjudicated and punished alongside adults. The laws of King Aethelbert, the earliest legal document written in the English language (circa 600 A.D.), made no special allowances for the age of the offender, and a number of recorded cases have come down through history of children as young as six or eight being hanged or burned at the stake. Children were also imprisoned along with adults. No segregated juvenile facilities existed. Neither the development of gaols (an old word for jails) in the thirteenth century nor the early English prisons provided any leniency on the basis of age.[15] In like fashion, little distinction was made between criminality and **delinquency** or other kinds of undesirable behavior. Problems such as epilepsy, insanity, retardation, or poverty were seen in the same light as crime,[16] and people suffering from these conditions were shut away in facilities shared by juveniles and adult offenders.

Court philosophy in dealing with juveniles derived from another early Roman principle called *patria postestas*. Under Roman law (circa 753 B.C.) children had membership in their family, but the father had absolute control over children, and they in turn had an absolute responsibility to obey his wishes. The power of the father extended to issues of life and death

Delinquency Juvenile actions or conduct in violation of criminal law, juvenile status offenses, or other juvenile misbehavior.

for all members of the family, including slaves, spouses, and children.[17] Roman understanding of the social role of children strongly influenced English culture and eventually led to development of the legal principle of *parens patriae*. *Parens patriae* allowed the king, or the English state, to take the place of parents in dealing with children who broke the law. *Parens patriae* held that the king was father of the country and thus had parental rights over all his citizens

By the Middle Ages, social conceptions of children had become strongly influenced by Christian Churches. Church doctrine held that children under the age of seven had not yet reached the age of reason and could not be held liable for spiritual transgressions. In adopting the perspective of the Church, English law of the period excepted children under the age of seven from criminal responsibility. Juveniles aged 7 to 14 were accorded a special status, being tried as adults only if it could be demonstrated that they fully understood the nature of their criminal acts.[18] Adulthood was considered to begin at age 14, when marriage was also allowed.[19]

Early English institutions placed a large burden of responsibility on the family, and especially the father, who, as head of the household, was held accountable for the behavior of all family members. Children, and even wives, were almost totally dependent upon the father and had a status only slightly above that of personal property. When the father failed in his responsibility to control family members, the king, through the concept of *parens patriae*, could intervene.

The inexorable power of the king, often marked by his personal and unpredictable whims, combined with a widespread fear of dismal conditions in English institutions to make many families hide their problem kin. The retarded, insane, and epileptic were kept in attics or basements, sometimes for their entire lives. Delinquent children were confined to the home or, if the family from which they came was wealthy enough, sent overseas to escape the conditions of asylums and gaols.

Juveniles in Early America

Early American solutions to the problems of delinquency were much like those of the English. Puritan influence in the colonies, with its heavy emphasis upon obedience and discipline, led to a frequent use of jails and prisons for both juveniles and adults. Legislation reflected the biblical Ten Commandments and often provided harsh punishments for transgressors of almost any age. For example, one Massachusetts law in the seventeenth century provided in part that

> If a man have a stubborn or rebellious son of sufficient years of understanding, viz. sixteen, which will not obey the voice of his father or the voice of his mother, and that when they have chastened him will not harken to them, then shall his father and mother, being his natural parents, lay hold on him and bring him to the magistrate assembled in Court, and testify to them by sufficient evidence that this their son is stubborn and rebellious and will not obey their voice and chastisement, but lives in sundry notorious crime. Such a son shall be put to death.[20]

Severe punishment was consistent with Puritan beliefs that unacknowledged social evils might bring the wrath of God down upon the entire colony. In short, disobedient children had no place in a social group whose life was committed to a spiritual salvation understood as strict obedience to the wishes of the Divine.

By the end of the eighteenth century, social conditions in Europe and America began to change. The Enlightenment, a highly significant intellectual and social movement, focused on human potential and generally rejected previously held supernatural explanations in favor of scientific ones. It was accompanied by the growth of an industrialized economy, with a corresponding move away from farming. Poor laws, lower infant death rates, and other social innovations born of the Enlightenment led to a reassessment of the place of children in society. In this new age, children were recognized as the only true heirs to the future, and society became increasingly concerned about their well-being.

The Institutional Era

The nineteenth century was a time of rapid social change in the United States. The population was growing dramatically, cities were burgeoning, and the industrial era was in full swing. Industrial tycoons, the new rich, and frontier-bound settlers lived elbow-to-elbow

Parens Patriae A common law principle which allows the state to assume a parental role and to take custody of a child when he or she becomes delinquent, is abandoned, or is in need of care which the natural parents are unable or unwilling to provide.

with immigrants eking out a living in the sweat shops of the new mercantile centers. In this environment, children took on new value as a source of cheap labor. They fueled assembly lines and proved invaluable to shop owners whose businesses needed frequent but inexpensive attention. Parents were gratified by the income-producing opportunities available to their offspring. On the frontier, settlers and farm families put their children to work clearing land and seeding crops.

Unfortunately, economic opportunities and the luck of the draw were not equally favorable to all. Some immigrant families became victims of the cities which drew them, settling in squalor in hastily formed ghettos. Many families, seeing only the economic opportunities represented by their children, neglected to provide them with anything but a rudimentary education. Children who did work labored for long hours and had little time for family closeness. Other children, abandoned by families unable to support them, were forced into lives on the streets where they formed tattered gangs—surviving off the refuse of the glittering cities.

The House of Refuge

An 1823 report by the Society for the Prevention of Pauperism in the City of New York called for the development of "houses of refuge" to save children from lives of crime and poverty. The Society also cited the problems caused by locking up children with mature criminals. Houses of refuge were to be places of care and education where children could learn positive values toward work.

In 1824 the first house of refuge opened in New York City.[21] The New York House of Refuge was intended only for those children who could still be "rescued," and sheltered mostly young thieves, vagrants, and runaways. Other children, especially those with more severe delinquency problems, were placed in adult prisons and jails. Houses of refuge became popular in New York and were quickly copied by other cities. It was not long before overcrowding developed, and living conditions in them deteriorated.

The 1838 case of *Ex parte Crouse* clarified the power which states had in committing children to institutions.[22] The case involved Mary Ann Crouse, who had been committed to the Philadelphia House of Refuge by a lower court over the objections of her father. The commitment was based upon allegations made by the girl's mother that she was incorrigible, that is, beyond the control of her parents. Mary Ann's father petitioned the court to release his daughter on the grounds that she had been denied the right to trial by jury.

The decision by the appeals court upheld the legality of Mary Ann's commitment. It pointed to the state's interest in assisting children and denied that punishment or retribution played any part in her treatment. The court also focused on parental responsibilities in general and stressed the need for state intervention to provide for the moral development of children whose parents had failed them. Most important of all, the court built its decision around the doctrine of *parens patriae*, taking what had previously been an English judicial concept and making it applicable to the American scene. The court wrote

> The object of the charity is reformation, by training its inmates to industry; by imbuing their minds with principles of morality and religion; by furnishing them with means to earn a living; and above all, by separating them from the corrupting influence of improper associates. To this end, may not the natural parents, when unequal to the task of education, or unworthy of it, be superseded by the *parens patriae*, or common guardianship of the community?[23]

The Chicago Reform School

Around the middle of the 1800s, the child savers movement began. Child savers espoused a philosophy of productivity and eschewed idleness and unprincipled behavior. Anthony Platt,[24] a modern writer who recognized the significance of the child savers movement, suggests that the mid-1800s provided an ideological framework combining Christian principles with a strong emphasis on the worth of the individual. It was a social perspective which held that children were to be guided and protected.

One product of the child savers movement was the reform school—a place for delinquent juveniles which embodied the atmosphere of a Christian home. By the middle of the nineteenth century, the reform school approach to handling juveniles was well under way. The Chicago Reform School, which opened in the 1860s, provided an early model for the reform

Young New York pickpockets in custody, circa 1900. Beginning in the late nineteenth century, juvenile courts had to consider what was in the child's "best interests." *Bettmann*

school movement. The movement focused primarily on predelinquent youth who showed tendencies toward more serious criminal involvement. Reform schools attempted to emulate wholesome family environments in order to provide the security and affection thought necessary in building moral character.

The reform school movement also emphasized traditional values and the worth of hard work. The movement tended to idealize country living, apparently in the belief that the frantic pace of city life made the transition from child to adult difficult. Some early reform schools were built in rural settings, and many were farms. A few programs even developed which tried to relocate problem children to the vast open expanses of the Western states.

The reform school movement was not without its critics. As one modern-day observer writes, "If institutions sought to replicate families, would it not have been better to place the predelinquents directly in real families?"[25] As with houses of refuge, reform schools soon became overcrowded. What began as a meaningful attempt to help children ended in routinized institutional procedures devoid of the reformer's original zeal.

In the 1870s, the Illinois supreme court handed down a decision that practically put the reform school movement out of business. The case of *People ex rel. O'Connell* v. *Turner*[26] centered on Daniel O'Connell, who had been committed to the Chicago Reform School under an Illinois law which permitted confinement for "misfortune." Youngsters classified as "misfortunate" had not necessarily committed any offense. They were, rather, ordered to reform school because their families were unable to care for them or because they were seen as social misfits. Because O'Connell had not been convicted of a crime, the Illinois supreme court ordered him released. The court reasoned that the power of the state under *parens patriae* could not exceed the power of the natural parents except in punishing crime. The *O'Connell* case is still remembered today for the lasting distinction it made between criminal and noncriminal acts committed by juveniles.

The Juvenile Court Era

An expanding recognition of the needs of children led the state of Massachusetts to enact legislation in 1870 which required separate hearings for juveniles.[27] New York followed with a similar law in 1877.[28] The New York law also prohibited contact between juvenile and adult offenders. Rhode Island enacted juvenile court legislation in 1898, and in 1899 the Colorado School Law became the first comprehensive piece of legislation designed to adjudicate problem children.[29] It was, however, the 1899 codification of Illinois juvenile law which became the model for juvenile court statutes throughout the nation.

Delinquent Child A child who has engaged in activity which would be considered a crime if the child were an adult. The term *delinquent* is applied to such a child in order to avoid the stigma which comes from application of the term *criminal*.

Undisciplined Child A child who is beyond parental control, as evidenced by his/her refusal to obey legitimate authorities, such as school officials and teachers.

Dependent Child A child who has no parent(s) or whose parent(s) is (are) unable to care for him or for her.

Neglected Child A child who is not receiving the proper level of physical or psychological care from his or her parent(s) or guardian(s), or who has been placed up for adoption in violation of the law.

Abused Child A child who has been physically, sexually, or mentally abused. Most states also consider a child who is forced into delinquent activity by a parent or guardian to be abused.

Status Offender A child who commits an act which is contrary to the law by virtue of the juvenile's status as a child. Purchasing cigarettes, buying alcohol, and truancy are examples of such behavior.

Status Offense An act or conduct which is declared by statute to be an offense, but only when committed by or engaged in by a juvenile, and which can be adjudicated only by a juvenile court.

The Illinois Juvenile Court Act created a juvenile court, separate in form and function from adult criminal courts. In order to avoid the lasting stigma of criminality, the law applied the term *delinquent* rather than *criminal* to young adjudicated offenders. The act specified that *the best interests of the child* were to guide juvenile court judges in their deliberations. In effect, the judge was to serve as an advocate for the juvenile, seeking to guide the development of the child in socially desirable directions. Concerns with guilt or innocence took second place to the betterment of the child. The law abandoned a strict adherence to the due process requirements of adult prosecutions, allowing informal procedures designed to scrutinize the child's situation. By sheltering the juvenile from the punishment philosophy of the adult system, the Illinois juvenile court emphasized reformation in place of retribution.[30]

In 1938 the federal government passed the Juvenile Court Act, which embodied many of the features of the Illinois statute. By 1945 every state had enacted special legislation focusing on the handling of juveniles, and the juvenile court movement had become well established.[31]

The juvenile court movement was based upon five philosophical principles which can be summarized as follows:

1. The belief that the state is the "higher or ultimate parent" of all the children within its borders.
2. The belief that children are worth saving and that nonpunitive procedures should be used to save the child.
3. The belief that children should be nurtured. While the nurturing process is underway, they should be protected from the stigmatizing impact of formal adjudicatory procedures.
4. The belief that justice, to accomplish the goal of reformation, needs to be individualized; that is, each child is different, and the needs, aspirations, living conditions, and so on, of each child must be known in their individual particulars if the court is to be helpful.
5. The belief that the use of noncriminal procedures are necessary in order to give primary consideration to the needs of the child. The denial of due process could be justified in the face of constitutional challenges because the court acted not to punish, but to help.[32]

Categories of Children in the Juvenile Justice System

By the time of the Great Depression, most states had expanded juvenile statutes to include the following six categories of children that are still used today in most jurisdictions to describe the variety of children subject to juvenile court jurisdiction:

1. **Delinquent children** were those who violated the criminal law. If they were adults, the word "criminal" would have been applied to them.
2. **Undisciplined children** were said to be beyond parental control, as evidenced by their refusal to obey legitimate authorities, such as school officials and teachers. They needed state protection.
3. **Dependent children** typically had no parents or guardians to care for them, or had been abandoned or placed for adoption in violation of the law.
4. **Neglected children** were defined as those who did not receive proper care from their parents or guardians. They may have suffered from malnutrition, not been provided with adequate shelter, or had not received a proper upbringing.
5. **Abused children** included those who suffered physical abuse at the hands of their custodians—a category which was later expanded to include emotional and sexual abuse, as well.
6. **Status offenders**, a special category which was to lead to many later disputes, embraced children who violated laws written only for children.

Status offenses include behavior such as truancy, vagrancy, running away from home, and incorrigibility. The youthful "status" of juveniles is a necessary element in such offenses. Adults, for example, may decide to run away from home and not violate any law. Runaway children, however, are subject to apprehension and juvenile court processing because state laws require that they be subject to parental control.

Status offenses were a natural outgrowth of juvenile court philosophy. As a consequence, however, juveniles in need of help often faced procedural dispositions that treated them as though they were delinquent. As a result, rather than lowering the rate of juvenile incarceration, the juvenile court movement led to its increase. Critics of the juvenile court movement quickly focused on the abandonment of due process rights, especially in the case of status offenders, as a major source of problems. Detention and incarceration, they argued, were inappropriate options where children had not committed crimes.

Explanation of Delinquency

As states implemented innovative efforts to handle problem children, researchers began to investigate the causes of juvenile misbehavior. One of the first comprehensive social scientific explanations for delinquency, advanced by Clifford Shaw and Henry McKay[33] in the 1920s, was known as **social ecology**. The social ecology approach focused on the misbehavior of lower-class youth and saw delinquency primarily as the result of **social disorganization**. Whereas social order is the condition of a society characterized by social integration, consensus, smooth functioning, and lack of interpersonal and institutional conflict, social disorganization exists when a group is faced with social change, uneven development, maladaptiveness, disharmony, conflict, and lack of consensus. Geographic areas characterized by economic deprivation were said to have high rates of population turnover and cultural heterogeneity, both of which were seen as contributors to social disorganization. Social disorganization weakened otherwise traditional societal controls, such as family life, church, jobs, and schools, making delinquency more likely in such areas.

Because of their influence on policymakers of the 1930s, the first large-scale delinquency prevention program grew out of the work of Shaw and McKay. Known as the Chicago Area Project, the program developed self-help neighborhood centers staffed by community volunteers. Each center offered a variety of counseling services, educational programs, camps, recreational activities, and discussion groups. Programs were intended to reduce social disorganization by bringing members of the community together to work toward common goals and by providing community members with the skills needed for success.

The approach of Shaw and McKay was replaced in the 1960s by a perspective known as **opportunity theory**. Opportunity theorists saw delinquency as the result of the lack of legitimate opportunities for success available to most lower-class youth. Richard A. Cloward and Lloyd E. Ohlin[34] described the most serious delinquents as facing limited opportunities due to their inherent alienation from middle-class institutions. Others have claimed that delinquency is a natural consequence of participation in lower-class culture. Even stable lower-class communities, these authors suggest,[35] produce delinquency as a matter of course. A combination of both approaches is found in the work of Albert K. Cohen,[36] who held that delinquency, especially gang-related activity, is a response to the frustration lower-class youth experience when they find they cannot share in the rewards of a middle-class lifestyle. According to Cohen, vengeance and protest are major motivators among deprived youth and may account for vandalism and other seemingly senseless acts.

Opportunity theory gave rise to treatment models designed to increase chances for legitimate success among lower-class youth. Programs such as New York City's Mobilization for Youth provided education, skills training, and job placement services to young men and women. Mobilization for Youth, through the federal funds it received, hired hundreds of unemployed neighborhood youths to work on community projects, such as parks conservation and building renovation.

Gresham M. Sykes and David Matza[37] at least partially recognized the role of individual choice in delinquent behavior in their description of the neutralization of responsibility as a first step toward law violation. The delinquent, according to Sykes and Matza,[38] typically drifts between conformity and law violation and will choose the latter when social norms can be denied or explained away.

Cohort analysis is a useful technique for identifying the determinants of delinquency. Cohort analysis usually begins at birth and traces the development of a population which shares common characteristics until they reach a certain age. One well-known analysis of a birth cohort, undertaken by Marvin Wolfgang during the 1960s, found that a small nucleus of chronic juvenile offenders accounted for a disproportionately large share of all juvenile arrests.[39] Wolfgang studied males born in Philadelphia in 1945 until they reached age 18. He concluded that a relatively small number of violent offenders were responsible for most of

Social Ecology An approach which focused on the misbehavior of lower-class youth and saw delinquency primarily as the result of social disorganization.

Social Disorganization A condition which is said to exist when a group is faced with social change, uneven cultural development, maladaptiveness, disharmony, conflict, and lack of consensus.

Opportunity Theory A perspective which sees delinquency as the result of limited legitimate opportunities for success available to most lower-class youth.

Cohort A group of individuals sharing similarities of age, place of birth, and residence. Cohort analysis is a social scientific technique by which such groups are tracked over time in order to identify unique and observable behavioral traits which characterize them.

the crimes committed by the cohort. Eighteen percent of cohort members accounted for 52% of all arrests. A follow-up study found that seriousness of offenses among the cohort increased in adulthood, but that the actual number of offenses decreased as the cohort aged.[40] Wolfgang's analysis has since been criticized for its lack of a second cohort, or "control group," against which the experiences of the cohort under study could be compared.[41]

Perhaps the most comprehensive study to date which has attempted to unveil the underlying causes of juvenile delinquency was begun in 1986, with early results reported in 1994 and 1995. The study, named the Program of Research on the Causes and Correlates of Juvenile Delinquency,[42] was sponsored by the U.S. Department of Justice's Office of Juvenile Justice and Delinquency Prevention (OJJDP). The study drew together data on 4,000 youths from three distinct but coordinated projects: (1) the Denver Youth Survey, conducted by the University of Colorado; (2) the Pittsburgh Youth Study, undertaken by University of Pittsburgh researchers; and (3) the Rochester Youth Development Study fielded by professors at the State University of New York at Albany. The survey sampled youngsters at high risk for serious delinquency and drug use and found that (1) "the more seriously involved in drugs a youth was, the more seriously that juvenile was involved in delinquency," (2) "greater risks exist for violent offending when a child is physically abused or neglected early in life," (3) "students who were not highly committed to school had higher rates of delinquency," (4) "poor family life exacerbates delinquency and drug use," and (5) affiliation with street gangs and illegal gun ownership are both predictive of delinquency. The study also found that "peers who were delinquent or used drugs had a great impact on [other] youth." Perhaps the most significant result of the study was the finding that three separate developmental pathways[43] to delinquency exist. The pathways identified by the study were

1. The *authority conflict pathway*, down which subjects appeared to begin quite young (as early as three or four years of age). "The first step," said the study authors, "was stubborn behavior, followed by defiance around age 11, and authority avoidance—truancy, staying out late at night, or running away."
2. The *covert pathway*, which begins with "minor covert acts such as frequent lying and shoplifting, usually around age 10." Delinquents following this path quickly progressed "to acts of property damage, such as firestarting or vandalism, around age 11 or 12, followed by moderate and serious forms of delinquency."
3. The *overt pathway*, in which the first step was marked by minor aggression such as "annoying others and bullying—around age 11 or 12." Bullying was found to escalate into "physical fighting and violence as the juvenile progressed along this pathway."

The study also identified youth who, having many risk factors, did not engage in delinquent behavior. The research identified six factors that strengthen juveniles so that they do not become delinquent. These elements are called protective factors and include

1. Commitment to school
2. Achievement at school
3. Continuance of education (no dropping out)
4. High levels of parental supervision
5. High levels of attachment to parents
6. Association with conventional peers and peers approved of by their parents

Other studies[44] have also indicated the importance of regular school attendance and commitment to success at school. A 1996 report by OJJDP, for example, found that "chronic absenteeism is the most powerful predictor of delinquent behavior."[45] A comprehensive 1997 task force report by the American Society of Criminology[46] similarly concluded that "strong evidence links early problem behavior to later adolescent delinquency and serious adult criminality" and suggested that early intervention is the key to preventing the development of chronic patterns of criminal behavior. Authors of the task force report wrote that "[T]here is clear indication that problem behavior often begins early in life, and there is strong evidence of substantial continuity between problem behavior in early childhood and later adolescent delinquency and serious adult criminality. 'An ounce of prevention is worth more than a pound of cure' is more than an old adage. Not only can early prevention and intervention reduce future crime and delinquency, but waiting until the mid-to-late teenage years to intervene in serious, persistent delinquency commonly results in an uphill and all too frequently fruitless battle."[47]

The Post-Juvenile Court Era

Juvenile court era philosophy continues to undergird the contemporary system of American juvenile justice. As a box in this chapter explains, however, the juvenile justice system in the United States today is in the midst of transition. Extensive media coverage of violent crimes in predominantly urban neighborhoods has fueled perceptions that violence committed by juveniles has reached epidemic proportions and that no community is immune to random acts of violence committed by young people—especially those involving a weapon. A 1996 report by the Office for Juvenile Justice and Delinquency Prevention, for example, found that the American public is now vitally concerned with rising rates of juvenile crime and with the increased levels of violence associated with those crimes. The OJJDP report noted that "the issue of youth violence has been at or near the top of nearly every state legislature and governor's agenda for the past several years."[48] The report's survey shows that "[n]early every state has taken legislative or executive action in response to escalating juvenile arrests for violent crime and public perceptions of a violent juvenile crime epidemic. These actions have significantly altered the legal response to violent or other serious juvenile crime in this country. In many states, change has occurred in each legislative session since 1992, with more rapid and sweeping change occurring in 1995 and still more expected in [the future]. This level of activity has occurred only three other times in our nation's history: at the outset of the juvenile court movement at the turn of the century; following the U.S. Supreme Court's *Gault* decision in 1967; and with the enactment of the Juvenile Justice Delinquency Prevention Act in 1974."[49]

An OJJDP analysis of the "sea change" now sweeping across the country in the handling of serious and violent juvenile offenders found five common themes in new state laws intended to target such offenders.[50] The five themes are: (1) changes in jurisdictional authority, such that violent juvenile offenders are being legislatively removed from the juvenile justice system in order that they might be prosecuted as adults in criminal court; (2) changes in sentencing authority which mandate the imposition of specified minimum sentences, extend juvenile court jurisdiction beyond the age of majority, and allow for the imposition of "blended sentences" that mix both juvenile and adult sanctions; (3) increased pressure on correctional administrators to develop programs to serve violent juveniles; (4) a revision of traditional confidentiality provisions in favor of more open juvenile proceedings and court records; and (5) inclusion of victims of juvenile crime as "active participants" in the juvenile justice process.

Changes at the federal level have been slower in coming. As this book goes to press, however, federal policy on juvenile justice appears poised to take a sharp turn toward punishment. Not only violent youths, but runaways and other status offenders as well may soon be subject to tougher treatment.

Senate leaders of both parties and President Clinton have recently introduced legislation to expand the role of the federal government in combating juvenile delinquency. Three federal legislative initiatives are under consideration at this time, at least one of which (with modifications) is likely to be passed into law. The three are (1) the Senate's Violent and Repeat Juvenile Offender Act; (2) the House-passed Juvenile Crime Control and Delinquency Prevention Act; and (3) another Senate proposal, the Youth Violence, Crime, and Drug Abuse Control Act.

While significant differences exist among the proposals (especially along partisan lines), the plans, taken as a whole, would increase penalties for young people involved in the juvenile justice system, transfer more juveniles to adult courts, build juvenile prisons at both state and federal levels, and send status offenders to boot camps.

The Violent and Repeat Juvenile Offender Act of 1997 would (1) require that a juvenile in federal court be tried as an adult if the juvenile is 14 years or older and is charged with a federal offense that is a crime of violence or that involves a controlled substance for which the penalty is not less than five years' imprisonment; (2) require that a juvenile in the federal

Juvenile arrests for violent crimes increased by 51% between 1988 and 1994. Recent statistics predict a doubling in juvenile arrests for violent crime by the year 2010 if the last decade's trends continue unchecked.
—OJJDP

There was nothing to do.
—Terrance Wade, age 15, on why he and his friends allegedly raped, stomped, stabbed, and ultimately murdered a Boston woman

The values and experiences of many children today are far different from those of the past, as this photo of female gang members shows. *Robery Yager, Tony Stone Images*

court system being tried as an adult be subject to detention in the same manner and extent as an adult; and (3) eliminate various "protections" now available to juveniles under federal law.

The Juvenile Crime Control and Delinquency Prevention Act of 1997 proposes establishment of a model federal system for holding juveniles accountable for their crimes, loosens restrictions on juvenile records, broadens the possibility of punishment as a judicial alternative, and provides $1.5 billion in incentive grants to the states to strengthen their juvenile justice systems. Under the bill, states would be required to prosecute as adults all juveniles 15 or older who commit violent crimes (those who have reached their thirteenth birthdays *could* be tried as adults) and to maintain records of repeat juvenile offenders that commit felonies.

In addition to Congressional proposals, a White House-led initiative has declared youth crime the administration's "top law enforcement priority." The Clinton Administration proposes to crack down on gangs and youth violence, ban handgun ownership and use for life by violent juveniles, require safety locks on handguns, and give federal prosecutors the power to transfer more juveniles to adult court. The President's proposal also suggests spending $500 million over the next two years on a variety of antidelinquency-related efforts, including $200 million for state and local antigang prosecution (part of which would involve hiring new federal prosecutors); $170 million to assist states in building juvenile prisons; $75 million to fight truancy and school violence; $60 million for after-school programs to keep youths off the streets; and $50 million for enhanced juvenile court and probation systems. The money would be available only to states that allow for more juveniles to be treated as adults, punish juveniles for every offense, and keep adult-type criminal records on them.

The Problems of Children Today

Besides delinquency, but in some ways contributing to it, are a vast array of other problems which face children today. Many of these problems are quite different from those that existed when the juvenile court was formed.

One general problem with which many of today's children must deal is felt lack of purpose. A few years ago, for example, New York citizens were outraged by the actions of a group of East Harlem teenagers who attacked joggers and cyclists in near-desolate sections of

Juvenile Justice Today—A System in Transition

The "get-tough"-on-crime philosophy, now so pervasive in America, has begun to heavily influence America's system of juvenile justice and is beginning to bring about sweeping changes in at least some jurisdictions. Our system of justice for juveniles was originally built upon a simple philosophy: that the fundamental purpose of all agencies charged with the care and handling of adjudicated juveniles should be to act in the best interests of the child. For the past 100 years this principle, which grew out of the nineteenth-century juvenile court movement, has provided the one major distinguishing feature between what we have come to think of as appropriate justice for juvenile law violators and justice for adult criminals in the United States.

Over time, however, an increasing number of juvenile court officials have come to realize that at least a few children represent a criminal threat to their communities which belies their years, and a growing viciousness among juvenile law violators has surprised policy makers into believing that a more punitive approach to the handling of delinquency is necessary. Much current thinking is based upon the fact that juvenile gangs, drugs, the ready availability of handguns and automatic weapons, weapons in schools, and a willingness to resort to violence to solve even minor problems are sadly characteristic of the contemporary generation of young people.

Throughout the past few years, the national media has been abuzz with the plight of a justice system which seemed to lack the resources or decisiveness necessary to deal with serious juvenile crime. Examples were easy to find. One widely publicized case was that of New Englander Craig Price. Price, known as the Iron Man to his friends because of his muscular build (at 5 feet 10 inches tall, he weighs 240 pounds), pled guilty a few years ago to the murder of two Rhode Island women and two girls. The girls

were ten and eight years old at the time they were killed. All of the victims had been beaten and stabbed—one as many as 58 times. At the time of his confession, Price was already on probation for assault and burglary—and he was only 14 years old. (He had been 13 at the time of the first murder.) Reporters covering the Price case were quick to point out that Rhode Island, like many other states, has no provision which would allow anyone who was under the age of 16 at the time their offense was committed to be tried as an adult. In addition, Rhode Island law requires that juveniles sentenced to incarceration be released on or before their 21st birthdays. Hence, following his plea of guilty to four murders and two burglaries, Craig Price was sentenced to the maximum the law allows—incarceration in the Rhode Island Training School until he reaches the age of 21.[1]

While sociologists, religious leaders, parents, and concerned citizens seek the causes of increased criminal violence among children, politicians, heeding the call of their constituencies, have begun to enact "get-tough" policies designed to reduce juvenile crime and to increase control over juveniles. In 1995, for example, Texas Governor George W. Bush signed into law a new juvenile justice bill "designed to make the system stricter from beginning to end."[2] "This new law," said the governor, "tells juveniles that violent behavior will be punished in Texas. Our goal is to save a generation of young people by making them accountable for their actions."[3] The new Texas law lowers the age at which juveniles can be tried as adults (from 15 to 14), eases restrictions on the fingerprinting and photographing of children taken into custody, opens most juvenile hearings to the public, and makes it possible for children committing serious violent crimes to be sentenced to up to 40 years in confinement—with transfer to an adult prison when they reach the age of 16.

Texas is not the only state getting tough on juvenile offenders. In 1995 Minnesota completed what was called "the biggest overhaul of its juvenile justice system in 50 years."[4] Minnesota's new law, which is intended to crack down on violent juvenile offenders, creates a special category of delinquency under which serious and repeat offenders can be labeled extended-jurisdiction juveniles. Those so categorized can be sentenced as both juveniles and adults. If they fail to abide by the conditions of their juvenile sentence, their adult sentence is activated—which usually means time spent in prison or jail. Extended-jurisdiction trials are also open to the public, and another significant feature of the Minnesota law is that it makes it easier to try juveniles as adults. Previously, attorneys for the state were required to convince hearing judges that juveniles should be treated as adults. Under the new law the burden has shifted to the juvenile and his or her attorney, who must show why the child should *not* be considered an adult for purposes of criminal trial.

In 1996 Michigan Governor John Engler signed into law a sweeping juvenile justice reform package of 21 new laws which he said would give his state "the toughest juvenile justice system in the nation." "No more excuses, no more slaps on the wrist," said Engler at the signing ceremony. "Young offenders will be held accountable for their crimes." Included in the new Michigan laws are measures to (1) require adult sentencing for juveniles convicted as adults for serious crimes, (2) lower the jurisdictional age to 14 for automatic waivers, allowing prosecutors to bypass juvenile court for youths accused of capital crimes, (3) expand sentencing options for judges dealing with young criminals, (4) require that the state Family Independence Agency demonstrate that youths have been rehabilitated before being released from custody programs, and (5) set stiff terms for juveniles convicted of using firearms during commission of any crime. Other states are joining the reform bandwagon. Tennessee recently eliminated any minimum age for trying some youths as adults, Oregon lowered its minimum age from 14 to 12, and Wisconsin put the age at which juveniles can be tried as adults at 10.

Many juvenile justice advocates, well versed in the traditional protectionist philosophy which has guided the American system of juvenile justice for the past century, fear that changes like those now occurring in Texas, Minnesota, Michigan, and elsewhere, may soon steamroll their way through state legislatures across the country—turning the juvenile justice system on its head and eradicating many of the significant differences between the juvenile and adult systems which developed during the last century. Recently, for example, the

prestigious and influential International Association of Chiefs of Police threw its weight behind the juvenile reform movement, calling for a "tougher approach to juvenile crime careerists."[5] Others, however, caution that much of today's concern is unrealistically built upon media overcoverage of isolated events. "One heinous case has everyone jumping up and down saying all kids are doing it,"[6] complains Edward Loughran, a former head of Massachusetts's juvenile corrections agency. "Bad cases make bad law," cautions Loughran.

QUESTIONS FOR DISCUSSION

1. Do you believe that the American system of juvenile justice should be concerned primarily with the best interests of the children who come before it? Or should it concern itself more with punishment? Defend your position.

2. How do you think the juvenile justice system of the future may differ from the system of today? Why?

[1]Price was later charged with extortion and assault and accused of threatening a guard while confined in a juvenile facility. Since the charges came after he had reached the age of 16, authorities were able to continue holding Price beyond the age of 21.

[2]*Criminal Justice Newsletter*, June 1, 1995, p. 7.

[3]Ibid.

[4]Carolyn Pesce, "Minnesota Puts 'Hammer' on Juvenile Criminals," *USA Today*, December 30, 1994, p. 2A.

[5]International Association of Chiefs of Police, *Murder in America: Recommendations from the IACP Murder Summit* (Alexandria, VA: IACP, 1995).

[6]Ted Guest and Victoria Pope, "Crime Time Bomb," *U.S. News & World Report* World Wide Web site, September 27, 1996.

Central Park.[51] Before their spree of intimidation and violence ended, the gang, which at one point numbered as many as 30 kids between the ages of 14 and 17, had attacked, raped, and viciously beaten a 28-year-old investment banker jogging through the area. The victim, who became known to the press as "the Central Park jogger" and was working her way through Yale business school at the time of the attack, suffered two skull fractures and serious brain damage. Following police questioning, the youngsters—who remained largely unrepentant—described how evenings spent "wilding" (the pack's slang term for violent mischief) had given vent to their frustrations. Said one psychologist attempting to explain the event, "Feelings of frustration and alienation are widespread, particularly among lower classes."[52] Today's "angry adolescents" have been described as sharing these traits: (1) aggressiveness, (2) immaturity, (3) susceptibility to peer pressure, and (4) a lack of accountability.[53]

How did the angry adolescent come to be a problem in America? Over half a century ago many of the problems encountered by juveniles grew out of their value as inexpensive laborers in the "sweat shops" and factories of the awakening industrial giant that was America. The economic prosperity which followed World War II, however, was based on a less labor-intensive form of production. Complicating matters still further was the need for the national economy to absorb millions of women who were entering the labor force. Juveniles, no longer needed for their labor, were thrown into a cultural limbo. Some, unable to meaningfully participate in the long educational process that was becoming increasingly necessary for future success, turned to delinquency and vandalism. For these disenfranchised youth, criminal activity became an alternative avenue to excitement and some limited sense of purpose.

By the 1960s a self-indulgent ethic had replaced the sense of personal responsibility among a goodly proportion of American youth. For lower-class youth, the ethic led to violence, theft, and increased participation in gangs. Middle-class youth, because they were more affluent, focused on what some authors at the time called the "automobile-alcohol-sex combination,"[54] rejecting middle-class values of social duty and personal restraint.

While much of the literature of delinquency focuses on the criminality of lower-class youth, there is evidence that middle- and upper-class youths today commit a fair number of delinquent acts. A recent study of the "lifetime delinquency" of Ivy League college students,

When young people are taken into custody, they are confined separately from adult offenders. Here, a teenager is arrested following a disturbance at a concert. *AP/Wide World Photos*

for example, found "substantial levels of involvement in a variety of serious offenses."[55] According to the study, 167 students admitted to 4,100 past offenses ranging from public intoxication to forcible rape.

Regardless of class background, there are a number of common problems facing juveniles today. Each is described in the sections that follow.

Drug and Alcohol Abuse

Many of today's adolescents have experimented with illegal drugs. While surveys showed some decline in drug use during the mid-1980s, the trend in drug use has increased over the last few years. The 1996 Monitoring the Future[56] survey, which measures drug abuse among high-school students, found that "substance abuse among young teens continues [to increase]... especially tobacco and marijuana—and that alcohol use also remains unacceptably high." According to Health and Human Services Secretary Donna Shalala, "The survey tells us that drug use among young people is at unacceptable levels; that the core of the problem is marijuana; and that we must fight aggressively to change these trends." According to the survey, indicators which measure marijuana use within the past month among 8th graders increased from 9 percent in 1995 to 11 percent in 1996. Past month marijuana use among 10th graders increased from 17 percent to 20 percent over the same one-year period. The survey also showed an increase in marijuana use of more than 250 percent since 1991 for 8th graders and over 150 percent for 10th graders since 1992. The survey found that the use of crack cocaine by youngsters (8th graders) is growing and that LSD use is showing some resurgence. According to the survey, about half of all high school seniors had used an illicit drug at least once in their lifetimes.

Young people abuse other substances as well. Surveys show that 20% of 8th graders have used inhalants at least once, while 28% of seniors, 21% of 10th graders, and 13% of 8th graders report binge drinking—consuming five or more alcoholic drinks in a row.[57] According to a 1996 RAND Corporation Drug Policy Research Center study[58] (1) about one out of every six high-school seniors averages at least one alcoholic drink every other day, (2) more than a quarter of all teenagers experience a drinking-related problem (such as missing school) on at least three occasions in any given year—or a more serious problem (such as a fight) at least once; and (3) about 25% of teenagers engage in two or more high-risk drinking activities (combining alcohol with other drugs, driving while drinking, etc.) at least once per year.

The current [juvenile justice] system, a relic from a more innocent time, teaches youthful offenders that crime pays and that they are totally immune and insulated from responsibility.
—The National Policy Forum

A teenage girl negotiates the price of crack in a run-down North Philadelphia neighborhood. The problem of drug abuse has been exacerbated by the decline of inner-city areas. *Eugene Richards, Magnum*

As Figure 14–3 shows, drug-related *arrests* of juveniles have recently been on the rise—indicating an increase in drug use among juveniles of all ages. In 1985, for example, 64,246 individuals under the age of 18 were arrested for drug offenses nationwide. By 1992, the figure had risen to 73,981, then more than doubled to 158,447 in 1996.[59] While some of the increase may be due to new get-tough enforcement policies, evidence indicates that a juvenile arrested today is far more likely to be using cocaine or crack cocaine than were juveniles in earlier periods. The most commonly abused drug in 1975 was marijuana.

Drug abuse may also lead to other types of crime. One recent study found that seriously delinquent youth were regular drug users.[60] The Bureau of Justice Statistics concludes: "The involvement of adolescent users in other destructive behavior is strongly associated with the number and types of harmful substances they use; the more substances they use, the greater their chance of being involved in serious destructive or assaultive behavior."[61]

Violence

Observers of the national scene have recently reported an apparent epidemic of violence among the nation's teenagers. While the numbers are still too small (there are approximately 3,000 homicides committed by juveniles annually) to significantly impact data such as that contained in the *Uniform Crime Reports*, there is little denying that childhood violence is growing. A few years ago, for example, 12-year-old Shanda Renee Sharer was bludgeoned, sodomized, tortured, doused with gasoline, and set afire by four other teenage girls. The killing, which took place in the small town of Madison, Indiana, appears to have been motivated by lesbian jealousies.[62] In an unrelated case that happened about the same time, two teenage Gulfport, Mississippi, girls were accused of choking their mother to death while the boyfriend of one of the girls stabbed the woman. The mother had punished the girls for sneaking away from the house at night.[63] Recently, two Chicago girls, aged 12 and 13, were arrested for planning to kill their English teacher at the end of class—by stabbing her in the chest with a fillet knife brought from home. The girls had apparently taken a few hundred dollars in lunch money bets from fellow students over whether they would be able to follow through.[64] Cases such as these have led some observers to conclude that girls are beginning to catch up with boys in the area of violence.

The recent spate of violence among children seems to know no religious, age, or geographic boundaries. In 1992, for example, devout Christians and community stalwarts

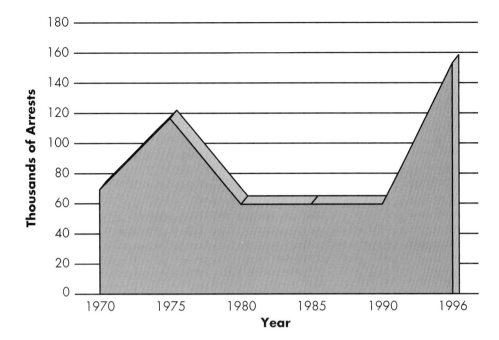

FIGURE 14–3 Drug-related arrests of juveniles, 1970–1996. *Source:* Federal Bureau of Investigation, *Crime in the United States* (Washington, D.C.: U.S. Government Printing Office, various years).

Harold Read and his wife Janet were killed in the small town of Madras, Oregon, by blasts from a 12-gauge shotgun—apparently fired by 12-year-old Jacob Colman, whom they had befriended and taken into their home.[65] About the same time a 22-month-old Savannah, Georgia, girl apparently killed her six-month-old baby brother by dragging him from bed and repeatedly biting him,[66] and in mid-1993 England was horrified by the kidnapping and killing of 2-year-old James Bolger—a crime committed by two 10-year-olds.[67]

A recent report[68] by the Office of Juvenile Justice and Delinquency Prevention (OJJDP) found that a significant "increase in the juvenile arrest rate for violent crimes began in the late 1980s," and concluded that "if trends continue as they have over the past 10 years, juvenile arrests for violent crime will double by the year 2010." Rates for murder and assault, said the report, will be even higher. The report also noted that, although all racial groups are showing increased violence among youth, "the rate of violent crime arrests for black youth was about 5 times the white rate."

Investigators are seeking to understand why the rate of juvenile crime has risen so notably over the last decade. One answer comes from Alfred Blumstein, who says: "This striking array of changes in juvenile crime since 1985—a doubling of the homicide rate, a doubling of the number of homicides committed with guns, and a doubling of the arrest rate of non-whites for drug offenses, all after a period of relative stability in these rates—cries out for an explanation that will link them all together. The explanation that seems most reasonable can be traced to the rapid growth of the crack markets in the mid-1980s. To service that growth, juveniles were recruited, they were armed with the guns that are standard tools of the drug trade, and these guns then were diffused into the larger community of juveniles."[69]

GANGS

Juvenile gangs have been an inner-city phenomenon for decades. Detailed descriptions of gang activities in the United States date from the 1920s and 1930s.[70] Recent gang activities, however, differ substantially from those early reports, reflecting, perhaps, the influence of "the rapid growth of the crack markets" identified by Blumstein as so influential on today's delinquency patterns. Whereas membership in early gangs served to provide some sense of personal identity in the immigrant's culturally diverse world, many of today's juvenile gangs have developed into financial enterprises. Their activities may center on drug running and on the acquisition and sale of stolen goods. Today's gangs rarely hesitate to use ruthless violence to protect financial opportunities. One study of an East Coast gang of the 1930s found that weapons of choice included milk bottles, flower pots, and banana tree stalks.[71] In contrast, some members of large-city gangs today brandish semiautomatic weapons and Uzi submachine guns.[72]

A 1995 study[73] of Los Angeles' two largest youth gangs, the Crips and the Bloods, determined through interviews with gang members that most young men who join gangs "grow up in dangerous family environments" and that members may affiliate with gangs "to escape the violence [of home], or drift away because they are abandoned or neglected by their parents." Mark Fleisher, author of the study, concludes that, as a consequence of unfortunate home lives, "these young men develop…a defensive world view, characterized by six attributes: (1) a feeling of vulnerability and a need to protect oneself, (2) a belief that no one can be trusted, (3) a need to maintain social distance, (4) a willingness to use violence and intimidation to repel others, (5) an attraction to similarly defensive people, and (6) an expectation that no one will come to their aid." Cincinnati Judge David Grossmann, president of a national juvenile judges' group, adds that "gangs have become the alternative to a nurturing family."[74]

Gangs exist in many of our nation's major cities, and evidence shows that they are spreading to still others. A 1996 NIJ report estimated a yearly incidence of 580,331 gang-related crimes—a "12-fold increase over the 46,359 gang crimes estimated to have occurred in 1991."[75] The same report estimated the number of juvenile gangs nationwide at 16,643, with memberships totaling 555,181. Another NIJ survey[76] found that most serious gang activity has a strong ethnic link. Most gang members (47.8%) were found to be African-American youth, while Hispanic youngsters accounted for 42.7% of reported gang members. Asian gang membership totaled 5.2% of all gang involvement, while whites accounted for only 4.4% of gang members nationwide.

Los Angeles is considered to be the "gang capital"[77] of the United States with more than 150,000 juveniles known to be participating in over 1,350 different gangs as of October 1, 1997.[78] During 1996 Los Angeles County saw 614 gang-related homicides, and over 2,000 injuries were directly caused by gang activity.[79] Drugs form the centerpiece of much Los Angeles gang activity, with large quantities of crack—a highly addictive form of cocaine—being produced and sold by many groups.

The Los Angeles County Sheriff's Department uses a computer system known as GREAT (Gang Reporting, Evaluation, and Tracking) to keep track of gang members, and Los Angeles-area police agencies have resorted to massive arrests in order to gain some control over the gang problem. The first LAPD sweep focused on city schools, where officers made 127 arrests, half of them for felonies. However, few arrested juveniles remain in custody for long. In California, one report found gang culture flourishing inside of California Youth Authority (CYA) institutions, with members of rival gangs forming branches for protection.[80]

Local police efforts may not be enough to stem gang violence. Current evidence indicates that many big city street gangs are expanding their drug activities into other cities across the United States. Authorities have been able to pinpoint L.A. gang involvement in drug transactions involving 45 American cities from Anchorage, Alaska, to Washington, D.C.[81] John M. Hagedorn's study[82] of Milwaukee gangs supports the findings of other researchers on the centrality of drugs to street gang activity. Hagedorn categorized those associated with gangs as: (1) "legits," former members who had matured out of the gang; (2) "homeboys," who alternately worked conventional jobs and took various roles in drug sales; (3) "new jacks," who regarded the drug game as a career; and (4) "dope fiends," who were addicted to cocaine and participated in the drug business as a way to maintain access to the drug.

A large-scale project of the National Gang Crime Research Center, known as Project Gangfact, provides a profile of gangs and gang members nationwide. The 1996 Gangfact report,[83] based on data collected by 28 researchers in 17 states, showed that (1) "gang members were significantly more likely than non-gang members to have…sold crack cocaine, and to be involved in organized drug dealing," (2) "gang members were less likely to come from an intact family," and more often came from a "dysfunctional family," (3) "gang members were significantly less likely than non-gang members to complete high school," (4) gang members tended to be more predatory (that is, to be bullies in school and to be risk takers). Among its dozens of intriguing findings, Gangfact also found that (1) the average age for

Los Angeles gang members display signs of membership in front of a street mural. *A. Reininger, Woodfin Camp & Associates*

joining a gang, nationally, was 12.8 years of age; (2) over half who joined gangs had tried to quit; (3) more than two-thirds of gangs have written rules for members to follow; (4) over half of all gangs hold regular weekly meetings; (5) nearly 30% of gangs requires their members to pay dues; (6) about 55% of gang members have been recruited by other gang members, while the remainder sought out gang membership; (7) most gang members (79%) said they would leave the gang if given a "second chance in life;" (8) four-fifths of gang members reported that their gang sold crack cocaine; (9) 70% of gangs are not racially exclusive and consist of members of various ethnic groups; (10) one-third of gang members report that they have been able to conceal their gang membership from their parents; (11) most gangs (83%) report having female members, but few allow female members to assume leadership roles; and (12) 40% of gang members reported knowing male members of their gangs who had raped females.

A comprehensive 1997 study of youth gangs by the Office of Juvenile Justice and Delinquency Prevention[84] concluded that communities might achieve a sustained reduction in gang-related problems via the use of a number of specific strategies. OJJDP researchers say that (1) community leaders must recognize the presence of gangs and seek to understand the nature and extent of the local gang problem through a comprehensive and systematic assessment of the gang problem; and (2) the combined leadership of the justice system and the community must focus on the mobilization of institutional and community resources to address gang problems. Among those resources, say researchers, community leaders must mobilize citizens and community groups and agencies; provide or enhance social and economic opportunities, including special schools, training, and job programs; develop and utilize youth outreach programs, and direct street gang members toward mainstream opportunities; and suppress gang activities via surveillance and enforcement activities.

In proposing a national gang strategy, Finn-Aage Esbensen reminds policy makers that many gang members are delinquent before they become associated with gangs.[85] Esbensen says "that concerns with gang suppression should not supplant efforts to implement effective delinquency intervention and prevention strategies."[86]

For the foreseeable future, American youngsters will be aware of the psychoactive potential of many drugs and, in general, will have relatively easy access to them. In the absence of reasons not to use, many are going to try them and a significant number will get into trouble with them.

—Monitoring for the Future study

Runaways

The U.S. Department of Health and Human Services puts the number of children reported missing each year at over 1.5 million.[87] A 1990 in-depth study[88] of missing children found that the largest subgroup (approximately 583,000) are runaways, while a sizable proportion (approximately 190,000) are "thrownaways"—children no longer wanted by their parents. Family abductions and children who are lost through accident, injury, or misadventure make up the remainder of all missing children. Although most runaway children eventually return home, there is evidence that runaway and thrownaway children are beginning to contribute to the increasing number of homeless on city streets.

Children run away for a variety of reasons. Some come from homes where there is little love and affection. Others clash with their parents over disputed activities within the home, problems in school, and because of difficulties with friends. Some are lured away from home by the promise of drugs or the money that drugs might bring. Official statistics show that one-third of runaways leave home because of sexual abuse,[89] while another half leave because of beatings.

If a child cannot go to school without fear of being raped, robbed, or even murdered, then nothing else the government does really matters.
—The National Policy Forum

Whatever the reason, the number of runaway children has become a problem of near-epidemic proportions. The Office for Juvenile Justice and Delinquency Prevention estimates that the vast majority of those children "who remain at large for a few weeks will resort to theft or prostitution as a method of self-support."[90] Of all children who do run away, only approximately 20% will ever come into official contact with police or social service agencies.[91]

The juvenile justice system is hampered by statute in its ability to deal effectively with runaways. Running away from home is not a criminal act. Under the 1974 Juvenile Justice and Delinquency Prevention Act, runaways are designated status offenders. As a result, although many runaway children are placed in unguarded group homes by police officers and social service workers, neither shelter workers nor the police have any legal authority to force a child to stay in the facility.

Short-term solutions to the runaway problem are being sought in clearinghouses for cataloging and disseminating information about missing and located children. The Missing Children Act of 1982 mandates that the parents, legal guardians, or the next of kin of missing children may have information about a missing child entered into the FBI's National Criminal Information Center (NCIC). The essence of these informational strategies is speed. The fast dissemination of information and the rapid reunion of family members with runaway children may provide the best hope that distraught children can be persuaded to return home.

Until the Juvenile Justice and Delinquency Prevention Act is amended to provide states and local jurisdictions with the needed authority to take runaway children into custody and safely control them, however, the problem of runaways will remain. The U.S. Attorney General's Advisory Board on Missing Children has called for just such a change,[92] and indications are that it won't be long in coming.

In recent years, the number of runaway children has become a problem of near-epidemic proportions. This adolescent runaway lives under a highway overpass in Hollywood, California. *Dorothy Littell, Stock Boston*

Sexual Abuse

Some parents exploit their children for personal gain. In a famous case of a few years ago, a mother living in Ft. Lauderdale, Florida, was sentenced to a year in prison and two years of house arrest for forcing her 17-year-old daughter to work as a topless dancer.[93] The daughter committed suicide.

All states have laws circumscribing the procuring of minor children for sexual performances. In recent years the sexual abuse of children has repeatedly made headlines. In some parts of the country, day care center operators have been charged with the sexual molestation of their charges, and many grade schools now routinely train young children to resist and report the inappropriate advances of adults.

Other Forms of Abuse

Most forms of child abuse are crimes that adults commit against children. For that reason we will not discuss them in detail in this chapter. All forms of abuse, however, are damaging to children and should be prosecuted. A 1997 study[94] conducted by the Child Welfare League of America found that "two of the surest predictors of a child likely to commit a crime [are] a child who has previously committed a crime and a child who has been victimized by child abuse and/or neglect." According to the League, "9 to 12 year old youth known to the child welfare system are 67 times more likely to be arrested than 9 to 12 year old youth from the general population of children."

Some forms of abuse, such as the instance of sexual procurement mentioned earlier, may lead directly to the child's involvement in delinquency. Parental encouragement of delinquency is a problem juveniles sometimes encounter who come from families already engaged in criminal activities. Prostitutes, for example, sometimes encourage their daughters to learn the profession. In families where the theft and sale of stolen goods is a way of life, children may be recruited for shoplifting or for burglaries which require wiggling into tight spaces where an adult might not fit.

Research has shown that children who are encouraged in delinquency by adults tend to become criminals when they reach maturity. More surprising, however, is the finding that abused children have a similar tendency toward adult criminality.[95] A recent National

PARENTS ON TRIAL

Faced with a significant increase in crime among juveniles, a number of jurisdictions have responded with laws which place responsibility for children's behavior squarely on the parents. California's Street Terrorism Enforcement and Prevention Act, one of the first of its kind in the nation, subjects parents of wayward youths to arrest. Gloria Williams, the first person arrested[1] under the law, was charged with neglecting her parental duties after her 15-year-old son was charged with rape. Police said photo evidence proved she had known her son was a gang member. Charges against her were dropped when she was able to show that she had taken a parenting course in an effort to gain better control over her son.

A number of other states now have similar laws. In 1989 Florida legislators enacted a statute which imposes a five-year prison term and a $5,000 fine on the parents of children who find and use guns left around the house, and in Wisconsin a 1985 law makes both sets of grandparents financially liable for a child born to unmarried minor children. Wisconsin also has a law which can cause welfare parents to lose their benefits if their children are habitually truant from school.

Local jurisdictions are beginning to follow suit. In 1995 the town of Silverton, Oregon (population 6,710), began enforcing an ordinance which holds parents responsible when their children break the law. Parents of wayward children in Silverton can be fined up to $1,000. The Silverton ordinance, which is called a "parental duty law," reads:

> A person commits the offense of failing to supervise a minor if the person is the parent, legal guardian or person with legal responsibility...of a child under 18 years of age and the child violates Silverton municipal code."

Soon after the Silverton law was passed, communities across the nation began asking for a copy of the ordinance, and more than 100 towns and cities were reported considering similar legislation.[2] Six months later, the Oregon state legislature adopted a parental responsibility law which stipulated that, after a warning, parents of delinquent children could be fined up to $1,000 and be required to attend parenting classes.[3]

Local parental duty laws are being tailored to the specific needs of individual communities. After 25 youngsters were killed in two years of gang violence, for example, Atlanta passed an 11 P.M. curfew for anyone under 17 enforceable by a $1,000 fine with which the parents of violators can be saddled.[4] In 1995, Washington, D.C., faced with a juvenile crime problem spiraling out of control, enacted a similar curfew requiring anyone under the age of 17 to be off the streets of the city by 11 P.M. The law requires teenagers found in public places during curfew hours to be held at designated police-run truancy centers until a parent or guardian claims them. Parents who are determined to be permitting or aiding teens to break the curfew law are subject to fines and community service.

Supporters of the new laws say they are trying to force parents to be parents. Critics claim that the statutes go "well beyond the pale of traditional law."[5] The American Civil Liberties Union, for example, objects strenuously to the idea that now people can go to prison for a crime committed by someone else. "[T]he crime is having a kid who commits a crime...," says Jay Jacobson, director of the Arkansas section of the ACLU. Similarly, in 1995, Arthur Spitzer, legal director for the American Civil Liberties Union national capital area chapter, claimed that the city's new law unfairly interferes with the rights of children. "We think it's a truly silly law because high-risk teenagers who are committing crimes...are not going to be deterred by a slap on the wrist for violating the curfew law,"[6] Spitzer said.

How the new laws will fare in court is not known. In 1993, however, the California supreme court, in the case of *Williams* v. *Garcetti*, unanimously upheld California's parental responsibility statute. Whether or not the new laws ultimately survive challenges to their constitutionality—which are bound to continue—they represent, for the moment at least, society's interest in using the familial bond as a mechanism of social control.

QUESTIONS FOR DISCUSSION

1. Do you agree with the basic philosophy of parental responsibility laws: that parents can and should be punished for the misdeeds of their minor children? Why or why not?

2. Do you believe that parental responsibility laws such as those described in this box will be effective in reducing the incidence of juvenile delinquency in the United States? Why or why not?

[1] "Now, Parents on Trial," *Newsweek*, October 2, 1989, pp. 54–55.

[2] Deeann Glamser, "Communities Seek to Stem Youth Crime," *USA Today*, February 21, 1995, p. 1A.

[3] "Oregon Will Punish Delinquents' Parents," *USA Today*, July 18, 1995, p. 3A.

[4] *ABC Nightly News*, December 17, 1990.

[5] "Now, Parents on Trial," p. 55.

[6] Kimberly A.C. Wilson, "D.C. Curfew," The Associated Press wire services, June 21, 1995.

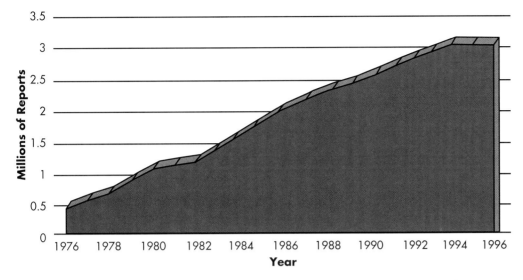

FIGURE 14–4 Reports of child abuse and neglect, 1976–1996. *Source:* The National Committee to Prevent Child Abuse.

Institute of Justice survey found that children "who had been abused or neglected…were more likely to be arrested as juveniles, as adults, and for a violent crime."[96] Although some recent studies[97] have questioned the strength of the relationship, maltreatment and delinquency appear to be intertwined. If so, early intervention into abusive environments may lead to an overall reduction in future criminality.

Unfortunately, however, some studies show that police officers called to the scene of child abuse situations are reluctant to make an arrest or even to report cases to social service agencies.[98] In an effort to support vigorous prosecution of child abuse cases, the National Center for the Prosecution of Child Abuse was formed in 1985.[99] The Center serves as a national clearinghouse for legal and other information on child abuse and publishes comprehensive training manuals and materials for prosecutors and police officers to use in attacking the child abuse problem. (See Figure 14–4.)

Teen Suicide

Children today face many stressors unheard of years ago. Drugs, peer pressure, parents' insistence on success, sexual and other forms of abuse, and violent and broken homes lead some children to take their own lives. In mid-1993, with her mother terminally ill, six-year-old Jackie Johnson of Dania, Florida, told friends she wanted to be with the angels—then calmly stepped in front of a speeding freight train[100] as her brother, sister, and cousin watched. In late May 1991, Susan Zingales and Julie Pallach, two 14-year-old girls, sat on train tracks outside of Chicago[101] with their knees drawn up and their hands covering their ears as they waited for a commuter train to come around a curve in the tracks. Both died at the scene as the train ran over them. The girls' suicides shocked suburban Round Lake, Illinois, where both had been on the Magee Middle School basketball team. The two left behind a suicide note which said that life had become unbearably stressful.

Suicide among teenagers is a quickly growing phenomenon. Only 475 teenage suicides were recorded across the nation in 1960, but by 1991, the most recent year for which reliable data are available, 1,899 such deaths were reported—bringing the suicide rate for 15- to 19-year-olds to 11.1 per 100,000.[102] According to the American Foundation for Suicide Prevention, suicide had become the fourth major cause of death among 5-to 14-year-old children by 1997.[103] Although no one is certain why suicide rates are on the increase, some warning signals have been identified. The American Academy of Child and Adolescent Psychiatry,[104] for example, cites the following indicators that a teenager may be suicidal: (1) changes in eating habits; (2) changes in sleep patterns; (3) withdrawal from friends, family members, and school activities; (4) rebellious or violent behavior; (5) running away; (6) drug or alcohol abuse; (7) disregard for personal hygiene; (8) decline in the quality of school work and grades; (9) frequent headaches, fatigue, and stomach aches; (10) constant boredom; (11) giving away favorite personal possessions; and (12) verbal clues, such as "This is the last time we will be together."

WHAT CAN BE DONE?

Although the problems facing children today are many and varied, there are those who believe that children in trouble share some characteristics in common. Broken homes, little parental supervision, poor role models, lack of educational opportunity, and poverty are seen as factors contributing to delinquency and later criminality. Recently, for example, the Office of Juvenile Justice and Delinquency Prevention (OJJDP) suggested that effective programs intended to reduce both the problems faced by children and the incidence of juvenile delinquency "must emphasize opportunities for healthy social, physical, and mental development." "Such programs," said OJJDP, "must involve all components of the community, including schools, healthcare professionals, families, neighborhood groups, law enforcement, and community-based organizations."[105]

Many who have studied the problems of juveniles come back to basics, such as the quality of family life, economic conditions within neighborhoods, proper socialization, and supportive social institutions when recommending solutions. Recently, for example, the Office of Juvenile Justice and Delinquency Prevention published a "Policymaker's Guide," based upon the findings of a metastudy,[106] which summarized many other studies which have been conducted over decades. The report concluded that (1) there is "a positive relationship between parental conflict and delinquency," (2) "the effect of broken homes on delinquency is real and consistent," (3) the tendency toward delinquency and other problems is enhanced for children living in low-income families, (4) "physical abuse of children leads them into violence later in life," and (5) "children who have criminal parents are at greater risk of becoming delinquent themselves." The study authors suggested that "a healthy home environment, one in which parents and children share affection, cohesion, and involvement, reduces the risk of delinquency," and of other childhood problems, within both one- or two-parent families, and "parental rejection appears to be one of the most significant predictors of delinquency." The report concluded that "parents play a critical role in moral development," and "the quality of [parental] supervision is consistently and strongly related to delinquency" and other childhood problems. As a consequence, said the authors, "parents must adequately monitor their children's behavior, whereabouts, and friends," and that they "must reliably discipline their children for antisocial and prohibited behavior, but must do so neither rigidly nor severely."

Some also suggest that the time has come for a reevaluation of the basic philosophy underlying juvenile courts,[107] so that the decisions of such courts might be more realistic and encompass the needs of the community and of victims—as well as the needs of the children who come before them. As the National Council on Crime and Delinquency explains it, "We believe a more promising direction for the future of U.S. juvenile justice is the rediscovery and updating of the juvenile court's historical vision."[108] Some say the court must make better use of the community resources that are available to it. In 1997, for example, the Office of Juvenile Justice and Delinquency Prevention published a study[109] of efforts by officials in Allegheny County, Pennsylvania, to deal with increased violence and heightened rates of offending among the county's juveniles. Allegheny County, with support from OJJDP, undertook a comprehensive approach to reducing juvenile crime. That approach, said Shay Bilchik, OJJDP administrator, replaced "the community's fragmented response to juvenile violence with a collaborative and coordinated approach." The approach recognizes, said Bilchik, "that juvenile crime is a societal problem that can be solved only with the cooperation of the entire community."[110] The program, which focuses on juveniles who are high risk of engaging in violent crimes, effectively coordinates the efforts of the law enforcement community, public and private agencies, grassroots organizations, and individual citizens. Such coordinated efforts seem to be paying off. Initial reports from the program show reduced rates of juvenile crime in Allegheny County, which exceed reductions in other parts of the state.

Perhaps the most comprehensive proposal yet to emerge for dealing with the problems of today's juveniles is the report of the national Coordinating Council on Juvenile Justice and Delinquency Prevention (CCJJDP). CCJJDP was established by Section 206 of the Juvenile Justice and Delinquency Prevention Act and is an independent organization in the executive

Many parents, driven by a significant increase in crimes against children, make special efforts to assist in the identification of their offspring. Here, a Concord, Massachusetts, policeman fingerprints a young girl. *Bruce M. Wellman, Stock Boston*

branch of the federal government charged with coordinating all federal programs that address juvenile delinquency, detention or care of unaccompanied juveniles, and missing and exploited children. The council is composed of 18 members. Nine are from the federal government and include the Attorney General; Secretaries of Health and Human Services, Labor, Education, and Housing and Urban Development; the OJJDP Administrator; the Director of the Office of National Drug Control; and others. Nine "civilian" representatives round out the Council's membership. The Council's 1996 book-length report, entitled *The National Juvenile Justice Action Plan*,[111] proposed an eight-point national strategy for combating juvenile delinquency, juvenile violence, and attendant problems. Each point is stated in terms of an "objective," as follows:

Objective 1: Provide immediate intervention and appropriate sanctions and treatment for delinquent juveniles. In support of this objective, the Council recommends widespread use of preadjudicatory assessment centers which could offer a "systematic and coordinated way for youth to enter or be diverted from the system…"

Objective 2: Prosecute certain serious, violent, and chronic juvenile offenders in (adult) criminal court. The Council says that "transferring to criminal court those targeted juvenile offenders who are the most chronic and who commit the most serious and violent crimes enables the juvenile justice system to focus its efforts and resources on the much larger group of at-risk youth and less serious and violent offenders who can benefit from a wide range of effective intervention strategies."

Objective 3: Reduce youth involvement with guns, drugs, and gangs. A strong relationship exists, says the Council, between delinquency and violence, and gun possession and drug use among juveniles.

Objective 4: Provide (enhanced) opportunities for children and youth. The Council recommends the development of "comprehensive neighborhood-based programs that help children develop positive life skills and minimize risk factors."

Objective 5: Break the cycle of violence by addressing youth victimization, abuse, and neglect. "Many violent juveniles," says the Council, "have themselves been victims of neglect, abuse, and violence." Hence, breaking the cycle of violence should lead to lower overall rates of offending.

We know that many [youths] who are on the streets are there as a result of sound rational choices they have made for their own safety and welfare, such as avoiding physical abuse, sexual abuse, or extreme neglect at home.

—National Council of Juvenile and Family Court Judges

Objective 6: Strengthen and mobilize communities. The Council observes that "juvenile violence stems in large part from a breakdown of family and community structures." Hence, "nurturing strong families, providing social support systems, and reinforcing healthy cultural norms and values" can do much in the fight against delinquency.

Objective 7: Support the development of innovative approaches to research and evaluation. Better research should lead to more reliable and more useful information in the fight against juvenile crime, says the Council.

Objective 8: Implement an aggressive public outreach campaign on effective strategies to combat juvenile violence. "A well-designed public information campaign is essential to the success of any juvenile violence reduction plan," says the Council. The Council recommends involving the media in creating "a public information campaign designed to persuade young people to avoid violence and dangerous lifestyles, to teach adults about proven antiviolence strategies, and to involve all segments of the community in the fight against juvenile violence."

Although only a few brief details can be provided here, the Council describes its book-length action plan as "a blueprint for community action designed to address and reduce the impact of juvenile violence and delinquency." It says the plan "presents a framework for the handling of delinquent offenders, including possible transfer of the most serious and violent offenders to the criminal justice system, and describes programs that increase opportunities for youth to have a stake in their future."

Significant Court Decisions Affecting Juveniles

Throughout the first half of this century, the U.S. Supreme Court followed a "hands-off" approach to juvenile justice, much like its early approach to prisons (see Chapter 13). The adjudication and further processing of juveniles by the system was left mostly to specialized juvenile courts or local appeals courts. Although one or two early Supreme Court decisions[112] dealt with issues of juvenile justice, it was not until the 1960s that the Court began close legal scrutiny of the principles underlying the system itself. In the pages that follow, we will discuss some of the most important U.S. Supreme Court cases in recent years relating to juvenile justice.

KENT V. U.S. (1966)

The U.S. Supreme Court case which ended the "hands-off" era in juvenile justice was *Kent* v. *U.S.*,[113] decided in 1966. The Kent case focused upon the long-accepted concept of *parens patriae* and signaled the beginning of the Court's systematic review of all lower court practices involving delinquency hearings.

Morris Kent, Jr., age 14, was apprehended in the District of Columbia in 1959 and charged with several house burglaries and an attempted purse snatching. Kent was placed on juvenile probation and released into the custody of his mother. In September 1961, an intruder entered a woman's Washington apartment, took her wallet, and raped her. At the scene police found fingerprints which matched those on file belonging to Morris Kent. At the time, Kent was 16 years old and, according to the laws of the District of Columbia, was still under the exclusive jurisdiction of the juvenile court.

Kent was taken into custody and interrogated. He volunteered information about the crime and spoke about other offenses involving burglary, robbery, and rape. Following interrogation, his mother retained counsel on his behalf. Kent was kept in custody for another week, during which time psychological and psychiatric evaluations were conducted. Reports from professionals conducting the evaluations concluded that Kent was a "victim of severe psychopathology." The juvenile court judge hearing the case did not confer with Kent, his parents, or their lawyer. The judge, however, ruled that Kent should be remanded to the authority of the adult court system, and he was eventually tried in U.S. District Court for the District of Columbia. The judge gave no reasons for assigning Kent to the adult court.

Kent was indicted in criminal court on eight counts of burglary, robbery, and rape. Citing the psychological evaluations performed earlier, Kent's lawyers argued that his behavior was the product of mental disease or defect. Their defense proved fruitless, and Kent was found guilty on six counts of burglary and robbery. He was sentenced to 5 to 15 years in prison on each count.

Kent's lawyers ultimately appealed to the U.S. Supreme Court. They argued that Kent should have been entitled to an adequate hearing at the level of the juvenile court and that, lacking such a hearing, his transfer to adult jurisdiction was unfair.

The Supreme Court, reflecting the Warren court ideologies of the times, agreed with Kent's attorneys, reversed the decision of the district court, and ordered adequate hearings for juveniles being considered for transfer to adult court. At such hearings, the Court ruled, juveniles are entitled to representation by attorneys who must have access to their records.

Although it focused only on a narrow issue, the *Kent* decision was especially important because, for the first time, it recognized the need for at least minimal due process in juvenile court hearings. The *Kent* decision set the stage for what was to come, but it was the *Gault* decision, to which we now turn our attention, that turned the juvenile justice system upside down.

In Re Gault (1967)

On June 8, 1964, Gerald Gault and a friend, Ronald Lewis, were taken into custody by the Sheriff of Gila County, Arizona, on the basis of a neighbor's complaint that the boys had telephoned her, and made lewd remarks. At the time, Gault was on probation for having been in the company of another boy who had stolen a wallet.

When Gerald was apprehended, his parents were both at work. No notice was posted at their house to indicate that their son had been taken into custody, a fact which they later learned from Lewis's parents. Gault's parents could learn very little from authorities. Although they were notified when their son's initial hearing would be held, they were not told the nature of the complaint against him. Nor could they learn the identity of the complainant, who was not present at the hearing.

At the hearing, the only evidence presented were statements made by young Gault and testimony given by the juvenile officer as to what the complainant had alleged. Gault was not represented by counsel. He admitted having made the phone call, but stated that after dialing the number he turned the phone over to his friend, Ronald. After hearing the testimony, Judge McGhee ordered a second hearing, to be held a week later. At the second hearing, Mrs. Gault requested that the complainant be present so that she could identify the voice of the person making the lewd call. Judge McGhee ruled against her request. Finally, young Gault was adjudicated delinquent and remanded to the State Industrial School until his twenty-first birthday.

On appeal, eventually to the U.S. Supreme Court, Gault's attorney argued that his constitutional rights were violated because he had been denied due process. The appeal focused specifically on six areas:

1. *Notice of charges.* Gault was not given enough notice to prepare a reasonable defense to the charges against him.
2. *Right to counsel.* Gault was not notified of his right to an attorney or allowed to have one at his hearing.
3. *Right to confront and to cross-examine witnesses.* The court did not require the complainant to appear at the hearing.
4. *Protection against self-incrimination.* Gault was never advised that he had the right to remain silent nor was he informed that his testimony could be used against him.
5. *Right to a transcript.* In preparing for the appeal, Gault's attorney was not provided a transcript of the adjudicatory hearing.
6. *Right to appeal.* At the time, the state of Arizona did not give juveniles the right to appeal.

The Supreme Court ruled in Gault's favor on four of the six issues raised by his attorneys. The majority opinion read, in part, as follows:

In *Kent* v. *United States*, we stated that the Juvenile Court Judge's exercise of the power of the state as *parens patriae* was not unlimited…. Notice, to comply with due process requirements, must be given sufficiently in advance of scheduled court proceedings so that reasonable opportunity to prepare will be afforded…. The probation officer cannot act as counsel for the child. His role in the adjudicatory hearing, by statute and in fact, is as arresting officer and witness against the child. There is no material difference in this respect between adult and juvenile proceedings of the sort here involved…. A proceeding where the issue is whether the child will be found to be "delinquent" and subjected to the loss of his liberty for years is comparable in seriousness to a felony prosecution. The juvenile needs the assistance of counsel to cope with the problems of law, to make skilled inquiry into the facts, to insist upon regularity of the proceedings, and to ascertain whether he has a defense and to prepare and submit it.[114]

There are no illegitimate children—only illegitimate parents.

—U.S. District Court Judge Leon R. Yankwich, in *Zipkin* v. *Mozon* (1928)

The Court did not agree with the contention of Gault's lawyers relative to appeal nor with their arguments in favor of transcripts. Right to appeal, where it exists, is usually granted by statute or by state constitution—not by the Constitution of the United States. Similarly, the Court did not require a transcript because (1) there is no constitutional right to a transcript and (2) no transcripts are produced in the trials of most adult misdemeanants.

Today, the impact of *Gault* is widely felt in the juvenile justice system. Juveniles are now guaranteed many of the same procedural rights as adults. Most precedent-setting Supreme Court decisions which followed *Gault* further clarified the rights of juveniles, focusing primarily on those few issues of due process that it had not explicitly addressed.

In Re Winship (1970)

At the close of the 1960s, a New York Family Court judge found a 12-year-old boy named Winship delinquent on the basis of a petition which alleged that he had illegally entered a locker and stolen $112 from a pocketbook. The judge acknowledged to those present at the hearing that the evidence in the case might not be sufficient to establish Winship's guilt beyond a reasonable doubt. Statutory authority, however, in the form of the New York Family Court Act required a determination of facts based only on a *preponderance of the evidence*—the same standard required in civil suits. Winship was sent to a training school for 18 months, subject to extensions until his eighteenth birthday.

Winship's appeal to the U.S. Supreme Court centered on the lower court's standard of evidence. His attorney argued that Winship's guilt should have been proven beyond a reasonable doubt—the evidentiary standard of adult criminal trials. The Court agreed, ruling that

the constitutional safeguard of proof beyond a reasonable doubt is as much required during the adjudicatory stage of a delinquency proceeding as are those constitutional guards applied in *Gault*…. We therefore hold…that where a 12 year old child is charged with an act of stealing which renders him liable to confinement for as long as six years, then, as a matter of due process…the case against him must be proved beyond a reasonable doubt.[115]

As a consequence of *Winship*, allegations of delinquency today must be established beyond a reasonable doubt. The court allowed, however, the continued use of the lower evidentiary standard in adjudicating juveniles charged with status offenses. Even though both standards continue to exist, most jurisdictions have chosen to use the stricter burden of proof requirement for all delinquency proceedings.

McKeiver v. Pennsylvania (1971)

Cases like *Winship* and *Gault* have not extended all adult procedural rights to juveniles charged with delinquency. Juveniles, for example, do not have the constitutional right to trial by a jury of their peers. The case of *McKeiver* v. *Pennsylvania*[116] (1971) reiterated what earlier decisions had established and legitimized some generally accepted practices of juvenile courts.

Joseph McKeiver, age 16, was charged with robbery, larceny, and receiving stolen property, all felonies in the state of Pennsylvania. McKeiver had been involved with 20 to 30 other juveniles who chased three teenage boys and took 25 cents from them. He had no previous arrests and was able to demonstrate a record of gainful employment. McKeiver's attorney requested that his client be allowed a jury trial. The request was denied. McKeiver was adjudicated delinquent and committed to a youth development center. McKeiver's attorney pursued a series of appeals and was finally granted a hearing before the U.S. Supreme Court. There he argued that his client, even though a juvenile, should have had the opportunity for a jury trial as guaranteed by the Sixth and Fourteenth Amendments to the Constitution.

The Court, although recognizing existent difficulties in the administration of juvenile justice, held to the belief that jury trials for juveniles were not mandated by the Constitution. In the opinion of the Court

> The imposition of the jury trial on the juvenile court system would not strengthen greatly, if at all, the fact-finding function, and would contrarily, provide an attrition of the juvenile court's assumed ability to function in a unique manner. It would not remedy the defects of the system.... If the jury trial were to be injected into the juvenile court system as a matter of right, it would bring with it into that system the traditional delay, the formality, and the clamor of the adversary system and, possibly, the public trial.... If the formalities of the criminal adjudicative process are to be superimposed upon the juvenile court system, there is little need for its separate existence.

McKeiver v. *Pennsylvania* did not set any new standards. Rather, it reinforced the long-accepted practice of conducting juvenile adjudicatory hearings in the absence of certain due process considerations, particularly those pertaining to trial by jury. It is important to note, however, that the *McKeiver* decision did not specifically prohibit jury trials for juveniles. As a consequence, approximately 12 states today continue to provide for the option of jury trials for juveniles.

Breed v. Jones (1975)

On February 2, 1971, a delinquency complaint was filed against Jones, age 17, alleging that he committed robbery while armed with a deadly weapon. At the adjudicatory hearing, Jones was declared delinquent. A later dispositional hearing determined that Jones was "unfit for treatment as a juvenile," and he was transferred to superior court for trial as an adult. The superior court found Jones guilty of robbery in the first degree and committed him to the custody of the California Youth Authority.

In an appeal eventually heard by the Supreme Court, Jones alleged that his transfer to adult court, and the trial which ensued, placed him in double jeopardy because he had already been adjudicated in juvenile court. Double jeopardy is prohibited by Fifth and Fourteenth Amendments to the Constitution. The state of California argued that superior court trial was only a natural continuation of the juvenile justice process and, as a consequence, did not fall under the rubric of double jeopardy. The state further suggested that double jeopardy existed only where an individual ran the risk of being punished more than once. In the case of *Jones*, no punishment had been imposed by the juvenile court.

The U.S. Supreme Court did not agree that the possibility of only one punishment negated double jeopardy. The Court pointed to the fact that the double jeopardy clause speaks in terms of "potential risk of trial and conviction—not punishment," and concluded that two separate adjudicatory processes were sufficient to warrant a finding of double jeopardy. Jones's conviction was vacated, clearing the way for him to be returned to juvenile court. However, by the time the litigation had been completed, Jones was beyond the age of juvenile court jurisdiction, and he was released from custody.

The *Jones*[117] case severely restricted the conditions under which transfers from juvenile to adult courts may occur. In effect the court mandated that such transfers as do occur must be made prior to an adjudicatory hearing in juvenile court.

Schall v. Martin (1984)

Gregory Martin, age 14, was arrested in New York city, charged with robbery and weapons possession and detained for more than two weeks in a secure detention facility until his hearing. The detention order drew its authority from a New York preventive detention law which allowed for the jailing of juveniles thought to represent a high risk of continued delinquency.

Martin was adjudicated delinquent. His case eventually reached the U.S. Supreme Court on the claim that the New York detention law had effectively denied Martin's freedom prior to conviction and that it was therefore in violation of the Fourteenth Amendment to the U.S. Constitution.

The U.S. Supreme Court upheld the constitutionality of the New York statute. The Court ruled that states have a legitimate interest in preventing future delinquency by juveniles thought to be dangerous. Preventive detention, the Court reasoned, is nonpunitive in its intent and is, therefore, not a "punishment."

While the Schall[118] decision upheld the practice of preventive detention, it seized upon the opportunity provided by the case to impose procedural requirements upon the detaining authority. Consequently, preventive detention today cannot be imposed without (1) prior notice, (2) an equitable detention hearing, and (3) a statement by the judge setting forth the reason(s) for detention.

Illinois v. Montanez (1996)

In 1996, in the case of *Illinois* v. *Montanez*,[119] the U.S. Supreme Court let stand a state court ruling which threw out a voluntary confession made by a juvenile suspect who had been tried as an adult. The confession was held inadmissible because it had not been made in the presence of a parent or other "concerned adult." The Chicago case involved a 15-year-old girl, Jacqueline Montanez, who admitted participating in two May 1992, execution-style slayings of rival gang members.

According to an eyewitness, Montanez and two female companions were laughing and giggling as Montanez forced a young male member of a rival gang into a men's room at Humbolt Park. The witness described hearing a "noise like a firecracker" and seeing Montanez emerge from the men's room alone. The witness also saw the two other girls kill a second rival gang member, according to court records. Montanez was seen to then kick the body, and the three girls ran off. Dead were Jimmy Cruz and Hector Reyes, members of the Latin Kings. Both boys had been shot in the back of the head at close range.

Police later arrested Montanez, said to be "a self-described chief of the Maniac Latin Disciples street gang…and two of her female gang underlings."[120] Montanez was charged as an adult and advised of her right to remain silent as well as to have a lawyer present during questioning. Her mother, who was present in another part of the police station, was not allowed into the interrogation room. Montanez refused a lawyer and made three incriminating statements to police during the course of an eight-hour late-night interrogation. A television videotape prepared for a local news program showed Montanez leaving the interrogation room the next morning flashing gang signs and repeating the phrase "K.K." According to police, "K.K." meant "King Killer," a status Montanez was said to have claimed.

Montanez was tried as an adult. Her confession was admitted at trial, and she was convicted of homicide. The Illinois Court of Appeals, however, reversed the judge's ruling, holding that since the girl's mother, a "concerned adult," was not allowed to be present at her daughter's interrogation, the confession obtained by police should have been suppressed. In refusing to hear the case, the U.S. Supreme Court indicated its agreement with the appellate court's finding.

Because the decision of the U.S. Supreme Court not to review a lower court's ruling in *Illinois* v. *Montanez* did not result in a written opinion, the case may be accorded less weight by jurists than the other cases cited here. Within the contemporary context of growing concern over violent juvenile crime, however, and given the ever increasing number of minors throughout the nation now being charged as adults, the *Montanez* case may prove especially important in the future.

A Summary of Differences in Adult and Juvenile Justice

The cases we've discussed have two common characteristics. They all (1) turn on due process guarantees specified by the Bill of Rights and (2) make the claim that adult due process should serve as a model for juvenile proceedings. Due process guarantees, as interpreted by the Court, are clearly designed to ensure that juvenile proceedings are fair and that the interests of juveniles are protected. Those interpretations do not, however, offer any pretense of providing juveniles with the same kinds of protections guaranteed to adult defendants. While the high court has tended to agree that juveniles are entitled to due process protection, it has refrained from declaring that juveniles have a right to all the aspects of due process afforded adult defendants.

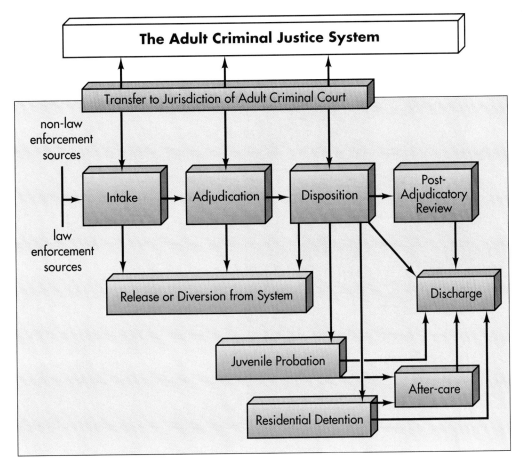

FIGURE 14–5 The Juvenile justice process.

Juvenile court philosophy brings with it other differences from the adult system. Among them are (1) a reduced concern with legal issues of guilt or innocence and an emphasis on the child's best interests; (2) an emphasis on treatment rather than punishment; (3) privacy and protection from public scrutiny through the use of sealed records, laws against publishing the names of juvenile offenders, and so forth; (4) use of the techniques of social science in dispositional decision making, rather than sentences determined by a felt need for punishment; (5) no long-term confinement, with most juveniles being released from institutions by their twenty-first birthday, regardless of offense; (6) separate facilities for juveniles; and (7) broad discretionary alternatives at all points in the process.[121] This combination of court philosophy and due process requirements has created a unique justice system for juveniles, which takes into consideration the special needs of young people while attempting to offer reasonable protection to society. The juvenile justice process is diagrammed in Figure 14–5.

As mentioned earlier, however, existing juvenile court philosophy has come under increasing fire in recent years by those who point to growing levels of violence among juvenile offenders. Recently enacted legislation in a number of states, and proposed legislation at the federal level, is beginning to shift the juvenile justice system away from its traditional emphasis on guidance and rehabilitation and towards the punishment of delinquents. As of this writing, it appears to be only a matter of time before a flood of new federal and state legislation, mandated by surging public demand for personal responsibility among adolescents, leads to a revamping of the present system. Hence, the juvenile justice system of the twenty-first century will, in many respects, likely be quite different from the one we know today.

Each year, tens of thousands of youngsters unnecessarily suffer the negative consequences of costly incarceration in overcrowded, unsafe juvenile detention facilities.

—Douglas W. Nelson, Executive Director, Annie E. Casey Foundation

OTHER LEGAL ASPECTS OF THE JUVENILE JUSTICE PROCESS

Most jurisdictions today have statutes designed to extend the *Miranda* provisions to juveniles. Many police officers routinely offer *Miranda* warnings to juveniles in their custody

A memorial to 12-year-old Polly Klaas, whose kidnapping and murder galvanized the nation. Children today are too often the victims of violent crime and abuse. *Bettmann*

If I were king, I would spend time looking at and helping to improve the juvenile justice system. One of the reasons we are now in this mess is that we have ignored the juvenile justice system for too long.

—Samuel F. Saxton, Director, Prince George's County (Maryland) Department of Corrections

prior to questioning. Less clear, however, is whether or not juveniles can legally waive their *Miranda* rights. A 1979 U.S. Supreme Court ruling held that juveniles should be accorded the opportunity to a knowing waiver where they were old enough and sufficiently educated to understand the consequences of a waiver.[122] A later high court ruling upheld the murder conviction of a juvenile who had been advised of his rights and waived them in the presence of his mother.[123]

An emerging area of juvenile rights centers on investigative procedures. In 1985, for example, the Supreme Court ruled in *New Jersey* v. *T.L.O.*[124] that schoolchildren have a reasonable expectation of privacy in personal property. The case involved a 14-year-old girl who was accused of violating school rules by smoking in a high-school bathroom. A vice principal searched the girl's purse and found evidence of marijuana use. Juvenile officers were called, and the girl was eventually adjudicated in juvenile court and found delinquent.

Upon appeal to the New Jersey supreme court, lawyers for Ms. T.L.O. were successful in having her conviction reversed on the grounds that the search of her purse, as an item of personal property, had been unreasonable. The state's appeal to the U.S. Supreme Court resulted in a ruling which prohibited school officials from engaging in *unreasonable* searches of students or their property. A reading of the Court's decision leads to the conclusion that a search could be considered reasonable if it (1) is based upon a logical suspicion of rule-breaking actions; (2) is required to maintain order, discipline, and safety among students; and (3) does not exceed the scope of the original suspicion.

Legislation Concerning Juvenile Justice

In response to the rapidly increasing crime rates of the late 1960s, Congress enacted the Omnibus Crime Control and Safe Streets Act of 1968. The act was to provide money and technical assistance for states and municipalities seeking to modernize their justice systems. The Safe Streets Act, in combination with monies funneled through the Law Enforcement Assistance Administration; the Youth Development and Delinquency Prevention Administration of the Department of Health, Education, and Welfare; and the Model Cities Program of the Department of Housing and Urban Development provided funding for youth services bureaus. Youth services bureaus had been recommended by the 1967 presidential commission report *The Challenge of Crime in a Free Society*. Such bureaus were to be available

Theory into Practice

A Comparison of Adult and Juvenile Justice Systems in the United States

Adult Proceedings	**Juvenile Proceedings**
Focus on criminality	Focus on delinquency and a special category of "status offenses"
Comprehensive rights against unreasonable searches of person, home, and possessions	Limited rights against unreasonable searches
A right against self-incrimination; a knowing waiver is possible	A right against self-incrimination; waivers are questionable
Assumed innocent until proven guilty	Guilt and innocence are not primary issues; the system focuses on the interests of the child
Adversarial setting	Helping context
Arrest warrants form the basis for most arrests	Petitions or complaints legitimize apprehension
Right to an attorney	Right to an attorney
Public trial	Closed hearing; no right to a jury trial
System goals are punishment and reformation	System goals are protection and treatment
No right to treatment	Specific right to treatment
Possibility of bail or release on recognizance	Release into parental custody
Public record of trial and judgment	Sealed records; may be destroyed by specified age
Possible incarceration in adult correctional facility	Separate facilities at all levels

QUESTIONS FOR DISCUSSION

1. Which of the differences between the adult and juvenile systems of justice shown in this box do you think should be maintained (or even enhanced)? Why?
2. Which differences, if any, between the adult and juvenile systems of justice do you think might best be eliminated (or minimized)? Why?

to police, juvenile courts, and probation departments in order to act as a centralized community resource in handling delinquents and status offenders. Youth services bureaus also handled juveniles who came to them from referrals by schools and young people themselves. Guidelines for setting up and running youth services bureaus were provided through the Youth Development and Delinquency Prevention Administration and the National Council on Crime and Delinquency. Unfortunately, within a decade after their establishment, most youth services bureaus had succumbed to a lack of continued federal funding.

In 1974, recognizing the special needs of juveniles, Congress passed the Juvenile Justice and Delinquency Prevention (JJDP) Act. Employing much the same strategy as the 1968 bill, the Delinquency Prevention Act provided federal grants to states and cities seeking to improve their handling and disposition of delinquents and status offenders.

Nearly all states chose to accept federal monies through the JJDP Act. States had to meet two conditions within five years:

1. Participating states were required to agree to a "separation mandate," under which juveniles were not to be held in institutions where they might come into regular contact with adult prisoners.
2. Status offenders were to be deinstitutionalized, with most being released into the community or placed in foster homes.

Within a few years, institutional populations were cut by more than half, and community alternatives to juvenile institutionalization were rapidly being developed. Jailed juveniles were housed in separate wings of adult facilities or removed from adult jails entirely. When the JJDP Act was reauthorized for funding in 1980, the separation mandate was expanded to include a new requirement that separate juvenile jails be constructed by the states. Studies supporting reauthorization of the JJDP Act in 1984 and 1988, however, found that nearly half the states had failed to come into "substantial compliance" with the jail removal mandate. As a consequence, Congress modified the requirements of the act, continuing funding for states making "meaningful progress" toward removing juveniles from adult jails.[125] In 1996, however, in the face of pressures toward punishment and away from treatment for violent juvenile offenders, the Office of Juvenile Justice and Delinquency Prevention proposed new rules for jailing juveniles. The new rules would (1) allow an adjudicated delinquent to be detained for up to 12 hours in an adult jail before a court appearance, and (2) make it easier for states to house juveniles in separate wings of adult jails.[126]

The Juvenile Justice Process Today

Modern juvenile court jurisdiction rests upon the offender's age and conduct. The majority of states today define a child subject to juvenile court jurisdiction as a person who has not yet turned 18. A few states set the age at 16, and several use 17. Figure 14–6 shows the upper ages of children subject to juvenile court jurisdiction in delinquency matters, by state. When they reach their 18th birthday, children in most states leave the purview of juvenile court and become subject to the jurisdiction of adult criminal courts.

Depending upon the laws of the state and the behavior involved, the jurisdiction of the juvenile court may be exclusive. Exclusive jurisdiction applies when the juvenile court is the only court that has statutory authority to deal with children for specified infractions. For example, status offenses such as truancy normally fall within the exclusive jurisdiction of

FIGURE 14–6   Limit of juvenile court jurisdiction over young offenders, by state.

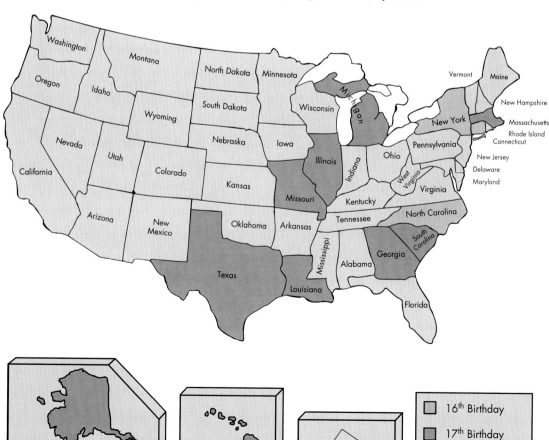

Female Offenders in the Juvenile Justice System

The appropriate treatment of female offenders by the juvenile justice system is a matter of increasing interest to policymakers, practitioners, and the public. Two 1996 studies by the Office of Juvenile Justice and Delinquency Prevention found that females today are entering the juvenile justice system more frequently than ever before—and that they do so at younger ages. According to one study, "[a]lthough male juvenile offenders still account for most delinquent acts, the relative growth in juvenile arrests involving females was more than double the growth for males between 1989 and 1993. While juvenile arrests for violent crimes increased 33% for males during that period, they increased 55% for females. In fact, the ratio of male juvenile arrests to female juvenile arrests declined from eight to one in 1989 to six to one in 1993." Analysis of 1993 and 1994 data (the latest available) from the FBI, the National Juvenile Court Data Archive, and the Children in Custody (CIC) census show that

1. In 1993 U.S. law enforcement agencies made an estimated 570,100 arrests involving females under the age of 18.
2. Between 1989 and 1993 the number of arrests involving female juveniles increased by 23% compared with an 11% increase in arrests of male juveniles.
3. The female proportion of all juvenile arrests grew from 21% to 24% between 1983 and 1993.
4. Juvenile courts in the United States handled an estimated 1,555,200 delinquency cases in 1994, 24% of which involved females.
5. Between 1985 and 1994 the number of juvenile court cases involving females charged with delinquency offenses increased by 54%, while the number of cases involving males increased by 38%.
6. Between 1985 and 1994 the number of female juveniles charged with person offenses (violent crimes) doubled, growing from 2.7% to 5.8% of all delinquency cases.
7. Delinquency cases involving females were less likely than those involving males to be processed formally, more likely to receive probation as the most restrictive disposition, and less likely to result in detention or out-of-home placement.

Sources: Jeffrey A. Butts, "Offenders in Juvenile Court 1994," An OJJDP *Bulletin*, October 1996; and Eileen Poe-Yamagata and Jeffrey A. Butts, *Female Offenders in the Juvenile Justice System* (Washington, D.C.: Office of Juvenile Justice and Delinquency Prevention, June 1996).

juvenile courts. Delinquency, which involves violations of the criminal law, however, is often not within the juvenile court's exclusive jurisdiction. All 50 states, the District of Columbia, and the federal government have judicial waiver provisions which allow for juveniles who commit serious crimes to be bound over to criminal court. Although in practice few such transfers occur, the number of delinquency cases judicially waived to criminal court is increasing. Today approximately 2% of all juveniles are bound over for trial in adult criminal courts.[127] Juveniles who commit violent crimes or who have prior records are among the most likely to be transferred to adult courts.[128] In a hearing which made headlines some years ago, Cameron Kocher, a 10-year-old Pennsylvania youngster, was arraigned as an adult for the murder of 7-year-old Jessica Carr.[129] Cameron, nine years old at the time of the crime, was alleged to have used his father's scope-sighted hunting rifle to shoot the girl from a bedroom window while she was riding on a snowmobile in a neighbor's yard. The two had argued earlier over who would get to ride on the vehicle. The case was resolved in 1992 when the Pennsylvania supreme court overruled Kocher's arraignment as an adult, and the boy was placed on probation.

Where juvenile court authority is not exclusive, the jurisdiction of the court may be original or concurrent. Original jurisdiction means that a particular offense must originate, or begin, with juvenile court authorities. Juvenile courts have original jurisdiction over most delinquency petitions and all status offenses. Concurrent jurisdiction exists where other courts have equal statutory authority to originate proceedings. If a juvenile has committed a homicide, rape, or other serious crime, for example, an arrest warrant may be issued by the adult court.

Some states specify that juvenile courts have no jurisdiction over certain excluded offenses. Delaware, Louisiana, and Nevada, for example, allow no juvenile court jurisdiction over children charged with first-degree murder.

Although institutionalized juveniles are housed separately from adult offenders, juvenile institutions share many of the problems of adult facilities. Here, recent arrivals at a California "boot camp" for juvenile offenders listen to what will be expected of them. *Tony Savino, JB Pictures Ltd.*

How the System Works

The juvenile justice system can be viewed as a process which, when carried to completion, moves through four stages. They are intake, adjudication, disposition, and postadjudication review. Though organizationally similar to the adult criminal justice process, the juvenile system is far more likely to maximize the use of discretion and to employ diversion from further formal processing at every point in the process. Each stage is discussed in the pages that follow.

Intake and Detention Hearings

Juvenile Petition A document filed in juvenile court alleging that a juvenile is delinquent, a status offender, or a dependent, and asking that the court assume jurisdiction over the juvenile, or asking that an alleged delinquent be transferred to a criminal court for prosecution as an adult.

Delinquent juveniles may come to the attention of the police or juvenile court authorities either through arrest or via the filing of a **juvenile petition** by an aggrieved party. Juvenile petitions are much like criminal complaints in that they allege illegal behavior. Petitions are most often filed by teachers, school administrators, neighbors, store managers, or others who have frequent contact with juveniles. Parents, unable to control the behavior of their teenage children, are the source of many other petitions. Crimes in progress result in other juveniles coming to the attention of the police. Three quarters of all referrals to juvenile court come directly from law enforcement authorities.[130]

Many police departments have juvenile officers, specially trained in dealing with juveniles. Because of the emphasis on rehabilitation which characterizes the juvenile justice process, juvenile officers usually have a number of discretionary alternatives available to them in the form of special programs, especially in the handling of nonviolent offenses. In Delaware County, Pennsylvania, for example, police departments participate in "Youth Aid Panels." Such panels are composed of private citizens who volunteer their services in order to provide an alternative to the formal juvenile court process. Youngsters who are referred to a panel and agree to abide by the decision of the group are diverted from additional handling by the juvenile court.

Real Justice Conferencing (RJC), another Pennsylvania program, provides another example of a diversionary program. Started in Bethlehem, Pennsylvania, in 1995, RJC is intended to serve as a model for other cities. RJC claims to be a "cost-effective new approach to juvenile crime, school misconduct, and violence prevention." It makes use of family group conferences (sometimes called "community conferences") in lieu of school disciplinary or judicial processes—or where that is not appropriate, as a supplement to those processes. The family group conference (FGC) is built around a restorative justice model and allows young offenders to tell what they did, to hear from those they have affected, and to participate in deciding how to repair the harm caused by their actions. Successful RJC participants may avoid further handling by the more formal mechanisms of the juvenile justice process.

Even youth who are eventually diverted from the system may spend some time in custody. One juvenile case in five involves detention prior to adjudication.[131] Unlike the adult system, where jail is seen as the primary custodial alternative for persons awaiting a first appearance, the use of secure detention for juveniles is acceptable only as a last resort. Detention hearings will investigate whether candidates for confinement represent a "clear and immediate danger to themselves and/or to others." Such a judgment, made through a detention hearing, is normally rendered within 24 hours of apprehension. Runaways, since they are often not dangerous, are especially difficult to confine. Juveniles who are not detained are generally released into the custody of their parents or guardians or into a supervised temporary shelter such as a group home.

Detention hearings are conducted by the juvenile court judge or an officer of the court, such as a juvenile probation officer who has been given the authority to make **intake** decisions. Intake officers, like their police counterparts, have substantial discretion. Along with detention, they can choose diversion and outright dismissal of some or all of the charges against the juvenile. Diverted juveniles may be sent to job training programs, mental health facilities, drug treatment programs, educational counselors, or other community service agencies. When caring parents are present who can afford private counseling or therapy, intake officers may release the juvenile into their custody with the understanding that they will provide for treatment. The National Center for Juvenile Justice estimates that more than half of all juvenile cases disposed of at intake are handled informally, without a petition, and are dismissed or diverted to a social service agency.[132]

Intake The first step in decision making regarding a juvenile whose behavior or alleged behavior is in violation of the law or could otherwise cause a juvenile court to assume jurisdiction.

Preliminary Hearing

A preliminary hearing may be held in conjunction with the detention hearing. The purpose of the preliminary hearing is to determine if there is probable cause to believe the juvenile committed the alleged act. At the hearing, the juvenile, along with his or her parents or guardian, will be advised of his or her rights as established by state legislation and court precedent. If probable cause is established, the juvenile may still be offered diversionary options, such as an "improvement period" or "probation with adjudication." These alternatives usually provide a one-year period during which the juvenile must avoid legal difficulties, attend school, and obey his or her parents. Charges may be dropped at the end of this informal probationary period, provided the juvenile has met the conditions specified.

Where a serious offense is involved, statutory provisions may allow for transfer of the case to adult court at the prosecuting attorney's request. Transfer hearings are held in juvenile court and focus on (1) the applicability of transfer statutes to the case under consideration and (2) whether the juvenile is amenable to treatment through the resources available to the juvenile justice system. Exceptions exist where statutes mandate transfer (as may be the case with first degree murder).

Adjudication

Adjudicatory hearings for juveniles are similar to adult trials, with some notable exceptions. Similarities derive from the fact that the due process rights of children and adults are essentially the same. Differences include

Adjudicatory Hearing The courtroom stage of a juvenile hearing, which is similar in substance to a criminal hearing or trial.

1. *No Right to Trial by Jury.* As we discussed in our review of the U.S. Supreme Court decision in the case of *McKeiver* v. *Pennsylvania*,[133] juveniles do not have a constitutional right to trial by jury.[134] Nor do most states provide juveniles with a statutory opportunity for jury trial.

    Some jurisdictions, however, allow juveniles to be tried by their peers. The juvenile court in Columbus County, Georgia, for example, began experimenting with peer juries in 1980.[135] In Georgia, peer juries are composed of youths under the age of 17 who receive special training by the court. Jurors are required to be successful in school and may not be under the supervision of the court or have juvenile petitions pending against

Juvenile court in action. Juvenile courts are expected to act in the best interests of the children who come before them. *Billy Barnes, Stock Boston*

them. Training consists of classroomlike exposure to the philosophy of the juvenile court system, Georgia's juvenile code, and Supreme Court decisions affecting juvenile justice.[136] The county's youthful jurors are used only in the dispositional (or sentencing) stage of the court process, and then only when adjudicated youths volunteer to go before the jury.

Another early program that has served as a model for many others can be found in Odessa, Texas. The Odessa Teen Court was started by the local Junior League in 1983. Since then it has handled thousands of cases, with all major courtroom participants— other than the judge—coming from the ranks of local juveniles. Youngsters fill the role of prosecutor, defense attorney, and a four-person peer jury. As in Georgia, the court does not decide guilt, but imposes sentences only. Defendants are selected by the police from among youngsters who have already pled guilty to relatively minor offenses. The court has been amazingly successful in reducing recidivism. Only 2% of defendants in Odessa's Teen Court go on to commit another crime. As a spokesperson for the Odessa Police Department put it, "It's one peer saying to another, 'This is not acceptable behavior.'…[T]he defendant cannot come back on the grown-up and say, 'You adults don't understand what I am going through.'"[137]

By 1997, 250 **teen court** programs were in operation in 30 states.[138] The Office of Juvenile Justice and Delinquency Prevention (OJJDP) notes that teen courts are "an effective intervention in many jurisdictions where enforcement of misdemeanor charges is sometimes given low priority because of heavy caseloads and the need to focus on more serious offenders."[139] Teen courts, says OJJDP, "present communities with opportunities to teach young people valuable life and coping skills and promote positive peer influence for youth who are defendants and for volunteer youth who play a variety of roles in the teen court process."

2. *Emphasis on Privacy.* Another important distinctive characteristic of the juvenile system derives from its concern with privacy. Juvenile hearings are not open to the public or to the mass media. Witnesses are permitted to be present only to offer testimony and may not stay for the hearing. No transcript of the proceedings is created. One purpose of the emphasis is to prevent juveniles from being negatively labeled by the community.

Theory into Practice

JUVENILE COURTS ARE VERY DIFFERENT FROM ADULT COURTS

The language used in juvenile courts is less harsh. For example, juvenile courts

- Accept "petitions" of "delinquency" rather than criminal complaints.

- Conduct "hearings," not trials.
- "Adjudicate" juveniles to be "delinquent" rather than find them guilty of a crime.
- Order one of a number of available "dispositions" rather than sentences.

Source: Bureau of Justice Statistics, *Report to the Nation on Crime and Justice*, 2nd ed. (Washington, D.C.: U.S. Department of Justice, 1988), p. 78.

3. *Informality.* While the adult criminal trial is highly structured, the juvenile hearing borders on informality. The courtroom atmosphere may give more the appearance of a friendly discussion than of adversarial battle. The juvenile court judge will take an active role in the fact-finding process rather than serving as arbitrator between prosecution and defense.

4. *Speed.* Informality, the lack of a jury, and the absence of an adversarial environment promote speed. While the adult trial may run into days, or even months, the juvenile hearing is normally completed in a matter of hours or days.

5. *Evidentiary Standard.* Upon completion of the hearing, the juvenile court judge must weigh the evidence. If the charge involves a status offense, the judge may adjudicate the juvenile as a status offender upon finding that a "preponderance of the evidence" supports such a finding. A preponderance of evidence exists when evidence of an offense is more convincing than evidence offered to the contrary. If the charge involves a criminal-type offense, the evidentiary standard rises to the level of "reasonable doubt."

6. *Philosophy of the Court.* Even in the face of strong evidence pointing to the offender's guilt, the judge may decide that it is not in the child's best interests to be adjudicated delinquent. The judge also has the power, even after the evidence is presented, to divert the juvenile from the system. Juvenile court statistics indicate that only 55% of cases disposed of by juvenile courts in 1994 were processed formally. Formal processing involves the filing of a petition requesting an adjudicatory or transfer hearing. Informal cases, on the other hand, are handled without a petition. Among informally handled (nonpetitioned) delinquency cases, half (50%) were dismissed by the court. Most of the remainder resulted in voluntary probation (28%) or other dispositions (22%), but a small number (1%) involved voluntary out-of-home placements.[140]

Disposition

Once a juvenile has been found delinquent, the judge will set a time for a **dispositionary hearing,** which is similar to an adult sentencing hearing. Dispositional hearings are used to decide what action the court should take relative to the child. As in adult courts, the judge may order a presentence investigation before making a dispositional decision. Such investigations are conducted by special court personnel, sometimes called juvenile court counselors who are, in effect, juvenile probation officers. Attorneys on both sides of the issue will also have the opportunity to make recommendations concerning dispositional alternatives.

The juvenile justice system typically provides the judge a much wider range of sentencing alternatives than does the adult system. Two major classes of dispositional alternatives exist: to confine or not to confine. Because rehabilitation is still the primary objective of the juvenile court, the judge is likely to select the "least restrictive alternative" available in meeting the needs of the juvenile while recognizing the legitimate concerns of society for protection.

Dispositionary Hearing The final stage in the processing of adjudicated juveniles, in which a decision is made on the form of treatment or penalty which should be imposed upon the child.

Juvenile Disposition The decision of a juvenile court, concluding a disposition hearing, that an adjudicated juvenile be committed to a juvenile correctional facility or be placed in a juvenile residence, shelter, or care or treatment program or be required to meet certain standards of conduct or be released.

Most judges decide not to confine juveniles in their dispositions. Juvenile court statistics[141] indicate that in more than half (53%) of all adjudicated delinquency cases, juveniles are placed on formal probation. Probationary disposition usually means that juveniles will be released into the custody of a parent or guardian and ordered to undergo some form of training, education, or counseling. As in the adult system, juveniles placed on probation may be ordered to pay fines or make restitution. In 15% of adjudicated delinquency cases, courts order juveniles to pay restitution or a fine, to participate in some form of community service, or to enter a treatment or counseling program—dispositions with minimal continuing supervision by probation staff. Because juveniles rarely have financial resources or jobs, most economic sanctions take the form of court-ordered work programs, as in the refurbishing of schools, cleaning of school busses, and so on.

One innovative probation program for juveniles, run by the Lehigh County (Pennsylvania) Juvenile Probation Office, uses a school-based probation program, which places juvenile probation officers in public schools. The officers function much like school counselors, paying special attention to the needs of their charges in areas such as tutoring, attendance, and grades. In-school probation officers work at addressing problems as diverse as getting students to school on time (by developing personal schedules), raising grades (through improving study skills, tutoring, and sitting in on classes), and successful involvement in extracurricular activities. The program, which began in 1990, has since been expanded through a federal grant to 29 other Pennsylvania counties.[142]

Of course, not all juveniles who are adjudicated delinquent receive probation. More than one quarter (29%) of adjudicated cases in 1994 resulted in the youth being placed outside the home in a residential facility. In a relatively small number of cases (3%), the juvenile was adjudicated delinquent, but the case was then dismissed or the youth was otherwise released.[143]

Secure Institutions for Juveniles

Juveniles who evidence the potential for serious new offenses may be ordered to participate in rehabilitative programs within a secure environment such as a youth center or training school. As of February 15, 1995, approximately 69,075 juveniles were held under custodial supervision in the United States.[144] This translates into an overall nationwide custody rate of 350 juveniles in custody per 100,000 juveniles.[145] Most confined juveniles are held in semisecure facilities designed to look less like prisons and more like residential high-school campuses. Most states, however, operate at least one secure facility for juveniles, intended as a home for the most recalcitrant youthful offenders. Halfway houses, boot camps,[146] ranches, forestry camps, wilderness programs, group homes, and state-hired private facilities also hold a proportion of the total number of juveniles reported under confinement. Children placed in group homes continue to attend school and live in a familylike environment in the company of other adjudicated children, shepherded by "house parents." Figure 14–7 shows juvenile custody rates by state.

Under our Constitution, the condition of being a boy does not justify a kangaroo court.

—In Re Gault, 387 U.S. 1 (1967).

The operative philosophy of custodial programs for juveniles focuses squarely on the rehabilitative ideal. Juveniles are usually committed to secure facilities for indeterminate periods of time, with the typical stay being less than one year. Release is often timed to coincide with the beginning or end of the school year.

Most juvenile facilities are small, with 80% designed to hold 40 residents or fewer.[147] Many institutionalized juveniles are held in the approximately 1,000 homelike facilities across the nation, which are limited to 10 residents or fewer.[148] At the other end of the scale are the nation's 70 large juvenile institutions, each designed to hold over 200 hard-core delinquents.[149] Residential facilities for juveniles are intensively staffed. One study found that staff members outnumber residents 10 to 9 on the average in state-run institutions, and by an even greater ratio in privately run facilities.[150]

Jurisdictions vary widely in their use of secure detention for juveniles. In 1995, juvenile custody populations ranged from a low of 24 in Vermont, to a high of 19,567 in California.[151] Such differences reflect population differences as well as economic realities and philosophical beliefs. Some jurisdictions, like California, expect rehabilitative costs to be born by the state rather than by families or local government agencies. Hence, California shows a higher rate of institutionalization than many other states. Similarly, some states have more firmly embraced the reformation ideal and are more likely to use diversionary options where juveniles are concerned.

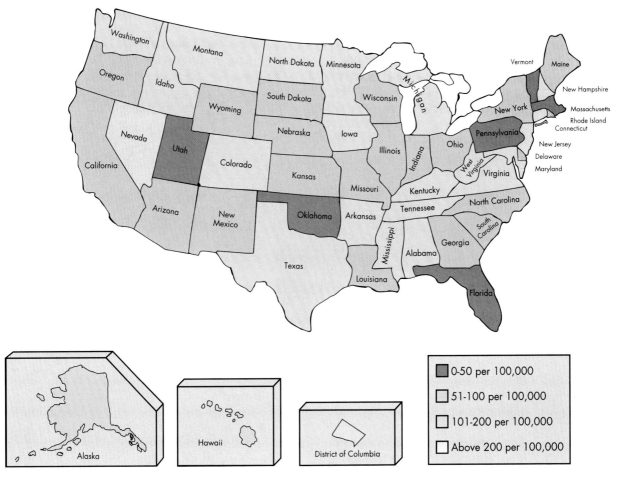

FIGURE 14–7 Juvenile custody rates by state.

Characteristics of Juveniles in Confinement

Institutionalized juveniles are a small but special category of young people with serious problems. A report on institutionalized youth by the Bureau of Justice Statistics found 12 striking characteristics: of the total,

1. 93.1% were male.
2. 46.8% were ethnic minorities or black.
3. 12.7% had completed the sixth grade or less.
4. 2.9% had completed high school.
5. 70% did not live with both parents while growing up.
6. 43% had been arrested more than five times, with over 20% experiencing more than ten arrests in the past year.
7. 39.3% were being held for a violent offense.
8. More than 60% used drugs regularly, and almost 40% were under the influence of drugs at the time of the commission of their offense.
9. 82.2% had previously been on probation.
10. 58.5% had previously been incarcerated.
11. The average age was 15.7 years, with 12.8 years as the average age at first arrest.
12. On average, institutionalized juveniles had spent 8.3% of their lives incarcerated.[152]

Overcrowding in Juvenile Facilities

As in adult prisons, overcrowding exists in many juvenile institutions. A recent survey[153] found half of all states reporting overcrowding in juvenile facilities, while 22 states were operating facilities at more than 50% over capacity. The most overcrowded juvenile correctional systems were reported operating in Maryland, California, Wisconsin, and Ohio—all of which were well over 200% of capacity (that is, holding more than twice the number of youthful offenders they were designed to hold) at the time of the study.

A recent national study[154] of the conditions of confinement in juvenile detention facilities conducted by the Office of Juvenile Justice and Delinquency Prevention (OJJDP) found that "there are several areas in which problems in juvenile facilities are substantial and widespread—most notably living space, health care, security, and control of suicidal behavior." Using a variety of evaluative criteria, the study found that 47% of juveniles were confined in facilities whose populations exceeded their reported design capacity, and that 33% of residents had to sleep "in rooms that were smaller than required by nationally recognized standards." To address the problem, study authors recommended the use of alternative placement options so that only juveniles judged the most dangerous to their communities need be confined in secure facilities. Similarly, because injuries to residents were found most likely to occur within large dormitory-like settings, the OJJDP study recommended that "large dormitories be eliminated from juvenile facilities." Finally, the study recommended that "all juveniles be screened for risk of suicidal behavior immediately upon their admission to confinement," and that initial health screenings should be "carried out promptly at admission." Other problems, which OJJDP found "still important enough to warrant attention," included education and treatment services. Further study of both areas, said OJJDP, is needed.

Private facilities are used by a number of states, and a recent survey found 13 states contracting with 328 private facilities—most of which were classified as halfway houses—for the custody of adjudicated juveniles.[155] In the past few years, admissions to private facilities (comprised primarily of halfway houses, group homes, shelters, and ranches, camps, or farms) have increased by more than 100%, compared with only about 10% for public facilities (mostly detention centers and training schools).[156] The fastest-growing category of detained juveniles involves drug and alcohol offenders. Approximately 12% of all juvenile detainees are being held because of alcohol and drug-related offenses.[157] Reflecting widespread socioeconomic disparities, an OJJDP report found that "a juvenile held in a public facility…was most likely to be black, male, between 14 and 17 years of age, and held for a delinquent offense such as a property crime or a crime against a person. On the other hand, a juvenile held in custody in a private facility…was most likely to be white, male, 14 to 17 years of age, and held for a nondelinquent offense such as running away, truancy, or incorrigibility."[158] The report also noted that "juvenile corrections has become increasingly privatized."

Postadjudicatory Review

The detrimental effects of institutionalization on young offenders may make the opportunity for appellate review more critical for juveniles than it is for adults. However, federal court precedents have yet to establish a clear right to appeal from juvenile court. Even so, most states do have statutory provisions that make such appeals possible.[159]

From a practical point of view, juvenile appeals may not be as consequential as are appeals of adult criminal convictions. Most juvenile complaints are handled informally, while only a relatively small proportion of adjudicated delinquents are placed outside the family. Moreover, because sentence lengths are short for most confined juveniles, appellate courts hardly have time to complete the review process before release occurs.

Dissatisfaction with Today's System

As noted throughout this chapter, the juvenile justice system is not without its critics, and a huge potential for reform of the system now looms on the horizon (see the box "Theory Into Practice" entitled "Juvenile Justice Today—A System in Transition" on page 577). An emerging recognition of the fact that a small number of "hard-core" delinquents are responsible for repeated serious criminal activity, combined with a concern for public safety, has laid the groundwork for a burgeoning reform movement which focuses on three areas: (1) lessening the degree of privacy which surrounds juvenile proceedings; (2) increasing penalties associated with certain kinds of delinquent acts; and (3) reducing diversionary opportunities for habitual, violent, and serious offenders. Modern critics of the juvenile justice system argue that it is time to replace a court philosophy ostensibly based upon achieving the best interests of the child with one which gives primacy to justice.[160] The overall thrust of the present-day juvenile justice reform movement is intended to bring about changes which would recognize the harm suffered by victims of delinquency and which would result in juveniles being treated more like adults.

While privacy may shield the juvenile from labeling, it does little to protect society from further victimization. A few years ago, for example, a 27-year-old teacher, pregnant with her first child, was stabbed repeatedly by a 14-year-old transfer student with a past record of violence and disruption.[161] School officials, however, had not had access to the child's previous record. To protect the public, the National School Safety Center recommends modifying state and federal laws to allow for a sharing of information about dangerous juveniles on a need-to-know basis.[162] The movement to lessen privacy is consistent with the Bureau of Justice Statistics' belief that "the nation's information policy (is moving) in the direction of enhancing the public's access to criminal history record information."[163] A number of states have since moved to open juvenile court hearings to the public, especially in serious cases. In 1995, for example, Pennsylvania opened juvenile court proceedings to the public for youths 14 years of age and older who have been charged with felonies.

Those who cite continued and frequent delinquent acts by a minority of adjudicated delinquents are in favor of stiffer penalties. The same critics argue that the present system is limited in its capacity to reform, often releasing dangerous juvenile offenders back to the streets. Evidence from the Habitual Serious and Violent Juvenile Offender Program, which targeted 13 cities for vigorous prosecution of violent and repeat offenders, tends to support such claims. The program combined careful case screening with victim/witness support to remove habitual juvenile offenders effectively from society.[164] Supporting the movement toward stiffer penalties for delinquent youth, sentencing guidelines for juveniles proposed by the Justice Department recommend that state legislatures adopt fixed penalties for certain law violations.[165] In a similar move, the Office of Juvenile Justice and Delinquency Prevention has developed a monetary and direct victim service restitution program for juvenile courts.[166] Called RESTTA (for Restitution Education, Specialized Training, and Technical Assistance Program), the program provides local juvenile courts with the information needed to make restitution a meaningful part of the dispositional process.

Given the continuing influence of the juvenile court movement and the principles it institutionalized within our judicial system, many are reluctant to directly impose "punishment" in the handling of juvenile offenders. Hence, those who would change the system stress a need for "accountability," "discipline," and "sanctions." OJJDP, for example, now calls for "a systemwide strategy of intervention, treatment, and rehabilitation for serious, violent, and chronic juvenile offenders that combines accountability and sanctions with increasingly intensive community-based intervention, treatment, and rehabilitation services if a juvenile reoffends."[167]

On the other side of the reform movement are those who argue for still greater protections on behalf of juveniles. Because they lack all the rights of adults, such critics say, juveniles are apt to be "railroaded" through a system which does not live up to its purpose of protecting children.[168] Others cite the criminalizing influence of juvenile institutions and suggest that juveniles should be kept from institutionalization wherever possible.

In 1993 the National Juvenile Corrections and Detention Forum, a group of leading juvenile correctional administrators from all 50 states, developed a list of recommendations intended to guide the juvenile justice system into the next century. Among the recommendations were[169]

1. Develop, introduce, and pass congressional legislation that guarantees due process rights and humane treatment to juveniles in pre- and postdispositional confinement.
2. Prohibit the use of detention as a dispositional (preadjudicatory) placement.
3. Develop and implement a juvenile justice philosophy of using the least restrictive placement that is consistent with providing for public safety.
4. Develop and implement quality assurance programs to ensure continuous quality of life and services in juvenile justice facilities.

Visit the *CJToday* Web page and click on "Web Chapters," then "Chapter 14." Follow the "find the facts" links in order to learn more about juvenile justice and the problems facing juveniles today.

SUMMARY

Children are the future hope of each mature generation, and under today's laws they occupy a special status. That status is tied closely to cultural advances which occurred in the Western world during the past 200 years, resulting in a reevaluation of the child's role.

Many children today lead privileged lives which would have been unimaginable a few scant decades ago. Others are not so lucky, and the problems they face are as diverse as they are staggering. Some problems are a direct consequence of increased national wealth and the subsequent removal of children from the economic sphere, which has lessened expectations for responsible behavior during childhood years. Others grow from the easy availability of illicit drugs—a fact which has dramatically altered the early life experiences of many children, especially in the nation's large cities. Finally, the decline of traditional institutions and the seeming plethora of broken homes throughout our country have combined with the moral excesses of adult predators interested in the acquisition of sexual services from children, to lead to a quick abandonment of innocence by many young people today. Gang involvement, child abuse and neglect, juvenile runaways and suicides, and serious incidents of delinquency have been the result.

In the face of these massive challenges, the juvenile justice system's commitment to a philosophy of protection and restoration has begun to crumble. The present system, for the most part, still differs substantially from the adult criminal justice system in the multitude of opportunities it provides for diversion and in the emphasis it places on rehabilitation rather than punishment. The professionalization of delinquency, however, the hallmark of which is repetitive and often violent criminal involvement of juveniles in drug-related gang activity, represents a major new challenge to the idealism of the juvenile justice system. Addressing that challenge may well prove to be the most significant determinate of system change as we enter the twenty-first century.

DISCUSSION QUESTIONS

1. How does the philosophy and purpose of the juvenile justice system differ from that of the adult system of criminal justice? In your opinion, should children continue to receive what many regard as preferential treatment from the court? Why or why not?

2. What was the impact of the *Gault* decision on juvenile justice in America? What adult rights were not accorded juveniles by *Gault*?

3. Describe the six categories of children found under the laws of most states. Do some of the problems faced by children today necessitate the development of new categories? If so, what might such categories be? If not, how are existing categories able to handle illicit drug use by juveniles or the repetitive and apparently vicious delinquency of some inner-city gang members?

4. In your opinion, is the concept of "status offenses" still useful in our system of juvenile justice? Should laws which circumscribe status offenses be retained or abandoned? Why?

5. One explanation given in this chapter for the rise in delinquency rates is the lack of meaningful roles for juveniles in modern society. Do you agree with this explanation? Why or why not?

6. One problem with secrecy in juvenile hearings and records is that innocent others throughout society are not protected from continued delinquency. Do you think that secrecy in the juvenile justice system is justified? Or do you think that those who stand to be injured by the future delinquency of adjudicated offenders should be forewarned? Why or why not?

7. What do you think of "parental-responsibility laws," described in this chapter? Do you think such laws are useful? Are they fair? Can they achieve their desired result? Would you change them in any way? If so, how?

 WEB WATCH

Access the *Criminal Justice Today* site on the World Wide Web by pointing your Web browser at http://www.prenhall.com/cjtoday. Once there, click on "Web Chapters" then select "Chapter 14: Juvenile Delinquency" in order to access electronic information and other sites of relevance to this chapter. You may also wish to enter the Global Town Meeting, which provides facilities for the posting of electronic messages for others to read. Messages are arranged by topic, with new topics constantly being added.

NOTES

1. Elliot Grossman, "Toughlove Parents Scared," *The Allentown Morning Call*, March 7, 1995, p. B1.
2. Kevin Johnson, "In a Gang, 'This Could Be You,'" *USA Today*, September 8, 1994, p. 3A.
3. Ibid.
4. Ibid.
5. FBI, *Uniform Crime Reports 1996* (Washington, D.C.: U.S. Government Printing Office, 1997).
6. Where "juvenile" refers to persons under 18 years of age.
7. Alfred Blumstein, "Systems Analysis and the Criminal Justice System" *Annals of the American Academy of Political and Social Science*, Vol. 474 (1967).
8. Howard N. Snyder and Melissa Sickmund, *Juvenile Offenders and Victims: A National Report* (Washington, D.C.: National Center for Juvenile Justice, 1995).
9. James Alan Fox, *Trends in Juvenile Violence: A Report to the United States Attorney General on Current and Future Rates of Juvenile Offending* (Washington, D.C.: Bureau of Justice Statistics, 1996).
10. "Young in Years, Old at Crime," *USA Today*, April 26, 1993, p. 2A.
11. Maria Eftimidaes, et al, "Why Are Kids Killing?" *People Weekly*, June 23, 1997, pp. 46–53.
12. For more details, see Carla Koehl, "Tragedy at the Prom," *Newsweek*, June 23, 1997, p. 64; and Janet Zimmerman, "'Prom Mom' Charged with Murder," *USA Today*, June 25, 1997, p. 1A.
13. Marc Peyser, "Death in a Dumpster," *Newsweek*, December 2, 1996, pp. 92–94.
14. A reform movement, now underway, may soon lead to changes in the way juvenile records are handled.
15. For an excellent review of the handling of juveniles through history, see Wiley B. Sanders, ed., *Juvenile Offenders for a Thousand Years* (Chapel Hill: University of North Carolina Press, 1970).
16. Robert M. Mennel, *Thorns and Thistles: Juvenile Delinquents in the United States, 1925–1940* (Hanover, NH: University Press of New England, 1973).
17. Arnold Binder, et al., *Juvenile Delinquency: Historical, Cultural, Legal Perspectives* (New York: Macmillan, 1988), p. 45
18. Thomas A. Johnson, *Introduction to the Juvenile Justice System* (St. Paul, MN: West, 1975), p. 1.
19. Charles E. Springer, *Justice for Juveniles*, 2nd printing (Washington, D.C.: Office of Juvenile Justice and Delinquency Prevention, 1987), p. 18.
20. Ibid., p. 50.
21. See Sanford Fox, "Juvenile Justice Reform: An Historical Perspective," in Sanford Fox, *Modern Juvenile Justice: Cases and Materials* (St. Paul, MN: West, 1972), pp. 15–48.
22. *Ex parte Crouse*, 4 Whart. 9 (Pa., 1839).
23. Fox, "Juvenile Justice Reform," p. 27
24. Anthony Platt, *The Child Savers: The Invention of Delinquency*, 2nd ed. (Chicago: University of Chicago Press, 1977).
25. Ibid., p. 29.
26. *People ex rel. O'Connell* v. *Turner*, 55 Ill. 280, 8 Am. Rep. 645.
27. Johnson, *Introduction to the Juvenile Justice System*, p. 3.
28. Ibid., p. 3.
29. Ibid.
30. Fox, "Juvenile Justice Reform," p. 47.
31. Ibid., p. 5.
32. Principles adapted from Robert G. Caldwell, "The Juvenile Court: Its

Development and Some Major Problems," in Rose Giallombardo, ed., *Juvenile Delinquency: A Book of Readings* (New York: John Wiley, 1966), p. 358.

33. Clifford Shaw, Frederick Zorbaugh, Henry McKay, and Leonard Cottrell, *Delinquency Areas* (Chicago: University of Chicago Press, 1929).

34. Richard A. Cloward and Lloyd E. Ohlin, *Delinquency and Opportunity: A Theory of Delinquent Gangs* (New York: The Free Press, 1960).

35. Walter B. Miller, "Lower Class Culture as a Generating Milieu of Gang Delinquency," *Journal of Social Issues*, Vol. 14, no. 3 (1958), pp. 5–19.

36. Albert K. Cohen, *Delinquent Boys, The Culture of the Gang* (New York: The Free Press of Glencoe, 1955).

37. David Matza, *Delinquency and Drift* (New York: John Wiley, 1964).

38. Gresham M. Sykes and David Matza, "Techniques of Neutralization: A Theory of Delinquency," *American Sociological Review*, Vol. 22 (December 1957), pp. 664–666.

39. Marvin Wolfgang, Robert Figlio, and Thorsten Sellin, *Delinquency in a Birth Cohort* (Chicago: University of Chicago Press, 1972).

40. Marvin Wolfgang, Terence Thornberry, and Robert Figlio, *From Boy to Man, From Delinquency to Crime* (Chicago: University of Chicago Press, 1987).

41. Steven P. Lab, "Analyzing Change in Crime and Delinquency Rates: The Case for Cohort Analysis," *Criminal Justice Research Bulletin*, Vol. 3, no. 10 (Huntsville, TX: Sam Houston State University, 1988), p. 2.

42. Stuart Greenbaum, "Drugs, Delinquency, and Other Data," in *Juvenile Justice*, Vol. 2, no. 1 (Spring/Summer 1994), pp. 2–8.

43. For another interesting analysis, see Robert J. Sampson and John H. Laub, *Crime in the Making* (Cambridge, MA: Harvard University Press, 1993).

44. For further information on the causes of juvenile delinquency, along with suggestions for control of delinquency, see *Critical Criminal Justice Issues: Task Force Reports From the American Society of Criminology* (Washington, D.C.: National Institute of Justice, 1997).

45. Eileen M. Garry, "Truancy: First Step to a Lifetime of Problems," *A Juvenile Justice Bulletin* (Washington, D.C.: Office of Juvenile Justice and Delinquency Prevention, 1996).

46. Marcia Chaiken and David Huizinga, "Early Prevention of and Intervention for Delinquency and Related Problem Behavior," in *Critical Criminal Justice Issues:*

Task Force Reports From the American Society of Criminology (Washington, D.C.: National Institute of Justice, 1997).

47. Ibid.

48. Patricia Torbet, Richard Gable, Hunter Hurst IV, Imogene Montgomery, Linda Szymanski, and Douglas Thomas, *State Responses to Serious and Violent Juvenile Crime* (Washington, D.C.: Office of Juvenile Justice and Delinquency Prevention, 1996).

49. Ibid., p. xi.

50. Ibid.

51. "Going 'Wilding': Terror in Central Park," *Newsweek*, May 1, 1989, p. 27.

52. "Angry Teens Explode in Violent Wilding Sprees," *USA Today*, April 27, 1989, p. 1D.

53. Marco R. della Cava, "The Societal Forces That Push Kids Out of Control," *USA Today*, April 27, 1989, p. 6D.

54. Ruth Shonle Cavan, *Juvenile Delinquency: Development, Treatment, Control*, 2nd ed. (Philadelphia: J. B. Lippincott, 1969), p. 152.

55. Alexis M. Durham III, "Ivy League Delinquency: A Self-report Analysis," *American Journal of Criminal Justice*, Vol. 12, no. 2 (Spring 1988), p. 188.

56. U.S. Department of Health and Human Services, *Monitoring the Future Survey* (Washington, D.C.: HHS, December 19, 1996).

57. Ibid.

58. Phyllis L. Ellickson, Kimberly A. McGuigan, Virgil Adams, Robert M. Bell, and Ron D. Hays, "Teenagers and Alcohol Misuse in the United States," *Addiction*, Vol. 91, no. 10 (1996), pp. 1489–1503.

59. *Uniform Crime Reports*, 1996.

60. Cheryl Carpenter, Barry Glassner, Bruce Johnson, and Julia Loughlin, *Kids, Drugs, and Crime* (Lexington, MA: Lexington Books, 1988).

61. M. R. Chaiken and B. D. Johnson, *Characteristics of Different Types of Drug-Involved Offenders*, p. 9, citing Delbert S. Elliott, David Huizinga, and Barbara Morse, "Self-reported Violent Offending: A Descriptive Analysis of Juvenile Violent Offenders and Their Offending Careers," *Journal of Interpersonal Violence*, Vol. 1, no. 4 (1986), pp. 472–514.

62. "Torture Killing," *USA Today*, January 29, 1993, p. 3A.

63. "Girls Just Catching Up to Boys," *USA Today*, July 9, 1992, p. 10A.

64. "The Knife in the Book Bag," *Time*, February 8, 1993, p. 37.

65. "Haunting Slayings in Oregon," *USA Today*, April 27, 1992, p. 3A.

66. "Child Kills Infant Brother," *The Robesonian*, September 8, 1992, p. 2A.

67. "Liverpool Boys Back in Court," *USA Today*, March 4, 1993, p. 4A.

68. Howard N. Snyder and Melissa Sickmund, *Juvenile Offenders and Victims: A Focus on Violence* (Washington, D.C.: Office of Juvenile Justice and Delinquency Prevention, 1995).

69. Alfred Blumstein, "Violence by Young People: Why the Deadly Nexus?" *National Institute of Justice Journal*, August 1995, p. 6.

70. See, for example, Frederick M. Thrasher, *The Gang* (Chicago: University of Chicago Press, 1927), and William Foote Whyte, *Street Corner Society, the Social Structure of an Italian Slum* (Chicago: University of Chicago Press, 1943).

71. "Young Urban Terrorists," *The Ohio State University Quest* (Fall 1988), p. 11.

72. For a good overview of the topic, see C. Ronald Huff, *Gangs in America*, 2nd ed. (Thousand Oaks, CA: Sage, 1996).

73. Mark Fleisher, *Sentenced to Life* (forthcoming), as reported in Kevin N. Wright and Karen E. Wright, *Family Life, Delinquency, and Crime: A Policymaker's Guide* (Washington, D.C.: Office of Juvenile Justice and Delinquency Prevention, 1994).

74. Ted Guest and Victoria Pope, "Crime Time Bomb," *U.S. News & World Report* World Wide Web site, September 27, 1996.

75. G. David Curry, Richard A. Ball, and Scott H. Decker, "Estimating the National Scope of Gang Crime from Law Enforcement Data," National Institute of Justice, August 1996.

76. G. David Curry, Richard A. Ball, and Robert J. Fox, "Gang Crime and Law Enforcement Recordkeeping," National Institute of Justice, April 1994.

77. *Criminal Justice Newsletter*, Vol. 19, no. 19 (October 3, 1988), p. 2.

78. "Telephone conversation with Mr. Michael Blake, Los Angeles County District Attorney's Office, October 7, 1997.

79. Ibid.

80. Paul Demuro, Anne Demuro, and Steven Lerner, *Reforming the California Youth Authority: How to End Crowding, Diversify Treatments, and Protect the Public—Without Spending More Money* (Bolinas, CA: Commonweal Research Institute, 1988).

81. "Los Angeles Drug Gangs Move into Other Cities, Police Told," *The Fayetteville Observer-Times* (North Carolina), July 16, 1988, p. 2A.

82. John M. Hagedorn, "Homeboys, Dope Fiends, Legits, and New Jacks," *Criminology*, Vol. 32, no. 2 (1994), pp. 197–219. See also John M. Hagedorn, "Neighborhoods, Markets, and Drug Gang Organization," *Journal of Research in Crime and Delinquency*, Vol. 31, no. 3 (1994), pp. 264–294.

83. National Gang Crime Research Center, *Achieving Justice and Reversing the Problem of Gang Crime and Gang Violence in America Today: Preliminary Results of the Project Gangfact Study* (Chicago: National Gang Crime Research Center, 1996).

84. James H. Burch II and Betty M. Chemers, *A Comprehensive Response to America's Youth Gang Problem* (Washington, D.C.: Office of Juvenile Justice and Delinquency Prevention, 1997). See also Bureau of Justice Assistance, *Addressing Community Gang Problems: A Model for Problem Solving* (Washington, D.C.: U.S. Government Printing Office, 1997).

85. Finn-Aage Esbensen, "A National Gang Strategy," in J. Mitchell Miller and Jeffrey P. Rush, eds., *Gangs: A Criminal Justice Approach* (Cincinnati: Anderson, 1996).

86. See Mary H. Glazier, a review of J. Mitchell Miller and Jeffrey P. Rush, eds., *Gangs: A Criminal Justice Approach* (Cincinnati: Anderson, 1996), in *The Criminologist*, July/April 1996, p. 29.

87. U.S. Attorney General's Advisory Board on Missing Children, *America's Missing and Exploited Children: Their Safety and Their Future* (Washington, D.C.: Office of Juvenile Justice and Delinquency Prevention, 1986), p. 11.

88. David Finkelhor, Gerald Hotaling, and Andrea Sedlak, *Missing, Abducted, Runaway, and Thrownaway Children in America* (Washington, D.C.: Office of Juvenile Justice and Delinquency Prevention, 1990).

89. "Runaway Children and the Juvenile Justice and Delinquency Prevention Act: What Is Its Impact?" *Juvenile Justice Bulletin* (Washington, D.C.: Office of Juvenile Justice and Delinquency Prevention, no date).

90. Ibid., p. 1.

91. Ibid., p. 2.

92. U.S. Attorney General, *America's Missing and Exploited Children*, p. 19.

93. "Teen Stripper's Mom Gets Year in Jail," United Press International, January 22, 1988.

94. Child Welfare League of America, "Sacramento County Community Intervention Program: Findings from a Comprehensive Study by Community Partners in Child Welfare, Law Enforcement, Juvenile Justice, and the Child Welfare League of America" (The League, June 19, 1997).

95. National Committee for Prevention of Child Abuse, *Child Abuse: Prelude to Delinquency?* (Washington, D.C.: Office of Juvenile Justice and Delinquency Prevention, 1986).

96. Charles B. DeWitt, *The Cycle of Violence* (Washington, D.C.: National Institute of Justice, October 1992), p. 2.

97. Matthew T. Zingraff, Jeffrey Leiter, Kristen A. Myers, and Matthew C. Johnsen, "Child Maltreatment and Youthful Problem Behavior," *Criminology*, Vol. 31, no. 2 (May 1993), pp. 173–202.

98. Cecil L. Willis and Richard H. Wells, "The Police and Child Abuse: An Analysis of Police Decisions to Report Illegal Behavior," *Criminology*, Vol. 26, no. 4 (1988), pp. 695–715.

99. See "The Role of the National Center for the Prosecution of Child Abuse," in *Prosecutors Perspective*, Vol. 2, no. 1 (January 1988), p. 19.

100. "Kids Struggle with Horror of Girl's Suicide," *USA Today*, June 17, 1993, p. 3A.

101. "Girls' Suicides 'Like a Bombshell,'" *USA Today*, May 22, 1991, 3A.

102. American Suicide Foundation, "Suicide Facts, 1994," (Pamphlet).

103. AFSP home page on the World Wide Web, http://www.afsp.org.

104. Ibid., p. 3A.

105. Michael A. Jones and Barry Krisberg, *Images and Reality: Juvenile Crime, Youth Violence and Public Policy* (San Francisco, CA: National Council on Crime and Delinquency, 1994), p. 41.

106. Kevin N. Wright and Karen E. Wright, *Family Life, Delinquency, and Crime: A Policymaker's Guide: Research Summary* (Washington, D.C.: Office of Juvenile Justice and Delinquency Prevention, 1994).

107. For an excellent true-to-life account of the functionings of the Los Angeles Juvenile Court, see Edward Humes, *No Matter How Loud I Shout: A Year in the Life of Juvenile Court* (New York: Simon and Schuster, 1996).

108. Barry Krisberg and James F. Austin, *Reinventing Juvenile Justice* (Newbury Park, CA: Sage Publication, 1993).

109. Heidi M. Hsia, "Allegheny County, PA: Mobilizing to Reduce Juvenile Crime," *A Juvenile Justice Bulletin* (Washington, DC: OJJDP, 1997).

110. Ibid.

111. Coordinating Council on Juvenile Justice and Delinquency Prevention, *Combating Violence and Delinquency: The National Juvenile Justice Action Plan* (Washington, D.C.: U.S. Government Printing Office, 1996).

112. See, for example, *Haley* v. *Ohio*, 332 U.S. 596 (1948).

113. *Kent* v. *U.S.*, 383 U.S. 541 (1966).

114. *In re Gault*, 387 U.S. 1 (1967).

115. *In re Winship*, 397 U.S. 358 (1970).

116. *McKeiver* v. *Pennsylvania*, 403 U.S. 528 (1971).

117. *Breed* v. *Jones*, 421 U.S. 519 (1975).

118. *Schall* v. *Martin*, 467 U.S. 253 (1984).

119. *Illinois* v. *Montanez*, No. 95-1429 (1996).

120. Michael Kirkland, "Court Rejects Juvenile Confession Case," United Press International wire services, June 10, 1996.

121. Adapted from Peter Greenwood, *Juvenile Offenders*, a Crime File Study Guide (Washington, D.C.: National Institute of Justice, no date).

122. *Fare* v. *Michael C.*, 442 U.S. 707 (1979).

123. *California* v. *Prysock*, 453 U.S. 355 (1981).

124. *New Jersey* v. *T.L.O.*, 105 S.Ct. 733 (1985).

125. "Drug Bill Includes Extension of OJJDP, with Many Changes," *Criminal Justice Newsletter*, Vol. 19, no. 22 (November 15, 1988), p. 4.

126. See "OJJDP Eases Rules on Juvenile Confinement," *Corrections Compendium*, November 1996, p. 25.

127. Melissa Sickmund, "How Juveniles Get to Criminal Court," *OJJDP Update on Statistics*, October 1994.

128. Ibid.

129. "Ten-Year-Old Faces Murder Trial as Adult," *The Fayetteville Observer-Times* (North Carolina), August 27, 1989, p. 5A.

130. Bureau of Justice Statistics, *Report to the Nation on Crime and Justice*, 2nd ed. (Washington, D.C.: U.S. Government Printing Office, 1988), p. 78.

131. Ibid.

132. Ibid.

133. *McKeiver* v. *Pennsylvania*.

134. Some states, such as West Virginia, do provide juveniles with a statutory right to trial.

135. Peer juries in juvenile court have been identified in Denver, Colorado; Duluth, Minnesota; Deerfield, Illinois; Thompkins County, New York; and Spanish Fork City, Utah. See Philip Reichel and Carole Seyfrit, "A Peer Jury in the Juvenile Court," *Crime and Delinquency*, Vol. 30, no. 3 (July 1984), pp. 423–438.

136. Ibid.

137. "In This Court, Teens Sit in Stern Judgment on Violators," *The Fayetteville Observer-Times* (North Carolina), May 3, 1992, p. 22A.

138. Sharon J. Zehner, "Teen Court," *FBI Law Enforcement Bulletin*, Vol. 66, no. 3 (March 1997), pp. 1–14.

139. Tracy M. Godwin, "A Guide for Implementing Teen Court Programs," (Washington, D.C.: Office of Juvenile Justice and Delinquency Prevention, August 1996).

140. OJJDP, "Juvenile Probation: The Workhorse of the Juvenile Justice System," *A Juvenile Justice Bulletin*, March 1996.

141. Jeffery A. Butts, Howard N. Snyder, Terrence A. Finnegan, Anne L.

Aughenbaugh, and Rowen S. Poole, *Juvenile Court Statistics 1994* (Washington, D.C.: Office of Juvenile Justice and Delinquency Prevention, December 1996).

142. Bethany Gardner, "Successful Pennsylvania School-Based Probation Expands," *Corrections Compendium*, Vol. 19, no. 8 (August 1994), pp. 1–3.

143. Butts, et al, *Juvenile Court Statistics 1994.*

144. *Juveniles in Public Facilities 1995* (Washington, D.C.: Office of Juvenile Justice and Delinquency Prevention, November 1997).

145. Where juveniles are defined as children aged 10 to the upper age of juvenile court jurisdiction (which varies by state).

146. See, for example, Blair B. Bourque, Robert C. Cronin, Daniel B. Felker, Frank R. Pearson, Mei Han, and Sarah M. Hill, "Boot Camps for Juvenile Offenders: An Implementation Evaluation of Three Demonstration Programs," *An NIJ Research In Brief* (Washington, D.C.: National Institute of Justice, 1996).

147. Ibid., p. 110.

148. Ibid.

149. Ibid.

150. Ibid.

151. *Juveniles in Public Facilities 1995.*

152. Allen Beck, Susan Kline, and Lawrence Greenfeld, *Survey of Youth in Custody 1987* (Washington, D.C.: Bureau of Justice Statistics, 1988).

153. Ibid.

154. Dale G. Parent, Valerie Leiter, Stephen Kennedy, Lisa Livens, Daniel Wentworth, and Sarah Wilcox, *Conditions of Confinement: Juvenile Detention and Corrections Facilities* (Washington, D.C.: Office of Juvenile Justice and Delinquency Prevention, 1994).

155. *Corrections Compendium* (December 1993), p. 14.

156. Ibid.

157. Ibid., p. 22.

158. Office of Juvenile Justice and Delinquency Prevention, *National Juvenile Custody Trends, 1978–1989* (Washington, D.C.: U.S. Department of Justice, 1992), p. 2.

159. Section 59 of the Uniform Juvenile Court Act recommends the granting of a right to appeal for juveniles (National Conference of Commissioners on Uniform State Laws, Uniform Juvenile Court Act, 1968).

160. Springer, *Justice for Juveniles.*

161. Bureau of Justice Statistics, *Open vs. Confidential Records: Proceedings of a BJS/SEARCH Conference* (Washington, D.C.: Bureau of Justice Statistics, November 1988), p. 42.

162. Ronald D. Stephens, "Access to Juvenile Justice Records," in *Open vs. Confidential Records* (Washington, D.C.: Bureau of Justice Statistics, 1988), p. 45.

163. Bureau of Justice Statistics, *Public Access to Criminal History Record Information* (Washington, D.C.: Bureau of Justice Statistics, 1988), p. 70.

164. American Institutes for Research, *Evaluation of the Habitual Serious and Violent Juvenile Offender Program: Executive Summary* (Washington, D.C.: Office of Juvenile Justice and Delinquency Prevention, 1988); and "Targeting Serious Juvenile Offenders for Prosecution Can Make a Difference," National Institute of Justice Reports (September/October 1988), p. 9.

165. "Federal Study on Youth Urges Fixed Sentences," *The New York Times*, August 29, 1987.

166. "Introducing RESTTA," *Juvenile Justice Bulletin* (Washington, D.C.: Office of Juvenile Justice and Delinquency Prevention, 1985).

167. "Allegheny County, PA," p. 8.

168. Greenwood, *Juvenile Offenders*, p. 2.

169. National Juvenile Corrections and Detention Forum, *Recommendations for Juvenile Corrections and Detention in Response to Conditions of Confinement: A Study to Evaluate the Conditions in Juvenile Correctional and Detention Facilities* (Laurel, MD: American Correctional Association, 1993).

chapter 15

DRUGS AND CRIME

If we fail, it means that what we have been saying is true—that drugs may represent to our civilization, to many of our cities, a life-or-death situation. If we don't get control of this drug problem, we may not go into the twenty-first century intact.[1]

—THE FIRST "DRUG CZAR,"
WILLIAM BENNETT

We cannot go into tomorrow with the same formulas that are failing today. We must not blindly add to the body count and the terrible cost of the War on Drugs, only to learn...30 years from now, that what we've been doing is wrong, terribly wrong.

—WALTER CRONKITE
THE CRONKITE REPORT, JUNE 20, 1995

The Drug Problem and the Criminal Justice System

Drug Abuse   Illicit drug use that results in social, economic, psychological, or legal problems for the user. *Source:* Bureau of Justice Statistics, *Drugs, Crime, and the Justice System* (Washington, D.C.: Bureau of Justice Statistics, 1992), p. 20.

Recently, Ross Deck, Senior Policy Analyst at the Office of National Drug Control Policy (ONDCP) opened his remarks to a yearly conference on controversies in criminal justice with these words: "First of all, we are not fighting a drug war anymore. To have a war you must have enemies. In this situation, we are our own enemy. And, we cannot declare victory simply because we killed ourselves."[2] In other words, seen from the federal level, **drug abuse** is so pervasive in American society, and the values which support it have become so entrenched among large segments of the American population, that the fight against drug abuse through the application of strict criminal justice sanctions seems bound to fail. Arrest, incarceration, and a national prison system filled with drug law violators no longer seem to hold the answer to winning the drug-control battle. As Deck explained it, "So, what can we do about the heavy drug users? Well, we tried incarceration, but we could not confine all of them…. Today, in contrast, we are looking at drug abuse from the user's perspective: we are looking at treatment and accepting relapse as inevitable. Along with relapse, We are looking at harm reduction for the first time."

A 1995 report by the National Assessment Program,[3] a federally sponsored survey which polls more than 2,000 criminal justice professionals across the nation to determine the system's most pressing needs, found that drug crimes are among the most costly in terms of system resources. Comments made by survey respondents include the following:

- A police chief said: "Alcohol and drug abuse play a major role in the majority of our cases of crimes against persons."
- A jail administrator noted: "Seventy percent of inmates are here due to drug-related commitments; 65 percent are repeat inmates."
- A prosecutor said: "Drug prosecutions are easily the largest contributor to our workload problems."
- A superior court judge observed: "Drug-related cases—especially possession, possession for sale, and small quantity sales—have overwhelmed the system. The congestion compounds caseload management and has resulted in the doubling of criminal cases without an increase in the number of judges."
- A trial court administrator said: "There continues to be a significant increase in workload resulting from drug-related cases. They involve more forfeiture hearings and more motions to suppress evidence than in the past. As a result, courtrooms are in use more often along with court reporters, the judge's time, and our law clerk's time."
- A probation agency director remarked: "In recent years the upsurge in arrests for drug offenses coupled with stagnant staffing levels has created major workload problems."

The dramatic increase in drug-related crime and the corresponding expansion of both drug laws and efforts at enforcement over the last few decades have had a significant impact

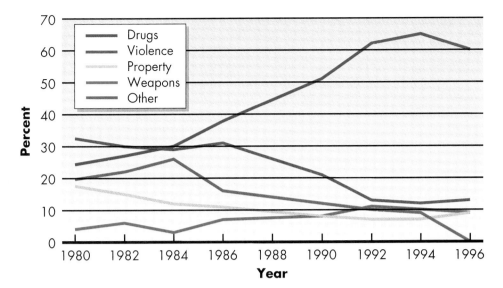

FIGURE 15–1 Federal inmates, by offense category, 1980–1996. *Source:* U.S. Department of Justice, Bureau of Justice Statistics.

on all aspects of our justice system. In some parts of the country, courts' dockets have become so clogged with drug charges that criminal case processing has ground almost to a halt. Prison populations also reflect the huge increase in drug crimes. As a writer for *The Washington Post* recently explained it, "The proportion of federal prisoners who are drug offenders has risen from 38% in 1986 to 58% in 1991 and, according to Bureau of Prisons current figures, 62% today. About 70% of all first offenders in the federal prisons are serving drug sentences. This is also true of 85% of the noncitizens and 66% of the women…"[4] (see Figure 15–1). As Ross Deck might put it, "we have met the drug enemy and they are us"…or at least they account for many of our prisoners and for a large portion of those processed by the criminal justice system today.

DRUG ABUSE: MORE THAN AN INDIVIDUAL CHOICE

Few criminal justice textbooks devote an entire chapter to drug-related crime. Most prefer, instead, to describe a general category of social order or victimless crimes. This book, however, directly addresses drug crime because it has such a pervasive and far-reaching impact, not only on the criminal justice system but also on all of society. This is so because

- Drug abuse accounts for a large proportion of present-day law violations.
- Drug abuse contributes to many other types of criminal activity, including smuggling, theft, robbery, and murder.
- Drug abuse has led to a huge number of arrests, clogged courtrooms, and overcrowded prisons.
- As a consequence, drug abuse has placed tremendous strain on the criminal justice system, and the fight against it has become one of the most expensive activities ever undertaken by federal, state, and local governments.

Drug crime may be *the* major challenge facing the nation's criminal justice system and state and federal criminal justice policy makers today.[5] The country's official *National Drug Control Strategy*, a White House publication, describes the problem this way: "Because it is linked to the Nation's efforts to promote economic growth, empower communities, curb youth violence, preserve families, and improve access to health care for all Americans, drug policy is a cornerstone of U.S. domestic policy in general and U.S. social policy in particular."[6]

Even though, as the White House statement admits, drug abuse is widespread, it is only one of a great number of social order crimes. As such it shares a number of characteristics with other victimless crimes, like prostitution, gambling, and the diverse forms of sexual deviance which occur among consenting partners. A hallmark of such crimes is that they

Drug trafficking is the number one crime problem facing our country and the world…

—Former Attorney General Richard Thornburgh, in an open letter to President Bush

involve willing participants. In the case of drug law violations, buyers, sellers, and users willingly purchase, sell, and consume illegal drugs. They do not complain to the authorities of criminal injuries to themselves or to others resulting from the illegal use of drugs. Few victimless crimes, however, are truly without an injured party. Even where the criminal participant does not perceive an immediate or personal injury, the behavior frequently affects the legitimate interests of nonparticipants. In many victimless crimes, it is society which is the ultimate victim. Prostitution, for example, may victimize the customer or his family through the spread of AIDS, other venereal diseases, and economic hardship due to the cost of illicit sexual services. Prostitution has many other negative consequences, including (1) lowered property values in areas where it regularly occurs, (2) degradation of the status of women, (3) victimization of the prostitute, and (4) the seeming legitimacy it lends to interpersonal immorality of all kinds.

Drug abuse has many equally or even greater destructive consequences, including lost productivity, an inequitable distribution of economic resources among the poorest members of society, disease, wasted human potential, fragmented families, violence, and other crimes. Some evidence has even linked drug trafficking to international terrorism and efforts to overthrow the democratic governments of the Western Hemisphere. Each of these consequences will be discussed in some detail in this chapter. We begin now with an analysis of what constitutes a drug, move through a history of drug abuse in America, and then describe the various categories of major **controlled substances**. Finally, the link between drugs and other forms of crime will be explained, and solutions to solving the problem of drug abuse described.

What Is a Drug?

Before we begin any comprehensive discussion of drugs, we must first grapple with the concept of what a drug is. Common usage holds that a **drug** may be any ingestible substance which has a noticeable effect upon the mind or body. Drugs may enter the body via injection, inhalation, swallowing, or even by direct absorption through the skin or mucous membranes. Some drugs, like penicillin and tranquilizers, are useful in medical treatment, while others, like heroin and cocaine, are attractive only to "recreational" users[7] or to those who are addicted to them.

In determining what substances should be called "drugs," it is important to recognize the role that social definitions of any phenomenon play in our understanding of it. Hence, what Americans today consider to be drugs depends more upon social convention or agreed-upon definitions than it does upon any inherent property of the "drugs" themselves. The history of marijuana provides a case in point. Prior to the early 1900s, marijuana was freely available in the United States. Although alcohol was the recreational drug of choice at the time, marijuana found a following among some artists and musicians. Marijuana was also occasionally used for medicinal purposes to "calm the nerves" and to treat hysteria. Howard Becker, in a now-classic study of the early Federal Bureau of Narcotics (forerunner of the DEA), demonstrates how federal agencies worked to outlaw marijuana in order to increase their power.[8] Federally funded publications voiced calls for laws against the substance, and movies such as *Reefer Madness* led the drive toward classifying marijuana as a dangerous drug. The 1939 Marijuana Tax Act was the result, and marijuana has been thought of as a drug worthy of federal and local enforcement efforts ever since.

Both the law and social convention make strong distinctions between drugs that are socially acceptable and those which are not. Some ingestible substances with profound effects upon the body and mind are not even thought of as drugs. Gasoline fumes, chemical vapors of many kinds, perfumes, certain vitamins, sugar-rich foods, and toxic chemicals may all have profound effects upon the mind and body. Even so, most people do not think of such substances as drugs, and they are rarely regulated by the criminal law.

Recent social awareness has reclassified substances like alcohol, caffeine, and nicotine as "drugs," although before the 1960s it is doubtful that most Americans would have applied that word to this threesome. Even today alcohol, caffeine, and nicotine are readily available throughout the country, with only minimal controls on their manufacture and distribution. As such, they are three drugs which continue to enjoy favored status in both our law and culture. Nonetheless, alcohol abuse and addiction are commonplace in American society, and anyone who has tried to quit smoking knows the power that nicotine can wield.

Controlled Substance A specifically defined bioactive or psychoactive chemical substance which is proscribed by law.

Drug Any chemical substance defined by social convention as bio- or psychoactive.

Mexican federal police guard a shipment of high-grade cocaine seized near Mexico City in 1995. Drug abuse is one of the most significant problems facing the criminal justice system and society today. *Miguel Castillo, MIC Photo Press/Sygma*

Occupying a middle ground on the continuum between acceptability and illegality are substances which have medical applicability but are usually available only on a prescription basis. Antibiotics, diet pills, and, in particular, tranquilizers, stimulants, and mood-altering chemicals (such as the popular drug Prozac® are culturally acceptable, but sometimes legally accessible only upon the advice of a physician. These substances are clearly recognized as drugs, albeit useful ones, by the majority of Americans.

Powerful drugs, those with the ability to produce substantially altered states of consciousness and with a high potential for addiction, occupy the "high ground" in social and legal condemnation. Among them are **psychoactive substances,** such as heroin, peyote, mescaline, LSD, and cocaine. Even here, however, legitimate uses for such drugs may exist. Cocaine is used in the treatment of certain medical conditions and can be applied as a topical anesthetic during medical interventions. LSD has been employed experimentally to investigate the nature of human consciousness, and peyote and mescaline may be used legally by members of the Native American Church in Indian religious services. Even heroin has been advocated by some as beneficial in relieving the suffering associated with some forms of terminal illnesses. Hence, answers to the question of "What is a drug?" depend to a large extent on the social definitions and conventions operative at a given time and in a given place. Some of the clearest definitional statements relating to controlled substances can be found in the law, although informal strictures and definitions guide much of everyday drug use.

Psychoactive Substance
A chemical substance which affects cognition, feeling, and/or awareness.

Alcohol Abuse

Although the abuse of alcohol is rarely described in the same terms as the illegal use of controlled substances, alcohol misuse can lead to serious problems with grim consequences. On June 19, 1995, for example, a pickup truck driven by Gallardo Bermudes, 35, of Cathedral City, California, rear-ended a car carrying 11 people near Beaumont, California.[9] Most of the occupants of the car were children of Jose Luis Rodriquez and Mercedes Diaz—the only adults in the car. Eight of the children burned to death in the Rodriquez-Diaz vehicle when

To those who use drugs— stop now! Drugs are unsafe and illegal.

—Donna E. Shalala, Secretary of Health and Human Services

Drug Use and Abuse—Commonly Used Terms

Drug: Any chemical substance defined by social convention as bio- or psychoactive. Not all "drugs" are socially recognized as such, while those which are may not be well understood. Among recognized drugs some are "legal" and readily available, while others are closely controlled.

Controlled Substance: A specifically defined bioactive or psychoactive chemical substance which is proscribed by law.

Drug Abuse: The frequent, overindulgent, or long-term use of a controlled substance in such a way so as to create problems in the user's life or in the lives of those with whom the user associates.

Psychological Addiction: A craving for a specific drug which results from long-term substance abuse. People who are psychologically addicted use the drug in question as a "crutch" to deal with the events in their lives. Also referred to as psychological dependence.

Physical Addiction: A biologically based craving for a specific drug, which results from frequent use of the substance. Also referred to as physical dependence.

Addict: Generally, someone who abuses drugs and is psychologically dependent, physically dependent, or both.

Soft Drugs: Psychoactive drugs with relatively mild effects whose potential for abuse and addiction is substantially less than for the hard drugs described below. By social convention,

soft drugs include marijuana, hashish, and some tranquilizers and mood elevators.

Hard Drugs: Psychoactive substances with serious potential for abuse and addiction. By social convention, hard drugs include heroin, Quaaludes, sopors, LSD, mescaline, peyote, psilocybin, and MDA. Cocaine and its derivative, crack, are often placed in the hard drug category.

Recreational Drug User: A person who uses drugs relatively infrequently and whose use occurs primarily among friends and within social contexts which define drug use as pleasurable. Most addicts began as recreational users.

Physical Addiction (or Physical Dependence) A biologically based craving for a specific drug, which results from frequent use of the substance. Dependence upon drugs is marked by a growing tolerance of a drug's effects so that increased amounts of a drug are needed to obtain a desired effect and by the onset of withdrawal symptoms over periods of prolonged abstinence. *Source:* Bureau of Justice Statistics, *Drugs, Crime, and the Justice System* (Washington, D.C.: Bureau of Justice Statistics, 1992), p. 21.

Recreational Drug User A person who uses drugs relatively infrequently and whose use occurs primarily among friends and within social contexts which define drug use as pleasurable. Most addicts began as recreational users.

it flipped and caught fire after being hit. Bermudes, who fled from the scene, had been convicted of drunken driving on three previous occasions. He later told police investigators that he had had "10 to 15" beers before the crash.

Recognizing the many problems attributable to the misuse of alcohol, alcohol abuse has been called "one of the nation's gravest health and social problems."[10] Indications are that it is a serious problem which shows few signs of abating. Although 30% of the American population are abstainers, surveys show that more Americans drink today than at any time since World War II, and those who drink, drink more excessively.[11] According to recent polls, 93% of high-school seniors have tried alcoholic beverages, and up to one-half of teenagers in the United States become intoxicated on the average once every two weeks.[12]

Per capita alcoholic beverage consumption in the United States exceeds 27.6 gallons yearly.[13] Some perspective on consumption can be gained by realizing that the typical American drinks 25.9 gallons of coffee per year, 27.1 gallons of milk, and 45.6 gallons of soft drinks.[14] The average American adult consumes 34.5 gallons of beer, 3.5 gallons of wine, and 2.5 gallons of liquor per year.[15] While some individuals are abstainers, others are especially heavy drinkers. It is estimated that one-half of all the alcohol consumed yearly in the United States is ingested by just 5% of the adult population.[16]

Alcohol, sometimes in combination with other drugs, is often a factor in the commission of crimes. Drunk driving is a crime closely associated with the use of alcohol. Most states define a blood alcohol level of 0.10% or more as intoxication and hold that anyone who drives with that amount of alcohol in his or her blood is driving under the influence (DUI) of alcohol.[17] Drunk driving has been a major social concern for some time. Groups such as Mothers Against Drunk Driving (MADD) and Remove Intoxicated Drivers (RID) have given impetus to enforcement efforts to curb drunk drivers. Between 1970 and 1992, for example, arrests for DUI increased 200% across the nation, while the number of licensed drivers grew by only 42%.[18] Today nearly one million drunk driving arrests are made annually—more than for any other offense except drug abuse and larceny-theft. The average driver arrested for DUI is substantially impaired. Studies show that he or she has consumed an average of

FIGURE 15–2 Percentage of inmates who had been drinking prior to crime commission. *Source:* Bureau of Justice Statistics, *Report to the Nation on Crime and Justice*, 2nd ed. (Washington, D.C.: U.S. Government Printing Office, 1988), p. 51.

six ounces of pure alcohol (the equivalent of a dozen bottles of beer) in the four hours preceding arrest.[19] Twenty-six percent of arrestees have consumed nearly twice that amount.

Driving under the influence is costly for both offenders and society. The National Highway Traffic Safety Administration estimates that as many as 250,000 people have been killed in alcohol-related motor vehicle accidents over the past decade. More than 650,000 persons are injured in such crashes yearly.[20]

Another offense directly related to alcohol consumption is public drunkenness. During the late 1960s and early 1970s, some groups fought to decriminalize drunkenness and treat it as a health problem. Although the number of arrests for public drunkenness reached 494,025[21] in 1996, law enforcement officers retain a great deal of discretion in handling these offenders. Many individuals who are drunk in public, if they are not assaultive or involved in other crimes, are likely to receive an "official escort" home rather than face arrest.

The use of alcohol may also lead to the commission of other, very serious, crimes. Some experts have found that use of alcohol lowers inhibitions and increases the likelihood of aggression.[22] A recent report by the National Institute of Justice concluded that "of all psychoactive substances, alcohol is the only one whose consumption has been shown to commonly increase aggression."[23] Studies show that about half of all prison inmates report that they had been drinking just prior to the crime for which they are serving time.[24] As Figure 15–2 shows, alcohol use has been found most often among individuals imprisoned for assault (60%), but tends to be less prevalent among property offenders (40%) and drug offenders (30%).[25] In self-reports, male prison inmates have revealed that prior to imprisonment they were three times as likely as other men to consume an ounce or more of alcohol each day.[26] Female inmates were five times more likely than women in general to consume that amount.[27]

Besides crime, alcohol abuse produces illnesses, on-the-job accidents, lost productivity, family problems, and a lowered quality of life. There are few reasons to think, however, that the legal environment surrounding alcohol consumption will change anytime soon. Cultural acceptance of alcoholic beverages remains high. Beer, wine, and mixed drinks are served at many parties, weddings, and funerals and are, of course, served in numerous homes and restaurants.

Lawmakers appear willing to deal with the problems caused by alcohol only indirectly. The American experience with prohibition is not one that legislators are anxious to repeat. In all likelihood future efforts to reduce the damaging effects of alcohol will continue to take the form of educational programs, legislation to raise the drinking age, and enforcement efforts designed to deter the most visible forms of abuse. Struggles in other areas may also

Psychological Addiction (or **Psychological Dependence**) A craving for a specific drug which results from long-term substance abuse. Psychological dependence upon drugs is marked by the feeling that drugs are needed to achieve a feeling of well-being. *Source:* Bureau of Justice Statistics, *Drugs, Crime, and the Justice System* (Washington, D.C.: Bureau of Justice Statistics, 1992), p. 21.

Alcohol abuse, especially in the form of drunken driving, has gotten considerable attention from lawmakers and enforcement agencies in recent years. This 1997 car crash in which Princess Diana was killed appeared to have been at least partially caused by her driver's intoxicated condition. *Jerame Delay, AP/Wide World Photos*

have some impact. For example, lawsuits claiming civil damages are now being brought against some liquor companies and taverns on behalf of accident victims, cirrhosis patients, and others. We can anticipate, however, that while concern over alcohol abuse will continue, few sweeping changes in either law or social custom will occur anytime soon.

I keep in my house a letter from Bill O'Dwyer, who once was the mayor of New York, and who wrote to me, 'There is no power on earth to match the power of the poor, who, just by sitting in their hopelessness, can bring the rest of us down.' It always sounded right, but I never saw it happen until crack came along. And with it, there are no more rules in American crime. The implied agreements on which we were raised are gone. You now shoot women and children. A news reporter is safe as long as he is not there. A cop in his uniform means nothing.
—Jimmy Breslin, *Crack*

A History of Drug Abuse in America

Alcohol is but one example of the many conflicting images of drug use to be found in contemporary American social consciousness. The "War on Drugs," initiated by the former Reagan administration and given added impetus by the former Bush administration, portrayed an America fighting for its very existence against the scourge of drug abuse. While many of the highly negative images which emanated from the "war period" may be correct, they have not always been a part of the American world view.

Opium and its derivatives, for example, were widely available in "patent" medicines of the 1800s and early 1900s. Corner drugstores stocked mixtures of opium and alcohol which were available for the asking. Traveling road shows extolled the virtues of these magical curatives which offered relief from almost any malady. Such "elixirs" were promoted as curealls and did indeed bring about feelings of well-being in almost anyone who consumed them. Although no one is certain just how widespread opium use was in the United States a hundred years ago, some authors have observed that even baby formulas containing opium were in use for feeding infants born to mothers who were addicted.[28]

Opium was also in widespread use among Chinese immigrants who came to the West Coast in the 1800s, often to work on railroads. Opium dens—in which the drug was smoked—flourished, and the use of opium quickly spread to other ethnic groups throughout the West. Some of the more affluent denizens of West Coast cities ate the substance, and avant-garde poetry was written extolling the virtues of opium.

Morphine, an opium derivative, has a similar history. Although it was legally available in this country almost since its invention, battlefield injuries during the Civil War dramatically heightened public awareness of its pain-killing properties.[29] In the late 1800s morphine was being widely prescribed by physicians and dentists, many of whom abused the substance

Careers in Justice

Working for the Bureau of Alcohol, Tobacco, and Firearms

TYPICAL POSITIONS. Special agent, explosives expert, firearms specialist, bomb scene investigator, liquor law violations investigator, fingerprint identification specialist, intelligence specialist, and forensic chemist.

EMPLOYMENT REQUIREMENTS. ATF special agent applicants must meet the same employment requirements as most other federal agents, including (1) successful completion of the Treasury Enforcement Agent Examination, (2) a field interview, and (3) a thorough background investigation. See the box on employment with the U.S. Secret Service for additional details on Treasury agent general employment requirements.

OTHER REQUIREMENTS. Other general requirements for employment as a federal officer apply. They include (1) U.S. citizenship, (2) an age between 21 and 35, (3) good physical health, and (4) eyesight of no less than 20/100 uncorrected, and corrected vision of at least 20/30 in one eye and 20/20 in the other. New agents undergo eight weeks of specialized training at the Federal Law Enforcement Training Center in Glynco, Georgia.

SALARY. A Bachelor's degree qualifies applicants for appointment at the GS-5 level, although some appointments are made at the GS-7 level. Depending on geographic area of assignment, this salary can be raised

from 16% to 30% above the established base level.

BENEFITS. Benefits include (1) 13 days of sick leave annually, (2) 2-1/2 to 5 weeks of annual paid vacation and 10 paid federal holidays each year, (3) federal health and life insurance, and (4) a comprehensive retirement program.

DIRECT INQUIRIES TO:
Bureau of Alcohol, Tobacco, and Firearms, U.S. Treasury Department
650 Massachusetts Ave., N.W.,
Room 4100
Washington, D.C. 20226
Phone: (202) 927-8423
Web site: http://atf.ustreas.gov

---

themselves. By 1896, when per capita morphine consumption peaked, addiction to the substance throughout the United States was apparently widespread.[30]

Heroin, the most potent derivative of opium ever created, was invented as a substitute for morphine by German chemists in 1898. When first introduced, its addictive properties were unknown, and it was marketed as a nonaddictive cough suppressant, also useful in treating morphine addiction.[31]

Marijuana, a considerably less potent drug than heroin, has a relatively short history in this country. Imported by Mexican immigrants around the turn of the twentieth century, marijuana use quickly became associated with marginal groups. By 1930 most of the states in the Southwest had passed legislation outlawing marijuana, and some authors have suggested that antimarijuana laws were primarily targeted at Spanish-speaking immigrants who were beginning to challenge whites in the economic sector.[32] As mentioned earlier, other writers have suggested that the rapidly growing use of marijuana throughout the 1920s and 1930s provided a rationale for the development of drug legislation and the concomitant expansion of drug enforcement agencies.[33] By the 1960s public attitudes regarding marijuana had begun to change. The Hippie generation popularized the drug, touting its "mellowing" effects upon people who smoked it. In a short time marijuana use became epidemic across the country, and books on marijuana cultivation and preparation flourished.

Another drug which found adherents among some youthful idealists of the 1960s and 1970s was LSD. LSD, whose chemical name is lysergic acid diethylamide, was first synthesized in Switzerland in 1938 and found limited use in this country in the 1950s for the treatment of psychiatric disorders.

Many drugs when first "discovered" had been touted for their powerful analgesic or therapeutic effects. Cocaine was one of them. An early leading proponent of cocaine use, for example, was Sigmund Freud, who prescribed it for a variety of psychological disorders. Freud was himself a user and wrote a book, *The Cocaine Papers*, describing the many benefits of the drug. The cocaine bandwagon reached the United States in the late 1800s, and various medicines and beverages containing cocaine were offered to the American public. Prominent among them was Coca-Cola, which combined seltzer water, sugar, and cocaine in

Legalization does not provide an answer to the problems of drug use and crime. Rather, it is a formula for self-destruction. The Administration is unequivocally opposed to any "reform" that is certain to increase drug use.
—The White House, *National Drug Control Strategy*

Legalization seems to many like too dangerous an experiment. To others, the War on Drugs, as it is now conducted, seems inhumane and too costly. Is there a middle ground?
—Walter Cronkite, *The Cronkite Report*, June 20, 1995

Cocaine, a controlled substance today, was commonly found in late nineteenth-century medicines and consumer products—as this early advertisement for cocaine-laced wine shows. *Bettmann*

a new soda advertised as providing a real "pick-me-up." Cocaine came out of Coca-Cola before 1910, but found continued adherents among jazz musicians and artists. Beginning in the 1970s, cocaine became associated with exclusive parties, the well-to-do, and the "jet set." Television shows and movies often portrayed the drug as glamorous, and cocaine soon became the drug of choice among the young and upwardly mobile. In testimony to both the cost of the drug and the economic success of some of its users, sterling silver "coke spoons" and rolled $100 bills became preferred paraphernalia. Words like "snorting" and "free-basing" entered common usage, and it was not long before an extensive drug underworld developed, catering to the demands of the affluent users. Crack cocaine, a derivative of powdered cocaine, became popular in the 1980s and is sold today in the form of "rocks," "cookies," or "biscuits" (large pieces of crack) which are then smoked.

Drug Use and Social Awareness

As we have seen, drugs were not strangers to the American social scene of the late 1800s and early 1900s. While drug use still permeates American society, there have been dramatic alterations over the last 100 years in the form such use takes and in the social consequences of involvement with drugs. Specifically, six elements have emerged which today cast drug use in a far different light than that of the past:

1. The conceptualization of addiction as a physical and/or medical condition
2. The understanding that drug use is associated with other kinds of criminal activity

3. Generally widespread social condemnation of drug use as a waste of economic resources and human lives
4. Comprehensive and detailed federal and state laws regulating the use and/or availability of drugs
5. A growing involvement with illicit drugs among the urban poor and the socially disenfranchised, both as an escape from the conditions of life and as a path to monetary gain
6. A shift from the definition of drug abuse as primarily a medical problem to the view that such abuse is a law enforcement issue

This last element is especially significant for what it means to the criminal justice system. In his classic study of the evolution of marijuana laws,[34] Howard S. Becker identified three American values which led to increased regulation of all drugs: (1) the belief "that the individual should exercise complete responsibility for what he does and what happens to him; he should never do anything that might cause loss of self-control"; (2) "disapproval of action taken solely to achieve states of ecstasy"; and (3) "humanitarianism."[35] Of humanitarianism, Becker said, "[R]eformers believed that people enslaved by the use of alcohol and opium would benefit from laws making it impossible for them to give in to their weaknesses."[36] Becker believed that these values rest upon the Protestant Ethic and a strong "cultural emphases on pragmatism and utilitarianism."[37]

The contemporary situation is based largely upon the values identified by Becker. In an insightful work[38] which clarifies the valuative basis of modern antidrug sentiments, Franklin E. Zimring and Gordon Hawkins examine three schools of thought which, they say, form the basis for current drug policy in the United States. The first is "public health generalism," a perspective which holds that all controlled substances are potentially harmful and that drug abusers are victimized by the disease of addiction. This approach views drugs as medically harmful and argues that effective drug control is necessary as a matter of public health. The second approach, "cost-benefit specifism," proposes that drug policy be built around a balancing of the social costs of drug abuse (crime, broken families, drug-related killings, etc.) with the costs of enforcement. The third approach, the "legalist," suggests that drug control policies are necessary in order to prevent the collapse of social order and of society itself. Advocates of the legalist perspective say that drug use is "defiance of lawful authority that threatens the social fabric."[39] According to Zimring and Gordon, all recent and contemporary antidrug policies have been based upon one or the other of these three schools of thought. Unfortunately, say those authors, it may not be possible to base successful antidrug policy on such beliefs, since they do not necessarily recognize the everyday realities associated with drug use. Nonetheless, antidrug abuse legislation and activities undertaken in the United States today are accorded political and ideational legitimacy via all three perspectives.

Drug Abuse Legislation

Antidrug abuse legislation in the Untied States dates back to around 1875 when the city of San Francisco enacted a statute prohibiting the smoking of opium.[40] A number of western states were quick to follow the city's lead. The San Francisco law, and many which followed it, however, clearly targeted Chinese immigrants and were rarely applied to other ethnic groups which may have been involved in the practice.

The first major piece of federal antidrug legislation came in 1914, with enactment of the Harrison Narcotics Act. The **Harrison Act** required persons dealing in opium, morphine, heroin, cocaine, and specified derivatives of these drugs, to register with the federal government and to pay a tax of $1.00 per year. The only people permitted to register were physicians, pharmacists, and members of the medical profession. Nonregistered drug traffickers faced a maximum fine of $2,000 and up to five years in prison.

Because the Harrison Act allowed physicians to prescribe controlled drugs for the purpose of medical treatment, heroin addicts and other drug users could still legally purchase the drugs they needed. All the law required was a physician's prescription. By 1920, however, court rulings had established that drug "maintenance" only prolonged addiction and did not qualify as "treatment."[41] The era of legally available heroin had ended.

Marijuana was not included in the Harrison Act because it was not considered a dangerous drug.[42] By the 1930s, however, government attention had become riveted on marijuana.

Harrison Act The first major piece of federal antidrug legislation, passed in 1914.

Controlled Substances Act Title II of the Comprehensive Drug Abuse Prevention and Control Act of 1970, which established schedules classifying psychoactive drugs according to their degree of psychoactivity.

At the urging of the Federal Bureau of Narcotics, Congress passed the Marijuana Tax Act in 1937. As the title of the law indicates, the Marijuana Tax Act simply placed a tax of $100 per ounce on cannabis. Individuals not paying the tax were subject to prosecution. With the passage of the Boggs Act in 1951, however, marijuana, along with a number of other drugs, entered the class of federally prohibited controlled substances. The Boggs Act also removed heroin from the list of medically useful substances and required the removal, within 120 days, of any medicines containing heroin from pharmacies across the country.[43]

The Narcotic Control Act of 1956 increased penalties for drug trafficking and possession and made the sale of heroin to anyone under age 18 a capital offense. However, on the eve of the massive explosion in drug use which was to begin in the mid-1960s, the Kennedy administration began a shift in emphasis from the strict punishment of drug traffickers and users to rehabilitation. A 1963 presidential commission[44] recommended elimination of the Federal Bureau of Narcotics, reduced prison terms for drug offenders, and stressed the need for research and social programs in dealing with the drug problem.

The Comprehensive Drug Abuse Prevention and Control Act of 1970

By 1970 America's drug problem was clear to almost everyone, and legislators were anxious to return to a more punitive approach to controlling drug abuse. Under President Nixon, legislation designed to encompass all aspects of drug abuse and to permit federal intervention at all levels of use was enacted. Termed the Comprehensive Drug Abuse Prevention and Control Act of 1970, the bill still forms the basis of federal enforcement efforts today. Title II of the Comprehensive Drug Abuse Prevention and Control Act is the Controlled Substances Act (CSA). The CSA sets up five schedules which classify psychoactive drugs according to their degree of psychoactivity and abuse potential.[45] The five schedules are described below and summarized in Table 15–1.

- Schedule I controlled substances have no established medical usage, cannot be used safely, and have great potential for abuse.[46] Federal law requires that any research employing Schedule I substances be fully documented and that the substances themselves be stored in secure vaults. Included under this category are heroin, LSD, mescaline, peyote, methaqualone (Quaaludes), psilocybin, marijuana,[47] and hashish as well as other specified hallucinogens. Penalties for a first-offense possession and sale of Schedule I controlled substances under the federal Narcotic Penalties and Enforcement Act of 1986 range up to life imprisonment and a $10 million fine. Penalties increase for subsequent offenses.
- Schedule II substances are defined as drugs with high abuse potential for which there is a currently accepted pharmacological or medical use. Most Schedule II substances are also considered to be addictive.[48] Drugs which fall into this category include opium, morphine, codeine, cocaine, phencyclidine (PCP), and their derivatives. Certain other stimulants such as methylphenidate (Ritalin®) and phenmetrazine (Preludin®) and a few barbiturates with high abuse potential also come under Schedule II. Legal access to Schedule II substances requires written nonrefillable prescriptions, vault storage, and thorough record keeping by vendors. Penalties for first-offense possession and sale of Schedule II controlled substances range up to 20 years imprisonment and a $5 million fine under the federal Narcotic Penalties and Enforcement Act. Penalties increase for subsequent offenses.
- Schedule III substances involve lower abuse potential than do those in previous schedules. They are drugs with an accepted medical use, but which may lead to a high level of psychological dependence or to moderate or low physical dependence.[49] Schedule III substances include many of the drugs found in Schedule II, but in derivative or diluted form. Common low-dosage antidiarrheals, such as opium-containing paregoric, and cold medicines or pain relievers with low concentrations of codeine fall into this category. Anabolic steroids, whose abuse by professional athletes is coming under increased scrutiny, were added to the list of Schedule III controlled substances by congressional action in 1991. Legitimate access to Schedule III drugs is through a doctor's prescription (written or oral) with refills authorized in the same manner. Maximum penalties associated with first-offense possession and sale of Schedule III controlled substances under federal law include five years imprisonment and fines of up to $1 million.

Table 15-1 Categories of Controlled Substances under the Federal Controlled Substances Act

Drugs	Schedule	Names	Physical Dependency	Psychological Dependency	Cost	Primary Sources of Supply
Narcotics						
Opium	II, III, V	Dover's powder, Paregoric, Parepectolin	High	High		Asia, Mexico
Morphine	II, III	Morphine, Pectoral syrup	High	High		Pharmaceutical diversion
Codeine	II, III, V	Codeine, Empirin compound with codeine, Robitussin A-C	Moderate	Moderate		
Heroin	I	Diacetylmorphine, horse, smack	High	High	$2.00 per milligram (or $100 per day for an average user)	Asia, Mexico, Afghanistan, Pakistan, Iran
Hydromorphone	II	Dilaudid	High	High		
Meperidine (pethidine)	II	Demerol, Pethadol	High	High		Pharmaceutical diversion
Methadone	II	Dolophine, Methadone, Methadose	High	High		
Other narcotics	I, II, III, IV, V	LAAM, Leritine, Levo-Dromoran, Percodan, Tussionex, Fentanyl, Darvon, Talwin, Lomotil	High-low	High-low		
Depressants						
Cloral hydrate	IV	Noctec, Somnos	Moderate	Moderate		
Barbiturates	II, III, IV	Amobarbital, Phenobarbital, Butisol, Tuinal, Phenoxbarbital, Secobarbital	High-moderate	High-moderate		Domestic production
Glutethimide	III	Doriden Optimil,	High	High		
Methaqualone	II	Parest, Quaalude, Somnafac, Sopor	High	High	$3.00-10.00 (retail)	Pharmaceutical diversion
Benzodiazepines	IV	Ativan, Azene, Clonopin, Dalmane, Diazepam, Librium, Serax, Tranxene, Valium, Verstran	Low	Low		
Other depressants	III, IV	Equanil, Miltown, Noludar, Placidyl, Valmid	Moderate	Moderate		
Steroids						
Anabolic steroids	III	Anabolin, Androlone, Dianabol, Kabolin, Winstrol	Low	High	$5-100 per day for an average user	Pharmaceutical diversion
Stimulants						
Cocaine	II	Coke, flake, snow	Possible	High	$800 to $2,100 per ounce (wholesale) $120 per gram (retail)	Peru, Bolivia, Colombia, Ecuador

Table 15-1 (continued)

Drugs	Schedule	Names	Physical Dependency	Psychological Dependency	Cost	Primary Sources of Supply
Stimulants (continued)						
Amphetamines	II, III	Biphetamine, Delcobese, Desoxyn, Dexedrine, Mediatric, crank, ice	Possible	High	$3.00 per dosage unit (retail)	Domestic production
Phenmetrazine	II	Preludin	Possible	High		
Methylphenidate	II	Ritalin	Possible	High		Pharmaceutical diversion
Other stimulants	III, IV	Adipex, Bacarate, Cylert, Didrex, Ionamin, Plegine, PreSate, Sanorex, Tenuate, Tepanil, Voranil	Possible	High		
Hallucinogens						
LSD	I	Acid, microdot	None	Degree unknown	$2.00-8.00 per dose	Clandestine laboratories
Mescaline and peyote	I	Mesc, buttons, cactus	None	Degree unknown		American Southwest
Amphetamine variants	I	2, 5-DMA, PMA, STP MDA, MMDA, TMA, DOM DOB	Unknown	Degree unknown		Clandestine laboratories
Phencyclidine	II	PCP, angel dust, hog	Degree unknown	High		
Phencyclidine analogs	I	PCE, PCPy, TCP	Degree unknown	Degree unknown		
Other hallucinogens	I	Bufotenine, Ibogaine, DMT, DET, Psilocybin	None	Degree unknown		
Cannabis						
Marijuana	I	Pot, Acapulco gold, grass, reefer, sinsemilla, Thai sticks	Degree unknown	Moderate	Marijuana, $60-130 per ounce (retail)	Domestic production, South America
Tetrahydro-cannabinol	I	THC	Degree unknown	Moderate	Sinsemilla, $165-210 per ounce (retail)	
Hashish	I	Hash	Degree unknown	Moderate		Southeast Asia
Hashish oil	I	Hash oil	Degree unknown	Moderate		

Sources: Adapted from the National Narcotics Intelligence Consumer's Committee, *The NNICC Report: The Supply of Illicit Drugs to the United States* (Washington, D.C.: NNICC, 1997); Drug Enforcement Administration, *Drugs of Abuse* (Washington, D.C.: U.S. Government Printing Office, 1997); and United States Pharmacopeial Convention, *United States Pharmacopeial Formulary* Vol. II, 11th ed. (Rockville, MD: USPC, 1991).

- Schedule IV substances have a relatively low potential for abuse (when compared to higher schedules), are useful in established medical treatments, and involve only a limited risk of psychological or physical dependency.[50] Depressants and minor tranquilizers such as Valium, Librium, and Equanil fall into this category, as do some stimulants. Schedule IV substances are medically available in the same fashion as Schedule III drugs. Maximum penalties associated with first-offense possession and sale of Schedule IV substances under federal law include three years in prison and fines of up to $1 million.

- Schedule V controlled substances are prescription drugs with a low potential for abuse, and with only a very limited possibility of psychological or physical dependence.[51] Cough medicines (antitussives) and antidiarrheals containing small amounts of opium, morphine, or codeine are found in Schedule V. A number of Schedule V medicines may be purchased through retail vendors with only minimal controls, or upon the signature of the buyer (with some form of identification required). Maximum federal penalties for first-offense possession and sale of Schedule V substances include one year in prison and a $250,000 fine.

Pharmacologists, chemists, and botanists are constantly discovering and creating new drugs. Likewise, street-corner "chemists" in clandestine laboratories churn out inexpensive designer drugs—psychoactive substances with widely varying effects and abuse potential. One designer drug now catching the attention of many is methamphetamine. Methamphetamine is a stimulant drug chemically related to other amphetamines, but with stronger effects on the central nervous system. Street names for the drug include "speed," "meth," and "crank." Methamphetamine is used in pill form, or in powdered form by snorting or injecting.[52] Crystallized methamphetamine known as "ice," "crystal," or "glass," is a smokable and still more powerful form of the drug. Effects of methamphetamine use include increased heart rate and blood pressure, increased wakefulness, insomnia, increased physical activity, decreased appetite, and anxiety, paranoia, or violent behavior. The drug is easily made in simple home "laboratories" from readily available chemicals, and recipes describing how to produce the substance circulate on the Internet. Methamphetamine appeals to the abuser because it increases the body's metabolism and produces euphoria and alertness, and gives the user a sense of increased energy. Methamphetamine, an increasingly popular drug at raves (all night dancing parties), is not physically addictive but can be psychologically addictive. High doses or chronic use of the drug increases nervousness, irritability, and paranoia.

The Controlled Substances Act includes provisions for determining which new drugs should be controlled and into which schedule they should be placed. Under the CSA, criteria for assigning a new drug to one of the existing schedules include[53] (1) the drug's actual or relative potential for abuse; (2) scientific evidence of the drug's pharmacological effects; (3) the state of current scientific knowledge regarding the substance; (4) its history and current pattern of abuse; (5) the scope, duration, and significance of abuse; (6) what, if any, risk there is to the public health; (7) the drug's psychic or physiological dependence liability; and (8) whether the substance is an immediate precursor of a substance already controlled. Proceedings to add a new chemical substance to the list of those controlled by law or to delete or change the schedule of an existing drug may be initiated by the chief administrator of the Drug Enforcement Administration, the Department of Health and Human Services, or a petition from any interested person—including manufacturers, medical societies, or public interest groups.[54]

In 1997 the "date rape drug" Rohypnol (discussed in Chapters 2 and 4) was proposed for addition to the list of Schedule I controlled substances by DEA officials. Rohypnol (whose generic name is flunitrazepam) is a powerful sedative manufactured by Hoffmann-LaRoche Pharmaceuticals. A member of the benzodiazepine family of depressants, it is legally prescribed in 64 countries for insomnia and as a pre-operative anesthetic. Seven to 10 times more powerful than Valium, Rohypnol has become popular with some college students and with "young men [who] put doses of Rohypnol in women's drinks without their consent in order to lower their inhibitions."[55] Available on the black market, it dissolves easily in drinks and can leave anyone who unknowingly consumes it unconscious for hours—making them vulnerable to sexual assault. The drug is variously known as "ropies," "roche," "ruffles," "roofies," and "rophies" on the street.

We cannot define what victory is. We cannot tell you which objectives to look at. We can only try to have policymakers at all levels of government working together to do what is right for this nation: reduce the impact of drug abuse and increase the strength of our families and communities. If we do that, we may still have a drug use issue, but we will have a healthier nation that can absorb that issue, that will reduce the harm of drug abuse.

—Ross Deck

As of this writing, Rohypnol is still officially classified as a Schedule IV drug. However, penalties for trafficking in flunitrazepam were increased under the Drug-Induced Rape Prevention Act of 1996,[56] effectively placing it into a Schedule I-type category for sentencing purposes. The U.S. Sentencing Commission then proposed modifying federal sentencing guidelines to raise the penalty for offenses involving trafficking in flunitrazepam to 20 years imprisonment for one gram of the substance—a proposal which is still pending as this book goes to press. The maximum sentence for importing and exporting offenses involving flunitrazepam was raised to 20 years imprisonment regardless of weight.

The Anti-Drug Abuse Act of 1988

In 1988 the country's Republican leadership, under then-President Reagan, capitalized upon the public's frustration with rampant drug abuse and stepped up the "war on drugs." The president created a new cabinet-level post, naming a "drug czar" who was to be in charge of federal drug-fighting initiatives through the Office of National Drug Control Policy (ONDCP). William Bennett, a former secretary of education, was appointed to fill the post. At the same time, the Anti-Drug Abuse Act was passed by Congress. The overly optimistic tenor of the act is clear from its preamble, which reads: "It is the declared policy of the United States Government to create a Drug-Free America by 1995."[57] The goal, which reflected far more political rhetoric than realistic planning, was both overly optimistic and incredibly naive.

Even so, the Anti–Drug Abuse Act of 1988 had plenty of teeth. Under the law penalties for "recreational" drug users increased substantially,[58] and weapons purchases by suspected drug dealers became more difficult. The law also denied federal benefits, ranging from loans (including student loans) to contracts and licenses, to convicted drug offenders.[59] Earned benefits, such as social security, retirement, health and disability benefits, are not affected by the legislation. Nor are welfare payments or existing public housing arrangements (although separate legislation does provide for termination of public housing tenancy for drug offenses). Under the law, civil penalties of up to $10,000 may be assessed against convicted "recreational" users for possession of even small amounts of drugs.

The legislation also included the possibility of capital punishment for drug-related murders. The killing of a police officer by offenders seeking to avoid apprehension or prosecution was specifically cited as carrying a possible sentence of death, although other murders by major drug dealers also fall under the capital punishment provision.[60] On May 14, 1991, 37-year-old David Chandler, an Alabama marijuana kingpin, became the first person sentenced to die under the law.[61] Chandler had been convicted of ordering the murder of a police informant in 1990.

One especially interesting aspect of the Anti-Drug Abuse Act is its provision for designating selected areas as high-intensity drug trafficking areas (HIDTAs), making them eligible for federal drug fighting assistance in order that joint interagency operations can be implemented to reduce drug problems. Using the law, former **Drug Czar** William Bennett, in 1989, declared Washington, D.C., a "drug zone." His designation was based in part upon what was then the city's reputation as the murder capital of the country. At the time of the declaration, over 60% of Washington's murders were said to be drug related,[62] and legislators and tourists were clamoring for action. Bennett's plan called for more federal investigators, prosecutors, and specially built prisons to handle accused drug dealers. The immediate results of the secretary's action, however, were squabbles between federal and city officials over who should be responsible for drug enforcement efforts within the city.

On June 9, 1995, more than six years later—and after interagency squabbles had been worked out—a new drug czar, Lee P. Brown, presided at the official opening of the Washington/Baltimore High Intensity Drug Trafficking Area program. The Washington-area HIDTA, funded for $12.6 million during fiscal 1995, became the seventh HIDTA to begin operation in the country (the others are in New York City, Los Angeles, Miami, Houston, the Southwest Border area, and Puerto Rico/U.S. Virgin Islands) under the Office of National Drug Control Policy. In 1996, former U.S. Army General Barry R. McCaffrey assumed directorship of the ONDCP.

Drug Czar   The head of the Office of National Drug Control Policy (ONDCP). A federal cabinet-level position that was originally created during the years of the Reagan presidency to organize federal drug fighting efforts.

Other Federal Anti-Drug Legislation

Other significant federal anti-drug legislation exists in the form of the Crime Control Act of 1990 and the Violent Crime Control and Law Enforcement Act of 1994. The Crime Control

Act of 1990 (1) doubled the appropriations authorized for drug law enforcement grants to states and local communities; (2) enhanced drug control and education programs aimed at the nation's schools; (3) expanded specific drug enforcement assistance to rural states; (4) expanded regulation of precursor chemicals used in the manufacture of illegal drugs; (5) sanctioned anabolic steroids under the Controlled Substances Act; (6) included provisions to enhance control over international money laundering; (7) created "drug-free school zones" by enhancing penalties for drug offenses occurring in close proximity to schools; (8) enhanced the ability of federal agents to seize property used in drug transactions or purchased with drug proceeds.

The Violent Crime Control and Law Enforcement Act of 1994 provided $245 million for rural anticrime and drug efforts; set aside $1.6 billion for direct funding to localities around the country for anticrime efforts, including drug treatment programs; budgeted $383 million for drug treatment programs for state and Federal prisoners; created a treatment schedule for all drug-addicted federal prisoners; required post-conviction drug testing of all federal prisoners upon release; allocated $1 billion for drug court programs for nonviolent offenders with substance abuse problems; and mandated new, stiff penalties for drug crimes committed by gangs. The act also tripled penalties for using children to deal drugs near schools and playgrounds and enhanced penalties for drug dealing in drug free zones near playgrounds, schoolyards, video arcades, and youth centers. Finally, the law also expanded the federal death penalty to cover offenders involved in large-scale drug trafficking and mandated life imprisonment for criminals convicted of three violent felonies or drug offenses.

Wake up, America. The drug war is over. We lost.
—David Nyhan, *Boston Globe* Columnist

The Investigation of Drug Abuse and Manufacturing

Investigation of the illegal production, transportation, sale, and use of controlled substances is a major area of police activity. Investigation of drug manufacturing activities has given rise to an area of case law which supplements the *plain view* doctrine which we discussed in Chapter 7. Two legal concepts, "abandonment" and "curtilage," while generally applicable elsewhere, have taken on special significance in drug investigations. Abandonment refers to the fact that property, once it has been clearly thrown away or discarded, ceases to fall under Fourth Amendment protections against unreasonable search and seizure. **Curtilage** is a legal term which describes the area surrounding a residence which can reasonably be said to be a part of the residence for Fourth Amendment purposes.

In 1988 the U.S. Supreme Court decided the case of *California* v. *Greenwood*,[63] which began when Officer Jenny Stracner of the Laguna Beach, California, Police Department arranged with a neighborhood trash collector to receive garbage collected at a suspect's residence. The refuse was later found to include items "indicative of narcotics use."[64] Based upon this evidence, Stracner applied for a search warrant, which was used in a search of the defendant's home. The search uncovered controlled substances, including cocaine and hashish. The defendant, Greenwood, was arrested. Upon conviction, Greenwood appealed, arguing that the trash had been placed in opaque bags and could reasonably be expected to remain unopened until it was collected and disposed of. His appeal emphasized his right to privacy with respect to his trash.

The Supreme Court disagreed, saying that "[a]n expectation of privacy does not give rise to Fourth Amendment protection unless society is prepared to accept that expectation as objectively reasonable…[I]t is common knowledge that plastic garbage bags left on or at the side of a public street are readily accessible to animals, children, scavengers, snoops, and other members of the public." Hence, the Court concluded, the property in question had been abandoned, and no reasonable expectation of privacy can attach to trash left for collection "in an area accessible to the public." The concept of abandonment extends beyond trash which is actively discarded. In *Abel* v. *U.S.* (1960),[65] for example, the Court found that the warrantless search of a motel room by an FBI agent immediately after it had been vacated was acceptable.

Curtilage, a concept which initially found clear recognition in the case of *Oliver* v. *U.S.* (1984),[66] refers to the fact that household activity generally extends beyond the walls of a residence. People living in a house, for example, spend some of their time in their yard—an area which they probably think of as private and under the control of their household. Territory within the curtilage of a residence has generally been accorded the same Fourth Amendment guarantees against search and seizure as areas within the walls of a house or apartment. But

Curtilage A legal term which describes the area surrounding a residence which can reasonably be said to be a part of the residence for Fourth Amendment purposes.

Theory into Practice

DRUGS: WHAT'S IN A NAME?

Drug names have been a source of confusion to many people attempting to grapple with the drug problem. A single drug may have a dozen or more names. Drugs may be identified according to

BRAND NAME: The name given to a chemical substance by its manufacturer. Brand names are registered idioms and are often associated with trademarks. They are used to identify a drug in the pharmaceutical marketplace and may not be used by other manufacturers. Psychoactive substances with no known medical application or experimental use are not produced by legitimate companies and have no brand name.

GENERIC NAME: The chemical or other identifying name of a drug. Generic names are often used by physicians in writing prescriptions which are less costly than when brand names are specified. Generic names are also used in most drug abuse legislation at the federal and state levels in order to specify controlled substances. Generic names are sometimes applicable only to the psychoactive chemical substances in drugs and not the "drugs" themselves. In marijuana, for example, the chemical tetrahydrocannabinol, or THC, is the active substance.

PSYCHOACTIVE CATEGORY: Psychoactive drugs are categorized according to the effects they produce on the human mind. Narcotics, stimulants, depressants, and hallucinogens are typical psychoactive categories.

STREET NAMES: Street names are slang terms. Many of them originated with the pop culture of the 1960s, and others continue to be produced by modern-day drug subculture. Street names for cocaine include "coke," "flake," and "snow," while heroin is known as "horse," "smack," or "H."

"PCP," AN EXAMPLE: "PCP" and "angel dust" are the street names for a veterinary anesthetic marketed under the brand name Sernylan. Sernylan contains the psychoactive chemical phencyclidine. Phencyclidine is classified as a depressant under the Controlled Substances Act.

The drug problem did not develop overnight; it took years and years to get to this point as a result of misguided attitudes and a mindset that drug usage, at least using cocaine and marijuana, was all right. Dealing with the drug problem involves changing attitudes, and that takes time.

—Judge Reggie B. Walton

just how far does the curtilage of a residence extend? Does it vary according to the type or location of the residence? Is it necessary for an area to be fenced in order for it to fall within residential curtilage?

A collateral area of concern is that of activity conducted in fields, out of doors. The open fields doctrine began with the case of *Hester v. U.S.* (1924),[67] in which the Supreme Court held that law enforcement officers could search an open field without need for a warrant. The *Oliver* case extended that authority to include secluded and fenced fields posted with No Trespassing signs.

In *U.S. v. Dunn* (1987),[68] the U.S. Supreme Court considered a Houston-area defendant's claim that the space surrounding a barn, which was located approximately 50 yards from the edge of a fence surrounding a farmhouse, was protected against intrusion by the Fourth Amendment. The Court rejected the defendant's arguments and concluded that, even though an area may be fenced, it is not within the curtilage of a residence if it is sufficiently distant from the area of household activity which attends the residence.

Other, related decisions, have supported seizures based upon warrantless aerial observation of marijuana plants growing in the backyard of defendant's homes[69] and those based upon naked-eye sightings from helicopters of the contents of greenhouses.[70] The Court's reasoning in such cases is that flights within navigable airspace are common. Where no comprehensive efforts to secure privacy have been made, there can be no reasonable expectation of privacy—even within areas that might normally be considered curtilage. Were sophisticated surveillance techniques to be employed by law enforcement authorities, however—such as the use of drone aircraft, satellite, or infrared photography—the Court's decision would be in doubt because such devices extend beyond the realm of "normal flight."

The sale of illegal drugs is a $57 billion annual industry in the United States.[71] Some perspective can be gained on this figure by recognizing that Americans spend approximately $44 billion on alcohol products and another $37 billion on tobacco products annually.[72]

According to a federal study released in 1997,[73] 13 million Americans were "current" users of illegal drugs—defined as those "having used an illicit drug in the month before the survey." Ten million people reported using marijuana, and 6 million of those were found to be "frequent" marijuana users (defined as "use on at least 51 days during the past year"). Around 1.75 million used cocaine in various forms, and 608,000 were classified as "hardcore" cocaine addicts. Many users reported using more than one drug, either alone or in combination, while the illegal use of inhalants, hallucinogens, heroin, and the nonmedical use of psychotherapeutics accounted for the remainder of the total number of reported users.

Of the 13 million reported total illicit drug users, 2.2% were between the ages of 12 and 13; 15.6% were 16-17 (which was the age range showing the highest rate of illicit use); and 20% were 18–20. Rates of use declined with age, and only about 1% of those over age 50 reported current illicit drug use. The study also found that a total of 77 million Americans (37% of persons aged 12 and older) had used an illegal drug at least once; with 70 million reporting marijuana use, 23.5 million the use of cocaine, 4 million reporting the use of crack-cocaine, 2 million heroin usage, and 18 million the consumption of hallucinogens. All these figures represent a considerable decline from 18 years earlier—or 1979, the year in which the highest levels of drug abuse ever recorded in the United States were reported (the number of adults reported abusing drugs in 1979 was 24.3 million), although figures for recent years have shown a gradual increase in drug use (especially that classified as "occasional use"). As the Office of National Drug Control Policy points out, however, federal studies typically underestimate the number of hard-core drug abusers in the country because they fail to survey the homeless, prisoners, people living at colleges, active-duty military personnel, and those in mental and other institutions. ONDCP estimates that there are 2.1 million hard-core cocaine addicts and 600,000 heroin addicts in the country[74]—figures well above those provided by the survey.

Another way to measure the size of the drug problem in America is to analyze the dollars spent to combat it. In 1981, for example, total federal spending for all drug control efforts, including enforcement activities, educational programs, and treatment, totaled $1.5 billion. By 1989 the figure had risen to $6.7 billion and reached $12.2 billion in 1993. Fiscal year 1998 federal expenditures on drug control activities stood at $16 billion.[75] State budgetary allowances for drug control activities, which are considerable, are not included in these figures.

A number of agencies report on the amount of various types of drugs which enter the country or are produced here. One such group, the National Narcotics Intelligence Consumers Committee (NNICC), was established in 1978 to coordinate the collection and analysis of foreign and domestic strategic drug-related intelligence.[76] Members of the NNICC include the DEA, FBI, CIA, IRS, INS, Coast Guard, and other federal agencies charged with drug law enforcement. NNICC data describe the availability and use of marijuana, cocaine, PCP, and heroin. Other dangerous drugs and the money laundering schemes of drug traffickers are also a focus of NNICC activity. NNICC and DEA data for each of the major drug categories are described in the paragraphs that follow.

MARIJUANA

Marijuana, whose botanical name is *cannabis sativa L.*, grows wild throughout most of the tropic and temperate regions of the world.[77] Marijuana commonly comes in loose form, as the ground leaves and seeds of the hemp plant. Also available to street-level users are stronger forms of the drug, such as sinsemilla (the flowers and the leaves of the female cannabis plant), hashish (the resinous secretions of the hemp plant), and hash oil (a chemically concentrated form of delta-9-tetrahydrocannabinol, or THC, the psychotropic agent in marijuana).

In this crime-weary, drug-infested nation, it now appears that any tough-on-crime proposal goes, no matter how dangerous it may be to individual rights.

—USA Today editorial

Smoking marijuana in a San Francisco, California, clinic. In 1996 voters in California and Arizona passed ballot initiatives legalizing the use of marijuana for medical purposes when approved or prescribed by a doctor. Michael Sullivan, left, and David Shull of San Francisco share a pipe in the smoking lounge. Both men have AIDS and go to the CHAMP office to smoke pot to make them feel better. *Fred Mertz*

Marijuana is usually smoked, although it may be eaten or made into a "tea." A recent report[78] by the ONDCP, however, found that the use of inhalants, such as spray paint and solvents, in combination with marijuana is growing in popularity. Low doses of marijuana create restlessness and an increasing sense of well-being, followed by dreamy relaxation and a frequent craving for sweets.[79] Sensory perceptions may be heightened by the drug, while memory and rational thought are impaired (see Table 15–2). Marijuana's effects begin within a few minutes following use and may last for two to three hours.

Although marijuana has no clearly established medical use, medical acceptability of the usefulness of marijuana as a supplemental medication in cases of on-going chemotherapy (where it seems to reduce nausea); glaucoma (where it may reduce pressure within the eye); anorexia and "AIDS wasting" (where it may increase appetite and lead to weight gain); and sleep disorders is increasing.[80] In 1996 voters in California and Arizona passed ballot initiatives legalizing the use of marijuana for medical purposes when approved or prescribed by a doctor (see box on page 651). Even before the proposition was brought to ballot boxes, however, the *Drug Enforcement Report* found that marijuana was being openly used for medicinal purposes throughout San Francisco with the tacit approval of local officials and with no interference from federal enforcement agencies.[81]

Most illicit marijuana users, however, do not use the substance for medicinal purposes. The majority of users are young people, with many less than 20 years old. In 1996, for example, 23% of eighth-graders had tried marijuana at least once in their lifetimes, and 11.3% were current users, according to the U.S. Department of Health and Human Services.[82]

Intelligence shows that domestic production accounts for about 19% of all marijuana in the United States. Most marijuana brought into the United States comes from Mexico[83] and Colombia.[84] Of all the marijuana entering the country or produced domestically, approximately one quarter, or 4,000 metric tons, is seized or lost in transit.[85]

Cocaine

Cocaine (cocaine hydrochloride) is the most potent central nervous system stimulant of natural origin.[86] Cocaine is extracted from the leaves of the coca plant (whose botanical name is *Erythroxylon coca*). Since ancient times the drug has been used by native Indians through-

Table 15-2 Major Controlled Substances: Their Uses and Effects

Substances	Legitimate Use	Street Use
Narcotics, including opium, morphine, heroin, codeine, Dilaudid	pain relief, antidiarrheal, cough suppressant	pleasure, euphoria, lack of concern, general feelings of well-being
Stimulants, including amphetamines such as Dexedrine and Benzedrine, and other drugs such as cocaine, crack, crank, methamphetamine, and ice	increase alertness, reduce fatigue, control weight	produce excitability, feelings of competence and power
General depressants, including sedatives and tranquilizers such as Nembutal, Seconal, Phenobarbital, Quaalude, Sopor, Valium, Librium, Thorazine, and Equanil	release from anxiety, mood elevators, treatment of psychological problems	in high doses to produce intoxication, also used to counter the effects of other drugs or in the self-treatment of withdrawal
Marijuana, including hashish, cannabis, sinsemilla, and hashish oil	none fully recognized; possible use in cancer chemotherapy for treatment of nausea	euphoria, relaxation, intoxication, time distortion, memory alterations, focused awareness
Hallucinogens, including LSD, mescaline, psilocybin, peyote, and MDA	none	to produce hallucinations and distortions of reality
Inhalants, including nitrous oxide, gasoline, toluene, amyl nitrite, and butyl nitrite	some are used as medical sedatives	to produce a "rush" or sense of lightheadedness
Anabolic steroids, including nandrolene, oxandrolene, oxymetholone, and stanozolol	weight gain, treatment of anemia, breast cancer, and angioedema	to build muscle mass and increase strength (in weightlifters, professional athletes, others)

Note: Each drug may have a variety of effects or may produce different effects on individual users. Drugs used in combination with one another may have unpredictable effects.

Source: Adapted from Drug Enforcement Administration, *Drugs of Abuse* (Washington, D.C.: U.S. Department of Justice, 1997); and U.S. Pharmacopeial Convention, *Drug Information*, 15th ed. (Rockville, MD: USP, 1995).

---

out the highlands of Central and South America, who chew the leaves of the coca plant to overcome altitude sickness and to sustain the high levels of physical energy needed for rigorous mountain farming.

Cocaine has some medicinal value as a topical anesthetic for use on sensitive tissues such as the eyes and mucous membranes. Throughout the early 1900s cocaine was valued by physicians for its ability to anesthetize tissue while simultaneously constricting blood vessels and reducing bleeding. Recently, more effective products have replaced cocaine in many medical applications.

A recent report by the ONDCP classifies cocaine users into three groups: "1) the younger, often minority crack user; 2) the older injector who is combining cocaine HCL with heroin in a speeedball; and 3) the older, more affluent user who is snorting cocaine HCL."[87] Cocaine generally reaches the United States in the form of a much-processed white crystalline powder. It is often diluted with a variety of other ingredients including sugar and anesthetics such as lidocaine. Dilution allows sellers to reap high profits from small amounts of the drug.

Cocaine produces intense psychological effects, including a sense of exhilaration, superabundant energy, hyperactivity, and extended wakefulness.[88] Irritability and apprehension may be unwanted side effects. Excessive doses may cause seizures and death from heart failure, cerebral hemorrhage, and respiratory collapse. Some studies show that repeated use of cocaine may heighten sensitivity to these toxic side effects of the drug.[89]

NNICC data indicate that cocaine has become the country's most dangerous commonly used drug. During a recent year, nearly 100,000 hospital emergencies involving cocaine abuse were reported across the country.[90] At the time of the NNICC report, cocaine was available in all major American metropolitan areas and most small communities. The cocaine derivative crack, manufactured by numerous street-level laboratories, was available primarily in large urban areas. A recent DEA survey, however, found that "crack dealers are expanding their markets to target potential users in small towns and rural areas across the United States" because "crack distribution and use appears to have reached the saturation point in large urban areas."[91] The Federal-wide Drug Seizure System reports the seizure of around 300,000 pounds of cocaine throughout the United States annually.[92]

Most cocaine enters the United States from Peru, Bolivia, or Colombia. Together, these three countries have an estimated annual production capability of around 760 tons of pure cocaine.[93] During the 1980s, most cocaine coming into the United States was controlled by the Medellin Cartel, based in Medellin, Colombia. Multinational counterdrug efforts had crippled the cartel by the start of the 1990s, however, and the Cali Cartel (based in Cali, Colombia), a loose organization of five semi-independent trafficking organizations, took over as the major illegal supplier of cocaine to this country. According to the DEA, "the Cali Cartel has grown into the most powerful international drug trafficking organization in history." "Each year," said the report, "the Cali Cartel smuggles hundreds of tons of cocaine into the United States and Europe and launders billions of dollars in drug proceeds."[94] Recent arrests of the Cali Cartel's top leaders, Gilberto Rodriguez and his brother, Miguel, however, are said to have sounded the death knell for what may have been the world's most successful drug trafficking organization ever.[95]

A key response to drug use and drug trafficking is an aggressive and coordinated law enforcement effort. Americans have the right to feel safe in their homes and secure in their communities.

—The White House, National Drug Control Strategy

HEROIN

Classified as a narcotic, heroin is a derivative of opium—itself the product of the milky fluid found in the flowering poppy plant (*Papaver somniferum*). Opium poppies have been grown in the Mediterranean region since 300 B.C.[96] and are now produced in many other parts of the world as well. Although heroin is not used medicinally in this country, many of the substances to which it is chemically related—such as morphine, codeine, hydrocodone, naloxone, and oxymorphone—do have important medical uses as pain relievers.

Heroin is a highly seductive and addictive drug which, when smoked, injected underneath the skin (skin popping), or "shot" directly into the bloodstream (mainlining), produces euphoria. Because tolerance for the drug increases with use, larger and larger doses of heroin must be injected to achieve the pleasurable effects desired by addicts. Heroin deprivation causes withdrawal symptoms which initially include watery eyes, runny nose, yawning, and perspiration. Further deprivation results in restlessness, irritability, insomnia, tremors, nausea, and vomiting. Stomach cramps, diarrhea, chills, and other flulike symptoms are also common. Most withdrawal symptoms disappear within seven to ten days,[97] or when the drug is readministered.

Street-level heroin varies widely in purity. It is often cut with powdered milk, food coloring, cocoa, or brown sugar. Most heroin sold in the United States is only 5% pure.[98] Because of dosage uncertainties, overdosing is a common problem for addicts. Mild overdoses produce lethargy and stupor. Larger doses may cause convulsions, coma, and death. Other risks, including infectious hepatitis and AIDS, are associated with self-administered heroin through the use of dirty needles. The National Institute on Drug Abuse (NIDA) notes that the number of intravenous drug users with AIDS is doubling every 14 to 16 months.[99] The causes of such spread include sharing "dirty" needles containing small amounts of contaminated blood left from other users in groups or at parties, and in "shooting galleries" where drug paraphernalia may be passed among many people. Likewise, the Centers for Disease Control and Prevention (CDC) estimates that almost one-third of AIDS cases are associated with intravenous (IV) drug use.[100] The CDC also reports that, as of late 1995, almost 60% of children under the age of 13 with AIDS contracted the disease from mothers who were IV drug users or who were sex partners with IV drug users.

Heroin abuse has remained fairly constant over the past few decades. Some indicators point to an increased availability of heroin in the last few years.[101] Street-level heroin prices have declined in recent years, while nationwide heroin-related emergency room admissions have reached almost 40,000 per year.

Most heroin in the United States comes from Southwest Asia (Afghanistan, Pakistan, and Iran), Southeast Asia (Burma, Laos, and Thailand), and Mexico. According to data from the

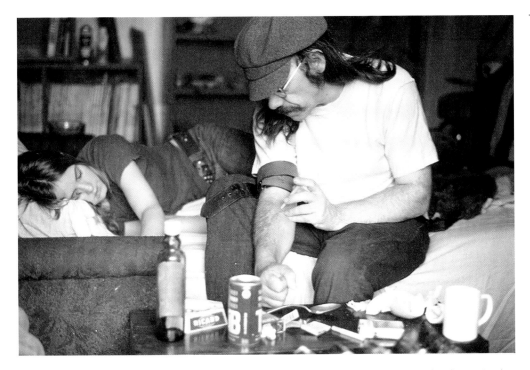

The sale and consumption of illicit drugs comprise a multibillion-dollar annual industry in the United States. Here, a heroin addict shoots up. *Alan Mercer, Stock Boston*

Heroin Signature Program (HSP), which uses chemical analysis of the trace elements in heroin supplies to identify source countries, 62% of all heroin entering the U.S. comes from South America.[102] The Federal Drug Seizure System reports the seizure of approximately 2,500 pounds of heroin throughout the United States annually.[103]

Evidence indicates that the heroin abuse picture is changing. Although, according to a recent ONDCP report,[104] older users still dominate heroin markets in all parts of the country, increasing numbers of non–inner-city young users (under 30 years of age) are turning to the drug. Additionally, because high-purity powdered heroin is widely available in most parts of the country, new users seem to be experimenting with heroin inhalation, which often appears to lead to injection as addiction progresses. Treatment programs report that the typical heroin user is male, over 30 years old, and has been in treatment previously.[105] Alcohol, cocaine, and marijuana remain concurrent problems for heroin users in treatment.

Drugs, Crime, and Social Problems

The drug problem in the United States is not simply one of drug use. The manufacture, possession, sale, and use of controlled substances are related to a variety of criminal activities and produce other large-scale social problems. Some of these problems are examined over the next few pages.

Drugs and Crime

The link between drugs and crime has at least three dimensions: (1) the possession, use, or sale of controlled substances which directly violates antidrug laws; (2) crimes committed by drug users in order to obtain more drugs, or crimes committed by persons whose judgment is altered by drugs; and (3) organized criminal activities in support of the drug trade and associated money laundering activities.

As Figure 15-3 shows, 970,200 persons over the age of 18 were arrested in 1996 for drug law violations (excluding alcohol) in the United States.[106] Seventy-five percent of all arrests nationally were for possession of controlled substances; the remainder were for sale, possession, or manufacture.[107] Arrests for heroin or cocaine possession accounted for 25.6% of all

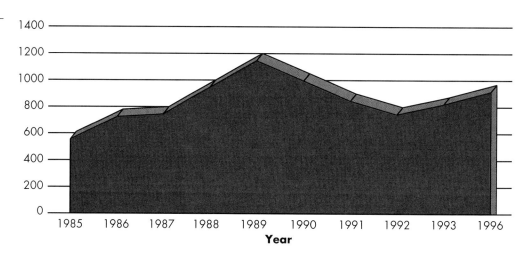

FIGURE 15–3 Adult arrests for drug law violations, 1985–1996. *Source:* Federal Bureau of Investigation, *Crime in the United States* (Washington, D.C.: U.S. Department of Justice, various years).

possession arrests, while 36.3% of such arrests were for marijuana possession.[108] Possession of PCP, LSD, amphetamines, and tranquilizers accounted for only a relatively small number of arrests.

A close examination of official statistics reveals considerable regional variation. Marijuana arrests in the Western states, for example, were less frequent than arrests for cocaine or heroin possession. Midwestern states, on the other hand, reported 100 percent more arrests for marijuana than they did for possession of cocaine and heroin.[109] The rate of drug law violations also varies greatly from region to region. Arrest rates are highest in the Western part of the country (682 per 100,000) and lowest in the South (506 per 100,000).[110]

After experiencing a decline from 1979 to 1992, the number of persons arrested for drug law violations is once again increasing. Moreover, as the data at the start of this chapter indicate, much of the overcrowding in federal and state prisons today is due to an accompanying increase in convictions for drug law violations.

Drugs and crimes are linked in other ways, as well. A recent report[111] by the Office for National Drug Control Policy, for example, claims that 5.2% of all homicides are "related to narcotic drug law" violations. "Reducing drug use will have a direct and positive impact on reducing criminal activity," says ONDCP. "Drug users often commit criminal offenses, such as theft and prostitution, to support an existing drug habit."

The link between drugs and other types of crime came into clearer focus at the end of 1987 with the establishment of the federal Data Center and Clearinghouse for Drugs and Crime, a part of the National Institute of Justice. A recent NIJ study[112] of 201 heroin users in Central and East Harlem (New York City) found that *each* daily user committed on average about 1,400 crimes per year. Of these offenses, 1,116 were directly drug related, involving primarily drug sales and use. Another 75 were relatively minor crimes such as shoplifting, but the remaining 209 offenses committed by each user involved relatively serious violations of the law such as robbery, burglary, theft, forgery, fraud, and the fencing of stolen goods. A separate study which followed the daily activities of 354 Baltimore heroin addicts over a nine-year period found that they had committed a total of nearly 750,000 criminal offenses.[113]

One of the most promising means of reducing the supply of drugs is a strong source country strategy.

—The White House, National Drug Control Strategy

A comprehensive effort designed to gauge the degree of drug use among criminal offenders is the NIJ's Drug Use Forecasting (DUF) program. DUF utilizes voluntary urine specimens and analyzes anonymous interview data from randomly selected male and female arrestees in 25 cities across the country. The percentage of sampled arrestees testing positive for any drug, including marijuana (but not alcohol) in selected cities during 1996 is shown in Figure 15–4. DUF data for 1996 range from a high of 83% of sampled female arrestees in Manhattan, to a low of 35% of arrested females in New Orleans who either tested positive for or admitted to recent drug use.[114] Cocaine was the most widely abused drug among arrestees in most cities, although there is evidence that its use may be declining.

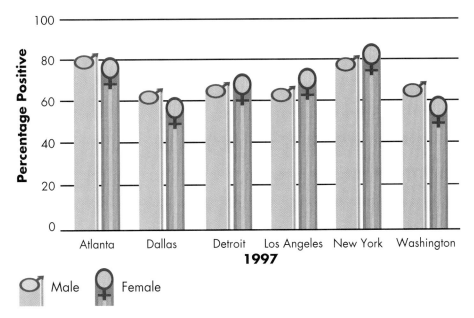

FIGURE 15–4 Percentage of arrestees testing positive for any drug in selected cities. *Source:* National Institute of Justice, *Drug Use Forecasting* (Washington, D.C.: NIJ, 1997).

A number of cautions should be held in mind when interpreting Figure 15–4. First, although the tendency among some who view the statistics is to conclude that drug use *causes* crime, it could be that both crime and drug use are the result of some other factor such as poverty, socialization, and so on. Second, given the rising number of drug arrests, it is not entirely surprising that many arrestees have drugs in their systems. Many of those arrested were arrested for drug sales, possession, or use. Third, self-reports of state correctional facility inmates, while still indicating a high level of drug use prior to criminal activity, do not necessarily support the data available through the Drug Use Forecasting Program. A survey of state prison inmates showed, for example, that 43% had been involved in daily drug use in the month before their current offense, while "only" 19% were using a major drug (heroin, methadone, cocaine, PCP, or LSD) on a daily or near-daily basis.[115]

MONEY LAUNDERING

Because cash can flow into the hands of dealers in huge amounts, it can be difficult to spend. Few people buy houses, cars, and other "big-ticket" items with cash, and cash transactions arouse suspicion. **Money laundering** is the name given to the process used by drug dealers to hide the source of their revenues[116] in order to avoid taxes and to disguise the financial evidence of drug dealing. Drug profits are laundered by converting them into other assets, such as real estate, stocks and bonds, racehorses, diamonds, gold, or other valuables. The NNICC says that millions of dollars in drug monies are laundered through commercial banks and other financial institutions each year, with major money laundering operations flourishing in South Florida and Los Angeles.[117] Other estimates put the laundered amount as high as $300 billion.[118] The Police Executive Research Forum (PERF) estimates that profits in excess of $100 billion a year are generated in the United States through narcotics trafficking and related underworld activities.[119] PERF also points out that successful money laundering can be accomplished only with the cooperation of lawyers, accountants, stockbrokers, realtors, and other investment advisers.[120]

A few years ago, U.S. Customs agents in Tampa, Florida, arrested seven high-level banking executives who had been lured back into U.S. jurisdiction from other countries.[121] "The Cash Cleaners," as the men were dubbed, were arrested after allegedly laundering $14 million for narcotics agents in a "sting" operation. Estimates were that many times that amount had been laundered for real criminals.[122] Indictments named 80 individuals and the first banking company ever charged with money laundering under U.S. law. The company, Bank of Credit and Commerce International, based in Luxembourg, was the seventh largest pri-

Money Laundering The process of converting illegally earned assets, originating as cash, to one or more alternative forms to conceal such incriminating factors as illegal origin and true ownership. *Source:* Clifford Karchmer and Douglas Ruch, "State and Local Money Laundering Control Strategies," *NIJ Research in Brief* (Washington, D.C.: NIJ, 1992), p. 1.

"Drug loot" confiscated in a joint **NYPD-DEA** operation. The cash take from illegal drug sales must be laundered before it can enter the flow of legitimate transactions. *Nola Tully, Sygma*

vately owned financial institution in the world.[123] BCCI was closed in 1991 by international banking regulators.

In an effort to catch money launderers, U.S. banking law requires financial institutions to report deposits in excess of $10,000. Traffickers attempt to avoid the law through two techniques known as smurfing and structuring.[124] Smurfers repeatedly purchase bank checks in denominations of less than $10,000, which are then sent to accomplices in other parts of the country who deposit them in existing accounts. Once the checks have cleared, the funds are transferred to other banks or moved out of the country. Structuring is very similar and involves cash deposits to bank accounts in amounts of less than $10,000 at a time. After accounts are established, the money is withdrawn and deposited in increments elsewhere, making it difficult to trace. Countries which have secrecy laws protecting depositors are favorites for drug traffickers. Among them are Switzerland, Panama, Hong Kong, the United Arab Emirates, and the Bahamas.[125]

Recently, the U.S. Supreme Court made the task of catching money launderers more difficult. In the 1994 case of *Ratzlaf* v. *U.S.*[126] the court ruled that no one can be convicted of trying to evade bank reporting requirements unless authorities can prove that offenders knew they were violating the law.

Although federal law prohibits the laundering of money, only two states—California and Georgia—have strict laws against money laundering.[127] As a consequence, many local enforcement agencies are reluctant to investigate money laundering activities in their states. To counteract this reluctance, the federal government is moving to facilitate interagency activities of its enforcement personnel. The federal task force, the Financial Crimes Enforcement Network (FINCEN), formed to coordinate the fight against money laundering, began to pay off shortly after it was formed. In December 1989, in one of the network's first major successes, it effectively traced records contained on computer disks which had been captured by the Colombian government, to bank accounts in the United States, Luxembourg, Switzerland, Austria, and Britain. As a result, over $60 million in assets belonging to Colombian drug lord Jose Gonzalo Rodriguez Gacha were frozen.[128]

NARCOTERRORISM

Some authors have identified a link between major drug traffickers and terrorist groups.[129] A number of South American traffickers appear especially willing to finance the activities of terrorist groups as a way of purchasing protection for themselves and their operations. The insurgents with whom they deal have their own political agendas, including the disruption of society, the overthrow of constitutional governments, and the spread of radical political ideas. A little over five years ago, for example, the Colombian government became involved in what can only be described as a civil war, involving the constitutionally elected government, on the one hand, and armed representatives of the Medellin, Cali, and Bogotá drug cartels, on the other. While the government sought to close down drug laboratories and money laundering operations, the cartels threatened to topple the government and targeted opposing judges, newspaper editors, and government officials for assassination. By 1990, Colombian cartels had succeeded in murdering 11 Colombian Supreme Court justices, over 30 other judges, two powerful newspaper editors, the country's attorney general, and hundreds of Colombian national police officers, and in forcing the resignation of the minister of justice.[130] In 1993, in an attempt to hide criminal activities behind a political facade, Colombian narcotics kingpin Pablo Emilio Escobar-Gaviria created an antigovernment armed revolutionary group called the "Antioquian Rebellion." During the last six months of 1992, Escobar assassins killed more than 50 of the country's police officers; the drug kingpin was himself shot to death by government forces in December 1993. The battle continues. In late 1995 charges of corruption in Colombian government led to the resignation of the defense minister and sparked an investigation into accusations that President Ernesto Samper's campaign organizers had taken drug money.

The link between drug traffickers and insurgents has been termed **narcoterrorism**.[131] Narcoterrorism, simply defined, is the involvement of terrorist organizations and insurgent groups in the trafficking of narcotics.[132] The first documented instance of an insurgent force financed, at least in part, with drug money, came to light during an investigation of the virulent anti-Castro Omega 7 group in the early 1980s.[133] Clear-cut evidence of modern narcoterrorism, however, is difficult to obtain. Contemporary insurgent organizations with links to drug dealers probably include (1) the 19th of April Movement (M-19) operating in Colombia, (2) Peru's *sendero luminoso* (shining path), (3) the Revolutionary Armed Forces of Colombia, and (4) the large Farabundo Marti National Liberation Front (FMLN), which has long sought to overthrow the elected government of El Salvador.[134]

The symbiotic relationship which exists between terrorist organizations and drug traffickers is mutually beneficial. Insurgents derive financial benefits from their support role in drug trafficking, while the traffickers themselves receive protection and benefit from the use of terrorist tactics against foes and competitors.

Narcoterrorism, because it is a relatively new phenomenon, raises a number of questions. James A. Inciardi summarizes them as follows:[135]

1. What is the full threat posed by narcoterrorism?
2. How should narcoterrorism be dealt with?
3. Is narcoterrorism a law enforcement problem or a military one?
4. How might narcoterrorism be affected by changes in official U.S. policy toward drugs and drug use?
5. Is the international drug trade being used as a tool by anti-U.S. and other interests to undermine Western democracies in a calculated way?

Unfortunately, in the opinion of some experts, the United States is ill prepared to combat this type of international organized crime. In 1994, testifying before the Senate's Foreign Relations Subcommittee on Terrorism, Narcotics, and International Operations, William J. Olson, a National Strategy Information Center senior fellow, told Congress that more than $1 trillion (equivalent to one-sixth of the U.S. gross national product), is generated yearly by organized criminal activities like those associated with narcoterrorism. "We must recognize that the rules of the crime game have changed," said Olson. "International criminal organizations are challenging governments, permeating societies. They're running roughshod over weak institutions and exploiting gaps in the U.S. and international response. They have the upper hand at the moment and they know it," he said.[136] Other experts testified that a comprehensive national strategy—one which goes far beyond law enforcement and criminal prosecution to include diplomacy and organized international efforts—is needed to combat international organized criminal enterprises before they can co-op global markets and worldwide financial institutions.

Narcoterrorism A political alliance between terrorist organizations and drug supplying cartels. The cartels provide financing for the terrorists, who in turn provide quasi-military protection to the drug dealers.

Antidrug strategies must be supported by knowledge gained from research.
—The White House, National Drug Control Strategy

Lost Productivity and Police Corruption

Drug abuse has many personal and social costs that extend beyond its impact on the criminal justice system. Among them are lost productivity (estimated at as high as $60 billion annually[137]), poor job performance, medical claims, the corruption of public officials, the loss of human life, and disease. In 1995, for example, 531,800 drug-related hospital emergency room episodes were reported to the Drug Abuse Warning Network (DAWN), and many others probably went unreported. The most frequently cited reason for a drug-related emergency room visit was "overdose," while "unexpected reaction" and "chronic effects" were the next most cited reasons.

Studies of postal service workers have shown that applicants who tested positive for drug use in preemployment screening, but were hired anyway had 43% higher rates of absenteeism and were 40% more likely to be fired than were other workers.[138] The same study suggested that absenteeism and job turnover are only two of many areas that drug use among workers can affect.[139] Job quality and on-the-job safety, although not measured by the study, are probably also hurt by employee drug abuse. A poll conducted by the Institute for a Drug Free Workplace found that one in four U.S. workers have personal knowledge of coworkers using illegal drugs on the job.[140] The Institute also found that 97% of workers agree that drug testing at work can be appropriate under some circumstances.

The potential for official corruption posed by widespread drug abuse is another area in which social costs may be substantial. In 1995, for example, former Justice Department attorney and Harvard Law School graduate Michael Abbell was indicted by federal prosecutors in Miami and charged with multiple counts of racketeering activity—charges which stem from his alleged support of the cocaine-smuggling operations of the infamous "Cali cartel," the major source of cocaine in the United States.[141] Justice Department officials insist that Abbell knowingly served international drug traffickers at the highest-level for years, conniving illegally to beat federal prosecutors, and that he distributed cartel monies to underlings to keep them from testifying against their bosses.

Similarly, a few years ago, the judge executive of Morgan County, Kentucky, and the Morgan County sheriff were found guilty of accepting $5,000 monthly payments to protect a large cocaine distribution ring.[142] Over the past few years, seven sheriffs and two former sheriffs in the Eastern Federal District of Tennessee have been convicted of accepting bribes from drug dealers.[143] Some analysts of police behavior have cited a new generation of police officers who have come of age in environments where drugs are generally accepted—and the huge amounts of money drug kingpins have at their disposal create a potentially lethal mix in the fight to keep enforcement agents honest.[144]

Solving the Drug Abuse Problem

As this book goes to press, American drug control strategies are caught in a kind of limbo between conservative "supply reduction through strict enforcement and interdiction" policies of the conservative Republican majority now controlling congress, and Clinton administration–initiated policies stressing "demand reduction through education, treatment, and counseling." In February 1997, the White House Office of National Drug Control Policy (ONDCP) released its *National Drug Control Strategy*,[145] a yearly publication outlining the current drug abuse situation in the United States and detailing a drug-fighting strategy intended to guide the nation's criminal justice agencies in the battle against drugs. The 1997 *National Drug Control Strategy*, touted as a "bipartisan commitment to reducing drug abuse and its destructive consequences," enumerated five specific policy goals which it called a "dynamic, comprehensive plan for the Nation" to follow in the fight against drug abuse. The five goals set forth by the *Strategy* are to: (1) educate and enable America's youth to reject illegal drugs as well as alcohol and tobacco; (2) increase the safety of America's citizens by substantially reducing drug-related crime and violence; (3) reduce health and social costs to the public of illegal drug use; (4) shield America's air, land, and sea frontiers from the drug threat; and (5) break foreign and domestic drug sources of supply.

Politics aside, any problem as complex and as large as drug abuse is unlikely to yield to simple strategies[146]—however well meaning. Among the many methods for attacking the drug problem that have been proposed, six general types of strategies can be identified. They

U.S. Customs officers with seized cocaine. Lower photo: Officer Rick Dallent shows how four tons of packaged cocaine were hidden in hardwood boards designed for pic-nic tables shipped from Honduras to Florida. *Bob Sherman, Time Magazine* and *UPI/Bettmann*

are (1) strict enforcement, (2) asset forfeiture, (3) interdiction, (4) crop control, (5) educa-tion and treatment, and (6) legalization or decriminalization. Each of these strategies will be discussed in the following pages.

STRICT ENFORCEMENT

Trafficking in controlled substances is, of course, an illegal activity in the United States—and has been for a long time. Conservative politicians generally opt for a strict program of antidrug law enforcement and costly drug sentences, with the goal of removing dealers from the streets, disrupting supply lines, and eliminating sources of supply. Unfortunately, legal prohibitions appear to have done little to discourage widespread drug abuse. Those who look to strict law enforcement as a primary drug control strategy usually stress the need for secure borders, drug testing to identify users, and stiff penalties to discourage others from

I do think it would likely reduce the crime rate if drugs were legalized.

—Former U.S. Surgeon General Jocelyn Elders

drug involvement. A U.S. Coast Guard policy of "zero tolerance," for example, which was highly touted in the late 1980s, led to highly publicized seizures of multimillion-dollar vessels when even small amounts of drugs (probably carried aboard by members of the crew) were found on board.

Calls for harsh punishments of drug law violators are being heard from many corners. Even rural areas and some traditional "liberal" enclaves have joined the bandwagon, believing that drug abuse may lead to other forms of criminal activity and social disruption. Officials in the state of Minnesota, for example, have attributed at least 75% of major crimes in that state over the past few years to drug abuse and have considered reinstatement of the death penalty to quell drug-related violence.[147] The federal Violent Crime Control and Law Enforcement Act of 1994 mandated the hiring of 100,000 new police officers under the Community Oriented Policing Services (COPS) program. According to a 1995 report by the White House, many of these "police officers will work to identify drug use and drug trafficking trouble spots, coordinate crisis intervention services, and encourage community residents to come forward with information pertinent to criminal investigations and transfer intelligence information to drug enforcement personnel."[148]

But strict enforcement measures may be only a stop-gap strategy—and may eventually lead to greater long-term problems. As James Q. Wilson observes, "…it is not clear that enforcing the laws against drug use would reduce crime. On the contrary, crime may be caused by such enforcement because it keeps drug prices higher than they would otherwise be."[149]

Some U.S. enforcement strategies attempt to enlist the help of foreign officials. Because drug exports represent extremely lucrative sources of revenue, however, and may even be thought of as valuable "foreign trade" by the governments of some of the world's major drug-producing nations, effective international antidrug cooperation is hard to come by. In 1991, for example, partly in response to pressures from cocaine-producing cartels within the country, Colombia outlawed the extradition of Colombian citizens for any purpose—making the extradition and trial of Colombian cocaine kingpins impossible. "Furthermore," as the DEA recognizes, "the unprecedented economic, political, and social power and influence wielded by [cocaine] kingpins inside Colombia make it difficult to bring these drug lords to justice in their own country."[150]

Forfeiture

Forfeiture (also **Asset Forfeiture**) The authorized seizure of money, negotiable instruments, securities, or other things of value. In federal antidrug laws: the authorization of judicial representatives to seize all monies, negotiable instruments, securities, or other things of value furnished or intended to be furnished by any person in exchange for a controlled substance, and all proceeds traceable to such an exchange.

RICO An acronym that stands for "Racketeer Influenced Corrupt Organization" and refers to a federal statute which allows for the federal seizure of assets derived from illegal enterprise.

Forfeiture, as an enforcement strategy that federal statutes and some state laws support, bears special mention. Antidrug forfeiture statutes authorize judges to seize "all monies, negotiable instruments, securities, or other things of value furnished or intended to be furnished by any person in exchange for a controlled substance…(and) all proceeds traceable to such an exchange."[151] Forfeiture statutes find a legal basis in the relation-back doctrine. The relation-back doctrine assumes that because the government's right to illicit proceeds relates back to the time they are generated, anything acquired through the expenditure of those proceeds also belongs to the government.[152]

The first federal laws to authorize forfeiture as a criminal sanction were both passed in 1970. They were the Continuing Criminal Enterprise statute, commonly called the CCE, and the Organized Crime Control Act. A section of the Organized Crime Control Act, known as the **RICO** statute (for Racketeer Influenced Corrupt Organizations), was designed to prevent criminal infiltration of legitimate businesses and has since been extensively applied in federal drug smuggling cases. In 1978, Congress authorized civil forfeiture of any assets acquired through narcotics trafficking in violation of federal law. Many states modeled their own legislation after federal law and now have similar statutes.

The newer civil statutes have the advantage of being relatively easy to enforce. Civil forfeiture requires proof only by a preponderance of the evidence, rather than proof beyond a reasonable doubt as in criminal prosecution. In civil proceedings based upon federal statutes, there is no need to trace the proceeds in question to a particular narcotics transaction. It is enough to link them to narcotics trafficking generally.[153]

Forfeiture amounts can be huge. In a recent 15-month period, for example, the South Florida-Caribbean Task Force, composed of police agencies from the federal, state, and local levels, seized $47 million in airplanes, vehicles, weapons, cash, and real estate.[154] In a single investigation involving two brothers convicted of heroin smuggling, the federal government seized a shopping center, three gasoline stations, and seven homes worth over $20 million in New York City.[155]

A 1991 Virginia forfeiture case may hold special interest for college and university students. In March of that year, federal agents seized three University of Virginia fraternity houses and indicted 12 students on charges of drug distribution. The 12 were allegedly involved in a series of small sales of illegal drugs to undercover agents over the months preceding the seizure. The action was part of an effort by law enforcement agencies to counter charges that enforcement activities had been focused only on inner-city areas. Following the arrests, E. Montgomery Tucker, U.S. attorney for the Western District of Virginia, said "[these arrests show] there are no safe havens, no safe places, to conduct illegal drug trafficking." Fraternity members were allowed to return to the houses, which are now owned by the federal government.

Although almost all states now have forfeiture statutes, prosecutions built upon them have met with less success than prosecutions based on federal law. The Police Executive Research Forum[156] attributes the difference to (1) the fact that federal law is more favorable to prosecutors than most state laws, (2) greater federal resources, and (3) the difficulties imposed by statutory requirements that illegal proceeds be traced to narcotics trafficking.

In 1993, in *U.S.* v. *92 Buena Vista Ave.*,[157] the U.S. Supreme Court established an "innocent owner defense" in forfeiture cases, whereby the government was forbidden from seizing drug transaction assets that were later acquired by a new and innocent owner. In the same year, in the case of *Austin* v. *U.S.*,[158] the Court placed limits on the government's authority to use forfeiture laws against drug criminals, finding that seizures of property must not be excessive when compared to the seriousness of the offense charged. Otherwise, the justices wrote, the Eighth Amendment's ban on excessive fines could be contravened. The justices, however, refused to establish a rule by which excessive fines could be judged, saying, "[T]he Court declines to establish a test for determining whether a forfeiture is constitutionally 'excessive,' since prudence dictates that the lower courts be allowed to consider that question." The *Austin* ruling was supported by two other 1993 cases, *Alexander* v. *U.S.* and *U.S.* v. *Real*.[159] In *Alexander*, the Court found that forfeitures under the RICO statute must be limited according to the rules established in *Austin*, while in *Real*, the Court held that "[A]bsent exigent circumstances, the Due Process Clause requires the Government to afford notice and a meaningful opportunity to be heard before seizing real property subject to civil forfeiture."

On the other hand, in 1996 the U.S. Supreme Court upheld the seizure of private property used in the commission of a crime, even though the property belonged to an innocent owner not involved in the crime. The case, *Bennis* v. *Michigan*,[160] involved the government's taking of a wife's car used by her husband in procuring the services of a prostitute. In effect, the justices ruled, an innocent owner is not protected from criminal conviction-related property forfeiture.

Also in 1996, in the case of *U.S.* v. *Ursery*,[161] the U.S. Supreme Court rejected claims that civil forfeiture laws constitute a form of double jeopardy. In *Ursery*, the defendant's house had been seized by federal officials who claimed that it had been used to facilitate drug transactions. The government later seized other personal items owned by Ursery, saying that they had been purchased with the proceeds of drug sales and that Ursery had engaged in money laundering activities to hide the source of his illegal income. The Courts of Appeals, however, reversed Ursery's drug conviction and the forfeiture judgment, holding that the double jeopardy clause of the U.S. Constitution prohibits the government from both punishing a defendant for a criminal offense and forfeiting his property for that same offense in a separate civil proceeding. In reaffirming Ursery's conviction, however, the U.S. Supreme Court ruled that "a forfeiture [is] not barred by a prior criminal proceeding after applying a two-part test asking, first, whether Congress intended the particular forfeiture to be a remedial civil sanction or a criminal penalty, and, second, whether the forfeiture proceedings are so punitive in fact as to establish that they may not legitimately be viewed as civil in nature, despite any congressional intent to establish a civil remedial mechanism." The high court concluded that "civil forfeitures are neither 'punishment' nor criminal for purposes of the Double Jeopardy clause." In distinguishing civil forfeitures and criminal punishments, the majority opinion held that "Congress has long authorized the Government to bring parallel criminal actions and…civil forfeiture proceedings based upon the same underlying events…, and this Court consistently has concluded that the Double Jeopardy Clause does not apply to such forfeitures because they do not impose punishment."

The 11th Commandment: Thou Shalt Not End the War on Drugs.
—Anonymous

Drug interdiction, which involves efforts aimed at stopping drugs from entering the country, is an international strategy. Here, a drug dog alerts on a bag at Moscow's international airport. *Reuters/Bettmann*

Interdiction

A few years ago, a single Los Angeles drug bust amazed investigators with the size of their catch. In a warehouse in a quiet section of the city, police seized 20 tons of cocaine, valued at up to $20 billion on the street.[162] Found along with the cocaine was $10 million in cash. Other large caches have also been uncovered, including nine more tons of cocaine in a house in Harlingen, Texas; six tons on a ship in the Gulf of Mexico; and more than five tons hidden in barrels of lye in New York City.[163] Annual seizures of cocaine in the United States total about 140 tons (with an estimated wholesale value of $50 billion). All such seizures, however, reflect a failure to interdict drugs at the nation's borders.

Interdiction involves efforts aimed at stopping drugs from entering the United States. The Coast Guard, Border Patrol, and Customs agents have played the most visible roles in interdiction efforts over the last few decades. Interdiction strategies in the fight against drugs, however, are almost doomed to failure by the sheer size of the task. Although most enforcement efforts are focused on international airports and major harbors, the international boundary of the United States extends for over 12,000 miles. Rough coastline, sparsely populated desert, and dense forests provide natural barriers to easy observation and make detection of controlled substances entering the country very difficult. Add to this the fact that over 420 billion tons of goods and more than 270 million people cross over the American border annually and the job of interdiction becomes more complicated still.[164] Because even minute quantities of most drugs can be highly potent, the interdiction strategy suffers from the proverbial "needle in the haystack" predicament.

In 1993 the Clinton administration issued a Presidential Decision Directive (PDD) which included a new National Interdiction Command and Control Plan intended to enhance U.S. interdiction operations and which created the position of Interdiction Coordinator within the ONDCP.[165] The PDD also called for a controlled shift in the focus of cocaine interdiction operations away from borders and transit zones to source countries. In keeping with this policy, government reports show that interdiction operations along the American border may be faltering. In 1995, for example, the Coast Guard spent a mere 9% of its operating budget on interdiction operations—down from 24% in 1989. Allocations for fiscal year 1996, under the Coast Guard Authorization Act for 1996, were about the same, reflecting

Interdiction The interception of drug traffic at the nation's borders. Interdiction is one of the many strategies used to stem the flow of illegal drugs into the United States.

TYPICAL POSITIONS. Criminal investigator, special agent, customs inspector, canine enforcement officer, and import specialist. Support positions include intelligence research specialist, computer operator, auditor, customs aide, investigative assistant, and clerk.

EMPLOYMENT REQUIREMENTS. Applicants must (1) be U.S. citizens, (2) pass an appropriate physical examination, (3) pass a personal background investigation, (4) submit to urinalysis for the presence of controlled substances, (5) have at least three years of work experience, and (6) be under 35 years of age. Appointment at the GS-7 level also requires (1) one year of specialized experience (for example, "responsible criminal inves-tigative or comparable experience"), (2) a Bachelor's degree with demonstration of superior academic achievement (a 3.0 grade point average in all courses completed at time of application or a 3.5 grade point average for all courses in the applicant's major field of study, or rank in the upper third of the applicant's undergraduate class, or membership in a national honorary scholastic society), or (3) one year of successful graduate study in a related field.

OTHER REQUIREMENTS. Applicants must (1) be willing to travel frequently, (2) be able to work overtime, (3) be capable of working under stressful conditions, and (4) be willing to carry weapons and be able to qualify regularly with firearms.

SALARY. Successful candidates are typically hired at federal pay grade GS-5 or GS-7, depending on education and prior work history.

BENEFITS. Benefits include (1) 13 days of sick leave annually, (2) 2-1/2 to 5 weeks of annual paid vacation and 10 paid federal holidays each year, (3) federal health and life insurance, and (4) a comprehensive retirement program.

DIRECT INQUIRIES TO: Office of Human Resources, U.S. Customs Service
1301 Constitution Ave., N.W., Room 220
Washington, D.C. 20229
Phone: (202) 634-2534
Web site: http://www.customs.treas.gov

what conservative congressional analysts criticized as an intentional shift away from drug interdiction efforts by the Clinton administration.

In contrast to Clinton administration policies, a number of hard-line suggestions have surfaced recently on expanding interdiction efforts. Some would supplement current U.S. Border Patrol (USBP) and Coast Guard efforts with Armed Forces personnel and equipment. Advanced AWACS radar surveillance airplanes, helicopter gunships, naval vessels, and infantry soldiers could be called upon to identify, track, and search all vessels bound for the United States.

Opposition to the use of the military in the war against drugs, however, comes from many corners. One is the Posse Comitatus Act of 1878, which forbids American military forces from enforcing civilian law. The Pentagon and the Joint Chiefs of Staff are themselves opposed to military involvement in drug interdiction activities, except for a limited role in support of law enforcement efforts. Speaking in 1995, Joints Chiefs of Staff Chairman John Shalikashvili said that "our role is that of support to law enforcement agencies; support such as logistic support or informational support. But the issue of enforcement belongs to the properly constituted law enforcement agencies, and not the military."[166] Military estimates of costs for a full-scale interdiction operation, were it to be ordered, include $14 billion for additional surveillance aircraft and $6.2 billion yearly to physically patrol the border.[167]

Interdiction as a drug control policy has itself come under fire recently. Recently, for example, Attorney General Janet Reno questioned the effectiveness of federal interdiction efforts in Florida, pointing out that only approximately 15% of drugs entering Dade County, Florida, are interdicted.[168] About the same time, U.S. Representative Charles E. Schumer, chairman of the House Judiciary Committee's Subcommittee on Crime and Criminal Justice, said, "The international eradication and interdiction effort has been a near-total failure," and added "We should seriously consider eliminating almost all spending on foreign eradication and overseas interdiction."[169] Schumer advocated a change in government expenditures, with the lion's share of the federal antidrug budget going to fund education,

treatment, and prevention programs, rather than law enforcement or military interdiction efforts. In keeping with that sentiment, the anti-drug strategy of the Clinton administration deemphasized interdiction and shifted resources toward democratic institution building in source countries.

Crop Control

Crop control strategies attempt to limit the amount of drugs available for the illicit market by targeting foreign producers. Crop control in source countries generally takes one of two forms. In the first, government subsidies (often with U.S. support) are made available to farmers to induce them to grow other kinds of crops. Sometimes illegal crops are bought and burned. The second form of control depends upon aerial spraying or ground-level crop destruction.

Source country crop control suffers from two major drawbacks.[170] One is that the potentially large profits which can be made from illegal acreage encourage farmers in unaffected areas to take up the production of crops which might have been destroyed elsewhere. Another derives from the difficulties involved in trying to get foreign governments to cooperate in eradication efforts. In some parts of the world, opium and coca are major cash crops, causing considerable reluctance on the part of local governments to undertake any action directed against them at all.

Some international efforts have been successful, however. Operation Snowcap, for example, a program operated by the DEA, involves efforts by 12 Latin American countries working in conjunction with U.S. agents to reduce the flow of cocaine into the United States. In 1991, in Peru alone, Operation Snowcap resulted in the seizure of the largest cocaine laboratory outside of Colombia as well as several metric tons of chemicals used in the processing of cocaine.[171]

Education and Treatment

Although every proposed solution to the drug crisis has its difficulties, many people believe that education, aimed at preventing drug abuse, provides the best solution to the problem. The ONDCP's *National Drug Control Strategy* says, "[U]ltimately it is prevention efforts that will bring about a long-term solution to the Nation's drug abuse problem."[172] "To accomplish

A dorm room drug party. Drug abuse extends to all social groups and can be found among all ages. *Lynn Eskenazi, Comstock*

this," says the plan, "communities, jails, and prisons must provide effective drug treatment." The report notes, however, that "[c]urrent treatment capacity…falls well below the level of resources needed to address the problems of chronic, hardcore drug use."

Michael S. Goodstadt of the Addiction Research Foundation[173] groups drug education and treatment programs into three categories: (1) those that provide factual information about drugs; (2) those that address feelings, values, and attitudes; and (3) those that focus directly on behavior. Most modern programs contain elements of all three approaches.

Drug education programs can be found in schools, churches, and youth groups and may be provided by police departments, social service agencies, hospitals, and private citizens groups. Media advertisements against drugs also make use of educational principles. An example of a school-based program provided through the use of police resources is the School Program to Educate and Control Drug Abuse (SPECDA), which began in New York city in 1984.[174] SPECDA began with 50 officers selected to provide anti–drug abuse instruction to students in the city's fifth and sixth grades. The program, which elicits parental involvement, consists of 16 45-minute classroom sessions dealing with such topics as the dangers of drug abuse, self-awareness, peer pressure, decision making, leadership, and drug refusal strategies.[175]

Project DARE (the Drug Abuse Resistance Education Program), the nation's preeminent school-based antidrug education program, began as a cooperative effort between the Los Angeles Police Department and the Los Angeles Unified School District in 1983. It uses uniformed law enforcement officers to conduct classes in elementary schools and, like SPECDA, focuses on decision-making skills, peer pressure, and alternatives to drug use.[176]

A 1994 study, however, cast the effectiveness of the DARE program into doubt amidst charges that officials in the Clinton administration chose not to recognize the study's results. The study, published in the *American Journal of Public Health*, reviewed DARE programs in six states and British Columbia and found that "the popular drug prevention program does not work well and is less effective than other drug prevention efforts targeted at students."[177] Defending the DARE program, Justice Department officials questioned the study's methodology, and published their own version of the study's results which showed that "user satisfaction" with the DARE program is high. The same study, according to Justice Department interpreters, found substantial grass-roots support for the DARE program and led to the conclusion that DARE "has been extremely successful at placing substance abuse education in the nation's schools."[178] Drug abuse education may not necessarily be effective at preventing drug use, however, and a 1997 review of numerous DARE studies concluded that the program's "effects on drug use, except for tobacco use, are nonsignificant."[179]

Each of us has a responsibility to work toward reducing the demand for drugs in this country. We should expect nothing less from our government. The Congress, the media, communities, schools, churches, families, and every single citizen in this country must make living in a drug-free society their top priority.

—Dr. Lee P. Brown, Former Director, Office of National Drug Control Policy

Other studies also show that there is little evidence to support the belief that education will produce the desired effect upon problem drug users or those at risk of beginning drug use.[180] Studies analyzing state-by-state spending on school-based drug education, for example, show little relationship between the amount of money spent on drug education and the number of hard-core cocaine users.[181] To be effective, programs will probably also have to acknowledge the perceived positive aspects of the drug experience, as well as cultural messages that encourage drug use.[182] Until they do, many recipients of today's messages may discount them as conflicting with personal experience.

A few years ago, in a separate effort designed to measure the effectiveness of educational efforts to combat drug use, the ONDCP implemented the Monitoring the Future (MTF) study, which provides information on drug use trends and patterns among students in the eighth, tenth, and twelfth grades. As early as 1991, MTF surveys showed that attitudes among youngsters against the regular use of marijuana were weakening. This attitude change was followed by an increase in reported drug use in 1993, a trend which ONDCP says "is continuing into the present." "Unless the increased marijuana use by the Nation's youth is reversed," says ONDCP, "it is likely that new, younger users will progress into more severe and debilitating drug use."[183]

The treatment of individual drug abusers, combined with community antidrug efforts, provides another potentially promising avenue for policymakers to pursue. In 1994, the National Institute of Justice reported on case studies involving 13 grass-roots citizen responses to illegal drugs.[184] The study attempted to measure the success of each local antidrug program by assessing "improvement in the quality of life in the neighborhood with respect to the drug trade" which the programs had been able to achieve. Programs were grouped into three categories, according to the tactics used: (1) grass-roots vigilance programs, in which citizens collect information about drug use in their neighborhoods and then communicate it to the police; (2) street presence programs, in which citizens conduct patrols and marches against drugs; and (3) neighborhood advocacy programs, through which citizens ask the police and other authorities for enhanced assistance in combating drugs. The comprehensive NIJ survey came up short of a conclusive recommendation, saying that further study of antidrug grass-roots programs is needed. "It is essential to…initiate a program of research that can identify what works best under what conditions," said the study authors. "If we can evaluate community drug-fighting efforts and assess the kinds of interventions that work best in particular drug markets, then we can offer concrete, practical advice to citizens, police officials, and policymakers for the most effective strategy to defeat drugs neighborhood by neighborhood."

A 1997 study by the RAND Corporation's Drug Policy Research Center (DPRC) found education to be the most efficacious alternative for dealing with drug abuse. DPRC researchers focused on the use of alternative strategies for reducing cocaine abuse. They mathematically modeled the market for cocaine and projected a number of possible scenarios. They concluded that "Mandatory minimum sentences are not justifiable on the basis of cost-effectiveness at reducing cocaine consumption or drug-related crime. Mandatory minimums reduce cocaine consumption less per million taxpayer dollars spent than spending the same amount on enforcement…And either enforcement approach reduces drug consumption less, per million dollars spent, than putting heavy users through treatment programs. Mandatory minimums are also less cost-effective than either alternative at reducing cocaine-related crime. A principal reason for these findings is the high cost of incarceration."[185]

One of the most hopeful antidrug treatment programs is the drug court. Modern drug courts, or court-based drug abuse treatment programs, are often modeled after a Dade County (Florida) innovation begun in 1989 which has come to be known as the "Miami Drug Court model." Nonviolent first-time drug offenders are routinely diverted to mandatory treatment programs, with required periodic drug testing. A failure to comply with court-ordered treatment, or a return to drug use, results in harsher punishments, including imprisonment. An evaluation of Miami's Drug Court found a high rate of success, with few clients rearrested, lowered incarceration rates, and a lessened criminal justice system burden.[186] The success of the drug court model led to $1 billion worth of funding through the Violent Crime Control and Law Enforcement Act of 1994, to be spent over six years for similar court initiatives throughout the nation. Under the legislation, nonviolent offenders with

Twenty-First Century Criminal Justice

A Trend Toward Drug Legalization?

In 1996 California and Arizona voters passed resolutions in their respective states legalizing the medical use of marijuana under certain circumstances. Some saw the legislation as indicative of changing sentiments toward the role of controlled substances in American society and suggested that legal restrictions on other drugs should also be relaxed throughout the United States in the near future. The thrust of California Proposition 215, which the voters approved, is contained in the following language taken from the proposition:

(A) To ensure that seriously ill Californians have the right to obtain and use marijuana for medical purposes where that medical use is deemed appropriate and has been recommended by a physician who has determined that the person's health would benefit from the use of marijuana in the treatment of cancer, anorexia, AIDS, chronic pain, spasticity, glaucoma, arthritis, migraine, or any other illness for which marijuana provides relief.

(B) To ensure that patients and their primary caregivers who obtain and use marijuana for medical purposes upon the recommendation of a physician are not subject to criminal prosecution or sanction.

Although the California law permits possession of marijuana for valid medicinal purposes, buying and selling the drug remain illegal—meaning that legitimate users may have to grow their own supply or buy it on the black market. Arizona law requires prescribing physicians to write a scientific opinion explaining why the drug is appropriate for a specific patient, and a supportive second opinion is required before the drug can be administered.

Following passage of the resolutions, Attorney General Janet Reno warned that physicians who prescribe marijuana to their patients could be arrested under federal laws. In addition to arrest, Reno suggested that prescribing physicians could be barred from treating patients covered by government-financed medical care, such as Medicaid and Medicare. They might also have their privileges to prescribe medications revoked by the DEA (the agency with which physicians must register in order to legally write prescriptions).

Source: Kevin Johnson, "Medical Marijuana Rejected as 'Hoax,'" *USA Today*, December 31, 1996, p. 4A.

---

substance abuse problems will be intensively supervised, given drug treatment, and subjected to graduated sanctions—ultimately including prison terms—for failing random drug tests. By mid-1997 more than 200 drug courts were functioning in 33 states.

Finally, in an effort to reach hard-core drug addicts, the federal Violent Crime Control and Law Enforcement Act of 1994 authorized a total of $13.5 million for substance abuse treatment programs in federal prisons and another $26.7 million in new funds for similar programs in state prisons. Such funding formalizes the important link between the activities of the criminal justice system and treatment programs designed to reduce dependence on drugs.

Legalization and Decriminalization

Often regarded as the most "radical" approach to solving the drug problem, decriminalization and legalization have been proposed repeatedly and in recent years seem to be gaining at least a modicum of respectability. Although the words decriminalization and legalization are often used interchangeably, there is a significant difference. Legalization refers to the removal of all legal strictures from the use or possession of the drug in question. Manufacture and distribution might still be regulated. Decriminalization, on the other hand, substantially reduces penalties associated with drug use, but may not eliminate them entirely. States such as Oregon, which have decriminalized marijuana possession, for example, still consider simple possession of small amounts of the substance a ticketable offense similar to jay-walking or improper parking.[187] Hence, decriminalization of a controlled substance might mean that the drug "would remain illegal but the offense of possession would be treated like a traffic violation, with no loss of liberty involved for the transgressor."[188]

Legalization (of drugs) Eliminates the laws and associated criminal penalties that prohibit the production, sale, distribution, and possession of a controlled substance.

Decriminalization The redefinition of certain previously criminal behaviors into regulated activities, which become "ticketable" rather than "arrestable."

Many suggest that any solution to the American drug problem must begin at home. In this photo, young boys search through hundreds of crack vials dropped by a drug dealer as he fled from a competitor on a Philadelphia street. *Eugene Richards, Magnum*

Arguments in support of both legalization and decriminalization include the following:[189]

1. Legal drugs would be easy to track and control. The involvement of organized criminal cartels in the drug distribution network could be substantially curtailed.
2. Legal drug sales could be taxed, generating huge revenues.
3. Legal drugs would be cheap, significantly reducing the number of drug-related crimes committed in order to feed expensive drug habits.
4. Since some people are attracted to anything "taboo," legalization could, in fact, reduce the demand for drugs.
5. The current war on drugs is already a failure and will be remembered as one of history's follies.[190] Prohibiting drugs is too expensive in terms of tax dollars, sacrificed civil liberties, and political turmoil.
6. Drug dealers and users care little about criminal justice sanctions. They will continue their illegal activities no matter what the penalties.
7. Drug use should ultimately be a matter of personal choice.

Modern advocates of legalization are primarily motivated by cost–benefit considerations, weighing the social costs of prohibition against its results.[191] The results, they say, have been meager at best, while the costs have been almost more than society can bear.

Opponents of legalization argue from both a moral and a practical stance. Some, like New York city mayor Rudolph Giuliani, believe that legalization would only condone a behavior that is fundamentally immoral.[192] Others argue that under legalization drug use would increase, causing more widespread drug-related social problems than exist today. Robert DuPont, former head of the National Institute on Drug Abuse, for example, estimates that up to ten times the number of people who now use cocaine would turn to the substance if it were legal.[193]

A compromise approach has been suggested in what some writers call the limitation model. The limitation model "would make drugs legally available, but with clearly defined limits as to which institutions and professions could distribute the drugs."[194] Hence, under such a model, doctors, pharmacists, and perhaps licensed drug counselors could prescribe controlled substances under appropriate circumstances, and the drugs themselves might be taxed. Some claim that a more extreme form of the limitation model might be workable. It could be one under which drugs are sold through designated "drugstores" with distribution systems structured much like those of "liquor stores" today. Controlled substances would be sold to those of suitable age, but taxed substantially, and the use of such substances under certain circumstances (such as when operating a car) might still be illegal. Regulation and taxation of controlled substances would correspond to today's handling of alcoholic beverages.

Another example of the limitation model, already tried in some countries, is the two-market system.[195] The two-market approach would allow inexpensive and legitimate access to controlled substances for registered addicts. Only maintenance amounts (the amounts needed to forestall symptoms of drug "withdrawal") of the needed drugs, however, would be available. The two-market approach would purportedly reduce the massive profits available to criminal drug cartels while simultaneously discouraging new drug use among those who are not addicted. Great Britain provides a modern example of the two-market system. During the 1960s and 1970s, British heroin addicts who registered with the government were able to receive prescriptions for limited amounts of heroin dispensed through medical clinics. Because of concern about system abuses, clinics in the late 1970s began to dispense reduced amounts of heroin, hoping to "wean" addicts away from the drug.[196] By 1980 British policy replaced heroin with methadone,[197] a synthetic drug designed to prevent the physical symptoms of heroin withdrawal. Methadone, in amounts sufficient to prevent withdrawal, does not produce a heroinlike high.

It is doubtful that the two-market system will be adopted in the United States anytime soon. American cultural condemnation of major mind-altering substances has created a reluctance to accept the legitimacy of drug treatment using controlled substances. In addition, cocaine is much more of a problem in the United States than is heroin. The large number of drug abusers in the country, combined with the difficulty of defining and measuring "addiction" to drugs such as cocaine, would make any maintenance program impractical.

SUMMARY

Drug crimes and drug-related crimes account for a large proportion of all crimes committed in this country. While the manufacture, importation, sale, and use of illegal drugs account for a substantial number of law violations, many other offenses are also linked to drug use. Among them are thefts of all kinds, burglary, assault, and murder.

Drug-related crimes derive from the fact that drugs are both expensive for users and extremely profitable for suppliers. The high cost of drugs forces many users, some of whom have little legitimate income, into the commission of property crimes to acquire the funds necessary to continue their drug habits. On the other hand, users of illicit drugs who have substantial legitimate incomes may indirectly shift the cost of drug use to society through lowered job productivity, psychological or family problems, and medical expenses.

The widespread use of illegal drugs in America today carries with it other social costs. Many criminal enterprises, for example, are supported by street-level demand for drugs. Some of these illegitimate businesses are massive international cartels which will stop at nothing to protect their financial interests. Kidnapping, bribery, extortion, torture, and murder are tools of the trade among drug kingpins in their battle to continue reaping vast profits.

Any realistic appraisal of the current situation must admit that the resources of the criminal justice system in dealing with drug crime are strained to the limit. There are simply not enough agents, airplanes, equipment, or money to entirely remove illegal drugs from American communities. The justice system faces the added problem of corruption inherent in any social control situation where large amounts of money frequently change hands. Until attitudes supportive of drug use are modified or replaced by more sanguine values, law enforcement can only hope to keep the problem of drug abuse in America from becoming worse—and from losing sight of its fundamental mandates in the process.

Visit the *CJToday* Web page and click on "Web Chapters," then "Chapter 15." Follow the "find the facts" links in order to visit the federal government's Substance Abuse and Mental Health Services Administration home page.

DISCUSSION QUESTIONS

1. Why have drugs become a large-scale problem in the United States today? In your opinion, are there identifiable elements of contemporary American culture which support drug use? If so, what might they be?

2. What commonly used legal substances might qualify as drugs, even though they are generally not recognized as such? Why do people use such substances?

3. Why does drug use tend to lead to other types of crime commission? What kinds of crimes might be involved?

4. How would you deal with the problem of illicit drug use facing American society today? Discuss the strategies cited in this chapter, listing the "pros" and "cons" of each.

5. What characteristics does drug use share in common with other social order or "victimless" crimes? Should social order crimes be legalized and left to individual choice? Why or why not?

If I were king, I would find a civil way to allow citizens to sue the drug dealer for selling drugs to their children.

—Samuel F. Saxton, Director, Prince George's County (Maryland) Department of Corrections

We must fight crime at the critical points of origin. Crime that originates in Europe harms the United States just as our own crime problems cause harm when they find their way overseas.

—FBI Director Louis J. Freeh

 WEB WATCH

Access the *Criminal Justice Today* site on the World Wide Web by pointing your Web browser at http://www.prenhall.com/cjtoday. Once there, click on "Web Chapters," then select "Chapter 15: Drugs and Crime" from the selection box in order to access electronic information and other sites of relevance to this chapter. You may also wish to enter the Global Town Meeting, which provides facilities for the posting of electronic messages for others to read. Messages are arranged by topic, with new topics constantly being added.

NOTES

1. Interview with William Bennett, *USA Today*, March 20, 1989, p. 11A.
2. Ross Deck, "A New Way of Looking at the Drug War," in *Enhancing Capacities and Confronting Controversies in Criminal Justice—Proceedings of the 1993 National Conference of the Bureau of Justice Statistics and the Justice Research and Statistics Association* (Washington, D.C.: Bureau of Justice Statistics, 1994), p. 12.
3. Tom McEwen, *National Assessment Program: 1994 Survey Results* (Washington, D.C.: National Institute of Justice, April 1995).
4. "Who Is in Federal Prison?" *The Washington Post* wire services, October 3, 1994.
5. For an excellent overview of the issues involved, see Doris Layton MacKenzie and Craig D. Uchida, *Drugs and Crime: Evaluating Public Policy Initiatives* (Thousand Oaks, CA: Sage, 1994).
6. The White House, *National Drug Control Strategy: Executive Summary*, April 1995, p. 1.
7. The term *recreational user* is well established in the literature of drug abuse. Unfortunately, it tends to minimize the seriousness of drug abuse by according even hard drugs the status of a hobby.
8. Howard Becker, *Outsiders: Studies in the Sociology of Deviance* (New York: The Free Press, 1963).
9. Jay Tokasz, "Eight of 11 People in Car Die in Crash," *USA Today*, June 20, 1995, p. 2A.
10. James B. Jacobs, "Drinking and Crime," an NIJ *Crime File Study Guide* (Washington, D.C.: National Institute of Justice, no date), p.1.
11. Ibid.
12. Ibid.
13. *Statistical Abstracts of the United States 1987* (Washington, D.C.: U.S. Government Printing Office, 1988), Table 181.
14. Ibid.
15. Steven Olson and Dean R. Gerstein, *Alcohol in America: Taking Action to Prevent Abuse* (Washington, D.C.: National Academy Press, 1985), p. 13.
16. Ibid.
17. In most states individuals may also be arrested for "driving under the influence" of other drugs and controlled substances, including prescription medicines.
18. Bureau of Justice Statistics, "Drunk Driving," a BJS *Special Report* (Washington, D.C.: U.S. Government Printing Office, 1988), p. 1, and Federal Bureau of Investigation, *Crime in the United States 1992* (Washington, D.C.: U.S. Government Printing Office, 1993).
19. Ibid.
20. Ibid.
21. U.S. Department of Justice, *Crime in the United States 1996* (Washington, D.C.: U.S. Government Printing Office, 1997).

22. Bureau of Justice Statistics, *Report to the Nation on Crime and Justice*, 2nd ed. (Washington, D.C.: Department of Justice, 1988), p. 50.

23. Jeffrey A. Roth, "Psychoactive Substances and Violence," a National Institute of Justice *Research in Brief* (February 1994), p. 1.

24. Bureau of Justice Statistics, *Report to the Nation on Crime and Justice*, 2nd ed., p. 51.

25. Ibid.

26. Ibid., p. 51.

27. Ibid.

28. Howard Abadinsky, *Drug Abuse: An Introduction* (Chicago: Nelson-Hall, 1989), p. 32.

29. Charles E. Terry and Mildred Pellens, *The Opium Problem* (New York: The Committee on Drug Addiction, 1928).

30. Ibid.

31. Ibid., p. 76.

32. David Musto, *The American Disease: Origins of Narcotic Control* (New Haven, CT: Yale University Press, 1973).

33. Becker, *Outsiders*.

34. Ibid.

35. Ibid., p. 136.

36. Ibid.

37. Ibid.

38. Franklin E. Zimring and Gordon Hawkins, *The Search for Rational Drug Control* (New York: Cambridge University Press, 1992).

39. Ibid., p. 9.

40. The President's Commission on Organized Crime, *Organized Crime Today* (Washington, D.C.: U.S. Government Printing Office, 1986).

41. *Webb* v. *U.S.*, 249 U.S. 96.

42. Michael D. Lyman and Gary W. Potter, *Drugs in Society: Causes, Concepts, and Control* (Cincinnati, Ohio: Anderson, 1991), p. 359.

43. Drug Enforcement Administration, *Drug Enforcement: The Early Years* (Washington, D.C.: DEA, December 1980) p. 41.

44. White House Conference on Drug Abuse, *Commission Report* (Washington, D.C.: U.S. Government Printing Office, 1963).

45. For a good summary of the law, see Drug Enforcement Administration, *Drugs of Abuse* (Washington, D.C.: U.S. Government Printing Office, 1997).

46. Drug Enforcement Administration, *Drug Enforcement Briefing Book* (Washington, D.C.: Drug Enforcement Agency, no date), p. 3.

47. A number of states have now recognized that marijuana may be useful in the treatment of nausea associated with cancer chemotherapy, glaucoma, and other medical conditions.

48. DEA, *Drug Enforcement Briefing Book*, p. 3.

49. Ibid.

50. Ibid., p. 4.

51. Ibid.

52. Much of the information in this section comes from the National Institute on Drug Abuse's World Wide Web site at http://www.nida.nih.gov.

53. DEA, *Drugs of Abuse*.

54. Ibid.

55. "'Rophies' Reported Spreading Quickly Throughout the South," *Drug Enforcement Report*, June 23, 1995, pp. 1–5.

56. Public Law 104-305.

57. Anti-Drug Abuse Act of 1988, P.L. 100-690, Sec. 5251.

58. This provision became effective on September 1, 1989.

59. "Congress Gives Final OK to Major Antidrug Bill," *Criminal Justice Newsletter*, Vol. 19, no. 21 (November 1, 1988), pp. 1–4.

60. Ibid., p. 2.

61. "Drug Lord Sentenced to Death," *USA Today*, May 15, 1991, p. 3A.

62. Ibid.

63. *California* v. *Greenwood*, 486 U.S. 35, 108 S.Ct. 1625 (1988).

64. Ibid.

65. *Abel* v. *U.S.*, 363 U.S. 217 (1960).

66. *Oliver* v. *U.S.*, 466 U.S. 170 (1984).

67. *Hester* v. *U.S.*, 265 U.S. 57, 44 S.Ct. 445 (1924).

68. *U.S.* v. *Dunn*, 480 U.S. 294, 107 S.Ct. 1134 (1987).

69. *California* v. *Ciraolo*, 476 U.S. 207, 106 S.Ct. 1809 (1986).

70. *Florida* v. *Riley*, 488 U.S. 445, 109 S.Ct. 693, 102 L. Ed. 2d 835 (1989).

71. "ONDCP Finds Americans Spent $57 Billion in One Year on Illegal Drugs" (Office of National Drug Control Policy, 1997).

72. Office of National Drug Control Policy, *What America's Users Spend on Illegal Drugs* (Washington, D.C.: ONDCP, 1991) p. 4.

73. U.S. Department of Health and Human Services, *National Household Survey on Drug Abuse: Main Findings 1996* (Washington, D.C.: U.S. Government Printing Office, 1997).

74. Carolyn Skorneck, "Drug Use," The Associated Press wire services, July 20, 1994.

75. ONDCP, *National Drug Control Strategy 1997*, February 1997, p. 63.

76. National Narcotics Intelligence Consumers Committee, *The NNICC Report 1996* (Washington, D.C.: Drug Enforcement Administration 1997), preface.

77. DEA, *Drugs of Abuse*, p. 45.

78. ONDCP, *Pulse Check: National Trends in Drug Abuse* (Washington, D.C.: The White House, 1995), p. 11.

79. Ibid.

80. See Anita Manning and Andrea Stone, "How States Will Face Regulating Marijuana as Medicine," *USA Today*, November 7, 1996, p. 3D.

81. "Marijuana Used Openly as Medicine in San Francisco," *Drug Enforcement Report*, March 23, 1995, pp. 5–6.

82. Department of Health and Human Services, "Substance Abuse: A National Challenge," *An HHS Fact Sheet*, August 6, 1997.

83. National Narcotics Intelligence Consumers Committee, *The NNICC Report 1996* (Washington, D.C.: Drug Enforcement Agency, 1997).

84. Ibid.

85. Ibid.

86. Ibid., p. 37.

87. ONDCP, *Pulse Check: National Trends in Drug Abuse* (Washington, D.C.: The White House, 1995), p. 9.

88. *The NNICC Report 1996.*

89. Ibid.

90. Ibid.

91. DEA, *Crack Cocaine Drug Intelligence Report 1994.*

92. National Institute of Justice, JUSTINFO on-line, July 5, 1995.

93. *The NNICC Report 1996.*

94. DEA, *The Cali Cartel: The New Kings of Cocaine* (Washington, D.C.: Drug Enforcement Agency, 1994), foreword.

95. Sam Vincent Meddis, "Arrests 'Last Rites' for Cali Cartel," *USA Today*, August 7, 1995, p. 1A.

96. DEA, *Drugs of Abuse*, p. 14.

97. Ibid., p. 12.

98. Ibid., p. 15.

99. Ibid., p. 54.

100. *National Drug Control Strategy: Executive Summary*, April 1995, p. 13.

101. DEA, *Drugs of Abuse.*

102. NNICC, *The NNICC Report 1996.*

103. National Institute of Justice, JUSTINFO on-line, July 5, 1995.

104. ONDCP, *Pulse Check: National Trends in Drug Abuse* (Washington, D.C.: The White House, 1997), p. 3.

105. Ibid.

106. Federal Bureau of Investigation, *Crime in the United States 1996* (Washington, D.C.: U.S. Government Printing Office, 1997).

107. Ibid.

108. Ibid. Unfortunately, UCR data combine arrests for heroin and cocaine possession into one category. They do the same for sale/manufacture arrests.

109. Ibid.

110. Ibid.

111. *National Drug Control Strategy: Executive Summary*, April 1995, p. 12.

112. Bernard A. Gropper, "Probing the Links Between Drugs and Crime," a National Institute of Justice *Research in Brief* (February 1985), p. 4.

113. J. C. Ball, J. W. Shaffer, and D. N. Nurco, "Day to Day Criminality of Heroin Addicts in Baltimore: A Study in the Continuity of Offense Rates," *Drug and Alcohol Dependence*, 1983, p. 12.

114. National Institute of Justice, *Drug Use Forecasting 1996: Annual Report on Adult and Juvenile Arrestees* (Washington, D.C.: National Institute of Justice, December 1997).

115. Bureau of Justice Statistics, "Drug Use and Crime: State Prison Inmate Survey, 1986," a BJS *Special Report* (Washington, D.C.: Bureau of Justice Statistics, 1988), p. 1.

116. For a true-life account of money-laundering activities, see Nick Tosches, *Power on Earth: Michele Sindona's Explosive Story* (New York: Arbor House, 1986).

117. NNICC, *The NNICC Report 1996.*

118. Clifford L. Karchmer and Douglas Ruch, "State and Local Money Laundering Control Strategies," *NIJ Research in Brief* (Washington, D.C.: National Institute of Justice, 1992), p. 1.

119. Clifford L. Karchmer, *Illegal Money Laundering: A Strategy and Resource Guide for Law Enforcement Agencies* (Washington, D.C.: Police Executive Research Forum, 1988), p. iv.

120. Ibid.

121. "The Cash Cleaners," *Time*, October 24, 1988, p. 65.

122. Ibid.

123. Ibid.

124. NNICC, *The NNICC Report.*

125. Ibid., p. 85.

126. *Ratzlaf* v. *U.S.*, 114 S.Ct. 655, 126 L. Ed. 2d 615 (1994).

127. Karchmer, *Illegal Money Laundering*, p. 5.

128. Jonathan Beaty and Richard Hornik, "A Torrent of Dirty Dollars," *Time*, December 18, 1989, p. 50.

129. Daniel Boyce, "Narco-Terrorism," *FBI Law Enforcement Bulletin* (October 1987), p. 24; and James A. Inciardi, "Narcoterrorism: A Perspective and Commentary," in Robert O. Slater and Grant Wardlaw, eds., *International Narcotics* (London: Macmillan/St. Martins, 1989).

130. Office of the Attorney General, *Drug Trafficking*, p. 19.

131. A term reportedly invented by former Peruvian President Fernando Belaunde Terry; see James A. Inciardi, "Narcoterrorism," a paper presented at the 1988 annual meeting of the Academy of Criminal Justice Sciences, San Francisco, p. 8.

132. Boyce, "Narco-Terrorism," p. 24.

133. Ibid., p. 25.

134. U.S. Department of State, *Terrorist Group Profiles* (Washington, D.C.: U.S. Government Printing Office, 1989).

135. Ibid.

136. "U.S. Government Lacks Strategy to Neutralize International Crime," *Criminal Justice International*, Vol. 10, no. 5 (September/October 1994), p. 5.

137. Jack Kelley, "Poll: On-Job Drug Use Is Significant," *USA Today*, December 13, 1989, p. 1A.

138. Associated Press (Washington), "High Firing, Absentee Rates Tied to Drug Use," preliminary report of a study conducted by the National Institute on Drug Abuse for the U.S. Postal Service, January 14, 1989.

139. Ibid.

140. Ibid.

141. See "A Turncoat in The Drug War," *Newsweek*, June 26, 1995, pp. 26–27.

142. "High Firing, Absentee Rates Tied to Drug Use," p. 4.

143. Ibid.

144. Todd S. Purdum, "Drugs Threatening Integrity of New York Police," *The New York Times*, November 12, 1988, p. 10Y.

145. Office of National Drug Control Policy, *National Drug Control Strategy 1997* (Washington, D.C.: U.S. Superintendent of Documents, 1997).

146. To more fully explore the complexities of the issues involved, see Franklin E. Zimring and Gordon Hawkins, *The Search for Rational Drug Control* (New York: Cambridge University Press, 1995).

147. "Hardening Their Hearts: Minnesota Gets Tough," *Newsweek*, April 3, 1989, p. 28.

148. *National Drug Control Strategy*, April 1995, p. 25.

149. James Q. Wilson, "Drugs and Crime," in Michael Tonry and James Q. Wilson, eds., *Drugs and Crime* (Chicago: University of Chicago Press, 1990), p. 522.

150. *The Cali Cartel*, p. 10.

151. 21 U.S.C. § 881 (a) (6).

152. Michael Goldsmith, *Civil Forfeiture: Tracing the Proceeds of Narcotics Trafficking* (Washington, D.C.: Police Executive Research Forum, 1988), p. 3.

153. *U.S. v. $4,255,625.39 in Currency*, 762 F.2d 895, 904.

154. Bureau of Justice Assistance, *Asset Forfeiture Bulletin* (October 1988), p. 2.

155. Ibid.

156. Ibid., p. 1.

157. *U.S. v. 92 Buena Vista Ave.*, 113 S.Ct. 1126, 122 L. Ed. 2d 469 (1993).

158. *Austin v. U.S.*, 113 S.Ct. 2801, 15 L. Ed. 2d 448 (1993).

159. *Alexander v. U.S.*, 113 S.Ct. 2766, 125 L. Ed. 2d 441 (1993); and *U.S. v. James Daniel Good Real Property*, 114 S.Ct. 492, 126 L. Ed. 2d 490 (1993).

160. *Bennis v. Michigan*, 116 S.Ct. 1560, 134 L. Ed. 2d 661 (1996).

161. *U.S. v. Ursery*, 116 S.Ct. 2135, 135 L. Ed. 2d 549 (1996).

162. "Drug Raid Called Biggest Ever," *The Fayetteville Observer-Times* (North Carolina), September 30, 1989, p. 1A.

163. "Cocaine Found Packed in Toxic Chemical Drums," *The Fayetteville Observer-Times* (North Carolina), November 5, 1989.

164. Mark Moore, *Drug Trafficking*, a National Institute of Justice Crime File Study Guide (Washington, D.C.: U.S. Government Printing Office, 1988), p. 3

165. ONDCP, *National Drug Control Strategy*, April 1995, p. 33.

166. "Briefly," *Drug Enforcement Report*, March 23, 1995, p. 7.

167. "Is the War on Drugs Another Vietnam?" *Newsweek*, May 30, 1988, p. 38.

168. "Officials Raise Doubts About Drug Interdiction Efforts," *Criminal Justice Newsletter*, May 17, 1993, pp. 1–3.

169. Ibid.

170. Moore, *Drug Trafficking*.

171. NNICC, *The NNICC Report 1991*.

172. ONDCP, *National Drug Control Strategy*, April 1995.

173. Michael S. Goodstadt, *Drug Education*, National Institute of Justice Crime File Study Guide (Washington, D.C.: U.S. Government Printing Office, no date), p. 1.

174. See Wilhelmina E. Holliday, "Operation SPECDA: School Program to Educate and Control Drug Abuse," *FBI Law Enforcement Bulletin* (February 1986), pp. 1–4.

175. Ibid.

176. Ibid.

177. "DARE Not Effective in Reducing Drug Abuse, Study Finds," *Criminal Justice Newsletter*, October 3, 1994, pp. 6–7.

178. The government version of the study was first reported as "The DARE Program: A Review of Prevalence, User Satisfaction, and Effectiveness," *National Institute of Justice Update*, October 1994. The full study, as published by NIJ, is Christopher L. Ringwalt, et al., *Past and Future Directions of the DARE Program: An Evaluation Review* (Washington, D.C.: National Institute of Justice, 1995).

179. Fox Butterfield, no headline, *The New York Times* wire services, 7:06 EST, April 16, 1997, citing Office of Justice Programs, *Preventing Crime: What Works, What Doesn't, What's Promising* (Washington, D.C.: U.S. Department of Justice, 1997).

180. Goodstadt, *Drug Education*, p. 3.

181. *USA Today*, September 6, 1990, p. 8A, citing a report by the U.S. Senate Judiciary Committee.

182. Ibid.

183. *National Drug Control Strategy: Executive Summary*, April 1995, p. 9.

184. Saul N. Weingart, Francis X. Hartmann, and David Osborne, "Case Studies of Community Anti-Drug Efforts," A National Institute of Justice *Research in Brief*, October 1994.

185. Rand Corporation, Drug Policy Research Center, *Are Mandatory Minimum Drug Sentences Cost-Effective?* (Santa Monica, CA: Rand, 1997).

186. John S. Goldkamp and Doris Weiland, "Assessing the Impact of Dade County's Felony Drug Court," A National Institute of Justice *Research in Brief*, December 1993.

187. Paul H. Blachy, "Effects of Decriminalization of Marijuana in Oregon," *Annals of the New York Academy of Sciences*, Vol. 282 (1976), pp. 405–415. For more information on the decriminalization of marijuana, see James A. Inciardi, "Marijuana Decriminalization Research: A Perspective and Commentary," *Criminology*, Vol. 19, no. 1 (May 1981), pp. 145–159.

188. Arnold S. Trebach, "Thinking Through Models of Drug Legalization," *The Drug Policy Letter* (July/August 1994), p. 10.

189. For a more thorough discussion of some of these arguments, see Ronald Hamowy, ed., *Dealing with Drugs: Consequences of Government Control* (Lexington, MA: Lexington Books, 1987).

190. See Kurt Schmoke (*Washington Post* editorial author), "Considering Decriminalization: War on Drugs, Policy of Folly?" reprinted in *The Fayetteville Observer-Times* (North Carolina), May 16, 1988, p. 4A.

191. "Should Drugs Be Legal?" *Newsweek*, May 30, 1988, p. 36.

192. Ibid., p. 37.

193. Ibid., pp. 37–38.

194. "Thinking Through Models of Drug Legalization," p. 10.

195. For a more detailed discussion of the two-market system, see John Kaplan, *Heroin, an NIJ Crime File Study Guide* (Washington, D.C.: National Institute of Justice, no date)

196. Ibid., p. 3.

197. Ibid., p. 4.

chapter 16

MULTINATIONAL CRIMINAL JUSTICE

...[O]ur indebtedness to American criminology is immense and lasting, but non-American countries possess not only their own crime problems but also their own criminological literature....[They] have to be interpreted more independently and without a wholesale take-over of American ideas.

—HERMAN MANNHEIM[1]
UNIVERSITY OF LONDON

NEW SCOTLAND YARD

The International Perspective

In June 1997, Japanese police arrested a 14-year-old boy after he confessed to beheading a fellow student. The head of his 11-year-old victim, Jun Hase, was discovered by a custodian at the gate of a junior high school in the city of Kobe. Hase's eyes had been gouged out and his mouth had been slashed from ear-to-ear. In place of his tongue, police found a taunting note, which called investigators "fools" and boasted that the killer enjoyed seeing people die.[2] The suspect in the case, whose name has not been released, told police he killed Hase, brought the severed head home, washed it in a bathroom, and hid it overnight in the attic above his room. The next morning he carved the head on his desk, then placed it near the school. Police who later searched the boy's room found horror videos, knives, and a book about the Zodiac serial killings which took place in San Francisco in the 1960s. Investigators also reportedly found notebooks recording details of other attacks, and the boy then confessed to two assaults on young girls and to two other attacks in which one girl was beaten to death and another stabbed.

The editor of Tokyo-based *Focus* magazine, which published a yearbook photo of the confessed killer in violation of Japanese law, held a news conference, saying "The suspect in this case does not fit a typical juvenile model presupposed under the juvenile law."[3] Under Japanese law, children under 16 cannot be sentenced as criminals. Delinquent children must either be sentenced to probation or reform school—where offenders are likely to go free after a year or two, even for the most serious crimes.

The gruesome murder of young Hase was the latest in a series of demoralizing incidents that have caused many Japanese to question what is happening to their society. Motoo Sakai, 34, a Kobe hotel doorman, was one of many upset by the beheading. "I'm worried that more and more crimes are being committed by youngsters. I just wonder where Japanese society is headed,"[4] he said.

Only a few years earlier, Japan had seemed safe from violent crime, and fear of crime was at the bottom of citizens' concerns. That sense of security largely disappeared in 1995 when cult leader Shoko Asahara was arrested and charged with masterminding a nerve gas attack on a Tokyo subway station. The attack left 12 dead and injured more than 5,500 others. Intense Japanese media coverage of the Asahara arrest and pending trial made the event the Far Eastern equivalent of the O. J. Simpson trial, which received extensive coverage in American media. Unlike Simpson, however, who quickly assembled a "dream team" of defense attorneys anxious to share the media spotlight during his double-murder trial, Asahara, leader of the 10,000-member Aum Shinri Kyo (Supreme Truth) sect, was initially unable to find a lawyer to represent him. As one Japanese legal expert put it, "This is nothing like the O. J. Simpson case. Every lawyer in town is running for cover."[5] "There are no lawyers to defend (Asahara)," Japan Bar Association Chairman Koken Tsuchiya told reporters,[6] explaining that it would be dishonorable for an attorney to argue innocence for a person who appeared to be guilty of such a horrendous crime.

The inability to find a lawyer proved to be a daunting hurdle for Asahara. "Japan's legal system is completely different from that of the United States and Europe," said Masaki Nibe of the Japan Bar Association.[7] Japan does not have a system of public defenders and a suspect can go through a series of hearings until a lawyer is appointed as trial is about to begin. "Unless he finds his own lawyer, he will be in a bad position because no one but lawyers can really understand Japan's complicated legal procedures," Nibe said.

Prior to the Asahara case, Japan had long been renowned as a sanguine and relatively crime-free nation. Since the end of World War II Japanese crime rates have been the lowest

Japan, once regarded as a country with a very low incidence of serious crime, has recently weathered a series of traumatizing criminal episodes. Here, Japanese police officers prepare to search the headquarters of the militant Aum Shinri Kyo sect, suspected in nerve gas attacks on Tokyo subways. *Itsuo Inouye, AP/Wide World Photos*

among developed countries. The annual rate of serious crime is only about 1,400 per 100,000 people in Japan—one quarter the rate found in the United States. Violence has been even more rare. Murder rates in the United States, for example, are 17 times what they are in Japan. If recent events are any guide, however, Japan may be catching up to the United States in criminal activity. In 1995, for example, Japan's top police official, Takaji Kunimatsu, was shot four times in front of his condominium building by unknown assailants.[8] About the same time, an airline hijacking by a political radical further rattled the nerves of Japanese citizens. One local commentator bemoaned the growing social disorder in Japan and noted that "The Japanese who had been proud of a safe and orderly culture started worrying aloud that now anything could happen to anyone at any time."[9] Nobuhiko Shima, a popular TV news reporter, put it this way: "In the past three months, Japan's myths have completely crumbled."[10]

As Japanese citizens began adjusting to a lessened sense of personal security, some suggested that officials there could learn something from the experience of the United States and other industrialized countries in which criminality is rampant. A few even suggested that comparing Japanese troubles with understandings of what had historically contributed to high crime rates in America might produce effective strategies to head off further crime and social disorder in Japan.

Criminologists who study crime and criminal justice on a cross-national level are referred to as **comparative criminologists,** and their field is called comparative criminology or **comparative criminal justice.** Comparative criminal justice is becoming increasingly valued for the insights it provides. By contrasting native institutions of justice with similar institutions in other countries, procedures and problems which have been taken for granted under one system can be reevaluated in the light of world experience. As communications, rapid travel, and other technological advances effectively "shrink" the world, we find ourselves in a nearly ideal situation of being able to learn firsthand about the criminal justice systems of other countries and to use that information to improve our own. This chapter explains the value of comparative criminology for students of criminal justice, points to the problems which arise in comparing data among and between nations, and explores three criminal justice sys-

Comparative Criminologist One who studies crime and criminal justice on a cross-national level.

tems in other parts of the world: those of China and England, and Islamic criminal justice. International police agencies are also described, and the role of the United Nations in the worldwide fight against crime is discussed.

Ethnocentrism and the Study of Criminal Justice

Ethnocentrism The phenomenon of culture-centeredness, by which one uses one's own culture as a benchmark against which to judge all other patterns of behavior.

Like most other human beings, we Americans often assume that the way we do things is the best way to do them. Such belief is probably part of human nature. As a consequence of this attitude, however, the study of criminal justice in the United States has been largely **ethnocentric.** The word *ethnocentric* literally means centered on one's own culture. Because people are socialized from birth into a particular culture, they tend to prefer their own culture's way of doing things over that of any other. Native patterns of behavior are seen as somehow "natural," and therefore better, than foreign ones. The same is true for values, beliefs, and customs. People tend to think that the religion they were born into holds a spiritual edge over other religions, that their values and ethical sense are superior to those of others, and that the fashions they wear, the language they speak, and the rituals of daily life in which they participate are somehow better than comparable practices elsewhere. Ethnocentric individuals rarely stop to think that people elsewhere in the world probably cling to their own values, beliefs, and standards of behavior with just as much fervor as they do. Hence, ethnocentrism is not a uniquely American phenomenon.

Only in recent years have American students of criminal justice begun to examine the justice systems of other cultures. Unfortunately, not all cultures are equally open, and it is not always easy to explore them. In some societies even the *study* of criminal justice is taboo. As a result, data gathering strategies taken for granted in Western culture may not be well received elsewhere. One author, for example, speaking about China, has observed, "The seeking of criminal justice information through face-to-face questioning takes on a different meaning in Chinese officialdom than it does generally in the Western world. While we accept this method of inquiry because we prize thinking on our feet and quick answers, it is rather offensive in China because it shows lack of respect and appreciation for the information given through the preferred means of prepared questions and formal briefings."[11] Hence, most of the information available about Chinese criminal justice comes by way of officialdom, and routine Western social science practices like door-to-door interviews, participant observation, and random surveys might produce substantial problems for researchers who attempted to use such techniques in China.

Problems with Data

Similar difficulties arise in the comparison of crime rates from one country to another. The crime rates of different nations are difficult to compare[12] because of (1) differences in the way a specific crime is defined, (2) diverse crime reporting practices, and (3) political and other influences on the reporting of statistics to international agencies.

Definitional differences create what may be the biggest problem. For cross-national comparisons of crime data to be meaningful, it is essential that the reported data share conceptual similarities. Unfortunately, that is rarely the case. Nations report offenses according to the legal criteria by which arrests are made and under which prosecution can occur. Switzerland, for example, includes bicycle thefts in its reported data on what we call "auto theft" because Swiss data gathering focuses more on the concept of personal transportation than it does upon the type of vehicle stolen. The Netherlands has no crime category for "robberies," counting them as thefts. Japan classifies an assault that results in death as "assault" or "aggravated assault," not homicide. Greek rape statistics include crimes of sodomy, "lewdness," seduction of a child, incest, and prostitution. Some communist countries report only robberies and thefts which involve the property of citizens, since crimes against state-owned property fall into a separate category.[13]

Social, cultural, and economic differences among countries compound the difficulties we have identified. Auto theft statistics, for example, when compared between countries like the United States and China need to be placed in an economic as well as demographic context. While the United States has two automobiles for every three people, China has only one car per 100 citizens. For the Chinese auto theft rate to equal that of the United States, every automobile in the country would have to be stolen nearly twice each year!

Reporting practices vary substantially between nations. INTERPOL (the International Police Organization) and the United Nations are the only international organizations which regularly collect crime statistics from a large number of countries.[14] Both agencies can only request data and have no way of checking on the accuracy of the data reported to them. Many countries do not disclose the requested information, and those that do often make only partial reports. In general, small countries are more likely to report than are large ones, and nonsocialist countries are more likely to report than are socialist nations.[15]

International reports of crime are often delayed. Complete, up-to-date data are rare since the information made available to agencies like the United Nations and INTERPOL is reported at different times and according to schedules which vary from nation to nation. In addition, official United Nations world crime surveys are conducted only infrequently. To date, five such surveys have been undertaken. Selected preliminary data from the fifth survey are shown in Table 16–1.

Crime statistics also reflect political biases and national values. Some nations do not accurately admit to the frequency of certain kinds of culturally reprehensible crimes. Communist countries, for example, appear loathe to report property crimes such as theft, burglary, and robbery because the very existence of such offenses demonstrates felt inequities within the communist system. After the breakup of the Soviet Union, Alexander Larin, a criminal justice scholar who worked as a Russian investigator during the 1950s and 1960s, revealed that "Inside the state security bureaucracy, where statistics were collected and circulated, falsification of crime figures was the rule, not the exception." "The practice was self-perpetuating," said Larin. "Supervisors in the provinces were under pressure to provide Moscow with declining crime rates. And no self-respecting investigator wanted to look worse than his neighbor....From the top to the bottom, the bosses depended on their employees not to make them look bad with high crime statistics."[16]

On the other hand, observers in democratic societies showed similar biases in their interpretation of statistics following the end of the cold war. Some Western analysts, for example, reporting on declines in the prison populations of Eastern and Central Europe during that period attributed the decline to lessened frustration and lowered crime rates brought about by democratization (in one country, Hungary, prison populations declined from 240 inmates per 100,000 persons in 1986 to 130 per 100,000 in 1993, with similar decreases in other nations).[17] The more likely explanation, however, appears to have been the wholesale post-*perestroika* release of political dissidents from prisons formerly run by communist regimes.

The Chinese Justice System

The People's Republic of China (PRC), with a land area of 3,691,502 square miles and a population of more than 1.2 billion people, is arguably the largest nation on earth. Some people predict that in the twenty-first century, as the Chinese economy awakens and its massive military might makes itself felt, it will become the world's most important nation. For that reason students of criminal justice should have some understanding of the Chinese justice system and of the cultural assumptions which underlie it.

In the spring of 1989, the world focused its attention on China, where students and workers supported mass demonstrations favoring freedom and democracy. Tiananmen Square, in the center of Beijing, became the rallying point for protesters. The huge and famous portrait of Mao Zedong, China's revolutionary communist leader, which overlooks the square, was defaced with paint. Students even constructed a small replica of the Statue of Liberty on the bricks of the square. As the world looked on, the Chinese Red Army, acting on orders of party leader Deng Xiaoping and members of the Chinese Communist Party Central Committee, moved decisively to end the demonstrations. On June 4, 1989, at least 800 people died in a hail of rifle fire directed at the protesters. It is estimated that thousands more perished in the weeks that followed.[18] Some were victims of government action to suppress continuing demonstrations, while others were summarily tried and executed for inciting riots and for plotting against the government. While the Chinese democratic revolution of 1989 did not succeed, it gives evidence of the sense of single-minded purpose so characteristic of Chinese society. It is that shared sense of purpose which underlies the Chinese legal system today.

Table 16-1   Crimes in Selected Countries, 1994

Country	Murder	Assault	Rape	Robbery	Theft	Burglary	Drugs
Austria	283	33,667	553	2,442	127,076	90,162	11,963
Belarus	1,029	3,221	672	7,013	72,372	20,525	1,441
Belgium	343	33,329	899	1,448	275,484	154,659	14,959
Bolivia	1,687	NA	2,261	11,543	28,396	NA	118
Bulgaria	948	1,079	903	6,597	161,811	NA	NA
Canada	596	225,616	31,690	28,888	1,003,322	387,877	60,594
Chile	626	45,383	961	72,058	17,576	NA	8,799
Columbia	27,130	28,748	1,930	28,486	80,519	8,533	13,812
Costa Rica	298	2,052	294	16,067	15,995	12,704	423
Croatia	367	1,168	94	389	31,081	18,232	857
Cyprus	12	976	7	14	990	1,291	135
Denmark	263	9,881	481	4,880	206,278	106,338	15,661
Ecuador	2,073	2,958	935	21,814	26,882	7,917	16,112
Egypt	871	108	9	375	1,760	5,772	88,022
Finland	533	19,836	387	2,122	115,234	98,656	5,926
France	NA	NA	6,526	73,310	2,573,074	484,901	53,892
Greece	298	7,566	258	812	57,343	37,123	2,531
Hong Kong	98	7,203	100	6,269	31,136	13,509	4,618
Hungary	477	11,077	828	2,570	135,620	78,877	259
Israel	389	15,351	550	450	9,815	2,953	8,807
Italy	3,040	20,873	869	29,981	1,333,089	NA	38,290
Jamaica	743	13,855	1,070	5,461	12,992	1,461	5,895
Japan	1,746	24,032	1,616	2,684	1,310,077	247,661	23,059
Jordan	298	14,946	36	500	6,567	1,622	NA
Kuwait	940	1,523	9	162	171	1,552	2,109
Lithuania	560	956	165	806	38,580	7,355	334
Madagascar	63	1,158	50	31	3,396	1,289	321
Malaysia	NA	2,846	965	6,072	51,159	21,553	10,350
Malta	11	83	10	33	4,095	1,909	246
Mauritius	36	12,862	34	767	11,111	960	1,882
Nicaragua	1,128	8,991	1,323	13,325	7,655	117	986
Northern Ireland	341	3,633	208	1,567	33,233	16,902	1,286
Panama	323	2,763	290	3,662	16,270	NA	2,978
Rep of Korea	4,514	NA	6,173	4,580	NA	1031	1,725
Romania	1,732	6,733	1,391	4,161	104,033	30,386	267
Russia	34,302	NA	13,956	148,546	1,314,788	NA	74,798
Scotland	113	5,917	569	5,297	238,233	88,394	19,281
Singapore	51	601	81	812	26,943	2,459	1,844
Slovakia	205	NA	213	1,244	58,807	43,069	88
Slovenia	111	1,816	240	294	15,763	10,422	407
Spain	NA	12,129	1,211	55,678	72,313	140,723	NA
Sudan	1,002	NA	610	846	NA	78,025	1751
Sweden	1,050	53,665	1,812	5,331	506,642	141,278	30,785
Switzerland	NA	3,612	275	1,954	195,409	66,466	40,144
Syrian Arab Rep	174	72	100	18	202	1,624	2,692
Turkey	1,794	32,245	503	1,542	75,054	NA	2,339
England & Wales	726	210,311	5,067	59,765	2,501,778	1,257,916	NA
United States	23,330	1,113,180	102,220	618,950	9,419,100	2,712,800	NA
Zimbabwe	1,779	67,598	3,091	12,378	164,724	57,943	10,487

NA = Not available.

Source: United Nations, *Fifth United Nations Survey of Crime Trends and Operations of Criminal Justice Systems* (Vienna, Austria: UN Crime Prevention and Criminal Justice Branch, 1997).

Individual Rights Guaranteed Under the Constitution of the People's Republic of China

(Adapted December 4, 1982 by the Fifth National People's Congress, Beijing)

Right	Guaranteed by
1. Equality Before the Law	Article 33
2. Freedom from Unlawful Detention	Article 37
3. Right Against Unlawful Personal Searches	Article 37
4. Protection from Unlawful Arrest	Article 37
5. Right Against Unlawful Searches of a Residence	Article 39
6. Right to a Public Trial	Article 126
7. Right of Defense in a Criminal Trial	Article 126
8. A Right to Use One's Native Spoken and Written Language in Court	Article 134

MAOIST JUSTICE

Under party Chairman Mao Zedong, criminal justice in the People's Republic of China was based upon informal societal control. Mao abhorred bureaucratic agencies and procedures and, during his reign, accused offenders found themselves turned over to the populace for a hearing and punishment.[19] The infamous Chinese Cultural Revolution, which began in 1966 and lasted until 1973,[20] was intended to integrate Maoist teaching and principles into Chinese society. During the revolutionary period, Mao called upon his hordes of fanatical followers, known as Red Guards, to "smash the police and the courts." One of Mao's most popular sayings intoned: "Depend on the rule of man, not the rule of law."[21] Because of Maoist thinking the People's Republic of China had no criminal or procedural legal codes, no lawyers, and no officially designated prosecutors until after 1978. Under Mao, the police were replaced by military control with arrest powers residing in the People's Liberation Army.

According to the concept of "class justice" taught by the Cultural Revolution, the severity of punishment an offender received depended upon his or her social and political identity. Consistent with the tenor of the times, a Chinese textbook of the late 1960s proclaimed, "The point of our criminal law is chiefly directed toward the enemies of socialism."[22] Wealthy, successful, and educated people, because of their high status under previous regimes, were automatically suspected of crimes and were often summarily tried and severely punished for the vaguest of allegations. Following Mao's death, the Cultural Revolution was denounced by the Central Committee of the Chinese Communist party as "responsible for the most severe setback and the heaviest losses suffered by the party, the state, and the people since the founding of the People's Republic."[23]

CHINESE JUSTICE AFTER MAO

In 1978, two years after the death of Chairman Mao, another wave of reform swept China. This time a formalized legal system, based upon codified laws, was created and a radically revised Constitution was given life on December 4, 1982. Predictability and security, especially for the potentially most productive members of society, became the goal of the new National People's Congress. The Congress sought to ensure internal stability, international commerce, and modernization through legislation. The Chinese Constitution now contains 24 articles on the fundamental rights and duties of citizens[24] and guarantees equality before the law for everyone.

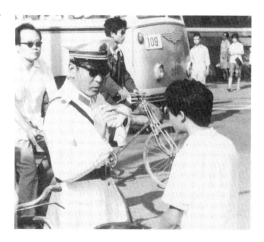

China: A police officer lectures a young man. Chinese society expects conformity in ways foreign to the Western mind, permitting Chinese officers to act as the conscience of the community even when no law has been broken. *Office of International Criminal Justice*

The Chinese Justice System

The modern Chinese justice system is structured along jurisdictional lines similar to those in the United States. At the highest level, the Chinese justice system is built around four national offices: the Ministry of Public Security, the Supreme People's Court, the People's **Procuratorate**, and the Ministry of Justice. Article 5 of the Chinese constitution specifies that the procuratorate is directly responsible for supervising the administration of criminal justice throughout the country, including the investigation of crimes, the activities of the courts, the police and correctional institutions, and to initiate prosecution.[25]

Chinese police agencies, which fall under the authority of the Ministry of Public Security, are often regarded as technologically backward. Some, however, are beginning to apply twenty-first-century technology in the fight against crime. In 1995, for example, Chinese officials announced[26] that police forces in more than 20 provinces had begun to use DNA fingerprinting as a method of criminal identification. Also in 1995, the China Criminal Information Center, a computerized national network designed to provide police forces throughout China with rapid interprovincial information on criminal offenders, began operating in 11 provinces along China's east coast. Officials said they hoped that the new computer system will allow for improved control over China's huge migrant population,[27] estimated at between 60 and 80 million people—especially members of that group who are involved in criminal activity.

Courts in China are hierarchically organized. The Supreme People's Court is the highest court in China. It deals with cases which may have an impact on the entire country.[28] Most cases come before the Court on appeal. The Court is divided into three sections: criminal court, which deals with felony violations of the law, mostly on appeal, and death penalty reviews; civil affairs court; and economic court.

At the opposite judicial extreme, the Basic People's Court operates at the county level as the court with original jurisdiction over most criminal cases. Two judicial levels—the Intermediate People's Courts and the Higher People's Courts—stand between the Basic Court and the Supreme Court. Both function as courts of appeal, although Intermediate Courts have original jurisdiction in criminal cases with the potential for sentences involving death or life imprisonment. They also hear criminal charges brought against foreigners.

Defendants may choose to be represented in Chinese courts by an attorney, a relative, or a friend, or may choose to represent themselves. If they desire, a lawyer will be appointed for them. Attorneys in China, however, have a far different role from that of their American counterparts. While they work to protect the rights of the defendant, attorneys have a responsibility to the court which transcends their duties to the accused. Defense lawyers are charged with helping the court render a just verdict.[29] The Chinese believe that vigorous defense strategies such as those found in the adversarial framework of Western justice can lead to criminals escaping responsibility.[30]

A visit by a delegation of the American Bar Association to Shanghai determined that 78% of the work load of Chinese attorneys consisted of defending accused criminals. The remaining 22% was divided about equally between family practice (wills, divorces, adoptions,

Procuratorate (also **Procuracy**)   A term used in many countries to refer to agencies with powers and responsibilities similar to those of prosecutors' offices in the United States.

inheritance, etc.) and civil suits.[31] The legal profession in China is not, on the whole, well trained. While most lawyers probably have some formal legal education, many simply meet the conditions of Article 8 of the Chinese constitution, which requires persons who wish to engage in the practice of law to "have the cultural level of graduates of institutions of higher learning, and be suitable to be lawyers."

The Chinese justice system has a built-in system of checks and balances which, in theory, operates to prevent abuses of power. Arrests made by the police, for example, must be approved by the local procurators office. If a decision is made to prosecute, the court may conduct its own investigation prior to the start of trial to determine whether prosecution is warranted.

The official Chinese crime rate is astonishingly low—only 56 crimes per every 100,000 citizens (versus 5,600 per 100,000 people in the United States). In 1994 the Chinese government reported only 624,000 major crimes[32] (including murder, assault, rape, robbery, and theft) throughout the country. Although the official figure was said to reflect a 15.6% increase over the previous year, the number of officially reported crimes is amazingly low for a country with such a huge population.

One special area of concern to outsiders has been China's wholesale violation of intellectual property rights by profiteers who reproduce foreign movies, compact disks, tapes, and software, and resell them in China and throughout Asia without paying permission fees or royalties. U.S. industry spokespersons estimate that Chinese copyright, trademark, and patent violations cost American companies alone up to $1.0 billion a year in lost sales.[33] In response to stiff international pressure, China has recently taken steps to criminalize such activities, including the establishment of special courts to prosecute those who violate laws governing intellectual property[34] and the enforcement of new antipiracy laws seems to be speeding up.

Organized crime is another problem in China. Chinese gang roots can be traced to secret societies, called triads, that fought to restore the Ming Dynasty, which was overthrown in 1644. Beginning in the early 1900s, the triads which still survived became increasingly involved in criminal activities. In 1949, after the communist takeover, China's gangs and underworld secret societies were either eradicated or forced into hibernation. In recent years these "black societies" have made a strong comeback, manufacturing and selling guns, running illegal gambling operations, smuggling, forcing women into prostitution, and fighting gun battles with local police. In 1995 Chinese officials announced a major crackdown on organized crime throughout the country, vowing to execute any gang bosses who could be identified. Military Police Colonel Zhang Dingxing was blunt in his assessment of the situation. "All leaders of black societies will be executed without exception,"[35] he said, announcing the crackdown.

Illegal drug use, another area of criminal activity within the country, was said to have been virtually eliminated by the communist government in post–World War II China. In recent years, however, drug abuse, often supported by organized crime, is reported to be making a strong comeback. In 1993, for example, more than 1,000 people were sentenced to death for drug trafficking,[36] although most of the sentences were later suspended and commuted to life in prison. Recently,[37] authorities in the central Chinese province of Shaanxi reportedly formed a special antidrug trafficking force to combat organized gangs who were importing heroin from the Golden Triangle area of Thailand, Laos, and Burma. Reports said that 20 people had been arrested and that education programs were being started to assist addicts and prevent others from becoming addicted.

Once arrested, suspects face a high likelihood of conviction. Records show only a 1% acquittal rate in Chinese criminal courts (versus 31% in the United States).[38] A crime problem of growing concern to the Chinese, however, is juvenile delinquency. Juvenile gang activity is on the increase, with gang members often coming from the families of high communist party functionaries.[39] Some officials have also suggested that international gang-related drug trafficking is on the rise in the People's Republic of China. However, although China has had a history of problems with opium abuse, actual consumption of illicit drugs by Chinese citizens probably occurs at a rate much below that of the Western world.[40]

Mediation Committees

One reason for the low official crime rate is the Chinese system of People's Mediation Committees. By virtue of the large number of cases they resolve, **mediation committees** may

Mediation Committees Chinese civilian dispute resolution groups found throughout the country. Mediation committees successfully divert many minor offenders from handling by more formal mechanisms of justice.

Women prisoners sewing in a Chinese prison. *Courtesy Thomas McAninch and Sgt. Jeff Sanders*

be the most important component of justice in modern China. Mediation committees generally consist of from five to seven people, with judicial assistants assigned to them by the Bureau of Justice, the courts, and the procuratorates.[41] They are officially guided by law and government policy. Their power, however, comes from the force of public opinion.[42] Education and persuasion are their primary tools.[43]

Committees function informally based upon the belief that minor disputes and misdemeanor offenses such as minor assaults, thefts, and vandalism can be best handled at local levels without unnecessary protocol. Mediation committees are also believed to play a significant role in crime prevention by resolving disputes before they evolve into serious altercations. That is why housing disputes, divorce cases, and land sharing problems also commonly come before such committees.

People's mediation committees are everywhere in China—in factories, on farms, in schools, and in businesses. According to some authorities, over 800,000 Chinese mediation committees functioning on a regular basis handle over 8 million cases per year.[44] In contrast, only 3,000 regular courts are in existence at all levels throughout the entire country.[45] Mediation committees serve to divert a large number of people from processing by county and provincial courts. They also serve to unintentionally, but dramatically, lower the number of officially reported offenses throughout China.

One item of special interest in international criminal justice circles involves the reversion of Hong Kong to China which occurred on July 1, 1997. After the turnover, Chinese officials worked toward creation of Chinese-like criminal justice agencies throughout the former British territory, including a separate supreme court of Hong Kong. The new court, called the Court of Final Appeal for Hong Kong, replaces London's Privy Council as the former territory's supreme judicial agency.

Chinese Criminal Punishments

The punishment of offenders in China can be severe in cases which go beyond mediation and enter the court system. Thirty-eight percent of convicted offenders in China are sentenced to more than five years in prison,[46] and repeat offenders are subject to harsh punishments. Widespread use of the death penalty, usually carried out with a single bullet to the back of the head, is characteristic of contemporary China. Executions are often preceded by a public rally during which the prisoner's name, crime, and punishment are announced to the crowd, while the prisoner is forced to stand with head bowed and hands tied. Following execution, the offender's family is routinely ordered to pay for the cost of the bullet. The number of people executed each year is a state secret. Amnesty International, however, says that more people are executed in China each year than in all of the rest of the world. In 1996, observers for Amnesty International recorded 6,100 death sentences and 4,367 Chinese executions,[47] although the organization believes the real number may have been far higher. Amnesty International also says that a recent *Yanda*, or anti-crime campaign aimed at combating major crimes, such as murder and robbery, led to 1,014 death sentences between April and June of 1996— resulting in over 800 immediate executions.[48]

In China, capital punishment can be imposed for a wide variety of crimes. One man was recently executed, for example, for publishing pornographic books; and four others were put to death for faking tax receipts. "The death penalty is apparently used to deter people from actions that interfere with economic development," said one Western observer.[49] Widespread use of the death penalty, while expected to deter others, is admittedly not based upon studies of the punishment's effectiveness as a deterrent. As one Chinese diplomat said, "We don't feel the death penalty is based on research but on common sense arguments and primal response."[50] Although death sentences must be reviewed by the Supreme People's Court, the court may rule on the legality of a case before a defendant is sentenced, which clears the way for speedy executions.

Executions which occur out of the public view are often widely publicized. In 1995, for example, South China's Guizhou province executed Yan Jianhong, the formerly powerful chairwoman of Guizhou International Trust and Investment Corporation. Jianhong had been convicted of embezzling, illegally lending huge amounts of public money, and receiving kickbacks. Her death sentence was given extensive coverage, reflecting the government's strategy of using particularly serious cases as warnings to officials tempted by corruption. The Chinese government called her crimes grave and warned that other corrupt officials would face the same punishment.[51]

Some international human rights organizations have recently called attention to the claimed unethical use of organs taken from executed prisoners in China. According to Amnesty International, "There is abundant evidence that organ harvesting from the bodies of executed prisoners is a common practice in China. The retrieval of organs from prisoners accounts for the vast majority of transplants in China,"[52] says the human rights organization. Worse, "the deplorable lack of safeguards in the Chinese legal process provides little guarantee that the decision to impose or to implement death sentences will not be influenced" by the need for transplanted organs, says Amnesty. The organization also claims that foreigners visiting China routinely arrange to purchase the organs of dead prisoners for use in planned transplant operations.

According to authorities there, Chinese prisons hold 1.28 million inmates in 685 prison units. Western authorities, however, doubt that official Chinese statistics are correct. Independent research into Chinese arrest and sentencing patterns, and accounts by former prisoners, lead some to conclude that as many as 16 to 20 million people are confined in 990 labor reform prisons—that is, prisons set aside for inmates whose only crime may be speaking out against the dictatorial aspects of Chinese government.

Many Chinese prisons are notoriously primitive. Typical cells, which range in size from 36 to 60 square yards, hold 30 to 50 inmates, who sleep on hard woven mats covering the floor. Cells, which are unheated in the winter, are fitted with only one latrine and are lit with a single light bulb.

For all its seeming harshness, the Chinese justice system is based upon a strong cultural belief in personal reformation. As one author has observed, "Repentance, which means reclaiming individuals for society, is at the heart of Chinese justice."[53] Confucius taught that "Man is at birth by nature good,"[54] and Chinese authorities seek to build opportunities into their criminal justice system which allow offenders to change for the better. Even persons sentenced to death are generally granted a two-year period during which they may repent and attempt to demonstrate that they have changed. If they can successfully convince the court that they have reformed, their sentence will be commuted.[55]

Prison sentences in China allow for parole after completion of one-half of the time imposed (ten years for life sentences).[56] Violation of prison rules may result in extended incarceration, solitary confinement, or "group criticism." The study of communist policy, according to official Chinese interpretation, is required of all inmates. Such study is the focal point of prison treatment programs.[57] Political prisoners are subjected to *laogai*,[58] or "thought-reform-through-labor," and are required to work at prison farms, factories, and the like.

A female prisoner gardening at a Chinese "reeducation center." *Xinhua, Gamma—Liaison, Inc.*

Official parole eligibility comes only after the offender has shown repentance and performed "meritoriously" while in prison. In practice, however, parole may be granted routinely after half the sentence has been served. Chinese parole follows the institutional model, in which individual confinement facilities recommend parole to the court, which then makes the final decision. Parole officers are unknown in China, but parolees are supervised by local police agencies and by citizens groups.

The philosophy which underlies Chinese corrections is well summed up in the words of a western observer who recently visited prisons there: "Inmates are expected to conform not to benefit themselves, but to benefit their families, villages, and even their country. Crime is not a reflection of individual failure, but instead is considered a reflection of the family, the community, and even the larger society. It is for the good of society, it is for the good of the communist structure that one must reform one's self. The individual is punished, but he is punished as a member of the group."[59] Faith in repentance, a fundamental doctrine in Chinese corrections, is apparently well placed. The official rate of recidivism in China is only 4.7% for serious offenders.[60]

In December 1994 China's legislature, the National People's Congress, passed the National Prison Reform Law. The new law guarantees prisoners dignity, safety, the right to a legal defense, a right of appeal, and freedom from physical abuse. The law also prohibits forced confessions and the illegal confiscation of property and holds prison officials responsible for ensuring that inmates serve their full sentences. The 1994 law officially codified a decade-old set of Chinese administrative guidelines for prisons. The guidelines, originally approved in 1982, had been largely ignored by prison administrators and remained unenforced—allowing Chinese prisons to become the target of international human rights groups which have strongly criticized prisons there. "Establishing a modern prison system is a key goal of the recently enacted prison law," Justice Minister Xiao Yang said. Under the law, each province was ordered to build "at least one modern prison before 1996 and two to five before 1998," Xiao said.

Islamic Law A system of laws, operative in some Arab countries, which is based upon the Muslim religion and especially the holy book of Islam, the Koran.

Islamic Criminal Justice

Although the subject of much curiosity, justice in Islamic countries is often not well understood by westerners. In an insightful analysis,[61] Sam Souryal and Dennis W. Potts describe the four aspects of justice in Arab philosophy and religion. Islamic justice, say Souryal and Potts, means

- a sacred trust, a duty imposed on humans to be discharged sincerely and honestly. As such, these authors say, "justice is the quality of being morally responsible and merciful in giving everyone his or her due."
- mutual respect of one human being by another. From this perspective, a just society is one which offers equal respect for individuals through social arrangements made in the common interest of all members.
- an aspect of the social bond which holds society together and transforms it into a brotherhood in which everyone becomes a keeper of everyone else and each is held accountable for the welfare of all.
- a command from God. Whosoever violates God's commands should be subject to strict punishments according to Islamic tradition and belief.

As Souryal and Potts observe, "the third and fourth meanings of justice are probably the ones most commonly invoked in Islamic jurisprudence," and form the basis of criminal justice practice in many middle eastern countries.

The *Hudud* Crimes

Islamic law (or *Shari'ah* in Arabic, which means "path of God") forms the basis of theocratic judicial systems in Kuwait, Saudia Arabia, the Sudan, Iran, and Algeria. Other Arabic nations, such as Egypt, Jordan, and Iraq, recognize substantial elements of Islamic law in their criminal justice systems, but also make wide use of Western and nontheocratic legal principles. Islamic law is based upon four sources. In order of importance these sources are (1) the Koran (also spelled "Quran" and "Qur'an"), or Holy Book of Islam, which Muslims believe is the word of God, or "Allah"; (2) the teachings of the Prophet Mohammed; (3) a consensus of the clergy in cases where neither the Koran nor the prophet directly address an issue; and (4) reason or logic which should be used when no solution can be found in the other three sources.[62]

Islamic law recognizes seven *Hudud* (sometimes called *Hodood* or *Huddud*) crimes—or crimes based on religious strictures. *Hudud* crimes are essentially violations of "natural law" as interpreted by Arab culture. Divine displeasure is thought to be the basis of crimes defined as *Hudud*, and *Hudud* crimes are often said to be crimes against God (or, more specifically, "God's rights"). Four *Hudud* crimes for which punishments are specified in the Koran are (1) making war upon Allah and His messengers, (2) theft, (3) adultery, and (4) false accusation of fornication or adultery. Three other *Hudud* offenses are mentioned by the Koran, for which no punishment is specified—(1) "corruption on the earth," (2) drinking of alcohol, and (3) highway robbery—and the punishments for these crimes are determined by tradition.[63] The seven *Hudud* offenses and associated typical punishments are shown in Table 16–2. "Corruption on Earth" is a general category of religious offense, not well understood in the West, which includes activities such as embezzlement, revolution against lawful authority, fraud, and "weakening the society of God."

The religious aspect of Islamic law makes for strict punishment of moral failure. Sexual offenders, even those who engage in what may be considered essentially victimless crimes in Western societies, are subject to especially harsh treatment. The Islamic penalty for fornication, for example, is 100 lashes. Men are stripped to the waist, women have their clothes bound tightly, and flogging is carried out with a leather whip. Adultery carries a much more severe penalty: flogging and stoning to death.

Under Islamic law even property crimes can be firmly punished. Thieves who are undeterred by less serious punishments may eventually suffer amputation of the right hand. In a reputedly humane move, Iranian officials recently began the use of an electric guillotine, specially made for the purpose, which can sever a hand at the wrist in one-tenth of a second. For amputation to be imposed, the item stolen must have value in Islam. Pork and alcohol, for example, are regarded as being without value, and their theft is not subject to punishment. Islamic legal codes also establish a minimum value for stolen items which could result in amputation being imposed. Likewise, offenders who have stolen because they are hungry, or are in need, are exempt from the punishment of amputation and receive fines or prison terms.

Slander and the consumption of alcohol are both punished by 80 lashes. Legal codes in strict Islamic nations also specify whipping for the crimes of pimping, lesbianism, kissing by an unmarried couple, cursing, and failure of a woman to wear a veil. Islamic law provides for

Hudud **Crimes** Serious violations of Islamic law regarded as offenses against God. Hudud crimes include such behavior as theft, adultery, sodomy, drinking alcohol, and robbery.

Table 16-2 Crime and Punishment in Islamic Law: The Iranian Example[1]

Islamic law looks to the Koran and the teachings of the Prophet Mohammed to determine which acts should be classified as crimes. The Koran and tradition specify punishments to be applied to designated offenses, as the following verse from the Koran demonstrates: "The only reward of those who make war upon Allah and His messenger and strive after corruption in the land will be that they will be killed or crucified, or have their hands and feet on alternate sides cut off, or will be expelled out of the land" (Surah V, Verse 33). Other crimes and punishments include the following:

Offense	Punishment
Theft	Amputation of the hand
Adultery	Stoning to death
Fornication	One hundred lashes
False accusation (of adultery or fornication)	Eighty lashes
Corruption on Earth	Death by the sword or burning
Drinking alcohol	Eighty lashes; death if repeated three times
Robbery	Cutting off of hands and feet on alternate sides

[1] For more information, see Sam S. Souryal and Dennis W. Potts, "The Penalty of Hand Amputation for Theft in Islamic Justice," *Journal of Criminal Justice*, Vol. 22, no. 3 (1994) pp. 249–265; and Parviz Saney, "Iran," in Elmer H. Johnson, ed., *International Handbook of Contemporary Developments in Criminology* (Westport, CT: Greenwood, 1983), pp. 356–369.

the execution, sometimes through crucifixion, of robbers. Laws stipulate that anyone who survives three days on the cross may be spared. Depending upon the circumstances of the robbery, however, the offender may suffer the amputation of opposite hands and feet, or simply exile.

Rebellion, or revolt against a legitimate political leader or established economic order, which is considered an aspect of "corruption on earth," is punishable by death. The offender may be killed outright in a military or police action or, later, by sentence of the court. The last of the *Hudud* crimes is rejection of Islam. The penalty, once again, is death, and can be imposed for denying the existence of God or angels, denying any of the prophets of Islam, or rejecting any part of the Koran.

In a recent example, on August 22, 1995, a court in Tehran, Iran, sentenced a man to death for what is believed to be the biggest bank fraud case in Iranian history.[64] The defendant, Fazel Khodadad, was convicted of embezzling $21.7 million from state-run Bank Saderat. Khodadad was sentenced under Islamic laws, which allows capital punishment for "sabotaging the country's economic system." Khodadad was also sentenced to 50 lashes for other illegal activities, including drug abuse, and 99 lashes for an illegal sexual relationship with a woman involving "touching, kissing, and lying next to each other." The woman, identified only as M.H., received a sentence of 99 lashes, which was suspended for two years.

Hudud crimes can be severely punished, Souryal observes, because "punishment serves a three-tiered obligation: (1) the fulfillment of worship, (2) the purification of society, and (3) the redemption of the individual." However, Souryal adds, the interests of the individual are the least valuable component of this triad, and may have to be sacrificed "for the wholesomeness and integrity of the encompassing justice system."[65]

Tazirat Crimes Minor violations of Islamic law, regarded as offenses against society, not God.

All crimes other than *Hudud* fall into an offense category called **tazirat**. *Tazir* crimes are regarded as any action not considered acceptable in a spiritual society. They include crimes against society and against individuals, but not against God. *Tazir* crimes may call for *Quesas* (retribution) or *Diya* (compensation or fines). Crimes requiring *Quesas* are based on the Arabic principle of "an eye for an eye, a nose for a nose, a tooth for a tooth," and generally require physical punishments up to and including death. *Quesas* offenses may include murder, manslaughter, assault, and maiming. Under Islamic law such crimes may require the vic-

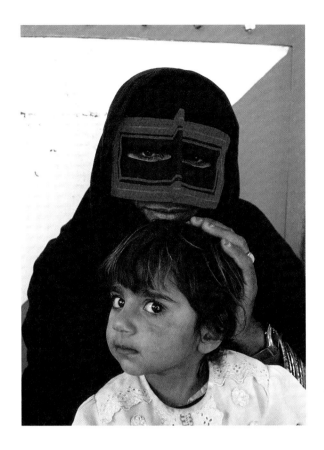

Islamic tradition and Muslim law strongly influence the style of dress worn by this woman in Oman. Islamic law is based upon the teachings of the Koran and the sayings of the Prophet Mohammed. *A. Johannes, Sygma*

tim or his representative to serve as prosecutor. The state plays a role only in providing the forum for a trial and in imposing punishment. Sometimes victims' representatives dole out punishment. In late-1997, for example, 28-year-old taxi-driver Ali Reza Khoshruy, nick-named "The Vampire" because he stalked, raped, and killed women at night after picking them up in his cab, was hung from a yellow crane in the middle of Tehran, the Iranian cap-ital.[66] Before the hanging, prison officials and male relatives of the victims cursed Khoshruy and whipped him with thick leather belts as he lay tied to a metal bed. The whipping was part of a 214-lash sentence.

ISLAMIC COURTS

Islamic courts typically exist on three levels.[67] The first level hears cases involving the poten-tial for serious punishments, including death, amputation, and exile. The second level deals with relatively minor matters, such as traffic offenses and violations of city ordinances. Special courts, especially in Iran, may hear cases involving crimes against the government, narcotics offenses, state security, and corruption. Appeals within the Islamic court system are only possible under rare circumstances and are by no means routine. A decision rendered by second level courts will generally stand without intervention by higher judicial authorities.

Under Islamic law, men and women are treated very differently. Testimony provided by a man, for example, can be heard in court. The same evidence, however, can only be provided by two virtuous women—one female witness will not be sufficient to have the evidence heard.

While Islamic law may seem barbaric to many Westerners, Islamic officials defend their system by pointing to low crime rates at home and by alleging near anarchy in Western nations. An early criticism of Islamic law was offered by Max Weber at the start of the twen-tieth century.[68] Weber said that Islamic justice is based more upon the moral conceptions of individual judges than it is upon any rational and predictable code of laws. He found that the personality of each judge, what he called "charisma," was more important in reaching a final legal result than was the written law. Weber's conclusion was that a modern society could not develop under Islamic law because enforcement of the law was too unpredictable. Complex social organizations, he argued, could only be based upon a rational law, which is relatively unchanging from place to place and over time.[69]

More recent observers have agreed that "Islamic justice is based on philosophical principles which are considered alien, if not unconscionable, to the Western observer." However, these same writers note, strict punishments such as hand amputation, "may not be inconsistent with the fundamentals of natural law or Judeo-Christian doctrine. The imposition of the penalty in specific cases and under rigorous rules of evidence—as the principle requires—may be indeed justifiable, and even necessary, in the Islamic context of sustaining a spiritual and peaceful society."[70]

Criminal Justice in England and Wales

The country of England is quite small—only a little larger than the state of New Jersey, but with a population of nearly 40 million people. One of the original participants in the industrial revolution, it remains a highly industrialized nation. England is linked closely to its neighbors—Wales, Scotland, and Northern Ireland—an alliance which created the political entity of "Great Britain" and which today is officially known as the "United Kingdom of Great Britain."

Our American heritage, both legal and cultural, has been strongly influenced by Great Britain. Chapter 4 describes the way in which British common law formed the basis of our own legal traditions, and Chapter 5 shows how American police forces and other criminal justice agencies in their formative periods drew upon earlier English experience. Because England is a much more open society than either China or Iran, a far greater amount of descriptive detail is available about the criminal justice system there.

Rates of Crime

British crime surveys mirror their American counterparts, and the Research and Statistics Department of the Home Office makes reports of crime freely available to researchers. Major crimes in England and Wales are termed "notifiable offenses," the counterpart of "Part I" or "Index Offenses" in the United States. In recent years public opinion polls have identified crime as the number one concern of the British voting public. By any measure, crime would appear to be high in England. In 1996,[71] for example, approximately 5 million criminal offenses were recorded by police forces throughout England and Wales—about one for every ten members of the population. Another 9 million crimes went unreported, according to data gathered by the British Crime Survey. Reported crimes included 1.16 million burglaries, 2 million larcenies, and 1.4 million vehicle thefts. Ninety-two percent of reported crimes in England and Wales during 1996 were against property, while 8% were violent crimes. Overall violent crime increased by 33,000 offenses, or 11%, over the previous year. However, vehicle theft fell by 3%, and burglaries decreased by 6% from 1995. Since 1973, however, crime rates in England have risen nearly 900%.[72] In 1996, 27% of all offenses were "cleared up" (solved).

The British Political System

Parliament The British legislature; the highest law-making body of the United Kingdom of Great Britain.

England is a country without a constitution in the strict sense of the word. The legal basis of English government, however, can be found in at least three significant documents: (1) the Magna Carta, (2) the Bill of Rights, and (3) the Act of Settlement. The Magna Carta, written in 1215, was forced upon the king by English nobility and the upper classes. It guarantees a number of legal rights to British citizens accused of crimes, including the right to due process of law and a hearing before one's peers. The English Bill of Rights, passed by Parliament in 1688, established the two houses of Parliament (the House of Lords and the House of Commons), guaranteed free elections, and placed Parliamentary authority in statutory matters over that of the sovereign. As a consequence, although modern England still has a royal family whose members perform ceremonial functions, the real power to make laws and run the nation lies in the hands of the two houses of Parliament and the prime minister. In 1700 the Act of Settlement reinforced the powers of Parliament and made clear the authority of judges and other officials.

As Richard Terrill points out,[73] at least three major differences can be found between the British and American systems of government, all of which bear significance for the administration of criminal justice:

British "Bobbies." Uniformed English police officers have a recognizable appearance rooted in the time of Sir Robert Peel. *Comstock*

- The British system, unlike the American, makes no provision for judicial review of Parliamentary action. Acts of Parliament are the law of the land and cannot be overruled by any court.
- In Britain a unity of powers, rather than a separation of branches, characterizes the government. Executive, legislative, and judicial authority all ultimately rest in Parliament.
- England is a unified nation. No separate state legislatures or state governmental offices exist. Parliamentary law applies at both the national and local level.

Modern Criminal Law in England

In 1967 Parliament passed the Criminal Law Act, a sweeping piece of legislation which substantially altered English criminal procedure. The old distinction between "felonies" and "misdemeanors" was eliminated in favor of two new offense categories: "arrestable" (or indictable) and "nonarrestable" (or summary) offenses. Under English common law, the arrest powers of the police without a warrant were limited to treason, felonies, and breaches of the peace. The Criminal Law Act broadened arrest powers in the absence of a warrant to all offenses "for which (a) sentence is fixed by law," and to attempts to commit such offenses. The 1967 act also gave private citizens the power to arrest offenders they caught engaging in criminal activity or whom they had reasonable suspicion to believe had committed an arrestable offense.

In November 1994, a powerful nationwide conservative emphasis led to passage of the Criminal Justice and Public Order Act 1994. The 1994 Criminal Justice Act (CJA) marked a return to a get-tough English anticrime policy. British Home Secretary Michael Howard explained why the bill was passed in these words: "In the last 30 years the balance in the criminal justice system has been tilted too far in favor of the criminal and against the protection of the public. The time has come to put that right."[74]

The CJA selectively criminalized what had previously been especially serious violations of the civil law, made it easier to catch and convict criminals, made it harder for repeat offenders to get bail, and restricted, at least to some degree, the rights of criminal defendants. Prior to the new legislation, for example, police officers in England were required to caution detained persons with the admonishment: "You do not have to say anything unless you wish to do so, but anything you say may be given as evidence." Criticisms of the British right to silence were effectively promoted in the national media by law enforcement agencies which cited difficulties in obtaining convictions when a suspect's silence went unquestioned. Such criticisms found their way into the 1994 legislation, and English courts are now permitted to draw "such inferences as are appropriate" from a suspect's silence. Today, an English police officer arresting someone is required to say: "You do not have to say anything, but it may harm your defense if you do not mention when questioned, something which you later rely on in court. Anything you say may be used as evidence." When preparing to question a suspect, officers are enjoined to admonish: "I must warn you that if from now on you refuse to account for a fact, a court may draw their own conclusions why you have not done so." Hence, under modern British law, a suspect's refusal to answer questions (specifically to account for one's presence at a given location or to account for the possession of objects, substances, and bodily injuries) can be used later by a court to infer his or her guilt. The CJA also gives British courts wider powers to sentence persistent offenders between the ages of 12 and 14 and effectively doubles the maximum possible sentence youthful offenders can receive.

A 1997 election victory by Labor Party Prime Minister Tony Blair may soon produce substantial change in the English criminal justice system. Blair, the first Labor Party prime minister to take office in nearly 20 years, favors the creation of sentencing guidelines for major offenses, and stricter punishment for repeat offenders involved in serious crimes. Blair also supports the creation of an anti-drug czar position in his cabinet and wants a total ban on the ownership of handguns by civilians.

Police in England

The historical development of police forces in nineteenth-century Britain is described in Chapter 5. By World War II 183 police departments—some large, some very small—existed throughout England and Wales.[75] Each was headed by a chief constable, and jurisdictional disputes between departments were common. Major efforts to consolidate police departments culminated in the Police Acts of 1946 and 1964, to which contemporary British policing owes its structure. The Local Government Act of 1972 further reduced the number of police forces throughout England and Wales until the combined forces numbered just 43. The smallest police agency in Britain today has over 600 officers—a good-sized department by American standards. Approximately 128,000 sworn police officers are employed throughout Britain, and 55,000 civilians serve police forces there.[76]

The police of Britain are subject to civilian control through local commissions called police authorities. Two-thirds of each police authority is comprised of elected civilians, while one-third of the authority's members are judicial officers elected by fellow magistrates. Each police authority appoints a local chief constable—with overall authority for the daily operations of the police—and an assistant chief constable. In 1994, Parliament passed the Police and Magistrates Courts Act, legislation which emphasizes the important role local communities play in setting the goals of police service. In tones reminiscent of the American emphasis on community policing, British Home Secretary Michael Howard described the new law this way: "I believe that an active partnership between government, the public, and the police is the way forward. The Police and Magistrates Courts Act gives us the framework for the future."[77]

Beyond the local level, the British home secretary has statutory authority to intervene in police administration, police discipline, and suspected cases of corruption and mismanagement. The home secretary also provides for the coordination of police services throughout Britain, runs the Police College and local police training centers, maintains forensic laboratories, and is ultimately responsible for information management, including national databases and telecommunications.

Britain does not have a national police force.[78] The Metropolitan Police District, with 26,000[79] members, however, serves many centralized functions. The Metropolitan Police District encompasses 32 boroughs and portions of four counties surrounding London. Headquartered at **New Scotland Yard**, perhaps the most famous address of any police force in the world, the Metropolitan Police serve as a national repository for information on crime statistics, criminal activity, fingerprints, missing persons, and wayward and delinquent juveniles. The agency also maintains links with INTERPOL and handles requests for information from police agencies in other countries.

In 1992 the National Criminal Intelligence Service (NCIS), charged with intelligence gathering and record-keeping, began operation[80] in England. Likened by some to the

Theory into Practice

Arming the British Police

In a tradition dating back to the days of the "Wild West," American law enforcement officers routinely carry guns. Expertise with a handgun or rifle has long been regarded as a sign of accomplishment among police ranks. The development of a well-financed and often brutal drug subculture within the country, however, has left many police officers feeling outgunned. In a tragic Florida shootout a few years ago, three FBI agents were killed by heavily armed bank robbers. The agents' traditional sidearms were no match for the robbers automatic pistols and machine guns. Since then, many federal law enforcement agencies have increased the "firepower" available to their agents by issuing 9mm semiautomatic pistols and Uzi-type machine guns. As a consequence, American law enforcement officers today, especially on the federal level, are routinely well armed.

In contrast to the American situation, the police of England (with the exception of those guarding international airports and a few highly sensitive locations) do not carry weapons beyond a simple "billy club." The typical British municipal police department, which may have as many as 380 officers, will probably maintain no more than six handguns under lock and key for use only in emergencies.[1] In fact, only a small percentage of British officers are authorized to use a weapon under any circumstances, and firearms practice is not a routine part of law enforcement training in England.

The 1993 opening of the "Chunnel," a tunnel linking France and England under the English Channel, became another focus for the British aversion to armed police. Under an agreement between the two countries, French police, typically armed, may not carry weapons on tunnel trains and are permitted to have weapons only in a controlled zone at the tunnel mouth. They have to surrender their weapons if they leave the area.[2]

There are a number of significant reasons for the British reluctance to arm their police. Of greatest significance may be the fact that British citizens are themselves unarmed. The "right to bear arms" is foreign to English law, and very few guns are in private hands in any part of the country.

People Killed by Handguns in 1994[3]

Britain	63
Canada	90
Japan	46
Switzerland	68
United States	12,769

QUESTIONS FOR DISCUSSION

1. What might happen if American police were unarmed? Would there be more crime? More violence? Why or why not?

2. Do you think it will be necessary for most British police officers to eventually carry handguns? Why or why not?

[1]"CBS Early Morning News," March 17, 1989.

[2]"Chunnel Patrol," *Criminal Justice Europe* (March/April 1992), p. 3.

[3]Handgun Control, Inc., telephone conversation, September 17, 1997.

American FBI, few real similarities exist—primarily because NCIS agents do not have an operational role but function only as staff officers to exchange information on criminal activity with other police agencies throughout England.

In 1948 the Police College opened at Ryton-upon-Dunsmore. The Police College was designed to enhance professionalism among the nation's constables. The training it provided made possible professional advancement within police ranks. In 1960 the college relocated to Bramshill. Known today by its new name, the Police Staff College at Bramshill serves as an international model for police management training.[81]

Traditionally, British police officers have gone on patrol unarmed, except for a nightstick or billy club. Events in the 1980s, especially terrorist attacks on civilian targets including London's Heathrow Airport, led to a reassessment of traditional policy. That reassessment continues today, although most beat constables remain unarmed. Weapons are kept on hand in local police stations and can be issued upon the order of senior police personnel. Officers who routinely patrol highly congested areas, including those with considerable international traffic such as major airports, are now armed with handguns and automatic weapons as a precaution against terrorist attack. In emergencies, local chief constables are authorized to call upon the military for armed assistance. Even so, support continues to grow for British police to routinely carry sidearms as part of their everyday equipment. Former Scotland Yard chief Ken Hyder warns that "carrying guns as a normal part of equipment will lead to acci-

James Bulger, the two-year-old
English boy whose 1993 murder by
two ten-year-olds, came to symbolize
public concern in England over rising
crime. Bulger's young killers, Robert
Thompson and Jon Venables, were
both sentenced to terms requiring
them to serve at least 15 years of
detention. *Mercury Press, SIPA Press*

dental shootings of bystanders as well as suspects." "Arming the police in a routine way," says Hyder, "would have two other effects—it would distance them from the public, whom they need to provide them with information and support, and it would encourage more villains to arm themselves."[82]

Evidentiary standards, such as the American exclusionary rule, do not apply to the British police. Unlike their American counterparts, British courts have not utilized precedent-setting decisions to carve out individual rights for citizens who face apprehension and criminal prosecution. What they have done, through judicial conferences, is draw up "directions" for acceptable police procedure. A key document to emerge from such conferences was the *Judges' Rules and Administrative Directions*, drawn up in 1964. Rules such as this have the weight of law even though they are technically only administrative regulations. Although offenders may not be released when incriminating evidence is gathered inappropriately, as happens in the United States, improper actions by police officers can be grounds for reprimand or dismissal.

In 1995 British police began using the world's first national DNA database, which was hailed as "the biggest advance in the fight against crime since the use of fingerprints." Although the database, which may have uses other than in the field of criminal investigation, currently holds only around 135,000 records, plans are to expand it to more than 5 million records within a decade. Records in the database will come from convicted criminals and from unsolved crimes. The 1994 CJA gives police officers the authority to collect and retain "nonintimate" biological specimens without the consent of anyone charged with a crime.

Courts in Britain

Nonarrestable (summary) offenses are minor matters which are tried in magistrates courts. Magistrates are members of the local community, but have little legal training and are unpaid. Magistrates' courts are staffed by underpaid lay justices who are not required to have formal training in the law. Magistrates sit as a body, usually in groups of three or more, and hear cases without a jury. While they generally try less serious cases in summary fashion, criminal defendants charged with certain major crimes may waive the right to trial by jury and be tried in magistrates' court. It has been estimated that the approximately 900 magistrates' courts[83] throughout Great Britain handle 98% of all criminal cases in the Kingdom.

The hand-made, curled horsehair and silk wigs that English judges and barristers wear while in courtrooms first became fashionable in the 1680s. Many traditionalists claim that wigs lend authority to practitioners of the law, while others say that they're mere remnants of a bygone formal era and should be discarded. Like most social institutions in Britain, however, the legal profession is steeped in tradition, and tradition dictates that—in addition to wigs—gowns, robes, breeches, stockings, court shoes, and buckles must be worn by criminal court judges.

A recent poll of British jurors found most feeling more confident about judicial proceedings when seeing wigs worn in court. Even so, many now suggest that it is time for courtroom personnel to adopt modern forms of dress. Still others suggest that a shift of focus is in order. "You would think with so much wrong with the criminal justice system they would have more important things to worry about," says barrister Michael Mansfield. "If they can't change the dress, it doesn't give you confidence that they can change anything else," he adds.

Most of the wigs today's judges wear are made by a small company specializing in handcrafting named Ede and Ravenscroft. Located in London's Chancery Lane since 1726, the company produces about 1,000 wigs a year at a cost of between $500 and $2,500 each depending upon the style. Techniques for making the wigs, including the length of time required for a permanent curl to set in the horsehair, remain closely guarded secrets.

QUESTIONS FOR DISCUSSION

1. If you were a British citizen, do you think you would vote to retain traditional modes of dress for British judges and barristers? Why or why not?
2. Could American courts benefit from greater formality—perhaps following the English example of wigged justices? On the other hand, might less formality in American courtrooms be better? Why?

Within the magistrates' courts, certain courts are designated "youth courts" and process the majority of youthful offenders who are apprehended for criminal law violations. Although English common law originally provided for hearings before a grand jury, the grand jury system was abolished by parliamentary action in 1933. Magistrates' courts have taken over some of the functions of the grand jury, including that of binding over serious offenders for trial by higher courts. Magistrates are limited in their sentencing authority to a maximum of six months' imprisonment. In serious cases, however, they are able to refer convicted defendants to higher courts for sentencing.

Arrestable (indictable) offenses involve more serious crimes. Indictable offenses require a preliminary hearing in front of magistrates who decide whether there is substance to the charges against the defendant. If an indictment is issued by the magistrates, then the defendant comes before a Crown Court and may be tried before a jury. Created in 1971, Crown courts are headed by justices appointed by the king or queen on the recommendation of the lord chancellor. Twelve-member juries hear Crown court cases. Conviction requires only a majority consensus, not unanimous agreement among jurors

A third category is that of "mixed offenses." Mixed offenses involve certain cases of theft, burglary, and other crimes which are less serious than indictable offenses. Depending upon circumstances, mixed offenses may be tried by jury (in a Crown court) or before magistrates.

Tradition dictates considerable formality at all court levels. Crown court judges and counsel both wear white powdered wigs and black flowing robes. Verbal give and take is highly structured and polite. Sharp exchanges between the bench and counsel almost never occur, and lawyers are expected to treat one another with respect.

Crown courts also hear appeals from magistrates' courts. Appeals are heard without a jury. Petitions from magistrates' courts which concern questions of law sometimes go directly to an appellate court called the high court. The high court is divided into three divisions: (1) the Queen's Branch, (2) Family Court, and (3) the Chancery. The Chancery Division deals with matters of inheritance, trusts, property, and so on, while the Family Division of the Court concerns itself with marriages, divorces, adoption, and the like. The

Visit the *CJToday* Web page and click on "Web Chapters," then "Chapter 16." Follow the "find the facts" links in order to learn more about international criminal justice and the role of the United Nations.

The court system in the United Kingdom is highly dependent upon tradition. Three principal judicial officers ensure the effective functioning of the courts. They are

The Lord Chancellor. The lord chancellor is appointed by the monarch upon recommendation of the prime minister. Tradition calls for an appointee well versed in the law. The lord chancellor presides over the House of Lords, one of the two houses of the British Parliament. Because the House of Lords is the highest English court, the lord chancellor is also the high-est judicial officer in the kingdom. The lord chancellor recommends for appointment all members of the judiciary.

The Attorney General. Appointed by the prime minister, the attorney general is legal advisor to the monarch and Parliament. The attorney general officially serves as "guardian of the public interest" and handles most controversial legal issues affecting the government-both criminal and civil.

The Director of Public Prosecutions. The director of public prosecutions is charged with advising police agencies involved in criminal investigations, and with coordinating the activities of prosecutors throughout the kingdom. Appointed by the home secretary, and supervised by the attorney general, the director is a lawyer in charge of a staff of professional "solicitors" who specialize in criminal law and procedure.

Source: Julia Fionda, *Public Prosecutors and Discretion: A Comparative Study* (Oxford: Clarendon Press, 1995); and Richard J. Terrill, *World Criminal Justice Systems: A Survey* (Cincinnati, OH: Anderson, 1984).

section of the high court which focuses on criminal matters is the divisional court of the Queen's Branch. Like other divisions of the high court, the Queen's Branch sits without a jury when hearing criminal appeals.

Another intermediate appellate court occupies a level above the high court. Called the court of appeals, it has two branches: one civil and one criminal. The court of appeals consists of 16 lord justices of appeal and is headed by a judge called the master of the rolls. Criminal appeals not resolved by the high court may go to the court of appeals. Appeals involving the sentencing decisions made by magistrates' or crown courts can go directly to the criminal division of the court of appeals.

At the apex of the appellate process stands the House of Lords, one of the houses of Parliament. The House of Lords may hear appeals from both the Queen's Branch and the criminal division. An appeal to the House will be heard only by those members who specialize in the appeals process. Although the House of Lords is the highest appellate court in Britain, it has nothing like the power of the U.S. Supreme Court. Acts of Parliament are inviolate and cannot be "struck down" or significantly modified by judicial interpretation.

Corrections in England

The British correctional system operates under the Prison Act of 1964 and the Young Offenders Institution Statutory Instrument, passed in 1988. The correctional system is under the administrative control of the home secretary who makes appointments to the national Prison Board, which in turn sets policy for the Prison Department. The Prison Department oversees the activities of the nation's prisons, the parole board, and probation and after care services. A separate agency, the Board of Visitors, permits lay volunteers to serve as hearing boards attached to individual prisons. Each Board of Visitors is empowered to hear alleged violations of prison regulations and is expected to prepare a yearly report on prison conditions.

Three kinds of prisons exist in England: short term, medium term, and long term. Short-term institutions house offenders serving less than 18 months, while medium-term institutions hold persons sentenced to between one-and-a-half and four years. Long-term prisons hold prisoners sentenced to more than four years. Inmates in all British prisons are expected to work, although meaningful work programs are not available for everyone.[84]

In the face of growing crime fears, members of Parliament have come under increasing pressure to require longer and more frequent prison sentences for many offenders. Growing

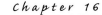

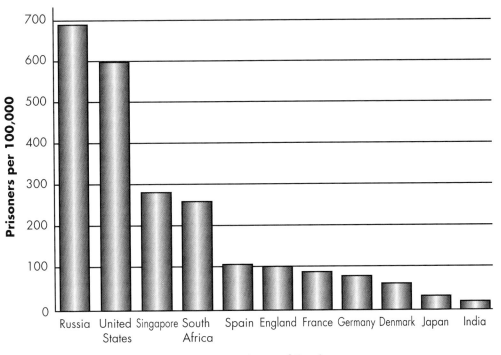

FIGURE 16–1 International incarceration rates, selected countries, 1995. *Source:* The Sentencing Project, *Americans Behind Bars* (Washington, D.C.: The Project, 1997).

crime rates, high levels of unemployment, increased drug use, and the development of poverty-ridden ghettolike areas in many of the nation's large cities have all contributed to a public perception of unnecessary leniency in the criminal justice system. The 1994 CJA, passed in response to growing public concerns about crime, mandates increased sentences for a variety of crimes, and the building of six new privately run prisons to handle the increase in prison populations expected to result.

As in the United States, which sports the second highest incarceration rate among democratic nations (see Figure 16–1), the call for longer sentences has come up against the reality of prison crowding. The British prison population as of June 30, 1997, was 61,467 inmates, the highest level ever recorded.[85] Of the total, 2,300 were women. Reflecting growing incarceration rates, government spending on prisons tripled between 1978 and 1990—from £231.8 million to £870.3 million (about $1.5 billion)[86] and reached £1.522 billion by 1997. The Home Office estimates that prisons throughout England and Wales will hold 71,800 inmates by 2002—an increase of 17% over current levels.

While an active prison reform movement exists in Britain, it faces many barriers. Many British prisons are antiquated, and some have been described as "…dilapidated to the point of hazardousness."[87] Unfortunately, the financial difficulties which the country has experienced for the past few decades provides little hope for widespread and extensive modernization of existing prisons.

International Criminal Justice Organizations

The first international conference on criminology and criminal justice met in London in 1872.[88] The London conference evolved out of emerging humanitarian concerns about the treatment of prisoners. Human rights, the elimination of corporal punishment, and debates over capital punishment occupied the conference participants. Although other meetings were held from time to time, little agreement could be reached among the international community on criminal etiology, justice paradigms, or the philosophical and practical bases for criminal punishment and rehabilitation. Finally, in 1938 the International Society for Criminology (ISC) was formed to bring together people from diverse cultural backgrounds who shared an interest in social policies relating to crime and justice. In its early years, membership in the ISC consisted mostly of national officials and academicians with close government ties.[89] As a consequence, many of the first conferences (called International Congresses) sponsored by the ISC strongly supported the status quo and were devoid of any significant recommendations for change or growth.

Throughout the 1960s and 1970s the ISC was strongly influenced by a growing worldwide awareness of human rights. About the same time, a number of international organizations began to press for an understanding of the political and legal processes through which deviance and crime come to be defined. Among them were the Scandinavian Research Council for Criminology (formed in 1962), the Criminological Research Council (created in 1962 by the Council of Europe), and other regional associations concerned with justice issues.

A number of contemporary organizations and publications continue to focus world attention on criminal justice issues. Table 16–3 lists some of the better known organizations. Perhaps the best-known modern center for the academic study of cross-national criminal justice is the International Center of Comparative Criminology at the University of Montreal. Established in 1969, the center serves as a locus of study for criminal justice professionals from around the world and maintains an excellent library of international criminal justice information. The University of Illinois at Chicago's Office of International Criminal Justice has also become a well-known contributor to the study of comparative criminal justice. In conjunction with the University's Center for Research in Law and Justice, the office publishes the newsletter *Criminal Justice International* and sponsors study tours of various nations.

Many sources of contemporary information on criminal justice agencies and activities around the world are now being published. They include (with their sponsor/publisher) *International Annals of Criminology* (ISC), *International Review of Criminal Policy* (United Nations), *International Journal of Criminal Policy* (United Nations), *International Journal of Penal Law* (International Association of Penal Law), *International Journal of Comparative and Applied Criminal Justice* (Wichita State University), *International Journal of Criminology and Penology* (Academic Press), *Victimology: An International Journal* (National Institute of Victimology), *Howard Journal of Criminal Justice* (Howard League for Penal Reform), *International Review of Criminal Police* (INTERPOL), and *International Security* (UNISAF Publications Ltd.).

In 1995 Mitre Corporation in McLean, Virginia, began an Internet service on the World Wide Web to provide information about the United Nations Crime Prevention Branch. Called UNOJUST, for United Nations Online Justice Information System, the service holds much promise as an on-line provider of international criminal justice information. A link to the site is provided at the *Criminal Justice Today* World Wide Web site.

Table 16-3 *Historical and Modern International Criminal Justice Organizations*

The International Society of Criminology
The International Federation of Senior Police Officers
Scandinavian Research Council for Criminology
Criminological Research Council (Council of Europe)
International Association of Youth Magistrates
International Commission of Jurists
International Association of Penal Law
International Society of Social Defense
Amnesty International
International Chiefs of Police
International Criminal Police Organization (INTERPOL)
International Prisoners Aid Association
Howard League for Penal Reform
United Nations Crime Prevention and Criminal Justice Program

The Role of the United Nations in Criminal Justice

The United Nations (UN), composed of 184 member states and based in New York City, is the largest and most inclusive international body in the world. From its inception in 1945, the UN has been very interested in international crime prevention and world criminal justice systems. A United Nations' resolution entitled the International Bill of Human Rights supports the rights and dignity of all persons who come into contact with the criminal justice system.

One of the best-known specific United Nations' recommendations on criminal justice is its Standard Minimum Rules for the Treatment of Prisoners, adopted in 1955 at the first United Nations Congress on the Prevention of Crime and the Treatment of Offenders. The rules call for the fair treatment of prisoners, to include recognition of the basic humanity of all inmates and set specific standards for housing, nutrition, exercise, and medical care. Follow-up surveys conducted by the United Nations have shown that the rules have had a considerable influence upon national legislation and prison regulations throughout the world.[90] Although the rules do not have the weight of law, unless adopted and enacted into local legislation, they carry the strong weight of tradition, and at least one expert claims that "there are indeed those who argue that the rules have entered the *corpus* of generally customary human rights law, or that they are binding…as an authoritative interpretation of the human rights provisions of the United Nations charter."[91]

A more recent, but potentially significant, set of recommendations can be found in the UN Code of Conduct for Law Enforcement Officials. The Code calls upon law enforcement officers throughout the world to be cognizant of human rights in the performance of their duties and specifically proscribes the use of torture and other abuses.

The United Nations World Crime Surveys, which report official crime statistics from nearly 100 countries, provide a global portrait of criminal activity. Seen historically, the surveys have shown that crimes against property are most characteristic of nations with developed economies (where they constitute approximately 82% of all reported crime), while crimes against the person occur much more frequently in developing countries (where they account for 43% of all crime).[92]

Complementing the official statistics of the World Crime Surveys are data from the International (crime) Victim Survey (IVS). The IVS, conducted in approximately 50 countries around the world, has been coordinated by the Ministry of Justice of the Netherlands and, more recently, by the United Nations Interregional Crime and Justice Research Institute, located in Rome, Italy. To date three IVS surveys have been conducted—in 1989, 1992, and 1996.

Through its Crime Prevention and Criminal Justice Program, the United Nations continues to advance the cause of crime prevention and to disseminate useful criminal justice information. The Program's 40-member State Commission on Crime Prevention and Criminal Justice, and its secretariat, the Crime Prevention and Criminal Justice Branch of the United Nations Offices at Vienna, provide forums for ongoing discussions of justice practices around the world. The Program has regional links throughout the world, sponsored by supportive national governments which have agreed to fund the Program's work. The European Institute for Crime Prevention and Control (HEUNI), for example, provides the Program's regional European link in a network of institutes operating throughout the world. Other network components include the United Nations Interregional Crime and Justice Research Institute (UNICRI) in Rome, Italy; an Asian regional institute (UNAFEI) in Tokyo, Japan; ILANUE, based in San Jose, Costa Rica, which focuses on crime problems in Latin America and the Caribbean; an African institute, (UNAFRI) in Kampala, Uganda; Australia's AIC in Canberra; an Arabic institute (ASSTC) in Riyadh, Saudi Arabia; and other centers in Siracusa, Italy, and in Vancouver and Montreal, Canada.[93]

At its formation, the Crime Prevention and Criminal Justice Program announced as its goals: "1) the prevention of crime within and among states; 2) the control of crime both nationally and internationally; 3) the strengthening of regional and international cooperation in crime prevention, criminal justice, and the combating of transnational crime; 4) the integration and consolidation of the efforts of member states in preventing and combating transnational crime; 5) more efficient and effective administration of justice, with due respect for the human rights of all those affected by crime and all those involved in the criminal justice system; and 6) the promotion of the highest standards of fairness, humanity, justice and professional conduct."[94]

In 1995 the United States signed an agreement with the United Nations Crime Prevention and Criminal Justice Branch, intended to facilitate the international sharing of information and research findings. According to Jeremy Travis, director of the National Institute of Justice, the agreement will boost "international cooperation on dissemination of knowledge on crime and justice."[95] Under the agreement, NIJ joined 11 other criminal justice research organizations throughout the world as an associate UN institute.

Continuing a tradition begun in 1885 by the former International Penal and Penitentiary Commission, the United Nations holds an international congress on crime every five years. The first UN crime congress met in Geneva, Switzerland, in 1955. Crime congresses provide a forum via which member states can exchange information and experiences, compare criminal justice practices between countries, find solutions to crime, and take action at an international level. The Ninth UN Congress on the Prevention of Crime and the Treatment of Offenders was held in Cairo, Egypt, in mid-1995. Delegates to the meeting agreed that transnational organized crime is now a "major force in world finance, able to alter the destinies of countries at critical stages of their economic development." Participants in the conference identified the world's major crime clans as the (1) Hong Kong-based Triads, (2) South American cocaine cartels, (3) Italian Mafia, (4) Japanese Yakuza, (5) Russian *Vory v Zakonye*, and (6) West African crime groups—each of which extends its reach well beyond its home country. The Cairo meeting also included workshops on terrorism, violent crime, spreading urban crime, crime among young people, violence against women, and crimes against the environment. Conference organizers recognized that old-fashioned laws often do more to protect international criminals than to bring them to justice; and officials hoped the meeting might help persuade governments throughout the world to adopt a UN Model Treaty on Extradition which would ease the cross-national extradition of known offenders. The Tenth UN Congress will be held in South Africa in 2000.

INTERPOL

INTERPOL An acronym for the International Police Association. INTERPOL began operations in 1946 and today has 137 members.

The International Police Association (INTERPOL), headquartered in Lyon, France, traces its origins back to the first International Criminal Police Congress of 1914, which met in Monaco. The theme of that meeting was international cooperation in the investigation of crimes and the apprehension of fugitives. INTERPOL, however, did not officially begin operations until 1946, when the end of World War II brought about a new spirit of international harmony.

Today, 137 nations belong to INTERPOL. The U.S. INTERPOL unit is called the "U.S. National Central Bureau" (USNCB) and is a separate agency within the U.S. Department of Justice. USNCB (also called INTERPOL-USNCB) is staffed with personnel from 12 federal agencies. Among them are the DEA, Secret Service, FBI, Immigration and Naturalization Service, IRS, ATF, and the Federal Law Enforcement Training Center. Through USNCB, INTERPOL is linked to all major U.S. computerized criminal records repositories, including the FBI's National Crime Information Index, the State Department's Advanced Visa Lookout System, and the Immigration and Naturalization Service's Master Index.

INTERPOL's primary purpose is to act as a clearinghouse for information on offenses and suspects who are believed to operate across national boundaries. The organization is committed to "promot(ing) the widest possible mutual assistance between all criminal police authorities within the limits of laws existing in…different countries and in the spirit of the Universal Declaration of Human Rights."[96] INTERPOL does not intervene in religious, political, military, or racial disagreements in participant nations. As a consequence, a number of bombings and hostage situations were not officially investigated until 1984, when INTERPOL pledged itself to the fight against international terrorism. More recently, the world traffic in illegal drugs has also become a major focus of INTERPOL's efforts.

INTERPOL does not have its own field investigators. It draws, instead, upon the willingness of local and national police forces to lend support to its activities. The headquarters staff of INTERPOL consists of around 250 individuals, many with prior police experience, who direct data gathering efforts around the world and who serve to alert law enforcement organizations to the movement of suspected offenders within their jurisdiction.

In 1995 the 15 European Union member nations agreed to form Europol,[97] an integrated police agency that will facilitate the sharing of crime information between European countries and INTERPOL. Although Europol is just starting operations, it is anticipated that it will become a significant agency in the fight against international crime and terrorism by the year 2000.

SUMMARY

The international perspective has much to contribute to the study of American criminal justice. Law enforcement agencies, court personnel, and correctional officials in the United States can benefit from exposure to innovative crime prevention and investigative and treatment techniques found in other parts of the world. Policymakers, through a study of foreign legal codes and the routine practice of criminal justice in other countries, can acquire a fresh perspective on upcoming decisions in the area of law and justice.

A number of barriers, however, continue to limit the applicability of cross-national studies. One is the continuing unavailability of sufficiently detailed, up-to-date, and reliable international information on crime rates, victimization, and adjudication. Another, more difficult limit is imposed by ethnocentrism. Ethnocentrism, a culturally determined hesitancy on the part of some people to consider any personal or professional viewpoints other than their own, reduces the likelihood for serious analysis of even the limited international information which is available in the area of criminal justice.

Given enough time most barriers are overcome. Although political, economic, and ideological differences will remain dominant throughout the world for many years, the globe is shrinking. Advances in communications, travel, and the exchange of all types of information are combining with an exponential growth in technology to produce a worldwide interdependence among nations. As new international partnerships are sought and formed, barriers to understanding will continue to fall.

DISCUSSION QUESTIONS

1. What benefits can be had from the study of criminal justice systems in other countries? Are there any potentially negative consequences of such study?

2. If you were to study the criminal justice systems of other countries, which nations would you select for analysis? Why?

3. What is "ethnocentrism"? How does it develop? What purpose does it serve? How can it be overcome? Should it be?

4. What are some of the limitations facing the international study of criminal justice today? Do you see any way in which those limitations can be overcome?

5. Do you think that police in England should carry guns, like their American counterparts? Why or why not?

 WEB WATCH

Access the *Criminal Justice Today* site on the World Wide Web by pointing your Web browser at http://www.prenhall.com/cjtoday. Once there, click on "Web Chapters," then select "Chapter 16: Multinational Criminal Justice" in order to access electronic information and other sites of relevance to this chapter. You may also wish to enter the Global Town Meeting, which provides facilities for the posting of electronic messages for others to read. Messages are arranged by topic, with new topics constantly being added.

NOTES

1. Herman Mannheim, *Comparative Criminology* (Boston: Houghton Mifflin, 1967), pp. x–xi.

2. Joji Sakurai, "Arrest Made in Japan Beheading," The Associated Press wire services, June 28, 1997.

3. Mari Yamaguchi, "Japan Orders Withdrawal Of Magazine," The Associated Press wire services, July 4, 1997.

4. Shizuo Kambayashi, "Beheading Arrest Shocks Japan," The Associated Press wire services, June 29, 1997.

5. Teruaki Ueno, "Japan Cult Leader Cannot Find Lawyer," Reuters wire services, May 19, 1995.

6. Ibid.

7. Ibid.

8. In 1996 a police officer confessed involvement in the shooting.

9. David Thurber, "Japan-Doomsday Cult," The Associated Press on-line, April 15, 1995.

10. Ibid.

11. Robert Lilly, "Forks and Chopsticks: Understanding Criminal Justice in the PRC," *Criminal Justice International* (March/April 1986), p. 15.

12. Adapted from Carol B. Kalish, "International Crime Rates," a Bureau of Justice Statistics *Special Report* (Washington, D.C.: Bureau of Justice Statistics, 1988).

13. Ibid.

14. Ibid.

15. Ibid.

16. Lee Hockstader, "Russia's War on Crime: A Lopsided, Losing Battle," *The Washington Post* wire services, February 27, 1995.

17. Roy Walmsley, *Developments in the Prison Systems of Central and Eastern Europe*, HEUNI papers no. 4 (Helsinki, 1995).

18. "China: The Hope and the Horror," *Reader's Digest*, September 1989, p. 75.

19. This section draws heavily upon Shao-Chuan Leng and Hungdah Chiu, *Criminal Justice in Post-Mao China: Analysis and Documents* (Albany, NY: SUNY at Albany Press, 1985).

20. Various authorities give different dates for the ending of the Cultural Revolution. We have chosen 1973 because it represents the date at which military control over law enforcement finally ended.

21. *China Mainland Magazine*, No. 625, September 3, 1968, p. 23.

22. Central Political-Judicial Cadre's School, *Lectures on the General Principles of Criminal Law in the People's Republic of China* (Peking, 1957), as cited by Leng and Chiu, *Criminal Justice in Post-Mao China*, p. 21.

23. "On Questions of Party History," *Beijing Review*, Vol. 24, no. 27 (July 6, 1981), p. 20, as quoted in Leng and Chiu, *Criminal Justice in Post-Mao China*.

24. Leng and Chiu, *Criminal Justice in Post-Mao China*, p. 42.

25. For an excellent review of the role of the prosecutor in China, see He Jiahong and Jon R. Waltz, *Criminal Prosecution in the PRC and the USA: A Comparative Study*, English edition (Beijing: China Procuratorial Press, 1995).

26. "China uses technology to tackle soaring crime," Reuters wire services, December 18, 1994.

27. Ibid.

28. Zhenxiong (Joseph) Zhou, "An Introduction to the Present Legal System of the People's Republic of China," *North Carolina Criminal Justice Today*, Vol. IV, no. 6 (Salemburg: NC Justice Academy, 1987), pp. 8–15.

29. Robert Lilly, "Forks and Chopsticks: Understanding Criminal Justice in the PRC," *Criminal Justice International* (March/April 1986), pp. 14–15.

30. Ibid., p. 14.

31. Leng and Chiu, *Criminal Justice in Post-Mao China*, p. 75.

32. Benjamin Kang Lim, "China Declares War on Organized Crime," Reuters wire services, February 23, 1995.

33. Jeffrey Parker, "China, U.S. Push Hard to End Trade-War Threat," Reuters wire services, February 23, 1995.

34. "China Vows to Enhance Copyright Protection," Reuters wire services, March 13, 1995.

35. Lim, "China Declares War on Organized Crime."

36. Dick Ward, "Drug Crackdown Nets Citizens and Foreigners, But Punishments Differ," *Criminal Justice International* (November/December 1993), p. 3.

37. "Anti-Drug Unit Forms in Shaanxi," *The Fayetteville Observer-Times* (North Carolina), December 28, 1990, p. 14B.

38. Statistics on arrest, conviction, and imprisonment in China are taken from Robert Elegant, "Everyone Can Be Reformed," *Parade*, October 30, 1988, pp. 4–7.

39. Leng and Chiu, *Criminal Justice in Post-Mao China*, pp. 141–142.

40. Zhu Entao, "A Perspective on Drug Abuse," *Criminal Justice International* (January/February 1987), pp. 5–6.

41. Zhou, "An Introduction to the Present Legal System of the People's Republic of China," p. 13.

42. Ibid.

43. For more information, see Lening Zhang, Dengke Zhou, Steven F. Messner, Allen E.

Liska, Marvin D. Krohn, Jianhong Liu, and Zhou Lou, "Crime Prevention in a Communitarian Society: *Bang-Jiao* and *Tiao-Jie* in the People's Republic of China," *Justice Quarterly*, Vol. 13, no. 2 (June 1996), pp. 199–222.

44. Ibid.

45. Leng and Chiu, *Criminal Justice in Post-Mao China*, p. 64.

46. Elegant, "Everyone Can Be Reformed," p. 5.

47. Seth Faison, "In Surge of Death Sentences, China Doomed 6,100 Last Year," Simon and Schuster Newslink, August 26, 1997.

48. Amnesty International, "At Least 1000 People Executed in 'Strike Hard' Campaign against Crime," Amnesty International World Wide Web site, http://www.amnesty.org. (October 2, 1997.)

49. "Executions an Every Day Event in China," Reuters wire services, March 17, 1995.

50. Ibid.

51. Jeffrey Parker, "Provincial Chinese Leader Executed for Graft," Reuters wire services, January 16, 1995.

52. Ruth Youngblood, "Organ Removal at Chinese Prisons Decried," United Press International wire services, northern edition, March 21, 1995.

53. Elegant, "Everyone Can Be Reformed," p. 6.

54. Ibid.

55. Constitution, People's Republic of China, Article 13.

56. E. Eugene Miller, "Corrections in the People's Republic of China," in *International Corrections: An Overview* (College Park, MD: American Correctional Association, 1987), pp. 65–71.

57. Ibid., p. 69.

58. Harry Wu, "A Prisoner's Journey," *Newsweek*, September 23, 1991, p. 30.

59. Jeff Sanders and Thomas McAninch, "A Communist Prison Experience," *American Jails* (November/December 1994), p. 87.

60. Elegant, "Everyone Can Be Reformed," p. 5.

61. Sam S. Souryal, Dennis W. Potts, and Abdullah I. Alobied, "The Penalty of Hand Amputation for Theft in Islamic Justice," *Journal of Criminal Justice*, Vol. 22, no. 3 (1994), pp. 249–265.

62. Parviz Saney, "Iran," in Elmer H. Johnson, ed., *International Handbook of Contemporary Developments in Criminology* (Westport, CT: Greenwood, 1983), p. 359.

63. This section owes much to Matthew Lippman, "Iran: A Question of Justice?" *Criminal Justice International*, 1987, pp. 6–7.

64. Sharif Imam-Jomeh, "Iran Court Sentences Man to Death for Bank Fraud," Reuters, wire services, August 22, 1995.

65. "The Penalty of Hand Amputation for Theft in Islamic Justice," *Journal of Criminal Justice*, Vol. 22, no. 3 (1994), pp. 249–265.

66. Afshin Valinejad, "Iran Flogs, Hangs Serial Killer Known as 'The Vampire,'" *USA Today*, August 14, 1997, p. 11A.

67. For additional information on Islamic law, see Adel Mohammed el Fikey, "Crimes and Penalties in Islamic Criminal Legislation," *Criminal Justice International*, 1986, pp. 13–14; and Sam S. Souryal, "Shariah Law in Saudi Arabia," *Journal for the Scientific Study of Religion*, Vol. 26, no. 4 (1987), pp. 429–449.

68. Max Weber, in Max Rheinstein, ed., *On Law in Economy and Society* (New York: Simon & Schuster, 1967), translated from the 1925 German edition.

69. Ibid.

70. "The Penalty of Hand Amputation for Theft in Islamic Justice," *Journal of Criminal Justice*, Vol. 22, no. 3 (1994), pp. 249–265.

71. Home Office, Research and Statistics Department, World Wide Web server, October 1, 1997.

72. "Putting Crime in Perspective," *World Press Review* (January 1995), and "Crime Falls in England, Wales for Second Year," Reuters wire services, April 11, 1995.

73. Richard Terrill, *World Criminal Justice Systems* (Cincinnati, OH: Anderson, 1984), p. 3.

74. Alan Wheatley, "Howard Promises Crackdown on Crime," Reuters wire services, October 6, 1994.

75. Philip John Stead, *The Police of Britain* (New York: Macmillan, 1985), p. 94.

76. Home Office, Research and Statistics Department.

77. "Police and Magistrates Court Act Aids British Service," *Criminal Justice International* (May/June 1995), p. 7.

78. Exceptions might include the Transport Police who supervise the operation of the nation's ports and secretive intelligence gathering agencies such as "M.I.5."

79. "An Interview with Sir Kenneth Newman, Commissioner of the Metropolitan Police," *Criminal Justice International* (November/December 1986), p. 17.

80. "New Intelligence Service Begins Operation," *Criminal Justice International* (July/August 1992), p. 3.

81. For a good discussion of the curriculum at Bramshill, see Dennis Rowe, "On Her Majesty's Service: Policing England and Wales," *Criminal Justice International* (November/December 1986), pp. 9–16.

82. Ken Hyder, "Beware LA Law," *Criminal Justice International* (May/June 1995), pp. 10–11.

83. Stead, *The Police of Britain*, p. 147.

84. Terrill, *World Criminal Justice Systems*, p. 71.

85. Home Office, Research and Statistics Department.

86. Apex Trust et al., *A Joint Manifesto for Penal Reform* (London, 1989), as cited in Mike Carlie, "Prison Reform in England: An Overview," paper presented at the annual meeting of the Academy of Criminal Justice Sciences, Nashville, Tennessee, March 1990, p. 11.

87. Sean McConville, "Some Observations on English Prison Management," in *International Corrections*, p. 37.

88. Paul Friday, "International Organization: An Introduction," in Johnson, ed., *International Handbook of Contemporary Developments in Criminology*, p. 31.

89. Ibid., p. 32.

90. Gerhard O. W. Mueller, "The United Nations and Criminology," in Johnson, ed., *International Handbook of Contemporary Development in Criminology*, pp. 74–75.

91. Roger S. Clark, *The United Nations Crime Prevention and Criminal Justice Program: Formulation of Standards and Efforts at Their Implementation* (Philadelphia: University of Pennsylvania Press, 1994).

92. Ibid., pp. 71–72.

93. "International News," *Corrections Compendium*, June 1995, p. 25.

94. Resolutions adopted on the reports of the Third Committee at The Forty-sixth Session of the United Nations General Assembly.

95. Khaled Dawoud, "U.N. Crime Meeting Wants Independent Jail Checks," Reuters wire services, May 6, 1995.

96. "INTERPOL at Forty," *Criminal Justice International* (November/December 1986), pp. 1, 22.

97. "Europol Will Not Solve All EU's Crime Ills," Reuters wire services, July 3, 1995.

chapter 17

THE FUTURE OF CRIMINAL JUSTICE

The rise of a new kind of America requires a new kind of law enforcement system.

—ALVIN TOFFLER

You bring me a select group of hackers, and within 90 days I'll bring this country to its knees.

—JIM SETTLE, RETIRED DIRECTOR OF THE FBI'S COMPUTER CRIME SQUAD

It's just a matter of time before we have a cyber Pearl Harbor.

—JAMIE GORELICK, DEPUTY U.S. ATTORNEY GENERAL

Terrorism is going to join the omnipresence of crime as one of the things we have to worry about in American cities.

—BRUCE HOFFMAN RAND CORPORATION

Introduction

…technology throughout history has been a double-edged sword, equally capable of enhancing or endangering democratic values.

—John H. Gibbons, Director, Office of Technology Assessment, U. S. Congress

On June 28, 1993, Kirk Bloodsworth walked out of a Jessup, Maryland, prison a free man[1]—after serving nine years for a murder he did not commit. Standing before media cameras, Bloodsworth sobbed for his mother, who had died before seeing him cleared. Bloodsworth had been convicted in 1984 of the rape-murder of nine-year-old Dawn Hamilton and sentenced to die. He had consistently claimed he'd never met the girl. Shortly before his release, an FBI DNA test of semen found on the girl's underwear showed that Bloodsworth could not have been the killer. Were it not for modern technology, Bloodsworth would have remained imprisoned or been put to death.

Cases like Bloodsworth's are rapidly growing in number. On July 17, 1997, lawyers for David Milgaard, 45, held a news conference in Toronto to announce that DNA tests on a semen sample preserved since 1969 proved conclusively that Milgaard was not a rapist.[2] Milgaard had served 23 years in prison for the sex killing of a Canadian woman, Gail Miller. Miller, a 20-year-old nurses' aide had been raped, stabbed, and left to die in a dark, snow-covered alleyway in Saskatoon, Saskatchewan on January 31, 1969. DNA testing was not available at the time the crime was committed, and Milgaard, a small-time drug dealer had been arrested near the scene of the rape-murder after his car broke down. He was convicted on circumstantial evidence.

Also in 1997, attorneys for Illinois death row inmate Ronald Jones asked the Illinois supreme court to throw out his first-degree murder conviction.[3] At the time, Jones had already spent eight years on death row following his conviction on rape and murder charges in the killing of 28-year-old Debra Smith. Attorneys said that new DNA tests on semen recovered from the victim's body 12 years earlier proved that Jones could not have been the killer. Although Cook County state's attorney's office officials acknowledged the validity of the DNA test results, they announced that they would seek a retrial based on a confession Jones made following his arrest. That confession, claimed Jones' lawyer, had been coerced.

Emerging technology, like that of DNA "fingerprinting," will change many of the practical aspects of the criminal justice system of the twenty-first century—from the way in which evidence is gathered to the development of innovative forms of sentencing. Even so, the criminal justice system of the next century will look much like the system we know today. It will rest upon constitutional mandates and will be responsive to court precedent. The system itself will remain recognizable through its backbone of subsystems: the police, courts, and corrections. Deterrence, apprehension, and reformation will continue to serve as the philosophical trilogy guiding the day-to-day operations of criminal justice agencies. New issues will arise, but most of them will be resolved within the context of the question which has guided American criminal justice since its inception: how to ensure public safety while guaranteeing justice in a free society.

7. LEFT INDEX

Fingerprinting, which became widespread as a crime fighting technique in the late 1800s, provided one of the first nearly foolproof methods of identification available to investigators. The fingerprint shown here provides an example of a "tented arch"—a particularly distinctive characteristic. *Courtesy of the FBI*

Coming changes in the fabric of American society will necessitate some predictable, large-scale system responses. Many demographic, ideological, and behavioral transformations, such as widespread illegal drug use and a greater social acceptance of certain victimless crimes, have already occurred and are now firmly rooted in substantial segments of American society. In the area of drugs, much is already known. Drug culture has been studied, the impact of drug abuse on society is becoming clear, and the economic and human costs of drugs have been charted. Because the battle lines in the "war on drugs" are firmly drawn, a picture of drug abuse and the system response to it can be provided, as we have done in an earlier chapter. Only the final outcome of the "war" is still unknown.

Less clear, however, are changes yet to come, changes we can only now begin to discern. This chapter attempts to identify some of these coming changes and to predict what impact they will have on American criminal justice. Perhaps the two most significant sources of change will be technology and the continuing evolution of society. Throughout history, the interplay between technology and culture has been weighted in favor of cultural norms and ideals. Scientific advances often came before society was ready for them. When they did, they were denied or suppressed. Today, however, the situation is reversed. Technology is now often the prime mover, unable to be denied, forcing social change when it occurs. Because technology may be the most important harbinger of change in the modern world, it is upon the opportunities and threats that technology represents to the justice system that this chapter focuses.

Technology and Criminal Justice

Two years ago Chicago police arrested an alleged prostitute after arranging an illicit rendezvous via an on-line computer service.[4] Officers responded to an on-line advertisement offering sex for sale and arranged through electronic mail to meet the woman. The on-line account used by investigators had been temporarily borrowed from a volunteer. About the same time, Leslie Isben Rogge, a fugitive who had been on the FBI's Ten Most Wanted list for six years, surrendered to U.S. authorities in Guatemala after his picture was seen on the FBI's web site by a 14-year-old American living in the tiny tourist village of Antigua, Guatemala.[5] Rogge had earned a living by working as a handyman in Guatemala after escaping from an Idaho prison 11 years earlier. The FBI said that Rogge's arrest was the first time that a listing on the World Wide Web had led to the capture of one of its "most wanted" fugitives.

As these stories illustrate, we live in a world governed by rapid change. Technology and science are the modern-day engines of change, and they continue to run relentlessly forward. The impact of change on all areas of human life has been dramatic. The automobile and the airplane have made the world a smaller place, and journeys that would have required months

The future comes one day at a time.

—Dean Acheson (1893–1971)

a century ago can now be made in a day. Radio and television have transformed the planet into a "global village," in which every human being can be in touch with events of importance as they happen anywhere around the globe. Computers have dramatically altered the rate at which information is being produced, so much so that precedence is given today to storing information rather than using it. Future computers, it is hoped, will sort through the accumulated information, allowing us to distinguish the significant from the mundane and permitting us to make use of that which is of interest.

Advancing technology, along with legislation designed to control it, will create crimes never before imagined. The future will see a race between technologically sophisticated offenders and law enforcement authorities as to who can wield the most advanced skills on either side of the age-old battle between crime and justice.

Technological advances signal both threats and opportunities for the justice field. By the turn of the twentieth century, police callboxes became standard features in many cities, utilizing the new technology of telephonic communications to pass along information on crimes in progress or to describe suspects and their activities. A few years later, police departments across the nation adapted to the rapid growth in the number of private automobiles and the laws governing their use. Motorized patrol, VASCAR devices, radar, police helicopters, and aircraft were all called into service as solutions to the need for a rapid response to criminal activity. Today's citizens' band radios, often monitored by local police and highway patrol agencies, and cellular car telephones with direct numbers to police dispatchers, are continuing the trend of adapting advances in communications technology to police purposes.

Technology impacts criminal justice in many areas. The National Law Enforcement Technology Center (NLETC), formerly known as the Technology Assessment Program Information Center (TAPIC), of the National Institute of Justice's Office of Science and Technology performs yearly assessments of key technological needs and opportunities facing the justice system. The Center is responsible for helping to identify, develop, manufacture, and adopt new products and technologies designed for law enforcement, corrections, and other criminal justice applications.[6] NLETC concentrates on four areas of advancing technology: (1) communications and electronics, (2) forensic science, (3) transportation and weapons, and (4) protective equipment.[7] Once opportunities for improvement are identified in any area, referrals are made to the Law Enforcement Standards Laboratory (LESL)— a part of the National Bureau of Standards—for the testing of available hardware. The Justice Technology Information Network (JUSTNET), a service of NLETC, acts as an information gateway for law enforcement, corrections, and criminal justice technology and notifies the justice community of the latest technological advances. JUSTNET is accessible via the World Wide Web and lists the web sites of technology providers. An affiliated organization, the Office of Law Enforcement Technology Commercialization (OLETC), is a joint project of the National Institute of Justice, the National Aeronautics and Space Administration, and the National Technology Transfer Center.

While federal justice technology assessment programs concentrate primarily on facilitating suspect apprehension and the protection of enforcement personnel, other authors have pointed to the potential held by emerging technologies in the area of offender treatment. Simon Dinitz, for example, has suggested that novel forms of biomedical intervention, building upon the earlier practices of castration, psychosurgery, and drug treatment, will continue to be adapted from advances in the biological sciences and serve as innovative treatment modalities.[8] The possibilities are limited only by the imagination.[9] Chemical substances to reform the offender, drugs to enhance the memories of witnesses and victims, and microchip extensions of the personality all appear to be on the horizon of applicability.[10] In 1995, for example, medical information on a U.S.-sponsored cocaine immunization project came to light during discussions between Drug Policy Director Lee P. Brown and officials of the Home Department of the United Kingdom.[11] Although details of the program were not released, it is but one more indication of the potential that scientific advancements have on impacting crime prevention and control.

Criminalistics: Past, Present, and Future

Criminalistics The use of technology in the service of criminal investigation; the application of scientific techniques to the detection and evaluation of criminal evidence.

The use of technology in the service of criminal investigation is a subfield of criminal justice referred to as **criminalistics**. Criminalistics applies scientific techniques to the detection and evaluation of criminal evidence. Police crime scene analysts and laboratory personnel versed

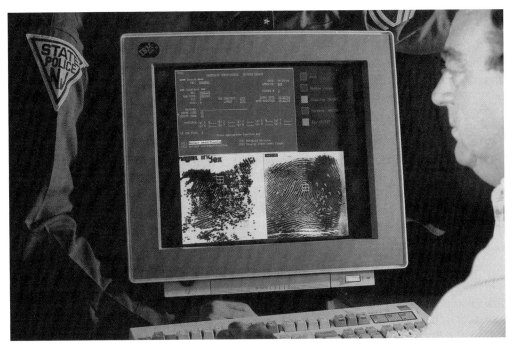

An automated fingerprint ID system in operation. Technology has been a boon to police investigations, although high-tech criminals have often more than kept pace with advances in investigative technology. *Jacques M. Chenet, Gamma—Liaison, Inc.*

in criminalistics are referred to as **criminalists**. Modern criminalistics had its beginnings with the need for the certain identification of individuals. Early methods of personal identification were notoriously inaccurate. In the 1800s, for instance, one day of the week was generally dedicated to a "parade" of newly arrested offenders during which experienced investigators from distant jurisdictions would scrutinize the convicts, looking for recognizable faces.[12] By the 1840s the Quetelet system[13] of anthropometry was making itself known. The Quetelet system depended upon precise measurements of various parts of the body to give an overall "picture" of a person for use in later identification.

Criminalist The term applied to police crime scene analysts and laboratory personnel versed in criminalistics.

The first "modern" system of personal identification was created by Alphonse Bertillon.[14] Bertillon was the director of the Bureau of Criminal Identification of the Paris Police Department during the late 1800s. The Bertillon system of identification made the assertion that certain bodily aspects, such as eye color, skeletal size and shape, and ear form, did not change substantially after physical maturity had been reached. It combined physical measurements with the emerging technology of photography. Although photography had been used previously in criminal identification, Bertillon standardized the technique by positioning measuring guides beside suspects so that their physical dimensions could be calculated from their photographs and by the use of both front views and profiles.

Fingerprints, produced by contact with the ridge patterns in the skin on the fingertips, became the subject of intense scientific study in the mid-1840s. While their importance in criminal investigation today seems obvious, it was not until the 1880s that scientists began to realize that each person's fingerprints were unique and unchangeable over a lifetime. Both discoveries appear to have come from the Englishmen William J. Herschel and Henry Faulds, working in Asia.[15] Some writers have observed that Asiatic lore about finger ridges and their significance extends back to antiquity and suggest that Herschel and Faulds must have been privy to such information.[16] As early as the Tang Dynasty (618–906 A.D.) inked fingerprints in China were being used as personal seals on important documents, and there is some evidence that the Chinese had classified patterns of the loops and whorls found in fingerprints and were using them for the identification of criminals as much as 1,000 years ago.[17]

The use of fingerprints in identifying offenders was popularized by Sir Francis Galton[18] and officially adopted by Scotland Yard in 1901. By the 1920s fingerprint identification was in use in police departments everywhere, having quickly replaced the anthropometric system of Bertillon. Suspects were fingerprinted and their prints compared with those lifted from a crime scene. Those comparisons typically required a great deal of time and a bit of luck to produce a match. Over time, as fingerprint inventories in the United States grew huge, including those of all persons in the armed services and certain branches of federal employment, researchers looked constantly for an efficient way to rapidly compare large numbers of prints. Until the 1980s most effective comparison schemes depended upon classification methods which automatically eliminated large numbers of prints from needed comparisons. As late as 1974, one author lamented "Considering present levels of technology in other sciences…[the] classification of fingerprints has profited little by technological advancements, particularly in the computer sciences. [Fingerprint comparisons are] limited by the laborious inspection by skilled technicians required to accurately classify and interpret prints. Automation of the classification process and potentially comparison as well, would open up fingerprinting to its fullest potential."[19]

Within a decade, advances in computer hardware and software made possible CAL-ID, an automated fingerprint identification system (AFIS) belonging to the California State Department of Justice, which used optical scanning and software pattern matching to compare suspect fingerprints. Such computerized systems have grown rapidly in capability in the past few years, and links between systems operated by different agencies are now routine. The latest technology employs proprietary electrooptical scanning systems which digitize live fingerprints, eliminating the need for traditional inking and rolling techniques.[20] Other advances in fingerprint identification and matching are also being made. The use of lasers in fingerprint lifting, for example, recently allowed the FBI to detect a 50-year-old fingerprint of a Nazi war criminal on a postcard.[21] Computerization and digitization improve accuracy and reduce the incidence of "false positives" in ongoing comparisons.[22] The Los Angeles Police Department, which also uses an automated fingerprint identification system, now estimates that fingerprint comparisons which in the past would have taken as long as 60 years can now be performed in a single day.[23] Computerized fingerprint identification systems took a giant step forward in 1986 with the introduction of the American National Standard for Information Systems—Fingerprint Identification—Data Format for Information Interchange.[24] This electronic standard makes it possible to exchange data between different automated fingerprint identification systems. Prior to its invention, the comparison of fingerprint data between AFIS systems was often difficult or impossible. Using the standard, cities across the nation can share and compare fingerprint information over telephone lines linking their AFIS systems.[25] Recently, the FBI announced plans to develop an integrated automated fingerprint identification system (IAFIS) as part of NCIC-2000 (see box in Chapter 5). IAFIS will integrate state fingerprint databases and automate search requests from police agencies throughout the country.

Ballistics The analysis of firearms, ammunition, projectiles, bombs, and explosions.

Forensic Anthropology The application of anthropological principles and techniques in the service of criminal investigation.

Modern criminalistics also depends heavily upon **ballistics**, the analysis of weapons, ammunition, and projectiles; medical pathology, to determine the cause of injury or death; **forensic anthropology**, to reconstruct the likeness of a decomposed or dismembered body; **forensic entomology**, or the study of insect behavior to determine issues such as the time of death of a corpse; the photography of crime scenes (now often done with video or digital cameras); plaster and polymer casting of tire tracks, boot prints, and marks made by implements; polygraph (the "lie detector") and voice-print identification; as well as a plethora of other techniques. Many criminal investigation practices have been thoroughly tested and are now accepted by most courts for the evidence they offer (polygraph and voiceprint identification techniques are still being refined and have not yet won the wide acceptance of the other techniques mentioned).

Emerging Technologies in Criminalistics

The future will see criminalistics aided by a number of technologies now in their infancy. They include

- DNA profiling and new serological/tissue identification techniques.
- on-line clearinghouses for criminal justice information.
- computer-generated psychological profiles and crime scene analysis.
- computer-enhancements of photographs, images, and other types of evidence.
- forensic animation (computer simulations of criminal activity).

Justice in American Context

The Most Pressing Problems Facing the Criminal Justice System Today

Results from the 1994 National Assessment Program (NAP) survey of over 2,500 directors of criminal justice agencies indicate great concern about the impact that violence, drugs, firearms, and troubled youths are having on society and the criminal justice system. In this regard, the views of the directors probably epitomize those of most Americans today. But because these directors deal with these problems on a day-to-day basis, their opinions are valuable in pointing out the needs of their agencies and in identifying programs and strategies that might be effective in addressing these prevailing important issues.

Police chiefs point to problems in combating violent crimes such as homicides, rapes, assaults, domestic violence, and child abuse. Prosecutors reflect on the difficulties in obtaining convictions for gang-related crimes in which victims and witnesses are reluctant to testify. Judges point to the backlog of cases in their courts and the increase in trials in some jurisdictions. Directors of probation and parole agencies are concerned about alcohol and drug treatment programs and the impact of new initiatives—such as day reporting centers and boot camps—on the workloads of an already overburdened staff.

Respondents to the 1994 NAP survey repeatedly expressed concern about young people, both as victims and offenders. A police chief from a large western city wrote, "Numerous social problems, especially with young adults and juveniles, have caused an escalation in the level of violence that youths are willing to commit on each other." Another chief commented, "The national phenomenon seems to be an exponential increase in youth violence and criminality, for which no one seems to have a feasible solution." A judge in a southern state had similar comments about the "dramatic rise in youth crime demonstrated by marked increases in transfers from juvenile court to adult court."

Use of firearms in crimes committed by juveniles and adults was yet another problem cited by many respondents. One police chief wrote about firearm involvement in 40 of the city's 49 homicides in 1993. Another stated that whereas last year showed an overall decrease in crime, "the number of violent crimes has increased, including cases involving firearms." In total, 83% of the responding police chiefs and sheriffs indicated that crimes committed with firearms contributed to workload problems in their agencies.

Finally, alcohol abuse and illegal drug abuse continued to clog the criminal justice system with offenders. Respondents across the system gave comments on the impact these offenders have had on their agencies. Criminal justice agencies face many other problems and needs that were identified in the 1994 NAP survey, including:

- How can police respond better to an increasingly culturally diverse society?
- To what degree are today's jails and prisons crowded?
- What kinds of programs have police departments established for at-risk youths?
- How are criminal justice agencies responding to mentally ill offenders?
- What kinds of information systems should agencies establish to support their activities?

Although survey results cannot provide solutions, they do indicate the extent to which heads of agencies believe their efforts need improvement and key areas in which strategies need to be established.

Source: Adapted from Tom McEwen, *National Assessment Program: 1994 Survey Results* (Washington, D.C.: National Institute of Justice, April 1995).

- chemical and microscopic examination of fibers and other materials using advanced techniques.

A brief description of these technologies, including their current state of development and the implications they hold for the future, is provided in the paragraphs that follow.

DNA Profiling

DNA (deoxyribonucleic acid) profiling, also termed DNA fingerprinting,[26] makes use of human DNA for purposes of identification. DNA is a nucleic acid found in the center of cells. It is the principal component of chromosomes, the structures that transmit hereditary characteristics between generations. Each DNA molecule is a long, two-stranded chain made up of subunits, called nucleotides, coiled in the form of a double helix. Because of the fact that genetic material is unique to each individual (except in the case of identical twins or

DNA Profiling The use of biological residue found at the scene of a crime for genetic comparisons in aiding the identification of criminal suspects.

clones), it can provide a highly reliable source of suspect identification. A new investigative technology, DNA profiling began as a test for determining paternity.

DNA profiling requires only a few human cells for comparison purposes. One drop of blood, a few hairs, a small amount of skin, or a trace of semen usually provide sufficient genetic material for comparison purposes. Because the DNA molecule is very stable, genetic tests can be conducted on evidence taken from crime scenes long after fingerprints have disappeared. The process, diagrammed in Figure 17–1, involves the use of a highly technical procedure called electrophoresis, which has not yet been universally accepted in American courts, although courts in 49 states have admitted DNA evidence in hundreds of trials and hearings.[27] Many of those trials, however, have involved civil suits. Maine, Rhode Island, North Dakota, and Utah have still to accept DNA evidence in criminal trials.[28]

Forensic use of DNA technology in criminal cases began in 1986 when police asked Dr. Alec J. Jeffreys (who coined the term "DNA fingerprints"[29]) of Leicester University (England) to verify a suspect's confession that he was responsible for two rape-murders in the English Midlands. DNA tests proved that the suspect could not have committed the crimes. Police then began obtaining blood samples from several thousand male inhabitants in the area to identify a new suspect.[30]

In a 1987 British case, 32-year-old Robert Melias became the first person ever convicted of a crime (rape) on the basis of DNA evidence.[31] Melias was convicted of raping a 43-year-old disabled woman, and the conviction came after genetic tests of semen left on the woman's clothes positively identified him as the perpetrator.[32]

In November 1987, in one of the first uses of DNA in a criminal case in the United States, the Circuit Court of Orange County, Florida, convicted Tommy Lee Andrews of rape after DNA tests matched his DNA from a blood sample with that of semen traces found in a rape victim.[33] Virginia's 1989 multiple murder trials of Timothy Wilson Spencer were the first cases in the United States where the use of DNA evidence led to guilty verdicts resulting in a death penalty. The Virginia supreme court upheld the murder and rape convictions of Spencer, who had been found guilty on the basis of DNA testing that matched his DNA with the semen found in several victims.[34]

In 1993 the U.S. Supreme Court, in the civil case of *Daubert* v. *Merrell Dow Pharmaceuticals, Inc.*,[35] revised the criteria for the admissibility of scientific evidence by rejecting a previous admissibility standard established in the 1923 case of *Frye* v. *United States*.[36] The *Daubert* Court ruled that the older *Frye* standard requiring "general acceptance" of a test or procedure by the relevant scientific community "is not a necessary precondition to the admissibility of scientific evidence…" The baseline rule for the admissibility of scientific evidence, said the Court, is established by Rule 402 of the *Federal Rules of Evidence*, which was published after *Frye* and supersedes it. Rule 402 says that, in a trial, "[A]ll relevant evidence is admissible, except as otherwise provided by the Constitution of the United States, by Act of Congress, by these Rules, or by other rules prescribed by the Supreme Court pursuant to statutory authority." The Court went on to say that although "the *Frye* test was displaced by the Rules of Evidence, [that] does not mean…that the Rules themselves place no limits on the admissibility of purportedly scientific evidence. Nor is the trial judge disabled from screening such evidence. To the contrary, under the Rules the trial judge must ensure that any and all scientific testimony or evidence admitted is not only relevant, but reliable." The real test for the admissibility of scientific expert testimony, said the Court, is for the trial judge to decide "at the outset…whether the expert is proposing to testify to (1) scientific knowledge that (2) will assist the trier of fact to understand or determine a fact in issue." The Court concluded that the task of the trial judge is one of "ensuring that an expert's testimony both rests on a reliable foundation and is relevant to the task at hand. Pertinent evidence based on scientifically valid principles," said the Court, "will satisfy those demands."

Daubert **Standard**   A test of scientific acceptability applicable to the gathering of evidence in criminal cases.

The plaintiffs in *Daubert* did not argue the merits of DNA testing, but claimed, instead, that the drug Bendectin caused birth defects. Nonetheless, the *Daubert* **standard** eased the criteria for the introduction of scientific evidence at both civil and criminal trials—and effectively cleared the way for the use of DNA evidence in the courtroom.[37] Specifically, the *Daubert* Court found that the following factors may be used to determine whether any form of scientific evidence is reliable:

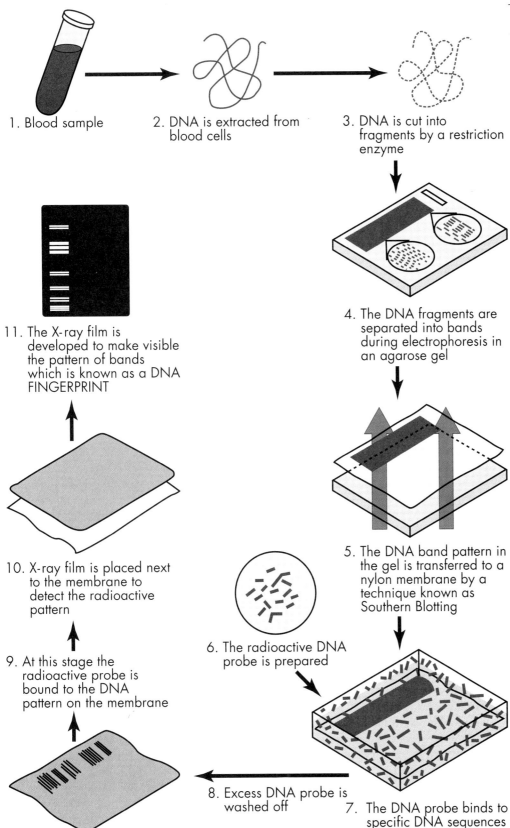

1. Blood sample

2. DNA is extracted from blood cells

3. DNA is cut into fragments by a restriction enzyme

4. The DNA fragments are separated into bands during electrophoresis in an agarose gel

5. The DNA band pattern in the gel is transferred to a nylon membrane by a technique known as Southern Blotting

6. The radioactive DNA probe is prepared

7. The DNA probe binds to specific DNA sequences on the membrane

8. Excess DNA probe is washed off

9. At this stage the radioactive probe is bound to the DNA pattern on the membrane

10. X-ray film is placed next to the membrane to detect the radioactive pattern

11. The X-ray film is developed to make visible the pattern of bands which is known as a DNA FINGERPRINT

FIGURE 17–1 The DNA fingerprinting process. *Source:* Cellmark Diagnostics, Division of ICI Americas, Inc. Reprinted with permission.

- whether it has been subject to testing
- whether it has been subject to peer review
- known or potential rates of error
- the existence of standards controlling application of the techniques involved

In 1994, a section of the federal Violent Crime Control and Law Enforcement Act entitled the "DNA Identification Act of 1994"[38] provided substantial funding to improve the quality and availability of DNA analyses for law enforcement identification purposes. The act also provided for establishment of a "DNA Index" for law enforcement purposes which would allow investigators to produce quick matches with DNA samples already on file, and limited accessibility of DNA samples to investigators, court officials, and personnel authorized to evaluate such samples for purposes of criminal prosecution and defense.

A few years ago, an authoritative study on the forensic uses of DNA, conducted by the National Research Council of the National Academy of Sciences, noted that, "The reliability of DNA evidence will permit it to exonerate some people who would have been wrongfully accused or convicted without it. Therefore, DNA identification is not only a way of securing convictions; it is also a way of excluding suspects who might otherwise be falsely charged with and convicted of serious crimes."[39]

In 1996, the most comprehensive report to date on the applicability of DNA testing to criminal case processing was released by the National Institute of Justice. The report, entitled *Convicted by Juries, Exonerated by Science,*[40] provided statistical support for the earlier observation made by the National Academy of Sciences. The report called DNA testing "the most important technological breakthrough of twentieth-century forensic science" and provided a detailed review of 28 cases in which postconviction DNA evidence exonerated defendants who had been sentenced to lengthy prison terms. The 28 cases were selected on the basis of a detailed examination of records which indicated that the convicted defendants might have actually been innocent. The men in the study had served, on average, seven years in prison, and most had been tried and sentenced prior to the widespread availability of reliable DNA testing.

In each of the 28 cases, which involved 14 states and the District of Columbia, the imprisoned defendant obtained, through an attorney, case evidence for DNA testing and consented to a comparison to his own DNA sample. In each case, the results conclusively showed the lack of matching DNA, and the defendant was ultimately set free. Sexual assault was the most frequent crime for which the defendants had been sentenced. In six of the cases, the victims had also been murdered. All but one case involved a jury trial.[41] Of the cases where the time required for jury deliberations was known, most verdicts had been returned in less than a day.

The 28 wrongful conviction cases shared several common themes in the evidence presented during and after trial, including (1) eyewitness identification—all cases, except for homicides, involved victim identification both prior to and at trial; (2) an alibi defense—most defendants had presented an alibi defense, frequently corroborated by family or friends; (3) the use of forensic evidence other than DNA-testing, including the examination of nonvictim specimens of blood, semen, or hair at the crime scene; (4) the testimony of prosecution experts who explained the reliability and scientific strength of non-DNA evidence to the jury; and (5) alleged government malfeasance or misconduct—including perjured testimony at trial, police and prosecutors who intentionally kept exculpatory evidence from the defense, and intentionally erroneous laboratory tests and expert testimony admitted at trial as evidence.

One provocative finding of the NIJ report was that "Every year since 1989, in about 25% of the sexual assault cases referred to the FBI where results could be obtained (primarily by State and local law enforcement), the primary suspect has been excluded by forensic DNA testing....The fact that these percentages have remained constant for seven years, and that the National Institute of Justice's informal survey of private laboratories reveals a strikingly similar 26% exclusion rate, strongly suggests that postarrest and postconviction DNA exonerations are tied to some strong, underlying systemic problems that generate erroneous accusations and convictions."

The report concluded that "momentum is growing, spurred in part by the public's education from the Simpson trial, for DNA testing in criminal cases. Juries may begin to ques-

Our "can-do" spirit as Americans generates tremendous fascination with technology and what it can do for us (as a society). But at the same time we have an innate and healthy skepticism, perhaps even a fear, of what technology can do to us as individuals.

—Mark H. Gitenstein, Executive Director, The Foundation for Change

tion cases where the prosecutor does not offer 'conclusive' DNA test results if the evidence is available for testing. More defense attorneys in court-appointed cases may file motions for DNA testing and request the State to pay for the tests…"

Commenting on the NIJ report and on the future of DNA-testing, Attorney General Janet Reno said: "By highlighting the importance and utility of DNA evidence, this report presents challenges to the scientific and justice communities. Among the tasks ahead are the following: maintaining the highest standards for the collection and preservation of DNA evidence; ensuring that the DNA testing methodology meets rigorous scientific criteria for reliability and accuracy; and ensuring proficiency and credibility of forensic scientists so that their results and testimony are of the highest caliber and are capable of withstanding exacting scrutiny."[42]

As standards develop, DNA identification techniques continue to evolve. Notably, the amount of DNA needed for accurate identification continues to grow smaller. In 1997, for example, Australian forensic scientists reported success in obtaining useful amounts of DNA from the surface of objects that people touched for as little as five seconds as much as one year previously. In their tests, researchers at the Victoria Forensic Science Center in Victoria, Australia, used swabs to recover DNA-laden material from partial fingerprints found on gloves, glasses, mugs, pens, car keys, briefcases, knives, locker handles, and telephone handsets. Moreover, in one in four cases, they also were able to recover DNA that was transferred from one person to another while shaking hands. The technique developed by Australian forensic scientists uses "naked DNA," such as that found on the surface of skin, rather than the DNA found inside of cells.[43]

The need for consistently high standards in DNA testing is illustrated by the case of Kerry Kotler. Kotler was freed in 1992 after spending 11 years in prison on charges he raped an East Farmingdale, New York, woman in 1978 and again in 1981. Although the woman repeatedly insisted that Kotler was her attacker, DNA tests seemed to show that he was not guilty. In 1996, however, Kotler was arrested again and charged with first-degree rape and second-degree kidnapping. A 20-year-old college student told police that Kotler posed as a police officer, abducted and raped her, then used a water bottle to try to wash traces of his semen from her body.[44]

On-line Clearinghouses

As we have seen in earlier chapters, computers and the personnel who operate them are an integral part of most police departments. Police department computers perform such routine tasks as word processing, filing, record keeping, printing reports, and scheduling human resources and facilities. Computers which serve as investigative tools, however, have the greatest potential to impact criminal justice in the near future. The automated fingerprint technology discussed earlier is but one example of information-based systems designed to help in identifying offenders and solving crimes. Others include the nationwide National Crime Information Center (NCIC) and Violent Criminal Apprehension Program (VICAP) databases, state-operated police identification networks, and specialized services like METAPOL, an information sharing network run by the Police Executive Research Forum (PERF). Electronic facsimile systems (fax machines) now provide for easy hands-on distribution of on-line information. NCIC and PIN-type networks furnish a 24-hour channel to information on suspects, stolen vehicles, and other data and can be accessed through computers installed in patrol cars. In 1993 William Sessions, then-director of the FBI, announced the creation of the Criminal Justice Information Services Division (CJIS) within the FBI. The CJIS, Sessions said, "will provide state-of-the-art identification and information services…and will act as a focal point for the continual advancement of existing information systems and the development of new information services."[45]

Computer-Aided Investigations

Some police departments have begun to build and use large computer databases with the ability to cross-reference specific information about crimes in order to determine patterns and identify suspects. One such program, HITMAN, developed by the Hollywood, California, Police Department in 1985, has since been adapted by the entire Los Angeles Police Department to help detectives solve violent crimes. In a similar use of computers, the LAPD keeps track of a target population of over 60,000 gang members.[46]

More money has been stolen at the point of a fountain pen than at the point of a gun.
—Woody Guthrie

Expert Systems
Computer hardware and software which attempt to duplicate the decision-making processes used by skilled investigators in the analysis of evidence and in the recognition of patterns which such evidence might represent.

The developing field of artificial intelligence uses computers to make inferences based upon available information and to draw conclusions or make recommendations to the system's operators. **Expert systems**, as these computer models are often called, depend upon three components: (1) a user interface or terminal, (2) a knowledge base containing information on what is already known in the area of investigation, and (3) a computer program known as an "inference engine" which makes comparisons between user input and stored information according to established decision-making rules.

A number of expert systems already exist. One is being used by the FBI's National Center for the Analysis of Violent Crime (NCAVC) in a project designed to profile violent serial criminals. The NCAVC system depends upon computer models of criminal profiling to provide a theoretical basis for the development of investigative strategies. A number of other systems are under development, including some which focus on serology analysis, narcotics interdiction, serial murder and rape, and counterterrorism.[47]

Similar to expert systems are relational databases, which permit fast and easy sorting of large records. Perhaps the best known early criminal justice database of this sort was called Big Floyd. It was developed in the 1980s by the FBI in conjunction with the Institute for Defense Analyses. Big Floyd was designed to access the more than 3 million records in the FBI's Organized Crime Information System and to allow investigators to decide which federal statutes apply in a given situation and whether investigators have enough evidence for a successful prosecution.[48] In the years since Big Floyd, other "bad-guy" relational databases targeting malfeasants of various types have been created—including computer systems to track deadbeat parents and quack physicians. In 1996 President Clinton ordered the Department of Justice to create a computerized national registry of sex offenders. The national sex offender registry is being developed as a part of an overhaul of the FBI's computer systems and is scheduled to be on-line in mid-1999.[49]

Some systems are even more problem specific. For example, ImAger, a product of Face Software, Inc., uses computer technology to artificially age photographs of missing children. The program has been used successfully to identify and recover a number of children. One of them was only six months old when he disappeared and was found after ImAger created a photo of what the child was predicted to look like at age five. The photo was recognized by viewers who called police after it was broadcast on NBC television.[50] Another composite imaging program, Compusketch by Visatex Corporation, is used by police artists to create simulated photographs of criminal suspects.[51]

NCAVC says that expert systems and relational databases:[52] (1) help eliminate useless investigative paths, (2) store information that might otherwise be forgotten or not shared among investigators, (3) train beginning investigators to think like experienced profilers, and (4) are not subject to human failings such as the need for rest.

Computer-Based Training

Computers provide an ideal training medium for criminal justice agencies. They allow users to work at their own pace, and they can be made available around the clock to provide instruction on-site to personnel whose job requirements make other kinds of training difficult to implement. Computer-based training (CBT) is already well established as a management training tool. It is now under development by criminal justice education specialists for specific applicability in the field of law enforcement.[53] CBT has the added advantage of familiarizing personnel with computers so that they will be better able to use them in other tasks.

Some of the more widely used computer training programs include shoot/no-shoot decision-based software and police pursuit driving simulators. The Atari Mobile Operations Simulator (AMOS), firearms training simulation (FATS), and ROBBEC'S JUST (Judgment Under Stress Training) are just a few of the contemporary products available to police training divisions. Recent innovations in the field of virtual reality (a kind of high-tech-based illusion) have led to the creation of realistic computer-based virtual environments in which law enforcement agents can test their skills.[54] Other high-technology-based training is available via the Law Enforcement Satellite Training Network (LESTN), a privately owned company operating out of Carrollton, Texas.

We have mentioned some of the most prominent uses of technology in criminal justice, but they are by no means all of them. Laser fingerprint lifting devices, space age photography, video camera-equipped patrol cars, satellite and computerized mapping,[55] advanced

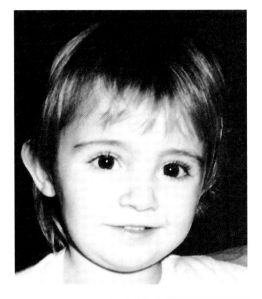

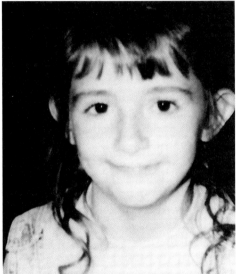
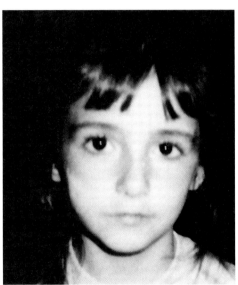

Computer-aged image of a missing child. The child, Autumn Jade Young, is shown at the time of her disappearance in the upper left photo when she was three years old. Computer imaging updated her appearance in the right photo to what she might be expected to look like at age nine. Shortly after the image was released, Autumn (bottom photos) was returned to her family. *The National Center for Missing and Exploited Children*

chemical analysis techniques, and hair and fiber identification are all crime fighting techniques of the future that enforcement agencies are already using. Refinements in technology, lower costs, and better training will see many of these technologies become common investigative tools. Field test kits for drug analysis, chemical sobriety checkers, and hand-held ticket-issuing computers, have already made the transition from high-technology to widespread use. As one expert has observed, "Police agencies throughout the world are entering an era in which high technology is not only desirable but necessary in order to combat crime effectively."[56]

Problems in Implementation

Technological innovations, however, do not represent all smooth sailing for several reasons. First, the speed with which justice agencies successfully adapt to the opportunities brought by technology may be limited. Some writers have observed that "law enforcement has been slow to utilize new technology,"[57] and a study by the International Association of Chiefs of Police found that only 10% of police departments are innovative in their use of computers.[58]

The industry that most lags in the distribution of computing is government, and the most needy is probably the criminal justice system.

—Dr. Alfred Blumstein, Dean, School of Urban and Public Affairs, Carnegie-Mellon University

As anyone knows who has bought a computer recently, technology changes rapidly, making equipment quickly out of date and obsolete. Just the sheer amount of choice involved may also be daunting, as can the dependability of some high-technology vendors' claims about their products. And line staff and decision makers within police departments may lack the personal experience and knowledge to use technology effectively. Equally significant, the future legal acceptability and social applicability of specific technologies is uncertain.[59]

A second area of concern arises from the "supersleuth" capabilities of some high-technology items. As high-tech gadgetry becomes more commonplace in criminal justice agencies, we can be sure that the courts will watch for potential violations of individual rights. The use of photographic techniques developed for the space program, for example, which permit enlargement of details never before thought possible, or the use of superlistening devices, such as those now used to isolate and amplify the voices of referees and quarterbacks on weekend television, may extend investigative capabilities beyond previous understandings of limited search and seizure.

Finally, it must be recognized that the investigative and other opportunities created by technology for the agents of criminal justice have their flip side in the threats represented by the products of modern science in the hands of criminals.

Cybercrime: The New White-Collar Crime

Cybercrime Crime committed with the use of computers. Another term for computer crime.

The flip side of high technology, as far as the justice system is concerned, is the potential it creates for committing old crimes in new ways, or for the commission of new crimes never before imagined. Sometimes in today's high-tech world it's even difficult to tell when a crime has occurred. In 1995, for example, University of Michigan student Jacob Alkhabaz (A.K.A. Jake A. Baker), 20, became the first person ever indicted for writing something on the Internet when he was arrested by the FBI and charged with five counts of interstate transmission of threats.[60] Alkhabaz had posted a series of stories on the Internet about his fantasy of torturing, raping, and murdering a female classmate. One of his messages contained the phrase, "Just thinking about it anymore doesn't do the trick. I need to do it." Another note read: "Torture is foreplay, rape is romance, snuff (killing) is climax."[61]

Although he might have been punished by a sentence of up to five years in prison, Detroit U.S. District Judge Avern Cohn threw out the charges after Alkhabaz had spent 29 days in jail.[62] Cohn ruled that Alkhabaz's violent-sounding Internet writings were protected under the free speech clause of the U.S. Constitution. In contrast, the government had argued that true threats are not so protected and maintained that Alkhabaz's naming of a specific woman had raised the threats to the level required for violation of federal criminal law. Under the law, however, federal prosecutors would have had to prove that Alkhabaz intended to carry out his threats, something the judge did not believe could be done.

Opinions about the case varied greatly. Susan McGee, executive director of the Domestic Violence Project in Washtenaw County, Michigan, said the ruling "shows the judicial system in the United States is more interested in men's rights to torture, beat, and harass women than it is in women's right to live their lives in peace and safety."[63] American Civil Liberties Union representative Paul Denenfeld, however, said, "I think Judge Cohn did the right thing. The language was offensive but not an imminent threat to anyone. People should not have to stand trial for private thoughts and fantasies."[64] As a security manager with the Boeing Corporation observed, "The main problem...with computer crime prosecution has been lack of clear legal definitions and the resultant difficulty in convincing a judge or jury of the crime."[65]

White-Collar Crime

White-Collar Crime Nonviolent crime for financial gain committed by means of deception by persons having professional status or specialized technical skills during the everyday pursuit of their business endeavors.

Because of the skill and knowledge required by their crimes, most, but not all, today's high-tech offenders can aptly be labeled white-collar criminals. The term **white-collar crime** was coined by Edwin Sutherland in his 1939 presidential address to the American Sociological Society.[66] Sutherland later defined the term to include crimes committed by persons in authority during the normal course of their business transactions. White-collar crimes include embezzlement, bribery, political corruption, price fixing, misuse and theft of company property, corporate tax evasion, fraud, and money laundering (which obscures the source of funds earned through illegal activities, allowing them to enter the legitimate financial arena). White-collar crimes tend to be committed by financially secure, well-educated,

Nicholas Leeson, accused of losing more than $1 billion in illegal securities trading activities. Arrested in Germany, Leeson was extradited to Singapore. Security trading under the control of Leeson destroyed Barings, an English bank. *Bernd Kammerer, AP/Wide World Photos*

middle- or upper-class persons. Sutherland claimed that the prevalence of white-collar crimes shows that "The theories of criminologists that crime is due to poverty or to psychopathic and sociopathic conditions statistically associated with poverty are invalid."[67] Anyone, said Sutherland, is capable of committing a crime, but many crimes are overlooked when committed by powerful people.

A broad, and somewhat more modern, definition of white-collar crime might be "nonviolent crime for financial gain committed by means of deception by persons having professional status or specialized technical skills during the everyday pursuit of their business endeavors."[68] The insider-trading scam of stock market tycoon Ivan Boesky, which was estimated to have netted $250 million[69] for Boesky and his friends, and the $600 million fine levied against junk bond king Michael Milken in 1990 for securities fraud provide two recent examples of white-collar crime. Another can be found in the savings and loan fiasco of the late 1980s and early 1990s, which has been called "the biggest white-collar crime in history."[70] The S&L disaster was a long time in the making. While the boom days following World War II were lucrative for the savings and loan industry, hard times set in during the 1970s, when low-interest long-term housing loans made by member institutions were costing the industry more than it could earn. Then, falling interest rates and a surge in land development combined with decreased federal regulation to produce a climate in which savings and loan institutions could quickly turn big profits by signing increasingly risky loans. Following deregulation, made possible in part by Congress's passing of the Depository Institutions Deregulation and Monetary Control Act of 1980, organized criminal groups began working the S&L market. As Frank Hagan notes, "[T]he S&L scandal reflected increased criminal opportunity due to an economic crisis that was taken advantage of by greedy insiders who collectively looted financial institutions and left the bill to the U.S. taxpayers."[71]

As individual savings and loans closed, costs began to mount. The bankruptcy of Charles Keating's California-based Lincoln Savings and Loan Association cost taxpayers around $2.5 billion, while the collapse of Neil Bush's Silverado Banking S&L in Denver cost nearly $1 billion.[72] Once called the "granddaddy of all S&L crooks,"[73] Donald Dixon, the former chief of Vernon Savings and Loan (in Vernon, Texas) is typical of the fraudulent operators who enriched themselves via S&L mismanagement. Dixon, through the help of personally approved high-risk loans, spent tens of millions of dollars for jets, fast cars, prostitutes, and a 110-foot yacht. While paying himself a multimillion-dollar salary from 1981 to 1987, Dixon bought Ferraris and million-dollar beach houses in Del Mar and Solana Beach, California. When the Vernon S&L was finally shut down in 1987, 96% of its loans were delinquent. Dixon was finally convicted on December 20, 1990, of 23 counts of misappropriation of funds—including $42 million spent on, among other things, a 5,500-square-foot beach house and a party where prostitutes were provided for guests.[74] Estimates are that the total S&L debacle will cost American taxpayers nearly $500 billion over the next 30 years—an amount far larger than that lost in all bank robberies throughout the course of American history.

A more recent white-collar crime appears to have been involved in the bankruptcy of Canadian gold prospector Bre-X Minerals Ltd. In the mid-1990s, Bre-X officials claimed that assayed ore from the company's Busang mine in Indonesia proved that it owned what was likely to be the world's largest gold reserve. In what some have called "the greatest stock fraud of the century," shares of the company's stock soared from pennies to a value of $206 each. After a number of debacles, including the suspicious death of the company's chief geologist who fell from a helicopter over the Indonesian jungle, the company admitted in 1997 the truth of an independent report which showed that the company's claims were based on falsified data.[75] Bre-X shareholders were left with worthless stock certificates, while the company's vice-president of exploration filed for residency status in the Cayman Islands where he owns about $6 million dollars worth of beachfront homes.

Also in 1997, shares of Mercury Finance Company tumbled when the company revealed that it would have to lower its reported earnings over the previous four years by about $90 million, due to accounting irregularities. After the announcement, Mercury defaulted on millions of dollars in debt and was served with a search warrant by FBI agents seeking financial records. The company lost more than $2 billion in market capitalization when the stock plunged following the earnings announcement. Investigations into the actions of officers of Bre-X and Mercury Finance are ongoing at the time of this writing.

White-collar criminals tend to be punished less severely than other offenders. In the 1930s and 1940s Edwin Sutherland studied the 70 largest corporations of his time and found that 547 adverse court and regulatory agency decisions had been made against them—an average of 7.8 decisions per corporation.[76] Although this should have been evidence of routine corporate involvement in white-collar criminality, almost no corporate executives were sentenced to prison. More recent studies have shown that about 40% of convicted federal white-collar offenders are sentenced to prison versus 54% of non-white-collar criminals.[77] When prison sentences are imposed, white-collar offenders are sentenced to only 29 months on average, versus 50 months for other inmates.[78] As other authors have noted, "[F]or some reason our system has seen nothing unjust in slapping an 18-year-old inner-city kid with a 20-year prison sentence for robbing a bank of a couple of thousand dollars while putting a white-collar criminal away for just two years in a "prison camp" for stealing $200 million through fraud."[79]

Occupational Crime

Occupational Crime Any act punishable by law which is committed through opportunity created in the course of an occupation that is legal.

Criminologists were quick to realize that if persons of high socioeconomic status could commit crimes during the course of their business, then so could persons of lower social standing.[80] The term *occupational crime* was coined to describe the on-the-job illegal activities of employees. Thefts of company property, vandalism, the misuse of information, software piracy which occurs in the workplace, and many other activities come under the rubric of occupational crime. The employee who uses company phones for personal calls, the maintenance worker who steals cleaning supplies for home use, and the store clerk who lifts items of clothing or jewelry provide other examples of occupational criminality. The Council of Better Business Bureaus estimates that one-third of all plant and office workers steal from their employers.[81] Total losses are said to be in the range of $10 to $20 billion per year.[82] The council believes that one-third of all business failures are directly attributable to employee crime.[83]

In a recent book on occupational crime,[84] Gary S. Green defines occupational crime as "any act punishable by law which is committed through opportunity created in the course of an occupation that is legal."[85] Green has developed the following typology which considerably broadens the classification of occupational criminality: "(a) crimes for the benefit of an employing organization (organizational occupational crime); (b) crimes by officials through the exercise of their state-based authority (state authority occupational crime); (c) crimes by professionals in their capacity as professionals (professional occupational crime); and (d) crimes by individuals as individuals (individual occupational crime)."[86]

James Coleman provides a further distinction between types of white-collar crime.[87] Coleman points out that some white-collar crimes affect only property while others endan-

The Terminology of Computer and High-Technology Crime

SOFTWARE

Computer programs or instructions to machines which control their operations. Software is generally found in magnetic storage media, but can be reproduced on paper or held in either machine or human memory.

HARDWARE

Computer machinery, including keyboards, disk or tape drives, optical scanners, "mice," video monitors, printers, central processing units, modems, terminals, add-on boards, peripherals, and so on.

CPU

Central processing unit. That part of the computer which houses the microprocessor and performs data manipulations.

MODEM

A telecommunications device used to link computers. A modem is generally used by hackers to gain illegal access to other computers.

HACKERS

Computer hobbyists or professionals, generally with advanced programming skills. The term *hackers* is often used to describe computer operators involved in "computer trespass."

INTERNET

The world's largest computer network. The Internet permits access to the World Wide Web (www) and to many other forms of data exchange.

PIRACY

The unauthorized duplication of software or the illegal transfer of data from one storage medium to another. One of the most prevalent computer crime problems is the unauthorized duplication of copyrighted software.

ILLEGAL ACCESS

Unauthorized entrance into a computer's files or operating system. Entrance may be made through the use of private information (a password), physical trespass, or electronically via a modem and software. In legal terminology, illegal access is often referred to as "computer trespass."

THEFT BY COMPUTER

The illegal use of a computer to transfer money, valuables, software, data, or other property from one account or machine to another.

THEFT OF COMPUTER SERVICES

The illegal use of computer time or of information or other services available on-line or directly. Employees of computer-based industries may use machines for personal purposes (such as check-book balancing, games, etc.), while hackers may acquire on-line services illegally by circumventing security and fee systems.

VIRUS

A computer program which is designed to secretly invade systems and modify either the way in which they operate or alter the information they store. Viruses are destructive software which may effectively vandalize computers of all sizes. Other destructive programs include *logic bombs, worms*, and *Trojan horse* routines, which hide inside of seemingly innocent software or disks.

FEDERAL INTEREST COMPUTER

A computer owned by the federal government or a financial institution or one which is accessed across state lines without prior authorization. Federal Interest Computers are defined by the Computer Fraud and Abuse Act, as amended in 1986.

CYBERCRIME

Crime committed with the use of computers, or another term for computer crime.

---

ger the safety and health of people. The knowing sale of tainted food products or medicine are examples of the latter type of crime. Coleman has also suggested that the term organizational crime is useful to distinguish those offenses which are designed to further the goals of corporate entities, from business-related crimes committed by individuals to further their own desires.[88] Organizational crimes are the "crimes of big business." Sometimes, however, it pays to remember that all crimes are committed by people and not by institutions.

Some authors maintain that occupational and **corporate crime** are a way of life in American businesses.[89] Examples abound.[90] Government investigations in the late 1950s revealed that the General Electric Company was heavily involved in price fixing.[91] In 1975 Allied Chemical Corporation was fined $5 million and agreed to donate another $8 million to a cleanup fund after it was revealed that former Allied employees had arranged to establish a small, seemingly independent business to supply Allied with the highly toxic chemical

Corporate Crime A violation of a criminal statute by a corporate entity or by its executives, employees, or agents acting on behalf of and for the benefit of the corporation, partnership, or other form of business entity.

Computer Crime Any crime which takes advantage of computer-based technology in its commission. This definition highlights the manner in which a crime is committed more than it does the target of the offense. Hence, the physical theft of a computer, or of a floppy disk, would not be a computer crime, while the use of computer software to analyze a company's security operations prior to committing a robbery might be.

Cybercrime Crime committed with the use of computers.

Hackers Computer hobbyists or professionals, generally with advanced programming skills. Today the term *hacker* has taken on a sinister connotation and includes those hobbyists who are bent on illegally accessing the computers of others or who attempt to demonstrate their technological prowess through computerized acts of vandalism.

Computer Viruses A small computer program which is designed to secretly invade systems and modify either the way in which they operate or alter the information they store. Viruses are destructive software which may effectively vandalize computers of all sizes.

Software Piracy The unauthorized duplication of software or the illegal transfer of data from one storage medium to another. Software piracy is one of the most prevalent computer crimes in the world.

Kepone.[92] Workers in the Kepone manufacturing facility became seriously ill, and the St. James River near the plant was badly contaminated. Most readers of this volume will recognize the acronym "PCBs" and the role of such chemicals in cases of criminal contamination of the environment. A few may remember the infamous "Love Canal Incident" or the exploding gas tanks on Ford Pintos which were manufactured between 1971 and 1976. There is evidence that Ford executives may have known of the defects before the Pinto was even put into production.[93] The Ford Motor Company ultimately paid more than $100 million in recall fees and civil settlements directly related to the gas tank coverup.[94]

More recent examples of corporate crime come from the $10 billion 1985 mail and wire fraud scheme of E. F. Hutton[95] and the 1988 stock fraud case of Wall Street giant Drexel Burnham Lambert, Incorporated. In 1988 Drexel agreed to pay $650 million in fines and restitution and pleaded guilty to six felony counts involving securities law violations.[96] Government prosecutors used the case to prove other wrongdoings on the part of some of the nation's best-known corporate traders.[97]

White-collar, occupational, and corporate crime provide the subject matter of the National White Collar Crime Center (NWCCC). Formed in 1992, the NWCCC provides a national support system for the prevention, investigation, and prosecution of multijurisdictional economic crimes, including investment fraud, telemarketing fraud, securities fraud, commodities fraud, and advanced-fee loan schemes. From 1978 to 1992 the Center was called the Leviticus Project and operated as a multistate association of law enforcement, prosecution, and regulatory agencies banded together to fight criminal activity in the coal industry and, subsequently, in the oil, natural gas, and precious metals industries. In 1992 the Center expanded its mission to include all economic crimes. Today, the Center provides training, research, and information sharing (computer database) services to local and state law enforcement, prosecution, and regulatory agencies throughout the United States. The Center also provides specialized training at locations across the country on a variety of white-collar crime topics. The National White Collar Crime Center, which is located in Morgantown, West Virginia, is funded by the federal Bureau of Justice Assistance.

Computer and High-Technology Crime

During Sutherland's time, political corruption and corporate bribery were serious concerns. Although both offenses exist today, computer crimes are rapidly becoming the white-collar crime *par excellence* in the modern world. **Computer crimes**, sometimes called **cybercrimes**, use computers and computer technology as tools in crime commission. Thefts of computer equipment, although sometimes spectacular, are not computer crimes, but are instead classified as larcenies. In 1995, for example, armed robbers clad in sports coats and ties robbed Centon Electronics, a computer chip distributor based in California's Silicon Valley, of more than $12 million in computer chips, after tying employees up.[98] At the time of the heist, the stolen chips, consisting primarily of 32-megabyte memory modules, were worth more per pound than gold.

"True" computer criminals, however, go beyond the theft of hardware, focusing instead on the information stored in computer systems and manipulating it in a way which violates the law. In 1995, for example, the arrest of computer expert Kevin Mitnick, known as the "FBI's most wanted hacker,"[99] alarmed security experts because of the potential harm represented by Mitnick's electronic intrusions. The 31-year-old Mitnick allegedly broke into an Internet service provider's computer system and stole more than 20,000 credit card numbers. Although Mitnick appears to have been arrested before the numbers were sold or clandestinely distributed, experts feared that others with similar high-tech skills might be tempted to enact copycat schemes—costing credit card-issuing companies millions of dollars. Mitnick was caught with the help of Tsutoma Shimomura, whose home computer Mitnick had also attacked and who assisted FBI experts in tracking him through telephone lines and computer networks to the computer in his Raleigh, North Carolina, apartment.

Another form of cybercrime, the unauthorized copying of software programs, also called **software piracy**, appears rampant. According to the Software Publishing Association (SPA), global losses from software piracy totaled $11.2 billion in 1996.[100] According to the SPA, 46% of all software in use in the world has been copied illegally. Some countries have especially high rates of illegal use. Of all the computer software in use in Vietnam, for example, it is estimated that 99% has been illegally copied. On a dollar basis, most piracy occurs in

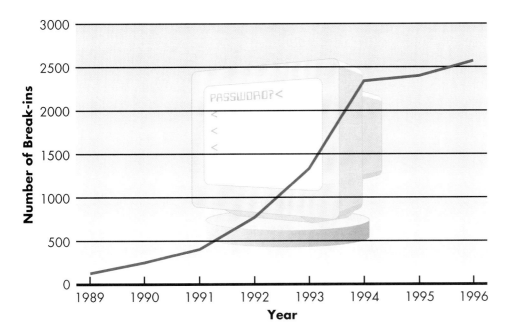

FIGURE 17–2 Number of computer break-ins. *Source:* Software Engineering Institute, Carnegie-Mellon University.

Asia and Pacific rim countries ($3.7 billion), while Western Europe (at $2.5 billion) and North America (at $2.7 billion) also account for substantial losses in software manufacturers' revenue.

Prosecution of Computer and High-Tech Crime

Twenty years ago, computer crimes were virtually unheard of (see Figure 17–2), and as little as a decade ago few states had computer crime laws. Crimes using computer technology had to be prosecuted, if at all, under laws intended for other purposes. Burglary laws sometimes served to prosecute illegal entry into computer systems, laws against theft were applied to the stealing of digitized information, and embezzlement statutes were applied to illegal electronic fund transfers. Thirty years ago, for example, an employee of Texas Instruments Corporation who stole more than 50 typewritten copies of software programs was convicted of theft under Texas law.[101] Had the software been stolen in electronic form, or through the use of a modem, prosecution under the state larceny statute would have been much more difficult. In another early case, Wisconsin authorities found themselves at a loss as to how to prosecute the "414 gang"—a teenage group of computer hackers based in Milwaukee who had infiltrated the computers of 60 businesses, including government computer systems, the Los Alamos National Laboratory, the Sloan-Kettering Cancer Center, and the Security Pacific National Bank in Los Angeles.[102] At the time of the offense (1983), neither Wisconsin nor the federal government had specific legislation applicable to the hackers' activity, and they had to be arraigned under a law pertaining to telephone mischief.

Because existing laws were often not adequate in the prosecution of computer crimes, most states and the federal government moved rapidly to create computer and high-technology criminal statutes. In October 1984 the first federal computer crime law was enacted.[103] Called the Computer Fraud and Abuse Act (CFAA), it made unauthorized access to government computers or to computers containing information protected under the Federal Privacy Act a crime.[104] It also defined unauthorized interstate entry into any computer as illegal. In 1986 Congress modified the Computer Fraud and Abuse Act[105] and expanded the penalty for illegal access to computers which represent a "unique federal interest." **Federal interest computers** are those that (1) are the property of the federal government, (2) belong to financial institutions, or (3) are located in a state other than the one in which the criminal perpetrator is operating. Under the CFAA, which has been revised a number of times since it was first passed, convicted offenders face penalties of up to ten years imprisonment and fines which can extend to twice the amount of the "unlawful gain."

Federal Interest Computers Are those which (1) are the property of the federal government, (2) belong to financial institutions, or (3) are located in a state other than the one in which the criminal perpetrator is operating. Federal Interest Computers are defined by the Computer Fraud and Abuse Act, as amended in 1986.

Today, high-tech criminals may be prosecuted under a variety of other federal legislation. One authority estimates that as many as 40 different sections of the federal criminal code may be applicable to thefts which occur through the use of a computer.[106] Applicable federal statutes include the Computer Abuse Amendments Act of 1994 (a part of the Violent Crime Control and Law Enforcement Act of 1994); aspects of the Electronic Communications Privacy Act of 1986; the National Stolen Property Act;[107] the Federally Protected Property Act;[108] the Federal Trade Secrets Act;[109] the amended Copyright Act of 1980;[110] and various federal wire, mail, and bank fraud statutes.[111] All can support prosecutions of high-tech offenders.

Following the lead of the federal government, most states have developed their own computer crime laws. The New York state Computer Crime Act is an example of such legislation.[112] Enacted in 1986 it created six crime categories involving software and computer misuse. The law specifically prohibits the duplication of copyrighted software and makes the possession of illegally duplicated software a felony. Other activities defined as illegal under the law include the "unauthorized use of a computer," "computer trespass," and "theft of computer services." The New York bill also created sweeping amendments to existing laws. Theft laws were modified to specifically include "computer program" and "computer data" under the definition of "property," and computer terminology was incorporated into forgery laws. Most state computer crime laws impose punishments proportional to the damage done, although California bases penalties on the number of violations.

Types of Computer Crime

One problem in the development of comprehensive laws is lack of legislative appreciation for the potentially wide variety of crimes which can be perpetrated using a computer. While a comprehensive typology of computer-based crime has yet to be developed,[113] the categories which follow probably encompass most such offenses today.

Unauthorized Access to Data   An old adage says that "knowledge is power." Information stored in today's magnetic and laser-read media is often sensitive (like personnel records) or necessarily secret (such as corporate marketing plans or the detailed technical description of a new product). Unauthorized access to data can lead to lawsuits over patent infringements, loss of a competitive edge, and the need to redo many hours or even months of work.

The frequent need for access to computer-based data, and the routine use of telephone lines for data transfer, make such information particularly susceptible to snooping. Four techniques are used today to prevent the compromise of sensitive data:

- *Physical security*. Locked disk files, key-operated hard disks, removable storage media, and limited access computer rooms are all physical security measures which can be taken to thwart the potential viewing or theft of information.
- *Passwords or other forms of identification*. Individual computers and networks sometimes require users to properly enter a password or other form of identification to gain access. Some advanced systems use optical imaging to recognize the unique network of blood vessels on the retinas of users requesting access to highly secure computer networks. "Eyeball scanners," voice recognition units, hand geometry scanners, keyboard rhythm recognition units, and other high-technology gadgetry—known in the trade as biometric security devices—are not readily available to most businesses because of cost.
- *Data encryption methods*. Data encryption uses either hardware or software to turn information into gibberish until it is uncoded by authorized users.[114] Data encryption techniques may be either unique to an individual company and peculiar to its products or may use the Data Encryption Standard (DES) of the National Bureau of Standards. DES makes it possible for banks and other businesses to freely exchange and decrypt coded data even when the computer systems used in the exchange differ substantially.
- *Screen blanking*. Screen blanking lacks the sophistication of some of the other methods we have described. It depends upon a relatively simple technology which causes video monitors to go blank after a set period of nonuse. Hence, data entry stations left unattended cannot be casually viewed by unauthorized personnel.

Data Encryption
Methods used to encode computerized information.

Willful Destruction of Data As computer systems grow in complexity, they challenge the inventiveness of sophisticated hackers, or computer buffs. Some are tempted to try their skill at invading highly protected systems. Such top-level invaders typically leave some sign of their accomplishment. It may be something as simple as a message which appears in printed documents or on the screens of legitimate users. Hackers may also introduce a set of hidden instructions that cause the computer to destroy its data or alter its software instructions. The sophisticated but destructive computer programs involved in this modern kind of vandalism are called computer viruses. Viruses spread from one computer to another through disk swapping or over data lines that link one machine to another (such as the Internet).

As society becomes more dependent upon computers, the damage potential of viruses increases. Computer viruses were brought to public attention in 1988 when the "Pakistani" virus (also called the "Pakistani brain" virus) became widespread in personal and office computers across the United States.[115] The Pakistani virus had been created by Amjad Farooq Alvi and his brother Basit Farooq Alvi, two cut-rate computer software dealers in Lahore, Pakistan. The Alvi brothers made copies of costly software products and sold them at low prices to mostly Western shoppers looking for a bargain. Through a convoluted logic, the brothers hid a virus on each disk they sold in order to punish buyers for seeking to evade copyright laws.

A more serious virus incident affected sensitive machines in NASA, nuclear weapons labs, federal research centers, and universities across the United States in late 1988.[116] The virus did not destroy data. Instead it made copies of itself and multiplied so rapidly that it clogged machines and effectively shut them down within hours after it invaded them. Robert Morris, creator of the virus, was finally sentenced in April 1990 to 400 hours of community service, three years probation, and a fine of $10,000.[117] Since then, many other virus attacks have made headlines, including the infamous Michaelangelo virus in 1992 and the intentional distribution of infected software on an AIDS-related research CD-ROM distributed about the same time.

The first criminal prosecution of a person accused of creating a virus was that of 40-year-old Fort Worth, Texas, programmer Donald Gene Burleson. Prosecutors claimed Burleson infected a former employer's computer with a program that erased over 168,000 business records.[118] Burleson's alleged motive was revenge for office disagreements.

Computer viruses have become increasingly sophisticated. Although early viruses were relatively easy to detect with hardware or software scanning devices which looked for virus "signatures," new viruses called "stealth viruses" and "polymorphic viruses" change form with each new "infection" and are much more difficult to locate and remove. Moreover, while older viruses infected only executable programs, or those that could be run, newer viruses (such as the Word for Windows "Macro" virus, also called the "Concept virus") attach themselves to word processing documents and to computer codes that are routinely distributed via the World Wide Web (including Java and Active-X components used by web browsers).

Data Manipulation Data manipulation may be the most serious kind of computer crime. People who are able to effect an unauthorized entry into computer files are often able to modify the data they contain. Students who access university administrative computers in order to change records of their grades are one example of data manipulation. A few years ago a 17-year-old Chicago high-school student broke into a computer system operated by AT&T and stole communications software valued at over $1 million.[119] Other skilled operators may transfer funds between private accounts, download trade secrets, hide the evidence of embezzlement, or steal customer lists. The hit movie *The Net* depicted a scenario in which a computer user enters a web of intrigue after accidentally discovering clandestine messages on the Internet. Computer experts have warned of the real-life potential for international terrorism through computer sabotage.[120]

What may be the largest computer crime in history (in dollar amounts) happened rather early in the computer age. In 1984 a ring of employees at Volkswagen's Wolfsburg, West Germany, headquarters modified files in the company's computers to hide the theft of $428 million.[121] Some experts say that banks around the world routinely transfer over $3 trillion a day through electronic media.[122] Such huge amounts represent potentially easy prey to technologically sophisticated criminals.

That's funny. I could have sworn that computer hacker got five years and $50,000 in fines. But here it is—six months suspended and five bucks. *Reprinted by permission of NEA, Inc.*

Combating Computer Crime

Computer criminals are generally young, well educated, aggressive, and technically sophisticated.[123] They commit their crimes for various reasons. Some seek personal riches, while others are attracted to the offense by the technical challenge it represents. A study of computer felons showed that they saw themselves as pitted against the computer.[124] The computer criminal is the type of person who would probably resist the temptation to commit most other types of crimes. Because the offense is against a machine, however, this otherwise conformist type of personality may deny that they are involved in crime commission.

Computer criminals are highly skilled, and the crimes they commit are often difficult for the technically uninitiated to detect. Many large corporations employ experts to detect unauthorized access to data processing equipment. A growing cadre of consultants serve the computer security needs of smaller companies. Police departments have been hard-pressed to keep pace with the growing sophistication of computer equipment and the criminals who prey upon it. Among law enforcement agencies, expertise in computer crime investigations is rare. Some agencies, such as the FBI, maintain substantial investigative capabilities in the computer area. Others, however, must rely upon personnel minimally trained in computer crime investigation. Given the wide range of expertise demanded of today's law enforcement personnel, it is probably unrealistic to expect detectives to be experts in the investigation of computer crime. Some authorities have suggested that competent criminal investigators today should at least be able to recognize that a computer crime has occurred.[125] Once the offense has been recognized, investigators can then call upon the services of persons skilled in combating it.

Terrorism A violent act or an act dangerous to human life in violation of the criminal laws of the United States or of any state to intimidate or coerce a government, the civilian population, or any segment thereof, in furtherance of political or social objectives. While we usually think of terrorism as involving bombings, kidnappings, and hijackings, other forms of terrorism might include attacks on the information systems of financial institutions and threats to reveal trade or industry secrets. Crimes which lack the ideological component necessary to qualify as terrorism can be described simply as murder, vandalism, blackmail, and so on.

Terrorism

The American criminal justice system of the twenty-first century will be buffeted by the expanding power of politically oriented endemic groups with radical agendas. Throughout the 1960s and 1970s, domestic terrorism in the United States required the expenditure of considerable criminal justice resources. The Weathermen, Students for a Democratic Society, the Symbionese Liberation Army, the Black Panthers, and other radical groups routinely challenged the authority of federal and local governments. Bombings, kidnappings, and shootouts peppered the national scene. As overt acts of domestic terrorism declined in frequency in the 1980s, international terrorism took their place. The war in Lebanon, terrorism in Israel, bombings in France, Italy, and Germany, and the many violent offshoots of the Iran-Iraq and Gulf wars occupied the attention of the media and of much of the rest of the world. Vigilance by the FBI, CIA, and other agencies largely prevented the spread of terrorism to the United States.

After incidents such as the terrorist attacks on Rome's Leonardo da Vinci airport in 1987 and the 1988 bombing of Pan American's London-to-New York flight, however, Americans began to realize that international terrorism was knocking on the domestic door. Pan American flight number 103 was destroyed over Scotland by a powerful two-stage bomb as it reached its cruising altitude of 30,000 feet, killing all the 259 passengers and crew aboard.

The "FBI's most wanted hacker," Kevin Mitnick. The 31-year-old Mitnick was arrested in 1995 and charged with breaking into the computer system of an Internet service provider and stealing more than 20,000 credit card numbers. *Bob Jordan, AP/Wide World Photos*

Another 11 people on the ground were killed, and many others injured as flaming debris from the airplane crashed down on the Scottish town of Lockerbie. Any doubts that Americans are being targeted by terrorists were dispelled by the June 25, 1996 truck bomb attack on U.S. military barracks in Dhahran, Saudi Arabia. Nineteen U.S. Air Force personnel were killed and more than 250 others injured in the blast that destroyed the Khobar Towers housing complex. A 40-person Pentagon task force headed by retired U.S. Army General Wayne Downing later concluded that the Pentagon had failed to take threats seriously.

The 1993 bombing of the World Trade Center in New York City and the 1995 conviction of Sheik Oma Abdel-Rahman and eight other Muslim fundamentalists on charges of plotting to start a holy war and conspiring to commit assassinations and bomb the United Nations[126] indicates that the threat of international terrorism has become a part of daily life in America. According to some terrorism experts, the bombing of the World Trade Center, which left four dead and a 100-foot hole through four subfloors of concrete, ushered in an era of serious domestic terrorism. Robert Kupperman of the Center for Strategic and International Studies says,[127] "We're in for very deep trouble. The terrorism infrastructure operating in the United States is altogether deeper than what we've thought so far."[128] Many now suspect that sleeper agents, planted by nations as diverse as Libya, Syria, North Korea, Cuba, Iran, and Iraq, have taken up residence throughout the United States and are awaiting the appropriate signal to attack. Siddig Ibrahim Siddig Ali, one of the eight terrorists convicted in the Trade Center bombing, seemed to confirm such suspicions when he told reporters following his arrest, "We can get you anytime." The United States has lax security according to Philip Jenkins, a counterterrorism expert. "In Europe," says Jenkins, "if you leave a bag at a railroad station, it will be blown up when you come back 30 minutes later. Here, it will be taken to lost and found."[129]

The technological sophistication of state-sponsored terrorist organizations is rapidly increasing. Handguns and even larger weapons are now being manufactured out of plastic polymers and ceramics. Capable of firing Teflon-coated armor-piercing bullets, such weapons are extremely powerful and impossible to uncover with metal detectors. Evidence points to the black market availability of other sinister devices, including liquid metal embrittlement (LME). LME is a chemical which slowly weakens any metal it contacts. It could be applied easily with a Magic Marker® to fuselage components in domestic aircraft, causing delayed structural failure.[130] Backpack-type electromagnetic pulse generators may soon be available to terrorists. Such devices could be carried into major cities, set up next to important computer installations, and activated to wipe out billions of items of financial, military, or other information now stored on magnetic media. International terrorists, along with the general public, have easy access to maps and other information which could be easily used to cripple the nation. The approximately 500 extremely high-voltage (EHV) trans-

In 1998, Larry Wayne Harris, 46 and William Leavitt Jr., 47, were arrested and charged with possession of a dangerous biological agent. FBI spokespersons initially said that the two had planned to unleash military-grade anthrax in the Las Vegas area. Later tests showed that the bacteria in their possession was relatively harmless. Even so, the arrests alerted citizens and enforcement agencies to the threat of biological terrorism. *Chris Farina, Sygma*

Once you're convicted of committing a felony, we should frankly say you're barred from having a gun the rest of your life, and we should enforce it. And I think if we did that, people would feel relatively safe.

—House Speaker Newt Gingrich

formers on which the nation's electronic grid depends, for example, are entirely undefended, but specified with extreme accuracy on easily available power network maps.

Equally worrisome are domestic underground survivalist and separatist groups and potentially violent special interest groups, each with their own vision of a future America. In 1993, for example, a confrontation between David Koresh's Branch Davidian followers and federal agents left 72 Davidians (including Koresh) and four federal agents dead in Waco, Texas.

Exactly two years to the day after the Davidian standoff ended in a horrific fire that destroyed the compound, a powerful terrorist truck bomb devastated the Alfred P. Murrah federal building in downtown Oklahoma City, Oklahoma. One hundred sixty-eight people died and hundreds more were wounded. The targeted nine-story building had housed offices of the Social Security Administration, Drug Enforcement Administration, the Secret Service, the Bureau of Alcohol, Tobacco, and Firearms, and a day care center called "America's Kids." The fertilizer and diesel fuel device used in the attack was estimated to have weighed about 1,200 pounds and had been left in a parked rental truck on the 5th Street side of the building. The blast, which left a crater 30 feet wide and 8 feet deep and spread debris over a ten-block area, demonstrated just how vulnerable the United States is to terrorist attack.

In 1997, a federal jury found 29-year-old Timothy McVeigh guilty of 11 counts, ranging from conspiracy to first-degree murder, in the Oklahoma City bombing. Jurors concluded that McVeigh had conspired with Terry Nichols, a friend he had met while both were in the Army, and with unknown others to destroy the Murrah Building. Prosecutors made clear their belief that the attack was intended to revenge the 1993 assault on the Branch Davidian compound. Following the guilty verdicts, McVeigh was sentenced to death.[131] If executed, he will be the first person under federal jurisdiction to be put to death since 1963. Terry Nichols was later convicted of conspiracy in the bombing and eight counts of involuntary manslaughter.

Some experts believe that the Oklahoma City attack was modeled after a similar bombing described in the *Turner Diaries*, a novel used by extremist groups to map their rise to power.[132] Just as Hitler's biography *Mein Kampf* served as a call to arms for Nazis in Europe during the 1930s, the *Turner Diaries* describes an Aryan revolution which occurs in the United States during the 1990s in which Jews, blacks, and other minorities are removed from positions of influence in government and society. Also unsolved as of this writing is the 1996 Olympic Centennial Park bombing in which one person died and 111 were injured—an attack which many antiterrorism experts believe was the work of a separatist organization.

Active fringe groups include those espousing a nationwide "common law movement," under which the legitimacy of elected government officials is not recognized. An example is the Republic of Texas separatists who took neighbors hostage near Fort Davis, Texas, in 1997 in order to draw attention to their claims that Texas was illegally annexed by the United States in 1845. While not necessarily bent on terrorism, such special interest groups may turn to violence if thwarted in attempts to reach their goals.

Sometimes individuals can be as dangerous as organized groups. In 1996, for example, 52-year-old Theodore Kaczynski, a Lincoln, Montana, recluse, was arrested and charged in the Unabomber case. The Unabomber (so called because the bomber's original targets were universities and airlines) had led police and FBI agents on a 17-year-long manhunt during a series of incidents which involved as many as 16 bombings, resulting in three deaths and 23 injuries. Kaczynski pled guilty to federal charges in 1998, and was sentenced to life in prison without possibility of parole.

The current situation leads many observers to conclude that the American justice system of today is ill prepared to deal with the threat represented by domestic and international terrorism. Intelligence gathering efforts focused on such groups have largely failed. Military-style organization and training are characteristic of the groups that are known, making them difficult to penetrate. The armaments at their disposal include weapons of mass destruction, which the firepower and tactical mobility of law enforcement agencies could not hope to match, although new federal antiterrorist legislation is on the horizon.

Even more frightening is the prospect of cooperation between international terrorist organizations and disaffected domestic groups. Such joint activities have already occurred. In 1986, for example, around the time of the Libyan crisis which led to the American bombing of Tripoli, the FBI intercepted communications between a Chicago-based drug gang and the Libyan government. The gang, seeing the opportunity for fast profit, proposed to engage in acts of domestic terrorism for the Libyans. Gang leaders were sentenced to prison for the scheme.

Rules of Terrorism

According to criminologist Gwynn Nettler, any terrorism, domestic or international, has six characteristics.[133] They are

- *No rules.* There are no moral limitations upon the type or degree of violence which terrorists can use.
- *No innocents.* No distinctions are made between soldiers and civilians. Children can be killed as easily as adults.
- *Economy.* Kill one, frighten 10,000.
- *Publicity.* Terrorists seek publicity, and publicity encourages terrorism.
- *Meaning.* Terrorist acts give meaning and significance to the lives of terrorists.
- *No clarity.* Beyond the immediate aim of destructive acts, the long-term goals of terrorists are likely to be poorly conceived or impossible to implement.

Controlling Terrorism

Terrorism represents a difficult challenge to all societies. The open societies of the Western world, however, are potentially more vulnerable than are totalitarian regimes such as dictatorships. Democratic ideals of the West restrict police surveillance of likely terrorist groups and curtail luggage, vehicle, and airport searches. Press coverage of acts of terrorism encourage copycat activities by other fringe groups or communicate information on workable techniques. Laws designed to limit terrorist access to technology, information, and physical locations are stop-gap measures at best. The federal Terrorist Firearms Detection Act of 1988 is an example. Designed to prevent the development of plastic firearms by requiring handguns to contain at least 3.7 ounces of detectable metal,[134] it applies only to weapons manufactured within U.S. borders.

In 1996, President Clinton signed the Antiterrorism and Effective Death Penalty Act into law. The Act

- Limits federal appeals in death penalty cases.
- Bans fund-raising and financial support within the United States for international terrorist organizations.

The Threat of Nuclear Terrorism

In 1997, two Lithuanian nationals, 28-year-old Alexander Porgrebeshski and 36-year-old Alexander Darichev, were arrested in Miami and charged with trying to sell Soviet-era nuclear weapons to federal agents posing as arms brokers for drug dealers. The two were caught on videotape negotiating the sale of Bulgarian-made tactical nuclear weapons. Dennis Fagan, chief agent at the U.S. Customs Service in Miami, said that the incident "shows there are people out there who have the ability to move weapons—strategic weapons—around the world."

Today's loose control over nuclear weapons and weapons-grade fissionable materials is the direct result of the collapse of the Soviet Union at the close of the 1980s. That country's dissolution seriously lessened the ability of Russian and former East-bloc authorities to retain control over cold war stockpiles of nuclear weapons. Evidence of such lack of control continues to surface. A few years ago, for example, German police asked Stuttgart's State Center for Environmental Affairs to examine a gritty substance confiscated from the garage of an accused counterfeiter in the small town of Tengen-Weichs in southwestern Germany. They were surprised to find that the material was superpure plutonium 239—a key ingredient needed in the manufacture of atomic bombs. Officials at the European Institute for Transuranium Elements, where the plutonium was sent for further analysis, were able to determine through the identification of "chemical footprints" unique to the material, that it had come from one of three top-secret Russian nuclear weapons laboratories—each of which had been among the most strictly guarded sites in the former U.S.S.R.

Destruction of 30,000 nuclear warheads under arms control agreements now in effect between the United States and Russia have further loosened controls over bomb-grade plutonium. And there is plenty of money available to reward nuclear smugglers. While the average Russian worker in the country's top-of-the-line nuclear facilities is paid only $113 per month, experts estimate that oil-rich Middle Eastern countries, controlled by fanatical and dictatorial regimes, are willing to pay as much as $100 million for the plutonium needed to make one bomb—an amount that can be smuggled out of a secure area in a briefcase or even the pocket of an overcoat.

The implications for Western nations concerned with controlling the spread of nuclear terrorism may be particularly dire. On a trip to Russia a little over a year ago, FBI director Louis Freeh told senior law enforcement officers there that, "[O]ne criminal threat looms larger than...others: the theft or diversion of radioactive materials in Russia and Eastern Europe." While Russian officials denied that any material has disappeared, they eagerly accepted Freeh's offer of U.S. aid in helping to prevent nuclear smuggling.

In the post-*perestroika* era, however, other officials are more willing to speak openly. Deputy chief of St. Petersburg's organized crime unit Vladimir Kolesnik, whose unit has been making at least four arrests per year of Russians trying to sell stolen nuclear material, says: "The problem is that security standards have slackened, and virtually everybody who has access to nuclear materials could steal something."

Of crucial concern to security experts are what weapons makers call "pits," or baseball-sized plutonium spheres, the end result of an exacting, highly technical, and very expensive manufacturing process. Anyone with even a rudimentary knowledge of bomb making can build an atomic bomb capable of wiping out a large city using stolen plutonium "pits." Pits can also be manufactured by processing plants operating in many places throughout the world from even small amounts of plutonium, weighing a gram or less. Hence, the continued pilfering of minute quantities of weapons-grade plutonium and the resale of such materials on a world-wide black market could soon lead to the construction of powerful terrorist weapons. As one writer explains it, "Nuclear weapons in the hands of extremists willing to use them would produce terrorism of a wholly new magnitude. The central logic of terrorism is to maximize horror and shock, producing a blaze of publicity and attention for the cause it represents. By that measure, the crudest of fission bombs set off in a modern city, vaporizing entire blocks, would make the crimes of [traditional terrorists] rank as little more than pinpricks."

QUESTIONS FOR DISCUSSION

1. What potential consequences does nuclear terrorism hold for the United States? For the American criminal justice system?

2. Is nuclear smuggling an activity with which American law enforcement agencies are well equipped to deal? If not, how might they be better equipped?

Sources: Catherine Wilson, "Two Accused in Nuke Sale Sting," The Associated Press wire services, June 30, 1997; James O. Jackson, "Proliferation: Nightmare in a Vial of Dust," *Time, Inc.,* wire services, July 28, 1994; Steve Komarow, "Nuclear Smuggling: A Bomb Waiting to Go Off," *USA Today,* August 17, 1994, p. 6A; and Bruce W. Nelan, "Formula for Terror," *Time, Inc.,* wire services, August 26, 1994.

- Provides $1 billion for enhanced terrorism-fighting measures by federal and state authorities.
- Allows foreign terrorism suspects to be deported or to be kept out of the United States without the need to disclose classified evidence against them.
- Permits a death sentence to be imposed upon anyone committing an international terrorist attack in the United States, if a death occurs.
- Makes it a federal crime to use the United States as a base to plan terrorist attacks overseas.
- Orders identifying chemical markers known as taggants to be added to plastic explosives during manufacture.
- Orders a feasibility study on marking other explosives (except gunpowder).

Sponsors of the 1996 legislation, a direct response to the 1995 Oklahoma City bombing, had originally proposed mandating the addition of taggants to all powerful explosives during the manufacturing process, as well as to chemical compounds which could be used to make such explosives. It was also proposed to include a powerful wiretap provision which would have made it easier for government agents to listen in on conversations of alleged terrorists. A political coalition led by the National Rifle Association and the ACLU, however, was successful in excluding both provisions from the final version of the legislation.[135] Other special interests were successful in adding a separate provision to the act mandating the creation of a five-member committee to study the activities of federal law enforcement agencies in dealing with right-wing groups.

There are no signs that either international or domestic terrorism will abate anytime soon. If diplomatic and other efforts fail to keep terrorism at bay, the criminal justice system may soon find itself embroiled in an undeclared war waged on American soil. The system, whose original purpose was to resolve disputes and to keep order among the citizenry, cannot be expected to adequately counter well-planned, heavily financed, covert paramilitary operations. As long as terrorists can find safe haven among sympathizers antagonistic to the rule of law, their activities will continue. As Nettler has observed, "[T]errorism that succeeds escalates."[136]

And say, finally, whether peace is best preserved by giving energy to the government, or information to the people—this last is the most certain, and the most legitimate engine of government. Educate and inform the whole mass of the people.

—Inscription on the atrium wall, Jefferson Hall, FBI National Academy, Quantico, Virginia

Technology and Individual Rights

The Office for Technology Assessment of the U.S. Congress notes that, "What is judicially permissible and socially acceptable at one time has often been challenged when technology changes."[137] When agencies of the justice system use cutting-edge technology, it inevitably provokes fears of a future in which citizens' rights are abrogated to advancing science. Individual rights, equal treatment under the law, and due process issues all require constant reinterpretation as technology improves. However, because some of the technology available today is so new, few court cases have yet to directly address the issues involved. Even so, it is possible to identify areas which hold potential for future dispute.

TECHNOLOGY AND THE FIRST AMENDMENT

One of the most revered covenants in the U.S. Constitution protects free speech. Found in the first Amendment, the relevant phrase reads, "Congress shall make no law…abridging the freedom of speech, or of the press…" In 1996, amidst fierce debate, the U.S. Congress passed and President Clinton signed, a law intended to control the availability of obscene materials on the Internet. Entitled the Communications Decency Act (CDA), the new law was part of the Telecommunications Act of 1996. The CDA made it a federal offense for anyone to distribute "indecent" or "patently offensive" material to minors (anyone under 18 years of age) over computer networks such as the Internet or commercial on-line services. The law provided for prison terms of up to two years and a $250,000 fine if indecent material was transmitted to minors.

Opponents of the law claimed that it unconstitutionally restricted free speech because it is not technologically possible for providers of access or content on the Internet to prevent

Many people worry that government intrusion may reduce rights otherwise supported by the Constitution. This National Rifle Association member is demonstrating in support of the Second Amendment's guarantee that "the right of the people to keep and bear arms shall not be infringed." *Donna Binder, Impact Visuals Photo & Graphics, Inc.*

minors from obtaining indecent materials intended for adults. "The senders…have no ability to ensure that their messages are only available to adults," said Harvard University computer consultant Scott Bradner.[138] "It is also not possible for an Internet service provider…to screen out all or even most content that could be deemed 'indecent' or 'patently offensive,'" added Bradner.

In mid-1996, a three-judge federal panel agreed with opponents of the CDA and issued a preliminary injunction barring enforcement of portions of the act. The unanimous decision held that speech over the Internet should be given the broadest possible constitutional protections—much like that now accorded to newspapers and magazines—as opposed to the tighter restrictions on broadcast media, such as television. "As the most participatory form of mass speech yet developed, the Internet deserves the highest protection from governmental intrusion," said U.S. District Judge Stewart Dalzell, a member of the judicial panel.[139] "Just as the strength of [the] Internet is chaos, so the strength of our liberty depends upon the chaos and cacophony of the unfettered speech the First Amendment protects," Dalzell wrote.

In 1997, in the landmark case of *Reno* v. *ACLU*,[140] the U.S. Supreme Court upheld the lower court's ruling, effectively invalidating enforcement provisions of the CDA. Writing for the majority, Justice John Paul Stevens said: "It is true that we have repeatedly recognized the governmental interest in protecting children from harmful materials. But that interest does not justify an unnecessarily broad suppression of speech addressed to adults." The ruling effectively accorded Internet content the same level of constitutional protection previously afforded print media, such as newspapers and magazines.

Technology and the Second Amendment

The Second Amendment to the U.S. Constitution reads "[a] well regulated Militia, being necessary to the security of a free State, the right of the people to keep and bear Arms, shall not be infringed." Many interpret the words of this amendment as a complete and total ban on gun control by the federal government. The National Rifle Association (NRA), long a proponent of individualized gun ownership is the strongest, most vocal, and best organized group in the nation opposing gun control. The NRA claims that efforts to legislate controls over gun ownership, and specifically the Brady Handgun Violence Prevention Act of 1993,

The principle all…moralists out there should remember is that when you erode one individual's rights, it can come back to attack you and your family at a later time.

—Sandra Craig, following her conviction on 53 counts of assault, child abuse, and perverted sexual practices

are unconstitutional. The Brady law, named after former President Ronald Reagan's White House press secretary Jim Brady, who was shot in the head during John Hinckley's 1981 attempted assassination of Reagan, provides for a five-day waiting period before the purchase of a handgun.[141] The law also created a national criminal background checking system, which is to be contacted by gun dealers before the sale of any firearm. Under the law, firearms dealers must register with the federal government and must disapprove the purchase of handguns by felons, by those awaiting trial on felony charges, or by fugitives. In 1997, a portion of the Brady Handgun Violence Prevention Act, which required the "chief law enforcement officer" of each local jurisdiction to conduct background checks and perform related tasks on an interim basis until a national checking system became operative, was struck down by the U.S. Supreme Court as unconstitutional. The Court, in the combined case of *Printz* v. *U.S.* (1997)[142] and *Mack* v. *U.S.*,[143] held that the constitutional principle of "dual sovereignty" prohibits direct federal control over state officers.

Another direct result of get-tough crime control attitudes in the United States is the Violent Crime Control and Law Enforcement Act of 1994, which increases federal control over firearms through a ban on the manufacture of 19 military-style assault weapons. Other new gun laws may also be in the works. Following passage of the Brady law, President Clinton said that he was intrigued by an idea raised by New York City Mayor Rudolph Giuliani, "calling for either the federal government or the states to establish gun licensing and training systems for potential gun owners, similar to current licensing requirements for motorists."

Opponents of gun control, many of whom continue to be quite vocal today, are not convinced it will reduce crime. They believe, instead, that a waiting period and other controls impose burdens only on those who obey the law and that even an assault weapons ban contravenes liberties guaranteed under the Second Amendment.

In the area of gun control, as in many others, technology and individual rights have the potential for conflict. While government agents fear the manufacture of nondetectable handguns and other weapons, makers of such guns have been quick to fight government restrictions on the manufacturing process. As mentioned in this chapter's terrorism section, handguns and even larger weapons, which are capable of firing nonmetallic projectiles, are now being manufactured (especially overseas, where legislative controls are lax) out of plastic polymers and ceramics. Such weapons can be extremely powerful and impossible to find with metal detectors. Agencies of control, which would ban the manufacture, importation, and possession of such easy-to-hide weapons, have suggested the adoption of international treaties requiring gun manufacturers to embed special transponder chips in each weapon made for civilian use so that it could be tracked anywhere in the world. Such miniaturized computer chips would be detectable by a variety of high-tech means, as well as through a network of geosyncronis satellites circling the earth, which could pinpoint the location of a specific weapon to within ten feet.

Advocates of gun ownership are bothered by such suggestions since they see efforts at further control as an infringement upon Second Amendment rights. Weapons which are easily detectable, they argue, could be just as easily confiscated and would no longer address the concerns of Second Amendment authors who seemed to contemplate a citizen-led defense against foreign invasion. As both technology and efforts at control advance, advocates of both gun ownership and control will find themselves in the midst of an ideational and political fray which will probably last for years.

Technology and the Fourth Amendment

The Fourth Amendment to the U.S. Constitution guarantees "[t]he right of the people to be secure in their persons, houses, papers, and effects, against unreasonable searches and seizures." Given the electronic network which permeates contemporary society, today's "houses" are far less secure from prying eyes than were those of the 1700s. Modern dwellings are linked to the outside world through phone lines, modems, fax machines, electronic mail, and even direct radio and television communications. One highly significant question centers on where the "security" of the home ends and the public realm begins.

Complicating matters still further are today's "supersnoop" technologies which provide investigators with the ability to literally hear through walls (using vibration detectors), listen into conversations over tremendous distances (with parabolic audio receivers), record voices

Computers can be broken into. If they're on the Internet, [they] might as well have a welcome mat.

—Kevin Mitnick
(As quoted in Jonathan Littman, "In the Mind of 'Most Wanted' Hacker, Kevin Mitnick," *Computerworld*, January 15, 1996, pp. 87–89).

in distant rooms (via laser readings of windowpane vibrations) and even look through walls (using FLIR—or "forward-looking infrared" devices, which can detect temperature differences of as little as two tenths of one degree). In 1994, in a case which many think bodes ill for traditional Fourth Amendment guarantees, the U.S. Supreme Court refused to review a case in which police used a helicopter-mounted thermal imaging device that allowed them to discover heat-producing drug manufacturing activities taking place inside of a suspect's house. Armed with such high-tech observation equipment and with evidence of exceptionally high electric bills at the targeted residence, detectives obtained a search warrant, entered the home, and confiscated drug-producing equipment. The high court upheld convictions resulting from the investigation, even though police officials admitted that "the infrared device actually produced imagery of what was on the interior [of the house]."[144] FLIR devices are used today by police departments in 40 cities, and a recent Tulsa, Oklahoma, study found that criminal apprehensions in that city rose 800% after two police helicopters were "armed" with FLIR.[145]

Another question concerns the Fourth Amendment's guarantee of secure "papers and effects." The phrase "papers and effects" takes on a much wider meaning when we enter the world of modern technology. Although the framers of the Constitution could not envision electronic databases, their admonition would seem to apply to such records. Databases may already be the repositories of more information than is routinely stored on paper. Tax listings, records of draft registrants, social security rolls, health reports, criminal histories, credit bureau ratings, and government and bank logs all contain billions of items of information on almost every man, woman, and child in the country. Most agree that official access to such information should be limited. A report to the U.S. Congress asks "whether the new technology is making everyone subject at all times to an electronic search even where traditional police searches would require a warrant issued on the basis of probable cause."[146]

A third question centers on the privacy of various kinds of information, the proper legal steps to be used in acquiring information for investigative purposes, and the types of information that can be appropriately stored in criminal justice data repositories. The kinds of information which can be appropriately stored in criminal justice databases, along with considerations of who should have access to such data, are both legal and ethical questions. In 1974, the Justice Department established the "one-year rule," prohibiting the FBI from disseminating criminal records more than a year old. The department was concerned about the potential for inaccuracy in older files.

Even "official" records may be misleading or incomplete. A study of FBI criminal records databases, for example, recently concluded that about 50% of arrest entries do not show the disposition of cases.[147] Inquiring agencies using such records could be falsely misled into prejudging the "guilt" of an offender against whom earlier charges had been dropped. The same study also found that as many as 20% of the arrest-dispositional data contained in FBI records may be erroneous. Evidence seized as the result of an arrest based upon inaccurate NCIC information can be suppressed.[148] Half of all requests for criminal records made to the FBI, however, are from employers and licensing agencies. If an applicant is refused employment or rejected for licensing (or bonding) on the basis of criminal record inaccuracies, he or she may needlessly suffer.

The U.S. Supreme Court has not yet directly addressed database management in criminal justice agencies (see, however, the 1995 case of *Arizona* v. *Evans* in Chapter 7). A number of lower courts have held that criminal justice agencies have a duty to maintain accurate and reliable records.[149] In one important decision, the Federal Court of Appeals for the District of Columbia found, in *Menard* v. *Saxbe* (1974), that the FBI has a duty to be more than a "mere passive recipient" of records. The court held that the FBI should avoid unnecessary harm to people listed in its files.[150] In answer to critics, the FBI has implemented NCIC-2000, a project designed to introduce more than 60 upgrades to the agency's computer operations.[151]

Technology and the Fifth Amendment

As we have discussed throughout this book, the Fifth and Fourteenth Amendments to the Constitution require that an accused receive "due process of law" prior to the imposition of any criminal sanction. Due process necessitates a presumption of innocence, and lawful prosecutions must proceed according to the standards of the Sixth Amendment.

What may be the greatest potential threat to the due process guarantee comes not from the physical sciences but from psychology, sociology, and other social scientific approaches to the study and prediction of human behavior. Social science research generally involves the observation of large numbers of individuals, often in quasi-experimental settings. Many studies produce results of questionable validity when applied to other settings. Even so, the tendency has been for social scientists to create predictive models of behavior with widely claimed applicability. Worse still, legislatures and criminal justice decision makers have often been quick to adopt them for their own purposes. Behavioral models, for example, are now used to tailor sophisticated law enforcement investigations, such as those based on the FBI's criminal profiling program. Statutory guidelines,[152] including the Federal Sentencing Guidelines,[153] are written with an eye to predictive frameworks which allegedly measure the danger potential of certain types of offenders. The justice system's growing use of behavioral models demonstrates a heightened faith in the reliability of the social sciences, but also holds the danger of punishment in anticipation of a crime.

The major threat from the social sciences to individual rights comes from the tendency they create to prejudge individuals based upon personal characteristics rather than facts. Persons who fit a conceptual profile defined as dangerous may be subject to investigation, arrest, conviction, and harsh sentences solely on the basis of scientifically identified characteristics. In effect, some social scientific models may produce a veiled form of discrimination. This is especially true when the predictive factors around which they are built are mere substitutions for race, ethnicity, and gender.

As an example, some early predictive models from studies of domestic violence tended to show that, among other things, the typical offender was male, unemployed or with a record of spotty employment, poorly educated, and was abused as a child and/or came from a broken home. Because many of these characteristics also describe a larger proportion of the nation's black population than they do whites, they created a hidden tendency to strongly accuse black males suspected of such offenses (and sometimes to suspect them even when they were not accused).

With these considerations in mind, social scientific models may nonetheless prove to be useful tools. The most acceptable solution would treat individuals on a case-by-case basis, looking to the general predictive models of social science only for guidance once all the facts became known.

The Fifth Amendment raises a second issue—this one outside the purview of social science. The amendment reads, "No person shall be held to answer for a capital, or otherwise infamous crime, unless on a presentment or indictment of a Grand Jury,…nor shall be compelled in any criminal case to be a witness against himself."

Statements made under hypnosis or during psychiatric examination are generally protected by court decision and are not available as evidence at trial.[154] However, modern technological procedures appear to make self-incrimination a possibility even in the absence of any verbal statements. The Supreme Court has held that suspects must submit to blood-alcohol tests under certain circumstances[155] and that samples of breath, semen, hair, and tissue may also be taken without consent when the procedures used do not "shock the conscience."[156] Technological advances over the next few decades are anticipated to increase the potential for incriminating forms of nontestimonial evidence.

Technology and the Sixth Amendment

The Sixth Amendment guarantees the right to a public trial by an impartial jury. The meaning of the words "public" and "impartial," however, have been rendered ambiguous by advancing technology. A famous author once coined the term "global village" to describe how advances in communications technology have increased the ready availability of information for us all. Are public trials ones in which TV cameras should be allowed? Would broadcasts of trials be permissible? Although courts in some jurisdictions now allow video recordings of trials with great public interest, courts at higher levels have yet to address the question.

Also at issue is the expanding use of scientific jury selection techniques, which are discussed briefly in Chapter 9. This new "technology" attempts to predict the outcome of jury deliberations based upon an assessment of the economic, social, cultural, and demographic characteristics of individual jurors.[157] Using jury selection techniques, some lawyers attempt

The Internet threatens to give every child a free pass into the equivalent of every adult bookstore and every adult video store in the country.

—U.S. Justice Department attorney, Seth P. Waxman arguing before the U.S. Supreme Court in *Reno* v. *ACLU* (1997)

to choose jurors likely to be predisposed to a finding in favor of their client.[158] The constitutional merits of scientific jury selection techniques have yet to be decided by the high court.

The Sixth Amendment allows an accused person to "be confronted with the witnesses against him." Some courts now permit only an indirect confrontation, through the use of television, videotapes, and the like. Abused juveniles, for example, appear to jurors in some jurisdictions only on television screens to spare them the trauma and embarrassment of the courtroom. Although such strategies may appear to be an "end run" around the Sixth Amendment, they are complicated by claims that justice is better served by an articulate witness rather than a frightened one and by the fact that most such testimonial strategies involve juveniles as witnesses.

Technology and the Eighth Amendment

The Eighth Amendment is the most concise statement in the Bill of Rights. It reads, "Excessive bail shall not be required, nor excessive fines imposed, nor cruel and unusual punishments inflicted."

Modern technology brings with it the possibility of a host of new treatments for the criminal offender. Most of these treatments can also be considered punishments because the courts impose them upon unwilling subjects. Examples of unusual "punishments" today might include drug and hormone therapy or the use of electronic bracelets to monitor the public movements of convicted offenders. A few years ago authorities in Arapahoe County, Colorado,[159] decided to experiment with an electronic system that alerts the potential victim via an alarm when a convicted stalker approaches. Although similar bracelets have been used to monitor compliance with probationary sentences of home confinement, some claim that the public use of such devices lends credence to the "brave new world" form of authoritarianism feared by many as undue governmental intrusion on privacy.

Drug therapy is another area under scrutiny. Two innovative drugs already in use are Antabuse® and Depo-Provera.® Antabuse® is utilized in the treatment of alcoholics. It produces nausea and vomiting when alcohol is ingested. Depo-Provera® is the trade name given by the Upjohn Company to its brand of medroxyprogesterone acetate, a synthetic form of the female hormone progesterone. Depo-Provera® has been shown to reduce the male sex drive and is sometimes administered to sex offenders by court order. A recent survey found that 14% of rehabilitative programs across the nation specializing in the treatment of adult sex offenders had used Depo-Provera® on an experimental basis.[160] In 1997 California became the first state to require twice-convicted child molesters to get weekly injections of Depo-Provera® upon release from prison (see the box in Chapter 11 on "chemical castration").

Drugs such as Antabuse® and Depo-Provera®, and surgical procedures like castration and lobotomy may soon run afoul of the Eighth Amendment's ban on cruel and unusual punishment. In most cases where these alternate treatments are contemplated by the court, criminal offenders are offered a choice between prison or a chemical or surgical remedy. The American Civil Liberties Union, however, has argued that the use of Depo-Provera® and other drugs in the treatment of criminal offenders is a form of coercion. The ACLU claims that the offered alternative, prison, is so dangerous as to force acceptance of any other choice.[161]

As with many emerging issues, drugs like Antabuse® and Depo-Provera® have not yet been subject to Supreme Court scrutiny. A few lower court cases have, however, begun to provide some general guidance in judging what treatments are permissible. For example, in the 1970 case of *Holt* v. *Sarver*,[162] the federal court for the Eastern District of Arkansas defined cruel and unusual punishment to be that which is "shocking to the conscience of reasonably civilized people." Whether "chemical castration" falls into such a category, and whether the U.S. Supreme Court will apply the *Holt* standard to such cases, are questions which remain unanswered.

Technology and the Fourteenth Amendment

Section One of the Fourteenth Amendment to the U.S. Constitution concludes with the phrase, "No state shall…deny to any person within its jurisdiction the equal protection of the laws." Modern technology, because it is expensive and often experimental, is not always equally available. Criminal justice programs which depend upon technology that is limited in its availability may contravene this Fourteenth Amendment provision. Court-ordered confinement, for example, which utilizes electronic monitoring and house arrest is an alternative much preferred by offenders. The technology supporting such confinement is, however, expensive, which dramatically limits its availability. Although the Court has yet to address this particular topic, it has ruled that programs which require the offender to bear a portion of the cost of confinement are unconstitutional when their availability is restricted to only those offenders who can afford them.[163]

SUMMARY

Old concepts of criminality, and of white-collar crime in particular, have undergone significant revision as a result of emerging technologies. Science fiction–like products, already widely available, have brought with them a plethora of possibilities for new high-stakes crimes, including computer crimes and "cybercrime." The well-equipped technologically advanced offender in tomorrow's world will be capable of property crimes involving dollar amounts undreamed of only a few decades ago. At the same time, the ability of law enforcement agencies to respond to everyday crimes will be enhanced by the advantage of "cutting-edge" technology.

Barring global nuclear war or world catastrophe, advances in technology will continue to occur. Citizens of the future will regard as commonplace much of what is only fantasy today. Gradual lifestyle modifications will accompany changes in technology and result in taken-for-granted expectations foreign to today's world. Within that changed social context the "reasonableness" of technological intrusions into personal lives will be judged according to standards tempered by the new possibilities technology has to offer.

Coming social changes, combined with powerful technologies, threaten to produce a new world of challenges for criminal justice agencies. Domestic and international terrorism, widespread drug running, and changing social values will evolve into a complex tangle of legal and technological issues which will confront the best law enforcement minds of the future. Only through a massive infusion of funds to support the purchase of new equipment and the hiring and training of technologically sophisticated personnel can tomorrow's enforcement agencies hope to compete with technologically adept criminals.

DISCUSSION QUESTIONS

1. How has technology affected the practice of American criminal justice over the past 100 years?

2. What future benefits and threats to the practice of criminal justice can you imagine emanating from technological advances which are bound to occur over the next few decades? What new forms of cybercrime do you envision?

3. What threats to civil liberties do you imagine advances in technology might create? Will our standards as to what constitutes admissible evidence, what is reasonable privacy, and so on, undergo a reevaluation as a result of burgeoning technology?

4. What are the major differences between the concepts of "white-collar crime" and "occupational crime"? How have advances in technology created new opportunities for white-collar or occupational criminals? What is the best hope of the criminal justice system for coping with such criminal threats?

5. Has criminal law kept pace with the opportunities for dishonest behavior created by advancing technology? What modifications in current laws defining criminal activity might be necessary in order to meet the criminal possibilities inherent in technological advances?

 Web Watch

Access the *Criminal Justice Today* site on the World Wide Web by pointing your Web browser at http://www.prenhall.com/cjtoday. Once there, click "Web Chapters," then select "Chapter 17: The Future of Criminal Justice," in order to access electronic information and other sites of relevance to this chapter. You may also wish to enter the Global Town Meeting, which provides facilities for the posting of electronic messages for others to read. Messages are arranged by topic, with new topics constantly being added.

Notes

1. "DNA Evidence Spells Freedom," *USA Today*, June 19, 1993, 3A.
2. "Canada—Sex Killing," The Associated Press wire services, July 18, 1997.
3. "DNA Test May Free Death Row Convict," United Press International wire services, July 10, 1997.
4. "The Oldest Profession Goes Hi-Tech," *Computerworld*, September 23, 1996, p. 134.
5. "Kid Finds Fugitive On-Line," *The Washington Post*, June 7, 1996; and "Fugitive Surrenders After Picture Shows Up on the Internet," The Associated Press, May 20, 1996.
6. National Law Enforcement Technology Center, electronic press release, April 7, 1995.
7. Lester D. Shubin, "Research, Testing, Upgrade Criminal Justice Technology," *National Institute of Justice Reports* (Washington, D.C.: U.S. Government Printing Office, 1984), pp. 2–5.
8. Simon Dinitz, "Coping with Deviant Behavior Through Technology," *Criminal Justice Research Bulletin*, Vol. 3, no. 2 (Huntsville, TX: Criminal Justice Center, 1987).
9. See, for example, Laurence P. Karper, Alexander L. Bennett, Joseph J. Erdos, and John H. Krystal, "Antipsychotics, Lithium, Benzodiazepines, Beta-Blockers," in Marc Hillbrand and Nathaniel J. Pallone, eds., *The Psychobiology of Aggression: Engines, Measurement, Control* (New York: The Haworth Press, 1994), pp. 203–222.
10. See, for example, L. R. Tancredi and D. N. Weistub, "Forensic Psychiatry and the Case of Chemical Castration," *International Journal of Law and Psychiatry*, Vol. 8 (1986), p. 259.
11. "Drug Policy Director Signs Historic Agreement with Great Britain," *Justinfo* (an electronic publication of the National Institute of Justice), April 25, 1995.
12. Harry Soderman and John J. O'Connell, *Modern Criminal Investigation* (New York: Funk and Wagnalls, 1945), p. 41.
13. Invented by Lambert Adolphe Jacques Quetelet (1796–1874), Belgian astronomer and statistician.
14. For a summation of Bertillon's system, see *Signaletic Instructions* (New York: Werner, 1896).
15. Robert D. Foote, "Fingerprint Identification: A Survey of Present Technology, Automated Applications, and Potential for Future Development," *Criminal Justice Monograph Series*, Vol. 5, no. 2 (Huntsville, TX: Sam Houston State University, 1974), pp. 3–4.
16. Soderman and O'Connell, *Modern Criminal Investigation*, p. 57.
17. Ibid.
18. Francis Galton, *Finger Prints* (London: Macmillan, 1892).
19. Foote, "Fingerprint Identification," p. 1.
20. U.S. Congress, Office of Technology Assessment, *Criminal Justice: New Technologies and the Constitution: A Special Report* (Washington, D.C.: U.S. Government Printing Office, 1988), p. 18. Electrooptical systems for live fingerprint scanning were developed on a proprietary basis by Fingermatric, Inc., of White Plains, New York.
21. T. F. Wilson and P. L. Woodard, U.S. Department of Justice, Bureau of Justice Statistics, *Automated Fingerprint Identification Systems—Technology and Policy Issues* (Washington, D.C.: U.S. Department of Justice, 1987), p. 5.
22. Los Angeles Police Department *Annual Report 1985–1986*, p. 26.
23. Ibid., p. 27.
24. American National Standards Institute, *American National Standard for Information Systems—Fingerprint Identification—Data Format for Information Interchange* (New York: ANSI, 1986). Originally proposed as the *Proposed American National Standard Data Format for the Interchange of Fingerprint Information* by the National Bureau of Standards (Washington, D.C.: National Bureau of Standards, April 7, 1986).

25. Dennis G. Kurre, "On-Line Exchange of Fingerprint Identification Data," *FBI Law Enforcement Bulletin* (December 1987), pp. 14–16.

26. As of this writing, Cellmark Diagnostics has applied to register the phrase "DNA Fingerprinting" as a trademark.

27. John T. Sylvester and John H. Stafford, "Judicial Acceptance of DNA Profiling," *FBI Law Enforcement Bulletin* (July 1991), p. 29.

28. Edward Connors, Thomas Lundregan, Neal Miller, and Tom McEwen, *Convicted by Juries, Exonerated by Science: Case Studies in the Use of DNA Evidence to Establish Innocence After Trial* (Washington, D.C.: National Institute of Justice, 1996).

29. See Alec J. Jeffreys, Victoria Wilson, and Swee Lay Thein, "Hypervariable 'Minisatellite' Regions in Human Nature," *Nature*, 314 (1985):67; and "Individual-Specific 'Fingerprints' of Human DNA," *Nature*, 316 (1985):76.

30. Peter Gill, Alec J. Jeffreys, and David J. Werrett, "Forensic Application of DNA Fingerprints," *Nature*, 318 (1985), p. 577. See also Craig Seton, "Life for Sex Killer Who Sent Decoy to Take Genetic Test," *The Times* (London) (January 23, 1988), p. 3. A popular account of this case, *The Blooding*, was written by crime novelist Joseph Wambaugh (New York, N.Y.: William Morrow & Co., Inc., 1989).

31. Bureau of Justice Statistics, *Forensic DNA Analysis: Issues* (Washington, D.C.: U.S. Department of Justice, Bureau of Justice Statistics, June 1991).

32. "Genetic Fingerprinting Convicts Rapist in U.K.," *The Globe and Mail*, November 14, 1987, p. A3.

33. *State* v. *Andrews*, 533 So.2d 841 (Dist. Ct. App. 1989).

34. *Spencer* v. *State*, 384 S.E.2d 775 (1989).

35. *Daubert* v. *Merrell Dow Pharmaceuticals, Inc.*, 509 U.S. 579, 113 S.Ct. 2786 (1993).

36. *Frye* v. *United States*, 54 App. D.C. 46, 47, 293 F. 1013, 1014 (1923).

37. For the application of *Daubert* to DNA technology, see Barry Sheck, "DNA and *Daubert*," *Cardozo Law Review*, 15 (1994), p.1959.

38. Violent Crime Control and Law Enforcement Act of 1994, Section 210301.

39. National Research Council, National Academy of Sciences, *DNA Technology in Forensic Science* (Washington, D.C.: National Academy Press, 1992), p. 156.

40. *Convicted by Juries, Exonerated by Science.*

41. The nonjury case involved a guilty plea from a defendant who had mental disabilities.

42. *Convicted by Juries, Exonerated by Science.*

43. Stephen Strauss, "Fingerprints Leaving Fingerprints of Their Own," Simon and Schuster NewsLink, June 20, 1997.

44. David Stout, "Man Cleared of Rape by DNA Is Implicated in a Second Case," *The New York Times*, April 9, 1996, p. B5.

45. William S. Sessions, "Criminal Justice Information Services: Gearing Up for the Future," *FBI Law Enforcement Bulletin* (February 1993), p. 2.

46. Ibid., pp. 181–188.

47. *Criminal Justice: New Technologies and the Constitution*, p. 29.

48. Ibid., p. 29.

49. Craig Stedman, "Feds to Track Sex Offenders with Database," *Computerworld*, September 2, 1996, p. 24.

50. "Saving Face," *PC Computing*, December 1988, p. 60.

51. *Omni* Magazine, February 1988, p. 12.

52. David J. Icove, "Automated Crime Profiling," *FBI Law Enforcement Bulletin* (December 1986), pp. 27–30.

53. John C. LeDoux and Henry H. McCaslin, "Computer-Based Training for the Law Enforcement Community," *FBI Law Enforcement Bulletin* (June 1988), pp. 8-13.

54. See, for example, Jeffrey S. Hormann, "Virtual Reality: The Future of Law Enforcement Training," *FBI Law Enforcement Bulletin* (July 1995), pp. 7–12.

55. See, for example, Thomas F. Rich, "The Use of Computerized Mapping Crime Control and Prevention Programs," National Institute of Justice, July 1995.

56. Matt L. Rodriguez, "The Acquisition of High Technology Systems by Law Enforcement," *FBI Law Enforcement Bulletin* (December 1988), p. 10.

57. William L. Tafoya, "Law Enforcement Beyond the Year 2000," *The Futurist* (September/October 1986), pp. 33-36.

58. Ibid.

59. See Rodriguez, "The Acquisition of High Technology Systems by Law Enforcement," pp. 11–12.

60. Brian S. Akre, "Internet-Torture," *The Associated Press* wire services, February 10, 1995.

61. Ibid.

62. Jim Schaefer and Maryanne George, "Internet User's Charges Dismissed—U.S. Criticized for Pursuing U-M Case," *Detroit Free Press* wire services, June 22, 1995.

63. Ibid.

64. Ibid.

65. Charles B. Carkeek, "Ensuring Computer Security," *FBI Law Enforcement Journal* (October 1986), p. 5.

66. James William Coleman, *The Criminal Elite: The Sociology of White Collar Crime*, 2nd ed. (New York: St. Martin's Press, 1989), p. 2.

67. Edwin H. Sutherland, "White-Collar Criminality," *American Sociological Review* (February 1940), p. 12.

68. This definition combines elements of Sutherland's original terminology with the definition of "white-collar crime" as found in the *Dictionary of Criminal Justice Data Terminology*, 2nd ed. (Washington, D.C.: Bureau of Justice Statistics, 1981). It recognizes the fact that the socioeconomic status of today's "white-collar criminals" is not nearly so high as Sutherland imagined when he coined the term.

69. "Tennis, Anyone? Ivan Boesky Does Time," *Business Week*, April 25, 1988, p. 70.

70. Frank E. Hagan and Peter J. Benekos, "The Biggest White Collar Crime in History: The Great Savings and Loan Scandal," paper presented at the annual meeting of the American Society of Criminology, Baltimore, Maryland, 1990.

71. Ibid., p. 4.

72. "Silverado Suit Tentatively Settled for $49.5 Million," *The Fayetteville Observer-Times* (North Carolina), May 30, 1991, p. 4A.

73. "Dixon Faces Sentence Today," *USA Today*, April 2, 1991, pp. B1–2.

74. Ibid.

75. James Cox, "Gold Dust or Bust," *USA Today*, April 17, 1997, p. 1B.

76. Edwin H. Sutherland, "Is White Collar Crime Crime?" *American Sociological Review* (April 1945), pp. 132–139.

77. *White Collar Crime*, a Bureau of Justice Statistics *Special Report* (Washington, D.C.: Bureau of Justice Statistics, 1987).

78. Ibid., p. 1.

79. Stephen Pizzo, Mary Fricker, and Paul Muolo, *Inside Job: The Looting of America's Savings and Loans* (New York: McGraw-Hill, 1989), p. 284.

80. See Gilbert Geis and Robert F. Meier, eds., *White Collar Crime*, 2nd ed. (New York: The Free Press, 1977).

81. "The Venture Survey: Crime and Your Business," *Venture* Magazine, February 1986, p. 26.

82. Ibid.

83. Ibid.

84. Gary S. Green, *Occupational Crime* (Chicago: Nelson-Hall, 1990).

85. Ibid., p. 16.

86. Ibid.

87. James William Coleman, *The Criminal Elite: The Sociology of White Collar Crime* (New York: St. Martin's Press, 1989), p. 9.

88. Ibid.

89. William J. Chambliss, *Exploring Criminology* (New York: Macmillan, 1988), p. 64.

90. See, for example, M. David Ermann and Richard J. Lundman, eds., *Corporate and Government Deviance: Problems of Organizational Behavior in Contemporary Society*, 3rd ed. (New York: Oxford University Press, 1987); and Stuart L. Hills, ed., *Corporate Violence: Injury and Death for Profit* (Totowa, NJ: Roman and Littlefield, 1987).

91. Gilbert Geis, "The Heavy Electrical Equipment Antitrust Cases of 1961," in Gilbert Geis and Robert Meier, eds., *White Collar Crime*, rev. ed. (New York: The Free Press, 1977), p. 123.

92. Coleman, *The Criminal Elite*, p. 34.

93. "Ford Pinto Scored in Coast Magazine on Peril from Fires," *The New York Times*, August 11, 1977.

94. Coleman, *The Criminal Elite*, p. 41.

95. As cited in Gwynne Nettler, *Criminology Lessons* (Cincinnati, OH: Anderson, 1989), p. 116.

96. "After Drexel: Are Raiders Next Target?" *USA Today*, December 23, 1988, p. B1.

97. Ibid.

98. Tom Bradford, "$12 Million High-Tech Heist One of Largest Ever," *USA Today*, May 19, 1995, p. 3A.

99. "Are you Vulnerable to Cybercrime?" *USA Today*, February 20, 1995, p. 3B.

100. Software Publishers Association and the Business Software Alliance, "Global Study Shows Increase In Software Units Pirated," SPA World Wide Web site http://www.spa.org/piracy/releases/96pir.htm (Web posted May 7, 1997).

101. *Hancock* v. *State*, 402 S.W.2d 906 (Tex. Crim. Appl. 1966).

102. Stanley S. Arkin et al., *Prevention and Prosecution of Computer and High Technology Crime* (New York: Matthew Bender, 1988), 3.05.

103. The Computer Fraud and Abuse Act. (Public Law no. 98–473, Title II, Section 2102 (a), October 12, 1984.) The Computer Fraud and Abuse Act was substantially revised in 1986 and again in 1988.

104. William J. Hughes, "Congress vs. Computer Crime," *Information Executive*, Vol. 1, no. 1 (Fall 1988), pp. 30–32.

105. Because of significant modifications introduced into the legislation in 1986, the law is often referred to as the "Computer Fraud and Abuse Act of 1986."

106. Arkin, *Prevention and Prosecution of Computer and High Technology Crime*, 3.05 [B].

107. 18 U.S.C. 2311.

108. 18 U.S.C. 641.

109. 18 U.S.C. 1905.

110. 17 U.S.C. 101, 117.

111. 18 U.S.C. 1341, 1343, and 1344.

112. N.Y. Penal Law, sections 156.30 and 156.35.

113. For a recent list of suggested computer crime categories, see David L. Carter,

"Computer Crime Categories: How Techno-Criminals Operate," *FBI Law Enforcement Journal*, July 1995, pp. 21–26.

114. For information on specific software programs used for data encryption, see Ted Chiang, "Data Encryption: Computer Security with Data Encryption Programs," *Profiles* (December 1987), pp. 71–74.

115. "Invasion of the Data Snatchers!" *Time*, September 26, 1988, pp. 62–67.

116. "Virus Infects NASA, Defense, University Computer Systems," *The Fayetteville Observer-Times* (North Carolina), November 4, 1988, p. 19A.

117. *Raleigh News and Observer*, April 27, 1990.

118. "Invasion of the Data Snatchers!"

119. Hughes, "Congress vs. Computer Crime," p. 32.

120. "Crime in the Computer Age," *MacLean's Magazine*, Vol. 101, no. 5 (January 25, 1988), pp. 28–30.

121. Ibid.

122. Ibid., p. 29.

123. August Bequai, *Computer Crime* (Lexington, MA: Lexington Books, 1978), p. 4.

124. Ibid.

125. Bill D. Colvin, "Computer Crime Investigations: A New Training Field," *FBI Law Enforcement Bulletin* (July 1979).

126. Bruce Frankel, "Sheik Guilty in Terror Plot," *USA Today*, October 2, 1995, p. 1A. Sheik Abdel-Rahman and codefendant El Sayyid Nosair were both sentenced to life in prison. Other defendants received sentences of between 25 and 57 years in prison. See Sascha Brodsky, "Terror Verdicts Denounced," United Press International wire services, January 17, 1996.

127. "Wouldn't Be Hard to Hit U.S. Target," *USA Today*, June 25–27, 1993, p. 1A.

128. Ibid.

129. Ibid.

130. Technological devices described in this section depend upon G. Gordon Liddy, "Rules of the Game," *Omni* Magazine (January 1989), pp. 43–47, 78–80.

131. The death penalty was imposed for the first-degree murders of eight federal law-enforcement agents who were at work in the Murrah building at the time of the bombing. While the killings violated Oklahoma law, only the killings of the federal agents fell under federal law, which makes such murders capital offenses.

132. Michael E. Wiggins, "Rationale and Justification for Right-Wing Terrorism: A Politico-Social Analysis of the Turner Diaries," paper presented at the annual meeting of the American Society of Criminology, Atlanta, Georgia, October 1986.

133. Gwynn Nettler, *Killing One Another* (Cincinnati, OH: Anderson, 1982).

134. The actual language of the bill sets a standard for metal detectors through the use of a "security exemplar" made of 3.7 ounces of stainless steel in the shape of a handgun. Weapons made of other substances might still pass the test provided that they could be detected by metal detectors adjusted to that level of sensitivity. See "Bill Is Signed Barring Sale or Manufacture of Plastic Guns," *Criminal Justice Newsletter*, Vol. 19, no. 23 (December 1, 1988), pp. 4–5.

135. See Robert Burns, "Clinton—Terrorism," The Associated Press wire services northern edition, April 20, 1996.

136. Nettler, *Killing One Another*, p. 253.

137. *Criminal Justice: New Technologies and the Constitution*, p. 51.

138. Randall Mikkelsen, "U.S. 'Cybersmut' Suit Gives Glimpse of Internet Future," Reuters wire service, March 21, 1996.

139. Randall Mikkelsen, "U.S. Court Blocks New Internet-Indecency Law," Reuters wire service, June 12, 1996.

140. *Reno* v. *ACLU* (1997), No. 96-511. Decided June 26, 1997.

141. The five-day waiting period will be phased out after a planned national instant background checking system becomes fully operational.

142. *Pritz* v. *U.S.*, No. 95-1478. Decided June 27, 1997.

143. *Mack* v. *U.S.*, No. 95-1503. Decided June 27, 1997.

144. *Pinston* v. *U.S.*, declined for review on December 12, 1994.

145. Mark Powell, "Orwellian Snooping: Infrared Sees Through Crime, and Your Bedroom Walls," *USA Today*, April 2, 1996, p. 13A.

146. *Criminal Justice: New Technologies and the Constitution*, p. 20.

147. Ibid., p. 47.

148. *United States* v. *Mackey*, 387 F.Sup 1121, 1125 (D. Nev. 1975).

149. See Louis F. Solimine, "Safeguarding the Accuracy of FBI Records: A Review of *Menard* v. *Saxbe* and *Tarlton* v. *Saxbe*," *University of Cincinnati Law Review*, Vol. 44 (1975), pp. 325, 327.

150. *Criminal Justice: New Technologies and the Constitution*, p. 47.

151. William S. Sessions, "The FBI and the Challenge of the 21st Century," *FBI Law Enforcement Bulletin*, Vol. 58, no. 1 (January 1989), pp. 1–6.

152. The Bail Reform Act of 1996 allowed magistrates to consider elements of the offender's background, such as family ties and prior offenses, in setting bail. Factors

cited by the act were based in part on social scientific findings at the time.

153. See U.S. Sentencing Commission, *Sentencing Guidelines and Policy Statements*, submitted to Congress April 13, 1987, with amendments submitted April 13, 1987.

154. *Estelle* v. *Smith*, 451 U.S. 454 (1981).

155. *Schmerber* v. *California*, 384 U.S. 757, 86 S.Ct. 1826 (1966).

156. *Rochin* v. *California*, 342 U.S. 165 (1952).

157. For a discussion of such techniques, see Patrick Moynihan, "Social Science and the Courts," *The Public Interest*, No. 54 (Winter 1979), pp. 12–31.

158. Arnold Urken and Stephen Traflet, "Optimal Jury Design," *Jurimetrics* (Journal of the American Bar Association), Vol. 24 (Spring 1984), p. 218.

159. "Stalkers Get Electronic Guard," *The Fayetteville Observer-Times* (North Carolina), September 20, 1992, p. 16A.

160. *Criminal Justice Newsletter* (June 16, 1986), p. 6.

161. *Criminal Justice: New Technologies and the Constitution*, p. 43.

162. *Holt* v. *Sarver*, 309 F.Sup 362 (E.D. Ark. 1970).

163. *Bearden* v. *Georgia*, 461 U.S. 660 (1983).

Glossary

The 17 chapters of *Criminal Justice Today* contain hundreds of terms commonly used in the field of criminal justice. This glossary contains many more. All concepts, wherever they appear in the book, are explained, whenever possible, according to definitions provided by the Bureau of Justice Statistics under a 1979 mandate of the Justice System Improvement Act. That mandate was to create a consistent terminology set for use by criminal justice students, planners, and practitioners. It found its most complete expression in the *Dictionary of Criminal Justice Data Terminology*,[1] the second edition of which provides many of our definitions. Others (especially those in Chapter 2) are derived from the FBI's Uniform Crime Reporting Program and are taken from the *Uniform Crime Reporting Handbook*.[2]

Standardization is becoming increasingly important because of the fact that American criminal justice agencies, justice practitioners, and involved citizens now routinely communicate over vast distances about the criminal justice system itself. For communications to be meaningful, a shared terminology is necessary. Standardization, however desirable, is not easy to achieve. In the words of the Bureau of Justice Statistics, "It is not possible to construct a single national standard criminal justice data terminology where every term always means the same thing in all of its appearances. However, it is possible and necessary to standardize the language that represents basic categorical distinctions."[3] Although this glossary should be especially valuable to the student who will one day work in the criminal justice system, it should also prove beneficial to anyone seeking a greater insight into that system.

1983 lawsuits   Civil suits brought under Title 42, Section 1983 of the United States Code, against anyone denying others of their constitutional rights to life, liberty, or property without due process of law.

abused child   A child who has been physically, sexually, or mentally abused. Most states also consider a child who is forced into delinquent activity by a parent or guardian to be abused.

acquittal   The judgment of a court, based on a verdict of a jury or a judicial officer, that the defendant is not guilty of the offense(s) for which he or she has been tried.

actus reus   An act in violation of the law; a guilty act.

adjudication   The process by which a court arrives at a decision regarding a case; also, the resultant decision.

adjudicatory hearing   In juvenile justice usage, the fact-finding process wherein the juvenile court determines whether or not there is sufficient evidence to sustain the allegations in a petition.

ADMAX   Administrative maximum; the term used by the federal government to denote ultra-high-security prisons.

admission (corrections)   In correctional usage, the entry of an offender into the legal jurisdiction of a corrections agency and/or physical custody of a correctional facility.

adult In criminal justice usage, a person who is within the original jurisdiction of a criminal, rather than a juvenile, court because his or her age at the time of an alleged criminal act was above a statutorily specified limit.

adversarial system The two-sided structure under which American criminal trial courts operate and that pits the prosecution against the defense. In theory, justice is done when the most effective adversary is able to convince the judge or jury that their perspective on the case is the correct one.

aftercare In juvenile justice usage, the status or program membership of a juvenile who has been committed to a treatment or confinement facility, conditionally released from the facility, and placed in a supervisory and/or treatment program.

aggravated assault Unlawful intentional causing of serious bodily injury with or without a deadly weapon, or unlawful intentional attempting or threatening of serious bodily injury or death with a deadly or dangerous weapon.

aggravating circumstances Circumstances relating to the commission of a crime which cause its gravity to be greater than that of the average instance of the given type of offense.

alias Any name used for an official purpose that is different from a person's legal name.

alibi A statement or contention by an individual charged with a crime that he or she was so distant when the crime was committed, or so engaged in other provable activities, that participation in commission of that crime was impossible.

alter ego rule A rule of law that, in some jurisdictions, holds that a person can only defend a third party under circumstances and only to the degree that the third party could act on their own behalf.

alternative sanctions See **intermediate sanctions**.

appeal Generally, the request that a court with appellate jurisdiction review the judgment, decision, or order of a lower court and set it aside (reverse it) or

modify it; also, the judicial proceedings or steps in judicial proceedings resulting from such a request.

appearance (court) The act of coming into a court and submitting to the authority of that court.

appellant The person who contests the correctness of a court order, judgment, or other decision and who seeks review and relief in a court having appellate jurisdiction, or the person in whose behalf this is done.

appellate court A court of which the primary function is to review the judgments of other courts and of administrative agencies.

appellate jurisdiction The lawful authority of a court to review a decision made by a lower court.

arraignment I. Strictly, the hearing before a court having jurisdiction in a criminal case, in which the identity of the defendant is established, the defendant is informed of the charge(s) and of his or her rights, and the defendant is required to enter a plea. II. In some usages, any appearance in court prior to trial in criminal proceedings.

arrest Taking an adult or juvenile into physical custody by authority of law, for the purpose of charging the person with a criminal offense or a delinquent act or status offense, terminating with the recording of a specific offense.

arrest (UCR) In *Uniform Crime Reports* terminology, all separate instances where a person is taken into physical custody or notified or cited by a law enforcement officer or agency, except those relating to minor traffic violations.

arrest rate The number of arrests reported for each unit of population.

arrest warrant A document issued by a judicial officer which directs a law enforcement officer to arrest an identified person who has been accused of a specific offense.

arson The intentional damaging or destruction or attempted damaging or destruction, by means of fire or explosion of the property of another without the consent of the owner, or of one's own property or that of another with intent to defraud.

arson (UCR) In *Uniform Crime Reports* terminology, the burning or attempted burning of property with or without intent to defraud.

Ashurst-Sumners Act 1935 federal legislation which effectively ended the industrial prison era by restricting interstate commerce in prison-made goods.

assault Unlawful intentional inflicting, or attempted or threatened inflicting, of injury upon the person of another.

assault on a law enforcement officer A simple or aggravated assault, where the victim is a law enforcement officer engaged in the performance of his or her duties.

atavism A condition characterized by the existence of features thought to be common in earlier stages of human evolution.

attendant circumstances The facts surrounding an event.

attorney A person trained in the law, admitted to practice before the bar of a given jurisdiction, and authorized to advise, represent, and act for other persons in legal proceedings.

Auburn style A form of imprisonment developed in New York state around 1820 that depended upon mass prisons, where prisoners were held in congregate fashion. This style of imprisonment was a primary competitor with the Pennsylvania style.

backlog (court) The number of cases awaiting disposition in a court which exceed the court's capacity for disposing of them within the period of time considered appropriate.

bail I. To effect the release of an accused person from custody, in return for a promise that he or she will appear at a place and time specified and submit to the jurisdiction and judgment of the court, guaranteed by a pledge to pay to the court a specified sum of money or property if the person does not appear. II. The money or property pledged to the court or actually deposited with the court to effect the release of a person from legal custody.

bail bond A document guaranteeing the appearance of the defendant in court as required and recording the pledge of money or property to be paid to the court if he or she does not appear, which is signed by the person to be released and any other persons acting in his or her behalf.

bail bondsman A person, usually licensed, whose business it is to effect release on bail for persons charged with offenses and held in custody, by pledging to pay a sum of money if a defendant fails to appear in court as required.

bailiff The court officer whose duties are to keep order in the courtroom and to maintain physical custody of the jury.

bail revocation The court decision withdrawing the status of release on bail previously conferred upon a defendant.

balancing test A principle developed by the courts and applied to the corrections arena by the 1974 case of *Pell* v. *Procunier*, which attempts to weigh the rights of an individual as guaranteed by the Constitution, against the authority of states to make laws or otherwise restrict a person's freedom in order to protect its interests and its citizens.

ballistics The analysis of firearms, ammunition, projectiles, bombs, and explosions.

Battered Woman's Syndrome (BWS) A series of common characteristics that appear in women who are abused physically and psychologically over an extended period of time by the dominant male figure in their lives; a pattern of psychological symptoms that develop after somebody has lived in a battering relationship; or a pattern of responses and perceptions presumed to be characteristic of women who have been subjected to continuous physical abuse by their mates.[4]

behavioral conditioning A psychological principle which holds that the frequency of any behavior can be increased or decreased through reward, punishment, and/or association with other stimuli.

bench warrant A document issued by a court directing that a law enforcement officer bring the person named therein before the court, usually one who has failed to obey a court order or a notice to appear.

bias crimes See hate crimes.

Bill of Rights The popular name given to the first ten amendments of the U.S.

Constitution, considered especially important in the processing of criminal defendants

bind over I. To require by judicial authority that a person promise to appear for trial, appear in court as a witness, or keep the peace. II. The decision by a court of limited jurisdiction requiring that a person charged with a felony appear for trial on that charge in a court of general jurisdiction, as the result of a finding of probable cause at a preliminary hearing held in the limited jurisdiction court.

biological school A perspective on criminological thought that holds that criminal behavior has a physiological basis. Genes, foods and food additives, hormones, and inheritance are all thought to play a role in determining individual behavior. Biological thinkers highlight the underlying animalistic aspect of being human as a major determinate of behavior.

Bivens action The name given to civil suits, based upon the case of *Bivens* v. *Six Unknown Named Defendants*, brought against federal government officials for denial of the constitutional rights of others.

Bobbies The popular name given to members of Sir Robert (Bob) Peel's Metropolitan Police Force.

booking A law enforcement or correctional administrative process officially recording an entry into detention after arrest, and identifying the person, the place, time, and reason for the arrest, and the arresting authority.

broken windows thesis A perspective on crime causation which holds that physical deterioration in an area leads to increased concerns for personal safety among area residents and to higher crime rates in that area.

Bureau of Justice Statistics (BJS) A U.S. Department of Justice agency responsible for criminal justice data collection, including the annual NCVS.

burglary I. By the narrowest and oldest definition, trespassory breaking and entering of the dwelling house of another in the nighttime with the intent to commit a felony. II. Unlawful entry of any fixed structure, vehicle, or vessel used for regular residence, industry, or business, with or without force, with intent to commit a felony or larceny.

burglary (UCR) Unlawful entry of any fixed structure, vehicle, or vessel used for regular residence, industry, or business, with or without force, with intent to commit a felony, or larceny.

capacity (legal) In criminal-justice usage, the legal ability of a person to commit a criminal act; the mental and physical ability to act with purpose and to be aware of the certain, probable, or possible results of one's conduct.

capacity (prison) See **prison capacity**.

capital offense I. A criminal offense punishable by death. II. In some penal codes, an offense which may be punishable by death or by imprisonment for life.

capital punishment Another term for the death penalty. Capital punishment is the most extreme of all sentencing options.

career criminal In prosecutorial and law enforcement usage, a person having a past record of multiple arrests or convictions for serious crimes, or an unusually large number of arrests or convictions for crimes of varying degrees of seriousness.

carnal knowledge Sexual intercourse, coitus, sexual copulation. Carnal knowledge is accomplished "if there is the slightest penetration of the sexual organ of the female by the sexual organ of the male." (*State* v. *Cross*, 200 S.E.2d 27, 29.)

case law That body of judicial precedent, historically built upon legal reasoning and past interpretations of statutory laws, which serves as a guide to decision making, especially in the courts.

caseload (corrections) The total number of clients registered with a correctional agency or agent on a given date or during a specified time period, often divided into active supervisory cases and inactive cases, thus distinguishing between clients with whom contact is regular and those with whom it is not.

caseload (court) The number of cases requiring judicial action at a certain time or the number of cases acted upon in a given court during a given time period.

certiorari See **writ of *certiorari***.

change of venue The movement of a case from the jurisdiction of one court to that of another court which has the same subject matter jurisdictional authority but is in a different geographic location.

charge In criminal justice usage, an allegation that a specified person(s) has committed a specific offense, recorded in a functional document such as a record of an arrest, a complaint, information or indictment, or a judgment of conviction.

child abuse The illegal physical, emotional, or sexual mistreatment of a child by his or her parent(s) or guardian(s).

child neglect The illegal failure by a parent(s) or guardian(s) to provide proper nourishment or care to a child.

circumstantial evidence Evidence that requires interpretation, or that requires a judge or jury to reach a conclusion based upon what the evidence indicates. From the close proximity of a smoking gun to the defendant, for example, the jury might conclude that she pulled the trigger.

citation (to appear) A written order issued by a law enforcement officer directing an alleged offender to appear in a specific court at a specified time in order to answer a criminal charge, and not permitting forfeit of bail as an alternative to court appearance.

citizen's arrest The taking of a person into physical custody by a witness to a crime other than a law enforcement officer for the purpose of delivering him or her to the physical custody of a law enforcement officer or agency.

civil death The legal status of prisoners in some jurisdictions who are denied the opportunity to vote, hold public office, marry, or enter into contracts by virtue of their status as incarcerated felons. While civil death is primarily of historical interest, some jurisdictions still place limits on the contractual opportunities available to inmates.

civil law That part of the law that governs relationships between parties.

classical school A perspective on criminological thought that centered on the idea of free will and held that punishment, if it was to be an effective deterrent, had to outweigh the potential pleasure to be derived from criminal behavior. Classical thinkers, who had their roots in the intellectual enlightenment which swept Europe a few centuries ago, highlighted the role that rationality and free choice play in determining human behavior.

clearance (UCR) The event where a known occurrence of a Part I offense is followed by an arrest or other decision which indicates a solved crime at the police level of reporting.

clearance rate A traditional measure of investigative effectiveness that compares the number of crimes reported and/or discovered to the number of crimes solved through arrest or other means (such as the death of a suspect).

clemency In criminal justice usage, the name for the type of executive or legislative action where the severity of punishment of a single person or a group of persons is reduced or the punishment stopped, or a person is exempted from prosecution for certain actions.

closing argument An oral summation of a case presented to a judge, or to a judge and jury, by the prosecution or by the defense in a criminal trial.

cohort In statistics, the group of individuals having one or more statistical factors in common in a demographic study.

comes stabuli Nonuniformed mounted early law enforcement officers in medieval England. Early police forces were small and relatively unorganized, but made effective use of local resources in the formation of possees, the pursuit of offender, and the like.

commitment The action of a judicial officer ordering that a person subject to judicial proceedings be placed in a particular kind of confinement or residential facility for a specific reason authorized by law; also, the result of the action, the admission to the facility.

common law Law originating from usage and custom rather than from written statutes. The term refers to an unwritten body of judicial opinion originally developed by English courts, and which is based upon non-statutory customs, traditions, and precedents.

community-based corrections (also community corrections) A sentencing style that represents a movement away from traditional confinement options and an increased dependence upon correctional resources which are available in the community. More specifically, the use of a variety of court-ordered programmatic sanctions permitting convicted offenders to remain in the community under conditional supervision as an alternative to active prison sentences.

community corrections See community-based corrections.

community policing "A collaborative effort between the police and the community that identifies problems of crime and disorder and involves all elements of the community in the search for solutions to these problems."[5]

community service A sentencing alternative that requires offenders to spend at least part of their time working for a community agency.

comparative criminologist One who studies crime and criminal justice on a cross-national level.

compelling interest A legal concept that provides a basis for suspicionless searches (urinalysis tests of train engineers, for example) when public safety is at issue. It is the concept upon which the Supreme Court cases of *Skinner* v. *Railway Labor Executives' Association* (1988) and *National Treasury Employees Union* v. *Von Rabb* (1989) turned. In those cases the Court held that public safety may provide a sufficiently compelling interest such that an individual's right to privacy can be limited under certain circumstances.

complaint I. In general criminal-justice usage, any accusation that a person(s) has committed an offense(s), received by or originating from a law enforcement or prosecutorial agency, or received by a court. II. In judicial process usage, a formal document submitted to the court by a prosecutor, law enforcement officer, or other person, alleging that a specified person(s) has committed a specified offense(s) and requesting prosecution.

computer crime (also **cybercrime**) A popular name for crimes committed by use of a computer or crimes involving misuse or destruction of computer equipment or computerized information, sometimes specifically theft committed by means of manipulation of a computerized financial transaction system, or the use of computer services with intent to avoid payment.

computer virus A computer program which is designed to secretly invade systems and modify either the way in which they operate or alter the information they store. Viruses are destructive software which may effectively vandalize computers of all sizes.

concurrence The coexistence of an act in violation of the law and a culpable mental state.

concurrent sentence A sentence that is one of two or more sentences imposed at the same time after conviction for more than one offense and to be served at the same time, or a new sentence imposed upon a person already under sentence(s) for a previous offense(s), to be served at the same time as one or more of the previous sentences.

conditional release The release by executive decision from a federal or state correctional facility of a prisoner who has not served his or her full sentence and whose freedom is contingent upon obeying specified rules of behavior.

conditions of probation and parole The general (state-ordered) and special (court- or board-ordered) limits imposed upon an offender who is released on either probation or parole. General conditions tend to be fixed by state statute, while special conditions are mandated by the sentencing authority and take into consideration the background of the offender and circumstances surrounding the offense.

confinement In correctional terminology, physical restriction of a person to a clearly defined area from which he or she is lawfully forbidden to depart and from which departure is usually constrained by architectural barriers and/or guards or other custodians.

conflict model A perspective on the study of criminal justice that assumes that the system's subcomponents function primarily to serve their own interests. According to this theoretical framework, "justice" is more a product of conflicts among agencies within the system, than it is the result of cooperation among component agencies.

consecutive sentence A sentence that is one of two or more sentences imposed at the same time, after conviction for more than one offense, and which is served in sequence with the other sentences, or a new sentence for a new conviction, imposed upon a person already under sentence(s) for previous offense(s), which is added to a previous sentence(s), thus increasing the maximum time the offender may be confined or under supervision.

consensus model A perspective on the study of criminal justice which assumes that the system's subcomponents work together harmoniously to achieve that social product we call "justice."

constitutive criminology The study of the process by which human beings create an ideology of crime that sustains it (the notion of crime) as a concrete reality.

contempt of court Intentionally obstructing a court in the administration of justice, or acting in a way calculated to lessen its authority or dignity, or failing to obey its lawful orders.

controlled substance A specifically defined bioactive or psychoactive chemical substance which is proscribed by law.

Controlled Substances Act Title II of the Comprehensive Drug Abuse Prevention and Control Act of 1970, which establishes schedules classifying psychoactive drugs according to their degree of psychoactivity.

conviction The judgment of a court, based on the verdict of a jury or judicial officer, or on the guilty pleas or *nolo contendere* pleas of the defendant, that the defendant is guilty of the offense(s) with which he or she has been charged.

corporate crime A violation of a criminal statute either by a corporate entity or by its executives, employees or agents acting on behalf of and for the benefit of the corporation, partnership, or other form of business entity.[6]

corpus delicti The "body of crime." Facts which show that a crime has occurred.

correctional agency A federal, state, or local criminal or juvenile justice agency, under a single administrative authority of which the principal functions are the intake screening, supervision, custody, confinement, treatment, or presentencing or predisposition investigation of alleged or adjudicated adult offenders, youthful offenders, delinquents, or status offenders.

corrections A generic term that includes all government agencies, facilities, programs, procedures, personnel, and techniques concerned with the intake, custody, confinement, supervision, or treatment, or presentencing or predisposition investigation of alleged or adjudicated adult offenders, delinquents, or status offenders.

corruption Behavioral deviation from an accepted ethical standard.

Cosa Nostra Organized crime of Sicilian origin. Another word for "Mafia."

counsel (legal) See **attorney**.

count (offense) See **charge**.

court An agency or unit of the judicial branch of government authorized or established by statute or constitution, and consisting of one or more judicial officers, which has the authority to decide upon cases, controversies in law, and disputed matters of fact brought before it.

court calendar The court schedule; the list of events comprising the daily or weekly work of a court, including the assignment of the time and place for each hearing or other item of business, or the list of matters which will be taken up in a given court term.

court clerk An elected or appointed court officer responsible for maintaining the written records of the court and for supervising or performing the clerical tasks necessary for conducting judicial business; also, any employee of a court whose principal duties are to assist the court clerk in performing the clerical tasks necessary for conducting judicial business.

court disposition For statistical reporting purposes, generally, the judicial decision terminating proceedings in a case before judgment is reached, or the judgment; the data items representing the outcome of judicial proceedings and the manner in which the outcome was arrived at.

court-martial (also **courts-martial**) A military court convened by senior commanders under authority of the Uniform Code of Military Justice for the purpose of trying members of the armed forces accused of violations of the Code.

court of record A court in which a complete and permanent record of all proceedings or specified types of proceedings is kept.

court order A mandate, command, or direction issued by a judicial officer in the exercise of his or her judicial authority.

court probation A criminal court requirement that a defendant or offender fulfill specified conditions of behavior in lieu of a sentence to confinement, but without assignment to a probation agency's supervisory caseload.

court reporter A person present during judicial proceedings who records all testimony and other oral statements made during the proceedings.

credit card fraud The use or attempted use of a credit card in order to obtain goods or services with the intent to avoid payment.

crime Conduct in violation of the criminal laws of a state, the federal government, or of a local jurisdiction, for which there is no legally acceptable justification or excuse. Also, an act committed or omitted in violation of a law forbidding or commanding it for which the possible penalties for an adult upon conviction include incarceration, for which a corporation can be penalized by fine or forfeit, or for which a juvenile can be adjudged delinquent or transferred to criminal court for prosecution.

crime control model A criminal justice perspective that emphasizes the efficient arrest and conviction of criminal offenders.

Crime Index In *Uniform Crime Reports* terminology, a set of numbers indicating the volume, fluctuation, and distribution of crimes reported to local law enforcement agencies, for the United States as a whole and for its geographical subdivisions, based on counts of reported occurrences of UCR Index Crimes.

crime rate The number of index offenses reported for each unit of population.

criminal homicide The causing of the death of another person without legal justification or excuse.

criminal homicide (UCR) The name of the UCR category that includes and is limited to all offenses which cause the death of another person without justification or excuse.

criminal incident In National Crime Victimization Survey terminology, a criminal event involving one or more victims and one or more offenders.

criminalist The term applied to police crime scene analysts and laboratory personnel versed in criminalistics.

criminalistics The use of technology in the service of criminal investigation; the application of scientific techniques to the detection and evaluation of criminal evidence.

criminal justice In its broadest sense, those aspects of social justice which concern violations of the criminal law. In the strictest sense, the criminal (penal) law, the law of criminal procedure, and that array of procedures and activities having to do with the enforcement of this body of law.

criminal justice system The aggregate of all operating and administrative or technical support agencies that perform criminal justice functions. The basic divisions of the operational aspect of criminal justice are law enforcement, courts, and corrections.

criminal law That branch of modern law that concerns itself with offenses committed against society, members thereof, their property, and the social order. Another term for criminal law is **penal law**.

criminal negligence Behavior in which a person fails to reasonably perceive substantial and unjustifiable risks of dangerous consequences.

criminal proceedings The regular and orderly steps, as directed or authorized by statute or a court of law, taken to determine whether an adult accused of a crime is guilty or not guilty.

criminology The scientific study of crime causation, prevention, and the rehabilitation and punishment of offenders.

cruel and unusual punishment Punishment involving torture or a lingering death, or the infliction of unnecessary and wanton pain.

culpability I. Blameworthiness; responsibility in some sense for an event or situation deserving of moral blame. II. In Model Penal Code (MPC) usage, a state of mind on the part of one who is committing an act, which makes him or her potentially subject to prosecution for that act.

curtilage A legal term which describes the area surrounding a residence which can reasonably be said to be a part of the residence for Fourth Amendment purposes.

custody Legal or physical control of a person or thing; legal, supervisory, or physical responsibility for a person or thing.

cybercrime Crime committed with the use of computers. Another term for **computer crime.**

danger laws Those intended to prevent the pretrial release of criminal defendants judged to represent a danger to others in the community.

dangerousness The likelihood that a given individual will later harm society or others. Dangerousness is often measured in terms of **recidivism,** or as the likelihood of additional crime commission within a five-year period following arrest or release from confinement.

data encryption Methods used to encode computerized information.

date rape Unlawful forced sexual intercourse with a female against her will which occurs within the context of a dating relationship.

deadly force Force likely to cause death or great bodily harm.

deadly weapon An instrument designed to inflict serious bodily injury or death, or capable of being used for such a purpose.

deconstructionist theories Emerging approaches which challenge existing criminological perspectives to debunk them and which work toward replacing them with concepts more applicable to the postmodern era.

decriminalization The redefinition of certain previously criminal behaviors into regulated activities, which become "ticketable" rather than "arrestable."

defendant In criminal justice usage, a person formally accused of an offense(s) by the filing in court of a charging document.

defense counsel (also **defense attorney**) A licensed trial lawyer, hired or appointed to conduct the legal defense of an individual accused of a crime and to represent him or her before a court of law.

defenses (to a criminal charge) Evidence and arguments offered by a defendant and his or her attorney(s) to show why that person should not be held liable for a criminal charge.

defensible space theory The belief that an area's physical features may be modified and structured so as to reduce crime rates in that area and to lower the fear of victimization which area residents experience.

delinquency In the broadest usage, juvenile actions or conduct in violation of criminal law, juvenile status offenses, and other juvenile misbehavior.

delinquent A juvenile who has been adjudged by a judicial officer of a juvenile court to have committed a delinquent act.

delinquent act An act committed by a juvenile for which an adult could be prosecuted in a criminal court, but for which a juvenile can be adjudicated in a juvenile court or prosecuted in a court having criminal jurisdiction if the juvenile court transfers jurisdiction. Generally, a "felony" or "misdemeanor"-level offense in states employing those terms.

delinquent child A child who has engaged in activity that would be considered a crime if the child were an adult. The term *delinquent* is applied to such a child in order to avoid the stigma that comes from application of the term *criminal.*

dependent A juvenile over whom a juvenile court has assumed jurisdiction and legal control because his or her care by parent, guardian, or custodian has not met a legal standard of proper care.

dependent child A child who has no parents or whose parents are unable to care for him or her.

design capacity (or **bed capacity**) The number of inmates which a correctional facility was originally designed to house, or currently has the capacity to house as a result of later, planned modifications, exclusive of extraordinary arrangements to accommodate overcrowded conditions.

detainee Usually, a person held in local, very-short-term confinement while awaiting consideration for pretrial release or first appearance for arraignment.

detention The legally authorized confinement of a person subject to criminal or juvenile court proceedings, until the point of commitment to a correctional facility or until release.

detention hearing In juvenile justice usage, a hearing by a judicial officer of a juvenile court to determine whether a juvenile is to be detained, continue to be detained, or be released, while juvenile proceedings in the case are pending.

determinate sentencing (also called **fixed sentencing**) A model of criminal punishment in which an offender is given a fixed term that may be reduced by good time or earned time. Under the model, for example, all offenders convicted of the same degree of burglary would be sentenced to the same length of time behind bars.

deterrence A goal of criminal sentencing that seeks to prevent others from committing crimes similar to the one for which an offender is being sentenced.

deviance (also **deviant behavior**) A violation of social norms defining appropriate or proper behavior under a particular set of circumstances. Deviance often includes acts which are criminal.

diminished capacity (also **diminished responsibility**) A defense based upon claims of a mental condition which may be insufficient to exonerate a defendant of guilt, but that may be relevant to specific mental elements of certain crimes or degrees of crime.

directed patrol A police management strategy designed to increase the productivity of patrol officers through the application of scientific analysis and evaluation to patrol techniques.

direct evidence Evidence that, if believed, directly proves a fact. Eyewitness testimony (and, more recently, videotaped documentation) account for the majority of all direct evidence heard in the criminal courtroom.

direct supervision jails (also called **podular/direct** and **new generation jails**) Temporary confinement facilities that eliminate many of the traditional barriers between inmates and correctional staff. Physical barriers in direct supervision jails are far less common than in traditional jails, allowing staff members the opportunity for greater interaction with, and control over, residents.

discharge In criminal justice usage, to release from confinement or supervision or to release from a legal status imposing an obligation upon the subject person.

discretion The opportunity that individual law enforcement officers have for the exercise of choice in their daily activities. The decision whether to effect an arrest or release a suspect is a primary example of discretion in law enforcement activity.

disposition In criminal justice usage, the action by a criminal or juvenile justice agency which signifies that a portion of the justice process is complete and jurisdiction is terminated or transferred to another agency, or which signifies that a decision has been reached on one aspect of a case and a different aspect comes under consideration, requiring a different kind of decision.

dispositionary hearing A hearing in juvenile court, conducted after an adjudicatory hearing and subsequent receipt of the report of any predisposition investigation, to determine the most appropriate form of custody and/or treatment for a juvenile who has been adjudged a delinquent, a status offender, or a dependent.

dispute resolution centers Informal hearing infrastructures designed to mediate interpersonal disputes without need for the more formal arrangements of criminal trial courts.

district attorney See **prosecutor**.

diversion I. The official suspension of criminal or juvenile proceedings against an alleged offender at any point after a recorded justice system intake but before the entering of a judgment and referral of that person to a treatment or care program administered by a nonjustice or private agency; or II. no referral.

DNA profiling The use of biological residue found at the scene of a crime for genetic comparisons in aiding the identification of criminal suspects.

docket See **court calendar.**

double jeopardy A common law and constitutional prohibition against a second trial for the same offense.

drug Any chemical substance defined by social convention as bio- or psychoactive.

drug abuse Illicit drug use that results in social, economic, psychological, or legal problems for the user.[7]

drug czar The head of the Office of National Drug Control Policy (ONDCP). A federal cabinet-level position that was originally created during the years of the Reagan presidency to organize federal drug fighting efforts.

drug law violation The unlawful sale, purchase, distribution, manufacture, cultivation, transport, possession, or use of a controlled or prohibited drug, or the attempt to commit these acts.

due process of law A right guaranteed by the Fifth, Sixth, and Fourteenth Amendments of the U.S. Constitution, and generally understood, in legal contexts, to mean the due course of legal proceedings according to the rules and forms which have been established for the protection of private rights.

Due process model A criminal justice perspective that emphasizes individual rights at all stages of justice system processing.

ECPA An acronym for the Electronic Communications Privacy Act.

element of a crime (1) Any conduct, circumstance, condition, or state of mind which in combination with other conduct, circumstances, conditions, or states of mind constitutes an unlawful act; (2) the basic components of crime; (3) in a specific crime, the essential features of that crime as specified by law or statute.

embezzlement The misappropriation, or illegal disposal, of legally entrusted property by the person(s) to whom it was entrusted, with intent to defraud the legal owner or intended beneficiary.

emergency searches Those searches conducted by the police without a warrant that are justified on the basis of some immediate and overriding need, such as public safety, the likely escape of a dangerous suspect, or the removal or destruction of evidence.

entrapment An improper or illegal inducement to crime by agents of enforcement. Also, a defense that may be raised when such inducements occur.

equity A sentencing principle, based upon concerns with social equality, which holds that similar crimes should be punished with the same degree of severity, regardless of the social or personal characteristics of offenders.

espionage The "gathering, transmitting or losing"[8] of information related to the national defense in such a manner that the information becomes available to enemies of the United States and may be used to their advantage.

ethnocentrism The phenomenon of culture-centeredness, by which one uses one's own culture as a benchmark against which to judge all other patterns of behavior.

evidence Anything useful to a judge or jury in deciding the facts of a case. Evidence may take the form of witness testimony, written documents, videotapes, magnetic media, photographs, physical objects, and so on.

exclusionary rule The understanding, based on Supreme Court precedent, that incriminating information must be seized according to constitutional specifications of due process, or it will not be allowed as evidence in criminal trials.

excuses A category of legal defenses in which the defendant claims that some personal condition or circumstance at the time of the act was such that he or she should not be held accountable under the criminal law.

expert systems Computer hardware and software which attempt to duplicate the decision-making processes used by skilled investigators in the analysis of evidence and in the recognition of patterns which such evidence might represent.

expert witness A person who has special knowledge recognized by the court as relevant to the determination of guilt or innocence. Expert witnesses may express opinions or draw conclusions in their testimony, unlike lay witnesses.

ex post facto Latin for "after the fact." The Constitution prohibits the enactment of *ex post facto* laws, that make acts punishable as crimes which were committed before the laws in question were passed.

extradition The surrender by one state to another of an individual accused or convicted of an offense in the second state.

federal court system The three-tiered structure of federal courts, involving U.S. district courts, U.S. courts of appeal, and the U.S. Supreme Court.

federal interest computers Those that (1) are the property of the federal government, (2) belong to financial institutions, or (3) are located in a state other than the one in which the criminal perpetrator is operating.

felony A criminal offense punishable by death or by incarceration in a prison facility.

feminist criminology A developing intellectual approach which emphasizes gender issues in the subject matter of criminology.

filing The initiation of a criminal case in a court by formal submission to the court of a charging document, alleging that one or more named persons have committed one or more specified criminal offenses.

fine The penalty imposed upon a convicted person by a court, requiring that he or she pay a specified sum of money to the court.

first appearance (also **initial appearance**) An appearance before a magistrate which entails the process whereby the legality of a defendant's arrest is initially assessed, and he or she is informed of the charges on which he or she is being held. At this stage in the criminal-justice process, bail may be set or pretrial release arranged.

fleeting targets exception An exception to the exclusionary rule that permits law enforcement officers to search a motor vehicle based upon probable cause but without a warrant. The fleeting targets exception is predicated upon the fact that vehicles can quickly leave the jurisdiction of a law enforcement agency.

forcible rape (UCR) The carnal knowledge of a female forcibly and against her will. See, also **carnal knowledge**.

forensic anthropology The application of anthropological principles and techniques in the service of criminal investigation.

forfeiture (also **asset forfeiture**) The authorized seizure of money, negotiable instruments, securities, or other things of value. In federal antidrug laws, the authorization of judicial representatives to seize all monies, negotiable instruments, securities, or other things of value furnished or intended to be furnished by any person in exchange for a controlled substance, and all proceeds traceable to such an exchange.

forgery The creation or alteration of a written or printed document, which, if validly executed would constitute a record of a legally binding transaction, with the intent to defraud by affirming it to be the act of an unknowing second person; also the creation of an art object with intent to misrepresent the identity of the creator.

fraud offense The crime type comprising offenses sharing the elements of practice of deceit or intentional misrepresentation of fact, with the intent of unlawfully depriving a person of his or her property or legal rights.

frivolous suit A lawsuit with no foundation in fact. Frivolous suits are generally brought by lawyers and plaintiffs for reasons of publicity, politics, or other nonlaw-related issues and may result in fines against plaintiffs and their counsel.

Fruit of the Poisoned Tree Doctrine A legal principle that excludes from introduction at trial any evidence eventually developed as a result of an originally illegal search or seizure.

general deterrence A goal of criminal sentencing which seeks to prevent others from committing crimes similar to the one for which a particular offender is being sentenced by making an example of the person sentenced.

good faith A possible legal basis for an exception to the exclusionary rule. Law enforcement officers who conduct a search, or seize evidence, on the basis of good faith (that is, where they believe they are operating according to the dictates of the law) and who later discover that a mistake was made (perhaps in the format of the application for a search warrant) may still use evidence seized as the result of such activities in court.

good time In correctional usage, the amount of time deducted from time to be served in prison on a given sentence(s) and/or under correctional agency jurisdiction, at some point after a prisoner's admission to prison, contingent upon good behavior and/or awarded automatically by application of a statute or regulation.

grand jury A body of persons who have been selected according to law and sworn to hear the evidence against accused persons and determine whether there is sufficient evidence to bring those persons to trial, to investigate criminal activity generally, or to investigate the conduct of public agencies and officials.

grievance procedure Formalized arrangements, usually involving a neutral hearing board, whereby institutionalized individuals have the opportunity to register complaints about the conditions of their confinement.

Guilty But Mentally Ill (GBMI) Equivalent to a finding of guilty, a GBMI verdict establishes that the defendant, although mentally ill, was in sufficient possession of his faculties to be morally blameworthy for his acts.

guilty plea A defendant's formal answer in court to the charge(s) contained in a complaint, information, or indictment, claiming that he or she did commit the offense(s) listed.

guilty verdict See **verdict**.

habeas corpus See **writ of** *habeas corpus*.

habitual offender A person sentenced under the provisions of a statute declaring that persons convicted of a given offense, and shown to have previously been convicted of another specified offense(s), shall receive a more severe penalty than that for the current offense alone.

hackers Computer hobbyists or professionals, generally with advanced programming skills. Today, the term *hacker* has taken on a sinister connotation and includes those hobbyists who are bent on illegally accessing the computers of others or who attempt to demonstrate their technological prowess through computerized acts of vandalism.

hands-off doctrine An historical policy of nonintervention with regard to prison management that American courts tended to follow until the late 1960s. For the past 20 years the doctrine has languished as judicial intervention in prison administration has dramatically increased, although there is now growing evidence of a return to a new hands-off doctrine.

Harrison Act The first major piece of federal antidrug legislation, passed in 1914.

hate crimes Criminal offenses in which the defendant's conduct was motivated by hatred, bias, or prejudice, based on the actual or perceived race, color, religion, national origin, ethnicity, gender, or sexual orientation of another individual or group of individuals.

hearing A proceeding in which arguments, witnesses, or evidence are heard by a judicial officer or administrative body.

hearsay Something that is not based upon the personal knowledge of a witness. Witnesses who testify, for example, about something they have heard, are offering hearsay by repeating information about a matter of which they have no direct knowledge.

hearsay rule The long-standing American courtroom precedent that hearsay cannot be used in court. Rather than accepting testimony based upon hearsay, the American trial process asks that the person who was the original source of the hearsay information be brought into court to be questioned and cross-examined. Exceptions to the hearsay rule may occur when the person with direct knowledge is dead or is otherwise unable to testify.

hierarchy rule A standard UCR scoring practice in which only the most serious offense is counted in a multiple-offense situation.

high-technology crime Violations of the criminal law whose commission depends upon, makes use of, and often targets, sophisticated and advanced technology. See also **cybercrime** and **computer crime**.

home confinement (also **house arrest**) Individuals ordered confined in their homes are sometimes monitored electronically to be sure they do not leave during the hours of confinement (absence from the home during working hours is often permitted).

homicide See **criminal homicide**.

***Hudud* crimes** Serious violations of Islamic law regarded as offenses against God. *Hudud* crimes include such behavior as theft, adultery, sodomy, drinking alcohol, and robbery.

hung jury A jury that after long deliberation is so irreconcilably divided in opinion that it is unable to reach any verdict.

hypothesis I. An explanation that accounts for a set of facts and that can be tested by further investigation. II. [S]omething that is taken to be true for the purpose of argument or investigation.[9]

illegally seized evidence Evidence seized in opposition to the principles of due process as described by the Bill of Rights. Most illegally seized evidence is the result of police searches conducted without a proper warrant or of improperly conducted interrogations.

illegal search and seizure An act in violation of the Fourth Amendment of the U.S. Constitution: "The right of people to be secure in their persons, houses, papers and effects, against unreasonable searches and seizures, shall not be violated, and no warrants shall issue but upon probable cause, supported by oath or affirmation, and particularly describing the place to be searched and the persons or things to be seized."

incapacitation The use of imprisonment or other means to reduce the likelihood that an offender will be capable of committing future offenses.

inchoate offense One not yet completed. Also, an offense that consists of an action or conduct that is a step toward the intended commission of another offense.

incident-based reporting A less restrictive and more expansive method of collecting crime data (as opposed to summary reporting) in which all the analytical elements associated with an offense or arrest are compiled by a central collection agency on an incident by incident basis.

included offense An offense that is made up of elements that are a subset of the elements of another offense having a greater statutory penalty, and the occurrence of which is established by the same evidence or by some portion of the evidence that has been offered to establish the occurrence of the greater offense.

incompetent to stand trial In criminal proceedings, the finding by a court that a defendant is mentally incapable of understanding the nature of the charges and proceedings against him or her, of consulting with an attorney, and of aiding in his or her own defense.

indeterminate sentence A type of sentence to imprisonment where the commitment, instead of being for a specified single time quantity, such as three years, is for a range of time, such as two to five years or five years maximum and zero minimum.

indeterminate sentencing A model of criminal punishment which encourages rehabilitation via the use of general and relatively unspecific sentences (such as a term of imprisonment of "from one to ten years").

Index crimes See **Crime Index**.

indictment A formal, written accusation submitted to the court by a grand jury, alleging that a specified person(s) has committed a specified offense(s), usually a felony.

individual rights Those rights guaranteed to all members of American society by the U.S. Constitution (especially as found in the first ten amendments to the Constitution, known as the Bill of Rights). These rights are especially important to criminal defendants facing formal processing by the criminal justice system.

individual rights advocate   One who seeks to protect personal freedoms within the process of criminal justice.

industrial prisons   Those which flourished during the industrial prison era, and whose intent it was to capitalize on the labor of convicts sentenced to confinement.

information   In criminal justice usage, a formal written accusation submitted to the court by a prosecutor, alleging that a specified person(s) has committed a specified offense(s).

infraction   A minor violation of state statute or local ordinance punishable by a fine or other penalty—but not by incarceration—or by a specified, usually limited term of incarceration.

inherent coercion   Those tactics used by police interviewers that fall short of physical abuse, but that, nonetheless, pressure suspects to divulge information.

initial appearance   In criminal proceedings, the first appearance of an accused person in the first court having jurisdiction over his or her case. See also **first appearance**.

initial plea (also **first pleas**)   The first plea to a given charge entered in the court record by or for the defendant. The acceptance of an initial plea by the court unambiguously indicates that the arraignment process has been completed.

insanity defense   A defense which claims that the person charged with a crime did not know what they were doing or that they did not know that what they were doing was wrong.

institutional capacity   An officially stated number of inmates that a confinement or residential facility is or was intended to house.

intake   The process by which a juvenile referral is received by personnel of a probation agency, juvenile court, or special intake unit and a decision is made to close the case at intake, refer the juvenile to another agency, place him or her under some kind of care or supervision, or file a petition in a juvenile court.

intensive supervision   A form of probation supervision involving frequent face-to-face contacts between the probationary client and probation officers.

intent   The state of mind or attitude with which an act is carried out; the design, resolve, or determination with which a person acts to achieve a certain result.

interdiction   The interception of drug traffic at the nation's borders. Interdiction is one of the many strategies used to stem the flow of illegal drugs into the United States.

intermediate appellate court   An appellate court of which the primary function is to review the judgments of trial courts and the decisions of administrative agencies and whose decisions are in turn usually reviewable by a higher appellate court in the same state.

intermediate sanctions (also **alternative sanctions**)   The use of split sentencing, shock probation and parole, home confinement, shock incarceration, and community service in lieu of other, more traditional, sanctions such as imprisonment and fines. Intermediate sanctions are becoming increasingly popular as prison crowding grows.

INTERPOL   An acronym for the International Police Association. INTERPOL began operations in 1946, and today has 137 members.

interrogation   The information gathering activities of police officers that involve the direct questioning of suspects. The actions of officers during suspect interrogation are constrained by a number of Supreme Court decisions, the first of which was *Brown* v. *Mississippi* (1936).

Islamic Law   A system of laws, operative in some Arab countries, which is based upon the Muslim religion and especially the holy book of Islam, the Koran.

jail   A confinement facility administered by an agency of local government, typically a law enforcement agency, intended for adults but sometimes also containing juveniles, which holds persons detained pending adjudication and/or persons committed after adjudication, usually those committed on sentences of a year or less.

jail commitment   A sentence of commitment to the jurisdiction of a confinement facility system for adults which is administered by an agency of local government and of which the custodial authority is usually limited to persons sentenced to a year or less of confinement.

judge An elected or appointed public official who presides over a court of law and who is authorized to hear and sometimes to decide cases, and to conduct trials.

judgment The statement of the decision of a court that the defendant is acquitted or convicted of the offense(s) charged.

judgment suspending sentence A court-ordered sentencing alternative that results in the convicted offender being placed on probation.

judicial officer Any person authorized by statute, constitutional provision, or court rule to exercise those powers reserved to the judicial branch of government.

judicial review The power of a court to review actions and decisions made by other agencies of government.

jural postulates Propositions developed by the famous jurist Roscoe Pound that hold that the law reflects shared needs without which members of society could not co-exist. Pound's jural postulates are often linked to the idea that the law can be used to engineer the social structure to ensure certain kinds of outcomes (such as property rights as embodied in the law of theft do in capitalistic societies).

jurisdiction The territory, subject matter, or persons over which lawful authority may be exercised by a court or other justice agency, as determined by statute or constitution. See also **venue**.

jurisprudence The philosophy of law; the science and study of the law.

juror A member of a trial or grand jury, selected for jury duty, and required to serve as an arbiter of the facts in a court of law.

jury panel The group of persons summoned to appear in court as potential jurors for a particular trial, or the persons selected from the group of potential jurors to sit in the jury box, from which second group those acceptable to the prosecution and the defense are finally chosen as the jury.

jury selection The process whereby, according to law and precedent, members of a particular trial jury are chosen.

just deserts As a model of criminal sentencing, one which holds that criminal offenders deserve the punishment they receive at the hands of the law and that punishments should be appropriate to the type and severity of crime committed.

justice The principle of fairness; the ideal of moral equity.

justice model A contemporary model of imprisonment in which the principle of just deserts forms the underlying social philosophy.

justifications A category of legal defenses in which the defendant admits committing the act in question, but claims it was necessary in order to avoid some greater evil.

juvenile In the context of the administration of justice, a person subject to juvenile court proceedings because a statutorily defined event or condition caused by or affecting that person was alleged to have occurred while his or her age was below the statutorily specified age limit of original jurisdiction of a juvenile court.

juvenile court The name for the class of courts that have, as all or part of their authority, original jurisdiction over matters concerning persons statutorily defined as juveniles.

juvenile court judgment The juvenile court decision terminating an adjudicatory hearing, that the juvenile is a delinquent, status offender, or dependent, or that the allegations in the petition are not sustained.

juvenile disposition The decision of a juvenile court, concluding a disposition hearing, that an adjudicated juvenile be committed to a juvenile correctional facility; placed in a juvenile residence, shelter, or care or treatment program; required to meet certain standards of conduct; or released.

juvenile justice agency A government agency, or subunit thereof, of which the functions are the investigation, supervision, adjudication, care, or confinement of juvenile offenders and nonoffenders subject to the jurisdiction of a juvenile court; also, in some usages, a private agency providing care and treatment.

juvenile justice system Government agencies that function to investigate, supervise, adjudicate, care for, or confine youthful offenders and other children subject to the jurisdiction of the juvenile court.

juvenile petition A document filed in juvenile court alleging that a juvenile is a delinquent, a status offender, or a dependent, and asking that the court assume jurisdiction over the juvenile or that an alleged delinquent be transferred to a criminal court for prosecution as an adult.

Kansas City Experiment The first large-scale scientific study of law enforcement practices. Sponsored by The Police Foundation, it focused on the practice of preventive patrol.

kidnapping Transportation or confinement of a person without authority of law and without his or her consent, or without the consent of his or her guardian, if a minor.

landmark cases Precedent-setting court decisions, often recognizable by the fact that they produce substantial changes in both the understanding of the requirements of due process and in the practical day-to-day operations of the justice system.

larceny Unlawful taking or attempted taking of property other than a motor vehicle from the possession of another—by stealth, without force, and without deceit—with intent to deprive the owner of the property permanently.

larceny-theft (UCR) Unlawful taking, carrying, leading, or riding away by stealth of property, other than a motor vehicle from the possession or constructive possession of another, including attempts.

law A rule of conduct, generally found enacted in the form of a statute, which proscribes and/or mandates certain forms of behavior. Statutory law is often the result of moral enterprise by interest groups that, through the exercise of political power, are successful in seeing their valuative perspectives enacted into law.

law enforcement The generic name for the activities of the agencies responsible for maintaining public order and enforcing the law, particularly the activities of prevention, detection, and inves-

tigation of crime and the apprehension of criminals.

law enforcement agency A federal, state, or local criminal justice agency or identifiable subunit of which the principal functions are the prevention, detection, and investigation of crime and the apprehension of alleged offenders.

law enforcement officer An employee of a law enforcement agency who is an officer sworn to carry out law enforcement duties.

lawyer See **attorney**.

lay witness An eyewitness, character witness, or any other person called upon to testify who is not considered an expert. Lay witnesses must testify to facts alone and may not draw conclusions or express opinions.

legal cause A legally-recognizable cause. The type of cause that is required to be demonstrated in court in order to hold an individual criminally liable for causing harm.

legalistic style A style of policing that is marked by a strict concern with enforcing the precise letter of the law. Legalistic departments, however, may take a "hands-off" approach to otherwise disruptive or problematic forms of behavior that are not violations of the criminal law.

legalization (of drugs) Eliminates the laws and associated criminal penalties that prohibit the production, sale, distribution, and possession of a controlled substance.

lex talionis The law of retaliation, often expressed as "an eye for an eye," or like for like.

mala in se Acts that are regarded, by tradition and convention, as wrong in themselves.

mala prohibita Acts that are considered "wrongs" only because there is a law against them.

mandatory sentence A statutory requirement that a certain penalty shall be set and carried out in all cases upon conviction for a specified offense or series of offenses.

mandatory sentencing A structured sentencing scheme which allows no leeway in the nature of the sentence required and under which clearly enumerated punishments are mandated for specific offenses, or for habitual offenders convicted of a series of crimes.

maximum sentence I. In legal usage, the maximum penalty provided by law for a given criminal offense, usually stated as a maximum term of imprisonment or a maximum fine. II. In correctional usage in relation to a given offender, any of several quantities (expressed in days, months, or years) which vary according to whether calculated at the point of sentencing or at a later point in the correctional process, and according to whether the time period referred to is the term of confinement or the total period under correctional jurisdiction.

mediation committees Chinese civilian dispute resolution groups found throughout the country. Mediation committees successfully divert many minor offenders from handling by the more formal mechanisms of justice.

medical model A therapeutic perspective on correctional treatment that applies the diagnostic perspective of medical science to the handling of criminal offenders. Rehabilitation is seen as a cure, and offenders are treated through a variety of programs in order to reduce their antisocial tendencies.

mens rea The state of mind that accompanies a criminal act. Also, guilty mind.

Miranda **rights** The set of rights that a person accused or suspected of having committed a specific offense has during interrogation and of which he or she must be informed prior to questioning, as stated by the U.S. Supreme Court in deciding *Miranda* v. *Arizona* and related cases.

Miranda **triggers** The dual principles of custody and interrogation, both of which are necessary before an advisement of rights is required.

Miranda **warnings** The advisement of rights due criminal suspects by the police prior to the beginning of questioning. *Miranda* warnings were first set forth by the Court in the 1966 case of *Miranda* v. *Arizona*.

misdemeanor An offense punishable by incarceration, usually in a local confinement facility, for a period of which the upper limit is prescribed by statute in a given jurisdiction, typically limited to a year or less.

mistrial A trial that has been terminated and declared invalid by the court because of some circumstances which create a substantial and uncorrectable prejudice to the conduct of a fair trial or which makes it impossible to continue the trial in accordance with prescribed procedures.

mitigating circumstances The opposite of aggravating circumstances. Circumstances surrounding the commission of a crime which do not in law justify or excuse the act but which, in fairness, may be considered as reducing the blameworthiness of the defendant.

mixed sentence One which requires that a convicted offender serve weekends (or other specified periods of time) in a confinement facility (usually a jail), while undergoing probation supervision in the community.

M'Naghten Rule A rule for determining insanity which asks whether the defendant knew what he was doing or whether he knew that what he was doing was wrong.

Model Penal Code A generalized modern codification of that which is considered basic to criminal law, published by the American Law Institute in 1962.

money laundering The process of converting illegally earned assets, originating as cash, to one or more alternative forms to conceal such incriminating factors as illegal origin and true ownership.[10]

moral enterprise The process undertaken by an advocacy group in order to have its values legitimated and embodied in law.

motion An oral or written request made to a court at any time before, during, or after court proceedings, asking the court to make a specified finding, decision, or order.

motive A person's reason for committing a crime.

motor vehicle theft (UCR) Unlawful taking or attempted taking of a self-propelled road vehicle owned by another, with the intent to deprive him or her of it permanently or temporarily.

murder and nonnegligent manslaughter (UCR) Intentionally causing the death of another without legal justification or excuse, or causing the death of another while committing or attempting to commit another crime.

narcoterrorism A political alliance between terrorist organizations and drug supplying cartels. The cartels provide financing for the terrorists, who in turn provide quasi-military protection to the drug dealers.

National Crime Victimization Survey (NCVS) An annual survey of selected American households conducted by the Bureau of Justice Statistics (BJS) in order to determine the extent of criminal victimization throughout the U.S.—especially unreported victimization.

natural law Rules of conduct inherent in human nature and in the natural order which are thought to be knowable through intuition, inspiration, and the exercise of reason, without the need for reference to man-made laws.

NCVS An abbreviation for National Crime Victimization Survey.

neglected child A child who is not receiving the proper level of physical or psychological care from his or her parents or guardian or who has been placed up for adoption in violation of the law.

negligence In legal usage, generally, a state of mind accompanying a person's conduct such that he or she is not aware, though a reasonable person should be aware, that there is a risk that the conduct might cause a particular harmful result.

negligent manslaughter (UCR) Causing death of another by recklessness or gross negligence.

new police Also known as the Metropolitan Police of London, were formed in 1829 under the command of Sir Robert Peel. Peel's police became the model for modern-day police forces throughout the Western world.

night watch An early form of police patrol in English cities and towns.

nolle prosequi A formal entry upon the record of the court, indicating that the prosecutor declares that he or she will proceed no further in the action. The terminating of adjudication of a criminal charge by the prosecutor's decision not to pursue the case, in some jurisdictions requiring the approval of the court.

nolo contendere A plea of "no contest." A no contest plea may be used where the defendant does not wish to contest conviction. Because the plea does not admit guilt, however, it cannot provide the basis for later civil suits that might follow upon the heels of a criminal conviction.

not guilty by reason of insanity The plea of a defendant or the verdict of a jury or judge in a criminal proceeding, that the defendant is not guilty of the offense(s) charged because at the time the crime(s) was committed the defendant did not have the mental capacity to be held criminally responsible for his or her actions.

nothing works doctrine The belief, popularized by Robert Martinson in the 1970s, that correctional treatment programs have little success in rehabilitating offenders.

no true bill The decision by a grand jury that it will not return an indictment against the person(s) accused of a crime(s) on the basis of the allegations and evidence presented by the prosecutor.

occupational crime Any act punishable by law that is committed through opportunity created in the course of an occupation that is legal.

offender An adult who has been convicted of a criminal offense.

offense I. a violation of the criminal law, or, in some jurisdictions, II. a minor crime, such as jaywalking, sometimes described as "ticketable."

offenses known to police (UCR) Reported occurrences of offenses, which have been verified at the police level.

opening statement The initial statement of an attorney (or of a defendant representing himself or herself) made in a court of law to a judge, or to a judge and jury, describing the facts that he or she intends to present during trial in order to prove his or her case.

operational capacity The number of inmates a prison can effectively accommodate based upon management considerations.

opinion The official announcement of a decision of a court together with the reasons for that decision.

opportunity theory A perspective which sees delinquency as the result of limited legitimate opportunities for success available to most lower-class youth.

organized crime The unlawful activities of the members of a highly organized, disciplined association engaged in supplying illegal goods and services, including but not limited to gambling, prostitution, loansharking, narcotics, labor racketeering, and other unlawful activities of members of such organizations.[11]

original jurisdiction The lawful authority of a court to hear or act upon a case from its beginning and to pass judgment on the law and the facts.

parens patriae A Latin term that refers to the legal basis upon which delinquent children may be removed from the home and supervised by the state. It means, in effect, that the state assumes responsibility for the welfare of problem children.

Parliament The British legislature; the highest lawmaking body of the United Kingdom of Great Britain.

parole The status of an offender conditionally released from a prison by discretion of a paroling authority prior to expiration of sentence, required to observe conditions of parole, and placed under the supervision of a parole agency.

parole board A state paroling authority. Most states have parole boards (also called commissions) that decide when an incarcerated offender is ready for conditional release and that may also function as revocation hearing panels.

parolee A person who has been conditionally released by a paroling authority from a prison prior to the expiration of his or her sentence and placed under the supervision of a parole agency, who is required to observe conditions of parole.

parole revocation The administrative action of a paroling authority to remove a person from parole status in response to a violation of lawfully required conditions of parole including the prohibition against commission of a new offense, and usually resulting in a return to prison.

parole supervision Guidance, treatment, or regulation of the behavior of a convicted adult who is obliged to fulfill conditions of parole or conditional release. Parole supervision is authorized and required by statute, performed by a parole agency, and occurs after a period of prison confinement.

parole supervisory caseload The total number of clients registered with a parole agency or officer on a given date, or during a specified time period.

parole violation An act or a failure to act by a parolee that does not conform to the conditions of parole.

paroling authority A board or commission which has the authority to release on parole adults committed to prison, to revoke parole or other conditional release, and to discharge from parole or other conditional release status.

Part I offenses (also called Major Crimes) Include murder, rape, robbery, aggravated assault, burglary, larceny, and motor vehicle theft as defined under the FBI's Uniform Crime Reporting Program.

Part II offenses In *Uniform Crime Reports* terminology, a set of offense categories used in UCR data concerning arrests.

peacemaking criminology A perspective which holds that crime control agencies and the citizens they serve should work together to alleviate social problems and human suffering and thus reduce crime.

penal code The written, organized, and compiled form of the criminal laws of a jurisdiction.

penal law See **criminal law**.

penitentiary A prison. See also **Pennsylvania style**.

Pennsylvania style A form of imprisonment developed by the Pennsylvania Quakers around 1790 as an alternative to corporal punishments. The style made use of solitary confinement and resulted in the nation's first penitentiaries.

peremptory challenge The right to challenge a juror without assigning a reason for the challenge. In most jurisdictions each party to an action, both civil and criminal, has a specified number of such challenges and after using all his peremptory challenges he is required to furnish a reason for subsequent challenges.[12]

perjury The intentional making of a false statement as part of testimony by a sworn witness in a judicial proceeding on a matter material to the inquiry.

perpetrator The chief actor in the commission of a crime, that is, the person who directly commits the criminal act.

petition A written request made to a court asking for the exercise of its judicial powers or asking for permission to perform some act where the authorization of a court is required.

petit jury See **trial jury**.

phenomenological criminology A perspective on crime causation that holds that the significance of criminal behavior is ultimately knowable only to those who participate in it. Central to this school of thought is the belief that social actors endow their behavior with meaning and purpose. Hence, a crime might mean one thing to the person who commits it, quite another to the victim, and something far different still to professional participants in the justice system.

physical addiction (or **physical dependence**) Dependence upon drugs marked by a growing tolerance of a drug's effects so that increased amounts of a drug are needed to obtain a desired effect, and by the onset of withdrawal symptoms over periods of prolonged abstinence. Also, a craving for a specific drug which results from long-term substance abuse. Dependence upon drugs is marked by a growing tolerance of a drug's effects so that increased amounts of a drug are needed to obtain a desired effect and by the onset of withdrawal symptoms over periods of prolonged abstinence.[13]

piracy See **software piracy**.

plaintiff A person who initiates a court action.

plain view A legal term describing the ready visibility of objects that might be seized as evidence during a search by police in the absence of a search warrant specifying the seizure of those objects. In order for evidence in plain view to be lawfully seized, officers must have a legal right to be in the viewing area and must have cause to believe that the evidence is somehow associated with criminal activity.

plea In criminal proceedings, a defendant's formal answer in court to the charge contained in a complaint, information, or indictment, that he or she is guilty or not guilty of the offense charged or does not contest the charge.

plea bargaining The negotiated agreement among the defendant, prosecutor, and the court as to what an appropriate plea and associated sentence should be in a given case. Plea bargaining circumvents the trial process and dramatically reduces the time required for the resolution of a criminal case.

police community relations (PCR) An area of emerging police activity that stresses the need for the community and the police to work together effectively and emphasizes the notion that the police derive their legitimacy from the community they serve. PCR began to be of concern to many police agencies in the 1960s and 1970s.

police culture (also **subculture**) A particular set of values, beliefs, and acceptable forms of behavior characteristic of American police and with which the police profession strives to imbue new recruits. Socialization into the police subculture commences with recruit training and is ongoing thereafter.

police ethics The special responsibility for adherence to moral duty and obligation inherent in police work.

police management The administrative activities of controlling, directing, and coordinating police personnel, resources, and activities in the service of crime prevention, the apprehension of criminals, and the recovery of stolen property, and the performance of a variety of regulatory and helping services.

police professionalism The increasing formalization of police work and the rise in public acceptance of the police which accompanies it. Any profession is characterized by a specialized body of knowledge and a set of internal guidelines which hold members of the profession accountable for their actions. A well-focused code of ethics, equitable recruitment and selection practices, and informed promotional strategies among many agencies contribute to the growing level of professionalism among American police agencies today.

police working personality All aspects of the traditional values and patterns of behavior evidenced by police officers who have been effectively socialized into the police subculture. Characteristics of the police personality often extend to the personal lives of law enforcement personnel.

postconviction remedy The procedure or set of procedures by which a person who has been convicted of a crime can challenge in court the lawfulness of a judgment of conviction or penalty or of a correctional agency action, and thus obtain relief in situations where this cannot be done by a direct appeal.

postmodern criminology A brand of criminology which developed following World War II and which builds upon the tenets inherent in postmodern social thought.

precedent A legal principle that operates to ensure that previous judicial decisions are authoritatively considered and incorporated into future cases.

preliminary hearing The proceeding before a judicial officer in which three matters must be decided—whether a crime was committed, whether the crime occurred within the territorial jurisdiction of the court, and whether there are reasonable grounds to believe that the defendant committed the crime.

presentence investigation The examination of a convicted offender's background prior to sentencing. Presentence examinations are generally conducted by probation/parole officers and submitted to sentencing authorities.

presentment Historically, written notice of an offense taken by a grand jury from their own knowledge or observation; in current usage, any of several presentations of alleged facts and charges to a court or a grand jury by a prosecutor.

presumptive sentencing A model of criminal punishment that meets the following conditions: (1) the appropriate sentence for an offender in a specific case is presumed to fall within a range of sentences authorized by sentencing guidelines that are adopted by a legislatively created sentencing body, usually a sentencing commission; (2) sentencing

judges are expected to sentence within the range or provide written justification for departure; (3) the guidelines provide for some review, usually appellate, of the departure.

pretrial detention Any period of confinement occurring between arrest or other holding to answer a charge and the conclusion of prosecution.[14]

pretrial discovery In criminal proceedings, disclosure by the prosecution or the defense prior to trial of evidence or other information which is intended to be used in the trial.

pretrial release The release of an accused person from custody, for all or part of the time before or during prosecution, upon his or her promise to appear in court when required.

prison A state or federal confinement facility having custodial authority over adults sentenced to confinement.

prison argot The slang characteristic of prison subcultures and prison life.

prison capacity The size of the correctional population an institution can effectively hold.[15]

prison commitment A sentence of commitment to the jurisdiction of a state or federal confinement facility system for adults, of which the custodial authority extends to persons sentenced to more than a year of confinement, for a term expressed in years or for life, or to await execution of a death sentence.

prisoner A person in physical custody in a confinement facility or in the personal physical custody of a criminal justice official while being transported to or between confinement facilities. A person in physical custody in a state or federal confinement facility.

prisonization The process whereby newly institutionalized individuals come to accept prison lifestyles and criminal values. While many inmates begin their prison experience with only a modicum of values supportive of criminal behavior, the socialization experience they undergo while incarcerated leads to a much wider acceptance of such values.

prison subculture The values and behavioral patterns characteristic of prison inmates. Prison subculture has been found to have surprising consistencies across the country.

private prisons Correctional institutions operated by private firms on behalf of local and state governments.

private security Those self-employed individuals and privately funded business entities and organizations providing security-related services to specific clientele for a fee, for the individual or entity that retains or employs them, or for themselves, in order to protect their persons, private property, or interests from various hazards.[16]

private security agency An independent or proprietary commercial organization which provides protective services to employers on a contractual basis and whose activities include employee clearance investigations, maintaining the security of persons or property, and/or performing the functions of detection and investigation of crime and criminals and apprehension of offenders. Also known as **private protective services**.

privatization The movement toward the wider use of private prisons.

probable cause A set of facts and circumstances that would induce a reasonably intelligent and prudent person to believe that a particular person had committed a specific crime; reasonable grounds to make or believe an accusation. Probable cause is needed for a "full blown" search or arrest.

probation A sentence of imprisonment that is suspended. Also, the conditional freedom granted by a judicial officer to an adjudicated or adjudged adult or juvenile offender, as long as the person meets certain conditions of behavior.

probationer A person who is placed on probation status and required by a court or probation agency to meet certain conditions of behavior, who may or may not be placed under the supervision of a probation agency.

probation revocation A court order in response to a violation of conditions of probation, taking away a person's probationary status, and usually withdrawing the conditional freedom associated with the status.

probation termination The ending of the probation status of a given person by routine expiration of probationary period, by special early termination by court, or by revocation of probation.

probation violation An act or failure to act by a probationer that does not conform to the conditions of his or her probation.

probation work load The total set of activities required in order to carry out the probation agency functions of intake screening of juveniles cases, referral of cases to other service agencies, investigation of juveniles and adults for the purpose of preparing predisposition or presentence reports, supervision or treatment of juveniles and adults granted probation, assisting in the enforcement of court orders concerning family problems such as abandonment and nonsupport cases, and other such functions as may be assigned by statute or court order.

problem-solving policing (also called **problem-oriented policing**) A style of policing which assumes that many crimes are caused by existing social conditions within the community and that crimes can be controlled by uncovering and effectively addressing underlying social problems. Problem-solving policing makes use of other community resources such as counseling centers, welfare programs, and job training facilities. It also attempts to involve citizens in the job of crime prevention through education, negotiation, and conflict management.

procedural defense A defense which claims that the defendant was in some significant way discriminated against in the justice process or that some important aspect of official procedure was not properly followed in the investigation or prosecution of the crime charged.

procedural law That aspect of the law that specifies the methods to be used in enforcing substantive law.

procuratorate (also called **procuracy**) A term used in many countries to refer to agencies with powers and responsibilities similar to those of prosecutor's offices in the United States.

professional criminal See **career criminal**.

property crime An offense category that, according to the FBI's UCR program, includes burglary, larceny, auto theft, and arson. Since citizen reports of criminal incidents figure heavily in the compilation of "official statistics," the same critiques apply to tallies of these crimes as to the category of violent crime.

property bond The setting of bail in the form of land, houses, stocks, or other tangible property. In the event the defendant absconds prior to trial, the bond becomes the property of the court.

proportionality A sentencing principle which holds that the severity of sanctions should bear a direct relationship to the seriousness of the crime committed.

prosecution agency A federal, state, or local criminal justice agency or subunit of which the principal function is the prosecution of alleged offenders.

prosecutor An attorney who is the elected or appointed chief of a prosecution agency and whose official duty it is to conduct criminal proceedings on behalf of the people against persons accused of committing criminal offenses. Also called district attorney, DA, state's attorney, county attorney, and U.S. attorney and any attorney deputized to assist the chief prosecutor.

prosecutorial discretion The decision-making power of prosecutors based upon the wide range of choices available to them in the handling of criminal defendants, the scheduling of cases for trial, the acceptance of bargained pleas, and so on. The most important form of prosecutorial discretion lies in the power to charge, or not to charge, a person with an offense.

prostitution Offering or agreeing to engage in, or engaging in, a sex act with another in return for a fee.

psychoactive drug A chemical substance that affects cognition, feeling, and/or awareness.

psychoanalysis A theory of human behavior, based upon the writings of Sigmund Freud, that sees personality as a complex composite of interacting mental entities.

psychological addiction (or **psychological dependence**) A craving for a specific drug which results from long-term substance abuse. Also, dependence upon drugs marked by the feeling that drugs are needed to achieve a feeling of well-being.[17]

psychological manipulation Manipulative actions by police interviewers, designed to pressure suspects to divulge information, which are based upon subtle forms of intimidation and control.

psychological school A perspective on criminological thought that views offensive and deviant behavior as the products of dysfunctional personalities. The conscious, and especially the subconscious, contents of the human psyche are identified by psychological thinkers as major determinants of behavior.

psychopath or sociopath A person with a personality disorder, especially one manifested in aggressively antisocial behavior, which is often said to be the result of a poorly developed superego.

psychopathology The study of pathological mental conditions, that is, mental illness.

psychosis A form of mental illness in which sufferers are said to be out of touch with reality.

public defender An attorney employed by a government agency or subagency, or by a private organization under contract to a unit of government, for the purpose of providing defense services to indigents; also, occasionally, an attorney who has volunteered such service. The head of a government agency or subunit whose function is the representation in court of persons accused or convicted of a crime who are unable to hire private counsel and any attorney employed by such an agency or subunit whose official duty is the performance of the indigent defense function.

public defender agency A federal, state, or local criminal justice agency or subunit of which the principal function is to represent in court persons accused or convicted of a crime(s) who are unable to hire private counsel.

public safety department An agency organized at the state or local level of government incorporating at a minimum various law enforcement and emergency service functions.

radical criminology A conflict perspective that sees crime as engendered by the unequal distribution of wealth, power, and other resources which it believes is especially characteristic of capitalist societies. Also called "critical criminology."

rape (generic) Unlawful sexual intercourse, achieved through force and without consent. Broadly speaking, the term *rape* has been applied to a wide variety of sexual attacks and may include same-sex rape and the rape of a male by a female. The term *forcible rape* has a more concise meaning. See also **forcible rape** and **sexual battery**.

rated capacity The number of inmates that a correctional facility can house without overcrowding, determined by comparison with some set of explicit standards applied to groups of facilities.

real evidence Evidence consisting of physical material or traces of physical activity.

reasonable doubt (in legal proceedings) An actual and substantial doubt arising from the evidence, from the facts or circumstances shown by the evidence, or from the lack of evidence.[18] Also, that state of the case which, after the entire comparison and consideration of all the evidence, leaves the minds of the jurors in that condition that they cannot say they feel an abiding conviction of the truth of the charge.[19]

reasonable doubt standard That standard of proof necessary for conviction in criminal trials.

reasonable force A degree of force that is appropriate in a given situation and is not excessive. The minimum degree of force necessary to protect oneself, ones' property, a third party, or the property of another in the face of a substantial threat.

recidivism The repetition of criminal behavior.

recidivist A person who has been convicted of one or more crimes and who is alleged or found to have subsequently committed another crime or series of crimes.

reckless behavior Activity which increases the risk of harm.

recreational drug user A person who uses drugs relatively infrequently and whose use occurs primarily among friends and within social contexts which define drug use as pleasurable. Most addicts began as recreational users.

reformatory concept A late-nineteenth-century correctional model based upon the use of the indeterminate sentence and belief in the possibility of rehabilitation, especially for youthful offenders. The reformatory concept faded with the emergence of industrial prisons around the turn of the century.

regional jails Jails that are built and run using the combined resources of a variety of local jurisdictions.

rehabilitation The attempt to reform a criminal offender. Also, the state in which a reformed offender is said to be.

release on recognizance (ROR) The pretrial release of a criminal defendant on their written promise to appear. No cash or property bond is required.

reprieve An executive act temporarily suspending the execution of a sentence, usually a death sentence. A reprieve differs from other suspensions of sentence not only in that it almost always applies to temporary withdrawing of a death sentence, but also in that it is usually an act of clemency intended to provide the prisoner with time to secure amelioration of the sentence.

research The use of standardized, systematic procedures in the search for knowledge.

reasonable suspicion 1. That level of suspicion which would justify an officer in making further inquiry or in conducting further investigation. Reasonable suspicion may permit a simple "stop and frisk." 2. A belief, based upon a consideration of the facts at hand and upon reasonable inferences drawn from those facts, which would induce an ordinarily prudent and cautious person under the same circumstances to generally conclude that criminal activity is taking place or that criminal activity has recently occurred. See also **probable cause.**

resident A person required by official action or his own acceptance of placement to reside in a public or private facility established for purposes of confinement, supervision, or care.

residential commitment A sentence of commitment to a correctional facility for adults, in which the offender is required to reside at night, but from which he or she is regularly permitted to depart during the day, unaccompanied by any official.

restitution A court requirement that an alleged or convicted offender pay money or provide services to the victim of the crime or provide services to the community.

restoration A goal of criminal sentencing that attempts to make the victim "whole again."

restorative justice A sentencing model which builds upon restitution and community participation in an attempt to make the victim "whole again."

retribution The act of taking revenge upon a criminal perpetrator.

revocation The cancellation of a probationer's or parolee's freedom. Revocation usually results from the violation of at least one of the conditions of probation or parole and may be ordered only by a special hearing board constituted for that purpose.

revocation hearing A hearing held before a legally constituted hearing body (such as a parole board) in order to determine whether or not a probationer or parolee has violated the conditions and requirements of his or her probation or parole.

RICO (Racketeer Influenced Corrupt Organization) A federal statute that allows for the federal seizure of assets derived from illegal enterprise.

rights of defendant Those powers and privileges which are constitutionally guaranteed to every defendant.

robbery (UCR) The unlawful taking or attempted taking of property that is in the immediate possession of another by force or threat of force.

rules of evidence Rules of court which govern the admissibility of evidence at a criminal hearing and trial.

runaway A juvenile who has been adjudicated by a judicial officer of juvenile court as having committed the status offense of leaving the custody and home of his or her parents, guardians, or custodians without permission and failing to return within a reasonable length of time.

schizophrenics Mentally ill individuals who suffer from disjointed thinking and, possibly, delusions and hallucinations.

scientific jury selection The use of correlational techniques from the social sciences to gauge the likelihood that potential jurors will vote for conviction or acquittal.

scientific police management The application of social scientific techniques to the study of police administration for the purpose of increasing effectiveness, reducing the frequency of citizen complaints, and enhancing the efficient use of available resources.

search warrant A document issued by a judicial officer which directs a law enforcement officer to conduct a search at a specific location, for specified property or persons relating to a crime(s), to seize the property or persons if found, and to account for the results of the search to the issuing judicial officer.

searches incident to an arrest Those warrantless searches of arrested individuals which are conducted in order to ensure the safety of the arresting officer(s). Because individuals placed under arrest may be in the possession of weapons, courts have recognized the need for arresting officers to protect themselves by conducting an immediate and warrantless search of arrested individuals without the need for a warrant.

security The restriction of inmate movement within a correctional facility, usually divided into maximum, medium, and minimum levels.

self-defense The protection of oneself or one's property from unlawful injury or the immediate risk of unlawful injury; the justification for an act which would otherwise constitute an offense, that the person who committed it reasonably believed that the act was necessary to protect self or property from immediate danger.

sentence The penalty imposed by a court upon a person convicted of a crime. The court judgment specifying the penalty imposed upon a person convicted of a crime. Any disposition of a defendant resulting from a conviction, including the court decision to suspend execution of a sentence.

sentencing The imposition of a criminal sanction by a sentencing authority.

sentencing dispositions Court dispositions of defendants after a judgment of conviction, expressed as penalties, such as imprisonment or payment of fines; or any of a number of alternatives to actually executed penalties, such as suspended sentences, grants of probation, or orders to perform restitution; or various combinations of the foregoing.

sentencing hearing In criminal proceedings, a hearing during which the court or jury considers relevant information, such as evidence concerning aggravating or mitigating circumstances, for the purpose of determining a sentencing disposition for a person convicted of an offense(s).

sequestered jury A jury that is isolated from the public during the course of a trial and throughout the deliberation process.

service style A style of policing that is marked by a concern with helping rather than strict enforcement. Service-oriented agencies are more likely to take advantage of community resources, such as drug treatment programs, than are other types of departments.

sex offenses In current statistical usage, the name of a broad category of varying content, usually consisting of all offenses having a sexual element, except forcible rape and commercial sex offenses. All unlawful sexual intercourse, unlawful sexual contact, and other unlawful behavior intended to result in sexual gratification or profit from sexual activity.

sex offenses (UCR) The name of the UCR category used to record and report arrests made for "offenses against chastity, common decency, morals, and the like," except forcible rape, prostitution, and commercialized vice.

sexual battery Intentional and wrongful physical contact with a person without his or her consent that entails a sexual component or purpose.

sheriff The elected chief officer of a county law enforcement agency, usually responsible for law enforcement in unincorporated areas and for the operation of the county jail.

sheriff's department A local law enforcement agency organized at the county level, directed by a sheriff, which exercises its law enforcement functions at the county level, usually within unincorporated areas, and operates the county jail in most jurisdictions.

shock incarceration A sentencing option that makes use of "boot-camp"-type prisons in order to impress upon convicted offenders the realities of prison life.

shock probation The practice of sentencing offenders to prison, allowing them to apply for probationary release, and enacting such release in surprise fashion. Offenders who receive shock probation may not be aware of the fact that they will be released on probation and may expect to spend a much longer time behind bars.

simple assault (UCR) Unlawful threatening, attempted inflicting, or inflicting of less than serious bodily injury, in the absence of a deadly weapon.

smuggling Unlawful movement of goods across a national frontier or state boundary or into or out of a correctional facility.

social control The use of sanctions and rewards available through a group to influence and shape the behavior of individual members of that group. Social control is a primary concern of social groups and communities, and it is the interest that human groups hold in the exercise of social control that leads to the creation of both criminal and civil statutes.

social debt A sentencing principle which objectively counts an offender's criminal history in sentencing decisions.

social disorganization A condition said to exist when a group is faced with social change, uneven development of culture, maladaptiveness, disharmony, conflict, and lack of consensus.

social ecology An approach which focused on the misbehavior of lower-class youth and saw delinquency primarily as the result of social disorganization.

social justice An ideal which embraces all aspects of civilized life and which is linked to fundamental notions of fairness and to cultural beliefs about right and wrong.

social order The condition of a society characterized by social integration, consensus, smooth functioning, and lack of interpersonal and institutional conflict. Also, a lack of social disorganization.

social order advocate One who suggests that, under certain circumstances involving criminal threats to public safety, the interests of society should take precedence over individual rights.

Social-Psychological School A perspective on criminological thought which highlights the role played in crime causation by weakened self-esteem and meaningless social roles. Social-psychological thinkers stress the relationship of the individual to the social group as the underlying cause of behavior.

sociopath See **psychopath**.

software piracy The unauthorized duplication of software or the illegal transfer of data from one storage medium to another. Software piracy is one of the most prevalent computer crimes in the world.

specific deterrence A goal of criminal sentencing which seeks to prevent a particular offender from engaging in repeat criminality.

speedy trial A trial which is held in a timely manner. The right of a defendant to have a prompt trial is guaranteed by the Sixth Amendment of the U.S. Constitution which reads, "In all criminal prosecutions, the accused shall enjoy the right to a speedy and public trial…"

Speedy Trial Act A 1974 federal law requiring that proceedings in a criminal case against a defendant begin before passage of a specified period of time, such as 70 working days after indictment. Some states also have speedy trial requirements.

split sentence A sentence explicitly requiring the convicted person to serve a period of confinement in a local, state, or federal facility followed by a period of probation.

stare decisis The legal principle which requires that courts be bound by their own earlier decisions and by those of higher courts having jurisdiction over them regarding subsequent cases on similar issues of law and fact. The term literally means "standing by decided matters."

state action doctrine The traditional legal principle that only government officials or their representatives in the criminal justice process could be held accountable for the violation of an individual's constitutional civil rights.

state court administrators Coordinating personnel who assist with case flow management, budgeting of operating funds, and court docket administration.

state court systems State judicial structures. Most states have at least three court levels, generally referred to as trial courts, appellate courts, and a state supreme court.

state highway patrol A state law enforcement agency of which the principal functions consist of prevention, detection, and investigation of motor vehicle offenses, and the apprehension of traffic offenders.

state police A state law enforcement agency whose principal functions usually include maintaining statewide police communications, aiding local police in criminal investigation, police training, and guarding state property; may also include highway patrol.

state-use system A form of inmate labor in which items produced by inmates are salable only by or to state offices. Items that only the state can sell include such things as license plates and hunting licenses, while items sold only to state offices include furniture and cleaning supplies.

status offender A child who commits an act that is contrary to the law by virtue of the juvenile's status as a child. Purchasing cigarettes, buying alcohol, and truancy are examples of such behavior.

status offense An act or conduct which is declared by statute to be an offense, but only when committed by or engaged in by a juvenile, and which can be adjudicated only by a juvenile court.

statutory law Written or codified law. The "law on the books," as enacted by a governmental body or agency having the power to make laws.

stay of execution The stopping by a court of the carrying out or implementation of a judgment, that is, of a court order previously issued.

stolen property offenses The unlawful receiving, buying, distributing, selling, transporting, concealing, or possessing of the property of another by a person who knows that the property has been unlawfully obtained from the owner or other lawful possessor.

stop and frisk The detaining of a person by a law enforcement officer for the purpose of investigation, accompanied by a superficial examination by the officer of the person's body surface or clothing to discover weapons, contraband, or other objects relating to criminal activity.

strategic policing A style of policing which retains the traditional police goal of professional crime fighting, but enlarges the enforcement target to include nontraditional kinds of criminals such as serial offenders, gangs and criminal associations, drug distribution networks, and sophisticated white-collar and computer criminals. Strategic policing generally makes use of innovative enforcement techniques, including intelligence operations, undercover stings, electronic surveillance, and sophisticated forensic methods.

street crime A class of offenses, sometimes defined with some degree of formality, as those which occur in public locations, are visible and assaultive, and thus constitute a group of crimes which are a special risk to the public and a special target of law enforcement preventive efforts and prosecutorial attention.

strict liability Liability without fault or intention. Strict liability offenses do not require *mens rea*.

structured sentencing A model of criminal punishment that includes determinate and commission-created presumptive sentencing schemes, as well as voluntary/advisory sentencing guidelines.

subculture of violence A cultural setting in which violence is a traditional method of dispute resolution.

subpoena A written order issued by a judicial officer, prosecutor, defense attorney, or grand jury requiring a specific person to appear in a designated court at a specified time in order to testify in a case under the jurisdiction of that court or to bring material to be used as evidence to that court.

substantive criminal law That part of the law that defines crimes and specifies punishments.

superpredators Members of a new generation of juveniles "who are coming of age in actual and 'moral poverty' without the benefits of parents, teachers, coaches, and clergy to teach them right from wrong and show them 'unconditional love.'"[20] The term is often applied to those inner-city youths who meet the criteria it sets forth.

supervised probation Guidance, treatment, or regulation by a probation agency of the behavior of the person who is subject to adjudication or who has been convicted of an offense, resulting from a formal court order or a probation agency decision.

suspect An adult or juvenile considered by a criminal justice agency to be one who may have committed a specific criminal offense, but who has not been arrested or charged.

suspended sentence The court decision to delay imposing or executing a penalty for a specified or unspecified period, also called "sentence withheld." A court disposition of a convicted person pronouncing a penalty of a fine or commitment to confinement, but unconditionally discharging the defendant or holding execution of the penalty in abeyance upon good behavior.

suspicionless searches Those searches conducted by law enforcement personnel without a warrant and without suspicion. Suspicionless searches are permissible only if based upon an overriding concern for public safety.

***Tazirat* crimes** Minor violations of Islamic law, which are regarded as offenses against society, not God.

team policing The reorganization of conventional patrol strategies into "an integrated and versatile police team assigned to a fixed district."[21]

TEMPEST A standard developed by the U.S. government that requires that electromagnetic emanations from computers designated as "secure" be below levels that would allow radio receiving equipment to "read" the data being computed.

terrorism A violent act or an act dangerous to human life in violation of the criminal laws of the United States or of any state to intimidate or coerce a government, the civilian population, or any segment thereof, in furtherance of political or social objectives.[22]

testimony Oral evidence offered by a sworn witness on the witness stand during a criminal trial.

theft Generally, any taking of the property of another with intent to deprive the rightful owner of possession permanently.

theory A series of interrelated propositions that attempt to describe, explain, predict, and ultimately control some class of events. A theory gains explanatory power from inherent logical consistency and is "tested" by how well it describes and predicts reality.

tort A private or civil wrong or injury. The "unlawful violation of a private legal right other than a mere breach of contract, express or implied."[23]

total institutions Enclosed facilities, separated from society both socially and physically, where the inhabitants share all aspects of their lives on a daily basis.

transfer to adult court The decision by a juvenile court, resulting from a transfer hearing, that jurisdiction over an alleged delinquent will be waived and that he or she should be prosecuted as an adult in a criminal court.

treason "A U.S. citizen's actions to help a foreign government overthrow, make war against, or seriously injure the United States."[24] Also, the attempt to overthrow the government of the society of which one is a member.

trial The examination in a court of the issues of fact and law in a case for the purpose of reaching a judgment. In criminal proceedings, the examination in a court of the issues of fact and law in a case, for the purpose of reaching a judgment of conviction or acquittal of the defendant(s).

trial *de novo* Literally, a new trial. The term is applied to cases that are retried on appeal, as opposed to those which are simply reviewed on the record.

trial judge A judicial officer who is authorized to conduct jury and nonjury trials and who may not be authorized to hear appellate cases, or the judicial officer who conducts a particular trial.

trial jury A statutorily defined number of persons selected according to law and sworn to determine, in accordance with the law as instructed by the court, certain matters of fact based on evidence presented in a trial and to render a verdict.

truth in sentencing A close correspondence between the sentence imposed upon those sent to prison and the time actually served prior to prison release.[25]

UCR An abbreviation for the Federal Bureau of Investigation's *Uniform Crime Reporting* program.

unconditional release The final release of an offender from the jurisdiction of a correctional agency; also, a final release from the jurisdiction of a court.

undisciplined child A child who is beyond parental control, as evidenced by their refusal to obey legitimate authorities such as school officials and teachers.

vagrancy (UCR) The name of the UCR category relating to being a suspicious character or person, including vagrancy, begging, loitering, and vagabondage.

vandalism (UCR) The name of the UCR category used to record and report arrests made for offenses of destroying or damaging, or attempting to destroy or damage, the property of another without his consent, or public property. Definition does not include burning.

venue The particular geographical area in which a court may hear or try a case. Also, the locality within which a particular crime was committed. See also **jurisdiction**.

verdict In criminal proceedings, the decision of the jury in a jury trial or of a judicial officer in a nonjury trial.

victim A person who has suffered death, physical or mental anguish, or loss of property as the result of an actual or attempted criminal offense committed by another person.

victim assistance program An organized program which offers services to victims of crime in the areas of crisis intervention and follow-up counseling and which helps victims secure their rights under the law.

victim impact statement The in-court use of victim- or survivor-supplied information by sentencing authorities wishing to make an informed sentencing decision.

victimization   In National Crime Survey terminology, the harming of any single victim in a criminal incident.

vigilantism   The act of taking the law into one's own hands.

violation   I. The performance of an act forbidden by a statute or the failure to perform an act commanded by a statute. II. An act contrary to a local government ordinance. III. An offense punishable by a fine or other penalty but not by incarceration. IV. An act prohibited by the terms and conditions of probation or parole.

violent crime   An offense category which, according to the FBI's *Uniform Crime Reports* (UCR), includes murder, rape, aggravated assault, and robbery.

warden   The official in charge of operation of a prison, the chief administrator of a prison, or the prison superintendent.

warehousing   An imprisonment strategy based upon the desire to prevent recurrent crime but which has abandoned any hope of rehabilitation.

warrant   In criminal proceedings, any of a number of writs issued by a judicial officer, which direct a law enforcement officer to perform a specified act and afford him protection from damage if he performs it.

watchman style   A style of policing that is marked by a concern for order maintenance. This style of policing is characteristic of lower-class communities where informal police intervention into the lives of residents is employed in the service of keeping the peace.

weapons offenses   Unlawful sale, distribution, manufacture, alteration, transportation, possession, or use or attempted sale, distribution, manufacture, alteration, transportation, possession, or use of a deadly or dangerous weapon or accessory.

white-collar crime   Nonviolent crime for financial gain committed by means of deception by persons whose occupational status is entrepreneurial, professional, or semiprofessional and utilizing their special occupational skills and opportunities; also, nonviolent crime for financial gain utilizing deception and committed by anyone having special technical and professional knowledge of business and government, irrespective of the person's occupation.

witness   In criminal justice usage, generally, a person who has knowledge of the circumstances of a case; in court usage, one who testifies as to what he or she has seen, heard, otherwise observed, or has expert knowledge of.

work release   A prison program in which inmates are temporarily released into the community in order to meet job responsibilities.

workhouse (or **brideswell**)   A form of early imprisonment whose purpose it was to instill habits of industry in the idle.

writ   A document issued by a judicial officer ordering or forbidding the performance of a specified act.

writ of *certiorari*   A writ issued from an appellate court for the purpose of obtaining from a lower court the record of its proceedings in a particular case. In some states this writ is the mechanism for discretionary reviews. A request for review is made by petitioning for a writ of *certiorari* and granting of review is indicated by issuance of writ.

writ of *habeas corpus*   In criminal proceedings, the writ that directs the person detaining a prisoner to bring him or her before a judicial officer to determine the lawfulness of the imprisonment.

youthful offender   A person, adjudicated in criminal court, who may be above the statutory age limit for juveniles but is below a specified upper age limit, for whom special correctional commitments and special record sealing procedures are made available by statute.

NOTES

1. Bureau of Justice Statistics, *Dictionary of Criminal Justice Data Terminology*, 2nd ed. (Washington, D.C.: U.S. Government Printing Office, 1982).

2. Federal Bureau of Investigation, *Uniform Crime Reporting Handbook* (Washington, D.C.: U.S. Department of Justice, 1984).

3. *Dictionary of Criminal Justice Data Terminology*, p. 5.

4. *People v. Romero*, 8 Cal.4th 728, 735 (1994); and *People* v. *Dillard*, 96 C.D.O.S. 3869 (1996).

5. The Community Policing Consortium, "What Is Community Policing?" (1995).

6. Michael L. Benson, Francis T. Cullen, and William J. Maakestad, *Local Prosecutors and Corporate Crime* (Washington, D.C.: National Institute of Justice, 1992), p. 1.

7. Bureau of Justice Statistics, *Drugs, Crime, and the Justice System* (Washington, D.C.: Bureau of Justice Statistics, 1992), p. 20.

8. Henry Campbell Black, Joseph R. Nolan, and Jacqueline M. Nolan-Haley, *Black's Law Dictionary*, 6th ed. (St. Paul, MN: West, 1990), p. 24.

9. *The American Heritage Dictionary and Electronic Thesaurus on CD-ROM* (text copyrighted, 1987 by the Houghton Mifflin Company).

10. Clifford Karchmer and Douglas Ruch, "State and Local Money Laundering Control Strategies," *NIJ Research in Brief* (Washington, D.C.: National Institute of Justice, 1992), p. 1.

11. The Organized Crime Control Act of 1970.

12. *Federal Rules of Criminal Procedure*.

13. Bureau of Justice Statistics, *Drugs, Crime, and the Justice System* (Washington, D.C.: Bureau of Justice Statistics, 1992), p. 21.

14. National Council on Crime and Delinquency, National Assessment of Structured Sentencing (Washington, D.C.: Bureau of Justice Statistics, 1996), p. xii.

15. Bureau of Justice Statistics, *Prisoners in 1990* (Washington, D.C.: Bureau of Justice Statistics, May 1991).

16. *Private Security: Report of the Task Force on Private Security* (Washington, D.C.: U.S. Government Printing Office, 1976), p. 4.

17. Bureau of Justice Statistics, *Drugs, Crime, and the Justice System* (Washington, D.C.: Bureau of Justice Statistics, 1992), p. 21.

18. *Victor v. Nebraska*, 114 S. Ct. 1239, 127 L. Ed. 2d 583 (1994).

19. As found in California Jury Instructions.

20. The term *superpredator* is generally attributed to John J. DiIulio, Jr. See John J. DiIulio, Jr. "The Question of Black Crime," *The Public Interest*, Fall 1994, pp. 3–12.

21. Sam S. Souryal, *Police Administration and Management* (St. Paul, MN: West, 1977), p. 261.

22. Federal Bureau of Investigation Counterterrorism Section, *Terrorism in the United States 1987* (Washington, D.C.: FBI, December 1987).

23. General Statutes of Georgia, 51-1-1.

24. Daniel Oran, *Oran's Dictionary of the Law* (St. Paul, MN: West, 1983).

25. Lawrence A. Greenfeld, "Prison Sentences and Time Served for Violence," *Bureau of Justice Statistics Selected Findings*, No. 4, April 1995.

List of Acronyms

ACJS	Academy of Criminal Justice Sciences
ADMAX	Administrative Maximum
AFIS	Automated Fingerprint Identification System
AIDS	Acquired Immune Deficiency Syndrome
AO	Administrative Office of the United States Courts
ASC	American Society of Criminology
ASIS	American Society for Industrial Security
BJA	Bureau of Justice Assistance
BJS	Bureau of Justice Statistics
BOP	Federal Bureau of Prisons
BWS	Battered Women's Syndrome
CCJJDP	Coordinating Council on Juvenile Justice and Delinquency Prevention
CDA	Communications Decency Act
CDC	Centers for Disease Control and Prevention
CFAA	Computer Fraud and Abuse Act
CIC	Children in Custody
CJIS	Criminal Justice Information Services Division (FBI)
CLEA	Commission on Accreditation for Law Enforcement Agencies
CPOP	Community Police Officer Program (New York City)
CPO	Certified Protection Officer
CPP	Certified Protection Professional
CPTED	Crime Prevention Through Environmental Design
CSA	Controlled Substances Act
DARE	Drug Abuse Resistance Education Program
DEA	Drug Enforcement Administration
DPIC	Death Penalty Information Center
DPRC	Drug Policy Research Center (RAND Corporation)
DUF	Drug Use Forecasting
DUI	Driving Under the Influence (of drugs or alcohol)
ECPA	Electronic Communications Privacy Act
FBI	Federal Bureau of Investigation
FCC	Federal Correctional Complex

FCI	Federal Correctional Institution
FINCEN	Financial Crimes Enforcement Network
FLETC	Federal Law Enforcement Training Center
FLIR	Forward-Looking Infrared
FOP	Fraternal Order of Police
FPC	Federal Prison Camp
FTCA	Federal Tort Claims Act
FDSS	Federal-wide Drug Seizure System
FGC	Family Group Conference
GBMI	Guilty But Mentally Ill
HIDTA	High-Intensity Drug Trafficking Area
IACP	International Association of Chiefs of Police
IAD	Internal Affairs Division
IAFIS	Integrated Automated Fingerprint Identification System (FBI)
IDRA	Insanity Defense Reform Act (1984)
ILEA	International Law Enforcement Academy
INTERPOL	The International Police Organization
IVS	International Victim Survey (UN)
JUSTNET	Justice Technology Information Network
JJDP	Juvenile Justice and Delinquency Prevention (Act)
LEAA	Law Enforcement Assistance Administration
LEAP	Law Enforcement Availability Pay
LEEP	Law Enforcement Education Program
LESL	Law Enforcement Standards Laboratory
LESTN	Law Enforcement Satellite Training Network
MCFP	Medical Center for Federal Prisoners
MDC	Metropolitan Detention Center
MSBP	Munchausen Syndrome by Proxy
NAP	National Assessment Program
NCAVC	National Center for the Analysis of Violent Crime
NCCD	National Council on Crime and Delinquency
NCCS	The National Computer Crime Squad (FBI)
NCIC	National Crime Information Center (FBI)
NCIC-2000	National Crime Information Center-2000 (FBI)
NCSC	National Center for State Courts
NCVS	National Crime Victimization Survey
NIBRS	National Incident-Based Reporting System (FBI)
NIDA	National Institute on Drug Abuse
NIJ	National Institute of Justice
NLETC	National Law Enforcement Technology Center
NNICC	National Narcotics Intelligence Consumers Committee
OBTS	Offender-Based Transaction Statistics
OJARS	Office of Justice Assistance, Research, and Statistics
OJJDP	Office of Juvenile Justice and Delinquency Prevention
OLETC	Office of Law Enforcement Technology Commercialization
ONDCP	Office of National Drug Control Policy
PCC	Police Cadet Corps (New York City)
PCR	Police Community Relations
PERF	Police Executive Research Forum
PLRA	Prison Litigation Reform Act

RESTTA	Restitution Education, Specialized Training, and Technical Assistance Program
RICO	Racketeer Influenced Corrupt Organizations
RISE	Reintegration Shaming Experiments (Australian Institute of Criminology)
RJC	Real Justice Conferencing
SBI	State Bureau of Investigation
SCU	Street Crimes Unit
SPECDA	School Program to Educate and Control Drug Abuse
UCR	Uniform Crime Reports
UNOJUST	United Nations Online Justice Information System
USBP	United States Border Patrol
USP	United States Penitentiary
USNCB	U.S. National Central Bureau (INTERPOL)
VAWA	Violence Against Women Act
VCAN	Victim's Constitutional Amendment Network
VICAP	Violent Criminal Apprehension Program
VOCA	Victims of Crime Act
WWW	World Wide Web

Index

Case Index

Name Index

Subject Index